KHOTANESE TEXTS

I–III

KHOTANESE TEXTS

I

EDITED BY

H. W. BAILEY

SECOND EDITION

CAMBRIDGE UNIVERSITY PRESS

CAMBRIDGE

LONDON NEW YORK NEW ROCHELLE

MELBOURNE SYDNEY

Published by the Press Syndicate of the University of Cambridge
The Pitt Building, Trumpington Street, Cambridge CB2 1RP
32 East 57th Street, New York, NY 10022, USA
296 Beaconsfield Parade, Middle Park, Melbourne 3206, Australia

Library of Congress Catalogue Card Number: A45-4291

First published 1945
Second edition 1969
Reprinted 1980

First printed in Great Britain at the
University Press, Cambridge
Reprinted in Great Britain by George Over Ltd
Rugby

ISBN 0 521 06961 0

CONTENTS

PREFACE TO THE SECOND EDITION

The three volumes *Khotanese Texts* I, II and III are out of print. In this new edition the anusvāras of the first three texts of *KT* I have now been inserted: they had been omitted to lighten the transliteration. It has also been possible on the basis of photographs not accessible at the time of the first edition to distinguish rr and r in the text of P 3513, the Bhadracaryā-deśanā and part of the Suvarṇabhāsa-sūtra. The mark = has been used in Jātakastava 31*r*1 kājenesār=re to indicate the division of the akṣara rr between two words; it occurs also in *FM* 25, 1, *b*2 k⟨ä⟩mīr=ro from kämīrä rro. In Siddhasāra 141*v*5 prihar-ra has the suprascript -r- over ra. Photographs of the Paris texts which were not to hand for *KT* I and for four pieces in *KT* III (p. v, footnote 1) were later obtained. The system of sigla has not been changed in these three volumes.

Additions have been made. The Sanskrit texts from the Cikitsā-sthāna of the Caraka-saṃhitā (identified by J. Filliozat in *Journal asiatique* 1946–7, 135) have been added for their importance to Gostana-Sanskrit. New texts since the publication of *KT* V include two pieces of the Saṃghāṭa-sūtra (here printed with the original Sanskrit text from Gilgit Manuscript 37) and some documents. One piece Kha 1. 219, 1, a variant to E 21. 30–41, was missed previously.

Since the publication of *KT* I 1945 the full text of Siddhasāra P 2892 has been printed in *KT* V 315–24. A text, translation and glossary of the Jātakastava has been published (1955) by Mark J. Dresden, and of the Bhadracaryā-deśanā by Jes P. Asmussen (1961). Four texts of *KT* II, P 2790 and P 5538*a*, P 2787, P 2958, have been translated in *Asia Major*, n.s., XI 1–26, 1964; 101–119, 1965; and BSOAS 30, 1967, 95–104. Four facsimile volumes entitled *Saka Documents* have been published in the *Corpus inscriptionum iranicarum* (1960, 1961, 1963, 1967).

I have to thank the Director of the National Archives, New Delhi, for a microfilm of the Sanskrit Saṃghāṭa-sūtra from which parts have been printed here.

Work towards a dictionary has been in progress since 1934; and a translation is in preparation. A first volume of a grammar of Saka by my former pupil R. E. Emmerick is now accepted for the London Oriental series.

H. W. BAILEY

1968

FOREWORD

It is hoped that the present volume will be the first of a series to contain texts in the Khotanese language. Five texts are given here. The first three, Ch ii 002, ii 003 and 00274, have been published in facsimile in the *Monumenta linguarum Asiae maioris*, vol. II: *Codices Khotanenses* (1938).

1. Siddhasāra of Ravigupta. A fragment of this text is comprised in P 2892 (165 lines),[1] from which variants are quoted in footnotes, marked P. The Khotanese is rendered from a Tibetan text (see *BSOS*, x, 600 ff.) corresponding to the Tanjur, *Rgyud*, vol. *do*, 138 ff. (= Cordier, *Catalogue du fonds tibétain de la Bibliothèque nationale*, III, 501). This has accordingly been placed opposite. Folio 100 of the Khotanese text has not been identified: it is perhaps from another medical treatise. The Sanskrit original follows. This text is found in photographs of two Nepalese MSS in the Indian Institute, Oxford.[2] Only the passages preserved in the Khotanese have been given. For one long passage (B 62*r*4–63*r*1) and for several short passages B is the only testimony. Added is the additional part of the Sanskrit text which corresponds to the Turkish version published, unidentified, by Rachmati, *Zur Heilkunde der Uiguren*, II, 20 ff. I have not had the Tibetan of this part. Both MSS are corrupt and differ extensively. The left ends of B are broken or rubbed off. The spelling has been adapted to normal Sanskrit usage. A critical edition with all variants has not been sought. If one MS has the correct text, errors in the other are not noted. If both are corrupt, the variants are given. A few passages have defied interpretation. I have been able through the kindness of Prof. E. H. Johnston to use the photographs in Cambridge. It has not been possible to read over my transliterated copy of the Tibetan with the printed text, so that a few uncertainties, indicated by italics, remain. Errors in the Khotanese text are noted in footnotes. Subscript letters have not been noted.

2. Jīvakapustaka.[3] The MS is bilingual, Sanskrit and Khotanese. The Sanskrit text is mainly in ślokas. At first the sentences are alternate, later long passages succeed, each containing a medical prescription. The two texts have been separated and set opposite for easy comparison. The Sanskrit,

[1] P = fonds Pelliot, Bibliothèque Nationale.

[2] T. R. Gambier-Parry, *A Catalogue of Photographs of Sanskrit MSS* (1930), no. 49, cited as A, and no. 50, cited as B. My attention was first directed to these photographs by Prof. F. W. Thomas.

[3] This name has been given as a simple form of reference.

in Khotanese orthography, as used for Sanskrit words also in the body of Khotanese texts, is often faulty. The late Dr A. F. Rudolf Hoernle had begun a study of part of this text. Some six years ago I saw the MS on one afternoon, but when about two years later I wished to examine it, it was not to be found. I have not seen it again and do not know what Dr Hoernle had done. Mr Pargiter's note (*JRAS*, 1923, p. 551) evidently refers to this manuscript.

3. Jātakastava.[1] The Khotanese is a translation from a language unknown. The original text has not been found. The Jātakastava edited in *BSOS*, IX, 851 ff. is different.

4. Bhadracaryādeśanā. This text is part of P 3513 (fol. 43 *v* 1–58 *r* 2), quoted already for a few forms of words by Prof. Pelliot in 1913, *Mém. Soc. Ling.* XVIII, 105 ff. It would have been acceptable to have given here the Buddhist-Sanskrit original. But it must suffice to refer to the easily accessible text in Suzuki and Idzumi, *Gaṇḍavyūha sūtra* (1934–6), IV, 543 ff. I have had my transliterated copy of P 3513, made in 1938, but the photograph I had hoped to have has not reached me. A few uncertainties, indicated by italics, therefore remain.

5. Suvarṇabhāsasūtra.

(*a*) Or. 9609 in the British Museum (in parts badly rubbed and broken). These eleven folios belong to the same MS as that from which Prof. Sten Konow edited twelve other folios in *Zwölf Blätter einer Handschrift des Suvarṇabhāsasūtra in Khotan-Sakisch* (1935). I have had a photograph, but it has been impossible to make a fresh examination of the MS.

(*b*) P 3513, 59 *v* 1–75 *v* 2, Deśanā-parivarta (= ed. Nobel, cap. III). A part was edited by Prof. Pelliot in *Mém. Soc. Ling.* XVIII, 89 ff. down to verse 25 (59 *v* 1–64 *r* 1) and partly again by Ernst Leumann in *Buddhistische Literatur, Nebenstücke*, 57 ff.

(*c*) Stein MSS, fragments, of which most have been identified (Kha I. 198, E I. 33 ends lost; Kha 0012 beginnings lost; Kha I. 119 almost complete; others central pieces).

For the transliterated Khotanese text it is to be noted:

1. P 3513 has both the double dotted *ä* (rarely apart from *lä*) and the later fused sign. In the present texts the two separate dots are found (apart from regular *lä*) in 59 *v* 1 *baudhisatvä* and 63 *v* 1 *duṣä'caidye*.

[1] In the summary of Jātakas of this text (*Codices Khotanenses*, XIII) *jala haraṣṭai* was misunderstood: the story is that of Dīpaṃkara. Kājenesārre can now be recognised as Sanskrit Kāñcanasāra, and in 16 *r* 4 must be added the story of Kalyāṇaṃkara and Pāpaṃkara.

2. *ǵya* is used (P 3513, 43*v*4) for the *gya* with ornamental flourish (see *BSOS*, x, 602 note 1): it can be seen in the Staël-Holstein roll 32, 40.

3. For initial *i, e, ai, o, au* made on the akṣara *a*, I have used, as before, *i̇, ė, ai̇, ȯ, au̇*. Once, Jīvakapustaka 95*v*3, *'a* (that is, the akṣara *a*) is written over *v*: *a͡vī* for the usual *u͡vī*.

4. *rr*. In my early transcripts medial *-rr-* was used for all cases where the *r*-curve turned back. Some of these, however, where the back-curve is at the tip and slight, should be rather *r̦*. Where I have had no photograph, this could not be changed.

5. The raised comma represents the Khotanese subscript curve.

6. In some akṣaras *u* and *ū* are hardly if at all distinguished, in others, as *ŭ, rŭ, kŭ, dŭ, śŭ, gŭ*, the signs are quite distinct. In cases of doubt the macron has not been used.

7. The subscript hook stands for unetymological anusvāra. In the texts given in facsimile in *Codices Khotanenses*, to lighten the transliteration, unėtymological anusvāra is not indicated, but the hook is put for the anusvāra (in Ch ii 002 and Jātakastava) which stands wrongly for the double dot, and in *ą̄* for older *o, ŭ, au*. Note also *eṃ, iṃ* (*ę*) for older *ai* (once, Ch ii 003, 80*v*4, *äṃ*). In Ch ii 003 *ttila* has been adopted throughout (=Sanskrit *taila*).

8. In loan-words from Sanskrit *tt* has been used even where it might be *nt* for Sanskrit *nt*. Possibly in *jīvatta* and *dravatti* (Ch ii 003, 73*v*3; 78*v*3; 80*r*2; 81*v*2) a newly formed conjunct akṣara for *nt* is used.

9. ⟨ ⟩ indicates insertions, and [ ] deletions; × × in Khotanese lost or broken akṣaras; the single dot . the MS ⁓; : the MS: and ≈; : : for more elaborate MS punctuations.

It will be seen that in the course of several years' further study of these texts advances have been made, and a few errata in the List, *BSOS*, VIII, 117 ff. (1936), have been disclosed.

I have finally the pleasant task of thanking the Librarian of the India Office, Dr H. N. Randle; the Keeper of Oriental MSS at the British Museum (now retired), Dr L. D. Barnett; Prof. Paul Pelliot for the use of the MSS of his collection; Prof. F. W. Thomas, Prof. Sten Konow, and Prof. E. H. Johnston for various kindnesses. It has also been a pleasure to know the accurate work of the Cambridge University Press.

H. W. BAILEY

1941

POSTSCRIPT

In September this year while reading the proofs of this book I received Prof. Sten Konow's monograph, *A Medical Text in Khotanese*, 1941 (*Avhandlinger utgitt av det Norske Videnskaps-Akademi i Oslo*, II, Hist.-Filos. Klasse, 1940, no. 4). He has edited with English translation the Khotanese part of Ch ii 003, but has omitted the Sanskrit verses. We were unfortunately not able to correspond about this work and I did not hear of it till my manuscript was in the hands of the printer. I have been able to avoid certain errors by the use of it, but it will be seen that I have preferred different readings in some places (apart from the unimportant matter of *ä* and *i*, on which full agreement is hardly attainable). The *Khotansakische Grammatik*, mentioned on p. 8, has not yet come into my hands, but in July 1939 I read through the rough draft of it when Prof. Konow was my guest in Cambridge.

1945

Other manuscripts of the Sanskrit text of the Siddhasāra have been found (R. E. Emmerick, BSOAS 37, 1974, 628–54) and an improved text is now possible (notes, where however for 'misread' it would be desirable to read 'edited', are given in R. E. Emmerick's article in BSOAS 34, 1971, 91–112). A full edition from all the manuscripts would be valuable for the Khotanese text, although the Khotanese version is from a Tibetan text of which four editions are extant.

1978

I

SIDDHASĀRA

1r 54 pattra sedasārą

1v1 | siddhaṃ
aurga tsūṃ raṃnāṃ drriṃnä ṣadi jsa brīya
mahaiśvarä brahmāṃ: tti ma āysda yināṃde .
2 khu ttu śāsträ | byūttä yinūṃ nva arthä 1
siddhasārä śāsträ cu mara vījye myą̄ña :
kamalä mą̄ñaṃdä cu kṣyāṃ iṃdrryau jsa uspurrä .
3 pichaṣṭu jsīñi hūrākä da|khāṃ jinākä .
anāhāṃ mu'śdī'nai mahāsamudrrä 2
ṣi' maṃ śāsträ hīdvāṃ ye pvī'stai arthäna .
4 tta ttai sājīra udaiśä' pīsą̄ brrāṃ|be .
ihīye phara jsa garkha vyaṃjaṃ pātcä .
dasta berä ttidä muhye harye akīrä 3
daṃdä tsve khu ri maṃ dva drrayi ni ya .
5 cu jsāṃ pū|śākä ṣi' jsāṃ ttaṃdī śau .
hāysi dīṣṭāṃdä vīja sājaka baiśä .
daiṣṭa-karma pastrīyāṃdä hanaśa tsvāṃda 4
1 bis r1 yauga mālyo jsa yuḍāṃ|dä śau kṣīrä krra .
apaysāṃdä āchai cvai nayä ni bvīra .
viysä[1] dūṣä' kālä u rve haṃdari pātcä .
pijsanīrą aprrasama arve muḍa phari satva 5
2 | ttiña beḍa tcaisyāṃ ye paḍą ttanä nąma :
tu śāsträ byaudi khąṇḍä ttāgūttau phari jsa :
samīśe pīḍai khve ṣi' hamye uspurrä .
3 byūttä vaskai ra ni ya | bvą̄ma hota 6
ṣi' tu śāsträ jsą̄ṇakyi ṣṭāṃ rrvī vī haiṣṭe .
miṣḍi gyastī mu'śdi' udiśä hamaiyi ttu .
ttāgūtto ṣṭāna uspurrä ṣe' pasti byūte
4 | ustimāṃjsyāṃ satvāṃ kį̄ṇä cu āchinuḍa 7
cu maṃ ye drrą̄ma arve pvīstye dä .
ttayi śī mistä vījä ttye śāsträ bvāką .

[1] viysaṃ.

5 ṣi' hā pā gīsti vinau mātsarä śi | rkä
rarūyi māśti uspurrä dāśe ṣi' 8
priṇahą̄na basta vasva mu'śdi' udiśä .
yinīde ustimye kālä satvāṃ krra .
1 *bis* v1 krre beḍa vījä āchinakä | jsa haṃtsa .
miṣḍi gyastuṃ a ttī vari byāti hamą̄ne 9
drrainä raṃnąnä hīye hąṭhi jsa ttyāṃ .
gyamūñe[1] mu'śdi' jsi u ṣadi jsa pātcä .
2 dva padya niṣi' | māde āchā biśä .
ba'ysūśtä byehīṃde tta tta khvaṃ kṣą'mä 10 || ||

[1] gyastūñe.

3 | || hīdvāṃgye vīje u krre hīvī sịdhasārä nạma śāsträ ||
aurga ī ṇe' biṃdä rrāysanaudä vīrāṣṭä ||
4 ttye vīje vī || piṣkalä haṃbistāṃdä . | u śūridirsą padidāṃdä || tta tta
khu ttanvạme hīvī piṣkalä || arvāṃ hīyāṃ gāṃ' hīvī piṣkalä hvaḍä
5 khaṣṭä hīvī piṣkalä śirkāṃ | u viśụ'nāṃ gūnāṃ hīvī piṣkalä || ttavai
hīvī piṣkalä || aviysārä hīvī piṣkalä || hụñä phehāme hīvī piṣkalä ||
2*r*1 kṣayä | hīvī piṣkalä || gą'mä hīvī piṣkalä || dūvarä hīvī piṣkalä ||
pramīhä hīvī piṣkalä kuṣṭä hīvī piṣkalą : arja u bagaṃdalä hīvī
2 piṣkalä . ysī | ḍai āchai hīvī piṣkalä : haika u ūysna āphārä hīvī
piṣkalä || phāhä hīvī piṣkalä : bąmä ttarä hīvī piṣkalä || bīysma kaśāme
3 hīvī pi | ṣkalä || pvaiskyāṃ haṃbaḍāme hīvī piṣkalä : ātmādä u avas-
4 mārä hīvī piṣkalä || beta hīvī piṣkalä || mąñä dīrä hīvī piṣkalä || || vī | sapä
hīvī piṣkalä : haśa hīvī piṣkalä || kaṃmä hīvī piṣkalä || tcimañāṃ
5 hīvī piṣkalä || be' jehụme hīvī piṣkalä || riysāyenāṃ śū'hyąma | u
dahośta aspaśdākä piṣkalä : vitkavīje hīvī piṣkalä paṃjāṃ kīrāṃ hīvī
piṣkalä : tta tta khu vimaṃ u vrrī u haysgvā u vastä u anavāysana
2*v*1 krre hīvya pi | ṣkica āstaṃna :
aträ raṣa'yä hīvī pūrä || harbiśāṃ hye vaṃgārä[1] harbiśa bvākye
2 hālai aúrga tsue || ttāhirai hye padīmākä sidhasārä || ravagūptä | ācārī
jsa biraṣṭä ||

kąma ttika cu baka bvąka .
jsīña bvāṣṭīña mahāsamudrra trąmąmata kṣa'ma .
cu hā ni traṃdä himāre ||
3 ttyāṃ vaska | ttā ṣā' biysąnąme udiśāyä
śāstrrä hīya haspara hvata hame .
tvā jsīña hīvya bvāṣṭya .
brahmānī jastvā ṣṭāṃ hve .
4 pacaḍą jsai kā | śā janavāṃ bisāṃ rruṃdāṃ hālai ||
u biṣṭāṃ hālai biraṣṭe :

viña ttā ttye padā ttanvąme hīvī piṣkalä padā uysdīśāṃ || ttye hīya
5 haḍi aṃga || tcimañāṃ hī | ya krra ttaraṃdarä hīya krra || sparśä'
pverąma śalyāharttä || ba' īśāma jīñi[2] huṣąñąma || vitkavīja || u śūkrrä
huṣąñąme jsa || hasta aṃga ||
3*r*1 cu hve' ṣṭe ṣe' | mahābhūta bu'jsā ūysąnai ṣṭe || u āchāṃ va pārahā
ṣṭe || tta tta khu ttaraṃdaraja āchā || u aysmvaja āchā : u āvaṃdva
2 āchā u haṃtsa-ysā | tāṃ āchāṃ āstaṃna busta ṣṭāre :
cu ttaraṃdaraja āchā . ttavai u kuṣṭa āstaṃna || cu aysmvaji āchā

[1] hye ⟨hā⟩vaṃgärä. [2] jsīñi.

138r2 || sman dpyad gces grub ces-bya-ba lehu sum-bcu-rća-gcig-pa bźugs ||

3 rgya-gar skad-du | SIDDH̱ASARA | bod skad-du sman dpyad gces-pa grub-pa źes-bya-ba || || bam-po daṅ-poho || sman dpyad-kyi gźuṅ hdi-la lehu bsdus-pa sum-cu-rća-gcig yod-de | rgyud-kyi lehu daṅ | sman gyi sde-ćhan gyi lehu daṅ | zas-kyi lehu

4 daṅ | hchi ltas-kyi lehu daṅ | rims-kyi lehu daṅ | hkhru-bahi lehu daṅ | khrag lud-pahi lehu daṅ | gcoṅ chen-pohi lehu daṅ | skran-gyi lehu daṅ | dmu-rjiṅ-gi lehu daṅ | gcin sñi-bahi lehu daṅ || mje nad-kyi lehu daṅ | gźaṅ-hbrum daṅ | mćhan-

5 par rdol-bahi lehu daṅ | skya-rbab-kyi lehu daṅ | skyigs-bu daṅ | dbugs mi-bde-bahi lehu daṅ || lud-pahi lehu daṅ | skyug-pa daṅ | skems-pahi lehu daṅ | gcin sri-bahi lehu daṅ | rtug-skam-gyi lehu daṅ | smyo-byed daṅ | brjed-byed-kyi lehu

6 daṅ | rluṅ-nad-kyi lehu daṅ | chaṅ-nad-kyi lehu daṅ | me-dbal-gyi lehu daṅ | skraṅs-pahi lehu daṅ | rma gso-bahi lehu daṅ | mig-sman-gyi rgyud-kyi lehu daṅ | dug gso-bahi rgyud-kyi lehu daṅ | sman-bcud-kyi len daṅ | ro ća-bahi rgyud-kyi lehu

7 daṅ | byis-pahi rgyud-kyi lehu daṅ | las rnam lṅahi lehu daṅ | cho-gahi lehu rnams-so || bgrod-par dkah-bas bsruṅs-pahi bus || kun-phan kun-mkhyen phyag bćal-te || yaṅ-dag phan-pa gces grub hdi | ñi-mas bsruṅs-pas bśad-par

138v1 bya blo chuṅ-ṅu gaṅ-dag ćhehi rig-byed-kyi rgya-mćho brgal-bar mi-nus-pa de-dag-gis khoṅ-du chud-par bya-bahi phyir | rgyud-kyi gźuṅ hgrol-bar hdi byas-so || ćhe hjin-pahi rig-byed hdi ni || ćhaṅs-pas mtho-ris-su bśad-do || rim-gyis yul ka-śihi rgyal-pos mi-

2 rnams-la bśad-do || de-la rgyud-kyi lehu bśad-par bya-ste | hdihi yan-lag ni mig-sman daṅ | lus gso-ba daṅ | gdon bsal-ba daṅ | mćhon bug-rdu dbyuṅ-ba daṅ | dug-las bsruṅ-ba daṅ | ćhe bsruṅ-ba daṅ | byis-pa bsruṅ-ba daṅ | khu-chu hphel-bar bya-baho |

3 hbyuṅ-ba chen-pohi yon-tan-gyi raṅ-bźin-can-gyi mi ni | nad-kyi gźi yin-te | de yaṅ lus-kyi nad daṅ | sems-kyi nad daṅ | glo-bur-gyi nad daṅ | lẖan-cig skyes-pahi nad-rnams yin-par hdod-do || de-la lus-kyi nad ni rims daṅ | mje-la sogs-paho ||

3 tti ysura āstaṃna || cu āvaṃdva āchā | tti gvachā tti gvahaiyi jsa panata : cu hatsa-ysyāta āchā tti kṣu u ysirą̄ñi āstaṃna ||

4 cu kālą tte niśtä paḍāta hīrāña ustama hī | rāñai pā niśtä || vaskalyą̄mata mase raysga āstanuta gūnai || ttye hīya piṣkistä jsa ttā biraysāre : rve kṣa' biraṣṭe ||

5 haṃdyaji māśtä u rarūya | ṣi' hamāñā rva ṣṭe ||

cu ttāṃjāra u brakhaysdya . ṣā' paśāṃ'jsya rva ṣṭe :

cu mutca'ci māścä u mụñaṃja ṣi' ysumą̄ña rva ṣṭe ||

3v1 cu skarhvāra māśtä u rrāha | ja ṣi' ysumi ṇa'styi bisā rva ṣṭe ||

cu cvātaji māśtä u kaja ṣi' pasālya ||

cu hamārīji māśtä u siṃjsīṃja . ṣi' ṇa'styi pasālä bisā rva ṣṭe ||

2 pātcä | śau pacaḍä .

cu haṃdyaji myāṃ māśti āna aủdä ttāṃjeri myāṃ māśti bure ṣi' hamą̄ña rva ||

ttāṃjeri myāṃ māśti āna aủdä mutca'ci myāṃ māśti bure ṣi' paśāṃ'jsya rva ||

3 | mu'tca'ci myāṃ māśti ą̄na ỏdä skarhveri myāṃ māśti bure ṣi' ysumą̄ña rva ||

skarhveri myāṃ māśti āna aủdä cvātaji myāṃ māśti bure ṣi' ṇa'stya ysumāṃ bisā rva ||

4 cvā | vaji myāṃ māśti ą̄na ỏdä hamārīji myāṃ māśti bure ṣi' pasālya rva ||

hamārīji myāṃ māśti ą̄na audä haṃdyaji myāṃ māśti bure . ṣi' ṇa'scyi pasālāṃjsya rva

5 khu u | rmaysdi hauda rrichāṃ pa jsāte u rravye pa jsāte . dvyāṃ paṃdāvāṃ paṣṭą̄me jsa . varṣā'vāysä . u ysumą̄ñā u hamāṃ varṣā'vāysä

4r1 u ysumāṃ . | u hamāṃ ttavaṃdya . u śilīṣāṃ u beta vī bure paśä' u pasālä āphirāre . āchai hīvī haṃkhīysä u rvāṃ hīvī haṃkhīysä tti

2 śūją̄ña sameyā | ñä ||

cu bāta ttye pa'śa'raṃjsī kālä khu hvaḍä khaṣṭä gvaśte u ṇa'styi biraysde ||

cu ttavaṃdya ttye śva' haḍā u śva' ṣave . hvaḍä khaṣṭä gvachą̄me

3 vī bira | ysde ||

cu śilīṣāṃ' ṣi' khāysä hvaḍä ỉdä u byūsacä ysai ysai biraysde ||

tta tta dvyāṃ u drrayāṃ hīye piṣkici jsa ||

4 dūṣi' āphiḍa ṣṭāna vasū | ją̄ñä dūṣāṃ' . u dhāttavāṃ . u rīmañāṃ dijsākä satvāṃ hīvī ttaraṃdarä ttaraṃdarä gūrśte || khu ttika

5 hamaṃga hamāṃde āchai va ni hame : ttī jiga u huṣą̄ma | himāde . ttī āchā himāre || ttyāṃ āchāṃ hīya pārahā bāva u ttavaṃdya u śilīṣā ||

4 sems-kyi nad ni khro-ba-la sogs-paho || glo-bur-gyi nad ni gnod-
pa-las byuṅ-bahi nad-do || lẖan-cig skyes-pahi nad ni bkres-pa daṅ |
skom-pa daṅ rga-ba-la sogs-paho || dus ni thog-ma daṅ tha-ma
med-pa-ste mig hjum-bahi yud-ćam-la sogs-pahi mćhan-ma-
5 can-no || dehi rgyun-gyi rnam-pa dbye-ba ni | dus-ćhigs-rnam
drug-tu bśad-de | de-la dbyar-zla tha-chuṅ daṅ | ston-zla ra-ba gñis
ni dbyar-gyi dus-so || ston-zla hbriṅ-po daṅ | ston-zla tha-chuṅ
gñis ni ston-gyi dus-so || dgun-zla ra-ba daṅ | dgun-zla hbriṅ-po
gñis ni
6 dgun-gyi dus-so || dgun-zla tha-chuṅ daṅ | dpyid-zla ra-ba gñis
ni dgun-smad-kyi dus-so || dpyid-zla hbriṅ-po daṅ | dpyid-zla tha-
chuṅ gñis ni dpyid-kyi dus-so || dbyar-zla ra-ba daṅ | dbyar-zla
hbriṅ-po gñis ni sos-kahi dus-so || ñi-ma byaṅ phyogs-su hgro-ba
7 daṅ | lẖo-phyogs-su hgro-źiṅ lam gñis-su hjug-pahi phyir de-la char
hbab-pa graṅ-bahi dus daṅ | ćha-bahi dus-su gyur-paho || char
hbab-pa daṅ | graṅ-ba daṅ | ćha-bahi dus-su mkhris-pa daṅ | bad-kan
daṅ | rluṅ-rnams gsog-ciṅ | ston daṅ
139r1 dpyid daṅ dbyar hkhrug-par gyur-te | nad-kyi graṅs daṅ | nus-kyi
graṅs rim bźin-du so-sor sbyar-ro || rluṅ-nad ni phyi-hbyed-kyi dus
daṅ | khu-zas źu-bahi mjug-tu ldaṅ-ṅo || mkhris-pahi nad ni ñi-mahi
guṅ daṅ | nam-phyed daṅ
2 kha-zas hju-bahi ćhe ldaṅ-ṅo || bad-kan ni zas-zos ma-thag daṅ
srod daṅ | sṅa dro ldaṅ-ṅo || de bźin-du gñis-kyi cha hdus-pa daṅ
gsum-gyi cha hdus-pahi bye-brag-gi nad gźi hkhrug-pa sbyaṅ-byaho
|| nad-gźi nad | lus-zuṅs daṅ | dri-mahi gnas-
3 kyi lus ni lus źes-bya-ste | de-dag cha mñam-na ni nad-med-do |
śas che chuṅ-du gyur-na ni nad-du hgyur-ro || de-la nad-gźi ni
rluṅ-nad mkhris-pa daṅ bad-kan-rnams-so || lus-zuṅs ni bdun-te |
daṅs-ma daṅ | khrag daṅ | śa daṅ | ćhil daṅ | rus-pa
4 daṅ | rkaṅ daṅ | khu-chu-rnams-so || dri-ma ni phyi-sa daṅ | gcin
daṅ | rṅul-la sogs-paho || rluṅ ni graṅ-ba daṅ | yaṅ-ba daṅ | cha
phra-ba daṅ | mkhraṅ-ba daṅ | rćub-pa daṅ | mi-brtan-pa daṅ |
stobs che-ba daṅ | dbugs rgyu-bar byed-pa daṅ | ṅag

cu ttaraṃdarä . ṣi' raysä u hụñä u gūśta u pī u āstai u mijsā u
4v1 śū | krrä || cu rrīmạñä ṣi' saṃnä u bīysma āstaṃna || cu bāta ṣi' sāḍa
u raysga . u jsiṃṇa u ysīra u lokṣä || u eṣṭavana u hauvana ||
2 cu āṃ ūysna | trāme u nirạme u ttī jsāṃ āṃ vā phara naṣpaśde'
u raṣṭa paṣṭạma || rrīmañä naṣpaśdāme āstaṃna piṣkici jsa haṃphve ||
3 ttavadya āhvarrja . u dijsaṃca : u ttau | da : u ūśä' gvachạñāka .
ttīśä' u heṃji che padīmāka
cu śilīṣä' ṣṭi ṣi' hvarä u pūrä[1] u tcārbạ u garkhä u cihajsä ||
4 cu bāva ṣi' krriṃga-rūvya u hala-brāṃgvā pā | rotta :
cu ttavaṃdya ṣi' bụ'ñe haṃdrri vya veha[2] pārautta ||
cu śilīṣāṃ ṣṭe ṣi' khāysānya u garśa u eha u kima'ña āstaṃna
ūskyāṣṭä hamarvā pārauttä ||
5 khu dūṣä' hī | vī hīvī thāṃ rūyīye || kāmye dūṣi' vīra pārauttä ṣṭāna
varai krra tcerai || kāṃ dūṣä' purrdä hamāte . tta ttai śirä nirīkṣạ'ñä ||
5r1 u krravai || . | gạmạña tcerai ||
hvarä āstaṃna . rrāysa[3] kṣa' . tti pā dūṣä' hīvī piṣkici jsa || drrūne
va hettä . biśä bure sīvāñä ||
2 ttī tta tta ni yan | īye . ttī vai āchā panamāre . dajsaṃdai u ttīrä .
u byaṃjsä raysä . tti maṃ bāta āphirạñāre . dạjsaṃdai u āhvarai u
3 pūrä[1] raysä . tti maṃ ttavaṃdya ā | phirīdä || cu hvarä āhvarai u pūrä[1]
tti maṃ śilīṣāṃ āphirīdä || ttī tti raysa paribyūttä herna sīvạme jsa .
4 cvai va āchā hamāṃde | jihạme vīrai tsīdä || cu jsāṃ drrụnä himāṃde .
ttyāṃ jsāṃ suhä va hettä hame . cu hvarä raysä ṣi' tceña śirä īdä u
5 dhāttava pa'jsa padīme | u huṣa bāye || cu āhvarai ṣi' vāta nva ṇi'ma'ysä
viśte u haṃbusä || khāysạ gvāchākä u pajsākä dai haṃjsulyākä . cu
5v1 ṣūrä ṣi' . | vasūjākä u pajākä u gvāchākä u nvātạña padīmākä . cu
dạjsaṃdai ṣi' sturä hirạñe u dīḍe . u ba' jinākä u dai haṃjsulyākä u
2 pajsākä . cu | ttīrä ṣi' ttavai u ttarä āchai jinākä || u dai haṃjsulyākä
u vasūjākä . u rrīśi' prahājākä || cu byaṃjsä raysä ṣi' ttaraṃdarä
3 haṃthrrajākä u pū'haṃjākä | u strrajạñākä . u saṃnä haṃbīṭhạkä . u
kamāṃ haṃbrạñākä || cu ṣi' arva rraysä u hauva u gvāchä pārajsye
4 jsa || pīrmāttama ttyāṃ rriysāṃ | āstaṃna haṃdara pātcä . ạstaṃ
astaṃ . uskātta uskātta hī ṣaṣāme jsa || hva hva ttyāṃ bijairma hirāñä ||
5 raysä gvāchä haṃdrri vya ṣṭūkä || arvāṃ | dijsāme pārajsye jsa . sāḍä
ttauda stabhāvai[4] vī . ā vī ttye arve hīya hauva ysūṣṭa ṣṭe || cu rraysa
6r1 ttyāṃ gvāchä nvaiya . | hvarä u dajsaṃdai dva padya hame . ttyāṃ
dvyā haṃdrri vya hvarä garkhä u dajsaṃdai raysgä

[1] ṣūrä. [2] neha. [3] rraysa. [4] svabhāvai.

5 hbyuṅ-bar byed-pa daṅ | legs-par hjog-pa daṅ | bskyod-pa daṅ |
dri-ma hbyin-pa rnams-kyi bye-brag daṅ ldan-paho || mkhris-pa ni
skyur-ba daṅ | ro ćha-ba daṅ | drod ćha hur-ru-ru byed-pa daṅ |
hjug-par byed-pa daṅ | mdaṅs bskyed-pa daṅ | bźin-
6 mdog dmar-pahi rgyu byed-paho || bad-kan ni mṅar-ba daṅ | lan-
ćhvahi ro bro-ba daṅ | hjam-pa daṅ | lci-ba daṅ | śin-tu hbyil-baho ||
rluṅ ni gźaṅ daṅ | sgu-do daṅ | hdoṅ-mohi bar-gyi naṅ-na gnas-so ||
mkhris-pa ni loṅ-gahi naṅ-na gnas-
7 so || bad-kan ni pho-ba daṅ | lkog-ma daṅ | mthoṅ-ga daṅ | mgo
daṅ ćhigs-rnams-kyi naṅ-na gnas-so || nad-gźi rnams nor-bar byuṅ-
na | gnas de-ñid-kyi cho-ga bźin-du byaho || ćhabs che-bar gyur-na
yaṅ bye-brag phyed-par byas-la |
139*v*1 cho-ga bya-ba bsmyur-te byaho || mṅar-ba-la sogs-pa ro rnam-pa
drug-po-rnams kyaṅ | nad-gźi de-dag-gi bye-brag-las nad-med-pahi
rgyu gaṅ yin-pa rtag-tu bzah-bar byaho || de-ltar ma-byas-na nad-du
hgyur-ro || ćha-ba daṅ kha-ba daṅ | bska-ba-rnams-kyis ni rluṅ
hkhrug-par
2 hgyur-ro || ćha-ba daṅ | skyur-ba daṅ | lan-ćhva-rnams-kyis ni
mkhris-pa hkhrug-par hgyur-ro || mṅar-ba daṅ | skyur-ba daṅ |
lan-ćhva-rnams-kyis ni bad-kan hkhrug-par hgyur-ro || nad-gźi de-
dag źi-bar bya-bahi phyir de-dag-las ldog-ste | zos-na nad
3 yod-pa rnams ni sos-par hgyur-ro || nad-med-pa rnams-la ni
bde-bahi rgyur hgyur-ro || ro mṅar-ba ni mig-la phan-te | lus-zuṅs
hphel-bar byed-do || skyur-ba ni phyi-sa bźaṅ-ba hkhru-bar byed |
sñiṅ-la phan-pa daṅ | zas hju-ba daṅ | ćhos-par byed-
4 ciṅ drod skyed-par byed-do || lan-ćhva ni hkhru-ba daṅ | ćhos-par
byed-pa daṅ | hju-ba daṅ | śa slo-bar byed-do || ćha-ba śa che-ba
daṅ | sñom-pa daṅ | dug-rnams sel-ciṅ drod bskyed-ciṅ ćhos-par
byed-do || kha-ba ni rims daṅ | skom-pahi nad sel-pa daṅ |
5 drod bskyed-pa daṅ | hkhru-bar byed yi-ga hbyed-par byed-do ||
bska-ba ni śa na-bar byed-pa daṅ | śa hbri-ba daṅ | rtug-skams-su
byed | hkhru-ba gcoṅ rma bćo-bar byed-do || sman ni ro daṅ nus-pa
daṅ | źu-ba rnams-kyi rten yin-pas-na gćo-bo yin-no || ro-
6 la sogs-pa gźan-rnams kyaṅ || phyi-ma phyi-ma-la | sṅa-ma sṅa-ma
ldan-par yod-pas-na | phyi-ma phyi-ma-la gćo-bo yin-no || de-la
nus-pa ni ro źu-bar ma-gyur-pahi bar-ma-la byas-te | rjas-la gnas-
śiṅ brten-la | graṅ-ba daṅ ćha-bahi mćhan ñid-do || yaṅ-na rjas-
7 kyi mthu ñid-la yaṅ byaho || ro-rnams ni źu-bahi hog-tu mṅar-ba

2 vījä arva : āchanai . u vaṭhą̄narä . tti tcaura hamāṃde tti krre | hīya
aṃga ṣṭāre . ttī va ttika ni himāṃde sijāṣcye vīra ni jsāte . cu vījä
3 hīya aṃga ṣṭāre . ṣi' drrāṃ śtāka cu śāsträ u drriṣṭa-karmä | bautte .
u arvāṃ jsa kīrä butte . u puñuda dastai u vasva bvą̄mai u baka
4 kṣamä . cu āchinai hīya aṃga ṣṭāre . ṣi' jsāṃ a | rthäna haṃphve
śtāka . u jsį̄ñi jsa . u ysira bise hota jsa haṃphve cu jeha-vīyi āchā
u asthų̄mājsä āchinai ttikyāṃ jatte ||
5 cu a | rve hịvī aṃgä . ṣā' śira śaṃdai ysāta śtāka || cuai śirä rraysä
aśtä || u pīrmāttama . u bāḍāna śirna haṃdāḍa ||
6v1 cu vaṭhą̄na . | rä hīvī aṃgä . pi'[1] surakä u alobä . u brorä . u bu'ysa
aysmu u abyaṃdä . u hauta jsa haṃphve . khvai krra āstañe . u kīrä
2 ịṃdä . diśai' spā | śą̄ñä u bāḍä u kālä . u jsīna . u ttaraṃdarūṃ dai . u
ñuska . u pura[2] . u purva[3] . u ttaraṃdarä u ysira bi[4] hauva eṣṭą̄ma . u
3 āchai | khu ttika dye ịdä u ttīvai āstañą̄ñä . cu diśa' . kuṣṭa pharāka
4 utca hame u gara u bahya . u ganaistä hālai . ṣā' diśa' śilīṣā . u ba' | va
jsa va āchā panimāre . astaucä kuṣṭa utci baka u bata bahya diśa'
5 huña āphārä jsa hamya u ttavaṃdye jsa hamyava āchā pana | māre ||
haṃbairstau gų̄nyau jsa haṃphva diśi' haṃbajsya busti ṣṭe . cu
jsį̄na hīvī haṃba[5] ṣi' drrai padya ṣṭe || aysdau ⟨hi⟩rą̄ñi jsa u myą̄ñāvi
7r1 ysāḍi hīrą̄. . | ñi jsa [u[6] myą̄ñāvi ysāḍi hīrą̄ñi jsa][6]. khu śau salä vī bure
ṣvīdą jsa . u khāysą jsa jū u vara ą̄na kṣasä salä vī buri aysdo gūrśte
2 u vaḍą̄ṣṭä | hodāta salä vī bure myānai gūrśte || u ttina uskātta ysāḍä
gūśte || ttye hīye pacaḍä jsa śilīṣāṃ : u ttavaṃdya u beta hīye buḍara
3 masvą̄ñi jsa tta tta | khu haṃkhīysä hva ṣṭe hva hva hā haṃphīśą̄ñä .
cu aysdau u ysaṃgarä . ttye kṣārāṃ arvā u dai u hų̄ñi paśą̄me khiṇḍai
4 krra striha ni tcerā || krravai ho | ga tcerā . ttaraṃdarä hīya jsāṃ
piṣkici drrai padya uysdīśa ṣṭe . cu ttaraṃdarä godä ttye gūśti
5 huṣą̄ñą̄ñä || cu gūśta mista ttye gūśti pārīsą̄me | hīya krra tcerai || cu
ttaraṃdarä hīya gūśti samą̄na : ahamici jsai kāña krravī tcerai : cu
7v1 hova ṣṭe haṃdara ttuṃna u baka hova pā ịdä : u hadara gauda u hau | va
jsa haṃphva pā ịdä . sthyauśte u drrauphāme u garkha-aysmu styūdä
bvą̄ñä cuai hauva ahamaista he[7] || vyaysaṃ vai himāte . ā vī iskhajsä
2 hīscya beḍa : anvathā . mista aủtsālhą ttye hauva jsa haphve . hve
kuṣṭai ñuska . hvaḍä khaṣṭä āstaṃna . prara ttyāṃ ṣai viysama
himāte : suhä hālai hamāṃde . ṣā' ñuska tta tta bvą̄ñä . biṃna-vrrarä
3 āchai | nai hve . ṣi' aṃgä jsa gaudä u ysīrä . ttaṃga tcaṃjsai . drrāvā

[1] ṣi'. [2] P prrara. [3] P arva. [4] P pe'.
[5] P haṃbā. [6-6] om. P. [7] P hame.

daṅ | ćha-ba rnam-pa gñis-su hgyur-te | de gñis-kyi naṅ-na sṅa-ma
ni lci | phyi-ma ni yaṅ-ṅo || sman-pa daṅ | sman daṅ | nad-pa daṅ |
nad g-yog daṅ | hdi bźi-na ldan-pa ni gso-bahi yan-lag
140*r*1 yin-te | de-dag daṅ mi-ldan-pa ni mi-hgrub-pa yin-no || de-la
sman-pahi yan-lag ni sman-dpyad-kyi yi-ge kha-ton-du bslabs-śiṅ
don śes-pa daṅ | sman-gyi las śes-pa daṅ | lag gsod-pa daṅ | *gćaṅ*-źiṅ
re-ba med-paho | nad-
2 pahi yan-lag ni nor daṅ ldan-pa daṅ | ćhe ma-zad-pa daṅ | sñiṅ
stobs daṅ ldan-pa daṅ | raṅ dam daṅ ldan-pa gsor ruṅ-ṅo || sman-gyi
yan-lag ni sa bzaṅ-po-nas skyes-pa daṅ | ro ćha-ba daṅ | mchog-tu
gyur-pa daṅ | dus-su legs-par brṅas
3 paho || nad g-yog-gi yan-lag ni gćaṅ-źiṅ re-ba med-pa daṅ | yi
raṅ-ba daṅ | bag yod-pa daṅ | stobs daṅ ldan-paho || sman btaṅ-bahi
las bya-na | yul daṅ | dus daṅ | na-ćhod daṅ | me-drod daṅ | goms-pa
daṅ | raṅ-bźin daṅ | sman
4 daṅ | lus daṅ | sñiṅ stobs daṅ | ñams-stobs daṅ | nad daṅ hdi rnams
mthoṅ-nas gdod byaho || de-la yul ni chu maṅ-pa | nags-ri-can ni
gśer-bahi phyogs źes-bya-ste | bad-kan daṅ rluṅ-gi nad bskyed-do ||
skam sa ni chu ñuṅ-źiṅ śiṅ
5 ñuṅ-bahi yul-na | khrag-las gyur-pa daṅ | mkhris-pa-las gyur-pahi
nad bskyed-do || yul skam gśer-gyi cha hdren-ma ni nad kyaṅ hdren-
mar hgyur-ro || na-ćhod kyaṅ rnam-pa gsum-ste | byis-pa daṅ |
bar-ma daṅ | rgan-poho || de-la lo
6 gcig-gi bar-du ho-ma daṅ | kha-zas-kyi hćho-ba-nas | lo bcu-drug-
gi bar-du ni byis-pa źes-byaho || de-nas lo bdun-cuhi bar-du ni
bar-ma źes-byaho || de phan-ćhad ni rgan-po źes-byaho || dehi rim-pa
bźin-du bad-kan daṅ | mkhris-pa daṅ | rluṅ
7 śas che-bar hgyur-te | graṅs bźin-du so-sor sbyar-ro || byis-pa
daṅ rgan-po-la ni thal sman ćha-ba daṅ | me bćah daṅ | gtar-ka
lta-buhi dpyad drag-po mi-bya-bar dpyad hjam-po byaho || lus-kyi
bye-brag kyaṅ rnam-pa gsum-du hdod-de | lus skem-pa
140*v*1 . . . . | śa che-ba-la ni śa dbri-bahi sman byaho || lus-kyi śa
rnam-la mi-hgyur-bar bsruṅ-bahi cho-ga byaho || ñams-stobs ni la-la
śa che la | ñams-stobs chuṅ-ba yaṅ yod || la-la śa skem-la ñams-stobs
daṅ ldan-pa yod-
2 pas-na | sran yod-pa daṅ | rćol phod-pa daṅ | sgyur dgar-źiṅ sra-ba
rnams-las nan-tan-du rtogs-par byaho || sñiṅ stobs ni mi-hgyur-bar
byed-pa-ste | sdug-bsṅal-bar gyur-tam | mthos-par gyur-na | de daṅ
ldan-pas sro śi-ba daṅ | ẖa-caṅ dgah-
3 bar mi-hgyur-ba ni | sñiṅ stobs daṅ ldan-pahi mi yin-no || goms-pa
ni gaṅ-la zas daṅ | skam-la sogs-pa raṅ-bźin-gyis mi mthun-pa yin

aysmu . asthye . phara bijāṣä . cu āśi' tsṳ̄mamḍai aysą̄nā daittä huña ||
4 kāṃ hve ttavaṃ | dyūḍä . abāḍai tcaṃjsä śīyi nirą̄mīṃdä u chavī jsāṃ
śīya hime . āhisinuḍä . chāṃgä . ysurrjä iṃdrrāṃ jsä . hṳñi ra jsāṃ
5 dai vijsaiṣḍe || cu śilīṣą | majsa-vrrarä : eṣṭavana aysmu śira aṃgai .
phara purai . tcaṃjsai sataidä[1] . hṳña ūtci vijiṣḍi || dūṣā' dvyāṃ
8r1 drrayāṃ nvaiya . tsūka . hvaṇḍye haṃbairstāṃ gṳ̄nāṃ | jsa dyāñä ||
dūṣä' śe haṃdarye hamą̄me jsa || ṣi' utvaḍarvacä[2]-vrrarä bustä ṣṭe .
cu ttaraṃdarū dai hīya grauttā . ṣi' śilį̄ṣāṃ u ttavadye u beta hīye
2 utvaḍare | jsa . ttye tco-padya hamaṃgą̄ñi jsa . ttaraṃdarū dai nvārri[3]
jsai viysä[4] . tcau-padya hame . nva pacaḍä hva hva haṃphīśą̄ñä . khu
3 vara dai hamaṃgä hame : tta tta khu ni khauysde . ką̄' | me vaskai krra
tcairai . viysamye dai bita ṇiha'ją̄ma tcerai . strihą dai ttavaṃdye
krra tcerai . nvā dai śilīṣāṃ vasūją̄ma tcerai . ttī vai khāysä ni gvachāve
4 u | dai vahąnī harbiśāṃ āchāṃ hīya pārahā hame . ttye hīvī gūnai
haṃdaṃna bā'stä[5] jsahārä hime || ttīra ṣahe . cuai va agvahą harśtä
5 u nāṣṭä ni nirą̄me | ṣi' gūnai tco-padya āme jsa va pvāma hame . u
khorga nirą̄mīda u ysairä biṃdä ttodā hame u ṣahe nirą̄mīda . alasahą
8v1 āchai āstaṃna hame vara āra u namvīje u | ci jsa jaiṣṭa[6] haurāñä u
bamą̄ñą̄ñä . ttīrāṃ ṣahāṃ nama'śä' jsāṃ ttīrä rūjai hame u ga'sā .
2 u vausai . u ttarai hime . varai ūtci jṣą̄'ñą̄ñä u pvāva haurą̄ñä . u |
padaṃ hālai nāṣṭä ñą̄ñä || pātcä ą̄mä rasa ną̄ma . aṃgvā vīne || u
kamalä garkhä . khu khāysä vijiṣḍe u kṣame u ttyą̄nä ą̄staṃnai gṳ̄nā
3 hamāre || ttye vīra haḍāya husą̄|ñä u nahārośtä[7] biṃnāṃ hirāṃ jsa
phīśą̄ñä || viṣṭabdä ą̄mä . cu nāṣṭä straji u vinai himāre mą̄ṇḍa . u
4 saṃnä u bīysma kaśą̄ma . ṣi' āha | sāñą̄ñä u khīṣṭai pura[8] ūtca haurą̄ñä ||
tta tta ahaṃbusanāṃ hvaḍāṃ khaṣṭāṃ jsa : āchā panamāre . ttye
5 hirä pracaina ahaṃ.| busana hvaḍa khaṣṭa patsą̄ñä . nijsaḍna[9] u
9r1 haṃbusata[10] varāśą̄'ñä || tti buiri viysama hvaḍa khaṣṭa . murāsä u : |

[1] P sanaidä. [2] P utvaḍarvatä. [3] P nvāri. [4] viysaṃ.
[5] P bve'stä. [6] P jaiṣṭa khīṣṭä. [7] P anah°.
[8] ṣura. [9] P nijsaḍäna. [10] P haṃbusäna.

yaṅ | bde-ba ñid-du hgyur bde ni goms-pa źes-bya-bar śes-so || mi
rluṅ-gi raṅ-bźin-can ni | lus
4 skem-źiṅ rćub-pa daṅ | skra srab-pa daṅ | sems rgod-pa daṅ | lus
nad-pa daṅ | s⟨gra⟩-ba maṅ-ba daṅ | rmi-lam nam-mkhah-la ldaṅ-ba
yin-no || mi mkhris-pahi raṅ-bźin-can ni || dus-la ma-bab-par skra
dgar-ba daṅ | śa mdog dkar-ba daṅ | rṅul sñi-ba |
5 daṅ | spro thuṅ-ba daṅ | sems rno-ba daṅ | rmi-lam-du me hbar-ba
mthoṅ-ba yin-no || mi bad-kan-gyi raṅ-bźin-can ni | sems brtan-pa
daṅ | lus grims-pa daṅ | bu maṅ-ba daṅ | skra snum-pa daṅ | rmi-lam-
na chu daṅ | dkar bag rmi-ba yin-no || nad-
6 gźi cha gñis hdus-pa daṅ | cha gsum hdus-pahi raṅ-bźin-can-gyi
mi ni || hdus-pahi mćhan-mas rtogs-par bya-ste | nad-gźi gźan dag
yod-du zin kyaṅ | gaṅ śas che-bahi raṅ-bźin yin-par bśad-do || khoṅ-
na yod-pahi mehi drod ni bad-kan
7 daṅ | mkhris-pa daṅ | rluṅ-rnams re-re-nas śas che-bar gyur-pa
daṅ | śas mñam-par gyur-pahi bźi las mehi drod kyaṅ śas chuṅ-
ba daṅ || śas che-ba daṅ | drod ma-sñoms-pa daṅ | drod sñoms-
pa daṅ | rnam-pa bźir hgyur-te | go-rim bźin-du so-
141 r1 sor sbyar-ro || de-la mehi drod sñoms-na ni de-las mi-hgyur-bar
bsruṅ-bahi cho-ga byaho || drod ma-sñoms-pa-la ni rluṅ bsal-bar
byaho || mehi drod śas che-ba-la ni mkhris-pa bsal-bahi cho-ga
byaho || drod chuṅ-ba-la ni bad-kan sbyaṅ-
2 bar byaho || kha-zas ma-źu-nas mehi drod byi-ba ni | nad-do-cog
skye-bahi gźi yin-te | dehi mćhan-ma ni khoṅ ltam-ltam-por gyur-pa
daṅ | kha-chu skyur-ba daṅ | bcud daṅ daṅs-ma ma-źu-bar lus-pa
daṅ | bźaṅ gci thur-du ma-hbyuṅ-ba daṅ | rnam-pa bźiho |
3 de-la khoṅ ltam-ltam-por hdug-pa de-las ni | gsud-pa daṅ mchil-
ma maṅ-du hbyuṅ-ba daṅ | bad-kan mer-mer-por byed-pa daṅ |
yan-man-du mi-slon mi-sbo-bar hkhyil-ba de-la ni | śu-dag daṅ
lan-ćhva chuhi naṅ-du skol-ba blud-de skyug-tu gźug-go ||
4 kha-chu skyur-ba-las ni sgregs-pa skyur-ba daṅ | mgo hkhor-ba
daṅ skyug-pa daṅ | skom daṅ che-bar hgyur-te | de-la ni chu skol-te
graṅs-pa blud-la bser-bu phyogs-su hdug-par byaho || bcud daṅ
daṅs-ma ma-źu-bar lus-pa ni lus sñom-te | bya-
5 smyaṅ byed-pa daṅ | mgo yor-yor-pa daṅ | kha-zas mthoṅ-na
yid-du mi-hoṅ-ba-la sogs-par hgyur-te | de-la smyaṅ-bar bya-ba
daṅ | ñin-par thun-hgah ñal-na hjuho || zas smyaṅ-ba drags-na rluṅ-
naṅ mi-ldaṅ-bahi ran ćam-du byaho || thur-du mi-
6 hbyuṅ-ba-las ni ltor zug-ciṅ na-ba daṅ | behu-snabs-su hbyuṅ-ba
daṅ | phyi-sa daṅ gcin hgag-par hgyur-te | de-la ni lu mes bya-źiṅ
ćha-chu blud-do || hdi-ltar kha-zas mi-hphrod-pa zos-pa-las | nad-
do-cog byuṅ-bas-na | dehi phyir mi-hphrod-
7 pa de-dag spaṅs-la phan-ba-rnams bzah-bahi rigso || de-la kha-zas
mi-hphrod-pa ni | rma-bya daṅ sreg-pa daṅ | srog-chags godha daṅ |

ysara || tti buri ŧraṃdīnai rruṃ jsa saṃkhaista u ŧraṃdīnai bisu jsa
vaha ni hvarą̄ñä || gvīhä rruṃ u ṃākṣī hamaṃgä vistāta ṣṭą̄na ni
2 hverai : gvīhä rruṃ paṃjilīña bā|jinaña dasau haḍā vistā līkä ni
hverai : mākṣī ttaudye uci jsa ni khāśą̄'ñä || bārūtcä jsa haṃbairstä
ṣṭą̄na ni khāśą̄'ñä : pātcä mākṣī . u pā'śi[1] gūśta u trihe jsa pātcä haṃtsa
3 ni hverai ba|le[2] hīya gūśta haṃtsa mauna ni hverai || ñye jsa haṃtcą
krrigīña gūśti ni hverai . hvāṣa śą̄ñīje gūlä jsa haṃtsa haṃbirsta ni
4 hverai || kava sārmāṃ jsa haṃtsa ni hverai : hą̄mīnā ku|jsa jsa
haṃbersta rrų̄ña vaha khāysa mau āstaṃna āhvaryau raysyo jsa ni
hvairai : kava gūlä jsa hatsa ni hverai : māsta hvāṣe u āhvarāṃ hīyāra .
5 u kuṃjsārgye u kulastä . namve|jsa ŧrhve . u ñye . kava[3] . tti buri hera
buḍa ṣvīdä jsa ni samīdä haṃtsa ni hverai : priyaṃgīnai ka'kä jsa
saṃkhaista aṃgä . ṣṭāna ṣapā ni hverai : korakä hīya gūśta śaśvānīnai
9v1 rruṃ | jsa haṃtsa ni hverai . kava hīvī pī jsa haṃtsa papalä haṃbirstä
ni hverai || . haṃbirstą līkä rrīysu u kuṃjsa māṃgä u drrāma ttīma
2 jsa . u mo u rīysvą̄nai ṣapā | haṃtsa ni khāśą̄'ñä . kavīña gūśta u
rīysva gūrva u rruṃ u biśī haṃtsa haṃbirstä ṣṭą̄na ni hverai . kāṃ
hve viysama[4] rraysa[5] hauva[5] hvaḍāṃ khaṣṭāṃ jsa didrrą̄ma-vadya
3 ką̄|ma tte jaḍī jsa varāśą̄'te . ṣi' āchāṃ jsa haṃthrrīśtä . ā vā mīḍe .
tta tta aprisamāṃ hvaḍāṃ khaṣṭāṃ jsa : āchā himāre ttye va vrrī
4 u vimaṃ jsa vasūją̄ñä || ñuska u ttaraṃ|darū dai strihä hamāte u
hauva jsa haṃphve hamāte . anvaśtāvai ni hime[6] .

ttaṃtrādhyāyä paḍauysä ||

5 ttiña pacīḍa arvāṃ hīyāṃ ga'[7] hīya piṣkalä biraṣṭä hi|me ||
sālaparṇä . aúśta bāta . ŧraṃde . sachi bāta . rapabhakä[8] . jīvakä :
10r1 drrāṃgūlye śirāve . priśnaparṇä . bidārä . lākṣä . || . | vāttāka . brihatta
dva : kąṇḍārya . vrrīstya . maudgaparṇä . u mārpaparṇä[9] . gūrmä . u
ātmagaupta . ṣā' arvą̄na ga'[10] || naṣṭausai . u gą̄'mä u bāva . u ūysna
2 āphārä . u phāhä . | ttavaṃdye jsa hamya āchā jiṃdä .

bahyä ñagrodhä . udūbarä . palakṣä' . u madhukä . u aśvattä .
ttiṃdūkä . payālä baraśīṃja pārthä[11] . naṃdīvṛkṣä . aṃbrä . bī palāśä .
3 sunāha . bha|lāttaka . ttejana[12] . lodrrä . jaṃba drraya jābi[13] u jala
jaṃbi u mahājaṃbä || ṣā' arvą̄na ga'[14] hīya hamālā hų̄ñä bamą̄me
4 hīvī āchai u primīhä : ṇihejāka . u | viranāṃ haṃbrą̄ñāka . aṃgāṃ
ttodā u purą̄ña bisā āchā ṇiheje ||

[1] P pve'śä. [2] P u bale. [3] P u kava. [4] P viysamau.
[5-5] P vaṃ. [6] P himā. [7] P ge'. [8] raṣa°.
[9] P māṣa°. [10] P ge'. [11] P pārthavä. [12] P ttejava.
[13] jaṃbi. [14] P ge'.

goṅ-ma sreg daṅ | hdi-rnams ėraṇḍahi mar-gyis bskus-te | 'eraṇḍahi
śiṅ-gi mes bcos-pa mi-bzah | mar daṅ

141*v*1 sbraṅ rći cha-na ñams-te mi-bzah | mar mkhar-bahi snod-kyi naṅ-
du źag bcu phan-chad lon-pa mi-bzah | sbraṅ-rći chu dr⟨o⟩n-pas
hphul-źiṅ mi-bzah | char-bahi chu daṅ yaṅ sbyar-źiṅ mi-bzah | de
bźin-du sbraṅ-rći daṅ | phag-śa daṅ | la-phug daṅ yaṅ lh̲an-cig mi-
2 bzah | chu-skyar gyi śa⟨. .⟩daṅ lh̲an-cig-tu mi-bzah | źo daṅ bya-
gag-gi śa lh̲an-cig-tu mi-bzah | ldum-bu kaćamaća daṅ bu-ram lh̲an-
cig-tu mi-bzah | ña-śa daṅ ldum-bu 'upoḋa ⟨daṅ⟩ lh̲an-cig-tu mi-
bzah | phag-phye daṅ til-mar bsres-pahi snum-khur | rća-bas lh̲an-
3 cig mi-bzah | ña-śa daṅ bu-ram lh̲an-cig mi-bzah | ldum daṅ | rdad
daṅ | śiṅ-tog skyur-bahi bag daṅ | til-gyi ćhigs-ma daṅ | rgya-
sran daṅ | lan-ćhva daṅ | smyig-mdehu daṅ | źo daṅ | ña śa daṅ |
hdi-rnams śas cher ho-ma daṅ mi-mthun-te

4 lh̲an-cig mi-bzah | priyaṃkuhi lde-gus lus-bskus bźin-du | hbras-
kyi ho-thu mi-btuṅ | thi-bahi śa yuṅs-mar-gyis bskus-te | g-yos-pa
rnams mi-bzah | ñahi źag daṅ pipiliṅ lh̲an-cig mi-bzah | sbyar-thug
ces-bya-ba hbras daṅ | til daṅ |

5 mon-sran sṅehu bsres-pahi thug-pa daṅ | chaṅ hbras-kyi ho-thug
rnams lh̲an-cig mi-bzah | ña-śa daṅ | yos daṅ | mar daṅ | dar-ba
rnams lh̲an-cig spags-te mi-bzah | mi gaṅ-gis ro daṅ nus-pa mi-
mthun-pahi zas hdi lta-bu daṅ cha hdra-ba dag | ma-

6 śes-te zos-par gyur-na | de ni nad-kyis ñam-thag-pa ham | yaṅ-na
hchi-bar hgyur-ro || de-ltar kha-zas mi-mthun-pa zos-pa-las nad-du
gyur-pa-la ni | bkru-sman daṅ | skyug-sman-gyis bsal-bar byaho ||
goms-pa daṅ | mehi drod ćha-ba daṅ |

7 ñams-stobs che-ba-la ni gnod-par mi-hgyur-ro ||

rgyud-kyi lehu-ste daṅ-po rjogs-so ||

|| de-nas sman-gyi sde-ćhan-gyi lehu bśad-par bya-ste | sman tira
daṅ | ba-spru-ba daṅ | 'eraṇḍa daṅ | jh̲aśa daṅ | zad rći-ba daṅ |
jibaka daṅ | gze-ma

142*r*1 daṅ | ñehu śiṅ daṅ | laṅguli daṅ śira bidari daṅ | hānsa-pādika daṅ |
prih̲ati daṅ | dri | cikali daṅ | dve pah̲eba daṅ | sran-ma 'atmakupta daṅ
| sman-gyi sde-ćhan hdi-rnams ni | skem-pahi nad daṅ | sran daṅ

2 rluṅ-nad daṅ | dbugs mi-bde-ba daṅ | lud-pa daṅ | mkhris-pa-las
gyur-pahi nad sel-to || śiṅ nyagroda daṅ | 'udumbara daṅ | plakṣa
daṅ | maduka daṅ | 'aśvattha daṅ | tinduka daṅ | pilaya daṅ | rgya-śug
daṇ || padara daṅ | pārtha

3 daṅ | naṇḍa daṅ | brikṣa daṅ | 'amra daṅ | lcaṅ-ma daṅ | palāśa

pipalä . u citrai . u āra : vatsāvīśi' ttī . baraśīje . pipala-mūlä
5 buhane . u ttāṃgara | sūkṣmela . pravaṣe' . hiraṇva . bądarą . u
mirimjsya . u sąnā . khavari bā . ālavāya . mistä ciṃgāṃ ttīrai hīvī
10 v1 hīyārä ā vā perä . triphalä . aủṣai . u śī | śaśvāṃ . aṃgūṣḍä . kalyarū-
hana . viṇḍaṃga . ṣā' arvāṃ hīya ga'[1] hīya[1] hamālā . bāta u śilīṣāṃ
jināka ||

2 sūkṣmela . ttagarä . buhane . hiraṇva . tvacä : śaṃ | dhapaträ[2] śī
caṃdaṃ . kurkuṃ . cauraką . caṃdaṃ . hīśä[3] hīya hīsuṣka u ysairai .
nāgapuṣpä . devadārä sthąṇeyakä bu' . gūrgūlä bu' . syaucä bu' .
3 syaucä[4] bu'[4] . kava hī | vī gū . śrirṣai'[5] bu' . jąmaką . śī bu' . vyāgrinakä .
gīri bisai buśąnai . kuṣṭä . ṣā' arvāṃ hīye ga' . ilāda[6] hīya hamālā
4 khaysme u isye[7] . u ba'[8] u | bāta : u śilīṣāṃ jināka .

viśāla . arkakä kīrä . śirāve ttāṃgare . aủṣai . karkaṭa-śrigä .
5 sahacara . ysāysä ṣṭe : kąṇḍārya u vāttāka cika | lä u drraucä . puttī
karäjä[9] . śīyi mirimjsya . papalä . halīrai . agnapaṃthä[10] . ttīrä
11 r1 ahauḍä . citrai . nahtta:māla karaṃjä . ā. | lavāya . ṣā' arvāṃ hīya ga'[11]
hīya[11] hamālā . haṃdaṃna khajsā[12] u śilīṣāṃ u jsahera pī hī⟨vī[13]⟩āchai
u gąmä u kamala rrāhä jināka :

2 rrājivṛkṣä u caitrai . māśa'kye[14] . ka | ṇḍārya . ciṃgāṃ ttīrai hīya
perä u pāṭala u ālavāya . gihauṭa u gūluśä' . u madąnä . u pāṭha .
cirāttaikvai[15] . paṭaulä . karaṃja dva . vatsāvīśa' ttī sahanara[16] . ttīttä
3 hī | ya ttīma . aśphąṇḍä ṣā' arvāṃ hīya ga'[17] hamālā . prrimīhä . u
kuṣṭa . u ttavai . bąmä . be . śilīṣāṃ jināka .

4 lodrra dva . śaubarai u paṭkā lodrrä . parapelava . aśaukä | kadalä
bahyä : sālāsä ṣṭe . elavālokä . hama'ysä[18] . rrūnai . kaśmīrye . gūluśä' .
ṣā' arvāṃ hīya ga' hīya hamālā : ṣā' ga' raudrrąda nāma . śilīṣāṃ
5 u jsa | hera pī hīvī āchai hvaiñe[19] . u purāña āchā jiṃdä u kama jiṃdä
u strajāñāka u harbiśe ba'[20] pahaiśā'ka :

11 v1 pāṭha . sauthara spya | kä : lodrrä : samaṃga . viysä khīysarä
mahābuṃjä . saunākä[21] . belä . ṣā' arvāṃ hīya ga' hīya hamālā pahä
aviysārä jiṃdä ||

2 ąmalai . halīrai . pipalä citrai ṣā' | arvāṃ hīya ga'[22] hīya hamālā
śilīṣāmajsāṃ ttavai āstaṃna harbiśāṃ āchāṃ jināka . ni pa'jsä vrriṣa-
ṇīya . ni pa'jsą dai aspaśtāka[23] ||

[1-1] P om. [2] gaṃdha°. [3] hīśaṃ. [4-4] P om.
[5] P śrriṣṭai. [6] P ėlāda. [7] P ā'sye. [8] P be'.
[9] karaṃjä. [10] et P; °maṃthä. [11-11] P om. [12] P khajsāṃ.
[13] P hīvī. [14] P māśä'kye. [15] °ttaihtai. [16] P sahacara.
[17] P ge'. [18] P hame'ysä. [19] P hvęñe. [20] P be'.
[21] P syaunākä. [22] P ge'. [23] aspaśdāka.

daṅ | go-byed daṅ | śveta daṅ | gseṅ-phrom daṅ | jambu daṅ |
sman-gyi sde-ćhan hdi ni mkhris-pa daṅ | khrag lud-pahi nad daṅ |
sloṅ-pa daṅ | myos-pahi nad sel-to || rma daṅ
4 mṅal-gyi nad sel-to || gcin nad sel-źiṅ | rma daṅ lus ćha-ba daṅ |
mṅal-gyi nad sel-to || pipiliṅ daṅ | kru-trug-tres daṅ | śu-dag daṅ |
dug-mo-ñuṅs daṅ | rgya-śug daṅ | badara daṅ | pipiliṅ-gi rća-ba
daṅ | gla-sgaṅ daṅ | bcah-
5 sga daṅ | sug-smel daṅ | bo-ṅa dkar-po daṅ | h̲araṇyeka daṅ |
dbyi-moṅ daṅ | na-le-śam daṅ | la-la-phud daṅ | gabrahi rća-ba
daṅ | murva daṅ | mah̲animbahi hbras-bu daṅ | go-sñod daṅ |
yuṅs-kar daṅ | śiṅ-kun daṅ | pu-će-śel daṅ | byidaṅka
6 daṅ | sman-kyi sde-ćhan hdi ni rluṅ daṅ bad-kan sel-to || sug-smel
daṅ | rgya-spos daṅ | gla-skaṅ daṅ | h̲areṇyaka daṅ | śiṅ rća daṅ
gandh̲apatra daṅ | ćandan dkar-po daṅ | gurkum daṅ | bcah-ba daṅ |
ćandan daṅ | yascala daṅ | nāgapuṣpa
7 daṅ thaṅ śiṅ daṅ | guććha rasa daṅ | gugul daṅ sraći pog daṅ ña
phyi-sa daṅ | radh̲i daṅ | dh̲ya[illegible]a daṅ | pog dkar-po daṅ | byegh̲ranakha
daṅ | stag-gi sder-mo daṅ | spaṅ-spos daṅ | ru-rta daṅ | sman-gyi
sde-ćhan hdi ni | phol-mig daṅ | g-yan-pa
142v1 daṅ | dug daṅ rluṅ daṅ bad-kan sel-to || baruna daṅ | ’artagala
daṅ | ñehu śiṅ daṅ bcah-sga daṅ | go-sñod daṅ | biśanika daṅ |
sahireya daṅ | brih̲atī rnam gñis daṅ | rćva darba daṅ | sputaka daṅ
śigruka daṅ | ’arura daṅ | ’agnamanta daṅ | balba daṅ kru-trug-
2 tres daṅ nagtamala daṅ | sasmorta daṅ | sman-gyi sde-ćhan hdi
ni | khoṅ hbras daṅ | bad-kan daṅ ćhil rgyas-pas nad daṅ | skran
daṅ klad-pa na-ba sel-to || doṅ-ka daṅ | kru-trug-tres daṅ |
śārṃgasta daṅ kaṇḍakari daṅ | nimpa daṅ | patala daṅ | murba daṅ |
gh̲on-
3 ta daṅ | sle-tres daṅ | raṭa daṅ pag-tha daṅ | rća mkhris-pa daṅ |
kulaka daṅ karañja daṅ spyi-bźur śun-pa daṅ | dug-mo-ñuṅ daṅ |
sehireya daṅ | ’uśabī daṅ ba-hgal daṅ | sman-gyi sde-ćhan hdi ni |
gcin nad daṅ | mje daṅ | rims daṅ | skyug-pa daṅ | bad-
4 kan daṅ dug sel-to || gseṅ-phrom rnam gñis daṅ | plaba daṅ
’aśoka daṅ | chu śiṅ daṅ | pala daṅ | ’elabaluka daṅ | kadamba
daṅ | jigini daṅ | śriparṇi daṅ | sle-tres daṅ | sman-gyi sde-ćhan hdi
ni | bad-kan daṅ | ćhil rgyas-pahi nad skems śiṅ | mṅal-
5 gyi nad sel-te | rma hćho-bar byed-la | hkhru-ba gcod dug thams-
cad sel-to || ’ambh̲astha daṅ | dh̲ataki daṅ | gseṅ-phrom daṅ | samaṅga

3 triphalä ṣi' cu halīrai . u vihīlai : u āma|lai viysä[1] ttavai jiṃdä .
tciṃña śirä īdä . dai haṃjsulī primīhä . u kuṣṭä . u ttavaṃdya :
śilīṣāṃ jidä .
4 brihattä . u kaṇḍārya . pāṇa[2] . mahābuṃjä . vatsāvī|śi' ttī . ṣā'
arvāṃ hīya ga' hīya hamālā pajsāka . dūṣāṃ' drrayāṃ karyaustā
jināka ||
5 paṭolą[3] . śī caṃdaṃ . ālavāya . kalyarūhana . pāṭha | gūluśä' . ṣā'
arvāṃ hīya ga' hīya hamālā . ttavaṃdya u śilīṣāṃ u hīśau' bąmą u
ttavai . ā'syāṃ . u be[4] pahaiśā'ka :
12r1 gūluśä' . u ciṃgāṃ ttīrai hīye pirä | hīysimāṃ . mahābāṃjä . śī
caṃdä[5] . ṣā' arvāṃ hīya ga' hīya hamālā . ttarä hīvī āchai u aṃgvā
ttaudā . hīśau' . bąmą : u ttavai harbiśä pīraurākä ||
2 kā|kauṭä kṣīra-kākauṭa mahābāṃjä . karkaṭa-śrigä . meda u mahā-
meda : jīvakä . raṣabakä . pripuṇḍarī : gūra raidä . vrraidä . ttukākä
3 kṣīrä . maudgaparṇä . pvīdā[6] . puṣṭarä . gū|luśä' . ṣā' arvāṃ hīya . ga'
hīya hamālā pa'jsä[7] ttąñāka . pvīdä[8] huṣąñāka . jsīñi bu'ysa padīmāka .
4 dahauśti padīmāka . u huṃjuḍä phāhä u beta ji|nāka
sumana śāriva ṣi' cu sụmaṃ hīya bāva puṣṭarä . uśai'rä . madhuka-
puṣpa . śī caṃdaṃ . u hainai caṃdaṃ . kaśmīrye . mahābāṃjä . ṣā'
5 arvāṃ hīya ga'[9] hīya | hamālā hụñi bamąme hīvī āchai rraysgä vīra
jiṃdä . ttarä hīvī āchai avyaucä ṇa'heje . ttavaṃdyūḍye ttavai mistye
12v1 ttaude hatcañāka . cu aṃgvā pa'jsä ttaudā | tvā jiṃdä .
tciṃña bisā aṃjana . cuvaṃ . priyaṃgä . nāgakyesarä . u padma-
kyesarä mahābāṃjä . ṣā' arvāṃ hīya ga'[10] ⟨hī⟩ya[10] hamālā . hụña
2 bamąme hī|vī āchai u ba'[11] . aṃgāṃ ttaude ṇihejākä .
āra . buhane . halīrai . devadārä[12] . ttāṃgare . privaṣe' . halaidrrä .
3 priśtaparṇä . ysālva . mahābāṃją . vatsāvīśi' ttī . | ṣā' arvāṃ hīya
⟨ga'⟩[13] hamālā vacāda nāma u haraidrrāda āstaṃna . tti dvī ga' .
dūṣāṃ' pajsākye . ahahä[14] aviysārä niṣe'me . tcījsvā bisā āchā vasūji .
4 | mirimjsya . sidalū . ysamye dvī . śā puṣkīja u śā hauṣṭa . aṃgūṣḍä
5 śīlājattä . muḍāsaṃgä . ṣā' arvāṃ hīya ga'[15] hīya hamālā . pī huṣą|
ñąme hīvī āchai jidä sairkhą jsa haṃtsa panīysau u saṃgä cuai
pathīśtä u jiṃdai :
vīravṛkṣä bahyä ṣṭe : agnapaṃthä[16] . hacana bāta vrrikṣā'dänä u

[1] viysaṃ. [2] P pāṭha. [3] P paṭaulä. [4] P be'.
[5] caṃdaṃ. [6] P mārṣaparṇä . ṣvīdā. [7] P om.
[8] ṣv°. [9] P ge'. [10-10] P ge' hīya. [11] P be'.
[12] P detadārä. [13] P ge'. [14] apahä. [15] P ge'.
[16] P °maṃthä.

daṅ | padmahi ze-ba daṅ | śiṅ mṅar daṅ | 'aralu daṅ | bilba daṅ |
sman-gyi sde-ćhan hdi ni | źu-bahi ćhad-pa hkhru-ba
6 sel-to || skyurura daṅ | 'arura daṅ | barura daṅ | pipiliṅ daṅ |
kru-trug-tres daṅ | sman-gyi sde-ćhan hdi ni | bad-kan-gyi rims-kyi
gnod-pa thams-cad sel-te | ro ća-ba daṅ | me-drod śin-tu che-bar
byed | h̲a-caṅ ro ća-bar byed-la | h̲a-caṅ mehi drod che-bar
7 yaṅ mi-byed || hbras-bu gsum źes-bya-ba | 'arura daṅ | barura
daṅ | skyurura rnams ni | rims ldaṅ dub-can sel-źiṅ || mig-la phan-te
drod-pa skyed-la | gcin-nad daṅ | mje daṅ mkhris-pa daṅ | bad-kan
sel-to || brih̲atī daṅ | dh̲ataki daṅ | pāthā daṅ śiṅ
143*r*1 mṅar daṅ | dug-mo-ñuṅ daṅ | sman-gyi sde-ćhan hdi ni | ćhos-par
byed-pa-ste | nad-gźi gsum-las gyur-pahi gcin-nad sel-to || patoli
daṅ ćandan dkar-po daṅ | murba daṅ pu-će-śel daṅ | pātha daṅ
sle-tres daṅ | sman-gyi sde-ćhan
2 hdi ni | mkhris-pa daṅ bad-kan daṅ | yi-ga hchus-pa daṅ | skyug-pa
daṅ rims daṅ | g-yah-ba daṅ dug sel-to || sle-tres daṅ [ni] nimpa
daṅ | hosuhi hbras-bu daṅ | śiṅ mṅar daṅ ćandan dkar-po daṅ |
sman-gyi sde-ćhan hdi ni | skom-pahi nad daṅ |
3 lus ćha-ba daṅ yi-ga hchus-pa daṅ | skyug-pa daṅ rims thams-cad
sel-to || bu-ćhaṅ-rto daṅ | ra-mñe-ba daṅ śiṅ dkar daṅ | bu-bran
śiṅ daṅ meda daṅ | mah̲ame⟨da⟩ daṅ | jibaka daṅ | zad-rći-ba daṅ |
prapuṇḍarīka daṅ | rgun daṅ | raddh̲i daṅ | brih̲atī
4 daṅ | smyig skaṅ daṅ | sah̲a rnam gñis daṅ | payassya daṅ | śug-pa
daṅ sle-tres daṅ | sman gyi sde ćhan hdi ni śin-tu śa skye-ba daṅ | nu-
źo hphel-ba daṅ | ćhe riṅ-ba daṅ ro ća-bar byed-de | khrag lud-pahi
nad daṅ | rluṅ-nad sel-to || thal-tres daṅ śug-
5 pa daṅ | pu-śel-će daṅ madh̲uga daṅ | ćandan rnam gñis daṅ
ti-pal daṅ | śiṅ mṅar daṅ sman-gyi sde-ćhan hdi ni | khrag lud-pahi
nad myur-du sel-źiṅ | skom-pahi nad mi-bzad-pa źi-bar byed-de |
mkhris-pahi rims drag-po hjoms-la | lus śin-tu
6 ćha-ba sel-bar byed-do || mig-sman skyer-khaṇḍa daṅ | rća śyama
daṅ | naga-gesar-gyi ze-ma daṅ | padmahi ze-ba daṅ śiṅ mṅar daṅ |
sman-gyi sde-ćhan hdi ni | khrag lud-pahi nad daṅ | dug daṅ lus
ćha-bahi nad sel-to || śu-dag daṅ gla-sgaṅ daṅ | 'arura daṅ |
7 thaṅ śiṅ daṅ li doṅgra daṅ boṅ-ṅa dkar-po daṅ | yuṅ daṅ kalaśi
daṅ | skyer-ba daṅ | śiṅ mṅar daṅ | dug-mo-ñuṅ daṅ | sman-gyi
sde-ćhan śu-dag-la sogs-pa hdi rnams gñis ni | nad-gźi chos-par
byed-pa daṅ ma-źu-ba hkhru-bar byed-ciṅ | nu-mahi
143*v*1 nad sbyoṅ-ṅo || na-le-śam daṅ | rgyam ćha daṅ | nag-ćhur rnam
gñis daṅ | śiṅ-kun daṅ bag-źun daṅ spaṅs-ma daṅ | sman-gyi sde-
ćhan hdi ni | ćhil rgyas-pahi nad sel-źiṅ | gcin bsdus-pa daṅ | rdehus
hgags-pa sel-to || ra-mñe-ba daṅ | 'agnimanth̲a daṅ | śiṅ

13r1 gīsā bāva . ālavāya śirā | ve . saumarrāśā' . syaunākä . drrāṃgūlye .
vasauka[1] . vasīra[2] . drraubhä sahacara ysāysä mara [3]aśtä[3] . pāṣāṇa-
2 bhedakä . ṣā' arvāṃ hīya ga'[4] hīya hamālą cu bī | lysma na nirąme cu
va sairkhä hame u saṃgä . u bināṃ āchāṃ jināka .
mauṣkakä bahyä ṣi' cu cąṇä . triphalä . madąna . citrai vatsātīśa' ttī
3 sudākä kṣīrä . śīja palāśä . śe pacaḍä | ja[5] : ttyāṃ arvāṃ hīya ga' hīya
hamālā . pī huṣąme hīvī āchai . u arja . u mūtra kaicha . u cvai va
saṃgä haṃbette tvā naṣe'me ||
4 sāläsä . sphaṃdąna bahyä | kālīyakä . śīja . sarrjarasä bu' kīśaukä .
arrjāṃ asąnä . śirīṣä haiśū' . śīśapä . brāṃjä . kharä cikalä . śī caṃdaṃ
5 u hainai caṃdaṃ . kadalä . aśvakarṇä rrūnai | karaṃja dva . buttī
karaṃjä u nahva[6] . mālā karaṃjä . aśvagaṃdha . krriṣṇāgarä . ṣā'
13v1 arvāṃ hīya ga'[7] hīya hamālā . śilīṣāṃ . u ysīḍai āchai u ku | ṣṭä . u
primīhä āchai jiṃdä
spyakä upalä . u kumauda . u ttarū vaiysä . śī viysä . upalä hainai .
māhābuṃjä . ṣā' arvāṃ hīya ⟨ga' hīya⟩[8] hamālā . huñi bamąme hīvī[9] .
2 | u ttarä hīvī āchai u be' . u bąmä[10] jiṃdä :
tralo u śā . hīśaṃ . daujsä . ysīrrä ājsa . ttyāṃ hīya ysā'yä[11] . ṣā'
3 arvāṃ hīya ga'[12] || dūṣāṃ' drrayā jsa hamye līkä | gąmä drrai padya . u
ysīra dūva u ysīḍai u primīhä u haṃbairstä be[13] pahaiśā'ka .
4 surasä . nīro . jaṃbvīrä . kūlīrai . śaṃdyāñä . hīysaṃ[14] . hī | na .
puño . śauve . apaucalīkä[14] . jsokai . makala śāhą haspye[15] . sahamarai .
viṇḍaṃga . haryąsa śąñe . śīyi mīraijsya . drrivattą . kaśmīrye ṣā'
5 a | rvāṃ hīya ga'[16] hīya hamālā . pirąnāṃ hīvī āchai u śilīṣāṃ u phāhä
u hīśau' . u mālaigä u uysna āphārä jiṃdä u virana vasūje ||
14r1 pārūṣä . drrąma ttīma ve | gūra : kaśmīrye . aṃbrä hīyārä . rrājā-
dana . ąmalai . kanaka phalä . ṣā' arvāṃ hīya ga'[17] hīya hamālā . bāta
2 ṇa'hejāka : ysairä biṃdä śirä ṫdä u rīśä' pra | hāje . ttarä hīvī āchai . u
primīhä jidä .
buhane . u pāṭha halaidrrä . ysālva . kalya-uhana[18] . gīrąna ṣvīdā .
3 āra . sūkṣmela . śīyi pravaṣe' . kuṣṭä bhalāttakye . triphalä | māśi'kye .
ṣā' arvām hīya ga'[19] hīya hamālā śilīṣąmajsa āchā jiṃdä u vasūjāka . u
pajsāka : ttījsvā[20] ṣvīdä buḍa padīmāka : purąña bisāṃ āchāṃ
4 pi | rorāka .

[1] P vāśaka. [2] P vatsakä-bījä. [3-3] P ṣṭe. [4] P ge'.
[5] P śīṃja. [6] nahta; P nahtta. [7] P ge'. [8] P ge' hīya.
[9] P hīvī āchai. [10] P bamąme. [11] P yseya.
[12] P ge' hīya hamąlā. [13] P be'. [14-14] P om.
[15] P haskye. [16] P ge'. [17] P ge'. [18] P °rūhana.
[19] P ge'. [20] tcījsvā.

2 ⟨ka⟩śa daṅ brikṣadani daṅ । rćva kuśa daṅ morata daṅ । ñehu śiṅ daṅ lcam-pa daṅ । tuntuka daṅ gze-ma daṅ । basuka daṅ basira daṅ । rćva dh̲ārba daṅ sehiraya daṅ । srusruhi rća-ba daṅ । sman-gyi sde-ćhan hdi ni । gcin rdus-pa daṅ । gcin sri-ba daṅ rdehus hgags-pa
3 daṅ । rluṅ-nad-kyis ñam-thag-pa sel-to ॥ mus-ska daṅ hbras-bu gsum daṅ । śiṅ raṭa daṅ । kru-trug-tres daṅ । sguh̲i daṅ dh̲aba daṅ । palaśa daṅ । śiśapa daṅ sman-gyi sde-ćhan hdi ni । ćhil rgyas-pahi nad daṅ gźaṅ hbrum daṅ । gcin-nad daṅ । rdehus hgags-
4 pa sel-to ॥ śiṅ sala daṅ spandana daṅ kaliya daṅ dh̲aba daṅ । sraći pog-gi śiṅ daṅ । 'arjuna daṅ 'asana daṅ । śiriśa daṅ śiśapa daṅ । stag-pa daṅ । seṅ-ldeṅ daṅ ćandan rnam gñis daṅ । kadala daṅ । bajikarṇa daṅ karañja daṅ । jehu khyed-
5 kyi śiṅ daṅ । 'agaru daṅ । sman-gyi sde-ćhan hdi ni । bad-kan daṅ । skya-rbab daṅ । mje daṅ । gcin-nad sel-to ॥ me-tog 'utpala daṅ । kumuda daṅ । padma daṅ । kalh̲ara daṅ । 'utpala dmar-po daṅ । ru-rta daṅ sman-gyi sde-ćhan hdi ni । khrag lud-pahi nad daṅ
6 s⟨k⟩om-pahi nad daṅ । dug daṅ skyug-pa sel-to ॥ ćhon-mo-steṅ daṅ । zaṅs daṅ । lcags daṅ । ra-ñe daṅ । gser daṅ । dṅul daṅ । de rnams-kyi g-yah daṅ । sman-gyi sde-ćhan hdi ni । nad-gźi gsum-las gyur-bahi s⟨k⟩ran rnam gsum daṅ । sñiṅ na-ba daṅ । skya-rbab na-ba
7 daṅ । gcin-nad daṅ । sbyar-bahi dug sel-to ॥ byehu-rug-pa daṅ । kasamarda daṅ । panitja daṅ । zin-thig-la daṅ । ske-ćhe daṅ । nirgunthi daṅ । surase daṅ । paji daṅ । kolah̲ala daṅ । sugandh̲ika daṅ । jehu-khyab daṅ । kalamala daṅ । biśamuti daṅ । pra-
144r1 ćibila daṅ । byidaṅka daṅ । kaćamaći daṅ । maduka daṅ । muśa-karṇika daṅ । śrībari daṅ । sman-gyi sde-ćhan hdi ni । srin-buhi nad daṅ । bad-kan sel-ciṅ । lud-pa daṅ yi-ga hchus-pa daṅ । cham-pa daṅ । dbugs mi-bde-ba
2 hjoms-te rma sbyoṅ-bar byed-do । paruśaka daṅ । bal-pohi sehu daṅ । rgun daṅ ti-pal daṅ kaśihi hbras-bu daṅ । raja⟨da⟩na daṅ । skyurura daṅ । kaṇḍakarı daṅ । sman-gyi sde-ćhan hdi ni । rluṅ-nad sel-ciṅ sñiṅ-la phan-te । yi-ga hbye-bar byed-la । skom-
3 pahi nad daṅ । gcin-nad rnams sel-to ॥ gla-sgaṅ daṅ । patha daṅ । yuṅ-ba daṅ । skyer-pa daṅ । pu-će-śel daṅ । bya-nu daṅ । śu-dag daṅ । drabini daṅ । bo-ṅa dkar-po daṅ । ru-rta daṅ go-byed daṅ । hbras-bu gsum daṅ । śarṃgastha daṅ । sman-gyi
4 sde-ćhan hdi ni । bad-kan gyi nad sel-te । sbyoṅ-ba daṅ । chos-par

prriyaṃgä . dattä hīya bāta . drrivattä . sudā kṣīrä . śāmyā[1] ttrolä .
gūlūśä' traulä . sättala . ñāna spyakä . ttejava . rājavrrikṣä . lodrrä .
5 kaṃpīlai : | karaṃjä . gīrąna ṣvīdā . ṣā' arvāṃ hīya ⟨ga' hīya⟩[2] hamālā
udāvarte . dūvarä u nāṣṭä ga kaśte . u be[3] . u gąmä jiṃdä ||
14v1 belä agnamaṃthä . syaunākä[4] . kaśmīrye . pā|ṭala . ṣā' arvāṃ
ga'[5] hīya hamālā . paṃcimulä gūrśte mistä . dai haṃjsulyākä . śilīṣā
u beta jinākä .
2 priśnaparṇä . sālaparṇä[6] . īraṃde . brihatta dva . ṣā' arvāṃ hī|ya
ga' hīya hamālā vilakä paṃcimulą gūrśte . tvąñe . bāva . u ttavaṃdya
jiṃdä .
bidārä . sumana śārava . karkaṭa-śrigä . gūlūśä' . ysālva . ṣi' grū-
3 ṣkīnai | hamye paṃcamulä . parīysmä kaśāma u ttavaṃdya u bāta jidä.
haskye . śauve . drrāṃgūlye . sahacara . makala śąhä . khiṃtyau[7]
4 jsa hamye paṃcimulä . | śilīṣāṃ . bāva[8] jiṃdä .
gīsā bāte . hacana bāva . dva drraubha . khaṇauśä' gaysä hīya
5 bāva . ysāysyau hīyāṃ bātyau jsa hamye paṃcimulä . ttavaṃdye u |
mūtri kai⟨cha⟩ āchi jinākä u panīysau vasūjākä .
vījä pīrmāttąmye mą ṣā' piṣkica tta tta tcerai . arvāṃ hīya ṣā' ga'
15r1 hamālā kuṃjsavīnai rrūṃ jsa pajsąma . u gvī'|hä rruṃ jsa pajsāma u
agvā pisalyąma u khāśą'ma ā kāṃ ⟨saṃ⟩ himāve krra nva bvāṣcye
tcerai . arvāṃ jsa kaṣā' padīmāñä jiṣṭä beḍa u kṣasą cāśa utca niśąñä
2 u tcūrä[9] bhāgä | vāthaṃjąñä cu rrūṃ hīye jṣā'ñąme beḍa . tcau
bāga hā kaṣā' niśąñä u śau bāgä rrūṃ . daṃdä jṣą'ñąñä khu ra va rrū
3 ⟨harśtä⟩ : ttī ṣvīdä jsa haṃbirstä hamāte . caṃdä rrū hamāve daṃdä
hā ṣvīdä | niśąña arve hīye kekä beḍą . ttiña rrụña tcuraṃ bhāgä jsa
niśąñä . cu rrūṃ hīvī bhāgä ṣi' drrai bhāga u tcūraṃ hā bhāgä ṣe'
4 hīvī viśtąñä u jṣą'ñąñä daṃdä khu ṣi' cu ṣā' dī|ṣḍa u arvāṃ hīye
kaṣi' le⟨ha⟩ haṃbaḍāre . bvąñä se pahä ||
cu khaśi'-vīya jä u vastäva . ttyāṃ ttyāṃ va hamaṃgä jsāte .
5 pa' jsä strihä ni pajsąte . pa' jsä strehä ni pajsąñä . cu a|gāṃ makṣąme
u ṣi' śirä pajsąñä . cu haysgvā ṣṭä ṣi' ttakye jsa dilakä nvātta pāchai .
tti drrai pacadą ysūnąme jsa u kīrä paryąme jsa u śū'hyąme jsa
habajsya ttä hvata ṣṭe .
15v1 a|rvāṃ u gāṃ' hamāle hīvī piṣkalä śe' ||
ttiña pacīḍa hvaḍāṃ khaṣṭāṃ hīye krre hīya piṣkalä birāśāṃ' .

[1] P śąmā. [2] P ge' hamālā. [3] P be'.
[4] P spyaunäkä. [5] P ge'. [6] P om.
[7] P khęn(*vel* t?)yāṃ. [8] P u bāva. [9] tcūraṃ.

byed-pa daṅ | nu-źo hphel-bar byed-ciṅ | mṅal-gyi nad sel-to ||
śaba daṅ | dandahi rća-ba daṅ | drabanti daṅ | sguḫi daṅ rća śyama
daṅ | sle-tres daṅ śiṅ ñe-roṅ daṅ | bya-rnuhi sa-bon
5 daṅ | śaṃgini daṅ | śas-ste daṅ doṅ-ka daṅ | tilvaka daṅ | kampilaka
daṅ | karañja daṅ bya-rnu daṅ | sman-gyi sde-ćhan hdi ni | rtug-
skam daṅ | dmu-rjiṅ daṅ | lto sbo-ba daṅ | dug daṅ skran sel-to ||
bilba daṅ | 'agnimantha daṅ | tunṭyaka daṅ | śi-
6 riparṇi daṅ | patala daṅ | sman-gyi sde-ćhan hdi ni | rća-ba lṅa-
pa chen-po źes-bya-ste | drod bskyed-ciṅ | bad-kan daṅ rluṅ sel-to ||
priṣṇaparni spir daṅ 'eraṇḍa daṅ | briḫatī rnam gñis daṅ | sman-gyi
sde-ćhan hdi ni | rća-ba lṅa-pa chuṅ-ṅu źes-bya-ste | śa
7 skye-bar byed-ciṅ | rluṅ daṅ mkhris sel-to || bidari daṅ thal-tres
daṅ | ćhagaśrigri daṅ | basadana yuṅ daṅ | hkhri śiṅ-gi rća-ba lṅa-
pa hdi ni | gcin sri-ba daṅ | mkhris-pa daṅ | rluṅ sel-to || gridḫya
daṅ | ḫala daṅ gze-ma daṅ | sehireya daṅ kara-
144*vi* mardika daṅ ćher-mahi rća-ba lṅa-pa hdi ni | bad-kan daṅ rluṅ
sel-to || rćva kuśa daṅ | kaśa rnam gñis daṅ | ⟨dar⟩bḫa daṅ | hdam-bu
daṅ rćvahi rća-ba lṅa-pa hdi ni | mkhris-pa daṅ | gcin sri-ba sel-ciṅ |
chu-so sbyoṅ-ṅo || sman-pa mchog-gis bye-brag phyed-par bya-ste ||
sman-
2 gyi sde-ćhan hdi dag til-mar-gyis bćo-ba daṅ | mar-gyis bco-ba
daṅ | lus bsku-ba daṅ | btuṅ-ba yaṅ ruṅ-ste || cho-ga ji-lta-ba bźin-du
byaho || sman-gyi khu-ba dbyuṅ-źiṅ bskol-ba ni | chu-sman gyi
bcu-drug hgyur-du byas-la | bźi cha gcig lus-par byaho ||
3 sman mar skol-ba ni | sman-gyi khu-ba bźi cha lus-pa de-las mar-
gyi bźi hgyur daṅ | skol-te mar ñe-ce lus-par byaho || ho-ma daṅ
sbyar-ba ni | ho-ma mar daṅ phyed mar bya-ste | ho-ma du-bar
byaho || phye-mahi sman skol-ba ni || sman-gyi phye-ma-las | mar
bźi
4 hgyur-du bya | mar-las kyaṅ | sman-gyi khu-ba bźi hgyur-du
byas-te skol-la | sman-gyi khu-ba du-nas | sman-gyi phye-ma legs-par
hdres-par gyur-na ćhos-pa yin-no || de-la btuṅ-ba daṅ | mas btaṅ-ba
gñis ni hdra-ste | ćhos ran ćam-du byaho || lus
5 bsku-ba ni ćhos rab-tu byaho || sman blugs-pa ni ćhos-pa ñid-du
mi-bya-ste | gsum char yaṅ bćags-nas spyad-par bya-ba hdi ni |
spyihi cho-gar bstan-pa yin-no ||

sman-gyi sde-ćhan-gyi lehu-ste gñis-paho ||

|| kha-zas daṅ | btuṅ-ba ma-

2 anau hvaḍä khaṣṭą satvāṃ juva ni hime . ttye pracaina śirä | u darä hīye piṣkica ttāhirā birāśāṃ'

cu hiṃnā-grūṣkai rrīysu u mistä rrīysu u kalama śālä rrīysu . tti
3 hvara u śūkrrä padīmāka u tcārba u bāta bakä padīme | u saṃnä .

cu ttikyāṃ haṃdrra vya hiṃnā-grūṣkai rīysu . dūṣi' krra hīye ṇa'tcīphe . ttarą hīvī āchai u pī hīvī āchai jiṃda .

cu mistä rrīysu pīrmāttaṃ ṣi' bihī vrriṣaṇī
4 | cu kalama śālä rrīysu ṣi' śilīṣāṃ u ttavaṃdye jinākä cu ṣi'kä rrīysu cu kṣa'ṣṭä haḍā daśde' śī . ttye ysvye hvarä u pvā u garkhä gvaśde drrayi dūṣi' pi'tcīphe .

5 cu ṣi' | rrīysu cu kṣa'ṣṭyā haḍāṃ jsa daśde' cuai kaṃga haryāsa hame . uskātta bise raysa jsa u gvāchą u hauvi jsa dilakä ñaḍa .

16r1 cu bįmīysā ṣi' gaudä padīme u bāta hu.|ṣąñe . śilīṣāṃ u ttavaṃdye jinākä .

cu gau'sä u ėysä[1] u drrąśā ṣi' pā tta tta hvava ṣṭe .

cu rrūsa ṣi' sāḍa u bāta pharāka padīme u saṃnä . ttavaṃdya u
2 śilīṣāṃ | jiṃdä .

cu ganaṃ ṣi' pvā u garkha-gvāchä u hverä . vrriṣaṇī . u beta jinākä .

cu māṃgä ṣi' byaṃjsä u hvarä . u rraysga-gvāchą śilīṣāṃ u ttavaṃdye u hųña āphärä jinākä .

3 cu | skārä māṃgä ṣi' tcārbi u garkhä u grāṃ u nauyvā viranvā rrīma pharāka padīme u vrriṣaṇī . u be pi'rąrākä .

4 cu śī māṃgä ṣe' avrriṣaṇī . śilīṣāṃ u ttavaṃdye jinākä . u | beta padīmākä ||

cu kūlastä ṣi' uysni āphārä u haikye u arrde[2] . u śilīṣä u śūkrrä u beti jinākä .

cu haryāsakä māṃgä ṣi' pvā || drrāṃ ttavai cu hųñą bame tū
5 jaidä |.u styūda padįme .

cu viṇakä[3] gūrmä . ṣi' aviṣaṇī bvąñä . hųña āphärä āchai u śilīṣāṃ u ttavaṃdya tti jiṃdä u bāta padīme ||

16v1 cu nīysva ṣi' sāḍa u hvara nāṣṭä | ga styūdä padīme śilīṣāṃ u ttavaṃdya jiṃdä .

cu salīca . u nīysva 'ti pā hamye raysą jsa bvāñä

cu gurmä cu ttikyāṃ jsa hamaṃgä ṣṭe u bāta haḍi pa'jsa padīme .

2 cu kuṃjsa ṣṭe ttye ysve deläka suce | hīvī u hvarą u grāṃ . hauva u ttavadya huṣa bāye .

[1] ėysaṃ. [2] arrje. [3] ci°.

6 gtogs-par | hgro-ba rnams-kyi hćho-ba gźan med-pahi phyir | dehi phan-gnod-kyi bye-brag des-par bśad-do || de-la hbras salu śun-lpags dmar-po daṅ | salu chen-po daṅ | salu kalama rnams ni m⟨ṅ⟩ar-ba yin-te | khu-chu maṅ-bar byed-pa daṅ | snum-

7 pa daṅ | hphyen chuṅ-źiṅ | phyi-sa ñuṅ-bar byed-do || dehi naṅ-na yaṅ salu śun-lpags dmar-po ni | nad-gźi gsum hjoms-par byed-ciṅ skom-pahi nad daṅ | ćhil rgyas-pahi nad sel-to || salu chen-po mchog-tu ro ća-bar byed-do || salu galama

145r1 ni bad-kan daṅ | mkhris-pa sel-to || hbras źag drug-cus smin-pa dkar-po ni ro mṅar-la bsil-źiṅ lci-ba yin-te | nad-gźi gsum hjoms-par byed-do || hbras źag drug-cus smin-pa śun-lpags nag-po ni | sṅa-ma-las ro daṅ |

2 źu-bahi mthu cuṅ zad ćam-gyis chuṅ-ṅo || khre-rgod ni rćub-pa yin-te | skem-par byed-ciṅ rluṅ bskyed-la | bad-kan daṅ | mkhris-pa sel-to || khre daṅ ci-će daṅ koraduśa rnams kyaṅ de daṅ hdra-bar bśad-do || nas ni bsil-ba yin-te | hphyen cha-źiṅ phyi-sa

3 maṅ-la | mkhris-pa daṅ bad-kan sel-bar phyed-do || gro ni bsil-źiṅ lci-la mṅar-ba yin-te | ro ća-bar byed-pa rluṅ sel-to || || mon-sran-sṅehu ni | bska-źiṅ mṅar-ba yin-te | yaṅ-la bad-kan daṅ mkhris-pa daṅ | khrag-nad sel-

4 to || || mon-sran-grehu ni snum-źiṅ lci-la drod che-ste | hjag sgo dguhi dri-ma maṅ-ba daṅ | ro ća-bar byed-ciṅ rluṅ sel-to || mon-sran dkar-po ni | ro ća-bar mi-byed-ciṅ | bad-kan daṅ | mkhris-pa sel-la | rluṅ-gis ñam-thag-par byed-do ||

5 || rgya-sran ni dbugs mi-bde-ba daṅ | skyigs-bu daṅ | gźaṅ hbrum daṅ | bad-kan daṅ | khu-chu daṅ rluṅ sel-lo || mon-sran na-gu ni | bsil-ba yin-te | khrag lud-pahi rims sel-źiṅ | phyi-sa hgags-par byed-do || mon-sran caru ni | ñal-po bźan-par

6 byed-ciṅ khrag-gi nad daṅ | bad-kan daṅ | mkhris-pa sel-la | rluṅ bskyed-par byed-do || sran-chuṅ ni bsil-źiṅ ro mṅar-te | phyi-sa hgag-par byed-ciṅ | bad-kan nad | mkhris-pa sel-to || sran-chuṅ ni sran-cuṅ daṅ hdra-bar bśad-do || sran yaṅ de daṅ

7 hdra-ba-las | lẖag-par rluṅ bskyed-par byed-do || til ni thal-bahi ro bro-ba daṅ | mṅar-źiṅ kha-la drod che-ste | ñam-stobs daṅ |

cu saṃbīraustä buśuña pacaḍa jsāra īde tte pvāta u lokṣa' hauva
pāraṃgä padīmāka .
veña ttā guśti hīya peṣkeci uysdīśa .
3 | buysīña guśta . ni bihī pvāta . ci pa'jsä garkha-gvācha . ne pa'jsą̈
tcārba u duṣe' ni padīme u nitcīphą :
cu mi'ña guśta . ṣi' hvara u pvāta u garkha-gvācha u ga' straj-
4 ą̄ñāka u tvą̄ñā|ka
cu mahairṣą' hīya guśta ṣe' tcārba u garkha u hunä padīme u
śukrrą padīme u tvāñāka .
5 cu pā'śa guśta ṣe' garkha . vrreṣaṇīya . beva jenā|ka u ⟨ā⟩has-
āñāka .
cu sahaicä hīya guśta ṣe' dai hajsulī u śelīṣā u ttavaṃdya jedä .
17r1 bāta jiṃdä ū ni padīme . ṣi' : || | ni tta bisā ṣṭe
cu āskä hīya gūśta . ṣi' pvāva ṣṭe . drrayāṃ dūṣā' niṣę'māka u
saṃnä u bīysma strajākä :
2 cu murāsä hī⟨ya⟩ gūsca ṣi' beta jināka u gvaña räysga padīme | u
tciña rrijsai u cha śirka u bijāṣä jiṣä jihą u śūkrrä pharākä padīme :
cu krriṃgä hīya gūśta ṣi' tcārba u garkha u grą̄ma ṣṭe . bāta
jiṃdä vrriṣaṇīya ||
3 cu ttarä hīya gūsta : ṣi' ni | pa'jsä garkha-gvācha u[u] ni . bihī
grāma ni pa'jsä hvara . dūṣa' haḍi harbiśä jidä .
⟨cu⟩ ą̄ṇaka u khaukeja u baḍye hīya gūśta dai hajsulyākye saṃ-
dvęnā ācha jinākye :
4 cu | biṃji hīya gūśta ṣe' sadvinä āchai jināka śilīṣā u śukrrä
huṣą̄ñāka ||
cu ysara hīya gūśta . pvāva ṣṭe u rraysga śilīṣāṃ u huña bamāme
hīvī āchai jiṃdä ||
5 | cu gīri bisai aṣṇai hīya gūśta ṣi' pvāta u garkha hụñä bamāeme[1]
hīvī āc̣hai jiṃdä :
⟨cu⟩ āṣai aṣṇai u kaurakä hīya gūśta ṣi' dilaka rraysga-gvāche ||
17v1 cu āci hīya | gūśta ṣe' dilaka raysga-gvāche .
cu āci hī⟨ya⟩ guśta ṣe' tcārba u grą̄ma u garkha . vrreṣaṇīya u beta
u ttavaṃdye jenāka . ttekyāṃ haṃdrre vya sya pa' vrriṣaṇīya tti-
2 merāṃ u | beta jenāka
cu kavīñe guśta ṣe' tcārba u garkha-gvācha . beta jenāka u rahna-[2]
pettä padīmāka .

[1] bamāme. [2] rahta.

mkhris-pa bskyed-do | spyir-na gaṅ-bu-can sna-ćhogs rnams ni |
bsil-źiṅ rćub-pa yin-te | ñam-stobs hbri-bar byed-do || da ni śahi
145 *v*1 bye-brag bśad-de | ra-śa ni h̲a-caṅ bsil-ba yaṅ ma-yin | h̲a-caṅ
lci-ba yaṅ ma-yin | h̲a-caṅ snum-pa yaṅ mi-yin-te | nad-gźi bskyed-
par mi-byed-ciṅ sel-bar byed-do || lug-śa ni mṅar-źiṅ bsil-la | lci-ba
yin-te | phyi-sa hgag-pa daṅ | śa skye-bar byed-do || mah̲ehi śa ni
2 snum-źiṅ lci-ba yin-te | ñid hoṅ-bar byed-la | khu-chu maṅ-bar
byed-ciṅ | śa skye-bar byed-do || phag-śa ni lci-ba yin-te | ro ća-bar
byed-ciṅ rluṅ sel-la | rṅul sñi-bar byed-do || ri-boṅ-gi śa ni me-drod
bskyed-ciṅ | bad-kan daṅ mkhris-pa sel-la | rluṅ ni bskyed brir mi-
3 byed-de tha-mal-paho || khar go-śol-gyi śa ni bsil-ba yin-te |
nad-gźi gsum sel-źiṅ | phyi-sa daṅ gcin sri-bar byed-do || rma-
byahi śa ni rluṅ sel-źiṅ | rna-ba gsaṅ-ba daṅ | mig rno-ba daṅ | śa-
mdog bzaṅ-ba daṅ | skad sñan-pa daṅ | khu-chu hphel-bar byed-do ||
bya-
4 gag-gi śa ni | snum-źiṅ lci-la drod che-ba yin-te | rluṅ sel-ciṅ ro
ća-bar byed-do || sreg-pahi śa ni | h̲a-caṅ lci-ba yaṅ ma-yin | h̲a-
caṅ drod che-ba yaṅ ma-yin | h̲a-caṅ mṅar-ba yaṅ ma-yin-te | nad-
gźi thams-cad sel-to || hur-pa daṅ | co-ga daṅ | bartaka rnams-
5 kyi śa ni | drod bskyed-ciṅ hdus-pahi nad sel-to || mchil-pahi śa
ni | hdus-pahi nad sel-ciṅ | bad-kan daṅ | khu-chu hphel-bar byed-
do || goṅ-ma sreg-gi śa ni bsil-źiṅ yaṅ-ba yin-te | bad-kan daṅ |
khrag lud-pahi nad sel-to || phug-ron-gyi śa ni
6 bsil-źiṅ lci-ba yin-te | khrag lud-pahi nad sel-to || phug-ron
sṅon-po daṅ | thi-bahi śa ni de-las cuṅ zad ćam-gyis yaṅ-ṅo || chu-
bya rnams-kyi śa ni | snum źiṅ drod che-la lci-ba yin-te | ro ća-bar
byed-ciṅ rluṅ sel-to || de-dag-gi naṅ-na | bya ṅaṅ-pahi śa
7 ni ro ća-bar byed-ciṅ | śas-cher rluṅ sel-to || ña-śa ni snum-la
drod che-źiṅ | lci-ba yin-te | rluṅ sel-ciṅ mkhris-pahi nad daṅ |

cu uce ⟨bi⟩sā kurmä . karkaṭą āstaṃna ttyā hī⟨ya⟩ guśta ṣe' bāta u
3 ttavaṃdya jināka . u vrreṣa|ṇīya .

viña ttā hvāṣāṃ pūharāṃ hīya piṣkeca hvīde .

haryāsa śą̄ñe hvāṣa drrayi duṣe' jiṃdä .
kharaṃbette ttījsāṃ[1] ṣvīdä huṣāñāre . vrreṣaṇīya .
4 cukurīkīji śilīṣā | u bāta jinīdä .
śaśvānīje hvāṣe . harbiśą dūṣi' na jinīdä .
bāstulai . sārme . tcādare . palaigä . hiṃja mījidä . tti bure tcāve
5 bāte śelīṣā jinīdä . saṃnä | hargä padīmāre cu huñä bame tte āchā
niśti herą̄ña vīra bāyīdä .
18r1 ttrehe tte hāma ṣṭāna duṣe' huṣa bāyīdä . pahe ṣṭāna bāta ū . |
śilīṣāṃ jinīdä . cu vilakyi paha līkyi hetri[2] harbiśi dūṣi' jinīṃdä
ysirä u garśa vasūjākye
2 kākauṭīṃji . u vāttāka . u paṭaulīṃja . u makala śāhīṃjä . tti bure |
kuṣṭä u primīhä u ttavai . uysna āphārä . phāhä ttavaṃdya śilīṣāṃ
jinākye .
maṃgiṇdä ṣe' harbiśä dūṣi' jiṃdä . ysirä vī śirä īṃdä . phiysgāṃ
vasūjākä .
3 lā trūysāṃ hiyāra . alhoḍa . ttavaṃdye jināka . beta padīmāka .
trūysa u byāra tti bāta u śilīṣāṃ padīmāre u ttavaṃdya jinīṃdä .
4 īrhve . u śirāve . u ysba hīvī nauhä cījau . tti buri tta|vadye u
śilīṣāṃ jinīdä .
viysä hīya bāta u viysa ttīma . u khoje . u murau u aśe . tti buri
5 garkha-gvācha u pvāva . huñi bamąme hīvī āchai jinīdä . vrriṣaṇī|ya .
tcījsvā ṣvīdä vasūjidä .

viña ttā hiyārāṃ hīya piṣkici birāśāṃ' .

drrāmä ttīma . ṣi' saṃnä haṃbīṭhe u bāta jiṃdä śilīṣāṃ u ttavaṃdye jsa aviysa paṣṭe .
18v1 cu ą̄malai | ṣi' pā tta tta khiṇḍī . khvai hvaḍą īdä . hvarä raysä jsa
duṣe' jedä . vrriṣaṇī .
haṃga . ṣe' gą̄'mä u bāta u śilīṣā u ūysna āphārä . phāhä jenākä .
2 kapaittą hīvī hīyārą dīṣṭä | ṣi' ni garkhä . ga haṃbīṭhe . u dūṣe' u bi
jiṃdä .
cu aṃbrrä hīyārä . ṣi' beti ṇehejākä u tvą̄ñe u ⟨śu⟩krrä huṣāñe
guśta u cha u hauta ysyą̄ñe .
3 jaṃbrą hīyārą ṣe' beta padīmą̄|ką śelīṣā u ttavaṃdye jenākä u ga
styada[3] padīme heysgīyā padīme .

[1] tcījsāṃ. [2] trehi. [3] styūda.

khrag lus-pahi nad bskyed-do || chuhi srog-chags buluki daṅ | rus-
sbal daṅ | karkaṭa rnams-kyi śa ni rluṅ daṅ | mkhris-pa sel-
146r1 źiṅ | ro ća-bar byed-do || || da ni ldum daṅ sṅod-kyi bye-brag
bśad-de | ldum kakamaći ni | nad-gźi gsum sel-to || kalama ni
nu-źo hphel-ba daṅ | ro ća-bar byed-do || ćigeri ni bad-kan daṅ |
rluṅ sel-to || yuṅs-kar-gyi lo-mas ni
2 nad-gźi thams-cad bskyed-do || rgya-snehu daṅ | snehu chulli
daṅ | snehu-rgod daṅ | mon-snehu dmar-ru daṅ | hdi-rnams ni
rluṅ daṅ | bad-kan sel-źiṅ | phyi-sa bde-bar hbyuṅ-ba daṅ | khrag
lud-pahi nad med-par byed-do || la-phug rjen-pa ni nad-gźi bskyed-
3 par byed-do || bćos-pa ni rluṅ daṅ | bad-kan sel-to || la-phug
gźon-nu ni nad-gźi thams-cad sel-źiṅ | sñiṅ daṅ lkog-ma-la phan-
no || karkaṭaka daṅ | bārtaka daṅ | patola daṅ | karbelaka daṅ | hdi-
rnams ni | mje daṅ gcin-nad daṅ | dbugs mi-
4 bde-ba daṅ | lud-pa daṅ | mkhris-pa daṅ | bad-kan sel-to ||
kuśmamaḍa ni | nad-gźi thams-cad sel-źiṅ | sñiṅ-la phan-te chu-so
sbyoṅ-ṅo || kaliṅkahi hbras-bu daṅ | ku-ba ni mkhris-pa sel- źiṅ |
rluṅ bskyed-do || gru-sa daṅ | ga-gon ni | rluṅ daṅ |
5 bad-kan bskyed-la | mkhris-pa sel-to || smyig-mdehu daṅ | ñehu
śiṅ daṅ spahi to-rto daṅ | kebuka daṅ | hdi-rnams ni bad-kan daṅ |
mkhris-pa sel-to || padmahi rća-ba daṅ | śāluka daṅ | śriṃkāṭa daṅ |
maluka daṅ | kaśeruka daṅ | hdi-rnams
6 ni lci-źiṅ bsil-te | khrag lud-pahi nad sel-źiṅ | ro ća-ba daṅ | nu-
źo hphel-bar byed-do || || da ni śiṅ-tog-gi bye-brag bśad-de | bal-po
sehu ni phyi-sa sri-bar byed-ciṅ | hkhru-ba gcod | rluṅ sel-la | bad-
kan daṅ mkhris-pa daṅ yaṅ
7 mi-hphrod-pa ma-yin-no || skyurura ni de daṅ hdra-ba-las | zos-
pahi rjes-la ro mnar-bar hgyur-źiṅ | nad-gźi hjig pa daṅ hkhru ba
daṅ | ro ća-bar byed-do || kha-luṅ ni skran daṅ | rluṅ daṅ bad-kan
daṅ | dbugs mi bde-ba daṅ | lud-pa rnams sel-to ||
146v1 kabitthahi śiṅ-tog smin-pa ni | lci-ba yin-te | phyi-sa sri-bar
byed-ciṅ | nad-gźi daṅ | dug sel-to || śiṅ-tog ’amra ni rluṅ sel-źiṅ | śa
skye-ba daṅ | khu-chu hphel-ba daṅ | śa-mdog bzaṅ-ba daṅ | ñams-
stobs skye-bar byed-do || jambuhi śiṅ-tog ni | rluṅ

ttemdūką hīyārä śilīṣā u ttavaṃdye jenākä .
4 baraśīji hīvī hīyārä bāta | u ttavaṃdya jidä .
belä hīvī hīyārä bāta padīme nāṣṭä ga bañe .
pelāyālä hīyārä ṣe' beti jinākä .
5 cu ttālä hīyārä u rājādhąnä | u gechane . u banāte u nālakera hīyāra tte hvara u tcārbe u garkha-gvācha śukrrä u guśte padīmāka .
19r1 gura u madhukä u khajū|rā u kaśmīrye u pārūṣā . tti bura hīyāra bāta ttavaṃdya . hųñe āphārä jsa āchā jenīdä saṃnä nvaśtä naṣphaśdākä .
śama nāma hīyāra tti tcaṃjsä haṃtrāñāre .
2 kauśāṃttaka | u abrra u banāte u daṃda śaṭha u makala śāhą hīvī hīyārä tti bure . hųña bamąme hīvī āchai padīmāka bvāñą .
pīlu hīyārä . gąmä jināką .
3 viña ttā khāśi' bisā arvā | hīya niṣkeca uysdīśāṃ
ttuṃgare . mirijsya pipalą . śilīṣā u beta jenāka .
cu mīrimjsya ṣe' kūri vanvāñe .
ttāṃgarä u pipalä tti dva pa'jsä aspaśdā'ka .
4 aṃguṣḍä . gā'|mä u jsahera vīne u cu nāṣṭä ga baitte ttu prahāje . bāta śilīṣā pahaiśe' .
cu sānā u hīysemāṃ u aūṣai . ṣi' bāti ṣilīṣā jenāme va pīrmāttaṃ .
5 veña | ttā namvā hīya ni⟨ṣke⟩ci uysdīśāṃ .
sidalūṃ ṣe' tciña śirä īdä u vrriṣaṇī . drrayā dūṣā' niṣe'mākä ṣṭe .
spaju ṣe' grāṃ cu basta ga hamāte . u yserä bidä vīna tvā jiṃdä
19v1 | bidalūṃ ṣi' grąma u rriscya . ysairä bidä vīna jedä u bāta nva nį'ma'ysä veśte .
cu rrājā namva ṣe pātcä tta tta khendya . dilakai hauta ñaḍara .
2 cu ūcā nimva | . ṣi' garkha-gvācha u khāysä gvāchāka .
cu yava-kṣārä ṣe' ysairä bidą vīna u ysīḍai āchai u garśa bisāṃ āchāṃ jenākä u dai haṃjsulyākä
3 svarrjeka kṣā|rä . ṣe' strehą ṣṭe rrejsai cu aṃgvā ttaudā padīme u ttaraṃdarū dai strehą bāye . kaṃga padaśdą'.
veña ttā khaśā' hīya piṣkici birāśāṃ
4 cu bārä hī|ya utca ṣi' raysgą . dūṣe' jiṃdä ysairą biṃdą śirą īṃdä u bi jināka .
cu bārą hīya utca . cirąminai bhājaṃ vīra pārautta u hva piṣkette .
5 u ttekye ttekye hī|vī raysä u hauva pātcą hva hva biysaśte .
cu tsūmaṃce utca ṣe' lokṣa' u bāti huṣāñe .

2 skye-bar byed-la | bad-kan daṅ mkhris-pa sel-te | phyi-sa sri-źiṅ sbo-bar byed-do || tindukahi hbras-bu ni | bad-kan daṅ mkhris-pa sel-to || rgya-śug-gi śiṅ-tog ni | rluṅ daṅ mkhris-pa sel-to || bilbahi śiṅ-tog ni | rluṅ bskyed-ciṅ thur-du mi-hbyuṅ-bar

3 byed-do || piyalahi śiṅ-tog ni rluṅ sel-to || śiṅ tala daṅ | rājādana daṅ | chu-śiṅ-gi hbras-bu daṅ | panasa daṅ | nalikera rnams-kyi śiṅ-tog ni | mṅar-źiṅ snum-la lci-ba yin-te | khu-chu daṅ śa skye-bar byed-do || rgun daṅ | madhuka daṅ | bra-

4 go daṅ | tri-bal daṅ | paruśaka daṅ | hdi-rnams-kyi hbras-bu ni | rluṅ daṅ mkhris-pa daṅ | khrag-gi nad sel-la | phyi-sa bde-bar hbyuṅ-bar byed-do || śamihi śiṅ-tog-gis skra hbyi-bar byed-do || kośamamra daṅ | ñoti daṅ | dantaśatha daṅ | karmarda

5 daṅ | śiṅ-tog hdi-rnams ni | khrag lud-pahi nad bskyed-par śes-par byaho || piluhi śiṅ-tog ni skran sel-to || || da ni spod-kyi bye-brag bśad-de | bcah-sga daṅ | na-le-śam daṅ | pipiliṅ ni bad-kan daṅ rluṅ sel-to || de-la na-le-śam

6 ni ro ća-bar mi-byed-do || bcah-sga daṅ pipiliṅ gñis ro ća-bar byed-do || śiṅ-kun ni | skran-nad gzer-ba daṅ | phyi-sa hgags-pa sel-ciṅ | rluṅ daṅ bad-kan hjoms-par byed-do || la-la-phud daṅ | hosuhi hbras-bu daṅ | go-sñod ni rluṅ daṅ | bad-kan

7 sel-bahi mchog yin-no || || da ni lan-rćvahi bye-brag bśad-de | rgyam-ćha ni mig-la phan-źiṅ ro ća-bar byed-la | nad-gźi gsum źi-bar byed-do || kharu-ćha ni drod che-ste | phyi-sa hgags-pa daṅ | sñiṅ na-ba sel-to || ćabs-ru-ćha ni drod che-źiṅ

147*r*1 rno-ba yin-te | sñiṅ na-ba sel-źiṅ | rluṅ daṅ hphrod-do || ćha kha-ra ni | de daṅ hdra-ba-las cuṅ zad ćam-gyis mthu chuṅ-ṅo || rgya-mćhohi lan-ćhva ni lci-ba yin-te | kha-zas hdrul-bar byed-do || nas ćhig hkhus-pahi thal-ba ni | dug daṅ |

2 sñiṅ na-ba daṅ | skya-rbab daṅ | lkog-mahi nad sel-ciṅ | mehi drod-pa skyed-do || spacikahi thal-ba ni | rno-ba yin-te | lus ćha-bar byed-ciṅ | khoṅ-bahi drod bskyed-la | pags-pa hjig-par byed-do || || da ni btuṅ-bahi bye-brag bśad-de | char-

3 pahi chu ni yaṅ-ba yin-te | nad-gźi sel-źiṅ sñiṅ-la phan-te | dug sel-to || char-pahi chu sa-gźi daṅ | snod sna-ćhogs tha-dad-pa daṅ | phrad-pa-las ni | dehi rehi bye-brag daṅ | mthu yaṅ tha-dad-par hgyur-ro || hbab-chu ni rćub-pa yin-te rluṅ bskyed-do |

4 mćhohi chu ni mṅar-la yaṅ-ṅo || rjiṅ-buhi chu ni rluṅ daṅ bad-kan sel-to || lteṅ-kahi chu ni rluṅ bskyed-do || chu-mig-gi chu ni

cu āṣeṃjā ūtca ṣi' hvara u rraysga-gvācha :
20r1 cu vilysāṃjvā bisā utca ṣi' bāta u śilīṣāṃ jiṃdä
u tcātakvā bisā utca bāta padīme .
cu guryā ūtca ṣe' lokṣa' u ttaraṃdaru dai padīme .
2 cu garą beṃdä āna nāṣṭä vahaiysana utca | ṣe' raysga-⟨gvā⟩cha u
śelīṣā jināka .
cu gachā utca ṣe' dai haṃjsulyāka . u bāta byehaṃje .
cu gīmā ūtca ṣe' tavadye jenāka . cu āyauṣṭa u pīrūḍa ā va hvāṣā
3 jsa bijautta ṣe' ni | ysūṣṭa . ni khāśā'ñä . cu hā pā urmaysdāṃ bā'yä
ni hīsīṃdä ṣe' ni asthajāñä . vina ttikye cuai va gaṃjsa ni heme ṣe'
asthająñä .
4 khu utca' jṣāñīdä ttavai u uysna āphārä | pī hīvī āchai . ū bāta
śilīṣā jināka . śuma jeṣṭa aysdauda . ṣe' drraya duṣe' jeṃdä . tti śā
ṣava trvāyīye . ttī duṣä' padīme .
5 veña ttā ṣvīdą hīya pi|ṣkeca birāśā' .
cu gvīhä ṣvīdą ṣe' tcārbą u garkha-gvāchä u bāta u ttavaṃdya
jidä ⟨dā⟩ra-jsīna padīme .
cu mahairṣī'ñä ṣvīdä ṣe' gvīhä ṣvīdä jsa dilakä garkha nvārerä .
20v1 | u tcārbä ttaraṃdarū dai jinākä .
cu buysīñä ṣvīdą ṣe' hụñīnę aviysārą jinākä . u phāhä . u naṣṭausai
2 u ttavai pahaiśā'ką . vāśerū biṃdą bijsāñä u vāśerụną jsa | jīye .
cu miñą ṣvīdą ṣe' ttavaṃdya u śilīṣā byihaṃje .
cu ulīñä ṣvīdą ṣe' haśä u duvarä u āvāhä[1] u pirąnā u arrje . u
śilīṣā u bāva ṇiheje .
3 cu hvī ṣvīdä | ṣi' tciña śirä īdä u tcemañāṃ vasūjākä khvai tceña
paśīṃde : ā vā haysgvā . huñe bamąme hīvī āchai jeṃdä .
4 cu ñye ṣe' hauve padīme u bāve jidä . u | vrreṣaṇī ttavaṃdya u
śilīṣā padīme
amāstą ñye . drraye duṣe' padīme
cu ñyetutcą ṣe' srrauvāṃ vasūjākä .
5 cu nīyakä ṣe' jsahera vīne u arrja u pakṣāhakattą | cvai kurä gesārä
hame ttu jedä .
cu ṣvīdä haṃdarye paryāyä jsa . phrrūmä churba vī bure . tte
garkha-gvācha . kuṣṭä āchai aspaśde'
beśī māstą draya duṣe' jiṃdä .

* * * * *

[1] ānāhä.

rćub-pa yin-te | mehi drod bskyed-do || brag-mthon-pahi kha-nas
bab-pahi chu ni yaṅ źiṅ bad-kan sel-to || khron-pahi chu ni drod
che-
5 bar byed-ciṅ | rluṅ bskyed-do || chu-mig hphar-bahi chu ni
mkhris-pa sel-to || chu sñog-ciṅ srin-bu daṅ | ña cig yod-de | ma-
ruṅ-bar gyur-ciṅ | ñi-ma mi-mthoṅ-bahi chu ni blaṅ-bar mi-
byaho || skyon de-dag med-pahi chu ni blaṅ-bar byaho || chu skol-ba
ni rims
6 daṅ | dbugs mi-bde-ba daṅ | ćhil rgyas-pahi nad daṅ | rluṅ daṅ |
bad-kan sel-to || chu skol-te bsgraṅs-pas ni nad-gźi gsum sel-lo ||
de ñid źag lon-par byas-na nad-gźi bskyed-par byed-do || || da ni
ho-mahi bye-brag bśad-de
7 bahi ho-ma ni snum-źiṅ lci-ba yin-te | rluṅ daṅ mkhris-pa sel-źiṅ
ćhe riṅ-bar byed-do || maẖehi ho-ma ni bahi ho-ma-bas lci-źiṅ
snum-pa yin-te bye-brag-tu drod hbri-bar byed-do || rahi ho-mas
ni khrag-ćhad sel-źiṅ | lud-pa daṅ | sk⟨e⟩m-pa daṅ | rims
147v1 med-par byed-la | dreg na-bahi steṅ-du blugs-na dreg med-par
hgyur-ro || lug-gi ho-mas ni mkhris-pa daṅ | bad-kan bskyed-do ||
rṅa-mohi ho-mas ni skraṅ-ba daṅ | dmu-rjiṅ daṅ | lto sbo-ba daṅ |
srin-bu daṅ | gźaṅ-hbrum daṅ | bad-kan daṅ | rluṅ sel-to || bud-
2 med-kyi ho-mas ni lci-la phan-pa daṅ | mig-tu glugs-na mig-la
phan-pa daṅ | snar blud-na khrag lud-pahi nad sel-to || źo ni ñams-
stobs bskyed-ciṅ rluṅ sel-te | ro ća-bar byed-la | mkhris-pa daṅ |
bad-kan bskyed-do || źo ma-laṅs-pa nad-gźi gsum
3 bskyed-do || źo kha-chu ni hjag sgo sbyoṅ-bar byed-do || mar ni
pho-bahi nad daṅ gźaṅ-hbrum daṅ | bźin g-yo-ba daṅ | mjiṅ-pa yo-
bahi nad sel-to || ho-ma-las sna gźan-du bskyur-ba | phyur-ba-la
sogs-pa ni lci-ba yin-te | mje-nad-kyi rgyur hgyur-ro || dar-
4 bahi ho-ma ni nad-gźi gsum sel-źiṅ | pho-bahi nad daṅ skraṅ-ba
daṅ | gźaṅ-hbrum daṅ | skya-rbab daṅ | hkhru-ba daṅ | skran hjoms-
par byed-do ||

* * * * *

100r1 I cu ṣpaijai āchanai ṣā'vī arva . phaṃñā garṣva . ū bāṇā ṣavarą . aṣṇūha . puṣṭąrāna . hauṣkārä hāmai : tta arve noką ārąñą hamagye .
2 gvīhą rrūna u I ysauyąña mauna paherąña u pęṇḍai padīmąñä ttīvī beṃda sadalūṃ parkūnāñä ṣpaijai biṃdä bañąñä jatte II

3 cu khaiya hame ṣā'vī arva . āra . huraṣṭa . aùlṣai . bāvattī . ysīḍā spye ysaraṃjsa . kuṃjsa . kharaśpe . kūṃjsavīnai rrū ṣi' khaiya vaska peṇḍai :

khu hvaṃḍye jsahera ttauda sāḍa gūysma bāta hame . dvyā
4 kve'ysvā vī avyauca I vīna himāre ttīvai jsāṃ aha ācheja hame u jare ṣā'vai krrya . drrāṃgūlya bāva : aiśca bāva . sacha bāva . haryāsa sacha bāva . dajūna sacha bāva . laṃgara bāva . mahāḅāṃją . tta
5 alrve paṃjsa paṃjsa sera jehąñą haysñąñą hāña tcerai pajsa bāga vasva . tta arve hā nīśąñą . daṃdä jṣe'ñąñä khu ra va śau ṣaṃgą harśtą . ṣi' raysą thaṃjąñä u ysūnąñä .

100v1 khu pe'sauśtą paskyāṣṭą hā tcerai hallīrai . vihīlai . āmalai hīṃdvāṃgą ttuṃgara tta tcahora hālai hālai serą papalä drai mācāṃgye . mīrejsya śā mācāṃga kaśmīrye paṃjsa . pārūṣā daso . dūma-hauṣṭa gūra śā gauśtą . tta arve naukąārāñą . ttaña hā I
2 kaṣą'ña śau śiṃgą gvīhą: rrūṃ tcerai . u śau śegą kuṃjsavīnai . tta arve vimathąñą ṣa' rrū nvā daina pāchai daṃdą jṣe'ñąñą khū rrūṃ hīye pāchą vī hīśtą samāṃ vahaiśą'ñą

3 khu ysve hameta āną hā dasau śakara I kūṭāñä u śo serą golä u śau serą mākṣī' khu ṣa' rrūṃ haṃbairstą hame pape'śā' drrai prūyą khāśą'ñą co śvī cauhna ttai uskālta bīsā āchā jāre . dājsaṃdai hīya
4 ttīma āra tceñą sumaṃ ttye jsa piṇḍai I padīmāñą āstya bisā vīna jidą gai'sanai hai jṣe'ñą'ñą ttye jsa piṇḍai padīmąña āstya bisā vīna jidä .

kāṃjsa kāṃbā tciña sumaṃ āra sadalūṃ koṣṭą gąnā pattoda
5 mījsāka ysaṃbaste bejūha aṣṇūha mulaṣkīña' ttīrą ñe salma-bhāga hamaṃgą vīśtąña u naukąkūṭąñą ṣa' vīna ca ttorąna yaṃde āstya bisā ttraikṣa vīna jidą :

bā . kāṃjsa . hatsa kūṭāñą hvī ṣvīdąna 'peṇḍai padīmąñą phorą biṃdą bañąñą ṇaheje .

biji kūṭąñą ṣkūṭa sapala naṣphaśtąñą anvaśtą vīnaustą phorą bidą bañąñą vīna jidą

[Khotanese Texts I 101: the original text of this folio, in spite of intensive search, has not yet been found.]

101 *r*1 | . rū[1] krriṃga-rūvai nirąme . bīysmai pi'hīśtä . ttyāṃ āchā jiṃdä .
kalyarūhanāda ga' diśamūlä cu uskātta hva dvyāṃ āṃ śau kāṃ
2 saṃ hamāte . madanaphalą . | mahābuṃjä . bāvattī kuṣṭä gaṃdha-
prriyaṃgä . buhane . sidalūṃ āstaṃna cuṇya . ttavaṃdya u beta jsa
hamya āchāṃ hīvī pacaḍä spāśąñä ||
3 gvī'ha: rruṃ ā vā kuṃjsavīnai rruṃ dvyā āna śau kāṃ va | śau
haṃbusaṃ ṣṭāte śe jsa ṣvīdä u ūci jsa jṣą'ñąñä khu ri va rruṃ harśtä
ttye jsa anavāysina tcerai striha ||
4 khu arja vinosti hame u hunai vā nirąmī . hųñi bamąme hīvī ā | chai
hīya krra cu ttā thyątta hvata tcerai vī āsñi arvāṃ hvaḍāṃ khaṣṭāṃ
āstaṃna . ttīrāṃ rriysāṃ jsa . haṃbairsta ṣṭāna hverai . dai vai
5 pattīśtä . u dūṣai' jsāṃ pachāre . huṃjuḍa arrja hīya . pajsā | kyāṃ
arve ||
ūśī'rä . nigapaträ[2] . ysālve hīya grūṣkyi āstaṃna haṃtsi jṣą'ñąñä .
kaṣā' uysdimąñä ā vā pātcä . tuṃgara śī caṃdaṃ . cirāttaihtai .
101 *v*1 dūrālabha āstaṃna jṣą'ñąñä u kaṣā' u | ysdaimąñä u khīṣṭi haurą⟨ñä⟩ :
pātcä hauṣka arji hīvī āchai vī hųñä niṣe'māka ||
cigāṃ ttīrai hīya grūṣka u vitsāviśi' ttīṃ cuvaṃ : privaṣi' āstaṃna
2 cuṇya hakṣī[3] rrīysutcä hīvī rraysä jsa haṃbrīhąñä khīṣṭa hau | rąñä
samaṃga : nīlotpalą . gichanāṃ hīvī raysä lodrä kuṃjsa caṃdä
āstaṃna cuṇyą . buysäñä ṣvīdä jsa haṃbrīhąñä u khāśą'ñä drrąma
3 arja cvai vā hųñä nirąme jiṃdai : pātcä huṃjuḍye arji vą khāysą |
buysįñä ṣvį'dą jsa haṃphva hverai :
vitsāvīśä' hīya grūṣka . mākṣī' gūlą hīvī khavä ā vā gūlą jsa haṃ-
brīhāña hverai :
4 pātcä apāmaurgä || mākṣī' . rrīysutcą hīvī raysä haṃbrīhąñä ā vā |
pātcä viysä hīvī khīysarä mākṣī' jsa u nīyakä jsa haṃbrīhąñä hverai :
u pātcä viysä hīvī khīysarä śikara jsa haṃbrīhāñä hverai : cu drrąma
arja cvai vā hųñä nirąme ṣe' jatte :
5 badarä hīye perä | ttālīsapaträ mirijsye āstaṃna śau śau serä .
pipalą . pipala mulą . dva dva saira tcauri buśąñä . tvacą . sukṣmelą .
gaṃdhapaträ nāgakyesarä . ūśī'rä āstaṃna dvī dvī mācāṃga :
tūṃgare . drrai saira : gūlä hā drrai śū'ba śtāka . habrīhąñä u gūlye
102 *r*1 padīmąñä . ttyāṃ | hīya nāma . ttālīsāda gūlye hvañāre tti samąnakyi
varāśą'ñä . mau . u ttye hīvī raysä u gūśti hīvī raysä u ṣvīdä ñyevutcä
2 kuṃjī āstaṃna kāṃ saṃ hamāte . dū | ṣā' jsa spāśąñä si kāṃ va

[1] ū? [2] nāga°.
[3] mākṣī.

186r6 gźaṅ-hbrum daṅ | gźaṅ na-ba daṅ | gcin hgag-pa rnams sel-to ||
pu-će-śel-la sogs-pahi sde-ćhan daṅ | rća bcu-sṅar bśad-pa hdi
gñis-las gaṅ yaṅ ruṅ-ba daṅ | po-son-cha daṅ | śiṅ mṅar daṅ | śu-ti
daṅ | ru-rta

7 daṅ | gandha-priyaṅku daṅ | gla-sgaṅ daṅ | rgyam-ćha rnams-kyi
phye-ma | mkhris-pa daṅ | rluṅ gaṅ-las gyur-pahi nad-kyi skabs daṅ
sbyar-te | mar daṅ | til-mar gñis-las gaṅ hos-pa źig daṅ | ho-ma
chuhi naṅ-du skol-te | mar-ram | til-mar ñi-ćhe lus-

186v1 pas | bkru-sman drag-po mas btaṅ-bar byaho || gźaṅ-hbrum na-ba-
la khrag hjag-par rtogs-na khrag lud-pahi nad-kyi cho-ga bźin-du
bya-źiṅ | thog-ma sman daṅ | kha-zas-la sogs-pa kha-bahi bag-las
sbyar-źiṅ zos-na | mehi drod bskyed-ciṅ nad-gźi ćhos-

2 par byed-do || khrag nad-kyi gźaṅ-hbrum-can-la ćhos-par byed-
pahi sman pu-śel-će daṅ | yarita daṅ | skyer-pahi śun-lpags rnams
lhan-cig-tu skol-bahi khu-ba bsgraṅs-pa ham | yaṅ-na bcah-sga daṅ |
ćandan daṅ | rća mkhris daṅ | byi-ćher

3 rnams skol-bahi khu-ba bsgraṅs-pa blud-do || yaṅ-na skoms-pahi
nad daṅ khrag-nad źi-bar bya-bahi phyir | nimpahi śun-lpags daṅ |
dug-mo-ñuṅ-gi hbras-bu daṅ | skyer-khaṇḍa daṅ | bo-ṅa dkar-po
rnams-kyi phye-ma | sbraṅ-rći daṅ | hbras bskus-pahi khu-ba daṅ

4 sbyar-ba blud-do || samaṃga daṅ | 'utpala daṅ | chu-śiṅ-gi hbras-bu
daṅ | tirita daṅ | til daṅ | ćandan rnams-kyi phye-ma rahi ho-ma daṅ
sbyar-te hthuṅs-na yaṅ gźaṅ-hbrum khrag hjag-pa sel-to || yaṅ-na
khrag nad-kyi gźaṅ-hbrum-can-la | kha-zas rahi

5 ho-ma daṅ ldan-par bzah-źiṅ | sman dug-mo-ñuṅ-gi śun-lpags
daṅ | sbraṅ-rći daṅ | bu-ram-gyi sbu-ba rnams sbyar-ba ham | yaṅ-
na sman mayurakahi phye-ma | sbraṅ-rći daṅ | hbras bskus-pahi
khu-ba daṅ sbyar-ba ham | yaṅ-na padmahi ze-ba sbraṅ-rći daṅ |
mar-sar daṅ

6 sbyar-ba ham | yaṅ-na padmahi ze-ba kha-ra daṅ sbyar-ba zos-
na | gźaṅ-hbrum khrag hjag-pa bde-bar hgyur-ro || dbyi-mohi lo-ma
daṅ | bal-buhi lo-ma daṅ | na-le-śam rnams-las sraṅ re-re daṅ |
pipiliṅ daṅ | pipiliṅ-gi rća-ba sraṅ gñis-gñis daṅ | dri-sna

7 bźi źes-bya-ba | śiṅ rća daṅ | sug-smel daṅ | gandhapatra daṅ |
nāgagesar rnams daṅ | pu-śel-će daṅ | hdi rnams-las źo gñis-gñis
daṅ | bcah-sga sraṅ gsum daṅ | bu-ram sman spyir bsdoms-pahi sum
hgyur daṅ | hdi-rnams sbyar-te ri-lur

187r1 byas-pahi miṅ ni | bal-buhi ri-lu źes-bya-ste | hdi-las ran-par
zos-la | chaṅ daṅ | khu-bcud daṅ | śa-khu daṅ | ho-ma daṅ | źo kha-

strihä: tta ṣṭe . haṃbrīhąñä u horąñä . dai pattajīdä arji harbiśä
3 jinīṃdä . bąmä . ysira rāhä . phāhä gą'mä ttavai āstaṃna | jinīṃdä .
khvai . ttye krri jsa na niṣi'māte . drrāṃ imaṃgala vījä cu thyau tta
4 dirṣṭä-karmä dye . āchainai hīya pā uskyāṣṭä haṃgrīhāñä u bañą|ñä
daṃdä . khvai vā krriṃga-rūvai drrāṃ hami cu vā daitte u drrąmai
vą saṃña tcerai u tvāvī arja biśä tta tta spāśąñä se kuṣṭi ṣṭe . ā vā
5 ṣvįnai ā vā hīśąnai | yaṃdrrä padīmāñä nokalakä gvī'hye || hīśi'me
mąñaṃdū . ttori vī hvāhä: tte tcau ho'śä' . u buśde' pajsa ho'śä' .
102v1 kve'ysvā vī hā mista khųṇe padīmąñä drriye | tcauri bure u rīyai hā
puṇvąñä . u kālanāṣṭä arji hamāte khųṇe hāṣṭä paśąñä . khu vą ṣi'
arrji biśä ttyāṃ khųṇāṃ haṃdrri vya nirąme .
2 cu beta jsa u śilīṣāṃ jsa hamya | līka arrja hamāte ttai mąṇḍaka
nauṣṭarą jsa pyįhąñä . u tvā pyihaca hīśinakä jsa padajsāñä . ā vā vī
3 ā pyihasti ā na padajsąñä . ā vā kṣi' pacaḍa arja kā|ma saṃ hamāve .
ttai vā mąṇḍaka . ttiña khųṇyāṣṭä niṣpaśdą'ñä . u arvāṃ jsa u kṣā'rāṃ
jsa haṃbrīhąñä . u saṃkhalyąñä .
4 cu arrja jsä vinaustä . cī saṃ hamā|te paḍāvī hvąṇḍye hīya hota
padįmąñä beta ṇihejākye arve u hvaḍa khaṣṭa kąminā saṃ hamāṃde :
āchai spāśąñä u krravī tta tta tcirai .
5 cu arja jsä | ttye hva hva dūṣi' āphirąme va hvaḍa khaṣṭa . styūdāṃ
āysināṃ biṃdä ñąma . aysdrraphai brāma[1] : saṃnä . u bīysma pihe-
103r1 jąma . aśä āstaṃna bārrāṃ bvąma ttye | jsai phīśąñä ||
bagadalä || viña ttā gųnāṃ haṃdrri vya nirasaṃdai āchai hīya
piṣkalä biraysde .
ṣi' krriṃga-rūvai hīyai ttaurä vī dvī ho'śi' diśi' vī kvā'śa' kha-
2 ⟨ysma⟩ vi|nosta . khaysma ākrre herä hame . ṣi'kä nirauśtä . ṣi'
bagaṃdalä bvąñä . ttye ąstaṃna paṃjsa padya biraṣṭä ṣṭe ||
3 cu beta jsa hamye līkä khaysme ttye nąma si . ssa ttu|rai viraṃ
śittapāṇakä gūrśte . chavį heṃji hame pa'jsą vinostą hame khaiyai
trāmāre u ttauśtä .
cu ttavaṃdye jsa hamye līkä ttye nąma si . ȯṣṭagrīvakä u hvaṃno |
4 | vī ūla gīsārä ną⟨ma⟩ . chavai heje hame u pasujsaṃdai dai mąñaṃ-
dū ttaudä haṣṭe .
cu śilīṣā jsa hamye līkä ttye nąma chāṃbakāvartai nąma u hvaṃnau
5 vī ną|ma . si baiśä vīra ysųnaṃdai . chavī śīyi hame . u kahaittai tta
tta biraṣṭä ṣṭe .
cu drayā dūṣāṃ' jsa hamye līkä . ttye nąma si ga'saṃdai śaṃgä .

[1] ñāma.

chu daṅ | rćabs rnams-la gaṅ yaṅ ruṅ-bas nad-gźi gaṅ śas che-ba
daṅ sbyar-te phul-na | mehi
2 drod bskyed-ciṅ gźaṅ-hbrum thams-cad daṅ | skyug-pa daṅ |
sñiṅ na-ba daṅ | lud-pa daṅ | skran daṅ | rims-rnams sel-to || cho-ga
de-rnams-kyis kyaṅ źi-bar ma-gyur-na | sman-pa mkhas-śiṅ ston
byed-pa mthoṅ-bas | nad-pa rkaṅ-pa dgug-ciṅ
3 bciṅ-ba-la sogs-pa ci-nas kyaṅ gźaṅ-ltar snaṅ-bahi thabs byas-te |
hbrum-bu-ga-la hdug-pa brtag-na | rva ham | lcags-kyi sbubs
hjam-po || bahi nu-sor-gyi dbyi-bas hdra-ba | khahi sboms sor bźi |
srid-du sor lṅa yod-par byas-la | glo-
4 logs-su bu chen-po gsum-ćam byas-te | rkub-tu brjaṅs-la | glohi
bu-gur hbrum-bu-ga-la yod-pahi thaṅ-kar gtad-de | hbrum-bu
sbubs-kyi naṅ-du byuṅ-baho || rluṅ daṅ | bad-kan-las gyur-pahi
gźaṅ-hbrum źig yin-na | hbrum-bu mćhon-
5 gyis bcad-la | hphro-lcags-kyis bsreg-go | yaṅ-na mi-bcad-par
bsreg-go | yaṅ-na | gźaṅ-hbrum rnam-pa drug-po gaṅ yaṅ ruṅ-ste |
hbrum-bu-gaṅ-gi naṅ-du byuṅ-ba-la | sman mukakahi thal-ba phrad
daṅ sbyar-bas bsku-bar byaho || gźaṅ-hbrum na-ba-
6 la ni mdor-na gaṅ ci yaṅ ruṅ-ste | mihi stobs bskyed-pa daṅ |
rluṅ daṅ hphred-pahi sman daṅ | kha-zas daṅ | btuṅ-ba gaṅ yin-pa
de hbah-źig-las ćha-bas che-chuṅ daṅ sbyar-źiṅ btaṅ-bar byaho ||
gźaṅ-hbrum-can-gyis ni nad-gźi so-sohi hkhrug-par hgyur-
7 bahi kha-zas daṅ | stan mkhraṅ-po-la hdug-pa daṅ | ćog-ćog-pur
hdug-pa daṅ | phyi-sa daṅ | gcin phro bźin-du mnags-pa daṅ | rta-la
sogs-pa źon-pa rnams spaṅ-bar byaho || || da ni mćhan-par rdol-
bahi bye-brag bśad-par bya-ste | rkub-kha-
187*v*1 nas sor gñis-kyi ćhu-rol-gyi glo-logsu ñam-thag-par byed-pahi
phol-mig hbyuṅ-ste | de brdol-bahi miṅ ni mćhan-bar brdol ces-
bya-ste | de yaṅ rnam-pa lṅa yod-par bśado || de-la rluṅ-las gyur-
pahi phol-mig-gi miṅ ni rma-kha brgya-pa źes-bya-ste | mdog
2 dmar-la mi-bzad-par zug-ciṅ na-ba yin-no || mkhris-pa-las gyur-
pahi miṅ ni | rṅa-mo mgrin źes-bya-ste | mdog dmar-la me hbar-ba
bźin-du ćha-ba yin-par bśado || bad-kan-las gyur-pahi miṅ ni |
kun-tu hjag-pa źes-bya-ste | mdog dkar-la g-yah-
3 ba yin-par bśad-do || nad-gźi gsum hdus-pa-las gyur-pahi miṅ ni |
duṅ hkhyil-ba źes-bya-ste | thams-cad-kyi mćhan-ma daṅ ldan-pa

103v1 u harbiśāṃ gūnāṃ | jsa haphve hame . cvai hā hvīḍiña gvihaiya
jsäherä kaśte u hvīḍai u pyaḍai jsāte u ttye jsa hamye nąmai tta
tta si pyaḍa tsuką . ttyāṃ āstaṃna .
2 cu drrayāṃ dūṣā' jsa hame . u | ttī jsāṃ gvihaiyä jsa hamye līkä tti
dva paṃtsąñä .
cu harīyijāṃ ttyāṃ āstaṃna jihume va anvaśta u jihāri haḍa .
3 cu paḍauysä khaysmi sarbe u adīṣṭa hamāte . cu jsā | va īñakä
rrāṃ vīra[1] hųñą nirāme . u ṇihejākyi hā saṃkhaluna pisalyąñä .
4 kāmye dūṣä' jsa hamye līkä ṣṭāte prisimye vī hā arve jsa jiṣṭa līka |
kaṣā' niśąñä kąmai va haṃbusina ṣṭāte kuṃjsavįnai rruṃ cu ttyi
āchai jsa prisa⟨māṃ⟩ arvāṃ jsa haṃbairstä pisalyąñä u pasamąṇ-
5 ḍąñä . kuṣṭi burai jsāṃ vrrī haurīdä tti|ña myāñai nva haṃbusaṃ
krra tcerai .
cu bągaṃdalä hīya krra ṣi' ttā viña pacaḍakä jsa birāśāṃ' ||
khu āstaṃ vī khu nirauśtä ṣai' kaṃmą cä mäsu bāñä ṣṭe u kālanāṣṭai
104r1 niraṃdä ṣṭe . u nąkala|kye hīśąnīṃje śimuṣai jsai spāśąñä . kāla-
nāṣṭai kaṃmä hīvī pacaḍä hamāve bi'ṇą'ñä u arvįnāṃ vī hā kṣā'ri
2 saṃkhalyąñä . u padajsąme āstaṃna . nva | pacaḍä uspurāṃña vīra
haysąñä tta tta khu kaṃmä jihāme hīye krre nva hva u pātcī tta tta
nirīkṣąñä se kąmye dūṣä' jsai vā pana . kāmye jsai pana ṣṭāte presama
3 pri|samai hā krra tcerai cu kaṃmą jihąme hīya krra .
rrājivrrikṣą' . halaidrrä . baraśīji . āstaṃna cuṇya . gvī'hä . rruṃ
4 u mākṣī haṃbrīhąñä . u bīysma nirąmąme hīvī | kaṃmä u bagaṃ-
dalä ⟨biṃ⟩dą saṃkhalyąñä kaṃmä jīye . u ni ra jsāte ||
trolä . ttejivattä . dattä . ā vā bāta . rūnai . halaidrrä . ysālva .
5 cuvaṃ . cigāṃ ttīrai hīye perä | āstaṃna . habrīhąñä . u saṃkhaly-
āñä . nālāvīraṃ jiṃdä :
bagaṃdalä āchai va . karavīrai . ṣi' īrū hīya bāta ṣṭe . halaidrrä .
104v1 dattä hīya bāva . preśnaparṇä . se|dalū . citrai . īrhva hīvī raysä .
rrustira hīvī baurkhä . vitsāvīśi' ttīṃ āstäna jṣą'ną⟨ñä⟩ u kaṣā'
kuṃjsavīnai rruṃ jsa .
2 ttyāṃ arvāṃ hīya ga' . jṣą'ñąñä daṃdä khu ri va rruṃ ha|rśtä .
u ysunāñä . kaṃmä biṃdä . saṃkhalyąñä .
cvai bagaṃdalä āchai hami ṣi'kä hvt' khvai kaṃmä jīye . śā salī
3 burai bvā⟨me⟩ jsa parehąñä u strīyi jsa . u rraphai jsa . u | drāṃ-
phāme jsa . u garkhāṃ hvaḍāṃ khaṣṭāṃ jsa āstaṃna parehąñä ||
arja u bągadalä āchai hīvī piṣkalä drraisaṃ || ||

[1] dīra?

yin-no ‖ kha-zas zug-rṅu daṅ bcas-pa zos-te | gan ni hoṅ-bahi
sbubs-su zug-pa-las gyur-pahi miṅ ni | log-par soṅ-
4 ba źes-bya-ste | hdi-rnams-las nad-gźi gsum hdus-pa-las gyur-pa
daṅ | zug-rṅu zug-pa-las gyur-pa gñis ni spaṅ-bar byaho ‖ lhag-ma
rnams ni gso dkah-ba yin-no ‖ de-la phol-mig daṅ-po byuṅ-ste ma-
smin-pa-la ni | dehi ñen-hkhor ham rća-nas khrag
5 hbyuṅ-ba daṅ | nan-rćis bsku-ba daṅ | nad-gźi gaṅ-las gyur-pa
daṅ | hphrod-pahi sman skol-bahi khu-ba graṅ-dro gaṅ hos-pas |
steṅ-du blugs-pa daṅ | til-mar daṅ | nad daṅ hphrod-pahi sman
sbyar-bar bsku-źiṅ mñe-ba daṅ | bsku sman btaṅ-bahi bar-du
6 cho-ga rim bźin-du byaho ‖ brdol-bar gyur-pahi cho-ga yaṅ
bśad-par bya-ste | daṅ-por brdol-bahi rma zabs ci-ćam yod-pa daṅ |
srol gaṅ logs-su byuṅ-ba | lcags-kyi thur-ma hjam-pos brtag-pa
daṅ | rmahi srol gaṅ gyur-par dral-ba daṅ | sman
7 muskaka-la sogs-pahi thal-bas gdab-pa daṅ | bsreg-pa-la sogs-pa
go-rim bźin-du mthar-gyis byas-nas | rma gso-bahi cho-ga bźin-du |
nad-gźi gaṅ-las gyur-pa daṅ yaṅ sbyar-źiṅ mthun-mthun sman
byaho ‖ de-la rma gso-bahi cho-ga ni | doṅ-ka daṅ |
188r1 yuṅ daṅ | rgya-śug-gi hbras-bu rnams-kyi phye-ma | mar daṅ |
sbraṅ-rći daṅ sbyar-te | gcin hjig-pahi rma mćhan-par brdol-la
bskus-na | rma sbyoṅ-źiṅ mi-mched-par hgyur-ro ‖ śiṅ ñe-roṅ daṅ |
tejobati daṅ | dandahi rća-ba
2 daṅ | bcod daṅ | yuṅ daṅ | skyer-pa daṅ | skyer khaṇḍa daṅ |
nimpahi lo-ma rnams sbyar-bas bskus-na yaṅ rma hkhrims-pa sel-to ‖
mćhan-par brdol-gyi nad-la | karabira daṅ | yuṅ daṅ | dandahi rća-
ba daṅ | laṅkahi li daṅ | rgyam ćha daṅ | kru-
3 trug-tres daṅ | kha-luṅ daṅ | ’arka daṅ | dug-mo-yuṅs rnam |
skol-bahi khu-ba daṅ | til-mar-gyi naṅ-du | sman de-dag ñid-kyi
phye-ma skol-la | til-mar ñe-ćhe lus-pa bćags-pa rma-la bskus-par
byaho ‖ mćhan-par rdol-gyi nad yod-pahi
4 mis ni | rma sos-pahi hog-tu yaṅ lo gcig-gi bar-du phyugs źon-
pa daṅ | ñal-ba daṅ | stobs hgyed-pa daṅ | brćal-ba daṅ | kha-zas
lci-ba rnams śin-tu bsgrims-te spaṅ-bar byaho ‖
gźaṅ-hbrum daṅ | mćhan-par brdol
5 gso-bahi lehu-ste bcu-gsum-pa rjogs-so ‖ ‖

4   ttiña pacīḍa ttā ysīḍai āchai jihą̄me va krre I hīvī piṣkalä biraysde .

cu ysīḍai āchai ṣṭe ṣi' rrjjsāṃ hvaḍā khą̄ṣṭā āstaṃna u ttīra u ṣura :

5   añuta hvaḍa khaṣṭa : aůysma hvarāme āstaṃna u phara hvaI rą̄-
me jsai . ysīḍai āchai hame . ṣi' pā drrayāṃ dūṣāṃ' vī hva hva śe śe
dūṣä' jsa hame saṃdviṃnä haṃbirstāṃ dūṣāṃ' jsa hamye līkä hīya
piṣkici āstaṃna tcau-padya hame II

105*r1*   I cu beta jsa hamye līkä ysīḍai āchai hīya gūnā . aṃgai haryā-
saurga hamāre . beta hīya gū̄nā . beta jsa perā āvaṃdvāṃ āchāṃ jsa
hame .

2   cu ttavaṃdye jsa hamye I līkä ysīḍai āchai hīya gūnā . ttavaṃdye
hīya vī hā āchā nitcāṣṭā nirą̄mą̄re. tci'mą̄'ñä u ttą̄ñä . saṃnä bīysma
āstaṃna ttai ysīḍā hamāre :

3   cu śilīṣāṃ jsa haI mye ysīḍai āchai hīya gūnā . cvai cha ṣai' śīyaurga
hame . śilīṣāṃ jsa hamya līkāṃ āchāṃ jsa haṃphve hą̄me II

4   cu drrayāṃ dūṣā' jsa hamye līkä . ysīḍai āchai hīI ya gū̄nā .
harbiśāṃ gūnāṃ jsa haṃphve bvą̄ñä beśai va hamāre .

cu ttye ysīḍai āchai hamāte . hųñai jīye . svīvai cha vrrasti hamāre .

5   gūśtai jīye . bą̄mai hame I u haśä . hauṣkä hame .

cvai va haṃdare perā āchā hamāre . ccai¹ hā śīyi śīyi hira āyīṃde u
vajsyāte ṣi' mīḍe II

105*v1*   cu ysīḍai āchai harbiśau vī . āsñi pa. I ha rruṃna khāśą̄'ñä u khvai
jsihārä hau'gä hame . ttikye nimaśai' dūṣāṃ' jsa spāśą̄ñä u haṃphī-
śą̄ñä . uskyāṣṭī vimaṃ haurą̄ñä . u nāṣṭai jsāṃ strihä: vrrī horą̄ñä II

2   tti vā aI rve rruṃ hīye . ālavāya . kalyārūhana . halaidrrä . dūrālabha : u pipalä . caṃdä . ttiṣcya . trāyimą̄ṇä : vatsāvīśi' ttī . cirāt-

3   taihtai . paṭolä . buhane I detadą̄ra āstaṃna cuṇya dvī dvī mācāṃga
gvī'hä: rruṃ dvāridirsä saira ṣvīdä rruṃ jsa tcau śūṃ'ba byą̄ñä

4   daṃdä jsą̄'ñą̄ñä . khu ri va rruṃ harśtä . ysuną̄ñä . u [si] I simauci jsa
khą̄śą̄'ñä . ysīḍai āchai u ttavai khaysme . haśä . arrja . cu hųña bame
tti biśä jiṃdä II

triphalä . gūlūśä' . vāśika . kalyarūha⟨na⟩ . cirāttihttai ciṃgāṃ

5   ttīrai hīye I piri āstāmna jsą̄ñą̄⟨ñä⟩ uysdimą̄ñä mākṣī jsa haṃbrīhāñä
u khāśą̄'⟨ñä⟩ . ysīḍai āchai . ką̄'malä harbiśä jiṃdä II

106*r1*   pātcä ysīḍai āchai va . halīrā . gvī'hä bīysma . I haṃbrīhą̄ñä .
hvaḍa khaṣṭai jsāṃ ṣvīdä jsa haṃbairsta hverai . pātcä hīśaṃ ⟨hīya⟩
hīsuṣka u gvīhye: bīysma jsa bį̄ną̄ją̄ñä dvī māṣṭä buri hverai u biṃdai

2   hā ṣvīdä jsa vahaI ją̄:ñä :

¹ cvai.

de-nas skya-rbab-kyi nad gso-bahi lehu bśad-par bya-ste | skya-rbab-kyi nad ni | kha-zas-la sogs-pa rno-ba daṅ | skyur-ba daṅ | lan-ćhva daṅ | sṅon ma-goms-pahi kha-zas daṅ |
6 źab rnams-las | ẖa-caṅ maṅ-du zos-pa-las | skya-rbab-kyi nad-du hgyur-te | de yaṅ nad-gźi gsum so-sor-nas gyur-pa daṅ | kun hdus-pa-las gyur-pahi bye-brag-gis rnam-pa bźir hgyuro || de-la rluṅ-las gyur-pahi skya-rbab-kyi mćhan-
7 ma mi lus-kyi mdog-gnag-la | rluṅ-gi mćhan-ma daṅ | rluṅ-nad-kyi bla-gñan rnams daṅ yaṅ ldan-pa yin-no || mkhris-pa-las gyur-pahi skya-rbab-kyi mćhan-ma ni | mkhris-pa las-pa rnams hbyuṅ-źiṅ | mig daṅ | pags-pa daṅ |
188*v*1 phyi-sa daṅ | gcin rnams ser-ba yin-no || bad-kan-las gyur-pahi skya-rbab-kyi mćhan-ma ni | mdog dkar-la bad-kan-las gyur-pahi nad rnams daṅ ldan-pa yino || nad-gźi gsum hdus-pa-las gyur-pahi skya-rbab-kyi mćhan-ma ni | thams-cad-kyi mćhan-ma
2 daṅ ldan-par śes-par byaho || de-la skya-rbab-kyi nad yod-la | khrag zad-pa daṅ | glo hgrams-pa daṅ | śa zad-pa daṅ | skyug-pa daṅ | skam-pa-la sogs-pahi bla-gñan yod-pa daṅ | mdog ser-źiṅ snaṅ-ṅo-cog dkar-por mthoṅ-ba ni | hchi-bar hgyur-ro ||
3 sbyar-ba bya nad thams-cad la | daṅ-por ni sman-mar btuṅ-bas khoṅ hjam-por byas-la | dehi hog-tu nad-gźi daṅ sbyar-źiṅ | gyen-du skyug-pa daṅ | thur-du bkru-bahi sman rnon-pos sbyar-bar byaho || dehi sman-mar ni murba daṅ | pu-će-śel daṅ | yuṅ daṅ | byi-
4 ćher daṅ | pipiliṅ daṅ | ćandan daṅ | skra-lo daṅ | khyi-lce-ba daṅ | dug-mo-ñuṅ daṅ | rća mkhris daṅ | patola daṅ | gla-sgaṅ daṅ | thaṅ śiṅ rnams-kyi phye-ma źo gñis-gñis | mar sraṅ sum-cu-rća-gñis daṅ | ho-ma mar-gyi bźi hgyur-gyi naṅ-du skol-te |
5 mar ñi-ćhe lus-pa bćags-pa-las | ran-par hthuṅs-na | skya-rbab daṅ | rims daṅ | hbrum-bu daṅ | skraṅ-ba daṅ | gźaṅ-hbrum daṅ | khrag lud-pahi nad rnams sel-to || hbras-bu gsum daṅ | sle-tres daṅ | baśaka daṅ | pu-će-śel daṅ | rća mkhris daṅ |
6 nimpa rnams skol-bahi khu-ba bsgraṅs-pa sbraṅ-rći daṅ sbyar-te hthuṅs-na yaṅ | skya-rbab-kyi nad daṅ | mig-ser daṅ can-du sel-to || yaṅ-na skya-rbab-kyi nad yod-pa-la | ’arura daṅ | ba-gcin daṅ sbyar-ba btuṅ-źiṅ | kha-zas ho-ma daṅ ldan-par bzah-bar byaho || yaṅ-
7 na lcags-kyi phye-ma ba-gcin-gyi naṅ-du yun riṅ-du sbaṅs-pa bzah-źiṅ ho-mas dbul-lo || hbras-bu gsum daṅ | kru-trug-tres daṅ | gla-sgaṅ daṅ | byidaṅga daṅ | ćha-ba gsum rnams-kyi phye-ma daṅ | lcags-kyi phye-ma daṅ | sman de-rnams spyir bsdoms-pahi

pātcä triphalä . citrai . buhane viṇḍaṃga . trikaṭokä āstaṃna
cṳṇya . hīśaṃ hīya hīsuṣka u haṃ bāḍä arve hamaṃgä viśtą̄ñä
3 mākṣī' . u gvī'hä : rruṃ jsa haṃ | brīhą̄ñä u hverai . ysīḍai āchai . u
ką̄'malä . u haśä u primīhä jiṃdä :

pātcä kuṃjsa u trikaṭokä baraśīję . veṭa-mākṣaukä āstaṃna cṳṇyą
4 hīśaṃ | hīye hīsuṣkyi jsa caṃdaṃ haṃ bāḍä arve daṃdä hā hīsuṣka
tcerai hamaṃgä viścą̄ñä ttyāṃ āstaṃna mākṣī' jsa habrīhą̄ñä murą̄ña
5 samą̄nakä hvarą̄ñä strehä ysī|ḍai āchai u haśä jiṃda . cu ką̄'malä
āchai ṣṭe ṣi' ysīḍai āchai jsa parśtä u harśtä . ysaiysai āphiḍe . u
ką̄'malä āchai hame . ṣi' pā viña hvīṃde : ttai gṳ̄nā : tci'mą'ñä aṃga
106v1 ttai ysī|ḍā hamāre ||

cu mistä ką̄'malä āchai ṣṭe ką̄'malä jsa harśtä u parśtä . u biysą̄nai
mistä hame . ttyāṃ dvyāṃ vīra drrāṃ tcārbä vrrī haurą̄ñä ||
2 sicha bāta halaidrrä . ci|gāṃ ttīrai hīye perä . triphalä mahābujä
āstaṃna hamaṃgä viśtą̄ñä u ṣvīdä u mahairṣī'ñä gvī'hä: rruṃ ttye
3 jsa jṣą̄'ñą̄ñä khu ri va rūṃ harśtä u ysuną̄ñä samāṃ khā|śą̄'ñä ṣe'
ką̄'malä āchai jiṃdä ||

gūlūśä' . triphalä . ysālva . cigāṃ ttīrai āstaṃna kāṃ saṃ hamāte
4 ttye hīya kaṣā' mākṣī' jsa haṃbrīhą̄⟨ñä⟩ u ysai yāṃdä khāśą̄'|ñä .
ką̄'malä āchai jiṃdä ||

hīśaṃ hīya hīsuṣka . ysālva . halaidrrä . triphalä . kalyarūhana .
mākṣī' jsa u gvī'hä rruṃ jsa haṃbrīhą̄ñä hverai ką̄'malä nvaśtä
5 ha|me

ą̄malai . hīśaṃ hīya hīsuṣka . trikaṭaukä . halaidrrä . ysālve
āstaṃna cuṇya mākṣī' gvīhä: rruṃ u śikarä jsa haṃbrīhą̄ñä u hverai
107r1 ką̄'malä biysą̄nai mistä ā|chai jiṃdä ||

pipalä . badara phūkä . pipala mulä . citrai . są̄nā . mirijsya .
sidalūṃ . viṇḍaṃga . triphalä . hīysimāṃ . baraśīje . aủṣai . kharaśpa
2 ttīṃ āstaṃna cuṇya śau śo se|rä . ttrolä hīya cuṇya . kuṃjsavīnai
rruṃ haṣṭa haṣṭa saira . ą̄malai hīya kaṣā' kṣi'rinau saira . gūlä
3 pajsāsä saira ttye āstaṃna haṃtsi jṣą̄'ñą̄ñä . ttye hīya ną̄ma | ṣi'
arvā jsa līhä kalyą̄ṇai nāma . ṣi' samą̄nakä hvairai . ysīḍai āchai . u
ką̄malä . [u ką̄malä .] u arrja . haṃbairstä biśä jiṃdä primīhä :
4 kuṣṭä . ttavai | uysni āphārä . grihaṇī-padau ṣā' āstaṃna jidä ṣi'
jsāṃ rriysāyaṃ ṣṭe . cu drrāṃ strihä . ką̄'malä vī . mākṣī' hīvī
rraysä vasve tciṃña pa'jsä śirä ĩda :

5 pātcä | halaidrrä . svaṃna gīrai . ą̄malai hīya cṳṇya naukä haṃ-
bairsti ṣṭą̄na saṃkhalyą̄ña ||

189r1 ćhad daṅ mñam-pa daṅ I hdi-rnams sbraṅ-rći daṅ mar daṅ sbyar-te zos-na yaṅ I skya-rbab daṅ I mig-ser daṅ I skraṅ-ba daṅ I gcin-nad sel-to II til daṅ I ćha-ba gsum daṅ I rgya-śug-gi hbras-du daṅ I drub-mar-caṅ rnams-kyi phye-

2 ma daṅ I lcags-kyi phye-ma I sman de-rnams spyir bsdoms-pahi ćhad daṅ mñam-pa daṅ I hdi-rnams sbraṅ-rći daṅ sbyar-te ma-brjis-pa-las I ran-par zos-na yaṅ I skya-rbab-kyi nad drag-po daṅ I skraṅs-pa sel-to II mig-ser-gyi nad ni I skya-rbab-kyi nad yal-bar

3 bor-ba-las I mkhris-pa hkhrugs-nas I mig-ser-gyi nad-du gyur-pas-na I de yaṅ skabs hdir bśad-de I dehi mćhan-ma ni I mig daṅ lus-kyi mdog-ser yino II mig-ser chen-po źes-bya-ba yaṅ I mig-ser-gyi nad-pas bor-bor-nas

4 ćhabs chen-por gyur-pa-las hbyuṅ-ste I de gñis-la ni snum-pahi bkru-sman btaṅ-ṅo II bala daṅ I yuṅ daṅ I nimpa daṅ I hbras-bu gsum daṅ I śiṅ mṅar rnams cha mñam-ste I btags-la ho-ma daṅ I maẖehi mar daṅ I skol-nas mar ñi-ćhe

5 lus-pa bćags-pa-las ran-par hthuṅs-na yaṅ mig-ser-gyi nad sel-to II sle-tres daṅ I hbras-bu gsum daṅ I skyer-pa daṅ I nimpa rnams gaṅ yaṅ ruṅ-bahi khu-ba sbraṅ-rći daṅ sbyar-te I naṅ-par bźin rtag-tu hthuṅs-na yaṅ I mig-ser-gyi

6 nad sel-to II lcags-kyi phye-ma daṅ I yuṅ daṅ I skyer-pa daṅ I hbras-bu gsum daṅ I pu-će-śel rnams-kyi phye-ma I sbraṅ-rći daṅ I mar daṅ sbyar-te zos-na yaṅ I mig-ser-gyi nad sel-to II skyurura daṅ I lcags-kyi phye-ma daṅ I ćha-ba gsum

7 daṅ I yuṅ rnams-kyi phye-ma sbraṅ-rći daṅ I mar daṅ I kha-ra daṅ sbyar-te bros-na I mig-ser ćhabs chen-po yaṅ myur-du sel-to II pipi-liṅ daṅ I pipiliṅ chen-po daṅ I pipiliṅ-gi rća-ba daṅ I kru-trug-tres daṅ I la-la-phud daṅ I na-le-śam daṅ I

189v1 rgyam-ćha daṅ I byidaṅga daṅ hbras-bu gsum daṅ I husuhi hbras-bu daṅ I rgya-śug-gi hbras-bu daṅ I go-sñod daṅ I nu śiṅ-gi hbras-bu rnams-kyi phye-ma sraṅ re-re daṅ I śiṅ ñe-roṅ-gi phye-ma daṅ I til-mar sraṅ brgyad-brgyad daṅ I skyururahi khu-bahi sraṅ dgu-bcu-

2 rća-drug daṅ I bu-ram sraṅ lṅa-bcu daṅ I hdi-rnams lẖan-cig-tu skol-bahi miṅ ni I sman-gyi lde-gu dge-ba śes-bya-ste I hdi-las ran-par zos-na yaṅ I skya-rbab daṅ I mig-ser daṅ I gźaṅ-hbrum daṅ I sbyar-bahi dug-rnams sel-ciṅ I gcin-nad daṅ I mje daṅ I

3 rims daṅ I dbugs mi-bde-ba daṅ I phog-źi-nad rnams med-par byed-la I sman-bcud-kyi len-du yaṅ hgyur-ro II mig-ser-gyis ñam-thag-pa ni I sman dronapuśipahi khu-bahi mig bzaṅ-ṅo II yaṅ-na yuṅ daṅ bćag daṅ I skyururahi phye-ma źib-mo sbyar-bas

pātcä . kākoṭä krrasanīcä hīye bāta jsa cuṇya . jilabhaṃgä hīya
107v1 cuṇya . | haysgvā paśą̄ñä ||

pātcä ką̄'malä biysą̄nai āchai va . ṫraṃda . pipalä hīya cṳ̄ṇya pātcä haysgvā pąśą̄ñä .

2 cu gvā ysirūṃ āchai . ṣi' beta jsa . u ttavaṃdye jsa hame | ttye hīya gṳ̄ṇą aṃgāṃ hīya vī cha gvā ysirṳ̄na hame u śī āṣana . dilakä ysīca . ttave . u ttarai hame . ttaraṃdarū vai dai huṣute[1] . nvāvai
3 aṃga hamāre . uvī vai | haniśīṃdä . u hṳñä . ysīḍai āchai pā vara hame ttye jsa hame . ṣi' hvarāṃ hvaḍāṃ khaṣṭāṃ jsa u beti . u ttavaṃ-
4 dye jinākyāṃ arvāṃ jsa purrdä hame . ką̄'malä . | ysīḍai āchai hīya ttā krra tta tta khvai biraṣṭa . gvą̄ ysirūṃ āchai halīmakä ttye jsai pā haṃphīśą̄ñä .

ysīḍai āchai krre hīvī piṣkalä tcaulasä || ||

5 ttiña | pacīḍa ttā haika āchai . u ūysnai āphārä āchai hīvī piṣkalä biraysde ||

cu haika u ūysni āphārä . ṣi' āṃ bāta ttavadye hīvī thāṃ jsa parśtä . u śilīṣāṃ nima'śä' paṣṭe |

108 deest.

109r1 |ysūṣṭa ṣṭe .

cu haika āchai jihāme va krra .

baraśīji hīya mejsāka . cuvaṃ . rrīysva gurva haṃtse haṃbrī-hāñä . kalyarūhana svaṃna gīrai āstaṃna haṃtse haṃbrrīhāñä :

2 pipa|lä āmalai . śikarä . ttugara āstaṃna haṃtse haṃbairste ṣṭą̄na .

pātcą hauṣṭą śriṣṭai bu' haṃtce haṃbrrīhāñä . pāṭala haṃtse hiyārą u spyakä jsa haṃtse haṃbrrīhāñä :

3 pātcą pipa|lą . khajūrā mejsāka . haṃtse haṃbairste ṣṭāna . tte kṣa'yau gattyāṃ āstaṃna kāṃ saṃ śau hamā⟨te mā⟩kṣī jsa haṃbrrī-
4 hą̄ñą . līha padīmą̄ñä u hverai . haikye hīvī āchai jiṃdä mahā|bujä mākṣī' jsa habairstä . pepalą śekarą jsa habairstä .

pātcą ttugara gulä jsa haṃbairstą ṣṭāna

tte drraye ga kāṃ saṃ śau hamāte . haysgvā paśą̄ña haika āchai jedä

5 mā'ta vattala | u hvī' ṣvīdą ā skaphai hīvī rraysä kāṃ saṃ hamāte haṃbrrīhāñä . ā vā śī caṃdä . hvī ṣvīdāna sauyāñä u haysgvā paśą̄ñä haika āchai jīye :

[1] n?

4 kyaṅ bsku-bar byaho ‖ yaṅ sman karkotakahi rća-bahi phye-ma
ham | jalinahi hbras-buhi phye-ma snar blugso ‖ yaṅ-na mig ser-
gyis ñam-thag-pa-la | ’eraṇ⟨ḍ⟩a daṅ | pipiliṅ-gi phye sbyar-ba snar
blugso ‖ nad ljaṅ-gu kha źes-bya-ba ni | rluṅ-nad mkhris-pa-la
hbyuṅ-ste |
5 dehi mćhan-ma ni | lus-kyi mdog ljaṅ-gu khar hdug-pa daṅ | sṅo
saṅs daṅ | ser-ba daṅ | rims-kyis hdebs-pa daṅ | skom daṅ che-ba
daṅ | mehi drod chuṅ-bar byed-ciṅ | sgyid lug-pa daṅ | sñom-pa
rnams yin-te | skya-rbab-kyi nad yod-pa-la hbyuṅ-ṅo ‖ da ni kha-
6 zas daṅ | skom mṅar bag daṅ | rluṅ daṅ mkhris-pa sel-bahi sman
rnams-kyis thub-par hgyur-te | mig-sėr daṅ | skya-rbab-kyi nad-kyi
cho-gar bstan-pa bźin-du | nad ljaṅ-khu kha hdi-la yaṅ sbyar-bar
byaho ‖

skya-rbab-kyi nad gso-bahi lehu-ste bcu-bźi-pa rjogs-
7 so ‖ | de-nas skyigs-buhi nad daṅ | dbugs mi-bde-bahi nad gso-bahi
lehu bśad-par bya-ste | skyigs-bu daṅ | dbugs mi-bde-ba-la ni | rluṅ
mkhris-pahi nad-las hdas-te | bad-kan-gyi rjes-su hbraṅ-bar gyur-
pa-las | skyigs-bu daṅ | dbugs
190r1 mi-bde-ba drag-po skye-bar hgyur-ro ‖

* * * *

190v1 rid-ciṅ ñam chuṅ-ba-la ni źi-bar bya-bahi sman bya-bar bśad-do ‖
skyigs-buhi nad gso-bahi cho-ga ni | rgya-śug-gi
2 ćhig-gu daṅ | skyer khaṇḍa daṅ | hbras-yos rnams lh̲an-cig-tu
sbyar-ba daṅ | pu-će-śel daṅ | bćag lh̲an-cig-tu sbyar-ba daṅ |
pipiliṅ daṅ | skyurura daṅ | kha-ra daṅ | bcah-sga rnams lh̲an-cig
sbyar-ba daṅ | nag-ćhur daṅ | pog dkar-po lh̲an-cig-tu sbyar-ba daṅ
3 śiṅ paṭalahi hbras-bu daṅ | me-tog lh̲an-cig-tu sbyar-ba daṅ |
pipiliṅ daṅ | bra-gohi yal-gahi thor-to daṅ lh̲an-cig-tu sbyar-ba
daṅ | sman-gyi sbyor-ba rnam-pa drug-po hdi-rnams-las gaṅ yaṅ
ruṅ-ba | sbraṅ-rći daṅ sbyar-la sman-gyi lde-gur byas-te zos-na |
skyigs-
4 buhi nad sel-to ‖ śiṅ mṅar daṅ sbraṅ-rći daṅ sbyar-ba daṅ |
pipiliṅ kha-ra daṅ sbyar-ba daṅ | bcah-sga bu-ram daṅ sbyar-ba hdi
gsum-las gaṅ yaṅ ruṅ-ba snar blugs-na yaṅ skyigs-buhi nad sel-to ‖
sbraṅ-mahi rtug-pa bud-med-kyi nu-źo ham | le-brgan rćihi
5 khu-ba gaṅ yaṅ ruṅ-ba daṅ sbyar-ba ham | yaṅ-na ćandan dkar-po
bud-med-kyi nu-źo-las bdar-te | snar blugs-na yaṅ skyigs-buhi nad

109*v*1 ā vā pātcä hai|kyi āchai neṣā'mä va y⟨s⟩īrā . gvīhą ṣū . kuṣṭä .
sarrjerrasä bu' . gīsai hīya bāta kāma saṃ hamāte gvīhä. rrū jsa
2 haṃbrīhąñä . pajukīnai bājaṃ haṃdrre vya padają|ñä u śįñą
khūṇya ąna dūmä raṣṭa haysgvā u ėha paśąñä u haika āchai jīye .
gvīhą. rru dva sera . byājąñä . jṣą'ñąñä serä sedalūṃ hā tce⟨rai⟩ śau
3 serä . ā vā ye|va-kṣā'rą . gvīhä. rruṃ jṣąñąñä śirä u hā niśąñä . u
khāśą'ñä . haika āchai beysąnai jedä . uysne āphārä āchai jehāme va
krra .

4 durālabha . pipalä . gu|ra . karkaṭa-śreṃgä . halīrą āstaṃna
kūṭāñą mākṣī' gvīhä. rrū jsa haṃbrrīhāñą hverai . uysne āphārä .
phāhä . beta jsa āchā upattaṃtrąką āchai jedä .

5 gulą . | merejsya . halaidrrä . laṃgara bā . gura . pipalä āstaṃna
kuṃjsavīnai rru jsa haṃbrīhāñä hverai . uysne āphārą āchai beśä
jedä .

pātcą mākṣī' . u gvī'hä . rru u

110–120 desunt.

121*r*1 |grąma arve kuṭąñä . cuṇya gvīhye. bīysma āstaṃna grąmāṃ
raysā jsa pesalyąñą ysālva jṣā'⟨ñā⟩ñä gvīhye . bīysma jsa haṃbrī-
2 hąñä u khāśą'ñä . pī huṣąme jsa hamye | dānāṃ nirāme hīvī āchai vī
āhąsāñąñä . surisādą ga' āstaṃnaką nauką kūṭāñą . ūce jsa haṃ-
3 brrīhāñä u saṃkhelyāñą ci bīysme jsa hamye āchai ⟨ā⟩sñai śe|lakä
āhä.sāñąñä . u na śilakä besai vī pū'mā vī narująñä varī vī tvā
4 khụṇā ne haṃbrąñąñä u pīlīrū vī hā viśtąñä u bvę'śda' paśąñä | khu
vā buḍa ysauttä . ce rrutāṃ jsa narṣṭīką cvai āchai nuvarä[rä] hame u
pharākai ni dāśä varṣṭe ṣe'|dą jsa padijsąñä . bete jinąkyāṃ arvāṃ jsa
krra tcerai

5 cu pa|dī hīya krra ṣṭe . khvai padī ïdä . khu sä[1] kaṃmä krra
haṃbusaṃ ṣṭāṭą krravī tta tta yenąñä .

mūtre kicha āchai hīvī peṣkalą haṣṭūsä :

121*v*1 ttiña pacīḍa ttā : | ūdāvarttāṃ āchai jihume hīvī peṣkala beraysde .
ce udāvarttāṃ hīvī āchai ṣṭe rrīma naṣphaśtākä padaṃ khāysąña
2 ṣṭukä āphīḍe . huṣuttye jsa . saṃną hau|ṣḍe . ū nāṣṭą tsūme hīvī
paṃda pe'hīśtä . uskyāṣṭä dvyīṃdä udāvarttāṃ hīvī āchai hame . tta
tta biraṣṭä ṣṭe . ttai vā gųnā . ysirä . jsiṃnä brihä: kve'ysa . u phiysgā |
3 hasu . paṣkausā vī hame . bijāṣai pasauṣḍe' . garśai va galā hamāre .
ttave bąmai hame . dyąkyai kaśāre u gva' . u ttarä āchai āstaṃnakä .

[1] saṃ.

sel-to || yaṅ-na skyigs-buhi nad źi-bar bya-ba-la | ldoṅ-ros daṅ | ba-
laṅ-gi rva daṅ | ru-rta daṅ | srarćihi pog daṅ | rćva kuśa
6 rnams-las gaṅ yaṅ ruṅ-ba mar daṅ sbyar-te | snod-kha sbyar-gyi
naṅ-du bsregs-la | huhi naṅ nas dud-pa draṅ-źiṅ | kha snar brṅubs-
na yaṅ skyigs-buhi nad sel-to || mar bzaṅ-po sraṅ gñis bźu-ste |
chos-par byas-la | rgyam-ćha sraṅ gcig daṅ sbyar-ba ham
7 yaṅ-na nas ćhig hkhus-pahi thal-ba | mar bzaṅ-po bźus-te chos-
par byas-pahi naṅ-du btab-pa hthuṅs-na yaṅ skyigs-buhi nad-kyis
ñam-thag-pa sel-to || dbugs mi-bde-bahi nad gso-bahi cho-ga ni |
byi-ćher daṅ | pipiliṅ daṅ | rgun daṅ | bu-bran
191r1 śiṅ daṅ | 'arura rnams źib-tu btags-la | sbraṅ-rći daṅ | mar daṅ
sbyar-te zos-na | dbugs mi-bde-ba daṅ | lud-pa daṅ | rluṅ-nad
rmugs-byed rnams sel-to || bu-ram daṅ | na-le-śam daṅ | yuṅ daṅ
rārna daṅ | rgun daṅ pipiliṅ
2 rnams btags-la | til-mar daṅ sbyar-te zos-na yaṅ daṅ dbugs mi-
bde-bahi nad drag-po sel-to || yaṅ-na sbraṅ-rći daṅ | mar daṅ ga-
brahi rća-ba daṅ | śiṅ mṅar-gyi phye-ma sbyar-te bzah-bar byaho ||

* * * * *

197r4 || bad-kan-las gyur-pa-la ni | sman drod che-ba btags-pahi phye-
ma ba-gcin daṅ sbyar-ba bsrin-pos bsku-źiṅ skyer-pahi rća-ba skol-
bahi khu ba-gcin daṅ sbyar-ba btuṅ-bar
5 byaho || ćhil rgyas-pa-las gyur-pahi rlig-rlugs-kyi nad-la ni | dugs
bya-ba daṅ | byihu-rug-pa-la sogs-pahi sde-ćhan źib-tu btags-te
chu daṅ sbyar-bas bsku-bar byaho || gcin-las ma gyur-pa-la ni | daṅ-por
rlig-pa dugs
6 byas-pahi rjes-la rlig-pahi hog-gi srubs-nas brtol-te re-źig rna-
rći mi-sbyar-bar gcehus bsu-źiṅ riṅ-du hjag-tu gźug-go | rgyu-ma
rlugs-pa-las gyur-pahi rlig-rlugs da-duṅ ćhabs chen-por gyur-pa-la
ni | bsreg-pa
7 daṅ | rluṅ sel-bahi sman-rnams byaho || bsreg gcig-la ni bsregs-
pahi hog-tu rna-la cho-ga ji-ltar bya-ba bźin-du byaho ||
gcin sri-bahi nad sel-bahi lehu-ste bco-brgyad-pa rjogs-so || ||
de-nas rtug-skam-
197v1 gyi nad gso-bahi lehu bśad-par byaho || rtug-skam-gyi nad ni |
dri-ma hbyin-pa źes-bya-bahi rluṅ loṅ-ka-na gnas-pa hkhrugs-te
śas che-bar gyur-pas phyi-sa bskams-nas thur-du hoṅ-bahi lam
hgags-te gyen-du hkhyil-bar gyur-pa ni rtug-
2 skam-gyi nad bskyed-par bśad-do || dehi mćhan-ma ni sñiṅ daṅ

4 tti buri āchā | beśä ttyā udāvarttāṃ jsa panamāre . cvai udāvartta
āchai hame . āsñai aṃgą tcārbe makṣą̄ñä u bīṭhą̄ñä . āhä.sāñą̄ñä
5 arvījai hā ṣvaka krreṃga-|rūvya veśtāña u strehä . tcārbä vastä
yinąñä . khīṣṭai arvīnā rruṃna haurą̄ñä u anavāysena . strehä . vrrī
haurą̄ñä ṣā' arvīje ṣvakye hīye krre vī .

122r1 madanaphalä | hīhä daumä . vidilūṃ . trikaṭaukä . gūlä . tvā
cuṇya . gvīhye: bīysmi haṃdrri vya pajsą̄ñä . ṣvakyi padī̄mą̄ñä āṣṭye
2 āṣṭye mase gvīhä: rruṃ jsa gūmalyāñä u | hā viścą̄ñä . saṃni
⟨ni⟩rāme . paṣkosā naṣi'me u vina jsāṃ jiṃdä .

pātcä hīhä. daumä papalä madinaphalä . śī śaśvāṃ . gūlą āstaṃna
3 cuṇya gvīhye: bīysmi haṃdrri | vya daṃdä jṣą̄'ñą̄ñä khu syai .
thyotta bisāṃ khiṇḍä ṣvakyi padīmą̄ñä hā viśtą̄ñä pe'jsi śirä ī̆nīdä :

4 pātcä agūṣḍä . ārra . kų̄ṣṭä . svarrjika kṣārä . vidilūṃ āstaṃ|nakä .
āstaṃ vī bisai haṃbāṃ jsa hą̄dva dva bhāga byą̄ñä kūṭą̄ñä . u grą̄mye
jiṣṭe uci jsa . haṃbrīhą̄ñä khą̄śą̄'ñä . paṣkosā . vīnai u khaiye . ysīri
5 rā|hä . gomä āstaṃna jiṃdä . dva bhāga trolä . u tcau bhāga papalä .
halīrā . paṃjsa bhāga kūṭāñä naukä : niśą̄ñä hā gūlä kṣį'mä bhą̄gäna
122v1 hamaṃgä . pajsāñä śirä | yāṃdä . khu haṃdrrīśtä simānä gūlye
śū'hyą̄:ñä hvaḍä vaskimāṃde . varāśą̄'ñä śā śā tvā ysai brū nvaśtä .
2 hauṣkä saṃnä hīya biśä āchā jiṃdä . ttaraṃdarä ttai thyo | nvaśtä
suhye. pą̄dīme . hvīḍai jsāṃ hauma rrusa hau'vīṃdä ṣvīdä jsa . ā vā
ysumi jsa kąmye jsa saṃ hamāte haṃtsi hverai . bvīyi pā yuḍä ī̆dä :
3 khvai bāti paname . u | saṃnä paheją̄ñe ttikye jsa perā āvaṃdva .
ttavaṃdye . śilīṣā āstaṃnakä . perā āchā hamāre . ttye dvyāṃ vaski
4 dvyāṃ yaugāṃ jsa vastä tcerai . biti jsa ha|mye līką saṃnä pihīsąme
vī . phį̄ysgāña vina hamāre . ttavaṃdye jsa hamye . nehä. ttauśama
5 hame . śilīṣā jsa hamye . ysīri rrāhä: hame vanāsā|ma . ėhä: ą̄nai
jsām vā ṣaha nirāme . drrayāṃ dūṣā' jsa saṃdvainä jsa hamye .
harbiśāṃ gūnāṃ jsa hamphve hame . ṣi' paṃtsą̄ñä ni jatte cū beti jsa

mkhal-sked daṅ | rćib-logs na-ba daṅ | lgaṅ-ba chu-so skraṅ-ba daṅ | lto sbo-ba daṅ | skad hgag-ciṅ | lkog-naṅ lẖa-hor-du hgyur-ba daṅ | rims-kyi ma-hdebs-śiṅ

3 skyug-pa daṅ | mig ldoṅs-śiṅ hon-par hgyur-ba daṅ | skom-pahi nad-la sogs-pa nad-kyi sna-graṅs hdi-rnams skye-bar hgyur-te || rtug-skam-gyi nad yod-pa-la ni daṅ-por lus-skam-gyis bsku-źiṅ dril-ba daṅ | dugs byas-la sman-gyi reṅ-

4 bus gźug-pa daṅ | bkru-sman d⟨r⟩ag-po mas btaṅ-ba daṅ | sman-mar btuṅ-ba daṅ | hjam-rći mas btaṅ-ba daṅ | bkru-sman btaṅ-bahi las rnams byaho || de-la sman reṅ-bu mas btaṅ-bahi cho-ga ni po-son-cha daṅ | khyim-gyi du-ba daṅ |

5 ćabs ru-ćha daṅ | ćha-ba gsum daṅ bu-ram rnams-kyi phye-ma ba-gcin-gyi naṅ du | khaṇḍa ćhos-pa ćam-du skol-te reṅ-bu mthe-bo ćam-du byas-nas mar-gyis bskus-te mas btaṅ-na phyi-sa hbyuṅ-bar hgyur-la lto sbo-źiṅ na-ba yaṅ sel-to || yaṅ-

6 na khyim-gyi du-ba daṅ | pipiliṅ daṅ | po-son-cha daṅ | yuṅs-kar daṅ | bu-ram rnams-kyi phye-ma ba-gcin-gyi naṅ-du khaṇḍa ćhos-pas ćam skol-te sṅa-ma bźin-du reṅ-bur byas-pa yaṅ bzaṅ-ṅo || yaṅ-na śiṅ-kun daṅ | śu-dag daṅ |

7 ru-rtas daṅ | svarćikahi thal-ba daṅ | ćabs ru-ćha rnams yas-kyi rim bźin-du daṅ-pohi cha gñis-kyis skyed-de btags-la chu skol-ba dron-po daṅ sbyar-te hthuṅs-na yaṅ lto sbo-ba daṅ | zug-ciṅ na-ba daṅ | sñiṅ na-ba daṅ | skran-rnams

198r1 sel-to || śiṅ ñe-roṅ cha gñis daṅ | pipiliṅ cha bźi daṅ | 'arura cha lṅa-rnams btags-te de-rnams sbyar-ba bsdoms-pahi ćhad daṅ mñam-pahi bu-ram-gyi naṅ-du khaṇḍa ćhos-pa ćam-du skol-la ril-lur

2 byas-pa de ni phyi-sa hgags-pahi nad sel-bar byed-do || kha-zas-su ni nas rjen-pa khram-khrom-du btags-pahi chan ho-ma ham śa-khu daṅ ldan-pa ham | gźan yaṅ gaṅ de daṅ hphrod-pahi kha-zas rnams bzah-bar byaho || de lta

3 rluṅ-gi g-yos phyi-sa hgags-par gyur-pa-las mkhris-pa daṅ bad-kan bla-gñan-du gyur-pa-la ni de gñis-la phan-pahi sman mas btaṅ-ba rnam gñis byaho || rluṅ-las gyur-pahi phyi-sa hgag-pahi nad ni chu sor zug-par byed-do |

4 mkhris-pa-las gyur-pa ni lte-bahi phyogs ćha-ba yin-no || bad-kan-las gyur-pa ni sñiṅ na-ba daṅ | daṅ-ka mer-mer-po daṅ | kha-nas chu hbyuṅ-bar byed-do || nad-gźi gsum char hdus-pa-las gyur-pa ni mćhan-ma thams-cad

123r1 hamye līka I saṃnä pe'hīsąme hīvī āchai vī . sąną . aṃgūṣḍą' .
sidilūṃ . yavihä:kṣārä spaju . halīrāṃ āstaṃna cuṇya . ysaujsä
2 mauna haṃbrīhąñä . u khąśą' I ñä biśä jiṃdä .

pātcä spaju . ārra : aủṣai . mirejsyę āstaṃna uskātta bisai nva
byehä . thyątta thyątta bisā arva hā⟨dva⟩ daṃdä byąñä kuṭāñä .
3 cuṇya . ȋrhva raysä I vālaiga raysä jsa habrīhąñä murāña : gūlye
padįmąñä hvarąñä . beti jsa hamye saṃnä pihīsąme hīvī ttu āchiṃ
jiṃdä II

4 pātca beta jsa I hamye saṃnä pe'hīsąme hīvī āchai vī . suttä .
aṃbalavettä raysä . haṃga ṣṭe . trikaṭokä . sidilūṃ . spaju . vidalūṃ
5 āstaṃna cuṇya . vālaiga raysä I jsa haṃbrīhąñä . gūlye padīmąñä
hverai . ttaṃbīrä . halīrā . aṃgūṣḍä . huraṣṭa . vidalūṃ . sidilūṃ spaju
123v1 āstaṃna cuṇya u rrusa jṣą'ñąñä . I ttye hīye raysä jsa haṃbrīhąñä
khāśą'ñä cu beti jsa . saṃnä pi'hīśtä . gau'mä . upattaṃtrakä
2 nā⟨ma⟩ āchai jiṃdą . ttavaṃdye jsa hamye . saṃnä pe'hīsąme hi I vī
āchai . aủmalai hīya kaṣā' . bidārä hīya kaṣā' . trāyimųṇä hīya kaṣā' .
3 gūrāṃ hīya kaṣā āstaṃna . kąmī ji hamāte . śikarą jsa ha I brįhąñä
khāśą'ñä . ttavaṃdya varī sä[1] jiṃdä .

pātcä aủma[ma]lai . hīya cuṇya . mākṣī' jsa haṃbrīhąñä . rrīysva
4 gūrvāṃ hīya . caṇya . śi I karä . mākṣī jsa haṃbrįhąñä . śilīṣāṃ jsą
hamye . saṃnä pi'hīsąme hīvī āchai . ārra . buhąne . citrai halīrā .
5 kalyarūhine . āstaṃna . I cuṇya gvīhye: bīysmi jsa haṃbirstä ṣṭāna .
ā vā belāda ga' āstaṃna jṣą'ñąñä . grąma kaṣā' . yavahä:kṣā'rä jsa
haṃbirstä ṣṭāna khāśą'ña .

124r1 . viña ttā ysī I ra rāhä. hīya piṣkici . birąśāṃ'
cu ysira rāhä . ṣi' beta āstaṃna drrayāṃ dūṣā' jsa . hva hva śe śe jsa
2 hame . u pīrąnāṃ hīye gajsa jsa hamye paṃjsa pa I dya . ṣi' harbiśä .
khaiyuḍä u vinaustä . piṣkistä jsa pirąnāṃ jsa hamye līkä . y⟨s⟩irä
biṃdai kahai hame . cu beti jsa hamye ysīri rrāhä . āhvarā ttīra
3 ā I vā suttä . kāṃ ⟨saṃ⟩ hamāte āyvąñä . u vara hā kuṃjsavįnai rruṃ .
u sidilūṃ āstaṃ⟨na⟩ niśąñä . u khāśą'ñä . ā vā pātcä kuṃjsavįnai rru
4 jṣą'ñą I ñä. u gvīhä . hā bīysmi haṃbrīhąñä khāśā'ñą . gau'mą . vīne .

[1] saṃ.

5 daṅ ldan-pa yin-te spaṅ-bar byaho II de-la rluṅ-las gyur-pahi phyi-sa hgag-pahi nad-la ni I la-la-phud daṅ I śiṅ-kun daṅ I rgyam-ćhva daṅ I nas ćhig hkhus-pahi thal-ba daṅ I kha-ru-ćhva daṅ I 'arura rnams-kyi phye-ma chaṅ źim-po

6 daṅ sbyar-te hthuṅs-na sel-bar byed-do II yaṅ-na kha-ru-ćhva daṅ śu-dag daṅ I go-sñod daṅ I na-le-śam rnams yas-kyi rim bźin-du I sṅa-ma sṅa-ma-las ñis hgyur-du bskyed-de btags-pahi phye-ma kha-luṅ-gi khu-ba daṅ sbyar-te

7 brjis-pahi ril-bu zos-na yaṅ rluṅ-las gyur-pahi phyi-sa hgag-pahi nad sel-to II yaṅ-na rluṅ-las gyur-pahi phyi-sa hgag-pahi nad-la I ćhva daṅ star-bu daṅ I ćha-ba gsum daṅ I la-la-phud daṅ I rgyam-ćhva daṅ I kha-ru-ćhva

198v1 daṅ I ćabs ru-ćha rnams-kyi phye-ma I kha-luṅ-gi khu-ba daṅ sbyar-te ri-lur byas-pa bzah-bar byaho II ldum-bu seyaba daṅ I 'arura daṅ I śiṅ-kun daṅ I ma-nu daṅ I rgyam-ćhva daṅ I kha-ru-ćha daṅ I ćabs ru-ćha rnams-kyi phye-ma-nas bćos-pahi khu-ba daṅ

2 sbyar-te hthuṅs-na yaṅ rluṅ-las gyur-pahi phyi-sa hgag-pa daṅ skran daṅ I rluṅ nad I rmugs-byed rnams sel-to II mkhris-pa-las gyur-pahi phyi-sa hgags-pahi nad-la ni I skyururahi khu-ba daṅ I bidarihi khu-ba daṅ I khyi lce-bahi khu-

3 ba daṅ I rgun-gyi khu-ba rnams-las gaṅ yaṅ ruṅ-ba kha-ra daṅ sbyar-te hthuṅs-na de ma-thag-tu sel-to II yaṅ-na skyururahi phye-ma daṅ I sbraṅ-rći daṅ sbyar-bahi hbras brṅos-pahi phye-ma daṅ I kha-ra sbraṅ-rći daṅ sbyar-ba btuṅ-ṅo II bad-kan-

4 las gyur-pahi phyi-sa hgags-pahi nad-la ni I śu-dag daṅ I gla-sgaṅ daṅ I kru-trug-tres daṅ I 'arura daṅ I pu-će-śel rnams-kyi phye-ma ba-gcin daṅ sbyar-ba ham I yaṅ-na bilba-la sogs-pahi sde-ćhan skol-bahi khu-ba dron-mo-nas

5 ćhig hkhus-pahi thal-ba daṅ sbyar-ba btuṅ-bar byaho II II da ni sñiṅ na-bahi bye-brag bśad-par bya-ste I sñiṅ na-ba-la ni I rluṅ-la sogs-pa nad-gźi gsum so-so-las gyur-ba daṅ I kun hdus-pa-las nad-du gyur-pa daṅ

6 srin-buhi ñes-pa-las gyur-pa daṅ I rnam-pa lṅa yod-de I thams-cad kyaṅ zug-ciṅ na-ba yin-no II bye-brag-tu na srin-bu-las gyur-pa ni I sñiṅ g-yah-źiṅ na⟨ho⟩ I de-la rluṅ-las gyur-pahi sñiṅ na-ba-la ni I ćaṅ śu bsres-pahi naṅ-du I

7 til-mar daṅ I rgyam-ćha blugs-te btuṅ-bar byaho II yaṅ-na til-mar skol-ba ba-gcin daṅ sbyar-te hthuṅs-na I skran daṅ I zug-ciṅ na-ba

paṣkausā biśä . jiṃdä . ā vā paṃjsāśāṃ halīrāṃ hīyai ke'kä spaju dva
5 sairą . | gvīhä: rruṃ 32 saira . tcau bāga hā tvaḍa ūtci tcerai jṣą'ñąñä
khu ri va rruṃ harśtä . ysai ysai khāśą'ñä . ysiri rāhä . uysina āphārä .
124v1 go'mą āstaṃna jiṃdä . | ā vā pātcä tuṃgara : spaju . aṃgūṣḍä .
drrąma ttīma . aṃbalavetta raysä . haṃga raysä . ūci jsa jṣą'ñąñä
2 grāmye u haṃbrīhąñä u khāśą'ñä uysni ā|phārą . ysira rāhä. jiṃdä .

ttavaṃdye jsa hamye ysira rāhä. vī . pvātāṃ ārvāṃ[1] hīyāṃ kaṣāṃ'
3 jsa aṃga bijsąñä . pvāñä . pvątāṃ hvarāṃ līhā . arvāṃ jsa . | aṃga
pisalyąñä . u hvarāṃ arvāṃ jsai . caṃ tcerai .

pātcä kalyarūha:nāṃ hīya cuṇya . ā vā mahābuṃji hīya cuṇya
4 kāma hamāte . śika|rä ūci jsa haṃbrīhāñä u hā niśąñä khāśā'ñä .

sālaparṇä . stharādi ga' āstaṃna . kūṭąñä . cuṇya gvīhä. rruṃ tcau
5 bāga buḍana ūci jsa . u ṣvīdä | ękṣa' raysä . drrayvā āna śau kāṃ ⟨saṃ⟩
hamāte . rūṃ hīvī bāgą jsa hamaṃgä viśtąñä jṣą'ñąñä . khu ri va
125r1 śūmą rūṃ harśtä . ysuṇąñä . si.|mąnakä khāśą'ñä . ttavaṃdye jsa
hamye ysiri rāhä: jiṃdä .

śilīṣāṃ jsa hamye . ysiri rāhä. vīra . papalä . ṣalä . ārra . laṃgari
2 bā . ttuṃgara . halīrā . hu|raṣṭi āstaṃna cuṇya . gvīhye. bīysmi jsa
āyvąñä haṃbrīhąñä ū khāśą'ñä . ā vā tvā bīysmį daṃdä jṣą'ñąñä
3 khu ri va tcau bāgį ąna śau bhāgä harśtä khāśą'ña | drrayvāṃ
dūṣāṃ' jsa hamye līkä . ysīri rāhä. āstaṃ vī vai anahārośtä hīya krra
4 tcerai u ttye nima'śä' hauvi jsa haṃphve hamāte spāśąñä bātą |
ttavaṃdya śilīṣāṃ : kāṃ va dūṣi' purrdą hamāte ttye krra tcerā .
pirąnāṃ jsa hamye līkä ysiri rāhä. va.ṇḍaga kūṣṭa hīya cuṇya .
5 gvīhye: bīysmi jsa haṃ|brīhąñä . u khāśą'ñä .

ūdāvarttāṃ hīvī jehāme hīvī piṣkalä nausä : ||

125v1 ttiña pacīḍą ādāmādä u avisimārä āchai jįhųme hīvī piṣkalä |
biraysde :

cu ādimādä āchai ṣi' cvai va haṃdara viśų'na hiri yinīṃdä . u
hvaḍvā khaṣṭvā vī hā asurai herä hīśtä . u hvīḍai u khāśai' . pvą'nä
2 jsa . harīysā|me jsa u kāṣṭyi jsa . gąchąnāṃ jsa . aysmu u͡vī . byātaji
ttai paraṃjsa vaṣṭīdä u āphīrāre . ṣi' pā paṃjsa padya hame .

3 cu beti jsa hamye ādąmādä āchai ⟨hīya⟩ gūnā | satta dyū . nvāśe .
khīttä . nvāka huñe . u kṣi'mīdä . hve' . ttyāṃ āstaṃna bvąñä .

[1] arvāṃ.

daṅ I lto sbo-ba yaṅ sel-to II yaṅ-na 'arurahi hbrum-bu lṅa-bcuhi phye-ma daṅ I kha-ru-

199r1 ćha sraṅ gñis I mar sraṅ sum-cu-rća-gñis daṅ I chu-mar-gyi bźi hgyur-gyi naṅ-du skol-te I mar ñi-ćhe lus-pa-las ran-par hthuṅs-na sñiṅ na-ba daṅ dbugs mi-bde-ba daṅ I skran-rnams sel-to II

2 bcah-sga daṅ I kha-ru-ćha daṅ I śiṅ-kun daṅ bal-po sehu daṅ I star-bu rnams-kyi phye-ma chu skol-ba dron-po daṅ sbyar-te hthuṅs-na yaṅ dbugs mi-bde-ba daṅ I sñiṅ na-ba sel-to II mkhris-pa-las gyur-bahi sñiṅ na-ba-la ni I sman

3 bsil-bahi khu-ba-la sogs-pas lus-pa blugs-pa daṅ I sman bsil-bahi lde-gus bsku-ba daṅ I sman mṅar dag-gi bkru-sman btaṅ-ṅo II yaṅ-na pu-će-śel-gyi phye-ma ham I śiṅ mṅar-gyi phye-ma gaṅ yaṅ ruṅ-ba kha-ru chu daṅ sbyar-

4 bahi naṅ-du blugs-te btuṅ-ṅo II sman ster-la sogs-pahi sde-ćhan btags-pahi phye-ma I mar daṅ I chu-mar-gyi bźi hgyur daṅ I ho-ma daṅ I bu-ram śiṅ-gi khu-ba daṅ I rgun-gyi khu-ba gsum-las gaṅ yaṅ ruṅ-ba mar-gyi ćhad daṅ

5 mñam-pahi naṅ-du skol-te I mar ñi-ćhe lus-pa bćags-pa-las ran-par hthuṅs-na yaṅ mkhris-pa-las gyur-pahi sñiṅ na-bas sel-to II bad-kan-las gyur-pahi sñiṅ na-ba-la ni I pipiliṅ daṅ I li-zur-ba daṅ I śu-dag daṅ I rasna daṅ I

6 bcah-sga daṅ I 'arura daṅ I ma-nu rnams-kyi phye-ma ba-gcin bsros-pa daṅ I sbyar-ba btuṅ ṅam I yaṅ-na sman de-dag ñid ba-gcin daṅ skol-te bźi cha lus-pa btuṅ-bar byaho II nad-gźi gsum hdus-pa-las gyur-pahi sñiṅ na-ba-la

7 ni I thog-mar smyuṅ-bahi cho-ga byas-la dehi hog-tu ñam-stobs daṅ sbyar-źiṅ I rluṅ daṅ I mkhris-pa daṅ I bad-kan gaṅ śas che-bahi cho-ga byaho II srin-bu-las gyur-pahi sñiṅ na-ba-la ni I byidaṅga daṅ I ru-rtahi phye-ma ba-gcin daṅ

199v1 sbyar-te btuṅ-bar byaho II rtug-skam gso-bahi lehu-ste bcu-dgu-pa rjogs-so II II de-nas smyo-byed daṅ I brjed-byed-kyi nad gso-bahi lehu bśad-par byaho II de-la smyo-byed-kyi nad ni gźan-gyis ṅan-du byas-pa daṅ I bzas

2 daṅ I skom mi-gćaṅ bzos-śiṅ I hthuṅs-pa daṅ I hjigs-śiṅ sdaṅs-pa daṅ I mya-ṅan-gyis gduṅs-nas I yid daṅ I blo daṅ I dran-pa log-ciṅ hkhrug-pa yin-no II de yaṅ rnam-pa lṅa yod-par bśad-de I de-la rluṅ-las gyur-pahi

3 smyo-byed-kyi mćhan-ma ni I ṅaṅ-ñid-la ćham-rdam bye⟨d⟩-ciṅ

cu ttavaṃdye jsa hamye gūnä ysaurrjä hime . pvāśkai kṣi'me .
4 satta kṣeṃ'je ttyāṃ ąstaṃ | na hamāre

śilīṣāṃ jsa hamya gų̄ną . hųna māstä hame . u pharāka ni bijeṣe .
u mijṣe' vī kṣi'me . kṣi'je . khāysī ni kṣi'me .

5 cu saṃdvainä jsa hamye ṣi' harbiśāṃ gū | nā jsa haphve . ṣi' pa'jsä
anvaśtä paṃtsą̄ñą . ci āvaṃdū hirtha himye ādąmādä . ttye parvālāṃ
126r1 āstaṃna . u sparśä' . āphirāre u anvaśtāvī yinīṃdä . biśä hi. | rä butte .
ahvaṃḍi bvāṣṭyai hame . bvāṣṭyi vīrāṣṭä naysdä hame u pa'jsä hame .
bijāṣakä amaṃgalä . u śūrä āstaṃna gų̄nä jsa bvāñä :

2 ci beta jsa hamye līką | ādimādä . āstaṃ vīrai arvāṃ jsa haṃphva
rrūṃna khāśą̄'ñä .

ci ttavaṃdye jsa hamye līkä . āstaṃ vīra vrīca[1] haurą̄ñä .

3 ci śilīṣāṃ' jsa pana līkye . āstaṃ vīra vimana | haurą̄ñä .

tta tta hva hva krra thyautta yuḍa āstaṃna . khvai yuḍä īṃdä .
vastai tcerę . u ttī jsāṃ . anavāysināṃ āstaṃna nva pacaḍa krra
4 tcerai . ttikyi ni | ma'śą' halaidrrä ysālva . triphalä pṙiyaṃgä . ārra śī
śąśvāṃ . aṃgūṣḍi' : hai:śą' ttįma . śīyi buśa . rruṃnai . trikaṭokä .
5 devidārä . karäjä[2] āstaṃna cuṇya gvīha | rūṃ gvīhye. biysmi jsą
jṣą̄'ñą̄ñä daṃdä khu ra va rruṃ harśtä u ysųną̄ñä . simą̄⟨na⟩kä
khāśą̄'ñä ādämādä āchai jidä .

126v1 ā vā pātcä ttye hamye arve jsa cuṇya padįmą̄ñä | u gvīhä. rruṃ u
buysįñä bīysmi jsə jṣą̄'ñą̄ñä khu ri va rruṃ harśtä . u ttye hīya . nąma
sārasuttī nąma . ṣi' hvairai aviṣṣārä āchai be' jiṃdä .

2 pātcä pā | ṭha : halīrā . śīyi mįremjsya : trikaṭaukä . ārra . sidalūṃ
āstaṃna cuṇya . śau śau sairä . gvīhä. rruṃ 32 sairä buysįñä ṣvīdä
3 haṃdrryi vyai jṣą̄'ñą̄ñä daṃdä khu | ri va rūṃ harśtä ysunąñä ttye
nāma si biśtä padīmākä nąma . ṣi' simąnakä hverai . byāvarji brāvi
4 padįme aysmu rraṣṭä padīme . kārauśtä . u ėlai . bą | mä āstaṃna
harbiśą jiṃdä .

pātcą mahābuṃjä . ārra . aṃgūṣḍi ttagarä . hai.śū ttīma . ysaṃ-
bāste[3] . kuṣṭa ⟨ā⟩staṃna buysīñi bīysmi jsa sauyą̄ñä u ysųną̄ñä kaṣā'
5 ha | ysgvā paśą̄ñä u tcimañuā pisilyą̄ñä . ādämādä jsa biysī līkä ttye .

[1] vrīva? [2] karaṃjä. [3] ysaṃbaste.

rdig-pa daṅ | dub daṅ | rgod-pa daṅ | glu-len-pa rnams yin-par śes-
par byaho || mkhris-pa-las gyur-bahi mćhan-ma ni | khro-ba daṅ |
bsil-ba hdod-pa daṅ | sdigs-pa daṅ | sñigs-pa-
4 la sogs-pa rnams yin-no || bad-kan-las gyur-bahi mćhan-ma ni |
gñid che-ba daṅ | smra-ba ñuṅ-ba daṅ | bud-med-la dgah-źiṅ-
sñeg-pa daṅ | kha-zas mi-hdod-pa rnams yin-no || kun-hdus-pa-
las gyur-ba ni mćhan-ma thams-cad daṅ
5 ldan-te | ma-ruṅs-pa yin-gyis spaṅ-bar byaho || glo-bur-las gyur-
bahi smyo-byed ni | lh̲a-la sogs-pahi bdon hkhrugs-pas ṅan-du
byas-pa-las gyur-ba yin-te | mi ma-yin-pahi śes-pa daṅ | śes-ñen
daṅ | stobs daṅ | ćhig daṅ | dpah-ba-la
6 sogs-pa daṅ ldan-par śes-par byaho || de-la rluṅ-las gyur-bahi
smyo-byed-kyi nad-la ni | thog-mar sman-mar btuṅ-bar byaho ||
mkhris-pa-las gyur-ba-la ni | thog-mar bkru-sman btaṅ-ṅo || bad-
kan-las gyur-ba-la ni thog-mar skyug-sman btaṅ-
7 ṅo || de-ltar so-sohi cho-ga sṅar bya-ba rnams byas-pahi hog-tu
hjam-rći mas btaṅ-ba daṅ | bkru-sman drag-po mas btaṅ-ba-la
sogs-pahi cho-ga rim-bźin byaho || dehi hog-tu yuṅ daṅ | skyer-pa
daṅ | hbras-bu gsum daṅ | śiṅ ñe-roṅ daṅ |
200r1 śu-dag daṅ | yuṅs-kar daṅ | śiṅ-kun daṅ | śiriśa daṅ | kaṭabh̲i daṅ |
śveta daṅ | bcod daṅ | ćha-ba gsum daṅ | thaṅ-śiṅ daṅ | karañja
rnams-kyi phye-ma mar daṅ ba-gcin-gyi naṅ-du skol-te | mar ñi-ćhe
2 lus-pa bćags-pa-las ran-par hthuṅs-na smyo-byed-kyi nad sel-to ||
yaṅ-na sman de-dag-ñid-kyi phye-ma mar daṅ ra-gcin-gyi naṅ-du
skol-te | mar ñi-ćhe lus-pa bćags-pahi miṅ ni | sman gnod-sel ces-
bya-ste | hdi zos-na brjed-byed-
3 kyi nad daṅ | dug sel-bar byed-do || sman patha daṅ | 'arura daṅ |
śig-gru daṅ | śu-dag daṅ | ćha-ba gsum daṅ | rgyam-ćha rnams-
kyi phye-ma sraṅ re-re daṅ | mar sraṅ sum-cu-rća-gñis rahi ho-
mahi naṅ-du skol-te | mar ñi-ćhe lus-pa
4 bćags-pahi miṅ ni lce bde-bar byed-pa źes-bya-ste | hdi-las ran-
par zos-na | dran-pa gsal-ba daṅ | yid gźuṅs-par hgyur-źiṅ hon-pa
daṅ | dig-pa daṅ | lkug-pa rnams kyaṅ | dehi mthus sel-bar byed-do ||
yaṅ-na śiṅ-mṅar daṅ |
5 śiṅ-kun daṅ | śu-dag daṅ | rgya-spos daṅ | śiriśa daṅ | sgog-skya
daṅ | ru-rta rnams ra-gcin-gyi naṅ-du bdar-te bćags-pahi khu-ba
sṅar blugs-śiṅ | mig-tu bsku-bar byaho || || smyo-byed-kyis thebs-
pa-la | thog-mar ni |

āsñya bañāñä u dvyą̄ñä hāṣṭä vāṣcä ni paśą̄ñä haṃdrraṃją̄ñä .
127r1 biśūña pacaḍai pvį̄'ñą | ñä . ttiñä nvaiyai hā hau'gāṃ salą̄vāṃ jsa āspā
vą̄śą̄ñä . cvai hirthaṃ jsa hamye ādimādä āchai jsa biysī lokä[1] . ttye
2 surai alobhä vīji . devattāṃ pūjä tce | rai u bala . jaysñya pajsama .
havina . madrrāṃ jsa . aṃjināṃ jsa haysgvā paśą̄me āstaṃna . krra
nva dyą̄me pverāñä yiną̄ñä .

3 viña ttā avasmārä āchai hīya | piṣkici biraysde .

ci avasmārä ṣṭe ttāḍāvai aysmu ṇe'heje u āphiḍe . u dūṣi' hīye
4 utvaḍare jsa pa'tcautta byą̄varji hame u ysaurjä . a | vasmārä āchai tta
tta byāñä . ṣi' biysą̄nai . tcau-padya . bvą̄ñä . tta tta khu beti jsa
hamye līkä . u ttavaṃdye jsa . u śilīṣā' jsa hamye . gūnāvī haryāsą
5 cha ysīḍai | śī āstaṃna bvą̄ñä . nva pacaḍä hā haṃphīśą̄ñä cu buri
saṃ vijsyāte . ttye hīya hva hva gūnā . dya hamāre . drrayāṃ dūṣā'
127v1 jsa hamya līkä . avasmārä . | āchai . harbiśāṃ gūnāṃ jsa haṃphve
hame . jehą.me vaska pa'jsä anvaśtä . āsñai straha anavāysina tcerai
2 u ttikye nima'śä' vastä tcerai . u vimaṃ tcerai. u | ttikye nima'śä'
vrrī . ustaṃ haysgvā paśą̄ñä . krra āstaṃna paṃjsa tti kīra . khu saṃ
duṣä' hīvī gūnai hamāte . tta ttai hā paśą̄ñä .

3 cu beti jsa hamye līkä . ttye vastä tcerai | anavāysina tcerai .

cu ttavaṃdye jsa hamye līkä . vrrī haurą̄ñä .

śilīṣāṃ jsa hamye vimaṃ haurą̄ñä

4 cu haysgvā paśāma tvā nva dūṣä' arvāṃ jsa haṃ | phīśą̄ñä pañe vīra
saṃ śirä .

cu sadvainä jsa hamye . kāṃ va dūṣā' strehä: tta hamāte krra hā
ttikye hīya haphīśą̄ñä .

5 khvai ttye krre jsa ttaradarä agna surā ha | māre ttye nima'śai'
ādąmādä āchai pīraurāka krra tcerai .

·pātcä . ñāna spyakä . ārra . kuṣṭä āstaṃna cuṇya . āba hīya kaṣā' .
128r1 maṃgārä pharāka salä . gvī. | hä. rrūṃ jsą jṣą̄'ñą̄ñä khu ri va rruṃ
harśtä . ysuną̄ñä . semą̄naka khāśą̄'ñä . ādimādä u avismārä biśą
2 jidä . aysmu thāña viśte pīrmāttaṃ hva ṣṭe . gvīhä rruṃ u ku | jsavīnai
rruṃ 32 saira . ṣvīdą hā kṣa'sä [śu']śu'ba tvaḍa tcerai . jivīnīyā arve
dasau . cu ttā thyautta hvate ttyāṃ hīvī ka'ka śau serä jṣą̄'ñāñä .
3 gvīha: rrūṃ kuṃjsavį̄nai rru jsa | jṣą̄'ñą̄ñä daṃdą khu ri va rruṃ
harśtą ysuną̄ñä u khāśą̄'ñä . avasmārą jidą .

[1] līkä.

6 bciṅ-ba daṅ | rdeg-pa daṅ | gaṅ yaṅ mi-btaṅ-bar bsruṅ-źiṅ | thabs rnam-pa sna-ćhogs-kyis bsregs-la dehi hog-tu ćhig hjam-pos gźam-par byaho || glo-bur-las gyur-pahi smyo-byed-kyi nad-kyis thebs-pa-la ni | sman-pa gćaṅ-źiṅ re-ba maṅ-

7 bas mchod-pa daṅ | gtor-ma daṅ | ⟨sp⟩os daṅ | mchod-sbyin daṅ | sbyin-sreg daṅ | sṅags daṅ | mig-tu bsku-ba daṅ | snar blugs-pa-la sogs-pas cho-ga ji-lta-ba bźin-du bsal-bar byaho || || da ni brjed-byed-kyi bye-brag bśad-par bya-

200v1 ste brjed-byed ni | mun-pa hdra-bas sems non-nas nad-gźi śas-cher hkhrugs-pa-las dran-pa ñams-śiṅ khro-bar gyur-ba-la brjed-byed-kyi nad ces-byaho || de yaṅ rnam-pa bźi-ste ma-ruṅs-pa yin-par śes-par byaho || de-la rluṅ-l⟨as gyur⟩-ba daṅ |

2 mkhris-pa-las gyur-ba daṅ | bad-kan-las gyur-ba rnams-kyi mćhan-ma ni | mdog gnag-pa daṅ | ser-ba daṅ | dkar-pa rnams yin-te go-rim bźin-du sbyar-ba daṅ | ci mthoṅ-ṅo-cog kyaṅ de-dag so-sohi rnam-pa mtho⟨ṅ-bar⟩ yin-no ||

3 nad-gźi gsum car hdus-pa las gyur-bahi brjed-byed-kyi nad ni | mćhan-ma thams-cad daṅ ldan-pa-ste | gso dkah-ba yin | de-dag-la thog-mar ni bkru-sman drag-po mas btaṅ-ba daṅ | hjam-rći mas btaṅ-ba daṅ | skyug-sman btaṅ-ba daṅ |

4 bkru-sman btaṅ-ba daṅ | sman snar blugs-pa daṅ | cho-ga rnam-pa lṅa-pa hdi-rnams nad-gźi ji-lta-ba bźin-du btaṅ-bar byaho || de-la rluṅ-las gyur-pa-la ni bkru-sman drag-po mas btaṅ-ba daṅ | hjam-rći mas btaṅ-bar byaho || mkhris-

5 pa-las gyur-ba-la ni bkru-sman btaṅ-ṅo || bad-kan-las gyur-ba-la ni skyug-sman btaṅ-ṅo || sman snar blugs-pa ni so-sohi sman-las sbyar-na kun-la yaṅ phan-no || kun-hdus-pa-las gyur-pa-la ni | gaṅ śas che-ba daṅ yaṅ sbyar-źiṅ

6 cho-ga de-rnams-las gaṅ hos-pa btaṅ-bar byaho || cho-ga de-dag-gis lus rab-tu dag-par gyur-nas | dehi hog-tu ni smyo-byed-kyi nad bsal-bahi cho-gar bstan-pa bźin-du byaho || yaṅ-na sman śaṅge-puśipa daṅ | śu-dag daṅ | ru-rta

7 rnams-kyi phye-ma sman bram-mḫi khu-ba daṅ | mar rñiṅ-pa lo du-ma lon-pahi naṅ-du skol-la mar ñi-ćhe lus-pa bćags-te ci ran-par hthuṅs-na brjed-byed daṅ | smyo-byed-can sel-źiṅ yid gźuṅs-par byed-pahi mchog yin-no || mar daṅ til-

201r1 mar sraṅ sum-cu-rća-gñis-gñis daṅ | ho-ma mar-gyi bcu-drug-gi naṅ-du hćho-byed ces-bya-bahi sman sna bcu-lṅar bśad-pa rnams-kyi phye-ma sraṅ re-re skol-la mar daṅ til-mar ñi-ćhe lus-pa bćags-te ran-par hthuṅs-

śīye merejsya kụṣṭą . yserai . aúṣai . ysaṃ⟨ba⟩ste . trekaṭaukä
4 aṃguṣḍä āstaṃna cu|ṇya . buysīñe bīysme jsa . u kujsavīnai rru jsa
jṣ̄ą'ñąñä khu ra kujsavīnai rruṃ harśtą ysunąñä . haysgvā paśąñä .
avasmārä āchai jeṃdä .
5 cu ādemą|dä u avasmārä āchai ttye ūci jsa u dai jsa u baṃhyā.
jsa u garāṃ āstaṃna viysimāṃ thąni paṃtsąñä u parehāñä . aysmu
128v1 brā padīmākyāṃ . arvā hī|vī raysä jsa u raysāyānāṃ jsa ādarą
thająñä u yādą hverai .
ādimądä . avasmārä āchai hīvī jihụma hīvī peṣkalä bestä :
2 tteña pacīḍa ttā biti | jehāme . hīvī peṣkalą berāśāṃ'
cu beti jsa āchā tte haṣṭā hamāre . bāti āphirąme jsa hvata . ttyāṃ
3 haṃbąkyāṃ hīya gunā . vīnai hame . u ttausace vī|nauste . cu hā
neskaudą ịṃdä kheye aṃgāṃ ārīsāma . guśta u ė'hä . hvā mase muse
haṃthrrajīṃdä ma ā ā ñuṣṭịṃdą .
4 cu be'ti jsa ākṣī'pakä nāma | āchai cu yādą aga ne āhrrī ịdą u
gvamąnīdę
śe' beti jsa dhanụ skaṃdhą nāma āchai . kuysye duñe mąñaṃdụ .
5 didą bete jsa hālai aṃgä vīna padīmąme | nāma āchai . cvai hālai
aṃgą biśą vīnaustä hame .
tcuraṃ beta jsa ėkabāhau.ką nāma . cvai bāta sāmalā hīye re
ārraje tta tta bvāñä .
129r1 pātcä beta jsa graidhasą ną|ma āchai ṣe' dva-padya hame . cvai
hurāvuā bāta trāme . u ni ra butta tsai . u pārvā u haṃguṣṭāṃ
haṃdrrye vya bāta tti hīysde u paṣṭe . u ne ra tsva himye . bete jsa .
2 arrdettä nā|ma āchai . cvai bāta ttaurą śālanāṣṭä halīnai padịme .
krrauṣṭe śrirṣṭä nāma āchai cvai ysāṇve hasvīṃdä . ṣe' beta u huña
3 āphārä jsa ysāṇū hīya pārka hasu . ttyevī arvī|nāṃ rrūnāṃ jsa
makṣą'ma tcerai āhäsāñāñä vasva[1] tcerai . u haysgvā . tcārbai vrrī
haurąñä . hvaḍa khaṣṭai tcārba āhvarā . u ṣura u hvara . u vaṣeṇīya
4 |āstaṃnakä . beti jsa āchā jenāka .
sicha bāta jṣą'ñąñä u sahacera kāma saṃ hamāte pātcą tikyāṃ
5 hīvī ka'kä . kujsavịnai rruṃ u ṣvīdäna haṃtse jṣą'ñąñä | khu ri va
rruṃ harśtä . ysunąñä . khāśą'ñä . beta jsa āchā biśuña harbeśą jedä .
ā vā kuṃjsavịnai rruṃ . u ṣvịdä ssa 32 saira aśvagaṃdha pajsāsä sera
129v1 jṣą'|ñąñä u kaṣā' padīmąñä u rrụña neśąñä u vara hā buśąnai .
tvacą gaṃdhapaträ . rūṃnai drreyaṃttä surasą . ṣalä . secha bāta .
2 devidārä . sālaparṇä . mahābu|jä . laṃgara bā . sukṣmela . huraṣṭa .

[1] vasta.

2 na yaṅ brjed-byed-kyi nad sel-to ‖ śiṅ-kun daṅ | ru-rta daṅ | ldoṅ-ros daṅ | go-sñod daṅ | sgog-skya daṅ | ćha-ba gsum daṅ | śiṅ-kun rnams-kyi phye-ma ra-gcin daṅ | til-mar-gyi naṅ-du skol-bahi mar ñi-ćhe lus-pa bćags-te snar blugs-

3 na yaṅ brjed-byed-kyi nad sel-to ‖ smyo-byed-kyi nad daṅ | brjed-byed-kyi nad-la | chu daṅ | me daṅ | śiṅ daṅ | brag-la sogs-pa gnas ṅan-pa rnams ni spaṅ-bar byaho ‖ sems gsal-źiṅ yaṅ gźuṅs-par hgyur-bahi sman-bcud-kyis

4 len ni bsgrims-te rtag-tu bzah-bar byaho | smyo-byed daṅ | brjed-byed-kyi nad gso-bahi lehu-ste | ñi-śu-pa rjogs-so ‖ ‖ de nas rluṅ-nad gso-bahi lehu bśad-par byaho ‖ rluṅ-nad rnam-pa brgyad-cu ni | rluṅ hkhrugs-pa-las

5 hbyuṅ-ste | de-rnams spyihi mćhan-ma ni na-ba daṅ | yan-lag chag-pa sñam byed-pa daṅ | zug-pa daṅ | yan-lag hkhums-pa daṅ | śa skam-pa daṅ | drag-tu bcir-ba hdra-bar na-ba rnams yin-no ‖ de-la rluṅ-nad dam-po źes-bya-ba ni raṅ

6 dbaṅ-med-par lus hgul-ba yin-no ‖ rluṅ-nad sgur-po gźu-hkhums bźin-du hdug-paho ‖ rluṅ-nad gźogs-phyed na-ba źes-bya-ba ni | lus-kyi gźogs-phyed ril-gyis na-bar byed-paho ‖ rluṅ-nad lag-pa ya-gcig hjos-pa źes-bya-

7 ba ni | rluṅ-gis phrag-pahi rća hkhums-par byas-pa yin-par śes-par byaho ⟨‖⟩ rluṅ-nad dbyi mig man-cad zug-pahi *da* skran ni | brla man-chad-du na-ste | smyaṅ bskum mi-nus-te | rtiṅ-pa-las sor-mohi bar-du na-źiṅ hgro mi-śes-par byas-pa yin-no ‖ rluṅ-

201v1 nad kha-yon źes-bya-ba ni rluṅ-gis kha phyogs-gcig-tu yo-bar byas-pa yin-par bśad-do ‖ rluṅ-nad pus-mo skraṅ-ba źes-bya-ba ni | rluṅ-nad khrag rgyas-pas pus-mohi lẖa-ṅa skraṅ-bar byed-pa yin-no ‖ de-la sman-mar-gyis lus bsku-ba daṅ | dugs bya-ba

2 daṅ | sman mas-btaṅ daṅ | snar blugs-pa daṅ | snum-gyis bkru-sman btaṅ-ba daṅ | kha-zas snum-pa daṅ | skyur-ba daṅ | lan-ćhva daṅ | mṅar-ba daṅ | ro ća-bar byed-pahi bag-rnams ni rluṅ-nad sel-to ‖ sman ba-la daṅ | seriya gaṅ yaṅ ruṅ-ba skol-

3 bahi khu-bahi naṅ-du de-ñid-kyi phye-ma | til-mar daṅ | ho-ma lẖan-cig-tu skol-la | til-mar ñi-ćhe lus-pa bćags-te hthuṅs-na | rluṅ-nad-kyi sna-graṅs thams-cad sel-to ‖ yaṅ-na | til-mar daṅ | ho-ma sraṅ sum-cu-rća-gñis-gñis daṅ | sman

4 'aśvagandẖa sraṅ lṅa-bcu skol-bahi khu-ba mar-gyi bźi hgyur-gyi naṅ-du | spaṅ-spos daṅ | śiṅ ća daṅ | gandẖapatra daṅ | bćod daṅ |

ārra drrāṃgulye . kuṣṭä . puttī karaṃjä . bāta ttīṃ . ė'śte bāta .
3 kaṇḍārya . uśe'rä . ṣvīḍā bāta . kuṭąñä cuṅya dvī dvī | mācāṃgye
haṃtse jṣą'ñąñä . khu ra va rrū harśtä . ysunąñä . ttye nāma se
aśtagaṃdhādą[1] rūṃ . khāśą'ñä . aṃgą jsa makṣą'ñä . haysgvā vī
4 pąśąñä . anavā|ysena jsa tcerai . tcauraṃ jsa kīra beśą tcerā harb-
eśāṃ bināṃ āchāṃ natcīphāką

pātcą kuṃjsavīnai rruṃ u trehā hīvī raysä 32 sera ñye jsa . u
5 āhvarai raysä|na . u ṣvīdą āstaṃnakä . rruṃ jṣa tcau bāga tvaḍa
veśtąñä u vara hā . ārra . sechi bāva laṃgara bā . huraṣṭa ttuṃgara .
130r1 cetrai . śīye mereṃjsya . sedilūṃ . drrāṃgulye . | papalä āstaṃnakä
cuṇya jṣą'ñąñä khu ri va rru harśtä ysunąñä . ttye rru hīye tte arve
beti jsa āchā aharīna biysānā harbeśä jidä .

2 pātcą kuṃjsavīnai rruṃ u ṣvī|dä 32 32 sera sahacira ssa saira
jṣą'ñąñä . u kaṣā' padīmąñä u rruṃ jsa hā tcau śū'ba tvaḍa tcerai
ka'kä hā . jīvakä . raṣebhakä . meda . mahāmedą . kākūṭä . kṣī'ra-
3 kākụṭä | kūṣṭä . dva caṃdana . bāti ttī . devidārä . rrunai laṃgara bā
āstaṃna hīya cuṇya jṣą'ñąñä . khu re kujsavīnai rruṃ harśtą ysunąñä .
4 ttye jsa . vastä āstaṃna haṃphī|śąñä beṃnāṃ āchāṃ ṇe'hejāką
kujsavīnai rruṃ . ṣvīḍą 32 32 saira . drrāṃgulyā hīya kaṣā' . rruṃ
5 jsa tcau śu'ba tvaḍa tcerai . vara hā gulä . ttuṃgara hīya | cuṇya
haṣṭa haṣṭa sera . haṃtse jṣą'ñąñä . khu ri va rruṃ harśtä . ysunąñä .
semąnakä khāśą'ñä . ttye nima'śä' hā ṣvīdą khāśą'ñä khvai bitte .
130v1 nema'śai' . ttuṃgara . gula | jsa haṃtsi hverai . khvai ṣe' arva gvaśte .
ṣvīḍ̣naivī hvaḍa khaṣṭą varāśā'ñä . beti jsa biysąnā āchā harbiśą
jeṃdä .

2 gvīhä. rrü[2] ssa 28 serą ysaṃbasta ssa serą haṃtse jṣā'|ñąñä . kaṣā'
hā rruṃ jsa tcau śu'ba tvaḍa tcerai . ka'ką hā bądarä . cetrai . papalą
āstäna[3] cuṇya dvī dvī mācāṃgye . ttugara . aṃguṣḍä u paṃjsa nemve
3 ttyāṃ āstaṃna śau | śau serä . haga hīvī raysä hālai serä . ttyąna
āstaṃna haṃtse jṣą'ñąñä khu re va rruṃ harśtą . ysūnąñä . ttye

[1] aśva°. [2] rruṃ. [3] āstaṃna.

trabanti daṅ I byihu-rug-pa daṅ I jati daṅ I bala daṅ I thaṅ-śiṅ daṅ I stira daṅ I śiṅ-mṅar daṅ I rasna daṅ I

5 sug-smel daṅ I ma-nu daṅ I śu-dag daṅ I gze-ma daṅ I ru-rta daṅ I putika daṅ I śuti daṅ I purṇaṇaba daṅ I briẖatī daṅ I pu-śel-će daṅ I bariri rnams btags-pahi phye-ma źo gñis-gñis lẖan-cig-tu skol-te til-mar hbah-źig lus-pa bćags-

6 pahi miṅ ni 'aśvaganda-la sogs-pahi til-mar źes-bya-ste I btuṅ-ba daṅ I lus bsku-ba daṅ I snar blugs-pa daṅ I mas btaṅ-ba rnam-pa bźi-po dag-tu sbyar-na rluṅ-nad thams-cad sel-to II til-mar daṅ I la-phug-gi khuba sraṅ sum-cu-rća-gñis

7 . . gñis daṅ I źo daṅ I rćabs skyur-po daṅ I ho-ma rnams-las re-re yaṅ I til-mar-gyi bźi-hgyur bźi-hgyur daṅ I hdi-rnams-kyi naṅ-du I śu-dag daṅ I bala daṅ I rasna daṅ I ma-nu daṅ I bcah-sga daṅ I kru-trug-tres daṅ I śi-kru daṅ I rgyam-

202r1 ćha daṅ I gze-ma daṅ I pipiliṅ rnams-kyi phye-ma skol-la til-mar ñi-ćhe lus-pa bćags-pahi til-mar-gyi sman yaṅ rluṅ-nad-kyis ñam-thag-pa thams-cad sel-ba yin-no II til-mar daṅ I ho-ma sraṅ sum-cu-rća-gñis-

2 gñis daṅ I sman prasarani sraṅ brgya skol-bahi khu-ba til-mar-gyi bźi-hgyur daṅ I hdi-rnams-kyi naṅ-du sman jibaka daṅ I riśabẖaka daṅ I meda rnam-gñis daṅ I bu-ćhaṅ-rtoṅ daṅ I ra-mñe daṅ I ru-rta daṅ I ćandan rnam-gñis daṅ I śuti

3 daṅ I thaṅ-śiṅ daṅ I bćod daṅ I rasna rnams-kyi phye-ma skol-la til-mar ñi-ćhe lus-pa bćags-pa hdi-las mas btaṅ-ba-la sogs-par sbyar-na yaṅ rluṅ-⟨nad⟩ sel-to II til-mar daṅ I ho-ma sraṅ sum-cu-rća-gñis-gñis daṇ I gze-mahi

4 khu-ba til-mar-gyi bźi-gyur-gyi naṅ-du bu-ram daṅ I bcah-sgahi phye-ma sraṅ brgyad-brgyad lẖan-cig-tu skol-la til-mar ñi-ćhe lus-pa bćags-te ran-par hthuṅs-pahi hog-tu ho-ma hthuṅs-la thur-du hkhrus-pa chod-pahi rjes-la I bcah-sga daṅ

5 bu-ram sbyar-ba zos-nas sman sṅa-ma btaṅ-ba daṅ I źu-bar gyur-pahi hog-tu kha-zas ho-ma daṅ lẖan-cig-tu zos-na rluṅ-nad mi-bzad-pa thams-cad sel-to II mar sraṅ brgya ñi-śu-rća-brgyad daṅ I sgog-skya sraṅ brġya skol-bahi khu-ba mar-gyi

6 bźi-hgyur rnams-kyi naṅ-du dbyi-mo daṅ I kru-trug-tres daṅ I pipiliṅ rnams-kyi phye-ma źo gñis-gñis daṅ I bcah-sga daṅ I śiṅ-kun daṅ I lan-ćhva rnam-lṅa daṅ I hdi-rnams-las sraṅ re-re daṅ I star-bu sraṅ-phyed daṅ I hdi-rnams

4 nāma . si laśinādä rruṃ gurśte semąnaką khą|śą'ñä bete jsa āchā u
biti jsa śau aṃgą ruye . beti jsai hālai aṃgą purittä . gą'mą āstaṃna
5 āchā jeṃdä abyamai . badarä spaju . trikaṭauka śīyi | mirejsya .
sedelūṃ . hī'ysamāṃ āstaṃna . cuṇya dvī dvī mācāgye . gvīhą.
rruṃ 32 sera . ysirūnāṃ trihā hīvī raysą yserṳnāṃ ttūṃgarāṃ hīvī
131r1 raysą guśtą hīvī ra|ysä . suttä . āhvarai kuṃ.jī . ñetutcä . biśī
āstaṃna 32 32 saira . ttyāṃ āstaṃna jṣą'ñąñä khu ri va rruṃ harśtä .
2 ysunąñä semąnäką khāśą'ña beti jsa āchā be|śä jidä .
śų'mye beta vaska tcaura tcārba haurąñä . tta tta khu pī . mijsā .
gvīhä. rruṃ . kujsavīnai rruṃ āstaṃna krra tcerai . bete jsa pana
3 āchai beṃdą hā . śelīṣāmajsa u ttavaṃ|dyuḍą perā āchā ṣaide .
perāṃ āchāṃ paḍā krra tcerai . neṣ'āmą vaska baysąñą .
tteña pacīḍa śelīṣā krra tcerai . grāma arve rrestye haurąñä .
4 ustaṃ ttavaṃdye hva|rāṃ u pvātāṃ arvāṃ jsa krra tcerai beta jsa
āchai . cu śau aṃgä u śau pai rūye . u pātcą beti jsa ysāṇu hasu u
5 biśą paḍā vī huñä paśąñą . khve hųñä naṣphustä īdą|ttīvę beti
ṇe'hājāka biśuña pacaḍa krra tcerai . cve dvyāṃ hurāvuā hālaina
śelīṣā pīttą u pī āphirąme hīye hauvi jsa . beti hīya prara u paraṃ-
131v1 jsai . | ga'śīṃdä . u hurā pastrīsąme hīvī strehä . āchai hame . ttai
guną . pa'jsä garkhä hame harai gąrkhą hamāre . u ttye paḍā hvaśtī .
2 śelīṣāṃ neṣā'mą . lokṣāṃ arvāṃ| jsa krra yenąñä . ttiña pacīḍa hā
betä neṣą'mä udeśąyą harbiśä krra tcerai .
cū vāśeru ṣṭe . khu hve suhavarttai nittä . sųmārą ttiraṃdarą cve
3 daukhą ne paysemdą stā | āstaṃnaką . u ttī jsā strehāṃ kīrāṃ jsa
parauste . bāta . u hųñą āphirä[1] jse hame . āsñya pā dastāṃ vī vaṣṭe .
ustaṃ ttaraṃdarą beṃdä haraysde .
4 cū beta jsa | hamye vāśerū hīya gunā . venaustą . āstā vī hatcyadā
hamāre u beraṃdā . agai gauda hamāre u hasvīdä u ysīra u haryāsą
chava tta tta bvāñä .
5 hu|ñą jsa u ttavaṃdye jsa hamye līką vāśąrūṃ gunā . hiṃnā chą .
hąsu . vīnaustä . ttaudą . hau'gą . u ysīce utce ttaśtą u byaśde . u vīnę
132r1 trāmīdą u aṃgvā vī ttaudā hame | hau'gä hame . ttyāṃ āstaṃna
bvąñä .

[1] āphārä.

7 lhan-cig-tu skol-la mar ñi-ćhe lus-pa bćags-pahi miṅ ni sgog-
skya-la sogs-pahi sman mar źes-bya-ste | hdi-las ran-par hthuṅs-na
rluṅ-nad daṅ | rluṅ-nad rkaṅ zug ya-gcig hjas-pa daṅ | rluṅ-nad
gźogs-phyed na-ba daṅ | skran-la
202v1 sogs-pa sel-to || dbyi-mo daṅ | kha-ru-ćhva daṅ | ćha-ba gsum
daṅ | śig-gru daṅ | rgyam-ćhva daṅ | hosuhi hbras-bu rnams-kyi
phye-ma źo gñis-gñis daṅ | mar sraṅ sum-cu-rća-gñis daṅ | la-
phug-gi khu-ba daṅ | sgehu-gśer-gyi khu-ba daṅ | śa-khu daṅ
2 ćhva daṅ | rćabs skyur-po daṅ | źo-ga-chu daṅ | dar-ba rnams-las
sraṅ sum-cu-rća-gñis-gñis daṅ | hdi-rnams-kyi naṅ-du skol-la mar
ñi-ćhe lus-pa bćags-pa-las ran-par hthuṅs-na yaṅ rluṅ-nad sel-to ||
rluṅ ñi-ćhehi nad-la ni | snum rnam-pa bźi-
3 po | źag daṅ rkaṅ daṅ | mar daṅ | til-mar rnams-kyi sman btaṅ-
bar byaho || rluṅ yod-pahi steṅ-du | bad-kan daṅ | mkhris-pahi
bla-gñan-gyis thebs-pa-la ni re-źig bla-gñan bćan-par byas-te de
źi-bar bya-bahi cho-ga je byaho || de-la bad-kan la ni sman
4 drod che-źiṅ rno-ba rnams btaṅ-ṅo || mkhris-pa-la ni sman
mṅar-źiṅ bsil-bahi bag btaṅ-bar byaho || rluṅ-nad rkaṅ zug ya-
gcig hjas-pa daṅ | rluṅ-nad pus-mor skraṅ-ba-la ni | thog-mar gtar-
te khrag phyuṅ-la | de-nas rluṅ-nad sel-bahi cho-ga thams-cad
5 byaho || brlahi naṅ-na bad-kan daṅ | ćhil hdug-pa gñis ldan-pas
rluṅ non-te | brla reṅs-pahi nad drag-po bskyed-pahi nad-kyi mćhan-
ma ni śin-tu lci-bar gyur-ciṅ skyid lug-pa yin-te | de-la ni | thog-mar
bad-kan sel-bahi sman rćub-bo-cog-gi
6 cho-ga byas-la | dehi hog-tu rluṅ bsal-bahi cho-ga thams-cad
byaho || || dreg ni | mi skyeṅ-ṅe-bar hdug-ciṅ sdug-ma myoṅ-ba-las
ṅal-ba-la sogs-pa drag-śul-gyi bag byas-pas rluṅ daṅ khrag hkhrugs-
pa-las hbyuṅ-ste |
7 thog-ma ni rkaṅ lag-gi naṅ-na gnas-la phyi-sa lus-la hjug-par
hgyur-ro || de-la rluṅ śas che-bahi dreg-gi mćhan-ma ni | na-ba daṅ |
rus-pa grum-źiṅ hgas-pa daṅ | lus skam-pa daṅ | rćub-pa daṅ |
mdog gnag-pa rnams yin-par
203r1 bśad-do || khrag daṅ mkhris-pa-las rluṅ-bahi dreg-gi mćhan-ma
ni | mdog dmar-źiṅ skraṅ-ba daṅ | lhaṅ-lhaṅ-por na-ba daṅ | chu
ser hjag-ciṅ hjig-pa daṅ | na-ba daṅ | lus ćha-ba daṅ | mdog hjam-
pa
2 rnams yin-no || bad-kan-las gyur-pahi dreg-gi mćhan-ma ni | cher
mi-na-la | lus g-yah-źiṅ reṅs-pa daṅ | cher skraṅs-pa rnams yin-no ||

śilīṣā jsa hamye vāśurū gunā ni vīnaustä hame u kahaitte u aṃgai
pattīsīdä . u buḍa ttavai hasvaci hame .
2 cu dvyāṃ dvyāṃ dūṣā' jsa | hamye līkä u drrayāṃ dūṣāṃ jsa
hamye vāśirū hīya gunā . cu ttā uskātta hvata beśą śująña haṃbirstä
hamāre tta tta bvāñä .
3 cu śe ḍuṣą' jsa hamye vāśärūṃ nuvarä ṣe' | jehāme va nvaśtä .
cu dvyāṃ dvyāṃ dūṣā' jsa hamye . śā-saluṃ hvaḍāṃ khaṣṭā jsa u
arvāṃ jsa hama-kheṇḍī āhrrī. hame .
4 cu drrayāṃ duṣā' jsa hamye līkä . rauśtä u ysau|ttä cve āstai
gvaysde . kāmīnai hamāte ni ri jatte paṃtsąñä . ṣe' vā . vāśerūṃ
5 jehų.me va saṃñä . āsta⟨ṃ⟩ vīrai arvīnā rruna haurāñä u hauvai
padī|māñä u ttye nema'śä' vina beti jsa hamye aḍārye vāśeruṃ huñą
paśāñä . ttye nema'śä' kąmye duṣą' jsa hamāte haphīśąñä . va anavā-
132v1 ysäna . vamaṃ . vrrī | haysgvā . paṃjsa krre cu ttā thyauta hvate .
ttyāṃ āstaṃnakä kāmīnā haṃbusaṃ ṣṭāte tcerai . ce beti jsa hamye .
vastä hīya vī krra tcerā ttavaṃdye jsa hamye ttye . vrrī haurąñä .
2 śe|līṣā jsa hamye ttye vemaṃ haurąñą .
cve va beti hīya gunā hamāre . tcyauña . sumaṃ . buysį̄ñī ṣvīdą
haṃbrrīhauñą u pesalyąñä u jeṃda
3 pātcą kuṃjsa brrījsąñą | u cuṇya ṣvīdą haṃberstą ṣṭāna . ā vā
kuṃbā hīya cuṇya ṣvīda jsa haṃbirstä ṣṭā .
4 ā vā pātcą bātąttī jsa cūṇya ṣvīdą jsa ā vā ŧraṃdą ttī cuṇya ṣvīdä |
jsa hambersta . ttyāṃ āstaṃna kāṃ saṃ hamāte pesalyāñą vāśerū
bedą .
ucāṃ katāṃ āstaṃna sattā hīya guśtą kāma saṃ hamāte jseṇā
5 kuṭąñä khāśe' be|sä hā arva neśąñä . pāchę khū rraṣṭą paṃdą paśte u
vāśerū bedą peselyąñä
ttavaṃdye jsa hamye . vāśerū mahābuṃją hīya cuṇya gvīhä rruṃ
133r1 jsą u ṣvīdä jsa . ā | āḍä āstaṃna haṃbrīhāñä u līhä . padį̄mąñä u
pātcä hā pisilyąñä . pātcą jīvinīyi arve dasau tte pātcą kūṭąñä u
2 cuṇya gvīhä. rruṃ jsa haṃbrrīhāñä u | saṃkhelyąñä .
cve va śelīṣā buḍa hame . vāśerūṃ . aśvagaṃdha . kuṃjsa hīya
cuṇya . ā vā pātcą śī śąśvāṃ hīya cuṇya ā vā ėśta bāta u śīye mirejsye
3 jsa cu|ṇye āstaṃna kāma saṃ hamāte gvīhye. bīysme jsa saṃ-
khelyąñä .
cu buri saṃ aharīnaka vāśerū hamāte . halīrā u gulą haṃtsa

nad-gźi gñis-gñis hdus-pa daṅ | gsum char hdus-pa-las gyur-pahi
dreg-gi mćhan-
3 ma ni | mćhan-ma goṅ-du bstan-pa rnams cha hdres-pa-las rtogs-
par byaho || dreg nad-gźi gcig-las byuṅ-la | gsar-pa ni gso sla-ba
yin-no || nad-gźi gñis hdus-pa-las byaṅ-ba | lo gcig ćhun-chad lon-
pa ni | kha-zas daṅ
4 sman-gyi so ćam-du hjog nus-so || nad-gźi gsum char hdus-pa-las
byuṅ-la | rma rdol-ciṅ hjag-ste rus-pa hgas-pa gaṅ yin-pa ni | gsor
mi-ruṅ-ste spaṅ-bar byaho || de-la dreg gso-bahi thabs ni | thog-mar
sman-mar blud-de |
5 ñam-stobs bskyed-pahi hog-tu | rluṅ ñi-ćhe-las gyur-pa ma-gtos-
pa | gźan rnams-la gtar-ga gaṅ bciṅ khrag dbyuṅ-ṅo || dehi hog-tu
nad-gźi gaṅ yin-pa daṅ sbyar-źiṅ bkru-sman drag-po mas btaṅ-ba
daṅ | hjam-rći mas btaṅ-
6 ba daṅ | skyug-sman daṅ | bkru-sman daṅ | sman snar blugs-pa
daṅ | cho-ga rnam-pa lṅa-po sṅar bstan-pa hdi-rnams-las gaṅ hos
btaṅ-bar bya-ste | rluṅ-las gyur-pa-la ni | sman mas btaṅ-bahi cho-
ga byaho || mkhris-pa-las gyur-
7 pa-la ni | bkru-sman btaṅ-ṅo || bad-kan-las gyur-pa-la ni skyug-
sman btaṅ-ṅo || yaṅ-na rluṅ śas che-ba-las gyur-pahi dreg-la ni | bag-
che-mar daṅ | rahi ho-ma daṅ sbyar-bas bskus-na sel-bar hgyur-ro ||
yaṅ-na til brṅos-
203*v*1 pahi phye-ma ho-ma daṅ sbyar-ba ham | zar-mahi phye-ma ho-
ma daṅ sbyar-ba ham | śu-tahi phye-ma ho-ma daṅ sbyar-ba ham |
'eraṇḍahi sa-bon-gyi phye-ma ho-ma daṅ sbyar-ba gaṅ yaṅ ruṅ-bas
bsku-bar byaho || yaṅ-na chu-na gnas-pahi srog-chags ña-la sogs-
pahi śa gaṅ
2 yaṅ ruṅ-ba źib-tu brduṅs-pa-ste | spod sna-ćhogs-kyis btab-la
legs-par bćos-pas bsku-bar byaho || mkhris-pa śas che-ba-las gyur-
pahi dreg-la ni | śiṅ-mṅar-gyi phye-ma mar daṅ | ho-ma daṅ |
phye-rnams sbyar-bahi lde-gus bskuho || yaṅ-na
3 hćho-byed ces-bya-bahi sman sna bcu-po rnams btags-pahi phye-
ma mar daṅ sbyar-bas bsku-bar byaho || bad-kan śas che-ba-las gyur-
pahi dreg-la ni | 'aśvagandha daṅ | til-gyi phye-ma ham | yaṅ-na yuṅs-
kar-gyi phye-ma ham | yaṅ purṇarnaba daṅ | śi-
4 kruhi phye-ma daṅ | hdi-rnams gaṅ yaṅ ruṅ-ba | ba-gcin daṅ
sbyar-te bsku-bar byaho || dreg-go-cog-la ni 'arurahi phye-ma bu-

4 haṃberstä ṣṭāna hverai | pātcą gulūśą' jṣą'ñąñä kaṣā' khāśą'ñä .
pātcą papalą . ṣvīdą jsa haṃtse jṣą'ñąñä ṣe' raysāyaṃ hva ṣṭe .
5 khāś'ąñä kīrā . panūḍai vaṣṭä hā papalä byąñą paṃ|jsa paṃjsa
daṃdä khu ssīyā papalā. vī hīśtą u paskyāṣṭä panūḍai paṃjsa paṃjsa
pāraṃjsąñą . u paskyāṣṭä pajā papalā vī hīśtą pātcą tta tta kheṇḍī
133v1 uskyāṣṭą ėskhęjāñą u jṣą'ñą|ñä tvā krra tta tta tcerai u śirī jsāṃ
parehąñä . yāṃdī tta tta khāśą'ñą .
beta jsa āchāṃ hīvī jehāme hīvī peṣkalą śuribestaṃ .
2 tteña pacīḍa mau jsa āchāṃ jehų.|me vaṣkalą beraysde
cu be' ṣṭe ṣe' daśāṃ uysānāṃ jsa hva ṣṭe kąma ṣṭāte . ttye āstaṃna
pā beśą mau bedą idą . cve ne bvąre khāśä' duṣe' āphīrāñe tta tta
3 khu bā u tta|vaṃdya u śelīṣā ā[na]staṃna . u mau jsa vā streha
āchā panamāre .
ci beta jsa hamya gunā garkhą bejeṣe u pharākä bejeṣe hagavaṃdai
4 bejeṣe . hąṭhai | neśtä . hanāsai pharāką . aṃgai lok⟨ṣ⟩a hamāre . u
cha āṣana hame . u vau'saṃdai hame ttyāṃ āstaṃna bvąñä .
5 cu ttavaṃdye jsa ttai gunā chavai hija u ysīca | ysaurrją hame . jau
vī kṣą'me tteka busta ṣṭāre
ce śelīṣāmajsa hīya gunā pharāką ne bejeṣe salā haṃbirstä iṃdą
134r1 cedąma nastä chavī śīyau.|rga hauvi jsa ñaśikä hame .
cu jsāṃ drrayāṃ duṣā' jsa hamye līką . ṣe' harbeśāṃ gunāṃ jsa
haṃphve bvąñä .
2 ci be'ta jsa hamye līką mau jsa āchai hīya gunā . ysirä ki|mą'ña .
kvā'ysā vīne . agai strīsīṃdą haika biysaśte . phāhą . āstaṃna . ttavaṃdye jsa hamye mau jsa āchę hīya gunā ttarī hame . aṃgvā ttaudā .
3 āha.sāvī nerą|me . chavī ysīcą hame . vau'sai hiysda ysorrją āstaṃna
hvave ṣṭāre .
śelīṣā jsa hamye mau jsa āchai hīya gunā yserī vanāśtä u ṣahe
4 nerāmīdä | u hauśau'vī hame . bāmä agāṃ strīsāme āstaṃna
cu drayā duṣā' mau jsa hamye āchai gunā . harbeśāṃ gunāṃ jsa
haṃphve bvąñä .
5 ce beta jsa hamye mau jsa ā|chai vī . khu mau khāśe' khvai
gvahä. hame .
tteña pacīḍę hā mauya ⟨suttä⟩ spaju trekaṭauką jsa cuṇya . u dilaka
jsāṃ hā ūtce neśąñä haṃbrīhāñä khāśą'ñä jedä .
134v1 | ā vā pātcą . mauyä . suttä spaju . merejsya . kulīrai . sąnā ąstaṃna

ram daṅ sbyar-ba bzah-bar byaho ‖ yaṅ-na sle-tres bskol-bahi khu-
ba btuṅ-bar byaho ‖ yaṅ-na pipiliṅ ho-ma daṅ bskol-bahi
5 sman-bcud-gyis len btuṅ-bar bya-ste ‖ ñin gcig bźin-du pipiliṅ
lṅa-lṅas bskyed-de | pipiliṅ-gi graṅs brgyar phyin-nas | ñin gcig
bźin-⟨du⟩ pipiliṅ lṅa-lṅas phri-ste | pipiliṅ lṅa-la thug-nas yaṅ
sṅa-ma bźin-du bskyed-de | bskol-
6 ba deṅ lta-bu cho-ga legs-par bsruṅ-źiṅ | rtag-tu btuṅ-bar byaho |
rluṅ-nad gso-bahi lehu-ste | ñi-śu-rća-gcig-pa rjogs-so ‖

‖ de-nas chaṅ-nad gso-bahi lehu bśad-par byaho ‖ dug-la phan-
gnod rnam-pa bcu yod-par bstan-pa
7 gaṅ yin-pa de-rnams ni chaṅ-la yaṅ yod-de | de btuṅ ñes-pa-las
nad-gźi rluṅ daṅ | mkhris-pa daṅ | bad-kan rnams hkhrugs-nas |
chaṅ-nad drag-po skye-bar hgyur-ro ‖ de-la rluṅ-gis ćhul gyur-pahi
mćhan-ma ni | smra-ba thogs-
204*r*1 pa daṅ | maṅ-du smra-ba daṅ | smra-ba-la bskam-pa daṅ | ćhig
mi-brtan-ciṅ khral-khrul-ba daṅ | lus rćub-ciṅ mdog sṅon-por
hgyur-ba daṅ | dmar-por hgyur-ba daṅ | myos-pa rnams yin-no ‖
mkhris-pas ćhul gyur-bahi
2 mćhan-ma ni | mdog dmar-źiṅ ser-ba daṅ | khro-źiṅ hthab-par
dgah-ba yin-no ‖ bad-kan-gyis ćhul hgyur-bahi mćhan-ma ni |
smra-ba ñuṅ-ba daṅ | ćhig hphrel-ba daṅ | sems-pa daṅ | bźin-
mdog dpal skya-ba daṅ | rgyuṅ źan-
3 pa rnams yin-no ‖ nad-gźi kun-hdus-pa-las ćhul gyur-pa ni de-
dag thams-cad daṅ ldan-pa yin-no ‖ de-la rluṅ-las gyur-pahi chaṅ-
nad-kyi mćhan-ma ni | sñiṅ daṅ | klad-pa daṅ | rćib-log na-ba daṅ |
lus reṅs-pa daṅ | skyigs-
4 bus hdebs-pa daṅ | lud-pa lu-ba rnams yin-no ‖ mkhris-pa las
byuṅ-bahi chaṅ-nad-kyi mćhan-ma ni | skom daṅ che-ba daṅ | lus
ćha-ba daṅ | rṅul hbyuṅ-ba daṅ | mdog ser-por hgyur-ba daṅ | mi-
dran-źiṅ myos-pa rnams yin-no ‖ bad-
5 kan-las gyur-pahi chaṅ-nad-kyi mćhan-ma ni | mer-mer-po daṅ |
kha-nas chu hbyuṅ-ba daṅ | yi-ga hchus-pa daṅ | skyug-pa daṅ | lus
reṅs-pa rnams yin-no ‖ nad-gźi gsum hdus-pa-las gyur-pahi chaṅ-
nad ni | mćhan-ma thams-cad daṅ
6 ldan-par rig-bar byaho ‖ de-la rluṅ-las gyur-pahi chaṅ-nad-la ni |
chaṅ sṅa-ma hthuṅs-pa źu-bar gyur-pahi hog tu | chaṅ-gi naṅ-du
kha-ru-ćhva daṅ | ćha-ba gsum-gyi phye-ma daṅ | chu ñuṅ-zad-cig
blugs-te hthuṅs-na sel-bar byed-do ‖ yaṅ-na chaṅ-gi

cuṇya hā neśāñä . khāśą̄'ñä . beta jsa hamye mau jsa āchai strehä.
jidä .

2 pātcä beta jsa | hamye mau jsa āchai . piṣkelyāme va . mau jsa āḍe
jsa grauśe' padīmą̄ñä vara hā baraśīje . drrāma ttīma . ttittalīkä .
3 sānā . sedilū āstaṃna cuṇya neśą̄ñä | khāśą̄'ñä . ttīvī tta[ra]rä hamāte
īrmāṃ[1] hīvī raysä u drrāma ttīma . ttīrye ūce jsa murą̄ñä u khāśą̄'ñä
4 astaucä ysātāṃ u muñaṃdāṃ datāṃ | hīya guśta drrą̄ma ttauna .
sidalūṃ . drrą̄mä ttīma jsa haṃbrrīhą̄ñä khāśą̄'ñä . hvarą̄ñä pa'jse
śerą īdä .

5 ttavaṃdye jsa hamye mau jsa āchai vī . mau u śva' | utca haṃ-
brrīhāñä . mākṣī' hā neśą̄ñä . śekarä haṃbrrīhāñä khāśą̄'ñą ā vā
hvarāṃ arvāṃ hīyȧ kaṣā' śekarą jsa haṃberstä ṣṭāna . ā vā māṃgą
135r1 hīvī raysä śeka|rä jsa hambirstä ṣṭāna . ā vā hvarāṃ arvāṃ hīya
jiṣṭāna kaṣā' ysuma jsa haṃtsa ttyāṃ āstaṃna kāma saṃ hamāte
khāśā'ñą . tti harbeśą hvāta[2] ysūṣṭi ṣṭāre .

2 śilīṣā | jsa hamye mau jsa āchai vī . mau jsa vimaṃ hīye arve
haṃbrrīhāñä . bamą̄ñą̄ñą . ttiraṃdarna vī hauta spāśą̄ñä u ana-
3 hārauśta jsai krra tcerai ā vā grą̄māṃ de haṃ|jsulākyāṃ arvāṃ hīya
cuṇya tcerai u ⟨......⟩ habrrīhāñä khāśą̄'ñä u parehą̄ñą . cvai
hvīḍa rruśe jsa ⟨vadeṃda⟩ . hauṣkā ttrihā hīvī raysä kulastą hīvī
4 raysą . kā|sa hamāte . khą̄śi' bisā arva tcerai buḍatta . astaucą
muñaṃdāṃ datāṃ hīye apīye guśte jsa haṃtsa hvāysīmą hverai .

5 cu mau jsa āchai hīvī pracai kiṇā ttarą | āchai biysaśte u ttavai .
phāhä . kvā'ysva vī̜ne . avīysārą āstaṃna perā āvaṃdva haṃdara
āchā kāṃ saṃ hamāte ttyā hīya ttā krra hva hva beśä uskātta nva
135 v1 dūṣä' ha|phīśą̄ñä u neṣe'mą̄ñä . cu mau jsa aṃgāṃ bedä guśtä biśą
jīye . strehai . vastą tcerai u anavāysāna tcārbaṃdye jsai aṃga
2 makṣą̄'ñä u vameysą̄ñä u ysīną̄|hą̄ñą . arvīnā rrṳna u ṣvī̜da varāśą̄'ñä
u bują̄ñą̄ñä ṣe' vā rrūṃ śerāta . ėśtä bā . mahābuṃjä hīya cuṇya .
3 gvīha: rrūṃ . u tcau bhāga tvaḍa ūtce jsa jṣą̄'ñą̄ñä khu | ra va rrūṃ
harśtä . khāśą̄'ñä .

pātcą haryāsa sacha bāta jṣą̄'ñą̄ñä . kaṣą̄'ña hā ṣvī̜dą haṃbrrīhāñä

[1] īrhvāṃ. [2] pvāta.

7 naṅ-du ćhva daṅ I kha-ru-ćhva daṅ I na-le-śam daṅ I zim-thig-le
daṅ I la-la-phud rnams-kyi phye-ma blugs-te hthuṅs-na yaṅ I rluṅ-
las gyur-pahi chaṅ-nad drag-po sel-to II yaṅ-na rluṅ-las gyur-pahi
chaṅ-nad bsal-bahi phyir I chaṅ hol-kon-gyi
204v1 mar byas-bahi naṅ-du I rgya-śug-gi hbrum-bu daṅ I bal-po sehu
daṅ I tintilahi hbras-bu daṅ I la-la-bud daṅ I rgyam-ćhva rnams-kyi
phye-ma blugs-te ltuṅ-bar byaho II skom-du ni kha-luṅ daṅ I bal-po
sehu skyur-chuhi naṅ-du mñes-te btuṅ-bar byaho II ri-
2 dags skam-sa-na gnas-pahi śa-khu snum daṅ ldan-pa ham I
rgyam-ćhva daṅ I bal-po sehu daṅ I sbyar-ba yaṅ btuṅ-ba daṅ I
kha-zas spag-par bzaṅ-ṅo II mkhris-pa-las gyur-pahi chaṅ-nad-la
ni I chaṅ daṅ chu phyed mar byas-la I sbraṅ-rći daṅ I kha-ra daṅ
3 sbyar-te btuṅ-bar byaho II yaṅ-na sman-mṅar bag bskol-bahi
khu-ba kha-ra daṅ sbyar-ba ham I mon-sran sdehuhi khu-bcud kha-
ra daṅ sbyar-ba ham I sman-mṅar bag bskol-bahi khu-ba-las śa
bćos-te bsdus-pahi khu-ba rnams-las gaṅ yaṅ
4 ruṅ-ba btuṅ-bar bya-ste I thams-cad kyaṅ graṅ-mos byas-pa
yin-no II bad-kan-las gyur-pahi chaṅ-nad-la ni skyug-sman chaṅ
daṅ sbyar-te skyug-tu gźug-pa daṅ I ñam-stobs daṅ sbyar-te smyuṅ-
bahi cho-ga yaṅ byaho II yaṅ-na drod bskyed-
5 pahi sman-gyi phye-ma chaṅ daṅ sbyar-ba ham I hbras-bu gsum
bskol-bahi khu-ba I ćha-ba gsum-gyi phye-ma daṅ I sbyar-ba btuṅ-
źiṅ cho-ga bsruṅ-bar byaho II kha-zas ni nas-las byas-pahi kha-zas
la-phug skam-pohi khu-bcud daṅ I rgya-sran-
6 gyi khu-bcud gaṅ yaṅ ruṅ-bas spod ćha-bas śa skyed-de sbyar-ba
daṅ I ri-dags skam-sa-na gnas-pahi śa-snum bag chuṅ-ba daṅ I
lh̲an-cig-tu bzaho II chaṅ-nad-kyi rkyen-gyis bskos-pahi nad daṅ I
rim⟨s⟩ daṅ I lud-pa daṅ I rćibs-log na-ba daṅ I
7 hkhru-ba-la sogs-pahi nad bla-gñan gaṅ yaṅ ruṅ-ste I de-dag-la ni
so-sohi smin btaṅ-bas źi-bar byaho II chaṅ-gis lus-kyi śa zad-par
gyur-pa-la ni I bkru-sman drag-po mas btaṅ-ba daṅ I hjam-rći mas
btaṅ-ba daṅ I snum-gyis
205r1 lus bsku-źiṅ dril-ba daṅ I khrus bya-ba daṅ I sman-mar daṅ I
ho-ma bluṅ-ba rnams-kyis brta-bar byaho II de-la sman-mar ni
ñehu-śiṅ daṅ I purṇarṇaba daṅ I śiṅ-mṅar-gyi phye-ma mar chu
mar-gyi bźi hgyur-
2 gyi naṅ-du bskol-te I mar ñi-će lus-pa-las ran-par btuṅ-ṅo II yaṅ-
na bala daṅ I ’atilaba I bskol-bahi khu-ba ho-ma daṅ sbyar-ba

khāśą̄'ñä . kṣa'yą āchai jedä . ė'śte bāta jṣą̄'ñą̄ñä ka|ṣa'ña hā gvīhą.
4 rrū u ṣvīdä u mahābują hīya cuṇya neśą̄ñą .
pātcą jṣą̄'ñą̄ñä khu re va śumą rrū harśtą ysunāñą semānaką
5 khāśą̄'ñä . cve mau jsa cha bejette . pa|skyāṣṭa śerka hīya cha byehe: u hauta

mau jsa . āchai hīvī peṣkala dvārabestaṃ .

tteña pacīḍa ttā vesarpą jehųme hīvī peṣkala beraysde .

136r1 ci vesarpä . | ṣe' ṣurāṃ u āhvarāṃ u dijsaṃdāṃ u ttaudāṃ u
strahāṃ u trekṣāṃ' hvaḍā khaṣṭā āstaṃna yāṃdą sīvą̄me jsa u
2 varāśą̄'me jsa dūṣe' āphīrāre u ttye jsa . hauda-padya vesarpa|hame .
tta ttai bvą̄ñä cu visarṣą[1] ṣi' agvā harbeśāvī biraysde u trāme .
cu beti jsa hamye līką visarpą hīya gunā . vesarpä hau'ga hame u
3 hasva cha hasu . tta|ve . khe'yājsa āstaṃna
ci ttavaṃdye jsa hamye visarpä gunā . vesarpą hīya cha ysīca
hame u hiṃja . agai ttavāre . u ttavaivī hame . ttyāṃ āstaṃna
4 bvā|ñä .
ce śelīṣā jsa hamye vesarpą hīya gunā vesarpą cha śīya u khaysme
śīye . u kihaitte u śelīṣāmajsai hā ttavai ṣiṣḍä .
5 ce saṃdvęną jsa hamye | visarpä ṣe' harbeśāṃ gunāṃ jsa haṃphve
heme guhāme jsa hamye visarpä hųñä . u ttavaṃdye jsa dvyāṃ jsa
136v1 hame . visarpä hīya cha haryāsa u rrāṣa u hi|ji . u hasų . nerau .
aṃgai ttavāre u ttavai hā ṣiṣḍä . ttyāṃ āstaṃna hvata ṣṭāre .
dai mą̄ñaṃdä vesarpä . ṣe' beta jsa u ttavaṃdya jsa hamye . cu
2 vesarpą hīya cha drrą̄|mai hami si padīyā dai . īñakai ttaudą skarä
māñaṃdą . hainai u aṃga ttevāre . ttarai biysīśtä . u nāṣṭą tsų̄me
āstaṃnai gųnāṃ jsa bvāñä .
3 .cu khā'je mą̄ñaṃ|du vesarpą ṣe' śelīṣāṃ' u ttavadye jsa hamye .
cu vesarpą hīya cha ṣe' śīyaurga u heṃja u haryāsa u rrūsena rrīma
4 jsa pvīsta . venausta u īñakai | va ysīca ūtce khā'je kheṇḍä hame ttye
jsa bvą̄ñä .
cu drrayāṃ duṣā' jsa hva hva śe śe duṣā' jsa pana vesarpą jehume
5 va nvaśtä . harīyaja haṃdara ne jehāre . | ci aṃgāṃ haṃdaṃna u
netcaṃna nirą̄me . hamarāṃ biṃdą nirą̄me . ci hauda-pacaḍa ṣe' jsā
ni jatte

[1] visarpā.

hthuṅs-na zad byed-kyi nad sel-to ǁ punarnaba bskol-bahi khu-
bahi naṅ-du | mar daṅ | ho-ma daṅ |
3 śiṅ-mṅar-gyi phye-ma blugs-te | bskol-la mar ñi-ćhe lus-pa bćir-
ba-las ran-par hthuṅs-na yaṅ | chaṅ hthuṅs-pas mdaṅs med-par
byas-pa phyir brta-źiṅ sor chud-par byed-do ǁ
chaṅ-nad gso-bahi lehu-ste ñi-śu-rća-gñis-pa rjogs-
4 so ǁ ǁ de-nas me-dbal gso-bahi lehu bśad-par byaho ǁ me-dbal ni |
lan-ćhva daṅ | skyur-ba daṅ | ćha-ba daṅ | drod che-źiṅ rno-ba-la
sogs-pahi kha-zas rtag-tu zos-pas nad-gźi hkhrugs-par byas-pa-las
me-dbal rnam-pa bdun-
5 du śes-par bya-ste | me-dbal źes-bya-ba ni lus thams-cad-du
mched-ciṅ hjug-pa yin-no ǁ de-la rluṅ-las gyur-pahi me-dbal-gyi
mćhan-ma ni | hbrum-bu hjam-źiṅ mdog gnag-pa daṅ | skraṅ-ba
daṅ | rims-kyis hdebs-pa daṅ |
6 gzer-ba rnams yin-no ǁ mkhris-pa-las gyur-pahi me-dbal-gyi
mćhan-ma ni | hbrum-buhi mdog ser-źiṅ dmar-ba daṅ | lus-ćha
daṅ | rims-kyis hdebs-pa rnams yin-no ǁ bad-kan-las gyur-pahi me-
dbal-gyi
7 mćhan⟨-ma⟩ ni | hbrum-buhi mdog dkar-źiṅ dbal skya-ba daṅ |
g-yah-źiṅ bad-kan-gyi rims hdebs-pa yin-no ǁ kun hdus-pa-las
gyur-pahi me-dbal ni mćhan-ma thams-cad daṅ ldan-pa yino | glo
rdol-ba-las
205v1 gyur-pahi me-dbal ni | khrag daṅ | mkhris-pa gñis-las hbyuṅ-ste |
hbrum-b⟨u⟩hi mdog gnag-pa daṅ | sṅo-skyar hdug-pa daṅ | dmar-ba
daṅ | skraṅ-ba daṅ brnags-nas rdol-ba daṅ | lus ćha-ba daṅ | rims
bdo-bar byed-pa rnams yin-par
2 bśad-do ǁ mehi me-dbal źes-bya-ba ni | rluṅ daṅ | mkhris-pa dag-
las hbyuṅ-ste | hbrum-buhi mdog mes bsregs-pa hdra-la | ñen-bskor
me-mdag bźin-du dmar-źiṅ | lus ćha-ba daṅ | skom-dad che-ba
daṅ | hkhru-ba-la sogs-pahi
3 mćhan-ma-las rtogs-par byaho ǁ me-dbal rjab-hdra źes-bya-ba
ni | bad-kan daṅ mkhris-pa-las hbyuṅ-ste | hbrum-bahi mdog-dpal
skya-źiṅ dmar-ba daṅ | gnag-ciṅ hćher-te dri-mas g-yogs-pa daṅ |
ćha-źiṅ ñe⟨n⟩-skor-du chu-ser-gyi
4 hdam-źiṅ-du hdug-pa rnams yin-no ǁ de-la nad-gźi gsum so-so-
las gyur-pahi me-dbal ni gso sla-ba yin-no ǁ lẖag-ma gźan rnams ni
gsor mi-ruṅ-bar bśad-do ǁ lus-kyi phyi-naṅ gñis kar byuṅ-ba daṅ |
ćhigs-kyi steṅ-du

137r1 ci beta jsa pana vesarpä paṃje mulä hvata ṣṭāre paṃjsa : || |
paṃjsa uskātta ttyāṃ haṃdrre vya . ysāysį̄nāṃ bātāṃ jsa tcau ga'
paṃje mula kāṃta saṃ śau hemāte . aṃga jsa sakhalyą̄ñä . āchai
2 biṃdą hā baijsą̄ñä pahāṃ rrų̄nāṃ āstaṃna haṃ|phīśą̄ñä :

pātcą rrīysu rrusa . mahābuṃją āstaṃna cūṇya . gvīhä rru ṣvīdą
haṃdrre vya jṣā'ñą̄ñą . kai'vą jsa pajsą̄ñä u bidę hā pisalyą̄ñä ā vā
3 pātcą gvīhą ṣvī|dä jsa bejsą̄ñä . ā vā gvīhä rrū hīvī raysäna beją̄ñą .

ttavaṃdye jsa hamye visarpä . prripuṇḍarī . rruṃnai . puṣṭarä .
4 uśe'rä . caṃdaṃ . mahābujä . nī|lotpalą āstaṃna . cuṇya ṣvīdä jsa
haṃbrrīhāñä saṃkhalyą̄ñä . pātcą ñagraudhātta ga' āstaṃna cu ttā
5 uskātta hva ttye hīye kaṣe' jsa bejsāñä hīhä jsa | strīsāñą̄ñą u ssa juna
dvāñä khu śī hame . vara hā mahābuṃjä hīya cuṇya buḍatta neśą̄ñä
haṃbrrīhāñä u saṃkhalyą̄ñą .

137v1 pātcä srrauttų̄ja . uśe'rä | caṃdaṃ . buhane . mirāhe . kirkīyaṃ .
svana gīrai āstaṃna cuṇya gvīhä: rrūṃ u ṣvīdą jsa haṃbrrīhāñä u hā
saṃkhalyą̄ñä . ttavaṃdye jsa hamye visarpä jidä .

2 śi|līṣā jsa hamye vesąrpä vī . khara cikalä . aśäphauṇḍä . buhane .
śīja . rrājevṛkṣä . devidārą . īraṃdą āstaṃna sauysāñä u līhä padīmą-
3 ⟨ñä⟩ saṃkha|lyāñą āchā jedä .

pātcą mahābują trephalą . kākūṭä . haiśva ttī āstaṃna sīyą̄ñą u
līhą hā pīsalyą̄ñä .

4 pātcą śilīṣā jsa hamye vesarpä vī | vehīlāde ga' āstaṃna hā pisalyā-
ñä u kaṣe' jsa jsā bejsāñą u rrų̄vą jsa pajsą̄ñä pa'jsą śerą īdą

5 pātcą paṭaulä . cegāṃ ttīrai perä . ysālva . kalyaruha|ne trāye-
mų̄ṇḍą . mahābūją āstaṃna jṣā'ñāñä u kaṣā' khāśą̄'ñä vesarpä
harbeśą jedä .

138r1 pātcą buhąne . cigāṃ ttīrai hīye ⟨pe⟩rä . paṭaulą āstaṃna kaṣā' |
khāśą̄'ñä .

cu buri saṃ visarpą īye biśą jeṃdä .

pātcą aủmalai paṭaulą māṃgä āstaṃna jṣā'ñą̄ñä . kaṣā' gvīhä
2 rrūṃ jsa haṃbrīhāñä khāśą̄'ñą habistä nasą vi|sarpą vī āsña vemaṃ

5 byuṅ-ba ni | bdun char yaṅ lẖag-par gsor mi-ruṅ-ṅo || de-la rluṅ-las gyur-bahi me-dbal-la ni | rća-ba lṅahi sman-lṅa phugs-lṅa sṅar bśad-pahi naṅ-nas | rćahi rća-ba lṅa-pa ma-gtogs-par rća-ba lṅa-pa rnam-pa bźi-po rnam-las gaṅ

6 yaṅ ruṅ-bas lus bsku-ba daṅ | nad-kyi steṅ-du blugs-pa daṅ | sman-mar sbyar-ba-la sogs-pa byaho || yaṅ-na hbras daṅ | nas daṅ śiṅ-mṅar rnams-kyi phye-ma mar daṅ | ho-mahi naṅ-du bskol-te | thug-pa ćhos-par byas-pas na-bahi steṅ-du

7 bsku-bar byaho || yaṅ-na ho-mas na-bahi steṅ-du blugs-par byaho || yaṅ-na mar-gyi sñiṅ-pos steṅ-du blugs-par byaho || mkhris-pa-las gyur-bahi me-dbal-la ni | sman prapuṇḍarīka daṅ | bćod daṅ | śug-pa daṅ | bu-śel-će daṅ | ćandan daṅ |

206r1 śiṅ-mṅar daṅ | 'utpala rnams-kyi phye-ma ho-ma daṅ sbyar-te bsku-bar byaho || yaṅ-na śiṅ nyagrodẖa-la sogs-pahi sde-ćhan sṅar bśad-pas nad-kyi steṅ-du khu-ba blugs-pa daṅ | bsdu-ba daṅ | sman-mar sbyar-ba rnams

2 byas-na bzaṅ-ṅo || yaṅ-na mar gźu-źiṅ hkhyeg-du bcug-pa de-lta-bur | lan-brgyahi bar-du byas-te | rul-bar gyur-pahi naṅ-du | śiṅ-mṅar-gyi phye-ma śas cher blug-ste sbyar-bas bsku-bar byaho || yaṅ-na lig-bu-mig daṅ | pu-śel-ći daṅ |

3 ćandan daṅ | gla-sgaṅ daṅ | mu-tig daṅ | nor-bu rin-po che daṅ | bćags-rnams-kyi phye-ma | mar daṅ | ho-mar sbyar-te | bskus-na mkhris-pa-las gyur-pahi me-dbal sel-to || bad-kan-las gyur-pahi me-dbal-la ni | seṅ-ldeṅ daṅ | saptaparṇa daṅ |

4 gla-sgaṅ daṅ | śiṅ dẖaba daṅ | doṅ-ga daṅ | thaṅ-śiṅ daṅ | kuraṇḍa rnams bdar-bahi lde-gus bskus-na źi-bar hgyuro || yaṅ-na śiṅ-mṅar daṅ | hbras-bu gsum daṅ | bu-ćhaṅ-rto daṅ | śiriśa rnams bdar-bahi lde-gus bskuho || yaṅ-na bad-kan-

5 las gyur-pahi me-dbal-la | sman baruna-la sogs-pahi sde-ćhan-gyis bsku-ba daṅ | khu-bas blugs-pa daṅ | sman mar sbyar-ba-la sogs-pa byas-na bzaṅ-ṅo || patola daṅ | nimpa daṅ | skyer-pahi rća-bahi śun-lpags daṅ | pu-će-śel daṅ |

6 khyi lce-ba daṅ | śiṅ-mṅar rnams bskol-bahi khu-ba mthuṅ-na yaṅ me-dbal thams-cad sel-to || gla-sgaṅ daṅ | nimpa daṅ | patola rnams bskol-bahi khu-ba mthuṅs-na yaṅ | me-dbal-lo-cog sel-to || yaṅ-na skyurura daṅ | patola daṅ | mon-

7 sran-sdehu rnams bskol-bahi khu-ba mar daṅ sbyar-te btuṅ-bar byaho || mdor-na me-dbal-la ni | daṅ-por skyug-sman daṅ | bkru-

u vrrī jsa haphīśą̄ñä . huñai paśą̄ñä khvai tta tta krra yuḍą īṃdä . u
vesarpä daśte .

cu kaṃmä haṃbrrāme hīya krra hvata ṣe' harbeśą tcerā
3 visa|rpą jehāme hīvī piṣkalą drrerabestaṃ .
tteña pacīḍa ttā haśa āchai jehāme hīvī peṣkalą beraysde .
4 cu haśä āchai jata guśtą garkha-gvāchāṃ ā|hvarāṃ . śelīṣā'majsā
hvaḍāṃ khaṣṭā sīvą̄me jsa . duṣe' āphirāre . beysāja kṣe-padya haśą
5 āchai hame cu bure saṃ haśą īye gunaivī ṣai'kä cu askhaukara | hame .

cu ba'ta jsa hamya līka haśą gunā . ṣai hasvaca ttālanāṣṭä u
aḍāraṣṭą tsṳ̄maṃca hame . cve hā haṃguṣṭa jsa ṇehejīdä u dārą buri
138v1 va neca hame . chavī | haryāsa hame u heṃją u pa'jsä vinausta .

cu ttavaṃdye jsa hamye līkye haśa gṳnā . thyau parvaśte u berṣḍä
2 u hau'ga hame . u ysīca . u heṃja . u venausta u ttau|da . agvā vī
arādā hame .

śelīṣā jsa hamya līkye haśe gunā . chavī tcārba hame u śīya u
ysīcaurga . u styudai hame u kahaitte .

3 cu huña āphārä jsa | hamya u āvaṃdve haśa hīya gṳnā . ttavaṃ-
dyuḍe haśi hīyā gunā khaiṇḍe hamāre .

cu drrayāṃ dūṣā' jsa hamye haśa gṳnā harbiśāṃ jsa habajsya .
4 cvaṃ | duṣą' jsa hera hame . haṃdaṃna . pārahe . haśau khāysānai
jsa uskyāṣṭä pārautta hame khvai duṣe' myą̄ña pārautta hamāṃde .
5 hasvacai myāña hame ttī vai duṣä' | harbeśvą̄ agvā prattyaṃgvā
beśä vīra hą̄śä nirāme .

cu haśä āchai cū śe dūṣä' jsa hame cve va haṃda perai āvaṃdū
139r1 āchai ne hame khu hauvaṃ hve' ha|māte . u ttye nirāmīye ṣi' jehą̄me
vaska nvaśta hame . cu harbiśāṃ aṃgāṃ biṃdą nerāme . aůska āna
nāṣṭä una āna uskyāṣṭä hasu ṣe' pa'jsä anvaśta :
2 haśe ā|chai vīra vīją dūṣā' jsa haṃphīśą̄ñä . u hva hva dūṣā' hīyā
hīyā arvą̄nāṃ gāṃ' āstaṃna u arvīnā gvīha rrṳna śu'hyą̄ñä u kuṃ-
3 jsavīnā arvīną rrūna śu'hyāñä u | āchai biṃdą bijsą̄ñä u khīṣṭa
āstaṃna haṃphīśą̄ñä .

cu paṃjsa kīra . strehą vastä . anavāysena u vemaṃ . u vrrī
4 haysgvā paśāme āstaṃna strehä nvā | khu va saṃ haṃbusaṃ hamāte

sman-gyi sbyar-ba daṅ | gtar-źiṅ khrag dbyuṅ-ba rnams kyaṅ
byaho || cho-ga de-ltar byas-pa-las kyaṅ hbrum-bu
206v1 mnag-te rdol-ba-las gyur-pa-la ni | rma gso-bahi cho-gar bstan-pa
thams-cad byaho ||

me-dbal gso-bahi lehu-ste ñi-śu-rća-gsum-pa rjogso ||

|| sman-dpyad gces-pa grub-pa źes-bya-ba | bam-po drug-paho ||
de-nas skraṅ-bahi
2 nad gso-bahi lehu bśad-par byaho || skraṅ-bahi nad ni | mi zad-
pas | kha-zas lci-ba daṅ | skyur-ba daṅ | bad-kan skye-bar hgyur-bahi
zas zos-nas | nad-gźi rnams hkhrugs-pa-las skraṅ-bahi nad mi-bzad-
pa rnam-pa drug hbyuṅ-bar
3 hgyur-te | skraṅ-ṅo-cog-gi mćhan-ma ni gso sla-ba yino || de-la
rluṅ-las gyur-pahi skraṅ-bahi nad-kyi mćhan-ma ni | skraṅ-ba ñid
phan-chun-du hpho-źiṅ | gar mnan-pahi mal-śod ṅar hdug-pa daṅ |
mdog gnag-ciṅ dmar-ba daṅ |
4 mi-bzad-par na-ba rnams yin-no || mkhris-pa-las gyur-bahi
skraṅ-bahi mćhan-ma ni | myur-du smin-ciṅ rdol-ba daṅ | mdog
hjam-pa daṅ | ser-źiṅ dmar-ba daṅ ćha-ba daṅ | lus ćha-bar byed-pa
rnams yino || bad-kan-las gyur-pahi
5 skraṅ-bahi mćhan-ma ni mdog snum-źiṅ dkar-ba daṅ | dbal skye-
ba daṅ | khraṅ-ba daṅ | g-yah-ba rnams yino || khrag-las gyur-
pa daṅ | blo-bur-gyi skraṅ-bahi mćhan-ma ni | mkhris-pahi mćhan-
ma daṅ hdraho || kun hdus-pa-las
6 gyur-bahi skraṅ-bahi mćhan-ma ni | thams-cad daṅ ldan-pa yino ||
de-la nad-gźi pho-bahi naṅ-na gnas-na ni | ro-stod skraṅ-bar
hgyuro || nad-gźi loṅ-gahi naṅ-na gnas-na ni | ro-smad-du skraṅ-bar
hgyur-ro || nad-gźi bar-na gnas-na ni bar-du
7 ⟨skraṅ-bar⟩ hgyuro || nad gźi thams-cad-du khyab-na ni | lus-ril-
gyi skraṅ-bar hgyur-ro || de-la skraṅ-bahi nad-gźi gcig-las gyur-ba
yin-la | nad bla-gñan gźan-gyis kyaṅ ma-thebs-te | mi ñam-stobs
chen-po źig-la byuṅ-na ni gso sla-ba
207r1 yino || lus-ril-gyis skraṅ-ba daṅ | mas yar mched-de skraṅ-ba ni
ma-ruṅs-pa yino || skraṅ-bahi nad-la sman-pas nad-gźi daṅ sbyar
źiṅ nad-gźi so-sohi sman-gyi sde-ćhan rnams-kyis sman-mar
sbyar-ba daṅ
2 til-mar-gyi sman sbyar-ba daṅ | bsku-ba daṅ | nad-kyi steṅ-du
blugs-pa daṅ | btuṅ-ba rnams-su sbyar-bar byaho || las rnam-pa
lṅa-po bkru-sman drag-po mas btaṅ-ba daṅ | hjam-rći mas btaṅ-ba
daṅ | skyug-sman daṅ | skru-sman

haṃphīśą̄ñä . nva krre tcerai . vina ttekye ttā haṃdara haśe ächai
neṣā'mä va haṃbajsya krra berāśāṃ'
5 detadārä halīrā . ttuga|re . aủ'śte bāta hīya cụṇya uci jsa jṣą̄'ñāñä
u gr̦̄ama āna hā haṃbrrīhāñä . ā vā veṇḍaṃga prravaṣe' . vatsāvīśi'
139v1 ttī . ttuṃgare devadārä . mirijsye ā|staṃna cụṇya jeṣṭye gr̦̄aṃye ūce
jsa haṃbrrīhą̄ñą u ysunā̧ñą .
pātcą trikaṭaukä . hīśaṃ hīya hīsuṣka . yeva-kṣą̄rą . āstaṃna
2 cuṇya trephalą hīvī rraysä | jṣā'ñą̄ñä u kaṣā' haṃbrrīhāñä u khāśą̄'ñä
haśe āchai jedä .
pātcą kalyaruhana . hīśaṃ hīya hīsuṣka . tre⟨kaṭau⟩kä . traulą
3 āstaṃna cụṇya trephalą jṣāñą̄ñä | u kaṣā' haṃbrrīhą̄ñä .
pātcą gurgula bu' śīya cha gvīhye bīysma jsa haṃbairstä ṣṭāna :
pātcą papala hīya cụṇya ṣvīdą jsa haṃberstą ṣṭą̄na :
4 pātcą gulą | halīrāṃ hīya cūṇyą hamaṃgą veśtą̄ñą u haṃbrrīhāñą .
pātcą gulą u ttuṃgara hamaṃgą veśtą̄ñą u haṃbrrīhāñą : hverai .
5 pātca gula . yserūna | ttugara . samą̄nakä haṃbā jsa hverai .
cu ba'ta jsa hą̣myą haśe vī guśtīnāṃ rraysä jsa haṃtsa haṃbrrīhāñä u hverai
140r1 cū ttavaṃdye jsa hamye hvīḍai ṣvīdä jsa haṃbi.|rstä hverai .
cu śelīṣā jsa hamye vī . hvīḍai lokṣā' rraysä jsa . haṃtse hverai .
khvai tta tta krra yinīye haśe āchaí u naṣṭausai āchai . dūvarä .
2 ātmādä . gą̄'mä a|rrja . ūysna āphārä āstaṃna beśą jehāre .
detadārą . aủśte bāta . ttuṃgara . āstaṃna cụṇya ṣvīdą jsa haṃ-
3 brrīhāñä . ā vā pātcą cetre trekaṭaukä traulą de|tadārä āstaṃna
jṣą̄'ñą̄ñä u kaṣā' khāśą̄'ñä . haśą āchai jeṃdä .
śelīpadmą nā̧ma āchai pī u guśte vī pārautta dvavī pā hasvīṃdä ṣā
4 pā drrayā dūṣā' | jsa . buḍa va śelị̄ṣā purrdą ṣṭāna hame
peṣkece jsa drrai-padya hame . duṣā' hīya ttā hva hva gunā
5 nijsvāñāre ṣe' saṃ yāṃdä sāḍä hame ysīḍaurgä hame u sa|ni hauṣḍe
u huṣa jsāte . khvai śā salī parsīye ne ra jụttye vīre jehāme hīvī krre
vī dūṣā' jsa samaṃdva arvāṃ jsa sakhalụna saṃkhalyāñä u āhasāñą̄ñä
140v1 | u hụñai paśą̄me āstaṃnakai nejsaḍä .

3 daṅ sman snar blugs-pa rnams kyaṅ ćha-bas che-chuṅ daṅ sbyar-źiṅ cho-ga bźin-du btaṅ-bar byaho || de ma-yin-pa skraṅ-bahi nad źi-bar bya-bahi spyihi cho-ga gźan yaṅ bśad-par bya-ste | thaṅ-śiṅ daṅ | 'arura daṅ | bcah-sga daṅ

4 punarnaba rnams-kyi phye-ma chu bskol-ba dron-po daṅ sbyar-ba ham | yaṅ-na byidaṅga daṅ | boṅ-ṅa dkar-po daṅ | dug-mo-yuṅs-kyi śun-lpags daṅ | bcah-sga daṅ | thaṅ-śiṅ daṅ | na-le-śam rnams-kyi phye-ma chu bskol-ba dron-po daṅ

5 sbyar-ba ham | yaṅ-na ćha-ba gsum daṅ | lcags-kyi phye-ma daṅ | nas ćhig hkhus-pahi thal-ba rnams-kyi phye | hbras-bu gsum bskol-bahi khu-ba daṅ sbyar-te hthuṅs-na yaṅ skraṅ-bahi nad sel-to || yaṅ-na pu-će-śel daṅ | lcags-kyi phye-

6 ma daṅ | ćha-ba gsum daṅ | śiṅ ñe-roṅ rnams-kyi phye-ma | hbras-bu gsum bskol-bahi khu-ba daṅ sbyar-ba ham | yaṅ-na gu-gul dkar-po gcin daṅ sbyar-ba daṅ | yaṅ-na pipiliṅ-gi phye-ma ho-ma daṅ sbyar-ba btuṅ-bar byaho || yaṅ-

7 na bu-ram 'arurahi phye-ma daṅ cha bsñams-te sbyar-ba ham | yaṅ-na bu-ram gcah-sga daṅ cha bsñams-te sbyar-ba bzah-bar byaho || yaṅ-na bu-ram daṅ | sgehu gśer-ćhod ran-par bzaho || rluṅ-las gyur-pa-la ni kha-zas śa-khu daṅ

207*vi* lh̲an-cig bzaho || mkhris-pa-las gyur-ba ni kha-zas ho-ma daṅ lh̲an-cig bzaho || bad-kan-las gyur-pa-la ni kha-zas khu-ba bcud rćub-pahi bag daṅ lh̲an-cig bzah-bar byaho || cho-ga de-ltar byas-na skraṅ-bahi nad daṅ | skem-pahi nad daṅ | dmu-rjiṅ daṅ |

2 smyo-byed daṅ | skran daṅ | gźaṅ-hbrum daṅ | dbugs mi-bde-ba rnams hbyaṅ-bar hgyur-ro || thaṅ-śiṅ daṅ | punarnaba daṅ | gcah-sga rnams-kyi phye-ma ho-ma daṅ sbyar-ba ham | yaṅ-na kru-trug-tres daṅ | ćha-ba gsum daṅ | śiṅ ñe-roṅ daṅ | thaṅ-

3 śiṅ rnams bskol-bahi khu-ba hthuṅs-na yaṅ skraṅ-bahi nad sel-to || rkaṅ-hbams śes-bya-ba ni ćhil daṅ | śahi nad-las hgyur-te | rkaṅ-pa gñis bum-pa hdra-bar skraṅ-ba yin || de yaṅ nad-gźi gsum-la bad-kan śas che-ba-las gyur-

4 pahi bye-brag-gis | rnam-pa gsum yod-de nad-gźi so-sohi mćhan-mas bstan-to || de ni dus thams-cad-du graṅ-źiṅ ser che-la | skam-du mi-btub-pahi sar skye-bar hgyur-te | lo gcig lh̲ag-ba daṅ | rkaṅ-hbam grog-mkhar lta-bu ni mi-hćhoho⟨|⟩

5 de-la gso-bahi cho-ga ni nad-gźi daṅ hphrod-pahi sman-gyi bsku-ba daṅ | dugs bya-ba daṅ | gtar-te khrag dbyuṅ-ba-la sogs-pahi

haśa āchai jehāme hīya krra cu ttā biraṣṭa harbeśai khu saṃ ṣṭāte tcerai .

2 cu galą ṣṭe ṣe' beta jsa hame u pī huṣāme | jsa pā hame . śelīṣā jsa pā hame u peṣkece jsa drrai-padya hame .

cu beta jsa hamye līką gunā . chavī haryāsa hamye u heṃja u
3 arīśai' va bauśä hame ihai | va byaṃjsą hame :

cu pī jsa hamye līkä galą gunā . hau'ga hame u tcārbą .

śelīṣā jsa hamye līkä valą gunā pa'jsą mestä hame stadą nvaśtä ni
4 jīye | gaudāṃ hvaṇḍā hame . cu śā salī harśtą ṣe' ri ni jatte .

cu gąṇḍamāla ṣṭe . garśa śelīṣā u pī dvyāṃ jsa vehīlai hīye gech-
5 auka mase mą̄ṇḍakä hame pha|rākai tta tta ga'saṃdā hamāre . bu'ysą muñīdä u saṃna nerāmīdä .

cu galą jehų̄me va krra . vīją hva hva duṣā' jsa peṣkalyą̄ñä duṣā'
141r1 hīyā hva hva arvāṃ hī⟨yāṃ⟩ | gāṃ' jsa āhąsą̄ñāñą u saṃkhalyāñä u peṇdā jsa . hųñe paśą̄me jsa u vimaṃ jsa u vrrī jsa . kuṃjsavīnā arvīnāṃ rrųnāṃ khāśą̄'me āstaṃna galą nestä padīmą̄ñä

2 |cu gąṇḍamāla vī . tvacä hīya cųṇya . kujsavīnya rrųña uce jsa jṣą̄'ñāñą khu re va rruṃ harśtä ysunąñä .

3 ā vā pātcą cigāṃ ttīrai perä . karavīrai . buttanā|kecą āstaṃna cuṇya kujsavīnai rruṃ uce jṣāñą̄ñą khu re va rrū harśtä ysuną̄ñä . haysgvā paśą̄ñä .

4 cu adīṣṭa gąṇḍamāla vīra biṇāñä u ttu vā mą̄ṇḍa|ką thają̄ñą u kaṃmą padajsą̄ñä . cu jsā drāṃ dīṣṭą hamāte . mauṣkaką kṣą̄'rą hīye vai arve haṃbrrīhą̄ñą pisalyą̄ñä nvathą̄ñą̄ñä ttyāṃ haudvyāṃ vīri
5 saṃ kaṃmä hī|ya krra tcerai .

ā vā pāri vī āna dvāsą hau'śä' uskyāṣṭä . pīmą̄ñą u ttekye uskātta
141v1 bęṇą̄'ñä u mulāṃ hadrre vya mauṇḍaka pīvīnā kavīñą ā.|hā kheṇḍa hamāre ttyāṃ āstaṃna thaṃją̄ñä . kamä hīvī hā ttaurą padajsą̄ñä u kaṃmä jehą̄me hīya krra tcerā .

2 arbaudä nāma āchai ṣe' drrayāṃ dūṣā' jsa hame | huñe jsa u guśte jsa u pī āstaṃnaką . ttye hīya hva hva duṣā' hīyā nva guną bvą̄ñä .

cu hųñä jsa hamye u guśte jsa tte re ne jehāre .

3 cu guśte jsa hamye a|rbaudą na saṃñä . galą hīye krre kheṇḍä bųstą ṣṭe tta ttai tcerę .

ā vā bęṇą̄ñä u padajsāñą . arvīnā kṣā'rā jsa tcerai avī kuhaṃ.
4 thau jsa ā vā perāṃ jsa hā | hagunāñą .

cho-ga daṅ | skraṅ-bahi nad gso-bahi cho-gar bstan-pa thams-cad
kyaṅ | ci rigs-par bya-bar bśado || dbah-ba ni rluṅ-
6 las gyur-pa daṅ | ćhil-las gyur-pa daṅ | bad-kan-las gyur-pahi
bye-brag-gis rnam-pa gsum yod-de | de-la rluṅ-las gyur-bahi
dbah-bahi mćhan-ma ni | mdog nag-ciṅ dmar-ba daṅ | kha-dri mi-
źim-pa daṅ | rgan skam-par byed-pa yin-no || ćhil-las
7 gyur-pahi dbah-bahi mćhan-ma ni | hjam-źiṅ snum-pa yino ||
bad-kan-las gyur-pahi dbah-bahi mćhan-ma ni śin-tu che-źiṅ sla-ba
yino || de-la riṅ-ṅe-ba-la byuṅ-ba daṅ | lo gcig phan-chad lon-pa
ni | gsor mi-ruṅ-ṅo || hbras-kyi phreṅ-ba
208*r*1 źes-bya-ba ni | lkog-mar bad-kan daṅ | ćhil gñis-las skyururahi
rus-pa hdra-bar smin-bur gyur-pa maṅ-pos bskor-bahi miṅ ni | hbras-
kyi phreṅ-ba źes-bya-ste | yun riṅ-du mi-hbyaṅ-bar hdug-pa
yin-no || de-la dbah-
2 ba gso-bahi cho-ga ni | sman-pas nad-gźi daṅ sbyar-źiṅ | nad-gźi
so-sohi sman-gyi sde-ćhan-gyis dugs bya-ba daṅ | bsku-ba daṅ | lums
bya-ba daṅ | gtar-źiṅ khrag dbyuṅ-ba daṅ | skyugs-sman daṅ | kru-
sman btaṅ-ba daṅ | til-mar-
3 gyi sman btuṅ-ba rnams-kyis dbah-ba med-par byaho || hbras-
kyi phyed-pa-la ni | sman śa kotakahi śun-lpags-kyi phye-ma | til-
mar daṅ | chuhi naṅ-du bskol-te | til-mar ñi-ćhe lus-pa bćags-pa
ham | yaṅ nimpa daṅ | 'aśvama-
4 ra daṅ | nirgunti rnams-kyi phye-ma til-mar daṅ chuhi naṅ-du
bskol-la | til-mar ñi-ćhe lus-pa bćags-te snar blugso || yaṅ-na hbras-
kyi phreṅ-ba ma-smin-pa-la ni | dral-te smin-bu phyuṅ-la | rma-kha
sregs-so | smin-ciṅ rdol-ba-la ni sman mug-
5 kahi thal-bahi sman sbyar-bas bsku-źiṅ sbyaṅs-la | hdi gñis yaṅ
rmahi cho-ga bźin-du gso-bar byaho || yaṅ-na rtiṅ-pa-nas sor bcu-
gñis-kyi goṅ-du byin-pa dral-te | byin-pahi naṅ-na ćhil-gyi rmin-bu
ñahi sgo-ṅa hdra-ba hdug-pa rnams
6 phyuṅ-la | rma-kha sregs-te gso-bahi cho-ga bźin-du byaho ||
śa-rmen ni nad-gźi gsum so-so-las gyur-te | khrag daṅ | śa daṅ | ćhil
rnams-kyi rmin-bu yino || de ni nad bźi so-sohi mćhan-ma-las źes-par
bya-ste | de-la khrag daṅ
7 śa-las gyur-pahi śa-rmin ni | gsor mi-ruṅ-ṅo || śa-smin gso-bahi
thabs ni | dbah-ba gso-bahi cho-gar bśad-pa bźin-du byaho || yaṅ-na
dral-ba daṅ | bsreg-pa daṅ | sman-gyi thal-bas gdab-pa rnams kyaṅ
bya-źiṅ | ras-ma
208*v*1 ham lo-mas g-yog-par byaho ||

haśa āchę jehāme hīvī peṣkala tcaur-rabestaṃ .
tteña pacīḍa ttā kaṃmą jehume hīvī peṣkala berāśāṃ'
5 hamaiye agāṃ beṃdą neraṃda līkä | kaṃmą u ttī jsāṃ āvaṃdu
hairthaṃ jsa hamye āstaṃna dva-padya bvāñä . cu hamaiyi niraṃda
ṣe' dūṣā' jsa hamye bvąñä . ttiña pacīḍa bisai prihar-ra gvihaiye
āstaṃna ha⟨me⟩ .
142r1 | cu beta jsa hamye kaṃmä hīya gūnā . kaṃmä karvīnā lokṣä'
henai u rrāṣa cha hame . be'ti ysunaṃdaita vīnä vasve . pa'jsä ni
vinaustä hame .
2 cu ttavaṃdye jsa hąmye | kaṃmä gūnā . karä kaṃmä hainai
hame . u ysīḍai . u āṣeṃ ttaudai vā hera ysauttą aṃgvā vī ttaudā
hame .
3 cu śilīṣāṃ jsa hamye līkä kaṃmä gūnā styūdä hame u pa|rvaśte u
śīyi cha hame u ysauttä sāḍä u śī āstaṃna .
cu hūñi āphārä jsa hamye līkä kaṃmä gūnā . chavī heṃji hame u
huñai vā ysauttä
4 cu dvyāṃ dūṣā' | jsa hamye līkä u drrayāṃ dūṣāṃ' jsa hamye līkä
kaṃmä hīya gūnā . kąmye dūṣä' haṃbairsti īṃde . ttikyāṃ ttikyāṃ
5 hīyāṃ gūnāṃ jsa haṃbairsti bvąñä biśä paḍā khu ni | dāśi
byaśde' niṣe'mākyau arvāṃ jsa saṃkhaluna saṃkhalyąñä khu ākṣu
byaśde' ttī haṃdevāka krra tcerai . khu haṃdīṣṭä hame ttī nirūjąñä u
142v1 śau'ląñä arvāṃ jsa ysu kṣau'śtä vasujā|ñä piṣkalyąñä . u gūśti
ysyąñāka krra tcerai ||
ttī vā haṃdavąñāka arve . kuṃjsa tciṃña sumaṃ kuṃbā . kuṣṭä
2 āstaṃna cūnya . ārä[1] sidalū āstaṃna ttīrä ñye jsa murą.|ñä piṇḍai
padīmąñä haṃdevāką biśä pīrmāttä[2] biraṣṭä ṣṭe
ttai vā śva' haṃdīṣṭä hīya gūnā . tta ttai dā nirāme vinaustä hame
3 chavai hiṃji hame u hasu ttyāṃ ā|staṃnai gūnā uysdīśāṃ
cu haṃdīṣṭä hīya gūnā uskātta bisai śva' haṃdīṣṭä jsa . nauhä
4 ysurgą naittä tcinora hame . u śālanāṣṭä haṃbette | tta tta biraṣṭä ṣṭe :
tti vā nirūjākye arve dättä . sudākä kṣīrą . karaṃjä citrai āstaṃna
ga' .
pātcä citrai . aṣṇūha u krriṃgūha u bimjūhā āstaṃna cuṇya
5 haṃbirsti ṣṭāna ā | vā pātcä moṣkakä kṣā'rä hīye arve haṃbrīhąñä u
saṃkhalyąñä nirūjākyāṃ arvāṃ haṃdrri vya pīrmāttaṃ śo'lākyā
arvāṃ jsai ysu u kṣau'śtä pverāme vą saṃñą kuṃjsa sidalūṃ

[1] āḍä. [2] pīrmāttaṃ.

skraṅ-bahi nad gso-bahi leyu-ste ñi-śu-rća-bźi-pa rjogs-so ||
|| de-nas rma gso-bahi lehu bśad-par byaho ||
rma ni lus-ñid-las hbyuṅ-ba daṅ | blo-bur-du hbyuṅ-bahi bye-brag-gis
2 rnam-pa gñis yod-par rig daṅ byaho || de-la sṅa-ma ni nad-gźi rnams-las gyur-pa yino | phyi-ma ni mćhan-la sogs-pas rmas-pa yino || de-la rluṅ-las gyur-pahi rmahi mćhan-ma ni | rmahi ñen-skor rćub-ciṅ mdog dmar-la sṅo-skyar hdug-
3 pa daṅ | hjag-pa ñuṅ-źiṅ hdaṅ-ba daṅ | cher mi-na-ba rnams yino || mkhris-pa-las gyur-pahi rmahi mćhan-ma ni | rma daṅ | ñen-skor-gyi mdog ser-źiṅ dmar-la sṅo-ba daṅ | hjag-pa ćha-ba daṅ | lus ćha-ba rnams yino || bad-kan-las
4 gyur-pahi rmahi mćhan-ma ni | mkhraṅ-źiṅ dbal skya-ba daṅ | chu-ser skya-ba hjag-ciṅ graṅ la | sk⟨y⟩a-ba rnams yino || khrag-nad-las gyur-pahi rmahi mćhan-ma ni | mdog dmar-źiṅ khrag hjag-pa yino || nad-gźi gñis hdus-pa-las gyur-
5 pa daṅ | gsum hdus-pa-las gyur-pahi rmahi mćhan-ma ni | gaṅ daṅ gaṅ hdus-pa de daṅ dehi mćhan-ma hdres-pas bstan-to || de-la thog-ma ma-smin-pahi ćhe ni | źi-bar hgyur-bahi snan-rćis bsku ho || rnags-su ćha-ba-la ni smin-par
6 bya-bahi cho-ga byaho || rnags zin-pa-la ni brtol-te hjib-pahi sman-gyis rnag daṅ chu-ser dag-par bsal-nas | rmahi śahu-skyehi sman byaho || de-la rnags-par bya-bahi sman ni | til daṅ phabs daṅ | zar-ma daṅ | ru-rta rnams-kyi phye-
7 ma daṅ | phye daṅ | rgyam-ćha rnams źo skyur-po daṅ sbyar-te | brjis-pahi goṅ-bu ni smin-par byed-pahi mchog yin-par hdod-do || de-la rnagsu ćha-bahi mćhan-ma ni | ćha-ba hur-hur-por hdug-pa daṅ | na-źiṅ zug-pa daṅ | mdog dmar-ba daṅ
209r1 skraṅ-ba rnams yin-par bśad-do || rnags-pahi mćhan-ma ni goṅ-ma smin-du ćha-bahi mćhan-ma rnams rće gźil-bar hgyur-la | gñer-ma hdus-śiṅ phyogs-gcig-tu mthon-po cog-cog-por hbyuṅ-ba yino ||
2 rdol-bar bya-bahi sman ni | śiṅ ñe-roṅ daṅ | snuḫakīra daṅ | ’asmari daṅ | ćiri bilba-la sogs-pahi sde-ćhan daṅ | kru-trug-tres daṅ | thi-ba daṅ | bya-gag daṅ | mchil-pahi tug-pa rnams-kyi phye-ma sbyar-ba ham |
3 yaṅ-na muskahi thal-bahi sman sbyar-bas bsku-ba ni rdol-bar bya-bahi sman-gyi naṅ-na mchog yino || hjib-pahi sman-gyi rnag

143r1 mahābāṃją ciṃgāṃ ttīrai perą ha|laidrrä . ysālva . ñaulą[1] āstaṃna
cuṇya haṃbrīhąñä gvīhą rrūṃ jsa u piṇḍai baññä ||
ā vā pātcä ciṃgāṃ ttīrai perä kuṃjsa hīyą cųṇya mākṣī' jsa
2 haṃbrīhąñä u bañąña|kaṃmą vasūjąkä : tti vā gūśti ysyąñākyi arve .
rrūsāḍä . gvīha: rrūṃ mākṣī jsa haṃbrīhąñä banąñä kaṃmą gūśti
ysyąñe .
3 tti vā haṃburstą kaṃmä hīya gūnā hasvacai va ni | hame naukalakä
u hau'gä . biśāṃ' mąñaṃdä henai avīnä u ni ri ysauttä askhaukarī-
yāvai ri va ni hamä vasve baustä ṣṭe
4 cu beva jsa hamye līkä mą[2] | paṃcimulāda ga' mista u vilaka
haudvī harbiśe krre vīri hā haṃphīśąñä tcerai .
ttavadye jsa hamye līkä kaṃmä ñagraudāsa[3] ga' āstaṃna harbiśä
5 krra haṃphīśąñä u tce|rai .
cu śilīṣāṃ jsa hamye kaṃmą vī . rrājivrrikṣą'da ga' āstaṃna harbiśä krra haṃphīśąñä u tcerai ā vā nīlotpalą u sacha bāva ysālva meda
143v1 mahābuje śī caṃdä u samaṃ|ga . sauthara spyakä āstaṃna cuṇya .
gvīha: rrūṃ jsa haṃbrīhąñä u saṃkhalyąñä viraṃ haṃbrąñe .
pātcä ṣvīdaustāṃ bahyāṃ hīya chāṃ hīya cųṇya gvīha: rūṃ jsa
2 haṃbrīhąñä | ā vā pātcä triphalä . ñagraudä bahyä: hīye ysihe . u
chā . kharą cikalą : lodrrä . u caṃda āstaṃna cuṇya gvīhä : rrūṃ jsa
haṃbrīhąñä u saṃkhalyąñä kämą[4] haṃbrąñe
3 |pātcä arrjuṃ udūṃbarä . u aśtättä[5] . lodrrä . jaṃbrą bahyä. hīya
grūṣka . mahābāṃjä . kaṭaphalą . lākṣä' āstaṃna ṣi' cųṇya hoṣkakä[6]
4 niśąñä kaṃmä biṃdä gū|śti ysyąñe kalarū⟨ha⟩na . cirūttä . halaidrrä .
mahābāṃjä . nahta:makala karaṃjä hīvī hīyārä . u perä . paṭaulą .
5 śī sumaṃ ciṃgāṃ ttīrai hīye pera āstaṃna | cųṇya gvīhä rrūṃ j⟨s⟩a
ūci jsa jṣą'ñąñä . dädä[7] khu ri va rū harśtä . kaṃmą biṃdä śirä
īṃdä . ā vā pripųṇḍarī . mahąbāṃją . kākąṭä . kṣī'ri kākauṭä . caṃ-
144r1 dąna dva . cųṇya ṣvīdaustāṃ baṃhyä hīye kaṣā' | kuṃjsavīnai rrūṃ
haṃdrri vya jṣā'ñąñä khu ri va rrūṃ harśtä ysųñąñä . kaṃmä
häbrąñe[8] . khu hā kaṃmą biṃdä arva ṇa'stä yānīṃdä[9] . karaṃjä
2 bahyä: u palakṣą' u jaṃbrä āstaṃna baṃ|hyāṃ hīye hā perāṃ jsa
haṃgūnąñä . u ttye biṃdä hā kuhaṃ: thau jsa ñūṣṭąñä śirä īṃdä .
kamä haṃbrąñe jiṃdä ttī va kamaña pira hamāṃde surasāda ga'

[1] traulä. [2] [paṃ]. [3] °dāda. [4] kaṃmä. [5] aśva°.
[6] moṣkakä. [7] daṃdä. [8] haṃb°. [9] yan°.

daṅ | chu-ser bsal-bahi thabs ni | til daṅ | rgyam-ćha daṅ | śiṅ-mṅar
daṅ | nimpahi lo-ma daṅ |
4 yuṅ daṅ | skyer-pa daṅ | śiṅ ñe-roṅ rnams-kyi phye-ma mar daṅ
sbyar-te bsku-bar byaho || yaṅ-na nimpa-patra daṅ | til-gyi phye-ma
sbraṅ-rći daṅ sbyar-te bskus-na yaṅ rma sbyoṅ-bar byedo || rmahi
śahu-skye-bahi sman ni | nas rjen-par btags-
5 pahi phye-ma | mar daṅ | sbraṅ-rći daṅ sbyar-te | bskus-na rma
hdrub-par hgyuro || rma rub-pahi mćhan-ma ni | skraṅ-ba med-la |
hjam-źiṅ snum-par daṅ | lcehi mdog hdra-bar dmar-ba daṅ | na-
ba med-ciṅ hjag-pa chad-pa daṅ | rlob
6 med-pa rnams yin-te | rma dag-par hgyur-bahi rtag-su bśado ||
de-la rluṅ-las gyur-pahi rma-la ni | sman rća-ba lṅa-pahi sde-ćhan
che-chuṅ gñis cho-ga thams-cad-du sbyar-bar byaho || mkhris-pa-
las gyur-pahi rma-la ni | śiṅ
7 nyagrodha-la sogs-pahi sde-ćhan cho-ga thams-cad-du sbyar-bar
byaho || bad-kan-las gyur-pahi rma-la ni | doṅ-ga-la sogs-pahi sde-
ćhan cho-ga thams-cad-du sbyar-bar byaho || yaṅ 'utpala sṅon-po
daṅ | bala daṅ | skyer-pa daṅ | meda
209v1 daṅ | śiṅ-mṅar daṅ | ćandan daṅ | samaṅga daṅ | dhataki rnams-
kyi phye-ma mar daṅ sbyar-te bskus-na yaṅ rmahi śahu skye-bar
byedo || yaṅ-na śiṅ ho-ma-can-gyi myu-guhi phye-ma mar daṅ
sbyar-ba ham | yaṅ-na hbras-bu gsum daṅ | śiṅ batahi
2 yal-gahi thor-to daṅ | seṅ-ldeṅ daṅ | gseṅ-phrom rnams-kyi phye-
ma mar daṅ sbyar-bas bskus-na rma-kha hdrub-par hgyuro ||
yaṅ-na śiṅ 'arjuna daṅ | 'udumbara daṅ | 'aśvatha daṅ | gseṅ-phrom
daṅ | jambuhi śun-lpags daṅ | śiṅ-mṅar
3 daṅ katpala daṅ | rgya-skyags rnams-kyi phye-mas btab-pa-na
yaṅ | rmahi śahi bu skye-bar hgyuro || pu-će-śel daṅ | praćhila daṅ |
yuṅ daṅ | śiṅ-mṅar daṅ | naktamalahi hbras-bu daṅ | lo-ma daṅ |
malati daṅ | nimpahi lo-ma rnams-
4 kyi phye-ma mar daṅ chuhi naṅ-du bskol-te | mar ñi-ćhe lus-pa
yaṅ rma-la phan-pa yino || yaṅ-na prapuṇḍarīka daṅ | śiṅ-mṅar
daṅ | bu-ćhaṅ-rto daṅ | ramñe daṅ | ćandan rnams-kyi phye-ma |
śiṅ ho-ma-can bskol-bahi khu-ba daṅ | til-mar-
5 gyi naṅ-du bskol-te | til-mar ñi-ćhe lus-pa bćags-pa yaṅ rma hćho-
bar byedo || rma-kha sman-gyis bskus-pahi steṅ-du | śiṅ karañja
daṅ | plakṣa daṅ | jambu-la sogs-pahi lo-mas glan-la | dehi steṅ-du
ras-la sogs-pas dkri-ba ni

3 āstaṃna haṃbrīhąñä . | karä kaṃmä u kamaña pisalyąñä śirä ỉdä .
khu kaṃmä jatte u ni cu va hamāte . gaurmä . u āṣeṃ māṃgä
4 āstaṃna māṃgä hīye perä : cuṇya ūci jsa haṃbairsti | ṣṭāną ||

pątcä buvāṃ ttīrai u aṃbrāsä hīya cuṇya ūci jsa haṃbrīhąñä u
saṃkhalyąñä ṣi' nica haṃbaḍa hame ysu kṣo'śtä śā'lākyi hā arve
5 pisalyąñä u vasująñä | kaṃmä beṃdä gūrśti[1] ysaiye . arvāṃ āstaṃnai
kaṃmä hīya krra harbiśä nva vargą tcerai .

ttī va pa⟨ma⟩ṃthä harsī ttu pamaṃthä haṣkarä jsa haṃgąrąñä u
144v1 thaṃjąñä u kaṃmä jihume hīya vī jsāṃ hā krra nva | pacaḍä tcairai .
ttī vai ṣi' kaṃmä maṃgārä tsīye nālāviraṃ hamāte gaudä hame u
hauṣkä . tvąme hīya krra tcerai . āphaidä kaṃmä ịñakä karvīną hụñä
2 paśąñä . vimaṃ | horąñä u vrrī .

cu hairthä[2] vī āvaṃdū kaṃmä vī virī vai hā gvī'hä: rrūṃ mākṣī'
jsa haṃbrīhąñä u pisalyąñä u bañąñä . ttavaṃdya . u huñä āphārä u
3 ttaudä pāraṃjąñä pvā | vai krra tcerai .

ttī va āstai hatcyąve ā vā hamarä nirąmī bvākä vījä rrąśą'ñä
4 hamarai hā thąña viśtąñä u gvīhä : rrūṃ u mahābāṃjä pisalyąñä | śe
civarī jsa styūdä bañąñä . ṣvīdaustä baṃhyāṃ hīye grūṣkye jsa
sịmakyi bañąñä khu vā ni mvīre . tta tta jsāṃ hā ādarä tcerai u
5 parehąñä khu va ysu ni hamā⟨te⟩ kaṃmą u | hatcastä u borṣai-vī
hvīḍa . rrīysu . māṃgä . rruśi jsa vadida . astauci āṇaṃdāṃ datāṃ
hīya gūśta ysuṣṭa . ñye u ṣvīdä . ttīrä hirä u garkha-gvācha u mijṣe' vī
tsụma ttye jsa parehāñą

145r1 kaṃ | mä jehāme hīvī piṣkalä sparibistä :

ttiña pacīḍa tcimña bisāṃ ārvāṃ[3] hīvī piṣkalą birāśāṃ' .

cu tcimña bisāṃ arvāṃ hīvī śāsträ ṣṭe kāma ṣi' cu vaidaihī rruṃ-
2 dä | jsa hvata śākha ṣi' pa'jsä mista ya . mara ttā ṣā' harbiśä ni hvata
hamya . u nimve mąñaṃdai ttā bakalaka birāśāṃ' .

3 cu tciṃ hīya uysąną . aspāṃda hame heṃji | hame u śīya u hary-
āsa . tti pā paṃjsāṃ mahābuvāṃ jsa śaṃdā . u dai . ūtca . padaṃ

[1] gūśti. [2] hairthaṃ. [3] arvāṃ.

6 bzaṅ-ste | rma sbyoṅ-źiṅ hćho-bar byedo || rma-la hbu źugs-pa-la
ni byihu-rug-pa-la sogs-pahi sde-ćhan sbyar-bas rma-kha daṅ |
rmahi naṅ bskus-na phan-no || rma sos-pahi mal-śod-du gyur-pa-la
ni | sran-ma daṅ | mon-sran-sdehu-la sogs-
7 pa sran-mahi rigs rnams-kyi lo-mahi phye-ma chu daṅ sbyar-ba
ham | yaṅ-na śiṅ-tog kośa ham | śiṅ lbaṅ-ko btags-pahi phye-ma chu
daṅ sbyar-bas bskus-na slar gaṅ-bar hgyuro || rma hkhyims-pa-la
ni | cho-ga śes-pas rmahi bag
210r1 gaṅ byuṅ-ba brtags-te | mćhon-gyis dral-la dag-par bsal-źiṅ |
rnag daṅ | chu-ser hjib-pahi sman-gyis bskus-te myaṅ-ba-ste | rma-
ba śahi bu skye-źiṅ hdrub-pahi sman-la sogs-pa rmahi cho-ga thams-
cad
2 rim bźin-du byaho || rṅu-ba khoṅ-na yod-pahi rma-la ni | rṅu-ba
skam-pas draṅs-te phyuṅ-la | rma gso-bahi sman-gyi cho-ga bstan-
pahi rim[s] bźin-du byaho || rma rñiṅ riṅ-du lan-pahi rkyen-gyis śa
zad-ciṅ skam-par gyur-pa-la ni | śa
3 rta-bahi sman-gyi cho-ga yaṅ bya-źiṅ | rma yaṅ gso-bar byaho ||
rma raṅ-ba-la ni || rmahi ñen-skor gtar-źiṅ khrag dbyuṅ-ba daṅ |
skyug-sman daṅ | bkru-sman btaṅ | blo-bur-gyi rma-la | rma byuṅ-
bahi mod-la | mar daṅ sbraṅ-rći
4 daṅ sbyar-bas bskus-te | bciṅs-la | mkhris-pa daṅ | khrag-gi drod
ćha-ba dbri-źiṅ bsil-bahi cho-ga rnams byaho || rus-pa chag gam |
ćhigs byuṅ-ba-la ni | cho-ga śes-pas sraṅ-źiṅ | ćhigs bcug-la | mar daṅ
5 śiṅ-mṅar-gyis bskus-te | bciṅs-la ras-kyis dam-du dkris-la |
śiṅ ho-ma-can-gyi śun-lpags-kyis mi-mgul-bar dbaṅ-du byas-te |
ci-nas kyaṅ ma-rnags-par nan-tan-du bsruṅ-bar byaho || rma daṅ |
chag-
6 grugs daṅ bur-bahi kha-zas ni hbras salu daṅ | mon-sran-sdehu
daṅ | nas-la⟨s⟩ byas-pa daṅ | ri-dags skam-sa-na gnas-pahi śa rnams
bzaho || źo daṅ | ho-ma daṅ | skyur-bag daṅ | kha-zas lci-bahi bag
daṅ
7 ñal-po rnams spaṅ-bar byaho || rma gso-bahi lehu-ste ñi-śu-rća-
lṅa-pa rjogso || || de-nas mig-sman-gyi rgyud-kyi lehu bśad-par
byaho || mig-sman-gyi rgyud ces-bya-ba | lus-hphags-kyi rgyal-pos
210v1 bśad-pa gaṅ yin-pa ni rgya ches-pas-na | hdir de-dag thams-cad
mi-bśad-par cha ćam-źig bśad-par byaho || de-la mig-gi raṅ-bźin ni gaṅ
ruṅ hdug-pa daṅ | dmar-ba daṅ | dkar-po daṅ | gnag-pa yin-no || de
yaṅ hbyuṅ-ba chen-po sa daṅ

āstaṃna haphvą biraṣṭa . pārihā vą khuṇā ṣṭe . āvaśä' jsa va pā
4 haṃphve ṣṭe . ū beta . ttavaṃ|dya śilīṣā . hụñi āphārä āstaṃna
piṣkici jsa : abhaiṣānā nāma tciṃ'ña bisai āchai hame strihā . tcau-
padya . cu buri saṃ āchā |de biśä mahābuvāṃ jsa hamāre .
5 cu | beta hamye līkä ttiñä[1] āchai abhaiṣąnā hīya gūnā . āskyai sāḍi
hamāte . u ṣaukalai hauṣka hamāre u vinostą u bveci ttyāṃ āstaṃna
biraysdę .
145v1 cu ttavaṃdye jsa hamye | līka ściña bisai āchai abhaiṣąnā hīya
gūnā : āṣkyai ttauda hamāre . u ṣaukala ysīḍā ttaude u heṃde jsa
haṃphva āstaṃna hame .
2 cu śiliṣāṃ jsa hamye līkä tciṃña ā|chai abhaiṣąnā hīya gụnā .
ṣaukalai śīyi hamāre u āṣkyi śīye u ṣemāṃgye u kahaitte u hasu .
3 cu huñi āphārä jsa hamye līkä tciṃña āchai abhaiṣąnā hīya gụ|nā
tceṃ vai heṃnai hame u ttaudä . haijai kare . āṣkyai ttarụna hamāre .
khu hvīḍa viysama hame u ttī jsāṃ kālä jsa ni hvīḍä . ttye pracaina
4 tciṃña āchai abhaiṣąnā | hame biysąnai . ttye pārijsye jsai adhịmąñä[2]
nāma hame . ttai gūnā . tcịma'ñai u hālai kamalā pa'jsą vinaustä
5 hame . cvai gūnā khu ttā uskātta hva . dūṣāṃ' hīyā hva hva gụ|nā
jsa haṃphīśąñä u tta tta bvąñä ||
cu beta jsa hamye līkä tciṃña āchai jahąme hīya krra . śikarä :
146r1 lodrrä . sidalūṃ āstaṃna cụṇya hamąñe ūci jsa haṃbrīhąñä : u ysu|
nąñä kaṣā' ||
ā vā pātcä śikarä . ttuṃgąra . śobarai lodrrä āstaṃna krra tta tta
tcerai khu ttā uskātta hva tciṃña tcairai .
2 pātcä |raṃda hīvī spyakä . mahābāṃjä . śikarä ttūṃgare | āstaṃna
cụṇya . ñyetutcä jsa hamąñū[3] jsa haṃbrīhąñä ysunąñä ||
ā vā pātcä ttuṃgara sidalūṃ mahābāṃjä . lodrrä hīya cuṇya
3 gvī'hä . rrūṃ jsa aysbrījsąñä u rraysä | tciṃña niśąñä ||
ā vā pātcä mahābāṃjä . cadaṃ . rrūṃnai . lodrrą . svaṃna gīrai
āstaṃna cụṇya hamąñunye ūci jsa haṃbrīhąñä . u ysunąñä ||
4 ā vā pātcä belā|da ga' āstaṃna jṣą'ñąñä . tci'ma'ñą jsa bịjsąñä .
biysąnai tciṃña rrāhä . āchai jiṃdä ||
5 pātcä |raṃda hīya bāva . buysīñä ṣvīdä jsa jṣą'ñāñą hamāñụnakä
a|ysdęmąñä . u tciṃ byāśąñä . u śe surakä vāsti haṣkalakä jsa tciṃ

[1] tciñä. [2] °mamtha. [3] °ñūṃ.

2 chu daṅ I me daṅ I rluṅ rnams daṅ ldan-par bśado II gnas khuṅ-bu
yin-pas nam-mkhah daṅ yaṅ ldan-no II de-la rluṅ daṅ I mkhris-pa
daṅ I bad-kan daṅ I khrag-gi ñes-pa rnams-kyi bye-brag-las I mig-
nad mchi-ma hjag-pa źes-bya-ba I drag-
3 po rnam-pa bźir hgyur-te I de ni phal-cher mig-nad-do-cog
hbyuṅ-bahi gźi yino II de-la rluṅ-las gyur-pahi mig-nad mchi-ma
hjag-pahi mćhan-ma ni I mchi-ma graṅ-ba daṅ I rṅu-ma skam-po
yod-pa daṅ I na-źiṅ ẖa-re hdug-pa rnams yin-par
4 bśado II mkhris-pa-las gyur-pahi mig-nad mchi-ma hjag-pahi
mćhan-ma ni I mchi-ma ćha-ba daṅ I rṅu-ma ser-ba daṅ I ćha-ba
hur-hur-por hdug-ciṅ rća dmar-ba rnams yin-no II bad-kan-las
gyur-bahi mig-nad mchi-ma hjag-pahi mćhan-ma ni I rṅu-ma dkar-
5 pos yogs-pa daṅ I mchi-ma hbyar-hbyar-po daṅ I g-yah-źiṅ
skraṅ-ba rnams yino II khrag-gi ñes-pa-las byuṅ-bahi mig-nad
mchi-ma hjag-pahi mćhan-ma ni I mig dmar-źiṅ ćha-ba hur-hur-
por hdug-la I dmar-po śar-śar-por hbyuṅ-
6 źiṅ I mchi-ma rća dmar-ba rnams yino II kha-zas mi-hphrod-pa
zos-pa daṅ I dus bźin-du mi-za-bahi rkyen-gyis mig-nad mchi-ma
hjag-pa źes-bya-ba ćha-bas chen-por gyur-pa-la ni I mig-nad rduṅ-ba
źes-bya-bar gyur-te I mig daṅ klad-pahi phyed mi-
7 bzad-par na-bar hgyuro II dehi mćhan-ma yaṅ goṅ-du smos-pa
bźin-du nad-gźi so-sohi mćhan-ma daṅ sbyar-źiṅ rtogs-par byaho II
de-la rluṅ-las gyur-pahi mig-nad gso-bahi cho-ga ni I kha-ra daṅ I
gseṅ-phrom daṅ I rgyam-ćha rnams-kyi phye-ma chu hjam-ćam
211r1 daṅ sbyar-te bćags-pahi khu-ba ham I yaṅ-na kha-ra daṅ I bcah-
sga daṅ I śabarihi gseṅ-phrom rnams cho-ga goṅ-ma bźin-du byas-
te I mig-tu blugs-par byaho II yaṅ-na kuntahi me-tog daṅ I śiṅ-
mṅar daṅ I kha-ra daṅ I gcah-
2 sga rnams-kyi phye-ma źo kha-chu hjam-ćam daṅ sbyar-te
bćags-pa ham I yaṅ-na bcah-sga daṅ I rgyam-ćha daṅ I śiṅ-mṅar
daṅ I gseṅ-phrom rnams-kyi phye-ma mar-gyi naṅ-du brṅos-pahi
khu-bas mig-tu blugso II yaṅ-na śiṅ-mṅar daṅ I ćandan
3 daṅ I bćod daṅ I gseṅ-phrom daṅ I bćag yug-snam rnams-kyi
phye-ma chu hjam-ćam daṅ sbyar-te bćags-pa ham I yaṅ-na bilba-la
sogs-pahi sde-ćhan bskol-bas mig-gi naṅ-du blugs-na yaṅ mig-nad
mi-zad-par na-ba sel-to II
4 yaṅ-na 'eraṇḍahi rća-ba rahi ho-mahi naṅ-du bskol-te I hjam-
ćam-du bsgraṅs-la I mig gdaṅs-te I ras dkar-po gćaṅ-mas g-yogs-

pvīśą'ñä . tciṃ vī āna paysaṇu vīrāṣṭä aharṣṭä bįjsąñä . tcimąñāṃ
146v1 hīyāṃ arvāṃ haṃdrri vya ysve | jsa paśā⟨ñä⟩ biśa pīrmāttaṃ hva
ṣṭe ||
pātcä pipalä u hiravī mahābuṃjä . caṃdaṃ sidalūṃ āstaṃną
buysįñä ṣvīdä jsa jṣą'ñąñä u hamąñuṃ aysdimąñä . uskātta bisai
2 khi|ṇḍa ysuhakä jsa paśąñä . tciṃña bisā āchā bįysąnā vīne biśä
jiṃdä ||
pātcä hīśąnya bājinaña ā vā śāvįña . sidalūṃ ñye jsa haṃbrīhąñä ||
3 ā vā hīśąnīje ā | vā śāvīṃje bajsīha haṃdrri vya . paṃjilįnai .
bujsvārä jsa . halaidrrä pipalä naukä kūṭąñä u ñye jsa haṃbrīhąñä .
4 ttiña bajsīhaña śau haḍā śā ṣave śtąvįnai[1] ā | vā hīśąnīje pītcīyi jsa
isthaṃjąñä u tciña paśāñä . biysąnā tciṃña bisā āchā harbiśä jiṃdä :
ttavaṃdye jsa hamye tciṃña āchāṃ va pripuṇḍarī . mahābājä
5 ha|laidrrä . ąmalai . puṣṭarä āstaṃna jṣą'ñąñä . kaṣā' aysdemąñä u
mākṣī hā tcerai . u śikarä haṃbrīhąñä khu ttā uskātta hva ysunakä
147r1 jsa paśąñä aharṣṭä bijsąñä . tciña ā|chā jāre ||
pātcä caṃdaṃ . ciṃgāṃ ttīrai perä . mahābāṃjä . ysālva . sidalūṃ
āstaṃna cųṇya . pvāvye ūci jsa . haṃbrīhąñä u mākṣī' hā niśąñä u
2 śikari ysuhalakä jsa i|harṣṭa bįjsąñä :
śilīṣāṃ jsa hamye tciña āchāṃ vīra . hīha. dąmä . u halaidrrä .
śī śaśvāṃ . ysālva dva dva bāga tcerai . ttyāṃ āstaṃna cųṇya hamā-
3 ñųnye ūci jsa haṃbrī|hāña ysunä jsa paśąñä u ėhąrṣṭä bįjsąñä .
tciṃña bisā āchā cvai vā āṣkä beḍä jiṃdä :
pātcä ciṃgāṃ ttīrai hīye peri jsa pajukaustä bājaṃ haṃdaṃna
4 ė|salyąñä u tcau bāga lodrrä jsa pīha dąmä u śī śaśvāṃ . śo śo bāga
āstaṃna cuṇya iysbrījsąñä ū kūṭąñä hamāṃci rūci[2] jsa haṃbrīhąñä
5 u ysunakä jsa hā ėha|rṣṭa paśąñä u bįjsąñä :
huñi āphārä jsa hamye vī . śaubarai lodrrä . triphalä mahābāṃjä .
śikarä . śīyi buhane āstaṃna cųṇya pvāvye ūci jsa ysunakä jsa
147v1 paśąñą . iharṣṭä | ⟨bi⟩jsąñä . tciṃña bisai āchai cvai āṣkä beḍä jiṃdä :
lodrrä . mahābāṃjä . ysīrä . cuvaṃ āstaṃna cuṇya buysįñä ṣvīdą
jsa haṃbrīhąñä .
2 ā vā pātcä ysālva jṣą'ñąñą u | kaṣā' aysdįmąñä u mākṣī' jsa haṃ-
brīhąñä u pītcīyi jsa isthaṃjąñä u tciṃña pisalyąñä tciṃña bisā
āchā cvai āṣkä beḍä harbiśä jidä .
3 āstri[3] khvai tciṃña bisā āchā ha|māre vinausta virī vai saṃ

[1] śāvīnai. [2] ūci.
[3] āsñi.

pahi steṅ-du I mig hgram-logs-nas rgyun ma-chad-par blugs-pa ni I mig-sman ćhags-
5 las btaṅ-ba źes-bya-bahi mchog yino II yaṅ-na pipiliṅ daṅ I balaka daṅ I śiṅ-mṅar daṅ I rgyam-ćha mas rahi ho-ma daṅ bskol-te I hjam-ćam-du sgraṅs-pa sṅa-ma bźin-du ćhags-las btaṅ-bahi sman byas-na yaṅ I
6 mig-nad mi-bzad-pa na-ba sel-to II yaṅ-na lcags sam zaṅs-kyi snod-du rgyam-ćha daṅ I źo sbyar-ba ham I yaṅ-na zaṅs sam lcags-kyi gtun-gyi naṅ-du khar-bahi btun-bus ẏuṅ daṅ I pipiliṅ źib-tu brduṅs-la źo daṅ sbyar-te I
7 snod de-ñid-kyi naṅ-du źag lon-par bźag-pa zaṅs daṅ I lcags-kyi mig-sman-gyi thur-mas blaṅ-źiṅ mig-tu bskus-na I mig-⟨nad⟩ mi-bzad-par na-ba sel-to II mkhris-pa-las gyur-pahi mig-nad-la ni prapuṇḍarika daṅ I śiṅ-
v1 mṅar daṅ I yuṅ daṅ I skyurura daṅ I śug-pa rnams bskol-la bsgraṅs-pa sbraṅ-rći daṅ I kha-ras sbyar-te sṅar bstan-pa bźin-du I ćhags-las btaṅ-źiṅ rgyun-tu blugs-na mig-nad sel-to II yaṅ-na ćandan daṅ I 'ariśtahi lo-ma daṅ I śiṅ-
2 mṅar daṅ I skyer-pa daṅ I lce-myaṅ-ćha rnams-kyis phye-ma chu graṅ-mo daṅ sbyar-te I sbraṅ-rći daṅ I kha-ra daṅ ldan-pas byas-la ćhags-las btaṅ-źiṅ rgyun-tu blugso II bad-kan-las gyur-pahi mig-nad-la ni I dud-pa daṅ I yuṅs-kar cha-re daṅ I
3 yuṅ daṅ I skyer-pa cha gñis-gñis daṅ I hdi-rnams-kyi phye-ma chu hjam-ćam daṅ sbyar-te I ćhags-las btaṅ-źiṅ rgyun-tu blugs-na I mig-nad mchi-ma hjag-pa sel-to II yaṅ-na snod-kha sbyar nimpahi khu-ba bskus-pahi naṅ-du I gseṅ-
4 phrom cha bźi daṅ I dud-pa daṅ I yuṅs-kar cha-re rnams-kyi phye-ma ćhig-mar brṅos-te I btags-nas I chu hjam-ćam daṅ sbyar-ba yaṅ ćhags-las btaṅ-źiṅ I rgyun-tu blugs-par byaho II khrag-las gyur-pahi mig-nad-la ni I sman
5 tirita daṅ I hbras-bu gsum daṅ I śiṅ-mṅar daṅ I kha-ra daṅ I gla-sgaṅ chen-po rnams-kyi phye-ma chu graṅ-mo daṅ sbyar-te I ćhags-las btaṅ-źiṅ rgyun-tu blugs-na mig-nad mchi-ma hjag-pa sel-to II gseṅ-phrom daṅ I śiṅ-mṅar daṅ I
6 ldoṅ-ros daṅ I skyer-pa daṅ I skyer khaṇḍa rnams-kyi phye-ma rahi ho-ma daṅ sbyar-ba ham I yaṅ-na skyer-pahi khu-ba bsgraṅs-te I sbraṅ-rći daṅ sbyar-ba thur-mas blaṅs-la mig-la [la] bskus-na I mig-nad mchi-ma hjag-pa thams-cad sel-

lodrrä . u ąmalai ysīrą kūṭąñä u haṃbrīhąñä gvīhä: rrūṃ jsa iysbrī-
4 jsąñä u naukä kūṭąñä u ysīrā hā haṃbrịhąñi ūci jsa murąñä | karä
tcimañāṃ ttiña biṃdä saṃkhalyąñāṃ tciṃña hā ni paśąñä ||
pātcä cahä:ṣa: surakä balohä . haṃdrri vya bañąñä u nuvari niśā
5 gvī'hą: saṃnä hīvī rraysä | haṃdrri vya pāchai . khu śirä paśte . u
haryąsa grūṣka pahaiśą'ñä u hvaiñąñä naukä kūṭąñä u cụṇya nūyacä
śīṃ juṃ tciṃña niśąme jsa virī saṃ tciṃña besā biysānā āchā striha
148r1 niśte pa|dịme ||
pātcä strihä: tciṃña āchai vī śīyi mirimjsya śo bāgä u haṣṭa bāga
hā lodrrä tcerai u ysīrā drrai bāga ttyāṃ āstaṃna naukä kūṭąñä u
2 cụṇya haṃ|brịhąñä sura balohä: hā viśtąñä daṃdä khu ttu rraysä
khāśe' u ttye jsa dyaka haṃgūnąñä :
pātcä cuvaṃ . halīrā . ysālva svaṃna gīrai . sidalūṃ āstaṃna
3 haṃtsi bīnājąñä | u karä tcịmañāṃ ttaña biṃdä pisalyąñä u haṃ-
daṃna hā ni paśąñä cu buri saṃ tciṃña āchā iṃde bịśä jiṃdä .
4 cu tciṃña ṣaukala hamāre ttyāṃ vī harbiśāṃ vī | haṃdrrāṃji
hụñä paśąñä . khvai āṣkyi nirąmīṃdä . hva hva arvāṃ jsa krra khu
ttā thyątta hva tta tta tcerai . khu hā sąmīde . khvai hā haryāsye jaste
5 biṃdä śīyi kanā hamā|te ṣi' śūkrrä āchai ṣṭe . ṣi' śilīṣāṃ jsa hame .
tta tta bvąñä . cu tciṃ' hīye śīye jaste biṃdä heṃji kanā hamāte .
ṣi' arrjụnä nāma āchai ṣe' hụñi āphāra jsa hame
148v1 cu śūkrrä āchai cvai śī|yi kanā hamāte . ṣi' arjänā[1] nąma āchai
ṣṭe . ṣi' hụñi āphārä jsa hame .
cu śūkrrä āchai cvai śīye kanā hame . ttye va saṃñä . viṭa-mā-
2 kṣo'kä : mahābāṃjä hīvī rraysä | vihīlai hīvī mijsākä . sidalūṃ
āstaṃna kāṃ saṃ hamāte . cụṇya mākṣī jsa haṃbrīhąñä . tciṃña
pisalyąñä . śīyi kanā jiṃdä :
3 pātcä sedalūṃ . virūlya . mirimjsya : mahā|bāṃjä . u śaṃgä .
gūhä: hīvī daṃdai . sidalūṃ . ysīrā . śī caṃdä[2] . u śīye mirimjse
4 hīye kaṣe' jsa habrīhąñä u ṣkaka[3] padịmąñä . u sauyąñä u tciṃña|[ña]
pisalyąñä śīyi kanā jiṃdä : samądrri phịnä . krriṃgīñe āha hīvī dalai .
sidalūṃ . śīye mirijsye . u śaṃgä . āstaṃna cuṇya uci jsa haṃbrī-
5 hąñä u ṣvakyi pa|dịmąñä u sauyąñä u pisalyąñä śīyi kanāṃ āstaṃna
priharaṃ māñaṃdū istīdä jiṃdä .
149r1 krrigīñe āha hīya dalā . ysīrā . śaṃgä ūḍārä . śī caṃdä[2] | sidalūṃ .
āstaṃna cụṇya hamaṃga viścąñä tvā haṃbairca . tciṃña bise arve
hīye pītcīyi jsa tciṃña niśąñä . śīyi kanā u ārkhä āstaṃna āchā jiṃdä.

[1] arjąnä. [2] caṃdaṃ. [3] ṣvaka.

7 to ‖ thog-ma mig-nad-kyis btab-ste na-ba bod-pa-la ni | gseṅ-
phrom daṅ | skyurura khrel-bur sbyar-ba mar-gyi naṅ-du bsños-te |
źib-tu btogs-la | ldoṅ-ros daṅ sbyar-te | chu daṅ brjis-pas mig-gi
phyi-rol pags-pahi steṅ-du

212r1 bskuho ‖ yaṅ-na mig-sman ćakṣu ras gćaṅ-mahi naṅ-du phur-la |
ba-laṅ-gi lci-bahi naṅ-du bćos-te | chan-chos rab-tu gyur-pahi śun-
lpags med-par byas-te | bskams-la źib-tu btags-pahi

2 phye-ma ñal-gar-las cig rgya mig-tu blugs-pa rćam-gyis | de-ma-
thag-tu mig-nad mi-bzad-par bdo-ba yaṅ med-par byedo ‖ yaṅ-na
mig na-ste bdo-ba-la | śikruhi sa-bon cha gcig daṅ gseṅ-phrom cha
brgyad daṅ | ldoṅ-ros ćha

3 gsum daṅ | hdi-rnams źib-tu btags-pahi phye-ma sbyar-bas | ras
gćaṅ-ma-la źen-par btab-ste | mig g-yog-par byaho ‖ yaṅ-na skyer
khaṇḍa daṅ | 'arura daṅ | skyer-pa daṅ | bćag daṅ | rgyam-ćha
rnams lḫan-cig-tu

4 chu ṅags mar byas-la | mig-gi phyi-rol pags-pahi steṅ-du bskus-
na yaṅ mig-nad-do-cog sel-to ‖ mig-nad rduṅ-ba thams-cad-la ni
| dpral-rća gtar-te khrag phyuṅ-la | mig-nad mchi-ma hjag-pahi
skabsu so-sohi rkyen-tu | sman-

5 gyi cho-ga ji-ltar bstan-pa rnams kyaṅ mthun-mthun-du byaho ‖
mig-gi hbras-bu na-guhi steṅ-du dkar-pohi thig-le byuṅ-ba ni |
liṅ-tog ces-bya-ste | bad-kan-las gyur-par śes-par byaho ‖ mig-gi
sprin-gyi steṅ-du dmar-ba byuṅ-

6 ba ni | liṅ-tog dmar-po źes-bya-ste | khrag-gi ñes-pa-las hbyuṅ-
ba yino ‖ de-la liṅ-tog dkar-po źi-bar bya-bahi thabs ni | drub-mar-
chaṅ daṅ | me-tog madhukahi śiṅ-gi sñiṅ-po daṅ | badurahi ćhe-gu
daṅ | rgyam-ćha

7 rnams-las gaṅ yaṅ ruṅ-bahi phye-ma sbraṅ-rći daṅ sbyar-te | mig-
la bskus-na liṅ-tog med-par hgyuro ‖ yaṅ-na ga-bur daṅ | na-le-
śam daṅ | śiṅ-mṅar daṅ | duṅ daṅ | ba-laṅ-gi so daṅ | rgyam-ćha
daṅ | ldoṅ-ros daṅ |

212v1 ćandan rnams-kyis phye-ma śig-gruhi khu-ba daṅ sbyar-te ri-lur
byas-pas bskus-na yaṅ liṅ-tog dkar-po sel-bar byed-do ‖ rgya-
mćhohi sbu-ba daṅ | khyim-byahi sgo-ṅahi śun-pags daṅ | rgyam-
ćha daṅ | duṅ daṅ | śikruhi hbras-buhi ćhi-gu rnams-kyi

2 phye-ma chu daṅ sbyar-te ri-lur byas-pas bskus-na yaṅ liṅ-tog-la
sogs-pa gris bźogs-pa bźin-du med-par byedo ‖ khyim-byahi sgo-
ṅahi śun-lpags daṅ | ldoṅ-ros daṅ | duṅ daṅ | mchiṅ-bu daṅ |
ćandan daṅ | rgyam-ćha rnams-kyi phye-

2 pātcä śī cadaṃ | u sidalūṃ . halīrā . lākṣą' āstaṃna cụṇyą uskātta
bese nva pacaḍä . paḍauysye jsa . śa' dva bāga viśtą̄ñä u tta tta
3 khḹṇḍī hā byą̄ñä ū tcịṃña niśą̄ñä śīyi | kanā u ārkhi jsai āstaṃna u
hą̄nāṃ rrāhä kare biśä jiṃdä :
śī sumaṃ . lākṣą'. svaṃna gīrai . caṃdä[1] āstaṃna cụṇya hamaṃ⟨ga⟩
4 viśtą̄ñä ūci jsa haṃbrīhą̄ñä u | ṣvakyi paḍḹmą̄ñä u soyą̄ñä . ū
tcịṃña niśą̄ñä . tcịṃña hvaiya u kaṃmä u śīyi kanā hụñi āphārä jsa
biśä jidä .
5 cu tcịṃña heṃje kane va śaṃgä hīya cu | ṇya mākṣī' jsa haṃbrīhą̄ñä :
ā vā pātcä kanaka[2]-phalä . sidalūṃ jsa haṃbrīhą̄ñä . ā vā samą̄drri
phịnä śikarą jsa haṃbairstä āstaṃna . ką̄mā saṃ hamāte tcịṃña
149v1 niśą̄ñä . śī | sumaṃ hīya kaṣā' mākṣī' jsa cuvaṃ u halạidrrä . ysālva
hīya cụṇya āstaṃna haṃbrīhą̄ñä ||
pātcä papalä . surakaña baloha:ña pvīysakä bañą̄ñä u gvīhä:
2 saṃ | ną hīvī rraysä haṃdrri vya pajsą̄ñä u hvaiñą̄ñä u kūṭą̄nä . u
cụṇya tcịṃña niśą̄ñä . cu pa'śä' hālai ni vijsuiṣḍḹ tcịṃña bisā āchą
jiṃdä .
3 pātcä ysīrā halai | drrä sovīraṃjä . trikaṭaukä . gvīhä . ysaiysä
āstaṃna ūci jsa haṃbrīhą̄ñä
ā vā pātcä detadārä hīya cụṇya buysḹñe bīysma jsa paherą̄ñä u
4 hvai | ñą̄ñä u pharāka jụna bīnāją̄ñä u hvaiñą̄ñä u tciña niśą̄ñä :
cu tcḹ'mą'ñä āṣkyą̄ṣṭa haṃbīrīṃdä . āchā biśä jiṃdä .
5 pātcä ysirai : detadārą ⟨āra⟩[3] āstaṃna cụṇya . surasą | hīyāṃ
perāṃ hīye rraysä jsa haṃbrīhą̄ñä ṣvakyi padīmą̄ñä khu hā aurmaysdāṃ hīye bā'yą ni hīśca tcịṃña niśą̄ñą cu tcịṃña ysīci ūtci nḹrāme
150r1 āchā biśä jidä ysirai | sauvīraṃja . dva bāgā hā śā hīya hīsuṣka
niśą̄ñä ||
naukä kūṭą̄ñä cụṇya tcịṃña bise arve hīye pītcīyi jsa niśą̄ñä
pyą̄ṣṭāṃ āstaṃna āchā jiṃdä :
2 pātcä tri | kaṭokä . cuvaṃ ūci jsa haṃbrīhą̄ñä niśą̄ñä . cvai vā
āṣkä beḍä . biśä jiṃdä .
cu ttimīri vijiṣḍe harbiśä . haṃbaṃjsya gūnạ pa'jsä caṃbula
3 vijiṣḍe ṣi' bvą̄ña hva hva pi | ṣkici āstaṃna .
viña ttā bi⟨ra⟩ysde .
cu beta jsa hamye līkä ttamīre vijsyą̄me hīya gụ̄nā . cu buri saṃ
4 hira vijsyāte heṃnāta chava vijiṣḍe u khoysaṃdā u mvī | raṃdā
vijiṣḍe ṣi'kä ṣṭe .

[1] caṃdaṃ. [2] kataka. [3] Tib. śu-dag, Skt. vacā.

3 ma cha bsñams-pahi steṅ-du | mig-sman-gyi thur-ma bsgres-pas mig byug-na yaṅ | liṅ-tog daṅ | mig hjer-la sogs-pa med-par byedo || ćandan daṅ | rgyam-ćha daṅ | ’arura daṅ | rgya-skyags rnams-kyi phye-ma yas-kyi rim bźin-du

4 daṅ-pohi cha-res bskyede sbyar-bahi naṅ-du mig-sman-gyis thur-mas bsgres-pas mig byugs-na yaṅ | liṅ-tog daṅ | mig mjer-la sogs-pa med-par byed-do || sna-mahi me-tog kha ma-hbus-pa daṅ | rgya-skyags daṅ | bćag yug-snam daṅ |

5 ćandan rnams-kyi phye-ma cha mñam-la chu daṅ sbyar-bahi ri-lus mig bskus-na yaṅ mig snad-ciṅ rma byuṅ-ba daṅ | liṅ-tog rnams sel-źiṅ khrag-gyis rgyas-pa daṅ-bar byedo || liṅ-tog dmar-po-la ni duṅ-gi phye-ma sbraṅ-rći daṅ sbyar-ba

6 ham | katakahi hbras-bu rgyam-ćha daṅ sbyar-ba ham | rgya mćhohi dbu-ba kha-ra daṅ | sbyar-ba rnams-las | gaṅ yaṅ ruṅ-bas mig byug-par byaho || sna-mahi lo-mahi khu-ba daṅ sbraṅ-rći daṅ | yuṅ daṅ | skyer-pahi phye-ma daṅ | skyer khaṇḍa rnams-

7 kyi mig-sman nam | yaṅ-na pipiliṅ ras gćaṅ-mahi naṅ-du phur-te | ba-laṅ-gi lci-bahi khu-bahi naṅ-du bćos-la | skams-pahi phye-mas mig byugs-na | mćhan-mo mi-mthoṅ-bahi mig-nad sel-to || ldoṅ-ros daṅ | yuṅ daṅ s⟨taṅ-zil⟩

213r1 daṅ | ćha-ba gsum ba-laṅ-gi mkhris-pas sbrus-la | sran ćam-gyi reṅ-reṅ-po dral-la | chu-las bdar-ba ham | yaṅ-na thaṅ-śiṅ-gi phye-ma | ra-gcin-gyis sbaṅ-źiṅ bskam-pa de-lta-bur lan graṅs maṅ-du byas-

2 pas mig-bskus-na | mig mchi-mas gaṅ-ba sel-to || yaṅ-na | ba-bla daṅ | thaṅ-śiṅ daṅ | śu-dag rnams-kyi phye-ma | bye-rug-pahi lo-mahi khu-ba daṅ sbyar-te | ri-lur byas-la grib-mar bskams-pas mig bskus-na yaṅ

3 mig ćhag rñiṅ sel-to || ba-bla daṅ | staṅ-zil daṅ | de-gñis sdom-pahi gñis hgyur-gyi zaṅs rnams źib-tu btags-pahi phye-mahi naṅ-du | mig-sman-gyi thur-ma bsgres-pas mig byug gam | yaṅ-na ćha-ba gsum-gyi phye-ma

4 daṅ | skyer khaṇḍa daṅ | chu daṅ sbyar-te bskus-na yaṅ | mig ćhag-po sel-to || mig-nad rab-rib-tu gyur-pa thams-cad-kyi spyihi mćhan-ma ni | śin-tu zi-zi-por gyur-pa yin-par śes-par byaho || so-sohi bye-brag gźan ni

5 da bśade | de-la rluṅ-las gyur-pahi rab-rib-kyi mćhan-ma ni | ci mthoṅ-ṅo-cog rća dmar-źiṅ g-yo-ba daṅ | lo-loṅ-por sraṅ-ba yin-no | mkhris-pa-las gyur-pahi rab-rib-kyi mćhan-ma ni | kha-dog sṅon-po daṅ | ser-po

cu ttavaṃdye jsa hamyā ttimīrāṃ gū̯nāṃ vijsyā̯ma . ci tu vijsyāte
āṣana cha vijiṣḍe . u ysīḍā . u drrāṃ dā gūṃ khadyauttą prā̯ṇai
5 khi̯ṇḍä . byavi khi|ṇḍä vijiṣḍe u ttyāṃ āstaṃna hamāre .
cu śilīṣāṃ jsa hamya līka ttimī̯rā vijsyā̯me hīya gū̯nā . cu buri saṃ
150v1 rūta daiye tcārba vijiṣḍe u śīyi gū̯nä jsa u ni.|ṣāṃ'da vā dyāre
ttyāṃ āstaṃna hamāre .
cu drrayāṃ dūṣāṃ' jsa hamya ttamīrāṃ hīya gū̯nā . ṣi' harbiśāṃ
gūnāṃ jsa haṃphva vijiṣḍe .
2 cu hu̯ñi āphārä jsa hamya līkä ttimīrā | gū̯nā
cu ttu saṃ vijsyāte pa'jsä heṃnā nijiṣḍe[1] .
cu ttimīrāṃ hīyāṃ gū̯nāṃ jsa parśtä . u buḍa ttavai hame . ṣi'
3 pyā̯mą haṃgūstä gaurśte . ttye hīya gūnā āstri[2] ā̯na kā̯|mye dūṣą' jsa
hā̯mya līkāṃ hīya gū̯nā cu ttā ttimīrāṃ vīri hvata hama hamāre .
dilakä haḍi buḍatta āphiḍa hamāre . ttāḍā va hame buḍätta u tta tta
4 bvā̯|ñä .
ttyāṃ haṃdrri vya śilīṣā jsa hamye . tciṃ'ña āchai pyāmą .
jihāme vaski rrāvī khā̯ñä . u hu̯ñai paśā̯ñä .
5 cu ttamīrāṃ hīya krra . vihīlai hīya mijsāka . mahābāṃji . ā|malai .
mirijsya . muḍāsaṃgä āstaṃna ūci jsa ārrā̯ñä ṣvaka padī̯mā̯ñą u
sauyā̯ñä u pisalyā̯ñä . ttimīra jidä ||
151r1 pātcä trikaṭokä u hīśaṃ hīya hīsuṣka . sida|lū . trephalą
sauvīraṃją āstaṃna uce jsa śikalaka haṃbrīhāñä . u ṣvadyi[3] padī-
mā̯ñä tte ṣvakye haryāsa ṣvakye gaurśtāre . pisalyā̯ñä . ttemīrāṃ
jinākye .
2 pātcą ha|laidrrą . āmalai . pipalą . kanaka[4]-phale . śī śaśvā āstaṃna
cuṇya bārī hīye uce jsa haṃbrīhāñą u ṣvakye padīmā̯ñä paśā̯ñä
harbeśą tceña āchā jedä .
3 pātcą ka|ṇḍārya u buhane . aṃbrrą hīyārä . mahābują pepalą .
sedalūṃ āstaṃna cu̯nya śāvīnę bastä bājaṃ haṃdrre vya pharāka
4 haḍā buysīñą ṣvīdą jsa bīnājā|ñą u ṣvakye padīmā̯ñą . tceñą besā
harbeśā āchāṃ jenākye .
pātcą tcure-vā stura hīya daṃdā kāṃ saṃ hamāte . lākṣą'. karaṃją .
5 kaṇḍārya . kharīña āste . u ūlī|ñe āste . u kavā̯ñe . veṇḍaṃga .
trekaṭauką . kuṣṭą āstaṃna hamaga veśtā̯ñą . uce jsa haṃbrīhāñą u ṣvakye padīmā̯ñä . tte ṣvakye daṃdāṃ jsa vadeṃda
nā̯ma .

[1] vij°. [2] āsñi. [3] ṣvakyi. [4] kataka.

6 snaṅ-źin | me hbar-ba daṅ | srin-bu me-khyer daṅ | glog lta-bu mthoṅ-ba rnams yino || bad-kan-las gyur-bahi rab-rib-kyi mćhan-ma ni | mthoṅ-ṅo-cog mdog hjam-źiṅ skya-ba daṅ | bstan-par snaṅ sna-rnams yino || hdus-pa-las

7 gyur-pahi rab-rib-kyi mćhan-ma ni | mćhan-ma de-dag thams-cad lta-bur mthoṅ-na yin-no || khrag-las gyur-pahi rab-rib-kyi mćhan-ma ni | mthoṅ-ṅo-cog śin-tu dmar-bar mthoṅ-ba yino || mig-nad rab-rib ces-bya-ba yal-

213v1 bar bor-te | ćha-bas chen-po-las gyur-pa-las ni | mig-nad bris g-yogs-pa źes-bya-bar gyur-te | dehi mćhan-ma yaṅ thog-ma ni nad-gźi gaṅ-las gyur-pahi mćhan-ma rab-rib-kyi skabsu bśad-pa daṅ hdra-ba-las | phyir-źiṅ hkhrul

2 ćha-bas che-ba daṅ | mi-mthoṅ-bar hgyur-bar śes-par byaho || de-rnams-kyi naṅ-na bad-kan-las gyur-pahi mig-nad pris g-yogs-pa ni gso sla-ba yin-te rća gtar-źiṅ khrag phyuṅ-na bzaṅo || de-la rab-rib gso-bahi cho-ga ni | ’arurahi

3 ćhe-gu daṅ | śiṅ-mṅar daṅ | skyurura daṅ | na-le-śam daṅ | spaṅs-ma rnams chu ṅagsu byas-pahi ri-lus bskus-na mig-nad rab-rib rnams sel-to || ćha-ba gsum daṅ | lcags-kyi phye-ma daṅ | rgyam-ćha daṅ | hbras-bu gsum daṅ | staṅ-

4 zil rnams chu ṅagsu byas-te | legs-par sbyar-bahi ri-luhi miṅ ni | ri-lu nag-po źes-bya-ste | hdis bskus-na yaṅ mig-nad rab-rib sel-to || yuṅ daṅ | skyurura daṅ | pipiliṅ daṅ | katakahi hbras-bu daṅ | yuṅs-kar rnams-

5 kyi phye-ma char-pahi chu daṅ sbyar-te | ri-lur byas-pas bskus-na yaṅ | mig-nad-do-cog sel-to || byaghri daṅ | gla-sgaṅ daṅ | śiṅ-thog ’amra daṅ | śiṅ mṅar daṅ | pipiliṅ daṅ | rgyam-ćha rnams-kyi phye-ma zaṅs-kyi snod-kyi naṅ-du

6 rahi ho-ma daṅ sbaṅs-pahi ri-lus bskus-na yaṅ | mig-nad thams-cad sel-to || skaṅ bźi-pa phyugs-la sogs-pa gaṅ yaṅ ruṅ-bahi so daṅ | rgya-skyegs daṅ | karañjahi hbras-bu daṅ | priẖatīhi hbras-bu daṅ | gla-ba daṅ | rṅa-mohi

7 rus-pa daṅ | ña-rus daṅ | byidaṅkara daṅ | ćha-ba gsum daṅ | ru-rta rnams cha bsñams-te | chu ṅagsu byas-pahi ri-luhi miṅ ni | sohi ri-lu źes-bya-ste | hdis bskus-na mig-nad rab-rib daṅ | pris g-yogs-pa daṅ | mig-hjer daṅ

214r1 hbrum-ba byuṅ-ba daṅ | rma byuṅ-ba daṅ | liṅ-tog-la sogs-pa sel-to || ldoṅ-ros daṅ | rgyam-ćha daṅ | nag-ćhur daṅ | duṅ daṅ |

151v1 khu ttu tcemña [pa]|paśīṃdä ttimire u arbaudä āchai cve hā ne
hasvīdä . u ārkhä . pyāmä . u śīye kanā āstaṃna jidä .
ysīrā . sedalū . hauṣṭä . śaṃgä . trekaṭaukä cuvaṃ āstaṃna cuṇya
2 mā|kṣī' jsa haṃbairstą kaṣā' tceña paśą̄ñä . tceña besā āchā pyāmą
u śīyi kanā ārkhä u ttamīre jedä .
3 kapetta hīya kaṣā' u svaṃdū hīya cụṇya dva śu'ba habrrī⟨hā⟩|ñä .
ā vā sauvīraṃją hīya cuṇya u buhana drrai bāga jsa habrrīhāñä .
u gvehaiśkyẹ jsa ėsthajāñą . u tceña neśą̄ñä ttamīra jedä .
4 pātcą lavaṃgą śau bāgä . | śā dva bāga . sauvīraṃją drre bāga .
svadū paṃjsa bāga . nāgakyesarä dersą bāgą ttyāna āstaṃna cụṇya
5 bastą bājaṃ haṃdaṃna ėysbrrījsą̄ñą . u nauką kūṭą̄ñä tceña bi|se
arve hīye gvahaiśkye jsa ėsthaṃją̄ñä u yādą tceña neśą̄ñä .
pātcä sauvīraṃją aůmalai kā saṃ hamāte . cuṇya gvīhä . rrū jsa u
152r1 mākṣī' jsa haṃbrīhāñä hasī[1].|rąña ą̄na gichauka thaṃjāñä u tteña
ṣkāmakaña hā tvā arva viśtą̄ñä u darą hāmai jsa ėsalyāñä . baraśījā
2 hīvī besu jsa dą̄ña padajsą̄ñä . daṃdą khu hāmai suśtą u | dą̄mą jīye
u ėsūjāñä u aysdemą̄ñą . cu va halīrai jsehera arva hame ṣā' vāthaṃ-
3 jāñą u kuṭą̄ñą . halīrā hāyse dīśą̄ñą tcemña bese arvā hīye gvehai|śkye
jsa tceña neśą̄ñä . ttemīrā jenāka . pīrmāttaṃ hva ṣṭe .
pātca halaidrrą . u ysālva . halīrā . buśą̄nai kuṣṭä . pepalą āstaṃna
4 nauką kuṭāñä u cụṇya ttye nā|ma tta tta hva ṣṭe se jastä ba'ysą jsa
hva aṃja thyauta bese kheṇḍą tceña bese arve hīye gvehaiśkye jsa
asthaṃjāñą u tceña neśą̄ñą . tceña besā āchā beśą jedą .
5 pātcą | svaṃdụ . buśānai . gaṃdhapatrą hīya cuṇyą gvīha. rruṃ
jsa habrrīhāñä u haryāsą śaysdą . kamala pyahāñą tvā arva ėha
152v1 veśtą̄ñą u grīhą. jsa ttū kamalą darą ėsalyā.|ñä u phajiña viśtāñä .
daṃdä khu ṣe' grīhą. suśtä u paskyāṣṭą aysdemą̄ñä u tvā vā arva
thaṃją̄ñä u nauką kuṭą̄ñą tci'ña bese arve hīye gvehaiśkye jsa
2 asthajā|ña u tciña niśą̄ñä ttimīri jedą . vatsāviśe' ttī . gvīhą . rrūṃ
jsa haṃbrrīhą̄ñä u ñagraudą bahyą. hīyā perāṃ jsa ñuṣṭāñą uce
3 haṃdrre vya pajsą̄ñä daṃda khu paśte . ṣā' ka|ṣā' aysdẹmą̄ñä u
tceṃ vą jsi bijsą̄ñä ā vā pātcą vatsāviśe' ttī bāje astauci mụñaṃdāṃ
murāṃ hīye āhe ttata pajsą̄ñä khu ttā thyautta hva . u kaṣā' tcemña
4 bejsāña | tce'ma'ñai vasasīdą u prrehīsīdä .
pātce trephalą . hīśa hīya hīsuṣka mahābāje āstaṃna cuṇya

[1] halīraña.

ćha-ba gsum daṅ | skyer khaṇḍa rnams-kyi phye-ma sbraṅ-rći daṅ sbyar-bahi khu-bahi mig-

2 sman-gyis bskus-na yaṅ | mig-nad bris g-yogs-pa daṅ | liṅ-tog daṅ | mig-hjer daṅ | rab-rib rnams sel-to || śiṅ kapittahi khu-ba | mu-zihi khu-ba ñis-gyur daṅ sbyar-ba ham | yaṅ-na skyer khaṇḍa daṅ | staṅ-zil daṅ |

3 gla-sgaṅ-gi bźi-gyur-gyi phye-ma daṅ sbyar-bahi naṅ-du mig-sman-gyi thur-ma bsgres-te | mig byugs-na yaṅ rab-rib sel-to || yaṅ-na li-śi cha gcig daṅ | zaṅs cha gñis daṅ | staṅ-zil cha gsum daṅ | mu-zi cha lṅa daṅ || naga-ge-

4 sar cha gsum daṅ | hdi-rnams-kyi phye-ma snod-kha sbyar-gyi naṅ-du ćhig par brṅos-la źib-tu btags-pas mig-sman-gyi thur-ma-la mgo-źiṅ rtag-tu mig byug-par byaho || staṅ-zil lam | skyurura gaṅ yaṅ ruṅ-bahi phye-ma mar daṅ | sbraṅ-

5 rćis sbyar-te | ’arurahi sñiṅ-po phyuṅ-bahi skyin-par khoṅ-du bcug-la slar kha sbyar-te | pag-zan-gyis g-yogs-nas | rgya-śug-gi mehi naṅ-du sregs-la | bag-zan ćhig-ste dud-pa chad-nas slar byuṅ-ste | bsgraṅs-la | ’arurahi khoṅ-na sman |

6 hdug-pa btags-pahi phye-mas mig-sman-gyi thur-ma-la bsgo-źiṅ | mig byug-pa ni rab-rib sel-pahi mchog yin-no || yuṅ daṅ | skyer-pa daṅ | ’arura daṅ | spaṅ-spos daṅ | ru-rta daṅ pipiliṅ rnams źib-tu btags-pahi

7 phye-ma hdihi miṅ ni | saṅs-rgyas-pahi mig-sman źes-bya-ste | sṅa-ma bźin-du mig-sman-gyi thur-ma-la bsgo-źiṅ | mig-la byugs-na mig-nad thams-cad sel-to || yaṅ-na staṅ-zil daṅ | spaṅ-spos daṅ | gandha̱-patra rnams-kyi phye-

214*v*1 ma mar daṅ sbyar-la | sbrul nag-po śi-bahi mgo bcad-pahi khar bcug-la | hjim-pas g-yogs-te bsregs-la | hjim-pa ćhig-ste dmar-por gyur-nas phyuṅ-ste bsgraṅs-la | dehi naṅ-gi sman źib-tu btags-pahi phye-mas mig-

2 sman-gyi thur-ma-la bsgo-źiṅ mig byugs-na yaṅ rab-rib sel-to || dug-mo-ñuṅ-gi sa-bon mar daṅ sbyar-la | śiṅ batahi lo-mahi naṅ-du phur-mar byas-te | chuhi naṅ-du bskol-la ćhos-par gyur-nas | naṅ-gi khu-ba bsgraṅs-pa

3 mig-tu blugs-pa ham | yaṅ-na dug-mo-ñuṅ-gi sa-bon-gyi skyin-par bya skam-sa-na gnas-pahi sgo-ṅa sṅa-ma bźin-du bćos-pahi khu-ba mig-tu blugs-na mig blta-bar hgyuro || yaṅ-na hbras-bu gsum daṅ | lcags-kyi phye-ma

5 gvīhą. rru mą̄kṣī' jsa habrrīhā[ña] u nūyacą hverai . cu bu|ri saṃ
tceña āchā ḭde beśą jenīdą u ūrą bedą besā haṃguṣṭe stā vīśtīṃda .

trephalą jṣą̄ñāñą kaṣā' gvīha. ṣvīdą u gvīhą. rrų̄naña trephalą
153r1 hīya cuṇya jṣą̄'ñā|ñą daṃdä khu re va rrūṃ harśtä . pa'śā' hālai va
samą̄naką khāśą̄'ñä . thettyau[1] ttemīra beśą jedą .

lagarą bāta . trephalą deśamula āstaṃna jṣą̄ñą̄ñą kaṣā' tteña hā
2 rrūña jī|vanīye . daśau arvāṃ hīvī cụṇya jṣą̄ñą̄ñä khu ri va rru
harśtä . samānaką khāśą̄'ñą ttemīra jedä .

veña ttā gvaña āchāṃ hīye jehume hīya krra berāśą̄'ñą
3 | cu be'ta jsa hamyą gvaña besā āchā hīya gunā gvā vīna trą̄māre .
ne pyuṣḍe u nāyai vā nerą̄me u ysauttę .

4 ttavaṃdye jsa hamye līka gunā ttaudā vai ha|me
cu śelīṣā jsa hamye līka hīya gunā . hauṣka ysū . u arīśe' bauśa
hame . ttye hīya jehųme va arve . drrevaṃttą . kadalą śīye merejsya .
5 yseruna trehe u yse|runa ttuṃgara . ttyāṃ āstaṃna kāmenai saṃ
hamāte . kaṣā' . sedalū āstana habrīhāñą . u grą̄maką hā gvą'ña
pyąnāñą tta ttai hala khauśą̄'ñą khu hā haṃdäna[2] ñāme u khvę vā
153v1 asphī|rīye bvą̄ñą se śerai yuḍe .

sidalūṃ . kuṭą̄ñä . u rrustiri hīyvā ysīcvā pervā ñūṣṭyāñä . u
ttekyāṃ biṃdä hā netcaṃna rrustarinę bāgarą ñuṣṭāña hauda peṃ-
2 bara u pha|ja veśṭą̄ñä däda[3] paśą̄ñä khu ri va asuva śau beṣṭarą
bāgara harśtä . cu netcaṃna bese bāgara tti hāyse dīśą̄ñą u sedalūṃ
3 pā hāyse dīśą̄ñä u haṃdaṃna bese ysīce | perą cu hā arve hīvī
ṙaysą traṃdą ganaiste . tte kūṭą̄ñä u haṃthrajāñä cu vā ūtce nerą̄mī
ṣe' gvą̄ña paśą̄ñą gva'ña bisā āchā jeṃdä . belāda āstaṃna ga' |
4 detadārą pātcą tcārbą devadārą āstaṃna kāṃ saṃ hamāte . ttye
hīya askhauysa . ā vā detadārä . balohaña ñuṣṭą̄ñą . kujsavị̄ña rrų̄ña
5 ṣunāñą u padajsāña | u cve vā ṣe' rraysä ysauttą ṣe' paḍauysä hāyse
dīśą̄ñą u śe pacaḍą myāña besai grą̄maką gvą̄ña neśą̄ñą gvą̄ña āchā
jeṃdä . kuṣṭä . ttugara . āra

154 deest.

[1] thyautte. [2] haṃdaṃna. [3] daṃda.

daṅ | śiṅ-mṅar rnams-kyi phye-ma mar daṅ | sbraṅ-rći daṅ
sbyar-ba ñal-khar rtag-tu zos-na | mig-nad-do-cog sel-ciṅ | ro ća-bar
yaṅ hgyuro || hbras-bu gsum bskol-bahi khu-ba daṅ | ho-ma daṅ |
mar-gyi naṅ-du hbras-
5 bu gsum-gyi phye-ma bskol-te | mar ñi-ćhe lus-pa-las nub-mo
źiṅ ran-par hthuṅs-na yaṅ | riṅ-mo mi-thogs-par rab-rib sel-to ||
sman rasna daṅ | hbras-bu gsum daṅ | rća-ba bcu-pa rnams bskol-
bahi khu-ba
6 daṅ | mar-gyi naṅ-du sman hćho-byed ces-bya-ba | sna bcu-pahi
phye-ma bskol-to || mar ñi-ćhe lus-pa-las | ran-par hthuṅs-na yaṅ
rab-rib sel-to || || da ni rna-bahi nad-kyi cho-ga bśad-par bya-
7 ste | de-la rluṅ-las gyur-pahi rna-bahi nad-kyi mćhan-ma ni | rna-
ba gñisu zug-ciṅ na-la | hon-źiṅ sgra hbyuṅ-ba daṅ | hjag-pa rnams
yino || mkhris-pa-las gyur-pa ni ćha-ba hur-hur-por hdug-pa yino ||
bad-kan-las
215r1 gyur-pa ni rna-bahi nad skam-la dri mnam-pa yino || de-dag gso-
bahi sman ni | sman muraṃga daṅ | chu-śiṅ daṅ | śikru daṅ | la-
phug daṅ | sgehu-gśer rnams-las gaṅ yaṅ ruṅ-bahi khu-ba rgyam-
ćha daṅ |
2 sbyar-ba dron-pos rna-ba gaṅ-bar blugs-la | naṅ-du chub-par
bsgul-źiṅ phyir pho-na rna-bahi nad sel-to || rgyam-ćha btags-pa śiṅ
'arkahi lo-ma ser-pohi naṅ-du phur-la | dehi phyi-rol-tu yaṅ |
'arkahi lo-ma rim-bdun-gyis
3 g-yogs-te | me-mar-mur-gyi naṅ-du bcug-la | lo-ma naṅ-rim
ma-ćhig ćam-du bsregs-nas | lo-ma phyi-rim rnams kyaṅ bor | naṅ-
gi rgyam-ćha yaṅ bor-la | naṅ-rim-gyi lo-ma ser-po-la gśer bag yod-
pa bćir-bahi khu-
4 ba rna-bar blugs-na yaṅ rna-bahi nad sel-to || bilba-la sogs-pahi
sde-ćhan daṅ | thaṅ-śiṅ daṅ | sgron-śiṅ rnams-las gaṅ yaṅ ruṅ-bahi
śiṅ-buhi thor-to ras-kyis dkris-te | til-mar-gyi naṅ-du smyugs-la
bsregs-te | hbar-
5 du bcug-pahi khu-ba zags-pa dron-po rna-bar blugs-na yaṅ rna-
bahi nad sel-to || ru-rta daṅ | bu-bran śiṅ daṅ | śu-dag daṅ | thaṅ-
śiṅ daṅ | śu-ti daṅ | śiṅ-kun daṅ | rgyam-ćha rnams-kyi phye-ma ra-
gcin daṅ | til-mar-gyi
6 naṅ-du bskol-te | til-mar ñi-ćhe lus-pa dron-po rna-bar blugs-na
yaṅ rna-bahi nad-kyi ñam-thag-pa sel-to ||

* * * * *

155r1 caḍä krra tcerai .
pātcą mālaigą-vī . śirka buśe arve basta līkaña ṣadą̄naña[1] ṣyąnąñą
padajsāñä u dą̄ma haysgvā u ėha paśāñą .
2 pātcą tcauri buśą̄nā tta tta khu | tvacä sukṣmela . gaṃdhapatrą .
nāgakyesarą āstaṃna haṃtse haṃbrrīhāñą .
ā vā pātcą haryāsą aủṣai dīśte haṃphāją̄ñą haysgvā buśą̄ñą̄ñą .
3 pātcą ṣalą ttāmalaką u trekaṭau | ką hīya cụṇya gvī'hą. rrūṃ
haṃtse gulą jsa jṣą̄ñą̄ña u habrrīhāñą u hverai . mālaigą u stīyvā[2]
4 gvehaiya . kvā'ysvā vīne u ysera rrāhą u biṃga baṃdanvā | vīnāṃ
āstaṃna jedą .
kaṇḍārya u dattą ā vā bāva u āra u śīya meremjsya u surasą u treka-
ṭauka[ṭauką] sedalū āstaṃna ku⟨jsa⟩vīña rrūña uce haṃdrre vya
5 jṣą'ñą̄ñą khu ṛe va | rru harśtą . haysgvā ṣyanąñą . cve mālaigą jsa
parśtą haysgvā ānai vā ysu nerą̄me . ysunąme hīya āchā beśą jidä .
veña ttā beśā' hīya krra berāśāṃ' .
155v1 cu beśā' hīya | āchā tti drrai-padya hamāre .
cu beta jsa hamyata līka beśā' hīya āchā hvaḍā khaṣṭā hīvī ysvye
2 ne bautte . u baysgai biśā' hame u puṇauśtä aśauką bahyä hī | ye
peri mą̄ñadu hinai .
cu ttavadye jsa hamya gunā biśā'vī ysīrrä hame u ttaudāvī va
hame .
3 cu śilīṣā jsa hamye hīya gunā beśā'vī darą ysīrrä u ṣa' | lokṣą
hame . cu lokṣä biśā' hame beśā' va darą̄ñä banaji jsa cu va āche
jehụñą īye thaṃją̄ñä u kāmye duṣā' jsa ha [cu lokṣą beśā' hame beśā'
4 darą̄ | ñä banaje jsa cu va āche jehụñą īye thaṃjāñä u ką̄mye dūṣa'
jsa ha]mye īye haphīśą̄ñä . hva hva dūṣā' hīyā arvā hīyā ga' jsa
5 haysgvā paśą̄ñą u ė'ha | beysajāñą u paskyāṣṭą naṣṭvāña beśā'vą jsa
sakhalyāñä u tvāvą jsa krra tcerai .
veña ttā daṃdvā besā āchāṃ hīya krra berāśāṃ' .
156r1 cu daṃdvā besā āchā ttyāṃ khaiyi | trą̄mīdā u vinaustä hame u
pajyāre u byavāre . tti biti jsa hamāre . haudvyāṃ vīra saṃ gvī'hä.
rrūṃ ā vā kumjsavīnai . kaṃ saṃ ⟨ha⟩māte . beta jinākāṃ arvāṃ jsa
2 kaṣā' | grāmaka ā vā ka'kä ā vā kaṣe' jsa ttoṛä paṣoją̄ñä u paskyāṣṭä
naṣṭvą̄ñä:
ā vā pātcä ha kalyarūha⟨na⟩ buhane ⟨te⟩jiva . pāṭha . halaidrrä
3 ysālva laudrrä . kuṣṭą . sa | maṃga ā⟨staṃ⟩na cụnye jsa . daṃdāṃ

[1] padān°.
[2] svīyvā.

215v5 kha-zas ni ćha-źiṅ skyur-ba bzah-ba-la sogs-pa sman-pas cho-ga
bźin-du byaho || yaṅ-na cham-pa-la
6 ni sman dri źimo-cog snod kha-sbyar-gyi naṅ-du bsregs-pahi dud-
pa spyi hus draṅs-te | kha snar brṅub-par byaho || yaṅ-na dri sna
bźi źes-bya-ba | śiṅ-ća daṅ | sug-smel daṅ | gandẖa-patra daṅ |
naga-gesar rnams lẖan-cig-tu sbyar-bahi
7 yaṅ-na tha-phe nag-po phur-mar phur-te | snar snam-par byaho ||
li-zir-ba daṅ | tamala daṅ | ćha-ba gsum-gyi phye-ma mar daṅ bu-
ram-gyi naṅ-du bskol-te | sbyar-ba zos-na yaṅ cham-pa daṅ | glo
brdol-ba daṅ | rćibs-logs na-ba daṅ |
216r1 ṣñiṅ na-ba daṅ | mkhal-rkeṅ na-ba rnams sel-to || byagẖri daṅ
dandahi rća-ba daṅ | śu-dag daṅ | śikru daṅ | byihu-rug-pa daṅ |
ćha-ba gsum daṅ | rgyam-ćha rnams-kyi phye-ma til-mar daṅ |
chuhi naṅ-du bskol-te | til-
2 mar ñi-ćhe lus-pa snar blugs-na | cham-pa yal-bar bor-ba-las sna-las
rnag hjag-pahi lud sel-to || || da ni lce-nad-kyi cho-ga bśad-par bya-
ste | de-la lce-nad ni rnam-pa gsum-ste | rluṅ-las gyur-pahi lce-nad
ni | kha-zas-kyi
3 ro mi ćhor-źiṅ slo-slo-bor gyur-pa daṅ | hgags-pa daṅ | śiṅ
’aśokahi lo-ma bźin-du dmar-ba rnams yino || mkhris-pa-las gyur-
pahi mćhan-ma ni | lce rćub-ciṅ ćha-ba hur-hur-por hdug-la ćag-
ćag ćha-ba yino || bad-kan-las gyur-bahi mćhan-
4 ma ni | lce-ril-gyis stug-pa bem-bem-por hdug-pa yino || de-ltar
lce bem-bem-por gyur-pa-la ni | lce bźar-źiṅ naṅ khrag ṅan-pa
phyuṅ-la nad-gźi gaṅ-las gyur-pa daṅ sbyar-te | nad-gźi so-sohi
sman-gyi sde-ćhan-las snar blugs-pa daṅ | mkhur-ba
5 bkaṅ-źiṅ phyir dbo-ba daṅ || lce-la bsku-ba rnams-kyi cho-ga
byaho || || da ni so na-bahi cho-ga bśade | so-nad brug-ciṅ na-ba
daṅ | brće-ba rnams gñis ni | rluṅ-las gyur-pa yin-te | de-gñis-la yaṅ |
mar ram til-mar rluṅ
6 sman daṅ sbyar-ba dron-po ham | rluṅ sman bskol-bahi khu-ba
dron-pos kha bśal-źiṅ phyir dbo-ba ham yaṅ-na pu-će-śel daṅ | gla-
sgaṅ daṅ | tejobati daṅ | patha daṅ | yuṅ daṅ | skyer-pa daṅ | gseṅ-
phrom daṅ | ru-rta daṅ | samaṅga
7 rnams-kyi phye-mas so-druṅ-na | sohi druṅ g-yah-ba daṅ | so-
khrag hjag-pa daṅ | zug-ciṅ na-ba rnams sel-to || bcah ldan-źiṅ
kha-nas hbrum-ba ẖbyuṅ-ba ni | khrag daṅ mkhris-pa hkhrugs-pa-
las hgyur-te | de-la ni khrag hbyuṅ daṅ

bidą pisalyą̄ñä cu ārhvi kyihāre u hų̄ñä nirą̄me . u khaiyi trą̄māre .
vinostä hame ttyāṃ āstaṃna jimdä :
4 cu ttaude[1] jsa khaysmi nirą̄ | mīṃdä huñi jsa u ttavaṃdye āphirą̄me
jsa hamāre . ttyevī hų̄ñä paśą̄ñä . vrrī horāñä . gvī'hä. rrü[2] kuṃjsavīnai rruṃ u mākṣī' ṣvīdä gvīha bīysma āstaṃna kāṃ saṃ
5 hamāve . tto | rą jsa paṣaują̄ñä u paskyāṣṭä naṣṭvą̄ñä :
pātcä rrustirāṃ hīye ysīci perä u gūlūśä' . u gūra . dūrālabha
ysālva triphalą āstaṃna jṣą̄'ñą̄ñä u kaṣā' aysdimą̄ñą . mākṣī' jsa
156v1 haṃbrī | hą̄ñä ė'ha biysaṃją̄ñä u paskyāṣṭä nāṣṭvāñä cvai ttaudā
hame u ėha khaysma sarbīdä biśä jidä ||
2 paśtä phaṃnai . gūrakä hasvą̄me hīvī āchai . ṣi' śilīṣāṃ jsa u
hų̄ñä ā | phārä jsa hame . ṣi' pyihą̄ñä . trikaṭaukä . sidalūṃ āra .
mākṣīna haṃbrīhą̄ñä u ėha biysaṃją̄ñä u ṣaha paskyāṣṭä naṣṭvą̄ña u
śilīṣāṃ haṃgārą̄ñä
3 cu garśa bisai ā | chai ką⟨. . . . .⟩ ṭha śą̄ñä cu hagūṣṭi
biṃdä prihąraṃ jsa nirūją̄ñä pātcä uskātta bisai khiṇḍä sąmaṃdvāṃ
arvāṃ haṃjvą̄me u paskyā⟨ṣṭa⟩ naṣṭą̄ma tcerai .
4 cu garśa bisai āchai rohanī ną̄ | ma cu hadaṃna garśa chai khiṇḍä
tvaḍa gūrśta ysaiye ṣi' drrayāṃ duṣāṃ' haṃdrri vya śe śe dūṣä' jsa
hame . sadvịnä jsa . u hų̄ñä āphärä jsa pā hamāre . ttyāṃ hīya hva
5 hva gų̄nä narīkṣą̄'ñä | u paysą̄ną̄ñä . khu ttī ttyāṃ krra paiyi hamāte
u buḍatta huṣvīde jsiñi ṇa'styą̄ñä padīmāre gą̄mą̄ñä thyau krra
tcerai ||
ttyāṃ hīya krra harbiśāṃ saṃ hų̄ñä paśą̄ñä . ką̄mye dūṣä'

Marg. Sogd. čw kymš'n

deest caeterum.

[1] ttaure. [2] rruṃ.

216v1 bkru-sman btaṅ-ba daṅ | mar daṅ | til-mar daṅ | sbraṅ-rći daṅ |
ho-ma daṅ | ba-gcin rnams-las gaṅ yaṅ ruṅ-bas kha-bas kha bkaṅ-la
riṅ-du bźag-la phyir dboho || yaṅ-na sna-mahi lo-ma daṅ | sle-tres
daṅ | rgun daṅ byi-ćher daṅ | skyer-pa daṅ | hbras-
2 bu gsum-po rnams bskol-bahi khu-ba sgraṅs-pa sbraṅ-rći daṅ
sbyar-bas mkhur-ba bkaṅ-źiṅ phyir pho-na ćha ldan-źiṅ khar
hbrum-ba byuṅ-ba sel-to || rkan-gyi phug-nas lcehu chuṅ-ba
hdug-pahi skraṅ-bahi nad ni | bad-kan daṅ | khrag hkhrugs-
3 pa-las gyur-pa yin-te || de ni brtol-la | ćha-ba gsum daṅ | rgyam-
ćha daṅ || śu-dag daṅ | sbraṅ-rći rnams sbyar-ba khar bźag-ciṅ khu-
ba phyir dbo-bas bad-kan draṅ-bar byaho || || lkog-mahi nad
4 śaluka źes-bya-ba | lkog-mahi naṅ-du hbrum-ba rgya-śug-gi
hbras-bu hdra-ba ril-ril-por hbyuṅ-ba ni | bad-kan-las gyur-ba yin-
te | dehi cho-ga ni gtar-bahi dpyed mjub-mo bćags-bu phrehu
bciṅs-pas rtol-te | sṅa-ma bźin-
5 du de daṅ hphrod-pahi sman mur-źiṅ | khu-ba phyir dbo-bar
byaho || lkog-mahi nad roh̲ini źes-bya-ba | lkog-mahi naṅ-du | śa
lh̲ag myu-gu ltar skye-ba riṅ-po źig hbyuṅ-ba ni | nad-gźi gsum-po
re-re daṅ | kun-hdus-pa daṅ | khrag-gi ñes-pa
6 rnams-las gyur-ba yin-te | so-sohi mćhan-mahi sgo-nas rtogs-par
byaho || dehi cho-ga mchis-te cher skyes-na | srog-la yaṅ hbab-par
byed-pas-na cho-ga myur-te byaho || de-la cho-ga ni de-dag thams-
cad-la yaṅ gtar-ga bya-źiṅ khrag phyuṅ-
7 la | nad-gźi so-so gaṅ-las gyur-bahi sman sbyar-bas kha-na bźag-
bźag-ciṅ bad-kan draṅ-bar byaho ||

SANSKRIT TEXT.

A.

A1vi namaḥ sarvajñāya
sārvaṃ praṇamya sarvajñaṃ durgaguptasya sūnunā
saṃhitā siddhasāreyaṃ[1] raviguptena vakṣyate
āyur-vedodadhi-tantram aśaktā ye 'lpamedhasaḥ
2 teṣām iya|ṃ prabodhāya[2] vihitā tantra-paddhatiḥ
brahmā provāca yaṃ svarge vedam āyur-nibandhanam
śiṣyebhyaḥ kathayām āsa kāśi-rājo 'pi taṃ kramāt
3 tasya tv aṅgāni śālā|kya-kāya-bhūta-cikitsitam
śalyāgada-vayo-bāla-rakṣā-bīja-vivardhanam
puruṣo vyādhy-adhiṣṭhāna-mahābhūta-guṇātmakaḥ
4 śārīra-mānasāgantu-sa|hajā vyādhayo matāḥ
śārīrā jvara-kuṣṭhādyāḥ krodhādyā mānasāḥ smṛtāḥ
āgantavo vighātotthāḥ sahajāḥ kṣut-tṛḍ-ādayaḥ
5 anādi-nidhanaḥ kālo ni|meṣādika-lakṣaṇaḥ
vibhāgāḥ ṣaṭ samākhyātā ṛtavas tasya santatam
prāvṛṇ-nabho nabhasyau ca iṣo⟨r⟩jau ca śaran matau
6 mārga-pauṣau ca hemantaḥ śiśi|rau māgha-phālgunau
vasantaś ca caitra-vaiśākhau nidāghaḥ śuci-śukra-bhāk
ta ete varṣa-sītoṣṇā ravi-vartma-dvayāśrayāḥ
2ri vayo-varṣā himoṣṇeṣu pitta-śleṣma-na|bhasvatām
kopaḥ śarad-vasantāmbuvāha-kāleṣu kīrtitāḥ
vāyoḥ sāyāhna-kāleṣu jīrṇās tac ca visarpaṇam
pittasyāhar-niśasyārdhaṃ jīryamāṇe ca lakṣayet
2 bhukta-mā|treṇa pradoṣe ca pūrvāhne śleṣmaṇo bhavet
eka-dvi-tri-vibhāgena duṣṭān doṣān viśodhayet
doṣa-dhātu-maladhāra-dehināṃ deha ucyate
3 teṣāṃ | samatvam ārogyaṃ kṣaya-vṛddhī viparyayaḥ
rasāsṛṅ-māṃsa-medo'sthi-majja-śukrāṇi dhātavaḥ
vāta-pitta-kaphā doṣā viṇ-mūtrādyā malā matāḥ
B2vi vāyuḥ śīto laghuḥ sūkṣmaḥ kharo rukṣaḥ sthiro balī
prāṇāpāna-samānā ta. . vyāna-prabhedavān
A 4 pitta|m amlaṃ kaṭūṣṇaṃ ca pakty-ojo-rāga-kāraṇam[3]
madhuro lavaṇaḥ snigdho guru-śleṣmātipicchilaḥ

[1] A siddhi°. [2] A °dhama.
[3] A paktūjyotirāga°, B pakṣojorāga.

5 guda-śroṇy-āśritau vāyuḥ pittaṃ yaknāśaya-sthita | -m
kāyasyāmāśaya-sthāna-kaṇṭhoro-mūrdhni sandhayaḥ
doṣa-sthāna-gataṃ doṣa-sthānivat samupācaret
6 ādhikyaṃ ca paricchidya kriyā kāryāvilambi | tā
ṣaḍ rasā madhurādyāś ca sevitās te vibhāgaśaḥ
ārogya-hetavo nityam anyathā tu viparyayaḥ
kaṭu-tikta-kaṣāyāś ca kopayanti samīraṇam
2v1 kaṭv-amla- | lavaṇāt pittaṃ svādv-amla-lavaṇāt kapham
eta eva viparyastāḥ samā yeṣāṃ prayojitāḥ
bhavanti rogiṇāṃ śāntyai svasthānāṃ sukha-hetavaḥ
cakṣuṣo madhuro jñeyo raso dhātu-vivardhanaḥ
2 āmlo | 'nulomano hṛdyaḥ kledī pācana-dīpanaḥ
śodhanaḥ pācanaḥ kledī lavaṇaḥ śithilatva-kṛt
sthaulyālasya-viṣaghnaś ca kaṭur dīpana-pācanaḥ
3 dīpano jvara-tṛṣṇāghnas tiktaḥ śo | dhana-rocanaḥ
pīḍanā-lekhana-stambhī kaṣāyo grāhī ropaṇaḥ
rasa-vīrya-vipākānām āśrayād dravyam uttamam
uttarottara-saṃśleṣād itareṣāṃ pradhānatā
4 rasa-pākānta | ra-sthāpi dravyādhāra-vyapāśrayā
śītoṣṇa-lakṣaṇaṃ vīryam atha vā śaktir iṣyate
rasāṇāṃ dvi-vidhaḥ pāko madhuraḥ kaṭur eva ca
gurur ādyas tayor jñeyo laghutvam itarasya ca
5 | bhiṣag bheṣaja-rogārta-paricāraka-sampadaḥ
cikitsāṅgāni catvāri viparītāny asiddhaye
bhiṣak śāstrārtha-karmajño laghu-pāṇi-śucir mataḥ
6 dravyāyuḥ-satva-sampannaḥ sā | dhyo rogī sad-ātmavān
subhuja-surasaṃ śreṣṭhaṃ bhaiṣajaṃ kāla-saṃhṛtam
bhaktaḥ snigdho 'pramattaś ca balavān paricārakaḥ
deśa-kāla-vayo-vahni-prakṛti-sātmya-bhaiṣajam
3r1 deha-satva-ba | la-vyādhīn dṛṣṭvā karma samārabhet
bahūdaka-nago 'nūpaḥ kapha-māruta-rogavān
jāṅgalo 'lpāmbu-śākhī ca rakta-pitta-gadottaraḥ
saṃsṛṣṭa-lakṣaṇopeto deśaḥ sādhāraṇaḥ smṛtaḥ
2 vayo 'pi | tri-vidhaṃ jñeyaṃ bāla-madhyama-vṛddhataḥ
āṣoḍaśād bhaved bālo varṣāt kṣīrānivartanaḥ
madhyamaḥ saptatiṃ yāvat tatparo vṛddha ucyate
3 kapha-pittānila-prāyā yathā-saṃkhyam udīri | tāḥ
kṣārāgni-rahitā vṛddha-bāla-pravayasāṃ kriyāḥ

kṛśasya bṛṃhaṇaṃ kāryaṃ sthūla-dehasya karśanam
rakṣaṇaṃ madhya-kālasya deha-bhedās trayo matāḥ
4 sthūlo 'tyalpa-balaḥ kaś|cit kṛśaś ca balavān naraḥ
sthairya-vyāyāma-sāratvair boddhavyaṃ yatnato balam
avikāra-karaḥ satvaḥ [sa-]vyasanābhyudayāgame
5 aviṣādī mahotsāhas tad-yogāt sā|tviko naraḥ
pānāhārādayo yasya viruddhāḥ prakṛter api
sukhatvaṃ yāvat kalpānte tat-sāmyam iti gamyate
kṛśo rukṣo 'lpa-keśaś ca cala-citto 'navasthitaḥ
6 bahu-vā|g vyomagaḥ svapne vāta-prakṛtiko naraḥ
akāla-palitī gauraḥ prasvedī kopano budhaḥ
svapne ca dīptimat-prekṣī pitta-prakṛtir ucyate
sthira-cittaḥ subaddhāṅgaḥ suprajaḥ snigdha-mūrdhajaḥ
3v1 | svapne jala-sitālocī śleṣma-prakṛtiko naraḥ
san-miśrair lakṣaṇair jñeyo dvi-tri-doṣānvayā narāḥ
doṣaś cetara-sadbhāve 'py adhika-prakṛtiḥ smṛtaḥ
2 manda-tīkṣṇo 'tha viṣamaḥ samaś cai|va catur-vidhaḥ
kapha-pittānilādhikyāt tat-sāmyāj jaṭharo 'nalaḥ
samasya pālanaṃ kāryaṃ viṣame vāta-nigrahaḥ
3 tīkṣṇe pitta-pratīkāro mande śleṣma-viśodha|nam
prabhavaḥ sarva-rogāṇām ajīrṇa-vahni-sādanam
āmāmla-rasa-viṣṭambha-lakṣaṇaṃ ca catur-vidham
āmād[1] viṣūcikā kleda-hṛl-lāsālasakādayaḥ
4 vacā-lavaṇa-|toyena chardinaṃ tatra kārayet
śuktodgāro bhramo mūrcchā tṛṣo 'mlāt sampravartate
apāktvaṃ[2] tatra śītāmbu pānaṃ vāta-niṣevaṇam
5 gātra-bhaṅgaḥ śiro-jāḍya-bhakta-dve|ṣādayo rasāt
tasmin svāpo divā kāryo laṅghanaṃ vāta-varjanam
śūlānugranthi-viṇ-mūtra-saṅgāviṣṭambha-sūcanā
vidheyaṃ svedanaṃ tasya pānaṃ ca lavaṇodakam
6 |ahitāśana-samparkāt sarva-rogodbhavo yataḥ
tasmāt tad ahitaṃ tyājyaṃ nyāyāt pathya-niṣevaṇam
eraṇḍa-vahni-tat-tailaṃ bhṛṣṭau barhiṇa-tittirī
4r1 godhān kapiñjalān vāpi tyajyā|t tulyaṃ ghṛtaṃ madhu
daśa-rātra-sthita-sarpiḥ kāṃsa-pātre vivarjayet
uṣṇāmbu nānupānaṃ ca mākṣikasya nabho'mbhasaḥ
vārāha-piśitān nādyān[3] madhunā mūlakaṃ tathā

[1] A āmāmla. [2] A apāktvam, B avāktvā. [3] A pisitā nādyā.

2 valyakaṃ | cāpi madyena dadhnā ca saha kurkuṭān
kācamācīn guḍopetān matsyān upodakānvitān
saṣkulīm āraṇālena nādyān mīnaṃ guḍena ca
3 śākām!a-phala-piṇyāka-ku | lattha-lavaṇaiḥ saha
karīra-dadhi-matsyaiś ca prāyaḥ kṣīraṃ virudhyate
priyaṅgu-kalka-digdhāhvaṃ pāyasaṃ na samācaret
4 na jātu kaṭu-tailena bhṛṣṭān nādyāt kapotakān |
pippalī-matsya-tailena surā-kṛsara-pāyasān
nāśnīyād ekato mīna-dhānān sarpiṣy udaśvitā
viruddha-rasa-vīryāṇi dravyāṇy evaṃvidhāni yaḥ
5 bhukto mo | hāt sarogārtiṃ mṛtyuṃ vā prāpnuyān naraḥ
viruddhāśanajān rogān virekaṃ chardinair jayet
viruddhaṃ na bhavet sāmyād dīptāgner balavān[1] iva
6 iti tantrādhyāyaḥ pra | thamaḥ samāptaḥ

---

sthirā-punarnavairaṇḍa-jhaṣa-ṛṣabhaka-jīvakāḥ
śvadaṃṣṭrābhīru-lāṅgulī-bidārī-haṃsapādikā
bṛhatyau vṛścikālī ca dve sahe markaṭī-sahā
4v1 śo | ṣa-gulmānila-śvāsa-kāsa-pitta-haro gaṇaḥ
nyagrodhodumbara-plakṣa-madhukāśvattha-tindukāḥ
piyālā-badarī-pārtha-nandīvṛkṣāmra-vañjalāḥ
palāśāruṣka-śvetaṃ ⟨ca⟩ lodhra-jambu-trayo gaṇaḥ
2 | pittāsṛṅ-meha-nud vraṇya-dāha-yoni-gadāpahaḥ
pippaly-agni-vacā-vatsa-kolā-granthika-mustakāḥ
viśvailātiviṣā-kauntī-cavyoṣaṇa-yavānikīḥ
3 bhārṅgī-mūrvā- | mahānimba-phalājājyāḥ sa-sarṣapāḥ
hiṅgu-tikta-viḍaṅgaṃ ca vāta-śleṣma-haro gaṇaḥ
elā-vakrāmbu-kauntī-tvak-patra-hemāsra-corakāḥ
4 caṇḍāyaś cala-punnāga-dāru-gu | ccha-rasāḥ puraṃ
srajā-śukti-dadhi-dhyāma-kunda-vyāghra-jaṭāmayāḥ
elādiḥ piḍakā-kaṇḍu-viṣānila-kaphānta-kṛt
varuṇārtagalābhīru-viśvājājī[2]-viṣāṇikāḥ
5 | sairīya-bṛhatī-yugma-darbha-pūtika-śigrukāḥ
japāgnimantha-bimbāgni-naktamālāḥ sa-moraṭāḥ
vargāntarvidradhi-śleṣmā medo-gulma-śiro-'rti-nut
6 āragvadhāgni- | sāṅgaṣṭā-kaṇṭakī-nimba-pāṭalāḥ
mūrvā-ghoṇṭhāmṛtā-rāṭha-pāṭhā-bhūnimba-kūlakāḥ

[1] A °sān, B °gān. [2] A bilvācāja, B bilvājāvi.

karañjau vatsa-sairīya-suṣavī-saptaparṇakāḥ
meha-kuṣṭha-jvarā-chardi-viṣa-śleṣma-haro gaṇaḥ
5r1 | rodhra-dvaya-plavāśoka-rambhā-sālailavālukāḥ
kadambho jiṅginī caiva śrīparṇī sa-vasusravāḥ
vargo rodhrādiko nāma kapha-medo-viśoṣaṇaḥ
2 yoni-doṣa-haro vraṇya-stambhī-sarva-viṣāpa | haḥ
ambaṣṭhā-dhātakī-rodhra-samaṅgā-padmakesaram
madhukāralu-bilvaṃ ca pakvātisārahā gaṇaḥ
āmalakābhayā[1]-kṛṣṇā-citrakaś cety ayaṃ gaṇaḥ
3 sarva-jvara-kaphātma | hā nātivṛṣyo 'tidīpanaḥ
akṣa-dhātryābhayā hanti triphalā viṣama-jvaram
cakṣuṣmān dīpanī meha-kuṣṭha-pitta-kaphānta-kṛt
4 bṛhatī-dhāvanī-pāṭhā-yaṣṭī-ma | dhuka-liṅgakā
pācanīyo bṛhaty-ādiḥ kṛcchra-doṣa-trayāpahaḥ
paṭolaṃ candanaṃ mūrvā tikta-pāṭhāmṛtā-gaṇaḥ
pitta-śleṣmāruci-cchardi-jvara-kaṇḍū-viṣāpahaḥ
5 | guḍūcī-nimba-dhanyāka-madhuka-candanānvitaḥ
tṛṣṇā-dāhāruci-cchardi-pitta-jvara-haro gaṇaḥ
kākolyau madhukaṃ śṛṅgī mede ṛṣabhaka-jīvakau
6 prapauṇḍarīka-mṛ | dvīkā ṛddhi-vṛddhī tukā sahe
payasyā padmakaṃ chinnety eṣa vargo 'ti⟨bṛṃ⟩haṇaḥ
stanya-svajīvano vṛṣyaḥ pittāsrānila-nāśanaḥ
śārivā padmakośīra-madhukaṃ candana-dvayam
5v1 kā | śmaryaṃ madhukaṃ ceti śārivādir ayaṃ gaṇaḥ
rakta-pitta-jvara-cchardi-mahādāha-vināśanaḥ
añjana-tākṣaja-śyāma-nāga-paṅkaja-kesaram
2 | madhukaṃ cety ayaṃ vargaḥ pittāsṛg-viṣadāhanut[2]
vacā-mustābhayā-dāru-nāgarātiviṣā-gaṇaḥ
haridrā-kalaśī-dāru-niśā-madhuka-vatsakī
3 etau vacā-haridrādī gaṇau doṣa- | vipācanau
āmātisāra-śamanau stanya-doṣa-viśodhanau
uṣa-saindhava-kāsīsa-dvaya-hiṅgu-śilājatuḥ
tutthakaṃ ceti medo-ghnaḥ śarkarāśmari-nud gaṇaḥ
4 vīravṛkṣāgni | manthaś ca kāśa-vṛkṣādanī-kuśā
moraṭendīvarī-sūryabhaktā-dundūka-gokṣurā
vasuko vasiro darbhaḥ ⟨sa-⟩sairīyāśmabhedakaḥ
aśmarī-śarkarā-kṛcchra-mārutārti-haro gaṇaḥ

[1] A āmalakṛtayā, B om. [2] A viṣāpahaḥ.

5 | muṣkakas triphalā-rāṭha-vṛkṣāgni-snu⟨kma⟩hī-dhavāḥ
palāśa-śiṃśapā-vargo medo-'rśo-'śmari-mehahā
sāla-spandana-kālīya-dhava-sarjārjunāsanāḥ
6 śirīṣa-śiṃśapā-bhūrjā kha|dirāś candana-dvayam
kadaro vājikarṇaś ca karañja-kebuko guruḥ
vargo 'yaṃ kaphāpāṇḍutva-kuṣṭha-meha-vināśanaḥ
utpala-kumudaṃ padmaṃ kahlāra-lohitotpalam
6r1 madhukaṃ ceti pittāsṛ|k-tṛḍ-viṣa-cchardi-hā gaṇaḥ
trapus tāmramayaḥ sīsaṃ hema-rūpyaṃ ca tan-malā
vargas tu gulma-hṛd-roga-pāṇḍu-meha-gadāpahaḥ
surasa-kāśamardi[ka]ś ca phaṇijjhārjaka-bhūstṛṇam
2 nirguṇḍī-surasī-phāñjī-|kulāhala-sugandhakāḥ
kṣavakaḥ kālamālaś ca viṣamuṣṭi-pracīvalaḥ
viḍaṅga-kācamācī ca maruko mūṣikarṇikā
3 śrīparṇaś ceti vargo 'yaṃ krimi-śleṣma-vināśa|naḥ
kāsāruci-pratiśyāya-śvāsa-hā vraṇa-śodhanam
pharuṣo dāḍimaṃ drākṣā kāśmarī śāka-jambulam
rājādanaṃ sa-dhātrīkaṃ katakena samanvitam
4 pharuṣakādiko nā|mnā gaṇo 'yaṃ vāta-nigrahaḥ
hṛdyo ruci-pradas tṛṣṇā-mūtra-doṣa-vināśanaḥ
mustā-pāṭhā haridre dve tiktā-hemavatī vacā
drāmiḍy-ativiṣā-kuṣṭhī-bhallātaka-phala-trayam
5 sā|ṅgaṣṭhā ceti vargo 'yaṃ kapha-roga-nisūdanam
śodhanaḥ pācanaḥ stanyo yoni-doṣa-haro mataḥ
śyāmā danti-dravantī-snukmahā-śyāmāmṛtā trivṛt
6 saptalā śaṅkhinī śvetā | rājavṛkṣaḥ sa-tilvakaḥ
kampillakaḥ karañjāś ca hemakṣīrīty ayaṃ gaṇaḥ
udāvartodarānāha-viṣa-gulma-vināśanaḥ
bilvāgnimantha-duṇṭūka-śrīparṇī-pāṭalā-mahat
6v1 dīpanaṃ kapha-|vāta-ghnaṃ pañcamūlam idaṃ smṛtam
pṛṣṭaparṇī sthiraiaṇḍa-bṛhatī-dvaya-saṃyutaṃ
bṛṃhaṇaṃ vāta-pitta-ghnaṃ pañcamūla-kaniṣṭhakam
bidārī-śāriva-cchāga-śṛṅgī-vatsādanā-niśā
2 kṛcchra-pi|ttānilān hanyād vallījaṃ pañcamūlakaṃ
gṛdhrā-halī-śvadaṃṣṭrā ca sairīya-karamardikāḥ
ete śleṣmānilau hanti kaṇṭaja-pañcamūlakaṃ
3 kuśa-kāśa-dvayaṃ darbho naḍaś ceti | tṛṇodbhavam
pitta-kṛcchra-haraṃ pañcamūlaṃ vasti-viśodhanam

etais tailāni sarpīṃṣi[1] pralepāpānakāny api
gaṇair vibhajya kurvīta yathā-vidhir bhiṣag varaḥ
4 kvāthyā | c caturguṇaṃ vāri pādasthaṃ syāc caturguṇam
snehāt snehaḥ sama-kṣīraḥ kalkaś ca sneha-pādikam
saṃvartitauṣadhaḥ pāko vastau pāne bhavet samaḥ
5 kharo 'bhyaṅge mṛdur nasya sā | mānye 'yaṃ prakalpanā
iti dravya-gaṇādhyāyo nāma dvitīyaḥ

---

anna-pānād ṛte nānyad vartanaṃ jagato hṛtam
6 hitāhita-paricchittyai vidhiḥ samyaṅ[2] ni | gadyate
rakta-śāli-mahāśāli-kalamāḥ śālijātayaḥ
madhurāḥ śukralāḥ snigdhāḥ svalpa-māruta-varcasaḥ
rakta-śālis tri-doṣa-ghnas tṛṣṇā-medo-nivartanaḥ
7r1 mahāśāliḥ paro vṛ | ṣyaḥ kalamaḥ śleṣma-pittahā
śīto gurus tri-doṣa-ghno madhuro gaura-ṣaṣṭikaḥ
kiñcid vināśitas[3] tasmād aparo rasa-pākataḥ
2 śyāmākaḥ śoṣaṇo rūkṣo vātalaḥ śleṣma-pi | tta-hā
tadvat priyaṅgu-nīvāra-koradūṣāḥ prakīrtitāḥ
bahu-vāta-śakṛc-chītaḥ pitta-śleṣma-haro yavaḥ
vṛṣyaḥ śīto guruḥ svādur godhūmo vāta-nāśanaḥ
3 kapha- | pittāsra-jin muṅgaḥ kaṣāya-madhuro laghuḥ
māṣo bahu-malo vṛṣyaḥ snigdhoṣṇo vāta-hṛd guruḥ
avṛṣyaḥ śleṣma-pitta-ghno rāja-māṣo-'nilānta-kṛt
4 ku | latthaḥ śvāsa-hikkārśaḥ-kapha-śukrānilāpahaḥ
rakta-pitta-jvaronmāthī śī⟨to⟩ grāh⟨ī⟩ makuṣṭakaḥ
puṃstvāsṛk-kapha-pitta-ghnaḥ canako vātalaḥ smṛtaḥ
5 masū | ro madhuraḥ śītaḥ saṅgrāhī kapha-pitta-hā
saṭīnaś caivam[4] uddiṣṭaḥ kalāyaś cātivātalaḥ
sa-kṣāra-madhura-snigdho-balyoṣṇaḥ pitta-kṛt tilaḥ
6 bala-ghno | rūkṣaṇa-śītā vividhāḥ śimba-jātayaḥ
nātiśīta-guru-snigdhaṃ chāga-kravyaṃ adoṣalam
viṣṭambhi-madhuraṃ śītam āvikaṃ guru-bṛṃhaṇam
7v1 svapna-śukra-kara-snigdha-bṛṃha | ṇaṃ māhiṣaṃ guru
vṛṣyaṃ vāta-haraṃ māṃsaṃ vārāhaṃ svedanaṃ guru
vahni-kṛt kapha-pitta-ghno vāta-sādhāraṇasya saḥ
tri-doṣa-śamanaś caiṇaṃ baddha-viṇ-mūtra-śītalam
2 vāta-ghnaḥ | śrotra-dṛg-varṇaḥ svara-śukra-pradaḥ śikhī

[1] A sarpyādvi, B sappisi. [2] A ta nya. [3] A vinī°, B vino°. [4] A cedam.

uṣṇo vāta-haraḥ snigdho guru-vṛṣaṇyaḥ kurkuṭaḥ
gurūṣṇa-madhuro nāti tittiriḥ sarva-doṣa-hā
3 dīpanāḥ sannipāta-ghnā | lāva-vartīra-vartakāḥ
caṭakaḥ pitta-vāta-ghnaḥ kapha-śukra-vivardhanaḥ
śleṣmāsṛk-pitta-hṛc chaitya-lāghavārthī[1] kapiñjalaḥ
4 rakta-pitta-haraḥ śīto guruḥ pārāvato | mataḥ
tasmāl laghutaraḥ kiñcid dhārītaḥ sa-kapotakaḥ
snigdhoṣṇā gurukā vṛṣyā vāta-ghnā jala-pakṣiṇaḥ
haṃso vṛṣyataraḥ teṣāṃ prāyas timira-nāśanaḥ
5 sni|gdhoṣṇā guravo matsyā vāta-ghnā rakta-pittalāḥ
vāta-pitta-harā vṛṣyā cūlūkī-kūrma-karkaṭāḥ
2*vv.* A.
6 kācamācī tri-doṣa-ghnā stanyā vṛṣyā kalambukā
cāṅgerī kapha-vāta-ghnī sārṣapaṃ sarva-doṣalam
vāstukaḥ potikā cillī pālaṅkā taṇḍulīyakāḥ
8*r*1 manda-|vāta-kaphāsṛṣṭa-viṭkā-pittāsra-nāśanāḥ
mūlakaṃ doṣaṃ kṛtvāmaṃ svinnaṃ vāta-kaphāpahaṃ
sarva-doṣa-hara-hṛdyaṃ kaṇṭhyaṃ[2] tad bālam iṣyate
karkoṭakaṃ sa-vārtākaṃ paṭolaṃ kāra-vallakaṃ
2 ku|ṣṭha-meha-jvara-śvāsa-kāsa-pitta-kaphāpahaṃ
sarva-doṣa-haraṃ hṛdyaṃ kuṣmāṇḍaṃ vasti-śodhanam
kaliṅgālāvanī pitta-nāśanī vāta-kāraṇī
3 trapuṣairvāruke vāta-śleṣmale pi|tta-vāraṇe
karīrābheru-vetrāgra-kebukaḥ kapha-pitta-jit
viṣa-śālūka-śṛṅgāṭa-mālukaṃ sa-kaśerukaṃ
rakta-pitta-haraṃ vṛṣyaṃ stanyaṃ ca guru śītalam
4 vāta-ghnaṃ dāḍima|ṃ grāhi kapha-pittāvirodhi ca
tadvad āmalakaṃ vṛṣyaṃ madhurānurasa⟨ṃka⟩ram
gulma-śūla-kapha-śvāsa-kāsa-ghnaṃ bījapūrakam
5 kapitthaṃ grāhi doṣa-ghnaṃ pakvaṃ guru viṣā|pahaṃ
pakvāmraṃ vāta-nun māṃsa-śukra-varṇa-bala-pradam
vātalaṃ kapha-pitta-ghnaṃ grāhi viṣṭambhi jāmbaram
tindukaṃ ⟨ka⟩pha-pitta-ghnaṃ badaraṃ vāta-pitta-jit
6 viṣṭambhi vātalaṃ bi|lvaṃ piyālaṃ pavanāpaham
tālaṃ rājādanaṃ mocaṃ panasaṃ nālikerakam
śukra-māṃsa-karāṅy āhuḥ svādu-snigdha-gurūṇi ca
drākṣā-madhuka-kharjūra-kāśmaryaḥ sa-parūṣakam

[1] A °varcci°, B °vāca°. [2] A kaṇṭo, B kaṇṭhās.

8v1 vāta-pi|ttāsra-jid dṛṣṭaṃ keśa-ghnaṃ ca samī-phalam
kośāmrāmrātakaṃ dantaṃ śaṭhaṃ sa-karamardikam
rakta-pitta-karaṃ vidyād gulma-nut pīlujaṃ phalam
śuṇṭhī-marica-pippalyaḥ kapha-vāta-jito matāḥ
2 avṛṣyaṃ ma|ricaṃ vidyād itare vṛṣya-sammate
gulma-śūla-vibandha-ghnaṃ hiṅgu vāta-kaphāpahaṃ
yavānī-dhānyakājājyo vāta-śleṣma-nudaḥ param
cakṣuṣyaṃ saindhavaṃ vṛṣyaṃ tri-doṣa-śamanaṃ smṛtam
3 sau|varcalaṃ vibandha-ghnam uṣṇa-ḥrc-chūla[1]-nāśanaṃ
uṣṇa-śūla-haraṃ tīkṣṇaṃ viḍaṃ vātānulomanam
loṇakaṃ cānu tasya syāt sāmudraṃ kledanaṃ guru
4 hṛt-pāṇḍu-gala-doṣa-ghno yava-kṣārāgni-|dīpanaḥ
dahano dīpanas tīkṣṇaḥ svarja-kṣāro vidāraṇaḥ
doṣa-ghnaṃ nābhasaṃ vāri laghu hṛdyaṃ viṣāpaham
nānā-bhūpatra-saṃśleṣād bhidyate tad rasāntaraiḥ
5 nādeyaṃ vātalaṃ rūkṣaṃ sārasaṃ | madhuraṃ laghu
vāta-śleṣma-haraṃ vāpyaṃ tāḍāgaṃ vātalaṃ smṛtam
cauḍyam agnikaraṃ rūkṣaṃ kapha-ghnaṃ laghu nairjharam
dīpanaṃ vātalaṃ kaupyam audbhidaṃ pitta-nāśanam
5*vv*. A.
9r1 kaluṣaṃ krimi-śevāla-dūṣitaṃ sūrya-varjitam
agrāhyam udakaṃ grāhyam ebhir doṣair vivarjitam
2 uṣṇaṃ vāri jvara-śvāsa-medo-'nila-kaphāpa|ham
śṛta-śītaṃ tri-doṣa-ghnam uṣitānte ca doṣalam
go-kṣuraṃ vāta-pitta-ghnaṃ snigdha-guru rasāyanam
gavyād gurutaraṃ snigdhaṃ māhiṣaṃ vahni-nāśanam
3 chāgaṃ raktātisāra-ghnaṃ | kāsa-śoṣa-jvarāpaham
sekenānila-rakta-ghnaṃ pitta-śleṣmalam āvikam
auṣṭraṃ śophodarānāha-krimy-arśaḥ kapha-pitta-nut
4 cakṣuṣyaṃ jīvanaṃ strīṇāṃ rakta-pi|tte ca nāśanam
balya-vāta-haraṃ vṛṣyaṃ pitta-śleṣma-karaṃ dadhi
vṛṣyaṃ snigdhāsra-jit pitta-kapha-kṛd dadhi māhiṣam
5 tri-doṣaṃ manda-jātaṃ tu mastu sroto-viśodhanam |
grahaṇy-arśo-'rditārti-ghnaṃ navanītaṃ navodvṛtam
vikārāś ca kilāṭādyā guravaḥ kuṣṭha-hetavaḥ

* * * * *

59r4 pravāhikā-guda-bhraṃśa-śūla-mūtrāgrahāpaham

[1] A uṣṇa-śūla-, B usna-ḥrc-chula-.

5 tiktādyo yo gaṇo[1] vā syā|d vastir vā dāśamūlikaḥ
sa-kṣīra-lavaṇa-sneha-kalkair yukta-phalādibhiḥ
srāvaṇā-rakta-mālokṣa[2]-kriyā kāryāsra-paittikī
pūrvaṃ tiktopayogāś ca vahni-dīpana-pācanāḥ[3]
59*v*1 uśīrāriṣṭa-dārvī tvak kvāthaḥ syāc choṇitārśasām
śuṇṭhī-candana-bhūnimba-dhanva-yāṣa-bhavo 'tha vā
vṛkṣakasya tvacaṃ bījaṃ tākṣajātiviṣā-madhu
pibet taṇḍula-toyena tṛṣṇā-raktopaśāntaye
2 | samaṅgotpala-mocāhva-tirīṭa-tila-candanaiḥ
chāga-kṣīraṃ prayoktavyaṃ tad guda-śoṇitāpaham
ajā-kṣīrāśano yuktaḥ sa-kṣaudraṃ vṛkṣa-phāṇitam
3 mayūrakasya ka|lkaṃ vā raktārśī taṇḍulāmbhasā
sa-padma-kesara-kṣaudraṃ navanītaṃ navaṃ lihet
sitā-kesara-yuktaṃ vā śoṇitārśī sukhī bhavet
4 palikaṃ cavya-tālīsa-maricaṃ triguṇaṃ gu|ḍaṃ
sa-mūlā dvi-palā kṛṣṇā caturjāta-mṛṇālayoḥ
pṛthag akṣaṃ bhavec chuṇṭhyās tripalaṃ guḍikāgni-kṛt
sarvārśo-vāma[4]-hṛd-roga-kāsa-gulma-jvarāpahāḥ
5 guda-yantraṃ | bhavel lohaṃ śārṅgaṃ vā gostanākṛtiḥ
catur-aṅgulam āyāme nāhenāṅgula-pañcakam
chittvā vāta-kaphotthāni vahninārśāṃsi sādhayet
60*r*1 kṣīreṇaiva ca sarvāṇi dṛṣṭa-karmā bhiṣag | varaḥ
3*vv*. A, B.
pratyāditya gudaṃ kṛtvā paryaṅkaṃ nyase⟨t⟩[5] saṅgatam
2 2*vv*. A.
yantra-cchidreṇa niṣkrānta-vartyā sammṛjya vāyutaḥ
3 dadyāt kṣāraṃ sutīkṣṇaṃ hi yāvan-mātrā-s⟨u⟩saṅga|tam
tiṣṭhed yatnena yantrasya mukhaṃ pracchādya pāṇinā
balaṃ kṣārasya buddhvā hi[6] nirṇij⟨y⟩āt kṣārajaṃ malam
tuṣodakena sāmlena cukre vā mastunā 'tha vā
4 yaṣṭī-kalka-ghṛtākta|ṃ ca lepaṃ dadyāt suśītalam
vātajaṃ śleṣmajaṃ vāpi chittvā śastreṇa śastravit
23*vv*. A.
60*v*5 anna-pānaṃ yathāvasthaṃ tad yojyaṃ gudajāture
61*r*1 sva-doṣa-kopanaṃ | hy annaṃ kaṭhinotkuṭikāsanam
vega-saṃdhāraṇa-pṛṣṭhą-yānaś cārśī vivarjayet

[1] A tiktādyo yā ṣanā, B tiktādyā yā vano.
[2] A mālokṣa, B mālekṛ.
[3] A °aḥ, def. B.
[4] A vāpi, B bhrami.
[5] A konya, B kanyase.
[6] A budhvā ni, B budhvā.

arśo'dhyāyaś caturdaśamaḥ

gudasya dvy-aṅgule kṣetre pārśvataḥ piṭakārti-kṛt
2 bhinna-|bhagandaro jñeyaḥ sa ca pañcavidho mataḥ
tīvra-todāruṇa-vātāt piṭakaḥ śatapāṇakaḥ
pittāt tad-vyutthitā raktā śophauṣṭra-grīvakaḥ smṛtaḥ
3 kaphāt kaṇḍur mata|ḥ śvetaḥ parisrāvīti gadyate
tridoṣa-sarva-lingaḥ syāc chambūkāvarta-saṃjñakaḥ
unmārgī pañcamo jñeyaḥ śalyābhyavahṛte kṛte
4 tridoṣa-śalyajā tyājyā śeṣāḥ kṛcchra- | pratikriyāḥ
piṭakānām apakvānām apakarṣaṇa-pūrvakaṃ
karma kuryād vivekānāṃ bhinnānāṃ vakṣyate kriyā
eṣaṇā-pāṭanā-kṣāra-vahni-dāhādika-kramam
5 vidhā|ya vraṇavat kāryaṃ yathādoṣaṃ cikitsitam
āragvadhā niśā kālā cūrṇājyā kṣaudra-saṃyutā
mūtravṛtta-vraṇe yojyā śodhanī gati-nāśanī
61v1 trivṛt tejovatī dantī mañjiṣṭhā rajanī-dva|yam
tākṣajaṃ nimbapatraṃ ca lepo nāḍīvraṇāpahaḥ
karavīra-niśā-dantī-lāṅgalī-lavaṇāgnibhiḥ
mātuluṅgārka-vatsāhvaiḥ pacet tailaṃ bhagandare
10*vv*. A.
61v5 pṛṣṭha-yānāṅganā-yuddha-vyāyāma-guru-sevanam
rūḍha-vraṇaḥ prayatnena tyajet saṃvatsaraṃ nara
iti bhagandarādhyāyaḥ pañcadaśamaḥ

62r1 tīkṣṇāmla-lavaṇāsā|mya-mṛttikādi-niṣevaṇāt
syāt pṛthag yugapad doṣaiḥ pāṇḍurogaś caturvidhaḥ
kṛṣṇābho vāta-pāṇḍuḥ syāt tad-upadrava-saṅgataḥ
pitta-pāṇḍuś ca tad-rogī pīta-mūtrākṣi-viṭ-chaviḥ
2 śve|tābhaḥ kapha-pāṇḍutvaṃ tad-vikārānubandhanam
vijñeyaḥ sarva-rūpaś ca pāṇḍu-rogas tridoṣajaḥ
rakta-kṣayāsita-kṣīṇa-chardi-śophādy-upadravaḥ
3 pīta-bhāga-samālocī pāṇḍu-ro|gī jahāty asūn
snehita-sarpiṣā pūrvaṃ sarva-pāṇḍu-vikāriṇā
ūrdhvādhaḥ-śodhanais tīkṣṇair yathādoṣam upakramaiḥ
mūrvā-tiktā-niśā-yāsa-kṛṣṇā-candana-parpaṭaiḥ
4 trāya|ntrī-vatsa-bhūnimba-paṭolāmbuda-dārubhiḥ
akṣa-mātrair ghṛtaṃ prasthaṃ siddhaṃ kṣīraṃ caturguṇam

pāṇḍutā-jvara-visphoṭa-śophārśo-rakta-pitta-jit
5 phala-trikāmṛtā-vāsā | -tiktā-bhūnimba-vatsakaiḥ
kvāthaḥ kṣaudrayuto hanyāt pāṇḍurogaṃ sa-kāmalam
kṣīra-bhuṅ mūtra-saṃyuktāṃ pathyāṃ pāṇḍvāmayī pibet
kṣīreṇa loha-cūrṇaṃ vā gomūtreṇa subhāvitam
62v1 triphalāgny-abda-jantu- | ghna-vyoṣair loha-rajāḥ samam
līḍhaṃ kṣaudrājyavat pāṇḍu-kāmalā-śopha-meha-nut
loha-cūrṇa-tilair vyoṣa-kolās tāpyaṃ samaṃ samam
piṇḍī madhu-kṛtā ghora-pāṇḍu-śopha-nivāraṇī
2 jāya | te kāmalā pittāt pīta-netrāṅga-lakṣaṇāt
kumbhāhva-saṃpravṛddhasya tatra snigdhasya recanam
piṣṭair balā-niśā-nimba-triphalā-madhukaiḥ samaiḥ
3 sa-kṣīrair māhiṣaṃ sarpiḥ sādhitaṃ | kāmalāpaham
guḍūcyās triphalāyā vā dārvyā nimbasya vā rasaḥ
prātar mākṣika-saṃyuktaḥ śīlita-kāmalāpahaḥ
loha-cūrṇa-niśā-yugma-triphalā-kaṭu-rohiṇī
4 prali | hya madhu sarpirbhyāṃ kāmalāvān sukhī bhavet
dhātrī-loha-rajair vyoṣa-niśā-kṣaudrājya-śarkarāḥ
leho nivārayaty āśu kāmalām uddhatām api
5 kṛṣṇe dve granthikaṃ vahni | dīpyakoṣaṇa-saindhavam
krimi-ghna-triphalā-dhānyakālājyājy-ajamodakaḥ
palikāni trivṛc-cūrṇa-tailayoś ca palāṣṭakam
rasa-prastha-trayaṃ dhātryā guḍasyārdha-śataṃ pibet
63r1 etat kalyā | ṇakaṃ pāṇḍu-kāmalārśo-garāpaham
meha-kuṣṭha-jvara-śvāsa-grahaṇī-jid rasāyanam
añjanaṃ kāmalārtānāṃ droṇa-puṣpī-rasaṃ śubham
2 niśā-gairika-dhātrīṇāṃ cūrṇaṃ vā samprakalpa | yet
nasyaṃ karkoṭa-mūlasya ghreyaṃ vā jālinī-phalam
kāmalārtasya vairaṇḍa-pippalyau nāvanāñjanaiḥ
3 2*vv.* A.
harita-śyāva-pītatva-jvara-tṛḍ-vahni-māndya-kṛt
pāṇḍuḥ syāt sādanaṃ dravyo vata-pittād dhalīmakaḥ
4 madhurair anna | -pānais taṃ vāta-pitta-harair jayet
kāmalā-pāṇḍu-rogārtaṃ kriyāṃ cātra prayojayed
iti pāṇḍurogādhyāyaḥ ṣoḍaśaḥ

---

5 pitta-sthānam atikramya vāyu | ḥ kapha-purojavaḥ
hikkā-śvāsau karotīha tau ca pañcavidhau pṛthak

13vv. A.

63v4 hikkā-śvāsāture pūrvaṃ tailākte sveda iṣyate
ūrdhvādhaḥśodhanaṃ śakte durbale śamanaṃ matam
kola-majjāñjana-lājā-tiktā-kāñcana-gairikam
5 kṛṣṇā dhātrī sitā śuṇṭhī | kāsīsaṃ dadhi nāma ca
pāṭalyāḥ sa-phalaṃ puṣpaṃ kṛṣṇā kharjūra-mustakam
ṣaḍ ete pādikā lehā hikkā-ghnā madhu-saṃyutāḥ
madhukaṃ madhu-saṃyuktaṃ pippalī śarkarānvitā
64r1 nāgara-gu | ḍa-saṃyuktaṃ hikkā-ghnaṃ pādika-trayam
stanyena mākṣikā viṭkā nasyaṃ vā laktakāmbunā
yojyaṃ hikkā nirāsāya[1] phenyaṃ vā candanānvitam
2 nepālyā go-viṣāṇād vā kuṣṭha-sarjarasa | sya vā
dhūmaṃ kuśasya vā sājyaṃ pibed dhikkopaśāntaye
saindhavasya palaṃ dvābhyāṃ palābhyaṃ sarpiṣaḥ pibet
kṣāra-cūrṇāvakīrṇaṃ vā hikkārte sarpir uttamam
3 | durālambhā kṛṣṇā drākṣā śṛṅgī pathyāvacūrṇitāḥ
madhu-sarpir-yuto lehaḥ śvāsa-kāsopatantra-jit
guḍoṣaṇā niśā rāsnā drākṣā māgadhikā samāḥ
4 tailena cūrṇitā lī | ḍhā tīvra-śvāsa-nutaḥ smṛtāḥ
pralihyān madhu-sarpirbhyāṃ bhārṅgī-madhuka-saṅgatāḥ

* * * * *

71r5 añjanotpala-mañjiṣṭhā-candanośīra-gairikaiḥ
sa-yaṣṭī-padmakair lepaḥ ⟨××⟩[2]-kṣīrādi cokṣaṇam
dhavāśvakarṇa-mālānāṃ ⟨××⟩[3] lepaḥ kaphotthite
71v1 āragvadhādibhi | ḥ kvāthaḥ pariśeṣaḥ praśasyate
pāko rakṣyaḥ prayatnena śiśna-kṣaya-karo himaḥ
śastra-karmāṇḍa-pakṣe syād vraṇa-varcam upakramaḥ
kumudotpala-kahlāra-paṅkajāni prarohaṇī
2 masīvā | ntaḥ-pradagdhāyās triphalāyā ghṛtānvitā
rasāñjana-śirīṣeṇa pathyayā vā samanvitaṃ
sa-kṣaudraṃ lepanaṃ yojyaṃ sarvaliṅga-gudāpaham
3 balābalaṃ paricchidya doṣāṇāṃ sa | nnivāraṇaiḥ
upadaṃśa-dvayaṃ śeṣaṃ pratyākhyāya samācaret
mūtra-kṛcchropadaṃśādhyāyo viṃśatimaḥ

---

4 kruddha-pakvāśayopāno viṭkopāvartano | balī

[1] A °ārthaṃ. [2] A yaintī, B prette.
[3] A tvambhirlle°, B tvambhīrlle°.

 B56r3

ūrdhvago'dhaḥkha-saṃrodhī hy udāvarta[1]-karaḥ smṛtaḥ
hṛt-kukṣi-pārśva-rug-vasti-śophādhmāna-galagrahāḥ
jvara-cchardy-āndhya-bādhiryās tṛṣṇādyās tat-kṛtāgadāḥ
5 | udāvartinam abhyakta-svinna-gātram upācaret
vartikāsthāpanaṃ snehaṃ vasti-recana-karmaṇā
rāṭha-dhūma-viḍa-vyoṣa-guḍa-mūtre vipācitaiḥ
72r1 gude 'ṅguṣṭha-samāvartīn vidheyānāha | -śūla-nut
add. K, T.
rāmaṭhogrāmaya-svarjī-viḍa-bhāgā dvir uttarāḥ
cūrṇam uṣṇāmbunānāha-śūla-hṛd-roga-gulma-jit
trivṛt-kṛṣṇā-harītakyo dvi-catuḥ-pañca-bhāgikāḥ
2 guḍikā-guḍa-tulyā | s tāvad vibandha-gadāpaham
vāṭyaṃ kṣīra-rasaiḥ sevyam anyad yac cānulomanam
pitta-śleṣmānubandhe ca tad-dhitā vastayo matāḥ
3 vātād vastau bhavec chūlaṃ pittān nābhau vidā | hitam
kaphād vṛddhiṃ sa-hṛl-lāsaṃ sarva-rūpātmajaṃ tyajet
yavānī hiṅgu sindhūttha-kṣāra-sauvarcalābhayā
surā-maṇḍena pātavyā vāta-śūla-nisūdanā
4 sauvarcalāmla | kājājī maricair dvi-guṇottaraiḥ
mātuluṅga-rasa-śliṣṭā guḍikānila-śūla-hṛt
śuktāmla-vetasā-vyoṣa-yavānī-lavaṇa-trikaiḥ
5 bīja-pūra-rasopetā guḍi | kā vāta-śūlinaḥ
tumburūṇy abhayāhiṅgu pauṣkaraṃ lavaṇa-trayam
pibed yavāmbunā vāta-śūla-gulmopatantrakī
dhātrī-rasa-bidāryā vā trāyantrī-gostanāmbunā
72v1 pibet sa-śarkaraṃ | sadyaḥ pitta-śūla-pramardanaḥ
pralihyāt pitta-śūla-ghnaṃ dhātrī-cūrṇam sa-mākṣikam
śarkarā-mākṣikopetaṃ lājā-tarpaṇam āpibet
vacābdāgny-abhayā-tiktā-cūrṇa-go-mūtra-saṃyutaṃ
2 sa-kṣāraṃ vā | pibet kvāthaṃ bilvādi kapha-śūlavān

* * * * *

vātādibhiḥ pṛthak sarvaiḥ krimi-doṣāś ca pañcadhā

B56r1

2 hṛd-rogaḥ śūlavaj jñeyaḥ sa-kaṇḍvarti | . . . jaḥ
lavaṇāmla-yutaṃ tailaṃ hṛd-roge vātike pibet
siddhaṃ vā mūtravad gulma-śūlānāhādi-vāraṇam
3 pañcāśad abhayā-kalkāḥ sauvarcala-pala-dvayam |

[1] A hyād°, B hyad°.

⟨sarpiḥ-⟩prasthaṃ jale siddhaṃ hṛd-roga-śvāsa-gulma-jit
śuṇṭhī sauvarcalaṃ hiṅgu dāḍimaṃ sāmla-vetasaṃ
cūrṇam uṣṇāmbunā peyaṃ śvāsa-hṛd-roga-muktaye
4 sekā lepā himā I . . madhuraiś ca virecanam
piṣṭā vā kaṭukā peyā sa-yaṣṭyāhva-sitāmbunā
sthirādi kalkavat sarpiḥ kṣīreṇekṣya-rasena vā
5 drākṣā-rasena vā pakvaṃ pitta-hṛd-ro I⟨ga⟩. . -m
kṛṣṇā śaṭī vacā rāsnā śuṇṭhī pathyā sa-pauṣkarā
cūrṇitā vā śṛtā mūtre pātavyā kapha-hṛd-gade
6 tridoṣa-laṅghanaṃ pūrvaṃ yathāvasthaṃ kriyā matā I
. . . . piben mūtraṃ viḍaṅgāmaya-saṃyutam
ity udāvartādhyāya ūnaviṃśatimaḥ

---

duṣṭāmedhyānna-pānecchā bhaya-śokādi-samplavā
56v1 .[1] I . . . -ti vikopa unmādaḥ pañcadhā smṛtaḥ
vidyād āsphoṭanākranda-hasya-nṛtyair marud-bhavam
paittaṃ tu kopaśītecchā tarjanābhidravādibhiḥ
2 nidrālpa-bhā I⟨ṣa. . a⟩rocakaiḥ kaphajaḥ smṛtaḥ
sarva-liṅgānvito ghoro vivarjyaḥ sānnipātitaḥ
. . . . na vijñāno balavān vikramādibhiḥ
3 āgantu-pa I . . ⟨jñe⟩yo devādi-graha-dūṣaṇāt
vātike sneha-pānaṃ prāg virekaḥ pitta-sambhave
kaphajo vamanaṃ kāryaṃ paro vastyādikaḥ kramaḥ
4 niśā-yuk-triphalā-śyāmā-va I⟨cā⟩. . tha-hiṅgubhiḥ
śirīṣa-kaṭabhānvitā mañjiṣṭhā-vyoṣa-dārubhiḥ
sa-karañjair ghṛtaṃ mūtre siddham udmāda-nāśanam
5 apasmāra-viṣa-ghnaṃ ca basta-mūtre I . . . d ḥ
pāṭhā harītakī śigru vacā tryoṣaṇa-saindhavaiḥ
palāṃśaiḥ sarpiṣah prastham ajā-kṣīrāḍhake śṛtam
6 etat sārasvataṃ nāma smṛtim eṣāṃ viva I . .
jaḍa-gadgada-mūkatvaṃ prasabhād dhanti pānataḥ
yaṣṭī-hiṅgu-vacā-vakra-śirīṣa-laśunāmayaiḥ
sāja-mūtrair apasmāre sodmādair nāvanāñjane
57r1 bandha-tāḍa I⟨na⟩. . . . sanair vividhāśrayaiḥ
udmādinam upakramya paścāt sāntvair upācaraiḥ
pūjā-baly-upahāreṣṭi-homa-mantrāñjanādibhiḥ
jayed āgantum udmādaṃ yathāvidhi śucir bhiṣak

[1] kṣa *vel* ja.

2 I . . .⟨citta-⟩saṃra⟨m⟩bhau doṣād reka-hata-smṛte
apasmāra iti jñeyo gado ghoraś caturvidhaḥ
kṛṣṇa-pīta-sitā bhāvā vāta-pitta-kaphaiḥ kramāt
3 dṛśyante tad-vikārā vai sarvaiḥ kṛ I . . . . j ḥ
pañca karmāṇi tatrādau yathādoṣaṃ prayojayet
sarvataḥ śuddha-dehasya syād udmāda-harī kriyā
śaṅkha-puṣpī vacā kuṣṭhaḥ siddhaṃ brahmi-rase ghṛtam
purāṇaṃ ha. . . .odmādaṃ medhyam uttamam
8*vv*. B.
A73*r*2 taila-tulya-ghṛtaṃ prasthaṃ kṣīra-droṇe palāṃśikaiḥ
jīvanīyaiḥ śṛtaṃ pānād apasmāra-vināśanam
3 śigru-kuṣṭha-śilā I jājī-laśuna-vyoṣa-hiṅgubhiḥ
basta-mūtre śṛtaṃ tailaṃ nāvanaṃ syād apasmṛtau
4 2*vv*. A, B.
jalāgni-druma-śailādīn viṣamān parivarjayan
prayatnaḥ śīlayen medhyam apasmārī rasāyanam
ity unmādādhyāyo dvāviṃśatimaḥ

73*r*$^{4}_{5}$ aśīti vā I tajā rogā jāyante tasya kopataḥ
rug-bhaṅga-toda-saṅkoca-śoṣād veṣṭana-lakṣaṇaḥ
ākṣepako muhuḥ kṣepād vakṣaḥ[1]-stambhas tad-unnatiḥ
73*v*1 kṛtsna-dehārdharuk-kārī pakṣāghāto nigadya I te
mārutākuñcitā saṃsthā sirā jñeyaikabāhukam
gṛdhrasī śakthi-karma-ghnī saiva pārṣṇy-aṅgula-śritā
vaktrārdhaṃ vāyunā vakraṃ tad arditam udāharet
2 kroṣṭa-śīrṣaś ca jān⟨. . I śo⟩phaṃ vātāsra-sambhavam
abhyaṅgaḥ svedanaṃ vastir nasyaṃ sneha-virecanam
snigdhāmla-lavaṇaṃ svādu vṛṣyaṃ vātāmayāpaham
balā-niḥkvātha-kalkābhyāṃ tailaṃ pakvaṃ payo'⟨nvi⟩tam
3 I sarva-vāta-vikāra-ghnam eva sairīya-pācitam
16*vv*. A.
74*r*2 aśvagandhā tu lāvāmlā taila-prasthaṃ payo'nvitam
3 māṃsī-tvak-patraṃ-mañjiṣṭhā-I dravantī-surasā-jaṭā
balā-dāru-sthirā-yaṣṭī-rāsnailā-puṣkarā-vacā
śvadaṃṣṭrā-kuṣṭha-pūtīka-śatāhvā sa-punarnavā
4 vyāghrośīra-payasyā ca piṣṭair akṣā⟨ṃ⟩śitai I ḥ śṛtaḥ
sarvānila-gadādhvaṃsi caturdhā samprayojitam

[1] A vanta°, B uru°.

dadhy-amla-kāñjika-kṣīrair āḍhakāṃśair vacā-balāt
5 rāsnā-pau | ṣkara-viśvāgni-śigru-saindhava-gokṣurāt
kalkaṃ kṛtvā ca pippalyāḥ kṛtsna-vātārti-nāśanam
prasāraṇī śataṃ kvāthi tailaṃ prasthe payaḥ samam
74v1 jīvaka-ṛṣabhakau mede ⟨kākol⟩y⟨au⟩ | kuṣṭha-candanaiḥ
śatāhva-dāru-mañjiṣṭhā rāsnā piṣṭā vipācitam
vasti-pānādibhir yuktam etan māruta-roga-nut
taila-prasthaṃ payas tulyaṃ śvadaṃṣṭrā-surasāḍhake
2 guḍasya śṛṅgaverasya | pṛthaṅ mānī-śṛtaṃ pibet
kṣīrānu [s] tad-viriktaṃ ca khāded viśva-guḍānvitam
jīrṇe kṣīrānna-bhuk sarvān tīvrān vāta-gadān jayet
3 paced ghṛtāḍhakaṃ kvāthe laśunasya | śataṃ bhavet
karṣaś cavyāgni kṛṣṇānāṃ palike viśva-hiṅgunī
lavaṇā⟨ni⟩ pṛthak piṣṭvā palārdhaṃ cāmla-vetasām
gṛdhrasī-vāta-rug-gulma-pakṣāghātādi-vāraṇam
4 cavya- | sauvarcalā-vyoṣa-śigru-saindhava-dhānyakāḥ
akṣāṃśaiḥ sarpiṣaḥ prasthaṃ piṣṭaiḥ prasthonmitaiḥ pṛthak
5 mūlakārdraka-māṃsānāṃ rasaṃ śuktāmla-kāñjikaiḥ
mastu-takrayutaiḥ pakṣaṃ sadāgati-gadāpaham ||
vacā majjājya-tailāni vāta-vyādhiṣu yojayet
gṛdhrasyāṃ kroṣṭra-śīrṣe ca kṛtvā śoṇita-mokṣaṇam
75r1 | samīraṇa-haraṃ karma prayoktavyam aśeṣataḥ
śleṣmā medo'nvito jitvā vātam ūru-dvayāśritam
ūru-stambhaṃ karoty ugraṃ sāndra-gaurava-kāriṇām
2 sarvai rūkṣaḥ kramaḥ kāryas tatrādau | kapha-nāśanaḥ
paścād vāta-vināśāya kṛtsnaḥ kāryaḥ kriyā-vidhiḥ
praduṣṭa-sukumārāṇāṃ vāta-rakta-śramādibhiḥ
3 pūrvaṃ tat pāṇi-pādeṣu sthitvā dehaṃ pra | padyate
rug-bheda-śoṣa-pāruṣya-kārṣṇyād vātottaraṃ vadet
tāmra-śophātirug-dāha-mṛdutvai rakta-pittajaṃ
kaphena manda-ruk-kaṇḍū-staimitya-ghana-śophavat
4 dvandvataḥ sanni | pātāc ca liṅgair etaiś ca lakṣayet
ekadoṣaṃ navaṃ sādhyaṃ yāpyaṃ saṃvatsarotthitaṃ
5 tatrāsṛṅ-mokṣaṇa-pūrva-snigdho | vātottarād ṛte
tyājyaṃ tridoṣajaṃ bhinnaṃ sphaṭitaṃ *prasruñcayat
yathādoṣaṃ ca nirdiṣṭaṃ pañcakam āśraya-kramaḥ

A75r5–76r5 om. B, K.

A76r5 kaṇikyājā-payo lepaḥ sa-ghṛto vāta-rakta-jit
prabhṛṣṭaṃ kṣīra-nikṣiptaṃ tilair vā hy atha vomayā
śatāhvā kṣīra-sampiṣṭā bījaṃ vā vardhamānajam
76v1 pra | deho vodaka-kravya-veśavārāsu saṃskṛtaḥ
A76v1–5 om. B, K.
77r1 kalkaḥ śle | ṣmāture lepo vājigandhā-tilodbhavaḥ
śveta-sarṣapa-kalko vā varṣābhū-śigrujo 'tha vā
sarveṣu sa-guḍāṃ pathyāṃ guḍūcīṃ kvātham eva ca
2 pippalīṃ vardhamānāṃ vā śīlayet susamāhi | taḥ
iti vāta-vyādhi-cikitsādhyāyas trayoviṃśatimaḥ
ye viṣasya guṇāḥ proktās te madya-vipratiṣṭhitāḥ
3 tena mithyopayuktena bhavaty ugro ma | dātyayaḥ
add. K, T.
hṛc-chiraḥ-pārśva-ruk-stambha-hikkā-kāsair marudbhavaḥ
tṛḍ-dāha-sveda-pītatva-mūrcchābhiḥ paittikaḥ smṛtaḥ
4 hṛl-lāso rocakaś chardi-staimityaiḥ kapha-sambha | vaḥ
B60r2 jñeyas tridoṣajaś cāpi sarva-liṅgair madātyayaḥ
3 | . . ⟨sau⟩varcala-vyoṣa-yuktaṃ kiñcij jalānvitam
A77r4 jīrṇe madyāya dātavyaṃ vāta-pānātyayāpaham
śukta-sauvarcalaiḥ sāgni-śoṣaṇārjaka-dīpyakam
madyaṃ pītvā jayaty ugraṃ pavanotthaṃ madātyayam
5 ko | la-dāḍima-vṛkṣāmla-yavānī-lavaṇānvitā
pātavyā vāta-vicchittyai snigdhā madyena śaktavaḥ
yojayen mātuluṅgāmra-dāḍimaiḥ pānakāny api
77v1 snigdhoṣṇa-lavaṇāmlāṃś ca | rasān jaṅgalajān śubhān
paitte kṣaudra-sitā-yuktaṃ madyam ardhodakaṃ pibet
madhurauṣadha-niṣkvātha-yuktaṃ vā śarkarānvitam
muṅga-yūṣaḥ sitā-yuktaḥ svādur vā paiśito rasaḥ
2 | pitta-pānātyaye yojyāḥ sarvataś ca himā kriyā
vamana-dravya-saṃyuktaṃ madyānnollekhanaṃ matam
pāna-roge kaphodbhūtaṃ laṅghanaṃ ca yathābalam
3 dīpanīyauṣa | dhopetaṃ piben madyaṃ samāhitaḥ
triphalāyā rasaṃ vāpi vyoṣa-cūrṇa-samanvitam
śuṣka-mūlakajo yūṣaḥ kaulattho vā kaṭūtkaṭāḥ
4 yavānna-vikṛtir yo | jyā jāṅgalāny akṣatāni ca
sarvaje sarvam evedaṃ prayoktavyaṃ cikitsitaṃ
ye ca tṛṣṇādayo rogās te nivāryāś ca bheṣajaiḥ

5 madya-prakṣīṇa-dehasya vastayaḥ | sānuvāsanāḥ
abhyaṅgotsādana-snāna-sarpiḥ-kṣīra-niṣevaṇam
śatāvarī-sa-vṛścīva-yaṣṭī-kalkair ghṛtam śṛtaṃ
add. K, T.
balātibalayoḥ kvāthaṃ kṣīraiḥ pāna-kṣayāpaham
78r1 pa|yaḥ punarnava-kvāthaṃ yaṣṭī-kalkaṃ prasādhitam
ghṛtaṃ puṣṭi-karaṃ pānān madya-pāna-hataujasa
iti madātyayādhyāyaś caturviṃśatimaḥ

---

2 lavaṇāmla-kaṭūṣṇādi-saṃ|sevā doṣa-kopataḥ
visarpaḥ saptadhā jñeyaḥ sarvataḥ pravisarpaṇāt
vātāt kṛṣṇa-mṛdu-sphoṭā-śophavaj jvara-todavān
3 pittāt syāt pīta-raktābha-sphoṭa-dāha|-jvarānvitaḥ
B60v5 ka⟨phāt pāṇḍu-śve⟩ta-sphoṭaḥ kaṇḍu-śleṣma-jvaraiḥ smṛtaḥ
sannipāta-samutthaś ca sarva-rūpaiḥ samanvitaḥ
A78r3 kṣatajo rakta-pittābhyāṃ śyāva-lohita-śophavān
pāka-dāha-jvaro doṣī kṛṣṇa-sphoṭānvito mataḥ
4 agni-dagdhair avasphoṭaiḥ sahāṅgārāruṇā-|prabhāḥ[1]
dāha-tṛṣṇādayo jñeyā vāta-pittātmakāgnikāḥ
pāṇḍu-pītāruṇa-sphoṭo mecakī kapha-pittajaḥ
5 malinoṣṇāśraya-kledī kardamaḥ kardamopamaḥ |
ekadoṣās trayaḥ sādhyāḥ[2] śeṣāḥ sādhyetarā matāḥ
ubhayāntaḥśritāḥ sarve marmajāś ca viśeṣataḥ
tṛṇa-varjyaḥ prayoktavyaḥ pañcamūla-catuṣṭayaḥ
78v1 pradeha-seka-sarpirbhir | visarpe vāta-sambhave
lepanaṃ piṣṭa-saṃsiddhair yaṣṭī-sarpiḥ-payo-yutaiḥ
vātike kṣīra-seko vā ghṛta-maṇḍena vā smṛtaḥ
prapauṇḍarīka-mañjiṣṭhā-padmakośīra-candanaiḥ
2 sa-yaṣṭī|ndīvaraiḥ paitte kṣīra-piṣṭaiḥ pralepanam
sekālepājya-yogeṣu nyagrodhādi praśasyate
lepana-śata-dhautaṃ vā sarpir yaṣṭī-madhūtkaṭam
3 srotojośīra-śītābda-muktāmbu|maṇi-gairikaiḥ
sa-ghṛtaḥ payasā piṣṭair lepaḥ pitta-visarpa-jit
trāyantī-saptaparṇī-madhukāragvadha-dārubhiḥ
sa-kuraṇṭo bhavel lepo visarpe śleṣma-sambhave
4 madhuka-tri|phalā-vīrā-śirīṣair lepam ācaret
varuṇādir gaṇaḥ sapta kaphaje sarva-karmasu

[1] A sattā°, B satā°. [2] A yāyaḥ, om. B.

 A79v4

1v. B.

paṭolāriṣṭa-dārvī-tvak-tiktā-trāyantikāḥ śṛtāḥ
5 sa-yaṣṭī-madhukāḥ sarvaṃ visarpaṃ | ghnanti pānataḥ
mustāriṣṭa-paṭolānāṃ kvāthaḥ sarva-visarpa-nut
dhātrī-paṭola-muṅgānām atha vā ghṛta-saṃyutam
saṃśodhanaiś ca sarveṣu kāryaṃ śoṇita-mokṣaṇam

79r1 2vv. A.

iti visarpādhyāyaḥ pañcaviṃśati⟨maḥ⟩

79r2 kṣīṇa-māṃsasya gurv-amlaḥ sābhiṣyandānna-|sevayā
śophaḥ syāt ṣaḍvidho ghoro doṣair utsedha-lakṣaṇaḥ
calan syāt pīḍanān nimno vātāt kṛṣṇāruṇārti-kṛt
kṣipra-pākī mṛduḥ pittāt pīta-raktoṣma-dāhavān
3 | snigdhaḥ kāṭhinya-kaṇḍumāñ chukla-pāṇḍuḥ kaphodbhavaḥ
pittavad rakta-rūpaṃ[1] tu sarva-lingaṃ ca sarvajaḥ
upary āmāśayasthais tu pakvāśaya-gater adhaḥ
madhye madhya-gatair doṣaiḥ sarva-vyāpī ca sarvagaiḥ
vigatopadravaḥ sādhyo bala-sthasyaikadoṣajaḥ
4 śvayathuḥ sarvagaḥ kaṣṭo yaś cordhva|m upasarpati
pratyākhyāya kriyā kāryā tatrāpi *kurvate[2] parā
5 yathā|doṣaṃ gaṇaiḥ svaiḥ svaiḥ sarpis-tailāni kalpayet

8vv. A.

B61v5 pralepa-seka-pānāni bhiṣak śvayathu-rogiṣu
6 pañca karmāṇi | ...yathāvasthaṃ vidhānataḥ
A79v2 vakṣyante 'taḥ para-yogāḥ samānyāḥ śopha-nāśanāḥ
pibed uṣṇāmbunā dāru-pathyā-śuṇṭhī-punarnavāḥ
3 viḍaṅgātiviṣā-vatsa-viśva-dārūṣa|ṇāni vā
tryoṣaṇāyo-rajaḥ-kṣāraiḥ śophaṃ tu triphalā-rasam
kaṭukāyo-rajo-vyoṣa-trivṛdbhir vā samanvitam
puraṃ mūtreṇa saṃsevya pippalīṃ vā payo'nvitam
4 gu|ḍena vābhayā tulyā viśvaṃ vā śopha-rogiṇām
yuktā guḍārdrakaṃ sevyaṃ kṣīra-yūṣa-rasāśinām
śopha-śeṣodaronmāda-gulmārśaḥśvāsa-siddhaye

8vv. triṣṭubh A.

kṣīraṃ śopha-haraṃ dāru-varṣābhū-nāgaraiḥ śṛtam
peyaṃ vā citraka-vyoṣa-trivṛd-dāru prasādhitam

diff. A.

[1] A rūpan tu, B jāgantu.

[2] A kravate, B kruvate.

B62r4 medo-māṃsāśrayaṃ śophaṃ pādayoḥ ślīpadaṃ vadet
5 hastayoḥ karṇayoḥ kecit nāsāyā I .....
jvaraḥ pūrvaṃ bhavet tatra dehināṃ tu balārta-kṛt
sva-liṅgād arśibhir doṣais tat tridhā syāt kaphottaraṃ
samātītam asādhyaṃ syād dhalmīkākṛti-viśrutam
6 sarvaṃ tu I ....ta sthirodake
tantropanāhana-sveda-rakta-mokṣādi-kovidaḥ
sarvaś ca śopha-nirdiṣṭo yathāyogam udīritaḥ
trividho gala-gaṇḍo 'pi vāta-medaḥ-kaphānvayaḥ
B62v1 I ....⟨tā⟩lu-śoṣa-karo 'nilāt
medojaḥ syān mṛduḥ snigdhaḥ kaphajaś ca mahāsthiraḥ
kṣīṇasya ca samāhito gala-gaṇḍo na sidhyati
2 granthayaḥ śleṣma-me I .....pratimā-gale
gaṇḍa-mālā samākhyātā bahu-kālānubandhinī
svedopanāhanālepa-rakta-mokṣāviśodhanaiḥ
3 svair gaṇais taila-pānaiś ca gaṇḍa[1] I ⟨mālāṃ. . bhi⟩ṣak
gaṇḍa-mālāpahaṃ tailaṃ siddhaṃ sākhoṭaka-tvacāḥ
nimbāś ca māra-nirguṇṭhī sādhitaṃ vā. .nāvanam
4 sāruṣka-rasaṃ siddhārthā nimbapatraṃ ca dhyā I ⟨makaḥ⟩
⟨gaṇḍa⟩-mālāpaho lepaḥ chāga-mūtreṇa pīṣitaḥ
palam ardha-palaṃ vāpi sārdhaṃ taṇḍula-vāriṇā
kāñcanāla-tvacaṃ pītvā gaṇḍa-māla. .jayet
5 granthīn uddhṛtya I ...vahni-karma prayojayet
paktvā[2] kṣāreṇa saṃśodhya vraṇavat samupakramet
tyaktvendra-vastim āpādya[3] pārṣṇy-ūrdhvaṃ dvādaśāṅgulam
6 mīnāṇḍa-sadṛśa-medo hṛtvāvahṛtya I ...
. .pṛthag-doṣair asṛṅ mā.bhir jāyate 'rbudam
tat-sva-doṣa-vikāri syād asādhye rakta-māṃsaje
gala-gaṇḍa-kriyā tasyāvasthāpanādi-vastakaiḥ
B63r1 śastrāgni-kṣāra-ka I ......prayojayed
iti ślīpada-gaṇḍa-mālā-'rbuda-gala-gaṇḍa-śophādhyāyaś caturviṃśatimaḥ

B63r6 dvidhā vraṇaṃ parijñeyaṃ śārīrāgantu-bhedataḥ
A97v1 doṣair ādyas tayor anyaḥ śastrādi-kṣata-sambhavaḥ
vātād rūkṣāruṇa-śyāva-svacchālpa-sruti-vedanam
2 tīvroṣṇa-srā I vadāhādyaḥ pīta-nīlaś ca pittataḥ

[1] B r(*vel* c)aṇḍe. [2] B pakvā. [3] B māpādmā.

kaphāt pāṇḍuḥ sa-kāṭhiṇyaḥ śukla-śīta-ghana-srutiḥ
raktā-ratka-srutī raktād dvistrijāt[1] syāt tad-anvayaḥ
3 samānatva-vidagdha | sya vidagdhasya ca pācanam
pakvasya pāṭana-śuddhiḥ saṃrohaḥ syād vraṇasya ca
tila-kiṇvātasī-kuṣṭha-śaktūnāṃ lavaṇānvitā
4 dadhy-amla-marditā piṇḍī paraṃ pācanam iṣya | te
dāha-ruk-toda-rāgais tu vidagdha-śopham ādiśet
mandair etair vipakvaṃ ca valīmat piṇḍitonnataḥ
nikumbha-srukmayoś cāpi cira-bilvāgnikādayaḥ
5 kapota-da | kṣa-viḍ-yuktā kṣāro vā dāraṇam vraṇam
tila-saindhava-yaṣṭyāhvā nimbapatra-niśā-yutaiḥ
trivṛd-ghṛta-yutaiḥ piṣṭaiḥ pralepo vraṇaśodhanaḥ
98r1 nimbapatra-tilaiḥ kalko madhunā | kṣata-śodhanaḥ
ropaṇaḥ sarpiṣā yukto yava-kalke 'py ayaṃ vidhiḥ
nirutsaṅgī mṛduḥ snigdho jihvābho vigata-vyathaḥ
nirāsrāvo na cotsanno vraṇa-śuddhaḥ prakīrtitaḥ
2 pañcamūla-dvayaṃ vāte nya | grodhādiś ca paittikaḥ
āragvadhādiko yojyaḥ kaphajo sarva-karmasu
nīlotpala-balā-dārvī-meda-madhuka-candanaiḥ
samaṅgā-dhātakī-sarpir-yuktair lepaiḥ prarohaṇam
3 vra | ṇa-sandhāna[2]-kṛl lepo ghṛta-kṣīrī-drumāṅkuraiḥ
triphalā vaṭa-śuṅgāgragā[3]-patrī lodhrajo 'tha vā
arjunodumbarāśvattha-rodhra-jambū-tvacaḥ samāḥ
4 yaṣṭī-kaṭ⟨u⟩phalā-lākṣāś cūrṇi | tāḥ kṣata-rohaṇam
tiktā-śikṣa-niśā-yaṣṭī-naktāhva-phala-pallavaiḥ
paṭola-mālatī-nimba-patrair vraṇe ghṛtaṃ śṛtam
prapauṇḍarīka-yaṣṭyāhva-kākolī-dvaya-candanaiḥ
5 | tailaṃ siddhaṃ vraṇaṃ hanti kṣīra-vṛkṣa-kaṣāyavat
cailapaṭṭādibhir baddhvā vraṇa-śodhana-rohaṇam
karañja-plakṣa-jambvādi-patrādānaṃ ca śasyate
98v1 vraṇebhyaḥ krimi-juṣṭebhyaḥ surasādir ga | ṇo hitaḥ
kalāya-vidalī-patraṃ kośāmrāsthi ca pūraṇam
add. K, T.
nāḍīnāṃ gatim anviṣya śastreṇa pāṭya karma-vit
sarva-vraṇa-karma kuryāc chodhanā-ropaṇādikam
2 sa-śalyāc chalya | m āhṛtya kṣatā⟨t⟩ kaṅkāmukhena tu

[1] A dvistrijāḥ syā tad°, B dvītrijasyottad°.
[2] A sacona, B sanv(*vel* dh)āna. [3] A jyagā, def. B.

vraṇopasaṃhitaṃ kāryaṃ yathāvidhi bhiṣag g⟨h⟩itam
bṛṃhaṇīyo vidhiḥ kāryaś cirottha-kṣata-śodhanam
3 duṣṭa-vraṇeṣv asṛṅ-moktir ū|rdhvaṃ vādhaś ca śodhanam
baddhvāgantuṃ vraṇaṃ sadyo ghṛtaṃ kṣaudra-samanvitam
śītā kriyā prayoktavyā pitta-raktoṣma-nāśanī
4 kṣīrī-tvak-kuśikā-bandhaḥ sthiraḥ syād ghṛta-ce|lavān
bhinnāsthi-cyuta-sandheś[1] ca pāko rakṣyaḥ prakīrtitaḥ
śāli-muṅga-yavād adyāj jāṅgalaṃ ca sadā vraṇī
dadhi-kṣīrāmla-gurv-annaṃ maithunaṃ ca vivarjayed
5 iti | vraṇādhyāyas trayastriṃśatimaḥ

A80v5 yad videhādhipenoktaṃ tantraṃ śālākya-saṃjñakam
vistīrṇatvān na sarvoktas tasya leśo vidhīyate
B64r4 . . . ta jalaṃ vāyuḥ piṇḍaṃ rakta-sitāsitaṃ
sva-mārgaguṇam ākāśaṃ nayane *bhūta[2]-ta⟨d⟩-vidhiḥ
A81r1 vātāt pittāt kaphād raktād abhiṣyandaś ca|turvidhaḥ
prāyeṇa jāyate ghoraḥ sarva-netrāmayākaraḥ
śītāśru-śuṣka-dūṣikā-ruk-stambhair vātikaḥ smṛtaḥ
uṣṇāśru-pīta-dūṣikā-dāha-rāgaiś ca paittikaḥ
2 sitopadeha-pi|cchāśru-kaṇḍū-śophaiḥ kaphātmakaḥ
tāmrāśru-raktatā-dāhai raktajo rakta-rājimān
abhiṣyanda-pravṛddhaḥ syād adhimanthaḥ sva-lakṣaṇaiḥ
3 tīvra-mūrdhārdha-netrārti-viṣamāhita-| sevinām
sukhāmbu-piṣṭa-sambhṛtaiḥ śarkarā-lodhra-saindhavaiḥ
pūraṇaṃ vātike tadvat sitā-nāgara-śāvaraiḥ
kuruṇṭa-puṣpa-yaṣṭyāhva-sitā-viśvaiḥ sa-mastubhiḥ
4 śuṇṭhī-|saindhava-yaṣṭyāhva-lodhrair bhṛṣṭair ghṛtena vā
yaṣṭī-candana-mañjiṣṭhā-lodhra-kāñcana-gairikaiḥ
pūraṇaṃ tīvra-śūla-ghnaṃ tathā bilvādināmbhasā
5 eraṇḍena śṛta-kṣīraṃ | yojyam āścyotanaṃ param
śūla-ghnaṃ vā kaṇodīcya-yaṣṭī-saindhava-sādhitam
āyase tāmra-pātre vā saindhavaṃ dadhi-marditam
kāṃsa-ghṛṣṭe niśā-kṛṣṇe tv añjanaṃ vākṣi-śūla-nut
81v1 | badarī-patra-yaṣṭyāhva-tuccha-kālamakaiḥ samaiḥ
antardhūmaṃ kṣataṃ pakṣaṃ añjanaṃ kopa-hṛt param
prapauṇḍarīka-yaṣṭyāhva-niśāmalaka-padmakaiḥ
2 śṛtair madhu-sitā-yuktaḥ sekaḥ pittā|kṣi-roga-nut

[1] A sumbaś, B sandheś. [2] B bhukta ta.

candanāriṣṭa-patrāṇi yaṣṭī-darvyā sa-saindhavaiḥ
piṣṭāmbhasā bhavet sekaḥ paitte kṣaudra-sitānvitam
dvau dvau bhāgau rajanyau sva-bhāgikau dhūma-sarṣapau
3 ka | phābhiṣyanda-jid dṛṣṭaṃ piṣṭāścyotanam ambhasā
nimbākta-puṭa-sampakvaṃ lodhra-bhāga-catuṣṭayam
dhūma-sarṣapayor bhāgau kapha-sekaḥ sukhāmbunā
4 tirīṭa-triphalā | yaṣṭī-śarkarā-bhadra-mustakaiḥ
piṣṭaiḥ śītāmbunā seko raktābhiṣyanda-nāśanam
lodhra-yaṣṭī-niśā-dārvī-tākṣa-śailair ajā-payaḥ
5 dārvyā vā madhunā kvāthaḥ sarvābhi | ṣyanda-pūraṇam
lodhra-dhātryau ghṛtair bhṛṣṭau[1] piṣṭau dadyān manacchilām
pramṛjya[2] guḍikāṃ kṛtvā kupitaṃ locanaṃ bahiḥ
vastra-baddhaṃ śakṛd vāri svinnāraṇya-kulattha-jam
82r1 cūrṇaṃ sa | dyo 'kṣi-kopa-ghnaṃ niśīthe yojitaṃ sakṛt
bhāgaḥ syāc chigru-bījasya lodhrasyāṣṭau śilā-trayam
vicūrṇaṃ vastra-sambaddhaṃ guṇḍanaṃ kupitekṣaṇam
2 rasāñjanābhayā-dārvī-gairikaiḥ sai | ndhavānvitaiḥ
jala-piṣṭair bahir lepaḥ sarva-netrāmayāpahaḥ
A82r2–84r4 om. B.
A84r4 adhimantheṣu sarveṣu lalāṭe vyādhayec chirām
5 yathoktā ca prayoktavyā sā | bhiṣyandocitā kriyā
kṛṣṇa-bhāge sitaṃ binduṃ śukraṃ vidyāt kaphānvayam
raktaś ca śukla-bhāgas tu arjunaṃ śoṇitodbhavam
tāpyaṃ madhuka-sāro vā bījaṃ vākṣasya saindhavaiḥ
84v1 madhunāñjana- | yogāḥ syuś catvāraḥ śukra-śāntaye
A84 v1–2.
sphaṭikoṣaṇa-yaṣṭyāhva-śaṅkha-go-danta-saindhavaiḥ
3 sa-śilā-candanair vartiḥ śu | kra-ghnī śigru-vāriṇā
samudra-phena-dakṣāṇḍa-tvak-sindhūtthaiḥ sa-śaṅkhakaiḥ
śigru-vāri-yutair vartiḥ śukrādi śastraval likhet
4 dakṣāṇḍa-tvak-śilā-śaṅkha-kāca-candana | -saindhavaiḥ
tulyair añjana-yogo 'yaṃ puṣpārmādi[3]-viśodhanaṃ
candanaṃ saindhava-pathyā-palāśa-taru-śoṇitam
krama-vṛddham idaṃ vartiḥ śukrārmādi-vilekhanam
5 mālatī-kali | kā-lākṣā-giri-mṛc-candanaiḥ samaiḥ
kṣata-śukra-harī vartiḥ śoṇitasya-prasādanī

[1] A ghṛtād bhūto, B ghṛtair bhṛṣṭau.
[2] A °jyā, B °jyaṃ.
[3] A °pāmādi, om. B.

A85r4 śaṅkha-kṣaudreṇa saṃyuktaṃ kataka-saindhavena vā
sitāpārṇava-pheno vā yathā gañjanam añjane
B66v1 jātīpatra-rasa-kṣaudra-niśā-dvaya-rasāñjanaiḥ
2 naktāndham a | ....⟨sa⟩kṛt kṛtāḥ
A85v3 śilā-rasāñjana-vyoṣa-go-pittair vartir uttamam
pilla-ghnaṃ chāga-mūtreṇa bhāvitaṃ devadāru vā
ala-dāru-vacāḥ piṣṭvā surasā-patra-vāriṇā
4 chāyā-|śuṣkākṣatāvartiḥ klinna-vartma-nivāraṇī
ala-sauvīrayos tāmraṃ dviguṇa-ślakṣṇa-cūrṇitam
añjanaṃ pilla-roga-ghnaṃ sa-vyoṣaṃ vā rasāñjanam
5 sarve|ṣāṃ timirāṇāṃ ca dṛṣṭer ākulatā bhṛśam
sāmānya-lakṣaṇaṃ jñeyaṃ vaiśeṣikaṃ mataṃ param
calāvilāruṇābhāsaṃ rūpaṃ paśyen nabhasvatām
86r1 nīlaṃ pītaṃ ca pittena śikhi-khadyo|ta-vidyutaḥ
snigdha-śvetāni rūpāṇi timirāṇi vilāsataḥ
atiraktāni raktena sarvaiḥ sarvāṇi cekṣyate
timirāṇāṃ sva-rūpaiś ca kāryaṃ jñeyā tad-anvayā
2 kaphajas teṣu sādhyaḥ syād vyādha|naṃ tasya śasyate
akṣāsthi-madhya-yaṣṭyāhva-dhātrī-marica-tutthakaiḥ
jala-piṣṭaiḥ kṣatāvartis timirāṇi vyapohati
vyoṣāyaś-cūrṇa-sindhūttha-triphalāñjana-saṃskṛtā
3 guḍi|kā jala-piṣṭeyaṃ kokilā timirāpahā
haridrāmalakī-kṛṣṇā-kataka-śveta-sarṣapaiḥ
vyoṣa-vāri-yutair vartiḥ sarva-netrāmayāpaham
4 vyāghrī-yuktāmra-yaṣṭyāhva-pippa|lī-saindhavair yutam
aja-kṣīroṣitais tāmrair vartiḥ sarvākṣi-roga-nut
4vv. A, B.
A86r5 catuṣpada-dvijā-lākṣā-karañjā-bṛhatī-phalaiḥ
plavoṣṭra-matsyakāsthīni viḍaṅga-vyoṣam āmayam
86v1 ja|la-piṣṭair imais tulyair danta-vartir iti śrutā
timirārbuda-kācārma-vraṇa-śukrādi-nāśanī
śilā-saindhava-kāsīsa-śaṅkha-vyoṣa-rasāñjanaiḥ
sa-kṣaudraiḥ kāca-śukrārma[1]-timira-ghnī rasa-kriyā
2 ka|pittha-rasa-saṃsṛṣṭaṃ gandhaka-dviguṇa-rasāt[2]
añjanaṃ timira-dhvaṃsi sauvīraṃ cārdha-pādikam
nāga-śulvāla-vaṅgākhya-gandhakāñjanajair bhavet
3 triṃśad-vidhy eka-pañca-tri-bhāgai|ḥ pakṣaiḥ sadāñjanam

[1] A °krāma°, B °krārma°. [2] def. B.

sauvīram ājya-madhvāktā dhātrī digdhābhayodarau
badarānala-sampakvaṃ paraṃ timira-nāśanam
niśā-dvayābhayā-māṃsī-kuṣṭha-kṛṣṇā-vicūrṇitā
4 sarva-|netrāmayāṃ hanyād etat saugatam añjanam
B67v4 vadane kṛṣṇa-sarpasya saghṛtaṃ dagdham añjanam
māṃsī-patraka-saṃyuktaṃ cūrṇitaṃ timirāpaham
5 vaṭa-patra-yute kḷpta-kṣāliṃ ga|....cet
tad-rasas tarpaṇaṃ cākṣṇor eva syur jaṅgalāṇḍajāḥ
A86v4 triphalāyo-rajo-yaṣṭī-sarpiḥ-kṣaudra-samanvitā
dinānte śīlitā vṛṣyā sarva-netrāgadaṃ jayet
5 triphalā-kvātha-kalkena sa-pa|yaskaṃ ghṛtaṃ śṛtam
timirāṇy acirād dhanyāt pītam etan niśā-mukhe
4vv. A.
87r1 rāsnā-phala-traya-kvāthe daśamūlasya ca śṛtam
kalkena jīvanīyānāṃ ghṛtaṃ timira-nāśanam
2 | netra-rogādhyāyaḥ saptaviṃśatimaḥ

---

karṇayoḥ śūla-bādhirya-nāda-srāvāḥ samīraṇāt
pittoṣma-kapha-saṃśoṣāj jāyate karṇa-gūthakaḥ
3 muruṅgī-kadalī-|śigru-mūlakārdrakajaḥ pṛthak
rasa-⟨sa-⟩saindhavaḥ koṣṇaḥ pūraṇāt karṇaśūla-nut
lavaṇābaddha-pītārka-patraṃ tat-saptakāvṛtam
4 paktvā lavaṇam uddhūya tad-rasaḥ karṇaśūla-|hā
bilvāder deva-kāṣṭhād vā kāṇḍaṃ vā saralaṃ pṛthak
pradīpya caila-tailād [d] antaḥ-srāvaḥ karṇa-śūla-hṛt
kuṣṭha-śuṇṭhī-vacā-dāru-śatāhva-hiṅgu-saindhavaiḥ
def. K.
A88v1 vamanair ghṛta-pānaiś ca tāṃ bhiṣak samupakramet
2 pratiśyāyī pibed dhūmaṃ sarva|-gandha-samutthitam
cāturjātaka-cūrṇaṃ vā ghreyaṃ vā kṛṣṇa-jīrakam
4vv. A.
3 śaṭī-tāmalakī-vyoṣa-cūrṇaḥ sarpir-guḍaṃ śṛtam
4 uro-ghāta-pratiśyāya-pārśva-|hṛt-kukṣi-śūla-nut
4vv. A.
5 vyāghrī-dantī-vacā-śigru-surasa-vyoṣa-saindhavaiḥ
pācitaṃ nāvanaṃ tailaṃ pūti-nāsāgadaṃ haret
add. K, T.
A89v4 dantānāṃ toda-harṣau ca jāyate vātatas tayoḥ

uṣṇa-tailājyā vāta-ghnā niryūhā kavaḍa-grahāt
5 tiktā | bda-tejanī-pāṭhā-niśā-yug-lodhra-kuṣṭhajam
sa-samaṅga-rajonmārgād[1] danta-kaṇḍv-asra-toda-jit
10 *vv*. A.

90*r*3 mukha-pāko'sra-pittotthas tad-asṛṅ-mukti-recane
4 ghṛta-taila-madhu-kṣīra- | mūtraiś ca kavaḍa-grahāt
jātī-patrāmṛtā-drākṣā-yāṣa-dārvī-phala-trikaiḥ
kvāthaḥ kṣaudra-yutaḥ śīto gaṇḍūṣo mukha-pākavat
5 tālu-mūle kaphāsṛgbhyāṃ jāyate | gala-śuṇḍikā
chittvā tāṃ vyoṣa-sindhūttha-vacā-kṣaudraiḥ prasādhayet
6 *vv*. A.

A90*v*2 galaḥ syāt kaṇṭha-sālūkaḥ kolāsthi-pratimā-kaphāt
karmāsyāṅguli-śastreṇa pūrvavat pratisāraṇam
3 pṛthag-doṣaiḥ samastaiś ca śoṇitenāṅkurātmi | kā
svarūpe rohiṇī kaṇṭhe pravṛddhā hanti jīvitam
sarvāṃśāḥ śoṇita-srāvo yathāsvaṃ kavaḍa-grahāt
vātikā lavaṇaṃ yuktaṃ sa-kṣaudraiḥ pratisārayet

[1] A dmārṣā, B dmārṣār.

B.

A 30v3
4 vacā-bilva-kaṇā-viśva-|kuṣṭha-dīpyaka-kūlakam
sa-viḍaṅgaṃ jayet pītam āmam uṣṇāmbunā śṛtam
5 | pakvaḥ sakṛd atīsāro grahaṇī-mārdavād yadā
pravartate tadā kāryaḥ kṣipra-saṅgrāhiko vidhiḥ
samaṅgā-śālmalī-vṛnta-lodhraṃ pāṭhaḥ sa-dhātakī
6 amrā|sthi phalgunī padmā tirīṭī bilva-peśikā
valkalaṃ dīrgha-vṛntasya nāgaraṃ madhu yaṣṭikā
tvag-vṛkṣa-dāḍimaṃ lodhraṃ dhātakī gaṇḍamālikā
31r1 ete 'rdha-sammitā yogāś catvāro madhu-lehi|tāḥ
pakvātīsāra-nāśāya prayojyās taṇḍulāmbunā
pakvātīsāriṇo deyo musta-kvāthaḥ sa-mākṣikaḥ
lodhrāmb⟨r⟩aṣṭādikau vargau yojyāv etau mahāguṇau
2 kāśmarī-padma-patrāntāḥ pa|kvāḥ katvāṅga-valkalāt
sa-padma-kesaro grāhī syād raso mākṣikānvitaḥ
nyagrodhādi-gaṇā pūrṇāḥ puṭaṃ pakvasya tittireḥ
3 dravo madhu-sitā-yuktaḥ pīto hanty udarāmayam |
pañcamūlī vacā-viśva-dhānyakotpala-bilvajā
pittātīsāriṇo deyā peyāmlāmletarātha vā
kaṭphalātiviṣāmbhoda-vatsaka-nāgarānvitaṃ
4 śṛtaṃ pittātisā|ra-ghnaṃ pātavyaṃ madhu-saṃyutam
utpalaṃ dhātakī-puṣpaṃ śuṇṭhī dāḍima-valkalam
samaṅgotpala-padmāni lodhraṃ moca-rasas tilāḥ
5 śatakratu-yavā-mustaṃ bhūnimbaṃ sa-rasāñjanam |
mṛṇāla-candana-lodhram utpala-viśva-bhaiṣajam
pāṭha-durālambhā-viśvam āmra-jamb⟨r⟩āsthi-kaṭphalam
haridrā bilva dāru tvag dhanva-yāṣaḥ sa-vālakam
31v1 dhātaky ativiṣā śuṇṭhī vatsa-tva|k-phala-tākṣajam
kaṭphalaṃ madhukaṃ lodhraṃ dāḍimaṃ tvak-samanvitam
cūtasthi dhātakī-puṣpaṃ samaṅgā ca saroruham
sa-valka-vatsaka-dārvī pāṭha-granthika-nāgaram
2 vargāḥ ślokārdha-vicchedā da|śaite madhu-śālinaḥ
pītās taṇḍula-toyena pittātīsāra-nāśanāḥ
31v5 32r pittātīsāri|ṇaḥ pittam ahitāśana-sevanāt
sandūṣya ś[r]oṇitaṃ kuryā⟨d⟩ raktātīsāram uddhatam

tatra tūrṇa-kriyā kāryā rakta-pitta-nivāraṇī
ājyaṃ payaḥ prayoktavyaṃ pāna-bhojana-vastiṣu
2 paya|syā śārivā lodhraṃ śarkarā madhu yaṣṭikā
śītena payasā pītā sa-kṣaudrā rakta-nāśanāḥ
sallakī badarī jambū piyālām⟨r⟩ārjuna-tvacaḥ
3 pītāḥ kṣīreṇa madhvādyāḥ pṛthak | śoṇita-vāraṇāḥ
indīvaraṃ samaṅgā ca mocāhvāmbuja-kesaram
tilā sāvarakaṃ yaṣṭī samaṅgā śarkarotpalam
utpalaṃ śālmalī śleṣmā yaṣṭī sāvarakaṃ tilāḥ
4 yoga-|trayam ajākṣīra-kṣaudravad rakta-nāśanāḥ
candanasya priyaṅgor vā kalkaṃ sa-kṣaudra-śarkaram
pītvā rakta-śrute⟨r⟩ dāhān mucyate taṇḍulāmbhasā
5 j⟨y⟩eṣṭhāmbu-madhu-yuktena rakta-|hṛd vatsa-phāṇitam
madhukotpala-śankh[y]ānāṃ kalko vā śarkarānvitaḥ
kalka-tilānā⟨.⟩kṛṣṇā-śarkarā-pāñcabhāgikam
ājyena paya⟨s⟩ā pītaṃ sadyo raktaṃ niyacchati
32v1 pītvā sa-|śarkarā-kṣaudraṃ candanaṃ taṇḍulāmbunā
dāha-tṛṣṇā-pramehebhyo rakta-srāvaś ca sādhyate
vyatyāsena śakṛd raktaṃ sādhyamānaṃ virecayet
kṣīreṇa triphalāktena yuktyā sadyo[d]bhavena vā
2 | pūtīka-vyoṣa-bilvāgni-takra-dāḍima-hiṅgubhiḥ
bhojayet sambhūtair yūṣaiḥ śleṣmātīsāra-pīḍitaḥ

50v5 pānam iṣṭaṃ prameheṣu phalatraya-jalasya vā
prameha-piṭakānāṃ prāk kāryaṃ raktāvasecanam
51r1 pāṭa|naṃ ca vipakvānāṃ vraṇavat syāt kriyāvidhir
iti prame⟨hā⟩dhyāyo dvādaśamaḥ

---

pāpātmanāṃ trayo doṣāḥ kurvanty aśubha-bhojināṃ
2 tvaṅ-māṃsāsṛg-lasīkādya-kuṣṭhā|ny aṣṭādaśoddhatāḥ
audumbaraṃ tad-ābhāsaṃ śvitraḥ syāc chaṅkha-sannibhaḥ
kākaṇaṃ pakva-guñjābhaṃ carmākhyaṃ gajākṛtivat
pauṇḍarīkaṃ ca saṃjñābhaṃ mṛga-jihvaṃ ca nirdiśet

II

JĪVAKAPUSTAKA

44r1 I siddham

namau brrahmaṇe . namau saidha-vaidyādharą̄ṇāṃ .

2 bhagavāṃ brraṣmī I tta mai śrrūṇū ttā vakṣyą̄me jīvaką sarvąthā :

3 ye ke caitda I d agadā sine : jaṃbudvīpe vįṣāpaphā .

4 upary ąpari sarvi:ṣā' I ahaṃ vakṣyą̄mi ttat śrruṇū :

5 parapilavasyą catvāre : I catvārau nąladasya ca :

caṃdanasyą ca ⟨ca⟩tvāri : catvārau agarā bhavatte :

44v1 I tvacisyāpi va catvāri : catvārā kūkūmasya ca .

2 tta I thā vyāghrra-nakhasyāpi . dadyā bhāgaṃ catūṣṭīyi :

3 paṃcamautpale kūṣṭasya : I hīravīraṃ ca ąṣṭamaṃ :

4 paṃca sūkṣmelayā dadyā : I bhāgā suttalīna bhiṣaka :

5 aty attą̄na sarvāṇi : I pīṣayi vāraṇa saha :

45r1 ttattra maṃttra-padā sįdhā : I śrrūṇū vakṣyāma jīvaka :

II ttad yathā kiśi kiśi kiśa laṃbi hālī hilī

2 namau I baudhasya sįdhyąttū maṃttra-padą̄ni svāhā :

agattā yi × ttau × vi : imä maṃttram ūdāhari :

3 4 I śūca samāhyina būtvā pūṣya-yaugena I budamāṃ :

5 ttasya karma-gūṇā krraitsnā : I śrrūṇū vakṣyą̄ma jīvakä :

45v1 sarva-rauga-prraśamanī : samā I sāga-gattāttama :

⟨ ⟩ yiṣū rgoṣū bhiṣajya

2 I diva-gaṃdha⟨rva⟩-yikṣiṣū : prrītta-dārūṇā-rākṣasā :

3 I sarva-bhūtta-vakāriṣū : lalāṭim ūpa⟨lepa⟩ye :

4 I śą̄myatti sarva-vittāṇḍā : pūrnanākrraitta-vidhaka :

5 khākhau I dāś viva śą̄myatti : grrahā yau ca sudāraṇā :

46r1 sarvina I suprrayāttārthaṃ : agadā samūdāhyattä :

2 halāha'laiṣū saṃyūhttaṃ I vaṣa pīttaṣū dāraṇā :

3 pītta śīttana ttauyina : I sattyā ca vittä naravaṣaṃ :

4 banaviṭaṣū gāttriṣū : I āyū⟨dha⟩vaṣi dūṣattä

5 vrraṇālaipanä māttreṇa : I vrraṇadīṣā prramūcatta :

44r1 aúrga ttā brrahmāṃ hālai : aúrga ttā saidha-vaidhyādarāṃ raṣa'yā hālai :

2 jasta be'ysä tta tta hve sä ttū ttā mahā jsa : pū javā hvą̄ñū ttā harbaiśa padya :

3 ca bure heca agade : jaṃbvīyä bi pahiṃśā'kye .

4 uskātta u|skātta ⟨ha⟩rbīśāṃ agadāṃ myą̄ña : ayse ttā hvą̄ñū tvā pu :

5 parapilava tcau mā|cāṃgyi : tcahau mācāṃgyi gaṃdha nalądha :

44v1 caṃdaṃ tcau mācāṃga : tcahau | mācāṃgi agara hami :

tvaca pā tcahau mācāṃga : tcahau mācāṃgyi kųrkūṃ :

2 ttū padī vyāghrra-naka ṣai : haurą̄ña tcau mācāṃga :

3 paṃjsa mā|cāṃga nīlättpala u kauṣṭa : hīravī haṣṭa mācāṃga :

4 paṃjsa [mācāṃ] mācāṃ|ga sukṣmila hūrą̄ña . . nasäna hūvamāva tta arvi vījani :

5 | tta buri arvi harbiśa : uca jsa haṃtsa :

45r1 ca ra jsāṃ pīrmāttaṃ sįdavaṃda : | pū cve va hvāñūṃ tta vā tcaṃna tta arvi ṣā'ña u ṣā' agada :

2–3 ṣa' vīja ca āṃ tvā agada śū'hye : tta ą̄na yāṃda | ṣa' maṃdrra hvañai :

surai vī hūysīnautta hamāña vasvi samāhye : śinvā va nāsāñä

4 pväśa nakṣattra vīra bvāmaya vījina : ṣa' kīrä :

5 ttyi agadä hīyi kīra bviṃjsi aha|rīnaka . pū aysä ttā hvāñūṃ jīvā :

45v1 harbīśāṃ āchāṃ naṣiṃ'māka : | haṃbica jsa saṃ ṣā' agada pīrmāttama hvava

2 pū vįstharnai ttā hvāñāṃ : kāmyāṃ āchāṃ | vī ṣa' arva ɨ :

jasta gaṃdharvi yakṣa : prrīyi bīysą̄nā rakṣaysä :

3–4 harbīśāṃ būvajāṃ āchāṃ vīra . ṣā' agada haṃdrrauja pīsälyā|ña :

naṣa'māraṃ jsa harbįśa vittāla . būva u kūra hīra :

5 cāyūṃ jsa pātca biśa naṣa'māri : ką̄ma ra jsāna tta ggraha' cū bīhī bīysānā :

46r1 harbīśāṃ pahiją̄mi udaśāyä : ṣā' agada hvava ṣṭi :

2 cu halāhala bäna skva ɨde : cū vā ėha' ttraikṣa bi ā ɨ :

3 khāśā'ña | pvāyi ucana : ttanī thyau vīna be hamāre .

4 ca vā aṃga tta na|rva ha'tcasta u hvasta : prraharaṇḍyau jsa bi-vū-ḍau :

5 vīraṇāṃ bai|da sakhalyą̄ña masvą̄ña jsa : vīraṃ hīye gaṃjsa jsa gūśta :

46v1 jattavā ye ca drraiṣṭāsya : | yaurā[1] parame dārūṇā :
2 daheyū vaṣṭa māttrą̄ṇi : | ttiṣām apavaṣāvryā :
3 yasyä hasta gattā naittyaṃ : | pāpa ttasya na jāyatte :
4 sarva ca sādayi cārthaṃ : | pūna yäś ta na jāyätte :
5 yiva gaura vabai' däṣvai : vaṣa | ṣvastā suśą̄ṇättā :
47r1 tteṣāṃ kāka-padaṃ mū⟨r⟩dhaṃ : krraittvā dadyā⟨d a⟩|gadauttā :
mūkhanas tū ttrayau dadyā baidavau : nasta⟨ś ta⟩ ttraye :
2 | agadenavalīpenä : ttatta saṃjīvattą suptaṃ :
3 ttrabū kīdä ttą daṣṭä | lūttą mūṣaką veśte⟨kai⟩
4 nasya pą̄na⟨ṃ⟩ | janālaipā vadhąttā narvaṣe bhavä :
5 strīṇāṃ va mūcha[2] garbhāṇāṃ . | yauva-lepaṃ prradāpaye .
6 vasucakayāṃ ghaurāyāṃ : | dadyā⟨d u⟩ṣṇana vāraṇā :
rakṣakarṣū ca bālą̄nāṃ ⟨ ⟩
47v1 suprrają̄nāṃ prrajāyätte : | yāvąd artha varṣa pava :
2 narvaṣau kūrvattą kṣaprrä : | vrraikṣa' aidrrārthäna r yathā
3 bhagava|ttau bhāṣitta svastakaṃ nąma mahāgada samāptta

[1] gh°. [2] mūḍha.

46*v*1 ką̄ına ra jsą̄na āǀphīḍa prrą̄ṇā hamāṃde : bīysāṇā bīhī ttraikṣa :

2 cu hvą̄ṇḍa padaǀjsīda dūṣṭa masu : ttyāṃ hīyai pā be' pahaiśāę̄[1] :

3 ca ttye baida ṣa' agada ǀ hamāve : ttye herī vīśū'na hīra na hamāre :

4 harbīśai hāva saijīǀdä : pātca pātcī upadrrava na ysyāre :

5 cū bīysą̄nai be'na dūṣṭä : ǀ bi'na umya āphīḍe hū̄ña jsä :

47*r*1 ttyāṃ jsa vasalaka tcerā ttera baidä : ǀ tcerā ttera vīra haurą̄ñai ṣa'
    agada :

2 ėhi' drrai kane ṣa' agada haurą̄ña . haǀysgvā drrai kane :
    ttye agada sakhalyāñą̄me jsa : ṣa' bina mauḍa hve paskyāṣṭa būjvaiye :

3 gū̄ṇā ysyāsajā js[v]a dūrṣṭą̄ : cu vīśū̄'nyāṃ dūṣṭa u mūlāṃ drrvą̄ṇḍyau
    jsa :

4 haysgva khaśa' arja saṃkhalyūna dyenaṃ jsa vīnau be hame :

5 ką̄ma tta strīye cū haṃǀjsyāre maichāṃ ā vā maichīde . ttyāṃ
    pūrą̄ña saṃkhalyą̄ña u haurą̄ña :

6 ca vā pejsa vasuja ī : ǀ grrą̄mye uca jsa hū̄rą̄ña :

47*v*1 āysdärja tcairai ṣīkalakāṃ : śara śarą ǀ jsa pūra ysyą̄re cvai baida
    bīḍä :
    caṃdai kṣamī hamayi be' khāśe'

2 naṣa'be'vai padīme thyau ǀ haṣṭavī dīra na īdä : khu śakrrana paśā
    aśū'na bahya . bījeve tta ṣā' agada bījevākä :

3   jasta be'ysäna hvava svastaka ną̄ma agada dāśyā ::

---

[1] °śaka.

47v4 | siddhama
pūrvaṃ prraṇa⟨mya⟩ mūnaye : paramārthą-vahtrre
būdhāyai phūla-śatta-pattra-dala-kṣaṇāyai
5 dharmāyai cą̄myatta-ra | sāya-narāsrravāyä :
saṃghāyai cāryamara-pāragasāgya× ye :
ghrradvą-pākaṃ prravakṣyą̄me . sarpi parimaṃ baiṣija :
48r1 | sarva-raugą-haraṃ caivą sarviṣāṃ prrą̄ṇanā häta .
śattārdha ttūrūgadhā ca daśamūle pala pala :
2 balā punarṇavā rāsnā : de | vadārū mahauṣadha :
bidhārū ⟨pa⟩ttrasūdhāś ca ātmagūptą balāttakaṃ :
3 mājāttakā karkaṭa-śrraigī jaṭā raidhī śattā | varī :
vaṇḍaṃgā ttraphalā dve ca : bilvai dāḍama-bījaka :
jīvattīyą̄ṣadhaiś caiva prrathake rakṣa samaṃ bhave :
4 | kṣīra-mā⟨ṃ⟩sa-rasa-dvāthä[1] : ārūkaṃ ghrratta säpacettä
cättūrājätta palai krraiṣṇā : sattā madhū pale daśa :
5 jaye | nä sarveṣū raugeṣū : kāsa-śvāsä-kṣatta-kṣaye :
vaisvaryaṃ pārśa-śūle ca : gūlma-vātta-kaphāttmakä :
48v1 kaṭī-pyūiṣṭa-rūjā saidhaṃ prramehā' | vasta-ką̄ṇḍalai :
jvareṣū rāja-yekṣme ca vaiṣma-jvaraṃ vanāśanaṃ :
rasāyam idaṃ vṛittasya brrīhaṇa-bala-vardanaṃ
2 strī-vajaṃ alpa-śūkrrasya | pala-mättraṃ ca dāpaye :
vyaidhą̄nāṃ matha-bālą̄nāṃ kāla-mättraṃ ca dāpayettą
valī-palątta-nāśārthaṃ : ttatta para palatta-nāśą̄naṃ :
3 aśva | gaṃdādya nauma ghrrana samāptta .

49v5 kuṣṭelā vakrra ttālīsa daṃttī dārv elavālakā .
50r1 caṃdanautpala majäṣṭā vaśālā brrahattī-dvayä

[1] kv°.

48v3 aśvagaṃdha paṃjsāse sera : ttye jsa kaṣā' pāchai kṣa ṣaṃga utca
tcerā śau ṣaṃga thaṃjāña :
4 ⟨da⟩śa-mū | la śau śau sera [×]
bela-mūla agnamatha : syānāka : kaśmīrya mūla . pāṭala . sālaparṇa
brrahatta . kaṇḍārya . drrāṃgūlyai
5 ṣi' | ysīra kūṭąña tcahau ṣaṃga uca jsa jṣāñąña khu ra va śau ṣaṃga
harśta .
49r1 sächa bā aiśta bā . laṃgara bā . devadāra . bīdāra kṣīra : | tvaca :
suṣmela : gadhapattra . ättmagūtma . balättaka : mājättakye karkarṭa-
2 śrraiga . ttąmalaka : raidha . śarāve . vaṇḍaṃga . ttraphala . halī | rā
dva : vīhīlā . aumalai . śvąña gūra . kaśmīrya . pārūṣā . bela .
drrąma ttīma . jīvaka . rįṣabhakä . meda . mahāmeda . kākauṭa :
3 | mūdgaparṇa māṣaparṇa . jīvatta : mahābāṃja :
ṣa' baiśa hąmaṃga śtāka u māṃgī . ṣvīdä daṃda caṃda rūṃ .
4 gūśta hīvī | raysä . hvakhāṃdalaja ąstai hahvąña . kaṣāvaṃ jsa pāchai .
drrai ṣaṃga utca tcairai khu ra va haṣṭä śaiga harśca tta kaṣe' u arva
5 baiśa | hąña hąña tcerā . u śau ṣaṃga gvīha' rūṃ pāchai : khu paha'
hame . una āna hā
49v1 tvaca : suṣamela tcerai nāgapauṣpa . gaṃdhapattra | papala
śau śau sera nauka ārąña . hāña tcerai śakara paṃjsa sera . mākṣī
2 paṃjsa sera . ṣa' rūṃ harbaiśāṃ āchāṃ jsa paurda : | phāha' uysna
āphāra . paijvā gvahaiyi jsa naṣṭąsai . cū garśa pasauṣḍe
3 pesvā vīne . gąma baina . u śalīṣąmajsye ṣų | ña rāha' . u brraha
rāha' : hamarvā vīne prramīhä' phaiysgąña padąsāma . ttavai kṣayä :
vaiṣma jvara tta būra āchā jaida
4 | ṣa' raysāyaṃ dahauśte padīmāka u tvāñākä hauva hūṣąñākä .
strīyau jsa petcautta ttąraṃdara baka-śaukrra ttye śau sera
5 pa | mākye jsa haurąña : ysādāṃ u vaittakāṃ bāḍana ⟨ ⟩
aśvagaṃdhāya dāśe
50r5 kūṣṭi sūṣmela : ttagara : ttālīs-pattra : dattä | [datta] : devadārä :
èla-vālūkä : caṃdaṃ : nīląttapala : rrūṃnai vaiśāla : brrahatta
50v1 kąṇḍārya : halaidrra . ysālva caṃdana śārava . sumana śā | ravä :
sālaparṇä : prraśnaparṇä : haraṇvä . pauṣṭara : vīysa khīysāra :
2 vaṇḍaṃga : halīrā : vīhīlā : ąmalai prrayaṃgä : jāttīpū | ṣpi . drąma
ttīma .

haraidrre śarāva paṇyą̄ kauttī padama-kesaraṃ
2 vaḍagau ttraphalā śą̄ : mā jāttī- | pūṣpa sa-dāḍamä :
akṣā⟨ṃ⟩śe sarpaṣi prrastha paṃcattāyä cattūragūṇaṃ
ėtta kalyą̄ṇąkaṃ nąma bala-varṇä-prrajākara :
3 jva | rāpasmāra mihārśa śautha-mādä-vaṣāpaha :
pettāsṛiga-vātta-ttūtta gūlma : śvāsä-haikā grrai kyächanū :
4 jīvanīyaunva | ttra dva kṣīräṇa daśamūlava :
ąttadevākhalārttaghna mahā-kalyą̄ṇäkaṃ smrratta :

51 r^{4}_{5} sauvatcalaṃ : saidhavaṃ cä : bīṇḍa | k⟨ṣ⟩āraṃ sa-⟨ci⟩ttrakä .
paipalī śrṛaigaberaṃ cä . haigū kūṣṭābrravettasa :
ėraṇḍä pūṣkarā rāsnā śattą̄hvā dhą̄nyaka vacā
51*v*1 devadāra vīṇḍaṃgvā | cä sa-rūṣaṃ ttravattābhayā .
ėttą̄ne kalka paiṣṭą̄ne . bhaga akṣa sama prrīthagä :
kaṭūkä paṃcamūląsya . kūryā . palaṃ pala baiṣkä :
2 | kūrkūṭa-rasä vāra ca : kṣīra ttauyi cattūrguṇäṃ :
mahā-sauvatcalākhyāttaṃ sarpa vātta-jvarāpahä :
3 vaṣta-kauṇḍala graidāsī kaṭī prai | ṣṭi rūjāpahā :
pādauthä sädhają̄nāthaṃ urū-ska⟨ṃ⟩bha-vātta-gūlma-jetta :
ėkā⟨ṃ⟩gą-rauga-sadhāgnas⟨t⟩athā pakṣahīttąsya ca
4 bādharyaṃ | karṇa-śūlaṃ ca pārś⟨v⟩a-śūlam araucakä :
cattūrą-sthą̄na-gattą vāyū aśittą-vātta-raugakā .

ṣā' pąna arva dvī dvī mācāṃgye hālā : gvīha' rūṃ dva śaiga hālai.
3 ṣai' arva samāṃ kūṭāña : na nauka u na ysīra śau ṣaṃga | uca jsa
pāchai ṣa' rūṃ kalyāṇai nąma : hauva padīme u cha śairka. brrā-
4 vauśta jaida : hųna padīme : ttavai. apasmāra prramīha' : a|rja :
kṣaya utmādä be pīraurākä : cū baina hųña āphīḍe pąṇḍa-rauga :
5 gąma uysäna āphāra : haika : mūttra-kaicha : tta būra ā|chā baiśa
jaida :

khu hā ttī jīvanīya arve yänīdè : jīvaka raṣabhaka meda mahāmedā :
51*r*1 kākau⟨ṭä⟩ : kṣīra kākauṭa : mūdama-parṇa[1] : māṣapa|rṇa : jīvatta
mahābāṃja :

ṣā' pąna arva dvī dvī mācāṃgye : tta pā kekaña tcerā : hąmaṃga
rūṃ ṣvīda tcerai gvīha' : rūṃ u daśa-mūla jsa kaṣā' :
2 | bela-mūla : agnamatha : syąnāka pāṭala : kaśmīrya mūla :
sālaparṇa prraśtaparṇä[2] brrahatta kąṇḍāryi. drrāṃgūlyai :
3 tta hālai hālai sera : | kṣasä śaiga uca jsa jṣąñąña khu ra va tcahau
vasīyä harśta :

ṣa' beva va pīrmāttamye ra haṣṭā baina āchā jaida mahākal-
4 yąṇai | nąma bausta ṣṭe. ttara jaida u sparśa' jsa hamya āchā jaidā :
maṇḍalaña ąna pāchai kalyāṇī rūṃ

51*v*5 52*r*1 spajū : sadalū : bīdalū tcaittrai[3] : | papala ttāṃgara aṃgauṣḍi :
aṃbala vettarasä : īraṃde : hūraṣṭä laṃgara bā : śattapūṣpa hī-
2 ysamāṃ ārä : devadāra vaṇḍaṃgä mīraijsya. ttraula. ha|līrai

ṣa' hamīḍaka ārda ṣṭāna drrai mācāṃga. ysāysīnai hā paṃca-
mūlana kaṣā' śtākä :

3 ha'cana bāva : kāṃdarä gīsai hya bāva : drrąma bāva : | sauthaja[4]
gaysä hīyä bāva : khaṇauśa' gaysa hīyä bāvä

tta śau śau sera śtāka : ysīra kūṭąña drrai ṣaṃga uca jsa jṣąñąña
4 khu ra va | haṣṭa śaiga harśa[5] : hamayä mauḍa krraiga jsa ṣa' kaṣā'
pāchai ṣau ṣaṃga u hālai utca tcerā khu ra va paṃjsa śaiga harśta tta
5 kaṣe' tcahau śūṃ'ba u | ṣvīda drrai śaiga gvīha' : u hatca pāchai :
mahāsauvatcalāda nąma rūṃ :

baina ttavai pīrcḍa : vasta kūṇḍāla cu phaiysgąña mąṇḍa grrai-
52*v*1 dhasa brrąhą|ña ṣųñvā vīne jaida pāṃ dastāṃ vī : bīśvā hamarvā
hasvaca jaida urū-skabhä : baina gąma jaidä harbīśvā hamarvā va
2 ā śe aṃga vī pakṣā'|ha'ka : kārąña : gvąña vīne : pesvā vīne : arūśa' :
tcahaurvā sthąnvā tsūmaṃca bāvä : haṣṭā baina āchā : udāvartte

[1] mudga-. [2] prraśna-. [3] cai°.
[4] sauthara. [5] harśta.

5 uryāvatte [suttraṃ] udäreṣi : mūttra-kṛaicha prramū|catte
jayetta prramīhaṃ sarve[rve]ṣū śūdra-vastala-śaudhanä :
mahā-sauvarcalāda nąma ghrrata-rājaṃ samāptta .

$52v^{3}_{4}$ balā attabalāś taivą : tta|thā nāga-balāna ca :
parṇā cattūṣṭi dva meda . brrahattī kaṃṭākāraka :
kākąṭī kṣīra-kākauṭī raida rāsnā parūṣakā :
5 śanāvarī | paphasyā ca : jīvakā räṣabhakā caiva
bīdārī madhūka cākṣā kaśmīryąṇä ttrakaṃṭhakaṃ :
jīvata ātmagūptaṃ ca : tvag elāpattra kyesara
53*r*1 | kārṣakā dvai × ṇä kṣīra : ghrrattaṃ prrasthaṃ jvalą-dvaye :
sāda[ma]yät padūkā sąmya : nda saidąm avattāraya
2 śūca bāḍana dhāttavya śarkarā gūṇḍä dā|paya :
śarkarāgūrū dhūpayetta rū ⟨××××⟩ sthāpaye :
bala-garbhąm ittą khyąttaṃ sarpa⟨tta⟩d ätapūjattä :
3 ttarpaṇīyau madą śrṛaiṣṭä : brrīhąṇą-ba|la-vardanaṃ .
śrrṛaiṣṭaṃ rasāyąnaṃ caivą : valī-⟨pali⟩ttą-nāśąnaṃ :
⟨pa⟩kṣīhąttąnāṃ balānāṃ : vṛdhąnauś tāgną-vardhanaṃ
sthāpana : naṣṭinaidrrąnāṃ : vādhyąnāṃ cāpagarbada :
4 | garba-srrāva-hąnąś naivą : rahna-pettaṃ[1] asyaiga-dhara :
hṛaid-raugä ca hārau-rauga : karṇa-jehvāmąyaṃ kṣa'ye :
5 jvarija-rāja-yekṣmā ca : kṣana-kṣīṇe va|pārava :
cūdi kāsä ca gūlyārśä : halīma[mą]ka vanāśatta :
[m]aty-apasmāra-mūcchayā : vāttalaṃ sa-hṛdya ca :
53*v*1 vātta rahna[1] ca rāgeṣū atta|kheda madātyaye :
upadravaś ta garbaṇā : smṛātta-rädhā-kara para
bala-garbhi nąma ghrratta :

$54v^{1}_{2}$ harīttakī ttra|kaṭūka ca vacā kaṭūka-rąhaṇī .
sauvatcalaṃ yava-kṣāra viṇḍaga caittrakaṃ ttathā :
akṣa-prramąṇä r attas nai ghrrątta-prrastha vapaucayeta :
3 ttaratta sai|dha srrāvaye : tte vāttū pāyayīttą yathā

[1] rahta.

3 dūvara . mūttra-krraicha jsa | gūśta paurda : harbaiśa prramīha' śaukrra : phaiysgą̄ña āchā jaidä :

mahāsauvaracalāda nąma cąṇa

$53v^{1}_{2}$ śīya sacha bhāva u haija sacha bhāva : haryā|sa sacha bāvä : sā- laparṇa prraśaparṇa : mudgaparṇä : māṣaparṇä : medä : mahāmedä . brrahattä kąṇḍārya kākauṭa : kṣīra kākauṭa . raidha . laṃgara bā |

3 pārūṣṣā : śarāve : ṣvīdā bāve jīvakä raṣabhakä bīdāra mahābāṃja : kaśmīrye drrāṃgūlyai jīvatta : ātmagūpttä tvacä suṣamela gadhapa-

4 | tträ : nāga-kyesärä

ṣi' pąna arva dvī dvī mācāṃga hālā śtāka : gvīha' rūṃ dva śaiga hālai : ṣvīdā śau ṣagä : utca dva śūṃ'ba dva ṣaṃga : pāchai ṣa' rūṃ

5 | nvā daina : khu paha' hame ttī ysūnąña surąña padąnaña pyanąña [pyąnąña] : śakara paṃjsa sera : gaula paṃjsa sera : naukä ārąña rų̄ña

54r1 haṃ|brrīhą'ña : śakara kraiṣṇāgarä hālā hālā mācāṃga nąka ārąña ṣi' haḍa bagala padvąña kūṣṭa ttū rūṃ pyąnīda : khu padve hame ttī

2 hā rūṃ | pyąnąña :

balāgarba nąma :

maista hauvaṃ ṣa' rūṃ parvālāṃ jsa pajsamaḍä : paphąñāka :

3 pīrmāttaṃ tvąñāka hauva hūṣąñāka : pīrmāttaṃ ra|ysāyaṃ śīyāṃ ū tcanāṃ janāka : śajsāṃ paijvāṃ gvahaiye valakāṃ ysąḍāṃ aṃgyāṃ

4 jsa vārūḍāṃ haurąña ttyāṃ ca hūna panaṣṭāṃdä na ṣī|na-ṣīkāṃ na maista-ujāṃ maijṣyāṃ cvaṃ avastya vaṣprrīśta ttyāṃ haṃbūsaṃ :

rahna-petta jsāṃ asṛigadarä . ysīra rīysai kamala rāha' gvąña

5 vīna jai|da :

ttavai rāja-yäkṣa[1] ca maṃgāra naṣṭausai kṣayäna gausąma : bauma phāha' gūma arja halīmaka apasmāra : vaisai vāttaṣṭīla ysaira vīra

54v1 | ttūśātta : cū baina hų̄ña āphīḍe : ṣa' cū vāśarūṃ pe'jsa : mady- āttyaya byāvajä bvąmä padīmāka pīrmāttaṃ

balāgarba nąma :

4 halīrai : papäla : ttāṃgarä : mīraijsya : āra : kalyarūha'ne : spajū : yava-kṣārä : vaṇḍaṃga caittrai

5 ṣā' pąna | arva drrai drrai mācāṃgye . gvīha' rūṃ dva śaiga hālai ṣa' arva samāṃ kūṭąña hatca rūṃna hąña tcerai . u haṣṭi śaiga hā

55r1 ttīra ñe tcerai ṣä' rūṃ pāchai bā|va ṇaimeśa' vīśte . khāśāña nva hauvä : baina gąma jaida : ṣpaijai vasuje arjä jaidą phāhi' : uysāna

2 āphāra pīrąnā jaida u ysaira vīra bīsā ā|chā : daśāṃga nąma bausta

[1] yäkṣma.

balavāttū gūlma plīhārttau kāsä śvāsä krramīm ape :
4 daśāṃgaṃ nāma itt ṛhnaṃ hrrid-rraugaṃ vajrra|m eva ca :
daśāṃga nąma ghrratta :
$55r^2_3$ ttrapūsąnāṃ×śūṣkāṇi pa|lāny aṣṭau ca saṃharä :
ubhā cā paṃcamūlā [paṃcamūlą] cā prrathaką dva-palam āharä
4 ttripūsä rjarī kṛaitvā : jalai drrauṇe vapā|cayet :
sāsi-dhūma tti vigñeyą : cattūr-bāgā vīśeṣatta :
ttattra kalka kṛtta sādhyaṃ : sami-bhāgąnä sarväśa :
5 ttrapūsairvāra-bī|jāne : śattą-pūṣpābalavenasa
mūdgaparṇī mauṣparṇīś ta . haigū haigū śavāṭakī
dvi harädra vaḍaugā ca . śaṇą-mūla śanāvarī :
55v1 kū|lathaṃ ttraphala vyāghrrī : vaiśālaraṇḍam iva ca
vṛśä khadira-pūṣpāṇe : [stā] darbha-mūla ttrakaṭakä :
2 paipalī caittrakaṃ dattī . rai|da pāṣąṇa-bhedakaṃ :
śītta-vāra-bījąne ėty äva samūdāhare :
prrathaka akṣa' samaṃ bhāga gavā mūttreṇa bāvayetta :
3 ghrrattasya | āṇḍakaṃ vaidyaṃ : paṃcamyi dvāgtta-nāśaṇe :
ttata se[vyā]dhaṃ payi [ye kālī :] ėmācādhī na⟨ya⟩cchatte :
4 prramīhā vakṣaṇa-hana śarka|rā vasta-kāṇḍalā :
aśma-vṛṣaṇā-vardha⟨na⟩ṃ śara-vastū : pūjāpahaṃ
arśāse : pūṇḍa-raugaṃ cą mūttra kyaichaṃ : vadārūṇa
5 bhagaṃdarāyāṃ | dāttavya gūda-vyādha-rūjāpaha
tta : gūlma pa×py aṣṭąnāṃ nārīnāṃ ca sukhāvahaṃ :
56r1 kaṭī-pāśvä-rujā mūḍhaṃ gūlma-kąmalan āharä|t
ttrapūsādya nāma ghrratta :
56v5 paipalī dāṇḍama drākṣā palāṇḍä sa-mahauṣadha .
gūṇḍena sama-bāgauna ghrratta-prrastha vapācayet :
57r1 kṣīra-mā⟨ṃ⟩sä-rasąś taivą : ghrrąttaṃ | amrrattąm ūttamaṃ :
śvāsä-kāsä-prraśamana kṣatta-kṣīṇa-vanāśanä :
vaiṣma-jvaraṃ maṃjyanä.ttya madya sevya yikṛit jvare .
2 rahna-naiṣṭīvana-śauṣa : gūṇḍa-|ttūlyai sa-śarkara .
śīttauṭakaṃ pavä nanya : sahata prrīyikṛītti jvara :
gūḍa-sthānena : papalya sahasrrākṣa prrayūjayet :
3 prramihaṃ mūttra kṛai|cheṣā . vastä-kuṇḍalane hṛātta
gūḍa : dhāstrī madhū-meśra sahasrrākṣa prrayūjaye :

ṣṭe : vīśai'ra raṃna māñaṃda gara bauṣḍi tta tta ṣa' rūṃ tta āchā jaida :

daśāṃga nąma rūṃ ṣṭe :

56r1 hūṣka ttrūysi haṣṭa sera u haudva : paṃca-mūla : bela-mūla :
2 agnamathä syąnākä : kaśmīrya mūla : pāṭala : sālaparṇä . | prra-
śaparṇä bṛhattä : kąṇḍārya : drāṃgūlya

ṣa' dva dva sera śtāka : ttrūysna cha drasta padīmąñä : khu ysa-
3 rūna hamāṃde ysīra kūṭāña : tcau ṣaṃ⟨ga⟩ uca jsa | jṣąñąña khu
ra va śau ṣaṃga harśtä : tta būra hā kekaja arve tcerā sama-bhāga :
4 ttrūysāṃ byāra śattapūṣpi : aṃbala-vettarasä . mūdga | parṇä
māṣaparṇä : aṃgūṣḍi . śalaiṣmāttakye halaidrra ysālva vaṇḍaṃga :
śaṇa mūla : śarāve : kūlastä : halīrai vīhīlai ąmalai [kąṇḍā] . kąṇḍā-
5 | rya . vaiśāla : īraṃde : vāśakä khara dhāttakī-pūṣpi : laṃgara bā .
drūba hīyä bāva : drāṃgūlyę papala : caittrai : dattä raida : pāṣąṇa-
56v1 | bedaka : śī caṃdaṃ : vatsaka-bījä

ṣā' pąna arva paṃjsa mācāṃgye śtākä : ṣi' arva ārąña : na nauka na
2 ysīra gvīha' bīysma jsa dasau jųna ganīhąña u hvai | ñāña : arve u
keka ṣā' hąña tcerai : śau ṣaṃga gvīha' rūṃna hatsa pāchai nvā daina :
kālna khāśą'ña tta būra āchā jaida : prramīha' : hūṣvā vīne : śarkarya
3 | mūttra-kṛaicha . vasta kųṇḍala : aśmarya mūttra-kṛaichi ṣe' cū
hīyāra padausīdä : kameña phaiysgąña vīne : raidä : arja pūṇḍa-
4 | rauga : bhągaṃdala vīra haurąña : kṛaiga-rūvya ā:jṣyāṃ hūṃjīnai
gūma : pūrąña vīne ṣųñvā pesvā vīne gųma : bāva kąmala jaidä :
57r4 papala : drrąma ttīma . hūṣki gūra . ttūgare : śau śau sera . rīysvä
5 gūrva śīya | pau baista daṃdā . ṣa' arva samāṃ kūṭąña . pasīña
hvaśā . drrai ṣaṃga uca jsa [×] pāchai khu ra va haṣṭa śaiga harśta :
57v1 ṣvīda tcą śaiga gvīha' | rūṃ dva śaiga hāle baiśa hąña tcerai pāchai
khu paha' hame : ysūṇąña aysdaimąñä khu drrāṃ hami khu aspā
2 ttī hā tcahau sera gūla haṃbrrīhą | ña :

ṣa' rūṃ nva ttaraṃdarū dai varāśą'ña : u uysnä āphārä phāha'
jaidä : paijvā gvahaiye jaida [vai] vaiṣma jvara jaidä : cū avarāṃjsī
3 khaśa' u | mau sīve u jarī āchanai hame : u naṣṭausai hūjina vai
khaurga hamāre u pahvettā u ttara ttye hā gaulna hamaṃga śakara
4 tcerai jattai : cū sā | ḍa utca khāśī' yāṃda u ttīvai tta tta kasai hame
ṣpaijai prracaina ttī hā gaula thāña papala haṃbrrīhąña ṣpaijaivī
5 jatte : ca ttī prramīha' mū | ttra-kṛaicha vasta kųṇḍala : gaula ąmalai
mākṣī haṃbrrīhąña :

ṣa' sahasrrākṣa tta tta varāśą'ñä cū gauda ī ttū tvąñe java-hauva

4 krraśa-dūrbala-nāśaś ti . veṣma-jvara-vanāśa | naṃ :
sarpä : imaṃ srrahasrrākṣa brrīhąṇa-bala-vardanaṃ :
58r1 jīvattī madhūkaṃ vyāṣa śāravī : ⟨u⟩śīra caṃdanaṃ
2 padmaka-ttraphalā dārvī sthirā sāśūmattīs tha | ttā :
brrahattī-dhāvanīś tiva śvaidaṣṭrrā sa-pūnarṇavā :
dva midä dva ca kākauṭī jīvaką-raṣabhakāṃs thathā :
3 ātmagūpta-phalā rāsnā na⟨la⟩daṃ pa | dma-kesarä :
ttālīsa-pattrą maṃjaiṣṭhā : drrąkṣā nīlopala-balā .
ėttąne sama-bhāgauna kāraṣikąna samāharit :
4 kalka sucū | rṇatta paṣṭvā : ghrratta prrasthaṃ vapācayetą :
cattūragūṇäna yisyā⟨ṃ⟩śa nä mṛttranāttinā pącit
5 nāśaye : ttamira-kāca-paṭalaṃ : | arbūdąnāṃ ca
jätty-aṃdhauna maṇava paśṛtte . ttena sarpaṣā
ardha-bhäda adhīmaṃtha karṇa-śūlaṃ . ca nāśaye :
58v1 ye urdha-jattrūṇā | raugā prrattąśaye ⟨gala⟩-grraham
itty āstaṃbha-śąraṃ-śūlaṃ pala-mātträ⟨ṇa⟩ śąmitte :
dva-palaina mahābhāga laghū vyādhavya ⟨va ?⟩haṇittä
2 bālanāṃ atha vṛaidhą | nām itte syād ämrrattaupamaṃ :
mahāvedīhą ghrrattä :
59r5 daśamūla ha⟨ri⟩dri dvī vacā kaṭūka-rauha'ṇī :
ttraphalā : kūṭaja pāṭā ⟨maṃ⟩jaiṣṭā caittrakaṃ balā .
59v1 dūrālabhām atta | balā āragvadha-phala stharā :
ėṣā dva-palakā bhāgā padvāṃ pādāṃ vaśeṣattä
ilā hareṇḍakaṃ kūṣṭaṃ ttālīsaṃ caṃdana ttravet
2 śā | ravau jīva : || kaucąva daṃttī dārv-elavālūkā :
naçūlāna r vrraśāṃ bhārgä vaśāla paipalī nattaṃ
3 mā⟨ṃ⟩sī ttągä⟨ra⟩-drrayi . vā yivānī-phala [nī] | nīyena
āpāmārgā ca rahnākhyā ėttesya karṣa-saṃyūhttā :
ācā kaṣāyi-:kalkābhyā sarpä prrasthä vapācayetä
4 ghrratta tūlya da | dha kṣīraṃ gavā mūttra śakṛäd ra[ra]sa
ėna māhā pa⟨ṃ⟩ca-gavya pānīyā sarpaṣā para
viṣma-jvareṣū sarviṣū [di] dvattīyika cattūrthaka
5 | jvara cāttūrthaka śauṣa vaśeṇa⟨tta⟩ prraśasyattä
śauthārśāṃ kąmalā prramīha' krramī-māttratta śauṇatta

58r1 ttyāṃ hauva pa|dīme : vaiṣma-jvara jaida sahasrrākṣa nąma rūṃ
dāśe ::
58v2 jīvaka mahābūjä papala . ttūṃgarą : mīraijsya : caṃdana śārava :
3 sumąna śārava : uśai'ra | caṃdä pauṣṭarä halīrai vīhīle ąmalai :
ysālva : sālaparṇa : brrahattä kąṇḍārya . drāṃgūlyai : aiśta bāva :
4 mida [mahā] | mahāmeda : kākauṭa : kṣīra kākauṭa : jīvaka raṣabhaka .
⟨ā⟩dmagūpti : bela . lagara bāva . svarṇagūttaryāṃ būśąnai :
5 padma | kyesärä : ttālīs-pattra : rūṃnai : gūrä : nīlätpala[1] : sacha
bāva .
ṣi' pąna arva drrai drrai mācāṃga viśtąña u samāṃ kūṭąña . gvī.-
59r1 | ha' rūṃ dva śaiga hāle . ṣvīda śau ṣaṃgä . hatsa baiśa hąña tcairai :
nvā daina pāchai tta būri āchā jaidä pa⟨ṃjsa⟩ tcaimañāṃ kāśa' jaidä
2 ttamīra jaida | tcaiña paṭarä pyāṣṭi . ysāna hana hve . tcįmañī
prrahīsīda vījaiṣḍi : cū hālai kamala vī vīni : pejsa tcaiña rāha' :
3 gvaña vīna jai|da : uskātta garśä bīsā āchā : haysgye ttajsīda : garśa
4 rāhi' : cū paysaṇve strīsīḍä kamala rāhi' : śau śau sera khā|śą'ña :
baiśa būḍa dva sera : khvai śaira hamāve raysgä vīra āchā jaida valakāṃ u ysāḍāṃ ṣi' hamä ṇi mąñaṃdä :
5 mahāve|ṭī rūṃ :
60r1/2 belū-mūla : agnamathä syąnākä : pāṭa|la : kaśmīrya mūla . sāla-
parṇa . prraśnaparṇa . brrahatta : kąṇḍārya . drrāṃgūlye halaidrra .
3 ysālva . āra . kalya|rūhne : halīrai vīhīl[n]ai ąmalai . vatsaka-bīja .
4 pākṣa rūṃnai : caittrai sacha bāva dūrālaba . śīya | sacha bāva .
rājavrraikṣa . bela .
tta hamīḍa[ḍa]ka arve dva dva sera : śtāka ysīra kūṭąña . tcahau
5 ṣaṃga uca jsa jṣą|ñąña : khu ra va śau ṣaṃga harśtä :
suṣmel[n]a . hararṇvä kūṣṭi . ttālīsa-patträ . caṃda śārava : sumana
60v1 śāriva . jīva|[va]ka : raṣabhakä : datta . devadārä . ėlavālųka . nacūla .
2 vāśakä . khavare . vaiśāla : papala : ttāṃgara . sva|rṇagūttaryāṃ
būśąnai . vīṇḍaga . vatsāvīja ttī . sąnā . prrīyaṃga . būha'ne apā-
maurgä bīja : carāttaihttai :
3 tta baiśa arve | dvī dvī mācāṃga hālā samāṃ kūṭąñä kaṣā' u keka
4 baiśa hąña tcerai . u gvīha' rūṃ dva śaiga hāle gvīha' ñe dva śai|ga
hālai . gvīha' ṣvīda dva śaiga hālai : gvīha' bīysmä dva śaiga hāle .
gvīha' saṃna hīyai raysä dva śaiga hāla .
5 ṣa' | maista paṃca-gavyą khāśą'ña . ṣa' rūṃ pīrmāttaṃ : vīysaṃ
ttavai vīra : harbīśāṃ dūṣṭyau jsa hamye . kasai ca śe'ye haḍai .

[1] nīlą°.

bhagadala ca vaisarpa vaisvaryeṣū prraśasyatti .

60r1 | bala-varṇa-karaṃ ciṃvą alakṣmīnam anapara :

mahā-paṃca-gavya nąma grratta :

61r2 cavyā caittrakaṃ pākṣāyä . kṣārä kustūbūrū vacā

3 yi | vānī . paipalī-mūlaṃ utsa ca bīḍa saidhavaś

tättrakasyą ca mūlāne belva-madhya harīttakī

4 ėttā akṣa samā bhāga sami-piṃḍāṃ | ⟨×⟩ kārayetta :

cattūrgūṇāna dadhyenā ghrratta prra⟨s⟩tha vapācayettā

ttattau māttrā pabe kāla arśa-vyāda-sukhāvaha .

5 prramīhąṣū | vātta-gulmeṣū pārśveṣū śūlajeṣū ca :

pūjatta grrahaṇī dąṣaja śraiṣṭä cavyā ghrra⟨tta⟩m ūttama

cavyādhī ghrrata ||

61v4 haigū sauvatcalaṃ vyāṣi bīṇḍä [da] dāṇḍäma dīpyakai :

pūṣkarājāja dhąnyābdavaittasaṃ kṣāra caittrakai :

5 śaṭī vacą | jägaṃvelā . sūrsaś ta ghrrartta pacātä

vidhanānala-gūlmąghna śūlanāha-tavāreṇä

dādhayä ghrratta::

62r4 sahacare dve ttraphalā : haraidrre dve pūnarṇavā :

kāka-nāsa-gūṇḍūvīnā : rāsnā midā śattāvarī .

5 ėṣā dva-[pala] | palakā bhāgā ghrrarttaṃ p⟨r⟩astha vapaucayettā

akṣa māttrā pave . nārī yauna-vyāpada-pīḍattā :

62v1 ttena sā labhatte garbhä yauna cā | śū vaśūdhyatte

sahacārādyaṃ ghrrattaṃ

4 paṃca-kaulāmṛttā kṣądrrā devadārū dūrālabhā

5 bhūttī | kaṃ caṃdąnaṃ mūsta vā:śā parpaṭa-ttihttakā

drrąkṣā : dāḍamą bįjāne paṃca-gavya vapācayeta

63r1 bhūtta-kalyąṇakaṃ nąma vį | ṣmi-jvarą-vanāśanaṃ

61r1 | hame : cū tcurmye haḍai hame ca naṣṭausai ttyāṃ vīra ysūäṣṭä ṣṭe . harbaiśa arja . kāmala . ṣpaijai . jara . vāśarūṃ bhagaṃdala vīsärpa
2 ca garśa pa | sauṣḍe ttyāṃ haṃbūsaṃ : cha śaika padīme . asaṃbajāṃ vī pīrmāttaṃ

mahāpaṃcagavyi :

61r5 61v1 badara caittrai . pāṭa | yava-kṣāra . ttaṃbīra sąnā . papāla mūla : bīdalūṃ : sadalūṃ : īraṃdāṃ hīye bāve : bela : halīrā :
2 ṣa' baiśa paṃjsa mācāṃgye samāṃ kūṭąña | hatca haṃbrrīhāña : gvīha' rūṃ dva śaiga hālai : u ñe tcau śūṃ'ba śau ṣaṃga baiśa hatca haṃbrrīhą'ña : hąña tcerai daṃda pāchai khu ra va śūṃma rūṃ
3 harśta ysų | nąña : u pamākya jsa bāḍą [ḍū] khāśą'ñi arja jaida : u ṣpaijā rāhi' : baina gąma : kveysvā vīne : grrahaṇī padauṣṭa va pīrmāttaṃ
4 ca | vyāda nāma ::

61v5 62r1 aṃgauṣḍä . spajū . papala | ttāṃgara . mīraijsya . bīdalū . drrąma ttīma . sąnā . hūraṣṭi . aúṣai . hīysamāṃ . būhane : abala-vettaraysä .
2 yava-kṣāra . | caittrai ṣala : āra . aśvagaṃdha : sūṣmela : surasä

ṣā pąna arva drrai drrai mācāṃga śtāka gvīha' rūṃ dva śaiga
3 hāle . ttīra ñe śau ṣaṃga ṣa' | arva samāṃ kūṭąña hatca hąña tcerai . pāchai khāśą'ña . baina gąma jaida u vīna : ąnāha' basta prrahāje
4 dhāttī nā | ma rūṃ

62v1 sahacara : halīrā vīhīlā : gūra kaśmīrya pārūṣā halaidrra ysālva .
2 aiśta bā [kā] | kākanāsi : gūlūśa' laṃgara bāva . meda mahāmeda śarāve .

ṣā' pąna arva dva dva sera . gvīha' rūṃ dva śaiga hāle hatca
3 jṣą | ñąña . paṃjsa mācāṃgye maṇḍyāṃ varāśą'ñä pūrąña āchā jaida
4 u yąña vīne khvaṃ jsa āsā yaṃde pūraṃ jsa bye | he' : pūrāṃ vī vasauśta .

sahacārādya nąma rūṃ ::

63r2 papala : papala mūla : caittrai . ttāṃgara : badarä : gūlūśa' : kaṇḍyārya : devadāra : dūrālaba : carāttaihttai caṃdaṃ : būha'ni : vāśakä :
3 ttairṣṭya : kalyarūha' | ni gūra : drrąma ttīma [ttūma] :

ṣā' pąna arva tcau tcau mācāṃga samau kūṭąñä gvīha' rūṃ dva śaiga hālai gvīha' ñi dva śaiga hālai gvīha' ṣvīda dva śaiga hālai
4 gvī | ha' saṃna hīvī raysä dva śaiga hālai gvīha' bīysmä dva śiṃga hālai :

ṣi' pąna arva u raysä baiśa hąña tcairai pāchai ṣai' rūṃ bhūttakalyąṇai nąma .

sattatta sąnattauttiva dvattīyaka : ttrattīyakaṃ
jvaraṃ cattūrthakaṃ śąṣa pūrąṇä jvara-nāśanaṃ :
bhūtta-kalyāṇī ghrrattaṃ ::
63v1 ttrāyimąṇa-rasaṃ kūryä ttraphalā-rasäm iva ca
2 drrąkṣā parūṣakā vyā⟨×⟩ saṃryirabhi vapācayi | t .
garbharthä cauṣadha kūgā : jīvaka raṣabhakāv ibhāṃ
śaṭī pūṣkara vīryąṇi śṛgabhara sä-caittrakaṃ :
3 ttināsya vā⟨tta⟩-pittrautham ārthaṃ vagacchatte | lągū
sadhayau vāttasṛiga-gūlma-pakṣmāyitta-navāraṇā :
ttrāyamąṇḍādyaṃ ghrratta ::

64r4 drrūṣaṇi ttraphalā drrākṣā kaśmīryąṇi parūṣakā
dvi pāṭi sarālaṃ vyāghrrī svagūpttā caittrakiś cīra
5 dhā⟨nya⟩- | ttāmalakī medā kāka-nāsā śānāvarī :
ttrąkaṃṭhaka bīdārī ca bilvā karṣa-samaṃ ghrrattā[rthi]
prrasthaṃ cattūrgūṇaṃ kṣīra saidhakaṃ saṃhara pavetta :
64v1 | jvāra-gūlma-rūca-plīha-śarau-hṛt-pārśvā-raugakā
kąmalārśaunalaṣṭīla-kṣana-śauṣa-kṣayāpaha
drrūṣaṇā nąma vikhyāttam a⟨tad ghṛ⟩ttam anūttamä
2 . | ttraiṣaṇaṃ ghrratta || ::
65r1 paṃcamūla balā yaṣṭī : gūṇḍūcīnāṃ rasąḍhaka :
2 prrasthaṃ bidārī⟨×⟩ttraikṣi rasąnāṃ sarpaṣa | pavitta
prrasthaṃ cattūragūṇī kṣīra jīvanī⟨yau⟩ṣadha kalatta

5 I vįṣmä jvara janākä cū avarāṃjsī ttavi cū śa'-haḍāṃjsū cū drra-hadāṃjsų tcūra-haḍāṃjsų hamyi haḍiṃ viṃ kṣayi ca maṃgāra ttaviṃ
63v1 harbīśāṃ vī śaira I īda bīśūṃ jaida

bhūtta-kalyąṇī nąma rūṃ ::

3/4 ttrāyamąṇä kṣa serä ysīra kūṭąñä kṣa śaiga I utca tcerā daṃda jṣąñąña khū ra va śaiga harśta hālai : halīrai vīhīlai aủmalai
5 ṣi' śau śau sera ysīra kuṭąñä dvāsä śaiga utca I tcerā daṃda jṣąñąña khu ra vä dva śaiga harśta hauṣka gūra hāle śaiga tta grrąma uca
64r1 bīnauyä vīśtąña hama-ysāvaṃ jsa gūrūtca padīmąña . I śau ṣaṃga :
pārūṣā śau sera tta ysīra kuṭąña kṣa śaiga uca jsa jṣąñąña khū ra va śau śaiga harśtä :
2 jīvaka : raṣabhakä : ṣala : hūraṣṭa kākauṭä ttagara I cittrai ṣai' pąna arva kṣa mācāṃga samāṃ kuṭąñä tta kaṣi' kiki bįśa hąña tciṃrai dva śaiga hālai hā gvīha' rūṃ tcerai hatsa pāchai nvā daina
3 ṣi' rūṃ khāśą'ña . I bi'na pittana āchā panava ṣṭąna jahąme vīra tsīda raysgä vīra . harbīśvā hamarvā pąną vāśarūṃ u gąma jaida u
4 pakṣāha'ka ṇahe I je :

ttrāyämąṇāda rūṃ ::

64v2 papala ttāṃgara mīraijsya : halīrai vīhīlai ąmalai gūra kaśmīryi
3 pārūṣā pāṭha : lagara bāva : devadārä kąṇḍārya ā I tmagūpttai caitträ ṣąlą raidhä ttū[ma]malaka mida mahāmida kākanāsä śąrāvä drāgūlye bidārä bila
4 ṣi' pana arva dvī dvī mācāṃga hā⟨lā⟩ I samāṃ kūṭąñä : gvīhą' rū dva śiga hālę ṣvīda śau ṣagą hamīḍa hāñä tcerai ṣi' rū pāchai
5 nvā daina kąlana khāśą'ña phāhä jä I da ttavā gąmä arruśa' ṣpaijā rāha' : kamala rāha jaida ysara rāhą' kveysvā vīni arja dāttaṣṭīla[1]
65r1 paijvā gvahaiye naṣṭausai kṣayi I pīreḍa :

ttrūṣala nąma rūṃ bausta ṣṭe vįsthārī ::

3 sąlaparṇä prraśnaparṇä brrahatta kąṇḍārya . drrāṃgūlyai sącha bāvä mahābāṃja gūlūśa' .
4 ṣā' I pąna arva śau śau sera ysīra kūṭąña tcau ṣaṃga hąña utca tcerā daṃda jṣąñąña khu ra va śau ṣaṃga harśta :
5 bīdāra dva sera ąma I lai dva sira . aikṣa ā vā gaula dva serä ysīra kuṭąña . dvārabaista śaiga utca tcerā u kṣa śaiga thaṃjąña tta būra kekaja arve .
65v1 jīvaka : [ra] I raṣabhaka . mida . mahāmida kākauṭa kṣīra kāaukauṭa mūdgaparṇa . māṣaparṇä ttäjavänä mahābāṃja

[1] vätta°.

rasāyina[ka]m ida śauṣṭi kṣatta-śau⟨ṣa⟩-kṣayāpaha
3 jvara-pārśva-rūjā kāsä hṛid-rrauga-kṣatta-bi|ṣājä :
rasāyäna ghrrattä || ::

65v4 sa-mūla-phala-pattrāyāṃ kaṇḍvakārya-rasāḍhaka
ghrratta-prrastha balā-vyāṣa-vīdyaṃgą-śaṭha-ttrattrịriṃ
5 sau|vatcalai yava-kṣā'raṃ . pipalī-mūlaṃ pūṣkärä
vṛśtīva brrahattī pathyā yivānī dāḍamaṃ drrākṣyā
66r1 pūnarṇavā cavya dūrālabhā : aṃ|balavitta[ra]sä :
śragī ttąmalakī bhąrgī rāsnā gaukṣarakä pacättä
[ka]kalkis natta sarva-kāsäṣu : hikā-śvāsä vaśaṣyatti :
2 kaṃṭhakā|rī-ghrratta hyattra kapha-vārmä[1] vasūdattä :
kąṇvakā⟨rī⟩ grrattä :

66v3 nāgarā pipala-mūla cịttraką-hahva-pąpalī
śvadaṣṭyā pipalī dh[y]ąnya bilva pāṭhā yädhąnakā
4 cāgirī-sva-ra⟨sa⟩-sarpä ka|lka r ịṣā vapācayit
cattūgūṇina dagdhā ca t ghrrattaṃ kaphä-nātta-rcūt
5 ⟨a⟩rśāsi grrahaṇī dauṣā muu[2]-jicchā prravāha'|kā
gūda-bhrräśārttäm aunāha-hattam itta vyapauhatti
cāgīrī ghrrattaṃ

67r4/5 sättalā ttraphalā-kalka daśamūlaṃ | kaṣāyikä
'äräṇḍa-ttalādhayätta ghrratta kṣīrä dhattaṃ

[1] rm=t. [2] muttra.

2 tta paṃjsa paṃjsa mācāṃgyi samāṃ ku|ṭą̄ña u tta raysä u arvä
biśa hą̄ña tcirā u dva śiṃga hālai hā gvīha' rūṃ tcerā u śau ṣaṃga
ṣvīda
3 ṣa' rūṃ pāchai kālna khāśą̄'ña piṃ|jvā gvahaiyä jiṃda u na-
ṣṭausiṃ u kṣayi u ttaviṃ . u kviysvā vīni jaida : phāha' uystta[1] āphāra .
ysįra vī rīysiṃ kṣayi va pīrmāttaṃ
4 | raysāyaṃ nąma ::
66r2 haṃtsa biva jsa u hīyāra jsa kaṇḍārye ysīra kuṭą̄ña daṃda jṣą̄ñą̄ña
3 khu ra | va śau ṣaṃga harśta tcahau ṣaṃga uca jsa kaṇḍārya dasau
sirä śtā⟨ka⟩ : tta bura hā kikaja arvi tciriṃ sacha bāva papala ttāṃ-
4 gara | mīraijsya vīṇḍaga ṣala cįttriṃ spajū yava-kṣāra papala mūla .
5 hūraṣṭa brrahatta hąlīrai sąnā drrąma ttīma gūra aúśta bā | badara :
dūrālabha aṃbala-vittarasa karkä⟨ṭa⟩-śrriṃga. ttų̄malaka khavari
laṃgara bā : drrāṃgūlye
ṣā' pąna arva dvī dvī mācāṃgye hālā
66v1 | ṣa' arva samāṃ kuṭą̄ña gvīha' rūṃ dva śiṃga hālai baiśa hamīḍa
hą̄ña tciriṃ u ṣa' rūṃ pāchiṃ nvā diṃna harbįśa paṃjsa pacaḍa
2 phāha' jiṃ|dä u haika uysna āphārä kaṃṭhakāryādä nąma śalīṣą̄ma-
jsā u biṃnāṃ āchāṃ janākä bausta ṣṭi :
kąṇḍvakāryāda rūṃ ||
66v5 67r1 ttāṃgara papala mūlą cįttri gaja papala drrāṃgūlyai pa|pala
hīysamāṃ bila pāṭha sąnā
ṣā' pąna arva śau śau siri samāṃ kūṭą̄ñä cakūrīka . haṣṭa sira .
2 tcahau ṣaṃga uca jsa j⟨ṣ⟩ą̄ñą̄|ña khu ra va śau ṣaṃga harśtä u śau
ṣaṃga ttīra ñi dva ṣaṃgä hālai gvīha' rūṃ ṣa' bįśa haṃ bāḍa hą̄ña
3 tciri pāchiṃ : ṣa' rūṃ bāva jiṃda u śa|līṣāṃ u arja . grrahaṇī
padauṣṭa u mūttra-kṛichä u hatsa haṃthaṃga jsa paṃjsa pacaḍą
4 avīysāra jaida cū kṛiṃga-rū|viṃ narāmi cu aúnāha' kaśti ttyi jsa
harbįśa āchā jāri
cāṃgīrāda rūṃ ::
67v1 sāttala halīriṃ vīhīlai aúmalai ṣa' śau śau sära samāṃ kūṭą̄ñä
kika va
2 bila-mūla : agttamatha[2] syānāka pāṭala ka|śmīrya mūla sāla-
parṇä pṛiśtaparṇä[3] brrahatta kąṇḍārya drāṃgūlye śau śau sira
3 ysī⟨ra⟩ kūṭą̄ña tcahau ṣaṃga uca jsa jṣą̄ñą̄ña : | khu ra va śau ṣaṃga
harśtä īraṃdīnai rūṃ śau śiṃgä gvīha': rūṃ śau ṣaṃga ṣvīda tcau
4 śiṃga hatca hą̄ña tciriṃ pāchiṃ ṣa' rūṃ ṣpiṃ|jiṃna hamyi dūvara

[1] uysna. [2] agna°. [3] pṛiśna°.

67r5 plīha-vāttaudariśas ta vinā kṣīra kaphaudarä
67v1 samaudrra sādhanaṃ viṃ mūttra⟨×××⟩va | varjattä ::

68r1 sättalā papalī daṃttī : pathyā tvagä bīḍa dārūbhi
dagamūla ra⟨sa⟩ sįdha sarpä vāttaudarāpaha
sāttaladya dvayi ghrratta ||

5 pipalī dāḍamaṃ drrākṣā palāṇḍaṃ sa-mahauṣadha.
68v1 gūṇḍäna sama-bhāgau | ni ghrratta prrastha vapācayit
kṣīra mā⟨ṃ⟩sä ra⟨sa⟩ś tiṃva ghrrattaṃ amrrattam ūttamaṃ.
kāsa-śvāsä-prra⟨śa⟩manaṃ kṣatta-kṣayi-vanāśana :
2 prrlīhä gūlmārśä visarpaṃ | śvayäthā mūu[1]-nägṛhi
mūttra-kṛichaiṣva sarväṣū vastūrāgā rūjąpaha :
kṛiśa-dūrbala-nāścaś ta vįṣma-jvära-vanāśanāṃ
3 [śa]sarpa imä saha | srrākṣä : brrīhaṇą-bala-vardhana :
sähasrrākṣaṃ ghrrątta ::

69r4 amrratta-phalā paṃcamūlā : ttrāyattī mṛttä paṭālā
5 naba-dvąthänä[2] ghrra | ttaṃ sįdhaṃ payisā dvi-guṇānvicä
vātta-śauṇättaṃ vidradyąnmada pūṇḍaraugaś ta⟨thā⟩
kuṣṭa-kaṭha-pā⟨ṇḍu⟩-väsāphaṭakānahadya-śū⟨ṇatta⟩ :
69v1 amṛtta-ttahtākä | ghrrattä

5 mūvā ttaihttą naśā yāṣä kṛiṣaṇiṃ caṃdhanaṃ parpaṭiṃ
72r1 ttrāyanī vatsa bhūgįmṛ paṭālābūda dārū. | bhā

[1] mūttra.   [2] kv-.

jiṃda u biva jsa hamyi dūvara jiṃda ttyāṃ būra āchāṃ va ysūṣṭa
5 ṣṭi vīnau ṣvīda śalīṣąmajsä dūvara jiṃda ha|tca bīysma jsa vaha':
pīttį bīysma u īraṃdīniṃ rūṃ hatsa vaha': bīśāṃ dūvarāṃ jsāṃ
phīśąñä

68r1 sāttalāda rūṃ dūvara va pīrmāttaṃ | ::
2 | || sāttala papala : datta halīriṃ tvacä bidalū devadāra
tta paṃjsa paṃjsa mācāṃga ysīra kūṭāña ṣį' kika va
3 bila mūla | agttamatha[1] : syąnāka pāṭala kaśmīrya mūla sālaparṇa
prraśtaparṇä[2] brrahatta kąṇḍārya drāṃgūlya
4 tta paṃjsa paṃjsa | mācāṃga ysīra kūṭąña dva ṣaṃga uca jsa
jṣąñąña khu ra va paṃjsa śiṃga harśta bįśa hąña tciriṃ u śau ṣaṃga
5 gvīha' rūṃ hatsä pāchai | kālna khāśą'ñä biṃna dūvara jiṃda ||

sāttalāda rūṃ ::

68v3 pipala drāma ttīma gūra : ttāṃgare śau śau [śau] sira : gūrva līka
4 śīyä | pau 20 daṃdā ṣa' arva samāṃ kuṭąña :
pasīña hvaśā . ṣa' hahvāña driṃ ṣaṃga uca jsa pāchai khu ra va
5 haṣṭä . śiṃga harśta . ṣvīda tcau śiṃga gvīha' rūṃ | dva śiṃga : tta
bįśa hąña tcįrā u pāchai khu paha' hami ysūnąña aysdįmąña khu
69r1 drāṃ hami khu aspā ttī hā 4 sira gūla kuṭąña nauka u hā | hā
haṃbrrīhąña : ṣa' rūṃ nva ttaraṃdarū diṃ varāśą'ña : phāha' uysna
āphāra jiṃda piṃjvā gvahaiyi jiṃda : ṣpiṃjāṃ rāha' gąma arja
2 vīsä|rpä haśä cū pyatsī parīysma pīhīsta mūttra-kṛichi harbįśāṃ
dūṣyau' jsa phäysagąña āchā u vīniṃ tta būrä āchā bäśa jida : cū
3 gauda | ī ttū tvąñe cū bava-hauva ttyi śara-hauva padīmi viṣma jvara
jiṃda : ṣa' ca vīysaṃ ttaviṃ : ṣa' ttū sahasrrākṣa nąma śakrrana
4 | hva tvąñāka hauva padīmākä

sahasrrākṣä rūṃ ::

69v1 halīrai vīhīlai ąmale : sālaparṇa : brrahattä kąṇḍārya drāṃgūlye
2 ttrāyamąṇä gūlūśa' paṭaula ciṃgāṃ ttīrai hīye | pirä
ṣa' pąna arva śau śau sira hamīḍa ārąña śva' ysīrä naukyä jsa kika
3 padīmąña u ysīrye jsa kaṣ[ṭ]ā' pāchai drrai ṣaṃga utca | tcirā u
haṣṭa śiṃga thaṃjąña gvīha' rū dva śiṃga ṣvīda haṣṭa śiṃga
4 ṣa' rūṃ pāchiṃ . vāśarūṃ jaida khajsāṃ ādmāda ysī|ḍiṃ ttaviṃ
kauṣṭa cū aṃga kyahāri . ysūną kauṣṭa u khaysme tta būrä āchāi
5 jaida : vāśarūṃ va amrratta-ttįhttiṃ [nā] | nąma rūṃ ::
72r1/2 ālavāyi ka|lyarūhna : halaidra ysālva dūrālabha papala caṃdaṃ .
ttrirṣṭya ttrāyamąṇä vatsaka-bījä carāttįhttiṃ paṭāla hīravī divadārä

[1] agna°. [2] prraśna°.

akṣa-māttra ghrratta-prrasthi sidha kṣīraṃ cattūrgūṇi
maṇḍittā-jvara-viṣphāṭā- : śauthārśą̄-rahta-pi:tä-jittä
pūṇḍaraugaha smyattä :

4/5 hapūṣa[ṃbi] | m ilānala-vyą̄ṣa-cavya-dīpyąki-sādhava
⟨a⟩ją̄jī-grrathąkį-kālā-mūlakāṃbū-nūva-ghrratta
72v1 da⟨dhi⟩-kṣīra-yūhtį padva-gūlma-śūla-vībaṃdha- | nūtti
yauna-dą̄mā-varṣākārśau-śvāsa-hṛitta pārśva-śūla-jina
hamūṣādya ghrratta .

73r1/2 || daśamūlā-balā-rāsnā aśvagaṃdhā-pūna | rṇava
irąṇḍa-mūla-dvāthäna[1] kūrkaṭa-rasa-yaujanaṃ
jīvanīyauṣidhi-garga ghrrattam avāgnänā pącit .
3 visvaryą-śvāsa-kāsa- | ghna śari-pārśva-ujāpahä
mūttra-kṛichi-prramīhā'ś ca śūkrra-mähātta-garbhaṇī
sarvimū vātta-vyāvīnā vastä-śūla-vaśūdhanä
4 | kūrkaṭādya ghrratta :

74r1 ttraphalā-dvą̄tha[1]-kąlkaina : sahayiska ghrratta śrrattä :
ttamīrą̄ṇḍy ädhyanā pīrmam[2] itą ⟨ni⟩śā-myakhi
ttraphalādya ghrratta

[1] kv-. [2] rm=t.

3 ṣa' pąna arva paṃ|jsa paṃjsa mācāṃga samāṃ kuṭąña gvīha' rūṃ
dva śiṃga hālai . ṣvīda śau ṣaṃga bį̄śa hąña tcįriṃ pāchiṃ kālna
4 sämāṃ khāśą'ña ysīḍiṃ | āchiṃ jiṃda ttaviṃ khaysmi haśa : arja
ratta vṛätta jida ca iha . ⟨ha⟩ysgvā nāṣṭi hų̄ña narąmi

pąṇḍarauga va rūṃ ::

72v_2^1 hapūṣi : sūṣmila : cittri papala | ttāṃgara : mīriṃjsya badara
sąnā : sadalūṃ auṣi : papala mūla :

ṣā' pą⟨na⟩ arva paṃjsa paṃjsa mācāṃgya samāṃ kūṭąña baraśīji
3 | śau śiṃga rīysū hāle śäṃga śau ṣaṃga ūca jsa pāchiṃ khu ra va
4 śva' harśtä āysmāstąña padąnaña pyąnąña khu ttīra | hami dva
śiṃga pisūjąñä hūṣkyi ttrahi dasau ṣira kuṭąña kṣasa śiṃga uca jsa
5 jṣąñąña khu ra va dva śiṃga harśta : | stura drrąma bį̄sta hathrrająña
dva śiṃga drrąma raysä śtākä gvīha rūṃ dva śiṃga ñi dva śiṃga .
ṣvīda dva śiṃga . bį̄śa hąña tciriṃ u pāchai drriṃ drriṃ tcau tcau
73r1 prrų̄yi khā|śa'ña grrąmaka gąma jiṃda u aharīna vīni jsahira aṃgvā
hiṃga[1] padīmi

hapūṣāda rūṃ ::

73r4 bila-mūla : agnamathä : syąnāki pāṭala : kaśmīrya mūla . sāla-
5 parṇa prraśnaparṇa brrahattä kąṇḍārya | drrāṃgūlyai sächa bā .
lagara bā . aśvagaṃdha . iṃśta bā . iraṃdi bā .

ṣa' ⟨pa⟩na arva paṃjsa paṃjsa mācāṃga : ysīra kuṭąña drriṃ
73v1 ṣaṃga ⟨u⟩ca jsa jṣą'|ñąña . u haṣṭa śiṃga thaṃjąña : kṛiṃga śau
pāra u ṣkūṭa pā jsahira bīsā hīra tta bį̄śa hāysä dīśąña : hahvąña : u
2 kṣasä śiṃga | utca tcirā drriṃ śiṃga thaṃjąña . gvīha' rūṃ dva
śäṃga ṣvīdä dva śiṃgä bį̄śa hąña tciriṃ . tta būra hā kikaja arvä tciriṃ
3 jīvaka raṣabhäka mi|dä . mahāmida : kākauṭa kṣīra kākauṭa .
mūdgaparṇa māṣaparṇä j⟨ī⟩vatta mahābāṃja samāṃ kuṭąña pātca
4 hąña tci⟨rā⟩ | nvā diṃna pāchiṃ kālna sämāṃ khāśą'ña cu bījāṣa
pasuṣḍi uysttä[2] āphāra jiṃda kamala rāhä': kviysvā vīni ttyāṃ
5 janākä mū|ttra-krrį̄cha prramīha' arja ca vā raṣṭa pūraṣiṃdrrī
narąmi : mį̄sta-ujāṃ maṇḍyāṃ harbīśāṃ biṃnāṃ āchāṃ janāka
74r1 phiysgąña vīnāṃ | janākä

kurkūṭāda nąma rūṃ ::

halīri vīhīle ąmale dva dva sirä kuṭąña : śva ysīra padīmąña u
74r_3^2 naukyi jsa : kika padī|mąña u ysīryi jsa kaṣā' pāchiṃ drriṃ ṣaṃśa[3]
utca tcirā haṣṭa śiṃga thaṃjąña kika u kaṣā' hąña tcirā u dvą śiṃga
4 gvīha' | rūṃ u 4 śiṃga ṣvīdä hatsa pāchiṃ nvā dina tcįña ttamīra
5 jiṃda u bīśų̄ña āchā khu ttū rūṃ khāśīdi iha' rā|ha' jiṃda ::

[1] haśa. [2] uysna. [3] ṣaṃga.

74r5 māstā phala-ttrayi-kvāthaṃ daśamūlasya ⟨×⟩ śrratta
kalkenä jīva⟨nī⟩yąnį grattū : ttamīrä-nāśanī :
74v1 karṇayau śūla bāda⟨ryaṃ⟩ I nąsā vā⟨tta⟩-samīraṇaṃ
pittauṣa-kapha sa-śauṣā jāyätta karṇą-gūthakā : :

75r2 uśī'rä padmaka viśvä paṭāsä dūrālabhā
3 I niṃba kipilyakaṃ mū⟨r⟩vā karaṃjä dvi ssä-kąṭaphalā :
raudrra māttraka maṃjįṣṭām utpala surasaṃ cadaniṃ :
4 piṣṭā cä pala I kaṃ bhāgi mahāmidä palena ca :
madhūkąsya kāṣāyiṇä madhūchįṣṭa palaną cä
5 ghrratta prrasthaṃ sa-mālaiṇyaṃ : I mṛṃ rūpākä cä ttārayinä
brrahmąṇā nähittą sadya salvąnūḍä payāhattä
leha-līga-vakārāṣū visarpe-sphauṭākeṣū cä :
75v1 kṛma-kīṭeṣū kū I ṣṭeṣū vecarcaka thathiva ca .
bhäna-vṛidha-kṣyitta-kṣi'ṇi duṣṭe-ttāṇḍä-vṛṇäṣū cä :
ape dvādaśa-varṣiṇā vṛha'-rāhaṇäm ūttamä :
2 la[mą]ha-leįgādī[1] I ghrrattä : :

76r4 kaulāblā dāḍäma-rasiṃ : mättūlāgä-rasiṃ dädhara
śūṣkä mūląka naryahiṃ iṃva ardhāchakaṃ[2] pi⟨ci⟩ttä :
5 lavaniṃś ta paṃcabhį pā I ṭā yivąnī : paṃca kaulaki
svarjakä sa-yava-kṣārä : vaṇḍaṃgā śūṣka mūleḍhka
ghrratta-prrastha pącatdabhi gūlme vātta-kaphātmaki

[1] līg°. [2] °āḍhakaṃ.

$74v^{1}_{2}$ laṃgara bāva : halīriṃ vīhīlai āmalai bilva [mū] | mūla agnamathä
syąnākä : pāṭala : kaśmīrya mūla : sālaparṇa pṛstaparṇa[1] brrahatta :
3 kaṇḍārya drrāṃgulyi pąna arva hālai hāle | sira ysīra kuṭąña drriṃ
ṣaṃga uca jsa jṣąñąñä śau ṣaṃgä thaṃjąña tta būrä hā kikaja arvi
tciri :
4 jīvaka raṣabhaka mida mi | hāmidä kākauṭa : kṣīra kākauṭą :
mūdgaparṇä māṣaparṇä : jīvatta mahābaujä tta tcau tcau mācāṃgyi
5 samāṃ kuṭąña . | gvīha' rūṃ dva śiṃga . ṣvīda drriṃ śiṃga bįśa
hąña tcirā nvā diṃna pāchiṃ kālna sämāṃ varāśą'ñä ṣa' rū ttamīrāṃ
75r1 janąka . | gvąña vīna jiṃdä ca kāra ttyi gva prrahāji haysgvā bīsā
āchā jiṃda : pitta ttavaṃdyä śalīṣāṃ . jsa panava āchā : maṃgāra
2 naṣṭau | siṃ gisā gvaña vīni u ysū tta būra āchä biśa jiṃda :
ttraphalāda rūṃ ::
75v2 uśi'rä pauṣṭarä ttāṃgarä : paṭaule : dūrālabhä : ciṃgāṃ ttīriṃ
3 hīyi pirä kaṃpīlai . ālavāyä bāva : pūttī-karaṃja rmahtta-mā | la[2]
karaṃjä . kąṭaphale śąbariṃ . lāaudrä : māśa'kyi rūṃniṃ : nīlātpala :
. surasä : śī caṃdaṃ : hiṃniṃ caṃdaṃ :
4 ṣā' pąna arva tcau tcau mācāṃgä | samāṃ kūṭąña mahāmida śau
sira gvīha' rūṃ dva śiṃgä : mahābāṃjä dvāssä sira : kūṭąña drriṃ
5 ṣaṃga uca jsa jṣąñąña khu ra | va haṣṭi śiṃgä harśta : ṣvīda driṃ
śiṃga : bįśa hamīḍa hąña tcirā ṣa' rūṃ nvā diṃna pāchiṃ khu na
76r1 suśta ysūnąña dva sira hā carūtta haṃbrrīhą'ña | brrahmā jsa hvi
haṃbūsaṃ ṣa' rūṃ āchāṃ janākä satvąnū mviṃśdä' kįnä hija haśa
2 jiṃda . visarpa u hiṃja ttauca haśä biṃda khaysmä prrąṇḍyau | jsa
paśā bi jiṃdä tta khu śaysdä baṇāsīḍa drvīdä ttyāṃ vīra śįra ī īdä
drāṃ kūṣṭa jiṃdä cū ysautta : cū pyahasta khasta vīraṃ haṃbrrąñä
3 vīnau | sta nālāvīraṃ haṃbrrąñi maṃgāra dvāsä-salāṃjsų vīraṃ
haṃbrrįtta : maṃgāra āṣana haśa jiṃda ttyāṃ būra āchāṃ biṃda
4 sakhalyą | ñä ::
$76v^{1}_{2}$ baraśīji śau śiṃga rī | ysū hāle śäṃga hatsä pāchi khu paha' hamä
āysmāstąña bagalaña pyąnąña . khu māyi . pisująñä dva śiṃga
3 āhvariṃ | raysä dva śiṃga drrąma raysä dva sira vālaiga raysä dva
4 śiṃga ttīra ñi . haṣṭa sära hauṣkyi ttrahi : dvāsä śiṃga | uca jsa
. jṣąñąña khū ra va dva śiṃga harśta :
5 sadalūṃ bīdalūṃ spajū ucā namva rājā namva : pāṭa sąnā pa | pala
. papala mūla cįttriṃ ttāṃgara bądara svarjaka kṣāra vīṇḍaga hau-
77r1 ṣkyi ttrahi drriṃ drriṃ mācāṃga samāṃ kūṭąña gvīha' | rūṃ dva

[1] pṛśna-. [2] nahtta°.

76*vi* vātta | -vyādhį prramīha'rś tä hįkā śvāsä bhagaṃdarä
vįśvaryą-hitta-pārśvą-rūjāvadhmą̄nā-grrahaṇi-gada
śūṭī ghrratta :

77r^{2}_{3} : jīvaka raṣibhakä midā : drrākṣā są | mattī stharā :
nadagdhakā prrayaṃgā phalanī . vīṇḍa⟨ga⟩ mądhūką ⟨ba⟩lą
maṃjįṣṭā śarkarą rāsnā nīletpalaṃ ttraula kaṃṭakā :
4 prrapauṇarīkä pįpalyą : | vavābhu-lavaṇā tvaca
ittą̄ni sama-bhāgą̄ni kārṣaką̄ni samāharät
kalke sucarṇätta piṣṭvā ttila sarpä samāharät
5 cūttūrgūṇä | na payisā . padvam ȧtträyi narmättä :
pūttanāsyäm īdaṃ śrrįṣṭaṃ nättraupąlabda ma⟨×⟩dä
paṭala ttamira ką̄ca pilya naktā⟨ṃ⟩dha arbūdä
77*vi* jātty-a⟨ṃ⟩dhą ta | tti akṣa⟨× × ×⟩bala-varṇaṃ-kara
gala-gaṇḍä karṇa-śūla śīrṣa-rauga ni[rya]rasyatti
śvāsä-kāsą-hara hįkā : marttyą̄nāṃ amrrattaupamä :

78*r*2 : aśvagaṃdha palā tri⟨ṃ⟩śä . chą̄ga-mā⟨ṃ⟩sä-kaṣāyäkä :
3 kṣīra cattūrgūṇaṃ kyītvā ghrratta-prrasthaṃ vapāca | yi :
jīvakä-raṣabhakau midi drraukṣā' ridhī śanāvarī
balā bīdārī parṇau dvi : jīvattī madhūkä kaṇā
4 kākauṭī kṣīra-kākauṭī : svayi-gūpttā | bhalāttaka
sūkṣmila nāgara : śrigī kārṣakä ni⟨tya⟩m āharit
cattūṣpala śarkarā ca ttūlya mądhūna miśratta
5 śūcä-bhą̄ṇḍätą līḍhva syāt | maśtīyā vṛdha dubala
varṇä-kṣattą-kṣīṇä-vāttä-vyādhiṣū . ⟨× ×⟩ sarvaśa
aśvagaṃdhādya ghrrattä :

śiṃga . tta kaṣi' arva rūṃ bįśa hąña tciriṃ ṣi' rūṃ pāchiṃ gūma jiṃda bāva śalīṣąmajsa āchā aharīna biṃna āchā prramīhä' arja
2 hįka uysnä I āphārä bhagaṃdala ca bījāṣi jīyi ysīra rāhä' nariyi grrahaṇī prradauṣä tta būrä āchā jiṃ⟨da⟩

śūkṣī ghrratta :

$77v^{1}_{2}$ jīvaka : rįṣabhaka : mi I da : mahāmida : sālaparṇä prraśtaparṇä[1] brrahatta : kaṇḍārya prriyaṃgä mahābāṃja : sacha bāvi rūṃniṃ
3 śakarä laṃgara bāva . nīlątpala drrāṃgūlye prra I pūṇḍarī : papala iṃśta bāva sadalūṃ tvaca

ṣi' pąna arva bįśa hąmaṃga drriṃ drriṃ mācāṃga śtāka samāṃ
4 kūṭąñä śau ṣaṃga kūṃjsavīniṃ rūṃ u I śau śiṃgä gvīhi' ṣvīda haṣṭa śiga :

ṣi' arva rūṃ bįśi hąña tcirā ṣi' rūṃ nvā diṃna pāchiṃ mįstyi
5 āttriṃ raṣa'yina hva : cū haysgvā mattūṃna bau I śa narąmi ṣi' jiṃda ttyi va pīrmāttaṃ :

. nittraupalabū nąma tcįmąñāṃ va pīrmāttaṃ paṭala ttamīrį kāśa'
78r1 pyāṣṭyi ca ṣīyi na vījiṣḍi . cū ysā I na hąna ttyi tcįmiña prrahīsīda hauva cha śįrka padīmi : garśa haṃbva gvaña vīni kamiña vīni u
2 āchā jiṃda uysnā āphārä phāhi' . hika ttyāṃ būra āchāṃ I va ṇi mąñaṃda .

nįttraupalabū nąma rūṃ :

78^{r5}_{vi} : aśvagaṃdha 30 sira : ysīra kūṭą I ñä drriṃ ṣaṃga uca jsa jṣyą-ñāña khū ra va haṣṭa śiṃgä harśtä būysīña hvaśā hahvąña dva
2 ṣaṃga uca jsa pāchiṃ khū ra va kṣa śiṃga harśta I gvīha' rūṃ dva śiṃga hāle ṣvīda haṣṭa śāṃgä tta būra kikaja arvi

jīvaka raṣabhakä mida mahāmida gūra rįdha śarāvi sacha bāva
3 bī I dārä sālaparṇa jīvatta mahābauja . papala kākauṭa kṣīra kāīkauṭa
4 āttamagūpttį balāttakyi : sukṣmila : ttūṃgara : I karkaṭa-śri⟨ṃga⟩ .

ṣā' pąna arva drriṃ drriṃ mācāṃga ṣi' arva kaṣi' rūṃ ṣvīda hatsa
5 pāchiṃ ysūnąña aysdįmąña khū drāṃ hami khū hauṣkä a I spā : ttī hā tcahau sira mākṣī tcau sira ārda līka śakarä haṃbrrīhāñä suña
79r1 bagalaña pyąnąña : nva ttaraṃdarų diṃ varāśąña I ysāḍa paskyāṣṭi cista padīmi ahauvaṃ pijsa padīmi cha śįrka padīmi . piṃjvā gvahįyä
2 jiṃda kṣayi ca gauda āchiṃ jiṃda haṣṭā bäna I āchā jiṃda valaka

aśvagaṃdhādä rūṃ :

[1] prraśna°.

79*r*2 : daśamūla balā rāsnā śaṃkha-pūṣpī phalą-ttrakį
3 dvi mįda dhāttakī-pūṣpī vīḍagā kaṭa | ka-rahaṇī :
nīlaka vāstūkā-bījä kaṃpīlyāśna[1] punarṇävā
ābhyā kaṣāyä kalkābhyāṃ ghrratta-prrasthaṃ vapācayit
4 paṃca-gą̄lma | vaśiṣättä :
prramīha' vīśattaś tiva : nārīṇāṃ yaunanā padi
mahābiṃda ghrratta :

79*v*4 pāṣāṇä-bhida vṛṣakä śattāhvā pīlakī-phala
hiṃgv āblāvittasau : rbūkaṃ śvadaṣṭvā hapūṣā vacā
5 bhūkaucaka kharāśväś tä vi | śālā brrahattī dvayi
mūṣakarṇī śąṭa⟨×⟩ś tāś tathiṃva śītta vārikā
ttrapūsädhāḍä-bījāna dattī pāṭā harįttakī
80*r*1 ghrratta-prrasthaṃ vapakvavyä : | gavā mūdriṇä vāpayittä
įṣa r auṣadha cūrṇāś ta mākṣākaṃ līcham[2] iva vā
aśmarī śarkarā kyįchā vasta-kuṇḍäla narhyatta :
2 sarviṣāṃ | vātta-vyādhīnāṃ vastāttū mūttri-kṛich[ā]iṣā
kharpattī

80v_2^1 : nīlīkā ttrāphalā rāsnā ba | lā vyāghrrī pūnarṇavā
dhāttakī śaṃkha-pūṣpī ca vīḍaṃgā kaṭūka-rauhaṇī :
vāstūkasyą ca bīją̄ni ttathā kaṃpīlyakaṃ bhavitta
3 įtta | bhįda-ghrratta nāma arśāsā parä-mahauṣadha
paṃca mahā-gūlyaṃ⟨××⟩samāthą̄naṃ aṣṭau udakaṃ
4 yatti prramīhaṃ vī | śattąś tä vayanīdāṃ vīśiṣittä :

81r_3^2 jalai daśūgūṇä | sidha ttrāyamą̄ṇį cattūṣpala
kalka ttūma⟨la⟩kī vīrā jīvattī caṃdą̄ṇą̄tpala
4 kaṭūkā-rauha'ṇī mūsta ttrāyimāṇä | dūrālabhā
rasam āmalakīnā ca kṣīrāstha ca : ghrrattasyą ca
prrathakä aṣṭā⟨v a⟩ṣṭą̄ samya ⟨samya⟩ dva tvā vapācayät

[1] °āgna. [2] līḍham.

79r4–5 : bila-mūla agttamathä[1] syānāka pāṭala kaśmīrya | mūla sālaparṇä
prraśtaparṇa[2] brrahatta kąṇḍārya drrāṃgūlye
ṣā' pana arva śau śau sira ysīra kuṭāña . drriṃ ṣaṃga uca jsa
79v1 jṣą̄ñą̄ña khu ra va haṣṭi [śiṃ] | śiṃga harśta :
sacha bā laṃgara bā śaṃkha-pūṣpi hąlīriṃ vīhīle ą̄malai mida
2 mahāmidä dhāttakī-pūṣpa vīṇḍaga kalyarūhi'ni nīlai bāstū|lāe ttīma
kaṃpīlai iṃ'śta bāva .
ṣā' pąna arva dvī mācāṃgyi hālā : samāṃ kuṭą̄ña kaṣā' rūṃ biśa
hatsa pāchiṃ ysūną̄ña khāśą̄'ña :
3 ṣi' rūṃ paṃjsa-padya | gą̄ma jiṃda : haṣṭa pacaḍa dūvarä ma-
ṇḍyāṃ hūjīniṃ gą̄ma jiṃda bista pąacaḍa prramīhä' maṇḍyāṃ
ttąraṃdara vīni
mista bi'rmakitta rūṃ :
80r2 viśāla brra[tta]hatta kąṇḍāryä dravatti ṣala śī caṃdaṃ : ttrūysāṃ
3 byārāṃ datta pāṭa halī|riṃ
ṣa' pana arva dvī dvī mācāṃga : samāṃ kūṭą̄ñä gvīha' rūṃ dva
4 śiṃga hāle gvīha bīysmä haṣṭa śiṃga arva rūṃ bīysmä bį|śa hą̄ña
tcįriṃ ṣi' rūṃ pāchiṃ khāśą̄'ña aśmarya mūttra-kṛicha jiṃda :
5 phiẏsgāṃ vasta kuṇḍala jiṃda harbiśa biṃna āchā jiṃda tta | hama
arvi nauka ārāña cą̄ṇa⟨ṃ⟩ jsa padīmāña tta paḍā bīsā āchā jiṃda .
80v1 tta hama arvi nauka ārą̄ña ysūnāña | mākṣīna līha padīmą̄⟨ña⟩
ttavaṃdyi jsa hamyi mūttra-kṛįcha jiṃdä :
khaśpāda rūṃ mūttra-kṛįcha va pīrmāttaṃ :
80v4 : nīle halīriṃ vīhīlai ą̄malai laṃgara bāva sächa bā kąṇḍārya
5 äṃśta bā | dhāttakī-pūṣpi śaṃkha-pūṣpi viḍaga kalyarūha'na bāstūle
kaṃpīle .
81r1 ṣā' pąna arva drriṃ mācāṃga samāṃ kuṭą̄ña : gvīha' rūṃ | dva
śiṃga ṣvīda haṣṭi śiga bįśa hą̄ña tciriṃ ṣi' rūṃ pāchiṃ khāśą̄'ña
2 päśā' dvī dvī prrūyi arrja va pīrmāttaṃ : arva paṃjsi pacā̦ḍa gūma |
jiṃda haṣṭa pacaḍä dūvara bįsta pacaḍa prramīhä' aharīna maysją̄na
āchā biśa jiṃdä
biṃnakitta rrūṃ :
81r5 v1 : ttrāyimą̄ṇa | tcahiṃssä sära dva ṣaṃgä uca jsa jṣą̄ñą̄ña khū ra va
dva śiṃga harśtä aůmale tcahiṃssä sira kṣasa śiga uca jsa jṣą̄ñą̄ña
2 khu ra va | dva śiga harśa ṣvīda haṣṭi śiṃga na[3] būra kikaja arvi
ttą̄mala kākauṭä jīvattä caṃdaṃ nīlātpala kalyarūha'na būhani
3 ttrāyimauṇḍa dūrālabha tta arrvi dvī dvī mā|cāṃga hālai : tta kaṣi'

[1] agna°. [2] prraśna°. [3] tta.

5 pitta-gūlma [ra] I rahtä-pitta-visarpą pittakaṃ jvarä
hṛḍ-raugaṃ kaumala kauṣṭā hanyād itti ghrrattauttama
ttrāyamāṇā[da]dya ghrrattä :

81v4 : bhūnimba ttraphalą̄śīra ⟨pā⟩ṭhāṛiṣṭābda madhūkä
śārävį ttahtta ttrāyaṃttī caṃdanā krriṣṇā padmakaṃ
5 ṣaḍ-grathā I viśālaidrrimyi vā vṛiśā ⟨×××⟩
mū⟨r⟩chā paṭāla śamyāka parpaṭāt viṣā naśi 4 :
: sapttachąda śattāvaryā ätty iṣā pāda kalkattā
82r1 sarpär iṣṭi-gūṇa ttau I yi dvi gūṇāmalaka [d]risi 5 :
sādhattą vātta-pittauthaṃ kūṣṭa-visphą̄ṭa-pauṇḍä-jätta
mahāttįhtta jvarautmāda gąṇḍamālāpaham ittä :

82v^{1}_{2} : śūṭī grathakaṃ kṛiṣṇāgni cavya kṣāri palā I matti
ttūlyaṃ kṣīra ghrrattaṃ prrastha sādhanaṃ kapha-gūlma-nūt :
grrahaṇī-pāṇḍattā-plīha-kāsa-śvāsa-jvarāpaha
3 eittaṃ paṭ-palakāṃ[1] nąma śamadāvartta-nāśa I na :

82v5 : pitpalī nāgarą agną palāma dhānya dva dāḍäma :
83r1 [gū] I gūṇḍa cattūṣpala kṛitvā ghrrattaṃ prrastha vapācayitta :
kṣīraṃ cattūragūṇa sidhīn agrraṃtti-vāna-rauga-nūva :
2 brrīhaṇa harṣarṇä I balya kāsa-śvāsä-kṣayąpaha
viṣmä-jvaraṃ phārśva śūlaṃ ttriṣṇādāvartta pīṇḍattā
śvayithū-gūlya-mihārśa prralīhāṃ ttīkṣana biṣajä

83v1 jīvakä raṣabhakī vīryā jīvanī nāgarī śaṭī
cattū prra⟨śna⟩parṇī midā kākauṭī dva nąḍąhakā
2 I pūnarṇavä mūdhakisyā ātmagūpta śaṇāva⟨rī⟩
rīdhī parūṣkakaṃ bārgī mrrįkṣīkā brra⟨ha⟩ttī ttathā

[1] ṣaṭ.

u rrūṃ ṣvīdä biśa hatsa pāchi khu paha' hami khāśą̄'ñä pītta gą̄ma
4 jiṃdä rahna-pitta[1] vįsarpa pīttį ttaviṃ ysīra rīysiṃ ką̄mala kū | ṣṭi
tta būra āchā jiṃdä

ttrāyamą̄ṇāda rrūṃ :

82r2¹ : ą̄malai | 8 sira dva ṣaṃga uca jsa jṣą̄ñą̄ña khū ra va kṣa śiṃga
harśtä gvīha' rūṃ dva śiṃga tta būra kikaji arvi tcirā carāttįhttiṃ :
3 halī:ri vīhīlai ą̄male uśi'ra pāṭä niṃbä | būha'na dūrālabha mahā-
bāṃji caṃdą̄na śārava sūmana śārava kalyarūhni ttrāyamą̄ṇa śī
4 caṃdi hiṃniṃ caṃdaṃ gūlūśä' papala pauṣṭarä ṣä | ṇḍä grrathi
vįśāla vatsaka-bījä vāśakä ālavāya bāvi : paṭāla rāja-vṛākṣa ttirṣṭyva[2]
prravaṣi' halaidrra ysālva : [śa] aśphą̄ṇḍä śarāvi
5 ṣā' pą̄na a⟨rva⟩ dvī dvī | mācāṃga samāṃ kūṭą̄ñä kaṣi' u rūṃ bįśa
hą̄ña tciriṃ pāchiṃ nvā dina : tta būra āchā jiṃda biṃna u pīttana
82v1 āchā jiṃda kuṣṭi khaysmi ysīḍi āchiṃ jiṃdä | ṣa' mahāttįhttiṃ
ttaviṃ jiṃda u ātmāda . gaṇḍamāla pīriḍa aharīna isyi haśa lūtta

mahāttįhttiṃ rūṃ :

82v3 ttūṃgara papala . papala mūla cittriṃ bą̄darä yava-kṣāra
ṣā' pą̄na arva śau śau sirä [rrūṃ] gvīha rūṃ dva śiṃga hālai ṣvīda
haṣṭa śiṃga .
4 ṣį' arva sä | māṃ kūṭāña bįśa haṃtsa pāchiṃ khāśą̄'⟨ña⟩ grahaṇī
padauṣa pą̄ṇḍarauga ppiṃjā[3] rāha phāha uysnä āphāra ttavi bāva
5 naṣṭausiṃ u | dāvarttāṃ janāka .

ṣaṣṭapala ną̄ma rūṃ śalīṣāmajsa gą̄mä mūrāka :

83r3 papala ttāṃgara cittriṃ tta arvi śau śau sirä hīysmāṃ śau sira
drrą̄ma ttīma dva si⟨ra⟩ : gaula 4 sira gvīha' rūṃ dva śiṃga hāle :
4 ṣvīdä śau ṣaṃga biśa rūṃ arva ṣvī | da haṃtsa pāchiṃ khu paha' hami
aysdįmą̄ña drāṃ hami khu aspā ttī hāgau kūṭą̄ña ttaña rūṃña haṃ-
5 brrīhą̄ñä ahvaḍāṃdī tharka masi hviri haṣṭā biṃna āchā | jidi tvāñi
sīrauśi' hauva padīmi phāha' jida uysnä āphāra kṣayi gauda āchiṃ
jiṃdä : vīysaṃ ttaviṃ jiṃda kviysvā vīni udāvartti haśa gūma
83v1 prramīhä' arja | ṣpiṃjiṃ vīna jiṃda

paṃcapąlą rūṃ :

84r3 jīvaka . raṣabhakä midä mahāmidä . kākauṭa jīvattä . ttāṃgara :
4 ṣala sālaparṇä . prraśtaparṇa[4] . mūdgaparṇä māṣaparṇa kṣī | rakādä[5]
ką̄ṇḍārya . iṃśta bāva mahābāṃja . ātmagūpattä śarāvi : rįdhä
5 pārūṣā khavari . gūra brrahatti śrriṃgą̄ṭakyi . ttūmalakä ṣvī | dā
bāva . papala . sacha bāva baraśīji .

[1] rahta°. [2] °yca? [3] ṣp°. [4] prraśna°. [5] kā⟨kau⟩ṭā?

3 śriṃgaudaka ttāma|lakī payisyā pipalī balā
badarākṣąttra kha⟨r⟩jūrā : vąmāciṣarąn api
phalāna civam āttyąni : kalkaṃ kūrvīna kārṣikā
4 | dhāttra-rasä bīdārīkṣu chąga-mā⟨ṃ⟩sa-rasaṃ payi
kuryā prrasthātmitta ttäna ghrratta prrasthaṃ väpācayita
5 prrasthadha mūdhūną śittä : śakkarādhaṃ | ttūlaṃ ttathā
dvi kārṣakā ttä pattrįlā ttāga tvaka mäkacāna ca :
cūrṇattąnā vįnīyāsmā lehyā-māttrā sadāna
84r1 amṛtta-prrāśa ⟨ghra⟩ttäna nārąnāṃ | amrratta-ghrrattä .
prrāśa kṣīra mā⟨ṃ⟩sa rasā⟨nvita⟩ naṣṭa-nįdra kṣatta kṣīṇi :
dūrbala vyādha kąśittā strī prrasąkva kṛśā pūsā sū
hīnaś ta yi narā :
2 kā|sä hikā . jvarā śvāsä : dāha' tṛṣṇāsū pitta nū⟨tta⟩ :
pūttrada vama-mūcchā hṛna . yaunī mūttrāmayāpahā .
amrratra-prrāśä ghrrattä :
$85r^{3}_{4}$. akṣa va | sidhąva śūṭhī harīttakī vabhīttakī
aśvaga[ga]ṃdhā vacā hiṃgū pįpalī kuṣṭa cįttrakā
ląśūna divadārū cä mūla pauṣkaram iva cä
5 pūrą|ṇä ca ghrratta-prrasthaṃ dadhy ądhakaṃ cattūrgūṇä
pāyiyi mṛitta rāttäna ghrratta śiṣaṃ cäd udara
vįṣma-jvaraṃ aüja ghrraṣṭi ttathā adhāva bhidakį
85v1 adhąga | dvāyivā bhagni viṇḍaś ta yi narā ⟨××⟩
gridhasī upattadrra⟨ka⟩ś ta : ⟨śrau⟩ṇḍī graha'na pīḍattā
pāyiyi māttra yā kṣirau pa⟨×××⟩kāla balā
2 śana vastū-kärmąṇi ma|cyagas tāyū asthi gattānalena
hanyā vātta-vyādhī akṣāttāḍa nauma ghrrattä :
86r1 pūṣkarāhva śaṭhī drākṣā bilatmalą kaṇā pūṭā
2 jīvattī madū⟨ka⟩ : vyāghrrī | ttrāyittī yąṣa vatsakā :

ṣā' pạna arva dvī dvī mācāṃgyi samāṃ kūṭạñä ṣi' kikija arvi
84v1 ạmalai dva sira ịkṣa dva sira tta ha|mīḍa arvi drriṃ ṣaṃga uca jsa
jṣạñạña khu ra va haṣṭa śiṃga harśta . būysīña hvaśā hahvạña dva
ṣaṃga uca jsa jṣạñạña khu ra va tcau śiṃga harśtä : gvīha' rūṃ
2 dva | śiṃga hālai ṣvīda haṣṭa śiga bịśa hamīḍä hạña tciriṃ pāchiṃ
khu paha' hami : aysḍimạña khū drrāṃ hami khu aspā tta būrị hā
3 arva tciriṃ ārdä tharka mījsā . | khajūrā vāmīrā . aviṣa'kyi : mājāttakyi
tcau tcau mācāṃga : ttālīs-pattra sukṣmilạ nāgapūṣpa tvaca
4 lavaṃga ṣi' paṃjsa paṃjsa mācāṃga : śakara tcau si|ra ṣa' hamīḍakä
ārạña nauka rūṃña haṃbrrīhạña ṣi' rūṃ nva pạdaṃji nva ttaraṃ-
darụ diṃ pamākyi jsa khāśạ'ña biśa būri amrratta-prrāśä nạma
5 hva|ṇḍāṃ va ṇi māñaṃdä ṣa' rūṃ biṃdi hā ṣvīda tsạmạña ā vā grrạma
ysūmạ . ca ṣīya na hū yanīdä ttyāṃ hūnä padīmi cū kṣaya āchiṃ
85r1 pijvā gvahi|yi naṣṭausiṃ gisā ba-hauva śara-hauva padīmi āchiṃ
gauda tvạñä strīyạ jsa java-ttaraṃdarä śärä-hauva padīmi : java-
2 ttạraṃdara cviṃ dahauśta niśta | ttyi śara-hauva padīmi cū būījạṣa
ñaśa śira padīmä phāha' hikä ttaviṃ uysnä āphāra ttaudā . ttarä
3 rahta-pitta jiṃda cū pūra na hamārä | padīmị viṃsiṃ ysīra rīysiṃ
pūrạña āchā mūttra-krrịchi tta būra āchā jiṃda

amrratta-pārśa rūṃ raysāyaṃ :

85v2 ṣi' arva biśi vīhīlā masi sadalū ttägara halīr[ā]iṃ vīhīle aśva-
3 gaṃdha | ārä aṃgauṣḍä papala cịttriṃ ysaṃbasti divadāra papala
mūla hūraṣṭi

ṣi' pạna arva dvī dvī mācāṃgyi hālā maṃgāra gvīha' rūṃ dva
4 śiṃga hā|le ñivūtca haṣṭa śiṃgä ṣi' rūṃ nvā diṃna pāchiṃ khu ra va
śūṃma rūṃ harśti : vaṣma jvarä jiṃda ca uśa' vārä ca śāma halīja
5 jsāve cū śi hā|lena aṃga āchaniṃ . ciṃ aủṣta bīriṃda hvạṇḍāṃ
grradasa upattaṃttrakä ṣụñvā brrạhạña vīni khāśạ'ña kālna nva hauvi
86r1 u hays⟨g⟩vā paśạña | mạkṣạñạ jsa āstya bīsā bāva jiṃda biṃna āchā
jiṃda :

akṣattāṇḍa rūṃ :

86r^{2}_{3} hūraṣṭi . ṣala gūra . | sacha bā . nīlạtpaḷa ttạmalaka jīvatta .
mahābāṃja . kạṇḍārya . ttrāyamāṇä : dūrālabha . vatsaka-bīji .
drrāṃgulye . śī caṃdaṃ .

4 ṣā' pa|na arva driṃ driṃ mācāṃga samāṃ kūṭạñä dva śiṃga
hā⟨lai⟩ gvīha' rūṃ tciriṃ u haṣṭi śiṃgä ṣvīda .
5 ṣa' rūṃ pāchiṃ u kālna samāṃ nva ttạraṃdarū diṃ khāśạ'ña . | cū

śvadaṣṭvā śvätta : ttūlyā⟨ṃ⟩śä piṣṭaṃ pakvaṃ ghrratta jayit
ikādaśa-vīdä rūpa prriyaugätt rā⟨ja⟩-yikṣmaṇä :
86r5 v1 || paṭaula ttra | phalāriṣṭaṃ gūṇḍucī dhāvanī vṛśį
sa-karaṃjau ghrrata pakva kūṣṭi-hṛita vajrrakä spṛttä :
86v4 madhū yaṣṭī pąlą-ttrīśattä ttūlajaṃ vapācayitta
5 ta ghrratta-prra | sthaṃ paṃcądabhi caurakasya pąlą-ttrayi
sidha ghrrattaṃ rāja-yikṣma-śauṣa-kṣätta-vanāśanā
akādaśa-vīdha-rūpaṃ prräyaujā rāja-yikṣmaṇā
87r1 siṃdhanaṃ pį | palī bhārgą : : śṛiṃgabhira dūrālabhā
dāṇḍamā⟨ṃ⟩brrāsthaṃ jaṃbrrāsthi bhāgī nāgara ramaṭhūn
āpabitti badara sārdhām adarā dadha-mastūbhi .
2 śa | rasāsī dhąni sṛāvināyā hṛdaṃ śaumyatta
kāsina prrattiśū dhąpavįdyaṃ prrayaujayit :
87r5 v1 drākṣa mājättakyi vīrya kavaśtä phalą̄na | ca :
cūvikākṣāṇḍa pipalya . karkaṭācyā śināvarī
kākauṭyāṃ dāṇḍamaṃ midä jīvaką ṛṣabakāv abhau
2 bīdāryā gaukṣara śauṭhī . palā | rdhaṃ ca samāharit
ghrratta-prrasthaṃ paṃcadīrau dadha-kṣīra cattūrgūnaṃ
śūci-sthą̄na sthani śīlaṃ bhājä⟨na⟩ pārthavas [ta]
3 ttattra śarkąra mūkṣīkä khaḍa | gūṇḍi vamiśratta
aṣṭau maṃdhaṃ bhāvą̄ni . ttā līchä[1] kāką̄līṃ bhaujayit
strī vadyaṃ pūraṣaṃ śaṭhī alpa-śūkrraś ta dūrbalaṃ
4 navya saṃpadyatti | śūkrra varṇä ca balam ava ci
ttijasvanī mahābhāśa mūdra pūrūṣį sādhani
dīrghāyä yūvattī prramas trīśatti carrįtta mįthūnį
5 dyauthanį sta | bda śipani ca malāna na dūrbą̄lā
rasāyänam ida śrįṣṭą valī-palīttanąś⟨a⟩ta

mājättakādaṃ ghrrataṃ ::

88v1 siddhaṃ

2 mahättilaṃ prravakṣyą̄mi . | suryaudayi atti smṛttä :
būhū-rauga-vanāśārthaṃ mūśattąna prrakalpayittä

[1] lịḍhä.

maṃgāra naṣṭausiṃ strịhä' cvä śų̄dasä gų̄nā distä si nį ra jatti rāja-yikṣma ttyi rūṃ na jatti .

pūṣkarādya nąma rūṃ ||

$86v^{1}_{2}$ paṭaula halīriṃ . vīhīlai . ąmalai . ciṃgāṃ ttī|riṃ hya pira . gūlūśa' : kąṇḍārya . vāśaka . pūttī-karaṃja . nahna-mālā[1] karaṃjä .

3 ṣa' pąna arva hālai hąlai sira śtāka . gvīha' rūṃ śau śiṃga | hāle : utca tcau śiṃga ṣa' arva kūṭąñä arva u rūṃ hatca hąña tciriṃ daṃda

4 jṣāñąña khu ra va śūṃma rūṃ harśta thaṃjāña ysūnąña kauṣṭä | u ranīkāṃ biṃda pīsalyąña . pvā ttyāṃ va pīrmāttaṃ

vajrraka nąma rūṃ :

$87r^{2}_{3}$ sadalūṃ . papala . khavari . ttūgarä . dūrāla|bha drrąma ttīmi . aṃbala-vittarasi . aṃbrrāstha jaṃbrrāstha .

4 ṣą' pąna arva śā śā mācāṃga śtāka nauka ārąñä khavarutcana ā vā | ttāṃgarūtcana ā vā barāṃ śījāṃ hīyi raysna bārūtcana ā vā ñävutcana

5 khāśą'ña cu kamiña āchā gvąña ṣkala u panāyāma | u ṇiysūnąma u haysgvā u phāhä' mālaiga biśa jiṃdä ā vā ttyāṃ arvāṃ jsa dhų̄pąna tciriṃ :

87v5 88r1 hauṣka gūra mājāttakyi kākauṭa : ā|tmagūpttį iṃdrrahastä tharka mījsā . papala karkaṭa-śriṃga śarāvi kṣīra-kākauṭa drrąma ttīma

2 mida mahāmida jīvaka rṣabaka[ka] : bīdāra | drāṃgūlye ttūṃgara

ṣa' pąna arva hālai sira śtāka : gvīha' rūṃ dva śiṃga hālai ṣvīdä paṃjsa śiṃga

3 ṣa' rūṃ pāchiṃ khu paha:' hami aysdįmąñä khu strīha ⟨ha⟩|mi tta būra hāna ąna arvi tciriṃ nauka ārdi ysva līka papala . bīdārä

4 ttūṃgarä śakara khajūrā mākṣī . vąmavīrą aviṣa'ka mī|jsāka mājā-ttakyi

ṣį' pąna arva śau śau sira hatsa haṃbrrīhą'ña kālna śau śau sira varāśą'ña strīyau dahauśta śūkrra hūṣvąñi pūrį hami dauṣpyattā

5 jiṃdä | āstyä mījsā ysyąñi ṣaṭhį hami dahauśta hiḍa[2] chavaṃ jsa vasauśta hauva padīmi ttīśa'sta hami mista varāśą'niṃ bviṃysa-

88v1 jsīnī strīyāṃ brrī śī jūṃ yau|ga varāśą'mi jsa 30 jūṃ jsāvi

ṣi' gų̄niṃ biśa būra strįha' hami pastargä ṣa' pīrmāttaṃ tcanāṃ śīyāṃ janāka :

$90v^{2}_{3}$ vaña mįsta kūṃjsavīniṃ rūṃ | hvīdi sūryądaya nąma : bįśtaka pharākāṃ āchāṃ janāka :

4 : aśvagaṃdha dirsa sira : śarāvi paṃjsāsa ssira | tta ysīra kuṭāña

[1] nahta°. [2] hija.

tyaśat palāś ta ga⟨ṃ⟩dhāyās tū dhaṃtta śattāvarī
3 ulūkhayi sphauṭayi | tvā kaṣāyä kvāthayid bhaṣarkaṃ
avattārya kaṣāya ttū kalkāny ittą̄nä vāpayi
sukṣmilā ttagarä kūṣṭaṃ : caṃdana sa-hariṇāka
4 sidhārtha⟨×⟩ | apāmaurgä surasaṃ kṣịmakä gūṇḍä .
pṛyaṃgūm atha [prra] hrrīvira jīvattī jīvaka vacā
kayisthā ⟨ca vayisthā⟩ ca mūra yikṣä mūras tathā
5 śaṭhī pū | ṣkaraṃ mūla ca ⟨ta⟩thāca rajanī-dvayi
gaulamī bhūttanā-kiśī kākijaṇā palakaṃśä .
maṃjiṣṭā dabha⟨dā⟩rū ca näladaṃ jāmaka ghna⟨×⟩
89r1 śrī⟨ṣṭa gaṃdha⟩ vaḍagą̄ni : | sama-bhāgą̄ni pīṣayit
drravyą̄nä ttą̄nä sarvą̄ṇi gau-mūdrri gau-śakṛid rräsäṃ
ttila prrasthä ttū vapacit kṣīriṇä dva-gūṇina ttū
2 susịdham itta va | drriyi plakṣa pivịṣa dhą̄nakä
ttattaubhä maṃdryim attriṇa brrahmaṇā nąma jñeyāṃ :
avattārya ⟨tte⟩na ttila brrahmaṇä pūjayitta tti :
3 ttila[syā]sya gū | ṇā cittayit prravakṣyąma tta⟨thā⟩ śrūṇūi :
bhūtta-yik⟨ṣ⟩a-vakāriṣū . kākanī-ttrāsanīṣū ca .
4 kāṃbhaṇḍi ca [pa]paśaucịṃ va utmā[mā]da-ttamakịṣū | ca
chāyāpasmāra-bhūttịṣū gaṃdha⟨rva⟩-grraha-rākṣasā
nāga grrahāja bhakivā ttilābhya⟨ṃ⟩ga prraśasyatti :
5 yiva gārūṇḍakịṃ maṃttrịṃ : pūttrịṃ | vā mūdrakąs tathā
cakịtsa nyūna śakyątti : ttą̄ḍani dhūpattis tathā
89v1 ịda ttila varaṃ śrrịṣtą : satta grrahi- | vamaukṣaṇa
sarvi grrahāsya śrūṇḍitti vayąrjayitvā grāhā :
asādhyaṃ ttaṃ vajānīyāṃ bhāla bhāvā ca krrīḍatti
2 māttra grrahārivattī | ca ttathāpi mūkhū maṇḍakā
labaudarī labha-ttūjā laba-karṇī prra[ba]labakā
3 laba-sịcajā laba-nāsā labīṇḍaśī [tta] ttathā⟨pi ?⟩ | ci .
ittāharatte cai garbha parauvartta ca dārakā :
ąvajñātvā va bịṣajau ttälarät prradāpayet
4 asya ttela prrabhāvaina ṭirghā | yū janayet sūtta :
virauga caiva vaijñātvaṃ medhāvī prrīya-darśtana
śa:kyi sattū bhūyau tila maṃtta sadhāraṇā
5 kṛttyaṃ karmą | ṇā khākhaurdā dūlakvyā dūrattąnaṃ ca :
cattūrthąką tyattīyi ca sattattä jvari abhya⟨ṃ⟩gina
jvarā hąttī vṛkṣa mittrāśanär yathā śarau-rūja
90r1 śnā | rdha-bhada pārśva śūla thiṃva ca kaṃtṛkä ttraka

kṣa ṣaṃga uca jsa jṣą̄ñą⟨ña⟩ khu ra va śau ṣaṃga haśta tta būra hā
kikija arvi tcirịṃ .
5 sukṣmila ttāṃgarä kūṣṭa śī caṃ | daṃ . hiṃniṃ caṃdaṃ haraṇvä
śaśvāṃ apāmārga ttī . sūrasa . uśį'ri gaula . prrīyaṃga . hīravī .
91r1 jīvatta . jīvakä . āra . kayastha . vayistha gadhä mūrva . ṣala hūra | ṣṭa .
haledra . ysālva . būttanākiśi . kāka jīyä . hā'bä rūṃniṃ : divadāri
svarṇagūttaryāṃga būśauniṃ jāmaki : būha'ni : śrịṣṭiṃ bvī
vaṇḍaṃga :
2 | ṣā' pạna arva driṃ driṃ mācāṃgä samāṃ kūṭą̄ña kūṃjsąvīniṃ
rūṃ dva śiṃga hālai gvīha' ṣvīda dva śiṃga gvīha' ñi dva śiṃga
3 gvīha' saṃna hīvī raysa dva śiṃga gvīha' bīysmä | dva śiṃgä tta
būra hā kiṣa' cū hą̄ña tcirịṃ ṣį' rūṃ mạṇḍala nva pạdajä pāchiṃ
brraṃmanāṃ vī jsāṃ paṃjsa tci paṃjsi suttra hvą̄ñiṃ vara ṣṭāna cū
ttyi rūṃ bväjsi .
4 | tta ttā pvīryau khu paha' hami śā mācāṃga būha'ni ṣą̄'ña ttaña
rūṃña haṃbrrīhą̄ña būvyāṃ jsa u yikṣyāṃ jsa paśāva āchā rāṃdāṃ
5 hīvī harīysna paśā | va kūṃbhaṇḍāṃ u paśą̄cāṃ jsa paśāva utpādā[1]
apasmārä cū ṣi chāyä grraha' āstaṃ aharīna ṣikāna graha ttyi rūṃ
91v1 makṣą̄mi jsa aharīna jā | ri tta khu gą̄ḍūṇḍāna[2] maṃdrä paṃca-
sūttrį āstaṃna sūttrāṃ jsa rakṣa' maudrri khviṃ ttyāṃ jsa krra na
2 tcāraṇa hamāvi padvą̄mi jsa u dvyą̄mi u ha[r]thrrają̄mi āstaṃna | ttyāṃ
hīyi hauva pahīsī ttyi rūṃ mąkṣą̄mi jsa harbrriśä grrahaja āchā jāri
cū tta hauda baysāṃjı cū jsahira ą̄na ṣika graysą̄ñāri khū ysā hami
3 ttī | pharāka āchā bịḍa grahaja ttyi rūṃ makṣą̄mi jsa biśa jāri tta būri
baysāṃji cū jsahira ą̄na ṣika grraysą̄ñāri . laṃbaudara . baṃba[3]-.

[1] udmādä. [2] garūṇḍāna. [3] lamba°.

bhagni suyi cāttyi vātta śūlana śvayithauršiṣū
ttathā va pūṇḍa-raugaṇā halīmaki grṛdhāsī ca
2 ⟨ ⟩ ttilam i|ttatta prrayaujayit
śauṣä śvāsa kāsa cakṣi' ⟨×⟩ya gūlma vyapauhyątti
dhūpatti dhūpanāyi ca cūrṇattaṃ ttravidārthā
3 āthava rį maṃttra variṃ pīṇḍattā yiṃca mąna|vā
iṣąm īdaṃ ca kiṃ vi ttįlasyaryądayi nṛṇā
sarva rau⟨gi⟩ṣū dhāttavyam anṛāgam aparājätta
4 kṣīyi drayāṇā pūsąnā rįrttāṃ pahätta cāttą|sā
dīrga raugā⟨r⟩ttaṃ . bhūttąnāṃ [nä] närmāsānāṃ vaśiṣatta
ayi ttila vara śrrīmā balāṭūiṣū m ūpakrrami
5 pūryaudayinä vihyątta bala-varṇa-prra|dau nṛṇā
mauhanaṃ sarva-bhūttąnāṃ chāyāpasmāra ja bhani :
arnanaṣū ttriṇavaṣä sapttābhi pūttraka kṛitvā
90v1 pāka laikaṭāhakiṃ prra|kṣipttąvya au dārhaṃ ttrįlyąkṣä sphauṭanä
hūṃ phaṭ aum
namaḥ kapālana sūmūkhi krriṣṇa divyi hälīmi malī caccha gaccha
2 kāpālaka | mūka śastra viṣa pąnīyi sattyanūtta rāla aųma svāhā :
sūryaudaya nauma ttįla samāpta :
92r^{4}_{5} syąnākä : agnamaṃtha ca bilva mūlaṃ | ca pāṭalā
kaśmīrī sālaparṇīś ta . prraśnaparṇī nadignakā :
iraṇḍa mūla brrahattī palā⟨ṃ⟩śa yaujayi bhaṣakä
92v1 dva ṣalā⟨ṃ⟩śā balā rāsttā gau|kṣaraś ta nūtta sami
cattūra drąṇābhasā pāva cattūra bāga vaśiṣatta
ttila prrastha payis tūlyāt ttina kalya prravāpayit
2 hapūṣā ttraphalā śū|ṭī krrįṣṇā sukṣmilā grrathakäṃ
dāḍāma marāca vahni cavya cįttrakä-jīrakau
gūṇḍaṃ sīpyąkam akṣā⟨ṃ⟩śiṃ sįdha kṣīriṇa rauga-nūt
3 yaunī-dauṣa-haraṃ ba|lya . gūlmārgau cūrda-nāśanä
[kā]kāsa-śvāsä-haraṃ ciṃvą . vastū-śūla-viśūdhani :
pṛjāgarą hatta pū⟨ṃ⟩saṃ mūttra-kṛchiṃ ca pūjatta 5
4 | sarva-vātta-vikāraṇ rra grāṇī sthąna samāśvatta
jayi ajetta nāmā yi bharadvāje-prrakāśatta ttaila :
93v1 : ajagaṃdhāgnaṃ mṛįdvīkau śarkarā tṛphalāmrrattā
vyāghrra śauṣaṃ viṇḍaṃgą⟨ni⟩ ttrapūsirvāram iva ca

4 I bhūja laṃbakarṇa . prralaṃbakä labasphīja : labanāsä laṃbakyiśa . haṃdara miṃchą̄ñāri haṃdara vā haṃtsa āchāṃ jsa ysyą̄ñāri .
5 I ttyi rūṃ makṣą̄mi jsa ṣīka drų̄nä byihī'da u bviṃysa-jsīnä . bvą̄maya hamārä dyina śįka : najsą̄mą tcāraṇa hamāri khu ttyi rūṃ mąkṣą̄mi
92r1 jsa ṣīkau I biṃda bīśų̄ña grrahaja āchā paśä yanīdä hamya ṣṭą̄naṃ jsa ją̄ri :

tta khu cārthiṃ kasiṃ : ttrattīyikä . śa'-haḍāṃjsū panūḍą̄ṃjsī
2 mąkṣą̄mi jsa [ttaviṃ] I ttaviṃ āstaṃnaṃ jsa bįśa āchā ją̄ri : cū būri spa hamya tcahausi tcaura āchā biśa jārį . khu ṣa' rūṃ paha' hami
3 ttyi maṃdrana 7 jų̄na māṃga ṣą̄'ña . I u hā haṃbrrīhą̄ña :

aum dāphä ttrįlāaikyi sphauṭani hūṃ phaṭ
aumma nama kāpālani sūmūkhi kṛịṣṇä divya halīma caccha
4 gaccha kā I pāla : amakaṃ śastra viṣa pą̄nīyi satpanuttarāla
aumma svāhā .

sūryaudaya ną̄ma rūṃ dāśi :

92v_5^4 syaunākä aśnamatha[1] [be] I bila-mūla pāṭala kaśmīrya mūla . sālaparṇä . prraśnaparṇä brrahatta kąṇḍārya īraṃdä bāva
93r1 ṣā' pąna arva śau śau sira śtāka sacha bā laṃgara bā . I drrāṃgūlyai : tta hamaṃga dva dva sira śtāka . tcą̄ ṣaṃga uca jsa jṣą̄ñą̄ñä khu ra va śau ṣaṃga harśta ṣā' kaṣā' pisūją̄ña hāña tcirā dva śiṃga hālai hā
2 kūṃjsavīniṃ rūṃ tcįriṃ u dva ⟨śiṃ⟩Igä hālai gvīha' ṣvīda : tta būra hā nauka ārda kikaja arvi tciriṃ .

hapūṣi halīriṃ vīhīlai ą̄malai ttāṃgarä papala sūṣmila drą̄ma ttīma
3 mīriṃjsya cįttriṃ bądarä aù I ṣiṃ gūla sąnā .

ṣā' pąna arva dvī dvī mācāṃgyä hālā ṣa' rūṃ ṣvīdana u ttyi kaṣi' jsa pāchiṃ tta būra āchā jiṃda : pūrāṃ vasūjä u hauva padīmi :
4 I gą̄ma arja phāha' ji⟨ṃda⟩ : bą̄ma uysna āphāra jiṃda phįysgą̄ña vīnāiṃ vasūjāka pūrāṃ hūrākä dahauśta padīmāka ysūṣṭa ṣṭi śalī-
5 ṣą̄majsa prra I mīha' vī mūttra krrichi krriṃga rūya vīni ṣų̄ñvā vīni brrąhą̄ñä harbī⟨śāṃ⟩ biṃnāṃ āchāṃ vī pūrą̄ña āchāṃ pīraurāka pīrmāttaṃ

93v1 aji⟨tta⟩ nąma rūṃ bharatvā I ja raṣa'yina bīraṣṭä :
93v_3^2 kharaśpa I ttī cittri gūra śakari halīriṃ ą̄malai gūlūśa' kąṇḍārya papala ttūṃgara mīriṃjsya vīṇḍäga : ttrūysāṃ byārāṃ ysąraṃjsa . ysąraṃjsa ttī gū⟨la⟩
4 ⟨ṣa'⟩ I pąna arva tcau tcau mācāṃga kūjsavīniṃ rūṃ dva śiṃgä

[1] agna°.

2 kusābhaṃ cį tta bījaṃ ⟨ca⟩ | gūṇḍaṃ dvį-gūṇittaṃ payi
prrathaką akṣa prrayūttīva ttįlai prrastha vapācayit
śarkarā aśmarī krrichā yi śakṛṣūthā kharaśpādya ttila : ||
94r1 : aśvagaṃdā ttūlādhāṃbū ttilaṃ prrastha prrayaujayit
mā⟨ṃ⟩sī tvaga patträ maṃjįṣṭā : drravattī surasā jaṭā
2 balā dārā stharā | yaṣṭī rāsnilā pūṣkara vacā :
śvadaṣṭrrā kuṣṭa pūttīkī śattāhvā sa-pūnarṇavā
vyāghrrī ⟨u⟩śīra payasyāś [āś] tä piṣṭa rąkṣāśa kiṃśpharttaṃ
3 sarvā | nala-gąda-dhvasā cattūrthā sa⟨m⟩prriyaujayittā :
aśvagadyāda tila :
$94v^{2}_{3}$ || phalą-ttraka ga⟨ṃ⟩dha prrī | yādgabhaś ta
nīlāpalasyā madhū piṣṭikāś tä
kālaiyäkaś tä pūnarṇavą ca
kųṇḍąnasāraṃ nari māstū ttūrthā
4 balātta⟨ka⟩-bhṛga | rajīś ta . mā⟨ṃ⟩sī
sa-hasta-daṃttīm atha ttūbūrąṇi
draśīra ṣpṛkā saha nī⟨laka⟩ś ta
karpāsą maj⟨j⟩ā ttila pūṣpa lākṣā'
5 prrapąṇḍarīka : ca rasā⟨ṃ⟩jana [tta] | ś ta
kījalka sauvīra sa⟨mudra⟩-bhānā
samąna kṛitvā⟨r⟩dhāpalena ttīṣāṃ :
ttįlai pacitta krįṣṇā ttālasyą prrastha
dhāttīra sāmāḍhakam ūktam itta
95r1 svaki śātta ttattā | draṣṇā vāśauryamāṇā
ttįlaṃ pącitta jārā-palatta-nāśanā .
kiśa-rauhaṇā ttila ||
95r5 śratta rāsnā kaṣāyinā kalka śatta palai tmattina
95v1 ttila prrasthaṃ | vapakvavyā ; kṣīriṇā dvi gūṇina ttyā
pā⟨r⟩śvā pṛiṣṭa rrūjāṃ yautti udarautmāda-raugūṇāṃ :
2 cṛṭa-ttālai-śauṣa [pa]- dāha bhrramān api : pi⟨tta⟩-gūlmārśā | sā
pathyā śūkṛ-dauṣa-ha : rāsnādām āna vįdyāttā
rahta-gūlma navāsāna rāsnādyam anavāsanaka ttila ||
95v5 kuṣṭa mūstaṃ harįdrri dvi sįdhava mąracā ala
manā.śalā kāsīsa rasāṃjanā ttūrtha niṃba cā .
96r1 vįśālā arka käpīlyā viṇḍaṃgā sārṭapa | gva⟨×⟩
inātta sami kṛtvā ttilaṃ ttālasya vipācayittā
cattūrgūṇā gavā mądrriṃ . krrami kuṣṭa vacarcakā[ka]
2 pāma-carma-dala ttiṃvā | sarva-kuṣa-vanāśtām
abhya⟨ṃ⟩janaka ttįlai :

ṣvīda haṣṭa śiṃgä rūṃ ṣvīda hąña tciriṃ arva pā hąña tciri rūṃ
pāchiṃ kālai varāśą'ñä
5 śakkarya[1] ṣā' cū | va pūraṣāṃdrya drąma saṃgaka hamāri khu
kapāysa ttī u aśmarya mūttra . cū va utca ñasya hami pūrda carą
94r1 māñaṃdų śakrra aysūrāṃ jsa kharaśpādya | rūṃ samāsyi :
94r3 || aśvagaṃdha sparibista sira driṃ ṣaṃga uca jsa jṣąñą⟨ña⟩ khu
4 ra | va śau ṣaṃga harśta . tta būra hā kikaja arvi tciriṃ ttāgūttāṃ
būśąni tvaca ttālīspatta dravattä sūrasa ttauma⟨la⟩ka sacha bāva
5 divadāra sā | laparṇa mahābāṃjä laṃgara bāva sūṣmila : hūraṣṭä āra
drāṃgūlyai kūṣṭä pūttī-karaṃjä śattapūṣpä pūnarṇavä kaṇḍāryä
94v1 uśī'rä payi | sa
ṣi' pąna arva dvī dvī mācāṃga hālā śtāka vasvi kāṃjsavīniṃ rūṃ
dva śiṃga hālai ṣvīda dva śiṃga ṣa' haṃ bāḍa pāchiṃ ṣi' rūṃ tcau
2 pacaḍa varā | śąña hviriṃ haysg⟨v⟩ā tciriṃ makṣąña u anavāysąnaṃ
jsa tcirā harbīśāṃ biṃnāṃ āchāṃ natcīphākä
aśvagaṃdhādä rūṃ :
95r_2^1 || halīriṃ vīhīlai ąmalai gaṃdha prrīyaṃgä nīląktapala [ma] |
mahābāṇjä kālīyaka pū⟨na⟩rṇavi . kąṇḍąnasāra būha'nä mūḍā-
saṃga . bhalāttäka bhyägarajä ttāgūttāṃ būśąniṃ hasta-daṃdiṃ
3 ttaṃbīra uśī'ra | sparakä nīlai kapāysa ttī kuṃjsą dhāttakī-pūṣpa :
lākṣä prrapūṇḍārī . cūvaṃ vįysä khīysara . sauvīraṃja : samūdra phāna :
4 ṣa' pąna a | rva dvī dvī mācāṃga śtāka : haryāsa kāṃjsavī⟨nai⟩
rūṃ dva śiṃga hālai . driṃ sira ąmalai drriṃ ṣaṃga uca jsa : pāchiṃ
5 khu ra va śau ṣaṃga harśta ṣa' rūṃ pāchiṃ śįrkaṃ jsa | hīryāsa
tcaṃjsa hami śīyaṃ jsa jāri
makṣūnaja ysarūña janāka rūṃ ||
95v_3^2 ssa sira laṃgara bā jṣąñą | ña kṣa ṣaṃga utca tcirā kviysvā vīni
brrahaña pūrąñä dūtāra āchiṃ utmādä ttarä cviṃ phaṃni hūṣḍi
4 apasmāra ttaudä cū avī hana | śīdä gisā pi'ttä gąma įrja śūkrrä hīyi
gaṃjsį ttyāṃ pīraurāka pīrmāttä pūrąñä hūjīniṃ gūmä jīyi
rāsnāda nąmä ⟨rūṃ⟩ :
96r2 kauṣṭä būhani ysālva haledrrä sadalū śīya mīriṃjsya ysariṃ ysīrā
3 sūkṣmila ysamyä hau | ṣṭa cūvaṃ mūḍāsaṃgä niṃbapatträ viśāla
arka kṣīra kaṃpīle vaṇḍaṃga ysīḍiṃ śaśvāṃ sarjärasä
4 ṣa' pąna arva dvī dvī [mā] | mācāṃga śtāka kāṃjsavīniṃ rūṃ 4
śiṃga gvīha bīysmä jsa pāchiṃ
ṣa' rūṃ hatca pīryau jsa kuṣṭa jida vacatcika pāma carma dala
5 | āstaṃna kuṣṭa harbįśa jiṃda :

[1] tk?

96r5 jīvattī madhūkaṃ mịda: pịpalī madana vacā
96v1 balā srānā śarīṣaṃ bilva śattahvā sa-hari|drayi .
ittạnä sama-bhāgạnä ttila kṣīraṃ samaṃ ttatta
anūvāsanakaṃ ttilaṃ nasta-vyādha-nạsudänaṃ :

jīvattādyä ttile:

96v4 rāsnā ridha bal[v]ā bilva śatta pūṣpi śarśāvarī
pịpalī madhūkaṃ midhaṃ caṃdanaṃ mạdana . vacā .
5 ittạni drravya sa⟨ṃ⟩bhṛttyä akṣa-māttra samaṃ | ttattä .
yikiṃ ttila sarpibhyāṃ prrastha kṣīra cattūrgūṇä
anavāsanīka śrṛiṣṭä ạtta vāttānalemana [lạmana]
vātta-pitta-⟨vi⟩kāriṣū . kạṭī pṛiṣṭa rrūjāpahä
97r1 | jīrṇaṃ jvaraṃ śarä[ttä] śūla gūlmābhyā vasti-śūla-jat
arśa-vikāram ānāhi vasta-mạna-vaśaudhanä

rāsnādya ttịlaṃ ||

$97r^{4}_{5}$: kuṣṭa | śūṭhī vacā dārū . śattā⟨hva⟩ häṃgū sidhaviṃ :
vasta-mūttra śṛttä ttịlaṃ pūraṇä śṛvajārtti-jittä ||
97v2 lava⟨ṃ⟩gaṃ karpūra tvạg ilā ca ⟨caṃḍa⟩nä kuṣṭāmaṃ
gaṃdha prrayaṃga pịpalī kastūra mā⟨ṃ⟩sī agarä
sattạhvayi sparka natta ttịla ghrrattä vapācayittä .
3 śanāhvā śāka dva bätta ttrabhāgäka sị|dha sayā
kṣīraṃ cattūrgūṇaṃ saṃä nāsyāt ⟨××××××⟩
paräca.kṣūṣābhya karṇa śūlā⟨r⟩ttām adhā-bhạdaka : .
97v5 98r1 || kṣāra-|mūlakaṃ śūṭhīnāṃ śarttạhvā hiṃgū sidhaviṃ
śūdbha[1] cattūrgūṇaṃ kyatvā kabhis tịla vapācayit
bạdaryä karṇa-śūlaṃ ca pūṇasthāva ca karṇayit
2 krramaś ta⟨va⟩ vanāśạ|na ttịlasyāsya prrapūr⟨a⟩ṇä :
$98r^{3}_{4}$ || kṣāra-mūlaka-maṇḍūkä svarjī hiṃ|gū sa-nāgarä
śatti-pūṣpa vacā kuṣṭa dā[tt]ra śriga rasā⟨ṃ⟩jana .
sauva⟨r⟩tcala yava-kṣāra sarjakạ bịḍā siṃdhaviṃ :
bhūrja-grratha vastaṃ madhū śūdbha[1] ⟨mūla⟩ cättūgūṇä
5 | māttalāṃ⟨ga⟩-rasaś tiṃva kaṭalyā rasaṃ iva ca
ttịlam ittata pakvavya karṇä-śūlāpahaṃ paraṃ

[1] śūkta.

96v2 || jīvatta mahābāṃjä mida mahāmidä papala madana-phala āra
sacha bāva laṃgara bāva kākauṭä śattapūṣpi bilva ysālva halaidra
3 | ṣa' pąna arvä dvī dvī mācāṃga śtāka : kāṃjsavīnai rūṃ śau
śiṃgä ṣvīda tcau śiṃga
ṣi' rūṃ pāchiṃ anavāysanaṃ jsa tcirä phiysgąña āchā jiṃda :
$97r^{1}_{2}$ || lagara bā : ridha sacha bāva bi|la śattapūṣpä śarävi papala
mahābāṃjä : mida mahāmidä caṃdä āra
ṣä' pąna arva drriṃ drriṃ mācāṃga śtāka kuṃjsavīniṃ rūṃ śau
3 śiṃga gvīhä' rūṃ śau śiṃga ṣvīda | 8 śiṃga rūṃ pāchiṃ anavāysąnaṃ
jsa tcirä biva va pīrmāttaṃ nva ṇ̨imiysa vī śtāka biṃnā u pīttanāṃ
4 āchāṃ u brrąhąña vīnāṃ janāka maṃgā|ra ttaviṃ u kamäña vīni u
gąma u phiys⟨g⟩ąña vīni arjä uca ąnāhä kaśtä ttyāṃ būri āchāṃ
jänākä u pūrāṃ vasuji :
97^{r5}_{v1} kuṣṭä ttagärä ārä divadārä [rä] śattapūṣpi aṃ|gauṣḍa : sadalū
ṣa' pąna arva dvī mācāṃga śtāka . kuṃjsavīniṃ rūṃ häle śiṃga
būysīña bīysma dva śiṃga ṣa' rūṃ pāchiṃ gvąña paśąña gvąña vīna
jiṃda ||
97v3 || lavaṃgä kapūrä tvacä sukṣmila caṃdaṃ kurkāṃ prrīyaṃgä
4 [pa] | papala yausa ttāgūttāṃ būśąniṃ śakärä sparka ttagarä
⟨ṣa'⟩ pąna arva śā śā mācāṃga ś⟨t⟩āka kuṃjsavīniṃ rūṃ dva kaba
5 gvīha rūṃ dva kaba bāva sakala dva sira kṣa sira uca | jsa jṣąñąña
khu ra va śau śiga harśta maṇḍī ṣvīdana ṣi' rūṃ haysgvā paśąña ṣa'
rūṃ pīrmāttaṃ tcįmajāṃ āchāṃ va brrausira vīna jiṃda u gvaña
ttīmīri ardhāvabhidakä jiṃda ||
98r2 ttrahāṃ hīvī kṣārä ttūgara [ra] śattapūṣpi aṃgauṣḍi sadalūṃ
ṣā' drriṃ mācāṃga kuṃjsavīniṃ rūṃ myąña häle śiṃga mau
sautta śau śiṃga
3 ṣa' rūṃ pāchiṃ | gvąña paśąña cū kārąña gvąña vīni gvąña pvąma
u ṇäysūnąma u pīra bįsa jiṃdi gūvaṃ jsa bīrąñi ||
98v1 || hauṣkyāṃ ttrahau hīvī kṣārä hauṣka khuysiṃ svajaka kṣārä
2 aṃgauṣḍi ttūṃgara śattapūṣpi āra kuṣṭa divadārä śīya mi|riṃjsya
cūvaṃ spajū yava-kṣārä . sarjärasa bīdalū sadalūā brrāṃja hīya
grrathi vīṇḍagä būha'ni
ṣa' pąna arva śā śā mācāṃga śtāka kuṃjsavīniṃ rūṃ hālai
3 | śiṃgä mau sautta hālai śiṃga vālaiga raysa hīvī raysa hālai śiṃga
ttrahāṃ hīvī raysa hālai śiṃga
4 ṣa' rūṃ pāchiṃ papiṃśā' hauda kani hauda kani | gvąña paśąña
gvąña vīnāṃ janāka pīrmāttaṃ kāryi gva prrahāji gvąña ṣa'nā rāhä

bādharyaṃ karṇa-nādaś ta pūyä-srrāvaś ta dārụ̄ṇād
98v1 asya ttịlasya krra | mayi karṇäyau⟨×⟩ śṛttāpạhaṃ ||
98v5 || mūlaki-rasa prrastha ttila prrasthaṃ prasādhattä
dady abrra ką̄caka kṣīrar āḍhakāṃśa vącą̄ balā
rāsnā-riṣkara-viśvāś ta śigrū siṃdäva gą̄kṣarā .
99r1 | kalkaṃ kyätvā ca pịpalyaṃ kṛcha-vānārtta-nāśanä ||

99r5 || ttịlaṃ prrastha payis tūlya śvadaṣṭrrā svara sādhakiṃ :
99v1 gūṇḍä | sya śṛgabhirasya prratha-mą̄ṇī śratta pavittä
kṣīrāṃ nūtta[tta] va riktaś ta khādi viśva-gūṇḍānvattä[tti]
2 jīrṇä-kṣīranä bhū sarvās tīttṛ-vāttāgadā | yarjit

$99v^{3}_{4}$ || [ca]rā | snā cịttrakaṃ mūlą̄ni pịpa[pa]lī viṣva bhịṣajä
śą̄ṭhī pūṣkara mūla cä sarpar ita vapācayitta
5 hasta-pāda-gattā vātta kạṭī-pṛṣṭa- | uśrṛttāyą̄ ca
layāva khubjāś ta . sarvam inäna sādhayi ||

100r2 || vyāghrrī daṃttī vacā śrịgrū surasā vyāṣaṃ siṃdhava
pācananā⟨r⟩dhana ttila pū⟨ti⟩nasāgada harittä ||

4 ttrākṣās tạmalakī midā . papälī-mūla nāgarī .
cą̄malakī gratta siṃdhī hatta jīhva dvaki sūkhī ||

100^{r5}_{v1} sarpa⟨pa⟩ | higū kuṣṭaṃ ca : laśụ̄ṇą siṃdhava vacā :
nīla⟨ka⟩ vastri-mūttriṇä : hayasyą cä śakrrịtta-rasi
ttä sarpa-dvathina[1] vịdyā yikṣa-tarpaṇäm ūtta⟨maṃ⟩

[1] kv-.

jiṃda u ysū u ysīca utca khu va gvaña pīra hamāri ttyi rūṃ jsa
jāri ||

99r1 || hauṣkyi ttrahi śau thaṃga dvārabista śiṃga uca jsa jṣą̄ną̄ña khu
2 ra va dva śiṃga harśtä ñi dva śiṃgä drrą|māṃ hīvī āhvariṃ raysa
dva śiṃgä baraśīji śą̄ śiṃga rīysū hālai śiṃga kṣa śiṃga uca jsa śịra
3 pāchiṃ khu ra va dva śiṃga harśta āysmāstą̄ña bagalaña pyą|ną̄ñä
khu māyi ṣị' kāṃjä pātca kṣa śiṃga ṣvīda dva śiṃga :

āra sacha bāva laṃgara bāva hūraṣṭä ttūṃgara cittriṃ śīya
4 mīriṃjsya sada|lū drrāṃgūlyai papala

⟨ṣa'⟩ pą̄na arva dvī dvī mācāṃgyi śtākä kuṃjsą̄vīniṃ rūṃ dva
śiṃga haṃ bāḍāṃ ttyāṃ hīrpāṃ[1] jsa rūṃ pāchiṃ pamākyi jsa karavā
5 | khāśą̄'ña ca būra ttą̄raṃdara biṃda ttrịkṣa vīna ỉdi jsahira aṃgvā
bịśa jāri ||

99v2 kuṃjsavīniṃ rūṃ dva śiṃga hālai drrāṃgūlyai dvāssa sira
dvāradịrsa śiṃga uca jsa j⟨ṣ⟩ą̄ñą̄ña khu ra va haṣṭa śiga harśta .
ttūṃgara dva sirä

3. ṣa' rūṃ | pāchiṃ khāśą̄ñä ttrịkṣa biṃna vīna jiṃda khviṃ kṣamī
sa khu vrrī cāyūṃ ṣvīdaniṃ gūlya khāśą̄'ña . ttūṃgara pātca tta
āchā jiṃda ||

99v5 || laṃgara bā cịttri papala papala mūla ttāṃgara ṣala hūraṣṭa

100r1 ṣa' pą̄na arva tcau tcau [ysä] | mācāṃga śtāka gvīha rūṃ śau
śiṃga ṣvīda tcau śiṃga .

ṣa' rūṃ pāchiṃ varāśą̄'ñä ca dastvā u pā vīra tsūka bāva ỉ u
pūrāña brrą̄hą̄ña hūrāvvā aharīna biva ||

$100r^{2}_{3}$ || ką̄ṇḍārya dattä āra śīya mīriṃjsya : surasa : [pa]pa|pala[2]
ttāṃgari mīrijsya sadalū

ṣa' pą̄na arva drriṃ drriṃ mācāṃg⟨a ś⟩tāka kāṃjsavīniṃ rūṃ
hālai śiṃgi

4 ṣi' rūṃ pāchiṃ haysgvā paśą̄ña u vaśų̄'na bauśa | jiṃdä ||

$100r^{4}_{5}$ || gūra ttą̄malakä mida mahā|midä papala mūla ttāṃgara ą̄malai

ṣi' pą̄na arva tcau tcau mācāṃga śtāka : gvīha' rūṃ śau śiga ṣvīda
śau ṣaṃga ṣa' rūṃ pāchiṃ maṃgāra ttaviṃ jiṃdä ||

$100v^{2}_{3}$ || ysịḍiṃ śaśvāṃ aṃgauṣḍi kuṣṭa ysaṃbastä sa|dhalūṃ āra
rų̄sthara :

ṣā' pą̄na arva drriṃ drriṃ mācāṃga śtāka gvīha' rū śau śiṃga
4 cą̄kalīña bīysma dva śiṃga [pyaśa] aśa hīvī saṃna | hīva raysä

ṣi' rūṃ pāchä yakṣa-ttarpą̄na ną̄ma apasmāra graha āstaṃna

[1] ryāṃ. [2] la *ex* pa.

2 apasmā|ra-jūrautmādä : skaṃdhāyäś ta mahābalā
vịrakąma grahīttasya sattäm ittäna sādhayit ||
100v5 || rāsnā balātą ⟨gau⟩kṣara sidhava śrąttrūkā vacā
101r1 [cị] | cittrakaṃ śrägavira cä : pịpalį gaja-vipalī
bhalāttakā prrattaväṣā garbhinā ca vapācayit :
2 tilam ittaś ta śasyatti mūlakąnā | sarä hąttí
urū-skaṃbhi : kaṭī grāhā gradhasmavanaṃttraki
baśtācaṃ labha-garbha⟨×⟩ . pāttyāna cāpakarṣitti
3 vasta-kuṇḍalaṃ parvaṇā staṃbha | näprrasana ttathā
hānat mūlaka-ttiląsya rągānā ca nayichattä ||
101v2 || viśvąṣādha cịttrakaṃ mūląm ūgrä .
cavyā jamauda cä ditadārūr
itti ghrrattaṃ ttịlą sūsịdhaṃ arśą
sarvąṇä raugāṇä nahąttä śīghrraṃ ||
101v4 dvi-pa⟨ṃ⟩camūla vapącitta kaṣāya :
daṃttī vaṇḍaṃgā ttraphalās trabhąṇḍī :
5 suthā-payau nīla|na śaṃkha-pūṣpī :
pyąna sāttalā māgadhakau sa-mūla ||
r ittąni samąnätta [ku]kudā :
irąṇḍä-ttila vapącättä vajrrä :
102r1 ąnāha [baṃdha] varcä nyaka pakṣa|yąna
yaunī uirū-skä⟨ṃ⟩bhäm athānąlāsyaga
ma⟨j⟩jättąs tāyū gattäna lavą⟨×⟩ :
kṣīriṇa pita kaṇajä sa-mūtträ :
u-dau⟨ṣa⟩jä syāt traphala-rasina
2 saṃsargają chą|ga-rasäna dadyāttä
ịttāśna raugāsu būśtā yauthauktä :
svä⟨na⟩ prayaugäna ca raṇa hatti
irąṇḍa-ttila prravarakau bhārgau
3 vadha rājä-rasị mahā-irąṇḍa-|ttila :
102v5 || syātt vaṃcamūlaṃ ttraphalārdra dārų
[k]iraṇḍa mūlaṃ ttravittą nakuṃbhā
sudā-payau sāttalaṃ māgada cą
103r1 kaṃpīlya maṃ|jūṣtä samąna kṛtvā
irąṇḍa-ttila payisā⟨r⟩dha pācatt
aśītta vätt[ak]au kapha vīśanā ca
śrauṇā sa-miṇḍyaḍhyam atha ikabāhū
2 prrīhą|yi gūlmā vänāśanaṃ ca ||

5 graha jiṃda : ttavi unmāda skaṃda grrahä pharā | ka hauvana grrahaja āchā cịra kāmanī grraha āstaṃna grraha jiṃda ||

101r^{3}_{4} || laṃgara bāva drrāṃgūlye sadalū śīya | mīriṃjsya āra cịttriṃ ttāṃgara papala hasta papala bhalāttakyi prravaṣi'

5 ṣą' pąna arva dvī dvī mācāṃgä kāṃjsa | vīniṃ rūṃ dva śiṃgä hauṣkyi ttrahi dvāsä sira tcaurabịsta śiṃga uca jsa jṣąñąñä khu ra va haṣṭa śiṃga harśtä

101v1 ṣa' rūṃ pāchiṃ kālna varāśą'ña urūskabha ṣūña rā | hä grṛdhasä ca nāṣṭa aṃga rūyi cū maṇḍyi pūra na hami vasta kąṇḍala hamarvā strīsąma ttī ṇiysūnąma ṣa' mūlakā-ttịla nąma tta būra āchā jiṃdä ||

101v^{2}_{3} || ttūṃgara | cịttriṃ papala mūla bądarä kharaśpa ttī divadārä

ṣa' pąna arva tcau tcau mācāṃgä śtāka gvīhä' rūṃ hāle śiṃgä kuṃjsąvīniṃ rūṃ hālai śiṃga

4 ṣa' rūṃ pā | chiṃ varāśą'ña harbiśa arja paurda upadrava ||

102r3 bila-mūlą agnamathä syąnāką pāṭala kaśmīrya mūla . sālaparṇä prraśtaparṇä[1] brrahattä kąṇḍārya drāṃgūlye

4 ṣą' pąna arva | śau śau sira ś⟨t⟩āka drriṃ ṣaṃga uca jsa jṣąñąña khu ra va haṣṭa śiṃga harśta ttī hā dva śiṃga īraṃdīniṃ rūṃ tciriṃ u dva śiṃga ṣvīda

5 ṣa' būra kikaja ā | rda nauka arva dāttī vaṇḍaṃgä halīriṃ vīhīlai ąmale ttraula sudā-kṣīra nīlai śaṃkha-pūṣpi sāttala papala

⟨ṣa'⟩ pąna arva drriṃ drriṃ mācāṃga

102v1 ṣi' rūṃ | tta būra āchā jiṃda ąnāha' prrahāji gūmą dūvarä jidä narịyi haśa . prramīhä' ysira rāhä' brrąhąña rāha': ṣūña rāha'

2 khajsā gṛ | dhasa cū khāysąniṃ styūda cū parīysma kaśti pakvāhaka[2] . maṇḍyāṃ pūrąña āchā : urūskabhä : ca biṃna hūña āphīḍä mījsāya

3 | tsūmaṃca bāva āstyä pīttanāṃ āchāṃ vī ṣvīdana khāśą'[śą']ña

4 śalīṣąmajsāṃ vīra gvīhyi bīysma jsa ca drrayāṃ | dūṣāṃ' jsa hamya āchā ttyāṃ va ttraphala hīyi kaṣi' jsa biṃnāṃ āchāṃ vī būysīñä gūśta hīvī raysna khāśą'ña ||

103r2 || sālaparṇä prraśnaparṇä brrahatta kąṇḍārya drrāṃgūlye halīriṃ

3 vīhīlai ąmalai dävadārä īraṃdä bā . ttrau | la dätta sūdā-kṣīrä sāttala papala kaṃpīlai rūṃniṃ

ṣā' pąna arva drriṃ drriṃ mācāṃga śtāka īraṃdīniṃ rūṃ śau

4 śiṃga ṣvīdä tcau śiṃga ṣa' rūṃ | pāchiṃ khāśą'ña dvī dvī drriṃ drriṃ prrūya haṣṭä biṃna āchā jiṃda u bịsta śalīṣąmajsa ṣūñvā vīni

5 pūraṣidrriṃ biṃda īkabāha'kä jä | da ṣpiṃjiṃ jara vasūji gąma jiṃdä ||

[1] prraśna°. [2] pakṣā°.

103r5 phalą-ttrakä adhā-kṣīrī tṛvanāptä sama⟨ṃ⟩ bhavittä
103v1 iṛąṇḍä-ttila vapācittä : vātta-śauṇī | rma-vāraṇä ||

103v$^{2}_{3}$ || | ttraphalā paṃcamūlāgya paṃca kalaką parpaṭa
śįlājattū vaṇḍaṃgąna ttila iraṇḍą sarpaṣā
4 gau-mūttriṇa śrrattaṃ sa | rpi vyādhīnāṃ parąmąhauṣadä ||
|| aṣṭädarā paṃca-gulme [ca] nāśayit nāttra saṃśayi : ||

104r2 || paṃcamūla kaṣāyina . ttraphalā sāttalā gūṇḍaṃ
3 pipalī papala-mūlaṃ vā | stūkā-śaṃkha-pūṣpayau .
iṛąṇḍä-ttįla : : payisyā⟨× × ×⟩ca prryaujayittą
4 kaṭī śrąṇyā śrayayau śūlaṃ vātta-śauṇī-va | nāśanä :
iṛąṇḍa-ttila vātta-śauhṛta

104v$^{2}_{3}$ || jaląlā khāvara kāśa . bārgī [mū] | mūla sa-būṣkara
kṣūdrāttra kaṭū[ṭū]kä himgū . dvāra sauvarcala samaṃ :
ttir akṣä väpącitta ttila araṇḍa-jala ttūlyayau
4 kṣīra ttragū | ṇattaṃ kuryāta kaumala-śvayithū-nāśanī .
aśītta-vāttąjā raugā pavittrą mā⟨ṃsa⟩-räsįna cä ||

105r2 siddham svasti :
kątsūrā⟨ga⟩ra caṃdanā saha jalā . vyąṣä bhą nāgi tvaca :
3 tṛś ilā nakha kūkūmaṃ sa-näla | da : kākaula jāttīphala :
śilaiyä saha jīrakautpala ttūkā : ⟨spṛkā⟩ lava⟨ṃ⟩gābūdā :
4 kījalką sattä ṣaṇḍä-gūṇä sä⟨ta⟩-yūktä : śakrra-prra | kāśīkṛttaṃ :
kāsa papāsa ⏑ – ⏑ dāha-śamana : hṛt-kukṣa-kąṣṭāmayä

103*v*1 || halīriṃ vīhīle ąmalai sudā-kṣīrä ttraula
ṣa' pąna arva paṃjsa paṃjsa mācāṃga śtāka [×] ī̇raṃdīniṃ rūṃ
2 hālai śiṃga . gvīha' ṣvī | dä dva śiṃga ṣi' rūṃ pāchiṃ dvī dvī drriṃ
drriṃ prrūyi khāśą'ña ṣvīdana drrayau dūṣṭyau jsa hamyi vāśarūṃ
jiṃdä
i̇rąṇḍi ttįla ||
103*v*4/5 || halīriṃ vīhīlai ąmalai | sālaparṇa prraśtaparṇa[1] brrahatta
kąṇḍārya drāṃgūlyai papala mūla cittriṃ badarä ttāṃgari ttįṣcya
śalyājątti viṇḍaga
104*r*1 ṣā' pą | na arva paṃjsa paṃjsa mācāṃga śtākä ī̇raṃdīniṃ rūṃ
śau śiṃga gvīha' rūṃ śau śiṃga gvīha' bīysmä haṣṭa śiṃga
2 ṣa' rūṃ : pāchiṃ haṣṭa pacaḍa dū⟨va⟩ | ra jiṃda u paṃjsa padya
gąma abyąmiṃ ||
104*r*4 sālaparṇa prraśtaparṇa[2] brrahatta kaṇḍārya drrāṃgūlye
5 ṣa' pąna arva | śau śau sira śtāka kṣasä śiṃga uca jsa jṣąñąña khu ra
va tcau śāṃga harśta . ī̇raṃdīniṃ rūṃ śau śiṃga ṣvīda śau śiṃga tta
104*v*1 būra hā kikaja nauka ārda [a] | arvi tciriṃ halīriṃ vīhīlai ąmale
sāttala gūla papala papala mūla : bāstūlą śaṃkha-pūṣpä
2 ṣā' pąna arva dri mācāṃga śtāka ṣį rūṃ | pāchi dvī dvī prrūya
varāśą'ña brrąhąña ṣūñvā pijsa vīna jiṃdä . drayau dūṣyau' hamyi
vāśarūṃ ||
104*v*4/5 hīravī suṣamila : haulegą khavari | bāva hūraṣṭa kąṇḍārya papala
ttāṃgara mīriṃjsya aṃgauṣḍä yäva-kṣāra spajū
ṣa' pąna arva dvī dvī mācāṃga śtāka ī̇raṃdīniṃ rūṃ śau śiṃga
105*r*1 u | tca śau śiṃga . ṣvīda driṃ śiṃga gvīhä' rūṃ pāchiṃ dvī dvī
prūya ysama jsa khāśą'ña kąmąla jiṃda haśa jiṃdä haṣṭā biṃna
2 āchā jiṃdä śvayithū-nā | śana irąṇḍa ttila :
105*r*5 kapūra : kṛiṣṇāgara : caṃdaṃ : hīravī : papala . ttāṃgara .
105*v*1 mīriṃ | jsya . nāga-kyisara . cąnakavi . tvācä suṣmila . nakha . kūrkūṃ .
svarnagūttaryāṃga būśąniṃ : kākaula jāttīphala : śīlaiyikä . aụṣiṃ
2 nīlātpala ttūkā-kṣīra : spa[ra]rka . | lavaṃgä . būha'ni . viysa
khīysarä :
ṣä' pąna arva dvī dvī mācāṃga śtākä śakara śau thaṃga ṣi' cąṇa
śakrrana hva phāha' uysna āphāra jiṃdä ysira vī u jsahira arāṃdāṃ
3 jiṃda : ttą | raṃdarū diṃ strįha' padīmi harbįśa pahiṃśi' ttaviṃ vī
haṃbūsaṃ aṃgvā vīni u nvāva diṃ vąñä jiṃdä viṃsiṃ u aysmyāja

[1] prraśna°. [2] prraśna°.

ma⟨ṃ⟩dāgnī jvara śūla mūrca manasā saṃśrr̥̄ṣṭaṃ raktāṃdhanā[1] :
5 nįttyādāha yakr̥t prrī l līha śvayithū . chvardauttasāraṃ bhr̥ma
kąrpūrāryäm äda kṣatta-kṣayäna-cūrṇaṃ bala-vāhakä : :
$105v^{4}_{5}$ ll kr̥i l ṣṇāgaraṃ ttūṭa kaṇā marica varāṃga
pū⟨ṃ⟩nāga pūṣkaraṃ śaṭhīr ttūkāṃ ttaumalakaṃ
vr̥ikṣāmbla cąṇḍā surasā dala māttalāga
bārgī harįṇā . jala jīra śūṇvya jīvāṃ
106r1 l śīlaiyi kisaraṃ lava⟨ṃ⟩ga [kū]kṣīra māṃsī
kākąlaṃ jāttīphala dāṇḍima ttūla bhāgiṃ
samaṃ dūttąm ītta kr̥̄tvā śarkarā aṣṭa-bhāga .
2 arūcą ttamakaṃ śvāsa : kasa hrrid-rrauga l śauṣä
śvayithū gala rūcagna pārśva-hrritta vasta-śūla
apanayitta narąṇā : rau⟨ca⟩na-dīpanaś ta
pūhī-agarādyaṃ cūrṇaṃ :
106v2 agaraṃ ttūṭa varāṃga vįśva ttąlīs⟨a⟩-patträ
jaladä ◡ ◡ yivąṇī cąrakāṃ jīrakāś tä
⟨śa⟩ṭham adha dacä cīnāṃ pūṣkarā ttąmalakyi .
3 surākaṃ nakä l vāśīkąna rīpū cūrṇaṃ
sama dhr̥ttäm itta krr̥̄tvā śarkärā cāṣṭa-bāgā
arūcä nąmaka śvāsa kāsa hrr̥̄d-rąga śauṣaṃ
4 śvayithū gala rūcagnaṃ [pą] l pārśva ūru-stasta śūla :
apimayi narąṇā rącana-dīpanaś ta
agarādyä :
107r2 agarā pįpalīm iśā : śaṭhī caurakąm ūtpalai
3 l ttūkā-kṣīra sa-marąca bhārgī sauvarcalā ttathā
tvacaṃ naumalakī pattra māttalāṃga rasānvatä :
4 jīvattī surasaudīca ttīttalīkābrra l vattasa
nāgaramalakaṃ ttūlyai sūkṣma-cūrṇina kārayittä
cūrṇā cūttūragūṇättra prridayi sarga śarkarā
5 kāsa-śvāsarūca-hara pārśva l prr̥̄ṣṭi rūjā jayitä
madāgnä pauṇḍarąga cä padäyihyätta dāpayit
vātta-ślįṣma-vakärämū cūrṇām ittat yäthāmrrattä
107v1 bala varṇa l karäś tiṃvä : dīpanīyi rasāyina
agarādya cūrṇä :
107v5 : dvi caṃdanä sautpala nāga-pūṣpāṃ
108r1 ṣaṇḍī sa-kr̥̄ṣṇā l dälar traṃgam ilā :
vāsakā gūṇḍä ◡ ◡ ttramą nattä .
lava⟨ṃ⟩ga śriṃgī jala padra kisarä
pyäyigiṃ viś⟨v⟩auṣadha grrathakāghni

[1] *vel* t-t? nakt°.

4 śatcaphā jiṃdi hūña āphārna panava | āchā . ysira vī gvahiṃyi u kṣayä jiṃda ca varī ttaudä jarä ṣpiṃjiṃ vī vīna haśä bąma avīysāra gisā jiṃda hauva padīmi :

kapūrāda cąṇi : :

$106r^2_3$ kṛṣṇāgara : suṣamila . papala : mī|riṃjsya : tvacä nāgapūṣpi hūraṣṭa . ṣala : ttūkā-kṣīrä . ttą:malakä ttittalīka : surasä : cąṇakavi :

4 vālegä raysä khavara bā : harṇva : hīravī : aù|ṣiṃ : ttūṃgarä jīvattä : śīlaiyäka : nāga-kyisära : lavaṃga : karkaṭa-śrriṃgä : svarṇagūttaryāṃga būśąniṃ : kākaula jāttīphala :

5 ṣi' pąna arva dvī dvī mācāṃga | śnāka[1] : drrąma ttīma kṣa sirä śakara śau thaṃgä

ṣi' cąṇä pa tcịmañāṃ ttāḍā jidä : śịra uśa' padīmi phāhä uysnä

106v1 āphāra jiṃdä ysira rīysi u gauda āchiṃ | jiṃdä jsahira haśa u garśa rāha' āchā jiṃdä haṃdaṃna śịra ttąraṃdarū diṃ padīmi u phiysgąña vīna jiṃdä : śịra ttaraṃdarū diṃ haṃjsūly[ī]ā⟨ka⟩ :

2 mista agarāda | cąṇä :

106v4 : kṛṣṇāgara : sukṣmila : tvaca : ttūṃgara : ttālīspattra hīravī

5 | būha'ni sąnā cąrakä aùṣiṃ ṣalä papala cąṇakavi hūraṣṭi ttąmalaka surasa nāga-kyisara ttūkā-kṣīrä nāgapūṣpa

107r1 ṣa' pąna arva śā śā mācāṃga . | śakara tcau sira ṣi' cąṇä arūśa' jiṃdä phāha uysnä āphāra ysira rāhi jiṃda naṣṭausiṃ utvaḍari jsa

2 khąysąnya haśa jiṃda garśä haṃdaṃna ā|chā jiṃdä kviṃysvā u phiysgąña vīna jiṃdä uśä' haurāka : diṃ haṃjsūlyākä

agarāda cąṇä :

107v1 : kṛṣṇāgarä papala suṣmile ṣala cauraka nīlātpala ttūkā-kṣīra

2 | mīriṃjsya khavärä spajū tvacä ttūmalakä ttālīspattä vālega raysä

3 jīvata suräsä hīravī ttiṃttalīkä aṃbala-vittarasä ttagara | ąmale

ṣa' pąna arva śā śā mācāṃgyi śtāka . śakara paṃjsa sira ṣi' cąṇa

4 phāha' uysnä āphāra jiṃdä uśa' pa|dīmi kviysvā u brrąhąña vīna jiṃda nvāva diṃ vąña jiṃdä u pūṇḍärauga āchiṃ jiṃda bāva

5 śalīṣąmajsa āchā ṇahiji . ⟨ṇi⟩ | mąñaṃda hauva padīmi u chä diṃ haṃjsūlyāka

raysāyaṃ agarāda cąṇä :

108r4 hiṃniṃ caṃdaṃ . śī caṃdä : nīlātpala . nāgapūṣpa ṣala papala

5 cąṇakavi : su|kṣmila ttūkā-kṣīra kṛṣṇāgarä gūla kūrkāṃ ttagarä : lavagä karkaṭa-śriṃga hīravī ttālīspatträ nāga-kyisarä prrayaṃgä

108v1 ttāṃgara | papala mūla būhani uśi'rä samaṃga jāttīpattra

[1] śtāka.

2 sitya sąmaṃgā cä sa-ją|napatträ
käkaula tpagį ṣaṇḍa-gūṇä śa⟨r⟩karā⟨ṃ⟩bū
ttärṇäṣa tąṇḍāla dhāvanänäyä
bhäkta[1] pināthyaudha bhāgakä jvąrä
sadhāhinam ikiṣūśas ta ⟨× × ×⟩
3 | raktārśa pūṇḍätvaṃ ttrajaudamī śvāsa [sa]
hikāś ta pi⟨ttottha⟩-kąmalāpaha
gūlma sahitta tmaka śatkarąśma
4 prramihaṃ hṛihni yauna rūji|ṣū pūjatvä ||
|| mahī-caṃdanādä cūrṇaṃ
$108v^4_5$: caṃdana tta|gara mausta prrīyagī nāga-kisara
hṛivirāṃ padmakauśīra lava⟨ṃ⟩ga jātta-pattraki
109r1 sūkṣmilā agarā patträ tvacä madhūka | pūṣpayau
karṇāśąkiṃ sama-hṛįttiṃ : ttrūṣiṇä ttraphalādaka
tva kṣīrī pala saṃyūktaṃ[1] śakkarā[2] ṣaṇḍä-gūṇīkṛittä
2 tta | cūrṇä śvāsa-kāsa-ghnä hikā-dūrga⟨ṃ⟩dha-nāśanä :
viṣmi-jvarą-pārśva-śūla : kṛiṣṇāttīṣāraśaupuhā
3 mūtträ-kyächä vagątauvä : vadva|ttī paṃcagūlmayau
cūrṇayau vyādha haktā[1] ca⟨ṃ⟩danāda prrakīrttana :
caṃdanādyä cąṇä
109v4 || caṃdanautpala hrrīvirä papala māsta nāgarä
vaṇḍä⟨ṃ⟩ga tvaca sūṣmila śaṃkha ttąmalakaṃ śaṭhī :
5 surasīva sudā-|kṣīrä . dāṇḍamaṃ gūṇḍaṃ śarkarā
sama-bhāgąnä sarvąṇä . sukṣma cūrṇąna kārayitta
kāle mūthāyi bhūjītta cūrṇąm ittahä nāiśanä
110r1 | jvaraṃ lauhattäna cä . [m]arśä śvāsä ca kāsäyau
gūlmadaram ūdāvarttī grrahaṇī dauṣa maṇḍättā .
2 śvayithū ci kṛäṣṇä chadīr ca . a⟨ti⟩sāraṃ halīma|ka :
⟨a⟩nyāś ta dauṣā vividhā sarvāṇḍy ättä sādhayita
ca⟨ṃ⟩danādya śauthauhaṃ :
110r5 : caṃdanaṃ nalada lūdrä uśī'ra padma-kyisära :
110v1 nāga-pūṣpaṃ | ca b[v]ilva cä : bhadrä māsta sa-śarkarā :
hirivära· pāṭhaṃ cä kūṭajasyä phalai tvaca
gyägatära sättavirṣā dhāttäkī sa-ra⟨sāṃ⟩drinä :
2 amrrāsthä ⟨jaṃ⟩busā strä cänba | ttāthä mauca-räsą-yūttä :
nīlätpala samaṃgā cä : sukšmilā dāṇḍāmä tvacä
tcattūra-vīśattam ittąnä sama-bhāgąna kārayitta .
3 tta⟨ṃ⟩ḍūlā⟨ṃ⟩būnä sa⟨ṃ⟩yū|ktä[1] kṣądriṇau saha pīṣayittą[tä]

[1] *vel* t-t? [2] tk?

ṣi' pąna arva śā śā mācāṃga śtāka śakara kṣa sira ṣa' cąṇa rīysū-
2 | tcana khāśąña rahna-pitta[1] ṇihiji uskyāṣṭa nāṣṭa tsūkä ttaviṃ hatsa
3 ttavaṃdyi jsä ca pa tcįmañāṃ ttāra vīji⟨ṣḍi⟩ ṣi' jatti : | hūjīja arja
4 pūṇḍaraugä : uśi' hūṣąñāka uysnä āphārä hikyi kąmala pittä gąma u
śarkarya u | aśmaryä mūttri-kṛįchä prramīha : ysīra rīysiṃ pūrāṃ
vīnāṃ janāka

mįsta caṃdanāda cąṇa :

109r$^{3}_{4}$: caṃdaṃ ttagara bū|hni pṛiyaṃga nāga-kyisara hīravī pūṣṭarä
5 uśīra lavagä jāttīphala suṣmila kyiṣṇāgarä ttālīsa-[pa] | pattra tvaca
madūka-pūṣpa

ṣa' pąna arva śā śā mācāṃga papala ttūṃgara mīrimjsya drri
109v1 drriṃ mācāgyi ttūkā-kṣīrä | paṃjsa mācāṃga śakarä kṣa sira ṣi'
cąṇä phāha uysna ⟨ā⟩phāra jida u hika : cä ttūrana u haysgvā
2 vīśųna bauśa narą|mi u viṣma jvara u kti[2] vīni u ttara bįśa jiṃda jara
vasuji u vīni jiṃdi . harbiśa padya avīysāra jiṃda ca aṃga hvāri
3 ttyāṃ | va śįra īda mūttra-krricha jiṃdä ci aṃgvā vyāha' tsvä ī jatti
4 ci biṃda haṃbva īdi u jsahira vyāha' tta būra āchā jiṃ|hi[3] ||

110r$^{2}_{3}$: caṃdaṃ nīlātpala hīravī papala [bū] būhni ttūṃgarä vaṇḍa|gä
tvaca sukṣmila śaṃgä ttūmalaka : : ṣala surasä sudā-kṣīrä drrąma
ttīma . gūla śakärä : hąmaṃgyāṃ ttyāṃ arvāṃ jsa ṣi' cąṇä bāgna
4 samāṃ varāśą'|ña ttaviṃ lähalaigä haśä pitta rajsąna arjä uysna
āphārä phāha:' gąmä dūvarä udāvartti grrahaṇi prradąṣä . pūṇḍä-
5 raugau haśä ttara bhą|ma : avīysārä halīmakä u haṃdara bīśųña
āchā harbiśä ttyi cąṇa jsa jāri :

110v5 : caṃdaṃ svarnagūttariṃ būśąniṃ śaubariṃ lūdrä uśį'ra viysa
khīysāra nāgapūṣpä bilva būhni . śakarä : hīravī pāṭha . vatsäka-bījä :
111r1 ttūṃgarä prra|vaṣi' : dhāttakī-pūṣpä cūvaṃ . aṃbrrāsträ jaṃbrrasträ[4]
mauca-rasä nīlątpala samaga . sukṣmila drrąma dalai hamaṃgyāṃ
2 ttyāṃ arvyāṃ jsa ṣi' cąṇa rīysūtcana khāśą'|ña ā mākṣi hīyi uca jsa

[1] rahta°.
[2] t-ti? *lege* kviysvā.
[3] jiṃdi.
[4] str (*vel* sñ?): *recte* sth.

lehittī pīttaś ta [m] arśa-⟨śo⟩phā dvaratiṣū ca
⟨mū⟩rcchā bhrramaupasṛāṣṭąnā tṛṣāttānā[nā] ca dāpayat
4 a|nīsāra ca chvarda cä strīṇā cäṃvā asṛigadrrajä :
prrastrūrnānā[1] cä garbhąṇā strāpana[1] ⟨ca⟩ paramūcatti :
aśvattāṃ nąma nau yaugau : rahta-pittä-navāraṇi :
111r$^{3}_{4}$ || samaṃgā vālaka lū|drä kapithi bälvam iva ca :
sukṣmilā ttittalīka ca . pāṭhā vįśvauṣadhas tathā :
aṃbrrāsthaṃ civa jaṃbrrāsthä tvaca mauca-ra⟨sa⟩syä cä :
5 bädaraś ciṃva cāgä|rī dhāttakī-pūṣpa ttąṇḍūlā .
dāṇḍama ca sama cūrṇä dva-gūṇa śakkarā[2] bhavitta
amrratta ṣaṇḍävakaṃ nąma sarvąttäsāra-vanāśanä :
111v3 : aṃbrrāstha ja⟨ṃ⟩brrątmalam ivą śūṇvī
sa-dhāttakī mauca-rasa käpitta
sa-bilvam ilā tvaca māgadha ca .
4 | sa-ttittalīka dva-gūṇa ca dāṇḍama
diyā sattāṃ ga⟨r⟩karä ttūlyā bhāga
vavaṣū cattīsā⟨ra⟩ charda-nāśanä :
asṛigdhara sarva⟨-dauṣa⟩ bhava hatti ||
112r$^{1}_{2}$ || bilvasya madhya sa-kapithä | pįpalī
sa-nāgari mauca-rasa sama⟨ṃ⟩gā
ttirīṭam ūṣaṇa cavya ⟨ci⟩drrakau
sa-dhāttakī-pūṣpa varā⟨ṃ⟩gä mūsta
sukṣmala vatsa sa-lava⟨ṃ⟩ga jabū
3 abrrāsthaṃ pāṭhā sa-vi|ṇḍa⟨ṃ⟩ga-pūṣpa
saha kisariṇä
⟨sa⟩-pįpalī mūla samā⟨ṃ⟩śa kūryāt
dadyā sattāṣṭi-gūṇä sa ttūlānā
cūrṇä kṛttasya kkṛpa[2] dauṣa bhūjī
4 āṃmādä dū|ṣiṇä sa-māthānāyī
saṃvadānāpachayittāttasārā
hanṛąt drramī u⟨r⟩dh⟨v⟩am adha prravṛisidā :
112v3 || yavąnī pįpalī mūla cattūrjā⟨tā⟩nāgarā matta
marācāgna jalājājī : dyąna sauvartcalai samiṃ :
4 vṛibla | dhāttakī krrįṣṇā bilva dāṇḍamą-bījakiṃ :
tṛ-gūṇiṃ ṣaṇḍä-gūṇä sątttä kapithāiṣṭä-gūṇä kṛitta :
5 cūrṇāttasāra grrahaṇī yikṣa gūlmā | galāmayi :
kāsa śvāsāgna sādārśa pīnasā raucana jayit :
113r4 || karṣaupūniṃ ttūkā-kṣīrī carrjājaka dva kārṣakiṃ

[1] str (*vel* sñ?) : *recte* sth. rn *incert.* [2] tk?

haṃbūsaṃ . hiṃja haśa jiṃda u ysīcä arjä vī ttaviṃ [viṃ] u viṃsiṃ
3 vī gisi vī ttañāṃ hūña vasuji . ttara va śįra avīysāra bąmä u | strīyāṃ asṛigvara[1] jiṃda ṇiysūnāṃcā urāṃdāṃ avastha bañi aśvanyāhva[2] rahana-pitta[3] ṇähijākä ||
111^{r5}_{v1} samaṃga | hīravī . śaubari lūdrrä kapitta bilva sukṣamila ttiṃttalīka [ṣā'] pāṭha ttūṃgara aṃbrrāstha jaṃbrrāsthä tvaca : mauca-
2 rasä bądärä cakurīka dhāttakī-pū|ṣpä rīysva gūrvä śā śā mācāṃgyi śtāka drrąma ttīma haṣṭūäsa mācāṃgyi śakara tcau sira
3 ṣi' cąṇa amrrattā-ṣāṇḍava nąma harbīśi avīysāra va|sūjāka ṇvistyi bąma va pīrmāttaṃ :
$111v^{4}_{5}$ || aṃ|brrās⟨th⟩a jaṃbrrāsthą nīlautpala ttāṃgara : dhāttakī-pūṣpa mauca-rasä : kapithä bilva suṣmila tvacä papala ttiṃttalīka
112r1 ṣa' pąna arva śā śā [śā] mācāṃga drrąma | ttīma dva sira hāle : śakara tcau sira ṣa' cąṇa avīysāra jiṃda bąma vasuji harbiśau dūṣṭyau' jsa hamyi asrrįgdhara jiṃda ||
$112r^{4}_{5}$ || bilva kapithä : papala ttūṃgara mauca-ra|sä samaga : śaubariṃ lądrra mīriṃjsya badara : cįttri : dāttakī-pauṣpa tvacä būhni : sukṣmila vatsaka-bījä lavaṃga ⟨jaṃ⟩brrāsthä abrrā[sa]stha pāṭha
112v1 caṃdä nāgapūṣpä | viysa khīysarä papala mūla
ṣā' pąna arva śā śā mācāṃga śtāka śakarä kṣa sira
ṣi' cąṇa drräyau dūṣṭyau jsa paną ttara jiṃdä hanya[4] vīnyau jsa
2 avīysāra jiṃdä ca | bīysma vaṃdāya uskyāṣṭa nāṣṭa tsūka prrāṇā ṇvistyi vasujāka u ṇiysūnāmi ca hūña jiṃda śira ttąradarū diṃ
3 pądīmi biśa būra varāśą'|ñä
bilvādya cąṇa ||
112v5 : sąnā papala mūla tvacä sukṣmila nāgapūṣpi nāga-kyisāra .
113r1 | ttūṃgarä mīriṃjsya cittriṃ hīravī aùṣiṃ hīysamāṃ spajū
ṣi' pąna arva śā śā mācāṃga śtākä ttiṃttalīka dhāttakī-pūṣpä papala drrąma ttīma aùjaṃ
2 ṣi' pąna drriṃ drriṃ mā|cāṃga śtākä kaphitti haṣṭä [haṣṭä] sira śakara dasau sira
ṣi' ṇä bīśūñī avīysāra jiṃdä ṇvistyä bañä uskyāṣṭä grrahaṇī
3 padauṣa bañä . gauda | kṣayä . āchiṃ jiṃda gąma jida garśa bīśūña āchā jiṃda phāha uysna āphāra jiṃdä ttaraṃdarū diṃ strįha'
4 padīmi vīnausta arja jiṃ|dä haysga-ttājsiṃ jiṃda kapathāṣṭi[5] : ||
113^{r5}_{v1} : ttūkā-kṣīrä dvī mācāṃga hālai | tvacä suṣamila nāgapūṣpa nāga-

[1] asṛgdhara. [2] aśvatthāhva. [3] rahta°. [4] hatsa. [5] °ādya.

yivą̄nī dhą̄nyakajsājī grrathä vyą̄ṣa palā⟨ṃ⟩śakiṃ .
5 pa | lānau dāṇḍämāsyāṣṭau sarnāyiś ciṃka ttatta krrįttiṃ :
gūṇiṃ kapathāṣṭakaṃ ca tta cūrṇau[yi] dāṇḍamāṣṭāka :
113v2 [m]ilā śąṭhī papalī-mūla jaujī
3 dala ttūkā mau | ca-rasi yivą̄nī :
ttālīsa jāttīphala bīja-pūrakä
jūṭā surasyāmabhi ttättalīka
iṣā samā karṣakä : krįṣṇä śauṭhvī
4 pala kapi | tha papala dāṇḍamasya
aṣṭa-palā bhāgaṃ samāsattāś ca
mattä prrivāhaś ca kāsā prra hakā
yakṛttaś ca plīhä urattä chvarrdaṃ
5 gūdāma | yiṣā dīpanīyi cūrṇa :
114r^3_4 || sanāṣṭä bā | gā dva-paṭā sä-vyą̄mä
tvag ilā paṃcābla dva bhāmi yūjva
ajīrṇaṃ ma⟨ṃ⟩dāgnaṃ rūdham ąnya . m
5 arśaudarāṇāṃ prraśami pṛsa | hyä
sattāṣṭa bhāgä :
114v2 nāga-pūṣpaṃ tvacaṃ nala marācaṃ ila
3 ttālīsa-pattraṃ bhāgā⟨r⟩dha | śrriṃgabhirä
surūttamasa ttathā papälī kalka ttūlya
yāva cūrṇa prrayūhtä vimala dhrratta sarśā
4 aṣṭä bhātānṛ da | dyāt kūṣṭināṃ yįkṣmą̄ṇī
pūnar ipi ttathā kaumalai rakta-pitta
väsarpa kāsi śvāsinyi pi jvara śarasi :
5 hįka mūttra- | krrįchiṣą̄ pą̄ṇḍatvi agna
śauttī-rūca-karäm ūrdhą-jattrā
hasya cūrṇä chīvakina :
kṛtta matti amrrattä bäba sārasyä
115r1 | hīttū rāją̄nāṃ cūrṇā rājā magada .
janapadä māgada dīpattą̄ nąmāgada cūrṇā :
115r4 ttālīsa marąca śūṇvī krịṣṇā bhāgautta rādhyattā :
adhāśakiṃ tvag ilāś ta krịṣṇā aṣṭi-gūṇā satta .
5 | kāsä śvāsa rūcä plīha jvara śauṣāgta mādya-nūtta :
hṛdya cūrṇām attīsārä-⟨gū⟩lmārśa-chvarda-nāśanä :
115v^2_3 sūṣmilā tvaca [nā] | nāga-pūṣpa maracasyā pipalī nāgara .
itti bhāga
vivadhattį sama dhattiṃ sa mūdhattiṃ diyā sattā ṣaṇḍa-gūṇa

kyisärä tta paṃjsa paṃjsa mācāṃgyi sąṇā hīysamāṃ aủṣiṃ papala
2 mūla ttāṃgara mīriṃjsya tta śau śau sirä drrąma ttīma ha | ṣṭą sira
śakarä śau thaṃgä :

ttyi cąṇi anaśāsättakä ca kapathāṣṭi[1] vī hvavä dāṇḍamāṣṭi[2] cąṇä :
113v5 : sukṣamila . papala mūla ąṣiṃ . cąṇakavi ttūkā-kṣīrä mauca-rasä
114r1 sąṇā ttālīspatta jāttīphala vālega raysä | ttąmalakä surasa nāgapūṣpa
ttiṃttalīka

ṣa' pąna arvä śā śā mācāṃga ścāka :

papala ttāṃgara drriṃ drriṃ mācāṃga : kapätta śau särä drrąma
2 ttīma śau sira | śakara kṣa sirä ṣi' cąṇa ttaraṃdarū diṃ padīmi
khāysa vī rīśa' prrahāji drrāṃ avīysāra jiṃda ca pharāka aśūca jsāvi
3 u biṃda bīśūñī a | vīysāra arja jiṃdä u phāha' u jara ṣpiṃjiṃ vasujį
piṃjvā gvahiṃyi bąma ysịra vī bīsā āchā jiṃdä :

114r5 spajū : sadalūṃ papala ttāṃgara mīriṃjsyä tvacä sūkṣmila
114v1 ṣi' pąna śā śā [śā] mācāṃga baraśīji [drrą] | drrąma ttīma ttiṃttịlīki
cakūrīkä ⟨aṃ⟩bla-vittarasä

ṣä' dvī dvī mācāṃga śtāka śakara tcau sira
2 ṣa' cąṇa ągvāhi gvāchi ttaraṃdarū diṃ [śi] | śira padīmä khāysa
vī rīśa' prrahāji arja dūvara jiṃda [×] bāgiką

$115r^{1}_{2}$ || nāgapūṣpa tvaca cittri mīriṃjsya suṣmila | ttālīspattä śā śā
mācāṃgä ttūṃgara driṃ mācāṃga . papala nāṃ mācāṃga śakara 10
3 sira ṣi' cąṇä kuṣṭa kidarā yikṣma kąmala | rahna-pitta[3] vịsarpa
phāha uysna āphārä ttaviṃ ttara kamala rāha hịka mūttra-krriṃcha
4 pūṇḍarauga nvāva diṃ vąña khāysāṃ | vī rīśa' prrahāji māgadī :
115r5 ttālīspattä mīriṃjsya dvī dvī mācāṃgä : ttūṃgarä drriṃ mā |
115v1 | cāṃga : papala tcą mācāṃga tvacä suṣmila śā śā mācāṃga : śakarä
paṃjsa sirä ṣi' cąṇa phāha' uysna āphāra jiṃdä khāysāṃ vī rīśa'
2 padī | mi ṣpiṃjiṃ vasuji . ttaviṃ naṣṭausiṃ nvāva diṃ vąñä ṇahiji
ysaujsa ṣa' cąṇa avīysāra jiṃda maṃgāra arjä bąma jiṃdä :
$115v^{4}_{5}$ sūkṣmila śā mācāṃga tva | cä nāgapūṣpa : mīriṃjsya 4 papala 5
ttūṃgara 6 śaka[ka]ra 7 sirä

[1] °ādya. [2] °ādya.
[3] rahta°.

4 anaṃttaṃ cūrṇam ajī|rṇaṃ gūlma jaṭharä arśāsa hṛid-rāgā̤ṇā
kāsa śvāsäṣū rakta-pittaṣū sūlaṃ kaṇva-vakāraś ta yi :
116r_2^1 yivā̤nī rmitalīka cä : nāgara sābla|vittasä
dāṇḍama badhari cāṃbla kārṣka cauṣä kalpayita
dhā̤nya sauvartcala jājī varā̤na cādha-kārṣarka
3 pi̤palī cāśatti̤ka : | dvi nättä marīcasya ca .
śarkarāyās tū catvāri palā⟨ṃ⟩śä sūkṣama cūrṇayita
4 jihvā vaśūdhanä hṛdya cūrṇa bha|dva raucakatta
hṛt rraha[1] pārś⟨v⟩a gūlma-ghna vabaṃdhā̤⟨nā⟩ha-nāśanä
kāsa-śvāsa-hara grrāhī grrahaṇy ārśau-vakāra-nyatta
5 dva mariśa|tti̤kṣaṃ cūrṇaṃ :
116*v*4 hiraṇva cā̤rakā mūstā suṣmilā śaṭhi nāgarī
tvaca gattra pūṣkarā śraṃgī hrrīvira tū u kyisarä
5 | jīvattī malaka bhārgī pi̤palī surasa sanā
cattu catturgūṇä kṛtvā : tta cūrṇaṃ līḍham avā : ⟨× ×⟩
aṃna-pā̤na prrīyäauktavyä : bhakṣatti pakiṃ ⟨× × ×⟩

[1] t-prr?

116r1 ṣa' cą̄ṇa agvaha jiṃda dūvarä arjä ysịra vī bīsā āchā phā:|ha
uysna āphāra jiṃda rahna-pitta[1] stūra gatsauñä garśa bīsā āchā jida :
116r5 są̄ṇā ttiṃttalīka : ttūṃgara aṃbala-vittarasä drą̄ma ttīma bądara
vä vālaiga raysä
116v1 ṣa' pąna arva dvī dvī | mācāṃga hālā hīysamāṃ . spajū aůṣiṃ
tvacä ṣa' pąna śā śā mā⟨cāṃ⟩ga hālā . papala ssa ttīmä mīriṃjsya dvī
2 ssa ttīmä śakara 8 | ssira :
ṣa' cą̄ bīśą̄ya bīsā āchā jiṃda ca pā ḳaśti prrahāji khāysä vī rīśa'
3 prrahāji ysīrä rāha' ṣpijāṃ rāhä kviysvā vīnāṃ | jänāka ca parīysmä
kaśti u paṣkausä prrahājä : phāha' uysna āphāra jiṃda haṃbīṭhāka
4 grrahaṇī padauṣa arja tta | būra āchā jiṃda dva:marąśatti :

[1] rahta°.

Caraka-saṃhitā, *K.T.* I, 158
5 71 = Jīvaka-pustaka 72*r*4–72*v*1
hapuṣā-vyoṣa-pṛthivīkā-cavya-citraka-saindhavaiḥ
sājājī-pippalī-mūla-dīpyakair vipaced ghṛtam
72 sakala-mūlaka-rasaṃ sa-kṣīra-dadhi-dāḍimam
tat-paraṃ vāta-gulma-ghnaṃ śūlānāha-vimokṣaṇam
73 yony-arśo-grahaṇī-doṣa-śvāsa-kāsāruci-jvarān
basti-hṛt-pārśva-śūlaṃ ca ghṛtam etad vyapohati
iti hapuṣādyaṃ ghṛtam

Caraka-saṃhitā, *K.T.* I, 164
5 118 = Jīvaka-pustaka 81*r*2–5
jale daśa-guṇe sādhyaṃ trāyamāṇā catuṣpalam
panca-bhāga-sthitaṃ pūtaṃ kalkaiḥ saṃyojya kārṣikaiḥ
119 rohiṇī-kaṭukā-mustā-trāyamāṇā-durālabhā-
kalkais tāmalakī-vīrā-jīvantī-candanotpalaiḥ
120 rasasyāmalakānāṃ ca kṣīrasya ca ghṛtasya ca
palāni pṛthag aṣṭāṣṭau dattvā samyag vipācayet
121 pitta-rakta-bhavaṃ gulmaṃ vīsarpaṃ paittikaṃ jvaram
hṛd-rogaṃ kāmalāṃ kuṣṭhaṃ hanyād etad ghṛtottamam
iti trāyamāṇādyaṃ ghṛtam

Caraka-saṃhitā, *K.T.* I, 166–8
11 35 = Jīvaka-pustaka 83*v*1–84*r*2
35 jīvaka-ṛṣabhakau vīrāṃ jīvantīṃ nāgaraṃ śaṭīm
catasraḥ parṇinīr mede kākolyau dve nidigdhake

36 punarnave dve madhukam ātmaguptāṃ śatāvarīm
ṛddhiṃ parūṣakaṃ bhārgīṃ mṛdvīkāṃ bṛhatīṃ tathā
37 śṛngāṭakaṃ tāmalakīṃ payasyāṃ pippalīṃ balām
badarākṣoṭa-kharjūra-vātāmābhiṣukāṇy api
38 phalāni caivamādīni kalkān kuryīta kārṣikān
dhātrī-rasa-vidārīkṣu-cchāga-māṃsa-rasaṃ payaḥ
39 kuryāt prasthonmitaṃ tena ghṛta-prasthaṃ vipācayet
prasthārghaṃ madhunaḥ śīte śarkarārdhatulāṃ tathā
40 dvi-kārṣikāṇi patrailāhema-tvaṅ-maricāni ca
vinīya cūrṇitaṃ tasmāl lihyān mātrāṃ sadā naraḥ
41 amṛta-prāśam ity etan narāṇām amṛtaṃ ghṛtam
sudhāmṛta-rasaṃ prāśyaṃ kṣīra-māṃsa-rasāśinā
42 naṣṭa-śukra-kṣata-kṣīṇa-durbala-vyādhi-karśitān
strī-prasaktān kṛśān varṇa-svara-hīnāṃś ca bṛṃhayet
43 kāsa-hikkā-jvara-śvāsa-dāha-tṛṣṇāsra-pitta-nut
putradaṃ vami-mūrcchā-hṛd-yoni-mūtrāmayāpaham
ity amṛta-prāśa-ghṛtam

Caraka-saṃhitā, Cikitsā-sthānam, *K.T.* I, 152

39 = Jīvaka-pustaka 64*r* 4–64*v* 2
tryūṣaṇaṃ triphalāṃ drākṣāṃ   kaśmaryāṇi parūṣakam
dve pāṭhe devadārv ṛddhiṃ   svaguptāṃ citrakaṃ śaṭīm
40 brāhmī tāmalakīṃ medāṃ   kākanāsāṃ śatāvarīm
trikaṇṭakaṃ vidārī ca   piṣṭvā karṣa-samaṃ ghṛtāt
41 prasthaṃ caturguṇe kṣīre   siddhaṃ kāsa-haraṃ pibet
jvara-gulmāruci-plīha-śiro-hṛt-pārśva-śūla-nut
42 kāmalārśo-'nilāṣṭhīlākṣata-śoṣa-kṣayāpaham
tryūṣaṇaṃ nāma vikhyātam etad ghṛtam anuttamam
iti tryūṣaṇādyaṃ ghṛtam

Caraka-saṃhitā, *K.T.* I, 154

18 125 = Jīvaka-pustaka 65*v* 4–66*r* 2
sa-mūla-phala-patrāyāḥ   kaṇṭakāryā rasāḍhake
ghṛta-prasthaṃ bālā-vyoṣa-viḍanga-śaṭi-citrakaiḥ
126 sauvarcala-yavakṣāra-pippalī-mūla-pauṣkaraiḥ
vṛścīra-bṛhatī-pathyā-yavānī-dāḍimardhibhiḥ
127 drākṣā-punarnavā-cavya-durālambhāmlavetasaiḥ
śṛngī-tāmalakī-bhārgī-rāsnā-gokṣurakaiḥ pacet
128 kalkais tat sarvakāseṣu hikkā-śvāseṣu śasyate
kaṇṭakārī-ghṛtaṃ hy etat kapha-vyādhi-nisūdanam
iti kaṇṭakārī-ghṛtam

III
JĀTAKASTAVA

1v1 | siddhaṃ
1. jautti ṣai mistä pramuhä saheṃdrrä pųñä .
tta ttai ysīra kṣąmä pana ṣada uvāra .
2 | ci bura ī śau masi ba'ysä bu'jsä stavä .
3 si khvai biśä hva yuḍä yąnūṃ krrąñī ki | ḍna 1

2. khvaṃ hāḍę ė'drre vaña nyaśakyi ṣṭāre
asamāhye aysmu caṃcąlą haphārä .
4 vañą saṃ | vāśūṃ' stava ci buri himāṃde .
saṃ khuṃ hime mistä priyaugä ba'ysūśtāṣṭa 2

2r1 3. ṣā' jättaka sta.| vä śubhattrāttī garkhä .
gūraphusta vyaṃjana ṣai vṛttä anvaśta .
tta tta-ṃ ṣṭāṃ o'ste khu jsaṃ[1] hvaṃnau āya
2 | kṣīraṃ jsa hye himi mista śāśä[2] myąña 3

4. nimaṃdrrye jsauṇikyi ṣṭāṃ ṣadi jsa brīya :
3 ttrivīlai mestä | sāmanyąña bisaṃja
si vedyaśīlä nąma khu ācārī devä .
vyaṃjanvā daśtä tta tta khu kīvaṭä ucyą ⟨4⟩

4 5. | paryavūṃ va ttā vaña byūtti miḍąne
ba'ysūśti brīya puñāṃ tvāre kįną
2v1 śrī vīśa' śūrrä mistye . | rruṃdä hye udiśāyä
khvä[3] jsa vyachīṃdä kṣīra āchā pīle 5

2 6. śakrrä gyastä āstaṃ ci ra seṃdrro | peṃdrra .
ttī garaja . gyaśta daśāpāla hamīḍa .
3 haṃtsa parvārna lokapāla tca | haura .
biśā pyaṃtsāṣṭä huṣī pe' ttīśä' hauva :

4 7. miṣḍā gyastä hīya gyastų̄ | ña ttrivarga .
jsīna āysdaḍä kąṣṭa ī u padāḍa : .
3r1 | ssa bistä paśa' avaśä drrų̄nai īye .
biśī sūha brų̄na pajsamya byo byau tsīde

[1] jsāṃ. [2] śāśaṃ. [3] khvaṃ.

2 8. gyastä | rr̥̄na rr̥spuraka haṃtsa hamīḍa .
parvālyo hva hva āysdaḍa himāṃde .
3 mi | stä tcaisyā.nä gyastä hīya pārysā ą̄māca hamīḍa
4 śira dī. | ra myānya biśä kṣīrva hvąṇḍä .

9. huṣa tsī jsīna pīla harbiśä : vyąchī .
3v1 | khu ye mara āstaṃ vī pharākä birāśe' .
vyākṣīvastä bāḍä vī pha hva ni ysāṃde
2 vañą ttā | marṣya'rä ārrä ci tta tta ni bvą̄ne :

10. na ttye brītīnai dai nūṣṭhurä . staurä
3 ji. | ga heme harī nvāyā:ṣcya naṣā'mä
4 vanau dātīja ūca tvą̄ñe ba' | ysa
ttaną ttā ṣada adhīmāttra uvāra .

4r1 11. khu rre yai mahāpra | bhāsa . sarvą̄ña ba'ysa .
bala.cakrravarttä śire haṃphā mistä .
2 klaiśau' jsa byaudai saṃttą̄ña | piśārä
cu brrīyaustä hastä . pasve ayūlä ttrame'ste :

3 12. hastavā. | lena khu jsāṃ pyuṣṭe pātcä .
ba'ysų̄ña avīśaiṣakye bu'jse miste .
4 ne' raysāyana [ha] | hamaṃgä tvī ttiña beḍa .
romaharṣä pastā biśä aṃgāṃ vīra

4v1 13. khu vīrulya sphālya ysi | rra ā'jsa kvāysä .
gyasta kṣīryau jsa nahyaṃdā braha tterä .
2 sūmīrä garä mą̄ñaṃdä aha | mistä akhāṣṭä .
thu byaudę aysmu ba'ysūśtä varāṣṭa .

3 14. paṃjsa ge' nātai biśä haṃdara | mu'śde' .
styūda prraṇahą̄na cu ttī bastai ttāma .
4 buḍa ssa kūla yuḍai duṣkara kī[rī] | re .
tcana tvā byaude ba'ysūśtä uvāra :

15. dvārabistä byūrrä haṣṭa ysā[ra]ri pīrma .
5r1 ttirṣṭhaṃda pa | rśai' ba'ysųña tta rruṃde .
ni hatcastai haṭha cu hvai āstaṃ vīra .
2 ttane ttā orga buḍa ssa byū | rä juna .

16. haskye kṣa' śīya khu śägä ā vā ṣvīdä .
ā mīrāhīja karāśä ā vā bora
3 | paśāṃ'jsye purre hīvī ttīśä' . ysanākä .
cu tvī ya hastā rre ṣṭāna di śirka :

4 17. khu ttā ā . | ludrrai cu haska pajaiste :
kṣaṇa-māträ na yuḍai hīsä hai śira satva .
5v1 hīña ttūrre ke'.|caña ṣṭāṃ thīyę virśä'na .
saṃ khu praskąndha bahya thaṃja uysbāyä :

2 18. hamavaṃdä garna khu hve' vi|ysa bāthaṃje .
sīrä saṃduṣṭä muśda hīvī pve'hna .
daṃdīnā raṃna hāysa hauḍai rraysgäna
3 | cu pvestī pa'jsä kai kṣąmä na saije :

19. the maṃ bịśä bāḍa hamā pīsai hvāṣṭä .
4 thu muṃ ārū|va thu ma ttrāya miḍąne .
sarvalokä vīra biśe jva kṣīr-myāña .
āspātaṃ vina tvī niśtä pe' ysīra mista .

6r1 20. khu dyai ysā|ḍakä riṣa'yä dukhye anāhä .
hanāsai stāma jsa māstä duṣpye chāṃgä .
2 ttarrāye kṣųna pa|sūjsaṃdai dęna
si vaña pīttä vau'saṃdai śaṃdye bidä

21. tta khu bāśa' ysaṃgarä phuḍä bahyä pasūste .
3 khve rijsä | kṣīvi padaṃ pe'jsye pvehna .
dva pacaḍa daina cu ā hathrrī tvare
panate ttyevī mu'śdä' pajsa attrīma .

4 22. sahaica|kä ṣṭāna hamye drrātai tvare .
ka ni ṣa' hve mīḍe puñaudä kṣuna
6v1 ṣi' ąna parīdīvyai spāṣṭai cu ṣi' saṃñä | upāta .
vajsiṣṭai hala daina haṃbaḍa mista :

2 23. tta khu ttaudäna haṃthrrī satvä viysāṃji ysi|nāhe .
tta tta ttu mąñaṃdä śirye ādarä gīhna .
3 uysānā dīṣṭai ttiña dąna pasvą|ña
attajsādą eṣṭąme tvī ttā orga :

24. śakrrä hīvī bārai yai pīrūyä bāḍna
4 [a] | aśvarājä vālāhä śī aṃgna mistä .
ā'jsīja trạikha mīrāhḹnai gara .
7r1 purrä hī.| vyau bā'yo styerrījai ttīśä'na :

25. rakṣaśāṃ' baijāṃ ṣava-tsukāṃ myāña .
2 jabvīyā pa-sse sāṭīka anā | ha
staura hatharka buḍāṃdä bu'ysye bāḍna .
thvaṃ vāṣṭą nvā'stai biśä hamya ava'sta :

3 26. bīśe ttā | ṣaiṣṭi bīśāṃ aṃgā baida .
mu'śde jsa kāṣṭai khu ji pura paysāta .
4 āśā'ṣṭa satī khu | ji byata harrūñe .
ysamaśadai pveṇä pirorākye aurga :

7v1 27. rre brahmadattä khu pa'jsa . | yuḍi bāysä
cu ⟨śaṃ⟩dai khąstādä cū halahaja yuḍāṃdä .
2 ysirūṃ āṣṭaṃdi ṣkalāṃ davāṃ . | pva'ṇna
mu'śdi' jsa vaska jīye paṃtsyai pātcä :

28. ñāṃ ttāji ne'sto hī bāja hubastä :
3 pa | spuḍāṃdä tvąnai brrḹha garañāṣṭä sata .
ṣaṃbajsyau rrijsyau bi'stāṃde aga
4 guśta | ttąñä harṣṭa u āsvai natca ne'stä :

29. garāṃ rruṃdä mąñaṃdä ye śurī virśa'na
8r1 ėṣṭa | va krrąña kṣamau parārthä-cārä
gūysnā rre ṣṭāna yuḍai duṣkarä kīrä .
2 ttine śira satva . | muhu jsa pākvā orga .

30. barbīrye gūysna ja va mu'śda' jsa pātcä .
3 bukajä puṣa tsuai . | rruṃdāña hurāśña
cu didi pha ysairka yuḍą pąñe paṃna .
4 śau na ye vena tvī | cuai jīye hera :

31. pacīḍai dāśä hīsä staurä avasta
8v1 maraṇa-bhayä ttrikṣa pu. | ralakä pracaina
khu nā ahā āspāta himya avasta .
biśāṃ āspāta mamī ttā pā⟨kāṃ⟩ orga :

2 32. | nāta-śūṃ' nātai ysaṃthä mu'śda' pracaina .
ysurrīnai be'na pasūjsaṃdāṃ myą̄ña .
3 darrda.|rä nąma himyai nātau rre .
maittrīnai ne'na asphīraṃdai yāṃdä .

4 33. īyarai duṃdubha nā ṣā' | kīḍi pa'jsä
ahamñe ysīre hve ttrikṣa salāta
be'na saṃkhi'sta saṃ khu raijsā pųna
9r1 kṣamauttā aysmu ṣṭāne yuḍe | harga :

34. tta tta khu purra hīye bā'yä ni paśī hāysa .
2 kṣamottā mu'śdä' thi pā na yuḍai | harga .
eṣṭava muṃdai tta khu garä sumuīrä
ttane bra ba'ysa mahā jsa pākāṃ orga :

3 35. [na] | na'tcapha kāla tta khu huṣka samudrra .
pāttāla gaṃtsä bihī pve'styu tva.re
4 | gara ke'ca mą̄ñaṃdä vistārī mistä
bīysānai stūrū rakṣaysa miysirkä

9v1 36. śau śilo dā | udiśāyä ⟨ya⟩kṣä ėha
uysānā dīṣṭai gara ttraikhaña ṣṭąna .
ni himye pvąnä khu dyai bā'tai ttūrrä
2 āci-| ve'särä biśā' rrjjsā haskye :

37. hatsa-āspe hamya gyasto hvaṃḍä .
3 śakrrä āstaṃna . pha|re pajsama yuḍāṃda
rāja-riṣa'yä ṣṭāna yuḍai duṣka kīra
4 ttinā ma namasų|mä ba'ysa ṣadi jsa brrīya

38. kṣāṃttavādä ṣṭāne tvī kalabhu rre
apracai biṃdi garkha baśdā' byaudi
10r1 rhīnai | daina pasųjsaṃdai ṣṭąna .
ni pamūḍi vyaysaṃ cu ni bustä pa[na][1]daṃjya .

2 39. viysāṃ mą̄ñaṃdä tturrka tvą̄nā | gvaka
bra-vīyā śirkyi ysāra būjse haysgye
dasta pā ne'na raysāyana vadida
3 kāḍarna rejsai biśā | śadya hvaste :

[1] na deletum.

40. ne himye amanā śira satva puñauda .
same jsāṃ mu'śdä' himya ttyevī mista
4 vịra | ñau jse ṣvīdi naraṃdä vasve ūvārä .
hamya āspāta sarvasatvā mista :

10v1 41. śaṃdye jsa aiṣṭavañarą | aysmu hvarrä .
huṣāñai yāṃdä apramạṇyāṃ nvaiya
samudrrä mạñaṃdä himyai puñau śire jsa
2 | tvī hālai orga mamī pharāka jụna :

3 42. hvīya hụñä śūsta tcāra cu hvaḍi pha | rāka .
ttina himye ttaunä gukṣapä aṃgna maysirkä
4 maysdarvā paijvā urä jagyāṃ beṃ | da
burbulye ysāta khauṇḍa mauṇḍa pharāka .

11r1 43. be'saci mursala śeña dīśta maysi . | kä .
biysạṇai tcīri jsa tta khu vettālä spāśa .
bikṣistä rrīmajsä kaśaṭä haṣprrī tcaṃjsa
2 kalmāṣaṣā | da[1] sīha saudāysä rre :

44. viysä spulakä mạñaṃda sumārka vasuśka .
3 nauvari | nau rruṃdi kṣīrañau jsa pīrauḍe .
gara ke'ca khụṇāstā raṃgą viśų'na .
4 beśuṃ hā dī | ṣṭa pī jsā buysye bāḍna ||

45. ttai ya si jaysñä yanuṃ buvāṃ bala .
11v1 pathaṃjākī ra | thu yai śrūttasūṃ ṣṭāna .
sīrośā'dä śau jaṃbvī ḥarbiśä satva :
2 śakrrä ṣai āysaṃ khauṣṭä ttye śirä kī | rna .

46. vyaysanāṃ jigya naṣāmä hālai saṃña .
hi'ysda tvī pañe va hāvaṃgāra :
3 | cu mī dida kuśalai yai daśtä gumā .
ttine tsuṃ orga buḍa sa byūrä jụna :

4 47. gūha ysa | rnīja khu jsāṃ raṃnyau ūḍa
ṣi' haḍi mī haṃbaḍa śaysyau jsa bīysirka
ttī śirka strīya cu aysmu tte pīreḍe
12r1 ṣe' | hāḍa gaṃjsa cu hạmä hvaṃḍä nivartte :

[1] °pāda.

48. ttu māñaṃda śaṃdā tvā samudrra-na'scya
2 śau śilo dā udiśā | yä paṃtsai biśna
dharmāchāyä brraṃmaṃ ṣe' nāte darrona
3 didaṃde gaurava ya dāvī mista rre | ṣṭāna

49. karaṇāya ttu didi mistä dā udiśä
haudai haurä satvāṃ brrīya
4 ttini hamyai sarvaññä | bvāme jsa akhoṣṭä
ttane brra ba'ysa aurga pākāṃ dīna :

50. yamadattä rre ṣṭā brra ysuṣka manąbha[1]
12v1 śira | nąrä paṃnyai brra jīyena hamaṃga .
tta tta khu purra spāśa purṇa paṃjeśä' vīra
2 ttalottama raṃba sūja | rrījā ttīśna' .

51. bināsai yakṣä bihī pvestyaṃ tvare .
ṣai' tsodi haṃ jve brahyetī jseṇä .
3 śīvalya | pasta sūrā śaṃde beda .
ne khauṣṭä aysmu tta khu gara sumīrä .

4 52. virśī'nai styūdä kaśa | ṭä bastai pa'jsä .
ba'ysuśti brrīya sarvasatvāṃ kiṇa
sa khva parye yanuṃ biśo dukhyau jsa
13r1 virśau'da | ba'ysa ttere jse ttā orga :

53. śira bu'ysa bāysve tta khu vāsukä nā .
2 erakaña haṃphvai tta khu hīvī | purä .
naḍau arañä cu tvī sąnä himye .
3 cuai vāṣṭä thīyai gara ke'ce'.[ña][2]ña ṣṭą | na .

54. makalīñä barna parehaṃdai vrrastä .
4 śiraraṃ mistä cu yai deva-riṣa'yä | .
ttane tsuṃ orga paja-maṇḍalä ṣṭāna .
13v1 avaśu jāṃde āyauysa paca. | ḍna :

55. aṃttarrdāṃ dāśe tsai ba'ysāṃ dā
uysdīśākī ra na ye bu'ysye bāḍna
2 thvai vaska patsyai brrī jīye ysuṣkä
pasete rriscye gūhainä hvastāṃdä beda .

[1] manāta. [2] ña deletum.

3 56. hūṣāñai tvītvī virśä' ādarä thā.|ka
vyaysanāṃ jegi niṣā'mä hālaiyāṣṭa
duṣkarāṃ sa-yseryāṃ kīrāṃ vaska
4 himyai ā.|munä ttane pākvā orga

57. śīya viysa bāta khu baurīnai garä
drrāma śāhauja cu tvī beda buḍādä
14r1 tta|jsāḍai ttye jsa thu urmaysdāṃ ttīśna' .
caṃdäprabha ṣṭą̄na kamalä paṃtsyai ttą̄ma :

2 58. avīhyau raṃnyo brrų̄ña|dai maulna
ysānasta tcarṣu ttīśi' śire yanākä .
pyahaste brraṃmaṃ kāḍarną ttinī .
3 | didi śirka śą̄ma khu pura haṃbaḍa paśä' :

4 59. hä'jañe pastä kamalą jsauṇikyi ṣṭā|na
ba'ysuśti brrīya didrrāṃ huḍai haurä .
atyaṃtta ttyāgä cu drrą̄-mujse sāñe
14v1 kāṃ ṣi' | satva ba'ysa cu tvī orga ni jsāte :

60. cu ra kṣīra bārä ni pastä ttīma bajautta
2 hamye durbikṣä sa vaña | satva mīrāre
piṣkistai satvāṃ khą̄ysīnai nasä
nāvai thu śau bhāgä satvyau jsa hamaṃgä :

3 61. gesaṃdā | diśi' vī mi'ysdyų̄na pravaiya .
ustaṃ śau hamadā ā dukhye riṣa'yä
4 ttu bhāgä hīvī ttye hau|ḍi
pātcä thu mī sa uysānā huḍai

62. drrai māśtä āna bala-cakrravartta hvāṣṭä
15r1 śadye bida yuḍe ttu dūṣkarä kī|rä mu'⟨śdi⟩ jsa pātcä .
ysaujsa hvaḍa khaṣṭa tcaṃna āsaḍä yai
2 haṃbāya ni yuḍai tvī aurga mi|ḍą̄ne :

63. gara ttājä stāga bihīsadā jų̄na .
3 ābe'syau khvīyau vyaulasta bajā|ṣa .
varadā rraga baṃhya caṃbva ysāysa .
4 si vaña mu pacaḍni jidā . bā|ysąña baṃhya :

64. hvīyaṣai satva parauysaṃdai ysirkä
15v1 bīsaije baṃtve yuḍi du|kha-vī tvare
thu jsā ttiña bāśi' guysnä yai kiḍa śirkä
raṃnīnai haṃbīsä khiṇḍa tcarṣu

2 65. dyena ysire vā parabyūttä pa'|jsä mu'śdi jsa haṃtsa
vahaiṣṭī ttāja parauysandai vaska dukhä
karītte jsa śirye stāma jsa virśä'na
3 khu jsā ttā ājiṃdai | huṣkä vī rräja[1]

66. ttai hvai si hai naḍi khve śirka sastä īye
cu ni muḍī ūca jīye byaudai ysuṣkä
4 munā | tta hirṣṭai ṣva nąma ni huña . krraña
bhąga ąmuhä nāsä ṣanau tta maṃna :

16r1 67. ṣi' [vā].|vā niḍi tvī va ājīdi jsināka
ttina rruste ba'ysa ṣi' hvi hīya dasta .
2 [ru] rurä guysnä | ṣṭąna yuḍai duṣkarä kīrä .
ttanā namasū ṣadi gaurava thauña .

3 68. pharākye stāma | jsa vāthīyai vāṣṭä
hatcastye nauvi jsa sāṭīka samudrra .
4 raṃna vā nuḍai śira va|sva agaṃjsa
pāpaṃkārä brrāte paysä krrąñī kiṇa

69. apracai āna ṣi' tvī sānä himye
16v1 | husaṃdai ąne bre tcęmą'ña thīye
kharīja rraisvi gvahai'ñä cve ttā hvasve[2] .
2 lobhä pracaina ttauma raṃnāṃ | vaska .

70. ne hami'stä aysmu ttye brrābharä[3] vīra .
saṃ khu ātaśä' cu pauryau ni hamaitte
3 | krrąñīnai bhātai ttu haṃdara muśde' .
haṃdrrūṣa purrdai tvī aurga miḍąne

4 71. samu|drra tsuai nātāṃ bīśä hai thu miḍāni .
cidurä[4] āmācä ṣṭąna pārysai rruṃdą .
17r1 ysu|rri jsa sujsaṃdā ttu ra nāta viśu'na
duma jsa pvestyąna eha byava niraṃde 81

[1] rraṃja. [2] hvaste.
[3] brrātarä. [4] vidurą.

2 72. thu mī vara mudai | haṃtsa tcuramyai haḍai .
yuṃdā hvai gaṃbhīrą uvārä
ne' raysāyaṃna hamagä brrahma-vyahāra .
3 ra | ṣi'yānąhīvya śira nāṃdä padaṃja :

4 73. hajva bvąmaya parehaṃdā krramna | .
padeṃdai nāta daṃda aysmva biśä .
17v1 samudrrä mąñaṃdai yai bvau'me jsa miḍą. | ne .
tvī orga haṃ vī bāḍä ṣadi jsa brīya :

74. kṣu ttarrna duṣpya sujsaṃdā-jsaima .
2 ysīra . | grąñaṃca bīysīsaṃdai śąṇḍäna .
cu āṣṭā puraka hvarä vrrāghrraja strīya
3 yu. | ḍai ttyāṃ vīra mahākāruṇa uvāra .

75. ttye vrrāgri kįṇa garna pastī ttąma
4 khu | na hvīḍä hīya brra puraka vitka .
haṃthrrīyai aysmu ysamaśaṃdai vaska
18r1 ava' | ste haurākä tvī orga miḍāne :

76. khue kṣaudi mīḍi vasve ba'ysā dā
2 brrahä bedä kaṃga gurvai ṣadi jsa | brīya
hatcastę . āstai ırä mąñaṃdä śī
3 uysāñe bida kala śu'stai ttye jsa baṃda

77. jīvaina hamagä hųñä ttarų̄na .
4 narä udiśāya narrvai hīvye re .
dīdaṃ | de dāvī ya gaurava ṣada .
kelāsa garna häpaga[1] styūdā beda .
18v1 78. brahmadevä rre ṣṭāṃ . | dā brrīya uvāra .
dīdi staura ėṣṭyai ha⟨ṃ⟩tharka biysāṃja .
2 ttane gaṃbhīrä samudrrä mąñaṃ. | dä bvų̄ọcya
dukhya bajattye ttuṃñe tsų̄mī orga :

79. udvīyastä ysātī rāysāysña uska bihīvī
3 | pve'stī ttya rruṃdā byehä pharä salī
nvastä avyāyaṃdai bu'ysä⟨bāḍna⟩
4 tta tta muṃdai ma jve vaña āche | be.da

[1] haṃmaga.

80. śera nāma rrustai cue ya si sūnetträ .
mukä-paṃka nāma himyai ṣiṣṭa-biśā'
19r1 pravaje kṣaudā ha | spiscya parāhä .
parrīyastāni śirkye ą'me thāna :

2 81. yāva khue rrāśa' yuḍāṃdä hamai ri | ṣa'yä .
avamāva kūla parryai satva dukhyau jsa .
3 ba'ysa-vīrīñä yuḍai vara tte. | ña kṣīra :

82. hamya phara satva dhyąna-lābhya vrrasta :
4 aysmvījvā bīsvā bīsā baysga . | jaḍīja .
kūra dṛṣṭīja stura ttāḍā ttrikṣa .
19v1 dā hīyau bā'yau harahustai rraysga | na

83. tta tta khu urmaysdi paśa' bāḍū āśa'
tta khu viśi'rä pąna urvārīnai garä burṣḍä
2 vaṣprīśtä jīyabąñi | karya jsa tta tta bu'ysa bāḍna
3 magāra jaḍīja hatcastai ttāḍā tvī orga miḍāne : |

4 84. : strīya brrī kṣudai gvāysīnai dainą
naṣau' | dai aysmya tta khu pyaura mayserka .
utcīnai garkhä pāsä tcänā[1] buysvaiye . 10 .
20r1 | ysāysa kīśeṃja pana bāśa' ṣi' dai .

85. vījä yai daśtä gūmā keśavä nāma .
2 sañi jsa ttye | strīyi udiśä sve beṃdä
pātcä muḍa strīya bāstai garkhu bu'ysye bāḍna .
3 haṃdaryāṃ vya | ysana jai tsųme orga :

86. pajaṃdai braṃmaṃ viśpastī kiṇa .
4 behī bure pva'ste hatcañā | me vīra
sarvadattą rre ṣṭā cu haurä pajiste .
20v1 khve na ya haṃda haurāma vaska yu | ḍai

87. hārīscya hivī jīye biśna .
karāśi jsa bastadā hīya dasta .
uysānā haiṣṭai ttye braṃmaṃ ttāma
2 ṣi' | ahā puṣa bāsta sānä rruṃdā haiṣṭhe :

[1] tcaṃna.

88. keyuḍa ysarrnā sakyau jsa samartha
3 tti bāysve | ttą̄ma khu nārą̄yaṃ gyastä .
ttīśna' śūrīna śakrra muṃdai saṃ raudrra
4 se dyāma māttra haṣprrī sohna pu | ṣā

89. se āysaṃ bedä gorva kiṇa bīśų̄ña
brrų̄na pajsama cue ttā haiṣṭe
21r1 kṣamauttā pā.. | ysvīrä śāṃ brīya ysirastä .
cakrravartta jsą̄na himyai ṣai ttina ysaṃthäna

2 90. jīvīji pīhä ⟨haṃ⟩jsau | dai miste .
ttīśa'sta bu'jse ba'ysuśti pracaina .
himyai āspāta sarvasatvā mista
3 byūrä kū | la jų̄na mamī jsāṃ tta orga :

91. garä hīyau ttrikhyau piṣkistä samudrrä
4 hatcastye nauvi jsa . | sāṭīka anāha
mu'śda' jsa vaska jīye kṣīna yuḍai :
ṣaiṣṭa tvī beṃdä u rraṃjāṣṭą naraṃdą

21v1 92. | sāṭīkāṃ pvestī ka ni uci mīrāre .
tti vā bīsa byodāṃdä biśä dukhą naṣau'da
2 śuka tsai pari | lo ttyā keṇa ava'stä
ttine śira satva aurga pātce aurga :

3 93. vasve naṣo'dą ysīrrä māñaṃ | dä che jse :
kaṃga ya tvī bedä raṃnyo jsa najsata .
āta ttā tvī va asidūna jsanāka
4 bi'stā | de kaṃga biśā satvāṃ beda :

94. na uysaṃdī thu vāṣṭa hirṣṭai vīra
22r1 uysana be'-tuḍa ka na tti . | satva mīrāre .
nāgarājä ṣṭāna yuḍai duṣkarä kīrä .
2 ttanā namasųmä ba'ysa ṣadi jsa brrī | ya :

95. jaṃbuña cauṣkaña mura pura yuḍāṃdä .
tvī tteri beṃda ttą̄ma pīrūyä bāḍna
3 | drrai māśtä vina pveṇä vara ą̄ste kamą'ña .
ṣabajsyau rrijsyau tvī baistädä ttāra :

4 96. vratta | vaśca rṇä ni nvathātai gvāna
tta tta-ṃ kāṣṭe khu māta pura ki'ttä
22v1 virśīja pa'jsadi dūrā śira | styūda
dijsākye hālai tvī orga miḍąne :

97. āchaija gyauha mīrānī ya dukhya .
2 maiysyūna kṣuva anāspe | ta anāha
patsyai thu jīye brī ttye kiṇa aṃga .
vīni o'sä ṣṭāna rruśta vīra miḍąne

3 98. | mu'śda pracaina gyauhya drrųne kiṇa .
hauḍai thu hīyą hųña guśti jsa hatsa .
4 cu bure ysama | śaṃdya dukha-vīya uysnaura
thvaṃ śuka ttrāste tvī orga miḍąne :

23r1 99. ṣava-tsuka būva u. | kalaputtana baysgä
ājavaiṣa' ysurrja naṣpulaṃdā vāṣṭa
2 rakṣa[kṣa]ysāṃ myąña tta vā yakṣāṃ pyā | ña[1]
gara ttraṃdī thu nere drrąñī[2] kiḍna :

100. tsuai thu gyastāña kītha kiṃnara-dvīpa
3 ārāhye mistä | ttrāma kinara-rruṃdi
ājidai vāṣṭä rrīna kinara-kąña |
4 ttanā namasų | mä ba'ysa ṣadi jsa brrīya

101. crrāṃ mąñaṃdū purra brrųña vasve
23v1 āśa' vina myaurāṃ[3] nakṣāttrā[4] | myąña
tta tta ba'ysä ysāṃdī dīpaṃkarä brrūnä
khu dyai paṃdāya jsąna śāstārä ttu :

2 102. jala haraṣṭai | thu khājaña ttye va ttąma .
ṣadyāyä gauriva jsai pą⟨jsaṃ⟩ yuḍai .
āṣai upala harastai hā beda
3 | nātai thu vyāraṇa ba'ysuśta varāṣṭa :

103. avamāyau bu'jsyau bu'jsaudī ba'ysa .
4 bvākī | thu hastąmä nirvąnų paṃde
24r1 paphādai satva vasve dātī.ne... | ne'na :
ttaną ttā aurga ttāṣṭa gauravi thauña

[1] myāña. [2] krrañī. [3] pyaurāṃ. [4] nakṣattrā.

104. urmaysdā hīyau bā'yau jsa bajauttä
2 vīysịnai grau | nä khu paṃtsyāṃde satva
ttu mąñaṃdä paṃtsyai rruśtä dvīpā beda
3 ṣai hivī brrī jīye ttye dā . | kiṇa pātcä .

105. śe śilo kiṇa dāña ttraṃdī hāṣṭa .
viysīña paśtä sa khu hastä vahaiysde .
4 | niṣau'dai aysmya hagavąma hīsī .
ttarrai dā vaska ttine pākvā orga :

24v1 106. pura | ra pe'me'sti aysgaṃ rraijsai pneha[1] .
dva makala ṣīka cu ttā makalä paśāte .
2 ysīnīya tvīvī | āspeta jsa tvare bīhīye
aysmu kauṣṭä mu'śdi pracaina .

3 107. ustairṣṭai aṃgāṃ be | dä jsiṇakye chale
huṃjīja mista kane stura stura pha .
4 balą hā haiṣṭai ttyāṃ caska[1] uysgrī |
ṣanaumāyä khue jsā ttā paskyāṣṭä huḍe :

108. ysdāysa[2] hīyāra chaka bāgara hvāra
25r1 a | nattāgä nāma sarrau datā rre .
ttavaścaraṇī tta tta khu diva-riṣa'yä
2 śura virśau'dä ttine | pākvā orga :

109. sāṭīka paṃ-se mai'ysdyąna anāha .
hanaṣṭādä ttārä vīṣṣąmera alavä
3 | cu gaṃtsvā pasta garyau saṃgyau hvasta .
khaiṇuḍvā baṣkhvā tta khu prrīya narīya :

4 110. ttyā vaska | dasta pasvai mu'śda pracaina .
biśūṃ hagrīya dīryai kāṣṭa pacaḍna .
25v1 byaudāṃdä maśma[3] hvāha' | dukhą naṣau'da
hitteṣī ṣṭāna yuḍai duṣka kīrä

111. ttāḍeta kaṣṭye ysamaśaṃdai vaska
2 yuḍai upakārä | harrūñąma tvī
cirau mąñaṃdä himye pąñe pana
tcema'ñāṃ haurākye tvī ttā aurga :

[1] vaska. [2] ysāysa. [3] maśpa.

3 112. kū | ra-dṛṣṭīja ttāra kīśana baysga .
hanaṣṭāṃdä satva buysa bāḍä jaḍīna
4 thaṃ[1] vaska dā | tīnai cirau didai
tcaṃna byaudāṃdä vasve āryā paṃde :

113. pīha udiśāyä śirye ba'ysāṃ dā
26*r*1 nīlopa | lä mą̄ñaṃdä dvī tce'mą'ña ysuṣke .
sunaitträ rre ṣṭāna hāysa hoḍai brrīya .
2 ysamaśaṃdai tcema vadī tva | ttā orga :

114. dhyattarāṣṭrrä[2] ną̄ma syą̄nä rre yai hvāṣṭä
3 āṣaiṃjä haṃdrra śarāṃ mānasa | ną̄ma .
cu tvą̄na bu'jse dīśi' vīra biraṣṭe .
brrahmadattä juttai rruṃdä kāśāṃ kṣīrī :

4 115. | yāva tta khu ātī ttye panaka hāṣṭa .
uysāstā hvarrä khu ne' pejsīdä gvą'ña
26*v*1 āhu | rrja āśrīvādä vyasthānaiya biraṣṭai
śirkä va mū valmīkä āste ysūrrī

2 116. saṃttoña bu | ysna pathīsīdä na śiryau kīryau jsa
ṣi' hvī ysathä āspāte hācä himye
3 satvāṃ ysa. | maśaṃdya mistä .
ttanā ttā namasuṃ brra sarvaña ba'ysa :

4 117. baura pyą̄me jsa ysumana āṣṭi mi | rāṃ
hvīyeṣai āṣṭi mīrāṃ ttī jsāṃ kṣųna
thvai arrä ṣṭāna khu pye purakä ke'ttä
27*r*1 ėrakaña kāṣṭe jīyne[3] hmaṃ | ge .

118. ṣa' araña ṫyarai paṃda satva .
lobhe udiśāye byehāysāṃ pyaṃtsyą .
2 guḍe | ttanīyā tvīṣe yuḍāṃde buvāṃde guśta .
3 arnīñe dasti varī śaṃdya pasta | 40

119. kṣamauttā mu'śde' akhauṣṭe aysmu styūde .
4 ysīra puñaṃdai ttuṃña tta khu re | ne vīśe're .
ttuṣvā' tsve miste pajsaṃ byaudai suhve .
ttane tsu ȯrga ba'yse goreva thą̄ña

[1] thvaṃ. [2] dhṛ°. [3] jīyena.

27v1 120. | aśe yai āyạnī rruṃde subhadrre .
haysgema byaude ṣe' rre sạnā myạña .
2 peroḍai.yī | tha śirye mu'śde jse verśa'na .
ssa puna stāstā ce bestāṃde aga :

3 121. paraṃthaña verttai ve|re bāṇve baysge
veysvā ṣṭā drroṇve ṣeṣve tvī bede pa'jse .
4 raysgena veyse . | murdai ne cahaṃdī kheja .
paphvai rruṃde kīthe cevyai tvī ttā órga :

28r1 122. gode nạma prrāṇe yai | ysareguṃ che jsa .
samuvā ūḍāṃde raṃñau jse jsacaḍena[1] .
2 amu'śdye satvạ prrahareṇyo | jse beśe
śuḍvāṃde kuṣṭāde kaṃge pa'jsye lobhena .

123. pha drrvạṇe prrāṇā ca śau'vāṃde aṃga
3 | kṣemā bhāvyai saṃttāṃ akhoṣṭa .
ttī śā'dī huṣṭī saṃ pāśe're ṣṭāna .
4 mere pyare mạñaṃ|de tvī pākāṃ aúrga :

124. berāṣva veselakye kheḍe mista uvāra :
28v1 cekrravarttạna śerāṃ rruśte | jse suhena .
ttaraṃdare drrūnai pa'jsa dyạma śirkyạ .
tte tte khu pure spāśe purṇa paṃjeśe' vīra

2 125. | rre ṣṭāne padmake dyai satvạ dakhautta .
kṣụna āchaine anāspete śạtcaṃpha 1
3 keve ha|myai haije khu gūśtīne gara .
hvaḍāṃdā satvạ hemya drrụnạ pa'jsa .

4 126. ṣai sāne ha|medā ysera ṣṭe dī dyai .
ma ne rā vā pva'se ysuṣke bra bra hvạṇḍe
29r1 anā|ṣi'ṇe nāvai phare ysaṃthe veśụna .
prraṇạhānā kẹṇe nal[2] pakāṃ aúrgä :

2 127. pi'jse dai haṃ|ge'sta śeña kīśeña bāśa' .
baysaṃdai gāma paṃde vahī pvehna .
3 mạraṃ mạñaṃ|de phusti ge'sane dụmī jṣe .
ha bu'yse bvāysve ācīnā dasta .

[1] pacaḍena. [2] ttai.

4 128. tcane ā|ce ṣṭe bahya kīśeṃje beda .
mura data bāśa' pha are bīysīyai
29v1 viraṃdā | behya besaijaṃdā de
si muṃ vāttālä pane herthaṃ vīra

2 129. thu mī tteña bāśa' husure śe beṃhye | beṃda
ttere ṣīke āstīye bu'jsyau jse samartha .
ttre kūstai uce patcauttę pā bu'jsa .
3 tvī pu|ño harbeśą dai bu'ysva avīpa

130. ce ttu verśa' thīyai ce bede parāhi .
4 kṣamauttā mu'śde' sa|rvasatvāṃ vīre
ttene nve kṣama bu'ysvai dai dede miste de .
verśo'de ba'yse ttene pākāṃ aúrga 1

30r1 131. | beysīḍā śaysde pasųjsadā-neśte .
ba'-bhūḍe[1] haskye uysna tcęmąña aṃga .
2 beśųña prrą|ṇā kave khuysā meysairka .
mere myāña simądrre ttraṃdī śųka .

3 132. bāysvaje | hauve jsa saṃ hīvī virśe'na .
sāgare nā biśe tsvai raṃnāṃ vaska .
4 cettąmeṇe nu|ḍai raṃne jaṃbvī vīre .
neśācai ysarrvai[2] bāre satvā caska[3]

30v1 133. suhya beśe satvä hamya sa|jya hova .
tte khu striyestrīśa ce dukhą nąma na bvāre .
2 sarvārthaside ṣcąne yuḍe duṣkere | kīre .
hemyai ba'ysųña raṃna tvī ttā aúrga :

134. sāṭhīke pa-se āṣṭāde mīrāṃ
3 ce nauvi | byūtte pąda hīvī pvehna .
thaṃ natcāṣṭe ṇvāstai kurme prrąṇai ṣṭąna .
4 tte vā ahā [pa] | paskyāṣṭe jsāṃde ttaṃdā keṇa

135. sahyai saṃ ėṣṭyai āysįre udeśe .
31r1 cai dūrā kāle pamyę mu'śde' jsi |. śuste
hamaṃge aysmu sąne vīre u pure
śte[4] vā nąnuṃ[5] brra sarvaña ba'ysa :

[1] ba'-tūḍe. [2] ysarrnai. [3] va°. [4] tte. [5] vanuṃ.

2 136. kājenesār = re ṣṭā | dā brrīye uvāre .
suhavāysai[1] ttraikṣa' vīne jīye beṃda .
3 cvai ttaraṃdare narrvāṃde pha|rāke daiśe' .
pīlīrrvą stardāṃde rruṃ nīyāde hāṣṭą :

4 137. pasvāde dī-māla tteraṃda.|re beśe .
pasve haṃ bāḍe khu hauṣke brrāṃje pasuste .
31v1 ysemaśaṃdai kaiṇą yuḍai . | duṣka kīre .
ėṣṭevana ba'yse sime pākāṃ órga :

2 138. byehāyse rre guysve[2] udeśe pụna | paśāve .
ttī ahā bai'ste hasure vīysāṃje ṣṭāna .
3 mareṇą dve vīna tte na sąste | hugvą̄na
mire pyare udeśāye hvai' ysairka salāva

4 139. avījsyaṃdā ysāḍaka | dva mārā-pyara .
venai maṃ vure na ye haṃda kā'ke .
32r1 tta vaña muṃ khu ya.|nīde muṃ kṣụnę mīrāre
ysāysįña gvahąña ṣṭāṃ bāśe' ttuśąña .

2 140. śerā cede satvāṃ va ṣī|ve haḍāya
beśe bāḍe pvā'se ḍa[3] nạ dūkhya hamāre .
3 krrañīna vāyse yai śą̄ma|ke ṣṭāna .
verśāṃ'de ba'ysą ttere jsā ttā aúrga :

4 141. beysā deṇḍe caṇḍa rre yai śu.rī | ysurrje
ttīśa'stą khu dai spāśe paysairke[4] .
ttye rruṃde hīvī ye haste uvāre .
32v1 śure gaje-|gąṇḍą rrājevarrdaṃ nāma

142. saṃjaya mistye rruṃde brrīye tvare
2 śebīyā satvāṃ āspā|ve ysīrūva .
saninaṃ khenāṃ vamurāke jenāke .
3 dyą̄naṃ ce meste śerā ttye | kṣīre vaska .

143. veśvāṃttare ṣṭāne puṣai hauḍai haura .
4 rrude āstaṃne khauṣṭe śau kṣī|re hvąṇḍa .
vaṃke gīre muṃdai vare ttaṃttrya bāśa' .
na īṣṭī horana ttane aúrgą mīḍąne

[1] aha°. [2] guysne. [3] ka. [4] maysairke.

33r1 144. | śaysdyau jse kīśana anaṣāṃ'de atsāṣṭa:
dūma jsa byavyau jsa pasūjsaṃdā-ttīśa' .
2 bīhī | pva'scyąna ttrekṣe ysīra bajāṣe .
rakṣaysyo maryo khoysaṃdai skarbe .

3 145. haṃ vīre śurī śū | re puñau hīvī ttīśe'na .
vaspuḍai śaysdā beda hvāhye ysairena .
4 samųdrre ṣṭā nū | ḍai phare raṃne avīha' .
padedai satvą sūhya cū ya dakhautta .

33v1 146. mu'śde' vīrśä' śurī cū | haṭha parāhe' .
ttyāṃ vaske bājaṃ yai harbeśe ysaṃtha .
2 vīryabala ṣṭąna yuḍai | duṣkare kīra .
ttane ttā aůrga mūhu jsa pākāṃ dīna .

3 147. tte tte khu pura ysāṃde vesve | āvaśe' vīra
ā khu haṃdrrāṃje besā veselake spāśa .
4 keste keyure hāre grau | ne galąna .
ysīrrna raño jse mirāhyau jse samartha .

148. dyāne ve brrīyā ya śaṃde bede .
34r1 | ā māra-kąña ce uvī hośa' avīpa .
śīve rre ṣṭąne rrīna patsyai ysuṣka
2 dā udiśā | ye satvāṃ keṇe pātce órga :

149. aṣṇake ṣṭāne reṣa'⟨yä⟩ mu'śde' pracaina .
3 vekṣottai dāṃ | vaña saṃ khu kṣųna ne mīḍe .
ce āṃ pa'jse beṣṭā kṣu ttarna khejautte .
4 bāyāke pa | ñe satvä tvī ttā órga :

150. tte khu sumīre garna samudrre kauṣṭāṃde .
34v1 khu mī tteña ḅeḍe mista raṃthą | pana .
dedrrąmye tcephine drro mestye ṣkalana
tcure-ysąña hīne cu hā kṣịrāṣṭe ttraṃda

2 151. | tte tta khu mārīña hīne ā aysurąna .
prrahareṇyā kīśana pha satva vīśū'na
3 sta | rda beśe karvīnā pa'jsāṃde kaṃtha .
se veña ttye kṣīre yanīde ṇe'māṃ beśta .

4 152. na | raṃdī hāṣṭe tha ttye panake śūka :
tte khu dyūma baste sero spāśe pichaṣṭe .
35r1 naṣḍodai ttyāṃ | va śaṃge ce rrvī' thīye .
khu hvastai śaṃdā beśe śaṃdya pastą

2 153. gujsebrīyą hva hva deśe' vīre | tcabrrīya .
ave'stā byaude ṣe' kṣīre sāno beśte :
pha dāṃje byodai ttraśe rrespare ṣṭą̄na
3 | nāre ysāre ysuṣṭi rruṃde hį̄ya dūvą

154. tvī puñau satvä śerenīrą vestāva .
4 cekrreva | rtta jsāna hamyai vaṙe tteña ysītha .
karma-paha saṃvere node satva paceḍena
35v1 ttene ttā | auṙgą mu'hu jse pākāṃ dį̄na :

155. ajegarna pa'jse sāṭhe dukha-vī tvare .
2 cvai thu dyai alavāṃ jsāṃ mu' | śde' jse pātce .
saro rre ṣṭą̄na hayuṃ gurṣṭye hasta
bejeṣyai haṃtse yuḍai jį̄ye | kṣīna

156. hasta bede satī stai nauha kamala .
4 pāyve jsai gvaṣṭai ttāre bekhauṭe a | vīpa
sāṭhīke gūve jīye byaudāṃdą beśe
thvai hāḍa rrustai brrī hayuṃna haṃtsą .

36r1 157. | pharākę satvā hye suha' udaiśāya .
2 ahavāysai āyauyse beśe mu'śde' prra | caina
phare ysaṃtha ṣṭānę yuḍai duṣkere kīra .
3 ba'ysūśte brrīye ttene pākāṃ aụ̇ | rga :

158. pātce vā aṣṇai kaṇe bą̄'jsą vaska
ūstairṣṭai chala guśte agyāṃ beda .
4 uysgrī | udeśāye nai ācastai suha' .
cakrravarttą̄nai śerā cve ya miste .

36v1 159. cvā jse pe' l kūysdāṃde āspāta buḍāṃde .
beśāṃ tte tta gīstai khvaṃ āvaṃ sije .
2 mamī pā ttaṃdī pe' a | jse piḍą̄ne[1]
diśe'ną hori avaśe ba'yse himą̄ne :

[1] m°.

3 160. mu'śde' jse satve hamaṃge brra | ya beśe .
śere dīre myą̄ñā avaysą̄ñą paysą̄ña .
4 si ṣą sāne ṣi jsāṃ hayuṃ | ne ye
sañā ttane cu tvī dharmāṃ vīna satve saṃña .

161. khve vaska brraṃmaṃ ā ttaṃttrya bāśa' :
37r1 | pajeste pureke dva aysmu harṣa' .
cejelake[1] ramaña bravīya agaṃjsa .
2 ysaujsą | hvare hvą̄ña ṇe'ne śū'sti salāva

162. ttenīyuṃ hauḍai ba'ysūśte prracaina .
3 sahyai | purą̄na ñuska brīyā streha'
brraṃmanuṃ haudva habasta kīḍye jsa .
4 bu'yse khai | nuḍe kerāśe ttye jsaṃ hvaste

163. ce nvāśāṃde ṣanau yuḍāṃde dukha-vī tvare .
37v1 ysīrūṇe baṃ | tve maysdyūāne anāha .
hāyse burą pyuṣṭai ttyāṃ yserka salāta .
2 sumīre ga | re khaiṇḍe sahyai tvī ttā aủrga : || ||

3 164. cade mare bvāmai ṣṭā sarvaña ba'ysa | .
ttū darro thīyai tvī bujsāṃ vaska .
4 cvaṃ himye īye śā-thāña nejsa . | ḍana
tvā ttāṣṭe āṣe'ṇa yą mu'śde' prracnai[2]

165. ṣi' tvą̄nai bā'jsīnai mahāsamudrre
38r1 ano vara | nauhą ce bą̄ne paśte na byaide .
śakrra brahmāne lokepālo varūṇe .
2 tvī ba'yse bu' | jsye beśe ne hva yụḍāṃde .

166. caṃ naṣphajāṃde mamī puña avamāta .
3 ce ba'yse bvejse | hvi ṣąde jsa brrīya
pajse ge' satvāṃ trāyāke himāte .
4 dūkhyo parsīme avaśe | ba'yse himāne

167. ca ṣi' ci ttu sāje vārśe' āsā yaṃde .
38v1 saṃskāre drraya sūrā | agapya himāre .
vasusīdī̦ ėdrre śradhā-deye paṃjse :
2 byehi jsāṃ paṃde vasve ba'ysu | śtāṣṭi .

[1] vejelake. [2] prracaina.

168. karmaṃ jsāṃ jąre kleśa' ttaṃge himāre .
3 ysaṃthą vare nāste kūṣṭai āvaṃ . | aúste .
śere satve pyaṃtsāṣṭe . ttaraśvāna ne rūye .
4 pacedena ka | rśe' bhadrre-kalpya ba'ysa .

169. marṇe bhaye āstaṃ pha ptąṇe[1] harīysa .
39r1 upa | drrava āchā sparśa'stą vaśū'ne .
bīsä vyachīde puñā hīvī ttīśa'na .
2 devattai para | vālā āysde yenāre .
ṣi' cvai ttu pīḍe vasve ba'ysāṃ dā : ||

3 ttū jāttaką-stavä bįysų̄ñāṃ dāṣkarā kī | rāṃ hīvī agą
cā kīmäśąnä pasta pīḍai biysūśtä brrīyi ttye pūñä kūśalä-mūla pārrjsai jsa
4 cakavartta śai tcūnä aṇi'scyä rāśä' gavu ga-vaśiṣa hamāvä upa- | ttavaśeṣa sthąnä-vīśaiṣa haiysdi vīra jsā vīśä'rä rāśä' rādä bviṃysye jsīñä prrīyągä hamāvį : maiscyi aṇe'scyąnä bvaiysa
39v1 jsīna hamāvi kalpa jsa | hajsaidiṃ karma bįśdi' jādi bįśa pīrmą-ttama ttā baiysų̄śti parīdi vyechai
tta ṣṭāṃ pūñä padä śānä pyarä pūhyä cā pina jsa habrrīhū gavi
2 vasasīdä : mira hū | māṃ bveysa jsīnä hamāvä
tta ṣ⟨ṭāṃ⟩ pūñä pyara hīye paysāye brrąvära cā ttaiha tcainä kharūṣa jsa habrrīhū u pūrā dvarā jsa
3 ttu ṣṭāṃ pūñä naira kīma hva jsa habrrīhū u dvīra | rūpājīva jsa : dvīrä jvālakya jsa brrāvara ttravīlai sīdyakavarrda jsa ttravīlai darmajñā jsa
4 harbīśāṃ aśi'rya gāṭhā vajrrayaunyāṃ jsa biśä satva bi | ysūśtāṣṭä vyārṇa byehīdä
aysa ttā pā cā [ca] kīmäśanä byehīme thyau madrrāṃ sījāṣṭä baiysūśtä vyichīme **kymš'n**[2] paysāvye hvārakyä sūraimaitrra jsa

[1] pvąṇe. [2] Sogd.

IV

BHADRACARYĀDEŚANĀ

P 3513.43–58

43v1 | siddhaṃ
aurga tsūṃ āsña paḍā ṣadi jsa brrīya .
parimārtha-bhą̄ṇai hvāṣṭä maṃjūśrī .
2 kuṣṭa ysautta | ką̄me ṣā' myāṃja śirā .
samāhāṃ śamatha ṣi' saṃ maṃjūśrī . ⟨1⟩

3 baudhasatvä namasūṃ ttū samaṃtta|bhadrrä
pūri ba'ysą̄nä biśāṃ dūkhāṃ jinākä .
hamaṃgte dyą̄ma vara samaṃttabhadrä
4 | ttāharai aśtä avārauttä akhauṣṭä . ⟨2⟩

biśi ḡyasta ba'ysa baudhasatvyau haṃtsa .
44r1 tti vā viña haṃ bā|ḍä mahū āysda yināṃde .
khu byehū pyūṣṭi vasva bhadrra-cirya .
2 tcaṃna biśä karma anāvariṇa ha|māre 3

cu buri ysama-śaṃdya dasau diśi' vīra .
dri-bāḍva īṃde ba'ysūña sarauva .
3 tti ttā a|ysä vąnūṃ biśä aharįna .
ttaraṃdarna biśā'na aysmūna vasvena 4

4 harbiśvā kṣįttrvā parimau|ṇava grīca .
didaṃdyau tteryāṃ ttā tsūṃ biśä aúrga .
harbiśāṃ ba'ysāṃ ṣadyāyi ysīrastä .
44v1 pichaṣṭū | śą̄ma jsa aysmuna sakicä 5

khu śe parąmāṇavä nauhya: ba'ysa anaṃtta .
2 ba'ysä pūra karvįnä śāstärä | myą̄ña
tti vā aharįna dharma-dhāttä aṇe'styä
biśī ṣṭāṃ ba'ysyau haṃbaḍä ayaiṣṭhe 6

3 ająnä | bu'jsīnä mahāsamụdrra bijāṣa
svarä drāṃ khu vela mahāsamụdra .
4 avamāva bu'jse ttyāṃ ba'|ysāṃ biśä .
aysū ttā hvą̄ñū stava namasūṃ nąda 7

cu ra jsą̄na pīrmāttama pūjā-karma .
45r1 hvīya jastų̄ | ña raṃna vāstyau śū'sta
tti āṃ aysä ūvāra pariṇą̄mūṃ biśä .
są̄mūhāṃ ba'ysāṃ aysmūna vasvena 8

2 | ṣā' deśana bhadra-cirya vauḍā hauva
spye u pa'sārā cu ra buśą̄ñä uvāre .
3 saṃkhalūñāṃ jsa | u bį̄ną̄ñāṃ vyūhä:na
haiśų̄'mū ba'ysāṃ paṃji-mą̄ṇḍalä ṣṭą̄na 9

4 cu ri buśą̄ñä pīrmāttami | vāstyau haṃtsa .
sūmīrä garä mą̄ñaṃdä kuṣḍyāṃ' jsa cuṇyau jsa .
carauvyau bvą̄'ñāṃ śirkāṃ jsa bīśą̄nä .
45v1 pą̄ | metuṃ diśi' vī biśä są̄mūha : ba'ysa 10

hastamyāṃ nauhauysyāṃ ba'ysāṃ pātcä .
2 cu ra arrve pīrmāttami | atvaḍirūve .
raysāyana harbiśä cu ra ysaujsa bijairma .
3 ttyau jsa ṣṭāṃ pajsaṃ yanūṃ ba'ysāṃ biśä | 11

cu ra mahā jsa yuḍa īṃde kīra viśų̄'na .
biśä ysaṃtha brrīye ysūrri jaḍī rrāśa'
4 | ttaraṃdarrna biśā'na aysmuna asįdāna .
tta ṣṭāṃ aysä dīśūṃ' biśä ārrä paysą̄ne 12

46r1 cu da | sau diśi' vī hvaṃḍāṃ pūñi īṃde .
sājara cu ra vā ṣai dāśāṃdä kīri .
2 prrattyeka-budha ba'ysä pūra | uvāra .
biśä baudhasatvāṃ anamaudūṃ pūjä 12[1]

carauva dātīnā dasau diśi' vīra .
3 | biysą̄ną̄me jsa vinau byą̄nä bīysāṃda
tti aysä pātcä harbiśä ājīṣū' ba'ysa .
4 ge'śīṃ | de pīrmāttaṃ dāyī cakrrä 14

cu vā parinervāṃ dyą̄ma kṣama īṃde .
46v1 tti ṣṭāṃ aysä āyācu aṃ | jalä ṣṭą̄na .
cu kṣittrvā gruīca didaṃdä kalpa viṣṭīde .
ysama-śaṃdai hye suhi: kiṇa jsīna dijsāṃde . 15

[1] 13.

2 | aürgyi tsū̹me jsa pajsaṃ dīśą'me jsa .
pūñau ysvyą̄me jsa ājīṣą'me dāna .
3 namaṃdrą̄me jsa cu haṃ | jsāṃda ī pų̄ñä .
hanaimūṃ ba'ysūśtāṣṭi harbiśä aysä . 16

4 cu ji haṃjsimāṃde ma | mī mara pūña ttaṃda .
canka masi namasī ārūva jsa ba'ysa .
sī yinī ba'ysāṃ nva cirya padaṃja
47r1 | haṃba'rī bhadra-carya dāna parāhä:na 17

pajsamevye yinī̹me pīrūya tti ba'ysa .
2 cū vā tti ṣṭā̆ṃ da | sau dīśi' vīra īṃde .
cu vā ūstamāṃjsya panamāṃde nvaiya .
3 ba'ysūśtāṣṭä āvaṃ ṣą' ū | spūrä hamāve 18

cu dasau diśi' vī ttyāṃ īṃde kṣaittra .
4 śirka paräśaudha vasva tvari uvā | ra .
usahīṃdi baudha-vrraikṣä dīnāṣṭä
biśä ūspūra ttyāṃ śāśaṃ' ī ū ba'ysä pūra 19

47v1 cvaṃ ra | vainīyā dasau diśi' vīra .
biśä sūhya: īṃde drū̹nā u samartha .
2 ysama-śaṃdya satvāṃ pātcä dā | ya artha .
hvaraṃcī̹ñä si̹jīṃde āvama biśä 20

ba'ysū̹ña mista carya cu aysä carī̹me .
3 jā- | smarä ysyą̄ne aysä haṃ vī bāḍi .
harbīśvā ysaṃthvā kuṣṭa ysyą̄ne ha'cä .
4 vaysaṃbą ṣą̄ | mą̄ñä byehī̹me aysä 21

harbīśāṃ ba'ysāṃ nva sājaṃcä ṣṭą̄na .
48r1 haṃberaṃcä badra-carye dāna pa | rāhna .
ahatcastä naṣi'rrī̹mä īyāṃdä agaṃjsä .
paraustä yinīmä pīrmātta vasve parāhä: 22

2 | jastū̹ñe phari u nāvą̄nye ttī .
yakṣą̄nye kuṃbhaṇḍāṃ hvīye pātcä .
3 cu ri jsą̄na phara ī ysa | ma-śaṃdya biśä .
uysdīśī̹mi ba'ysāṃ dā pharyau jsa aysä 23

4 bāysdyaṃdai pārąmvā' ha|skauttä ṣṭąna .
baudha-cittä na hanāśįmä hairṣṭi gvąna .
cvaṃ asida kīra ịṃde byąnaṃgāra .
48v1 | tta harbiśä jāṃde pātci thyau aharįna 24

kleśāṃ' karmyāṃ mārä hīvī paṃde .
2 ysama-śaṃdai tsūma vara | gūscya carįme .
vīysa vasva ūca cu āṃ ni saṃkhalyāre .
3 ā khu urmaysdi u pūra āśa' a|kaṣṭa 25

biśä avāyāṃ gatti dukha niṣaṃ' yinįme .
4 u harbiśä satva sūhvā vistā yinį|me .
biśāṃ va harbiśä hye carye yinįme .
daṃdä tta khu kṣittrvā parimąṇava grruīca 26

49r1 cirye biśä | satvāṃ anūvarttąkä ịme .
biśä baudhasatva-carya vasve yinįme .
2 u diśañe bhadra-carye hauva | nijsvąne .
ustamāṃjsvā kalpvā biśä carye yinįme 27

3 cu hama-nasa ịṃde pātcä mahā | jsa carye jsa .
ttyau jsa aysi haṃgūjī haṃ vī bāḍä .
ttaraṃdarä biśā'na aysmuna paba :
4 | prraṇihąnāṃ cirya vasva haṃtsa himāṃde 28

cū ra hayuṃdauśti jsa maṃ hye nva tsīṃde .
49v1 ttyāṃ nijsvąñūąṣṭä | paṃdi bhadra-carye jsa .
ttyau jsa mąha vī haṃgūjsi hamāve .
2 tti jsāṃ aysä [ysä] ysathvā ma vi[rā]ra|me gvąna 29

dijsąne ba'ysāṃ sadharmä pabastä
3 śirka ba'ysūñä carya vasve yi⟨nī⟩[1]|me .
ñāpīyū bhadrra carye hīya hauva .
ustamāṃjsyāṃ kalpvā būrä vasva aharṣṭa 30

4 | ttirṣṭhāda daime biśä sąmuha: ba'ysä .
karvįnā ba'ysä pūryau parṣi' jsa haṃtsa .
50r1 ttyāṃ āṣaṃ' pū|jä pajsaṃ hairṣṭä yinįme .
ūstimāṃjsyūā kalpvā akhająme nvaiya 31

[1] broken out.

2 harbiśvā ysaṃthvā tta tta tsų̄macä jsą̄ | na
puñau bvą̄me jsa dāna hvani kaśą̄ne .
hajvattā u daśti saṃñä gūstyi samādha .
3 ajāṃ | ja pājęñä ī bu'jsyāṃ byauda 32

śe grīci nauhya : aciṃdya phari kṣaittra .
4 vara ri jsāṃ ba'ysa | aciṃdya avamāva .
karvį̄nā ba'ysä pūra ū myą̄ña ba'ysa .
aysū biśä baudha-carya daimi pichaṣṭä ⟨33⟩

50*v*1 | tta vā aharį̄na diśvā' vīdiśvā' biśä .
drau nauhya ttradhva avamāva tti ba'ysa .
2 samą̄drä mą̄ñaṃdä vara | tta kṣį̄ttra ū ba'ysa .
tti aysä ttrą̄mą̄ne carya kalpa samųdrä 34

3 khu śe svarä aṃgä phari jsa | ttrą̄mą̄me jsa .
brrahma-svarä hūvasve śirkä ba'ysāṃ pvą̄'ne
4 harbiśāṃ ba'ysāṃ nva āśayi | pve'hä:
ba'ysų̄ñä biśā'na dā pvā'ne aharṣṭä 35

vara ają̄nai ṣi' pvehä: vasve bijāṣä .
51*r*1 drä- | bā̦dvāṃ ba'ysą̄na ci vīrai pvą̄'ne .
dātīnai cakrrä najsadä ge'śą̄me jsa .
2 ba'ysų̄ñi hauva jsa aysä | ttraṃdi himą̄ne 36

u śe-kṣą̄ṇä ustamāṃjsya kalpa pharāka .
3 kṣaṇyau ttrą̄mą̄ma aysä ttraṃdä | himą̄ne .
cū ttradhva kalpa dri-bā̦dva ṣi' pamāka .
4 vara kṣą̄ṇäna ttrą̄mą̄ma uspūrä yinį̄ | me 37

cu ttradhva tsūka ttä ba'ysų̄ña sarauva .
tti aysä biśä diṃme śe k⟨ṣ⟩ą̄ṇä hamaṃgä .
51*v*1 ttyāṃ hīya | haṃjsara pātcä ttraṃdä himą̄ne .
cā'yi mą̄ñaṃdä gūscyi hauva prribhāvana 38

2 cu ttradhvāṃ kṣittrāṃ vyūhä: mi | sta vimuha:
tti aysä ṇvāyime śe grvīcika nauhya .
3 tti vā aharį̄na diśvā' vidiśvā' | biśä .
ttrą̄mą̄ne kṣittrāṃ vyūhi: ba'ysāṃ paṃna 39

4 ustamāṃjsya ysama-śaṃdya cärau-| dijsāka .
ttyāṃ biysą̄nīme aysi dāyī cakrrina .
nirvą̄ṇḍu daime naṣą̄'mä tsāṣṭä naṣāṃ'dä .
52r1 ā|speva jsa usahịme ba'ysāṃ paṃṇa 40

vara raidhāṃ pą̄'ñāṃ tta tta tsīme hamaṃgä .
2 mistä yą̄nä pę̄'ñāṃ | dāśą̄ma vījsyą̄ne .
carye pą̄'ñau jsa hamaṃgä bu'jsyau byaudä .
3 mittra pą̄'ñau jsa hamaṃgä tsų̄ma | tsịme . 41

pūñau pe'ñāṃ jsa vasvatte vī tsīme .
bvą̄me jsa rraṣṭä akaṣṭä tsų̄ma tsịme .
4 hajva|ttā u daśta saṃñä hūvasve pą̄'ñä .
ba'ysų̄ña hauva tvā haṃjsāṃdä yinīme 43[1]

52v1 cu karmāṃ hauva tvā | haṃjsāṃdä yinīme [43]
cu karmāṃ hauva tvā baiśä vasve yinīme .
2 kleśāṃ' hauva tvā biśä vamurrdä yi|nīme .
mārịña hauva vinau hauva yinīme .
haṃberī bhadra-carya hauva jsa biśä 43

3 vasūjī | kṣaittra tti ba'ysų̄ña samųdra .
haṃdają̄ñą̄ne satva dhāttä samųdrä .
4 vījsyą̄ne dātīnä mahā|samųdra .
bvą̄me jsa haṃbaḍä vahaiysą̄ne samųdrä 44

biśä baudhasatva samųdrä vasve yinịme .
53r1 | haṃberī prraṇihą̄nīnai ttū samą̄drä .
pichaṣṭū daime ba'ysų̄ñä samųdrä .
2 vina khają̄me jsa kalpa ci|rye yinịme 45

ba'ysų̄ña carya dri-bāḍū vī tsūka .
utvaḍa baudhacarya prraṇihą̄nyau jsa .
3 tti | ayoä haṃ bāḍä yinịme bisa aharịna .
bvą̄ne ba'ysūśtä vasve bhadra-carye jsa 46

4 hi|mą̄ne hvāṣṭä pūrä ba'ysāṃ biśä .
hamāvą ną̄ma tta tta khu samaṃttabhadrä .
53v1 byehịme hama-nasä | ttye carya u bvāṣṭya .
ttye nameśä' kūśala biśä kīra tcaḍāṃde 47

[1] 42.

ttaraṃdarä bīśā'na aysmūna vasvena .
2 ttye | vasvatte jsą̄ vasūsīṃde kṣittra .
cvai ną̄ma bvą̄ṣṭya vasva samaṃttabhadrä .
3 drą̄ma pātcä maṃ ī nva | aysmū bvą̄ṣṭya . ⟨48⟩

baudhasatvä maṃjūśrī śūrī bvą̄ṣcya .
ṣi' vā saṃ samaṃttabhadrä hauva pacīḍa .
4 | ttyāṃ nameśä' aysä biśä sājaṃdai īme .
uspūrä ra kīra kūśala carye yinīme 49

54r1 avamā | va vaisthārya carya himāte .
haṃkhīysä vaṣṭä parye bvaijse miste .
tta tvā avamāvą̄ñä haṃbāḍä yinīme
2 | bvą̄ne ba'ysų̄ñä tti prrahālye raidhä 50

khu burä ttaiṣṭhą̄ma ī āvaśä' prrare .
3 biśä sadhāttä | vasvattā tta tta āya .
vasūsīṃde satvāṃ biśä karma kleśa' .
4 vasva prraṇihą̄na mamī pā | tcä ma jāṃde 51

ci dasau diśi' vī raṃnīnā kṣittr a
ālaṃgrya baysāṃ aysä haiṣṭä yinīme .
54v1 ja | stų̄ña hvīya sūhaja pūjā-karma .
hauḍä yinī grīcyau kalpyāṃ jsa anaṃtta 52

2 ci tvā pariṇą̄ma | na rruṃdä mą̄ñaṃdä hvāṣṭa
pvā'kä hve cankai ji hā vauḍā ysyāte .
3 carye ba'ysų̄ñi āyi | mą̄nai ą̄na .
pīrmāttama tvaḍa ttye tta pūña himāre 53

4 avāyāṃ phīśą̄ma ñatau ttye | jsa .
asidyau ra hayų̄nyau phīśą̄ma pātcä .
thyau rraysgä vīra daitä armyāyi ba'ysä 54
55r1 ci | tvā pariṇą̄me bhadra-carya uvāra .

hā hūbyauda jsīna vasva ttyāṃ mara bvą̄ñä .
2 hūtsve tsvāṃdä | paṃda tta ttye hvī ysaṃthä vīra .
cirą̄mai vasva carya samaṃttabhadrä 56
3 ttai pātcä tta tta byehīṃ | dä rraysgä vī thyau .

ṣai anaṃttanarya bisā tsų̄ma ttrikṣa .
paṃjsa yuḍi | jaḍī tsų̄me rrāśa'
4 | tvā vasva bhadra-carya hvą̄ñaṃcä ą̄na 57
aharį̄nai rraysgä ttä karma harbiśä jāre .

55v1 rūna bvą̄|me jsa lakṣa'ṇyau jsa ṣi' biśä .
gūttairrna bu'jsyau haṃphve hami aủṣkä
2 aña-ttīrthyāṃ mārīñāṃ gau' jsa a|khauṣṭä . ⟨58⟩
pajsamaḍä jastyau hvą̄ṇḍyau jsa ttri-lą̄kä .

thyau jsāvi ba'ysų̄ñä rruṃdä dī bahyāṣṭä
3 | khu tsva hame satvāṃ hye udiśāyi naittä .
butti ba'ysūśtä dharma-cakrrä prravartte 59
4 gū|jsaba'ji mārä hīya tvā hį̄na viśū'na .

cu ṣi' cu tvā pariṇą̄mana bhadra-cirya .
56r1 daiysda ā|vāśe' haṃdarą̄nä bīrāśe' .
ttyāṃ pūñāṃ vīvāvina ba'ysäna butte 60
2 ba'ysūśtä bvāri tti byą|mā na ni tcerai .

cu ttradhvāṃ ba'ysyau ṣā' ysūṣṭa u hvata .
3 pariṇą̄mana diśina pīrmāttama u|ska .
aysī vyachīmi kūśala carya uvāra 61
ṣa' deśina bhadra-carya uspūra himāve .

4 | kāla krre ustamauysye tsų̄me biḍa .
āvaraṇa karma biśa aharī jāṃde .
56v1 pichaṣṭū daime ava|śä armyāyi ba'ysä ⟨62⟩
sūhāva kṣitträ vasve thyau hā tsį̄me .

vara tsva ą̄na tti prraṇihą̄na uvāra
2 cū bu|ri vā ha'cä yuḍai pyaṃtsä vaṣṭīde .
vyarą̄ma aysä vara byehīme akhauṣṭa 63
3 pichaṣṭū | są̄muhä: ttye armyāyi ba'ysna .

vasūsīyu bhadra-carya pyaṃtsāṣṭä vaska
4 prraṇihą̄na ha|rbiśä tta khu maṃjūśrī .
ustamāṃjsvā kalpvā biśä carye yinīme 64
haṃbīrī ma ṣā' krra biśa aharį̄na

57r1 | ba'ysṳ̄ñä mąṇḍalä ysą̄nastä uvārä .
vīysaña vara byehīme upapattä ysaṃthä .
2 vara ṣṭą̄na vyā|rṇa byehį̄me aysä 65
pichaṣṭū armyāyi ttye sarvąñä ba'ysna .

3 khu vyārṇa byaudi yinūṃ va|ra ṣṭāṃ aysä .
narmą̄ṇyau avamāvyau kūlyāṃ ttī .
4 ttyāṃ jsa aysä satvāṃ hāvä yuḍä yi|nīme 66
hauva bvą̄me jsa dīśāṃ' vīdaśāṃ' biśä .

bhadra-carye pariṇą̄mana jsa cū byauda ī̄ṃde .
57v1 pū|ña aṇe'scya pīrmāttami utvaḍirūve .
vyaysanvā vįma parauysaṃdā satva 67
2 ttyau pūñau tsīṃdä bai|śä armyāya kṣittra .

bhadra-carye prraṇihą̄nyāṃ hvą̄ñą̄me jsa .
3 cu mara haṃjsāṃdä pṳñä | ttinka namasūṃ .
śe kṣąṇä jsa harbiśa sijīdi maṃ .
himāṃde satvāṃ prraṇihą̄na vasva 68

4 tti|na pūñäna gaṃbhīrä dā bhāviña nvaiya
satva-dhāttä bvāve vasva aysmū prrara .
58r1 ci buri ttye | deśaña vī hamara rrihāsa .
vamasį̄me aysä avaśä ba'ysä himą̄ne nąda :

2 bhadra-|carya-deśana ūspūra samāsyā || ||

58v vacat.

V

SUVARṆABHĀSASŪTRA

(*a*) Or. 9609.

3r1 ro biśś × × × ste jsa . ṣā × gyasta ⟨balysa⟩ u bodhisatva vara u gyasta dīvate nara nāga yakṣa vara haṣḍä × nau dātīnau pajsamu maṅga-

2 lu dā × × × -ī . u dātīn⟨au⟩ aysmū dātīnau raysāyanu pajāysāro . ‖ ttätä jsa ttä pracā ttätäña sūtro ce käḍäna sūtrāṇu rre nāma .

3 balysānuṃ jsa × × × × -e . u śśuṃñahe jsa käḍä uvāra śśärna padīna u dātīnai jsa ttarandarä hvīnde gyastānu balysānu . u jsīñe padaṃgya a-

4 vamāta . u pūrvayaugga k⟨ä⟩ḍe duṣkara . u ṣāvai ⟨prattī⟩tä *bo*dhisatvä duṣkarä kīrä . u vyātaraṇe jsa pharākānu gyastaṣṣānu . u sta-

5 vaṃ jsa u dīśane u pariṇāmane . u armūvane u āyitane u ājīṣaṇe . u balysāna mästä hauta u dīrāṇu käḍyānānuṃ jsa jäṅga u ×

6 rañä u biśśānu uysnaurāṇu mara ttätäña sūtro mū-ysaṃthiya haṃdara-ysaṃthiya haṃdāra hvīnde . u rrundunuṃ jsa bvāmata hvīnde . kho kṣīña u-

7 ysnaura handāḍe . kho nä dātu vätä viśtīndä . ku ne ne avāyä tsīndä kho mū-ysaṃthīna härna haṃdāḍa hämāre . ṣätä ttätäña sūtro hva⟨nai cu⟩

3v1 ye vā āchänakānu uysnorāṇu ttarandarīya āchā vahāñätä ṣätä mara hvanai . ttäna ṣätä sūträ sūtrāṇu rre ggurśtä . biśśā⟨nu⟩

2 rro handarāṇu sūtrāṇu därjsākānu paderākä ttätä ṣei sūtrāṇu rre gurśtä . cūḍe vā suvarṇabhāysūttamä nāma . suvarṇä nāma

3 ysīrrä . bhāsä nāma bärūñāmata . kho ratänvo' ysīrrä hastamä hvatä bärūñāte . tta tta ṣätä sūträ ttyau ttandryāmyau pracyau . hastamä bärūñä-

4 te . ttäna suvarṇabhāysūttamä nāma cu hastamä . cu aysu ttu sūtru suvarṇabhāsūttamu parstaimä hvatanau pīḍe u paysāñvī

5 padandaimä ⟨cera puña u ce?⟩ra śäḍā hämāta īyä āstanna merä pīrä hvaräṇu brātaräṇu harbiśyau ysanyau hayūnyau kalyāṇamitryau

6 harbiśyau haṃtsa haṃbrīhe . u biśśäna hvatänä kṣīrna . u biśyau . hvataṃ kṣīryau uysnauryau haṃtsa haṃbrīhe . u ttu padī biśyau sarvasatvyau jsa ārī-

7 he . ttuto śśäḍo . u aysuṃ jsa avaśśä avachaudo bvāmato byehīñä . u ttuto rro śśäḍo u ttätä puña tcuīnu mästānu rrundän⟨u⟩ bāyīmä . u śrī-mahā⟨dī-⟩

4r1 ⟨vate rro⟩ ttānu mä mara ttätānu puñānu vätä biśśä hvāṣṭä nasä . a-

vaśśä ṣä tta sabajīyä balysānu bodhisatvānu puñyau kho ttätäña sū-
2 ⟨tro⟩ hvatu ṣṭe
siddhaṃ
tta mä pyūṣṭu ttye bāḍä gṛjakūlu ggaru vätä balysä dharmadhāttu
hasāya āstä natäña balysāña rahāśśa va-
3 sutānu arrīmajsānu bodhisatvānu hastamānu hvate ttu sūtrāṇu
rrundu . ysīrrä māñandä bärūñemäte natä pyū've'mäte jsa . u na-
4 tä nvaśtemäte jsa . diśvo' tcūruvo' balysyau atiṣṭhānyau ayäṣṭhätä
västätä akhvīhānau . akṣubhyä sarbandä hāle . rravye hālai
ratäna-
5 kīyä . nihujsandä hālai armätāyä . nyūvajsa dundubhisvarä . ttutu
hvāñīmä atiṣṭhānu viśtāmato maṅgalīyä hastamu hvanau biśye
6 dīrye härä jänje käḍäna dīrye käḍägānä jiṃgye yanāku biśye suhi
yanāku . biśye dukhi jiggo . bāgo balysūśte . ttāhä śśäratete jsa
7 biśśäñe śśäratete jsa āysätu . ce vā parchuta-indriyyau jsa uysnaura
ce vā jsīna jäta īyä o parrätatära īndä . kye vā ne vä × ×
4v1 śau vä näṣa'stä īyä o yä jsa vā dīvate paraṃjse īndä . kama jsa
vā manāva brya hva'ndä auṣṭa ysurgya yande o kāmiña biśśa o
ggalū gga ×
2 haysgamata īyä o kāṣca u vadravä īyo gārīvä o puvaṇä o ahvarīysä
īyä . kye vā grahyau nakṣatryau pīla īyä o cā'yyau dāru-
3 ṇä nuṣṭhurä o ce vā auśu hūnu daiye kuṃ jsa kāṣca u vadravä
hämäte . II ttye huysänauttäna suraiṇa pyū'vāñä hastamä sūträ kye
pyū-
4 vānde ttu sūtru natu balysānu rahāsu vasutäna śśärna aysmūna
suryo prahauṇyau āysätyau ttätä biśśä auṣku uvadrava hunuṣṭhu-
5 ra ttiśäna rrūndete jsa ⟨u ttäty⟩e sūtri käḍäna näṣamīndä biśśānu
uysnaurāṇu . hamatä lovapāla ttätä haṃtsa āmākyau haṃtsa hvāṣṭyau
6 pārysyau ttānu uysnaurāṇu rakṣo yanīndä anaṃkhäṣṭyau yakṣyau
ha⟨ṃ⟩tsa . sarasvatä mästä gyastä . trāmī rro nairaṃñä nätä vätä
āṇaṃkya
7 ⟨. u hā⟩räva dyūvānu ūśahārānu māta u styūda śśandye dīvata
brahmāna rrunde . u ttāvatrīśa rrunde . nātānu rrunde mästa hautana
kinnara-
5r1 rrunde aysurāṇu rrunde o suvarṇa-pakṣa-rāyānu rrunde . ttä hā
tsīndä haṃtsa hīñe jsa gīhäna bāryau ttānu rakṣo yanīndä ṣṣīvi
haḍāya
2 abätanda ttu sūtru uysdīśśīmä nato balysāno hajsaro rahāsu

5r2 biśśānu balysānu . duṣkara kūla kalpa vaṣṭa kye pyū'vānde ttu sūtru cai vā
3 handarye hvāñīndä . cai v⟨ā ha⟩l⟨c⟩*i*ndu hanu armūtīndä . cai ju vā pajsamu yanīndä ttä vā pajsama-jsera hämāre . anaṃkhäṣṭa kūla kalpa va-
4 ṣṭa gyastuvo' nāguvo' hva⟨ṃ⟩'duvo' kinnaruvo' aysuruvo' pārysyau puñīnai haṃbīsä avamātä aṣumuḍä atāṣṭä cu ttānu haṃjsaundä
5 hämäte . yäḍa-śśäḍānu uysnaurāṇu ttä nāta hīvya hämāre . balysyo daśvo' vidiśvo' nato tsūmato vätä tsūmandyau bodhisatvyau trāmī śśäre pra-
6 haune prahauyāña hubuśśānā prahauṇe däjsāña aysurrä hayūnauśtīnei aysmū vaṭhavāña . pajsamī tcerä abätaṃdä × × × × ×
7 arrīmajsä aysmū uysānye yanīru vasūjīru aysmū pyūvī'ru sūtru hastamu hutsutä ttye hva'ndye hubyaudī hvīyä hī⟨yärä juvīndä⟩
5v1 kye ttu sūtru pyūvā're . ustauda bärūñaṃce śśäḍye bāta ttānu pharākyau balysyau buljäta ttānu ṣei hvanei gguvo' pīttä . || suvarṇabhāysūttamä⟨na⟩
2 sūtrāṇu rrundäna āstanī päṣkalä näṣa'tä || [*Figura rotae.*] ttiye rro vā bāḍä ttye scätä rājagṛhä miśta kīntha ruciraketṭu nāma vätä bodhi-
3 satvä āstä ṣä paḍā⟨ṃ⟩jsyānu balysānu vätä yäḍa-vajsamä . kälstä väta śśärye härä bāta pharāka kūlai nayuta satä ysā-
4 re gyasta balysa ce pajsamu yäḍe vätä ttye tta hämätu cu ttīma u cū pracai cu gyasti balysi śśākyamunä tterä batu jsīñe pamāka
5 cu tta ttye × × se × ha⟨ṣṭātä⟩ salī . ttye bodhisatvä tta hämätu se hvate rro gyastä balysä dvī ttīmañä . u dva pracya bulyso dārajsīnyauñu varata . kāmä
6 dva . jsaṃgye jsa pathaṃka . u khāysä haurāmata . pātcu rro vā pharāka anaṃkhäṣṭa kūla nayuta satä ysāre gyastä balysä śśākyamunä jsaṃgye jsa .
7 pathīyä u yāva dasau kuśala-karma-paha hamaṅgu biśśīnda parauste u khāysu anaṃkhäṣṭ⟨u⟩ uysnaurāṇu hūḍe aṃdumaśu hīvī × × ×

24r1 āvuto rraysauya . o kho ṣä āvū tcam⟨ä⟩ña kṣāṣa' ttāṣe' ā're . aysmū ttu padī kṣāṣa' āysdatargye vä⟨tä patāro⟩tta . ha × × p × ṭt ⟨i-⟩
2 ndriyānu āysdatargye vätä rūva vätä u bajāṣṣa u buśśañä u ysvyañuvo' skaumavo' u dharma u aysmuī haṃjsare . aysmvī biśuvo' pa⟨ṃ⟩juvo'

3 indriyvo' muri māñaṃdu drāca tsūmata indriyyau traṃdye. kāmo
diśo kāmiye indriye vätä patärottä ttu indriyu haysānando padīmäte
4 uysānye. ttarandarä anārūhä u ayicä. u aneṣṭavanä u pracyānu
vätä patärottä. kūro kā'mato vätä hämätä trā-
5 mu ṣṭäte kho käḍägānīnei yaṃdrä o ttuśei āvū śśandā ūtca dai
bātä māñaṃdu kho ye āvuto ṣṭānä diśe diśe śśūjätäna trāmuṃ haṃ
6 vätä väruddha kho ājäväṣa ce hamiña biśśa ā're mahābhūtīnā
ājäväṣa tcohaurä padya dva uskālsto tsīṃdä. dva natālsto tsīndä
7 ⟨dva⟩ dva diśuvo' tsīndä. biśśä vā jyāre. ttätä mahābhūtīnā
ājäväṣa śśandeinei ājäväṣä ūcīnei ājäväṣä ttätä natālsto kṣī*n*⟨d⟩ä
24*v*1 ⟨rrūn⟩d⟨e⟩t⟨īn⟩ei ājäväṣä u bātīnei ājäväṣä ttä vā uskālsto ttuṣṣe
tsīndä aysmuī ⟨patä⟩rajsye jsa u viñāni. ysaṃtha kho handa-
2 ra-ysaṃthvai käḍägāne īndä. gyastuvo' hvaṃ'duvo' avāyuvo' kho
saṃ kīra yäḍe īyä. ttī ysaṃtha hämāre. cī śśālīṣmä u pättä jätä
3 hämäte. ttarandarä muḍä hämäte. bīysman*na u* panīys⟨au⟩ paskīna
atapyattetyau haṃbaḍä amanāva-vīyä ne vara hayirū-
4 ṇa śtä. kuṃ jsa pära u hajse hämāre. cīyä naṣphūstä hämäte
upalatāñe ggei'ha śśäte. dya ne thu dīvatä ttätä härа ce
5 marata ṣätä härä ce va satvä āya o pudgalä ttuśśā ttätä biśśä hära
jaḍī pracaina hämäta ttätä mästāñe hämemäte jsa
6 hämäta u mästāñe ahämemäte jsa. ahämätäna hämätäna hämäta
ne tta ttu hämāre. ttäna aysu ttätä mahābhūta nā-
7 ma yäḍaimä. cu härä ahämätänä gāvu niśtä. ahämätäye härä
pracaina hämāre ahämätäye yiḍä abustatete jsa

⟨*27⟩*r*1 ggurvīc⟨ ⟩ *n ñ* × × × päṣkal⟨ ⟩. biśśo ttuto tṛsahasro vätä cerä
ttä ggurvīcānu haṃkhäṣṭu īndä cu biśśānu uysnaurāṇu buvāmata u
ṣa ju tty⟨ ⟩ ×
2 × × × hämäta. u ttiñä buvemate jsa cu ttätä ggurvīca haṃkhīśäte
u tto ārdiyo buḍaru sarvasatvyau u bvāmatīyätaryau kho sarvasatva
3 biśśo ttätä ggurvī'ca haṃkhäṣṭu yanīndä. u ne balysāno bvāmato.
śye kṣaṇätä buvāmata hämäta tcamäna mäṣḍāna gyasta balysa bi-
4 śśu buvamätu riṣaya. anaṃkhäṣṭa kalpa kūla ne ye gāvu haṃkhäṣṭu
yīndä *nätā*tamu hālau gyastānu balysānu bvāmato. ||
5 suvarṇabhāysūttamäna sūtrāṇu rrụndänu rrundäna ttuśśāttete
päṣkalä näṣa'tä pūhä. || puñabuddhä parste pīḍe || [*Figura.*]
6 tta ttīyä vā vaiśśramaṇä mästä yakṣānu rre. u dhṛttirāṣṭrä. u
värūlei. u virūpākṣ⟨ä⟩ ttätä mästa yakṣānu rrunde ce nā-

7 ma hvīnde āysanyau vahäṣṭa śśau sutä vätä prahoṇe prahauṣṭāndä u *hvarandau ysānū śandya västāndä* hā gyasta balysa vara haṃ-
⟨*27⟩v1 ju dasta nāndä u namasätāndä mai u gyasti balysi tta hvatā⟨ndä⟩ ⟨mai . ṣätä⟩ gyasta balysa suvarṇabhāsūttamä sūtrāṇu rruṇd⟨ä⟩-
2 nu rre biśśānu gyastānu balysānu vūyätä . uysdätä biśśānu gyastānu balysānu āysdagäḍä u biśśānu bodhisatvānu namasanī . biśśā-
3 nu gyastūñānu ggäṣā'nu pajsama-jserä biśśānu gyastānu rrundänu sīratete yanākä . biśśi lovapāla stavätāndä buljätā-
4 ndä . ysūṣṭāndä . biśvo gyasta-kṣīruvo' bärūñāte . biśśānu uysnaurāṇu biśūnyānu suhānu haurākä biśśānu narīyānu
5 ttäryaśūnyānu śāmalovyānu dukhānu hvā'ñākä . biśśānu pva'ṇānu paltcīmphākä . biśśānu īṇātānu hīnauśānu īśśākä
6 biśye durbikṣīnai haṃdramä näṣemākä . biśye ācheinai alavi bajevākä . biśśānu grahānu nakṣatrāṇu ośānu patcīhākä hastame
7 tsāṣṭe -e × × × × ⟨o⟩śānu kāṣṭānu vadravānu näṣemākä . vicitrāṇu ahumārāṇu satä-yseränu vadravānu näṣemā⟨kä⟩

36r1 ñä vara ttu āysanu vätä nyāñu ku näṣa'stä hämäte ne rrundāñe māye jsa māstä hämāñu śtä . ne ju hārrustä n- × × × ⟨hämā-⟩
2 ñä śtä biśśāñe ṣkālśatete jsa bärrāṣṭattete jsa pahäṣṭāna aysmūna ṣätä suvarṇabhāysūttamä sūtrāṇu rrundänu ⟨rr⟩e ⟨pyū'vāñä⟩
3 u ttu rro dāta-hvāño vätä śāstāra-saṃña panemāña ttye hvą'ndānu rrundi ttye scātä ttye bāḍä rrīṇe u rräspūra varä u rrä⟨ysduīrä u⟩
4 biśo ro andīvärāṇo gäṣo' briyūnyau tcei'mañyau uysdiyāñe u byūṇyau[1] päjsäṣā'ñe u briyūnyau uysdyāñe rrī⟨ṇe u rräspū-⟩
5 ra u rräysduīrä pätāyāñuṃ jsa hau jsa haṃbrīhāñä bryūnäna salātäna biśśäna aṃdīvärna pätāyāñu nānā-vicitra dā⟨tä pyū've-⟩
6 mate käḍāna pajsama paryāña yäḍe atāṣṭa avamātäna sīravātīnaina suhäna uysānā paphāñāña akäṣā'ña ⟨u⟩ sīra-
7 vātīnaina suhäna suhäta tcerā uysānye mästä ttagatīnei hāvä maññä mästāñe sīratete jsai uysānā sīra padīmāña .
36v1 m⟨ä⟩stāñe uysānye sīravete jsa dāta-hvāñau patäna panamāñu u patäna tsūñau cīyä ṣätä tta tta hvatu ttīyä vā gyastä balysä tcuīnu
2 mästānu rrundänu tta hvate se ttī vā pātcu mästyau rruṃdyau ttye scātä ttye bāḍä ttye hvaṃ'dānu rrundi biśī śīya śśīphīsa nūvara dhyāna thauna prohau-
3 yāña nānā-vicitryau āysärūṇyau gyamānyau uysānā āysänāña . śīyä ro kṣaträ nāsāñä miśtāñe rruīye padaṃgye jsa ⟨miśte⟩

[1] bryūnyau.

4 rrvīye ṣkaugye jsa nānā-vicitryau maṃgalyau nātyau ttāna kūṣḍāna hālsto narāmāñu u dāta-hvāñei hā patätsuñau tta ce ⟨ttīmä-⟩

5 na cerä buro ṣä hvaṃ'dānu rre pve byālśāte ṣä tterä haṃkhīysgye jsa gyasta balysa kūla nayuta satä ysāre ārāhätä ⟨tterä haṃkhīysgye⟩

6 jsa rro kalpa kūla nayuta satä ysāre cvī rro saṃtsera ysaṃtha nāste sāñavatā*no* ne ne nāste . paskīnä bāyätä u tte⟨rä haṃkhīysgye⟩

7 jsa cakravarttoña rruīyānu kūṣḍānu kūlu nayutānu satä yseru byehandei hämäte cerä horna hā pve byālśāte tsīyä ⟨tterä haṃkhīysgye jsa⟩

---

53 *r*1 ⟨ka⟩ I naka-ggiri-suvarṇa-kāṃcana-prabhāsa-śrīr nāma tathāgatä -ä -ä tty⟨e⟩ balysä nāma ce pätä śśaṃdrāmata mästä gyastä puña haṃjsaund⟨ai⟩m⟨ä na-⟩

2 tä haspäta tcamäna vaysña kāmo diśo āysda yaṃde u kāmo diśo nvaśtät⟨i⟩ u kāmo diśo hā ⟨ts⟩ī ttye diśe anaṃkhäṣṭa kūla nayuta satä

3 ysāre uysnaura biśśūnyau ⟨suhā⟩vatānyau ⟨jsa⟩ hämāre avārūḍyatetu cevīndä hverä āstanna khaśä pattarre u ttagatä jsārä dīnāra

4 ysīrrä āljsatä mūryau märāhy⟨au⟩ värūlyau śaṃgyau īryau sakyau nānā-vicitryau ratanyau o padandä kīrna u biśśūnyau rro uvatāryau u biśśūnyau

5 saṃbāryau tsāta samartha ttä uysnaura hämāre śśaṃdremäte miśtä gyaśte prabhāväna ttye dastäna u ttye gyastä balysä pajsamä tcerä ggandavā-

6 rṣä vara tcerä u bū' vara paṭhāñä u śrī-mahādīvate miśtä gyaśte nāma usthaṃjāñä drai jūna u pajsamī tcerä buśañyau u spätyau rays⟨yau⟩

7 × × -i b⟨v⟩āñ × väk⟨ṣ⟩ivä ñānartha yanāña ne × × × × × × × -ä j⟨s⟩ārīṇei haṃbīsä h⟨u⟩ṣ⟨ṣ⟩ät⟨ ⟩ ×-o × hī -e × × -ä ×

53 *v*1 śśa⟨ṃ⟩dy⟨e⟩ × ⟨sī⟩ra hämāro gyasta dīvate hīyāra pīysgyau hāro × × × × × × × × × × × × × jsāra × × × × × × × × × ⟨suvarṇabhā-⟩

2 ysūttamä sūtrāṇu rrundänu rrundi nāma usthaṃjāñä u *h*vañä u ttätä rro uysnaura śśandrāmata mästä gyastä āysda yaṃde u miśtu nä rro śśärate-

3 tu heḍä hāva suha padīmäte . aṭavakanta kīntha puṇya-kusuma-prabhä nāma uryānä vara ttiña uryāña suvarṇa-dvaja nāma haudä-

4 ratanīgya bāśa śśaṃdrāmata āste ce ju halci hve' īyä ce jsārīṇai haṃbīsä huṣāñäte kṣamīyä ttye ṣa bäsa hugyastu gyehā-

5 ña ysänāhāñu śśuru su⟨śśīyä⟩ prrahauṇäna pamätäna u buśśāneina prahauṣṭä hämāñu . namas tasya bhagavato ratna-kusuma-guṇa-sāga-

6 ra-vaiḍurya-kanaka-giri-suvarṇa-kāṃcana-prrabhāsa-śrīr nāma tathāgatä ttīye gyasti balysi drrai jūna nāma hvañä śśandremäte gyaśte da-

7 stäna u ttye gyasti balysi pajsamä tcerä spätyau buśśañyau u vicitryau raysyau rro varata pajsamä tcerä uskośāña u ttye rro suvarṇabhā-

54r1 ysūttamä sūtrā⟨ṇu rru⟩ndänu rrundi drai jūna nāma usthaṃjāñä ⟨u rraṣṭä?⟩ dātä rro tcerä . u śśaṃdrematc miśte gyaśte pajsamä tcerä . sp⟨ä⟩ta u bu-

2 śśañä paṭhāña × × × × u nānā-vicitryau raysyau varata väkṣīvä tcerä ttye scātä ttye bāḍä śśandrāmata tto bäso byāta yande . u ttye mästu

3 jsārīṇau haṃbīsu huṣṣāñäte u ce vā hajsvätāte śandrāmato miśtu gyaśtu ātīmānä ttye hvaṃ'dä ṣā vījya hvaña u ttätä mandra-pata hvaña

4 namasīmä biśśä gyasta balysa hatäḍarāṃjsya vaysñaṃjsya ustamāṃjsya u ttānu aurgo tsutä hämäte . u ttuto mai vīgyo śūhī-

5 mä ṣā mamä vījya saṃbajätu . saryathedaṃ . pratipūrṇavare . samaṃta-darśane mahāvihāragati . samaṃta-nidhanāvatī . mahākā-

6 rya-prāpaṇe sarvārtha-samaṃta-suprapūre āyāna-dharmatā . mahāvigopite mahāmaitropasaṃhite . hite . mahāmaitropasaṃhite .

7 hiterṣi saṃgṛhīte samaṃtārthānupālane . svāhā . || ttätä tteru vätä aviṣijäta dātīnā man⟨dra⟩-pata īyānd*u* pätālye t⟨t⟩ä⟨t⟩ä

54v1 pata ajs⟨ī⟩raṇa ttätä pata . c⟨e⟩ myā⟨m⟩jo tsūmato tsīyä jsei'ṇu vät⟨ä⟩ hajuvānu dr⟨ai⟩śa tc⟨e⟩ra d⟨ä⟩jsāña h⟨au⟩d⟨aur⟩ṣṣ⟨ī⟩ v h⟨⟩ṇḍa vaṣṭa śśikṣāvatä⟨na⟩

2 hämāñu tṛkālä biśśānu gyastānu balysānu spätyau buśśañyau pajsamu yuḍu yīndä uysānye u sarvasatvānu rro balysūñe bvemäte haṃ-

3 bārāṣce kädāna pariṇāmaṃdei ṣṭānä ttätä ttandrāma hauva hväñätä mamä ttätä ātama saṃbajāṃdu thatau mä saṃbajändu . u tto bäso śśuru

4 padaṃdu tīndä u ā'mato o ārañāne gvīhä satanä vara kārṣa tcera buśśañä vara tcere u paṭhāñe rro u śśärä varata āysa-

5 nä viśtāñä baṣṭarrāñä spä⟨t⟩y⟨au⟩ jsa vara būm⟨e⟩ benda *nyāñä*

ttīyä mandrä hvañä śśandrāmata hā trāmäte u vara māñätä . ttätäna āstanna

6 vara ttiña biśśa ȯ āvuto o ārañāne ⟨o⟩ × × × ni tā*vu* ṣāta härna naṣṭa hämäte o dīnāryau o ysīrrna o ratanyau o ttaga-

7 täna o jsārañau biśśūnyau uvagāryau suha suhäta hämāre suha × puña yande biśpaḍā śśandremäte nasä haurāñä . śśandrāmata × ×

55r1 ⟨*circa* 11 *akṣara*⟩ r × -d n d t n⟨e⟩ p⟨achī⟩ysd⟨e.⟩ b⟨i⟩śś⟨ä⟩ rr⟨o⟩ ātama ttānu uy⟨s⟩n⟨au⟩r⟨ān⟩u ⟨hambe⟩räte . ‖ ⟨suvarṇa bhāysū-⟩

2 ttamäna sūtrāṇu rrundänu rrundäna śrī mahādīvata parivarttä nāma nomä näṣa'tä ‖ 9 . puñabuddhä parste pīḍe ‖ [*Figura.*] namasīmä na-

3 mo ratnaśśäkhu gyastu balysu ⟨na⟩masīmä namo vimalojvala-ratna-raśmi-prrabhāsa-kettu gyastu balysu . namasīmä suvarṇa-jaṃbudvaja-

4 kāṃcanābhu gyastu balysu . namasīmä svarṇa-śata-raśmi-pra-bhāsa-kettu gyastu balysu . namasīmä svarṇa-ratnākara-cchatra-kūṭu

5 gyastu balysu . namasīmä sva⟨rṇa-⟩puṣpojvala-raśmi-kettu gyastu balysu . namasīmä mahāpradīpu gyastu balysu . namasīmä ratna-ketu gyastu

6 balysu . namasīmä sarbandä hālai akṣubhyä nāma gyastä balysä . rravye hālai ratana-kīyä gyastu balysä . nihujsandä hālai armätāyä ⟨nā-⟩

7 ma gyastä ⟨ba⟩lysä . nyūvajsa duṃdubhisvarä nāma gyastä balysä . rucira-kettu nāma bodhisatvä . svarṇa-prabhä nāma bodhisat⟨v⟩ä . s⟨v⟩arṇa-⟨garbh⟩ä

55v1 nāma ⟨bodhi⟩satvä . sadā-praruditta nāma bodhisatvä . dharmod-gattä nāma bodhisatvä . ‖ ttīy⟨ä⟩ vā styūda ⟨b⟩ūma d⟨ī⟩va⟨ta⟩ gyasti balys⟨i⟩ tta hvatā⟨tä se⟩

2 ṣātä mäḍāna gyasta balysa suvarṇabhāysūttamä sūtrāṇu rrundänu rre . vaysña u ustamye bāḍä rro kāmiña āvuto o kīntha o parmiho

3 o ārañānä o garuvo' o a⟨la⟩*v*ä o rrundä kūṣḍu vātä nyāpīyä aysu mäḍāna gyasta balysa styūda śśaṃdye dīvata hā ttiña āguvo' o kīntha o

4 garuvo' ārañānuvo' o hve'tuvo' o rrundä kūṣḍu vātä aysu hā tsīmä kāmo diśo ṣātä suvarṇabhāysūttamä sūtrāṇu rrundänu

5 rre brūñāte bāraṣṭä vāstarna īyä ku halci mäḍāna gyasta balysa kāmo śśąndo ye dāta-hvāñei ṣṣamanä dharmāysanä baṣṭarrdä i-

6 yä kāmu āysanu vätä dāta-hvāñei nättä u ttu suvarṇabhāysūttamu
[sū] sūtrāṇu rrundänu rruṃdu västarna bärāśīyä uysdīśśīyä

7 × × × ⟨aysu⟩ mäḍāna gyasta balysa ⟨styū⟩da b⟨ū⟩ma dīva⟨ta⟩
t⟨tyau⟩ t⟨tyau⟩ ś⟨ś⟩aṃdye päṣkal⟨y⟩au' ā⟨'⟩mato yane *tta*täna dharm-
āysanui a -aṃ -ei × × ×

56*r*1 rna ttere jsa ttye dāta-hvāñei pānu ā'ye × × nīmä uysāno rro
ttätāña dāti pyū'vemate jsa u ttät⟨ä⟩na rr⟨o⟩ dātīn⟨ai⟩ ne'tīnei
rays⟨ä⟩na *y*sū-

2 ye jsa paphāñe u pajsamuī yanīmä *araṃ*dīśīmī . cīyä uysāno
paphāndu yanīmä u pajsamuī yuḍu yanīmä u sīruṣṭanvai pa-

3 daṃdu yanīmä ṣā haṣparekṣa⟨ṣṭ⟩ä sate ysāre gga⟨ṃ⟩pha śśandā
odä vaśirimgye śśaṃdye ā'ye āstanna śśaṃdye raysu huṣṣāñe u
haṃberīmī . biśśä

4 hālā odä mahāsamuḍrä tcalcānu ⟨u⟩ rro śśaṃdye raysu biśśu
tcārbu padīme u biśśo śśando tcārbäna raysäna haṃberīmä u
hasta-

5 rvai rū padīme tcamäna ttīye jaṃbvīyä biśśūnya raysāyana aruve'
kīśśängye bāysañä ysāyse biśśūnya hāro ūśäna hastara

6 hämāre häruvīndä biśśe paljsäte bāysañä banhya biśśä biśśūnya
bāggare späte hīyāra u jsārañä ūśäna hastara hämāre

7 ⟨buśśān⟩aiyatāra hämāre . tcārbätara hä⟨māre⟩ dyānatara u
mästara hämāre . u ttānu rro uysnaurāṇu hvera khaśa vicitra × × ×

56*v*1 *n*ya × × × *jsī*nana cchat⟨ä⟩ indr⟨i⟩ya p⟨ä⟩ṣa' huṣṣ⟨īndä⟩ hastara
h⟨ä⟩māre c⟨ī⟩y⟨ä⟩ tt⟨ī⟩ś⟨ä⟩na p⟨ä⟩ṣya⟨u⟩' chat⟨e⟩ jsa uspurra h⟨ä⟩m-
⟨ā⟩r⟨e⟩ ha⟨ṃ⟩phuta biśśūn⟨ī⟩na ⟨śśä-⟩

2 rna raysäna . ttīyä biśśūnya vicitra śśandau vätä jsānä pharāka-
padya kīre satä ysāre yanīndä panamāre haspäsīndä päta'garya
kīre ya-

3 nīndä . ttäna härna mäḍāna gyasta balysa ṣätä biśśä jaṃbvīyä
tsātä hämäte u samarthä hämäte . ramanī hämäte pharākyau .
uysnauryo kī-

4 śśänä hämäte . u hvą'ndä u ttä biśśä uysnaura suhäta hämāre u
biśśūnye hayirūṇe varāśāre . ttä uysnaura ttīśäna päṣa'ñyau

5 chate jsa dätäna uspurra haṃphuta hämāre . ttīye va suvarṇabhāysūttamä sūtrāṇu rrundänu rrundi śśāratete jsa ttānu ttīye sū-

6 trāṇu rrundänu rrundi däjsākānu ṣṣamanānu aśyānu dāta-
hvāñānu dharmabhānānu vätä āṇānu hā ttä vara tsūñau cīyä hā tsī-

7 ndä ttä uysnaura vasutäna aysmūna biśśānu uysnaurāṇu hāvä käḍäna hätä suhä käḍäna u ttä ju dāta-hvāñä ājīṣā⟨mato⟩

68*r*1 nä hā tsute bälsaṃghu varata yäḍe *nä* × × pūśe jsa balysānānu ṣṣāvānu ratnaucayu dharmabhāno ākṣutte hā pulsā*nu* ⟨se ku⟩

2 śtä ju marata ttätäña bälsaṃgya ṣä ṣṣamanä *rro* ratnaucayä nāma āya . ṣṣamanä *rro* ku buljsā-jserä *a*ndaryo ratnaucayä haṃdarña gu-

3 hya āstä ttu āṇu käṣṭe rāja-śśāstru nvaśtāmato vätä u haṃggei' tsāṣṭu āstä näjsaṣṭāndī ttīyä ttu ratnaucayu dāta-hvāñau dharmabhā-

4 nau uholañä haṃdarña guhya āṇä ttīśäna puñyau śśäratete jsa brūñandei ysānde ṣä ratnaucayä nāma dharmabhānai därysde natu gya-

5 stānu balysānu rahāsu ttu suvarṇabhāysūttamu sūtrāṇu rrundänu rrundu namasätai . päto' u ratnocayu dāta-hvāñau su-

6 saṃbhavä rre tta hvate se hvāña thu mamä haṃbaḍa purra tsargya . suvarṇabhāsūttamä sūtrāṇu rrundu . ahivāysäte . usahyäte

7 ratnaucayä dāta-hvāñei susaṃbhavi rrundi . biśśo trisahasryau lovadātu vätä . biśśī sīra hämäta gyasta dīvate surgyo diśo ha-

68*v*1 stamo añänāmo vasutäñe buśśāgye ūce jsa vatcäṣṭe . spätyau jsa śśando baṣṭarrde u ⟨pu⟩ṣpārūhu[1] yäḍe . vara āysanu västāte rre susaṃ-

2 bhavä āysäte ttu āysanu kṣatryau daśyau thaunyau ahumāryau yseryau nānā-vicitryau hastamyau buśśañyau cuṇyau vāysyo tcabrīye hā rre āysa-

3 nu vätä gyasta nāta aysura kinnara yakṣa u yakṣānu rrunde . gyastūñäna maṃdāravīneina spätainaina bāräna pajsamu yä-

4 ḍe ttye āysanä anaṃkhäṣṭa nayuta satä ysāre kūla cu hā dīvate haṃgrīye hā tsutändä dātä brīya . ce narāmandau ra-

5 tnaucayu dāta-hvāñau āśärī bendä berāñätändä hastama späte . ṣä ratnaucayä dāta-hvāñei huysänauttī ttarandarä . u su-

6 rau prahauṇu prahauṣṭä hā tsute ttu āysanu varata haṃju dasta näte namasätai mai gyastānu rrunde u gyasta dīvate mandārava

7 späte berāñätändä . anaṃkhäṣṭa satä ysāre bīnāña ākṣuttändä yanä u tta ṣṭāta ātāśo āysanu vätä naṣa's⟨t⟩ä .

[1] pu om.

(*b*) P 3513.

59*v*1 | siddhaṃ

ttī vā ruciraketta baudhisatvä ttina sūhäna sīrave jsa ų̄mye . hų̄ña
2 ysąrrnai kūsä dye . | biśä hālā brrų̄ñaṃdai . ttrą̄mä mą̄ñaṃdä khu
3 urmaysdāṃ vimą̄nä . biśvā ra diśvā' anaṃkhiṣṭa | jasta ba'ysa dye .
4 raṃnīnāṃ bahyāṃ dīna . vīrūlīnāṃ āysanāṃ biṃda ne'sta | parṣi'
jsa pe'jsata āre . vara ą̄na hvą̄ñīdä dā . brraṃmana-rūvai hvąṇḍä dye
60*r*1 si kūsä ṣṭāṃ ka'je . ttina ra | kūsä bijāṣṣäna . deśañi jsa gāha' narą̄-
2 maṃdā pyūṣṭe . cī rucarike'ttä baudhisatvä bīysāṃd⟨ä⟩ hą | mye . cī
ą̄na tvā deśana byāta yuḍe . ttye ṣīvi byūṣṭä . rājagṛhä kaṃthi jsa
3 naraṃdä . a | naṃkhiṣṭye yseryę uysnauryau haṃtsa ką̄mä hālai
4 gṛddhakūṭä garä . kuṣṭi jastä ba'ysä ā | ste hāṣṭä tsue . gyastä ba'ysä
pvā' śaṃdā haṃphve . pūjā-karmai haiṣṭe . drrai tcīrai tvaṃdaṃ
60*v*1 tsue u śi hā | lai ṇestä ką̄mä hālai jastä ba'ysä vye hāṣṭä aṃjalä dasta
yuḍe . namasye vī cuṃ hų̄ña gāha pyūṣṭi tta hve :

2 | śye ṣīvi ahaṃphiḍä śą̄na . hų̄ña dyai haḍara ba'ysa .
3 ysaragūnä tcarṣu kūsä . cu biśä hā | lā pattavīya 1

brrūñaṃdai khū ji urmaysdi . vīvīya harbiśä vīra .
4 harūñe biśä dīśä' vīra . | dyai ra biśä hālā ba'ysa 2

raṃnīnāṃ baṃhyāṃ dīna . vīrulīnāṃ āysanāṃ vīra .
61*r*1 paḍā ą̄ṇaṃdā ṇesta . | sa-yserye tvaḍa parṣe' 3

dye ra vara brraṃmaṃ rūväna . keją̄ma ttye śirä kūsä .
2 tti vā krrīsą̄me beḍa . śilāṃ | nvaysīra uvāra 4

ysīrä brrų̄ñaṃdai kūsäna . hastąmäna dūkha niṣa'māṃde .
3 biśe ttrri-saha | srre vīra . harbiśāṃ satvāṃ bida 5

avāyvā cu ra śa'ma-lāṃ . cu vā dukhättauñäna pātcä .
4 ysama- | śaṃdya mara dukha ī̆de . dṛ-haṣkalä biśä niṣa'māṃde 6

61*v*1 ttye kūsä pā'hą̄me jsa . ysama-śaṃdya vyaysa | na jaude .
hamāṃde satva ave'sta . ja-pve'ṇa saṃ khu ra ba'ysa 7

2 tti ra parīyastą̄ñau jsa . ṣṣahą̄nyau uspu | rra ī̆de .
saṃtsārū mahāsamudrrä . hajvatte vīnai pātcä 8

3 ttrą̄mä mą̄ñaṃdä himāṃde . ṣa | haunyau haṃbaḍa satva .
samāhą̄nyau jsa tta vātcä . baudhaugyau pe'nyau tsāta 9

4 ttina ra kūsä hīvī | pā'hna . brrahma-svara satva himāṃde .
bvāṃdi ba'ysūśtä uvāra . ge'śīde dāvī cakrrä 10

62r1 ttaiṣṭīde ka | lpa pharāka . hvą̄ñīde parimārthä dā .
ṇihejīde biśä kleśa' . naṣḍa'mīde dukha staura 11

2 ca | ja satva ṣṭą̄ṃde avāyä . pasva sūjsaṃdai diṃna .
3 pvāṃde ttye kūsä bijāṣṣä . nauda sādä | hva yinīde 12

jā-smara satva hamāṃde . sa ysaṃtha ysārū kūlä
4 biśä ba'ysa byāva yi | nāṃde . dāvuṃ jsa pvāṃde uvārä 13

cu jastāṃ hvąṇḍau īde . ṣai būvāṃ āvama au'sa .
62v1 ttye kūsä pvā | hą̄me jsa biśūṃ sįjīde madārä 14

cu tti satva cu narya ṣṭāre . sujsaṃdyāṃ garyau ṇi'hīya
2 ge'saṃdā yse | ra attrąṇa . ttina pā'hnä ṣi' dai būysvāve 15

3 cu ra satvāṃ ttriṃkṣa niraukṣa . narya prrīyvā du | kha īde .
ttrīyaśū' hvąṇḍāṃ pātcä . ttina pvehną biśä niṣa'māṃde 16

4 cu attruāsta cu bū | ri anāha cu ni pe' haṃdara niśtä .
hamą̄ne aysä ttyāṃ ttrąṇä ārūva hastama pīrma : ⟨17⟩

63r1 uha | rīde mūhu ba'ysa mu'śda'ṣṣauṇa śirna aysmūna .
cu ra dasau diśi' vī īde . ttirṣṭaṃda cu śi'vāvāṃ pīrma 18

2 | cu buri maṃ īde karma . yuḍa paḍā nūṣṭhura ysīra .
3 tti ṣṭāṃ biśä dīśūṃ' vaṃña . ttiṣṭaṃdāṃ ba'ysāṃ paṃ | na 19

cu ji meri vīra u pyarä . abustąñā ba'ysāṃ vīra .
4 śirye hirä vīra abvīya . asaidä | yuḍi īme he'cä . ⟨20⟩

gūttirrna īśvarī tsą̄ttauñä jsa u cistīye jsa .
63v1 ttye meva jsa ci māstä ṣṭąna asaidä yuḍi | īme aysä ⟨21⟩

duṣä'caidye duṣä'hva kāṇa . duṣa'yuḍāna kīrna ra pātcä .
2 āyinai cu cidyai īme asįdä | haṃjsaudai pātcä 22

vitkauñä bvą̄me nvaiya . jaḍīnai pyą̄mäna pātcä .
3 asidāṃ hayunāṃ rāśi'na . kleśāṃ' | jsa rristāna aysmūna 23

nahąryūnāṃ tcarkāṃ kiṇa . kāṣci ysūrri rāśä'na ra pātcä .
4 apaphaną̄ | me kiṇa . ttina cuṃ asida baśde' īde 24

auśa'raṇyau haṃtse jsa . cu arena hīsäna pātcä .
64r1 dukhättauñäna | cu ra śaṭhyau jsa . asidä hirä īmą hara 25

vyaysanvā cu hīsci beḍa . cu pva'stąñä cu ra vā ñaṣṭa
2 haṃ|darye kastarä ṣṭāna . cu ji dīrä yuḍi īme pātcä 26

3 cu drrāvai aysmū rāśa' . cu vā ysū|rri brrīye rāśä'na
kṣu ttarna haṃthrrī ṣṭąna ośä' hira yuḍi īme pātcä 27

4 cu ji hvīḍi kiṇau | khīṣṭe cu ra vā strīyāṃ kiṇa .
kleśī'nyau naṣṭāvyau jsa . biśų̄ñi baśde' pā'ste . 28

64v1 cu ttaraṃdaräna bīśā'|na aysmūna asidā ī
duṣa'tsūmą prracyau ttyau jsa . harbīśū dīśūṃ' vaṃña 29

2 cu dā prrakṣauttai īme . ava|raṃjsä rraṣṭä abvīya .
meri pyarä vīra abvīya . cu baśdā byaudai pātcä 30

3 cu ji ba'ysä | vīrau dā . ba'ysąnāṃ biṣṭāṃ vīra .
agauravä vyį ī pātcä . viñä ṣṭā dīśūṃ' biśä 31

4 prrattyeka-|budhāṃ vīra . baudhasatvāṃ vī pātcä .
agauravä yai ī pātcä . biśä dīśūṃ' ārä paysąne 32

65r1 vitkauña ṣṭą|na jaḍīna . cu ṣkāśī prracai mąnä .
ysūra brrīye jaḍī prracaina . ttu harbiśä dīśūṃ' vaṃña 32

2 pajsamevuṃ dī|śa' vī ba'ysa . dasau dīśi' vīra avamāva .
ttrāyīme harbiśä satva . diśi' vīra bīśyau dukhyau jsa 34

3 | pārīphī aysä biśä satva daśvā bhų̄mvā avamāva .
4 biśä daśvā bhų̄mvā ṣṭąna ba'ysa pana|māṃde madārä 35

śe śe ra satvä kiṇa mara . tti ra tsī khu kūlä kalpa
65v1 khu būrä na ra parya himāṃde . dukhī|nai mahāsamudrrä 36

uysdīśimä satvāṃ ttyāṃ gaṃbhīra deśana tvā .
2 suvarṇabhāsauttama nąma tcąmna | biśä jāre karma 37

ysārä kalpa cu ji yuḍa īde . bīysąnä nūṣṭūra karma
3 śau jų̄na khvai ye | bīrāśe' . biśä avīvävä hamāre 38

khvaṃ hva yinī tvā rraṣṭa . avaraṃjsa deśana śirka .
4 tcaṃna | thyau haṃgaśa byaide . bīśāṃ kīrāṃ byąnāṃ jaiga 39

tti viṣṭī bhūmvā gautträ . raṃna vaṃdāya hamaye .
66r1 ysaṃ | thīnai mahāsamudrrä ttrāyākä ba'ysä himą̄ne 40

ttye ra ba'ysų̄ñä samudrrä . cu bu'jsāṃ haṃphau mästä :
2 | ba'ysūñau bu'jsyau āṣṭä haṃberī sarvajñą̄nä 41

3 balyāṃ baudhyaṃgyau pa'jsä iṃdrryau jsa uvārañau | jsa .
samāhą̄nyau jsa balāṃdä . hamą̄ne sa-yseryāṃ jsa 42

4 ūharīde mūhū ba'ysa . āysda | rai śirna aysmūna .
nāsāṃde ma jsa biśä āra . mu'śdä'ṣṣaunä śirna aysmūna 43

66v1 cī ji asidä yuḍi | īme dikhu sīyvā kalpvā pīrma .
kāṣcinų̄ ttye kiṇa vaṃña . mu'śdä' vī haṃthrrī pveṇäna 44

2 asidą̄nä kīrāṃ | pvaimä . biśä bāḍą khīrai ysą'ña .
kuṣṭa kuṣṭai jä āṃ tsī ha'cä . rruṃdūni hirṣṭai niśtä 45

3 biśä mu' | śdi'ṣauna tti ba'ysa . biśä satvāṃ pveṇä jinąka .
4 nāsāṃde maṃ biśä ārra . gūchīde mūhū ttina | bayäna 46

karma kleśī'je rrīme . vauñāṃde maṃ biśä ba'ysa .
67r1 ysinājīde muhu ba'ysa . mu'śdī'je | ūci jsa pvāśkye 47

biśä baśde dīśūṃ' karma . cu jä paḍā yuḍi ī ha'cä .
2 cvaṃ ri hi'ysdāṃjsva īde . bīśū ṣṭā dī | śūṃ' vaṃña 48

pyaṃtsāṣṭä pathaṃka nāse . biśāṃ duṣä'yuḍyau hiryau jsa .
3 ni pacanūṃ baśde' gvą̄na . | cu burä maṃ duṣi'yuḍa īde 49

ttaraṃdarrna drra-vadya karma . cu ra tcahau-padya biśā'na .
4 a | ysmūna drra-vadya pātcä . bīśū ṣṭāṃ dīśūṃ' vaṃña 50

cu ttaraṃdaräna yuḍai biśā'na aysmūna caidyai pātcä
67v1 da | sa-vadya akūśala kīrä bīśū ṣṭāṃ dīśūṃ' vaṃña 51

dasau śira phīśę kīre hahrrīyai dasau dīra .
2 tti ṣṭāṃ bi | śä dīśūṃ' vaṃña . aharīna ba'ysāṃ paṃna 52

cu burä maṃ īde karma . tcaṃna vīvā hame ośä' .
3 tti ṣṭāṃ | biśä dīśū' vaṃña . są̄mūhāṃ ba'ysāṃ pyaṃtsä 53

4 cu burä maṃ ra jaṃbvī vīra . cu ri lą̄va-dāvuā pā | tcä
yinīde ṣṭāṃ śira kīre . tti ṣṭāṃ biśä armūvu hāṣṭä 54

cvaṃ ttaraṃdarrna bīśā'na aysmūna maṃ pūña īde
68r1 | haṃjsauda thyau jsa madārä ba'ysūśtä hastama bvāṃde 55

ysaṃthījau tsų̄mayau jsa . jaḍa bvą̄mai haṃthrrī jsą̄na
2 a|sịdä cu ji yuḍi ī he'cä . bīśūṃ viña dīśūṃ' ni aysä 56

3 ysaṃthīje cu haysgame jsa brrīvī|jau haṃtharkyau jsa
hagavą̄me jaḍī prracaina . vitkauśta dīśūṃ' ṣṭą̄na 58

4 cu drrātai aysmū kiṇa | asịdāṃ hayunāṃ gīhna .
haṃtharka pve'stai ṣṭą̄na . ysūri brrīye jaḍīna pyaudä . 61

68v1 ūvāśi' jsa haṃthrrī ṣṭą̄|na . bāḍä haṃtharki jsa pātcä .
pūñāṃ haṃjsą̄mäna vātcä . dīra hīra dīśūṃ' vaṃña 62

2 vą̄nų̄mä tti jasta ba'ysa . | bu'jsīnā mahāsamudrra .
ysaragų̄na saṃ khu sumīrä . tterä jsaṃ namasūṃ biśä 63

3 ysaragų̄na vi|rūlya-jsịma . ba'ysų̄ña urmaysdą̄ni .
mu'śdī'jau bā'yau jaidä . jaḍīnai ąndhākārä 64

4 niṣi'|rrīma tcarṣva vīvaṃdā aṃga . pūrä tti ba'ysų̄ñä vasva
69r1 pūra harasṭa-bā'yä niṣṭauda aysmva kleśī'nai | daina .
uysdaimīdä pvāśkäna bā'yīnai jālāna 65

dvāradairsä lakṣaṇa . ttyau āysyą aṃga .
2 anūvyaṃjanyau | tcarṣva biśä . jsiṇä vī ūḍa .
3 pūña śirā ttīśä' u brrų̄ñą̄ma bā'yä . brrūñāri hastari hastari |
ysama-śaṃdya ttyau jsa 66

arīmajsa vīrūlya vistārya gų̄na . biśų̄nya-padya śāvä byūsā gūna .
4 | ysaragų̄na sphālye mą̄ñaṃdau hiṃji . ttyau jsa brrų̄ñāri
khu sarbaṃdä urmaysde . ⟨67⟩

69v1 saṃtsārrva ttājä vya|ysanīnā vą̄ma . kāṣṭī̄ji īse u maraṇīją ūtca .
2 khvī ysarūñīji dukhīnā phara be'sa ysī|ra vegasta pahvą̄ñarī
biśna 68

3 namasų̄mä tti jasta ba'ysa . cu uysdva-chata ysaragų̄|na .
bvaime jsa vasva bijirma . lakṣaṇyau āysyą aṃga 69

4 khu avamā-kanyau samudrrä : khu ri śaṃdā paṃ|nakyau jsa .
khu ra malnä garä sūmīrä khu ri āvaśä' avamātä byą̄na 70

70r1 tta tta ba'ysāṃ gūṇi avamāve | ni tcāraṇa harbiśä satva .
avamāva kalpa gaṇāre . ciṃdā ra ne'śtą niśtä 71

2 biśä śaṃdā haṃtsa garyau jsa . haṃ|khiṣṭa hime ṣai aśka .
drrau nauhnä mahāsamudrrä . ni ba'ysāṃ bu'jse gvą̄na 72

3 ttrą̄ma biśä satva himāṃde | ṣṣahą̄nyau bu'jsyau ṣve jsa .
śira ttaraṃdarrnau dyena . lakṣaṇyau bījsanyau śū'sta 73

4 ttina ra aysä kuśalnä kī|rrna . ba'ysä panamą̄ni ma piṃya .
uysdīśī dā parämārthä . parījī satva dukhyau jsa 74

70v1 pūrrī mārä | hīñi jsa haṃtsa . parige'śī dāvī . cakrrä
ttiṣṭīmä kalpa avāṣṭa . pachāiśī' satva amrrena 75

2 pārą̄me uspuri | kṣa' haṃberī khu ra biśä ba'ysa .
damī dukha jinī kleśa' . jsinī ysurri brrīyā mauhä 76

3 haṃ vīra | jā-smarä ysyą̄ne . sa ysaṃtha ysārū kūlą .
4 biśä ba'ysa byāva yināṃde . dātūṃ jsa pvāṃdi ma|dārä 77

ttina ra aysä śirna kīrrna ba'ysyāṃ jsa haṃtsa himą̄ne
71r1 phīśīme asaidäna hirrna śira kuśala kī|ra yinīme 78

biśvā kṣittruā biśä vīra biśāṃ satvāṃ dukha niṣa'māṃdi .
2 ci būri vikalaidrrya satva . uspu|rą aṃga hamāṃde 79

āchinaka duṣpya gauda . śą̄naṃdā diśvā' attrą̄ṇa .
3 parsāṃdi āchau bi|śna . byehīde drrūnā pe'ñä 80

cu jsīñā rruṃdä parauya . vyaysanvā pveṇvā kaṣṭa
4 tti harbi|śä harga hamāṃde . byehīde pve'ṇyau gvaṣṭä 81

cu tti cu vā basta cu hvasta . haṃtharkvā vyasaña ṣṭāre
71v1 ha|ysgamevuṃ phari ysāri . biśų̄ña vyaula u kāṣṭye 82

gūsīde cu basta āre . bāja byehīdi cu dvyą̄ñä
2 | cu jsīñā tti haṃphūsīde . jīyina sūhya himāṃde 83

3 cu kṣųna ttarrna dukhauttä byehīde hvī|ḍi u khīṣṭe .
hą̄na daide u kāra pvāṃde . byehīde būnā vāsta 84

4 dukhya ñą̄nau | byehīde . spamasu jsārų̄ raṃna .
biśä satva suhya himāṃde ma jve dukha vedana bvāṃde 85

72r1 śira | dyena satva hamāṃde . dya-vīya prraysāvų̄na .
didi pūñūda khvaṃ biśä sįji . aysmų̄na hvīḍau khīṣṭe 86

2 | kṣąmä nvaiya biśą hamāṃde bīnąñä paṃca-tturyāṃga .
3 khāhi āṣaiji vīysāṃji . surutcā tcāva|ka śirka 87

samu aysmva masi pyaṃtsä . nirvarttī hvīḍi u khīṣṭe .
4 tti ālaṃgāra prrahauna . ysīrä | ā'jsa raṃna mīrāhi 88

dukhäna jve nąma ni bvāvi . anvaśtā ṣai śe satvä .
72v1 himāṃde satva ave'sta | brrų̄narā śūje vīra 89

cu buri mara pyālya hvīya ṣą' sijī cidañi vīra .
2 harbīśāṃ āvama rraysä . sįjī|de pūñāṃ prrabhāvna 90

pe'sārā buśąñä jimąne . hīsuṣkyi vāsta u spye .
3 drrai-bāḍa | bahyau vāṣṭa . bārīde satvāṃ vaska 91

yinīde ttye jsa uvāra . bīśūña pajsama vīcittra .
4 | diśi' vī ba'ysāṃ pūjä . hā baudhisatvāṃ pātcä 92

dīra ge' ma ni hā tsīde . phīśīde akṣaṇa haṣṭa .
73r1 ā|ysyāṃde ttu kṣaṇāṃ rruṃdä . ba'ysyau jsa haṃtsa himāṃde 93

2 bīsīvirā satva himāṃde . spamasve pāji|ñä tsāvi .
dyena cha bu'jsā suṣṭya . ttyau āysya pharāka kalpa . 94

3 strrīyi biśä tti daha hi|māṃde . śūra vairśāṃ'da u bvāka .
ba'ysūña carya carīde . pārąmvā haṃ vī auṣkä 95

4 diṃ|di dīśä' vī āṃ ba'ysa . vīrūlīnāṃ āysanāṃ vīra .
73v1 raṃnīnāṃ baṃhyāṃ dīna . dāvuṃ jsa pvāṃdi uvārä | 96

asida cvaṃ īde kīra . haṃjsāṃda ysaṃthvā pīrma .
aysūṣkye vīvā vaska . aharīna ttą biśä jāṃde 97

2 | cu tti satva cu basta ṣṭāre . ysaṃthīnyau ahyau jsa styų̄dä .
3 hajvatte vīnai dastäna . gūsīde ba'ysa | himāṃde 98

cu ṣṭāṃ mara satva vīcittre . biśų̄ñi śiḍi yināṃde .
4 cu ra dasau dīśi' vī pātcä | tti biśä armų̄vūṃ hāṣṭä 99

pūñāṃ armūviñi kiṇa . haṃjsauda cu ra maṃ īde
74r1 sįjīde biśä prraṇi|hąna . ba'ysūśti hastama bvąne 100

cu ṣi' cu namasī tta tta ba'ysa . stavīyuṃ biśna aysmūna .
2 pariṇą̄ | māñä ttye nva phīśe . avāyau jsa ṣi' kṣaṣṭä kalpa 101

3 ttyau śilą̄vyau cu stavī . kṣattrī brraṃmaṃ dahä | strrīya
aṃjalakä ṣṭą̄na tti ba'ysa . biśä ysaṃtha jā-smarä ysaiyi 102

4 uspurä idrryau | ysą̄nastä . pūñau bu'jsyau jsa huśū'stä .
74v1 hvaṃḍą̄nū rre pajsamaḍä . didrrāṃ hami kuṣṭi ha'cä ysyā | vi 103

ni tti satva śe ba'ysä vīra . puña pį̄rāṃdāṃḍä .
2 ni dvyą̄nä drrainä ni tcvīnä ni paṃjai vīra . ni | vā ṣai daśiṃ vīra 140

sa-ysiryiṃ ba'ysāṃ vīra . uspūra vīrā sabijäta .
3 pūña pį | rāṃdāṃḍä tti satva . cvaṃ ṣi' gvą̄ña deśina hīśtä 105

4 khu jastä ba'ysä tti gāha pyūṣṭä | yuḍi . ttī rucirakettä baudhisatvä
75r1 hālaiyāṣṭä sādhukārä hauḍi si śirä śirä bīsīvrrā | ṣṣā cu ysarrnai kūsä
hų̄ña dyai . caṃ jsa gāha' naraṃda . ba'ysą̄nū ttāhīre bu'jse . puñāṃ
2 pari | ṇą̄mana u deśana cuai pvāve . avamāvai pūña himāre . satvāṃ
3 va vī hye kiṇa birā | śī' ṣa' karmāṃ deśana byehi . amai vaña pvīryau
4 tvā karmāṃ deśana ṣā' . prraṇihą̄nāṃ hīya ha | harka hittä . biśāṃ
jastāṃ ba'ysāṃ hīvī ūhą̄nä ayiṣṭhą̄nä . khu jastä ba'ysä ttu hvanai
75v1 hva | yuḍe . harbiśä ṣā' mista parṣa' tvā dharma-deśana pyūṣṭāṃdä .
2 saṃdurṣṭa hamya ysuṣṭāṃdī suvarṇa | bhāsauttaṃ sūttrą̄nä rruṃdä
vīra eka-rāttri deśiñi vī hų̄nä pį̄ṣkalä tcuraṃ ne' ||

(*c*)

Kha. 1. 214 a (=ed. Nobel, p. 66)

recto

1 vasutyau tvatare-hve'yyau āysd⟨ ⟩

2 × mäḍāna gyasta balysa tcuīrnu mästā⟨nu⟩

3 -natä . ce buro ṣä mäḍāna gyasta

4 ī̆ṇāt⟨e⟩ jsa bvata.⟨t⟩īndä drubikṣīnaina ha⟨ṃ⟩drram⟨ä⟩na

5 ⟨vadrra⟩vyau . yseryau vadrravyau vadṛta häm⟨ā⟩nde .

verso

1 tt⟨ä⟩täye suvarṇabhāysūttamä sūtrāṇu

2 -ānu dāta-hvāñānu ṣṣamanānu pa × -ī

3 mäḍāna gyasta dāta-hvā⟨ñā⟩

4 ⟨ayi⟩ṣṭhānäna päta'jsu viśtemäte jsa u pa⟨ ⟩

5 ⟨usahyā⟩ro u ttutu ro suvarṇabhāy⟨sūttamu⟩

Stein Ė 1. 33 (=ed. Nobel, pp. 67–68 =30 b 1 ff. ed. Konow)

recto

1 × gyasta balysa buhu tc⟨ahaura⟩

2 ra biśśūnī suhāvatänäna u

3 × biśśyau rro uvatāryau uspu⟨rra⟩

4 *sū*trāṇu rrundunu däjsāka ṣṣa⟨mana⟩

verso

1 s ×

2 ⟨rru⟩nde ttu hvaṃ'dānu rrundu biśyau rru⟨ndyau⟩

3 × . u byāta-täḍätaru . ā̆ × ×

4 ⟨kṣīra⟩ñuvo yi rro buhu buljsā-jseru

5 -äna *s* × *ṇ* ×

Kha. 1. 119 (=33 b 2–3, ed. Konow; ed. Nobel, pp. 74–75)

recto

1 ttina hirna umānu tcuīnu mistānu rrundänu haṃtsa hīñi jsa u

2 ⟨ ⟩īyä subikṣä hime . ramanīyi himi pharākyau uysnauryau kīśśini hi⟨mi⟩

3 *ra* himi rve māśti u hala-māstä u s⟨ ⟩l⟨ ⟩ h⟨ ⟩ rraṣṭu bāḍāna haṃphve him⟨āre⟩

4 × × × urmaysde rraṣṭu *tsīndā* haura nāma h*i*m*i* haṃkhīysja bāḍāna bāta tsīndi u b⟨ ⟩

5 ⟨ ⟩īndä u biśśä jaṃbvīya uysnaura biśūnīna ttagatna tsāta himāri u ci bihīyu tsāta tti pa*tä*

verso

1 ⟨ ⟩*re* . daśyau karmapahyau uspurru hi⟨mā⟩ri ci tti hvaṃḍä cu mirārä ttānu śśira tsūma hime ha⟨ ⟩

2 thāna kīśśäna himāri ⟨u⟩ gyastyau u gyastaṣyau ci halci m⟨ä⟩styau rru⟨ṃ⟩dyau

3 ttye svarṇabhāysūttamä sūtrāṇu rrundänu rru⟨ṃ⟩dä pyūvā'kä himāte . āy⟨sda⟩

4 ⟨ ⟩rei hi × × u tti ju sūtrāṇu rrundänu rrundä dijsāka āśirya aśe ūvāysä

5 yane u hvā⟨ṣṭa⟩ paysānāte āysda ni yaṃdä . u pajsamu ni yanä . u umā̧nu

Kha. 1. 100 (=Kha. 1. 119)

recto

1 ⟨bihīy⟩u tsāta tt⟨ä⟩

2 ⟨hämā⟩re . ce ttä hvaṃ'dä c⟨e⟩

3 ⟨bi⟩śśä gyastānu thāna kīśśä⟨na⟩

verso

1 māte ce ttätäye suvarna

2 māte . u ttä ju sū

3 ⟨vä⟩tä yanä h⟨v⟩ā⟨ṣṭa⟩

Kha. 1. 115 (=ed. Nobel, pp. 80–81)

1 recto

1 ⟨suhā⟩nu byehānai himi . mistai pa'tä him⟨e⟩

2 ni hastamiñä che jsa haṃbaḍä jsa u

3 ⟨ka⟩lyāṇa-mitra rru byehi . avamātī

4 -ya va -e r*o* k*ä*ḍäna ttye hvaṃḍānu rrundä ṣih⟨āna⟩

5 rä ggaṃpha patä panamāñä patsuñau . ttu ru

verso

1 īmu mamä śākyamuni gyastä balysä kūṣḍu

2 pajsā*ñ*e . īmu aysu śśākyamuni gya*stä*

3 ⟨dā⟩tä pve īmu aysu ttina pyūṣṭäna dā⟨tä⟩

4 × īmu mamä muhu pharu kūlu nayva

5 hilysdājsyānu u ustamājsyānu gyastā⟨nu⟩

Kha. 1. 115 (=ed. Nobel, pp. 83–84)

2 recto

1 u tti sūtrāṇu rrundinu dijsāka ā⟨śirya⟩
2 ⟨*pa*⟩ysānāte aysmū ni ve yanāte
3 ve yanęme kiḍna . tta rruīyu kūṣḍä
4 ⟨pa⟩dīmāte u tu ru dātä pyūvāma mihyau
5 biśśānu rro dīvānu ciduku hanu ma⟨s⟩e

2 verso

1 ⟨ba⟩lysa ttye dāta-hvāñai āśirī dharmāysanu
2 citrä buśśañi paṭhāñä . ṣi miḍāni gyast⟨i⟩
3 kiḍna ttye nānā-vicitträ buśśañījä du -ī
4 × na mānu tcuīnu mistānu rrundänu hīviña
5 kṣaträ viśtä . hami ru ha'-vīyä buśśañi b⟨ ⟩

Kha. 1. 160 (=ed. Nobel, p. 99). Same folio as no. 3

1 recto

1 stavyāndä ⟨× ×⟩ stav- × -i
2 ⟨u⟩rmaysdānānu bā'yänu
3 trāme daṃdā khu kumuda
4 ⟨a⟩naṃkhiṣṭinu raṃnānu yanā
5 ⟨a⟩humāryau sīyau yseryau kīś⟨ś⟩

1 verso

1 ⟨ysā⟩ra-vā'sū . dastānu u pānu ce
2 ⟨ga⟩rānu rrundä balysu namasī⟨mä⟩
3 × cā'yä marīci māñaṃd⟨ä⟩
4 ⟨mist⟩ānu rrundänu ttye scye ggāhyau
5 ci dasau pa'tä ⟨× × ×⟩ nu l⟨ova⟩

Kha. 1. 160

4A

1 × ci ttu sūträ
2 mārai parṣi jsa haṃtsa ba
3 yakṣānu ci hvāṣṭu yi ×
4 -yau biśyau pahiṣṭä ni
5 ⟨tc⟩e'mañä tta ru bvām

Kha. 1. 160 (=ed. Nobel, p. 99)

3 recto

1 vasva
2 balysa ttrāme tce'mąñä khū vi⟨ysa⟩
3 ⟨gya⟩sta balysa mahāsamudr
4 ⟨sa⟩mudrrä bvāmatīji ū⟨ce⟩
5 muvo cakrrä ā -e

3 verso

1 ⟨māñaṃ⟩dä pānu jālä 3 ys⟨īrra⟩
2 ⟨mā⟩ñaṃdu vasva ūci pur⟨ra⟩
3 jsa balysu vąnīmä . ttī va
4 ⟨sū⟩ttrāṇu rre hastamä sva⟨rṇabhāysūttamä⟩
5 ⟨ ⟩ānu ⟨ ⟩ā -ä × ×

4 B

1 trr⟨i⟩sāhāsr*ye* biśśūñ

2 narya pharāka 9 cī

3 ⟨dhṛti⟩rāṣṭrä mistä rre . virūpā⟨kṣä⟩

4 ⟨pru⟩hauṣṭādä hvaradau ysānū

5 × -ä t⟨ty⟩e bāḍi ttyau pa

Kha. 1. 198 (=ed. Nobel, p. 101)

recto

1 ⟨ttū nijsaḍu?⟩ sūtrāṇu rre ṣa⟨hāna-suha haurāka⟩ *khu* raṃn⟨ān⟩u ttu

2 × × × × ttū nijsaḍu *ṣä* sūtrā⟨ṇu × × × × × sva⟩rṇabhāysūttamä ba⟨lys⟩na

3 hva⟨ṃ⟩'dānu pajsama-jserä u gyast⟨ānu rrundi⟩ namasīyä sūtrāṇu rre ⟨tcahau-⟩

4 ryau mistyau rru⟨ṃ⟩dyau cu ysama-śśaṃdai pā × × ni × balysa daśvā diśvā cuai ā × ⟨sūtrā-⟩

5 ṇu rruṃdu sūtträ hvāñaṃdu usāvañātī haurīndä gyasta balysa 3 yakṣa se-ys⟨ārä⟩

verso

1 hajva daśvā diśvā ci va ju pyūṣṭä hämāte sīruṣṭanä 5 ttīśu pa' virśu by-⟨×⟩

2 ndä u ttätäna mistäna ūśäna gyast*ānu* × *gäṣ*e' huṣṣa tsīndä 6 ttī vā ⟨vaiśśra-⟩

3 *vani* virūlai . virūpākṣä ca ⟨× × × × ×⟩ gyastä balysna tte ttidrā⟨me ggāhe⟩

4 pyūṣṭu u apyūṣṭu amañe u -ä ⟨× × × × × × ×⟩ himya . tti vā brīya-⟨. u⟩

5 sīra yäḍāndä rrīysä ⟨× × × × × × × × ×⟩ hataṃd*y*au a⟨ṃ⟩gyau ⟨× × × ×⟩

Kha. 1. 170 (=ed. Nobel, p. 102)

recto

1 ⟨dāta-hvā⟩ñai āśärī hvanai salāvä āysārūṇä prra⟨caina⟩

2 × salāta viśtīmä mistu ru ttye dāta-hvāñai *ā*⟨śärī⟩

3 *tca*rṣvattā ttiña svarṇabhāysūttamu sūttr

4 ⟨hā⟩m⟨u⟩rä himya īndä . tti aysu bi

5 × vāruṇi byātarj- -au

verso

1 rre dārburu jaṃbv⟨īya⟩
2 × *c*⟨i⟩ puñīṃju bātu kilstāṃdä u
3 sūtrāṇu rruṃdänu rruṃdu pvā'ru anaṃkhi⟨ṣṭu⟩
4 × × puñīnau haṃbīsu byehāru . avamā*ta*
5 *upāya* paysānāru . u kau ru biśśä śśāstra

Kha. 0012 (=Or. 9609 54*v*4–55*r*1, ed. Nobel, p. 118)

recto

1 mä sijāṃdu . kū tvā
2 ⟨sa⟩väna vara kārṣa' tce⟨ra⟩
3 baṣṭarrāñä spyau jsa va⟨ra⟩
4 -ä u vara māñe ttina
5 ⟨ha⟩me . o dīnāry⟨au⟩

verso

1 × ta biśūnyau *sū*
2 ⟨śaṃdre⟩me nasu haurāñä
3 × ni pachīysde . baśśi
4 ⟨bhā⟩ysūttamäna sūtrāṇu
5 10 || vaṃdakai parstä pīḍä

Kha. 1. 136 (=ed. Nobel, p. 124). See *K.T.* v, 152

1 recto

1 bise ×
2 nānā-vici⟨tra⟩
3 ttina miḍāna
4 avaśśa mai ya
5 mai paysā⟨n⟩

1 verso

1 × nā ×
2 dāta-hvāñ
3 -āṇu rrundi rru
4 bisvā aủvā kaṃ⟨th⟩
5 dātä

Kha. i. 99 (=ed. Nobel, p. 132)

1 A

1 × byāta yanä u
2 pakṣä vistāta
3 × -ej

1 B

1 ttu pū⟨ra ?⟩
2 padaṃgya hvat⟨a⟩
3 na devendra-sama⟨ya⟩

2 A

1 ⟨bh⟩āysūttamä sūtrāṇu rruṃ
2 × ra u mamä rro tta
3 nä ma

2 B

1 × t
2 ysā⟨ṃ ?⟩gye . ttā ×
3 śśaṃndau vätä hämäta śśa

Kha. i. 136 (=ed. Nobel, p. 123). See *K.T.* v. 151

2 A

1 × ru bi ×
2 × mäte . ttita ×
3 mata bihīy
4 × vaṃña at*i*
5 × varā

2 B

1 × uysdī
2 m*i* u paljsä
3 × tä ysyāñä ×
4 hare niśti
5 haphaṃ

Kha. i. 138 b

5 A

1 × × ×
2 × ryau sahyarä -ī
3 × vā × × ×

5 B

1 × u y⟨ ⟩e āysd
2 × ttamä sūttrāṇu
3 × × -au -ā ×

Kha. 1. 171

4 A

1 svarṇabhāysū
2 × × × ×
3 × yse ×

4 B

1 × × ×
2 himya
3 × × akaräṇī

3 A

1 ttamä sūtrāṇu rre
2 × × × × ×
3 tta × ×

3 B

1 × nai ×
2 indä o *kiḍ*
3 ñä ve haiśīmi u

INDO-SCYTHIAN STUDIES

BEING

KHOTANESE TEXTS
VOLUME II

EDITED BY
H. W. BAILEY

PREFACE

In this second volume of Khotanese texts are gathered up all the longer documents known to me. A few smaller pieces are added which will serve as examples of a fairly large collection of fragments to be published later. Of the religious texts only two pieces are incidentally included as being found in the same rolls with the documents nos. 1 and 57: the first, in lines 82–91, is a summary of part of the Sad-dharma-puṇḍarīka-sūtra, of which another copy is preserved in P 2782; the second is a legend of Kaṇaiska, edited in the *Journal of the Royal Asiatic Society* (1942), with translation and commentary.

Among these documents will be found those referring to the Chinese, the Turks and other peoples of Central Asia, in the eighth, ninth and tenth centuries A.D., from which some names and titles were published in *JRAS* (1939), 85ff.: to that list may be added the title *haṭtuna* 'khatun, queen', occurring once in no. 47, l. 48. No. 63 is a letter to an Altun Khan. In no. 57 is found a panegyric on the Khotanese king Viśa̮ Saṃgrāma and in no. 43 a shorter set of verses on king Viśa̮ Kīrtti, of which a first edition by Professor Sten Konow will be found in *A Volume of Eastern and Indian Studies presented to F. W. Thomas* (1939). No. 14 has reference to king Viśa̮ Dharma and no. 15 to king Viśa̮ Śūra to whom the Jātakastava, edited in *Khotanese Texts I*, is dedicated. The colophon of no. 68 alludes to king Viśa̮ Sabava, apparently as already deceased, and to Viśa̮ Śūra, who may be his successor. A prince Tcūṃ-ttehi: is named in no. 64, and a certain Tteyi-hvāṃ in no. 70. The documents are particularly rich in proper names. In nos. 11, 12 and 50, the texts are peculiar: scholastic exercises of alphabets and numbers with short texts interspersed. On no. 70 a Chinese seal occurs, repeated over the lines 34, 50, 63, 75, 76, 77, 79 and 80. Certain of the documents have already been published. So the Staël-Holstein roll, no. 45, by Professor Sten Konow in *Two Medieval Documents from Tun-huang* (1929) and my new edition in *Asia Major*, n.s. II; no. 3 partially, also by Professor Konow, in the *Norsk Tidsskrift for Sprogvidenskap*, XI (1938), pp. 21f.; the Itinerary, no. 14*a* by me in *Acta Orientalia* (1936); and Hoernle

143*a*, no. 34, by A. F. Rudolf Hoernle in *Manuscript Remains of Buddhist Literature found in Chinese Turkestan* (1916), pp. 400ff. New readings will be found in each of these in the present edition. An edition of no. 54 has been printed in *BSOAS* 12. 319–23, and again with full translation and commentary in *Asia Major*, n.s. 1 (1948); no. 9 has been edited with a preliminary translation in *BSOAS* 12. 616–24.

Since it is unlikely that any user of these documents will be satisfied without facsimiles, it is greatly to be hoped that this lack may be supplied at some future date. For the present there are to hand in the *Journal of the Asiatic Society of Bengal* for 1897 facsimiles of the Hoernle MSS.: no. 29 on plate iv, no. 30 on plate v, no. 31 on plate vi, nos. 32 and 33 on plate vii; in the volume for 1901, of no. 25 on plate vi, nos. 26 and 27 on plate vii and no. 28 on plate ii; and also in M. Aurel Stein's *Serindia* a facsimile of no. 18 on plate CXLVIII, of nos. 42, 43 and 44 on plate CLI and of no. 6, 1–37 on plate CXLVII.

As before, the MSS. are in Paris and London, and I am indebted, as in the first volume, to the kindness of Dr L. D. Barnett, Professor Paul Pelliot and Dr H. N. Randle for the use of them. I have also to add here the name of M. J. Filliozat, of the Bibliothèque Nationale. Of all the documents known to me in England, I have photostats. Of the Paris MSS., I had in 1942, when this second volume was first prepared, four in photostats, but in 1948 I received microfilms of the others. I have therefore been able to verify readings before this volume finally goes to Press, after so long a delay. The MSS. are written on Chinese paper, but nos. 3, 35, and 36 are on wood.

In this second volume the system of transliteration differs in the use of the subscript curve, as in *ba̜ysa*, in place of the apostrophe as in *ba'ysa*, used in Vol. 1. Since too the documents are not all so well preserved as the texts in rolls, a somewhat more elaborate apparatus has been used, according to the following scheme:

1. Clarendon (heavy) type represents supplements of the editor in broken passages.

2. Small capitals, only in nos. 67 and 70, indicate large script in the original MS.

3. Angle brackets ⟨ ⟩ enclose the editor's additions, where the MSS. show no lacuna, being conjectural supplements to the text.

4. Italic type indicates uncertainties of reading.

5. Broken parts are shown by ///. Occasionally the approximate number of lost akṣaras is shown by dots with strokes, as / . . . /.

6. Emendations are occasionally proposed in the footnotes.

7. Del. in the footnotes means 'deleted' by the scribe, usually by the drawing of a stroke through the akṣaras.

8. Words written below the line are marked 'subscript' in the footnotes; but larger subscript passages are given as 'interlinear'.

9. 'Inverted' is used when the lines start from the other end of the MS.

10. Small crosses ×× indicate that slight traces of lost akṣaras remain.

11. ( ) indicate uncertainty of part of an akṣara.

12. In punctuation the MS. ⌢ and occasional . are kept.

13. Blank spaces in the MSS. are indicated by a straight line ——.

14. [*Space*] indicates blank parts between lines.

A commentary on these texts and a Dictionary of Khotanese are in course of preparation, but it is desirable first to get the texts into print. In Vol. I no difficulty should be felt by the reader, except in the case of the Jātakastava, since the corresponding Tibetan or Sanskrit texts are either given or referred to. In this second volume no such aid can be found: here are original documents, many still containing serious difficulties and needing much explanation. Understanding of such texts is continually advancing but a complete interpretation is naturally not yet possible. The presence of foreign words, Chinese, Tibetan and Turkish, will at once be noticed, beside the usual words of Indian origin. An interesting trace of pre-Buddhistic Iranian cosmologic lore in Khotanese is to be noted in no. 57, l. 29, where *ākāśa-maṇḍäla haräysa vī gg̣isadai* 'the circle of the sky turning on the Haraysa', and l. 58 *mala ttraikha sūmīra gärǭnä rāṃda ttaira haraysä baidä* 'on the peak Mala of the king of mountains Sumeru, the ttaira Haraysa', contain the familiar Avestan Harā bərəz and the *taēra* 'peak' assimilated to Buddhist ideas of the world. In the Greater Bundahišn 55. 6 there is the *tērak ī harburz kē ān ī man xvaršēt ut māh ut stārak hač pas apāč vartēt* 'the peak of Harburz behind which my sun and moon and stars turn'. We cannot but regret that no more of this older Iranian background has survived.

H. W. BAILEY

CAMBRIDGE, 1953

CONTENTS

I

Or. 8212. 162

1 (traces of akṣaras)

2 /// -y *gīna* ⌢ tsāṣṭa ba ttai ⌢ tta ma le ⌢ dai ṣ̮ama le parya

3 /// ⌢ kūṣṭa parī tsve ⌢ ī̇ka śaina mi na khara ≈ m̤̄āṃ kṣvya[1] pha ḍī khara ṣa tsū ⌢ jū śa ⌢ parya

4 vą̄ paryai ⌢ tcūle ⌢ paryą ṇąiśtai ⌢ ××[2] ⌢ parya panīyai ⌢ haiya ⌢ a stā ≈ ḫaiya śai ḍa ⌢ a

5 stā kītha tsvāṃ : ḫaiya ga ḍai ra ⌢ kuṣḍau vī tsāṃ ≈ ḫaiyą u ḍai tcyau tta ma le : mā vą̄ bara ⌢ ˙hvą

6 śai haṃ tta mą le ≈ khī hvana ⌢ āṣą paryą yuḍai ⌢ tsaiyą ttą ma le ⌢ pūhara vā bara kva tta

7 ma le ≈ byāra vą̄ bara ⌢ hau kva tta ma le ttrruysa vā bara : kī tsaiyą ⌢ tcahąi ⌢ hū jñā

8 śa ⌢ a hauḍa vastya : ana khą le yą ⌢ draṣṭa yai ⌢ ca ḍīra : ṣą yai ≈ hąna ḍī ḫaiyą pa ḫai-

9 yą ⌢ caigāṃ bvą ā nai ⌢ haiya śą ttāṃ ≈ a stā bai [r] baiśa ≈ cī ma ttāṃ ⌢ bvaysną ⌢ pī pī ⌢ drai jsai ⌢ vara

10 hadarāṃ ⌢ i̇ra : kṣa mą huāṃ : pa ysą̄va ⌢ na kṣami ⌢ khavą ⌢ ttą̄ra ⌢ gana tcaimañai ⌢ śą tvą ⌢ gvą

11 pīra khumą ⌢ haysgyai ⌢ ttą̄ hvąra : raṃgya baida tcaṃjsa ≈ ttai bą ⌢ kāṃḫą thāṃ : ī̇ka ⌢ ttyai

12 ba ⌢ śą̄ vą̄ thāṃ pąrą̄thāṃ ≈ bai tsąva ≈ gīnū ⌢ śī ⌢ dasta ⌢ kyąḫą ≈ pā : ——

13 pva pvaisai saddhami ya tta magala sakala para ——

14 ‖ pvaisai ttā haṣḍä yūḍai janavai vīrāṣṭa : atvaḍarū maista bīsaga ——

15 : pvaisai ttā haṣḍä yūḍai janavai vīrāṣṭa : atvaḍa[3]ru[3]rū drraya rana vīra beysau śāśą : ṣą ttyai

16 dīśą vīra pūñūdyai u pāṣai : beysū[×]ñai vyārana nva hvasta mīḍauja kīla : ranījai ttā-

17 ja baida āvāysa śūstai : gūśądau cū rājagrrīhę [4]hīya[4] attīka : mūja ṣava ya parīyastā haudyāṃ

[1] Perhaps *kṣū*, or *tsū*.

[2] Two uncertain signs.

[3-3] Del.

[4-4] Subscript.

18 ttana kā̮le ā̮na va̮ña būrāṃ va ttaiṣṭyai : ca va na jārai ha̮jva [1]pūśīda[1] sā̮jīdä pūśīda ⁓ parā-

19 ha̮ paraihīda vasvai naṣa̮rīma̮ ṣadyū : haṃda̮rāṃ jsāṃ vyauca̮ ya̮nīda̮ ⁓ dara bīsaga̮ va : pūśīda

20 sājīda̮ askha̮jsa bā̮yīda śāśa̮ —— : mahāsama̮ rāṃda vī ā rāṃda dīryauda̮ rā̮śṭa̮ dā jsa

21 pūñā jsa̮ rā̮ja-vya̮stāṃ nvīya̮ hva hva̮ śū̮stāṃda̮ draina ranā̮na va̮ska sakhārma śairka̮ jaitta̮va jsa pakyairma̮

22 khvai hā[2] pārrva rā̮śṭa̮ janavai vīra : dvāsa sala āna̮ ṇaista̮ rā̮ysayaṃ baida . ttana kā̮lena̮ ya̮ ja-

22a [*interlinear but belonging to beginning of line* 22] śrī vījatta sagrauma rai hamyai pūñūda śura

23 nava̮ thā̮rsā̮va̮ bījā̮tta ⁓ ttaṃdī va̮ spara̮haudā̮ hīna na̮rada̮ ⁓ bāstai ttañai ba̮iḍa hīna jaṃbvī vīra ⁓ śūrī pai-

24 ñā jsa dara jabvī pā̮rrdai ⁓ khvai [3]mī[3] ā̮vastai karma baśdāṃ haṃjsāma̮ : [3]gumattīra vī āraṣṭa sakhārma ttā̮[3] daiśana̮ ā̮yīma̮ śū̮sta tcarṣū āvāysa

25 hūḍai hā haura vasva̮ arthū bauga : u gūśadāṃ[4] bīsa bīśa pharāka ⁓ vaña bura va draya rana̮ nvaśtā byaihī-

25a [*interlinear*] gu̮śa̮da nā̮ma jaittava jsa hamaga mista

26 da ⁓ cū va varā̮śā̮ra hvaḍa khaṣṭa panūḍai : ttā jsā āvā̮ysa māṇḍa bada̮ janai ṣa̮i ysīnī bā̮stai khva na jsāṃ va̮

27 harga ⁓ ttai ā̮ vaña kaida̮ ṇaistya śā̮śa̮ burakyai : tcaurrvā̮ śā̮mvā̮ pvā̮ha̮ kījsanū bvaiysa̮ ⁓ mista sīma mista̮

28 ayai valekyai pharā̮kyai ⁓ phaṣupāḍaññā nā̮lā̮ gaṃtsa mista̮ ⁓ ñānarthā̮ pāṣa prravaitta

29 ramanī tcaṣū paima bīsai jista ba̮iysa satvāṃ ttrvā̮yā̮ka : khvai vījsyāra̮ satta̮ naphanīda̮ tsāṣṭa

30 jsa ⁓ cīyai vījsyā̮vai ṣa̮ satsā̮ra jsa thyau gūśta : tcaurrvā śāmvā hvāhye mista saragyai ⁓ ba̮isu̮ bau-

31 spaujaññā̮ ranīnai stūpa̮ : cāvāṃ tta tta daitta̮ khu raṃnā male ttraikha : pū[va]ñūda va sa̮tta ysatha̮

32 upapattī nāsīdä ⁓ śajsā va̮ prravaja̮ nāda̮ prraṇa̮haunā [1]kaiṇa̮ prraṇa-haunā kaiṇa[1] : kaiṇa̮ u̮-

[1-1] Del.

[2] *hā* over *ttā*?

[3-3] Subscript.

[4] *gū* over *tt*.

33 stamājsī ka̮lyāka bā̮ḍa akhska̮jā̮ śā̮śa̮ khvau [2]ttā[2] vañau [1]ttā[1] kha̮stai va̮ṣṭa mistyau āśa̮ askhajāda̮ sakhā-

34 ra pañai haira jsa ⌢ jsīnā̮ hū̮ṣa tsī svahe̮[3] byau byau tsīdai ⌢ ttī vā̮ jsā hīra ba̮iśa nva kṣama̮ ha̮mādai . sa-

35 khārma daivā̮ttā̮ āṃ ysī[2]nī[2] ya̮nā̮vai[4] . bā̮ḍau sarbī khu ā̮rmaysda paḍā̮ byauṣṭa . jasta ba̮iysa dīvyai vā

36 āysda yanāṃdai . brruñā̮va śā̮śa̮ña̮ tta khu cadā̮va̮ña rana : phara sī bvā̮maya̮ ‥ hajū vā̮ysya̮-a-

37 ysmū draya pīle sīya̮ śāstra ṭīka[ka] vībā̮ṣā̮ . abīdarma yā̮gaśā̮strra hīṣṣṭai yāgasthauna ttu tta

38 bauttai sa kḥu hīya nā̮ma . [1]ttaya śī va̮maleśīle[1] . rrvī aysmū ārā̮hāka̮ pañai jsāṃ brrī . ttaya̮ śī vamale-

39 śīle bvaijsīnai rana : draya̮ pīla sīya̮ baida prrakā̮raṇa̮ haṣṭi . svārtha parā̮rtha vīra hajū nā̮-

40 hauysa naṣa̮ga̮ista . śāstrvā bīsai artha bā̮ya̮ daśa khaiṇḍa aha . gūttaira askhajā̮ka . dahū pañai hai-

41 ra jsa . hama ysā̮vaṣai brrā̮va̮ hūṣai tsīyai jsīna . ttaya̮ śī daivaisū bvaijsyā haphau : jsa̮iṇa̮ carya jsāṃ va̮ [1]pūñū

42 ma pañai ha[1] ahaṣṭa̮ saga̮krra̮ varttai . srīya̮[5] draya̮ pīle . śāsttra prrakaraṇa̮ ṭīka : [× ×] sāja pūśa ra-

43 ṣṭa̮ ahaṣṭa̮ bā̮vana̮ yadai : bāḍai sarbī . jsīna ṣā̮vai hūṣa tsī : pyara māñada̮ brrāva pa̮ysā̮ : hvaṇḍīnai

44 rana : nāgrābada thaiya̮ ttīka . ādara tta ya̮ : valaka aủna[6] [1]jsaiṇa baiysa śaiña .[1] ṣāmaña sakrra yāda tvā̮ hū-

śā̮ ṣa yāṃda

44a [*interlinear*] khu tsvai jsaiṇa padaja

45 ṣa bā̮ṣṭai sīyai jsāṃ dā̮ draina pīlvā ṣadyā̮ya̮ [2]tsāṣṭaka[2] . thaiya̮ ttīka daivacadra̮ : baiysūśta bvā̮ thyau : parā-

46 ha parā̮ste vasvai ba̮iysa̮ parā̮ya̮ : sagakrra̮ saumaña[7] ca̮rya̮ tvā hū̮ṣa bā̮stai āstaka mūdai valaka aủ-

47 na śā̮śa̮ña : ya ṣṭau pūña śaikyai ahaṣṭa̮ drayvā ranvā . cā̮ sa yai śai[2]ka[2] vīśu hatcā̮yai baiśa . prraṇahaunā̮

48 sagrā̮vā̮sa paijsa baysga̮ yai . ñaśa̮ prravai na mīrā nai pārśa̮ ttā dāśū : thaiya̮ ttīka bvaida-śīla arthāṃ

[1-1] Del.
[2-2] Subscript.
[3] *e* over *au*.
[4] *vai* over *sī*.
[5] Read *sīya*.
[6] *na* subscript.
[7] Read *ṣau*°.

49 haphā : vajrąyānī hajū thaiyą ttīka mista raijsai ṣadū dadą-idrai śakalaka . haiga ñahalmā khana-

50 dai . ų prraysą̄ u daidrąkarabhądrą thaiyą ttīka krrādaḍa raijsai vagastą : . brrą̄ra ñahalmā khanadai

51 dai u prraysā baiysā dą̄ sāja draina pīlvā ṣadyą̄yą : vajrrą̄yāna sīvą : ahaṣṭa ṣīyą ha-

52 ḍāya ṣadū śakalaka padī āśī hīyai . thaiyą ttīka dairāhasū hvaṇḍīnai rana : sagakrra

53 varttai ahaṣṭa ṣīya hąḍą̄ya . āstāka pūdai yāṃda sagasthāña kaḍą̄ṇabhadra nąma

54 ysāra bvaijsai prraumų̄hą baiysa yāna [1]dā[1] baidą rą̄ysnādą gūmā dąśta pajsa sūttra sīyą ttattrą

55 kailpe pharāka rāda hīyai kaḍą̄ṇamittrą jsīna pądairāka : daivarāca nąma . khu vajrasatta

56 spāśa : nāgrą̄ṣaikṣa brrą̄vą dąhų̄ raṣṭū śakalaka . bhvaiśą saidaśīle haigąleka ñahmāṃ . mattrā

57 vą̄dą dā bai⟨da⟩ rāysdādą amaṃgąle kṣaidrākarapą̄ña ttravīle drāśa[2]kūle[3]ra[3] ysīra tsūmaṃdai caistą

58 są̄jara brrą̄vai drayą pīle sīyą baida aủttara śą̄sttra vī ñīdai [3]jsai[3] dąra vartta sakrrą avąrī . ttunai

59 ysaira mūnai ysaira hama haira yai ⌢ gvaṣṭaṃdūṃ hairtha vī śujai jsa hva hva ⌢ hąspīsa namasą cąryą ṣauma-

60 ña tta rą̄śą tsrīyą garśa khā dadą-idrai mų̄ña : khvai tta jvīhį̄nai byāvaï-ra hamānai . ysīnī maṃ ttą̄ bą̄yą

61 ayīṣṭhya daiśa vānvą̄ . aśką̄ hama ṣika są̄hą cā thyautta yai : prrañaisū ttravīle jīyai ttą̄ gīha alā-

62 śva nvītha kuśale caryą pattaja . [3]stānaḍa prraumūha ttravīlā u dvīlā daryai bīsagną aủska aủ

63 nana burai ×[4] ñaśa prravai baka-vąrṣą̄ka baka-sī nāgąidravąrrda . hāysyai dīśą vīra brrīyą jūhaunai ṣṭā

64 ṣacū aủna sakaica tsūṃ ttą̄ṣṭa aủrga[3] hamārīja māśtą drairabaistamyai hądai . śvąi aủ bą̄stai hąḍā nakṣa-

65 ttra śattavaiṣa : nā hīya jsāṃ ttradą salī gvāysa ją̄ra . gvą̄ysū paiṣką̄cą cā pądaidą bą̄ḍa jsa

[1-1] Subscript.
[2] *śa* changed to *sa*?
[3-3] Del.
[4] Uncertain sign.

66 utvaḍarų samągrą bīsagą vara gūśądī [1]vara[1] . ca ya ñūska mūja
dadą salī vaṣṭa . pīruyā kī-
67 rāṃ hīyai pvaihą prracaina . haṣḍa yuḍai rāṃdą pyaṃtsą caigvą̄ haḍa
tsū . rrvīyāṃ ṣavāṃ *jsa*
68 hąraṣṭa mveśda āvaśą mą̄ñada . hva kaṣṭū haiysda hāysą cą̄rą̄na vījsai
parīya ñū-
69 vai dą̄ jsa satva pharāka : vyachara baiysūśta paryą̄va jsā byaudai
raysgą vī dą̄ya
70 rāśta . pūrą̄va jsāṃ māra tcahau hīña jsa hatsa : āra baiśą̄vą dą̄yī
cakrrą vainīyāva
71 parīją̄va satva aprraṣṭą nąravą̄ṇą kīthāṣṭa : paryą̄vą jsāṃ sīyai raysgą
vī vąjāysa
72 vyachāva jsāṃ bęysūśtą nąrāṃda nąrąpądą-śaiṣāṣṭa : ñaśa prrąvai
jąḍȧ abāstą byada
73 abvāmaya . baka valąka . bąką-sī . nāgędravarrda . pīḍaka ttą̄ hąṣḍi
yuḍai ṣacū
74 āna . daryai bīsagą vą aủska aủ naną burai . na hamyai ī̇yai drāṃ khų
bīsaja āṣą . ñaśa
75 prravai pąhvastą yai nāṃdą stā vąmāḍa : dara parą̄hą ājīde ṣacų kītha .
bąiysūña śaikṣą̄-
76 va jsaṃją hīya mista . tvā iṣṭai śaka na ra gatcañūṃ ną̄-ysathą . parāhą
paraihaume hī-
77 ya hauva mista ya . vīna sāna vīna gą̄ḍai mara āvūṃ drunai : utvąḍa-
rrvīā pīrmāttamā pū-
78 ñāṃ jsa rrvīyā . [2]ñaśa prravai na mīrā nai pāśą *ttā* dāśu[2] ca ttā ysūraiñai
mista ālo[3] jsą vąleka
79 ñaśa abausta aysmū kaiṇa cai na paysādai . prrahaja aysmū kląiśąu
jsa pvīstą ṣṭi . satsą̄ra jsāṃ kālāka *d*vai bvā- ka
80 mañāe ṣṭa . vaña aủ ttą̄ bąiysūña aysmū jsa kṣamiyūṃ : ca ttą̄ ⟨a⟩ysmū[4]
jsai ñaiysāra ttā na yąnīryāṃ ñaśa prravai na
81 mīrą̄ nai pārśą ttą̄ dą̄śų [5]ttaña *ka* ttā : ttāṃ ñaśa ——
82 : saidhama
aỉkayāṃ bārai śau bąiysūña [2]da[2] padai :
83 aủrga ī̇ tyai hālai ṣadyā I : ya vaña :
rahāsä kīḍa mesta tvara pūīstī garkha :

[1-1] Subscript. [2-2] Del. [3] *ā* with small *lo*.
[4] *au* over *ū*. [5] Change of hand.

84 draya padāvū hagrralthūi śau :
tta pyūṣṭä śāstāra śīña baiḍa
grradhakūṭä gara vī āstai[1] yai
85 maista[1] raṣayi gai bīlsagäjai karvīnạ mista :
phara ysāra baudhasatvä ūvāra
86 ttyāau hālai hauda-paldya sapatta hvai :
gabīra hvai vara dva maista rahāsa :
87 drayi vara śāvū niräl:vạṇva katha
pva pasvai bīśa mauñadū :
88 aủvama hvava ttyai pasvai bīśa jsa | :
cū aủ satsāra sūśtä pahaisīda ṣāvā :
89 kīḍa mvaiśdụ baka mvaiśdījai pyaura jsa | :
hā tta jasta bạiysa nīśīda satvau baidai
90 dāvīnai bārä pūra aủrmaysdau māñal:dū
bvaiya harūñīda dharma-pada[2] rāśīda
91 hamaga naravauṇa | bvaiya haspvaisū
ttā hāysye dīśạ vīra byūra jū ā
92 āśirī
:[2] uvārya garkhyau vaistārya pūñau kūśala-mūla : u garkhyai haura varāśạumai u bvamai
93 parāhạ jsa haphve u nva vīnī śaikṣāvau dījsạka : u bạysūñai parau paṣṭauñāka :
94 u bạysūñai jsaiṇai caryai tsāka : u lyāye lyākauttarye phara vīra tta ttye vīrā
95 u haiysdai daścai sañai[3] vīra gūmāva : u maistyai aủrmaysda mạñada jastāṃ bạysai hī-
96 ya attīka hīye ××[4] [5]nva[5] nva aysmū parau hagrāḥāka hama-vakṣau-nara ha-
97 ma-ysāvaṣau brrāvarau dharma-jñāna : kṣatta[6]pūña-javaidrākara-pūña vīdāśū-
98 ra-pūña hāysye dīśạ vīra naysdai grau brrīyausta jūhạunai aysmū jsa
99 ṣacū aủ aủrga drunā pvaisauma[7] pvaisū khu tta vaña haiysda vī ttyai śairkya ja-
100 sta bạysau jsa ayīkṣai vaṣạvāysaujsāṃ kāla vīra uvārrvā draiyvā saskhā-

[1-1] Subscript. [2] Change of hand. [3] *sa* subscript. [4] Blurred out.
[5-5] Del. [6] *nta?* [7] *sau* subscript.

101 rrvā u tcaurya mahābūvau[1] avaysamāśca hadra vya u pajsi skadau baida

102 śairka ṣṭāvai tsāṣṭa drunai ttyai kaiṇau ma ñaśa prravai āśa̮ jastāṃ jsa u dī

103 śadai nāvau jsa ttadī aisa āvattuka paijai khu tta sa ysāra salī vaṣṭa

104 śairkya hamai tsāṣṭa u drunai : jasta ba̮ysa dīvyavau āysda yanaudai jsī-

105 nau ḥūṣa tsī svahau bye bye tsīdai ttīvau jsāṃ harabaśa nva kṣama hamaudai

106 ma jsāṃ sa pūña spyaudai khvai jsa ṅa gvaiysai : ——

107 : uvārya garkhya vaistārya pūñau kūśala-mūla u garkhyai haura varā-

108 śa̮umai u hauva u śarī ttīśa̮ jsa haphvai u vrraśama yakṣana rauda hī-

109 ye ttīśa̮ jsa pakairma u[2] hīña bāyaumai vīra gūmā daścai u

110 kyaisara sarau mauñada ñauhīñai ttīśa̮sta [3]avamāvyau śāsa[3]nāvaca-

110a [*interlinear*] [3]u śau-ysā[3] : rrvī parau u śau-ysā pūra māñada rrvī aysmū ārā-

111 rya [3]dīhīñau bvajsāṃ gūṇa ṣahaunau jsa̮ [3]hā̮ka rājsa-dauda pakūṣḍä brrañadai

112 [3]haphvai ca[3] dā[2] [3]vaśa̮rana māñada[3] : —— sa ysārya pāraysau hadra vya

113 āśa̮ jastāṃ jsa u dī śadai nāvau jsa u hadra vya hvaṇḍä jsa ysūṣṭä u

114 bvaijai u[2] śau ysā pūra mā̮ñada ûvī aysmū ārāhāka u rāja-dau pakūṣḍä

115 sa ysārya pāraysau hadrai vya brrauñadai avamāvyau śāsanāvaca-

116 rya [2]dahīñau[2] bvaujsāṃ gūṇa ṣahaunau jsa haphvai ca [×] nvavara naṣkastyai vīysa

117 spūlaka mauñada : a[mū]ścu ⟨ī⟩ḍai ysīra kaścai he̮thīye . ca ṣṭāṃ vaña tta[4]

118 śca hauda kāla panvauḍai : aścai īḍa drai[2]kṣa[2] aścū gvaṣṭai[5] ysathūā : śā-janavai

119 hvaṇḍa ca brrī satva jsa hva hamya : ——

120 śā̮ haḍā ysāra jūna byāva tsūvalaka ñauysara[5] ṣaiṣṭai līka nvavara [×]

121 naṣkaista vīysa spūlaka mā̮ñada : ysāryau bvaujsāṃ jsa bvaujsāda : nva a-

[1] *mā* with *a* struck out. [2] Subscript. [3-3] Del.
[4] Uncertain, perhaps *ttu*. [5] *gve*, *yse* with *e* del.

122 ysmū hvaṇḍīnai rana : bakalakyai amanā kaiṇa : haiysde ysūra kaiṇa jīya-
123 ka padaida khu paradaiśai tcīrauka : khvai ṣṭāṃ spāśū jsīna ma pā pha naiśta
124 hasta khu mūḍa kṣīra khu [×] jve kṣīra vīnau sauha̮ : ——
125 rrvī vī haṣḍä yanau : drūttīrai prraumāha̮ ttathāgatta śrībhadra āstana āśa̮-
126 ryai : maihai ttā rrvī aysmū ārāha̮mai kaiṇa haṣḍa caiga kṣīrīrāṣṭa
127 u [1]khu mara[1] ṣacu āvadū rrvīye mvaśta jsāṃ ma ḍaikū pa̮ijsa śairka pasta spāṣṭai :
128 aủda vaña būrai : u pada hīye ma hairī pacaḍa na yai : khu tta ttaujai-
129 ra ma̮śta hva sa khuī gaisā ttī hā ḍaikū pyatsa haṣḍä yūḍādū sa [1]ca[1] maihai
130 ṣṭāṃ āśa̮ [2]ma̮ña[2] rrvī parau tta tta ṣṭai sa ca[1]da[1] anvaśta caiga kṣīrāṣṭa bāḍa hamāvai
131 ama āśa̮rya āda[3] yanīryau khu tsū hamīryau : ttīvau ḍaikū tta tta [1]pa[1]sta sa śaphī-
132 ḍa bāḍa ṣṭai ⁓ u kamacuvau hadrajīda : u drau haira hvañara ca na nyāṃda u na ṣṭau jai
133 ṣṭada u nau pasta paśāvai u ttī na bāysdaudū yauda hā haṣḍa yūḍādū sa
134 ma̮ñau parya paśāvai : u däda hā baṣṭadū khu draiyau kaṇa parau pasta sa dra-
135 ya tsūva u baiśa na tsvai hamīryau : u ttyau kaṇāṃ jsāṃ parau tta tta pasta sa khu aủ
136 na bāysdai tta tta khalavī vā padīmyaira sa khu tta āśa̮ avadāya kaśaudai
137 ca vā rrvī jsa āra na[1]rau[1]mīyai ama hagrīhyara : u khalavī hā padaidāṃdū
138 u āśa̮rya gākṣā hā akṣara nīśūdū : u draya tsūda gūśa̮dī thaiya
139 ttīka nāgaidravarda : u viśe̮sagrārmī dvīle sīvadākarauca : u gūmattī-
140 rai āśa̮rī vīrapūña brrakhaysda ma̮śtai : tsūdai : u ttī vā [ca][4] cvāvaja ma̮śta ja-
141 navai vī aủ haḍā āva ana vaijalaka u syau haḍai u parauvau ṣa ṣṭau[5] sa gaisīryau

[1-1] Subscript. [2-2] Subscript, read *māñada*.
[3] Read *ādara*, or *āda* shortened form.
[4] Blurred out. [5] *ai* and *au*.

142 parau [1]vā[1] na nījsąṣṭau[1]da[1] sa paḍā vā haira hūryaira cau vā śaikä parau ā[1]je[1]deṃ sa gaisara

143 u ḍaikūvau ysūmauñai bairai pasta hūḍai śā śā u hadavau ma haira na ye u

144 tta hā baira hūḍādū tcaurai u ttīvau ana vaijaleka tta tta hvai sa haira ba-

145 kala hamyai u adravā[ya][2]ysa vā ṇai *yu* u tta ttai hvadū sa paḍā vā parau

146 nījsāña : u parau vā nījsąṣṭai u parauvau tta tta ye kaumya padī jsa tsva hamāṃdai saña

147 tsīdī u ttau ra vā baịrai na hūḍai : u tta ttau hvai sa ama caiga kṣīra khu na tsūda u ttī-

148 vau ḍaikū vā śụ̄ vī hū[3][ñai][3]ḍaiga pasta hūḍai śą̄ u tta ttau hvai sa ttu vā vāsta hū-

149 ryara u nai hvaḍādū u tta ttau hvai sa vañau sa naṣka[4]ścū : u ttī maihai tta tta hvāṃdū

150 sa tsau maihai vā caiga kṣīrāṣṭa tsūdū : u tta hvāṃdū sa aủrāsa ha paśara maihai tsau

151 u aủrāsa hā paśauda : u ḍaikū va tta tta pasta sa khu draya āśą tsūda haudama mą̄śta

152 hairī vā phara na āva ttaka ra būḍa na paśā hamārai : u khu bausta sa ḍaikū va na pa-

153 sta paśāvai : u ttyau bairau kaṇa ḍaikū pasta pyūṣṭai u ysaura pasta yūḍai : u dīdai mā-

154 ścai vā hūḍai : u ttīvau [3]tta tta hvai[3] [1]jsa ma pha[1]rāka śa hvaiñū : u ttī jsāṃ ma gūmattīrai āśarī ye

155 dharmaidrākarapūña nauma : u nārai hā ṇaistai u ca va haiysda śāvī mūra ā-

156 ra haira ya ttu vai ysyai pvaica śā haiysdai kaumadai śai u hạḍa baista chā u cīva-

157 rau phaurthaka śau būśị̄nai śā pvaica āra u ttīvai jsi ttā janaivai vīrāṣṭa

158 khalavī padaidai śā baysgye kabala u ttī jsai ma kamacu-pa sīca yavanaidra-

159 ja nąma u ttu jsā ttā hāysa bāstai janavai vīrāṣṭai khalavī padädai pajsūsa

[1-1] Subscript. [2] Blurred out.
[3-3] Del. [4] Unusual shape of *ṣka*.

160 kabale u ttīvai hā a drūttīrai prraumą̄hą ttathāgatta śrībhadra pyāste sa tta

161 [a] kau aủ aśсai kaiṇa hāysa bāya : u māñau jsāṃ ma aśсai kaṇa paśa u pakūṣṭa

162 aủna kau baida tcauttai paijsāṃ arīśą avajsāmā yūḍai khu vaña haiysda vī

163 ttyai bąysau śāśą hīye āysāja parā spāṣṭai u ñaśau prravaiyau hī-

164 ye pārśą byāva paryā yūḍai khu vā śąi pada śai parau

*b*1 khu ma hadravyanajau khu ma hadravyanajau

2 hīya mvaśta haraysdai khva dada vī būrai ṅamyaina bīysajārai khu pada na

3 dāśau ma nāvai byaudai khva ma na aihąijīda

4 u ḍaikū maista hvaṇḍa pyūṣṭāṃda u tta tta hvada sa khu däda ṣada raiṣṭai cą aủ āśąu

5 ttira jsa parī aủryai ttī ṣa hvai āśąu baida khu tcauttai u vīśų̄ nauma ma padadai

2

Or. 8212. 186[1]

*a*1 parau tta tta ye khu pada sūrā ṣṭi **vā tsūva** ///

2 sa tsūva : ttīvau hvañīye sa mūñara pātca × ///

3 hväñīye[2] sa pada na sūrā -ai-au ///

4 rya pātca vā hāysa tsūva khu ///

5 hvañīye tta tta yada : parauvau tta tta **ye** ///

[*Space*]

6 ñaśe bīsa ——

7 : parau [3]vau[3] tta tta ye rrvī jsa aủ cega kṣīrāṣṭa na ///

8 ca pade ṣṭe ttye hīya aủ habā capasta ///

9 se tcerthūśī khu a [*ña*] ḍā ḥīsyara khū pa ///

10 ḍaikau habā bvāvai : īra u hūra u bvīysana ///

11 [3]nva[3] nauhya hīsīye : ttaka pārysā ca tta rrvī **vī** ///

12 ḍauda sa pārśąu aủ kṣama yūḍai caiga kṣīra js**a** ///

13 parau tta tta ye sa tsīda khu mara āvadū ka ///

[1] = P 2786, 172–239. [2] *hvī*°? [3-3] Del.

14 ḍa bījauda ye : raijsai[1] ma pada[2] hīya tsūma na ///
15 tta tta ya sa pada sūrā na ṣṭāvai pharākyaira ///
16 hīye kīra naiśta khvai jsāṃ sa ṣacū bīsa ḍe**kau** ///
17 ka hvañīye tta tta yaṇa pada hīye aủ habā ///
17a [*interlinear*] ṣacu ḍekau tta tta hve
18 re | ca pada hīye habā ṣṭe ṣa ī ///
ṣacu
19 [3]thai-śī ṣạ[3] jsāṃ ā drau kāla khu raysga ///
20 vaña būra haryadū [3]khu[3] ca jsāṃ vā ///
21 parau ā ṣạ jsāṃ tta tta ṣṭe sa khu sa ḍai**kau** ///
22 yada : ḍaikau jsāṃ tta tta hve[4] sa khu ///
23 rāṣṭa īra hīya u haura u bvīysana u -ai ///
24 na haraṣṭa ya ama pā hāysa tsāva ma**ra jsāṃ** ///
25 ma na hamīya [3]vaña ttā draya *māśta tsū*[3] ///
26 [3]vā phara na × ṣṭa × [3]vaña ra [5]ṣạ [5]rrvī śkyaise × ///
27 kṣīra na hīsīye ama ra pā hāysa na *tsū* ///
28 ca [5]tta[5] āśạrya rrvī vī haṣḍa yūḍauda **pārṣ̱au** aủ ///
29 caga kṣī tsai[6] ttyau va ttadī baida cīvara ye × ///
30 ra tsūe ca jsāṃ ñaśa bīsa : sagai ṣṭe ṣạ jsāṃ va ///
31 ye nva padajai na tsū hamye tta tta khu habū ///
32 parau tta ra haugrrau[5]tta[5] yanī tta[7]na pạijsa hatcasta ye ///
33 ra hā naspava[8] ca jsāṃ kamacu bāḍa ṣạ jsāṃ × ///
34 ranījai janavai hīya u ysarnai bāḍa hī ///
35 ṣạ jsāṃ maista ṣṭai khu ra[9] tta pvai tsūñai ha ///
36 sau varau nva bāḍa u janavai hīye ///
37 u aủhạvau va u **ɓ**īrukau va u mai**śta** ///
38 ṇḍa vī bura ca sa thautta rrvīya mva**śca** ///
39 ya ttyau vaskau varī śkyaisa jsạvai tta tta khu thautta ña**śau bī-**
40 sauhā hauvana yseye [3]khu ttā haṣḍā na[3]
41 ttā haṣḍa na darrvai ya bīsau parau na kṣa**ma** ///
42 ra baida hīsū khu tta rrvī vī jastuña a ///
43 sa khu ṣạ pada prrahīśta khu vā kamacu bāḍa ///
44 hīya mvaśca haraysde ttī va rrvīya mva ///
45 na ṣṭāvai ttī ma pāraysā ya ca ttā rrvī vī ///
pā

[1] *jsài* subscript.
[2] *da* subscript.
[3-3] Del.
[4] Corrected from *ysge*.
[5-5] Subscript.
[6] *ai* over *au*.
[7] *tta* del.
[8] *syava?*
[9] *ra* del.

46 sa caga kṣīra tsau [1]pāraśa̱ yanau[1] ca lā[2] ṣīkau sagīna ka ///
47 ye [1]ṣaumaña paśāva[1] [3]mārāpyarau[3] *va* u ṣaumaña paśāvai gākṣau ///
48 jsa tsvai mārāpyarau nāvai baiśa parāvai ///
49 sa caga kṣīra tsū rrvīya mvaśca nāvai u hāysa × ///
50 mau thāle tcūha̱ paṣa̱ ttā rrvī vī haṣḍä yūḍ ///
51 ra tsū chū bīra vīrāṣṭa hā hagaiṣṭa hūḍai × ///
52 na tsīnai rrvī vī hā kabala haiśū̱ ssa ca bū × ///
53 śau ye ṣa̱ bīsakvā bīse kadūja ye ×× ///
54 vai hā japha ṇaista kadūeja aủ thīgu hī*ya* ///
55 mvaśca haraṣṭa mvaśta hagrauttai u gaisāttā : ca ///
56 |[4] ja vaijalaka ye ṣa̱ ira parāvai u kūṣḍa vī ///
57 da haṣḍä ttā yūḍai sa caiga kṣīra tsū u ira ///
58 ra japha na hamye tcagalaṃ aủna jsā[5] gū rrvīya mva*śta* ///
59 hāysa ttā tsūe —— × [6]*byany*ami[6]
b1 /// ×× -e × na ye ttu ha̱u tcaisyau bīysī
2 /// × -ā -ā parau mūnai bīsa ṣṭe haṣḍä ttā yūḍe
3 /// × bīsa na hamū : jsaina ma jsā vā
4 /// -ū**sai** gubai re hīyau sturau baida u
5 /// ma mūñau ye u ysīḍa parau hīya
6 /// ×× **te** ca drūyāja kaira ḍaise
7 /// -ā a j*sa* drūyāja haṣḍä yūḍauda tta tta
8 /// × adā yūḍai : dadä śtāka
9 /// × byū[7]dau[7]dū ḍaise jsa aủna byai
10 /// **ṣṭa** pastauda naiṣkeśce khu ttyau drūyā
11 /// sāttā ca jsāṃ badalai hīye
12 /// ma : ttyai pā drayau śūma kenau hī
13 /// ye śūma kainau hīya mvaśta ha
14 /// -ā ca hagīñai khara painaka ye ttye
15 /// [3]h × *khu* mai na kraśīsa vīrāṣṭa parau ha[3] ///
16 /// *na*ñau tta parau hamyai tta tta sa caga kṣī
17 /// -au py**ūṣṭ**e gaisāttā khu va kamacu rrvī śkyai
18 /// *na* habūsana ṣṭāvai khu vā ttyau pā
19 /// śta haraysde ca va rrvī parau hagrīha̱u
20 /// -ai beda samaiyau ādara ya
21 /// dara hamai ——

1-1 Subscript. 2 *ā* or *ī*. 3-3 Del. 4 Stroke before beginning of line.
5 *jsā* subscript. 6-6 Small script. 7-7 *dau* Subscript.

3

Or. 9268

1

a1 || ttā pāḍa pharṣṣa bara pyaṣṭi u braṃgalä
2 || ṣā̮ pāḍa ttye pracai[1] cu
3 yagurä ūtca nāti draṃmā
4 ja pharṣa barana u braṃgalä
5 2000 500 mūri . phaṃnājā̮ñi āṣeṃji
6 jsa śau haḍā śā ṣṣava bastä ñāna ūtca dva
7 bā[2] ūtca pharṣa bara bāyi u śau bāgä yagurä
8 khu pharṣa bara hīvye mūri haurī ā vā phaṃnāja
9 yagurä nauhyä salye mūri 2000 500 nāsti saṃ bisalū-
10 ni nāsti u hi*vya* hve̮ himāte cu pyaḍa ūtca u-
11 ysgināte mūri śau dva heḍä tti buri va byāṃ vya pharṣa chuṃ-
12 gulä u malārrju̮nāṃ ṣṣanīrä u sucaṃdrä ⌢ ——

b1 || salī × māśtä 8 haḍā 27 ṣi̮ kṣu̮ṇä misḍāṃ gyastä hvaṃnä mistä rruṃ-
2 dänu rruṃdä viśa̮dharmä ttye scye ttiña beḍa sceyye ṣau hviṃdū salya mara
3 birgaṃdara auva ṣi̮ gvārä vye cu pharṣa bara u braṃgalä tta hvāṃdä si a-
4 śtä mānī hīvya ūtca phaṃnājā̮ñi āṣṣeṃji jsa śau haḍā śā ṣṣava ba-
5 stä ñāna ttuā ṣṭā̮na vaṃña draṃmāja viśtuṃ didä bāgä vī 2000 500 mūri nā-
6 timī yagurä ttuā ūtca draṃmāja hi̮vyau mūryau hi̮mya da̮myāṣṭa hāvä gārī-
7 na hauḍāmī ṣi̮ yagurä tti mūri 2000 500 ⌢ nāṃdu̮mūṃ mihi braṃgalä u saṃgaśū-
8 rai u puñadarınä tti mūri uspurri 2000 500 aurīṣṭa pharṣa bara u pyaṃtsä

c1 busvārāṃ āṃ gvārä tta tta padedāṃdä si hamya miṣa haṃtsa kīrä yanā-
2 dä paśä haṃbīśa 2 kūsa jsärä pharṣa bara nāsti u śau kūsä yagurä

[1] Read *pracaina*. [2] Read *bāga*.

3 nāsti khu phaṃnāja auvya ūtca uysgināṃde ttī vā yagurä hīvye mū-
4 ri 2000 500 nāsti ‿ u khu pātcä pharṣa bara hīvye mūri himāṃde ya-
5 gurä vā hīvye mūri 2000 500 nāsti samū haḍi bisalūni nāsti vi[1] pharṣṣa
6 bara haḍi vina phaṃnājāṃ yagurä mūri ni nāsti ṣi̮ gvārä haṃgrīma
ā vye pyaṃtsä pharṣa
7 chuṃgula[2] u pharṣa vikrạ̄ntadattä ‿ tti buri vara byāṃ vya parramai
ṣanīrä saṃgadattä
8 sucaṃdrä ‿ īrasaṃgä ‿ puñaudakä ‿ pạjä suvidattä ‿ phaṃnājä
buttạ̄nakä
9 ttī rä ṣạ̄ pāḍa prạmạ̄na himi khuī pharṣa bara pyaśdä

2

a1 || salī 17 māśtä mūdracaja haḍātū jsa 11
2 ttye scye ṣau vidyadatti salya mara birgaṃdara aủva ṣi̮
3 gvārä vye cu aśtä naḍi puñädattä ṣi̮ tta hve aśtä maṃ
4 pūri haryāsakä nāma ttū pūri permä haurū ne-
5 rä paysāye brātarä anāysä ttye pracaina cū ni
6 ạ̄spāta niśtä sä khu a ysājū miräci ṣai pāḍä
7 nātämī ṣi̮ aśnadāysä ttu puñadatti pūrä ha-
8 ryāsaki permä aủrīṣṭa aủva haṃdastä spāta
9 salmī u parramai aủśaki parramai dattaki parra-
b1 mai cegadattä parramai saṃgabudä u ttyāṃ hvaṃ⟨ḍāṃ⟩
2 pyaṃtsä āna uspurrä prahänaji hoḍi
3 u-ṃ dī mārāpyara pajistā⟨ṃdä⟩ mūri 500 u
4 drai chā śaṃcī 200 mūri ī haḍā āstaṃna hi-
5 ryāsakä ttye aśnadāysä pūri ne vara hadarye dā
6 cu ttū śūstä pedaudāna gvārä hamīhyī rruī va mū-
7 ri 200 heḍi u 50 daulaṃ nāstä u prahänaji śā
8 mūra 5 heḍä ttī ru ṣi perma-vāḍi pramā khuī parra-
9 mā pyaysīdä īysī pīḍe karä bi heri
10 puñadatti salāna haryāsaki salī 3

[1] Read *vina*? [2] °*ä*?

4

Or. 11252

2

1 || miṣḍāṃ ḡyastäna parau —— cira kṣvā aůvā piṣkalä tvā sa-
2 lī jsāra-haurā hvaṃḍä biśna 53 paṃñe hvaṃḍye ttāguttāṃ haudi śeṃgāṃ ṣaṃ-
3 gna jsārä pastä 11 kūsa 9 ṣaṃga —— biśna jsārä himi 600 ×
4 / . / × 7 ṣaṃga —— 225 kūsa 4 ṣaṃga rrusa [1]
5 / . . . / 4 kūsa ganaṃ || 221 kūsa 3 ṣaṃga gḁusä || hauda hvaṃ-
6 . -āṃ na tti śū̥mä gḁusä haurīdä biśnḁ gḁusä himi 83 kūsa 3 ṣaṃga
7 / . . . / visarrjāṃ 52 || vīṃgulḁ̄ña haskadarmä 29 || jīvvā khḁṣṭarāṃ
8 / . . . / × 2 || ysāḍḁ̄ña hvrrīviḍtä pūrä vismadatta 18 [1]
9 / . . . / × 34 || sividattä 35 || hvaṃḍä 46 tti jsārä drrai pila haurīdä
10 / . . . . / himi 547 kūsa 4 ṣaṃga ṣḁ 4 kūsa 9 ṣaṃga rrusa ||
11 / . . . / × na || 3 kūsa gḁusä || 225 kūsa 4 ṣaṃga rrusa || 200
12 / . . / 4 kūsa ganaṃ || 138 kūsa gḁusä || [1]
13 birgaṃdara mattiśkḁ̄ña ṣanīrakä 34 || ṣanīrakä 24 || vidarrjāṃ 20 ×
14 namaubudä || dumesalḁ̄ña hunakä || sahadattä || suhadāysä || suhīkā-
15 ña īrasaṃgä || spḁ̄ñi virgāṃ || mattiśkḁ̄ña naṃdakä || || śāṃdattä || śudeva
16 / . . . / × dattä || sḁ̄madattä pūrä daraukä || [2]bikiñḁ̄ña ṣanīrä || khau[2] spāña sīlāṃ
17 / . . . . . / mādāśi
ṣḁ sūlyḁ̄ña sudattä || kharajsajsä || puñaudā || sude || suda
18 / . . . / -ura puñiśela śī̥laṃ || altāṃ || svarrjāṃ || makalä || vasade || maṃ
19 . maysdakä || bḁsävī suhadāysä || puñide || phaṃña spḁ̄ñi sivi-
20 **da**ttä || se̥nilä || yseviḍtä || khaukulḁ̄ña sudattä || buttakḁ̄ña kharamurrai

3

a 1 —— pḁ sudi vara u sudatti vara u mānī chaska ba
2 dara stūra ājimyarä u śe hvaṃḍye chaski 2 ṣaṃga paśā a
3 / . . . . / hauḍa sejsīji 26 mye haḍai parau tta parī

[1] Chin. 行 *hing* 'approved'. [2–2] Del.

4 3 paṃdāta tsve himyi[1] u mānī va vārä paṃdāta ṣṭārä vañau va maṃ
5 ṣi khaudivā tsūva ttū āysaṃ drraśi̯rau khvau ttāgutta ni jsa
6 brattaṃdai suhade svarrnadi āskvī

b 1 bulu̯nä rma̯mä-śi̯rä tta parī ——
2 na u spāta vīsa vara hamīḍa hārvāṃ × ///
3 u mara ma phe̯ma ysaujsä mau niśtä vaña × × parau
4 khu śau mūrä ni himāte ttī dva kūsa puña ma yaṃ
5 bāysdai khu ma ttiña māśta 7 mye haḍai hī × -au ///
6 seṃjsīji 6 mye haḍai parau [2]spa . maṅ . pa[2] ///

4

a 1 || tti vā va vārä stūrä cu bīrrä barīdi sude | yīśedrrabhadrri | suhadāysi | jayabhadrri
2 pa̯ sudatti | gūha śā | śi̯laṃ | budarmä | spāta marṣa̯ | naṃdaki | makali | mādāśi | .
3 dabhadrri | suprabhadrri | īrasaṃgi gūha śā | śirgulā sahadatti gūhi / . / × ///
4 śau saṃgi | upadatti | budāṣṭiri śau senili | ysāḍadatti | pa̯ sa × ///
[*Writing inverted to above*]
5 ri hvāṣṭāna hvaṃḍi cu śera̯ña miḍāṃ jasti hīya 24 haubarai sīha̯i hīya paṃjamaki u aka̯na
6 haubarai tti ri stūrä hīvī nahva̯ni || yauvarāyi hīya 4 ganama-kirā 3 u hvurähvādi || sauvi
7 / . . . . / datti ||

b 1 spāta sudārrjuṃ tta parī —— pharṣa sāṃdarä vara vaña ā ṣä pa
2 / . . . / stūra pajīdä piravārāṃ va āṣṭaṃdādeṃ saṃ ī mara kīṃtha pajī ttī hā haṣḍä yuḍeṃ si ma
3 / . . . . / *dä* ttī tta parsti si khu maṃ kaṃthi vara pahājīdä u ni ma hīsīde kīrarā biśä dau
4 / . . . . / × ttā ysāḍadattä tsve stūrai va hā thyau sameva u śautī jsāṃ hā hvaṃḍä viśta drai
5 / . . . . / -īṃdä khu ma abyūṣṭä vīra kaṃthä hīsīṃdä piravārā vā pīḍakä hauḍāṃdä se
6 / . . . . . . / dūṃ haṃjsyārau hvaṃdä märāṃ kṣu̯na cvai tta jsārä ī cūḍai āṃ puṣa ni hajse̯mä hvāṣṭe va

[1] Or *himye*?   [2-2] Tibetan script.

7 *| . |* × bą̄ki yanāre khu parau pvą cve ra tta jsārä ỉ thyau thyautī parya däśtä khu tta hve nä ỉ biśai draṃmā naṣkāra
8 *| . . |* jsārä däthaḍai biśä cära paphve hime 副[1]

5

*a*1 || hiyaudä spāta sudārrjuṃ vara tta haṣḍi yu *|||*
2 rą̄na aủya hīye mahemattye ttājä jsa kṣa ysār *|||*
3 ttā śira kye sī budesa tsue u hvāṣṭāṃ hīya va *|||*
4 ni tcerā cuai pūrä ye cisti pąjsä ṣąi āṃ kīri ni ỉṃdä
5 h(ā)ṣṭä haśdä u pyarī dvī mastą̄ñä ỉṃdä u śi**rä** *|||*
6 āṃ kīri mą̄nī beṃda haśdä khu ysāḍa hvaṃḍi pa *|||*
7 śāḍi hvaṃḍi rama tti ỉṃdä cu āṃ hvāṣṭāṃ hīya × *|||*
8 yaudäna khu dā byehāṃ bulą̄ni maṃ śirä × *|||*
9 u spāta yąnividtä ma pūri ā *si* *|||*
10 haṃdara prrū tsue budesa haṃda**ra** *|||*
11 dara prrū tsve vidyabudä ṣị × *|||*

*b*1 *|||* śtä kṣasamye haḍai śę būkä hvaṃḍi āta
2 *|||* *s* lā ⟨||⟩ mulakä || aką̄nadatti ||
3 *|||* × × hvaṃḍi āta || ysevitti[2] || kharamurrai || maṣądatti
4 *|||* × ñä ||
[*Inverted*]
5 || spāta sudārrjuṃ

6

*a*1 *|||* m bajeṣirau hvāṣṭāṃ ėha ma salā niśtä ysiri tta ma haṃthraji ama vaña hvā
2 *| . . . |* haṣḍi yuḍeṃ sä kīrūṃ anvaśtä ṣṭä būki āṃ byehūṃ thu tta luni mąmi
3 *| . . . |* bajeṣi khvaṃ va tta ra kīri kūśą̄ puña-rucita hā hą̄ña khu ādari
4 *| . . . |* jsyau āṃ ttā pą̄sūṃ sa ttiṇa tta parīya byaudai ā na ra 副

*b*1 || spāta sudārrjuṃ tta parī —— pharṣa sāṃdarä vara makalä mau nai × *|||*
2 śāye vaña paśā naṃdaki biysīye ỉ āstaṃna kīri makalä parya naṃdaki ni ma × *|||*

[1] Chinese *fu* 'duplicate'. [2] *ḍti*?

3 u ttī ṣi jsāṃ naṃdaki spaśañañāṣṭi gvāri yuḍe u pyaḍai ṣi hā ṣapā̮ñä × / . . . /

4 parau pva̮ ṣapā̮ñä tti cu vaña hatcaste naṃdaki ṣapā̮ñä ni perri ya ṣapā̮ñä ttye / . . . /

5 peri ɨ tti ṣapā̮ñä cu vā vaña naṃdaki hīsīdi makalä parya 副 ——

7

a1 || spāta sudārrjuṃ tta parī ——

2 / . / × ña māśtä āstaṃ māśte tcaura vū hīśtä ///

3 / . / jsä kūysdai tta ne khu parau pva̮ śau khū rä ///

4 mi khu ttī nä hṳ̄ñä sä nä pyūṣṭeṃ u ttī jsāṃ tta ///

5 / . / tcahau kūśä rruäśä jsa āḍä khu ttā a × ///

6 / . . / cärā̮na biśä pāravārāṃ hauḍāṃ ///

7 ma̮mä śa̮urä pastä se birgaṃdara bisai ///

8 śau hvaṃḍä viśta kṣīrva-vīrai u spāta ya̮nävi ///

b1 /// dva tsuna āśi̮rī vimalidrrabha[1] khvī ra mau ///

2 /// hauḍi sa̮maṃ 20 ca mau rṣa̮[2] śte a ///

8

a1 bulā̮ni śa̮marrjai tta parī —— pharṣa sāṃdari vara haṃtsa kīraryau

2 jsa mara hīsa jsāre vāra ṣṭi cu jsāri biysīyi ɨ marai āji*ma* /// ××[3]

3 u rrūnai maṃ śtāka ṣṭi spāta ya̮niviṭi byāśta[4] ttā rrūnai keṇa paste baḍara vā na ×[3]

4 u ttī *pajī* ttā kapāysä ki ×× kūśä̮ va ttā girye vī mūca̮ci paḍauysye haḍai

b1 braṃgi | senili | naṃdaki || hvūrähvādi || sā̮madatti || kharr*jyā*ni || makali | ṣanīraki

2 aśnadatti /// li ×× sudarmä tti vā kavārma tsvāṃdi ṣanīrakä saṃgūlai ɨrvadatti

3 ɨrasaṃgi || suhadāysi || vaśi̮raki || kāgaki

4 [*Inverted*]

|| pharṣa sāṃda- —— rä hai- —— śā̮ñä

[1] Read *vimali bhadrra*.

[2] Uncertain.

[3] Uncertain marks: *thu ra spasaña?*.

[4] *bdā*o?

9

a1 / . . . . / staṃ vāta vistāta kaṃdvaji ṣanīrä 5 haḍā sividatti paṃjsa haḍā ——

2 / . . / paṃjsa haḍā svarrnade paṃjsa haḍā suhadāysi paṃjsa haḍā ——

3 / . . . / śau haḍājsya vāta vistāta maṃñe vāta 2 si vidyadatti vā 1 suhadatti vā

4 × k cā 2 || tti vā śę būki vāta vistāta altā ⌒ suhena ⌒ saṃgapuñi ⌒ gaudi ⌒

5 [*Inverted*]

|| tti bura kṣīrva-vīrā hvaṃḍi cu spaśi ni yanīdi suramarṣa̱ pahai || vidarrjāṃ ///

6 darmä niśtä || puñadatti kūṣḍi vī cira pāḍaka-barā 2 āskvīra pāḍaka-barā × ///

7 pi ṣi̱ śau budarmä sa̱madatti vilakä ——

b1 / . . . / hvaṃḍi vāra ya pa̱ sudatti vā 5 haḍā | ani rucira tsve || ṣanīrä thaiṣī paśāti

2 / . . . . paśāti ma̱ysdaki spaśaña tsve suhadatti spaśaña tsve khau si vidyada

3 tti / . . / tsve śirgu suhadatti spaśaña tsve sīlā spaśaña tsve | phaṃnāji suhadatti spaśa

4 ña / . . . / li spaśaña tsve ——

5 / . / sta*ṃ* hvaṃḍi vāra ya mādāśi | maṃñe ⌒ phaṃnāji si vidyadatti ⌒ ṣanīraki vā śau pyāravī ×

6 *tt* × svarrnade ⌒ marṣaḍatti ⌒ ī̆ysadatti ⌒ budadatti ⌒ ——

10

a1 /// × māśti sparäbistamye haḍai spaśaña tsīdi ——

2 /// . -ā . -i . × × × virgāṃ || makali || saṃgade || sūradatti ||

3 /// spaśaña tsīdi ysā[1]ḍādatti[2] | pu̱ysdaki || maṃñe || phaṃnāji suhadatti || kūca

4 lai || ṣanīrakä || khau si vidyadatti || yseviṭi || ——

5 /// tti || īrvadatti || darauki || śāṃdatti || birgaṃdara suhadatti || kharamurrai ||

[1] *ys* over *ṣ*. [2] Subscript *tti*.

b 1 /// th*a*ka hauḍāṃdi saṃgigūthaki ⌢ brūnade ⌢ sūradatti ⌢ budāṣṭiri gūñi śā senili ⌢

2 /// tti gūtheśe śāṃdatti ⌢ virgā ⌢ sīlāṃ ⌢ khau sudatti || darauki ⌢ ṣanīraki ⌢

11

a 1 /// ××× spāta śirīdatti ttā stūrā va parau buḍi 15 stūra pajīda

2 /// × k ⌢ si vidyadatti ⌢ śau jsā hā thu haura u chaski hā drraśīrau drrai stū

3 /// stūra haṃdara śtāka ×[1] ——

b 1 /// bera āḍä ma cakṣakä ye vidyada⟨tti⟩ nāma cu ǎ ///

2 /// -ai biysīyāṃdä u rrustāṃdī vaña ttā bisi bisi hvaṃḍāṃ bvāñä

3 /// dä biysaṃjārai 副 maṃñe vā paskyāṣṭa thyau hajṣ̤ema 副 ——

12

a 1 || spāta sudārrjā tta parī ——

2 kīrakāṃ u pa̤kisenā vara vaña thaiṣī bulā rma̤mi ///

3 miḍā jasti hīyā māśa-vīrā āstaṃna paśā a ///

4 ña viśtari khu umi parau pvīrau ttinī vā tti ṣapāñara samevya ///

5 vī būjāri tāgutta hvāṣṭa tti ṣapāñi va pa̤jsi ysurri yu ///

6 ñara hacasta mūca̤ci śūvarabistamye haḍai ttā ///

b 1 / . . . . / hasḍi yani —— a pharṣa sāṃdari

2 / . . . / ṣ̤apāñara sameva ttī jsā⟨ṃ⟩ paśā avaśāna cirāṣṭa śe

3 / . . . . / × spāta vīsa hīvī puñadatti ṣapāña viśta va

4 /// śa̤tāṃ bida kīri ni bāysdaitti paśāti bida ṣi kīri nä yīdi

5 / . / pa*r* ñauri ā vā vā ttāguttā parau parī hauḍi ttī jsāṃ vā śe j*au*

6 / . . . . / -ī ṣīya ysāḍa haysīru u vilaka u ṣanīri va

7 / . . . . / rau mūca̤ci haṣṭūsamye haḍai ttā hasḍi yuḍi

8 / . / × u ganaṃ haṃdāḍa yu spāta hajsaudāṃdi vaña ā parau

9 /// /// × naraṃda

13

a 1 || tti vaña [×] mūñaṃji māśti spa̤śara parstai samautti × ///

2 suhīkā ṣanīri || vilocaṃ || braṃgi || brūnade || sūra*da*tti ///

3 īysadatti || vidyabudi || [2]senili[2] || kharamurrai || īrvadatti
kāśaki

4 vidarrjāṃ phāji ṣi̤ paḍāda samautti ye ——

[1] Uncertain sign. [2-2] Del.

b 1 biśa braṃkhaysji 24 mye haḍai ttā hasḍä yuḍeṃ vaña ttā ///
2 dīśta vā salā na parya pa̱jsä ma bya̱mā ṣṭi ṣai khvai paṃdāya pa ///
3 pīḍa kuṣṭa buri padeṃda himya ‖ ā̱mācä mara ///
4 na ttiña māśta ×× hīsā ‖ ——

14

a 1 / . . / burä spaśara kharajsajsä ‖ ysevịḍti ‖ hunaki ‖ darau
2 **ki** ‖ /// rrjāṃ ‖ īrvadatti ‖ namaubudi ‖ suhe̱na | arsäli ‖ cira

b 1 ṣapāñara sirphūki | si vidyadatti | brīna | ṣanīri ‖ ha̱ttikaṃ | tt h ///
2 namaubudi | salaki sa̱madatti ‖ vidya̱datti | tti haṃtsa × ///
3 ustākaji ṣanīri | phaṃnāji sividatti bu̱ysi ṣanīri | sahadat**ti** ///
4 maṃgali ‖ mulaki ‖ akā̱nadatti ‖ vasade ‖ mādāśi haṃ**dastä** ///
5 upadatti | virgāṃ ‖ sīlāṃ ‖ śādatti ‖ budadatti tti ha*ṃ* ///

15

a 1 /// **mi**ḍā jasti vara tta hasḍi yanā̱maṃ —— kṣvā aủvā tsī ///
2 /// **su**dārrjāṃ u kṣā aủvā bisā hārva u hamīḍa pa̱kisina cu ra āma̱mi ///
3 /// piṣkali vī jva himāmaṃ ttaṃdī jasti puñau jsa cvau vā jasti biśi ba ///
4 /// parīdi ttye jasta vañau maṃ pharāka rrvīya kīrä ṣṭārä u stāna**ḍ**au ///
5 /// × ra maṃ drraya stānaḍa īdi ṣi jsā śau ysaṃgara ṣṭi ṣi̱ ni ṣṭāṃ rrvīya ///
6 /// × ttarau ṣṭāṃ haṃdira prū lyiba̱ pajīdi u tta ṣṭā rrvīya kīri ni ///
7 /// sti mu̱śdi parī byaudi khvau vā piṣkala paṃj**sa** ///

b 1 /// lä hīye ‖ rrvī thaṃgi kiṇa u kṣīrvāṃ kīrāṃ pracaina pa -ṃñai tsveṃ gvīrā ///
2 /// vīra vaña dvī jū̱na pīha hauḍi yiḍeṃ āysārā̱na hame̱ vaña āṃ ttā u[1] × ///
3 /// × paśū̱ṃ haṃtsa neri jsa u pūryau jsa pyaṃtsāṣṭa hiyaudi parśūṃ ×× māśta ///
4 /// × na va ttiña aủva satta ni didye vī di tsvā̱ naḍa va adāya ṣṭāre ///
5 /// kīra yuḍi yiḍeṃ khu pyaṃtsā paśā byehūṃ vañaṃ āspāta yidi ///

16

a 1 ‖ spāta sudārrjāṃ tta parī —— pharṣa sā**ṃdarä** ///
2 ja ya khu pravanai yanīra nama̱śā̱ hā kautaja mūrä ///

[1] *u* over *ī*.

3 maṃ pye pīḍakä hauḍä u ka̤ra sikha ysanaji vā hirä ha ////
4 tti mṵ̄rä paja paṃ-sa yina khu draiyvā haḍā mara hīsi -ī ////
5 kä̤ṇa̤ parau hauḍeṃ si i̇ma haṃgä vistāṃ vaña burä vā ////
6 rä hajse̤ma khve kākījā̤ña ni haurāñä himi phe̤ma ā ////
7 rīḍī ahā umā̤nī käṇa haṣḍi yuḍe si kīthai nāsī × ////
8 jsārä nä tvaryarä hamaiya jsā vā ttrāṃ jsārä k*va* 副 ——

b 1 paṃ**ja**maki || maṃgali || brīna || hary**ā**saki ||
2 saṃgaki mulaki vā paskyāṣṭi i̇ṣṭi ——
3 sparadirsamye kṣā mūca̤ci paṃjsūsamye
4 haḍai tte buri spaśara tsīdi ——
5 mādāśi[1] || vidyadatti || sirphūki sudarma[2]
6 akā̤nadatti || budarmä || pramuhā vasa-
7 di kharajsajsi || mūlaki sudatti i̇rasaṃga
8 suhadatti
9 suhadāysi
10 suhena[1]
11 virgā

[*Vertical*]

12 sarkā haṃguṣṭi
| | |
13 senili haṃguṣṭi
| | |
14 suhadatti haṃguṣṭi
| | |
15 vidyadatti haṃguṣṭi

17

a 1 || śa̤ṃmaji tta parī —— pharṣa sādari ////
2 ysä śtāka ṣṭi tvī vā paṃjsuśeṃ hvaṃḍā ka ma ////
3 ttū jsārä vā parya buḍä cira khu ma svī h**īśtä** ////

b 1 //// || ṣanīraki || virgāṃ || ṣanīraki | suhena
2 //// datti | sūradatti || ——

18

a 1 || spāta sudārrjāṃ tta parī —— aủ aủ aủva haṃda ////
2 u drrīma ttvaśdā vara ttāgutta hvāṣṭa tta parstāṃdi si hvaṃḍi vā bi**śi** ////

[1] Ring around *mādāśi* and *suhena*. [2] *rma* subscript at end of line.

3 ttvaśdyari khu parau pvīrau hvaṃḍi vā kītha ttvaśdyari brakhaysji kṣemye ///
mūñaṃji

4 parau tsve

b [*Written vertically*]
de āmāci ṣau viṣṇadattä haiśą̄ñi

19

1 /// spāta sudārrjāṃna parau ā si tcirrttū[1] vā haṃjsiṣḍi hīsi 10 kūsa ā
2 /// -aina tcahau kūsa[2] rruśi jsa āḍi paśā avaśānạ hvaṃḍi himya 52
3 / . . / māśa-vīrā birgaṃdara hvaṃḍi 27 phanāja hvaṃḍi 16

20

1 /// **spā**ta vidyadatti hīye vāra mūri ri ysā haṣṭa-se sūradatti hīvī ///
2 /// datti hīye vāra mūri drrai-se yseviḍti hīye vāra tcaṃna mau girye mūri × ///
3 / . . / ña śālyāni ——

21

1 || spāta sudārrjāṃ tta parī —— salya-bā ///
2 cira vaña vā miḍāṃ g̱yastäna parau ā haṃ bāḍa va śe*y*-ṃ ttye *thaṃ*[3] × ///
3 ysi dva chā hvāhị khu parau pvạ 10śvā haḍvā ttä thau haṃgạja tcahau ///
4 yaneṃ paja khve uspurri 23 chā himi ttī lse[4] śe kaṃ̣bala ///
5 kẹ khu ttāña māśta jsārä biśi hauḍä himi ttājerä 12 /// **pa**-
6 rau tsve 副 ——
7 [*fragments of akṣaras*]

22

1 || tti bura hvaṃḍi cu skarihvārä māśti didye haḍai spaśaña ///
2 datti || sudarmä || puñade || maṃgali || harāsaki ⟨||⟩ × ///
3 paṃjamaki || mulaki || jsajsaki | hunaki || burmaki || ——

[1] Uncertain akṣara.
[2] Subscript *sa*.
[3] *thau*?
[4] Uncertain.

23

1 tti vā drrai ysāri dvī-sa haṣṭāyī haṃbā mūri puḍa ——
2 upadatti haṃtsa yąnaki hīyau mūryau jsa mūri puḍi tcąhaų ysāri 4 ——
3 yaudari u mūri puḍi paṃ-se 20 ——
4 cira hvrrīviṭi dasau ysą ca-sa cąhausä ——
5 makali mūri vāra dvī ysā hauda-se tcąhausä ——

24

1 /// × svāṣṭi hvaṃḍi birgaṃdara mattiśkāña vidarrjāṃ II suhīkąña
2 /// rg II phaṃnāji kāśaki II u yaudari II āskvīra gūmaji vidyade 副

25

1 II spāta sudārrjāṃ tta parī —— pharṣa ///
2 rä vara khu parau pvą anarū ṣapąña ma ha[1] haysa × ///
3 13 mye haḍai parau 副 ——

26

1 tti vā rarūyi māśtä spaśaña tsvādi kharajsajsi II suhadāysi II saṃgade II virgāṃ II ///
2 salaki II sūradatti II kūcalai II sudatti pąji ——

27

1 budadatti I kāśaki I naṃdaki —— spaśara paṃjsūsi ——
2 II tti buri braṃkhaysji 16 mye haḍai tti bu⟨ri⟩ spaśaña tsīdi phaṃnāji sahadatti II
3 ṣanīraki ⌢ hvrrīviṭi ⌢ visarrjāṃ ⌢ kharamūrrai ⌢ marṣądatti ⌢ [2]śāṃdatti[2] ⌢ si vidyadatti ⌢ sa-
4 loki ⌢ maṃñe ⌢ sarkāṃ ⌢ [2]mulaki[2] ⌢ [2]makali[2] ⌢ īrvadatti ⌢ arsäli ⌢ [2]yaudari[2] ⌢

28

1 II tti hvaṃḍi khu pęmīnā thaunā va thaunaka hauḍādi ysevịḍti u /// **tca-**
2 haura śe hvaṃḍye pęmīnai thau vī hacaṃ śtāka drai chā -i tsuna spā ///

[1] Blurred. [2-2] Del.

3 hatsa kharajsajsäna u suramarṣa̤na īrasaṃ**gä** ///
4 suhena thau vāra paṃjsa chā sūradatti thau vāra paṃjsa ///
5 āskvīra nva thaunakā haca kṣasi chā phaṃnājā nva thaunakāṃ ha ///
6 thaunakāṃ hacaṃ nausä chā saṃgi thau vāra 12 chā × ///
7 /// chā ā /// /// **tca**hau chā hau ///

29

1 bulāni rma̤mi śa̤räna parau —— piracārā va nūvari jsārä śtāka ///
2 58 khara u 6 ṣaṃga drrai śega nūvarä khahāni haurāta ttīmä ttye jsārä ///
3 u guñi haysāka hvaṃḍi tta hā jsārä jseṇi hauḍa 64 khara kṣi ṣaṃga 2 *-ai* ///

30

1 35 mye kṣuṇi cira kṣvā aủvvā mista thauna himārä 32 u[1] 11 chā u vitt × ///
2 mūri 44 ysa̤ cya ṣau a̤ni kuhisyi ni nāsa̤ñi mista thauna hauda ///
3 u tsātā hvaṃḍāṃ bida himārä tsīṣī spāta sudārrjāṃ thauna 3 **h**au ///
4 ha̤usi chā spāta burmaki 20 chā spāta vīsa 20 chā ///
5 sādarä 15[2] chā pharṣa sāmadi 20 chā pa̤ sudatt ///
6 mattiśkāña ṣanīraki 20 chā kīrarā hvaṃḍi 44 mis**tä** *thau* ///
7 mūra himārä 44 -ā ×××× -au × 3 chā u mūrä ///
8 prū jsausīya parau ///

31

1 /// × yi yi 14 my⟨e⟩ haḍai paḍauysi būki kaṃthi vī kīri yanīdi ——
2 /// *sūr*ade ‖ maṃñe ‖ puñade ‖ ysāḍadatti ‖ sude ‖ gachauki ‖ sahadatti ‖ vilokä
3 /// ṣanīrä ‖ śirībudi ‖ sa̤madatti ‖ namaubudi ‖ anirudi[1] ‖ hunaki ‖ huni
4 /// × hi ‖ vidarrjāṃ ‖ sudaśta ‖ akānadatti ‖ sahadāysi ‖ svarrnade ‖ maṃgali
herrjaki
5 /// **hatti**kaṃ ‖ mādāśi ‖ paṃjamaki ‖ kalidrri ‖ budāṣṭiri ‖ gaudi ‖ suhena i‖ hvuri

[1] Subscript. [2] 5 subscript. [3] Ringed around.

6 /// **yau**dari II sāmadatti śude II sirphūki II si **vi**dyadatti khau II ṣanīraki spāta pūri

7 /// bīrra-barai puysadi II mulaki II śaṃphaki II śīlaṃ 副 ——

32

1 /// × rai pau tsī āstaṃdādi phimāña kītha paḍauysi būki hvaṃḍi

2 /// ri II **pu**ysdaki II sudivi II sudatti II gachauki II arsäli II kuca-

3 **lai** /// × rä II sīlāṃ II śāṃdatti II si vidyadatti II khau ṣanīrä II śirī

4 **datti** /// II hunaki II hunili II yulmahi II vidarrjāṃ II svarrnade[1]

5 /// **suha**dāysi II ——

6 /// -ā /// saṃg**u**lai II maṣida*tti* II b*u*dāṣṭiri II si vidyadatti II

7 /// /// *sal*aki II sirphū**ki** ///

8 /// **bha**drradatti II sal*aki* II ṣanīraki spāta ṣū II × /// t

9 /// × II kalidrrä II gaudi II svarrjāṃ II maṃgali II ——

10 /// **suha**dāysi makali II vasade II śīlaṃ II īrvadatti II brūnade II ——

11 /// de II sarkāṃ II naṃdaki II ṣarrnai II virgāṃ II upadatti II vasade II aśta[2]

12 /// × II haryāsaki II vidyadatti II buysi ṣanīrä II vaśiraki II

13 /// × buda II suhade II tti vā haṃdyaji 12 mye haḍai cirāṃna āta paḍauysi

14 /// ×× II saṃgalaki II saṃganaṃdi II yuduysi II matsarakīsä II

15 /// × II nahvani II tti vā śe būki naṃdaki II braṃgi II branaṃdi II īrvada

16 **tti** /// × datti II nine viṣali II arrjāṃ II budesa II skarai II phāji II tti vā di-

17 **dye** /// II ttīśani II saṃgabudi II sejhaṃ[3] II visarrjā II īraki II śirīde II

18 /// × II īysadatti II śirībudi II khāysadatti I vilocaṃ ysāḍi budesa

[*Inverted*]

19 II spāta sudārrjāṃ tta parī —— da -au ///

20 khu parau pvīrau cu burä hve ī cu ñāṃtca nāsāte biśū rrvīya ganī × ///

21 naṃ drrvārä rrvī ttājirä śeye haḍai ttā parau tsve 副 ——

33

1 /// **kaṃ**tha āsalyā tsīdi āskvīra sūra*d* ///

2 /// **tti** II śe paṃdi budarmä u saṃgada ///

3 /// arsäli II sahadatti —— birgaṃ ///

4 /// **s**īlāṃ II sāmadatti II mādāśi II dva × ///

[1] Ringed around. [2] *aśna*? [3] *ja* over *ha*.

5 /// | sahadatti || ḇuysi ṣanīri || hvaṃḍi dva ///
6 /// × || gaysāyī vaṃdyadatti || upadatti ///

34

a1 || tti vā sejsīji māśä[1] 8 mye haḍai spaśara tsīdi arsäli ×[2] || marṣạdatti ||
2 īrvadatti || khaukūlā sudatti || śāṃdatti || bärgaṃdara suhadatti || kharamūrrai | saloki
3 sīlā | ——
4 || tti vā śẹ būki spaśaña tsīdi kharajsajsi || suhadāysi || suhena || virgāṃ || naṃdaki ||
5 ṣanīraki || sūradatti || si vidyadatti || ṣanīraki || | ——
6 || tti burä vā diḍi būki spaśaña tsīdi śīlaṃ || pụysdaki || maṃñe || phaṃnāji suhada ///
7 kūcalai || sarkāṃ || saṃgade || khau si vidyadatti || pạ sudatti || [sign] ——
8 /// salī kṣeradirsä māśti rarūya haḍā śụ̄dasi ṣạ samauca ttye pracaina ca
9 aủvā hvaṃḍi haṃdira prū haṣḍa yuḍādi spaśarāṃ keṇa cirạna u seni ///
10 u makali || u naṃdaki || namaubudi || ṣanīraki || brūnade gachauki ///
11 nāṃdi sayī ṣaṃgi ttū ganaṃ vaña haraṣṭādi hvaṃḍi himya 58 ///
12 ganaṃ himye śau ṣaṃgi paṃjsa śega mātargä jsa āskūrya 15 ganaṃ ///
13 sa 3 ṣaṃga phaṃnāja u pạja 17 ganaṃ haurīda dva kūsa kṣi ṣaga birgaṃ ///
14 /// × ganaṃ haurīdi 3 kūsa 8 ṣaṃga spāta sudārrjā tta parī ——
15 /// || /// /// /// × na[3] ttye nva samauci pajitta rarūye spāta
16 parau [sign] ——

b1 /// × /// kīri uspurra dāśāṃ āspātau jastina ——

35

a1 /// hvaṃḍi cu mūñaṃji māśtä didye haḍai spaśaña tsuñai śarkāṃ | bāja vaśịraki jsā
2 /// dattä || budāṣṭirä || kaledrä || phāji cira || svarrnade māśa-vīrai
3 /// [4]śarkāṃ[4] māśa-vīrai || sūrade māśa-vīrai || saṃgapuñi || vidarrjāṃ
4 /// × salamai haubarai sīhai hīvī || brattaṃdai māśa-vīrai
5 /// ysaṃ[5] māśa-vīrai || ××j nahvạnä || [sign] vidarrjāṃ bāja svarrnade jsātä[6]

[1] Read *māśtä*. [2] Uncertain: *lśi*? or *śau*? [3] *naṃ*?
[4-4] Ringed about. [5] °*äṃ*? [6] *tä* subscript.

b 1 ‖ spāta sudārrjuṃ tta parī —— pharṣa sāṃdarä va parau ttā hauḍeṃ si
2 puṣa vā ttrāmīrau[1] haṣḍe yanạ̄maṃ ttye jsārä kịṇa ni ā vā ttrạ̄mīrau paya
3 ā himi thyau vā puṣi ttrạ̄mīrau haṃtsa gū̦hyau jsa cu bure tsīdä ṣapạ̄ñarāṃ āṃ vā
4 būka ni hīdä hvaṃḍe āṃ ma gvavạ̄na de jsārä thyau vā ṣapạ̄ñara haysa [ornament]

36

a 1 /// ä rarūyä māśtä 11 mye haḍai ///
2 /// aủva haṃ haṃdastä daraukä past ///
3 /// *-īṃ* darauki salā hauḍā si mạma aủva tsī*d* × ṣī k ///
4 /// × rä ṣarrnai ‖ svarrjuṃ ‖ ——
5 /// -āḍa spāñä upadattä brabudä ‖ hattäkaṃ āchänai ysaṃgarä aủ ///
6 /// **ā**chänai viśạ śīlä ysāḍä ttī ra prạmā khu hā darauki haṃguṣṭi viśti ——
I I
7 /// —— darauki haṃgu*ṣṭi* ///

b 1 /// samauca ṣau ani kukisyi ni paj**ittä** ///
2 /// di sūlī ganaṃ ni byaudi pīḍ ///
3 /// **spā**ta sudārrjā tta parī aủva haṃdastā × × ///
4 /// **rar**ūyi 11 mye haḍai parau [ornament] ——
[*Inverted*]
5 /// × × my r ttā**ṃ**jera 8 mye haḍai parau ‖ [2]phar śa : daṅ : spa[2] ///

37

a 1 /// —— pharṣa sāṃdarä vara vaña pravanā
2 /// × pa × maṃgārā kīrarāṃ vī khu śe hvaṃḍye kṣīrva-vīrai ×
3 /// ri ttājiri paḍauysye haḍai ttā parau tsve [ornament]
4 /// ‖ tti paṃjsa chā 2 tsuna buysde u na drrai chā ṣị cu nāṣṭa kaśti ——

b 1 /// × -i ra parī —— spāta sudā
2 /// kharrjā ṣapāña śera ganama-kerai ṣṭi yau
3 /// × ji 26 mye haḍai parau I [2]spa : sor : źoṅ : la : spa[2] .

[1] *ạ̄*? [2-2] Tibetan script.

38

1 II ṣi̯ vā haṣṭāyeṃ thau /// /// **paṃ**jsūsi ā̯māci sūlīna paphve thauna vā nāte dva

2 tca̯hausa chāya pe̯mī /// /// raki nāteṃ II thaunaka 3 brū̯nade nāte II thaunaka dva

3 nva mūrāṃ naraṃda ysā /// /// ka 53 tti sūlya nāṃdä haudyeṃ thau-

4 nāṃ va II pātci /// /// × va ttraṃda ysārī haṃbā va

39

1 /// ki ⁀ saṃgūlai ——

2 /// na u sarkāṃ -i × × bāja

3 /// × hunaki II anirudi II akā̯

4 /// × /// × tti śe̯ būki ṣanīraki

5 /// vā didi būk × × × tti II

6 /// × × khaukūlāna ṣanīraki

40

a 1 /// -au naṃdaki ///

2 /// īrva ///

b 1 /// *visa*rrj*ā* ///

2 /// la *jsā* ///

41

a 1 /// × ///

2 /// *h*a ḍā × ///

b /// r ///
-*u*

42

a 1 //// tt(a) *cu* × ////

2 [1]-i . sa . la[1] ///

b //// -u t ////
m

1-1 Tibetan script.

5

Or. 11344

1

1 ‖ tti bura hvaṇḍi cu rrāhaji māśta tcūramye haḍai spaśaña tsīdi āskīra nahvạni

2 sūrade ‖ maṃñe ‖ kharajsajsi ‖ pụysdaki ‖ saṃgapuñi | sarkāṃ ‖ saṃgadi ‖ khara[1]

3 ïrvadatti[1] ‖ brīna ‖ si vidyadatti ‖ jsajsaki ‖ vidyabudi ‖ hvrrīviḍti ‖
kucalai
ttāṃguysi

4 ‖ tti vā rrāhaji 21 mye haḍai spaśara tsīdi āskvīra sudatti ‖ saṃgūlai ‖ puñade ‖ *bu-*

5 rmaki ‖ [2]braṃgä ‖ ttāṃguysi[2] ‖ yaduysi ‖ paṃjamaki ‖ sudarmä ‖
sūradattä jsajsaki
mulaki ‖ vidyadatti ‖

6 sirphūki ‖ vidyadatti ‖ gaysātaji ‖ maṃgali ‖ ——

7 ‖ tti vā cvātaji kṣemye haḍai spaśaña tsvādi haryāsaki ‖ akạ̄nadatti ‖ tcaṃjsai

8 khau ṣanīrä ‖ vidyabudi ‖ cirāṃ ïrvadatti ‖ sūradi ‖ nahvạni ‖ gaudi *///*

9 śīlaṃ |! sude ‖ pa̱ sudatti ‖ si vidyadatti bāja kucalai ‖ saloki ‖
va ttāgutti tsve
sā ///

10 tti vā cvātaji 21 mye haḍai tsvādä kharajsajsi ‖ suhadāysi ‖ sūradatti ‖ ïrvadatti *///*

11 phaṃnā suhadatti ‖ marṣa̱datti ‖ arsäli ‖ virgāṃ ‖ śāṃdatti ‖ khau si vidyadatti ‖ suhena

12 ṣanīraki ‖ pātca śe̱ ṣanīraki | naṃdaki ‖ ——

13 ‖ tti vā kaji māśti haudamye haḍai tsvādi śīlaṃ ‖ pụysdaki ‖ maṃñe ‖ suhadatti ‖ kha⟨ra⟩mūrrai bāja[3]

14 kūcalai ‖ sarkāṃ ‖ saṃgade ‖ sudiva ttāgutti tsve ‖ sīlāṃ ‖ si vidyadatti khau ——

15 ‖ tti vā cvātaji māśtä 21 mye haḍai spaśaña tsīdi āskvīra kharajsajsä ‖ suhadatti *///*

[1] *khara* and *ïrvada* ringed around [2-2] Del.
[3] *ja* subscript.

16 phaṃnāji sūradatti ll īrvadatti ll suhadatti ll arsäli ll birgaṃdara suhadatti ///

17 śāṃdatti ll si vidyadatti ll marṣạdatti ll suhena ll ṣanīrakä ll ṣanīraki ll naṃdaki ///

18 ll tti vā [1]cvā[1] kaji māśtä pūhye haḍai spaśara tsīdi āskvīra śị̄laṃ ll pụysdaki ll

19 maṃñe ll kharamurrai ll si vidyadaltti kucalai ll sarkāṃ ll saṃgadi ll
suhadatti
sude l sudatti

20 visarrjāṃ ll hvrrīviṭi ll sīlāṃ ll sudatti ll naṃdaki salokä ——

21 ll tti vā kaji māśti haudamye haḍai spaśaña tsīdi śīlaṃ ll pụysdaki ll maṃñe ll suhadatti

22 kucalai ll sarkāṃ ll saṃgade ll sudi ll sīlāṃ ll si vidyadatti sudatti
va ttägutti tsve
pạji ——

23 tti vā kaji 23 mye haḍai spaśara tsī⟨di⟩ arsäli marṣạdatti ll saloki l
gaudiva
[2]ṣanīraki[2] l sivi ///
ars

24 sudatti khau l śādatti l suhadatti ll [2]suhena[2] l suhadatti ll kharamurrai
vaśiraki
bāja spaśaña tsve vaña /// **khara-**

25 murrai suhadatti bāja jsātä u [2]suramarṣạ[2] 副 ——
kharajsajsi

26 tti vā hamārrīji māśti haudamye haḍai kharajsajsi ll suhadāysi ll suhena ll virgāṃ ll naṃdaki ll ṣa**nīraki** ///

27 sūradatti ll īrvadatti l ṣanīraki pyāravī sudi śau paṃdi byāṣṭi ——

28 ll tti vā hamārrīji 19 mye haḍai spaśaña tsīdi śị̄laṃ ll pụysdaki ll maṃñe ll suhadatti 副

29 kūcalai ll sarkāṃ ll saṃgadai ll khau sa vidyadatti ll pạ sudatti ——

30 ll tti vā sejsīji 8 mye haḍai spaśara tsvādi arsäli ll marṣạdatti ll īrvadatti ll khau /// **vidyada-**

31 tti ll śāṃdatti ll śirgūlā suhadatti ll kharamūrrai ll sīlāṃ ll saloki ///

32 sejsīji 29 me[3] haḍai kharajsajsi ll suhadāysi ll suhena ll virgāṃ ll naṃdaki ll ṣanīraki ll ///

33 īrvadatti ll ṣanīraki ll pāravī sude śau paṃdi byāṣṭi ——

[1-1] Del. [2-2] Ringed around. [3] Read °*mye*.

2

1 || tti vā maṃ paḍauysi būki kaṃtha āsalyā hvaṃḍi ya ///
2 puñade || ysāḍadatti || puysdaki || sudi -i ///
3 pātci suhadatti || sīlāṃ || śāṃdatti ///
4 anirudi || hunaki || hunili || ///
5 || tti vā śa̱ hvaṃḍi sudatti || altāṃ || hvurihvādi || saṃgulai || ×× ///
6 paṃjamaki || sudarmä || mādāśi || śaṃphaki || hattikaṃ || mūla**ki** || s ///
7 sāmadatti śūde || samādrradatti || saloki || ṣanīraki || spā pūñibuda | ///
8 kaledrri || svarrjāṃ || maṃgali || ——
9 || tti vā śe̱ āstaṃ kaṃthi vī hi̯ysda hvaṃḍi ya maṃgali || śirībudi || su ///
10 mulaki || haryāsaki || darauki || ṣanīri || vidyadatti || × ///
11 rä || paṃjamaki || ysāḍadatti || saṃgapuñi || ××× ///
12 na || svarrjā || budadatti || tti vā cirā̱na ya *vi* ///
13 de || vidyabudi || khāhadatt**i** || yaduysi | ///
14 || tti vā maṃ haṃdyaji 23 mye haḍai hä̯ysda hvaṃḍi ya /// **sā̱**-
15 madatti || suhena || hvurihvādi || altāṃ || sudatti || ///
16 datti || kūcalai || kalidrrä || hunili || suda*gu* ///
17 vī haṃdara hvāṣṭi paśāti salamai vāta 10 haḍā tti × ///
[*Inverted*]
18 /// suhadāysi ⌢ [1]si vidatti[1] ⌢ [1]śe[1] būki tti buri vāta saṃgapuñi
19 /// × *ji* × haḍā || maṃñeṃ paṃjsa haḍā || phaṃnāji si vidyadatti 5
20 /// īysadatti | marṣadatti spaśaña ye | ṣanīraka spaśaña ye
21 /// rr**j**ā anirudi cira -ā ṣanīrä thai-ṣī paśāti || u svarrnade
22 /// ye *spaśaña* /// s**i** vidyadatti spaśaña ye || birgaṃdara
23 /// **spa**śaña ——

3

a1 || tti vā haṃdyaji māśti spaśaña tsvādi śīlaṃ || pu̯ysdaki || phaṃnāji sahadatti || maṃñe ///
2 kūcalai || sarkāṃ || saṃgade || khau si vidyadatti || ṣanīraki pyāravī ——
3 tti vā haṃdyaji paṃjsūsamye haḍai tsvādi arsäli || marṣạdatti || īrvadatti || khaukulā sudatti
4 śāṃdatti || birgaṃdara suhadatti || kharamurrai || saloki || sīlā || ——
pyāravī

[1-1] Half-ringed below.

5 tti vā rarūyi māśti spaśaña tsvādi kharajsajsi || suhadāysi || suhena || virgā ||

sudatti pyāravī

6 naṃdaki || saloki || sūradatti || si vidyadatti || sude drrai paṃdi byāśdi himye ——

7 tti pātci rarūyi māśtä spaśaña tsvādi kharajsajsi || suhadāysi || ///

8 virgāṃ || naṃdaki || tti pātci rarūyi māśtä śi̮laṃ | pu̯ysda**ki** ///

9 phaṃnāji suhadatti || kucalai || sarkāṃ || saṃgade || × ///

10 pa̱ sudatti || tti vā ttājirä māśtä tsvādi 10 haḍai arsäli || × ///

11 īrvadatti || khau sudatti śādatti || birga suhadatti || kharamurrai || ṣanī**ra** ///

12 **sīlā** ——

b 1 spāta sudārrjuṃ tta parī —— pharṣa sāṃdarä vara vaña vā hvaṃ**ḍ**ä

2 /// m āna tta ma hvāṃdä si pe̯vī tta paṃdä paskyāṣṭa[1] muttūṃ himye u tti ṣi jsāṃ tta birgaṃdara × ///

3 /// **paṃ**dä khu̯ṇā ṣṭe ṣi̯ cä ṣä̯ hirä ṣṭä cu āṃ hā hvaṃḍä haḍā kīrä jänīṃdä u paṃdä ā bu̯ma × ///

4 parau pva̱ hvaṃḍä hā bāya 10 vareṃ kīrä parya khu burä nä dāśīde bāra bāra hā gaysä

5 jsāṃ āṣaijä jä vī kaṃthä hālai narā̱macä pātcä bāra bāra gaysä parya näśāta || ///

6 *būra* hime khu tta hvāṣṭāna st**u**ra pānä hamāre u ttyau khu ttī nä hu̯ñä sä nä pyūṣṭe × ///

7 thai-**ṣ̯ī** bulāni rmạmi śi̯rä tta parī —— kṣvā aủvā ///

8 ×× *tta* salya bāyai pharṣa sāṃdari vara u kīrarā vara mara kītha kūsa × ///

9 ttī si umā̱nī ttā sī dyāña cī ra kūsi pasti pharṣa vida kūsi pattīyi umānī ///

10 × śi vā hirä haurāñi caṃda pajīde 33 kṣuṇi braṃkhaysji kṣemye haḍai ttā parau tsv ///

11 [*Tibetan script*]

[*Inverted*]

c 1 /// va tsvādi 28 jsajsaki || **vi**dyadatti || sū ×× || śa**kä** || budarmä || sudatt**i** || sudatti || puña

2 /// **dar**auki || ——

[1] Possibly *ä*.

4

1 *///* 5 mye kṣuṇi cira kṣvā aủvā kīrarā hvaṃ⟨ḍi⟩ tcahaura ca̯ha̯usi śe hvaṃḍye pe̯mīnai *thau* *///*

2 tti nva hva*ṃ*ḍā thauna himārä 25 u 12 chā —— tsī-ṣī u hārvāṃ u tsātā *///*

3 thauna himārä hauda u dirsä chā vaña nva kṣauvā hauḍa thauna himya 23 u *///*

4 *I* . *I* tsuna thauna dva hālai sūlya hauḍāṃdi kṣau na ra byaidi tti cu spāta śe̯maki *///*

5 thauna 3 tsī-ṣī spāta sudārrjāṃ haurāña u spāta ya̯niviṭi śau ca̯ha̯usä × *///*

6 di thau puḍi 20 chā ṣanīraki 20 chā budarmä 23 chā hrrīviṭi u visa*rrjāṃ* *///*

7 mūrai ysārä kṣe-se tcaha̯usä yaudarä hīye vāra —— mūri dvī ysārä dvī-sa paṃjsāsä sūradatti

8 vāra mūrä ysārä kṣi-se cahausi pa̯ sudatti vāra ——

5

1 II spāta sudārrju tta parī —— pharṣa *///*

2 spāta budarmä pīḍakä hauḍe se aśū̯ma pastādä gärye ha *///*

3 na hi̯ysda ya u tcahaura̯ majärma himya ttyāṃ va ma kāṃjsa *///*

4 jsāsī ṣaṃgä u kāṃjsa himye paṃjsūsi kusa śau ṣaṃgä *///*

5 paṃñe ā̯na *ttäkyāṃ* kāṃjsa pastä kṣasi ṣaṃga khu parau pva̯ ttu *///*

6 khu vā spāta budarmä pāra vaysnä ājäme khu ma hi̯ysd*a* *///*

7 *kaṃ*thi ni hime u khu jsāṃ stū̯rāṃ hvaiyä ni pajīdä nūvara *///*

8 parau tsve 副 ——

6

a 1 tti buri thau kīrirā paśāta cira phāji II salamai II īrvadatti u naṃdaki II saṃ

2 saṃgūlai II puñade II vasade bikināṃ mādāśi II saṃgaki II maṃgali II mulaki II *///*

3 ṣanīra II haryāsaki II vidyadatti II budarmä II *jsajsa*ki I *///*

3*a* [*interlinear*] ṣi̯ spaśaña puysdaki *///*

4 tti vā ttū *rruṃ*di hvaṃḍi harya kṣīrva-vīrā cu spaśaña ni tsvādi II × *///*

5 yaudari ⁀ vidyadatti ⁀ kharajsajsi ṣi̮ pyāravī āsti b̮uysī va himye ///
6 || hiyaudi spāta sudārrjāṃ vara tta haṣḍi yani —— ///
7 ttā ni ttā n̮āma pīḍaikāṃ pa*ste* haṣṭi thyau vā parau paśa maṃ pūra *tta tta* ṣṭāri ///
8 haura spaśarāṃ ra haḍā baka ī̇di khu cira buri spaśara tsī ///

b1 /// dudi | pu̮ysdaki || × × × × datti || suhada
2 /// ī̇rasaṃgi | puñadatti || suhi ×
3 /// sudatti || × sīlā || virgāṃ || saloki || vidarr̮jāṃ

7

1 || vaña vā miṣḍāṃ g̮yastina parau ā skarhveri māśti 15 mye haḍai si vaña āṃ sa khyeṣa × ///
2 rṣṭhi dramaji kūsi kaj̮īṃdä strihi vyaulä ṣṭe ——
3 || spāta sudārrjuṃ tta parī —— pharṣa sāṃdari vara vaña *p* ///
4 śd̮āṃ va khu parau pvī̮rau cu burau hva hva piṣkalaña aůya hvaṃḍi ī̇de bi*śa* ///
5 khve tta śau hve vā tsī u stūri nva vyasthāṃ garkhi āri daṃḍi byehi skarihveri ///

8

a1 || hvaṃḍi nau tti spaśaña tsvādi naṃdaki || ṣanīraki || virgāṃ | ṣanīraki || suhena || kharajsijs*i*
2 suhadāysi || ī̇rvadatti || sūradatti | hvaṃḍi 2 pāḍaka-barā[1] vasade || altāṃ || u mulaki
3 birgaṃdara spaśari ttāgutti vī ṣṭi ysiviḍti haṃdira prū tsve thaunā gvaṣce cira jsāra-barā 3
4 suhadatti || pu̮ysaki || ysāḍadatti || hvaṃḍi paṃjsa haḍa bisvā ṣṭāri hvaṃḍi 2 cira tsvādi an*i*-
5 rudi u svarrjāṃ hvaṃḍi 3 ṣau viṣṇadatti hīya vāra sūrade || sudatti || saṃganaṃdi ——
6 hvaṃḍi 5 yauvarāyi jasti hīya vāra aśtadatti[2] || kharrjāṃ || tcaṃjsai[3] || hvurihvādi || saṃgaki ——
7 hvaṃḍi 5 pahaisā suramarṣä̮ || vidarrjāṃ || haskadarmä || puñadatti || suma*tt* ///
8 hvaṃḍi 24 miḍāṃ jasti hīya kāṃjsata-kerā u ganama-kerā ——

[1] Or *-āṃ*? [2] Or *aśna*°? [3] *tcaṃ* (*caṃ*?) subscript.

b 1 kucalai rrusa[1] vāra 2 kūse[2] paṃjsa ṣaṃga ttye bāja ạysaṃ hauḍi ——
2 || ṣị vā phema bisai āysaṃ hatcaṃ cu phema kaṃdvāṣṭā buḍāṃdi paskāṣṭi phe ///
3 ñi 11 kūse 3 ṣaṃga ——
4 ganaṃ paṃjsūsi kūse[2] haṣṭa ṣaṃga ṣị cira haurạñi ——

9

a || pharṣa sāṃdari

b 1 /// parī —— pharṣa sāṃdarä vara cu vā pīḍakä hau
2 /// × nä himi khu tta ra ni byehe puṣa baḍä phẹma hvaṃḍä spāśä
3 /// dä yuḍä yuḍā*ṃ*dä u vara ạna jsāṃ vā pasi gẹnä ttaṃdī haḍä va
4 /// -īśa āskvīra tta mau ṣṭä paryatī pirśtä khu ni bajaittä
5 /// 10 mye haḍai narạmīṃdä u ṣị hirä biśä phaṃnājạñä āṣaiṃ
6 /// ×× hịysd*a* × viśta vaña mara hvāṣṭāṃ vaska hāṃ
7 /// ḍ*a* narāmī*ṃ*dä cu hạmai haurī*ṃ*dä vaña ttā hvaṃḍä paśātẹṃ dva
8 /// kaṃthä vīrāṣṭä āṃ tta hira pajīṃdä
9 /// /// āna hā jaṃ hā [illegible] ——

10

1 /// rä × jsāri barīdi makali śūhi[3] śau || budāṣṭiri ⌢ ṣanīraki ⌢ braṃgi ⌢ ×
2 /// ×× budadatti cirāṃ ⌢ ysāḍadatti ⌢ virśabhadrra ⌢ brabudi ⌢ hvrrīviṭi ⌢ bhadrra ///
3 /// *h*attikaṃ ⌢ darauki ⌢ virgāṃ ⌢ sude ⌢ śīlaṃ ⌢ budarmä ⌢ āśirī yīśe**drrabhadrri**
4 /// anirūda khara śā ⌢ suhadāysi ⌢ pharṣa sāṃdari ⌢ saṃgi ⌢ upadatti
5 /// *ni*datti ⌢ yadu gūhi śā || īrvadatti gūha śā ——
[*Inverted*]
6 || tti buri hvaṃḍi cu karera stūra haysīdi hunaki ⌢ ṣanīraki ⌢ sīlāṃ ⌢ *īrva* ///
7 datti ⌢ pụysdaki ⌢ kharajsajsi ⌢ ——
8 || tti buri stūra cu bīrri buḍāṃdi ṣanīraki haṣṭa sahadatti gūhi ⌢ -ī ///
9 /// sā*ṃ*dari ⌢ spāta marṣạ hīvī ⌢ viśudabhadrra ⌢ jayabhadrri ⌢ ——

[1] Akṣaras confused.
[2] Unusual shape of akṣara, without complete *s*.
[3] Read *gūhi*.

11

a1 /// —— pharṣa sāṃdarä vara vaña āṃ ma hvāṣṭä parsaṃ
2 /// **pa**jittä śau kūsi paḍāṃdare ttā parau hauḍeṃ nai vā hajsaudai khu ttā parau hī
3 /// **hvaṃ**ḍyi dīśta thyau hajsęma khu ma svī hīśtä pa[*sta*]rsaṃdai ma śtāka [1]la[1] ṣṭi ttāṃjeri
4 /// **pa**rau tsve 副
b1[2] × vā hvaṃḍye **gäryeṃ** × mūr ys**ā** tty**au** jsa u *mū* × js × ḍ **gäryeṃ** ///
2 vā [1]sudārrjāṃ[1] vạnā gäryeṃ mūrä haṣṭusi ttyau jsa jseṃṇa
3 /// mūrä haṣṭa ysārä ttyau jsa sudārrjuṃ va yābakajä thau gä**ryeṃ** ///

12

b1 || spāta sudārrju**ṃ** tta parī —— pharṣa sāṃdarä vara vaña vā śaṃ**dā** ///
2 rä kīṃtha āṃ naraṃdä dañai däthaḍai mara āskvīra bāḍa mau vā bara ha ///
3 jsāṃ vā haysa u kīrarä jsāṃ vā tsūva āskvīra u ttī jsāṃ tta āṣaijä vī pa × ///
4 hā ysai ysai hvaṃḍä bāya 20 baśạ baśạ hā gaysä näśarä u gaysä be × ///
5 būma jastä himi khu sala nä byehi u pęvī ṣ̨īrī pạjsä āṃ va aśa vahạnī ///
6 || āskūrī ha**ṃ**dasta ā ——
7 ysāḍadattä hīśvā padi parya jaśti āskūryạ̄ hīśạ pyähaitta 副
a1 /// śvarabhadrä śaṃdā haṃbujsai hụñūṃ —— spāta sudārrju*ṃ* cu ttā bu
2 /// kä vīrāṣṭä pīḍaka hauḍeṃ ttädīyū parya pạjsaude rrvī tta hāmai ṣṭä *dyā* ×
3 /// **pa**rya hajsaude u ttī jsāṃ tta mau ṣṭä paryatī pirśtä khu na bajaittä hvāṣṭa āṃ
4 /// **mā**śta 10 mye haḍai narạ̄mīṃdä paṃjsa ṣaṃga aśparä na ma vā pụsa 副

13

1 /// ji 18 mye haḍai spaśaña tsīdi [3]salamai[3] || [3]sagapuñi[3] || kharrjāṃ || [3]suhīkā ṣanīra[3]ki
2 /// braṃgi || brūnadi || sūrade || sāmadatti || saṃganaṃdi || [3]īysadatti[3] || vidyabudi ||

[1-1] Del. [2] Tops lost. [3-3] Ringed around.

3 /// × || kharamurrai va vāri spaśaña śau jū || īrvadatti va vārä spaśaña śau jūṃ || śirībudi ||

4 /// tti || va vāri spaśi śau ttī khvai va vidarrjāṃ 副 phāji || ttāṃguysi || 副

14

1 || tti vā hvrrīviṭi drrai ysārä dvī-sa haṣṭāyī haṃbā mūrä hauḍi pauḍauyse mūri hauḍi drrai ysārä drrai-si tti cvai la -i ///

2 u birgaṃdarajā śau thaunaki drrai ysārä mūrä u yąnaki hīye drrai ysārä drrai-se vī tti mūri nāti dasau ysą̄ ca śau dva na ——

15

1 /// ×× senili rrvī hirä buḍāṃdi pęmīnā thauna nau u śau cąhąu

2 /// × rau ysārä ——

16

1 /// tä[1] saṃttīrvā ttrraṃda u kṣauvā na ra py*ar* ///

2 /// nä sūlyau jsa paphūnva[2] nāne[3] rrāhaji

3 /// × brātarä haṃña biśa ——

17

a 1 || spāta sudārrjuṃ tta parī —— ///

2 rä aủva haṃdasti sudattä vara u pą suda ///

3 vaña vā miḍāṃ ḡyastäna parau ā si × ///

4 kīthi vā ysaṃgauñä huna parrya khu parau pvį̄rau svī pa*js* ///

5 mara ājumyarä paḍāṃdara ttā parau tsve khu vā ttina —— ///

6 spāta mirą̄ñū himi u dąula haṃdara skarähverä māśta ///

7 haḍai haṃdą̄maṃci parau 副 ——

[*Two small fragments*]

b 1 sāṃdari vara

18

1 pęmīnā thaunā hīya kṣauva u yserī haṃbā haṃda maṃ pīḍaki niśta ///

[1] *bh*? [2] Read *ka* for *nva*? [3] Read *nāte*?

6

Ch. 0043

01 [*pen trials*]

1 . . rrvī vī vara tta haṣḍi yana ña[1]śa[1] bīsa khuī hara ttā vaña × ///

1a [*Interlinear*: trials of *tsū* and *tsvā*]

2 va māra-pyara tta uca śadā ya rrvī[2]yau ja[2]phā käṇa parāva vą bva-

u ṭma

3 ysagāñaja hā bīsa hvā-cū masarīka gīrī [1]u[1] vaña ×

4 aủ tti jipha gvevona na bīḍa vaña rrvī vī āspāva khū tta japha

5 gvevāna ṣai hvā-cū masarīka bīḍa cą aủ ttya uca śadai kīra pa-

6 ra khva vā mūña bidā ṣau[3] na padi rä khū ra ca [4]khū khva[4] ——

7 khuī hará ttā na vara khū para hva-cū japha gvīvāna ṣṭi ra tte ṣį

8 stula masarīka bīḍā cū ā ttai uca śadi kīra para ca ttā

9 masta hvau-cū hīya vara tta haṣḍi yana ——

10 . . mistā puñā kuśala-[1]mūlā[1] jsā haphva vī bauḍa-dījsākyā [1]ña[5] ñaśä bīsa yū sa[1]

11 laka ña[1]śa[1] vā bīsa kamacū vā ṣṭau parā ṇasta sa gīrai-varā vā ye

12 u kṣaṣṭi kīṇa vastā [6]ñaśī basa[6] ahā[1]ḍa[1]ra pārda padāya ula mūḍa

arahaya

13 uca jsā ma nva aśa ya . . misti cigānyi ğyaśtä u mistai hvau-cu vara tta

14 . . mākṣī gula ttārji śakara mūvā agī mīrāhya dadāye śaga pi-

15 jsi huśịna jsīna kaṣṭi paśti hāda kāla panūḍi ṣį karavā castāña

16 ttiñā ysītha khva gīsta khva ttāḍū kṣāda vī bā*sti* kaṇa dvūnā ttāḍū

17 . . ttī vaṣṭi jauhya ñāysīraka pañä gāśti ttā ïniysi khyaṣe nāmi vī-

18 jilaka byīvīri miśtai kaniśta ā . . śūṣṭe ma ya aśi vīra śī aủ

19 hāḍa śtai ṣṭi ma ya mūva nāma nvaśa ā avi ttye[7] bajsi gvā[ḍa][8]ḍū u

20 ca na huru bajsā hāṣḍi āhāḍi hīysaka bitti . . hama ni

21 mu-ysītha sāhą ca ma ysīra aśti ysīri ysuṣkā [bhya][8] cya jsa ha-

22 ña kuḍi āvu hva vā kāmada disti śīyu hiji tturaka ttura-

23 ka jsa piji piji lā[×]nyā jsi śiṣejsā dasti kidi na śā ṣe jsi pīra-

24 ma parijuṣṭi nuye khū va drai cā dīśą harśta . . yādi ttā hva

25 ñusa huśąna ñūsa [×] hatsi ttā [×] hva [1]sa[1] ñūsa ñūsa na ñu vīśū vi

[1-1] Subscript.
[2-2] Written with *ja* between *y* and *au.va* above preceding *ya*.
[3] Read *ṣṭau*?
[4-4] Del.
[5] *ña* blurred.
[6-6] Read *ñaśa bīsa*.
[7] *stye*?
[8] Blurred.

26 vāñu da mi vi vā phustā śvū [× × ×] hīye *ḍa*ñī ttyai baida śtāeka[1] yi

27 . . rrvī vī vara tta haṣḍi yani ñaśi bīsa sanaka ñaśi bīsa vā parā ṇa-

28 sti sa ṣacu vijsvāñi a[na]kuśī̮ vāṣṭi parā ya sa aśi pamuhva vī bu-

29 rā śirka hajsāmīda vaña tsvaḍa pada hera hamai hira va na pa pūḍi

30 dā vaña rrvī vī āspāva khū ma tta akuśī bīsā ttāgava rrvī nyū parā hajsā-

31 mīda khu ttu rrvī parā hagrātta yainu khū na jsa mauma ——

32 . . maistyā ārmaysda mauñadā puñā kūśalya mulya jsa haphva vyāśā

33 guttira yuvarā⟨ya⟩[2] ārga drunā pvasāma haṣḍi yaini ñaśa ba-[3]

34 sa yu dāha̮ paḍi khū tta vaña ttya sālyaja kāla bāḍa vī śi-

35 rka dāvi drū[4]na[4] tsva ṣi̮ ttya kiṇā ma ñaśi bīsa : a dāna mīra ci ma

36 dā juha̮ka tti vi tti va jsā ttī nā dakhu kāra avyāca baye

37 haysgama ci amrre kaṇa bīdi khva [×] thāna hamāda khu śti

38 jsa hamāri : hīrāsakā iysīye basaka jsi mauña vīsa juhi̮

39 jsa kāṣḍvi āstikya nuyu ṣava krraga dā vā grusīda : ma ṣi ma ttya ñāña ysī-

40 raka [da][5] dā[4]va[4] hīri dara śu ṣi ka ca na juha̮ ca dā ju ṣi̮ tcyā kvä-khīmu cu nā-

41 ma naḍāna bvaysa haysga vaṇāsa darā īma phana ca cā tcyāṃ kvịna

42 cā tcyāṃ kvịna : rrvī vī vara tta haṣḍi yani ñaśa bīsa kharasanaña mistā tsve

43 syānā hvāṣa̮[6] vara tta haṣḍi yi ñaśa bīsa baramaija pacaka ñaśa bīsa va̮

7

Ch. 0048

1 pasa[7] salya cūvija māśti nāmai haḍā ṣi̮ byāvaja pīḍaka ttyi hira prracina cā ā baramyaja

2 ttūnakā panaka ṣi̮ cū haḍa tsvi u śā ma cigāna nāvi u tta tta jsa gvāra basti sa kṣīrā bāysda

3 —— u nārā padīmū bīśa bīsā jsā nāri naṣiphaśtu ttuka jsa gvāra tta tta basti ci ṣi̮ ×

[1] Read *śtāka*. [2] *yu* written as *yrra*. [3] Read *bīsa*. [4-4] Subscript.
[5] Blurred. [6] Read *hvāṣṭā*? [7] *pa* broken.

4 /// cigāna dāya na nā ttu ttyi jsā kṣādātma̮ prramākhva jsa vā ṣā panaka akṣara nīśä

5 : ṣi̮ ḃuri cīnä väjalakä ṣacū kīrä tcerai haṃtsa dū saṃgalakā āstaṃna ka̮mäcū tsuākāṃ u

6 ⟨su⟩dattä āstaṃna śvahvā̮ tsukāṃ haḍāṃ jsa haṃtsä kīrä tcerai khu ttā marä janävä vī ā̮nä tsvava

7 ttyā drai pacäḍa haḍa hīñä hīñä dīśtä bisā ysīḍā parauva dī ttye dī ttye hinā-pamūhai

8 haḍä baśtä sve bidä barīdä kuṣṭi saṃ va̮ysgede khu va bahyä nä hamāve virī baji ba-

9 ñāña u parauva aúski väśtāña u[1] ysai ysai panamāre biśä starāña u parauvā ānāñä

10 paḍauysä aśä parauvā va pathāñä dädä spāśāña khu parauva-bara bvā̮ttä u paḍā paḍā jsā

11 śau chā hīsyara parau tta tta [tva][2] tvarä khu thyautta : rrvī vī va tta haṣḍi yini : śidī ṣā̮ñä mau khaṣṭi vilakā i-

12 ysā ttī va [3]vā[3] byāva tha tsūāyi hirtha vīra varī panavu kamala rāha̮ pasāña ttā vi ttā tsvau

13 vara kuṣṭi thā phara bva ——

8

Ch. 0049

a 1 /// × sta tcāṃ tte hvā̮ṃ u ///

2 /// -ū yaṃ u śī kvai : ///

b 1 /// hūśa̮ina u khvau tta ṣṭe u sa-thū u mista rraispūra

2 /// × u ttaugä —— cā*ka* ėysa vaijalaka

3 —— u ėysa svaha̮ka

4 —— ll cā krraśīsa u kva ṣanīraka

5 —— amaga svanī u kīma ttehä śa-

6 —— nä u yā kī-tsena u la phadrū

7 —— hvā̮ṃ sa-ga u̮ sera hvai-jvai

[1] Possibly *dra* for *u*. [2] Blurred. [3-3] Subscript.

9

Ch. 00269

01*a* *III* × carä *ka* [*marks*]
01*b* *III III III* pīḍakạ
01*c* siḍa II gūha salya vā *III III* —— yuḍu ——
01*d* ḍa *lya*
01*e* gūhạ salya vā ——
01*f* yuḍa *salya* ——
01*g* —— guha salya ——

1 II mistai rraispū⟨ri⟩ tta parī hau kṣaṇyä —— uvāryau garkha ——
2 —— rya ka jsai kaiṇa ṣṭa
3 va cā rä kai harrda . . uvārya garkha pūñā krraña
ña
4 gūhạ salya vā —— haudya —— stai stai stai stai stai
5 . . haudyāṃ rrispūrāṃ rrvī vīrāṣṭā aủ⟨rrā⟩sä ha stai sta
6 : uvādā gakha : namayi śau ysatha ṣṭā ñāttipūrä . ra
7 uvāryā garkhā vaisthāryā pu —— ra ra ra ra
7*a* —— ū ū —— dū ——
8 āśạrī kaiṇa rr*va* va cạ ṣanīrä śvai : [1]××[1] prraphākaravarda ——
8*a* āśạ āśạ ——
9 . . uvāryāṃ garkhyāṃ pūñau vaisthā⟨ryau⟩ kūśala-mūlyā jsä haphvai ya mistai
10 sī thū ttaya-śī mārgạpadaiśai ttravīlai āśạrī prrañīdrākarava-
11 rrda dī pākā naysdä grāṃ brrīyạstā aysamū jsä aủrga drūnā
12 pūạisāma haṣḍä yanä ña⟨śa⟩ bīsa ttravīlai prravākaravarrda
13 khū vā ña⟨śa⟩ bīsä kṣīra ā dyāmai jsa gvaṣṭū āda ma vaña būrai hī-
14 yai hīye pūñau kuśalā-mūlyā jsa dākha [2]ma[2] naiśtä
15 : uvāryau garkha vaisthāryau pụ̄ñau kụśāla-mūlā jsa haphve yi mistye si thū tta-
16 yi-śī mārgabūde⟨śai⟩ ⁀ tträvīlai āśạ̄rī prrañaidrākaravarrda dī pākā aủ-
17 rga drūnā pvaisā . . śtä ṣṭā na mīre ca ma ṣṭā jūhạitte ve . ttī va jsā ttūā
18 dakhä ṣṭārä avyācä . II uvāryā garkhā vaisthāryā pūñā kuśạla-mū-

[1-1] Blurred. [2-2] Subscript.

19 lā jsā haphve : aủrrāsä ḥạṣḍä sī ca ——

19a [1]rrvī[1]

20 ñauysairä brrī pyarä ṣau staḍesä u mirä ėysājai vīdyehẹ u paysā-

21 va hvārakä ėysāja paḍa tcūkye . u ėysāja kha cūlye dī pākā aủrga

22 drrūnā pvẹsāma haṣḍä yanä ——

23 aủrrāsi ḥạṣḍä . . aủrrāsä haṣḍä stai [2]aủrrāsä haṣḍä[2]

24 . . aủrrāsä haṣḍä bīsä chikä gūlai u dūṃ saṃgalakā [ha][3] khu vā ña-

25 śāṃ bīsāṃ kạmäcū āṃ rrvī parau pastāṃdä si kạmäcū būrāṃ rrispūra

26 bāyạ̄ñä ⌒ u ñaśāṃ bīsāṃ tta tta parau nä ye si ami ttyāṃ tsvākāṃ rrispū-

27 rāṃ hīvī pamūhä: u stūra spāśarä u khu jsāṃ ñaśa bīsa radạ̄nahä : ā-

28 vaṃdūṃ khu spāṣṭāṃdūṃ stūra u śau ri va rrispūrāṃ hīvī ạṃmägạ ni mūṃde biśä

29 pahaiya cū stūra ttyāṃ jsāṃ hervī aśparä ni hauḍāṃdä u ñaśä ra ttā bīsa

30 vaṣṭi vī haṣḍä nä yuḍä yuḍāṃdūṃ si khu ttā haṣḍä yināṃ si stūra gauda

31 ṣṭāre ka ṇāṃ tta tta parī paśte si bīsāṃ āṃ nä kṣami tsve u nva parau tsvāṃdūṃ khu

32 jsāṃ paṃdāyi vistā hamyaṃdūṃ varä jsāṃ va väṣṭā hīya śaṃdā ni ya u paṃ-

33 dāyi sạ̄nāṃ hīvī pvạnä u khu jsāṃ stahä : biśị̄ āvaṃdūṃ varä ạ̄na cimū-

34 ḍāṃ jsa haṃgvāṃdūṃ aủdä ṣacū būrä cū paḍā paḍā bisā mahe yaṃdūṃ u rri-

35 spūra mahe svahä:kṣeṃ ṣacū āvaṃdūṃ cvāṃ va nū stūra harya vạstairma u hvạṇḍä

36 u herä u hvaihū:ra ttāṃ biśä cimūḍa hatcastāṃdä cū jsāṃ stūra ya ttāṃ jsāṃ

37 biśä paṃdāyi vạstā tsvāṃdä u tta tta āṃ harya ⌒ cū gūmattīrai rrispūrä hī-

38 ya drayi ula ya tta śau la[4] na parye hamye ttaṃdī ra ṣacū śe vạstairmä aśä jsa ā

39 cū śẹye rrispūrä stạmä hīya ula ya draya u aśa dva [5]tta[5] sị ttaṃdī ṣacū śau

40 aủlä ājiṃde ysbaḍäparrūṃ ạ̄na ṣacū būrä biśä pāyai tsve ⌒ cū rrispū-

[1-1] Subscript to *jsā*. [2-2] Red ink, subscript. [3] Blurred.
[4] Read *ula*. [5-5] Del.

41 rä thiyä tcų̄nä hī[1]vī[1]ya tcaura ula ya ṣį ttaṃdī ṣacū śau aủlä ā cvai cimūḍvā

42 gūmaistāṃdūṃ ⌢ cū rrispūrä yį̄nakä hīya kṣą ula ya ttä ṣacū drayi āva

43 u śau aśä ⌢ cū rrispūrä śvakalai hīyai ttaṃdī ṣacū śau aủlä ā ⌢ drvāttīrai

44 hiye hīvī aủlä cvai tcirthūśī jsa giryāṃdä ṣą ttaṃdī dva paḍyehä : śau haḍā

45 tsva hamye śau vai ra vā aśä ā ⌢ cū hirä śirä dīrä cū vā būḍāṃdūṃ cvāṃ

46 maṃ dīśta ye ttū cimūḍāṃ padaṃja hauḍāṃduṃ cvāṃ jsāṃ mvaṃ harye ttū jsāṃ cimūḍa ha-

47 tcastāṃdä u ṣacū ra ttūśā-dastā āvaṃdūṃ stūra jsāṃ vąstā tsvāṃdä u ja cū pā

48 gūmattīrai hiye hīvī draysä bidä ttūrkä uha: hīvī rrvī śkyesä ye ttū

49 pā biśä cimūḍa buḍāṃdä ⌢ khu vā ñaśāṃ bīsāṃ parau pastai ya paśte si

50 paṃdāyāṃ tta tta tta cimūḍa ṣṭāre ñaśa bīsai ñą̄msä phara bvį̄masti si tta ttāṃ

51 tsų̄ñī ttaṃdī vą̄ dasau[2] radą̄nahä: haḍā byaudāṃdūṃ ya śe tcaṃjsä biṃdāṃ maṃ

52 gārī ni hamīya ttaṃdī vą̄ gārī tta tta hamye cu śa paḍā yaṃdūṃ u vąstairma

53 dva u tta tta hatcastaṃdūṃ cū ttūra ttāttāhä: uhaḍpī tta ñą̄ña ñą̄ña hirä rau-

54 stāṃdä u haṃ bāḍä hvaihụ:ra jsāṃ vā drayi aśi ājiṃdāṃdä cū nayū chā-

55 rä ną̄ma sūlī ṣą jsāṃ vā śau tcaṃjsä ni ājiṃde ttye stūra biśä ja u herä garvā

56 pace khu rri hā ā u tcaṃjsä rä va ni byaude biśai cimūḍa thīyāṃdi bų̄nai ma ṣṭi

57 khu jsāṃ ṣacū vāṣṭä stūrāṃ kiṃṇa saṃgalakā parye varä jsāṃ va stūra biśä kämä-

58 cū hį̄ñä haṣṭāṃdä śau stūrä ni byaudeṃ ⌢ khu [3]ñaśa bīsa[3] ṣacū āvaṃdūṃ [3]cu hīna ya ttye śą māśtä ya[3] tta ñą̄ña dasau paṃ-

[1-1] Del.
[2] *da* corrected from *dra*.
[3-3] Subscript.

59 jsūsä haḍā parya u hi̥na ttī āva cu bḁgarakä attẹmä ūha: uha ya

59a [*interlinear* following 58 māśtä ya] khu kḁmäcū tsvāṃdä

60 vairä uha: uha: uha: u kḁ̄ṅūrapa sahḁ̄:nä uha: ⌒ u bīrūkä ci̥-

61 nä ttāhä:[1] u bīrūkä [2]tta vā baiśä mara[2] dūṃ ttāṃga u saraihä: chārä aha: cī
miṅamūkä[3] bīrūkä

62 tta vā ṣacū-pavḁ̄nye haṃtsä hīñä jsa pahaisā ṣacū vāṣṭä hāysa tsvāṃdä tta tta cū

63 pātcä kḁmäcū bisai khahḁ: nä jsāṃdi [ci][4] u ttaysī dagyi̥nä hā ṇḁstāṃdä ttī mīṃ

64 biśä bādū̥na ārrä ttyāṃ pahaisāṃ i̇ḍāṃdä si cu āṃ maṃ mḁ̄ñāṃ bāḍä vī ā-

65 phājä ni jāre amḁ̄nī ārrä ṣṭe ttī [2]jsāṃ bḁgarakä kḁmäcū bisā ha: hḁ: nä hī-[2]

66 [2]ya jaśtä sḁśe u maista-ujai hamya ttī jsāṃ ttā ṣacū bisḁ̄ hi̥na tta tta haṃgāre

67 si ci burä kḁmäcū hauvausta hvaihu: ra i̇ṃde tta biśä jsanāṃ u ajsāṃ sūhä:—

68 cū bisai uha: khi̥ṇḍä tcirthūśī ñi̥ u kaṃthi jsāṃ ṣacū vāṣṭä spāśe u ha:—

69 hḁ: na ra jsāṃ va nä hame u khvai bādū̥na ttū herä bausta[2] u tta vā hvḁṇḍä śaṃdā

70 tta tta paśāṃdä cvaṃ hvaihu: ra biśä āṣṭaṃdāṃdä jsḁnä cu hvaihu: ra tta baiśä

71 hama hamya natca kīthāṣṭä naraṃda kīthi ra va ttaṃdī dūṃta i̇ṃdä ttyāṃ jsāṃ [5]kītha[5] vī[6] nä

72 khāysä u nä stūra ⌒ viña maṃ śā tvaḍa māśtä hamya u hirvī ra vā phara na

73 ra hīśtä si kīthi va khu ṣṭe cu biḍagā sahḁ̄nä ṣḁ pā haṃtsa hvaihu: ⟨rāṃ⟩ jsa hamye

74 cu vā bḁgarakä jsa haṃtsa hvḁṇḍä pahaiya tta vā hirvī nārä pūra na pḁṃmḁ-

75 stä yudḁ̄ bū̥nā vā āva ⌒ cu jsāṃ kḁmäcū bādū̥na tta vaña drai pacaḍa ṣṭāre

76 cū ttūḍīśa u ttūrkä bayarkāva u hättäbara [5]u i̇cä i̇ṃjūva[5] tta yīpākī̥nā ttahä: u beḍä-

[1] *ttāttāhä:?* [2-2] Del. [3] *ṅa* or *ja?*
[4] Blurred. [5-5] Subscript. [6] *ī* del.

77 darūkä ṇąsta ṣṭāre ci buri hvaihu: ra tta biśä karattahä:[1] ṇąsta u karattaha

78 cu dūṃva u cahä:spata u sūlya tta jsāṃ kītha khu tta viña drai pacaḍa biśä haṃ-

79 tsa ni samīṃde kąmäcū hā hervī haḍä ni ttraṃdä [2]hame[2] śālai āphāje u śālai jsāṃ va

80 khāysä niśtä ⌢ khu [2]ṣacū[2] kītha [3]khu[3] hịna biśä āva hamya u khu hauda haṣṭa haḍā pa-

81 rye hamya ttī hā mahe tcirthūśī vīrāṣṭä u bągarakä vīrāṣṭä tta tta salā paśāṃdūṃ

82 si cū rrispūra ṣṭāre tti āśịrya ṣṭāre ttyāṃ hirvī sąnä niśtä mahe paḍā paḍā śau

83 dva kąmäcū vāṣṭä hvąṇḍä paśāṃ u śirä dīrä hīya vā phara spāśäere u mahe

84 pā tsāṃ ⌢ mara vā pā ṣacū tta tta hvāṃdä si hirvī va gaṃjsa niśtä paśarä hvąṇḍä u miśta

85 hvę ni jsāve u ganamai āṣṭaṃdāṃdūṃ haysä ⌢ u ttī vā bągarakä attęmä uha: dūṃ

86 saṃgalakā va hvąṇḍä haṣṭe u gurṣṭai biśāṣṭä u tta tta vā hvę si khu āṃ viña kąmäcū

87 vāṣṭä hvąṇḍä paśarä aśte vīra āṃ jsāve cu uhū:ysä uha: ye cu rrvī parau yi-

88 nīya u pharāka rrvīya muṣḍą nāve ṣị muḍä cu pā ttattayä uha: ṣị pā muḍä ca-

89 raihä: uha: jsāṃ kąmyāṃ garvā kūśịṃdä ajsāṃ u aha:cī ṣą ṣṭāṃ ṣacū ci jsāṃ hą:nä

90 ṣị jsāṃ vilakä ṣte ttye hīvī viña parau hamidā kathi vīra ni jsāve vina ttikye cu ttā hvę

91 jsāve u paṃdāyai ttattara [3]ni[3] jsanīṃ[2]dä[2] khu ī kąmäcū kąmyāṃ nitca kītha bisāṃ hvaihu:—

92 rāṃ jsa haṃgūjīṃde tti kṣụna mūḍa hvaihu:ra ṣṭāre tti viña hamidā hīya nūvarä

93 byehīṃde nvaśtai ni paśīṃdä kūṣṭä burä bāḍä hīya naiṣkaica ni hamāve hervī saṃ

94 śe hvąṇḍye paṃda niśtä ⌢ uha: tta tta hvę si ya āśịrya pā ttūśā-dastā tsīṃdä paṃdaṃ

[1] *sta* or *tta*?   [2-2] Subscript.   [3-3] Del.

95 cī bāye khu hvaihu:ra ni hamāṃde [1]cīyạ bāye[1] ⁓ haṃtsa aśte jsa tsīṃdä vina ⟨tti⟩kye cvaṃ na-

96 tca kītha bisā hvaihu:ra u cimuḍa ni jsanīṃde ttīvaṃ biśä pasa-vālā padịmāre haṃdi-

97 raṃ va pacaḍä naiśtä ⁓ tti rruṃdä hīya pūra ṣṭāre tta tta śtāka ṣṭāre khu ciṃgvā hīsīṃdä khvaṃ

98 va vira śikä hamāte ā viśū̆ṃ ṣạ mārā-pyarāṃ bāḍä ṣṭe mara hvaihū:rāṃ cimuḍāṃ hīya

99 bīsa hamāṃde tvāka viṣū̆na nạma cī bīḍä ⁓ paṃda hīvī maṃ pacaḍä daṃ-mäsū ṣṭe ña-

100 śāṃ jsāṃ vā bīsāṃ hairthaṃ vī paṃda hamya hirvī ra vā hirä ni paṃmuḍä yuḍāṃdūṃ cu jsāṃ vā

101 dilakä dilakä būḍä hamye ṣạ jsāṃ biśä cimūḍvā u ṣacū dva padaṃjä bāstä tsve hirvīvāṃ

102 ri maṃ herä niśtä ⁓ khu viña tta pve kạmäcū bāḍä hamāte biśä hā haṃdara bāḍa-

103 dījsā nūvara uha:va u bīrūka ñīṃdä ttyāṃ biśä śikạñä jsāve khu jsāṃ paṃda prri-

104 hīśtä ⁓ cu maṃgāra hvạṇḍä cu pharāka rrvīya mụśdạ nāṃdä tta baiśä ja ⁓ ttī jsāṃ mista

105 nạma ṣṭe si hauda vā rraispūra āva u ciṃgvāṣṭä mista haḍa u kṣạ-sse kịna īrä

106 u ni ra maṃ bāyịmai hirä rrispūrāṃ aśtä u nä haḍāṃ ⁓ [1]viña ttā[1] rrvī vī dva jastụ- khvāṃ vā viña

107 ñe bvạme śau parau hīśtä si khu dilakä herä nä hamāve vina herä ṣị paṃdä na

108 nirve hame ā pạjsä maṃ anvaśtä hamye ⁓ . . rrva vī vara ttạ haṣḍi yạne ñaśa

109 . . rrvī vī vara ttạ haṣḍi yạne —— : rra —— hve sagai ——

110 . . rrvī vī vạrä tta [hạ] hạṣḍi yanāṃ ——

111 . . haudä rrispūra ⁓ mähe vā rrvīye dyạme pyatsa aúna nạradadū si gūttauṣạnä tsāṃ

[*Change of hand*]

112 . . parauvāṃ tta tta ye sä ṣacū va bvaiysạ na mūñarä khu ttā cạpastạkä dīśtä haṣḍi yūḍāṃ-

[1-1] Del.

113 dūṃ ‿ kạmäcụ va viña būrikyä na ra raysde ‿ mạ̄ñāṃ jsāṃ stūrä baiśä jạ cīvarā jsāṃ je

114 nạ̄ma ⟨na ra⟩ stūrāṃ va aśtä herä u [1]na[1] cīvarä vaska ‿ na jsāṃ pā ṣạikä caṃ jsạ kamäcu [2]ā[2] naradä

115 hamāṃ ‿ cu jsāṃ pā ttayạ-śāṃ hīyạ stụ̄rä yạ tta pạ̄ jạ ‿ nạ rä stūrāṃ va aśtä herä

116 u nä cīvarä ‿ na ra jsāṃ ma chīkä prramāṃ ỉdä stụ̄ra ū nạ ḍū pūhạ : yạ ‿ khu pā

117 śvahvā hīsāṃ pātcāṃ maṃ na ciṃgä rruṃdä vaskạ śkyesä u nạ pīḍạkä ‿ hvaḍa khaṣṭä vaskạ he-

118 rä ṣṭāṃ pā hīye jsạ̄ve ‿ khvāṃ vạ̄ läkä mvạiśdä haraysde ‿ viña būrä va kamäcu pharāka

119 hvaṇḍä mūḍạ hamyạ ‿ na jsāṃ va hạṣḍa ‿ khāysä khu vā ttī parau hīsīye si [2]tsūṃ hva me ṣi[2]

120 khu dāña ttrāmāñä hamāte ạysạ̄nā paskyāṣṭä nạ bāyāṃ

10

Ch. 00270

1 ttaikṣada baiysa khaiṇḍa hīya mạ̄rga ——

2 [*uncertain writing*]

3 [*uncertain writing*]

4 tcaurya sagrāvasau jsa cu aủvvī[3] jsa phara satta : ysathūā ysathūā hūḍai

5 vasva hauḍa pharaka baista jsā hā prraṇahauna ysatha ysatha u[1]vā[1]ra :

6 pūñau jsai jsāṃ sījāṃda : tta prraṇahauna raysga vī : hamye ttaya-śī

7 baista tcaina pa-ṣạu pīsai *kūra* [*different handwriting*] cu aủ pīrī ja satta abrraṣṭa naravauṇa kītha-

8 ṣṭa : aska jsa bāye vā[1]ra[1] yauda khve na jsāvai va harga : vāra vaska maista pai ttaya-śī

9 pauṇe-prrasa : cau aủ pūrau khenḍi kai hūṣẹ jsīye jsīna : bvaysa bāḍa sauhạ

10 jsa : [2]māhā[2] lya ye phara vīra gū ×[4] danya vīrai : mahāyau dā [2]bāya raṣṭa[2]

[1-1] Subscript. [2-2] Del. [3] *dvī?* [4] Not clear.

11 [ba][1]bāya raṣṭa dasa khaṇḍa aihạ : vīnīyā *kū*[2]ñāṃ[2]je darya ysamaśadai vī

12 cva aů hā gītta pada naravauṇa [2]kī[2]tha ṣṭa : thaiya ttīka javaittapūña bīśau

13 bvejsāṃ ha[×]pha : brrā naṣạgaista prrabaudavada : hạra hvaña tcaṣu : prruña-

14 dai pañai brrī ṣadū śakalaka : thaiya ttīka pūñadrajaya bīśau bvajsāṃ

15 -au -āṃ ×

II

Ch. 00271

1 saddhaṃ ka kā ki kī

2 II ṣị burä ciṃgạ̄na phara II khava

ttaura

3 pīrakhu gạnä śạtva [*Numbers*]

haysgye tcai gva

4 II pa

5 haysgye

6 II [*Numbers*]

7 II maka⟨la sa⟩lya cvātaji māśtä 20 4 mye haḍai ⌢

8 . . parau —— 20 5 mye haḍi

9 II [*Numbers*]

10 —— haṃgīñai thyai tvạnä-kāṃ

11 khace vara ⌢ cu ttūnā mārā-pyạra yạ ttä śaunau

12 g̅yastāṃ rruṃdāṃ phạrākä pārśạ̈ yuḍāṃdä ⌢ khu

13 vā pā thā huṣāvī pātcä mārā-pyạrạ̄na pve tsve

14 śau nauhä pārśạ̈ vīrä västātī ⌢ viñe biṃdä

15 mụśdạ̈ pasteṃ byaude ⌢ śāṃ-śū hīya vettā biṃdä

16 mụśdạ̈ pasteṃ byaude ⌢ khu parau pyạ ī haḍā āstaṃ-

17 na pyaṃtsāṣṭä śāṃ-śūī hīvī kīrä yina ×

18 ādarä ya khve maṃ yaṃdrrye ni hame ⌢ cu jsāṃ va

19 haṣḍi yuḍe si thyautta va mārā-pyạrāṃ ///

20 ca rai saṃ*ña* kạñä ttū va × ///

21 jsāṃ aů jsa hvaṃ *d*i ///

22 / . . / -īṃ × ///

[1] Blurred. [2-2] Subscript.

12

Ch. 00272[1]

01 [*Covered and illegible*]
1 hvāṃ pi̯naka gūle h⟨au⟩ śvaikale h⟨au⟩ s ///
2 hvāṃ pi̯naka *u* hau gūle hau śvaikale hau saigūra ca ma *ttyai*
3 hvāṃ pä̯naka hau gvāle hau śvaikale hau saigvāra
4 . . a̯vimāvyāṃ g̯yastāṃ beysāṃ jsi a̯yīkṣye̯ ⌢ śūrū bvāmayi
5 bāḍi vīri dāṣkira ⌢ girkhye dī mveśdi̯ bāḍi ārāki ⌢ ji-
6 nivi̯ vī brrūñadā śūri dirrvājsa ⌢ jastā ysūṣṭā
7 siddhami [*Alphabet. Numbers*]
12 hvāṃ pä̯naka hau [2]gū[2]le hau śvaikale hau saigūra ñaśa saigūra āśa
13 siddhami̯ [*Alphabet. Numbers*]
17 [*Numbers*] sāja vakṣāyā thyau khu daula
18 na byai [*inverted*] (*b*) mārīja māśtaiña salye
19 [*inverted*] (*a*) parau jsīna matcakai vara ñava aủ haṃ-
20 siddhami [*Alphabet*]
37 : amaye saigūra
38 parau [2]hā[2]
39 —— jsīna matcakai vara va[2]ña[2] aủ ha̯-
40 mārīja māśtai dasamyi haḍai bä̯ḍa hīyai bvaiya hīne
41 hä̯ṣṭa parīda haṣrrīyai khū aủ hīnai ha parīda āvai u va-
42 ra aủnaka aủ khyaiṣṭūä̯ hīna parī bä̯śtai khū parau pva cuai tta
43 tta ra tcasyau pe̯ṣkala vīra bīsā bä̯ja pä̯yā hīñāṃ i̵-
44 dai tta be̯śa magä̯rau nva pīḍau bīśa bä̯ya tta bura
45 gūra aủva bisā bä̯ja pāyā hīñāṃ haubarau-
46 ña ḍāṃ tcaisyau gvaina śa̯ina u̯ ḍāṃ ḍīkau ana-śa̯ina u ḍāṃ
47 kīma-ttuna dra[3] ḍāṃ ana-kvai u ḍāṃ gvai-tcai u ḍāṃ gvaina-hū:
48 u hvāṃ tcaisyau yūautta-paḍa hvāṃ pe̯naka u śvaiña kaga
49 hau gūle hau śvaikale u māva jsai pūrakai: u vai cū hau
50 segūra tta būra pāyā hīñāṃ prrahauna ra āśi̯ u
51 hauṣka̯ gūrai khacai u a̯ra[2]ñāṃ[2] pe̯naka u gūle tcīca u
52 bä̯rai khacai u veṃja haukāṃ hīyai pūra śvakale:

[1] School exercise? [2-2] Subscript.
[3] *dra* written for *u*.

53 u saga̮ḍā̮ysa u vaja hau: ā hai vīṣ̌a̮ra saga u
54 sa gūle: staḍaisa ⁀ u mākṣaidabhadrra u sūpīyāña
55 ālaṣkau jsa gūlīnai u ālaṣkau jsa gūle u sagīna
56 na āle pe̮naka u hīrā̮sa nva kaurargai u vaijalaka
57 u śaiga māṣṭai pe̮naka u pathaiya ra khara cū: u
58 gaysañāṃ ḍaivūā kharuṣa u ṣacū u paḍa tsā̮ u vaija-
59 laka u paḍa-tsā u sagai u gaudaka u vīśa̮isa u ā-
60 rañāṃ sagai u pe̮[1]na[1]ka khū khyaiṣṭuāṃ hīsau khū va śau nva pa
61 rau hīñai vā̮yai hamāvai be̮ra [2]yera[2] śarā̮na ẏauḍa ida
62 pajsa pajsa pamūha̮ja kabala parīda pajaiśtai ——
63 parau ttā̮ thyaina hīja[3] tcaulasamyi kṣauṇa pvaisa sa-
64 lya kaja māśtai haṣpa[4]be̮stamyi haḍai rāṣ̌a̮ pa-
65 staudū yūḍai [5]hau sa gu amaye hau[5]
66 [6]hau sa gū pūra ḍai[6] ——
67 [*Sanskrit*] [Supplement]
69 [*Alphabet*]
71 hau gūle hau śvaikale hvāṃ pe̮naka hau sagūra ā [2]khyai[2] garu [2]tta[2] ra pvaisa
72 [*Alphabet. Numbers*]
78 [*Alphabet*]
83 [*Sanskrit*]
91 amaye hau sigūra ca ma dye sale mūdi
92 : amaye hau saigūra ca ma dye saile mūdi ha va
93 ya sca śa *pi* ——
94 : a̮maye hau saigūra cu ma ṣacu ba̮ista pvaica hā stai
95 : a : amaye hau saigūra cu ma ṣacu baista pvaica
96 hvā pe̮naka hau gūle hau śvaikale hau saigūra
97 ya ttugarā-baira para yūva yū*tt*iṃ kava baira nauva pūlaka
98 nau stue [7]stui[7] jsīna ma tca kai vara va[2]ña[2] aủ haṃ ——
99 ll parau jsīna ma ca ——
100 hau gūle hau śva[2]ka[2]le hvā pe̮naka ——
101 hau parau ——
102 hvāṃ gūle hau śvaikale hvāṃ sai ra hvāṃ pe̮naka
103 parau jsīna ma tca kai vara ña aủ ha̮- ——
104 mārīja māśtai dasamyi haḍai bā̮ḍa hīyai bvaiva hīne

[1-1] Small *na*, added. [2-2] Subscript. [3] *ja* for *ṅa*. [4] *ṣpa* from *ṣpara*.
[5-5] Suprascript scrawl. [6-6] Scrawl. [7-7] Suprascript.

105 hāṣṭa parīda haṣrrīyai khū aủ hīnai ha parīda āvai u va-[1]
106 ra aủnaka aủ hvāṃ saile hvāṃ pe̯naka hvāṃ sagūra hau gūle
107 hau śvaikale jsī pa ya sti śa sti

13

Ch. 00327

1 /// /// ttu × ×
2 /// /// haḍai ve narāmāña ha
3 m ū **cīka** gūl**ai** va̯ vā dū**ṃ** saṃgalakā par**au** pastā⟨ṃda⟩ sa kūṣṭa būrai vā parau na hī-
4 sīye kṣīrāṣṭa na tsva hama × × ttā saṃgalakā gā̯śta jsaiṇa vīra haṣḍa yū̯ḍai u
5 hervī va̯ vā parau na ā sa khvaṃ tcerai cū jsā ṣacū tcairthūśī ṣṭe ṣa̯ jsāṃ tta tti hve sä mā̯ñau vā he-
6 rvī tvī ka̯ṇä parau na ā sa khve tcerai aśtu̯ āṃ ya cū āṃ hāysa na tsai i̇ṇāva̯ña kṣīra
7 ra jsāṃ ma**ṃ** hera śte ū ttūṅa-śīyā āstaṃ jsā ma pharāka haḍa ṣṭāre khvā āṃ va pve-
8 sīda sa aśtū ā yaṃda̯ ca ā hāysa na tsūva hervī vai ā̯na khvai sa ca ttū va̯ hā hū-
9 ña kā̯mīnai jsāṃ aủvā [2]bāja vī thasai[2] thi̯nä-śī hīsīye ṣi̯ jsāṃ āṃ vā sćāna saṃ bāvana bīḍa he̯-
10 rvī vā̯ āṃ hva̯ṇḍe hakhīśa̯ na bīysaṃjāre [2]ttaka vā pā satta rrvī parau nva tsvāṃda[2] khvāṃ haṃbusaṃ ṣṭāve khvā vā parau hīśta sattä
11 tta̯ tcerai i̇ [2]hī[2]ye śaṃde bidä śäna avāyse ā ttä[3] na mīrā ⌢ majarūṣa gauśta ttā pā jsaiṇa
11 *a* [*Interlinear*] khu āṃ rrvī vī bīsa tta āra i̇da hamadā vai āṃ hā kveśa hva̯ṇḍi darvāre ñaśā ≂ āṃ vā bīsāṃ kveśa̯ hī[2]rvī hva̯ṇḍa na paśīda[2]
12 vī aủrrāsa haṣḍa yūḍādū khvā masa dūkha ṣṭāve ——

[1] With *va* above. [2-2] Subscript. [3] *ä* over *ā*.

14

Ch. i. 0021 *a*, *a*

1 || aủrga ı̇ bąysų̄ñä rāṃdātāṣṭä
āra-verūcä āstaṃnä hamīḍä
2 ttye vīśęra hīye gūtęra | jsa uskhąsta[1]
rana vī ysą̄ya abhįṣeką dījsāką 1
vīysñä ysą̄ vīysñą hamye tathatą̄-vrrara
3 attūśīlma nąmī bąysų̄ñä sąrau
harbīśāṃ bąysāṃ hye aủmaunä mista
cu ra baudasątva būma-prrą̄ptą̄ hvāṣṭa 2
4 | arahadä ṣāvā cu ra khąṇḍaką-vaṣą̄ṇä
cū parīda mūdä dharma-garbha hasą̄yą
5 dharma-dhātä | hīya dyaudha hajsara gūstyeṃ
tathatą-prrarastą śamatha-prrara vasva 3
6 narvakalpa hajsara vī | brrāva sųrā
bą̄dacaitta hīyę vīvā jsa naradä ⌒
sāṃbhaudha-kąyū narmauṇä ūvārä
7 pajsa gę vīlra sąrvasątvāṃ keṇä
mvįśḍījä bveya paśīdä ṇęva raysęṃ
8 khu nä tsīda satva avāya bveysye bālḍi
tti hadę dā jsa ūvą̄ra grą vą̄śįdi
bąysau jsa vyą̄rya mara nāsīdä ysathä
9 sąmyakä-drręṣṭä | vasve ġūtterä rrvī
mahāsaṃma rrāṃdä hyę gųtįrä jsa narädą
vrrīśmä ḡyasta aṣ̄ų ⌒ cayaṃ rre ⌒
10 ṣvīdä | hūrrāka būmä dīvya ḡyaśca
hūṣauñą̄ka āysdirai ką̄kä hadiṃ
valākäteśvarä baudasatvą
11 ūlvārä gaustamä-deśa ranīje
jīnäve vī rrą̄ścä hamya āṣą
ttye gą̄sta raudä bhala-cakrravartta
12 rāja rājęśvara rre[2] śūkä śāhają darye jabvī vī ttye raudä pūrāṃ pūrāṃ
śūrä darą̄ jsa

[1] *sta* small inserted. [2] Blurred.

13 harbīśāṃ rrāṃdāṃ hye vamurākä rre rāysanāṃ hvāṣṭä bīśāṃ rāṃdāṃ
biṃdä maittrai hye narmauṇa[1] ssa ysatha pīcha-

14 ṣṭä ttye śakrra brrąhmau ttī nārāya mįhaiśvarä skaṃdha varūṇä nāvau
rre haṣṭä baudasatva haṣṭä parvālā

15 jīvą-sabhava rāja dīvya jaścä cu rä dīśą̄pāla ną̄gapāla tcauhaurä
śūkhuṇa śakhīmä yakṣa dīśamū-

16 ka pātca grahavadatta būjsaju sthą̄nāva cu ra jasta dīvye parvą̄lā nāva
rrą̄śtä heṣṭāṃda rauja-lakṣa-

17 ṇä bįśa cakrravarttä hīya rājāga sąmartha haude rä ranä grahtä
parṇą̄yakä āhaurrja hvāṃdä a-

18 yīkṣyaude rāści raudą̄nä naumä vīśą̄ra rraśą̄ pūrą̄ysa śrī vīśą̄ dharma
baudasattū rre carau mauña-

19 dä strīyastrīśvāṃ jastvāṃ śakrra jasta brrūñīye jastāṃ myą̄ñä ttū
mauñadä jabvīyāṃ rādau myāṃ parīvāysau-

20 da śe-tcūnä miḍāṃjä ttye vīśą darma baudasatvāṃ rāṃdä kṣuṇi ye
pūha cū hīṅa kamala aśi rä bāstį

21 salī haudama māścä khu hā panä nva aysmų̄ jastuñä kṣamä rrīna
āyīma vasve ciṃgvą̄ ysą̄ye ttye

22 ysarnai rrvī gūttairä pabhä udeśä haḍi pasta haṣṭä vāṣṭä ṣacū vāṣṭä
aspūra ssą pajsāsą śū-

23 ra bīja hvą̄ṣṭą̄nä pūrä hvāṣṭä bįśa hamagä ṣahaunīya caistą padajūḍi
pūrā bvaijsāda śū-

24 rä pūñūda ṣadu sthyę gūttarasta kamalāysa ttyāṃ hvāṣṭāṃ hye āvasta
vīre biśa bāḍä naṣą̄ṃdä yāṃ thye-śī

25 bīśāṃ bvejsā byą̄dä ⌢ bvą̄me jsa ysā u bvemi jsa hųṣą̄ ysājsa hvārä
hvą̄ñä vīcakṣa ėdrrāṃ jsa śūrä

26 bāḍāñvą̄ phara-dyi hų̄dahų̄nä pūñūṃdä sera hvūṃ-śī haḍāṃ krraḍīñä
śę ⌢ ną̄ma-tsvä śūra tsāṣṭä verśą̄ṃ-

27 dä haiga cā kama-śī bīśāṃ bvejsā hvą̄ṣṭä nva parau tsvāṃda tta haḍi
ṣacū vāṣṭä jasta kṣīra mau-

28 ñadū ṣacū kathä carau mą̄ñädä vasve ssa vahä ysīrä ā khu ranīja ttrekha
tcaṣva śęrkä ttu mauña-

29 dä brrūñä ṣį kṣīrä rāṃda jsa hatsa pārahā mįsta kūśala vaską pūñāṃ
ttye darye jabvī vī janavi

30 kṣasa vara ˙idä katha kṣairähaṣṭą̄ ysą̄re ttye darye jabvī vī janavāṃ
bāḍvą̄na ˙ida ėdrrāṃ

[1] *ṇa* written below *mau*.

31 jsa kūśala-vīrā ṣada śūra bumaya haurä biṃdä darąjsa khu māje ysarne bāḍi vīrä

32 bīje ṣį pā vañä ṣacū gūmättīrä ṣṭe śairka-ysara garbha bįysa baudasatva ṣkāṃje bīhī

33 burä dąṣka duṣịṣkāṃdä da śerkä dąṣkara jsa ṣkaudä dąṣkare jsa vadedä pharākau ṣada ysą-

34 vä aysmya thyą cū dyāṃdu biysāṃ hya dyąma brrūnä jai vąrä bhaśje āyąysa naṣąṃdä kī-

35 ḍiṣą bīya karma ttāṃ baiśa jä ttyāṃ haḍāṃ hada vyi jaḍi abąstä tta tta khu śala

36 /// /// -idä khu vara byąśde sahecä

14*a*

Ch. i. 0021*a*, *b*

1 || vi janivi vī āṃ haṣṭimye haḍai kąśarapä hīsīdä hīśanijį katha vī āṃ ądi kau-

2 kvāṃ[1] burä katha ṣṭąrai tcąre caigąnä drai haḍāṃjsye śadi bidi paḍąysa katha

3 śaraḍūgä[2] nąmä ttye jsi pajsa haḍāṃjsye śadi bidä tcīnä haura lakä nąmä ttye jsa dva ha-

4 ḍvāṃjsye śadi bidi łcahana garä nąmä vara vi nąha gara driya sakhąrma ṣṭąre

5 ttye jsa dri haḍāṃjsye śadä bidä katha yabhagau nąmä hauhä ttājä hīye ttājä

6 hīye kamala bidä vara aủna tcūrmye haḍai kakvāha rtcai nąma kītha ṣṭe dī-

7 na āṣaija ttāja śä mistä ttye biṃdä ttājä śą mịsta garä u vara ṣį katha varä

8 aủ tcūrmyai haḍai prrūśavā hīyai bāḍi biṃdä hīsīdä vara va ysarnīje ū-

9 ca hīyai kamala naraume vạra va paḍąysa katha ṣṭe syadį nąmä nąha garä

[1] Or *dvā* or *jvā*? [2] Possibly *jū* or even *dū* for *ḍū*?

10 sakhārma va drayi vara aù kṣa haḍāṃjsye śadi biṃdä katha ṣṭe baurbura naumä sī-
11 na nauma va mista ttāja ṣṭe vara hvaṇḍa byaḍāṃ biṃdi ttrą̄mīdi sakhārma va tcaura
12 hvą̄na ttāja aùva karą̄nä ttye jsa ravya pa nva ttāje mista katha gīḍagīttä
13 ną̄mä sagījä vara va sakhārma haṣṭä rrāṃdä hīye aùmä varä tcaurvā bā-
14 ḍvā ttye jsa ravye pa hīdva kṣīrāṣṭä padi ttye ysarnījį nva ttājä vara va ttāja raga biṃda
15 mista kṣīrä ṣṭe śīlathasa naumä vara ttye hvānä ttāje aùva karą̄nä ttāji hye ra-
16 ga bidä drą̄mä pātca hā byaḍä jsa ttrą̄mīdä sīḍathasä aùnä aùdi ttī-
17 ḍī bhurai haṣṭa haḍāṃjsya śadä ṣṭe ravye pa vāṣṭa ttye nva ttāje tharkye hamāre
18 banāve ttī tta devadārä vara va makala mūñīdä ttīḍī va magala-cakrra nau-
19 mä rre mūñe ṣą padą̄ysa kaśmīrāṣṭä hīdvāṃga katha ṣṭe gara biṃdä vare śau
20 ravye pa mahuvi ttāja [1]ra[1]ga biṃdi ttīḍī ą̄nä ravye pa vāṣṭä hīdva kṣīrāṣṭä
21 dva haḍāṃjsya śadį bidä baurīne mista gara ṣṭe sargūṇi ną̄mä
22 ttu śą̄ haḍā vi[1]he[1]ṣṭä hame ttye dī satharä padą̄ysa aù ṣṭe markaṭa-gra-
23 ma ną̄ma vara va karą̄na drai-sse ttye jsa ravye pa dva haḍājsye śadi biṃdä ą̄ ṣṭe va-
24 rṇa-valā ną̄mä ttye raṣṭä aù bahauysna ṣṭą̄re mistä pa-sse ttye jsa ravye pa dva haḍāṃ-
25 jsa śadi bidi mista ą̄ ṣṭe manattapaurṇa ną̄mä vara bihą̄ysa śą̄ mista pajsa ysą̄ra va ka-
26 pīlye ṣṭą̄⟨re⟩ ttye jsa ravya pa drrai haḍājsya śadi bidi kṣīrä ṣṭe nalapaṭana naumä mista vara va bi-
27 hą̄ysa ṣṭe śą̄ haḍāṃjsye śadį bidi kapīlya va pajsa ysą̄rä ṣą bihą̄ysa vīysāje
28 hīye raga biṃdä sakhą̄rma va drrayi sagījä gavāṃ jsa ttye raṣṭä vīysāṃje kaśmīrą̄ṣṭa
29 ną̄va-vadāṃ padä adįṣṭädä kṣīrāṣṭä śą̄ haḍāṃjsvi vara katha adeṣṭä ttye adiṣṭānä kathe drayi

[1-1] Subscript.

30 śā̯mi̯ vīttasa nā̯mä ñā̯ hye ṣṭā̯re vara vi mistä nā̯vi bi̯sta ysā̯re ñūhūṃjsadä bīsā̯ vi jsā

31 śā̯ma katha hya vīysāṃja ṣṭe ṣa̯ katha śau haḍāṃj*s*a habistana va dirye kaśmīrä mista au̇va ṣṭā̯

32 re kṣaṣṭa ysāre ṣa̯ śau āṃ drai-sse ysā̯ karā̯nāṃ u śau karāṃ drai-sse kṣaṣṭyāṃ bīsā jsa va-

33 ra va mista damarāśā̯sta sakhā̯rma ṣṭā̯re pa-sse sagījā gavā jsa ñāttara sakhā̯rma

34 ahakhīysa rre va abi̯manyagauptä nā̯mä hasti pharāka hīna bāyā̯ve tcaurä

35 hīna ssa byūra ssa byūrä āysīrāṃjä biśä ——

15

Ch. 1. 0021*b*[1]

a[2] 43 di̯śanä cvai cā kīmä-śanä hīye aysmū jsa padaidai ūspā̯-
ra dāśā || || thyena tcūnä sūhye bāḍi̯ pūhye kṣuā̯ṇä pasa sälya ttaujji̯rä mā-

44 śtä hā̯dūsa̯mye haḍai nadā̯va kūṣḍvī ā̯nä dā rāysa̯nāṃdi baudhasa̯ttu vīśa̯ śūrä cai-

45 ga rāṃdānä rrādi hīye bveysyẹ ḡyastuñe ūvārye dra-vargye jsīña prrī ūdaśauya̯[2]

46 cā kīma-śanä hīye gauttra̯ aysmū jsa̯ ėdrai jsa śu̯ste u padaidai u pīḍai || ||

16

Ch. ii 001

a 1 | × pa ×× -i ni ya si kṣuṃdā̯sta ma majṣyä ysādä ⌢ u ḍekuṃ vā haṣḍi tta tta yu

2 /// × vīra hū mistye jaśta rrīña ṣi̯ būjsaṃja hastara ṣṭi āmūnā jsīna u

3 /// pastāṃdū si kṣūṃdausta ra āṃ vā ni ysye i̇nīdä ttī hā āśa̯irkyä kiṇä pyatsä ha-

[1] Religious text. [2] *au* for *ai*.

4 **ṣḍi** /// buḍāṃdū si khu ttakyi kṣuṃdausta ṣṭāre ni āvāysye hamāre
anvaśtä ṣe ttī vā

5 **āṣ̄irka** vā parya hauḍe cu ikṣuṃdā ṣṭe ~ si khu ma anvaśtä nä hame ~
u tta

6 × kiṃṇä jsāṃ vā phara tta tta ī̇ḍi si khu va ṣą̄ka śtāka ya ya ttī vā cigau

7 pakį jsa parau hīsīya ā vā hā sahą̈ : hvainä jsā vīrą̄ṣṭä u ārūku vī-

8 rāṣṭä salā jsa parau hąmīya ~ parauvāṃ hau ni niśāve ~ [1]u ttī hā ñaśa[1]

9 bīsa [1]panūḍai yaudä tsvāṃdū -ai *rā* ysi ttāṃ[1] *du* u tta tta vā paste
si pa × ///

10 -i -e -ā ×× ///

*b*1 /// /// × maysḍy × ///

2 ×××××[2] ye jsa kīthą̄ṣṭä ttraṃdadu ~ u khu pakuṣḍi āvadū [3]pyatsa
tsvāṃ[3]⟨dū⟩ u nva

3 rrvī parau hā biśä parau pastāṃdū [3]u ttugavāṃ jsi jsā tvai haṃgvāṃdu
~ bvestā bārāṃ āṃ pā[3] u cu ma pā ḍikau va u rrįspurä va u

4 śįna[4] va hva hva ñāṃ tcāṃ va u ttugavā va u ttūttūvā va tsanä-śīyāṃ

4*a* [*interlinear*] cīkä kaṃga ṣṭa tvai ñī

5 **ḍ**ikuṃ hā : sīnä ye ttū hā bīśä nva parauvāṃ u nva ėyāṃ paphvādū

6 /// hādimye haḍai pyatsä tsvāṃduṃ u ysinauśtä kiṇä hā parau
pastāṃdūṃ u pha-

7 **ra** -ā tta tta ī̇ḍä si [5]mahe ttā janave vīrāṣṭä haṣḍi vā nä hajsādāṃdu si
būjsaji[5] [1]bījeṣąma u pharāṃ ttā ī̇nāṃ u ttī hā svanaka[1]

8 **ñaś**ä bīsä kvāṃ pa lyehsakä u maśänä pau*ka* u rca paḍä tsā pācä
śą̄m u yinā
pyatsä tsvāṃ

9 /// tta tta parauta ciṃgāṃ hvanāṃ cvāṃ maśū cāṣṭä ya tti hā hā
pyatsä buḍāṃdū

10 /// -*ā* phara tta tta ī̇ḍe si mahe ma bijeṣāṃ u pharāṃ ttā ī̇nāṃ ~ u ttī
hagra-

11 /// dä u haṃgrįma vā salā ttūkä thīyāṃdä si ṣą̄ka ma āstaṃ satsārä

12 jsāvi u ttikyāṃ paṃjyāṃ ha u ṭya jsāṃ ma ttikye jsa hastara niśtä ~
u viña ttā

13 kä ttā bāḍä vī [1]haḍa hīsīdä[1] ḍikuṃ hīvī aủrrāsä haṣḍi hīstä u

14 ñaśāṃ bīsāṃ hīvī ~ [1]paskyā[1] vā × khvāṃ vā rraysgä vī haḍāṃ hī-

15 ya muṣ́dą harraysde khu kī svąña [6]-ū × pa[6] ṣṭi khu ttā paskyāṣṭä ttā-

[1-1] Del. [2] Bases of akṣaras. [3-3] Subscript.
[4] Akṣara above *śi*? [5-5] Subscript and del. [6-6] Broken.

16 ṣṭä gęsā hamāṃ u mūñajä māśta ttā . . -ä ājīmāṃ u khv*āṃ*
17 **ttā** paskyāṣṭä ttye krraśīsä hīya u ri*tsuya*rūṣä hīya u bvą̄mi
18 dārrjī hīya kvą̄ṃ pįnakä hīya u maṃdūysāṃ saṃgai hīya mųśdį
19 harraysde u maha mūṭtä hīya × khvāṃ jsāṃ vā pā katha jsa ysę-
20 rrī ysą̄ ñaśau drāṃ śirka parau hīśtä [1]. ×[1] āṃ vā tta tta yįnā ḍikuṃ
21 mahe pā rrvīye bīsa ṣṭāṃ u h*erv*ī /// /// × /// ·
22 nä harraysde -ṃ × ttī jsāṃ × /// ///

17

Ch. XLVI 0012*c*

3*a* 1 paysānāma kṣamī vajrracchaidakyi prrajñā-pārą̄me nva carya tsūma ttāra tçaca hīsą̄-
2 ma dharmamūkha mūkha niṣkalyāme hīya padaja ‖ cu prrajñāttīrṇa āśįrī mi-
3 styau jāyaryau gaṃbhīra jāryau gaṃbhīra jāyaka brraṣṭa ⁓ humädāṃ kītha ysāyī hāvä bujse
b 1 vīra anihvarrda biśä ysirrnai bąysą̄na bąysūśtä kṣąmä ṣį mī tvaḍa bistä salī garrvā mūṃde
2 vara ą̄na śūjye nva dva mārgaupadeśā parṣę parrīyasta cu biśe caigą̄nye jana-
3 ve vīra kalyą̄ṇamittra ya ⁓ hīya biśą̄yūṃ jsa tvā gaṃbhīra jāyaka pacaḍana ka ba

18

Ch. CVI 001

a 1 ‖ makala salya cvāvaja māśtä bistämye haḍai ṣą khalavī cu ratana-varaikṣä āśį u
2 prrakaittu būrä ṣacu vāṣṭä bauḍä va herä nauda ⁓ [2]gaḍā hvasta[2] thauracaihä bera śā
3 u śaca prraiysge bira śā u kabalīja baysgyi hvāhyä ką̄madä śe u hūḍaigä
4 ysīḍai attaravāysä śau u hūḍaiga ysīḍai lahäpī śau u ką̄ra kagä khau-
5 ṣa thą̄racaihä pabanā śa u khaucīja khauśka śā u įjīnai hī-
6 rāsä hvattarakīnai ūra-bada śau u gaḍā hvastä śīyi haysänā
7 līkä thauracaihä dva u mījī jūna baysgyi kabala dvī u haija mai-

[1-1] Broken. [2-2] Subscript.

8 stä kabala u pe u śīyi maistä kabala śā u aysūra-gūna da-
9 jūna baimya kamaiśkä śā u nämāya śau baraka u[1] hainai gaḍā hvastä
10 baysgi thauracaihä śau u haysnā līka gaḍā hvastä thauracaihä
11 dva u paha drau vī haysnā līkä śacī śau u haija baysgyi kabala
12 dvī u hainai thauna śacī u haysnā līkä thauna śaca dräya u śīya
13 baysgyi kabala tcaure u paima vīstā kabalīnai draijsai śau u gahai śau u
14 ×[2] [3]ė[3]ysnạ śā [3]maista[3] u dairśvā khaucvā drauhye bitcä dairsa u tcaurrvā starrvā ñū-
15 ṣṭye līka u śau barä khaucä pajsāsä sera u paima vīstāva thauna śacä ha-
16 darā śa u gaḍā hvastä thauracaihä jsa dā-gū baysgye paima jsa bira śā
17 u kagīja ṣkaumaka vīlaka śā hatca ttrraba jsa u dạrmīnai ṣkạma dale śau u
18 habastā gahā śa: gahai va maistä śau u valaka gahai śau u hatca hasạña jsa
19 aiysna śā u nauṣṭara śau u kabalījä bịrga kagyä karastä śe u kabalī-
20 nai rūśkagä thūḍa-pa śau u kaimeja ysīḍā-mejanya kamaiśka śā u hai-
21 ja baysgyä kabala pajse u hainā thauna: nāṃ u ysīra gū śacī śau u pai-
22 mīnā thauna tcaura u phrramaina kabala śā u kạra kagä khauṣa śa hatca
23 āvasakāṃ jsa u mījī jūna śadā kaimejä ṫśīma śa u [4]ysīcä spī-
24 yi drai gūna[5] kamaiśka śā[4] u painajä śī nama śau u thauna śacī nūvarä -e[2]
25 parekṣi śau u chava nū kāṃhä parakṣa śau u hainā śadā damarāśịnai [3]maista[3] kai-
26 mejä śau u śẹ āṣana śadā damarāśịnai maistä kaimejä śau u dai-
27 dä āṣana śadā śagīnai maistä kaimejä śau u paha drau vī sya-
28 dai hvaradai thauracaihä śau u haysnā līka hūḍaigä śau baysgi u hadā
29 naṣkūmāya namavīña thavalakañä khauca haudūsä sera pyaṣṭa līka
30 u hūḍaiga yạma-bakä śau u thauracaihä śūkyainä dva u hụnaugyä
31 jsaiṇyāṃ hīrāṃ jsa habaḍa pyaṣṭa līkya khadīrakya śe u pūstyạna tcairma

b 1 thavalaka śā u mījī junä thauracaihä birä śā u maistä pū-
2 stye śau u ėjsīnai vasīyikä śau u nūvarä barä u vatsāvīśị-
3 nai hamauka śau pajūka śau u būśaunāṃ barakä śau habaḍa u ūla ka-

[1] Subscript Tibetan *ya.ma.* [2] Blurred akṣara. [3-3] Subscript.
[4-4] Del. [5] Subscript Tibetan mnan *pa.*

4 gä baraka śau u nvadāvaunä aủramūṣa pajsa u g̱ahā śa maistä gahai
5 śau u valakä śau u thūra-ma śau u pūstyā̱nä : namavīja thavalakä śā
6 pūstyāṃ jsa habaḍa u badana dräya u ṣkā̱mye herä nāsākä ranavarai-
7 kṣä āśī̱ akṣärä □[1] u prrakai aḵṣärä □[1] byaunä kvāṃ ṣī-
8 thau āśī̱ akṣärä □[1] byauna būyunä śau-śū śvauñakä akṣärä □[1]

19

Envelope 417. 257

a1 /// miṣḍāṃ g̱yastä vara tta haṣḍi *y* ///
2 /// brātara̱ pramukhä āśi̱rī ra —— ///
3 /// paśāme *v v* g̱yasta —— ///
4 /// ttūdai viña̱ pūha sal ///
5 /// pūri ṣi̱ śiri saśi ginī ///
6 /// aủdi viñi burä mahā ///
7 /// vīni ā u ḍi-yeṃ ṣi̱ ///
8 /// pahai u jvī yi vā *s* ///
9 /// gi biysīye u *m* ///
10 /// muśdi[2] parī byaudä pa -ī ///

b1 / // merä u brātarä prra**muhä** ///
2 *ā*ṣmaṃttä bhadraśikṣä × ///
3 a maṃ pajsaṃ tterä vī pacūīmä ///
4 ya haṣḍa̱ yaḍi nai āṃ *be* ///
5 nai ttā dāśai yaṃ nva vī × ///
6 g̱amä vaska haṃda hālai thau ///
7 tceṃ mya ra̱ vā ttī ya̱ va jsāṃ × ///
8 tsve pa̱jsū̱me anvaśti ṣṭi ⌢ ci ///
9 tti cu bura̱ āṃ maṃ rrījāmi ā × ///
10 ysa buḍi ci maṃ hā kavī ///
11 na ra haṣṭi yīdä śiri × ///
12 māśtä 11 mye haḍai ttā ///
13 merä āṃ tta̱ u pramuih*ä* ///
14 nä ttunai rrvī tta śirkä × ///

[1] Marks.

[2] Read *śḍi*.

20

Achma

1 || hiyaudä ā̮mācä ṣṣau viṣṇadattä vara tta haṣḍi yane —— *aysä*

2 kṣā̮ aúvā bisai ysevidṭä hīye maṃ vā aḍāsvā̮na rrvīya thauna pastāṃdä

3 35 mye kṣuṇi skarihveri māśti haudamye haḍai ṣi̮ pīḍaki ttye pracaina cu ā phaṃnāji sinili

4 u birgaṃdaraji ṣanīraki pe̮mīnāṃ thauna nāṃdä u kāṃha thaunaka u ysārī haṃbā mūri makali thau

5 u yseviḍttä ——

6 tcahaurabisti chā spāta vidyadatti hīvī tca̮ha̮usi chā svarrjāṃ thau 23 chā puñaśālyā 20 chā -i -i

7 kāṃhi thaunaki [1]haṃtsa ysārī haṃbāna[1] ⌢ āskūryāna kāṃha thaunaka 20 u 2 [1]*ma*[1] nva mūrā sarkāṃ pe̮mīnai thau nausi chā bida śau thau-

8 naki || suhena pemīnai thau 20 chā u bida śau thaunaki haṃtsa mūryau jsa ysārī haṃbā u kāṃha thaunaka

21

Domoko A4

1 || spāta sudārrjāṃ tta parī —— salya-bāyai pharṣa sāṃda-

2 ri vara vaña mūra haṃgāṃ vara vaña ma haṃ[1]bā[1]ji mū̮ri pajistāṃdi bistä ysā̮

3 u cu ṣi tta va vāri ṣṭāri u cu ma̮śū̮ṃ draya hvaṃḍi vistāṃdi tti mū̮ri ysaṃ-

4 thaḍi pastādi śa jiśti haṣṭi mū̮ri sa khu tta parau hīśtä ttū̮ vā hiri thyau haṃ × ///

5 jari u ma ṣai vā hajse̮myari khu ttiña māśta paphve himi khu aḍa *-ā* ///

6 śta ysaṃthi ttä drā̮mi ttī jsāṃ vā kṣauva hajse̮myari thyau ttye hvaṃḍye dīśta cu va

[1-1] Subscript.

7 haṃbā buḍi paḍāṃda ttā parau hauḍeṃ kṣauvā kiṇa u nạ vā hauḍāṃda khu ×

8 hīsīdi makali vā hajsẹmyari lyibạ ạ̄ma pajīdä pa[*spu*]rsaṃdai ha-

9 jsẹmyarī vā aśau gänạ̄ña himi khu vā kṣauva u tti mūri paiya nä hīsī

10 □[1]

22

Domoko C[2]

1 kṣvā aủvā namaubudi thau hauḍä 36 chā kṣä tsuna nva thaunakāṃ spāta śẹṃma-

2 kä nātä u hū phạnä hvanä ——

23

Domoko D

1 kṣā aủvā budarma thau hauḍa drrarabista chā suradata th⟨au⟩ hau-

2 ḍa pajsa chā ——

24

Domoko F

1 /// cu 36 mye kṣuṇi ttāṃjiri 22 mye haḍai ėrma tsūkāṃ va hirä pajistādi

2 /// śāna śe hvaṃḍe haṃbā himye paṃ-se mūri mūra-haurā hvaṃḍi himya 46 mūri

3 /// ta × ri hvaṃḍi cu mūri haurīdi āskuvīra makali ⌢ pụysdaki ⌢ śị̄laṃ ⌢ svarrjāṃ ⌢

4 /// ysāḍadatti ⌢ saṃgūlai ⌢ suhadāysi ⌢ puñade ⌢ vasa-

5 **de** /// × × ǁ si vidyadatti ǁ kucalai ⌢ sarkāṃ ǁ pạ sudatti ⌢ sude ×

[1] Broken Chinese 副.

[2] Written between Chinese lines: Khotanese-Chinese bilingual.

6 /// birgaṃdara mādāśi ⁀ maṃgali ⁀ mulaki ⁀ sudatti ⁀ sirphūki ⁀ namaubu-

7 di /// **haryāsaki** ⁀ naṃdaki ⁀ ṣanīraki ⁀ vidyadatti ⁀ hunaki ⁀ budadatti ——

8 /// × ta ——

9 /// ka ⁀ īrvadatti[1] ⁀ nahvạni ⁀ visarrjāṃ ⁀ hvīviṭi śau ⁀ brạna ⁀ budesa

10 /// -ā tta parī —— pharṣa sāṃdari vara u darauki yseviṭi

11 /// -au tti nva samaucā hiri pajitta u pāra-vaysdānī hauḍa thyau ttāṃjiri

12 /// tsve 副

25

Hoernle 1

1 ‖ salī 17 māśtä skarhvārä haḍā 5 hvaṃnä rruṃdä viśạ vāhaṃ ttāña beḍa ṣị pīḍakä

2 ttye pracaina cū ā sīḍakä naḍau nāsti kṣīrū kīrä vī haṃtsa ūci śaṃdye jsa ci burä nvā sa-

3 lī pyaṃtsāṣṭa kṣīrū hirä pajīde sīḍakī heḍā pharākä bakä caṃdä pajīde u ci va vā-

4 ra maṃgāra ṣaṃga īde ttyāṃ brīyāsi u budarśạṃ chīyā yanīdä sīḍakä va gvārä näśtä

5 u vaña brīyāsi ceṃgāṃ jsārä hamayä hauḍä khu vā nauha salye bisai jsārä ttū sīḍakä he-

6 ḍä u brīyāsi bīḍä hamayädä u cvai vaḍāṣṭa pamūhi tsī ttūtī sīḍakä yīdä u bi-

7 salū nä naradä himi 30 haḍā vī narạmi ci vā trraṃdä ttī ra ṣị pīḍakä prạmāṃ hi-

8 /// × hä brīyāsi u budarśạṃ haṃguṣṭi viśtārä brīyāsi | haṃ | gu | ṣṭä

9 ttä burä vara byạna ya —— budarśạṃ | haṃ | gu | ṣṭä

10 puñargaṃ ‖ ci vaña ustaṃ brīyāsi jaṃpha himāde budarśạmnī hā chīyā yīdä sī

11 khau śyaṃ ‖ *tvaḍä* va gvārä näśtä —— puñargaṃ | haṃ | gu | ṣṭä

12 hatkaṃ ——

[1] ī, top lost.

26

Hoernle 2

1 || ṣṣau phvai hvuhi tta parī —— gayseta spāta sīḍakä vara u ttyāṃ hvaṃ-
2 ḍāṃ vara cu pe̤mīnā[1] thauna puḍaṃda u thauna ni hauḍāṃda vañau va mara hārū sā̤made u
3 harttākaṃ mūri jistādä dasau ysārya drai-se ttyāṃ mūryau jsa kāṃha thaunaka gvaṣcāṃdä
4 drai-se paṃsaya pe̤mīnaiyūṃ jsa thau gvaṣceṃ dirsä chā khu parau pvīrau tti mū-
5 ri haḍā ḥaṃgi puṣa hauḍa haṃtsa ysaṃthina khu śau dva na ni dāśīdä hime
6 ttāṃjerä 10 mye haḍai tta parau tsve □[2]

27

Hoernle 3

1 || 17 mye kṣāṇä ṣau ṣacū salya rrāha māśtä 17 mye haḍai gaysāta-
2 ja jsä ya cvātajä māśtū thaṃgä samauttāṃdä haurāka hvaṃḍä hä-
3 mya 55 thaṃgä 10 paṃ-ysärä paṃ-se mūrä [3]-e × -y ×× *pā* -e[3]
4 satāña haṃkhīṣa̤ ysāḍa hvaṃḍä 8 mara mūñaṃj*ä* māśta pa̤jsa
5 hauparadärsäna dasau hvaṃḍä dasau haṃba̤ [3]×××[3] hämya
6 55 □[2]

28

Hoernle 4[4]

1 /// bistamye salye kaji māśtä dasamye haḍai ṣi̤ pāra va
2 /// pracaina cu āna hvā cai-sai ttä mūri hāyi tti buru

[1] With *e* over *ī*. [2] Mark. [3-3] Broken.
[4] With 10 other unpublished lines, see J. A. S. Bengal, 1901, p. 40.

29

Hoernle 6

*a*1 || hiyaudi ā̮māci ṣṣau ///
2 ji mūra haṃgä puṣa *nva hau* × ///
3 hvarrnakä × × jsyāñā × ///
4 *r*āṃ *k*×ī pā *śi* ñ ///

*b*1 × nva × ///
2 *u* 20 hvaṃḍāṃ ///
3 mūrä ttā × ///
4 42 *tti* × ///

30

Hoernle 7

1 || salī 20 māśtä cvātaja haḍā 13 ttye hvaṃnä rrāṃdä väśa̮ vāhaṃ dädye ṣṣau vädya-
2 dattä gärya-vāḍä pīḍakä ttye pracaina cä bugura maṃdūsäna śaṃdā gärye avīmya
3 gaṃtsa kūḍai vīra drai kūśeṃ tcūrä-vāśa̮ra pīha ve murä ysārä ttä burä ttye śaṃdye hajsā-
4 ra̮ñä u cä jsai puñavärśä hīya -ṃ × ñūvä jsa sanekulä hīvī naḍa *kärä*ña
5 *sagaṃ* × khuī bugura tä kīra ka̮stä ídä khuai ttī maṃdūsä tcūrä-vāśa̮ra burä
6 iysgināte iysgede maṃgāḍara nä iysgärya hämä ttī ra ṣä pī**ḍakä** pra̮-
7 māṃ khu hā maṃdūsä haṃguṣṭä väśtä ttä burä vara bya̮na ya bye arsalaṃ bye /// **pa**-
8 rramai butta̮nakä bye *bau*ḍä □[1] —— maṃdū | sä | haṃ | **gu** | **ṣṭä** |

[1] Mark.

31

Hoernle 8

1 /// vā ///
2 /// nāte ——
3 /// × hvaḍī 10 × ///
4 /// ××× 50 hvaṃḍī 10 ///
5 /// 13 thauna hauḍä 13 vañi ///
6 /// **th**auna ḯdi 18 vañi *r* ///
7 /// × thauna ḯdi 11 ***vañi*** ///
8 /// × 4 u 2 chā 3 tsuna ///
9 /// × kä 3750 —— ///

32

Hoernle 9

1 /// × śa lā u phedūk⟨ä⟩ ///
2 /// **mā**śtä 13 mye haḍai ṣị pīḍaki ttye prracaina cu rruha
3 **datä** /// ḍi ye śau u nai hauḍi yūḍi vañai
4 /// daso chāya tī ri pr̥amāṃ hämi
5 /// **haṃgu**ṣṭi viśtä rruhada | tä | haṃ | guṣṭi
6 /// × puḍi ye śau u nai hauḍi yuḍi vaña
7 /// × ki thaunaka heḍi dva daso chāya
8 /// × hā r̥amaki haṃguṣṭi viśtä | | |
r̥amaki haṃguṣṭi

33

Hoernle 10

*a*1 /// × va -ū × ///
2 /// thauna haḍa 8 ///
3 /// × 9 —— ///

b 1 vā cā *u* ///
2 pharṣa puña ///
c 1 /// ××× ///
2 /// rrūśa̱ kaṃ ×× ///
d 1 /// /// u ///

[*Space*]

2 /// × ttä nva hvaṃḍāṃ mūrä himārä 62
3 /// la sa paṃjsāsī chātī ///
4 /// -ā × ——
5 /// -eṃ himārä -ooo 800 —— ///

34

Hoernle 143*a*

1 /// **spāta** rastaṃ -ā /// **haṣḍä** yani ⌢ ——
2 —— || āśi̱rī sureṃdra kṣī'a —— hvāṣṭyau pūri pā-
3 ḍai velakä a̱na aúdä ṣi̱ buri uvaysaṃbatī jsāṃ ṣṣāmañä gīstai u pa̱jsū avāysai himye dva drai jū̱na manu hastä *hve*
4 yiḍi drāma drāma̱ ahaṃbusa̱na salā hve cu pūrä na nä haṃbusīdä se ė̇ṣṭyai si kṣīra vaśū̱ bāḍä ṣṭi hvāṣṭāṃ
5 ttāṃ gvava̱na ni vistātai vaña ttā misali birgaṃdara tsvai si kīrä va yanīṃ khu pyaṃtsāṣṭa tsve himi cu va jsārä byaud*ai*
6 i̇me tvī tvītī vāṣṭa hajsaudai u ṣa̱ pūrä mara kṣīka̱najä su[1]**reṃdrä ā̱**[1] śi̱rī hīya mijṣe hīyausti khu vā birgaṃdara a̱-
7 na ātū vara biśa a̱nai byaudai cvaṃ pā hvaḍāṃda starrä niśāñä ye i̇ pā*tc*ī niśātai ttye mijṣe va vā ttāguttyau jsa
8 jaṃpha pravā panata u paṃtsai bista-serya thauna pajistādä u *prabhe* āśi̱rīyī vinīyabhavä gvārä nāte pīḍakä
9 padeṃdä si cu vā pracā panamāṃde aysī hā gvaścī i̇mi ra vā ttaṃdī drai kūsa ganaṃ hauryarä u drai kūsa mau u thau
10 bistä chā u ṣi̱ ni hā āśi̱rī vinīyabhatä ttāguttāṃ hirä *jsā* hauḍä u ṣa̱ pūrä sudana āśirī pūräna khara girye
11 śatcau baysga thauna ttāgutai drai thauna hatcastāṃdä vaña hā ṣa̱ pūrä vinau mau kṣaṣṭa cyaṃ mau hauḍä stūrä jsārä kṣi kūsa
12 [*tops of akṣaras*]

[1-1] Broken out.

35

F II 1. 006

1 tya pharṣavata vaṃña muho jsa amanā ma yanā aysä ra ttū sa-
2 lāvä paḍā mara kīntha bäśa anattī hvemä ttī miḍānä hvemä ttū bä-
3 sa miḍe maṃ nä hūḍe ttäna cu tu pyūṣṭämä se ttū bäsa rräspūrä kheysarä haṃ-
4 jsa̱rä haurä **vaṃ**ña ttā puñadāysä buḍe u miḍānāna ra ttä pāḍa bu-
5 / . / **ro** / . / × / . / hā karya sahyä cu vara hva̱ndä u stūra kuṃ nä hā puñadāysä pa-
6 / . . . . . / **pha**rṣavata ra hama pīre vā muh*au* vara pāḍa haure u cu ra *ma* ///
7 / . . . . / vā ha × mata hvāña pä ///

36

F II i. 1

a1 ‖ tta tta buri *bākare rrāva̱* . . . *cä*paśūrei ⌢ |
2 —— | budạkä | ⌢ kumaśūrei ⌢ ‖
3 | jsarsalä ⌢ | lāśūrei ⌢ ‖ bryaśnarä ⌢ |

b1 budäka ⌢ | *kuma*śūrei ⌢
2 ṣ*k*aṇḍäcä ⌢ | *k*uṣṭä ⌢
3 *buda*śudä ⌢ | mukaukä ⌢

37

Kha. 0013c, 10

a1 /// × 7 th**au**naka × × ///
2 /// śau paṃjilīnai nalaki | śau × ///
3 /// pīḍa hamauka tcahaura × ///
4 /// × hāna śau hīśaṃnai pharhyau ///
5 /// -irsa ⌢ khauca dirsa sai**ra** ///

38

Kha. 0013d, 1

1 || gulä ṣvīdina jñ̮ñ̮ñä ≈ grrā̮mä khāṣ̮ñ̮ñä bīysma prrahāje ///
2 naladä bhāga˙4 || kuṣṭi bhāga 4 || ——

39

Kha. 0013d, 2

a1 ganaṃ kha 6 viśa̮kāṃtta pīha hauḍā hamā ///
2 ganaṃ kūsi 2 haṃdara prū buḍāṃ āśi̮rya rrāhajä ///
3 gausi byaudä kūsa 12 ——

40

Kha. 1. 111

1 [*bases of akṣaras*]
2 /// g ×× khu hā akṣara ni
3 /// u akṣarä bhakṣa[1] spāta haryāsakä akṣarä
4 /// **aśi̮rī** suvikrāṃtta ja -ä akṣara ——

41

Kha. 1. 117, 1

a1 dra [*bases of akṣaras*]
2 draṃmaiyūṃ bäysī ///
3 sau kūsa āśi̮r ///
4 viṣṇeṃdrabhadrä ///
5 yāvi || ganaṃ drai ///
6 paṣetaka 25 ///
7 × ñeṃdrāna ///

[1] Vertical.

42

Mazar Tagh a. 1, 0033

1 ‖ spāta īramañi ⌢ neri śaṃdā haṃbajsai hų̄ñūṃ ⌢ īrasaṃgi āstaṃna ttā ṣīka pųsūṃ u jsijsīya u
2 vilāyi āstaṃna vitkä mistä na busvāra mąma śirkä ṣṭe drų̄nai khu nai khu tta umą̄nī śirkä
3 ṣṭą̄te drų̄nai a maṃ pajsa pachīśę bareṃja vaska tta ādari yanīrau khu tta jsārāṃ bāḍna ūtca
4 hauḍi yaṃda u mastą̄ñä kāṣṭi yaṃda pasāṃ āstaṃna stūra kąitta khvaṃ tta na panāśari ci tta
5 aśnesalą̄ña pąsīña drą̄ma ṣṭāri yāṃ kuṃ y- hauryari khu na hvą̄re vaña ttā kaṃdvaji ī-
6 raki tsve ganamī jsa ttā nāsīrau kṣa kūsa ganaṃ vā biśa bisai ārryari khu hą̄mai vasve hame
7 u dvāsä kūsa vā hą̄mai hajsęmyari khu vā hīya stūra tsvata hamāṃde ttītī vā hīyau stū-
8 rāṃ bida baḍa u śau jsāṃ vā hvę stūra haśdį na vā tsvata hamāṃde ttītī vā gvāraḍą̄na stū-
9 ra barīdä u khvau tta saṃ nvaśtyeri hamāte tta ttai yaṃda kuṃjsatīnai vā rrūṃ hajsęmari drai śiṃga huṣka
10 kūra drai ṣaṃga hālā pāraka gulä u dva thyeba khalavya u hāsą̄śka jsāṃ vā hauryari u cila-
11 ja namata baṃ ṣṭa dīśta ttā duna hauḍeṃ tta rai va tta śira ja girau u ṇāyarī hā ka nai hāṣą̄ka
12 jana same ci vā buḍāṃdä ī[1]ra[1]saṃgi jsāṃ vā ma tsa paṃdä vā ḅuysi ṣṭe u va[1]ra[1] śū saṃ tta biśa
13 ādari yaṃ hamārrīji māśti 10 6 mye haḍai ttā *pīḍ***akä** hauḍeṃ
14 ha ja ma ma rri śta[2]
15 [*verso*] spāta īramañä rāñä hau

[1-1] Subscript.
[2] In three vertical lines *ha ja, ma ma, rri śta.*

43

Mazar Tagh b. ii, 0065

1 : : cī ṣi̱ śiri bāḍä ye ttāma khu ṣi̱ bhadrra-kalpī mistä
2 miṣḍi ğyastä marä ysaṃthä nāte viśakīrttä pūlñāṃ prrabhāvina 1
subhikṣi mari paṃñe hirna rruṃdi hīyau [jsi] pūñau jsa
3 ttāguttyau hvāṣṭyau pātci ci ṣṭāṃ ttū hvaṃ I kṣīri kaidi 2
kṣasimī ṣṭāṃ tsve kṣuṇi panatai gaurivi mista
parvālāṃ pajsaṃ prracaina hā dharmä āhāri keṃṇa 3
4 I ṣi̱ mī vā ṣada jsi brī[1]ya[1] namaṃdrrye gari vīrāṣṭa
āśarya dva ṣi̱ ttū kālä rrāhaji āstaṃ māśte 4
5 kṣīri āysdarrji I prracaina haspisyari vari ā vāña
śā salī śiri apvaṣṭi khu vyachīṃdi harbaiśi pīle 5
6 ūpakaraṇi ci būlrāṃ śtā karaṇi harbäśūṃ vāṣṭi hajsau⟨dai⟩ ——

44

Mazar Tagh c. 0018

1 II salī tcahaura māśta rrāhaja haḍā haṣṭūsa hvaṃ-
2 na rrāda viśakīrtta ttya tcī-ṣī āmāca ṣṣau viśaraka sa-
3 lya /// × /// -i ××× -ī ×× /// × -e /// ×

45

Staël-Holstein roll

1 [2] *sarau viśa̱ saṃbha*ta rruṃdä 10 4 mye kṣuṇä krriṃgä salya ///// mā-
2 śtä 7 mye haḍai / . . . . / -ä herä haura u -erä ni ××
3 u *tcau*rä *pyaḍā* / . . / -ä / . / -ā -ä ja × nai × ṣä vā īste viña khu ī[1]ne[1]ṇ
4 -ī pyilyaiga ye 30 6 chā paṃjsa tsūna u rijī-jūṃ hūlyega
5 30 chā paṃjsa tsūna u hvāhä:tte 10 7 tsūna ——

[1-1] Subscript. [2] 1–3 hardly legible in facsimile.

6 . . ṣau śvą̄nakai biṃdä vāstä aśtä dva chā paṃjsū jsūna[1] ——

[*Space*]

7 . . sarau viśą saṃbhata rruṃdä 10 4 mye kṣųṇä krriṃgä salya kajä māśtä 10 2 mye haḍai

8 ṣį näṣkicä pīḍakä ttye herä prracaina cu maṃ ṣacū kīthä ttika burä haḍa ya .

9 bulųnä rrgyaḍä sųmä u ttāgutta kąrä ṣau ṣarrnädattä u hvaṃna kąrä ṣau ṣaṃdū u

10 naṃpajamñai ṣau śvą̄nakai u ttä burä kathä paysāṃdāṃdä . . phįmą̄na kaṃtha u

11 tsāḍīkāṃ bisā kaṃtha u paḍakä bisā kaṃtha u kąḍakä bisā kaṃtha u ysa-
nākä chittä-pū u nāhä : chū-

12 baḍä parrūṃ bisā kaṃtha . raurata kaṃtha u sucąnä kaṃtha u ṣacū
pū ḍūrtcī draya kaṃthe
kaṃtha u

13 śālahä: kaṃtha u hvinä tcvįnä kaṃtha u kvacū kaṃtha u sīnä śe
tcī dyaimä kaṃtha u ūnä kū kaṃtha ttūśā
kaṃtha

14 u kviyi kye kaṃtha u gākä mąnä kaṃtha u hvẹ ḍū kaṃtha u puṃ
ttūśā ttūśā ttūśā ttūśā
karä ḍaṃ-

15 tha u sauhä:cū kaṃtha u lāhä:puṃ kaṃtha u kyįnä kaṃ kaṃtha
ttūśā ttūśā
u lvainä

16 tsvainä kaṃtha . . kąmacū katha u laicū kaṃtha u śāhvā kaṃtha ——
ttūśā

17 . . tti burä secū bise kaṃthe . . īcū kaṃtha u kaųyākä kaṃtha u dapäcī katha

18 phūcąnä kaṃtha u śakāhä : kaṃtha u tsīrä kyepä kaṃtha u īśumä kaṃ-

19 tha u [2]ḍūkä cū[2] kaṃtha u hvẹ tsverä kaṃtha u ḍūkä cū kaṃtha
yūśumä
u ttiyākä kaṃ-

20 tha u tcyāṃ tsvainä kaṃtha u kautañai kaṃtha —— secū mistä kaṃtha —— paṃjä

21 kaṃthä —— hä:nä bihä:rakä nąma kaṃtha —— śaparä nąma kaṃtha u

22 yirrūṃcįnä kaṃtha —— cąmaiḍä baḍaikä nąma kaṃtha —— argīñvā bisā

23 kaṃtha —— ėrmvā bisā kaṃtha —— phalayākä kaṃtha —— tturpąnä kaṃtha

[1] Here *jsūna* for *tsūna*. [2-2] Del.

24 bapa̯nä kaṃtha

25 . . anä ttuṃga —— cā ttuṃga —— tsāṃ śāṃ-śī ca̯kä śāṃ-śī —— bya̯ yūṃ-śāṃ
cā ttuṃga

26 śī ——

27 'ijūva —— yahä : ḍaka̯rä —— aḍapahūttä —— bākū —— bāsä

28 kāttä —— kurabīrä —— kārähbarä ttä ttūlīsä ṣṭāre

29 . . iṃjū —— sīka̯rä —— ttaugara —— ayabīrä —— caraihä : yabū

30 ttäkarä —— añahä : ḍäpahūttä —— ⌢ karattaha-pata ttättarä dū sa-

31 hūta —— [1]sāḍāmīya[1] —— ttrūkä bayarkāta —— cūṇūḍa ——

[*different handwriting*]

32 . . salī 10 4 māśtä siṃjsīṃja haḍā 20 ⌢ ṣi̯ kṣuṇä misḍāṃ ğyastä hvaṃnä rruṃdä sarau

33 viśa̯ saṃbhatä ⌢ [2]ttiña beḍa[2] khū ṣṭāṃ yuḍa dāya rruśtä hvaṃ kṣi̯rä vīra ⌢ ttye rruṃdä īñakä bya̯ma-

34 yä pūñūdä hvaraṃdä vīrai iṃdrä jsä bijiṣṭä hvāṣṭä ye baḍä rrgyaḍä su̯mä

35 na̯ma harbīśvä paṃdāvvä kaṃthvä bvākä ⌢ ṣi̯ mī hvāṣṭä ⌢ rruṃdä hīye bya̯me u ttī-

36 śi̯ prribhāvana[3] hvaṃnya kṣi̯rä a̯nä ṣacū vāṣṭä paṃdä prrihīye kṣa̯ jū vā tsve u

37 [×] viña jsāṃ vā hauda jūnä haṃtsä [2]sa̯narau[2] ka̯ ṣau ṣaṃdū jsä u *n*va śau hayākä pātcä vā tsve

38 ṣacū ⌢ ttyāṃ nva vā pha arthä ā aùrya mista ⌢ tti burä jsāṃ haḍa ya ttye arthä jsa haṃ-

39 tsa cāṃ ttū-ttū u ka̯rä ṣau ṣarrnadattä u ṣau śva̯nakai u puśka-ka̯jai spā paḍä-dūsä u

40 ysarrarä kharuṣai u drau-vathaṃjai khrrī-rtta̯nänä ⌢ tti buri maṃ baudhasattä ğyastä

41 va u tte-pū va vistārya pūña prriyauga pa̯jsāṃḍāṃḍä ⌢ cāṃ ttū-ttū gūma-ttī-

42 rä ba̯sä paste padaide nūvarä śirkä 20 chāyavī pyaṃtsä haśirma u ttāgutta

43 ka̯rä ṣau ṣarrnadattä panūḍai pūstye vāśi̯ya śau u śau śārṣṭai tsīya ——

44 hvaṃna ka̯rä ṣau ṣaṃdū karä kaṃthä tsve ssa 20 1 u śārṣṭä paṃ-sse u dva śiṃgä rrūṃ jsä

[1-1] Del. [2-2] Subscript. [3] *v* over *t*.

45 dirye kaṃtha bäsvā u ayiṣṭhvā vḁnvā prriyaugä haiṣṭe u ṣau śvḁnakai śärṣṭä tsve

[46 *in smaller script*]

46 kāṃbaṃdä haurä haude śe u chāṃ-syū śau ——

47 —— puśka-kḁjai spāta tta padä-dūsä śārṣṭā tsve —— kharū-

48 ṣai jsāṃ maṃ ssa 30 haṣṭi byaṣṭe ˷ ttika buri ma śirä dauṣkarä dvā rruṃdāṃ va puña

49 prriyaugä pḁjsāṃdāṃdū cū rä vā padā ustaṃ hada hīsāta u mamaṃ pā ha-

50 sta padīna ādarä parīya yude puñau prrīyaugāṃ va haurä-maurä maṃ ni ī-

51 nīryau nāṃ sījīṃdä ustaṃ va vyaysaña kaśīryḁ ——

52 . . jūhḁnai bādä spyakyi ṣṭāṃ vā hārvaidä ˷

53 maṃ ṣḁ vala śtāka dye jsa śirka u būlśajsa ˷
maṃ ṣḁ vala dīśtä ṣṭḁnä pūmūda hamāte

54 maṃ rä būda ysīrä byājälkya spyakyi na śtāka ——
. . khvā nä vajsyḁne same paṃmarä bvḁne

55 hamarvā | vaṃ aṃgvā ṇe paṣṭa raysāya
drḁ-mḁjsakyä hva hva gvīracäkyä paṣṭīṃdä

56 ysīrakä | dravāśaṃ dai viña yaṃdä bḁjsakyä ˷
. . ttadī drḁmī khu śäkarīnai mūvai

57 ā vā | drḁmī sä sauhä: vaskā pādāṃdä
hvḁṇḍvā ysāvī ṣvīdä jastṳña khaṣṭai

58 vaña halmyai haña ysītha tçḭmḭśkyāṃ ysauhä ——

59 . . bastä hūbastä hvḁraṃdai ñauysirä grathä

60 ḁjsīṃjāṃ aůvya bastä ysarīṃje ñūcä jsä | pyaṣṭä ˷
tturkä viysä ysarrnā spyaka vasva biśä

61 hastama hvaṃdḭnä raṃna spaladā- | jsaimḁñä
viysä khīysarä ttaurrjä dädḁ ṣṭāṃ akhajaṃdai

62 jvḭhä khva rä maṃ hīye uvḭ | biṃdä nä īṃdä ˷
hai tha mūrä kakva jastṳña mūraka tcadä māhāsamḁdrä

63 | mḁñaṃdä krriṃgä ärrä pārä seśākä darau jsa ˷

64 nvīcä īdä agalakvā | hīye bḁjse drreha jsä brrīyikyä vīrāṣṭä

65 khu mī tha väña krrañakä | āye mahä ttä hayūṃ bīysaṃjä ˷

66 ma ttä ttū pvḁisai barä väla | kye brre vī
khvai hā hīśä vīrä hūña akakū akakū nḁtte

67 śä gaulśtä dajä-gūnä spūlakye brrīyilakä vā brraṣṭa

68 brrīyilalkā vā brraṣṭā khu tta pā nä harāśę

69 khū tta kā̦ma krrathä nä | gūche ma kaṇa ——

70 . . ttina kālna khū a paḍauśa̦ ahā rdyai vilalkä brrī
khva vistā ysirä biṃdä brrīvīnai ttaudä ayūlä

71 na̦ nä ṣṭā̦ṃ | aysmū rama kīrä nä u͡vī
vistātūṃ kīrä vanāsacau u͡vīśkyāṃ ⌢

72 ṣai khū ṣṭāṃ hūlsīme hūñä dai ėräkañä ṣṭā̦mä

73 mahe brrā̦ṃbe hatsa bīysā̦nū khvā | nä vijsye
välakä brrī mīrā ra̦ aṃgä hamarä gūsīṃdä bäśä

46

Godfrey 2

1 || 15 mye kṣu̦ṇi ṣi̦ buri gayseta hālai hvaṃḍye hiri pasti

2 || kamalaji haṃbā 606 mūri || u ysumā̦ña-vrrahau kā̦ṃhi thau

3 9 chā 2 tsūna haudāyī chātī va mūri himāri 616 ——

4 || u hamāña-vrrahaunī kā̦ṃhi thau pasti 8 chā 6 tsūna ttye va kṣaṣṭī chā-

5 tī va mūri himāri 516 || u hamā̦ña-vrrahaunī pi̦mīnai thau pa-

6 sti 1 chā 5 tsūna sa paṃjsāsī chātī va mūri himāri 225 || u hamā̦-

7 ña-vrrahau haṃbātī mūri **pa**sti 170 u hālai hvaṃḍye haṃba̦ci jsa mūri pa-

8 sti 2133 vina miṣḍā̦nāṃ haudi **chā**yi haṃbā □[1] ——

47

P 2024

1 *tta* kūysāṣṭa ///

2 hīyai u tcā̦ra tvana-**kau** **hī** ///

3 || tta būra pvaicai cū ttadrrvā[2] bāstadū[3] paḍā̦-

4 ysa padāya pvaica tsvā̦ śā u pyatsvā̦ śa̦-

[1] Mark. [2] *rrvā?* [3] Top of *sta* lost: read *stā?*

ña pvaica tsvą̄ śą̄ : tta śarai ma va· pvaica
tsvāṃda tcą̄rai u bīrūkāṃ śā u rūkyą̄
va śą̄ u maṇḍvai va tcą̄rai u aśa va haṣṭai
ttañä hakhīśa hą̄ tvana-kau hīyai pvaica
ttrrada dvī u [1]ḍīsaina hīyai × yai pvaicā
jaistādū[1] pātca śąiyai aśa vaską pvaica tsvau-
da haudai [1]drrayi nāve u tcą̄ra na ra nāstai[1] ×[2]
|| painakyaima baida pvaica tsvāda drra-
yai u kājanau va pvaica tsvā śā
cagalaka rūsa gīryāṃdū śā pvaica u
cąpastaka pvaica nāva drrayai u śai pvaica jsa
jsāṃ mūṣaka bīla padaide u śā jsāṃ pada-ba-
yai[3] ttāhą hūḍāṃdū pvaica śā jsā pvaica
masai dedū hūḍai *u*[4] śai pvaica jsa jsāṃ
drrai jsai ṣvādū śā jsā pvaica ula vau hūḍai
padāya kūysāṣṭa habaica jsa pvaica tsvāṃda baista dvāsa pauḍaina hīyai u haṣṭi tvana-
kau hīyai khu kūysa ttattara āvadū pātca ttara-
kana pauḍaina daurmīnai bagala haiṣṭa śau kṣa kīṇī
dvāsa śaca āra u ttaśį̄kau kāḍara śau drrai śaca āra u pvaica dvī u baicakama dva u pūna
drraya u dvī bīrūkau u śā pyatsauśąña u tvana-
kau hīyai ttarkana vaska pvaica haiṣṭe drrayai u
bīrūkau drrayai u habaica jsa pvaica tsvāṃda
haudvau hīyai tcahaisa pātca pvaica pāṣṭādū
śā pauḍaina hīya u pātca pauḍaina hīya pvaica pāṣṭādū śā cū vā aủpą dagyaina hīyai khāysa
būḍāda u dvī jsā yana i̊naḍa hūḍaudū u drraya jsāṃ pvaice aủpa dagyaina jsāda u śą̄ kaiṇa
hvala u śā jsā pvaica saukvara nāve gīrye va u tcą̄-
lasa jsāṃ ha-bāḍāṃ sūlyā śkyasa hūḍai u dvī pveca jsā mūṣaka va rīma gīryāṃdū u śā jsāṃ pveca cega
u pātca tvanakau hīya pvaica pāṣṭāṃdū śā pātca
pauḍaina hīya pvaica pāṣṭāṃdū śā u maṇḍvai baida pvaica tsvāṃda tcaurai u i̊naḍa ttāttāha pvaica nāva dvī
u śe haje pvaica jsa jsā maṇḍvai bīḍa padaidaudū u

[1-1] Del. [2] A mark. [3] Possibly *bā*. [4] Blurred.

41 dvauda śīyā pvaicāṃ jsa jsā yaḍama ṣvaudū u dvī jsau
42 paica[1] jsau pasa gīryāṃ[dū]dū u tcau pvaica jsāṃ painakyema
43 gīryāṃdū cva jsa pasa gīryādū u barsa ttāhạ
44 pvaica nāva dvī mūlāvī u yaragaka va pvaica
45 hūḍai drrayai u śā jsā pvaica pīhạja hūḍāṃdū
46 cū mūṣa kava yaragaka ṣvauda pātca tvana-
47 kāṃ hīya pvaca tsvạ̄ śā cū vā maśtara
48 hạttuna khaysa hajsādā u pātca pau-
49 ḍaina hīya pvaica pāṣṭādū śā cva jsa pasa gī-
50 ryādū śau u śā jsāṃ pvaica pāṣṭāṃdū cū kṣa yī-
51 ḍattā yaragaka baida hūḍāṃda pātca śạ̄ ī-
52 ḍattā painakyaima vī pasa gīrya śau pātca kalakāṃ vī
53 dva pātca tvanakau hīyai kạ̄cāhạra tsvai śạ̄ pātca
54 dva yīḍattā painakyama vī pasa gīryāṃdū
55 tcạ̄ra u hāḍaiha[2]hālai yīḍattā jsā painakyama sahạ-
56 naka hūḍāṃdū u śau yīḍattā vī jsā aürmaka gīryāṃ-
57 dū || u pātca śau kalakau vī pasa gīryāṃdū śau pātca tvana-
58 kāṃ hīya pvaica pāṣṭāṃdū śā pātca apacaka hāle
59 yīḍattā painakyaima pātca būhạra barsa hvala hū-
60 ḍaudū haṣṭā mūra pātca hāle yīḍattā painakyaima
61 vī padāya pasa gīryaudū śau ttuhạdī jūṣḍi kaga nā-
62 va śạ̄

Recto

a u tta mara thuhạdī hīyai aśa va śudasa u kamacū-pa hīye aśa va dasau baikara dva u śai aśa va dvāsa u khạ̄ṣara āśị̄ śau u pātca pasau va nau khu vā sahạracāka ạ̄vadū pasa tsvāda pajsūsa: [3]pātca pasa tsvāṃda dasau cū vā yaya mara tta ạ̄na gīryaudū[3]

b ||| **pā**tca śai jūṣḍi kaga vī pasa śau u yaragaka va dva u khạ̄śkya va śạ̄ u pātca pasau va dva u ttuhạdī bīrūka śạ̄ u yāsa baida śạ̄ u ha[4] u pātca dvāṃ jūṣḍi kagāṃ vī pasa gīryāṃdū dva u kamacū-pa miśta haḍa śau u śau jsā jūṣḍi kaga ttaṣakana [5]va[5] hūḍe haṣṭi jsā u dvī-sa mūle dvāṃ aśau va hūḍai ——

[1] Read *pvaica*.
[2] *ha* deleted and the next syllable written above.
[3-3] Del. [4] *ha* blurred. [5-5] Subscript.

48

P 2025

1 /// cā ḍīṃkāṃ ñaśau —— kīmä ṣī-thāṃ sagädatti : u kīmä śāṃ-khī
[1]hūśa̮ina hamāṃ tcūka[1]
2 /// vinä hya:nä kīmä śau-śī sagälakä ttrivīlai kaḍā̮nākarä ///
3 /// sagakä dārjī paḍa u bīrä tce pīḍakä śau : ḥuśa̮inä ña tcū-
4 kä saṃgīnā dvīlai [2]tta nāgrran( )dā[2] āśī̮ kaya maṃ gvaina ka gvai-
4*a* [*Interlinear, different hand*] tcarmaja tcakä hvaba-ḯna
5 ni tcūna saṃgakä kṣa hīrāsakä ḯrä sagidattä *m*alya pīḍakä ///
6 saka thājañä ṣau painakä hūśa̮ina būmā tcana̮ paḍä sā pīḍakä ///
7 (recto) amaya sū thaya pau cāva hyaina

49

P 2027

1 samādana̮ daivatta ṣa̮ **hūḍaudä**
2 mi̮stye rrīysdvīra̮ śa̮ttai hvī —— tcūsyau tcū ——
3 || mi̮stye rrīysdvīra̮ gvi̮na haṣḍa̮ yine —— rri̮spūra̮ tcūsyauṃ
4 maista ⟨rri⟩ysdvīrä mi̮stye rrīysdvīra̮ —— mistye mi̮stye rrīysdvīra̮
5 hāysye dīśa̮ vī naysda̮ grau aysm̀ū̮ jsa :
6 ma̮ra̮ ṣa̮cū ṣṭaunä | ttāṣṭä janavai[3] vīräṣṭa̮ ||
7 ysarnai bāḍa vī maista śāśa̮ṃ | baiysuña ||
ranījai janavai vī śāva̮khye kīthe : ——
8 bi̮ysa̮ bi̮ysūña̮ aysmū ttye jsī hīsī hī [×]
9 pyarä ṣau ṣa̮nīra ttra̮vīlai devaisīhā̮ ||
10 ṣau kharäsa̮nä ṣau śvā̮ñakä ai̮ysa | kharūṣai ||
dārjī paḍa̮ tcū tca̮ka̮ : svaḫa̮ka ||
11 ḍītcai śau gūttairä pūrau dvarau | thiyi ttaika̮
nāgaidrārmäsīḫa̮ ha̮yu maista̮ ||
12 nvīrä ttä[4] kṣāṃdai javaidaiva | ttravīlai :
ñā̮ysaira vāḍa vū va̮yu̮ drūpaḍä[5] ||

[1-1] Subscript below *kīmä śāṃ-khī*. [2-2] Blurred.
[3] *nai* with *ai* del. [4] Blurred. [5] *drū* written as if *drya*.

13 ṣạ mä aysdạrä aśạullaka svaḫạka ||
pye ṣau ṣạnīra khū vā paste ysāvai |
14 thū-khī [×] kṣailmye kṣūṇa śairka bāḍa vī ||
mārā-pyạrä saṃ kaitta gaurva jsa ṣạdyāyi ||
15 | pastai parśại khū ja⟨sta⟩ bẹysạ parśạ ysīrastạ ||
16 hūḍauda maista haurạ | ysathvā ysaṃthvā ||
bīsa biśa mūṣa mạstāña | ranū mūrä ||
17 | ttu ysīthạ̄ śairka hamye ysīra jsā baimeña ||
18 bīdauda mūṣījä | ttīmạ jästvā mūjä ||
kūśala pakṣa ttu [1]je[1] yaudi byāva yuḍaudi
19 | parāḫạ paraihaumạ tvā aḫạṣṭạ yūḍaudạ ||
20 artha-bauga nau | pā hajsādi vīstāvi ||
vaña ṣṭau yidi bẹysạ u śāśạṃ brrūnạ
21 | khvau tta vạña pvesạ sạlya ḫịmeña ṣṭāve ||
22 ttīvau jsā ṣạika kū | śala aḫạmaistạ ṣṭāvẹ ||
harbīśvạ bāḍvāvau śairka hamāve
23 | krraudirāja devattä nau avạrī kaide :
24 vaña ttā śau haṣḍạ yulḍai jūhại udiśāyi :
25 ñaśa ṣamaṃ javaidrākarạsīḫạ ṣacū ṣṭaulni ||
cū vā narädū mvīla guttarạ ṣṭaunä ||
26 jīye padaidai aṣạlnai parädeśai ||
na ja baṣṭū aysạ kūśala sājakyä vaskä ||
27 | āvāvä parṣ̌ạ̄ña yi mārā-pyạrä ||
28 nū byadī haṣkaude ttạ | karma baysgä ||
ysīnāḫạ ṣṭāṃ bvaiysạ pada ysīra ttạ brraijị ||
29 | ysathvāṃjsva kīra [×] cū vā aysạ pīrāṃdai ||
30 ā vā ttu ysītha kūlśala yaunạnạ sāhyai ||
karma-vapākä nạ nạ parśai māvụ pye :
31 | ssạmādauna daivạtta ṣạ hūḍaudä padi ||
32 (ma tta ścạ̄kạ ṣṭe khū | ttā pañai śau śau ||
33 vāstạ hajsāṃdi yauḍa yinū brrīye udiśālyi : ||
caigvāṣṭạ maṃ padi pamạraume vạskạ ||
34 herä ttuka bälṣṭạ hamye stūrụ cīvarä)[2] ||
35 khvau tta viña ñaśa bīsạ byāva hamaulnai ||
ttīvau jsā jvīhīnai pyara brrāvirau ||

[1-1] Subscript and uncertain. [2] Brackets in MS.

36 śau vä tta ysīnī ṣṭe pā|cūla naumą ||
kaitta rą ttą khū ttą paijsana habrrīśtą ||
37 ñaśa bīsą | na mīraunai saunau gauśtä ||
38 pyara brrāvąrau hīyā̮ pūñā̮ prrabāau|vana ||
ciga kṣīrä ṣṭauna ajai ttā hīsīnai ||
39 pyarä brrāvąrau hvā|räkyāṃ pārśā̮ dāśū ||
ttī ttā ttu ysītha ną hīsīnai kṣīra ||
40 | ttye hẹ̮rä prraciną jsīni hająḍą ǐyai
41 kaumye tta brrāvąrä a byā|va hamaunai ||
kveśā̮ṣṭe kaitta bīsą pūrą padaime ||
42 harbaiśau pū|ra dvarä ǐdą amauñāṃ ||
gvāysīne dai bvīryāṃ kāṣṭa ṣā̮kä ṣṭe ||
43 | ṣā̮ka[1] daukha garbaida[2] dīśa gara vā vaṣḍe
44 pācūla jsa gvā|ysīnai dai jsä ṣṭau mīrai ||
45 ysīra tta na vīśtarä paijsa kāṣṭaną | baḍą ||
śkaisau vā cūḍana aů mauñāṃ vaskä ||
46 ama pā ttye śkaisa jsa | maistą hauvana bvīryāṃ ||
a hą̮sta ye mūḍau hakhīśā̮ ttraṃdū ||
47 | uvāryau vịstā̮ryāṃ pūñā jsa haphva :
haura varāśā̮ume u kūśala yąnāka
48 | hāysye dīśā̮ vī naysdi grāṃ aysmū jsą :
49 ysāra jūna byāva tsvava ṣīva haḍā|yi :
pyara ṣau ṣanīra aůrga drrūnā pvaisū :
50 ysīnīvā[3] nāsīde harbaiśą | bā̮ysa :
haṣṭą baudhasątva haṣṭa jsā parvālā :
51 bẹ̮śna śvarą jastā jsāṃ | ysīnī nāsī :
ttravīlai devaisīhā̮ [4]khū ja vā ysāvī :
52 ṣada vịrśā̮ patsau|ma mvaiśḍą uvāri[4] :
—— drūnā[5] pvesū :
53 lāhūra āśī̮ jsa pakyai|rma daśta u gumā :
haura varāśā̮ume aysmū jsa ṣada jsa :
54 hvaṇḍīne rana | biśau bvaijsā haphvau :
ṣau kharasana : ṣau śvauñaka ai̇ysa kharūṣą :
55 dārjī paḍą | tcū tcaka svahā̮ką :
ai̇ysa ḍaitce śau gūttaira pūra dvara

[1] *ai* and *ā*. [2] Read *s*-. [3] *nāī* written.
[4-4] Del. [5] *drū* written as if *drya*.

56 drūnā ttā haṣḍa yilnū harbaiśą bāḍa :
ttravīlai javaidaiprraysādye jsą :
57 mvejdąṣauña hva aysmų̄ | śakalaka vīrai :
bvaijsaive pha gajsa tvāve śā nīśtą :
58 śau badraikalpe ṣą̄ jsīlną caḍāve :
ñāysaira vāḍa jvū va yau drūpaḍą :
59 ṣama sagaśīla tceną alysdeña svaḫāka :
ṣe̥ka avīśą mesta hamye mūña baidą :
60 cą̄ patsai hathrrą | vī āspāvau jai :
dārjī paḍa pācūlaka naumą pūra :
61 ysīnīvau nāsīldai haṣṭa pūyi jaśtą :
beṣajārāyi baudhasatva ysīnau hūrī :
62 khvau ttā byelhū tvā hų̄ra śauma khanaca :
ysathvaujsva haura ca pastāṃda hūḍai :
63 mārā-pyalra ysīrasta gauva jsa ṣadyāyi ‿
pastauda parśą̄i khva ja havī harīna
64 | parāhą̄ paraihauma tvā haṣṭa yuḍauda ||
65 kūśala-pakṣa ttu vau pā alvīhī ysīra aśta :
ttye pārjsai jsa jsīna arthą̄-baugą :
66 vīśe̥ra tha maulñadū aja vīstāvą
byūra ysatha vaṣṭā ṣą̄ jsīna hūṣīye

50

P 2028

1 rrvī vī hąṣḍi ‿ [×] j ñaśa bīsą paḍa tsā ——
7 netcūkä ha kṣa ṣä ttā pīrä hīye kṣya khvā ṣä dīna tvī ahā jsa brrau
8 hve̥ u ttye ḍi vaijalakä jsa ysiṣṭyerä hve naịśta ṣa gaurä ——
12*ff* ha kṣą sāja thyau asade haḍi ma na yana [*Frequently repeated*]
88 —— thyina hīña[1]
89 nāmye kṣuṇä aśi salya rarūyi māśta nau-
99 samye haḍi hīvyauṣṭyi gida[2]-vāḍi pīḍaka
91 ttyai pyocana[3] cu ḍī vijalada ——

[1] With ‿ before *ña*. [2] Read *rya*. [3] *pyo* for *prai*.

92 rrvī vī haṣḍį ⟨ya⟩ni ñaśa bīsa hvą̄ gvale ~ ñaśa ba[1]
93 ṣacu vā ttāṣṭa yuḍi sa ṣacu haḍa tsa tta tta ~
94 sa khva pārśą habāya pītta vaña rrvī vī ā-
95 spāva khvaṃ vā jastāna hīya mviśḍe hara[. .]
96 ysdai na
97 || bidi mvaśde pastada byaudi u śau śī hīya
98 vistāna rāśą pastāda yuḍa

51

P 2030

1 [*bases of akṣaras*]
2–3 || mistye haurä virāśāme jsa haṃphve ~ tcihauryāṃ dilśą̄ṃ jsa phirākvą̄
4 bāḍvā nąma-tsvata līka ~ pųñūṃdä | bvą̄mayi śūrä

52

P 2031

1 **haṣḍi yu**ḍādą si viña ma drai kamala haḍa ṣṭ**āre** cu **ciṃ**ga kṣīrāṣṭa bīsa haḍa ttyā**ṃ** viña
2 [2]-ī × -i[2] kūṣṭi buri naiṣkaica ni hamāve ni tsva hamāre ~ viña maṃ kąmäcū bisā [3]śau kamala[3] ha-
3 ḍa thyeṃ [4]× × ×[4] [3]paḍą-tsā[3] u thyeṃ [2]śāṃ-śī ṣṭāre[2] [3]haryāsakä[3] ~ u dva rrispūrāṃ bāyākä gūlai u saṃga-
4 lakä ā vā ami rrispūrāṃ kvą̄śą daṃdä mūñarä kūṣṭi buri ciṃgvāṣṭä paṃda ni
5 hamāve ā vā [3]vą[3] thyeṃ paḍä tsā u hīryāsakä jsa paphūjīrau cū va kąmäcū ni mūṃ-
6 dä iḍāṃdä [3]cvaṃ rä va ņastä hīvī pacaḍa na ye[3] vā stāva u kṣīrāṣṭä jsāṃ pā parau niśtä u ttaką kaṃdä rrispūra

[1] Read *bīsa*. [2-2] Del. [3-3] Subscript. [4-4] Not clear and del.

7 ⌒ u śau kamalä hāysa tsuva mą̄ñą maṃ baysgä haḍi ṣṭāre u paysdyi āṃ ttā ni dā-

8 śāṃ mahe jsāṃ maṃ drrai pacaḍa hiysda hvarāka hauparipaṃjsāsä yahi:ma-

9 līha: hvąṇḍä ṣṭāṃ u anvaśtāvą maṃ maista ṣṭe ⌒ khvāṃ vā parau hīśtä kaṃdyi[1]

10 ttā śau kamalä hāysa tsų̄ñī ṣṭāve tta ttā hāysa tsāṃ u dva kamala jsāṃ daṃdä

11 ñāṃ kūṣṭi buri ciṃgvāṣṭä paṃda hīya phara ni hamāve ⌒ [2]*ttai* khu jsāṃ maṃ tta ysyę[3]

12 ciṃgvāṣṭä paṃda hąmāve rrispūrāṃ ri maṃ vīna śe śe[4] bvą̄nai aśä hervī haṃda stū-

13 ri niśtä ną jsāṃ va vīna śau śau dva dva paṃjsä pamūha: haṃdara dīśta mū-varga *aśtä*

14 cvaṃ jsa hamidā śau khaysai kharä ghināre cvaṃ jsa dvaṃdā u pamūhä: barīṃdä

15 khvaṃ vā pā ttakye hīvī parau hīśtä si khvaṃ yināṃ ⌒[2] cu jsāṃ maṃ ñaśāṃ bīsāṃ

16 dilakä dilakä herä ye ttu haṃda cimuḍvā buvāṃdūṃ u haṃda jsāṃ ṣacū śkye-

17 sä u padaṃja buvāṃdūṃ ttī jsāṃ aśparä kamala gūmalāṃ rruṃ pasa ttą̄ pā bi-

18 śi girma ṣṭāre ⌒ ttī jsāṃ vā bągarakä attęmä uha: paḍauysą̄ñi jsa ssa kąmäcū-

19 pava āva u tta tta ciṃdyāṃdūṃ si khvaṃ śau khaysą ni yināṃ u khu ttā ttī kąmäcū a-

20 staṃ śūje haṃgūją̄mane khvaṃ ri hā spāśāṃ anvaśtā sahyāṃ:dūṃ pa-ssa u mau u

21 hą̄mai u rruṃ giryāṃdūṃ u śiką khaysą puḍāṃdūṃ khu bāḍä hīvī kamalä ni phai-

22 rtte ⌒ cāṃ ri maṃ dīśta dilakä dilaka mu-varga ya ṣą̄ jsāṃ pā hā draṃda ni ra maṃ

23 mu-varga mą̄ñāṃ u ni rispūrāṃ u nai āṃ bvāṃ si kālänāṣṭą tsų̄ñī hamā

[1] *dyi* broken, perhaps *dyau*.
[2-2] Del.
[3] *ysvę?*
[4] *śe* subscript.

53

P 2739

|| mistye harä[1] *va*rāśąme jsa haṃphve ⁓ tcihauryāṃ lokapālāṃ jsa āysdaḍä ysira garbä rrāysāyaṃ biṃdä pārautti līkye bala-cakrrivarttä ciṃgä rruṃdąnä rruṃdä hīvī ⁓ thyįnä-ṣī pharākä aủrga drų̄nā pųsąmą haṣḍį yine

[*Space*]

—— ñaśä bīsä yā pūhi:ya paḍai ⁓ khu tta viña haiysdä vī ttye śirkye pvāśąi kālai bāḍä bąḍa ū-vārvā baudhasątvąnvā drayvā saṃskārvā ⁓ tta ra hįña māśa suhą-je ąme bhaugä virāśąme hadra vya jastų̄ña aysmya śirkä ṣṭā-ve drų̄nai tsāṣṭä ttye kiṇä ma ñaśe hvąṇḍyė g̨yastāṃjsa aųsä āva ttaṃ-dī ṣąikä ṣṭe ⁓ khu tta harbiśvā bāḍvā bųysi jsįna u rrvīyi ga-rśi āvaśą mąñaṃdä mųśdą u māśä askhijsąme vī jsāve ⁓ ñaśe jsāṃ bīsä pųña spyāṃde khu iḍā ttayi-pū yūttyenä kuhä: jinave vī thyau rraysgä vī dyąma byehūṃ dye ⁓ viña ra ttā aśtū pharākä ttū-śā silāta haṣḍi yine ⁓ viña tta rraysgä vī gąmąñä kha-ysą paṃmarä pharāka ⁓ hīsāṃ ttā kṣąṣṭä bure ⁓ vęgasti hvā-ri diraujsa ⁓ bagalagvā śī śpaka-jsįma ⁓ ṣpaṭa garbā kusi jsihąra ⁓ hvīḍi tta pamarä rraysgä vī ⁓ būna śā tcarga mase ñūḍąji bąṣkala dvī-ssa ⁓ śau rraha: śīyi ttrihe : ttye nvaiyi ūspurä palaijä ⁓ g̨ysajä siṃjau dva dva bāgä śau maṃmä thau śau ⁓ kīḍakyä begąnä śau ⁓ grathä ttīlā vī burakyä ūspuri tcaṃgiḍai grąhe: mä jsa śų̄stä ⁓ śau pajūkä ttųna cīñaka ⁓ pa-ysauja pūha:ra hva hva : ñye tcįñä haṃga sų̄ttä ⁓ śaṃdyauña śi-yi nimva ⁓ ysirū pūha:rä ūspurä ⁓ ś̨ęmä pahä: hī-ysą nīrau ⁓ ysaṃbasta kaṃgai śī pau ⁓ ttyāṃ nvįyi iña iñakį ma ⁓ bīśūñāṃ arvāṃ jsa śų̄sta ⁓ grąma syalahä:ṣä ū thahä: cauhä: ⁓ ūstaṃ vī le thau jsįṇä nva ⁓ padaṃja biṃdä khaysą ⁓ ttye nva pasa tsīṃdä draya ⁓ aṇūtcä mau nau jsūre vāsta sūrä drai haṃkhīysą cu vā bąñä sąrvą dāja khve ni ī hauta khaysą va ⁓ haṣḍi vā yą mista ąna mų-śdą īnū khaysą va hajū ⁓ pvīysakä strīyai hvāṣṭa vi-ṣāmūlai jsa hūśų̄stä ⁓ dastaurä hauḍai [× ×] khara saṃnä ⁓ khvaṃ

[1] Read *haurä*.

32 nä bīḍä tvą̄ ttrvą̄ñä ñą̄ña ⁓ ṣę jsāṃ vā raṣṭakä gūḍe ⁓ kṣā-
33 rma haysgyi byaudai mista ⁓ hadarye bāḍä vī ą̄na ‖ baka sa-
34 stä ttū cī ịdä ⁓ khāysä mau kįṇḍä ịḍai kṣārma haysgya byaudai
35 mista pademḍai ⁓ ni haṃgū tva jsā bīśūñe ⁓ phą̄nä kyą-
36 nä hīye phūḍe ⁓ khaysą pamarä viña tvā kṣą̄rma ha-
37 ysdya *uysgyịnä* ⁓
: pvai

[*Space*]

38 : pvaisū ttā ñā ttä brrāvą̄rä
pharākau bvaijsau haphau :
39 dahų̄ṃ śūra | tcaṣū ysaunastą :
hvarä ąidrī ysą̄jsä salā ⁓
40 styauda bvaumaya dalrau jsa :
ṣą̄haunī pañai brrī :
maihaiśūra āṃ krrai dyainą
41 rauma raiṣma jsa | hamagaka
pañvą̄ kṣą̄ bą̄ḍvą̄ jāvūṃ :
tta bautta tta naule mą̄ñada
42 | gūjsabaija saunau raysme
nama hagrrīhāka śaira 3
43 [yū][1]| ttaya-pau yų̄ttyaina kūauhą
cakrravartta raudauna rauda
44 ą̄rą̄hą̄ka | aysmų̄ u͡vī :
parau hagrrīhą̄ka straiha 4
45 ca vą̄ vaña [2]ma vīra[2] | vā[ṣṭą][1]ṣṭą hajsādai :
brrī : ttū vaṣą̄mūle spūka[3] :
46 yą̄pūyą | ma vīrą̄ṣṭą
nva brrī yai [2]avainą̄vai[2] jvāhai thauña : 5 :
47 | jasta bąiysa parvą̄lą̄ ną̄va pacaḍa[jsa][1]na :
48 tcara lą̄kapą̄la | daśą̄pą̄lā hatsa :
padą̄rą̄ ysā garają jasta hamīḍa :
49 sa | jātta dīvyąṣmā[4] āysda yanąvai 6 :
50 ca vą̄ hajsāṃdai : khaysa hī | yai pīḍakä :
hīsīda ttą̄ kṣaṣṭa ṣīka bakai ṣṭą̄rai :

[1] Blurred. [2-2] Del. [3] Read *spūlaka*? [4] Read °*ṣṣā*.

51 mara vą̄ | bą̄ya ysą̄ra pa-sai hvą̄ṣṭą :
52 śara hvāra śara khą̄ṣą̄ : śara | da palyā bąiśa : 7 :

khaysa ma pamą̄ḍa aśta :
53 ttyai vaska daukhą | na jsāvai :
ysīra hathara pā rrvai dvī
kūṣų̄ byaihai pa-sai ysāra 8

54 | khaysną hvą̄ra bījīrma hvą̄ṣṭą
yūttaśa ttadī śūka
55 ṣacū [1]ka[1] kīra | na jsāvai :
hauva thaują pūra cī ysa jastvā 9 :

56 caigauna padalja jsaiṇa
khu mara vyasvaima na pī :
baiysai ra śą̄rą̄na ìda :
57 cą̄ ra | ttrvą̄ya ṣacū aùna 10

54

P 2741

1 || rrvī vī aùrāsä haṣḍä —— ñaśä bīsä thyai paḍä tsā ∽
2 || khu vā ñaśä bīsä pąsa mistye ysarrnīṃje jänave vī ą̄na [2]ysa[2] ką-
3 mäcū vāṣṭä ysarrnai parau nāteṃ ∽ khu garvā [2]hva:mäla[2] āvaṃdūṃ dasau
4 haḍā cimuḍāṃ [2]biṃdä[2] [1]haṃdryi vya[1] tsvāṃdūṃ ∽ cä cumuḍāṃ haṃdryi vya mistye bāḍä hī-
5 ya padaṃja ṣą̄ bisä tcerai hamya ∽ khu ṣacū āvaṃdūṃ ∽ viri vā didye
6 haḍai si-khūṃ cā śvāṃ-śį̄ haṣṭe si tvī kąmäcū vāṣṭä thyau närą̄mą̄ñä
7 hame ∽ cu ciṃga kṣīra bisā haḍä ṣṭāre tti viña ni tsva hamāre ∽
8 khū miri ṣacū āvaṃdūṃ haudamye haḍai [vā?] kąmäcū ą̄na stąnäcū
9 ā u barbajīyāṃ hīya sūlya ∽ ttīvī ñaśa bīsa brraṣṭāṃdūṃ si kąmä-
10 cū va bāḍä khu ṣṭe ∽ u ttä vā hve si kąmäcū va āphāji ṣṭāre ∽ cu thyautta-
11 nāṃjsī hą:nä ye ṣį paryе ∽ u cu jsāṃ hā viña ttrūkä bayarkāta u

[1-1] Subscript. [2-2] Del.

12 sahạ̄:nä aụ̆ga ttūkä nūvarä hạ:nä ṇẹstāṃdä ⌢ ttū jsāṃ āṃ va ttarrdā-
13 śāṃ [1]u śe aụ̆ga u bīrūkāṃ[1] āstaṃna dirsä dirsä hvaṃḍä papẹśạ̄ kịṃdä si khu ttrūkvāṣṭä ni pa-
14 haiśtä ⌢ u ttī jsāṃ va kaṃthi straihä: ṣamạñä ṣṭe ⌢ ñaśä bīsä skarhvẹri mā-
15 śti 28 mye haḍai ṣacū ạ̄na kạmäcū vāṣṭä niraṃdūṃ ⌢ rrāha:ji
16 māśtä paṃjsūsa haḍai kạmäcū āvaṃdūṃ ⌢ u didye haḍaivāṃ hạ:nä
17 pyaṃtsä bāstāṃdä ⌢ u cu maṃ hạ:nä va rrvīyi mụśdạ̄ ya tvā hā nva pa-
18 rau hauḍeṃ u svaṃna kalai hā aụ̆gavāṃ vīrāṣṭä parauta hauḍeṃ u mụ-
19 śdị ⌢ u khu busta si bāḍä hävī kīrä dāśe ⌢ ttī vā ttuḍīśä saḍä-
20 cī ttāttāhä: nạ̄ma bīrūkä tsve cu ñaśe bīsä hīvī kalātcyarai ye
21 u maṃgalī chārä ttāttāhä: u cịnä ttāttāhä: ⌢ ttaṃ vā ttä tta parau pa-
22 stāṃdä ṣi dasamye haḍaive āṃ närạ̄mạ̄ñä hame bụysä maṃ nä mūṃdä yaṃ
23 mạ̄ñāṃ maṃ drrạ̄ma āphāji ṣṭāre cu ri maṃ hvehva:rāṃ ṇẹstä va śaṃdā niśtä
24 viri hā ñaśä bīsä haṣḍi yuḍeṃ si khū vā aủrmaysdi guṣprrīsaṃcä bi-
25 sā ttuṃśīyi bāsteṃ u raṃnīṃje mistye jänave vī bisä thiṃśīya ⌢
26 u khu tti haḍi urmaysdi guṣprrīsaṃcāṣṭä nä paśä yinịme ⌢ [2]ysi[2]
27 ysarrnai mistye haurä pyaṃtsāṣṭä hā aủrāsä haṣḍi khu yine ⌢ u ttạ
28 vā hvāṃdä si cve maṃ haṃdana bisai parau hamāte ttūve ttā svī däthiḍai
29 paryāṃ ⌢ cu haḍi ṣṭāre ttä ri [1]nä[1] spāṣṭä yaṃ ⌢ tti viña ttäkye bāḍä vī phari
30 niśti si cu bāḍä niraṃdä hamāre ⌢ tvī rraysgä vī gạṣạ̄ñä hame ⌢
31 ttī vā kaji māśtä beraji vī kalātcyarai bīrūkä dīśti parau pastāṃdä si
32 viña āṃ [2]ga[2] ūhū:ysä aụ̆ga u barsä aụ̆ga āstaṃna hauda aụ̆gava [2]nya[2] tsīṃdä
33 u hauda bīrūka cu āṃ gūkäṃịnä ạ̄na ṣacū-pataṃ jsa bāḍä padịmā-
34 re u tvī pā tsụ̄ñai hame ⌢ khu rraysgä vī ysarrnai bāḍä vīrāṣṭä pharä gạste
35 u ttī vā ṣacū ạ̄na mājā hvaṃḍä pīḍakä hajsāṃdāṃdä si ṣacū-pata āṃ maṃ na
36 tta tti hụ̄ñīṃdä si khu vā kạmäcū ạ̄na thyai paḍä tsā hīśtä u cu maṃ ttikyāṃ

[1-1] Subscript. [2-2] Del.

37 āstaṃna haḍä ȋṃde daṃdą i̥hẹjāṃ kuṣṭi buri vā mājā haḍi ni hīsīṃde

38 cu jsāṃ va g̃yaśti hīya dyą̄ma ya tvā vą̄lai hų̄nvāṣṭä hajsāṃdāṃdä u pą-

39 jsä [1]maṃ[1] sāḍa-aysmva ṣṭāre ⌢ ttī ñaśä bīsä ttū pīḍakä hau ni niśāveṃ ⌢ u

40 ūhū:[2]jsi[2][1]ysä[1] ąủga mi biśāṣṭä gurṣṭe u ttī vā hve si ñaśä bīsä rrvīyi

41 myu̯śdą̄ pąjsä pharāka nā yuḍeṃ cu ṣacū bisā salāta ṣṭāre tti hauta ṣṭāre

42 viña ttikye paṃdä mų̄ña u ñaśä bīsai hā ttä hveṃ si śveri tta ṣacū bisā sa-

43 lāva ⌢ dva paciḍą ma ciṃga ḳṣīrāṣṭä haḍi ṣṭāre u kuṣṭi burą mari kąmä-

44 cū ą̄na viḍāṣṭä nä hajsāṃdä yiniֽme ni tsva hame ⌢ ttä hā aủgava paṃjsū-

45 samye haḍai āva u i̇ḍāri̥ jsāṃ hā ciṃgä rruṃdä hīvī haḍä śahvāṃ: ḍittū

46 kīthi bisai sūṃ śāṃ śū [×] u ṣi̥ hā ñaśe bīsä vīrāṣṭä hvaṃḍi haṣṭe

47 si yūttịnä kūhi: bisai maṃ haḍä ṣṭe khvaṃ jsi haṃgūjūṃ ⌢ u vaṣṭi[3] vīraṃ jsa ni

48 haṃgve ⌢ ttī hā hamārrīṃji [1]ṇẹ̄śti[1] māśti ṣacū bisā hịna āta u ttī jsāṃ hā spari-

49 bistä aủgava dvī ysārä [1]cumuḍą̄na[1] hịna ājīṃdāṃdä u dvī ssa ttattara ⌢ khu kąmäcū

50 ttraṃda didye haḍai buka hą:nä muḍä u nārä u dvī dvarä ⌢ haṣṭimye haḍai

51 hịna näraṃda u śaṃdąmä buri tsvāṃdä u ttrūkvä hā ni dirvāṃdä ⌢ u gą-

52 sāva ttī cumuḍa ysaurrä yuḍāṃdä tti hvāṃdä si cī hve:hva:rāṃ u ciṃgāṃ hīvī

53 thapsä ye ⌢ ci vā mą̄ñāṃ śā māśtāṃjsye śaṃde vī ą̄ni bāstāṃda u nau-

54 hyi: buri hịna ni bāstāṃda u hāysi tsvāṃdä ⌢ u ṣacū-pata jsāṃ kīthi

55 ṇẹsta u kṣi̥mye haḍai hā ttrūkä bayarkāvāṃ hīya hịna āta ⌢ u

56 paḍauysä nauhä: hā ūhū:ysä aủga u berakä ąttịmä ūha: āstaṃna hve-

57 hvu:rą̄na hịna āva u ūhū:ysä aủga āstaṃna va tcaurabistä hvaṃḍä mu-

58 ḍa u nva jsāṃ hā [2]ciṃ[2] ṣacū bisā hịna āva u khvaṃ ttrūkä bayar-kāvāṃ hī-

59 ya hịna dyā virī aśa u͡vī stāṃdä u ṇẹsta u ṣacū-pavą ri hā biṃda

60 ni dirvāṃdä ⌢ u drai haḍā ri va ṣacū-pata mūṃdāṃdä u haṃtsi vā

61 bẹgarakä attịmä ūga u ayavīrä ūga uha: ūga u ką̄ṅūrä

[1-1] Subscript. [2] Del. [3] *ve* with *e* del.

62 apa ūga u aha:cī u cįnä ttāttāhi: āstaṃna drayi bīrū-
63 kāṃ jsa hāysi tsvāṃdä u vīraṃ hā barsä uga tsve u ttą hve si āphāji
64 pharākyi ṣṭāre mą̄ñāṃ jsa haṃtsi hāysa tsa u haṃtsi vā ṣacū-patāṃ
65 jsa hāysi ni dirveṃ tsai si ärrä vī kaśe ⁓ u hamidā va drai māśti mūṃ-
66 deṃ u cu va kīthä aụgavāṃ āstaṃna ttūḍīśa ya tti ri va pā kīthi pha ni
67 mūṃdaṃdä u ttrūkaṃ vaski hā haṃtsi sahą̄:nä ūga jsa hįna ājīṃdāṃdä
68 u hau:rāṃ murāṃ jsa śūje va prrą̄ñī puḍāṃdä si mihe dva pacaḍa hve:hva-
69 ra u dūṃta śūje ni paśāṃ ⁓ cu maṃ bęgarä attįmä aụga āstaṃna
70 bāḍa-śipherā hvaṃdä ya tti ṣacū vāṣṭä hāysi tsvāṃdä u khu kīthi
71 bisā ttūḍīśa nitcä kīthi āta ttrūkāṃ jsa hami hamya ⁓ cu va pā
72 ttarrdāśāṃ hadri vya ịcīṃjūva ya ttä pā ttrūkvāṣṭä hāysä tsvāṃda
73 pātcä hā ttrūkvā bisā dasau miśtäri hvąṃḍä ttraṃda si bāḍāṃ padįmāṃ ⁓
74 u ttiña beḍi jsāṃ hā ñaśe bīsä vīrāṣṭä ṣacū ą̄na pīḍakä ā si
75 hauda vā prrivāsti rrispūra āta u haḍa cu āṃ gauthūśąnä tsīṃdä u
76 ttyāṃ daśāṃ hvaṃḍāṃ jsi haṃtsi ttrūkvāṣṭä thyai haryāsakä paśāveṃ si bā-
77 ḍi-dijsāṃ vā miśtirāṃ hvaṃḍāṃ jsa näṣkicä padįmä si tti rrispūra u
78 haḍi tsva hamāri ā ne ⁓ u haryāsakä tsve u ttauḍägarāṃ vī hā pyaṃtsä
79 dvī ysārrä hįna āta cu [×] karattahä: tsvā[1] ttarrdāśāṃ vī u haryā-
80 sakä biśāṣṭa [2]hā[2] hajsāṃdāṃdä u ttūrä[3] jsāṃ ttarrdāśvā bisā drai-sse
81 ula baḍä yuḍāṃ⟨dä⟩ u ttī jsāṃ ayavīrä aḍpä bękä cā bīrūkä
82 u ttarrdāśä ịttīyigąnä ttāttāhä: u saikairä ttrūkä chārä ā-
83 staṃna haudā bisa hvaṃḍä hāysi bāstāṃdä ⁓ khu vā viri āṃ tta gąsā-
84 ta u miri hā kīthi ą̄na haṃtsi ttarkąnä aụga jsa dūṃta niraṃda u haṃ-
85 tsi ttye aụga jsa hauparibistä kīthä bisā hvaṃḍä muḍa ⁓ haryāsakä jsāṃ
86 hā tti tti hvāṃdä si cu mihe dva pacaḍa hve:hvara ṣṭāṃ mahe haryāsa-[4]są̄[4]nā ha-
87 myaṃdūṃ bāḍä hīvī maṃ pacaḍä niśtä ⁓ khvąṃ vā ttarrdāśa vāṣṭä paśīṃ-
88 de u kīthi bisā hvaṃḍä mihe vą̄ pā paśä yināṃ ⁓ cu jsāṃ va ṣį ciṃ-
89 ga ķṣīrä bisai haḍä ye ttye jsi jsāṃ ñaśä bīsä haṃgviṃ u pīḍakä hā nä
90 dirveṃ haurä ⁓ salā jsai hā biśä guḍe si cu ịmājsā[5] haḍi ya tti

[1] With *e* del. [2-2] Del. [3] Read *stūra*. [4-4] Subscript. [5] Read °*jā*.

91 biśä ṣacū āva u mājā vā pā ḍittu pūhä:ya āstaṃna drayi
92 mista haḍa u nittastāṃ naḍām āstaṃna śų̄dasä hvaṃḍä tti pā
93 ṣacū āva ⁓ ttī vā brraṣṭi si ciṃga kṣḭ̄rāṣṭä vā rrvīyi muśdą̈
94 cilaka āva ⁓ ttai hā hveṃ si kṣḭ-sse kiṇa vā īrä rrāśą̈ pastāṃ-
95 dä yuḍe u ījīṃji ñūca u dva paśaṃjsana ⁓ u ttä vā hve si maṃ
96 vā pā ṣacū ą̄na cā ttäyä khī [1]āstaṃna ciṃgāṃ[1] hīvī pīḍakä tta tta ā ⁓ ṣḭ va pā ha-
97 ḍä dilakä mūṃde u haṃtsä ttaṃgātvā bisāṃ haḍāṃ jsa pahai u ttrūkvā
98 ttraṃdä u viri ą̄nä viḍą̄ṣṭä hāysi tsve cvai jsāṃ va ciṃgä rruṃ-
99 dä hīya hą:nä va muśdḭ ya tvāvī jsāṃ ttrūka biśä ysyāṃdä pī-
100 ḍäkä āstaṃna ⁓ khu durbikṣą̈ u āphāji pattīye u karä kīthi jsāṃ hā
101 są̄na haṃthrrīyāṃdä drai māśti ri kaṃthi viri ni prrihīyāṃdä ⁓ ttī hā
102 karattahä: ą̄na [2]caraihä[2]: ṣīyi caraihi: uha: u biḍigā
103 sahą̄:nä āstaṃna hvaṃḍä ttraṃda ⁓ cvaṃ hā dūṃvi tta tta hvāṃdä si mą̄-
104 ñāṃ āṃ khu yaṃda imi garvāṣṭä tcäbrrī yaṃda mahe kīthi ą̄na haṃ-
105 jsyāṃ kṣųna mīrä u karä kīthi jsāṃ maṃ są̄na ṣṭāre ⁓ ttī vą̄ jsāṃ maṃ yū-
106 ttḭnä bisā haḍä ṣṭāre miysdyų̄na cu haṃjsyą̄ri mīrāṃ u aśaṃ jsāṃ bi-
107 śä baḍä tsvāṃdä ⁓ cu hą:nä ṣṭe ṣḭ jsāṃ vilakä ṣṭe ⁓ ttāṃ vā haṃtsi hḭ̄-
108 ña jsi nätci bāstāṃdä u garvā ą̄nāṃ ṣacū vāṣṭä paśāṃdä
109 ttāṃ hvą̄ṃdä si cu hvehva:rāṃ bą̄ḍi ye ttū hīya tcḭmañä dyāṃda si tti
110 tta gatcastä tta tta burṣṭä ⁓ cu hą:nä ṣṭe u hve:hvara ttyāṃ ri maṃ nę-
111 stä va diśḭ niśtä tsvava khu drų̄nä tsva hamāta tsūva tti tsva hamā-
112 va mihe ri āṃ amājā śirki viśų̄na ną̄ma ni nā yināṃ ⁓
113 khu hā ñaśä bīsä ką̄mäcū ttraṃdūṃ u khu vā niraṃdū drai-sse haupari-
114 paṃjsāsä va hvaṃḍä muḍa ⁓ khu ttuṃjeri māśti kṣḭmye haḍai ṣacū ttraṃdūṃ
115 pātcä vā nva hvaṃḍä ātä si hamidā va ssa paṃjsāsä hvaṃḍä muḍa
116 u paṃjsāsä jsāṃ jūṃdā bāstāṃdä cvaṃ va pā kīthi dūṃvāṃ stūrä
117 ya ttą pā biśä baḍä yuḍāṃdä ⁓ cu jsārä ttū jsāṃ bakä ką̄istä yu-
118 ḍāṃdä u ttū jsāṃ nä haṃdāḍä yuḍāṃdä ⁓ cu viña buhä:thuṃ bisä ttatta-

1-1 Subscript. 2-2 Del.

119 ra ṣṭāre tta pā dva drai jṳ̄na karattahä: u ḍyau-tcvi̥nä bvāstāṃḍä ⁓ cu sūha:cū

120 ā̧na ḍyau-tcvi̥nä buri maśpa ṣi̥ ttattarāṃ jsa basta līkä ṣṭe ⁓ ḍyau-tcvi̥nä ā̧na jsāṃ

121 aủdi ka̧mäcū yīpäkị̄nä ttahi: buri vara jsāṃ ttardāśāṃ ttūḍīśāṃ u

122 ttūrkä bayarkāvāṃ hīya buḍämacīya cū jsāṃ mistāṃ hva̧ṇḍā ttyāṃ hīya

123 jsāṃ hauva ja u ñāttarāṃ hīya hīya hauva pattīya u

124 [1]viña ri āṃ śūja̧ña vina haṃdrauysī murä haṃdarye hva̧ṇḍye haḍä tsṳ̄[1]ma

125 [1]niśtä[1] ⁓ cu ciṃga kṣīrāṣṭä haḍāṃ hīya mista nā̧ma u rrispūrāṃ

126 hīya nā̧ma ṣi̥ pa̧jsi haraṣṭa khu tta tta bādṳ̄na śūja̧ña ni samīṃ-

127 de nva̧śtira maṃ paṃda hīvī pacaḍä niśtä ka̧mäcū bisai maṃ aủrrāsä

128 hasḍä ṣaikä ye ⁓ khu jsāṃ vā ñaśä bīsä mara ṣacū āvūṃ u didye

129 haḍai ma kathi-rāysi[2] pyatsä bāste u tta

130 ttaṃ vā hvȩ si rrvīve vā maṃ vīrāṣṭä tta tta parau ā si khve ttā ka̧-

131 mäcū āṃ paḍä tsā āstaṃna haḍa hīsīṃde raysgi vīraṃ vā vāṣṭi

132 hajsȩma ⁓ u gūlai saṃgalakā va̧ vā tta tta parau pastāṃḍä si kūṣṭi

133 buri vā ciṃgvā bisā haḍa na ga̧sāṃde u parauve vā ni hīsī nä tsva

134 hama ⁓ khvaṃ vā parau hīśtä si cilakaṃ : ra maṃ mṳ̄ñā̧ñä ā khvaṃ tcerai

135 [3] × vā -au -ī[3] parau āṃ maṃ spāśūṃ

55

P 2745

1 || khva tta tta h [*bases of akṣaras*]

2 | || pvau ñā̧hauji maṃ māśca
tte khu tsvaudū ṣacū
parya vau ṣa jsā ma
[4]dvī-ssa pajsāsä[4]
pātcä haḍä | [1]mistanāṃ būrakye[1] ⁓

[1-1] Del.
[2] Large broken part avoided by scribe between *thi* and *rā*.
[3-3] Not clear and del.
[4-4] Suprascript.

hvaḍaudū ṣa ma khāysa
kṣīrä aủnä vaña būre
4 pau I se kṣaṣṭi ṣąmāḍä jsä[1]
ysīre byamā janai ⌢
vaña ñanā byamā pvaisū
5 I kīmaśanä ( )eyacä[2]
khu vā ysāvī [3]ka[3]maśanä
6 salī calakya parye I tvī ⌢
culakye māśca parye tvī
haḍau vī būrä haiysda vī ⌢
7 calalkä khāysa hvaḍai thā
calakä nvaiya paraustai
8 vaña vā raysga I vī gverä
khva ṣą byamā jīye ⌢
salī va jä drairä baista
9 māśca dvī-lsa haudā ⌢
haḍā dvī ysārä kṣaṣṭä
ttārä ttakyā māścā baiśä vī ⌢
10 I khāysa drairbista ysā haṣṭa-se
u pajsāsä hvaḍai aủdä vaña būre

56

P 2786

1 II pvaisū ttā janävai vīrāṣṭa : utvaḍarū mistą hvāṣṭą śū-
2 ra darau jsä ——

[*Space*]

3 : rrvī vī chū-bīrä vīrąṣṭä haṃdanāṣṭä aủrąsą hąṣḍä :
4 drvāttīrai prraumauhą ttathągattą śąrībądra [4]āstaṃną āṣą-
5 rya[4] u anä saṃgai āstaṃna gākṣā : khu ttā märä ṣacū aủ ttau-
ñaśa bīsa āśąryą
6 jaira māṣtą naumyai hąḍai ḫvāṃ śau-śū narädä : mä[5]ra[5] vą ttąle kämä-

[1] *se . . . jsä* del., with subscript *dase pajsāsa nvaiya.*
[2] First letter probably *c.*
[3-3] Subscript: read *kī.*
[4-4] Del.
[5-5] Subscript.

7 cū aů: thai-śī ā hatcä ṣacū-pavāṃ hvąṇḍāṃ jsä: kämacū bīsai
māśta dvāsąmyai haḍai
8 rä vä ttakyāṃ hadarä vyä hąḍä ną yai : phąrä vą̄ ttä ttä ājīdau-
9 da saṃ mistą hąnä mauḍä : u [ḍā] maṃgą̄rä hąnä hīyai pų̄ra naistą
10 bāḍa vä ną rä räysdyąi : cą vä thai-śī āstaṃnä ṣacū-pavä hąḍą
11 yą ttą hątcästą : marä ra vā ttūśā āvä : namaiśą ra jsā vą̄
12 hadarä pharä na dą̄śā hīśą : [1]ttī ttā brrakha[1] : ttī mä mąrä ṣa-
13 cū būkä āstaṃna dva pacąḍa hąḍa yą : cą vā marä mauñāṃ jsa
ca ttattāha
14 thyautta dāśauda hīsą : ttī jsā mä dva pacaḍa sīcū-pavä vą yą
15 cą vā mauñāṃ jsā thyauttä dą̄śauda hīsą : u śau pacąḍa jsā
16 astaṃ āvą u ttakä maṃ yą kämacū vāṣṭä tsūmädą̄ : ttī hą̄
17 ñaśą bīsą ḍīkau pyaṃtsą hąṣdä yūḍāṃdū sa mauñāṃ maṃ pąrau
18 rrvī ttą tta są caṃdau saṃ ąnvąśtai bāḍa hąmävai cą āśąrya ṣṭā-
19 rai caraumyai padī jsä tsva hąmādai tsīdä ḍīkau vą̄ vā pąrau
20 tta tta pastą są bījsättä bāḍa ṣṭai u kaṇą āśąryą ą-
21 vädāyą käśārai u rrvī vī vä jastūña ąysmya ysą̄rä hąmai
22 āravā hīśtą : pada hīyai habā na baustī āśą ąśtai kaiṇą
23 paśāvai : u ttī hā drai tcą̄ jū yāṃdä byauttaudū khu baiśą na
rrvī pąrau pvaistaṃdū
24 tsvą hamādai khu dva drayą tsvą hāmąrai[2] : ttī vā ḍīkau ñaśāṃ
25 bīsāṃ ttą ttą hvai są khu aůna bāysdąittą khalīvī vā padai-
26 myą sąmātta āśą ąvaṃdą̄yą kaśaudai cą vā rrvī jsa ārą
27 hīsīyai japha ąmą baḍa ḍīkau vą japha naiśta : khalavī
28 padaidaudū ąkṣara hagauṣṭä hā nīśaudū cą saṃ āra hągrrī-
29 hą̄ña hamāvai mihai bąraucāṃ parau ttai : ttau hvā sa āśąrya
marau ttąña
30 hastrīsīdā drāṃ hairä hūñīdä sa cą na dryāṃdä na jsā pyū-
31 ṣṭaudä : āśąryau jsa ttą ttą khąlīvī padaidai są khu ttrāṃ hairą
32 ⟨hū⟩ñāvä ca na drāṃda na jsā vījaiṣṭaudä : ttū vą̄ vā rrvī jsa
33 līnvā baiśą parī pajaiśtą ttā ṣṭau ttā pīrīdä hąjsādai
34 ca jsā sahauna kaiṇą parau yai khu hīsyąrä pūhyai hąḍai vąrī
35 jsāvai ṣą pā na tsvą ⟨ha⟩myai khu tta hąḍä ca uską̄ttą ṣṭārai u sąhau-
36 na u mājā drayą āśą gūśąṃdī thaiyą ttīkä : u baḍārī
37 prrąmauhą sagai[3] sīdą̄kąrucą u gūmättīraį āśąrī vīrąpau-
38 ña : brraṃkhaysdyą māṣṭą haṣṭų̄ṣąmyai hąḍä tsvāṃdä : są̄hacū aů
39 ttāką vā pā mūtcaicą māṣṭai yai hąḍai mąrä ñaśai bīsa gauśtą
bīsą pīḍakä

[1-1] Del. [2] Read *ha*°. [3] Corrected.

40 ā pīḍakạña vä ttạ ttai yai sạ : mạrä sạ̄hạcū āvädū : [1]ttạ ttạ pyu-
41 ṣṭaudū sạ ka mājā maṃ pīrạ̄kạ ttārä dvi[1] tta āśạu jsa ttạ ttạ
42 pyūṣṭaudū caigạ kṣīrä aů vā rạ̄jārīmai yạ̄gadarāyaṃ
tta-śī narada
43 naumä u mauñāṃ kaiṇạ pyūṣṭä sạ hạḍa vā hīsaṃdạ̄ ṣṭārai
44 [1]śāmā śaumä sāṣṭai khu vā pai[1] khu ra vā mihai sāhạcū ā-
45 vadū tta tta pyūṣṭau⟨dū⟩ sạ dasau vai haḍā hạmyai khu caigạ kṣīrāṣṭạ
46 tsvai salā mä tta ttä paśāvai a vạ vā pyatsāṣṭä hvạṇḍạ paśū
47 mauñāṃ [jsā] vīrāṣṭä jsā vā gūśạṃdī thaiyạ ttīkä nāgai-
48 dravạrrda : pīḍakä jsa pharä ttạ ttạ hajsādä [×] kamạcū maṃ
49 bāḍa śaikä ṣṭai khu tvā ṣạ pharä hīśtạ vạrī vạ̄ tsūva : ttū jsā
50 pīḍäkä kamạcū-pa yaṃgai [nī][2] chāra ttūvạ chāra ājīdauda
51 mūtcaicạ māśtạ dvāsạmyai hạḍai cạ vā gīryai-vạrā tsvāṃdä ttạ
52 aůdä cvāväja māśta mạra mūdauda : vaña būra ra vā [1][-airī][1]
53 pharä na āvä : ca yaṃgai chārä raiyai u ttūvä chāra naumạ
54 u maṃgāra sīcū-pavä ca masạ mạrä ṣacū yạ kạmacū
55 vāṣṭä tsvākä yạ tta cvāvạja māśtai baistạmyai hạḍai tsvāṃda
56 śaula aů narädä kvacū na dāśaina ttraima hada[va][3]ra vyạvạhā
57 [4][drāva a][4] kamacū bīsā drāvä āvạ hairä ysyāṃdä u tta hvā⟨da⟩
58 sa tsūva kamacū vāṣṭä ca pā ṣacū-pavạ tsvāṃda haṃtca mạ̄-
59 jā āśạu jsa samaurai āstaṃna hauda tta vā pā na rä hīsīda
60 phara ca ma pā tcau ttūau-ttau āstaṃna ṣacū bīsā hạḍa tsvāṃ-
61 da paisa hadyaja māśtai haḍa ttyāṃ hadara vya bīsai vạ̄
62 tcā yāṃ-yīkä naumạ śau ā mūtcaica mā[1]śtai pātca vạña cvāvạ-
63 ja māśta tsvai ttakyai kaiṇai jsā na baustaṃdū sa khu tsvai khu vạ̄
64 īṣṭạ pasa kāṣṭa khu tsvai ttyai hyạ vā pā pharạ na ra hīśtạ[1]
65 phara vā tta tta ājīda : cạ kạmacū hana ttai ṣạ ttạ ttạ hvai sạ khu
66 hā mihai haḍa paśāṃdū yạ mūñāṃ vä[kä][4] vā pā hạḍa hīsī-
67 ra u hai ca hā ṣacū-pavä tta ttä aůräṣṭauda sạ kạmacū vāṣṭa
68 va haḍa na īdä na [5]jsā[5] śkyaisạ u yạ̄ga-darāyaṃ nau-
69 ma va rājārīmai tta-śī yai ttyai hana pharākä haira hūḍai
70 hatca tcahaisyau kamacū-pavā bīsā sūlyāṃ jsā aůska-vaṃ-
71 dā u hana pyaṃtsạ ṣạ ttayạ-śī ttạ hvai sạ a vā sījsī-
71a [*interlinear*] caiga kṣara tsvai ca śahvā na hīsīdä ——

1-1 Del. 2 Not clear. 3 Blurred *va*.
4 Blurred. 5-5 *jsā* over *tca*.

72 ja māśta hīsū kamacū mājā vā pā phara būḍai

[*Space*]

73[1] || rrvī vī chū-bīrä vīrāṣṭä hadanāṣṭä aủrāsạ haṣḍä :
74 drvāttīrai prramauha ttathāgattạ śạrībadrä ñaśa bīsạ ạna
75 sagai āstaṃna āṣ̱aryạ gākṣạ̄ : khu ttā mạrä ṣacū aủ ttaujairä
76 naumai hạḍai hvạ̄ṃ śau-śū narāda : mara vā ttāle kamạcū aủ māśta
77 dvāsạmyai haḍai : thai-śī ạ̄ hatcä ṣacū-pavāṃ hvạṇḍāṃ jsä : kạ
78 rrvī vī ——

[*Space*]

79 —— chū bīrä vīrāṣṭä hadanāṣṭä aủrāsạ haṣḍä
80 ca ma pā thai-śī ttai ṣạ ma pāna ra jsāvai ttạ ttạ aủ mä hūñī-
81 da kūṣṭạ būrai vā kamacū aủ hvạṇḍa na hīsīdai sạ mạrä
82 ma kamacū bāḍa raṣṭä tsa vā na jsāvai khvại vā sạ ł hvai hīsī-
83 yai sa kamacū mä bāḍa raṣṭä tsa vā vạrī sa jsāvai ñaśa pạ̄
84 bīsạ ādara łnau khu hatcạ tsvạ hạmạ : ——

[*Space*]

85 [2] : rrvī vī chū-bīra vīrāṣṭä hadanāṣṭa aủrāsạ haṣḍä : drvāttīrai
86 prramauhạ ttathāgatta śạrībadra ñaśạ bīsạ ạna saṃgai āstaṃna
87 āṣ̱arya [×] gākṣạ̄ khu ttā mạrä ṣacū aủ ttāṃjairä māśta
88 naumyai haḍai hvāṃ śau-śū narädä : mara vā ttāle kamacū aủ mā-
89 śtạ dvāsạmyai hạḍai [3]hyạ̄ṃ śau-śū nạ[3] ——
90 thai-śī ā hatcä ṣacū-pavā hvạṇḍāṃ jsä kamạcū bīsai ra
91 vä ttakyāṃ hadara vya haḍa na yai : phara vā ttạ ttä ājī-
92 daudä sạ mistạ hanä mauḍa : u magāra hana hīyai pūrä
93 naistạ : bāḍa vä na ra rạysdại ca vä thai-śī āstaṃna ṣạcū-pa-
94 va haḍä yạ tta hatcạstạ mara vā ttūśā āvä : namiṣ̱ạ
95 ra jsā vā hadara phara na dāśā hīsạ : ttī maṃ mạrä ṣacū
96 [3]būkacạ ttāttā[3]hạ āstaṃna haḍa yạ dva pa⟨ca⟩ḍä : ca vā mạ-
badạ
97 ra mauñāṃ jsa paḍā dāśaudä hīsạ : ttī jsā mä dva pacạḍä
98 sīcū-pavạ yạ cạ mä pā mauñāṃ jsā thyauttạ dāśaudä
99 hīsạ : u śau pacạḍa jsā vā ạsta āvä ttạkạ mä yạ kạ-
100 macū vāṣṭä tsūmaṃdạ̄ : ttī hā ñaśạ bīsạ ḍīkau pyaṃtsạ hạ-
101 ṣḍä yūḍāṃdū : mauñāṃ maṃ rrvī parau ttạ ttä cada saṃ ạnvạstạ bā-
102 ḍa hamāvai cạ āṣ̱aryạ ṣṭārai cạraumyai padī jsa tsvạ hạ-
103 mādai tsīdä ḍīkauvāṃ vā tta ttä pastạ sạ bījāttạ bạ̄ḍa
104 ṣṭai kaṇạ āṣ̱ạ ạvaṃdāyạ kaśārai[4] : rrvī vī vạ jastūña ạ-

[1] =3–7. [2] =3 ff. [3-3] Del. [4] *ka* half subscript.

ysmyą ysą̄ra hamai āravā hīśtą : pada hīyai habā na baustī ą̄śą ąśtai kaiṇą paśāvai : ttī ñaśą bīsą rrvī parau pvaistaṃdū drai tcā jū hā yāṃdä byauttaudū . khu baiṣą na tsvą hamāṃdai dva drayą tsīdä : ttī vą̄ ḍīkau ñaśau bīsą̄ tta ttä hvai są khu aủna bāysdaittä : khąlavī vā padaimyąrä sa : khu ttä ą̄śą ąvaṃdāyą kaśaudai : ca vā rrvī jsä ārä naraumāvai : japha ąmą bąḍą : ḍīkau vä japhą naiśtą : khąlavī padaidaudū ąkṣąra hagauṣṭa hā nīśaudū : cą saṃ āra hagrrīhą̄ña hąmāvai : mihai baraucāṃ parauttai : ḍīkauvāṃ tta tta hvai są ą̄śąryą hąstrīsīda : drāṃ hairä hūñīda cą na dryāṃda na jsā na jsā pyūṣṭaudä : ttī mī ñaśą bīsą āśąryą jsa tta khalavī padaidaudū są : khu drau hairä hųñāvā cą na dyauda na jsā pyūṣṭaudä : ttū vą̄ vą̄ rrvī jsa līnvā parīdä pajaiśtą ttā ṣṭau ttā parīdä hąjsādai : cą jsā sahauna kaiṇa parau yai kha hīsyąrä pūhyai hąḍai vąrī jsāvai ṣą pā na tsvą hąmyai : khų ttą haḍa cą ųskāttä ṣṭārai : u sahaunä u mājā drayą āṣą gūśąṃdī[1] thayą ttīkä nāgaidravąrrda : u baḍą̄rī prraumauhą sąḍą̄kąrraucą u gūmąttīrai ą̄ṣąrī vīräpauña : sąmaurai āstaṃna hauda ṣacų bīsā caigą : brraṃkhaysdya māśtą haṣṭūsąmyai hąḍai tsvāṃda : sāhącū āvä vąra aủ vā gūśadī thayą ttīkä nāgaidravąrrdaṃ pīḍakä hajsādai u ñaśai bīsą gauśtą pīḍäkä ā : pīḍäkąña vą tta ttą yai są mąra sāhącū āvädū phaimä maṃ pīrākä ą̄ṣą ṣṭārai ttyau āśau jsä ttą ttą pyūṣṭaudū caigą kṣīrä aủ vā tta-śī naradä rājāraimī yą̄gaṃdąrāyaṃ naumä : u mauñāṃ kaiṇą pyūṣṭai hąḍa vā hīsaṃdā ṣṭārai : khu vā mihai są̄hącū āvädū dasau vai haḍā parya khu caigą kṣīrāṣṭä tsvai salā mä tta tta paśą̄vą a vä vā pyaṃtsāṣṭä hvąṇḍą paśū : mauñāṃ vīrāṣṭä jsä vā gūṣadī thąyą ttīkä pīḍäkä jsa pharä tta tta hąjsāṃdai sa kamäcū mä bāḍa raṣṭä ttai khu ttā mūnā ṣa śvą phara hīṣṭą vąrī vā tsūvä : ttū jsā vā pīḍäkä kamącū pa yaṃgai chārä u ttūvą chārä nau[×]mä hvąṇḍą ājīdauda : mūtcaicä māśtą dvāsąmyai hąḍai cą vā gīryai-varā tsvaudä : tta aủda cvāväjä māśta būrä märä

[1] ī and *ai* with *d*.

141 mūdaudą vaña būrä ra vā phara na āvä : cą ⟨yaṃ⟩gai chā-
142 ra u ttuvą chārä u maṃgārä sīcū-pavä cą mąsą
143 mara ṣącū kamącū vāṣṭä tsvākä yą : cvāvąja māśtai
144 baistąmyai haḍai tsvāṃdä śaulakä aủ narāda kvącū na dą̄-
145 śauda hīsą hadara vyą vą hā kąmącū bīsā sąna ā
146 haira ysyāda tta hvādä tsūvä kämącū vą̄ṣṭä : cą maṃ
147 pā tcau ttu-ttau āstaṃ ṣaca bīsā haḍa tsvāṃda pąisą haṃ-
148 dyaja māśṭai ttyau vā hadara vya bīsai ra vā cā yāṃ-
149 -yīką naumą śau ā mūtcaicą māśtai : u ttą ttä vā pharä ājī-
150 dai : ca mä ṣacū-pavä hatcästą : tta mä tta ttä hatcästą cä mi-
151 stą hana mauḍa u nūra jsā hauva na dāśai byaiha : cą mä ką-
152 macū hanāsa yai ṣą̄ magārä hana vąṣṭä bīsai yai : khu
153 vaña ttu aủską pada pęmaistai na jsā utca parauṣṭā : ca bā-
154 ḍa ṣṭai ttu tta ttaṃdī jsā khu thyauttä yai tsa ṣacū-pąvą hā-[1]
155 ṣṭäkä mä tta ttą hvādä cą kamäcų̄ bāḍa sūrai na ra hamai
156 ca ttrūkä bayąkąvą̄ āstaṃna nakąra bādauna ṣą̄ hąi-
157 rī kītha hana jsa na ra hagūjaidä : pātcä ttą̄ cvāväja
158 māśtą draisamyai hąḍai tcyauvä aṃmäga āstaṃna haḍa tsvāṃda
159 pajsä : ttakyau gauśtą jsā hā kamącū vāṣṭä pīḍaką hajsāda
ḍīkau
160 tta tta są : ca magāra ąmanā ttu rau pā ą na kūśū na pvai-
161 sūṃ khvai śaikä bāḍa kṣąmīyai cai ttą būnā hvąṇḍą ī̆dai
162 bęśąvā vāṣṭä yaśą śauttä sąna ąhaijä : ttī jsā caigą kṣī-
163 rāṣṭä padä prrahājä : cą jsā mä mąrä hanaśīyą caigą
dva pacaḍa
164 ṣṭārai u hvąṇḍą bāḍa raṣṭa hąmai hvąṇḍā vā hąysą pātcä ttą̄
165 varī tsą ṣą̄ka vā vąña pharä na ra hīsta ——

[*Space*]

166 ca ma pā thai-śī ttai ṣa mä pā na rä jsāvai ttą tta aủ mä
167 hūñīda kūṣṭa būra vā [2]jä[2] aủ hvąṇḍa na hīsīdai sa
168 mara ma kamacū bāḍä raṣṭa tsa vā na jsāvai khvai vā
169 sa ī̆ hvai hīsīyai sa kamącū ma bāḍa raṣṭa tsa vā vą-
170 rī sa jsāvai ñaśą pā bīsa ādara ī̆nau khu hatca[3] tsvą
171 hamau ——

[*different handwriting*]

172[4] || ñaśau jsā bīsau : parau tta tta yai : rrvī jsā aủ : caigą kṣīrāṣṭä na pa-

[1] *h* not clear, read *tsā*.
[2-2] Del.
[3] *tca* changed to *tsa*.
[4] =172–239=Or. 8212. 186, a7–b21.

173 rīdä vījaiṣṭä : cą pada ṣṭai ttyai hīyą aủ habā ḍīkau bauttai u
174 capastąkä khu ⟨pa⟩ḍā hīsyąrä : khu pada sū[1]rā[1] ṣṭāvai ḍīkau habā
175 bvāvai : ȋrä u haurä bvīysnaṃ hąmịtcī nauhyą hīsīyai
176 tta pārysā cą ttā rrvī vī hąṣḍä yūḍāṃdä są pārśąṃ u kṣą-
177 ma yūḍą cegą kṣīrä jsä ttyau kaiṇą parau ttą ttä yai caigą
178 kṣīra tsīda : khu mara āvadū ‿ kamącū vä bāḍa bīją-
179 tta yai : raijsai mä pada hīye tsūmą na yą : parau jsau
180 tta tta yai są : pada sūrā na ṣṭāvai pharākyau hvąṇḍā hī-
181 yai ravä pā kīrä naiśtą khvai jsā sa ṣacū ḍīkau capastąkä hū-
181a [*interlinear*] mara ma hīna bāyąmai hīyai kṣīra ṣṭe
182 ñīyai tta tta yąną pada hīyai aủ habā ttakä bvārai : ṣa-
183 cū ḍīkau tta hvai są cą pada hīyai habā ṣṭai ṣą ȋmą
184 aśa naiśtą svī hąmai : u vąña būrä haryadū : ca jsā vā
185 vaijalakä gauśtą : parau ā : ṣą jsā tta tta ṣṭä sa khu sa ḍīkau hū-
186 ñīyai tta tta yadä : [×] ḍīkau jsā ttą hvai są khu vā rrvī jsā
187 caiga kṣīrāṣṭä ȋra hīyą u haurä u bvīysna u hąmatcī
188 hīyą : mvaiśdąna haraṣṭä yą : ama pā hāysą tsāvę
189 mara jsā vīśąu naumä na hąmīyą : vąña ra ṣą rrvī śkyaisą cą
190 ma aśtą caiga kṣīrä na hīsīyai : ąma pā hāysą na tsvą
191 hamīryau : ca ttā āśąryą rrvī vī haṣḍä yūḍāṃda pārśąṃ
192 aủ kṣamä yūḍai caigą kṣīra tsau ttau vā ttaṃḍī[2] bąida cīvī-
193 ra yai ṣą jsā magāra tsvai : ca jsā ñaśa bīsą sagai ṣṭai ṣa
194 jsā vā pā haḍa hīyai nva padaja na tsvą hamyai tta tta khu
195 habụsaṃ : u rrvī parau hagrrautta yanīna : pęjsa hatcastą yai
196 hauvą hänasyąvą : ca jsā kamacū bāḍa ṣą jsā śaphī-
197 ḍa ṣṭai : ca jsā ranījai janavai hīye u ysarnai bāḍa hī-
198 yą nauma ṣą jsā mistą ttai khu tta pvąi tsvauñī hąmāvai khu sau-
199 hacū hīsau varau nvą bāḍa janavai hyai naumai kamacū hana
200 va : aủhąvāṃ vą u bīrūkau vä u miśtauryau hvąṇḍā vī bū-
201 rai cą sa thyauttą rrvī vī mvaiśḍą hagrrauttau tta ȋyai ttyau vä vą-
202 rī śkyaisą jsāva : tta tta khu thyautta yai : ñaśau bīsau hā hauvä
203 nasyaiyą : vaṣṭä vī ttā haṣḍä na darrvai yą bīsāṃ pa-
204 rau na kṣama hagrrauttai u āra baida hīsūṃ khu tta rrvī vī jastū-
205 ña aysmya tta tta ȋyai sa khu ṣą pada prrahīśta khu vā kamacū
206 vāṣṭä lakyai śkyaisa hīyą mvaiśdą haraysdąi ttī vä rrvīyą mvaiśḍą
207 na habū⟨sa⟩na ṣṭāvai : ttī [3]ma[3] pārysā yą ca ttä rrvī vī haṣḍä yūḍāṃ-

[1-1] Small *rā*, added. [2] *ḍī* over *ttī*. [3-3] Subscript.

dä sa caiga kṣīra tsāṃ parśą yanau : calā ṣīkau sagīna yai ṣą
āśį̄ yai u ṣaumaña paśāvai gākṣau brrā[1]vą[1]rāṃ jsä tsvai mārā-pyarau nāvai bąiśa parāvai haṣḍä yūḍai sa caigą kṣīra tsūą̄ mvaiśdą nāvä hāysą ttā tsvai ca mauthāle tcūha paḍä
rrvī vī haṣḍä yūḍai sa caigą kṣīra tsūṃ: chū-bīrä vīrāṣṭä hą̄
hagauṣṭa hūḍai rrvī vī ttā kabala hąiśū ssą khu caiga kṣīrą
na tsīnai : vīna ttakyai hadana yai ca salā na hamąistai
parau na pacai : mara aů pā hvai sa parau vä hagrrīhāña
ttai : cą būnīyaṃja kharaśau yai ṣą bīsakvā bīsai kadvaja yai u kadvajä aů thī u bvaiysya nāvai hāysą ttā tsvai cą būnīyaṃjya vaijalakä yai ṣą ī-
ra parāvai : u kūṣḍa[2] vīrai bastauda u japhai āṣṭaṃdą
hamau japhai ra na hamyai u mvaiśdą hagrrauttai u gaisāttą̄
ca dārakau paḍa-tcaina yai : ttu hvą̄ṃ tcaisyau bīysīyai
tta tta sa mūnai bīsa ttą haṣḍä ttā yūḍa sa caigą kṣīra tsū khu bīsa na hamūṃ u tcaina ma jsā vā yai hamyai dasau kūsai gubąi raiyai hīyāṃ stūrau bąida u drai
māśtai tcaina ma mūñą̄ [ñā] yai rrvīyą ysīḍai parau hīyą mvaiśdą hagauttai gąisāttā ca drūyāṃja kairä ḍai-sai
yai ttyai kaiṇa ttā u jsa drūyāja haṣḍä yūḍāṃdä
tta tta sa cada hana paḍa-tsā ądā yūḍai ṣų̄ra drai jū
ttya[3] [4]ya[4] ḍa īḍai : paḍa-tsā jsä tsāṣṭą bīdaudū ḍai-sai jsa aůna byaihau rrvī jsai caigą kṣīrāṣṭa pastauda naiṣkaiśtai khu ttyau drū-
yājä adā jīyai : gąisāttā : ca badäle hīyai pū-
ra yai mvąkale naumä ttyai rrvī vī va[5]rāṣṭa drai śvakyaina japha yai
mvaśdą hagrrauttai u gęsāttā ca hagīñai khara pąinakä yai
ttyai hā tcā salī aů parau hamyai tta tta sa cąga kṣīrai tsūñī hąmai parau pyūṣṭai gaisāttā khu vā kamacū rrvī śkyaisa hyī mvaisḍą
na habūsana ttāvai khu vā ttyau pā jsā hīyą mvaiśḍą hąraysdai cą va rrvī parau hagrrīhāmivai haira tsīyai śūjai
bąida samaiyāṃ ādara yanau khu rrvī parau dara hamai
ttakä hvąṇḍą cą mä mara īdä : tta draumä ṣṭāvai khvaṃ ra hā [hī][3]
rrvīyai mvaiśdą jsä ḍīkau śā dvī māśtą śai śau pamūhą na hūrīyai
bāḍa [4]vīrāṣṭä ttā pąijsa mista viśų nauma jsāvai[4] ——
ttyāṃ pęjsa mistą kṣārma haysdą ttai : cą vā vāṣṭä tsvaudä tta vā

[1-1] Subscript. [2] *ḍ* over *ṭ*. [3] Not clear.
[4-4] Del. [5] Small *va*, added: read *vī*?

243 jairmā stūrau jsä tsvaudä : ca vä pabauna yai ttu jairmāṃ stūrau vą
244 pīhą hūḍāṃda : na ra ma stūrä ąśtą na bąida pamūhą
245 ca ma jīttai u brrāvä na tta caiga kṣīrāṣṭä ka kīrä na tsīda
245a [*interlinear, from ka of* 246] kya kaiṇa ḍīkau tta hūña sa
246 tta tta patta ttārai : ca jsā chvaṃ la ttai u sagąlakä tta jsā
247 stāna vaṣṭā hamāvai ‸ ca jsā caigą hvailā ttai

[*Space*]

verso

248 ṣą jsā aủna aspaura caigau bauttai na jsā hvaṇau bau-
249 ttai [1]na khu[1] vąñāṃ ttā rrvī vī ñąnararthā haṣḍä yą-
250 nai khu āra będa na hīsū haṣḍä vā [2]cūḍa[2] na īḍa
khu

57

P 2787

Śrī Viśą Saṃgrāma

1 ‖ sedhaṃ

2 vaysña ra hama-hauvą hamīryāṃ bįśa āśąryä ttų vą tcųtta. padī avą-| śerṣṭyā gāṭhāṃ dharma-śravaṇīyi.

3 cū būra vāṣṭa ūsahyāda ttye namāṃ gabhīra | paramārthą dūkha
4 [3]ja[3]ne ttrrīyąṇį nīr⟨v⟩āṇaka lakṣaṇa bąiysāṃ dąyvāje sājāmai | kęṇą bąiśa ra ttā sarvasattą ūysnaura vara maittra aysmū vasvąjīryāṃ
5 śai namau | jastā bąiysāṃ baudhasatvā devavau parvālā hīyai ū
6 pārasadyāṃ hīyai | ttā bvaijsąi gūṇa ṣahāna byāva yanīryąṃ.
7 ttaña pacīḍa ra gāṭhā dharma-śralvaṇīya tta hvāñara sa bąiysa ārva
8 jsąmanai : dā ārva tsvąmanai ‖ bīsaga | ārava tsāmanai :

cū drraina raṃnąna ārava tsvāṃdū : ma na ttā drrąyvā mįśtą
9 avālyvā ysatha na nāsąmanai vīnau prraṇąhaunau :
10 tta hvāñara dā khū ṣṭā vaysña mahai | ttū namauna gabhīra bęysāṃ dą pvāmanai
11 ttā būrai harbīśāṃ sarvasatta ūysnaurau | hastara avaistaivīnai
12 haura hvarau vīra pūṣa paśau sąna jvai na maññā na vīhīlā | dasāṃ maiśtā baśdąṃ jsa pathīsāṃ. dasau ra maista śalai samādāyī varttāṃ

[1-1] *na khu* deleted. [2-2] Deleted with *khu* subscript.
[3-3] Subscript.

13 drrai-pa|dya ttaradararna tcā̮-padya bīṣ̮āna . drrai-padya aysmūna
14 khū na[2] paḍāna hvāṃdū tta śe̮|na tta daina ūvai .
tta hvā̮ñara sa khū ṣṭā vaysña mahai ttye namāṃ gabhīra paramārtha
15 ba̮ilysāṃ dā [1]pvāme[1] k̮eṇa̮ ttu parāhi̮ nāṃdū
16 tta sabajī ttyāṃ pūñā kūśala-mulyä jsa khū | ma ra satsaira tsā̮manai
17 ma na ttā raṣṭa-haspyīsākyau avarajsa-bvā̮myau . sabūttyāṃ | pīsau
kaḍā̮ṇamaittrāṃ jsa hāysa na kaśā̮manai ma ttā be̮ysūña aysmū
18 panā̮śā̮|manai ma mvaiśda ū ma prraṇa̮hauṇa̮ ttū ra ttā jsā gabīra
19 paramārtha be̮ysāṃ dā bīśvā | bāḍvā bīśvā̮ ysathvā̮ āryāma̮ittrai jasta
20 be̮ysa paḍauysā̮ña jsa ttarṣṭaṃdā sau|mūhāṃ jastāṃ be̮ysau jsa ⌢
21 be̮ysūñuā parṣatta-maṇḍalvā ṣṭāna pītcīra pīchaṣṭū pyalṣṭa yāḍa yinā̮-
mā̮nai ū vyachai vamasyai bīśū vara aùna habīrāṃdai kṣautta būma
22 | pāraumai ū baudhadharma habaḍa āvana be̮śa sarvā̮satta ūysnaura
23 ysamaśadya be̮lysa hamāṃdai tta pā hamīḍaka gā̮ṭhā dharma-śravaṇī̮-
24 ya avīrmāttama be̮ysā|na be̮ysūśta bausta hamye hamaumanai ||
25 brrāhma̮ cūtta[vī]ra-vīdha pauṇya̮ kalpa sva|rga prrimādyattai ||
26 asakṣaittram asapūauṇyi bā̮hyana bījana yathā bīja 30 || | ɨ paiśā̮ mara
27 dīśa̮ vīdaśa̮ haṣṭa āvā̮ḍa̮ vaisthārya va pīrmāttama naṣi̮rīma | vasva
brrūñadā rrustäḍa klaiṣ̮īnā va pahaiṣṭa pasvaṇa̮ pavana nīhāra dūma
28 ṣkā̮|myai vasvaiyai
29 dharma-dhā̮ttīnai ākāśa-maṇḍāla harāysa vī [×] ga̮isadai haba|ḍai
māśta vīra habaḍai pūra hīyāṃ bvaiyāṃ jsa ūtvaḍarūttara brrūñadā̮
30 avachvasa|dā[3] ysūṣka śadā̮ va ttīśa saubhā̮ma[4]-kāyīnā va maṇḍā̮la
31 vamā̮na ysā̮ryai brrū|nyai nara[va]māṇä kāyījyā bvaiyyau jsa kūla sa-
32 ysairvā cā̮vadīvā̮ mahākā|raṇijyā sa-ysairyāṃ bvaiyāṃ jsa harūñā̮mai
33 jsa aharīnaka̮ anāstana kālä | bāḍa jaḍīnai adā̮kāra natcīphāka jasta kṣīra
34 vadā̮va ū bā̮dhakṣaittra vadā̮vau | nījsāñāka ba̮iysāṃ dāva hvā̮ñāma vīnai
35 aùrmaysdauna sauñā̮ma ṣṭai . śai-kū mīḍāṃ | jastä hīyai ājaṣi̮ nama-
36 drrū̮na dastana dạsau dīśa̮ vīra āṇaṃdyāṃ ttairṣṭadāṃ | saumūhāṃ
jastāṃ ba̮iysāṃ baiśa-pīrmā̮ttamyai aùttapa̮tta pūjāpasthāṃ ha̮iṣ̮ā̮mai
37 | ūdāśāya ⌢
38 ttūṣyi̮ bhavaña ā̮ṇādai śākai māhā̮dharmarā̮ja ācairrai[×]-prrā|pttai
āryāmaittrai baudhasatva paḍauysā̮ña jsä baiysairāṃ baudhasatvāṃ
39 nā̮rāṃ | paḍauysā̮ña jsa pūña bvā̮mavīnāṃ va hajsā̮mā ūspaurāṃ
40 prracaina būmā pā|rā̮māṃ vasvattai ke̮ṇa śakrra brramhāṃ tcā̮ryāṃ
41 läkapā̮lā jsa āstana ranījai ja|navai vī bīsāṃ ū [5]ranī[5] baiysāṃ ṣ̮ā̮śa̮

[1-1] Subscript. [2] Read *tta*. [3] Subscript *va*. [4] Read °*ga*. [5-5] Del.

42 hīyāṃ ką̄kāṃ āysdarāṃ daivattāṃ parvālā I grahavadatta nāvauna
43 rrūṃda paḍą̄ysauña jsa haṣṭūsa ysāryāṃ śāsäbhaiprrasanau I nāvauna
rāṃda būḍara masūña ūṣ̨a hūṣą̄ñą̄mai ūdaśāya
44 cū būra mara I maistyai ranījai janavai vīra āś̨a śadya āstaṃna asada
45 gūną̄ asada vīvālva asada ṣvai gārīya gą̄rīya-gą̄ra amagalīya-vadya hīra
46 śvą tcą̄ma śalarba : I pyatsą̄ṣ̨ta vaska baraijā bījaivāką ūpagāṃttaka
47 prracą̄ hajsą̄iṣ̨ta prrattaiṣ̨ta vastya ṣ̨tāṃdai I ttyāṃ vyachą̄mi parą-
varttą̄mai naṣą̄ma hīrą̄ña ūdaśāya : ūtvaḍaryai jsa marą ranījai
48 I janavai vīra rą̄ysanaunda ysara-gą̄ttyai tcą̄hauryą̄ lākąpālyāau jsa
49 āysdą̄ḍa : rą̄ysą̄yaṃ I baida : aúṇą̄ṃdai ysaraspūlyai rana-daśtą̄ttyai[1]
50 dajvanyai śāhauja dīna . śąkrrą jastą̄na I rūda mą̄ñada śaryai jsa
51 brrų̄ñadą̄va ttīś̨a pūhye lākapāla mą̄ñadū ysarnai bą̄ḍa ū I ranījai
janaivai vī āysdą̄rai : śī-kū śrī vījītta sagrāma rāṃdą̄na rāṃda ūvāryai
52 I jastūñai bvaiysyai ttrąvargyai jsīña paba ūskhäjsāmai ūdaśą̄yä .
53 ca būrai va ḡyasta ḡyalstūñai byaihą vīra . ḡyastuñai ttaradara baką̄
54 misai ṣ̨tą̄na āchai āstaṃna pīla ūpadrralva hīra hajsaiṣ̨tä prrattaiṣ̨ta
55 vastyą ṣ̨tādai khvą̄i harbaiśa vyachą̄mai paravarttą̄mai naṣą̄lma hīryą̄ña
vīra tsīdai kūṣ̨ta ranye ṣ̨tį̄di ūtca māhą̄samą̄drra myą̄ña ūskhastą
56 tcūra I rana ḵvaiysą nadyāṃ ūpanaṃdyāṃ ną̄vą̄nyāṃ raudyāṃ bastä
57 biną̄va pūra aúrmą̄ysdą̄na 30 I haṣ̨ṭi ya ma thai strīyastrīṣ̨ą̄na katha
58 khą̄rą̄va ttīṣ̨ą ḡyasta-bhävanyāṃja ttairṣ̨tasau[2] mala I ttraikha sūmīra
59 gärą̄nä rāṃda ttaira haraysä baidä pą̄rīyą̄ttaką̄bhidhāṃ ra jastūñe I
bahi̧ kalpāṃdāṃtta dai jsa apą̄itcą̄tta ṣ̨tą̄na mūñīyai . ū pauṇḍyi̧-kabala-
60 śaila īljījainai āysa baida va śakrrą ḡyastą̄na rai ḡyastuñai gą̄i jsa
61 pą̄ijsa ṣ̨tą̄na ḡyastų̄ñe saulhi̧-sapatta śarą̄ varą̄ś̨āvai ttā būrä marä
62 ranījai janavai vīra : śaina-kūna mi̧ḍāṃ jälstä śrī vīṣ̨ą sagrą̄ma hīyi
63 ṣ̨ą̄ cakrravarttą̄na rāṃdą̄na śärā brrūñīyai harbīśaivā I dāśvā dīśvūą̄
ḡyastä bą̄iysä tta tta ayīṣ̨ṭyādai khū tvā ranīja jänava dāna dīryai
64 yūḍą I īdä jaśtä rīñāṃ raispūrāṃ rraiysdyų̄rāṃ ttyau pāsa harbīśvą̄
65 bāḍvą̄ śarā tsą̄ṣ̨ṭą̄ drrūnā I bę̄maną̄ hamāvai mara ranījai janevai vīrä
66 śaryai dīryai myānī ysamaśadai harbīśāṃ dālyau barījāṃ sījāmai
sabają̄mai ūdaś̨āya :
67 ī pą̄iś̨ą̄ṃ mara āysñä gabhīrą paramārtha I bą̄iysāṃ dą̄ hvą̄ñāma ṣ̨ṭai :
kauma ṣ̨ą bą̄iysāṃ dā cū kūla nayū sa-ysairyāṃ pūrau aúrmaysdāṃ
68 I hīvī ttīś̨ana ūtvaḍarūttama brrūñadą̄ vamą̄na ttīś̨a śauma tcīra par-
69 bīra ysaunastyai ysa-lgų̄nya chai jsa vīvadāva avachūsadą̄vą dyaumai

[1] Read *-nyai*. [2] Read *dau*.

70 śrīvatsa māhā-pūraṣa-lakṣạnyau jsa ūlsphīsaryāṃ bvaiyau jsa pyaṣṭi
71 vajrrāysa ttīśạna dīga[ga]vạlyā jastāṃ bẹysā hīyai aủṣṭīlnāṃ vairyai
dadīnai kīśụka jsa ysạnastä ttūrīnai vīysa spūlakạ haṣprrīsaumai jsa
72 ṣị ganāyai | śauva-hamara aikaraysä gụstya ūysạnai mahākaraṇā-
73 naiṣanä naravạnāṣṭä bāyālmava ṇạista dūkhīnai ttāvạna naṣmāvā
74 ūysdaimākä asada drraiṣṭīyīnai pāttạla pahvạiñālkä drrạmyai mī ạnyai
bẹysāṃ dạ hvāñāmai bāvaumai haharkya pārajsyai jsa jasta bạiysa[1]
75 kūla sai-lysairrvā cạvadīvụạ sarvạkạrä vara jñānīnai maula pechvạmẹ
76 jsa ysạnastä avīrmạttama bẹlysūña dạya rạśta ahavạśdạ ū kṣyāṃ
77 pārạmvā jsa hūbastye narvạkalpa-jñānīnai ttāva jsa ttū | ysaira anạhạ-
ysamaśadai drraiṣṭīyīnai brrīvīnai ysathīnai jaḍīnai vạma jsa habaḍa
78 ūsphīlsaradạ ūtcyai drraiṣṭīyīnyāṃ daga-rakṣaysyāṃ jsa panādai
79 klaiṣīnyāṃ karyau bharṣyāṃ ttamattamagallā prrạṇā jsa ājaraista
haraysa-ūtcyāẹ drrai-padya aisīnai padäna navīsa tcạryāṃ tcaica
80 | vīsārai satsạrū māhāsamūdrrä myạña ūsphīsadai ttyai vū aủ nara-
81 vauṇḍūā āspara vīra | pārīphīda kūṣṭạ ạ va dạkhau panamạme hīyai
82 ūpāvana bīdai ⌢ tta tta mī ṣị avamāva-lbvaijsại bạiysāṃ dā ṣṭai
ca āṃ ttā [ttyai prra] hamīḍaka dharma-śravaṇīyāṃ hālaina ū ttyai
83 prralvạrṇajai ṣava vīra ūysdīśai hamai :
84 śai-kū miḍā jasta śrī vīśạ ⟨sa⟩grạma vā rai pīlrūyvā ysathvạ ttair-
ṣṭadāṃ sạmūhạu ğyastau bạiysau pyātsä ṣṭānä garkha vaistharya
85 prraṇihālna pastai baśti sa kaumvạ kṣịrañvā janavụạ ttye śākyamạna
86 ğyastä bạiysa hīyi ṣạ śāśạ[ña]lña vamạnīji bvẹyi ñāpaca ľye :
87 aysa vara prraṇihaunyau jsa rạysạyiña raudau | gūttaira vī ysatha
ū⟨pa⟩patti dyāñīme kaumye agäjsä ṣạ śạṣạ thūrsī ttakye ttakye agänai
88 a | padairū :
ttai prraṇihaunä jsa saijạme vī tsvāṃdi .
89 ū mara ranīṃje janave vīra ttū ūvālra raudāṃ byehị pastai ahạvạysye
90 vaña ra jsạnä aủṣkājsī dāvīnai ttaradara byehaume | vaskä pūñīje
ttīma pīrạnāme ūdaiśä ttū brrāṃhị pauña-kūśala-mūla kaiṇi ttū
91 vịlṣṇa-vakrrārma sakhāra kītha kärạnū vara mạñadi pastai ūśrīvye
92 ľyādve namadrūnä | jsai drrayā ranāṃ hālainạṣṭä pastai añạyai ū ttū
93 pīrmạtta tcạ-padya brrāṃhi pauña-kūśalla-mūla pastai haṣkāde aśtai
94 jsa āṃ śau kälpa brrahma-kạyvạ jastvā jastụña sauhị-salpattä śarạ parī
varaṣṭe tta tta rai ra śāstra hvāñạma ṣṭai sä brrạhmạ cūttāra-vīdha
95 pūṇyä kälpa svalrga prramūdyattai : sa brrāhmä tcạ-padya pauña-

[1] Subscript *ysa*.

96 kūśala-mūla ṣa̮ikä hamai cū sakha̮rma ārña̮na I padīme *ū* prravaiyāṃ
vaskä nvaśtä vīśtä ca ttye nara̮kṣi̮va ṣṭa̮na parī vaskä haspīsīdä ⁓
97 be̮lsa būspājä padīmīdä maittra āstanä tcaura aprramaṇä ja̮ye ū pa̮iṣkai-
98 stye bīsagä hama-lhauśte padīme ṣi̮ ma tca̮-paldya brra̮hmä pauña-
kūśala-mūla :
99 ū baudhasattä jastä ttū tcau-paldya brrāhmä pūña-kūśala-mūla
100 pastai haṣkāṃdai vaña jsāṃ aůṣkaujsī dāvīnai haura hūrāmai I ūdaiśa :
ttyai prrava̮rṇajai ṣa̮va vīra āysña gabīra be̮ysāṃ ḍā pastai ājaṣi̮
101 ttyai āṃ I da̮vasta cara̮ jsa vainīyau narava̮ṇāṣṭa padāva nījsāṣṭa II
60 II
102 prrava̮rṇa cī ṣa̮ I salā ṣṭe ṣi̮ cū harbeśe asadye jsä pathakä ū harbaśai
103 jsa pyatsa̮ṣṭa vaska namadrūna : I āṃ tta̮ prravārṇa hvīdai :
khvāṃ tta tta byamā mā hamāvai sa saittyai aů va prravāraṇa jsa cī
104 ṣa̮i I hāva hamai ū cūḍai ttī jasta be̮ysa ttāṃjairañā māśca pasta añāyai :
105 harbīśāṃ drabāḍvāṃ I jastāṃ be̮ysa tta tta padajä ṣṭai sa khū
106 be̮ysa̮na be̮ysūśca bva̮rai paña hala-māśca drrayi I ūsava haḍa̮
paraihīdi :
107 aṣṭai ū ca̮daśa pajai⟨śa̮⟩ ttī jsāṃ pajāṃ dāyau ṣaumañāṃ kīlrāṃ
ke̮ṇa drrai ma̮śta varṣa̮vāysa añāyida ū daśaina hāvāṃ ūdäśāyä ṇa̮istyai
108 valṣa̮vāysa [añāyī] pajaiśa̮ hadạ̄ vī prravārṇa añāyida
109 khū pā śākyamūna jalsta be̮ysa tvā avīrmāttama be̮ysūśta bāstä ṣa̮
110 pā pīrūyau jastāṃ be̮ysāṃ hīyai paldaji nvaiyi anavarttame̮ ūdaiśa
111 ttä drraya ūsava haḍa̮ pasta prrañavyai ū saijsījañā I māśta a̮na a̮da
ttāṃjairañā māśta būrai drrai māśca vaṣa̮vāysa pastāṃda nakṣa̮ttai
112 ū daśailna hāvāṃ ūdaiśa̮yi prravārṇa pasta añāye : paḍa̮ysa jsa hāva
113 ṣe̮ka hamaica I jsa bīsaga hama-hau hamai ū hama-hauva ṣṭāna dāya
114 ṣāmañāṃ avaśa-käraṇīya I kīra pa̮ijsaimīdä ⁓
śai va jsāṃ hāva ṣe̮ka hamaica jsa bīsaga hama-hauvyai śairyai jsa
115 hūṣa I jsāvai tta tta cū hama-hāvyä bīsaga pārajsyai jsa śa̮śa̮ña parūṣka
116 byahi̮-vīyi dharma ca I jsa prravaiyi be̮ysa-pūra śa̮śa̮nasthva najsaḍa-
117 nūna harga tsīda̮ tta naṣi̮ma̮rai ūvāra śa̮śa̮lsthvā bva̮ijsai jsa hūṣa tsīda
tta tta mī bīsaga śarai jsa haphattā dyāña :
118 śa̮ va jsa hāva ṣa̮lka hamaica jsa bīsaga nvaśtä sūha̮jä a̮mai jsa
119 pārajsyai jsa prraha-jana āśa̮rya palrī vaska haspīsavä parīyastanajsyā
120 samāha̮nyāṃ jsa tcarkya īnārai ca vasva-aysmva vīlnīyā hamādai khu
121 ttye bīsagi hīya haspīstya kūśala-pakṣa śairka carya pā pvārai I tta hā
aysmū vasvattā byaihīdä vasva-aysmū hamādä ttā ××× aysmū vas-

122 vattā | hūṣa jsāve akṣā̮rmarādāṃ paudgalā kūysdattā̮ byaihīdä
123 ū ṇīhīśa hamārai pa | /// hajanai jsa haphū pūñūda śarā sa*n*ā *n*vaśta
124 sūhi̮ja āmai hamai ū sanālña anamāna sīravā̮ anamāna pārajsyai jsa
125 dasama jsa hāva ṣa̮ika hamaica jsa ba̮ilysā śāśa̮ dā̮ra-ṣṭūka hamai : tta
126 tta mī ttyāṃ daśaina hāvau ūdaiśāyi jasta ba̮iysä prralvārṇa pasta
añāyai ttī vī cūḍa pajaiṣ̮ä haḍā vīra pasta añāyai ttyai prracaina
127 cū | ṣa̮ pajeśä haḍā̮ harbīśāṃ dāyāṃ ṣaumeñā kīrāṃ yinā̮mai vaska
128 p*ā*rṣa magalīlya ttyai prracaina pajaiśa̮ haḍā̮ vīra pasta añāyi . .
129 paḍā̮ysä vā prravā̮rṇa jasta | ba̮iysa vā̮rā̮ṇasem prravāryai raṣavadaña
130 bāśa̮ aù mrragadā̮pä davā̮ña pūña pacā | āśa̮ryāṃ āyīma dā̮yī dharma-
131 cakrra āra ba̮iśä khvai naravā̮ṇvai śarai vīra pārā̮ttai ilḍai . ttī mī hatsa
pacāṃ āśa̮ryāṃ jsa paḍāysä prravārṇa pasta paijsādai . .
132 śa̮ vā̮ prravālrṇa gajāśairṣa gara vī aùna pastai paijsādai ā̮rbala kā̮śava
133 āstana ysā̮ra jaṭala | brramana khva prravā̮sta iḍai ttī gajā̮śairṣai gara
134 vīra ā̮na drrayau prrahālyā jsa gra vā̮śi̮ | ū naravauṇvai śarai vīra
135 pārā̮ttai vara ā̮na ysā̮ryāṃ arahadyāṃ ba̮iṣṭyā jsa ṣa̮ prravārṇa | pastä
paijsādai . .
dīdä prravārṇa strrīyastrrīśvā jastvā̮ ā̮na pasta paijsādai khū maira
136 g̮yalśtä rrīña mahāmāye dā̮ ūysdīśai :
137 tcūrma vā̮ prravā̮rṇa jasti ba̮iysä jattavaña ālnä pastä paijsāṃdai
khvai vaska anāthapeṇḍī bīsa-dā̮rai sakhāra padaide :
138 pūhi̮ vā prravā̮lrṇa śū̮ra bīsä-dā̮rai bīśa ā̮nä pastä pa̮ijsādai :
139 kṣa̮ima vā̮ prravā̮rṇa vairaṇä aùva aùna̮ | pastä pa̮ijsāṃde khvai
vaska vairaṇai brramāna mattrai :
tta ttä mī ttyā̮na āstäna g̮yasta be̮ysa :
140 | sparatcahaisa prravā̮rṇa pasta pa̮ijsādai :
141 astämāysa vā̮ prravārṇa vailagrā̮ma ā̮nä | pasta pa̮ijsāṃdai :
tta tta mī kūṣṭa kūṣṭa jasta ba̮iysä tvā pārṣa prravā̮rṇa pasta
pe̮jsāde . .
142 | . . vara varä avamā̮ye ysamaśadai satvāṃ sauhi̮ śarā hūḍai ha̮dāra
143 satvāṃ avā̮yau jsa gūlvai hvī̮yai ga̮i vīra pārauttai hadā̮ra vā̮ satsā̮ranä
144 gū̮ve ū vasveye aysmū pārajsyena g̮yastaulñe ge̮ vī ysatha ūpapattä
naudä ||
145 hadara vā narvā̮ṇva śarā vyachāṃdä khvai ttä ttä ñāpa̮i pīrūlye
ñā̮pa tta drai ṣṭāṃ tta nai ñā̮pai :
kauma ṣa̮i yai iyai cū ma garkhyāṃ vaisthāryau puñāṃ kūśala-
146 | mūlyāṃ pārajsye jsa bala-cakrrävarttā̮na śarā dāra byauda i :

147 ttī hạdä hadarrvā kṣīrañvā | parauyä vīśćāme ke̮ṇa ū rāja-śāstra
148 vya̮sthā ārysdaje dara dījsāme ka̮iṇa : vaṣṭä | vī gajsa prrāṇāva hamya
149 ī : ttu̮ a̮ya̮ysä drayāṃ ranau panaka raṣṭa̮ dīśe̮ ī namạna- | jse̮ra ānai ṣa̮
150 asaida kīra ttagalaka hīrāña vī tsve ī : ū bakalakye asadye kīra | hīvī
harī varāśa̮ṃca ṣṭa̮ṇa̮ prravāraṇaja paiśa̮ vasvava aysmū ṣṭa̮na jsī paśāva
151 ī | u ttu̮ṣva̮ jastvā ysatha ūpapatta na̮va ī ūsta jsāṃ a̮rya̮maittrī g̮yas**tä**
152 b̮ai**ysä**[1] ××× ⟨vyā⟩|raṇa byauda īye ba̮iysūśca̮ṣṭä :
153 ttūvau aùnāṃ pīrūya pūrva-ya̮ga ××××× | dharma-śravaṇīyi aysmū
154 ñānarthe ke̮ṇa dada masū āstañāmanai hvāña̮māṃ vaska | tta̮ : ||
155 | || tta yathānūśru̮ya̮ttai . cūttara-śatta-varṣa : paravarttai : baudh-
156 yāṃ ba̮gavau bālhūlaka-vaṣäye : rra̮ja̮bhūtta̮ cadra kaṇaiskā naumä
157 parasainya̮vardhī būdhana | bagavattā vya̮krratta īttä vaiścaraṃ :
158 tta tta aù vā pyūṣṭi hamyi hamä sa khū jasta ba̮iysa | paranairvye
ttaña hadrra vya ssa salī parye ttana ka̮lna bāhulaka-vaṣayä ttahvāra-
159 | sthaima bala-cakrravarttāṃ rruṃdau gūttaira vī ysā śu̮re pūñūda
160 bva̮ṃa̮yi ttairṣṭada jasta | ba̮iysa jsa vārye bala-cakrravartta jabvi̮ya-rāja
161 rre pana cadrra käṇaiska naulmä
ṣi̮ mī rre pharaka se-yserye hīña jsa ū hīye ttaradajvye hauva pārajse
162 jsa | dara jabvi̮ dvīpa pa̮ra̮ya vīstāve pharāke̮ vā hvīyāṣā ū ttrīyaśu̮nyä
163 saltva parauya jīye rrustāṃdä :
164 hadaña be̮da mī ṣä rai kalāṇamaittrāṃ pārajsai jsa | ba̮iysāṃ śāśa̮ṃ
vīrä ṣada aysmū vasvattā byaudai . kūra draiṣṭa patsai ū raṣtyä drraiṣṭa
165 | pārajsyai jsa asadai jsa pathī haḍai haḍai aù drrayva̮ ranvā garkha
166 vaistha̮rya pūña-|kūśala-mūla yuḍai : tta ka̮lā bāḍāṃ parsa̮mai jsa
167 hamyai ṣi̮ rai tcūra-ysanyai hīña | jsa pa̮ijsa ṣṭa̮na gauda̮ra parmahai
168 vīra ā ttye vā tta tta kṣama pana sa a ttye dīśa̮ paiṣkalla vīra maista
vaistha̮rī sthūpa padīmāṃ tcūra-vadī bauganai habairū kūṣṭa aùna
169 va prralvaiya baiysa-pūra parī vaska haspīsīda :
170 ttaña baiḍa tca̮ra lākapāla ttyai rāṃda | hīyai aysmū ba̮sta ttai vaska
171 valakāṃ ṣikalakau hīyai rū yūḍāṃdä . ttai vaska vallakau ra ttyai
dīśa̮ vīra śau pha̮nīnai sthūpa[2] āstadāṃdä : khū rai tta ṣīka dyai
172 brraṣṭa sa | ca ttū aù yadä ttai ṣīka tta hvāṃda sä kaṇa̮iska sthūpau
173 padīmāṃ raiva jsa hā pyāstai tta hvai | sa cū ṣa̮ ttā pasta sä kaṇa̮iska
sthūpa ⟨pa⟩dīmīrya̮
174 ttanä ka̮lna tta ṣīkalaka hamailsta hīvī rū pai jsä va tca̮ra lākapāla

[1] Lower part of *b̮ai* broken away.
[2] *ya* written for *ū*.

175 pyatsa vīstạ̄va : khū rai tta lākapạ̄la ttyai[1] | pạijsa harīysāṃ bāraina
176 vaiysgaista pyatsa stai jsạ̄ṇakya vīstạ̄ pākau va aúrga śalraṇā va tsvai .
177 lākapāla jsa hā pyāstāṃda ttai hvāṃda sạ maista rrai va tvī bạiysūñe |
vyạ̄rṇana baiśạ sakhạ̄ra padīmạ̄ña hatsa vaisthạ̄rī sthūpa jsa ū hāṣṭai
178 hā śarīlra namadrrạ̄ña cai hạ̄ daryai jabvī dvīpa vī bīsạ̄ pūñūda śara
179 satva daivaltta parvālā barīda : cū ttā tta satta hamāṃdai ca ttyai
180 spyaka haiṣạ̄mava masai | sthūpa pajsa īnīdai tta ttạ̄ harbaiśa jasta-
181 kṣīrrvạ̄ ysatha nāsạ̄rai nauhạ vīra jsāṃ | baiysūśćāṣṭā vyạ̄rṇa byaihīda
182 ū ṣị jsāṃ sakhāra kāṇạiska vyahāra nạ̄ma halmai
khū mī rai ttyāṃ lākapālā hīya hvāñạ̄ma pyūṣṭā yūḍai ttaña baiḍa mī
183 ñarmyalrạ̄ aúmạ̄ca pasta gauṣṭai tta pasta sä pharạ̄ka vạ̄ kīragara
184 hvaṇḍa hagạijara | : mara ttyai dīśạ vīra sakhāra āstañara śau krrạ̄śā
185 ūskāṣkamai jsāṃ va damarāśạ | padī⟨mī⟩ryāṃ : ysīra ạijsa ranyāṃ
186 mīrāhyā jsa ūḍa : aúmāca pharāka kīragara | hvaṇḍā hagrīyāṃda vara
187 ttyai dīśạ paiṣkala vīra kaṇạiska sthūpa sakhāra | āstadāṃdā ha⟨tsa⟩
dämarāśạ jsa :
188 hadaña baiḍā mī ṣị rai ha⟨tsa⟩ aśagauṣa kalḍạ̄ṇamaittra tsā[2] : ttaña
189 kīrāṃja tsvai kūṣṭa āṃ ttū damarāśạ padaidāṃda : ttaña | baiḍa mī
190 ṣa aśagauṣa kaḍạ̄ṇamaittra śau ạ̄ysmīnai paiṇḍai ūsthīyai tta | tta
sattyāprrīyā ca yūḍā sa khū ttā a ttyai bhadrrai-kalpa baiysūśca bạ̄na
191 | avaśa ttyai pạiṇḍai dīśaumai jsa apūrve gụ̄nai caira hamāvi : ttyai
192 pạiṇḍai dīśaulmaiva masāmai : dadạ stụ̄ḍai bvạiśdai baiysūña prra-
193 baibạ̄i caira hamyai cada śālkyamūna jasta baiysa ///
194 | vasvai ṣị pātca śa ( )ai ///
195 | sāra pai a ///

58

P 2788

1 [*bases of akṣaras*]
2 rre khu ri tsāṃ ⌢ ttye vạ̄ [āṃ vā][3] jsāṃ tta tta hụ̄nīṃdā si cu haupari-
paṃjsāsā hvarā-
3 ka amī ṣṭīrau u haudā haṣṭā jsāṃ mistā ciṃga kṣịrā bisā haḍi ṣṭāre
tta vā

[1] Read *dyai*. [2] Read *jsa*. [3] Del.

4 pā mahe na nimaṃdryādūṃ u amạ vạ kṣīra ttaṃdī drai māśtä āhrrīyāṃda u māñāṃ

5 dida salī khu āṃ amājāṃ haḍāṃ hīya anvaśtā barāṃ cvaṃ āṃ parṣ̨āṃ [khu][1] tta

6 khu maṃ dilaka hvạṇḍä pārīsīṃdä hvarāka āvạ vä mụśdạ̈ hīśtä ṣacū vā-

7 ṣṭä u śikä śau parau anvaśtāvạ maṃ pạjsä maista ṣṭe ~ cu thyịnä kāṃcū ṣạ̄ vạ

8 āṃ hīyāṃ pūrāṃ jsa hvaḍä khaṣṭä panū kūysdä brraṣṭä jsa hasta kaittä ~ khu vā

9 pä thịnä kāṃcū u pūrāṃ nattalụ̄nāṃ va śau śau parau u[2] dilaka dilaka mụśdạ̈

10 hīśtä ttaṃdī vạ ạ̊usä ṣạikä ṣṭe khvāṃ vā nạ̄ma kiṃṇa rrvīya dilaka dilaka

11 mụśdạ̈ haraysde cu jsāṃ tta pā tta ṣacū bisā haḍä i̇ṃde khvaṃ hā dila-

12 kä hastara kyerȧ kalātcyarāṃ hīya muśdä[3] haraysde khu dilakä hasta kāṣṭ*a*

Verso

13 hamāre māñāṃ kāṃṇa āmä a⟨nva⟩śtā[4] maista barīdä ~

59

P 2789

1 me ṣa ttā vaña ttāṣṭa dalaka bauñā thau-

2 ña haṣḍi yūḍaudū [5]dalaka bauñạ̄ thauña[5]

hauda haṣṭa salā va ysī-

3 ḍā ttaye vāṣṭa[×]pā vā bauñāe hīsīda nau tta-

4 ya hauva tcā[×][6]ra ṇāśta u bạ̄ma ėdrre vạ̄ nvā-

5 vaye[7] hame aysamū jsāṃ mveysga ama ttaña haśạ abau-

6 maya hamarya

[*Inverted at end of roll*]

7 ttạ būra maṇḍvī cū bema nauda : ttāka ka āśị̄

[1] *khu* blurred out.
[2] Subscript.
[3] Base lost: read *mụśdạ̈*.
[4] Space left between *a* and *śtā*.
[5-5] Del.
[6] Blurred *ra*?
[7] *ye* blurred.

8 bema nāva pajsa pveca hīya [1]ttāde bema
9 nāva śā pveca[1] u mauyaka sakhyerma bīsā
10 āśi̮ka bema nā dvī pveca hīya u [×]
11 [1]gveśī bema nā śa pveca[1] u pātca sūka apa pveca
12 śā u ttūka apa śā pvaica pātca ttūka cū tteha̮
13 śā pveca u cā aṣītca bema nā dvī pveca
14 u [1]śā jsā vā heysda āva pātca cū śega hī-
15 ye ī bīśa bīsā maṇḍve bema nā śā pve-
16 ca pātca ttāde bema nā śā pveca[1] pātca ḍī-
17 ka īttī āśi̮ka bema nā dvī pveca u[1] pa-
18 jsa kīṇa jsāṃ kaucāha̮ra va hūḍaudū
19 pātca vā pvaica āva dvī heysde pātca vā āṣe kaucā-
20 ha̮ra āśau hatca ḍau svera jsa pātca namacī gīḍī aya-
21 kaña bīsa maṇḍve bema nā dvī pveca u pātca ⟨pa⟩jsa kī-
22 ṇa jsāṃ khve nau vaska hūḍaudū pātca sīḍīka be-
23 ma nā śā pveca pātca gahāvara bema nāva śā
24 pveca[1] ⁓ u ṣau hīrāsa hīya nāra bema
25 nā śā pvaca pātca ca marthava bema huḍau-
26 dū śau keṇa ——

[*Space*]

27 āśī hīye vā pveca āva drraye ⁓ ttāde
28 hīye śā u cāgvāe śega hīye śā pātca
29 dāde hīya śā pātca vā āśi̮ hīya pve-
30 ca āva śā ——

60

P 2790

01 (recto) pīḍaka
1 ā̮ haunä sai ye parauyi tta pā[2] aśtä ⁓ si khu hā aủrāśa*ka*
2 [1]ha[1] u pātcä hā sahä: kauvä ḍịnä ā u ṣi̮ ni bāysdye ttä
3 ttä hve si mā̮ñāṃ padaṃji niśtä si imā̮ñāṃ u hve:hvu:ra
4 haṃtsi ṇi̮yāṃ ⁓ ñaśa bīsa jsāṃ ttä tta hvāṃdūṃ si mā̮ñāṃ jsāṃ

[1-1] Del. [2] *pā* subscript.

5 padaṃji niśtä si haṃtsi vā tsvāṃdūṃ u hvavą jsi ñāṃ ⌢ u ttä
6 vą̄ jsāṃ parau tta tta ṣṭe ⌢ u ttī hā ttä tta hvāṃdūṃ si ysarrnai
7 bāḍä hīya āysāji ja ā cu āṃ nva parau ni tsūva ⌢ khu ką-
8 mäcū u ṣacū śūjąña bāḍä phaiḍi ttäka va ni ya ⌢ tti-
9 ka vā mistye ysarrnai bāḍä vī ą̄na āta ⌢ imą vā nä bī-
10 ysīyāṃdä[1] ⌢ khu hā mistye bāḍä vī ⌢ tteyi hvą̄ṃ: hīvī aủ-
11 rāsä ā si kąmäcū maṃ u ṣacū śūjąña bāḍä phaiḍä
12 u khu rrvī vī tteyi hvą̄ṃ: hīya āysāji ni pasti ya spāṣṭe
13 u ną va pastāṃdä ya paśāte imą ttī kuṣṭi byehāta ⌢
14 imi āṃ ttī ysarrnai mistye bāḍä hīya āysāji khu ni spāśī-
15 rau parau āṃ khu nä yaṃda ⌢ u ni bāysdyāṃdä ⌢ u saṃgalakä
16 dva ciṃga parahä: jsi aśä viḍāṣṭä haṃgāḍāṃdä u sahä:
17 kauti ḍinä jsāṃ ttaunä ttāttāhä: haṃdaṃnāṣṭä iysdāḍe si haṃ-
18 daṃna ttrāṃ urą̄nāṃ vī hā grīye ⌢ u ttaunä ttāttāhä: vā
19 saṃgalakä vīrāṣṭä tsāṣṭakä ttä tta hve: si nä ra hā brrūṣṭya
20 pharākä vā ñūrä haṃgrī ⌢ ṣį āṃ kauti ḍinä ysīrrä bije-
21 ṣe ⌢ u ni bāysdyāṃdä u hva vą̄ ṇistāṃdä u cu hve:hvu:-
22 rāṃ hīvī herä ttu vą hąña biśa biśä ją̄nvā ttuḍāṃdä
23 u pyaṣṭāṃdä ⌢ tturai ni ra bāyīṃdä u hve:hvu:rāṃ jsāṃ va
24 dā niśtä ⌢ khu ñaśa bīsa hamārrīṃji māśti 28 mye haḍai kī-
25 thi ttraṃdaṃdūṃ ⌢ u tcūrmye haḍai si-khūṃ jsi haṃgvāṃdūṃ ⌢
u pātcä
26 tti hvāṃ:dä si hve:hvu:ra ni haṃgūjīṃdä ⌢ u ñaśä bīsä
27 ni bāysdyeṃ tti hā hveṃ si khvāṃ hva hva ṇistāṃda u viña jsāṃ pā
28 si-khūṃ jsa ni haṃgūjīṃdä ⌢ ttī rraṣṭä paṃda ysarrnai bāḍä hī-
29 ya āysāji ja ā ⌢ u ttiña myą̄ña ri śau haḍā ni haṃgvāṃdūṃ
30 u didye haḍai haṃtsi hve:hvurāṃ jsa haṃgvāṃdū ⌢ u ñaśä bīsä
31 paḍā paḍā ttrvāstāṃdä u rrvī hā parau pasti yuḍeṃ u ttī hā u-
32 staṃ hve:hva:ra ttrvāstāṃdä ⌢ u khu haṃgve hamye pātcä hā
hve:hva:rāṃ ki-
33 ṇa hveṃ si haṃtsāṃ bāyarä u heraṃ jsāṃ hā paphūjīrau u ną vā
34 paśāṃdä u naṃ jsāṃ hā herä hauḍāṃdä ⌢ khu vā ñaśa bīsa āvaṃ-
35 dūṃ u pūhye: haḍai vā kąmäcū bisā haḍa āta u cu ttaunä ttā-
36 ttāhi: āstaṃna hve:hvu:ra tti hā iḍāryāṃ iñakä ni paśāṃdä
37 mą̄ñāṃ hā pā ni paśāṃdä ⌢ u khu kąmäcū bisā hve:hvura si-khūṃ
38 jsi haṃgvāṃdä u ttī vą ustaṃ i śūje paśāṃdä u khu ṣacū-pata bā-

[1] *d* with *ai* and *ä*.

39 ḍä bijeṣyāṃdä pātcą haudva pacaḍa kūṣḍvī ttrvāstāṃdä ⁀ cū ttika
nūva-
40 ra hve:hvu:ra cu vā kąmäcū ąna āta ⁀ tti maṃ pha ni paśāṃdä u pa-
41 skyāṣṭä gąsāta ⁀ u ñaśa pā bīsa haṃtsi ttikyāṃ jsa maṃjirūṣä
42 paśāṃdūṃ u saṃgalakā ⁀ siṃjsīṃji māśti 16 mye haḍai tsvāṃdä[1] ⁀
43 u cū vā ñaśe bīsä vīrāṣṭä nįña yų̄nä tcū-lyehsä: kąmäcū hą-
44 nä vīrāṣṭä śau ysīḍai parau ājiṃde u ñaśa bīsa tti tta paṃmu-
45 ḍāṃdū si şį ttye bāḍä phīrąme hīvī parau ṣṭe u āṣṭaṃdāṃdūṃ
46 mī hajsįmä u paskyāṣṭä tti tta ciṃdyāṃdūṃ si avädaṃji hame u
47 nai ri maṃ hajsāṃdāṃdūṃ ⁀ cū haḍi rrvī parau ttu hā salā jsa hąną[2]
48 u aų̆gavāṃ vīrāṣṭä pastāṃdūṃ si mistye ysarrnai bāḍä hī-
49 ya āysāja spāśīrau u bāḍä padįmīrau ⁀ cu mistye bā-
50 ḍä vī bisā haḍa ṣṭāre ⁀ tti maṃ mara āvaṃdūṃ ⁀ u khu āṃ ysarrnai bā-
51 ḍä hīya āysāji spāśāta khvāṃ vā haṃdyaji ąstaṃ māśti phara hī-
52 śtä ⁀ cu kąmäcū bisai śę haḍä ye ttuḍīśä ttiṃgaḍī ttāttāhä: şį
53 hā ñaśe bīsä biśa tsve u śūje haṃgvāṃdūṃ ⁀ u tti tta vā hvę si
54 miśtami vā ttāttāhä: haṣṭe si khu hīya tcįmąñä mistä haḍa vi-
55 jsya u ttī jsāṃ haṃgų̄ si ci ttuve ttā hūñe ⁀ u ñaśai hā bīsä
56 bāḍä kiṇa śirkä bijeṣyeṃ ⁀ ttai hā hveṃ si cu dvyāṃ bāḍāṃ hīya
57 śująña grauttā ṣṭe ⁀ tvā āṃ devatta parvālā ttutvī grąmyera pa-
58 dīmāre ⁀ u cu va imājai bāḍä vī bisā mājai bāḍä vī ha-
59 ḍa ya ⁀ tti vā viña vina gārai mara ṣacū āta ⁀ u tti tta śtā-
60 ka ṣṭe khu mistye ysarrnai bāḍä hīya nąma u tti haḍa rraysgä vī
61 kąmäcū hīsīṃdä ⁀ khu maṃ mara mąñāṃ ṣacū bų̄ysä ni hame ⁀
62 cu kąmäcu bisai bāḍi hīvī prracai şį maṃ tti tta hamye ⁀ cu ṣacū-
63 pata ṣṭāre tti āṃ maṃ biśų̄ña salāta bijeṣāre si kąmäcū va
64 khāysä duṣka ṣṭe u ttī jsāṃ va baśä-sīysa hvaṃdä ṣṭāre cu āṃ hą-
65 nä hīvī parau ni haṃgvāre ⁀ herä kiṇa kṣįra padaṃji jādä
66 u śūje hīya stūra biśä ttūdä yuḍāṃdä ⁀ ttika āṃ maṃ sa-
67 lāta ñaśa bīsa tcaṃjsi masi ysīra ni biysaṃjāṃ śau nauhä:
68 āṃ kąmäcū vāṣṭä paṃda kūśąṃ ⁀ ñaśa jsāṃ maṃ pā bīsa ṣacū u
69 kąmäcū bisai haṃbā spāṣṭāṃdūṃ si śūjąña āṃ bāḍä kąma bu-
70 ḍa kūśįṃdä u tti ttai āṃ ciṃdāṃ si khu mājai mistye ysarrnai bāḍä hī-
71 ya āysāji ni hamāte ⁀ kąmäcū bisā ri hvaṃdä bāḍä ni pa-
72 dįmāre ⁀ cu ṣacū-pata ṣṭāre ttyāṃ va ysira aśtä si khu bāḍä
73 padįmāre ⁀ khu vā maṃjärūṣä gąste u cū vā śika viśų̄na pha-

[1] With three subscript akṣaras *tsva*. [2] *-ä?*

74 ra ci vā ājịmī pātcä ttā biśä jsịṇi vī haṣḍi hajsịmāṃ ⌒ khvāṃ
75 vā parau hīśtä tti tta si khu ṣacū-pata tti mājā hve:hvu:ra paśīṃde
76 u ttukä herä cvaṃ [1]hā[1] pyaṣṭāṃdä u nạ hā paśīṃde khu tcerai u ttī bā-
77 ḍä ni hamāte ⌒ u ttika ciṃga cu va kạ[2]mä[2]cū īṃdä u nạ vā paśīṃde
78 ñaśāṃ pā bīsāṃ phara hamya [1]tta[1] si ni mạ̄ñāṃ paśīṃdä u ni hve:hvu-
79 ra ⌒ khvāṃ vā rraysgä vī parau hīśtä ⌒ ñaśa maṃ pā bīsa tsāṣṭakä tta
80 tta pyūṣṭāṃdūṃ si cu kạmäcū bisai hạ:nä u sīcū bisai śūjạña
81 bāḍä padiṃdāṃdä tti tta padiṃdāṃdä cu hā ṣacū ganama-drīyāṃ
82 bāḍä dva pacaḍa hịna haṃjsyāra bāyä ⌒ cu jsāṃ vā [1]cimuḍāṃ[1] [2]nạmäśạnāṃ[2]
83 kiṇa parau pastāṃdä paśte ⌒ si khvaṃ jsa tta ṣacū haṃgūjāta ⌒ śi-
84 rkaṃ jsa hā pyāyarä ⌒ ttyāṃ jsa maṃ haṃgvāṃdūṃ ⌒ paṃjsa maṃ aṳ̊ha:va ya
85 u ttyāṃ nimẹśạ̄ va ssa burä nạmäśạna ya ⌒ u mirä vā ñaśe
86 bīsä biśa śau śapättara [1]bu[1] bvạuḍä aṳ̊ga nạ̄ma aṳ̊ga [2]tsve[2] u tti tta hve
87 si thyautta mistye ysarrnai bāḍä hīya śirka nạ̄ma pyūṣṭāṃdūṃ ⌒ u
88 kṣạmạ̄mạ ṣṭe si khu puñaudä kṣịrä hīya śaṃdā paysạ̄nāṃ u viña
89 vā mistä haḍä āvī u cī ye tta mạ̄ñāṃ vīrāṣṭä parau aśtä si
90 khu tsạ̄mane mistye bāḍä vī va bijsạ̄mana nẹ ⌒ sārūpai thyautta
91 vạ̄ vā lyehsä:-pa ịnaḍa tti tta hve si mājai bāḍä hālai spāśā-
92 va hamisteṃ u haṃ bāḍä bā[1]dhā[1]nä jsa ni dāśāṃdūṃ bijeṣä
dā
93 u khu vā viña āvaṃdūṃ ⌒ cu lyes-pa ịnaḍi ṣṭe ṣị viña āchi-
94 nai hamye u haurä āṃ salā ni bijeṣe ⌒ tvīvī vā tti tta tsvāṃdūṃ
95 si khu va [1]śadā[1] śaṃdā byehạ̄:mane u mistye bāḍä vī va bijsạ̄ma-
96 ne ttī paḍā haḍa paśāṃ u khu ysarrnai hạ:nä hīya dyạ̄ma haṃgū-
97 jīṃdä u parau haṃgvāre u ttī ādarä yināṃ khu nva parau yuḍä
98 yināṃ ⌒ haṣḍi vā tti tta yuḍe ⌒ u khvai ñaśä bīsä baustūṃ si mājai
99 bāḍä vīrạ̄ṣṭä[3] aysmū grāṃ ṣṭe u kṣạmạ va aśtä u śirkaṃ jsi hā bi-
100 jeṣyāṃdūṃ u tti ttạ hvāṃdūṃ si cu ami ṣṭīrau imi drạ̄ma baysgä hvaṃḍä
101 ṣṭīrau u cu pharāka hvaṃḍä tti jsāṃ mistye ysarrnai bāḍä vī ysạ̄nāre
102 cu imạ̄ñāṃ va śaṃdā ṣạ̄ka [1]ttaka[1] śtāka ṣṭe khu mājā gara ṣṭāre ⌒
103 khvāṃ tta ysira īye chattạ̄ñarä u haṣḍi vā yanīrau ⌒ u a

1-1 Del. 2-2 Subscript. 3 ạ̄ with anusvāra del.

104 ysarrnai mistye bāḍä vīrāṣṭä haṣḍi hajsịmūṃ u khu haḍi paśā-
105 ta ttī viña rraysgä vī tsīṃdä ⌒ u ṣi̯ vā bva̯uḍi aủga haṣḍi tta tta yu-
106 ḍe si viñāṃ daṃdä śtāka ye khu mistä haḍä jsa haṃgvāṃdūṃ u ttī
107 jsāṃ pyūṣṭāṃdūṃ si haṃbāyāṃ [1]hā[1] ttā pastāṃda vistāte u viña
108 ga̯se u garvā tsūṃ u cira va drā̯ma bādā̯na īṃde cū ni ri bi-
109 jeṣāre bijeṣāṃ u khu paśā̯ tsvaṫa hamā̯mane phari vā ājị-
110 mūṃ ttī ni tsva hamā̯mane ttī haṃtsi mistye haḍä jsa haḍa paśāṃ ⌒
111 u ñaśi bīsai hā tti hveṃ si khu paśā̯ tsva hamāta ṣa̯ikä hasta ttī
112 ni tsva hamāta ⌒ ttī [1]ni tsva[1] haṃtsi mihā jsa buḍatta haḍa paśarä
113 mistye bāḍä [1]vī haḍä[1] vīrāṣṭä haḍa caṃdä buḍa hamāṃde
114 ṣa̯ikä śirkyerä hame ⌒ siṃjsīṃji māśtä 25 mye haḍai ttā ha-
115 ṣḍi haiṣṭāṃdūṃ ⌒ cu jsāṃ parau ye si ṣacū ā̯na ka̯mäcū vāṣṭä a-
116 ha:cī parśtä ⌒ ttukä hā pā gve̯tāṃ vistāṃdūṃ u nai paśāṃdä u
117 ttī ttaunä ttāhi:[2] āstaṃna haṃ bāḍä hvehvu:ra tti hvāṃdä si ttīhaḍpä
118 yiga̯nä jsāte ⌒ pātcai ni paśāṃdä u dūṃ ttattämīśä cīhä:-
119 śī haṣṭāṃdä u ttä ttai āṃ niśāṃ si pātca̯ va dūṃvāṃ jsa hau:rä
murä ṣṭe
120 u khu vā ka̯mäcū ā̯na tta tva phara ni hīsīye u ciṃga vā nä paśī-
121 ye virī hā hịna bāyīṃdä paṃmarārä ā̯ma̯ ⌒ ci pā cimūḍa ṣṭāre
122 tti maṃ pā mara ṣacū pa̯jsä baysgä ṣṭāre cu steṃna ṣacū bisā gara ṣṭā-
123 re tti biśä haṃbaḍa ṣṭāre ⌒ . . khu jsāṃ vā ñaśä bīsa hamārrīja māśti ⌒
124 28 mye haḍai mari ṣacū āvaṃdūṃ ⌒ siṃjṣīṃji māśtä haudūsamye
haḍai ttā
125 tsịnä tcutcä ā̯ṣṭaṃ[[1]dūṃ[1]]dāṃdūṃ ttāṣṭä paśä u ttī vā paḍäcu nameśā̯
126 parau ājiṃde sa ⌒ ——

61

P 2897

1–13 [*religious text*]
14 pvaisū ṣa ttā ṣacū aủ janavai vīrāṣṭa naysda grrau brrīyausta jūhūnai
aysmū jsa ysāra jva: atvaḍarū
15 ñauñau ysīraka yvamautcana māvara ẻysauja phyada samana bvaijsyā
haphyau śūra pūñūda rauma khe-

[1-1] Del. [2] Sic.

16 ṇḍa aidrrā sū̮rrai jsāka patsaunai brraura : raṣṭa aysmū śakalaka hvaṇḍīnai rana dahū padai hara jsa

17 ṣau kharaśau tcaista hayū byāva ma tta yaña: sakrra ṣaumaña-carya daiysda nva vīñī tsāṣṭa naṣa̮uda

18 pañai brrīvarja yanī bāya samādāṃ ahaṣṭa ṣīya haḍāya majaśūrī bauda[tta]satta hī-

19 yai naramauṇḍa ustamauysa śīlavarma pīsai āśį yūmautca hīyai pyai drunā pvaisū sūha̮ja aủma

20 tsāṣṭa ṣau kharaśau hīya nāra pharāka drunā pvaisū strrīya rana hvaṇḍī⟨nai⟩ rana uvāra aysūlya nauma

21 bīśau bvaijsā haphau[1] pūrau dva̮rau ṣṭau ttā pā drunā pvaisūau tta tta ra baysīryau khvau na hamāra āchanā

22 gūmattīrai pūra bīśau bvaijsyā āmauna : īśīdrāka-sū nauma raṣṭa aysmū śakalaka haysa

23 sa namasa jāya-śāṣṭā jsā tsa haira jsā sāja na tta paṣṭa ayakṣā yūmautca hīya nvaḍūdva ttī jsā

24 āśį drunā pvaisū bvaiysa bāḍa salī vaṣṭa : hauda gūttaira aủska aủ[na]na[2] būrai caigvāṣṭā na ka

25 hamaga drunā pvaisū khu na ṣṭāvai tsāṣṭa ttī jsā drunai tcaura mahābūva pajsa skada hamaga

26 ysāra salī vau tta sa śaikyaira hamāvai ⌄ ñaśa prravai pūña spaudai khvau jsa na gvaysū mara ma ṣacū pai

27 jsa śaika haira ttai cū būrakya [3]sauha[3] hvaṇḍai [4]va[4] sauḥ̮a ṣa̮uma mara aśta nau ṣṭau masai ttai vīnau hīyai janakai :

[4]ysaujsa khaśa̮ śaika brruna ttī jsa ñau tcai[4]

28 khvau vā sarbai ṣa̮ jūhūja ttavadya ttī jsā [4]magāra[4] ñūska śaika[5] aysmū hatca[6] tta tta ṣṭāvai saumīrai vau vā sa be-

śva̮ ṣava karavā ca vā sāṣṭauda śaika

29 ma ṣa tta prraṇahāna ya hatca āhā jsa [7]na ṣatta dāsyau sauha̮ hatca

nauhya na dāśauda hīsī kīra gvaṣṭūmā jsa

gvaṣṭūmā jsa[7] [7]rī hīyai pvai jsa varāśa̮u[7]

30 ysathvau jsai pūḍa nai kaiṇa mara ttu caigvā tta pvai mīrau nai ysatha ysathā gaiśū ——

31 yūmautcanā krraña sājū brraura kūṣṭa tta khāśa̮nvā śavāpaśama va aṣajvā[4]ma[4] na mīraudai hīsīdai tsā

32 pārśa̮ ttā dāśū ca ma mūña ysīra aśta ——

[1] *ha* subscript. [2] First *na* blurred. [3-3] Subscript *sauha*. [4-4] Subscript.
[5] Half-ringed. [6] *tc* with *s* over *c*. [7-7] Del.

33 jabvī dvīpa baida tcaurahaṣṭā ysārai katha ida janavai u kṣīraña maistai dī āvaśą naiśta khu va pā
34 haiysda vī māja pañai haira jsa sabajana u maista śūra pacaḍa hvaira hama jūnaka dāśīda
35 āṣą ttā yaña aiysa yūmautcanā hamārīja māśta drairabaistamyai haḍai śvąi aủ bāstai haḍā
36 nakṣattra śattavaiṣą nā hīya jsā ttrada salī gvāysa jāra gvāysū paiṣkaica cą̄ padaida bāḍa jsa
37 mauya hīya vīysama salī ttāṃjāra jsā māśta ahā jsa gvaṣṭū bvaiysa bāḍa salī vaṣṭa ——
38 vāya kaṣṭa-jsai ma anāspaivai jīyaka hamanai ṣąika sau khu ttā hīsū kyai vī ——
39 mauya salya ttāṃjairai māśta dīdyai haḍai ttā ṣacū aủ pīḍaka tsvai a ma svahąkṣai jsa āvū śau va aśa pa-
40 naṣṭa ttī jsā va aủla vaistā tsvai drunai haḍa āvū śaika ma ttai ttadī va ma daukha ṣąika ttai cau ra aủna vī jsā
41 khu ma ja pvaisū d⟨r⟩unai kaiṇa jsīna paśīnai prraṇahānau ttāṣṭa bañū janavai vīrāṣṭa mai haira ma gī-
42 ryai-vaḍā na iḍaudū drrau vara ma *ṣa*[1] śkyaisa na yai ca ttā hajsaimīna badalai ahącī hīyai
43 ttā pūra gauśta śau gūkyaina hajsādai hūḍaga ——
mvakalai gauśta
44 : u ——

62

P 2898

1 || rrvī vīrāṣṭā aủrrāsä haṣḍi
2 ñaśa bīsa thyai paḍa tsā
3 ñaśe vā bīsa bidä ysarrnai parau ṇesta sä kamacū thäna śītsä cū bāḍä hīyai kī-
4 /// × nva parau ⌢ dāśai cū hä:na u aủgąva [2]ū bīrūkāṃ[2] āstāna bāḍadījsāṃ miśtärāṃ hvąṇḍā
5 hīysda [2]ṇa[2] padaṃja [2]yä[2] ṣą̄ vą biśa tcerai hamya [3]tta tta[3] sa mistye bāḍa vī bisai haḍa ṣṭe ū aủgä

[1] *ṣa* blurred. [2–2] Subscript.

6 hīyai pūra cū biṃda pamūha: ū paraiṣṭā paśaṃjsa āstaṃna hera [[1]ttu[1]] stūra vā kamacū

7 ą̄na būḍa yūḍai haṣṭa-māśtāṃjsāṃ khāysä biśä gyerma ye [2]cvaṃ jsāṃ va stūra ya ttą̄ jsāṃ baḍa tsvāṃdä[2] cū āphāja jsā ū dū-

8 rabiha:kṣä u kära kītha sāna [2]tta jsāṃ hathrīyādä[2] ū cū jsā ha:na ye ṣą jsā parye [3]cū jsāṃ va[3] kī-

9 thä [1]sāḍämī[1] [2]jsāvä ttaṃdī[2] dūṃ ya tta jsāṃ tta hvą̄ sa tha mājai ha tsva na ṣṭi tha vā haḍa hī-

10 vī tsve u hvaihvarā aủgava ( )ī( )e[4] khu mīrāvä nvaśta vīnā hvaihva⟨ra⟩ barīdä *kīra*

11 ṣą aủrrāsa ttye nūä[[1]bīka[1]]vara ha:na pya[2]tsą[2] ā ṣą hā parau [2]hā[2] pasta tta hvąṇḍa ṣą āna mī-

12 re ca bāḍa hīya vaśų̄na nāma jsą̄ve [1]ttī ūvāṣa[1] u rrāṃdāṃ vā khu pąsa kaje **ra mā**-

13 śti ma kamacū āvūṃ ū tcerthūśī vā[5] [1]bau[1] sa ttä hve si pūhyai × ///

14 he /// /// -ā hä -i ///

63

P 2958

1–119 [*aśokāvadāna*]

120 ll mistye hauri virą̄ṣą̄me jsa haṃphve ⌢ haṃdrauysya tsų̄maṃdāṃ

121 g̱yastāṃ jsa haurä śirā byaudi līkä u tcihauryāṃ lokapālāṃ jsi

122 āysdaḍä ysira garbä rāysāyaṃ biṃdä pārauttä līkye bala-

123 cakrrivarttä ciṃgä rruṃdą̄nä rruṃdä hīvī ⌢ haṃdaṃnāṣṭä phirā-

124 kvą̄ bāḍvā bise tcįni hvau: haiśą̄kä u jsiṇye padaji jsä

125 haṣḍą̄ṃ aủrrāśākä ⌢ nätcāṣṭä aủdä mihāsimųdrä raṃgä vī

126 buri phirākvā bāḍvāṣṭä ysarnai parau paryākä ⌢

127 puñuṃdä ḇvą̄mayi śūrä mistye ysarnai bāḍä hīvī

128 ttyeṃ cīkāṃ mistä ṣī thau yā thayi uvī hvāṣṭa ką̄mai nąma

129 himāve ⌢ u hvū:ṣ̄įne ⌢ mistä śāṃ śū u haḍā-vaysāṃ

130 ṣī thau aủdä mistä ttyeṃ cakä vī burä ttikye spattä jsi pīrą̄-

[1-1] Del. [2-2] Subscript. [3-3] Ringed around.
[4] Not clear. [5] With *ä* through *ā*.

131 ñä ⁓ phirākä aùrgi drụnā pụsą̄mą haṣḍị yine ⁓

[*Space, one line*]

132 —— ñaśi hve kīmä ttų̄mą-śani

133 khu tta viña haiysdä vī ttye śirkye ttrimāysāṃjsī kālai bāḍi

134 bạḍa ūvārvā baudhasạtvą̄nvā drayvā saṃskārvā ⁓ tti

135 ra hīña māśą ⁓ suhaje ą̄me bauga viārāśąume[1] haṃdrya vyą g̱yastuą̄ña ą-

136 ysmyą śirkä ṣṭāve drūnai tsāṣṭi ⁓ ttye ḵiṃṇä maṃ ⁓ ñaśi hvạṇḍye ṣī-

137 yą hạḍāyi g̱yastāṃ jsa ịsą ⁓ āva ttaṃdī ṣẹka ṣṭe ⁓ khu ttą hạrbī-

138 śvā bāḍvā g̱yastuä[2]ña[2] ḅụiysä jsịna u rrvīyi garkhä āvaśị mą̄-

139 ñaṃdä mụśdą̄ u māśä iskhijsą̄me vī jsāte ⁓ ——

[*Space, one line*]

140 ‖ āhaurrji ą̄ ttā haṣḍị yine ⁓ harbäśä dvāridirsä sthą̄nā-

141 ttara siṃdra upiṃdra g̱yasta u aśvịna g̱yasta u ciṃgą̄nye jina-

142 ve hīya ką̄ki āysdarā haṣṭi baudhasạtva ⁓ haṣṭi parvā-

143 lā vrrīśmaṃ lokāpālai āstaṃna tcihauri lokāpāla ⁓ rrāji dī-

144 va g̱ya⟨sti⟩ u kūṣḍị dīva g̱yasti ysịnī nāsāṃde ⁓ hīvī jamni sa-

145 natsari prriṣṭą̄na saṃpạttakyi detatte ⁓ mistye ttikye kīrāstą̄nä nạ̄-

146 ma jsa hvāṣṭä u hvū:ṣ̄ịna hīvī g̱yastų̄ñä ttiraṃdarä iyaiṣṭhą̄

147 ārahä:ḵṣạ sịmābaṃdha haurīṃde ⁓ cu bure jsāṃ tta hasti-

148 mye pīrmāttimye bạysą̄na bạysūśti byehāṣṭyi kiṇa

[*Space, five lines*]

149 hana vā haṣḍä tta tta yūḍai sa bāḍa aśtai kaṇa jai khū thyautta ranījai janavai

150 vīra alattuna hana pasta yai u mista jasta u mara jsā [3]phā[3] [2]kamacū bą̄ḍa vīra[2] mista hana

151 yai śūjaña śaika bą̄ḍa ya khu śī-vą̄sta ranījai ja⟨na⟩vai vīra bīsa vą̄ haḍau

152 hīya mvaiśda kamacū bą̄ḍa vīrą̄ṣṭą haraysīya : alattuna hana vą̄ mai-

153 sta jasta vāṣṭa kamacū bą̄ḍa vīrą̄ṣṭa hana vaska daṣka daṣka pharą̄kyai haira

154 hīya mvaiśda haraysīya u kamacū hana jsā vą̄ ttą̄ ttą̄ṣṭa janavai vī-

155 rą̄ṣṭa haḍa paśīya u pharāka tcanahū alattu[2]na[2] hạna maista jasta va u

156 pharą̄ka salī vai hą̄ ranījai janavai vīra bīsai alattuna hana maista ja-

157 sta hīya mvaiśda haraysīya bą̄ḍa [×][4] śūjaña śaika bą̄ḍa yai khū

158 śī-vīsta u ṣvīda utca [3]u vaña są bāḍa aiśtai kaṇa jai khū vaña ranī-

[1] *viā°* read *vi°* for *va°*
[2-2] Subscript.
[3-3] Del.
[4] Uncertain.

159 jai janavai vīra alattuna hąna mesta jasta rauśta jsa pasta pachaysā-
160 vai u ma jsā kamacū bąḍa vī maista hana jsīna paśąvai [1]u śūja ṣą
161 bā⟨ḍa⟩ jai[1] ca ranījai ja⟨na⟩vi vīra bīsai alattuna ha[na][2]na maista jasta
162 pasta yai ṣą bąḍa hīyā bvaiyāṃ hīye pyai pasta yai ca jsā ka-
163 macū bąḍa[3] vīra bīsa maista hąna yai ṣą jsā mąjai maiśta brrąva ye
164 khū vaña [4]ranījai janavai vīra[4] bąḍa hī⟨ye⟩ bvaiya jastuña byaihą vīra pastāṃda pąrauttai
165 u mara jsā kamacū bąḍa vī a hana hamyi u vaña dasama salī khū
166 śūjaña ṣą bąḍa jai u hairī rāṃ vāi[5] ranījai janavai vīra bīsau haḍāṃ hīya
167 kamacū bąḍa vīrā[mva]ṣṭą mvaiśda na hąraysdai śaysda salya ttą [1]ttau haḍāṃ āṃ[1] haḍa
168 āṣą paśąvai dvą śau ttaya-ṣī u śau ttaya-ttaika u ranījai ja⟨navai⟩ vīra bīsai bą-
169 ḍa hīyāṃ bvaiya pyatsąṣṭa haṣḍą salā jsa u tcaihū makala śau ——
170 u vaña bura vą hairī śai haḍa hīya mvaiśda na haraṣṭą khū jsā vą ranījai
171 ja⟨nä⟩vī vī bīsāṃ caga kṣīra tsvaka kamacū bąḍa vīra ana sagai astana[6]
172 āśąrya gąkṣą haḍa ąva haudūsa āṣąrya śūdasa u gąkṣą kṣą u vā
173 vąṣṭa vą ranījai ja⟨na⟩vai vīra bīsai śau haḍa na ą kamacū bąḍa vīrāṣṭą
174 khū brraṣṭaudū sa vąṣṭa vą haḍa khu na āva tta tta vą hvā⟨ṃda⟩ sa ttai ca ma ra-
175 nījai ja⟨na⟩vī vīra bīsą hvāṃ capastaka astana[6] haḍa ya ca vą caga kṣī⟨ra⟩
176 aủna ąva mara hana hīya sala jsa raispųra gatcaustada u haḍa ra
177 vą na paste paśąvai tta tta sa khū aủ ttą haḍa paśau u kamacū va aủ hatca-
178 ñi kūṣṭą bura hą kamacū bīsą [4]haḍa[4] ranījai ja⟨na⟩vai vīra hatsa tcanahū jsa gā-
179 kṣą haḍa na hīsīdai bąḍa hīya vą ttą u haḍa hīya mvaiśda na hara-
180 ysdai khū ttą mara kamacū bīsą haḍa hīsīda hatsa padaja jsa u ttī thī pā
181 ranajai[7] janavai vī bīsa bąḍa hīya bvaiya haḍa parī paśąvai ——

[*Space*]

182 rrvī vī hąṣḍą yanai —— ñaśa prravai gūśąṃdī ttaya-ttaika prrañasū

[1-1] Del. [2] Blurred *na*. [3] *bāiṃḍa*. [4-4] Subscript.
[5] *ā* and *i*. [6] Read *ā*o. [7] Read *ranījai*.

183 u ana ḍaisai ñaśa bīsa ttą̄ rrvī pyatsa caiga kṣīrą̄ṣṭą haṣḍą yū⟨ḍe⟩ sa khva vą̄

184 caiga kṣīrą̄ṣṭą pa hīya mvaiśda haraysdai u mvaiśda vą̄ drrą̄ma haraṣṭą khū ra

185 ra sa bīsa baida bura mvaiśda na hamai ca vą̄ rrvīyāṃ parauvāṃ jsa mvai-

186 śda haraṣṭą tta tta sa [1][khū ṣu][1] kūṣṭai tta hvą hva hvaṇḍa vī hąira nąsauña

187 ṣṭą̄vai baśa pa jai ttu vą̄ hva hva hvaṇḍa śaikyai śauma jsa na hūḍauda u

188 vīśūąu jsa jsā na pajaista yūḍai tta tta sa kaṇa vyasuaima pī u pada

189 hīya ra parau na hagrautta yanva —— rrvīya mvaiśda jsa haṣṭausa ka-

190 bala alagīryai hīyai sakhyarma bīsa ttaya-ṣī jsa u ṣą radauna-

191 ka ā u na ra tsvai cai va pvaiya āchai yai u avai na paysauda khva aủ-

192 la ṇaista hau ttauḍau tta tta āvastai sa khū gaisīnai mīraña hama ttī pā tsīmai

193 hasta naiśtai khū mīrą̄nai khū padą̄ya aủ mī[2]rū[2] dī para aủda ṣacū bu-

194 ra sparatcaihąisa ha pą̄ya tsai ca śą̄ haḍą̄ hadrrauysī pąina ā:

195 rrvīyā pūñāṃ jsa ṣacū śaika āvūā ca ma śau dva khaca hąira yai ttu-

196 vą padą̄ya khaysa u ca va baiśa ją ttī ṣacū aủna kamacū āvadū

197 u vara aủna ma vą̄ ha jsa gaiśauda ca vą̄ hana hara paśą̄vai hauda

198 gą̄kṣą̄ haḍa kṣa ą̄śī śau jana⟨vī⟩ vīrāṣṭą ——

199 tcarrvą̄ dvīpvą̄ nama tsa-laka jabvī dvīpa baida rāauysanauda ranījai

200 janavai vīra maistyai caiga rauda —— vara tta haṣḍa yanai ñaśa prravai

201 śvahvāṃ raispūra hva pakyau ñaśa vą̄ bīsa vīrą̄ṣṭa rrvī parau ą̄ hvāṃ capa-

202 staka gauśta sa cai tta sa vasvai ȋra ȋya bīśai hą̄hą̄ ya ttyai capastaka

203 ȋra ma yai dairsa kīṇa u hą̄ stai ma hą̄ rrvī nva parau tta tta gvą̄ra basta

204 sa khū vą̄ gaisū [2]dva[2]-ssa śaca ttą̄ haira hūrū u ttyai ra vą̄ mūñai ȋ kaiṇa

205 śvahvāṃ vą̄ṣṭa na tsai ttą̄htta-vadą̄ pada narrvai ttą̄ṣṭa janavai vīrą̄ṣṭa hą̄-

206 ysa tsai ttu dvī-sa śaca hąira tha śa ttą̄ṣṭa hą̄ysa buḍai ttą̄ṣṭa ttą̄ ja-

207 navai vīrą̄ṣṭa tsamadai hvaina yai ca ttą̄ rrvī va tcainahū haṣḍą yanī-

208 na vaña ttā dvī-sa śaca ttu capastaka gauśta bīsai haira rrvī vī tcanahū

209 haṣḍą yūḍa ssa pajsāsa śaca rrvī vīrą̄ṣṭa parīya pajaiśtai u pajsā-

210 sa śaca [2]va[2] jsā maira khīvyana parya hūḍai khū vā haḍa tsīda khū vą̄ la-

211 kyai ȋra hīya mvaiśda haraysdai khū natca mvaiśda na hara sūttaysa

1-1 Blurred out. 2-2 Subscript.

212 nauma ttą̄ kamacū-pa hvaṇḍa gauśtau haṣḍą hajsādai rrvī vīrą̄ṣṭa : ca jsā vą̄
213 bą̄ḍa vīra bīsa ą̄śąrya ą̄va dva śau drrūttīrai u śau gūmattīrai tta
214 jsā caiga rauda pyatsa [bu] bą̄stai u caiga rauda hīya dyą̄ma dyada u paska
215 tta ṣva vą̄ gaisą̄va mara ṣṭą̄ra śvahvā hatsa maha jsa ——
216 ranījai janavai vīra maira hūśąina khīvyaina aůrga drrūṇą̄ pvaisauma haṣḍą
217 yanai śvahvāṃ raispūra hva pakyāṃ [khū] [1] khū tta vaña haysda vī śaika ṣṭāvai
218 tsāṃ u drrūna mara pą̄ śaika ṣṭai daukha ma ttadī ṣąiṣṭai ca ma hvāṃ capastaka
219 jsīḍai ca dairsa kīṇa vasvai ira jaistai u dvī-sa śaca va khalavī padai-
220 dai caiga kṣara aůna ra vą̄ṣṭą na tsai ttą̄httą-vadą̄ pada narrvai ttuva ttā
221 dva-sa śaca hara kṣīrą̄ṣṭa haysa būḍai vaña ttą̄ drrū śkyaisa na hajsā
222 yūḍai ca ma drrau ttą̄ṣṭa tsamadai hvaina ya vaña ttą̄ ttu dvī-sa śaca
223 hąira sa pajsāsa śaca [ysya?] [2] rrvī vīrą̄ṣṭa parīda pa[×]jaiśa ttcana-
224 hū u pajsāsa śaca jsā māva parya pajaiśtai khū vą̄ haḍa tsīdai laka
225 vā ira parya hajsādai ca jsā vą̄ āśąrya vą̄ dva śau drrūttīrai śau
226 gūmattīrai tta jsā hatsa mahą̄ jsa caga rauda pya⟨tsa⟩ bura ą̄va paską̄ vā
227 gaisą̄va u mara śvahvāṃ ṣṭą̄rai hatsa mahą̄ jsa

[*Recto in margin. Different handwriting*]

228 haḍūysa ją̄stau [3]ja[3]phā ra śūrā bāda pharākā bāḍā bāḍā misti ciga raudau hīyai bāḍa bīsi daną̄*ją* caina hvū̧

64

P 3510

7

4 mimī pye ysūṣka minā ⁀
śiṃ-kūṃ rruṃdą̄nä rre ⁀
5 cu yuḍi pha l śaḍe ūvāre
hūṣai tsī jsīnä ttrivargä 8 ⁀

[1] *khū* blurred. [2] Del. [3-3] Subscript.

6 māvä maṃ ysūṣka minālva
mista ciṃga̮ni ṣi̮ rri̮na ⌢
cva hūḍā tvā ge hvīya ⌢
7 hūṣīvī jsi̮lni ttravargä ⌢
rrispūrä rrīysdvarä pātcä
biśä bāḍä drūnā ide ⌢
8 | tti mu̮nā pārysā ysūṣka ⌢
cu ma ṣṭānä parśi̮dä brrīya
9 ttyāṃ pīla ālchā gvāysa
näṣa̮māṃde jvīde bvaiysi 40
10 mimī jsāṃ rrispūrä tcūṃ-ttelhi: pātcä ⌢
vyachīde harbaiśä pīle ⌢
upadravi āchā kāṣṭye ⌢

8

1 | sauhna jvīmä pharāka bāḍa ⌢ 41

65

P 3861

1–2 cā ḍaikau thū tcaina pasta pīḍai ba̮iysūśtä ⟨brrī⟩ya | baiśa satta ba̮iysa
3 hamauda aysa pā cā | ḍaikau ba̮iysa hamaunai nauda

66

P 4068

1 || sai jsaṃ ne sya kyitta ṣṭāṃ bīysirä mūṃ *///*
2 bāta vīrūlīja skaṃdä kāṃjana ysai**rr** *///*
3 garkhye haurä varāśa̮me u västārye bva̮me jsa haṃphve puña**au**dä bva̮maya śūra
4 jastāṃ jsa haurä śarā byauda-līkä puñau ba̮styа̮ña puñau ttye rä śūrāṃ mya̮ña *| . |*[1]

[1] Possibly one lost akṣara.

5 derä avamāvyau hvāṣṭa̱nyau śirkau bu̱jsyau jsa haṃphve tcūrvā hālaina mistvā bāḍvā

6 na̱ma tsvata-līkä vajrra̱mātä ttaraṃdarä ūdayä garä ttriṃkhvā nūtara[1] na-

7 ṣkha̱stye aúrmaysdāṃ ma̱ñaṃdä mistye tta tta na̱ma̱na hva̱ṇḍye hāysye diśi̱ vī ā-

8 na naysdä grau jūha̱nai brrīyaustä aysmū jsa pharākä aúrga dru̱nā pu̱sa̱-

9 ma̱ haṣḍi yine ˷ ñaśä hve̱ da̱nākūrakya̱ttä ˷

67

P 4091

1 ṣṭe śirki tta ṣṭi nai tsāṣṭä drūnai ā khve tta ṣṭe ˷ pastā ///

2 si śaike ṣä tta ṣṭi tsāṣṭä drūnai ˷ ttye kiṇa ma rrvī vī ggyast ///

3 saṃdauṣṭä pastāṃdū hamye ˷ ——

[*Space*]

4 || āstaṃ kalpä āṃ ssa hauparibistä byūra tcauhā /// ⟨pī-⟩

5 rmāttäma vāhä rrāysināṃdä askhijsye ///

6 . . PARAU ttā kha̱yi gvi̱nä askhijsye apvenye bāḍä śe̱ × ///

7 —— lya paḍauysye māśti haudämye haḍai rrāśi̱ ///

68

P 4099

435 ttu nīrāttamavattāra-sūttra rājārīmī thyaya-ttīka devedrraśū⟨ra⟩-sī⟨ha⟩ pī[ḍa]ḍe

436 ba̱sveśta udaśāya tta ṣṭa pūña paryá ya-śaina rradāna rrada vīśa̱ saba-

437 va jsa habrrīhe ba̱ysaśta brruva tta ṣṭa pūña hedava cakrravaratta rradá vīśa̱

438 śura jsa habrrīha jsana hūṣa̱ya tta ṣṭa pūñai : ṣacu ttavā jsa habrrīhe jsī-

[1] *nūvara?*

439 ne hūṣ̥aya : tta ṣṭa pūñe parye ye-śauna pīsā āśę tcaramaja prramāha ṃa-

440 ledaprraña jsa ga-vaśeṣ̥a ttā hamāva : tta ṣṭ̥ā pūña mere a̮ysaija hamātcana

441 jsa habrrīhe jsīne hūṣ̥a̮ ttsīya : pīle vyachai tta ṣṭā pūña hīye sakhyārma bī-

442 se paysāye brravara darmākarasīha jsa habrrīhū : u paysāyai hvarakye

443 yu drrau-paḍa jsa u paysāye hvarakya ḍīna-tce jsa: u paysāye hvarakyai ca-

444 pasta jsa [1]habrrīha[1] guma [×] ttīra basa śana jsa jsane hūṣa ttseya
u sa

445 cu ttaridi hīyi ysū

69

P 4649

1 : udayi garrä : gara ttraikhvā nūvara naṣakhastye ⌢ ā̮rmaysdāṃ mā̮ñadä maista *pa ā̮mā-*

2 ca ⌢ rraispūrä thayi tcūnä ⌢ hāysye diśi̮ vī ā̮na ⌢ naysdi aysmū jsa ⌢ ā̮rga̮ drrūnā̮ pua̮i-

3 sā̮ma haṣḍ*i* yane ——

4 —— ñaśä bīśä [2]/ . . . . /[2] khu tta̮

5 ttye ysarnai bāḍä vīra ⌢ śaikä ṣṭ̥āve tsā̮ṣṭä drrū̮nai ⌢ ñaśä ma bī̮śä ñaha̮lamā̮ aysmūna̮

6 pajsa ttę̮rra baida pachīśę̮ ≈ harbi̮śvā̮ ḅā̮ḍvā̮ satta̮ śaikyę̮rä hamāve ≈ bī̮śāṃ hvana kṣīra

7 kā̮kä tsvetta̮ : parvā̮lā̮ ysīnī nāsādę̮ ≈ rrāja dīvya̮ ḡyaśti ⌢ vrrīśama laikapālä ⌢

8 -āka bāysvā̮ uhā̮ paśīde ⌢ thau vā̮ ysarnai ḅā̮ḍä vīrāṣṭä ⌢ rrā̮jadā̮nä pakụ-

9 ṣḍi ttā̮ maha ṣä prrīhīye vaña masa̮ a*bv*eyi raysgä vīra pada yi nva aysmū̮ ttā̮ *p*e-

10 rä na hajsādä i̇ḍā ≈ śe ttā̮ thauna śacī jsa kaumade hajsādā̮ ≈ ā̮di̮ va ttā parya i̇-

[1-1] Del. [2-2] Blurred out.

11 ḍę ttraikṣa maṃ hamį hadādę ttadī hīyę hīyai ṣṭę cāṃ dyāma na vījsyę : arañī vī paste

12 vīstāve ca vą̄ śau pīḍakä na pastai hajsādę ⸗ tta tta pastäi hvai sä dvī salī tta kṣā̃ṃdai vī na

13 ysīra vaña b̨ų̄ra maṃ kṣā̃ṃdai vī na tsvą̄ ⸗ hīye jsā tta ysīra añą pastai bīysīye ×

14 ma jsā ma ṣįkä ārä naiśtä ⸗ hīña ysīra b̨ī*rr*ai ttą̄ bvąuma vīnai vą̄ parya prraysarye ha-

15 ra*kā* parya pīḍe : ×× -āṃ /// /// : kuṣṭa bų̄re ne sthā-[1]

16 ne sä hīyę hīyi dyą̄ma vaḍāṣṭä paśta vī rāha ṣą̄ rrvīyi kṣā̃ṃdai vī na darrvai tsai

17 kuṣṭa būre na mīrāṃ ne ttąkau ne vai ⸗ ju *n*ä hīye hīyi -ā ×× v ///

18 /// śe h -ai ś ///

19 /// ṣṭa bure × ///

20 /// pvaisāma haṣḍi yąne : śīña *kṣ*āmų̄ṃ jsa ttą̄ pātcä na ×

21 /// -āḍä tta dī pākä : pārysya bīśaka ysyāne ⸗ māre gīrye ×× ///

22 /// cä hā tsa vaḍāṣṭä yaulä jsa ——

70

P 5538*a*

1 ttaujerä māśti khyeṣvā kara hīna pastā̃ṃdū bāśte u viri bisā vā hvąṇḍä vāṣṭä

2 ttaujeri[2] māśta khyeṣvā kara hīna pastā̃ṃdū bāśte u virī bisā vā hvąṇḍi vā

3 māje bāḍä vīrāṣṭä sāṣṭā̃ṃdä ⸗ cu jsāṃ va māje vīśų̄na[3] ra ttąśįkä tcūṃ hyę : nä hī-

4 ye nere u pūrāṃ u hastä u vālāhä : mūlī aśä āstaṃna dauṣkari hīri *ya*

5 u īñakä bisā īysdą̄ra tti jsāṃ vā ——

6 RRVĪ vī haiṣṭā̃ṃdä ⸗ u ttī ą̄na pā saṃ aụdä naysdä sā*ta* burä bāḍä hīye ——

[1] *pvā?* [2] *-ī?* [3] *śāṃ* below *śūṃ*.

7 BĄ̄YI sįchvąnä ttayi kvainä pastāṃdū mūde ⁀ cu hā vaṣṭi vaṣṭi vī kara vāṣṭä khāysi

8 pastāṃdū hajsāṃde ⁀ cu karaji baysgä hvąṇḍä ṣṭāre u laka va khāysä dauṣka tsve u

9 ttī jsāṃ hā drai pacaḍä kaṃthi kāka pastāṃdū paśā yuḍe śau śau mistä tcaisyāṃ u ysārä

10 ysārä haṣṭi sse haṣṭi sse hįna u cu jsāṃ pā māje bāḍä vī bisā haṣṭi digyįna ṣṭą̄-

11 re ⁀ tti pā saṃ āstaṃ vī ą̄na viña buri viri ṣṭāre ⁀ cu pā mistye hįñi hīvī kālä

12 ṣį hā pā viña ni ri khaittä u bāḍä hīye haḍä āṃ 6 (ru / kṣa)

13 BĄ̄YÄ viña sįchvąnä ttąyi kvįnāṣṭä paryą̄mina haṣprrīye ⁀ cu hā ārrji paryą̄mi-

14 na hajsāṃde ⁀ cvai ṣä va cahä:rai hą:nä u ttąśįkä tcūṃ hye:nä āstaṃna satta pada

15 bīysīyāṃdä si khu hā hāṣṭä kara vāṣṭä ārrji ni rūyāṃ u tta tta āṃ paryą̄mi-

16 na haṣprrīye u ttūryāṃ haḍi bāḍä drą̄ṃ ni ṣṭe ⁀ cvai ri āhrrī: yinīdä ⁀ tteyi hvą̄ṃ

17 haḍä tta ysīri hatharä ni bara ⁀ mājā haḍi āṃ vā hvąṇḍä panūḍai vaṣṭä yāṃdä

18 vāṣṭä niradä[1] hamāre u hāṣṭä āṃ hā ttraṃdä[1] hamāre ⁀ khu ttā viña ttāṣṭä 6

19 PARAU· pastāṃdū pīḍe u ttye haḍai vā kara ą̄na hvąṇḍä āva u haṣḍä vā yuḍāṃdä si

20 cahä:rai hą:nä hā dvāsimye māśti hauparibįstamye haḍai kara kīthi hįna bāste u va-

21 ri ṣṭi karä kaṃthe u viña paḍauysye māśti tcūrmye haḍai buri vari ye karä kaṃthe u phirai ni

22 ri hami si caṃ-mäsū kari va ṇẹstä hame ⁀ ttye kiṇi āṃ bāḍä hīye 6

23 BĄ̄YÄ rraysgä vī paryą̄mina haṣprrīye u cu haḍi mari jinave vī bisā mista hįna ṣṭe

24 tvā āṃ viña ni paryą̄mina bāśte ⁀ sįchvąnä ttąyi kvainä va hįna aśtä ⁀ daṃ-misva cu va hį-

[1] With *tra* written below.

25 ñä hịñä hīvī kīrä hamāte cu hā spaiye ∽ cu ihīye kṣ̄rä ysīṇ̄me u bāḍä bīysaṃ-

26 jā̱me hīvī kīrä ṣṭe ṣị mistä ṣṭe u invaśtä u ināta stai haḍi ma pā uhaumä ni paryā̱-

27 mina yuḍe ∽ meri hīvī tta brrāta tcau tteyi hvā̱ṃ ysīri hatharä ni bara ∽ khu maṃ hamāte pātci ttā

28 PARAU hīśtä ∽ u ttī jsāṃ maṃ ttūnā ciṃga ya u bāḍä hīye[1] gha jsāṃ 6

29 BĀ̱YĀ bvą̄iysä nitci jinave pastāṃdū ye u khve maṃ lyāṃ āstaṃna nva haṃbūsaṃ kā̱maṃ ni bīdāṃ-

30 dä īye ∽ ysīri tta irīśą̄ ni biysaṃjä ∽ bāḍä biysaṃjā̱me hadärä vya maṃ harbīśe he-

31 rä hīya bāyā̱ma pẹjsä pharāka ṣṭe ∽ cu bāḍä biysaṃjā̱me vī heri hīye bā-

32 yā̱me vī buri invaśte ṣṭāre ∽ ttye kiṇai mū tteyi hvā̱ṃ bvą ∽ ttīve ttā pā saṃñä ni hīsīye

33 ysāḍa u miśtari hvą̄ṇḍä pvą̄isa u ttike ttā gverīdä ∽ hā āṃ hā herä phirākä jsāte u

34 hā jsārä u hā drąysi-barā stūra u hā hvą̄ṇḍä u hā hịna u viri jsāṃ āṃ va pharāka jauva

35 hamāre u hvą̄ṇḍä āṃ va mīrāre ∽ khu maṃ ttye bāḍä biysaṃjā̱me haṃdärä vya śā dvī silī

36 ttūnā ciṃga tta tta kā̱ma ni byehīṃ:de u ttāṣṭä jsāṃ ttā pā tta tta muśdą̄ ni hīsīye ∽ pa-

37 ḍā ā̱ne aù ttā paryāṃ paśte si invaśtä maṃ ttikye yaujsi ṣṭe ∽ khvāṃ tta tteyi hvā̱ṃ u ṣa-

38 cū kaṃthi jsi hvą̄ṇḍāṃ ysīri irīśą̄ ni biysīśtä ∽ khu bāḍä paryā̱mina biysī yu-

39 ḍe ∽ u khu maṃ saṃ ciṃga paryā̱mi nāte sāṣṭe u khu jsāṃ ttā saṃ ttāṣṭä muśdą̄ paryā̱-

40 mi nāte hajsāṃde ∽ hamaiyai tteyi hvā̱ṃ bvą ∽ viña maṃ sūrä pẹjsä 6

41 RRVĪ VĪ Ā̱YASTŪÑI aysmya irīśą̄ ṣṭe si khu hvā̱ṃ cū pastāṃdū ye u khu saṃ ttūnā ciṃga pa-

42 stāṃdū ī̱me sāṣṭe ∽ ttī jsāṃ ttā pā saṃ khu tteyi hvā̱ṃ vaski muśdą̄ pastāṃdū ī̱me hajsāṃ-

[1] *ya* below *ye*.

43 de ‿ ttye kiṇe tteyi hvą̄ṃ bịśä bausta līkä ṣṭe u khu pā 6———

44 GYASTŲÑI RRŲŚTI āṣąṃ pastāṃdū yuḍe u 6———

45 GYASTŲÑI aysmya tta tta pastāṃdū nīśāte si khu thyautta tteyi hvą̄ṃ vaski mụśdą̈ pa-

46 stāṃdū hajsāṃde u ciṃga pastāṃdū sāṣṭe ‿ viña hā bịśä ñą̄ña paryāṃ bīśte

47 ttī hā drāṃ herä khaste ‿ khu āstaṃ 6———

48 RRŲŚTI BĄ̄YÄ ttāṣṭä ṣạcū vā pastāṃdä haṣprrīye u mirä jsāṃ maṃ lakä

49 hį̄na bāyą̄ma pattīya ‿ u khu rä jsāṃ vā 6———

50 BĄ̄YÄ vāṣṭä pastāṃ⟨di⟩ haṣprrīye u viri jsāṃ vā ttąśį̄kvā ą̄na mājai vīṣ̨ų̄na ra

51 są̄nä ttąśį̄kä tcūṃ hyai:nä niraṃdä u ttī ą̄na maṃ viña buri hį̄na bāyą̄me āstaṃ-

52 na kīrä bịśä bīsti līkye rä ṣṭāre utvaḍira ‿ cu saṃ buḍa nitci jinave paryāṃ

53 ṣṭe ‿ viña maṃ haṣṭima salī hamya khu 6———

54 RRŲŚTÄ āṣąṃ pastāṃdū yuḍe u herī ttā saṃ merä hīvī brrātarä tteyi hvą̄ṃ saṃdauṣṭi ni

55 ri padaidä yināṃ ‿ ttye kiṇi cu maṃ ttye bāḍä biysaṃją̄me vī pvą̄yse phirākyi

56 ṣṭāre ‿ khu āṃ tta brrātarä tteyi hvą̄ṃ ysīri irīśą̈ bīysīsįye ‿ harbaiśä tti-

57 ka bāḍä bīysaṃją̄me āstaṃna kīrä paryāṃ nvīthye u tta tta ādarä paryāṃ yu-

58 ḍe khu brrātarä tteyi hvą̄ṃ saṃdauṣṭä paryāṃ padiṃdä yuḍe ‿ khu vā tcauta bava

59 tsīṃdä u jsịṇä vī vā pīḍakāṃ jsi haṣḍä yaṃ si aysmyave tta khu ṣṭe ‿ ysīre tta i-

60 rīśą̈ aśti ā si nva habūsaṃ va āṃ vā mụśdä ni hīśtä ‿ ā bāḍä biysaṃ-

61 ją̄me hīyaive tta saṃdauṣṭī ṣṭe ‿ hamidä [1]ma[1] ṣai ttye bāḍä bīysaṃją̄me kiṇä

62 miri kūṣḍvį̄ jaśtāṃ u rriysdvarāṃ u rrịspūrāṃ jsi ñą̄ma ni paryāṃ byaude ‿ cu maṃ

63 herī ūvāṣį nịśti ‿ ttī haḍä ma śau ṣạikä ṣṭe si ⟨ttye⟩ kiṇä tta tteyi hvą̄ṃ ysīri irīśį

1-1 Subscript.

64 hame ⌢ khve āṃ tta ysīri irīśą̄ hamāte ⌢ tcauti bavāṃ gauśti vā haṣḍä ya u ttiki bā-

65 ḍä bīysaṃją̄me hīya kīrä paryāṃ nvīthye u ttāṣṭä ttā tteyi hvą̄ṃ vaski mu̯śdį pa-

66 ryāṃ hajsāṃde ⌢ ttīve tta bāḍä bīysaṃją̄me kiṇä saṃdauṣṭī ṣṭāve ⌢ pātcä vā

67 haṣḍä ya u paryą̄mina hā pattīye ⌢ khu ttū bāḍä darä paryāṃ biysī yuḍe ⌢

68 viña ttā tteyi hvą̄ṃ vaski tvā buri mu̯śdą̄ pastāṃdū hajsāṃde ⌢ paḍauysä myą̄nī į-

69 rä śau dvāritcihaisä kīṇa u śę vasve irä dasau kīṇa u dįdä irä ha-

70 ṣṭi kīṇa hālai drai mą̄ṇḍi irä hamye kṣ̣aṣṭä kīṇi hālai u kaṃgīnai baṃgāṃ

71 śau u ṣvīnā daśtą̄nya byaṣṭi līka mārsalä śā u byaṣṭi līkä parąśą̄ śau

72 u bārai śau u kūsä śau ⌢ cu jsāṃ tta mājā rrispūra ṣṭāre u śįka ṣä āṃ tta kai u

73 hītalatsai ⌢ ttye kiṇä jsi maṃ 6————————[1]

74 RRVĪ JSA GYASTŲ̄ÑI aysmya pęjsä saṃdauṣṭä pastāṃdū hamye ⌢ khva tta hamidā śį-

75 kyerä kā u hīvalatsā ⌢ pātcā jsi ma 6————————

76 GYASTŲ̄ÑI aysmya saṃdauṣṭyerä[2] paryą̄mina hamye ⌢ ttīve vaski ttā ttąśįkä tcūṃ hyai:nä hīya

77 vari pastāṃdū hajsāṃde śā cvai daśtāṃ u gvą u khijsā tcīrika u nakhauṣai ęjsįnä ṣṭāre

78 ttīve vaski jsāṃ ttā iṃjīnai hūjsava pakai paśajsa pastāṃdū hajsāṃde śau ⌢

79 RRVĪ āṣą ——

勑[3]

80 || PARAU ttā thyęnä tcų̄nä sūhye: bāḍä tcūrmye kṣ̣ų̄ṇä aśä salya paḍauysye

81 māśti nąmye haḍai kvąniña ą̄na rrāśį pastāṃdū yuḍe ⌢

[1] Six akṣaras in different hand, (... *vastvama*). [2] Small *rä* inserted.

[3] Large Chinese character *ts'ī* 'rescript'.

71

S 2469

1 ll 24 mye kṣụṇä aśi salya hamārrījä māśtä 10
2 mye haḍai ⌢ baṃ mistä tcai-syāṃ pasti ye cva ma baudhasa-
3 ttä pasti pīḍe pharāka ma bal̮hä: haura pa-
4 sti hauḍe jastāṃ ba̮ysāṃ pyaṃtsä ā̮na karma-dīśę-
5 ni ttavę va ṣīka yaṃ khāṃ būkä saṃgakä u kharū-
6 ṣä u paḍai u tta hvaṃnä saṃgai vī burakye tti hā
7 pā puña-kuśilä-mūlä puḍāṃdä nva hvāṣṭä

On recto of roll, Chinese date:[1]

丙戌年五月十四日 'ping-hü year, 5th month 14th day'= 'June 7th (?) 746'

72

S 5212*b*

1 ll agaṣṭau brrau jsa i̇nīda kaṇa ma bīysajīda ttī jsā ṣadyai valakyai brrai
2 pvaisa kaṇai dvīda : chaugalakai aga a ñū caistaka jīyaka khvai ṣa pā ma kaiṇa
3 dvīda vīnai na hamai : brrī va ttā tsvai ttāṣṭa ṣacū kīthāṣṭa gīhyara vā cai-
4 ga ttī jsā hva[tta][2]na khva vā byaihai pada : kamacū kīthāṣṭa ama jsā ttyai
5 gīsta jsa maista baiysūśta bvīryau : × ll pharāka ya hvaṇḍa ttakyai
6 janavai vīra na ṣava basta aysamū ha-bāḍa śā ṣavai aysmū va tvī bai-
7 da basta valakā painā caṣṭā : vā ba brrīyā tta ysaiya śuḍa.
8 śuḍa ttaurai jsā dū khū nau pāra gaula hvīra: ——

[1] Kindly explained to me by Dr Lionel Giles. [2] Blurred.

INDO-SCYTHIAN STUDIES

BEING

KHOTANESE TEXTS
VOLUME III

EDITED BY

H. W. BAILEY

PREFACE

It has taken half a century since their discovery to place these texts of the Sakas in the hands of interested scholars. The Indo-Scythian portion of the Indo-Iranian field could not offer the striking novelty of the languages of Kucha and Karashahr, but yet comprises some vitally important material for the interpretation of early Iranian documents and also of problems of the Veda. This material has filled to some extent the gap in the knowledge of Asia between the Kušān period and the tenth century. For the history of Indian culture outside India and for 'Scythian' studies these texts are basic sources.

The present volume presents seventy-five texts, of which all except seven (Or. 11252.1, Hedin A, Ch. 00275, P 2801, P 2781, P 2783, P 5538*b*) and some lines of P 2892 and P 2893, are here published for the first time.[1] As in the three previous volumes *Khotanese Texts I* (1945), *Khotanese Buddhist Texts* (1951), and Indo-Scythian Studies, *Khotanese Texts II* (1954), the present volume contains transliterated texts. The cost of producing facsimiles is at present so high as to be prohibitive. Hence as far as possible a diplomatic text is printed here.

The contents are miscellaneous: Buddhist didactic prose and verse, love poems, medical texts, official documents,[2] bilingual texts in Chinese and Khotanese, and in Sanskrit and Khotanese, also Turkish. There are also Buddhist Sanskrit *dhāraṇīs* and a few verses.

This volume completes the publication of the Paris texts of the Pelliot Collection. From other collections there remain many smaller pieces which contain interesting data. It is hoped to publish these later. Every scrap adds a touch to the picture of these dark centuries. How heavy the losses of manuscripts have been can be judged in Khadaliq 1. 13 (in *Khotanese Buddhist Texts*) from which part of Folio 148 has survived, and Ch. lxviii 001, no. 9 below, of which one folio numbered 255 has reached us.

[1] No photograph has been available of the four no. 14 (P 1311), no. 49 (P 5536), no. 50 (P 5536*b*) and no. 53 (FM 25, 1). Hence the readings here depend upon transcripts of 1937–8.

[2] Some of these came into my hands too late to be put in *Khotanese Texts II*.

The critical apparatus has the following:

( ) round brackets for the editor's additions where the scribe has an omission.

[ ] square brackets for deletions, often simply ill-formed and blurred letters cancelled by the scribe.

⟨ ⟩ pointed brackets for insertions where the manuscript is broken or the letters are rubbed off.

The subscript hook is here indicated by a curve below.

Italics indicate uncertain readings.

× a cross shows the presence of a fragmentary letter.

/// three strokes indicate broken beginnings or ends of manuscript lines.

—— a stroke indicates unwritten space in a line.

Manuscript punctuation is shown by ⌐, ≂, the colon :, the two strokes ||, and the double colon ::.

The anusvāra has been noted by the angle below ⌞ where it does not continue an Older Khotanese nasal sound. As before, *ḡy* has been used for the *g* with lengthened *-y-*.

The initial letters *i, e, o, ai, au* are noted as 'independent'.

My thanks are due to the Bibliothèque Nationale in Paris for permitting me to read the Pelliot Khotanese manuscripts,[1] to the India Office Library, and to the British Museum. The text no. 1 was placed in my hands by the generosity of Prof. M. Leumann.

The task has taken a long time, far longer than I had anticipated when I began the work in 1934. Translation and Commentary are still needed, and a Lexicon is requisite. Both were in the plan from the beginning. A further volume containing a study, transliteration, translation and commentary of the Hedin texts has been with the editor of the volumes of the Sino-Swedish Expedition for four years and the printing has begun.

I have also to thank the Press for the careful and admirable printing of a difficult text.

H. W. BAILEY

CAMBRIDGE 1956

[1] This editing is referred to in *Journal asiatique* (1943–5), p. 480.

CONTENTS

I

Avalokiteśvara-dhāraṇī

Folio ⟨5⟩

Recto

1 āryāvalaukitteśvara mästye mụlysdīje ūce jsa. maṃ biśśä baśde karma klaiśa ba-
2 lysūśte byąna vasūja ⌢ binema ⌢ u pahaiśa āysda yanä hai muhu[1] mahāsatva
3 cu maṃ halcä anāstanī saṃtsāri cu ttāña ysīṃtha cu vā haṃdarvā ysaṃthvā
4 avamāvā ysaṃthvā aysä karma kiḍäyāne baśde yuḍe īmä ā vā haṃ-
5 darāṃ parstä īmä yuḍe ā vā haṃdarāṃ ggīste īmä yuḍe hā nva sīri hä-

Verso

1 my⟨e⟩ īmä hamaye baśdā haṣkaude īmä ā vā haṃdarāṃ parstä īmä haṣkaunde ⌢ drrai-
2 padya ttaraṃdarina tcahauri-padya biśāna drrai-padya aysmūna ⌢ dasau ka-
3 rma-paha bve īmä ā vā brrīye rrāśäna baśde yuḍä īmä ā ysurrä
4 rrāśäna ⌢ ā jaḍī rrāśäna ⌢ ā are jsa ⌢ ā aysmū bajevāme jsa ⌢ ā
5 ⟨d⟩iḍe jsa ⌢ ā bahauna ⌢ ā tvarīsce jsa ⌢ ā buṃḍīna ⌢ ā vā drraiṇi ratanāṃ

Folio 6

Recto

1 vīri śä-nūhyä aysmūna ⌢ ā yaulyau jsa ⌢ ā vā kṣārmä pakṣäre rrūyāme jsa
2 ā vā mästa-gvāroñä jsa ⌢ ā vā raṃbina ⌢ ā byaṃdīna ⌢ ā ṣkälsīna ⌢ ā
3 bihī uysāñe mañāme jsa ⌢ ā balysä vīra dātä vīra baudhisatvāṃ
4 vīra ā prrattyeka-buddhāṃ ā ṣṣāvāṃ ā mārā-pyarāṃ vīri ⌢ ā pīsāṃ kalyāṇa-
5 mäträṃ vīri ⌢ ā ysanāṃ busvārāṃ hayūnāṃ vīri ⌢ hamata karma kiḍyā-

[1] *muhu* below.

Verso

1 ne yiḍe īmä ā haṃdarāṃ parste īmä hā hama-hauvi hämye īmä ttä harbiśśä ka-

2 rma vaña aysä gyastāṃ balysāṃ baña u bodhisatvāṃ baña ⌒ dīśūṃ pacase ni nä pyūṃjūṃ

3 pyaṃtsāṣṭa pathaṃka vīra viṣṭūṃ nä śśäri yuḍẹme tta khu ṣi cu jaḍä ⌒ mūysaṃdai ⌒ aici[1]

4 araṃñä ⌒ aggumā ⌒ khu ṣä īndä tta tta aysä yuḍeme ⌒ u ne ne pātcä yane ⌒ biśśe drri-

5 bāḍva gyasta balysa byą̄ni hämāṃde u biśśä baudhisatva u biśä ṣṣāvā u biśśä ba-

Folio 7

Recto

1 lysą̄ni śśāśani parvālā prroda-phārra[2] nāta gyasta dīve nāva yakṣa aysura svarṇa-⟨pakṣa-⟩

2 rāya ggandharva kinara u mästa śśaysde tti mä biśśä byāvani hämāṃde khu aysä ⟨ttāña⟩

3 karyaustaña ⌒ dukhajaña ⌒ kāṣca-jseraña ⌒ saṃtsārīña alava-kaṃttera u

4 ttāña bārmaña kaṣṭūṃ u kūri paṃdā pastātūṃ uhu jsaṃ āspāta ⌒ thūṃ pāra-

5 hātī ⌒ thu trāyāki ⌒ thu ārūva ⌒ thu paṃde ⌒ thu pajsaṃ thu āspāta āysda ⟨ma⟩

Verso

1 yani hai mahāsatva muhu avą̄ste haurāka ⌒ āryāvalaukteśvara mästa mụy⟨s⟩ja-

2 ṣṣauna ma ma anāspetä paśśa pyụ̄ ma jsa ttä mụysdyūna salāva u baṃtve ttī v⟨ā ṣa⟩

3 dārañä hvañā tad yathā amaṭe ⌒ pramaṭe ⌒ vimaṭe ⌒ bharaṭe ⌒ saṃprrameyaṭe ⟨⌒⟩

4 ilini[1] ⌒ cilini ⌒ kilini ⌒ ārauhaṇi nirohaṇi ⌒ dharaṇi ⌒ patani

5 pani ⌒ avataraṇi ⌒ saṃ[va]taraṇi ⌒ saṃvāraṇi nivāraṇi ⌒ ni⟨vara-⟩

[1] Independent *ai* and *i*.

[2] *phārra* below.

Folio 8

Recto

1 ṇi ⌒ āva[va]raṇi[1] ⌒ saṃvaraṇi ⌒ lepani ⌒ ālepani ⌒ natapha ⌒ naphana gh . . .

2 naḍa ⌒ naḍanai ⌒ samṛdhyaṃtu me aśāmana pāripūrī dhāraṇyeyaṃ na⟨m⟩au ⟨āryāva-⟩

3 lokitteśvara ⌒ mahākāruṇika svāhā || ṣä vā ttye dārañä upavā⟨ysä⟩

4 araṇyi tsuñau pūrātä vara āna sähāña śśūki ḥaḍä ṣye ji ne vara brūṃbe

5 hvę ne paśśạñä śśā ṣṣava[2] śśo haḍā ṣa dārañä hvañä ttāña balśa kuṣṭa balysā-

Verso

1 na śśarīra u kuṣṭa āryāvalaukitteśvari bodhisatvä prrabiṃbai aśtä ⌒ kapī khāysä hve-

2 rai u kapī khaśä khāśāñä khuī ji hauva ī tta ttai būna spyau jsa ⌒ cirauna vara pajsaṃ

3 tceri abyaṃdi māñāñä ne phari pyāyāñä cu ttāña ysīṃtha anaṃttanarī ka⟨rmä⟩

4 ne yuḍe īyä ttänī avalaukitteśvari bodhisatvä pyaṃtsä viṣṭe biśśī ā. . . .

5 bere u ci ttye ttiña ysīṃtha anaṃttanarī karmä yūḍä ī tye[3] vā haṃdarye haḍai pyaṃtsä väṣṭe pātcī bi -× . . . .

Folio 9

Recto

1 kye ṣä īyä bisīvārāṣṣai o[4] bisīvārāṣṣaiña cu tta tta kṣamīyä se aysä amaṭe d⟨ārañä⟩

2 jsa upavāysä yanä ttye ṣa ttädrạma būspāṃja kūśạña kuṣṭa balysāna śśarīra u āry⟨āva-⟩

3 lokitteśvari baudhisatvä prrabiṃbai aśtä vara mī ttī gvīhä saṃna kārṣa padīmạña u śī caṃ⟨daṃ-⟩

4 nai śśāma tcera svena ṣä kārṣa biśśūnī pajsamäna āysänāña cu buri buḍari × .

5 śśīyä aggari ttaggarä kāḍānasārä ḅū padajsāñä haṣṭa vara raysa viśtāña kurkumī-

[1] *va* below. [2] small *va*.
[3] *tye* below. [4] Independent *o*.

Verso

1 nā surā prahaunä paṃjsa̮ña surai kapī hvīḍä khīṣṭe śtāka śśärna vasvena parāhäna uysā-

2 nā āysänāña tta tta mī tsuño araṇyi pūrā śśūka khvī jä ni īñakä śye hy̮e nạ̈ kaśtä ⌢ ttī

3 mī āstaṃ māśtä ą̄ṣṭaṃ vīra balśa nyāñä odi[1] paṃjeśä paṃjsa haḍā saṃ ṣvīdä tsā⟨mā-⟩

4 ñä codaśä paṃjeśä vīra anahārä māñāñä ⌢ ttī paḍā ttye dārañä jsa dvī āvarthä *hā*⟨ṣṭa⟩[2]

5 100 8 jūna śśā kerṣa niśśāña u śśā beṃda bera ‖ namau ratnatrayāya ⌢ namau ⟨āryā-⟩

Folio 10

Recto

1 valokitteśvarāya bodhisatvāya mahāsatvāya mahākāruṇikāya namas . . .

2 nāṃ saryathedaṃ sunākutmale svāhā ‖ khu tvā padaṃja yuḍi yaṃde ⌢ ttī hvaṃnye phari jsa ṣā āyā-

3 cana hvañā tcahau ju̮na bäśśä daśvā diśvāṣṭa b̮ū padajsa̮ñä āryāvalaukitteśvarä yse-

4 rkä bana̮ñä paradīvāñä tta ṣṭāṃ b̮ū padajsa̮ñä tta ṣṭāṃ herra herra tcahaurä hālā āyā-

5 cana hvañā ‖ aurgga[3] īyä muhu jsa punosari jsa[4] biśśāni gyastānä balysānä hālaiyāṣṭa u biśśāni

Verso

1 bodhisatvāni hālaiyāṣṭa namasūmä aysä namasūṃ namasūṃ ⌢ naunda naunda ava̮ste haurāka ā-

2 ryāvalokitteśvara baudhisatva mästa balysūñavūysā thu cu biśśāṃ dukhauttāṃ satva̮ni ā-

3 spete yanākī biśśe prrattiṃñä n̮vāyākī ⌢ biśśe drrä-haṣkalī ysamaśśaṃdai bisāṃ ⟨sa-⟩

4 tva̮nä trāyākī ggūchākī parrījäkī ⌢ paṃjvā ggavā gge̮saṃdānu satvāni nyūjäkī ⟨n̮vā-⟩

5 ya vā avalokitteśvara spāśśä vā muhu mu̮ysdyūni pyāya ma jsa haiśśä ⟨bajā-⟩

[1] Independent *o*. [2] Broken *hā*.
[3] Independent *au*. [4] *punosari jsa* below.

Folio 11

Recto

1 ṣṣa ⌢ mista bajāṣṣa mulysdaṣṣauna bajāṣṣa ⌢ hvarra bajāṣṣa ⌢ ysaujsa bajāṣṣa ⌢ ⟨..⟩

2 māñaṃda bajāṣina ⌢ brahmānä gyastä māñaṃda ⌢ karavīrai murä māñaṃda ⌢ śśära bajāṣṣa ⟨⌢⟩

3 vasva bajāṣṣa ⌢ pajsama-jsera mästa mulśdaṣṣauna ⌢ biśśāni pvạṇāṃ niṣemāka ⌢ biśśe

4 jaḍīje ttāḍe naṣḍamāka ⌢ brūñaṃdā rrūṃde yanāka ⌢ ḅāyāṃ paśśāka ⌢ ttāḍe jinā-

5 ka ⌢ satvāni närvāñāṣṭa rrahä bāyāka ⌢ nyūjāka āspāvä yanāka ⌢ biśśạ-

Verso

1 ni satvạni anulaṃbāka ⌢ hye yanāka ⌢ biśśāni satvāni iryāvahi[1] u carye anu⟨va-⟩

2 rrtāka ⌢ hai hai mahāsatva mista mulśdaṣṣauna ⌢ avạste haurāka ⌢ avalokitteśvara b⟨i-⟩

3 śśāni satvāni biśyau dukhyau ggūchāka ⌢ hai hai mahāsatva ⌢ ṇvāya vā tvā

4 paḍāṃjsya pratiña byātai yani ⌢ cu thu namau ratnaggarbhä gyastä balysä baña ⟨rr⟩i-

5 spūri ṣṭāna dikhautta satva ce saṃtsārīña haṃtharkaña kaṣṭa ⌢ vyay⟨s⟩a⟨ny⟩au ⟨jsa ttrā- ?⟩

Folio 12

Recto

1 ysasta bayasta haysgamasta pvạstā satva vainaiyā nāvai u ysinīya s⟨e⟩ a⟨ysä⟩

2 mäḍānä gyasta balysa daśvā diśvā biśśūnyau vyaysanyau jsa haṃthrīya pvạstā satva

3 biśśūnyau vyaysanyau jsa ggūchūṃ u parrījụmä ⌢ vaṃña mī hai mahāsatva tvā prra-

4 ttiṃña ṇvāya byā yani ma anaṃdīśśä ma hāmuri yana ma aña yana : biśna

5 aysmūna ṣṭāṃ aysä uhu jsa āspāta barūṃ ajsīraṇī thu mahāsatva ⌢ ttye ki-

[1] Independent *i*.

Verso

1 ḍāna maṃ uhu jsa āspāva ‿ ttrāstai ra thu paḍā ttiri sarva-satva uysnaura khu sīyvā

2 yservā kūlvā ggaṃgä nyāvā gruīcyau sye māñaṃda u ttrāyi ṣṭāṃ vaṃña pạnye kṣaṇi

3 avamāta aṣumuḍa sarva-satva ‿ tcārañī thu hai mahāsatva khu śśäña kṣa-

4 ṇa biśye saṃtsārīje haṃtharke jsa u saṃtsārīnaina bārmaṃna u saṃtsā-

5 rīnai kāṣce hīvī vyihārna biśśä sarva-satva parrījä ‿ cu ra ye vā muhụ jsa

Folio 13

Recto

1 pulśtä ‿ vaña muhu śśūka ma ṇiysānä ‿ ma ma parbava ‿ ma ma uysdvya ma *r* ⟨⟩s . .

2 nä nä thursūṃ ‿ ma ma naṣkalja ‿ ma ma naṣphaśta miśtye mulśdi jsa ‿ ma ma vatcīṃpha usthaṃ⟨ji⟩

3 ma biśśye janava-kāyä baña ma ma kṣera maṃ ni ysära tcauci yana vaṃña maṃ

4 vaṣṭa vīra jsāṃ ma thursa ma nvaṃthi ma vanāsa ‿ ma parājsạñä ‿ biśśäna a-

5 ysmūna maṃ uhu jsa āspāta ‿ cirāmyau aysä hai mahāsatva biśśūnyau karmyau *jsa*

Verso

1 klaiśyau āvaraṇyau baśdyau byanaṃggāryau hiryau āvrrye īmä cu prracaina aysä ttiña ttidrrā-

2 māña saṃtsārīña bārmaña kaṣṭä īmä u kāṣcīnya vyihera kaṣṭä īmä u pijsati

3 u piṣkistūṃ aysä biśye śśärate jsa iśvarīna[1] hvāṣṭauñä jsa u dāna u piṣkä-

4 stuṃ biśyau ysanyau busvāryau hayūnyau jsa ‿ u piṣkästuṃ aysä ttye mästye hovi

5 tcamna ye biśśāni draini ranạ̈ni uerä padī hamrraṣṭä pārśä pajsạmä īn⟨d⟩i ⟨pi-⟩

[1] Independent *i*.

Folio 14

Recto

1 ṣkästūṃ aysä biśśāni puñāni kuśala-mūlāni hīvye carye jsa ⁓ ni maṃ trāy⟨ā⟩k⟨ä a-⟩
2 śtä ne ārūva ⁓ ni pajsaṃ ⁓ ni paṃde ⁓ ni pārahā ⁓ u ni āspāta u ne cirau ⁓ thuṃ tträy⟨ā-⟩
3 kī ⁓ thūṃ ārūvai thūṃ pajsamī ⁓ thūṃ paṃdetī ⁓ thūṃ pārahātī ⁓ thu āspātai ⁓ thūṃ y⟨s⟩ā-
4 hä māñaṃdī ⁓ u thū cirau māñaṃdī ⁓ thūṃ pārajsākī ⁓ thūṃ isthaṃjākī āysda ma ya-
5 ni ⁓ hai muhu mahāsatva ⁓ ava̮ste haurāka ⁓ biśśāṃ pva̮ṇāṃ niṣe-māka ⁓ mästa muśda-

Verso

1 ṣṣā biśśāni satvāni āspāte yanāka ⁓ rrūṃde yanāka ⁓ hai mista mahā-kāru-
2 ṇika ⁓ gyastūñäna vasvena tce̮mäna vā muhu vyavalauva ⁓ u gyastū-ñäna vasvena
3 ggū̮na mamāne ttä mu̮ysdyūne baṃtve pyū̮ ⁓ u pa̮jsina āśayäna ⁓ maṃ kiḍä⟨na⟩
4 mästä ādarä yani ⁓ ttäna ma saṃtsārīnai bārmaṃna ttā muhu thyau parrīja biśśa-
5 bāḍva gyasta ba̮ysa byauji bāyūṃ ⁓ biśśe ttā tcahorä haṣ⟨ṭ⟩ā ysārä[1] dharma-skąndha dātä byauji bāy⟨ū⟩ṃ

Folio 15

Recto

1 biśśe ttā baudhisatva byauja bāyūṃ ⁓ biśśe ttyā srautāvaṃna·sakṛdā-gāma araha⟨n⟩da
2 prrattyeka-buddha byauja bāyūṃ ⁓ biśśe ttā riṣaya sidha-vidyādhara byauja bāyūṃ ⁓ bi-
3 śśe ttā brahmāni āstaṃna śśakṛ dvāradirśvā gyastakṣīrvā gyasta byauji bāyūṃ ⟨⁓⟩
4 biśśe ttā āśārya aśe ūvāysā ūvāysye byauja bāyūṃ ⁓ biśśe ttā śärata-
5 rana sarvasatva byauja bāyūṃ cu rraṣṭä pastāta śśärye hiri prraysaṃna īndä uhu .

[1] *tcahorä haṣ⟨ṭ⟩ā ysārä* below, in small letters.

Verso

1 raṃ byauja bāyūṃ haspījūṃ viñavūṃ avaśśä thu ttyāṃ kiḍna yana hai mahāsatva mästa mu-
2 lysjaṣṣauna avąste haurāka āryāvalokitteśvara[1] mistye mulśdīṃji ūci jsa maṃ biśśä ba-
3 śde karma klaiśa balysūśtä byąna vasūja binema u pahaiśa || āysda ma ⟨ya-⟩
4 ni hai muhu mahāsatva cu maṃ halci anāstanī saṃtsāri cu ttiña ysīṃtha cu vā
5 haṃdarvā ysaṃthvā avamāvā ysaṃthvā aysä karma kiḍäyāne baśde yuḍe ī⟨mä⟩

Folio 16

Recto

1 ā vā haṃdarāṃ parstemä īmä[2] yuḍe ā vā haṃdarāṃ gīstemä īmä yuḍe ⟨hā⟩ nva ⟨sīri⟩
2 himyęmä īmä ‿ hamaye baśdā haṣkaunde īmi ā vā haṃdarāṃ parstä īmä haṣkaunde
3 drrai padya ttaraṃdarina tcahau padya biśāna drai padya aysmūna ‿ dasau kuśala
4 karmapaha bveṃ īmä ā vā brrīye rrāśäna baśdā yuḍeṃ īmä ‿ ā ysurre rrā-
5 śäna ‿ ā are jsa ‿ ā aysmū bajevāme jsa ā dīḍe jsa ‿ ā bahauna ‿ ā tvatarīscä-

Verso

1 te jsa ‿ ā bụṇḍīna ‿ ā vā drraini ranāṃ vīra śi-nauhyi aysmūna ‿ ā yaulyau jsa ‿ ā vā kṣā-
2 rmä pakṣäre rrūyāme jsa ‿ ā vā mista-gvārauñe jsa ‿ ā vā raṃbina ‿ ā byaṃdīna ‿ ā ṣkā-
3 lśīna ‿ ā bihī uysāñe mañeme jsa ‿ ā balysä vīra dātä vīra ā
4 baudhisatvąnä vīra ‿ ā pratyeka-saṃbuddhąni vīra ‿ ā ṣṣāvąni vīra ‿ ā mārā-pya-
5 rąni vīra ‿ ā pīsāṃ kalyąṇa-mäträṃ vīra ‿ ā ysanāṃ busvārāṃ hay⟨ū⟩nāṃ ⟨v⟩ī⟨ra⟩

[1] *ryā* below. [2] Independent *i*.

Folio 17

Recto

1 hamayä karma käḍyān⟨e⟩ yuḍemä īmä ā vā haṃdarāṃ parstemä īmä hā ha⟨ma-hauvi ha-⟩

2 mye īmä ⌒ ttä harbiśśä karma vaña aysä gyastāni balysāni baña u bodhisatvā̱nä ⟨ba-⟩

3 ña dīśūmä pacase ni pyūṃjūṃ pyaṃtsāṣṭa pathaṃka vīra väṣṭūmä nä śśärä yuḍemä ⟨tta⟩

4 khu ṣä cu jaḍä mūysaṃdai aicä[1] ⌒ ataraṃñä aggumātä khu ṣä īndä tta tta aysä yuḍemä ⟨u ?⟩

5 nä ne pātcä pātcä yanūṃ ⌒ biśśūṃ dri-bāḍva gyasta balysa byāna hämände ⌒ u biśśä bau⟨dhi-⟩

Verso

1 satva u biśśi ṣāvā u biśśä balysāni śśāśani parvālā prroda-phārra gyasta n⟨ā⟩gga ya⟨kṣa a-⟩

2 ysura ggandharva känara svarṇa-pakṣa-rāya u mästa śśaysde ttä maṃ biśśä byāni hämānde ⟨khu⟩

3 aysä ttäña karyaustaña ⌒ dukhajaña ⌒ kāṣca-jseraña ⌒ saṃtsārīña alava-kaṃ⟨tte-⟩

4 ra u ttäña bārmaña kaṣṭūṃ u kuri paṃdā pastātūṃ uhu jsaṃ āspāta ⌒ thuṃ pāra⟨hā-⟩

5 tī ⌒ thuṃ trāyākī thuṃ ārūvai ⌒ thuṃ paṃdā-rāysī balysūśtāṣṭa ⌒ thuṃ pajsaṃ ⟨āspā-⟩

Folio 18

Recto

1 tai ⌒ āysda ma yani h⟨ai⟩ h⟨ai⟩ mahāsatva muhu avāste haurāka āryāvalaukätte⟨śvara⟩

2 mahā-kāru(ṇa)ka ⌒ mästa mulysjaṣṣauna ma ma anāspetä paśa ⌒ ma ma ttäjsera ma ma ggupha

3 ma ma ahamañä se ttädä karmaustä ttädi ahaura hauḍai ⌒ ttädi parvā-jseri ⌒ ttäde

4 naṣkrrīyä gyastāni balysāni pajsīma baudhisatvāni haṃkhīśa ttye prracaina jsa a⟨ysä⟩

5 vaña uhu āspāta nāse ṣṭāṃ ⌒ cirāme vaska ṣā mulysdi huṣṣāñāña īyä ttr⟨ā-⟩

[1] Independent *ai*.

Verso

1 ma huṣṣāñuṃ vaska mai pāraṃja ⌒ cirāme ṣi prrayaugä īyä ⌒ cirāma ṣ⟨i⟩ ādari īy⟨ä⟩

2 cve ṣi daśta saṃñä īyä khve thāka īyä ⌒ cve ttädirä śśärä byātarja u ttädi śśära ggum⟨ā-⟩

3 tä khu ye biśna padīna yseri mulysdyūni dukhauttä ttrāyä vaṃñe maṃ vaṣṭa vīra ⟨bā-⟩

4 ḍä ātä ⌒ ttrāya ma maṃni ysära tcauṃci yana ⌒ spāśśä ma uysdya ma pūya vā ⌒ vyava⟨lo-⟩

5 va vā kāmye buddhakṣetträ āye ⌒ samanvāhara vā kāmye deśättari[1] āye . .

Folio 19

Recto

1 tvī ṣṭāṃ hamaye gyastūñyau tcẹmañyau biśye dri-haṣkalī ysama-śśaṃdai benda vajsase muhu ⟨j⟩sa

2 ji dukhauttyeri karmaustyeri niśtä ttrāysa baya haysgame kāṣce upadrrava auysa[2] mu-[3]

3 ysdyūnauñä dukhittoñä biśśä padya pharāka pacaḍa āchā biśśä ttä dukha maṃ benda ⟨vau-⟩

4 nīha byondādi ⌒ paṃjsa anaṃttanarya karma yuḍemä ⌒ saddharma prrakṣīvai āryūpavā⟨d⟩ai

5 maṃ ttä mūlāvatta u biśśä padya hamayä pharākvā ysaṃthvā hauri nä hauḍemä .

Verso

1 ra hauḍāṃdä ttyām ra byạni yuḍemä ⌒ harbiśśä vaṃña ttä karma dukha ärra . . . . . .

2 te benda nijsāndä ⌒ śama-dūvạni rrāśa hämyemä ⌒ narya-vāla ma nṛhīśśāṃdi ⌒ śamä .

3 dīśta kaṣṭūṃ ⌒ cve vaṃña ṣä mästä ādarä īyä maṃ vaskai yani ⌒ cve karīttä īy⟨ä⟩

4 virśä īyä cve thāka īyä cve upāya īndi saña ttavaścaraṇa hauva rrāśa brrī-

5 yạni paśśāma vañaṃ biśśä ma beṃda nijṣvāñä ma thursa ma nvaṃthä ma vanāsa ma par⟨ā-⟩

[1] Or *nta*? [2] Independent *au*. [3] Base lost, *my* possible.

Folio 20

Recto

1 jsąñä ma ma ahamąñä ma ma kṣera maṃ ttuśśīma padīmä vaña ttrāya khu ra maṃ . . ⟨rrā- ?⟩

2 śa aśtä khu ra amaṭe dārañä jsa uhu namasye yanūṃ u nāme hva yanūṃ vaṃña ṣṣi-

3 naumä bve khu ma ttina ysaṃthäna ttrāyä khu ni buḍari balysūśtä jsa vastä ni × ×

4 *b*aṃña tvī beḍa vañe haṃggaśśa mästä mahākāruṇika cī maṃ ṣi ysaṃthi hamyātä ⟨ya-⟩

5 ni ttī *ka* haṃggaśśa[1] gvīḍä ⁓ padera tvā gyastāni balysāni baudhisatvāni haṃggaśśa gyastāni ⟨mä- ?⟩

Verso

1 ḍāni haṭhṭha se āryāvalaukitteśvari bodhisatvä biśśūnyau rūvyau biśśūnyau śśāmañyau bi⟨ś⟩śū⟨nī⟩

2 veṣäna ⁓ biśśūnyau iryāvahyau[2] biśśūnī ggūtträna ⁓ biśśūnye carye jsa ⁓ biśśūnīna daśtäna

3 sañäna ysera mulysdyūna dukhautta satva trāye ⁓ vaña tvā haṭhṭha u ttä mista prra-

4 ṇihāna byāñaṃ huṣṣāñu bihīśuṃ ma hāmuri yana ma aña yana ma anaṃdīśä ma

5 ma dīñä ma bahauji ma dārañā yana ⁓ crrāmä maṃ āśśayä bvā cirāmūṃ ggautträ ⟨īyä ?⟩

Folio 21

Recto

1 crrāmūṃ hettä īyä ttindrāmi rūvinạ veṣina iryāvahina[2] hai hai mahāsatva muhu ttr⟨ā-⟩

2 ya ku ne biśśye janava-kāyä eha[3] pīṃ se cu drrä-haṣkalī ysamaśśaṃdai satvä dukhauttyerä

3 vye anāspāyeri muysdyūnyeri ttū ahamañe kṣāḍai ṇaṣphūstai avalokitteśvarä

4 baudhisatvä ⁓ biśśąni drri-bāḍvāṃ gyastāni balysāni hīṭhṭhe jsāṃ namasūṃ bani ttrāya

5 biśśä balysāni dātä hīṭhe jsa ⁓ biśśāni tvī hama-vadaṃjāni baudhisatvāni hīṭhe

[1] *haṃ* below. [2] Independent *i*. [3] Independent *e*.

Verso

1 biśśāni haṭhṭha-hvāñāni hīṭhṭhe jsa ~ biśśāni riṣayāni hīṭhṭhe jsa ~ biśśān⟨i⟩ siddha-v⟨id⟩y⟨ā-⟩

2 ddharāni hīṭhe jsā ṣṭāṃ namasūṃ cu biśśä dāraña vījye maṃdrra sijāṃdi haṃtsa āspetä hä-

3 mya || tta tta maṃ amaṭe dārañä sijīyä āspātā jsa byehīmä || khu tvā tä āyā-

4 cana tcahauri hālā herra herra hvatä īndä pabastau bū̆ padaśdä ~ ttī ttye dārañä jsa

5 śśīya kapāysīṃja dasa baña̤ña ṣa cu anūḍa vrrīśe satä śśūvarebistä jūna dā⟨ra-⟩

Folio 22

Recto

1 ñä hvañā śśūvaribistä graṃthä viśtāña hvaraṃdai bāysū vīra bañāña ~ ttī baudhisa⟨t⟩v⟨ä⟩

2 hāṣṭa haṃggāḍä häme ≈ namau buddhasya ~ namo dharmasya ~ namo saṃghasya ~ nama ≈ sarvabu⟨ddh⟩e-

3 bhya ≈ nama āryāvalokitteśvara-prramukhebhyau baudhisatvebhya ≈ nama ≈ suvarṇa-prrabhāsa-

4 siṃha-vikrrīḍita-rājāya tathāgatāya ≈ nama ≈ amitābhāya nama ≈ śā⟨kya-⟩

5 munaye ~ nama ≈ sama ≈ ttaraśmä[1] atyudgata-śrīkūṭa-rājāya tathāgat⟨āya⟩ . .

Verso

1 prratiṣṭhäta-guṇamaṇi-kūṭa-rājāya tathāgatāya 5 nama ≈ samatt⟨āya 6 namau manju-⟩

2 śräye ~ 7 namo akṣubhyāya 8 namau samaṃttabhadrrāya 9 namau vairocanāya 10 na⟨ma ≈⟩

3 svabhāva-dharmauttara-niścātāya 11 namau amittābhāya ~ namo āryāva⟨lo-⟩

4 kitteśvarāya ~ namo āryāmahāsthāmaprrāptāya ≈ namo sukhāvatye laukadhātav⟨e?⟩

5 ebhyau[2] namaskṛtvā imāṃ[2] sukhāvatī vidyā prrayaujayāmä iyaṃ[2] me vidyā *s*⟨i-⟩

[1] Or *nta*? [2] Independent *e*, and *i*.

Folio 23

Recto

1 ⟨dhyat⟩u ‖ tad yathā hate ⁓ vihate ⁓ nihate ⁓ suhate ⁓ ahate ⁓ taskare ⁓ × . . .

2 r⟨e⟩ ⁓ śuddhe yukte ⁓ gupte ⁓ mukte ⁓ acyute ⁓ amṛte ⁓ staṃbhani jaṃbhani ⁓ vajrraṃbhanä ⁓ pūrṇe pū⟨rṇa⟩

3 manaurathe ⁓ paryyāpte ⁓ prakṛte ⁓ cirāvate ⁓ vidyate ⁓ paryāpte ⁓ serambhe ⁓ vi⟨ma-?⟩

4 ⟨ ⟩e ⁓ vimale ⁓ nirmale ⁓ nimiṣe ⁓ prabhasvare ⁓ prabhaṃkare ⁓ ālaukane ⁓ nilaukane ⁓ ālo⟨ka-⟩

5 n⟨e⟩ vilaukane ⁓ sarvasatva-vilaukane ⁓ rakṣa rakṣa mama puno-sarasya[1] sarvabhayebhya ≈ śānti vaśä[2] rakṣa . . .

Verso

1 haṃ ⁓ paritrā me karohi sarvvata sarvvadā ≈ sarvva-bhayebhya ≈ sarvvakāya-vāg-ma⟨naś-ca-?⟩

2 ⟨r?⟩itebhya ≈ sarvva-rāga-doṣa-mohebhya ≈ sarva-vyādhibhya ≈ sarvopadrravebhya ≈ sarva-ma⟨n⟩u⟨ṣ⟩y⟨ā⟩*ma*-

3 ⟨nu⟩ṣyebhya ≈ sarva-vāri taskarebhye varadāś ca me bhava deva-grahā ≈ nāga-grahā ≈ ya-

4 ⟨kṣa-gra⟩hā ≈ gandharva-grahā ≈ asura-grahā ≈ kinara-grahā ≈ mahauraga-grahā ≈ rākṣasa-

5 ⟨grahā⟩ ≈ preta-grahā ≈ piśāca-grahā ≈ kumbhāṇḍa-grahā ≈ pūtana-grahā ⟨≈⟩ . . . . .

2

Or 11252. 1

Verso 10 2si salya-bāyā u garaṇe

Recto

1 ⟨‖ salya-bā⟩yā 10 2 cu śiri dīri ī varai bva dvāsi salya-bāyā śau

2 ⟨haḍā bāy⟩īdi khu śau haḍā bāstä yanīdi ttī śā śā salī bāyīdi

3 ⟨‖ . .⟩ × paśā mūla ——

[1] *mama punosarasya* below.

[2] *śä* below.

4 ⟨||⟩ śva ṣṣava gūhi ——
5 ⟨|| . .⟩ byūṣṭi muyi ——
6 ⟨|| . . . .⟩ urmaysdā sahaici ——
7 ⟨|| . . .⟩ mase nā ysaiste ——
8 ⟨|| . . .⟩ svena mase śaysdä ——
9 ⟨|| . . .⟩ ḍā mase aśi ——
10 ⟨||⟩ paryai śva haḍā pasi ——
11 ⟨||⟩ maharadā bāḍi makalä ——
12 ⟨|| . .⟩ ṇa-vaśāri krregä ——
13 ⟨|| .⟩ × × ri hime ttā śve ——
14 ⟨|| . .⟩ ma hverāṃ pāsi ——
15 ⟨|| . .⟩ tti salya-bāyā śau kāla bāyīdi būna būna ——

[*Space*]

16 || paḍauysa mula mulä salya hve ysaiyi muysga-jsīnī hime u rrauḍi u
17 ⟨. . . .⟩ barīji ni śiri [hi] himāre u hve yaulajsi hime u sahautti
18 ⟨ni himi cu⟩ jvīdi ba-jsīnya himāre u trāvi pharāka himāre u hīni pha-
19 ⟨rāka ma⟩ śiri ——

[*Space*]

20 ⟨|| . .⟩ × śya ṣṣava cu gūhi salya hve ysaiyi sahautti hime u cuai ma pū-
21 ra himāde biśī sahautta himāre u cu barīja-kerai[1] śirai hime u stū-
22 ⟨ra pha⟩ rāka himāre u girye parā śirä yuḍi yaṃde u ūci jsai pyaṇi u dai

[*Space*]

23 ⟨|| muyi sa⟩lya hve ysaiyi bihāysä hime u jauysä u barījai ni śiri hi-
24 ⟨me u⟩ haphāra-salā hime u buysa-jsīnī ——

[*Space*]

25 ⟨|| sa⟩haici salya hve ysaiyi biśina sahautti hime mūryau jsa stūryau jsa aśau jsa
26 ⟨. . .⟩ biśau jsa biśina suhye hime u hāysai paṃdi ni himye u bedai āsye
27 ⟨himā⟩ri u khu barīja-keri śirai ni hime u biṣāna vaśū hime aysmūna

[*Space*]

28 ⟨va⟩śū hime grrahina mīḍe ——

[*Space*]

29 ⟨||⟩ nā salya bāri pha hime u braṃthi tsīdi u ūtca pha hime u hīni
30 pha tsīdi bāḍa hamyāri u biśi purrīdi u dai pītti daina pvaṇi

[1] *ai* over *ī*.

31 ⟨cu⟩ hve ysaiyi buysa-jsīnī hime ——
32 ⟨|| śaysdi sa⟩lya hvai ysaiyi ūtcai pha hime u bāri pha hime u ba-
33 ⟨rījai⟩ śiri hire ni himāre u āchai pha hime hvaṃḍi mirạ̄re u
34 ⟨daina⟩ pỵaṇi cu hve yṣyāte buysa-jsīnī hime ——

[*Space*]

35 ⟨||⟩ aśi salya hve ysaiyi hāysai añai hime u khu hiri ma ṣāyīdi
36 ⟨kīrī⟩ ni parsti īdi u hvaṃḍāṃ sāni pha himāri u ba dū haysīdi
37 ⟨...⟩ āchai hime mirāre ——

[*Space*]

38 ⟨|| pa⟩ sä salya hve ysaiyi sahautti hime̩ puñaudi biśe hirina sa-
39 ⟨hau⟩tti hime jsārina u mūryau jsa u āchinūḍi hime u ṃuysga-jsī-
40 ⟨n⟩ī bedai vaśuna āchā himāre u ạ̄syetī sarbīdi u vranī ka
41 ⟨mi⟩stä-ūri mijṣī mirāre u cu pura ysanīde muysga-jsīñya hi-
42 ⟨māre⟩ ——

[*Space*]

43 ⟨||⟩ makala salya hve ysaiyi hāysai śaṃdā añai hime u pūrai pha himāre
44 ⟨..⟩-aurina śiri hime bīsai pha himāri u aśa u khu hiri ma ṣā-
45 ⟨..⟩-i -ai ārhī īdi biśī ysīnīdi u pūryau jsa āspāta ni bye-
46 ⟨hīdi u⟩ tsīdi ā mirā(re) ——
47 ⟨|| krregä⟩ salya hve ysaiyi cuai pūra himāde biśī muysga-jsīñya hi-
48 ⟨māre⟩ u sahautta himāre rrusa ganaṃ aśa mūri paṃñe hirina sahau-
49 ⟨tta⟩ himāri u kīrī ni parstī yanīdi daina pỵaṇi u śạlarbi hīsī-
50 di jsāri hvarīdi ——
51 ⟨||⟩ śvā salya hve ysaiyi muysga-jsīnī hime u dikhau u cuai mū[1] pūra
52 ⟨ysyāre⟩ biśī muysga-jsīñya himāre u biṣāyina u haphāra-sa-
53 ⟨lāta u⟩ rrauḍa u śalarbi hīsīdi jsārä hvạrīdi ——

[*Space*]

54 ⟨||⟩ cu pāsi salya hve ysaiyi muysga-jsīnī hime u pūrai biśi mụysga-
55 ⟨.⟩jsīñya himāri u āchinūḍa kṣīra biśi āchai hime pharā-
56 ⟨ka⟩ u hīni ni tsīdi u biṣāna satta vaṣūna himāri u śalarbi
57 hīsīdi jsāri hvạrīdi ——

[1] Blurred *mū*, for *pū* of *pūra*.

3

Hedin A[1]

Folio 10

Recto

1 dijsāte ⌢ au[2] ye vāś̮īyä au[2] ye parṣi myāña haṃtsa arthäna hvāñīyä
2 ṣi̮ tyau puñyau atīsaṃdai himi hastamñi balysūśti jsa pātcä m̮anyuśrī
3 a̮ysā̮nai tta hvetä si ṣe̮ sūträ diś̮i diś̮i birāś̮ā̮ñä ā vā
4 ko śtātä kvī biśśä uysnaura pyūṣṭä yanīdä ⌢ pātcä m̮anyuśrī a̮-
5 ysā̮nai tta hve si ci ttū dātä śau jūna vāśīyä ttye uysānye rakṣa ⌢

Verso

1 cuī śe̮ jū̮na vāś̮i tye biśśä u tcārīmi rakṣa cai drrai jū̮na vāś̮īyä bi-
2 śānu ysañinu busvārāṇä rakṣa ⌢ cuai tcahau jū̮na vāś̮ītä harbi-
3 śye kṣīrä rakṣa ⌢ cuī paṃjsa jū̮na vāśītä biśānu balysañā-
4 nu rrudinu rakṣa ⌢ pātcä m̮anyuśrī a̮ysā̮nai tta hvetä si ⌢ ṣi dātä
5 härthu̮nä biśvā kṣīrañvā haurā̮ñä ttrāmī ttisä[3] ttrāmi bu̮vä

4

Ch. 0045

1 saka pāra tta pahā jsa pyūva × ///
2 vaṃña jsā va̮haiysda̮ vīra /// ⟨hū-⟩
3 ś̮ainä aspaurä pañe × ///
4 pāttärä va̮sta̮ : gītta̮ hā ///
5 sa khā rämaṃdai va̮ ttā ///
6 bvaiysa̮ jsīnä artha × ///
7 thanä va̮ ṣṭaudai : u ///
8 pūrākä : jāvā ttraumā /// ⟨ha-⟩

[1] Edited Helmer Smith, appendix, pp. 101–2, with facsimile, in Gösta Montell, *Sven Hedin's Archaeological Collections from Khotan*, Bulletin of the Museum of Far Eastern Antiquities, no. 10, 1938; Sten Konow, *Acta Orientalia* XVII (1938), p. 247. Original not now known to exist.

[2] Independent *au*.

[3] Broken *sä*, not *tä*.

9 ḍai sarbī khva aurmaysdạ ///
10 paḍạ̄ysauña jsa ha × /// ⟨su-⟩
11 hau ḃyau byau tsīdai ///
12 ysū[1] : ——

5

Ch. 00265

1 /// ××-rr ×× ah̯ana ārrdä mā⟨ṃ⟩-
2 gä paherạ̄ñä ⌢ heṃje haśä tcab̯ejạ̄kä pẹṇḍai :: īraṃde kuṃjsa hamaṃgä vī-
3 śtāñä ⌢ nauka ārạ̄ñä ⌢ ulị̄ñe tcāra jsä pẹṇḍai padị̄mạ̄ñä ⌢ paskyāṣṭä
4 h̯vạ̄ñạ̄ñä ⌢ gurgula b̯ū̯ u halīrai tti hā hamaṃgä vīśtạ̄ñä ⌢ ārạ̄ñä ⌢
5 hā haṃbrrīhạ̄ñä ⌢ gy̯īhye bīysma jsä paherạ̄ñä ⌢ ṣị pẹṇḍai āyvạ̄ñä ⌢ u
6 dirye urä biṃdä nīśạ̄ñä ⌢ dūvarä jiṃdä u haśä :: bah̯auyä ⌢ bauṇva ṣa-
7 varä hạmaṃgä viśtạ̄ñä ⌢ haṃtsä kūṭạ̄ñä ⌢ haśä biṃdä bañạ̄ñä ⌢ heji ha-
8 śä jiṃdä :: vạ̄mīrāṃ ⌢ ayṣ̯āyä ⌢ puṣṭarạ̄na ⌢ huṣkyä ttrahe ⌢ āḍä ⌢ hạ̄-
9 mai ⌢ biśä hạmaṃgä vīśtạ̄ñä ⌢ nauka ārạ̄ñä ⌢ mauna pāchai ⌢ yamai rūṃnä
10 gūmalyạ̄ñä ⌢ biṃdai sadalūṃ parkūnạ̄ñä ⌢ khāysạ̄ña bañạ̄ñä haijä ha-
11 śä jiṃdä ⌢ u paṣkāsā :: śvạ̄ña gūra ⌢ huṣkyi ttrahe ⌢ hamaṃgä viśtạ̄ñä ⌢
12 kūṭạ̄ñä ⌢ hạ̄mai hā haṃbrrīhạ̄ñä ⌢ mauna pāchai khāysạ̄ña bañạ̄ñä haśä
13 pẹṇḍai :: puṣṭirạ̄na ⌢ huṣkyä ttrahe ⌢ haṃga ⌢ mijsāka ⌢ āḍä ⌢ hạ̄mai ⌢ bauṇva
14 ṣavarä ⌢ rājānamva ⌢ dājsaṃdai ⌢ aṣṇ̣ū̯ha ⌢ kāṃjsạ ⌢ kāṃbā ⌢ tta biśä hạmagä
15 vīśtạ̄ñä naukä ārạ̄ñä mauna pāchai gū̯milyạ̄ñä ⌢ beṃdai ārä ⌢ hūraṣṭị parkū-
16 nạ̄ñä ṣị daśāṃgä nạ̄ma piṇḍai khāysạ̄ña bañạ̄ñä haśä jiṃdä :: huṣkyi ttrahe
17 ị̄raṃde ⌢ mujsāka ⌢ mau hīya purga ⌢ hạmagä viśtạ̄ñä ārạ̄ñä ⌢ mauna pāchai ⌢

[1] Different hand.

18 maṃgārä gy̮īḫa rūṃna gṳ̄malyą̄ñä ⁀ bidai kuṣṭi parkūną̄ñä ⁀ khāysą̄ña ba-

19 ñą̄ñä haśä jiṃdä u jsahera vı̮̄ne :: cu pā hasvīṃdä ṣi̮ va pı̮̄ṇḍai . ganı̮̄ma bī-

20 sai kuṃbā pattevą̄ña ⁀ u ārą̄ñä ⁀ paysāya bisā nāṃji tcerā ⁀ u maṃgā-

21 ra mau hīye purgyäna ṣi̮ pı̮̄ṇḍai pāchai ⁀ maṃgārä gy̮īḫa rūṃna gṳ̄malyą̄ñä ⁀ pāṃ biṃdä ba-

22 ñą̄ñä ⁀ hasvai jiṃdä :: īraṃdāṃ hīye pirä grą̄mūcä bı̮̄nāją̄ñä ⁀ kujsavīnai

23 rūṃna gūmalyą̄ñä ⁀ biṃdai sadälūṃ parkuną̄ñä ⁀ pāṃ biṃdä bañą̄ñä hasvai jidä

24 :: kuṃjsa ⁀ ysālva ⁀ mahābaujä ⁀ ysīḍā spye ⁀ hamaṃgā vīśtą̄ñä naukä ārą̄ñä ⁀ ba-

25 hauya[1] jsä paherāñä ⁀ tti ñye haśi jinākä pę̄ṇḍai :: śī pau ⁀ śī ḫṳ̄ ⁀ hamaṃgä vīśtą̄-

26 ñä ⁀ haṃtsä kūṭą̄ñä ⁀ gy̮īḫa rūṃnä mūrą̄ñä ⁀ heṃje ttaudye haśa biṃdāṣṭi pı̮̄ṃḍai ::

27 huṣkyä ttrahe ⁀ mau hīya purga ⁀ īraṃde ⁀ hamaṃgä vīśtą̄ñä ⁀ kūṭą̄ñä maṃgārä rrū

28 maunä ṣi̮ pę̄ṇḍai pāchai ⁀ maṃgārä gy̮īḫä rūṃna gṳ̄malyą̄ñä bidai hā kuṣṭä parkūną̄ñä ⁀

29 haśä jiṃdä hṳma bāva paśtä :: svaṃna-gīrai ⁀ hauṣkä gūra ⁀ gy̮īḫa : rūṃna hą̄maṃgä śtā-

30 kä ⁀ kuṭą̄ñä ⁀ gy̮īhye bīysmä jsa paherą̄ñä ṣi̮ peḍai hīya ttą̄ñä haśä jeṃdä styūda ::

31 arūva ⁀ raustarä ⁀ kuṃjsa ⁀ hauṣka gūra ⁀ pī hamaṃgä vīśtāñä ⁀ naukä kūṭą̄ñä gy̮ī-

32 ḫa rūṃna mūrą̄ñä ṣi̮ ysṳ̄rgä viranāṃ haśä jinākä peṃḍai :: tti vā jarä bidāṣṭä

33 pı̮̄ṇḍāṃ ⁀ būysı̮̄ña māstai ⁀ nīyakä ⁀ haṃtsä mūrą̄ñä biṃdä hā śakarä parkṳ̄ną̄-

34 ñä u hīśą̄ āṣkä ⁀ jarä biṃdä bañą̄ñä jatte :: būysı̮̄ña māstai ⁀ u śīlāja-

35 ttä haṃtsä haṃbrrīhą̄ñä kaṃgyä biṃdä ñṳ̄ṣṭyą̄ñä jara biṃdāṣṭä peṃḍai :: kuṃjsa ⁀ kuṃ-

36 bā ⁀ ysarūṃ maugä ⁀ rīysū ⁀ hą̄maṃgä vīśtą̄ñä ⁀ kūṭą̄ñä ⁀ ṣvīdana ṣi̮ peṃḍai pā-

[1] *ya* below.

37 chai ⌢ bidai śakarä parkūñ̮ñä haśä jiṃdä ū ūysa̮na āphārä : : īraṃde ⌢ tharka

38 mijsā ⌢ dū̮ma-hauṣṭä gūra ⌢ kūṃjsa ⌢ drrā̮ma ttī̮ma ⌢ ūlī̮ña tcāra ⌢ raustarä ⌢ bū-

39 ysī̮ña pī̮ ⌢ hamaṃgä vīśṭā̮ñä nauka kūṭā̮ñä ṣi̮ piṃḍai haṃbrrīhā̮ñä jarä biṃdä ba-

40 ñā̮ñä ⌢ hiṃja haśä jidä u phāha̮ä: :: gūra ⌢ kuṃjsa ⌢ hainai caṃda ⌢ rrīysū̮ ⌢ ha-

41 maṃgä vīśṭā̮ñä nauka kuṭā̮ña ⌢ ṣvīdana pāchai ⌢ jarrä biṃdä khaiya jinākä piṃḍai :

42 :: hauṣka gūra ⌢ rū̮nai ⌢ mahābaujä ⌢ haṃga ⌢ ha̮magä vīśṭā̮ñä -au × × × ×

6

Ch. 00275

1*a* [*variety of three hands*]

[*hand* 1]

1 30myä kṣauṇa gūha salyī hamārīja māścä pajsūsamyä āṣ̮irī[1] dasamyai māśca ttā kṣī

2 —— rrvī vī vī mūñaja māścai kabuäla jaista śā baysga dvāsa saira gvāra tta basta sasta

[*hand* 2]

3 tta ttū kalperāja-sūttra vīśa̮ ttīrai āśa̮rī savajaidākarä hi̮mña pasta

4 pauña pasta pīḍa —— [*hand* 3] haskasta śa̮ tta pasa × × × kṣa ttī prramākhva jsa vā akṣarä nī -e[2]

[*hand* 2]

5 —— [cha] rrvī vī vastūnvā[3] vajarachaidakä prrajñā-pārā(me) saddharma ——

[*hand* 3]

6 —— tta drrai padya namasu baysa ka *vaña* ska *sarvaña ha*

[1] *āṣ̮irī* written over a space.
[2] *vā akṣarä nī-e* at end of following line.
[3] *stū* uncertain; perhaps badly written *śū*.

1b 1 siddhaṃ̮
2 drrai padya namasu̮mä ḇaysä dṛbāḍva ṣadi jsa tva|rä
3 ttṛyā̮ṇī namasu̮mä dāta tti vā drrai padya | bisaṃgä ||
4 ttū padī namasu̮mä sūträ prajñā-pā|rā̮ma ḇaysā̮nä

2a 1 māta biśā̮nä pārā̮māṃ hvāṣṭä gabhī|ra pāraṣa uvāra 2
ḇaysūñe carye paḍauysa pīrmāttama ddharmā
2 bi|śäna paramārthä yaugä nijsvāka 3
3 kūṣṭa na karä kā̮ma niśtä hīyau|ścä tta vā parrūṣka ⌢
4 ttathatta āläbye[1] oṣkä[2] raysī tta tta khu ddharmakā|lyä ||
prajñā-pārā̮ma tvā haṃbistä sarvaṃña ḇaysä ⌢

2b 1 tvā ttṛśayä | vāṣṭä biraṣṭe cu ra vajrrachedäka nāma ||
2 biśä karma klaiṣ̮a u āvara|ṇä baśde garkhä
vaśa̮rä māñaṃdäna buṣḍä ttina vajrrachedäka nāma ≈
3 | cu bura ī ḇaysāṃ dātä ttrā̮mä biśä ttiña sūträ
4 ttye vajrra|chedakyi vīra ttina dadärä pārṣa uvāra ||

3a 1 cu tvā sājī dijsāti u | vāṣ̮ī pīḍä parī
2 biśī dātä sīyä pachīysdä huṣa jsāti biśna | śirä jsa ||
3 cirī puña mistä hamāri tta vā ttā sūträ hvañā|ri ⌢
ttana hajva hvaḍäna hamrraṣṭä ttina sūträ āsā tcaira ||
4 ttinai | aysä haṃjsye byūhä dā brrīya ṣada jsa vaña ⌢

3b 1 ka ma ḇaysä ālysdä yanāṃde khvai tta hva yanūṃ khu śtāka || ——
2 | siddhaṃ̮
3 orga[2] ī[3] harbiśā̮nä gyastā̮nä ḇaysā̮nä u baudhisatvāṃ ⌢ | hālaiyāṣṭä ||
4 tta tta ma̮mä pyūṣṭä śe stye śe styetä gyastānä gyastä | ḇaysä

4a 1 śrāvastä kṣīrä āstä vyä jīvä rrispūrä bāṣ̮a anā|thapiṇḍī hārū saṃ-
2 khyerma mistäna bi|sägäna[4] haṃtsa ⌢ dvāsi paṃjsā⌢|śau āṣ̮iryau
3 jsa ttī[5] gyastānä gyasta ḇaysä brrū haḍā navāysye | pättarä cīvara
4 pana nāti śrāvasta miśtä kītha piṇḍvā traṃda | ttī gyastä ḇaysä ttī
4b 1 gyastä ḇaysä kū śrāvastä mäśtä kītha piṇḍ(v)ā | vā tsuta hamyetä kū
2 khāysna kīrä yuḍä yuḍe hvaḍä khāysä kū | scetä paryeta hamye
3 pättara cīvarä pajsīṭhyi pā haysnätä | prañavyi āysaṃ vīra ṇastä bastä
4 palaṃgä rraṣṭä ttaraṃda|rana vistātä pyaṃtsä ttūśättetä byātajä
5a 1 vaṭhavyetä ⌢ ttītä | pharāka āṣ̮irya kā̮ma hālai gyastānä gyastä ḇaysä

[1] *lä* for *laṃ*. [2] Independent *o*-. [3] Independent *ī*. [4] *sä* for *saṃ*.
[5] Thin script across circle (hand 3 of fol. 1 *a*) *ttī hā pa ha sa*.

2 vyeta hāṣṭä tsuāṃldä kū vara hamya gyastānä gyastä b̮aysä pa̮ ttirä
3 jsa namasyāldä gyastä b̮aysä drrai tcīra hvaraṃcaiñä tva(ṃda)nä
4 tsuāṃdä u śau hāllai mī n̮asta ‿ ttye sce ra vātcä āṣ̮irī subhūta vara
5b 1 ttiña parṣa̮lña haṃgrī vyitä u n̮astä ttī āṣ̮irī subhūta āysaṃna
2 patata[1] | śau sve cīvarä ‿ prahauṣṭi u hvaraṃdai ysa̮nū śadya pārau- |
3,4 tti ka̮mä hālai ‿ gyastä b̮aysä āstä hāṣṭä aja̮lä dastä | yuḍai u gyastä
6a 1 b̮aysä tta hve sä duṣkarä miḍa̮na gyasta b̮aysa | cu ttira gyastānä
2 gyastä b̮aysäna ttāhirau hvāñākänä pajsa‿lmānä āṣa̮nna rraṣṭä biśä
3 hālä biysādä ahu jsa bauldhisatva mistä b̮aysūña-vūysä haṃdāḍa
4 [na] biśä pīrmālttamye haṃdārä jsa cu ttarä gyastä b̮aysäna ttāharä
6b 1 tsūkana ‿ | klaiṣ̮īna̮nä sāna̮nä tvīṣä yanākäna samna biśa̮nä hira̮nä
2,3 | vamasākana uhu jsa baudhisatvä mistä b̮aysūña-vūysä ysīlnīya
4 hauḍi biśa pīrmāttamye ysīnīya haura̮me jsa tta khu ‿ | vā miḍa̮na
7a 1 gyasta b̮aysä b̮aysūña-vūysaina baudhisatva-ya̮ña | haṃjsadaina mara
2 mahāya̮ñä viṣṭāña u khvai aysmū baysaṃja̮ñä | ttye hvaye hvanai
3 gyastānä gyastä b̮aysä āṣ̮irī subhūva | tta hve śirä śirä subhūva tta tta
4 ṣ̮i härä subhūta haṃdāḍä | gyasta b̮aysäna baudhisatva [b̮aysūña-
7b 1 vūysaina biśä pīrmāttalmye haṃdāra jsa cu ttirä gyasta b̮aysäna
2 ttāhirau tsūkana klaiṣ̮īlna̮nä sāna̮nä tvīṣä yanākäna samna baśa̮na
3,4 hira̮lnä vamasākäna uhu jsa baudhisatva mistä b̮aysūña-vūysailna
8a 1 ysīnīya hauḍä biśä pīrmāttamye ysīnīyä haura̮me jsa | tta khu vā
2 miḍa̮nä gyastä b̮aysä b̮aysūña-vūysaina baudhisatva-ya̮lña haṃjsa-
3 daina mara mahāya̮ña viṣṭāña u khuai aysmū nālsāñä ttye hvaye
4 hvanai gyasta b̮aysa āṣ̮irī subhūta tta hve | śirä śirä subhūta tta tta ṣ̮i
8b 1 hirä subhūta haṃdāḍa b̮aysana bauldhisatvä] biśä pīrmāttamä haṃ-
2 därä[2] jsa ysīnī hauḍä gyastä b̮aysäna bauldhisatva biśä pīrmāttamä
3 ysīnī haura̮me jsa ta ttina subhūta pyū ‿ | śiri subijī aysmya yaṃ ayse
4 hvāñīmä khu b̮aysūña-vū‿lysaina baudhisatva-ya̮ña ḫa(jsaṃ)daina
9a 1 mara mahāya̮ña viṣṭāñä u khuī | mara aysmu nāsāñä tta tta śirä gyasta
2 b̮aysa ttu näjsaḍä āṣ̮ilrī subhūta gyasta b̮aysäna pyūṣṭe gyastä b̮aysī
3 tta hve mara ‿ | subhūva b̮aysū ‿ ña-vūysaina baudhisatva-ya̮ña haṃ-
4 jsaṃdai | na tta tta aysmu upeva̮ñä cu burä satva satvāṃ nāsāme jsa
9b 1 haṃlkhīṣ̮a ysāya u āhya ysāta o[3] pūra̮ñä ysāta cu ganiśtä ysā(ta)
2,3 | cu ūvavā cu haṃtsä rūvina [rūvana] anau rūväna cu haṃltsa syāme
4 jsa cu anau syāme jsa cu vā tti satva cu ni haṃltsa syāme jsa anau
10a 1 syāmi jsa ku burä satvadāta prañavāñalmata[4] ñāpīya tti satva muhu

[1] Read *panatä*. [2] *dä* for *dā*. [3] Independent *o*. [4] For *-vañā-* or *-vāñā-*?

2 jsa harbiśä aharīna nirvāña pa|ranirvāña ⌢ dädirä avamāta satva ku
3 parinirvāye ⌢ | hamāti ⌢ na haḍi kāmu jä ṣai śau satva paranirvāye
4 | hämä tta ci härä kiḍna cī subhūta baudhisatva saṃña hä-
10b 1 | mātä ni ṣä baudhisatvä hvañai tta ci härä kiḍna ⌢ ni ṣi subhūta bau-
2, 3 | dhisatvä hvañai ci satvä vīra saṃña hamätä o[1] jvākä vīra | saṃña o[1]
4 pudgalä vīra saṃña häme ṣai haḍä vātca tti su|bhūta ni baudhi-
11a 1 satvana ātma-bhāvīnai vastä vīra pārauttä|na haurä haurąñä kuṣṭa
2 jä prattikārä vīra pārauttäna hau|rä haurąñä ⌢ ni rūvä vīra pārauttä
3 haurä haurąñä nä | bajāṣänä buśañāna ysvąñąni skvaumatąni dharmą-
4, 11b 1 |nä vīra pārauttäna haurä haurāñä tta tta subhūta baudhisa|tva haurä
2 haurąñä khu ni gūnä saṃña vīra hi(me) sä haurāka aśtä o[1] | vā nāsākä
3 o[1] vā haurä tta cu hirä kiḍna ci ṣi subhūta baudhisa|tva cu avārautta
4 ṣṭāna haurä hiḍi ttye sūbhūta baudhisatva puñī|nai haṃbīsä na
12a 1 huyuḍä pamāka nati ⌢ tta cue saittä sūbhūta hauyu|ḍä sarbaṃdä diṣä
2 hālai āṣi pamāka natä ⌢ āṣirī subhūtä tta hve | tä gyasta ḇaysa gyasta
3 ḇaysī tta hve tta tta rravyi pata nihujsädä[2] | nyūvijsa nāṣṭa uskyāṣṭä
4 daśvä diśvä huyuḍi ātaśą pamā|ka nitä āṣirī subhūta tta hve ni
12b 1 gyasta ḇaysa ḇaysī tta hve tta tta | ṣi härä subhūva tta tta ṣi hirä cu
2 ṣi baudhisatvä ci avārautta ṣṭāna | haurä hiḍä ttye puñīnai haṃbīsä
3 na huyuḍi pamāka ⌢ cu ha|ḍä vātca härä subhūta baudhisatva haura
4 haurąñä tta cue sai|ttä lakṣaṇījä pyālye jsa gyasta ḇaysä dyąñä*te*
13a 1 subhūta tta hve ta[3] kuṣṭä | burä subhūta lakṣąnä vara burä drrūja ttū
2 najsaḍä lakṣąṇä alakṣą|ṇä gyastä ḇaysä dyąñä ⌢ ttye hvaye hvanai
3 gyastä ḇaysä ⌢ | āṣirī subhūta tta hve aśta ni gyasta ḇaysä kāmu jä usta-
4 | mājsī bāḍä satva cu ttyāṃ didrrąmāṃ sūtrāṃ vīra kūra saṃña upevā-
13b 1 | ri gyastä ḇaysī tta hve ma thu subhūva tta tta hvāña hamāri ustamājsī
2 bā|ḍä ustamye paṃcāśai saddharma bijevaṃdai bāḍä (pare)haṃdā
3 ṣahā|nīya hajva na haḍi tti śau gyasta ḇaysä parśāṃdä ni śi gyastä
4 | ḇaysä vīra puña kūśalä mūlä pirādāṃdä ⌢ ttyāṃ sūtrāṃ vī-
14a 1 | ra śau kṣąṇä vasve aysmu byehīdi paysāṃda hamāri gyastä ḇaysä
2, 3 | na dya hamāri gyasta ḇaysana avamāta puñīnai haṃbīsāna | haṃphva
4 hamāri tta cue saittä subhūva ni ātma-saṃña pravarttä | o[1] na satva-
14b 1 saṃña ni jīva-saṃña ni pudgalä-saṃña pravarttä gyastä | ḇaysī tta
2 hve saittä subhūta ku ye kaulopąmä dharma-paryāyä bustä ⌢ | hämä
3 [bustä hamä] dātī ṣi hamadä paśāñä cu na ra vā adā|tä khu ṣi hve
4 cu ttāra tcacä kīrä khu burä ttäjä ni ra traṃdä ha|māti na vañā

[1] Independent *o*. [2] *jsä* for *jsaṃ*. [3] *ta* for *na*.

15a 1 drrāysä puṣa paśe khu traṃdä hamä nai na hamadā bīl|ḍä tta tta
2 ḅaysūña-vūysai ku na ra śirā butti ni vañā śarā vamal|śtä nai na
3 hamadā dā vīra hīyauṣṭyai tcairai ⌒ tta cue saittä su⌒|bhūta aśtä
4 nai ṣị dā cu gyasta ḅaysäna hvata āya bil|śau gyastyau ḅaysyau jsa
15b 1 hva āya ttina cu ārya-pudgalä nyāpaṃdā | gyastä ḅaysī tta hve cu
2 subhūta trisahasrrye mahāsahasrrye lovadāta haul|dyau raṃnyau jsa
3 haṃberi haurạ hiḍä tta cue saittä subhūta cu mani ṣị | bisīvrrāṣai o[1]
4 vā bisīvrrāṣaiñä pharāka puña ysyạ̄ñe su⌒|bhūtī tta hve bihī
16a 1 pharāka miḍạ̄na gyasta ḅaysa puñīnai haṃbīsä | ysyạ̄ñe cu haḍä härä
2 miḍạ̄na gyasta ḅaysa puñīnai haṃbīsä ahaṃbīl|sä gyasta ḅaysna ⌒
3 hvata cu ḅaysūśtä na ra pāraysdä khu dāta | ttye kiṇa gyasta ḅaysä
4 tta hve sä puñīnai haṃbīsä cu trasa⌒|hasrre mahāsahasrre lovadāta
16b 1 haurạ hiḍä śị vātca āya cu dharma- ⌒ | paryāyä tcūrạpatä śau gāhä
2 nāsāti sājīyä o[1] vā haṃdiryāṃ | vistarna birāṣ̥īyä ṣị haḍe ttina puñana
3 avamāta puña | ysyāñe anaṃkhiṣṭa tta cu hara kiṇa ttattīka naraṃda
4 gyastä | ḅaysa ḅaysānä ḅaysūśtä tta cue saittä subhūta cu mani ṣi
17a 1 srrauttā|vanä tta häme nä sä muhu jsa srrautāvaṃnā phārrä byaudä
2 tcamṇa ra vā ni | ī sä kāma dā(tä) ttä(na) āryāṣṭāga-mārgīnai ṇa-
3 ṃaysäna haṃphve subhū|tī tta hve ni miḍạ̄na gyasta ḅaysa ttinka
4 sa härna haṃphve ttina ⌒ | srauttāvaṃnä hvīdä ni rūvyau jsa haṃphve
17b 1 ni bajāṣyau ni buśañau jsa | ni skvaumayau na dharmyau jsa haṃphve
2 ttina sakṛttāgāmä[2] hvīdä cu mani ⌒ | ṣai sakṛttāgāma tta hamä sä
3 muhu jsa sakṛttāgāmā phārrä ⌒ | byaudä ⌒ tcạmna ra vā ni ī sä kạ̄mä
4 dāta ttana subhūvī tta hve sä | ni miḍạ̄na gyasta ḅaysa niśtä kāmu jä
18a 1 ṣị dharma cu sakṛttāgạ̄mä ḅalysī tta hve tta cue saittä subhūva cu
2 mani arahaṃdä hama nä sä muhu | jsa arahaṃdauñä byauda tcamna
3 klaiṣ̥īnā sāna ttūṣa yanūmä | subhūvī tta hve na miḍāna gyasta ḅaysa
4 niśta ṣị dharma cu arahaṃ|dauñä nāma āya cī arahaṃdä tta hama
18b 1 si muhu jsa arahaṃdau|nä ⌒ byaudä ṣị haḍä uysāñä nāsāma hamä o[1]
2 satva nāsāma jīva nāsā|ma pudgalä nāsāma gyasta ḅaysäna klaiṣ̥īnā
3 sānāṃ jau niṣạ̄mä ā|ṇadā biśä pīrmāttama hvata aysä arahaṃdūṃ
4 pahaiṣṭa brrīyai | jsa ni muhu gyasta ḅaysä vyira sä araṇā-vyihārai
19a 1 biśä pīrmāttama a|raṇä cu samāhāña āṇadai cu haṃdarye saṃttāña
2 klaiṣ̥īnai jau ni a|spaśde gyastä ḅaysä tta hve tta cue saittä subhūva
3 aśta nai ṣị dā cu mu|hu jsa dīpaṃkarä ⌒ gyasta ḅaysä īñaka nā āya
4 [āya] a|dhigama-svabhāvī dā ni nā hämä subhūvī tta hve sä miḍạ̄na

[1] Independent *o*.   [2] For *srauttāvaṃnä*.

19b1 gyasta ḇalysä niśtä kāmu jä ṣị dā cu thu dīpaṃgarä gyasta ḇaysäna
2 nā āyai ⌢ | ttana cu adhigama-subhāvä dāta na nā hamä subhūvī tta
3 hve sä | na miḍạ̄na gyasta ḇaysa niśti kāmu jä ṣị dā cu thu dīpakara
4 ḇalysäna īñakä nā āya cu subhūva tta huñī sa aysä buddha-kṣi-
20a1 | trā padaṃja piṣkalä naṣphāñū ṣị kūra hvāñe ci buddha-kṣitra-vyūhä
2 avyūhä | aviṣkastä arūpiṇä gyastä ḇaysäna hvata ⌢ ttye kiṇa subhūta
3, 4 | baudhisatva avārauttä aysmū śtāka ni rūvā vīra pārauttä | ni bajāṣā
20b1 ni buśañāṃ ni ysvạñā na skaumatā na dharmāṃ vīra hau|ra
haurạñä ⌢ ttrạmä mạ̄ñaṃ(dä) subhūva cī jä hve āya cu didaṃdä
2 ttaraṃda|rä āya khu sumīrä garä tta cue suaittä subhūta mistäna
3 ttaraṃdarä | na khu sumīrä gara bihī mistä miḍạ̄na gyasta ḇaysa
4 ḇaysī tta | hve abhāva ṣị ttaraṃdarä ttana ātma-bhāvä ḇaysạ̄nä
21a1 sābhaugī tta|raṃdarä anauṣkājsī kā(yä) na bajaitti gyasta ḇaysī tta
2 hve tta tta gaṃgä nyāya | gruīcyau sye didira ⌢ lovadāta hamāri ⌢
3 kạ̄mu jä dahä ā vā strī|ya haudyau raṃnyau jsa haṃbirä gyastāṃ
4 ḇaysạ̄nu haurä hiḍä caṃdī | puña kūśalä-mulä hamāri ttye dahä o[1]
21b1 vā strīyai cu ttye vajrrachedakyi | prajñā-pārạ̄mi vīra tcūrạpatī śau
2 gāhä dijsāti vāṣ̥īyä sājī | haṃdarạ̄ṇä vistarna uysdīśīya ttye pracainai
3 pharāka pu|ña kūśalä-mūlä hamāri ⌢ kāmye śadyi piṣkalä vīra ṣị
4 dā | ī pajsama-vīya ṣị diṣ̥ä hämä haṃtsa gyasta u hvaṃḍä ysama-
22a1 śaṃdaina kā|mña diśạña dā ī cittye mạ̄ñaṃdä ṣạ̄ diśạ pārṣạ hamä
2 tta tta hā mañạ̄ñä | sä śāstāra ttara āsti u hastamä pīrmāttạmä pīsai ⌢
3 ttye hvaye | hvanai āṣ̥irī subhuta gyasta ḇaysä tta hve ci nāma gyasta
4 ḇaysä | ṣị dā u khuai nāma dijsi ttye hvayai hvanai gyastä ḇaysä tta
22b1 hve prajñā- | pārạ̄ma nāma subhūva ṣị dāta tta ttai nāma dijsi tta ṣị
2 haḍi gyasta ḇalysäna apārạ̄ma hvata ⌢ tta cue saittä subhūva aśtä
3 nai ṣị dāta | cu gyasta ḇaysäna hva āya subhūvī tta hve khu aysä
4 miḍạ̄|na gyasta ḇaysa ttye hvanai arthä bve niśtä kāmu jä ṣị dā cu
23a1 biśau | gyastyau ḇaysyau jsa hva āya ḇaysī tta hve tta cue saittä
2 subhūva dvāradi|rsau mahā-puraṣa-lakṣaṇyau jsa gyasta ḇaysä dyạ̄ñä
3 nai subhūtī tta | hve na miḍạ̄na gyasta ḇaysa dvāradirsa hudihuna
4 gūnā | agūnā ḇaysäna hvata ttana cu dātīnai ttaradarä anavyaṃjanī
23b1 | nai rūpakāyä ttaraṃdarä ttina hvañāri dvāradirsä hudihūna
2, 3 | gūnā cu vā subhuva dahä ā vā strīya gaṃgä nyāya gruīcyau | sye
4 māñaṃdä ttaraṃdarä pasti śị jä vā āya cu ttye sūträ | vīra tcūrapatī
24a1 gāha pạ̄ti sājīyä haṃdarāṇu vistarna bi|rāṣ̥īyä buḍarī puñīnai haṃ-

[1] Independent *o*.

2 bīsai hame avamāta anaṃkhiṣṭyerä | ttī mī ā̤ṣirī subhūta ddharmavigana
3 ā̤ṣki cira yuḍe ālṣka mī ustaḍi gyasta ḇaysä tta hve bihī duṣkara
4 miḍā̤na gyalsta ḇaysä ṣi̤ dā kū jsa maṃ bvā̤ma panata[1] ni rā muhu
24b 1 jsa didira gaṃlbhīrä dā pyūṣṭä cu ṣā bhūtta-saṃña ṣā̤ haḍi abhūta-
2 saṃña natca ḇaysā śālśa̤ṃ ṣā̤ saṃña cu ttū dā ṣadahīdä pīrāttā[2] hā
3 yanāti ni ni ttyāṃ | uysā̤ñe vī saṃña prravarttä ni satva vīra saṃña
4 ni jvāka vī | na pudgalä vī saṃña na na ttyā̤nä nitcarīmai nāsākä
25a 1 arthä vīra | hanāsä aśtä ⌢ ttye hvaye hvanai gyastä ḇaysä ā̤ṣirī subhūta
2 tta hve | tta tta gyastä ḇaysä ⌢ pīrmāttama duṣkare jsa haṃphva
3 hvamāri[3] cu ttye sūträ | hvādä āna ni pvaidä ni harīysāri ni trāysä
4 byehīdä | pīrmāttama duṣkarä ṣā̤ pārā̤ma tvā pārā̤ma avamāta gyastä
25b 1 ḇaysä | hvādä ⌢ ttana kṣamauttitījä pārāma hīvyātca pamāka hämä ⌢
2 kāma bālḍana ma̤mä kalä rri ⌢ aga-prattyaṃga pa̤ste na ni ma̤mä
3 ttye stye ātma-⌢|saṃña vya ni satva-saṃña ni jīva-saṃña na
4 pudgalä-saṃña na maṃ ttū bālḍa saṃña vya u ni asaṃña cu maṃ
26a 1 ṣai ysura saṃña vya muśtä jsa ra haṃphva | maṃ saṃña hamīya
2 paysāni aysä subhūva byāta yani paḍā̤ṃjsyā̤nä bālḍānä pajsa-se
3 ysathä kāmä bāḍā̤nä aysä kṣāntavādä nāma vyi | raṣ̤iyä ttī ma̤mä ⌢ nä
4 ātma-saṃña vya ni satva-saṃña ni jīva-saṃlña ni pudgalä-saṃña
26b 1 ttye härä kiṇa subhūva baudhisatva mistä ḇaysṳ̄ña-|vūysai biśau
2 saṃñau jsa phīśāñä ⌢ u biśä pīrmāttamye ḇaysūśtä aysmū | upevā̤ñä
3 ni rūvāṃ vīra pārautta aysmu upevā̤ña ni bajā̤ṣä | na buśañāṃ ni
4 ysvā̤ñāṃ ni sk(vau)mavāṃ na dharmāṃ vīra ⌢ na kuṣṭai jä | pra-
27a 1 ttakärä vīra pārautta aysmu upevā̤ñä avārautta aysmuna | haurä
2 haurā̤ñä khu nä gūnā saṃña vīra ni pārahi biśāṃ satvānä śiri kilṇa
ṣā̤ saṃña skaddhvā ⌢ na bīdi ⌢ rraṣṭa hvāñe subhūva gyasta ḇaysa
3 haṭha | hvāñä vyāraṇai ni aña ttana cu' prajñai rraṣṭa śrāvaka-yāña
4 halṭha ysvīśe mahāyā̤ña ttāharä vyāraṇa ni aña ⌢ ṣi̤ ra subhūva cu
27b 1 | ṣi̤ dā cu ḇaysäna bustä ni vara haṭha u ni drrūja akṣaryau jsa hva artha
2 bilśä parī hālai gītti ⌢ ttrāmä mā̤ñaṃdä subhūva khu hve ttärä vi
3 traṃdä halmä ni nāmu[4] ja härä vajiṣḍi ttū najsaḍä pārahi pastä
4 baudhisatva | dyā̤ñä cu parī ni daittä ⌢ ttrāmä mā̤ñaṃdä subhūva khu
28a 1 tcaimauda hve byūṣṭe | ye ṣavi saye urmaysdāṃ biśūña rūva daittä
2 ttū najsaḍä ḇaysṳ̄ña-vūlysai dyāñä cu ni nāmye[5] härä vīra pārauttä

[1] *panata* with the stroke of *ta* added to *na*.
[2] *ttā* below.
[3] For *hamāri*.
[4] For *kāmu*.
[5] For *kāmye*.

3 ṣṭāna haurä häḍä ni ⁓ | parī dittä cu sūbhūva bisīvrāṣai o[1] vā bisī-
4 vrāṣaiñä ci ttū | dā dijsādi vą̄ṣ̨īdä paysāṃda hamāri gyastä ḇaysāṃ
28b 1 jsa o[1] dya hamā|ri avamāta puñīnai haṃbīsāna haṃphva hamāri ⁓
2 o[1] strīya o[1] vā da|hä brū haḍā gaṃgä nyāya gruīcyau sye māñaṃdä
3 ttaraṃdarä p̨aste śva ha|ḍä pa̧ş̣ārä didira ttaraṃdara p̨asti ttana
4 pacaḍana kūlä ka|lpä vaṣṭa āna haurä hiḍä ci ttū sūträ p̨āti nai
29a 1 prrakṣīvī ṣadahā | ⟨. . .⟩ttye pracaina buḍarä puñīnai haṃbīsä ysy̨āñe
2 avamāta a|naṃkhiṣṭä cu na ra vā ⁓ cuai pīrīdai buḍarä puñīnai
3 haṃbīsä ysyāñe | avamāta anakhiṣṭa cu na ra vā cue sāji o[1] vā haṃdarä
4, 29b 1 ulysdīśe ⁓ kūṣṭa ttu dā birā̧ş̣īdi pajsamavīya ṣ̨ā di̧ş̣a hamä ham|tsa
gyastä hvaṃḍä ysama-śaṃdaina vaṃnavīya hvaraṃcīñä tvaṃdanä
2 tsuñai | cittyä māñaṃdä ttye di̧ş̣a pajsaṃ tcerai ⁓ cu tti bisīvrrā̧ş̣ä o[1]
3 vä bisī|vrrāṣaiñä ci dädrrāma sūträ dijsādi vā̧ş̣īdi par̨āmīdi tti ⁓
4 | parabhūtta hamāri śirä haḍä parabhūtta hamāri tta ci härä kiḍna
30a 1 | tty̨ānä satv̨ānä paḍą̄ṃjsy̨ānä ysaṃthvä didrrāma karma ya tc̨amna
2 drrayvä avā|yvä ysaṃthä nāsāñä ye ttye sūträ prrabhāvana tti karma
3 harbiśä ⁓ | jāri thyau biśä pīrmāttama ḇaysūśta bvāri ⁓ byāta yani
4 su|bhūva paḍą̄ṃjsy̨ānä bāḍ̨ānä anaṃkhiṣṭ̨āna kalp̨ānä dīpaṃkarä
30b 1 gya|stä ḇaysä pīrmātt̨amä tcahaurä haṣṭä kūlä naysa[2] sa-ysārä gyasta
2 ḇaysä ⁓ | cu harbiśä muhu jsa ārāhya u ni virāhya ⁓ cu vā tti īdä
3 u|stamājsī bāḍä ustamauysye paṃcāśai cu tvā vajrrachedaka-sū-
4 | trä vā̧ş̣īdi o[1] parīdi pīḍi dijsādi ḇūna spyau jsai pajsama yanī-
31a 1 | di u śau śalo ustamāta pūjä pajsaṃ yanī ⁓ ttye bisīvrrāṣai puñī-
2 | nai haṃbīsai brrūbi sataṃ nasä ysāraṃ nasä kūlä nasä haṃkhī- ⁓
3, 4 | ysä masä uśm̨āna masi na ni kaśte ≈ ttī vā ā̧ş̣irī subhūtä gya|sta
ḇaysä tta hve khu vā miḍ̨āna gyasta ḇaysä baudhisatvä-y̨ānī marä
31b 1 | mahāyāña aysmū biysaṃj̨āñä gyastä ḇaysī tta hve mara subhūva
2 baudhisa|tva mästä ḇaysų̄ña-vūysaina tta tta aysmū upevāñä biśä
3 satva ahari|na paranirvāy̨āña ⁓ ni haḍi kāmu jä satva paranirvāña
4 | hāmä ⁓ tta ci härä kiḍna ⁓ cī subhūva baudhisatvä satva-saṃña
32a 1 hamāti | ni ṣ̨a baudhisatvä hvañai o[1] ātma-saṃña o[1] vā jīva-saṃñä
2 o[1] pudgalä-saṃña | hamāti ni ṣ̨ baudhisatva hvañai tta ci härä kiṇa
3 niśtä ṣ̨ dharmä | kāmu jä (cu) baudhisatva-y̨āñä haṃjsedai āya ⁓
4 aśtä nai ṣ̨ subhūva | dharmä cu gyasta ḇaysäna dīpaṃkarä gyasta
32b 1 ḇaysä īñaka biśä pīrmātta|mä ḇaysūśtä bustä āya ttye hvaye hvanai
2 ā̧ş̣irī subhūta gyastä ḇaysä ⁓ | tta hve sä niśtä mäḍ̨āna gyastä ḇaysä

[1] Independent *o*.

[2] For *nayva*.

3 kā̮mu jä ṣä̮ dharmä cu gyasta b̮aysä | na biśä pīrmāttama b̮aysūśtä
4 bustä āya ttye hvaye hvanai gyasta b̮alysä ā̮ṣirī subhūtä tta hve tta
33a 1 tta ṣi̮ härä subhūta niśtä kā̮mu jä ṣi̮ dharmä cu | gyasta b̮aysna
2 dīpaṃkarä gyasta b̮aysana b̮aysūśtä bustä āya cī subhūva | kāmu jä
3 ṣi̮ dharmä vya cu gyasta b̮aysana b̮aysūśtä bustä vya ni muhu | vyira
4 sä hama thu māṇavā ustamājsī bāḍä śākyamunä nāma gya˷|sta
33b 1 b̮aysä ˷ ttana cu ttūśāttä ṣi̮ b̮aysūśtä na ra vara haṭha na drrū̮jä | ttrā̮mä
mā̮ñaṃdä subhūva cī jä hve āya cue mistä ttaraṃdarä āya subhū-
2 | tī tta hve ṣi̮ miḍā̮nä ˷ gyasta b̮aysa ttaraṃdarä attaraṃdarä gyasta
3 b̮alysana hvata ˷ tta cue saittä subhūta aśtä nai ṣi̮ dharmä cu gyasta
4 b̮aysna | biśä pīrmāttama b̮aysūśtä busta āya subhūtī tta hve ni
34a 1 miḍā̮nä | gyasta b̮aysa niśtä kā̮mu jä ṣi̮ dharmä cu b̮aysū̮ña-vūysai
2 nāma āya | cu vina uysā̮ñe vina satvä vina pudgalä biśä hära ttū
3 nijsaḍa | vyachī ṣi̮ buddha-kṣitrā vyūha näṣphāñe ṣi̮ na b̮aysū̮ña-
4 vūysai hvalñai cu biśä hära vina uysā̮ñe vyachī ṣi̮ ttāharai baudhi-
34b 1 satva hva | tta cue saittä subhūva byaudi ni gyastä b̮aysä gūśtīji
2 tcaim̮a̮ñä ˷ su | bhūvī tta hve byaudai gyastä b̮aysä gūśtaijä tcaim̮a̮ñä ˷
3 ttī vā gya|sta b̮aysä ā̮ṣirī subhūta tta hve byaudi gyastä b̮aysä
4 gyastū̮ | ñä tcaim̮a̮ñä gyastä b̮aysä ā̮ṣirī subhūta tta hve byaudai gyastä
35a 1 b̮alysä gyastū̮ñä tcaim̮a̮ñä ˷ ttī vā gyastä b̮aysä ā̮ṣirī subhūta tta
2 hve | byaudai gyasta b̮aysä dātījä tcaim̮a̮ñä ˷ ā̮ṣirī subhūta tta hve
3, 4 | byaudai gyasta b̮aysä dātījä tcaim̮a̮ñä ˷ ttī vā ā̮ṣirī | sūbhūta gyastä
35b 1 b̮aysä tta hve īdä gyastāṃ b̮aysāṃ hajvattetījä | tcaim̮a̮ñä gyasta b̮aysä
2 ā̮ṣirī subhūta tta hve byaude gyasta b̮aysä ˷ | hajvattetīnai tcemä ˷
3 ttī vā ā̮ṣirī subhūta gyasta b̮aysä tta | hve īdä gyastā b̮aysāṃ dātījä
4 tcem̮a̮ñä ˷ gyasta b̮aysä ā | ṣ̮irī subhūta tta hve īdä gyastāṃ b̮aysāṃ
36a 1 dātījä tcem̮a̮ñä ˷ ttī | vā gyastä b̮aysä ā̮ṣirī sūbhuva tta hve īdä
2 gyastāṃ b̮aysāṃ b̮aysū̮ña tcai|[m̮a̮ña̮]m̮āñä īdä ā̮ṣirya subhūta
3 gyastāṃ b̮aysāṃ b̮aysū̮ña tcai|m̮a̮ñä ˷ ttī vā gyasta b̮aysä ā̮ṣirī
4 subhūta gūṣṭe u tta pastai | ci tvā tṛsahasrya mahāsahasrya lovadātä
36b 1 haudyau raṃnyau jsa haṃ|birä haura̮ hiḍi caṃdä ṣi̮ bisīvrrāṣai o[1]
2 bisīvrrāṣaiñä puña kūśalä-|mūlä ysyā̮ñe ā̮ṣirī sūbhūtä tta hve bihī
3 pharä miḍā̮nä gyastä | b̮aysa puñā kūśalä-mūlāṃ haṣkamä ysyā̮ñe ˷
4 cu vātcä haṃdā|rai bisīvrrāṣai cu tva vajrrachedaka-sūträ ustamāta
37a 1 śau tcūrapatī gāhä | pīrī sājīyā dijsāti vā̮ṣīyā b̮ū spyau jsai pajsaṃ
2 yanī ˷ ttye bisīvrrā|ṣaiñä buḍarä puñīnai haṃbīsä hämä ˷ sataṃ

[1] Independent *o*.

3 nasä ysāraṃ nasä | uśmą̄na masi hā ni kaśtä ⁓ ttī gyasta ḇaysä āṣ̨irī
4 subhūta tta | hve tta hve sä tta cve sai(ttä) āṣ̨arya subhūta tta ci härä
37b 1 kiḍna ni ṣ̨i subhūta sa | lakṣaṇīja pyālye jsa gyastä ḇaysä dyą̄ñä nai ⁓
2 āṣ̨irī subhūta tta hve | na miḍą̄na gyasta ḇaysa lakṣaṇījä pyālye jsa
3 gyasta ḇaysä dyą̄ñä ni | cīyä gyasta ḇaysa lakṣaṇīji pyālye jsa gyasta
4 ḇaysä vyä rri ṣą̄ | cakrravarttä ḇaysä hamīya ttana cakrravarta rruṃda
38a 1 lakṣaṇa-īji pyālye | jsa ḇaysä dyą̄ñä ⁓ ttī gyastä ḇaysä tta gāha hve ⁓
2 cu muhu ruvane deda cu | ma salāyau jsa mañāre
kūra cedą̄ma ttyą̄ṃ tta muhu herṣṭāya na deda
3 | dharmahe jsa ḇaysä dyą̄ña dātī dāvīne taraṃdara ttyą̄na
4 dū|ṣ̨abusta darmaha raṣṭa nai ye kara tcārą̄ṇa buśte ||
38b 1 tta cve setta sūbhūva|cu tta hvāñīye se ḇaysä ṣṭa au[1] vā hīśtä au[1] vā
2 biche [au[1] vā biche] | au[1] jsāve ṣ̨i maṃ hvāñą̄me artha baute cu haḍa
3 hera subhūva ḇaysä | tathāgata hvīde auṣkaujsī[1] cu na hamete jaḍa
4 haḍa ṣṭā kūra | nāsāre avyāsta ṣ̨a dharma-mūkhau jsa jaḍau praha-
39a 1 jañau jsa tta ce herä | kiṇa cu ṣ̨i ī subhūta cu tta hvāñī ḇaysäna hvata
2 uysą̄ñai vīra dyą̄lma adyą̄ma ṣą̄ gyasta ḇaysäna hvata ttina cu niśtūjä
3 uysą̄nā | dyą̄ma ttina gyasta ḇaysäna hvata avyāstä dharma jaḍyau
4 prahu|jañau jsa hvata kāmą̄ñä diṣ̨añä ttū sūtra birāṣ̨īdi tta tta hā
39b 1 ma|ñą̄ñä śāstārä ttara āsti u pīrmāttąmä ha[ma]stąmä pīsai ⁓ ttye
2 hvaye hva|nai āṣ̨irī subhūta gyasta ḇaysä tta hve sä cu nąma gyastä
3 ḇaysä ⁓ | ṣ̨i dā u khvai nāma dijsi gyastä ḇaysī tta hve prrajñā-pārą̄ma
4 nąlma subhūta ṣ̨i dātä tta ttai nāma dijsä ⁓ cu haḍi prrajñā-pārāma
40a 1 ṣ̨i gyastä | ḇaysana apārą̄ma hvata ⁓ tta cue saittä subhūta aśtä nai ṣ̨i
2 dā kū jsa | maṃ bvāma patata[2] dvāra[dira]dirśau mahāpuraṣa-
3 lakṣaṇyau jsa gyastä ḇalysä dyą̄ñä subhūvī tta hve na miḍą̄nä gyasta
4 ḇaysa agūnā gyastä | ḇaysäna hvata ⁓ gyastä ḇaysī tta hve tta tta subhūta
40b 1 baudhisatva-yą̄ña ḇajsaṃ|daina ḇaysūña-vūysaina harbiśä dharma
2 vyachą̄ñä khu dharma-saṃña vīra na pā|rahi ⁓ cu vā baudhisatva
3 ḇaysūñä-vūysai avamāta anaṃkhiṣṭa lo|vadāta haudyau ranyau jsa
4 haṃbiri haurą hiḍi ⁓ cu ṣ̨i bisīvrrāṣai cu ttye | vajrra-chedakyi prajñā-
41a 1 pārą̄me dā vīra ustamāta tcahaurapatī śau gāhä | nāsāti o[3] sājī haṃ-
2 daryą̄ṇä hālai uysdīśīyä ṣ̨i haḍi ttye puñīnai haṃ|bīsä buḍarä ysyą̄ñe
3 avamāta anaṃkhiṣṭä tta tta haḍi birāṣ̨ą̄ñä | khu hā uysnaurāṇa buhu-
4 mą̄nä ni bajaitti ādarä hā yanāri | o[3] garkhuṣṭānä tta tta hvīdi
birą̄ṣ̨ą̄ñä || ttī vā gyastä ḇaysä tti gāha hve

[1] Independent *au*. [2] For *panata*. [3] Independent *o*.

41b 1 khu ⊦jä oña[1] stārā dyāri ṣīvi brrūñāri hamrraṣṭä
2 cī byūśtä sarbä urmaysde | biśä narābhāsa hämāri ||
3 ttū padī indri[1] bvḁ̄ñä tcemä āstaṃna anilci ⌢
cī panami bvāma rraṣṭa ni jä nä āyāri hugvāna ||
4 crrḁ̄ma hve cu | tcaiña kḁ̄ṣä biśūña rūva vajseṣḍe
42a 1 ttai jä harä ttatva na īdä dyāri haḍi | kḁ̄ṣä pracaina ||
ttū padī rūva vicitra biśūña saidä jaḍḁ̄nä
2–3 | vina aysmū gvāna ni īdä saṃ aysmū kūrä halnāsä ≈
4 crrā mḁ̄ñaṃda uysnaura carau pracailna vījsyāri
42b 1 ttū padī ⌢ aysmu īña vaṣiyḁ̄nä ⌢ | dyḁ̄ma bvḁ̄ñä ||
saṃ khu praha gīsai nauhya bakä burä āstä u pīttä
2 tta | tta ⌢ ttaraṃdarä bata dasti m̥uṣ̥a buri pīttä ≈
3 saṃ khu khāysmūlā ucä | bāna paṣkauta asāra
4 tta tta varḁ̄ṣāma bvāñä suha dūkha ttalvā upekṣa ||
43a 1 saṃ khu hūsaṃdä uysnaura hūnä daittä khu vā beyseldyä
ni jä nä vara bhāvä ni drravyä samu byāta hamä ttū bāḍä ⌢
2 ttrḁ̄lmä tti ṣkaujä cu mara ye haittä bāḍä
3 samu ra ttī byāta ⌢ | hämä ttū bāḍä ||
4 trḁ̄ma mḁ̄ñaṃdä khu pyaura bāra berḁ̄lñä ttū bāḍa
43b 1 ttīmañāṃ pracai diysdai hārvaidä pryaurä prabhāvalna
tta tta ustamājsye ṣkaujä [ṣkaujä] cu ṣā vīpakajä bhrāntä
2 biśū̥ñä | ttīmḁ̄ñä diysedä hārvaidä pyaurä prabhāvana ||
3 ttū padī | ṣkaujä paṃtsḁ̄ñä nau padya khu mara najsūṣṭä
4 ttī vasve byehä ⌢ | rḁ̄ṣä saṃtsärä ṣi̥ baudhisatvä ×[2] •
44a 1 saṃtsira gvḁ̄nä ni jīyä ni | nirvāña yaṃdi prayaugä
2 na haḍi vara ni ṣi̥ mä gvāna tta tta alvārautta hamrraṣṭä

3 ttū burä hve gyastä ḅaysä sīrä hamye ḁ̄ṣilrī subhūta avaśiṣṭau ḁ̄ṣirya
4 ḁṣi ūvāysä ū(vā)ysye gyasta ⌢ | dīvitāna aysura-gḁndharvāṃ āstaṃna
44b 1 lovya parṣḁ gyasta ḅaysä ⌢ | haḍi vajrrachedaka ttṛśayä prajñā-pārḁ̄ma samāsye ||
2 | siddhaṃ
3 vajrrachidakyi hīya ttā diṣṭḁ̄nta | hvañāri ≈
paḍāṃjsyāṃ bāḍāṃ śiña kṣira śau lakṣa

[*Buddha figure in centre of folios* 1*b and* 44*b*]

[1] Independent *o* and *i*.

[2] Small sign, perhaps *na*.

7

Ch. 00276

Folio 3

*a*1 6 namau bhāṣma nā̮ma gyasta[1] b̮aysä namasūṃ 7 :
*a*2 namau aṣaṃgarājä b̮aysä namasūṃ 8
*b*1 namau mahāprrabhāsi gyastä baysä namasūṃ 9
*b*2 namau merū gyasta b̮aysä namasūṃ 10

Folio 4

*a*1 n(am)au agrākarä gyastä b̮aysä namasūṃ 1
*a*2 namau śrīgarbhakuṭi gyastä b̮aysa namasūṃ 2
*b*1 namau sarvārthasidhaśrī[1] gyastä b̮aysä namasūṃ 3
*b*2 namau hettauttaṃ gyastä b̮aysä namasūṃ : 4

Folio 9

*a*1 namau maitrai baudhisatvä namasūṃ ⌢
*a*2 namau ākāśagarbhä baudhisatvä namasū ⌢
*b*1 namau maṃjuśrī[1] baudhisatvä[2] namasūṃ ⌢ namau bhaiṣa-
*b*2 jirājä baudhisatvä namasūṃ ——

Folio 11

*a*1 namau piṃdūra bharadvāgya̮[3] sthīrä namasūṃ ⌢ ——
*a*2 namau kanakavatsi sthīra namasūṃ ⌢ ——
*b*1 namau kanaka-bharadhvājä sthīrä namasūṃ
*b*2 namau bhaiṣajä sthīrä namasūṃ ⌢ ——

Folio 12

*a*1 namau bakulä sthīrä namasūṃ ⌢ ——
*a*2 namau bhadrrika sthīrä namasūṃ ⌢ ——
*b*1 namau kāḍika̮[4] sthīrī namasūṃ ⌢ ——
*b*2 namau vajrraputrä sthīrä namasūṃ ⌢ ——

[1] With *sta* and *rī* below.
[2] *satvä* below.
[3] *gyaṃ* below.
[4] *kaṃ* below.

Folio 14

*a*1 namau vanavāsa¹ sthīrā namasūṃ ⌒ namau a-
*a*2 jittā sthīrā namasūṃ ⌒ namau cūḍa-pa-
*b*1 thai sthīrā namasūṃ ⪯ || gyastā ḅaysāṃ hī-
*b*2 ye nạ̈me u baudhisatvāṃ u mahā

Folio 18

*a*1 saddhaṃ namau sattaunā samya-sabauda kauṭīnā ttad-yathā cu le
　　　cu le cau
*a*2 tte svāhā || || namau aprattaprrabheva-mulagarbhe pratara baudhi-
　　　same
*a*3 sedhya sedhya mahāgarbhe ttūra ttūra svāhā oma² vapula ttāre hu || ||
b　　[*free*]

8

Ch. XCVI 0012*b*

*a*1 śamitha sị cụ naṣọma ⪯ vapaśana sị cụ dyạ̈ma dạ̈
*a*2 śamatha vapaśana vīra vä ⌒ ṣāvāṃ hīya u prra-
*a*3 ttīka-bodhā hīya ⌒ u bodhasatvāṃ hīya ⪯ u ⌒
*b*1 gyastā ḅaysā hīya ⌒ anakhaiṣṭa ⌒ samāhona
*b*2 hadrrīya ṣṭāre ⌒ hetti sạ̈ cụ parạ̈māṃ ⌒ nīvạ̈
*b*3 sạ̈ cụ ⌒ pvāmavīja bvama³ ⌒ u cidāmavīja bvạ̈ma

9

Ch. LXVIII 001 with Ch. XVIII 001

Folio 255

1 [*small hauda before line*] | bvāka hīrạ̈ñā vīra ⪯
　kạ̈mā āvaṣạ̈ paiṣkala narrujạ̈me hālai sājanai harbaiśā padya bvāka
　　hīrạ̈ñā vīra ⪯

¹ *sa* below.　　　² Independent *o-*.　　　³ Read *bvāma*.

2 kąma āvaş̣ä paiṣka⟨la⟩ | apanamąme hālai sājanai harbaiśä padya bvākä hīrąñä vīra ≈

kąmä aysmu paiṣkala jaiga hālai sājanai harbaiśa padya bvāka
3 ⟨hī⟩|rąñä vīra ≈

kąma aysmu paiṣkala avajsañąme hālai sājanai harbaiśä padya bvāka hīrąñä vīra ≈

4 kąma aysmva paiṣkala narū|jāme hālai sājanai harbaiśä padya bvāka hīrąñä vīra ≈

kąma aysmu paiṣkala apanamąme hālai sājänai harbaiśä padya bvāka
5 hī|rąñä vīra ≈

kąma abauste jaigya hālai sājanai harbaiśä padya bvāka hīrąñä vīra ≈

6 kąma abauste avajsañąme hālai sājanai | harbaiśa padya bvākä hīrąñä vīra

kąma abauste avajsañąme hālai narująme hālai sājanai harbaiśä
7 padya bvāka hīrą|ñä vīra ≈

kąma abauste apanamąme hālai sājanai harbaiśa padya bvākä hīrąñä vīra ≈

8 kąma ṣkāṃjāṃ (jai)gya hālai sāja|nai harbaiśä padya bvākä hīrąñä vīra ≈

kąma ṣkāṃjāṃ avajsañąme hālai sājanai harbaiśä padya bvāka hīrąñä vīra ≈

9 kąma ṣkāṃjāṃ | narrująme hālai sājanai harbaiśä padya bvākä hīrąñä vīra ≈

kąma ṣkāṃjāṃ apanamąme hālai sājanai harbaiśä padya bvākä
10 hīrą|ñä vīra ≈

kąma aysmu jaigya hālai sājanai harbaiśä padya bvāka hīrąñä vīra ≈

11 kąmä aysmu avajsañąme hālai sājanai harbai-|śä padya bvāka hīrąñä vīra ≈

kąma aysmu narrująme hālai sājanai harbaiśa padya bvāka hīrąñä vīra ≈

12 kąma aysmu apana|mąme hālai sājanai harbaiśa padya bvāka hīrąñä vīva[1] ≈

kąma nąma-rru jaigyä hālai sājanai harbaiśä padya bvāka hīrąñä vīra ≈

Verso

13 kąma | [kąma] nąma-rru avajsañąme hālai sājanai harbaiśa padya bvāka hīrąñä vīra ≈

[1] Read *vīra*.

14 kąma nąma-rū narūjąme hālai sājanai ha | rbaiśa ⟨padya⟩ bvāka hīrāñä
vīra ≈
kąma nąma-rru apanamąme hālai sājanai harbaiśä padya bvāka
hīrąñä vīra ≈
15 kąmä kṣyāṃ | tvārāṃ jaigya hālai sājanai harbaiśä padya bvāka hīrąñä
vīra ≈
kąma kṣyāṃ tvārāṃ avajsañąme hālai sājanai harbaiśä padya
16 bvā | ka hīrąñä vīra ≈
kąma kṣyāṃ tvārāṃ narrująme hālai sājanai harbaiśa padya bvākä
hīrąñä vīra ≈
17 kąma kṣyāṃ tvārāṃ apanamąme | hālai sājanai harbaiśä padya bvāka
hīrąñä vīra ≈
kāmä skvāme jaigyä hālai sājanai harbaiśä padya bvāka hīrąñä vīra ≈
18 kāmä skvąme | avajsañąme hālai sājanai ha ‿ rbaiśa padya bvāka hīrąñä
vīra ≈
19 kāma skvąme narrująme hālai sājanai harbaiśä padya bvāka | hīrąñä
vīra ≈
kąma skvąme apanamąme hālai sājanai harbaiśä padya bvāka hīrąñä
vīra ‿
20 kąma varąṣąme jaigyä hā(lai) | sājanai harbaiśä padya bvākä hīrąña
vīra ≈
21 kąmä varāṣąme avājsañąme hālai sājanai harbaiśa padya bvākä hīrąñä
vī | ra ≈
kąma varāṣąme narrująme hālai sājanai harbaiśa padya bvąka hīrąñä
vīra ≈
22 kąma varāṣāme apanamąme hālai sājanai | harbaiśa padya bvāka
hīrąñä vīra ≈
kąma ęsāṃ jaigya hālai sājänai harbaiśä padya bvāka hīrąñä vīra ≈
23 kąma ęsāṃ avajsañāme hālai sā | janai harbaiśä padya bvāka hīrąñä
vīra ≈
kąma ęsāṃ narrująme hālai sājanai harbaiśä padya bvāka hīrąñä vīra ≈
24 kąma ąisā apanam⟨āme⟩ | hālai sājanai harbaiśä padya bvąkä hīrąñä
vīra ≈
kąma pasujsanāṃ jaigyä hālai sājanai harbaiśä padya bvāka hīrąñä
vīra ≈
ką⟨ma.⟩ |

10

Ch. 00266

01 byūṣṭa vas[1]
1 byūṣṭa vasve juhaunau bāḍa pasailī
2 cu ṣṭā pa⟨......⟩mya | jūhai :
bīysāña ṣṭā casta hvaṇḍä śūja vaska :
3 seśīryau thyau pū[×]|ṣa spyakyā dāśāda :
phūmīdā[2] ṣṭā dīśa̯ vī brravīya padamaka
4 jū|hājaka thajīda ysera ṣa̯ca brīyekyä
5 maṣṭā tta tta setta ṣa̯ ṣṭā jabvī | hūrī
hūvāysañīda jūhaunai ttrakṣa̯ [kṣa] ma kiṇa
6 dīśa̯ vī pastā|va jasta māgadha māsta
ṣa̯śākā va ṣe̯rīda hamāranvā spyakvā
7 hvaṇḍā vī mūśa̯ yūḍāda mara pā dāśāda :
8 ustā karāśa | paiśkya u spūleka khīysara spyakye
9 kakva tcīrāka u papūśkya be|jakyä
tta mī bījeṣāre hada spyauysā bahyā
10 paijakya gvīthāre tta ma | jsāṃ hada karaśau :
sāha̯na gvīradā tsīda hada spyalakau[3] :
11 uska a|sphīraca jahvā sphālya-gūna
12 spyakīnai kāysvāka bīḍa pajsa-:|gu
aysdyäva ragā jsa gesta yada īsakye
13 panāyīda spyakya khū | ja bīna astana
spyakīnai pyauśa̯ka a̯iheja aysbanakvā
14 bī:|ysaśta tvā uska sāha jsa hā sāśe
15 nāṣṭa ttaśta spyakya habrrai|sta būśau jsa:
tta ā bījāṣe yeda khu jastūña gaysakye
16 mūai|śa̯ uysdaitta a̯isījā tcameśakyā jsa
17 aysmūryau jūhānai sāñīda pa|vanaka :
vaṣi̯cha khuīśakyā jsa raga spyakya bīysaśta
18 parageśa | skādaka samū brra māṇḍvā khai tta
19 ysarūne para bahyā samū gvaiva bā|stāda
ñāña spūlakīnā haphada āṣṭaka

[1] Half-written *s*. [2] *-dā* with *-au* deleted. [3] *ya* for *ū*.

20 ttarū lākṣa-gū khīysara | karvīnā
hanavä tta sa śūje paujsada paśąuda jsa
21 hadara haṣprraya | khu brrī vaka brrīyaka
ṇasta havrrīśace khu hale-beśkvā tsaba
22 khūau | ysa nūvara bādāha brrīyūna
23 sa kha jīśka māṇḍvā phastāre ca | pane
hadara ysanāra ṣaṣa brre hala-beśkvā
24 nā varūśara khu tcījsa | brrīyakya pejụā
chakanyau dadākyau skauda byahanīda
25 sa khu ja brra khī | tta skauda brrīyaka (va)ska ⸎
hadara ąijsava śīya ttarūna spyakye
26 pa | damyau phastāra brre garśa mīrāhę
27 pajarūṣṭīda śūje tta khu śatta | nvā pāyvā
ką(staka) ysānāra hatsa pajūṣṭa jsa
28 yyauvaka sāñada ttū spya | kūḍi pavakä
sāñīda ūskyāṣṭā yaka
29 sarbä paḍaura brrīyakyä | māśāṣṭa
brrīyūnakye cesta jīśke kṣaudā-bākve[1]
30 ūysdvīda kara | śā jsa vīyārastū śūje
31 khāṣ̨īdau ttū brrīvīnai ysaujsi ṇį | ka-raysä[2] ⸎
(kau)kalą īmūka tcāṣą karavī stārya
32 kakva papūśkyä beja | kya ysyama[3]
aṣṇā tcīrauka ū ttara ūcā mūraka
33 gąga tsīda bahyyūā | brrīya jsa śatcapha ⸎
hadara kṣįjīda [×] hada bahyā śūje
34 tta | ma jsā bvejsyau spyakya haññāre
35 yenāra ttū ysīra byāje hva | ra bījāṣàka
sa : khu pauśkya kęjīdaījījana nūvare
36 ṣādakye rrā | ysada hada hauṣkyā bahyā :
[×] karaka kąjī u thculasta hūḍūka
37 | cha rrvana pā u gesaca rrvasanakye
38 śūje pyatsa ñada pā gahvada ma grrau | sīda [×]
hagrrīsīda caurakya [dī] bauṇyakya spya
39 kakva [×] ṣęrīda jūhe | jsa khu ranīja bīna ṣkūī
gūjsabrrīsīda dīśą vī paskaṣṭa hā tsīde
40 baysara | nāyaca sa brrī pamara būsta

[1] For *bāḍve*. [2] For *eka-raysä*. [3] *-ya-* for *-ū-*.

cu ttye na ī gūscyanai āspara bada
41 nai ī | gvaḍa śą bhavanīja mva-varga
kāma-gūṇā hīya jsa gajsa na būāve
42 drāmya [ba] bāḍa | vī ā tta ——

11

P 2896

49 byą̄ṣṭä vasve jūhą̄nai bāḍa pasālī
50 cū ṣṭāṃ pa-sai tta brrāṃ hvą̄ṣṭau | aysmya juhąi
bīysą̄ña ṣṭāṃ caista hvaṇḍa śūje vaska
51 seśī | ryāṃ thyāṃ thyāṃ pūṣa spyakyāṃ dāśūda
52 phūmīda ṣṭāṃ dīśą vī | brravīya pädamaka
53 juhāṃjakya thajīda [×] ysīra se | ca brrīyäkye
maṣṭāṃ tta tta saitta ṣą ṣṭāṃ jabvī hūrī
54 hūvā(ysañīda jūhaunai) ttraikṣa | ma kaṇa
dīśą vī pastāva jasta mą̄gada mą̄sta
55 seśą̄ | kāṃ vaiṣąna hamą̄ranvā spyakya
hvaṇḍāṃ vī mvaiśdą ī

12

P 2956

1 ... ⟨se⟩śāk⟨ā⟩ṃ ha ....
2 ..... | .... ḍama vī ⁓
3 vaña vā dāś ..... | ⟨sp⟩ya⟨k⟩y⟨e⟩
⟨kak⟩va tcį̄rraukạ ū papūśkyä baijakye ⁓
4 tta mī bīje | ṣärrä hada spyauysau bahyau ⁓
5 tta ma jsā bvejsā jsa spyakya hą̄ñ(ā) | ñārre
są̄nä aysaṃvīrradā tsīda hą̄da spūläkau 4
6 ūska a | saphīräcą jahą sphālya-gūnä ⁓
7 spyakīnai kāysvą̄ka bīḍä | baida pajsa-gū ⁓
aysdyūva ragyau jsa gesta yäda īsakye ⁓
8 panāyīdä | spyakyä khu ja bīna astą̄na 5

spyakīnai byauśąuka ihęja aysbanvāi[1] ~
9 bīysa | śta tvā uską se haṃjsịṣḍai sänāṃ ≈
nvārī ttaśtą : spyakyau habịrstä būnau jvāṃ ~
10 tta āṃ bī | jāṣa yida khu jastuña gaysąkye 6
mvaiśą uysditta īsīja tcaimeśkyau jsa ~
11 | ąysmūryau jūhaunai ˢąñä pąvänakä ~
12 vaṣąicha khvauśkyāṃ jsa raga spyakya | bīysaśte ~
pargeśa skāṃda sä mū brre mąṇḍāṃ va khai 7
13 ysą-guna pera ba | hyau tta sä gvaiva bāstāṃdä ~
ñāña spūlakīnā haphada ąṣṭakye ~
14 tta | rūnä lākṣūna nauka khīysarrä kąrvī ~
15 hanava tta sa śūje pau | jsīda paśąudana 8
16 hadarra haṣaprrīya khu brrī vąska brrīya | ka ~
ṇesta havrrīśaca khu halą-baiśakvā tsabe ~
17 khauysadā nū | varra baudāha brrīyūnä ~
18 sa khu jīśkyą mauṇḍvā phastārra cā | paṇe (9)
khu hadarra ysaunārra khu ṣąṣa brre hala-baiśakvā ~
19 nāṣṭä | varūśārä khu tcaijsa brrīyakyą paijvāṣṭą ~
20 chakīnyauai[2] dadyākyau skau | da byahanīda ~
sa khu ja brra khītta skauda brrīyakä vaska 10
21 hadä | ājsava śī ttarūnyāṃ spyąkyau ~
22 padämyā phastāra khu brre garśa mīrā | hye ~
pajarūṣṭīdä śūje tta khu śattanvā pāyvā ~
23 kestaka ysąnā | ra hatca pajūṣṭāṃ jsa ~ 11
24 yąvaka sąñīdä ttū spyakūḍa patana | kä ~
sąñīdä uskyāṣṭa uysnāra tta ānaka ~
25 śīya-vrrahau sätta | khu dāśadai brrīyaką ~
26 sarba paḍaure śvą ṣave brrīyakye māśāṣṭa | 12
bachadā bahyą karāśą śūjañāṣṭa ~
27 brrīyūnakye cai | sta jīśkye kṣādvā-bāḍvāe[3] ~
28 aysdīda karāśau jsa vīyārastū śū | je ~
khāṣịda ttū brrīvīnai ysājsāṃ ika-räysä 13
29 kaukala | īmūka cāṣę karävīrä ~
30 stārye papūśakyä bīdye baijakye | ysūmä
aṣṇä ttā tcīraukä ū [tta[4] cuā] ttara ūcā mūrakä

[1] -*ā* and -*i* together.
[2] -*au* and -*ai* together.
[3] -*ā* and -*e*.
[4] *tta* below.

31 gẹgẹ tsīda | bahyau brrīye jsa śatcapha 14
32 hadara kṣaijīda hadä bahyāṃ | śūje
tta bajsāṃ bẏijsāṃ jsa spyakya hañāñāre ˷
33 yanāra | ttū ysīra byāji hvara bījāṣakä ˷
34 sa khu pauśkye kejīda ī|jīja nūvare 15
ṣaudakye rāysāra hada hauṣkāṃ bahyau ˷
35 | kargaka kejīdū [hū][1] u thvrrūcalaste hūlūka ˷
36 cha hvasta pākū | gesaca[2] rūsanakye śūje
37 pyatsa ñīdä pau gahvarda ma grrūsīdä | 16
hagrīsīdä cạṇakya bauṇvakya spyakyakvāṣṭa ˷
38 ṣịrī|da [×][1] jūhaunai hva bījāṣakä ˷
gūbrrīsīda dīśạ vī paskyāṣṭạ hāysa tsīda ˷
39 bä|ysāra nāyicạ sa brrī paṃmara bauste 17
40 cū ttye na ī gūstīnai āsparä | biṃdä ˷
nai ī gvaḍau śạ bāvạṇījī mū-varga ˷
41 kauma-gūṇāṃ hīya pijsāṃ gajsa na | bvāve ˷
drạmye bāḍa vīra āda*mād*ä bīysaśte 18
42 spyakyau ājsava be|ysa habäḍa phạysdve ˷
jạstūñe khaśạva isphīraciña hāysaiña ˷
43 yausa jsa | varkāṃdä būśaña spyakyau hīya ˷
arähaṃda vara śtāka ci ûvī tsāṣṭa dīrye īda ˷ ⟨19⟩
44 khu | piṃjakya gvīthāva kveśạ brrīyakya vaska ˷
hagyeḍa skaudä brraukalakīje vaṭākye ˷
45 ttūrakä ha|rrāśạdai vaña śạula auṣṭạkye ˷
jasta ḅaysa ttadī[3] śaca ra gū yanīda ˷ 20
46[4] | nai būśa vaṭākye tcanä[5] pajiḍa ûvīśkye ˷
narvaunū sạha cadä ys(au)sta ttye jsa aṃnä × ——
47 vatcakya pạysaṇvakyä khị|nai būśä vaiṭākye
nvärīda u vakṣesaca brrāsakye
48 | stiñe vaṭākye tcaṃna pajeḍä ûvīśkye
49 nervạṇū sauhä caṃ|dä ysausta
50 ttye jsa puñūda ạrähaṃda cū saṃtsārä nä|raṃdạ
nạ ysīra brrī aśtä na vā jūhai bvạ(re)
51 a | mụ̄śtu kīra yuḍeṃ haṃdara ysaṃthvạ

[1] Blurred. [2] *ca* below. [3] *dī* below.
[4] Line 46 deleted (=48), except *aṃnä* ×.
[5] With *nvākaka* below.

52 ca ma ṣṭāṃ jūhau | ni ri vyattive panūḍai 22
53 prrihajinyau hvąṇḍyau ąmi | byaṃdi na tsūivą
ṣkaujīnai sauhä bida pą̄jsä naṣiḍi
54 | saṃtsārä drrāma tti khu rai bida mīrica
55 āra-mārga | bāvyerä saṃtsāra näraumyara 23
56 ką̄ma tte ya pīrū|yau bāḍä prrihajinau satva
57 cū mara kīḍaśąu jsa ṣiṣṭi | ką̄ma-guṇāṃ bidä
58 avamāva b̨eysi paryi na rä | vījāṣṭāda
59 drrą̄myi sauha kaiṇa dūrā naryi vavada | 24
mādāttä rre vīna haṃkhīysi tsīda raṣṭe
60 pų|ñāṃ prribhāva nāva śakrrāṃ āysaṃ
61 ş̨ūrī pi̧ñau jsa | ū yserä biśä tcabrrīyi
62 ką̄(ma)-guṇvā avipha ṃ|di ṣṭā jsīna paśāve 25
63 jaustiña hauśä jastyau | pharä ysārä salī
64 vi( )āma[1] ⟨ya?⟩nīdū[2] sāna varai hau|ve pīhīya
65 ką̄ma-guṇāṃ keṇā dalīpa śaysdi pa|dīdą̄
kaucą̄ką ra rraispūra mauḍä drraupye kaiṇa 26
66 brrī|ye kaiṇa pauṇḍä hauda piṣkala ttāra gväṣṭä
67 sījsa u|daiśä diśagrrī kṣą pūnyau jsa ysira b̨aistä
68 gauttama śakrra | jasta ysurre jsa ahālya kaiṇa
69 jabvī vī jinavą mi|thūna-darmä kaiṇa 27
70 vyāsi rreṣąya pātcä kāśi-sā|dara ūdiśāyä
71 tcūrvāyi kīthāṣṭä rąhä kā|ḍä [×] gūhä khiṇḍä
72 b⟨rr⟩īvīje brrīthi jsa pajā|ḍä māsta ṣṭau
73 rauste a⟨bi⟩ñe pajsi ṣi̧ ādrrakä rą̄|ma ṣai 28
74 ūysirāvāsi kaṃthi pasvą stīyā udi|śāyä
gaupakä pyidau dahauśti[3] vāsile kaiṇa
75 si̧|na ū upaysauna tta dvā brrāvara hatca
76 ūma u de|vä śūje jsāṃdä tcaḍä simaudrra ṣṭā 29
77 para vrrāṃ | (*broken tops of syllables*).

[1] Letter broken out before *-ā*.
[2] First syllable broken out.
[3] Perhaps *ş̨i* written for *śti*.

13

Paris Y

1 II byūṣṭä vąsvai jūhaune bāḍä pasālī
2 cu ṣṭau paṃ saittä brr⟨ā⟩ṃ I hvąṇḍāṃ aysmyą jūhai :
3 bīysą̄ña ṣṭāṃ caistą hvāṣṭä śūjai vä I skä
śaiśīryau thyau thyau vaña spyąkau dāśauda : ——
4 I phūmīdä ṣṭāṃ dīṣą vīrä jästūñą padämäkä
5 jūhaujä I kyai thajīdä ysīrä sacä brrīyąkyai :
6 mąṣṭa ttä ttä saittä I ṣa ṣṭau jäbvī hūrī
hūvą̄ysąña jūhaunai ttraikṣą maṃ käṇą
7 I dīṣą vī pąstą̄vą̈ jästą mą̄gądä mą̄stą
8 saiśą̄kau vaiṣṇą I hamārāṇvā psyąkāṃ[1]
9 hvąṇḍā vī mvaiśdą yūḍāṃdä mą I ra pā dą̄śaudä
10 ustāṃ kärāiśą spyąkyai spūlakä khī(ysa) I rä spyąkyai :
ṣaudäkyą ysārą̄rä haṃdä hauṣkyau bähyau :
11 kä I rgakä kaijīdä u thūcälastą hūḍūka
12 śai rchä[2] hvū I pā[3] [pai][4] u gąisącä rūsąnä dyai
13 śūjai pyaṃtsä ñīdä I [paṃ] pau gąhvera dränä gūsīdä ::
14 uskä ąsphīrä I cä jaha sphālya-gūṇą
15 spyąkīne : kāysū nūvärä I pajsä-gū :
16 ąysadrųvą raṃgyau jsä gąistą īsąkyai yaṃ I dai
panāyadī pyauṣä khu bīnä ṣkīdä ąstāṃdä
17 I spyakyau ājsävä bvaiysą habäla phaysdyai
18 jästūñai I khaṣą̈ jsä ąsphīrätcaña hāysaiñä
19 yą̄są jsä vä I rkāṃdä bauśą spyąkyau hīyą
20 ąrähaṃdä vą śttākä cä ī I kṣą̄ṣṭä dīryai īda ——
21 I bąijakye drą̄hīdä haṃdä spyauysāṃ baṃhyau
22 tta maṃ jsā I bvaijsyau jsä spyąkä hąñą̄ñą̄rä
23 yīną̄rä ttų ysī I rä byą̄jai hvąrä bījāṣakä
24 saṃ khu pauśkyą kaijīdä I ījījä nūvąrai :
25 ttagyau khaivāṃ jsä pvīstą ttunāṃ aṃ I gä
mūvą̄ryau gąkyau ājsävä pąijäkyai :

[1] Read *sp*-.
[2] Blurred and uncertain.
[3] Two intertwined syllables.
[4] Blurred out.

26 ttaunäkä ṣū | ña pūhīmyau śatta śakyai pe̮jai
27 khvā daittä hvāṣṭä käṣa | harūyą ā panīśḍ̮ä :
28 jīśkyāṃ pą̄ ysīräkä paṃphīdä | brrau hvąṇḍāṃ vä :
29 śūjäñą̄ṣṭä phrrīnä paśīdä : saiśai vą | skä
thajī vā ysāṃjsä ysąrūṃ gūräṇai mau
30 ī śūjai | tsīdä spyąką khāṣ̮īdä gauṇe : ——
31 lākṣä-gūna[1] spyąkyai brra brrą jsā hvąṇḍ̮ą :
32 śūjäną̄ṣṭä nąl śa paśīdä jūhai udäśą̄yą :
33 gauṇai ×-audä[2] | haṣaprrīyą hąmāräne jsā dą̄śau :
34 ī śūjai tsīdä | [spyakye khāṣī][3] spyąkyai khāṣīdä haṃtcä :: ——
35 mūräkä ṣe̮rīdä hadä spyauysāṃ bahyau :
36 jūhai udä | śāyą bvaijsä kaujsä spyąkai jīdä
37 tha(jī) ttyau pą̄ṣą | hamą daukhą śaisai hīyai : ——
38 pūñūdä ąrähaṃdä ca satsą̄rä närädä
39 na ysīra | brrī aśtą na vā jūhai brārai :
40 ą mūśttū kīrä īḍai | ysaṃthvā ttraikṣä :
ą mūśttū -ī kīrä yūḍai ysaṃthvā ttraikṣa
41 | ca baśdai jūhaujara vyattaive panūḍai ——

14

P 1311

a1 /// × u drraya raysa śśīya u drraya śśīya khāysäna bala viśtāña u śśi upa. . u ṣį balsä

2 /// ⟨pa⟩ḍā hvaṣṭä biśśūnya vara spye viśtāña śśau śśau balä nauvaränau pacaḍa śtāka tca⟨hau⟩ra vara khā-

3 ⟨ysa⟩ /// ⟨bi⟩śśūnya vara upakaraṇa viśtą̄ña spye u ḇū tti vara viśtāña u tti mī dārañi ⟨hā⟩ p⟨īr⟩ā⟨ña⟩

4 /// × u ṣą̄ pātcä dārañä hā hamaṃga caittyä vīra sāñą̄ña u ṣį pātcä dārañä kalparāji vī

5 /// u ṣą̄ dārañi haṣparibistä jūna hvañā diśvā vidiśvā || namau navānavattī ną̄(ma) tathāga-

[1] With *gauṇe* below. [2] Three syllables struck out.
[3] *spyakye khāṣī* deleted.

6 ⟨ta⟩ /// l -nā samānāṃ auṃ[1] vipule vaipale pravare jinavare ⁓ sara⟨va⟩ra ⁓ sarva-ta ⟨thāgata⟩

*b*7 /// hva ci hämāte vajrrapāṇa bisīvrrāṣṣai o[1] bisīvrrāṣṣaiñi cu ṣṭā mistä *bū-*

8 /// kṣama haṃ bāḍä ttina bisīvrrāṣṣaina ṣi̮ kalparājä huysänautti pīrākä paryāñä pīḍä u

9 /// na pajsemina u manātī hvaḍä khaṣṭäna u śau ravi jsa pajsaṃ tcerai u ṣa̮i kalparājä ttī va

10 /// ñä ttī tti tcahaura miste dārañä hva hva śā śā nauvarenau jū̮na pīrāña ⁓ u buśañau saṃ

11 /// ×di raṃnī dakṣiṇä pīrākä pajsaṃ tcerai ⁓ ttī mī tcūrasa saṃnīja kārṣa *tc*erā u tcūrn⟨ ⟩

12 /// padā̮ni viśtā̮ña u b̮vasca vara viśtāña u surā vara bājana viśtāña kuṣṭa spye viśtā⟨ña⟩

15

P 2022

1 sa khu jä hīsīdä vīrä va̮ra pajsadā̮
2 dīśta̮ ga̮tca̮sta̮ ṣa̮ | käle tcāraṃpha̮ gub̮ā[2]
tha kṣaisttai tcaṃjsä gaudä naumä haura̮
3 | vā-ttarya̮ ra̮ śaiśākau sa̮ttau pāca̮rya̮ dī ttrauma̮ :
4 | sa khu ja hvāṣṭa̮ pyatsa̮ hāysa̮ haṣḍä raisvai
5 da̮khavīya̮ | käśaumä haiysda̮ pasakyāṣṭa̮ gaistai :
6 nīysīśta̮ mūkū̮vā | śa u parädīvaṃ haysgamästa̮
7 sttrīyāṃ nva̮ tsūkä ysärä jūna ba̮ | ya̮styairä :
maudättä rai vīnä hakhīysa̮ jsīnä va̮räṣṭai
8 | pūñāṃ prrabāva̮nä nāva̮ śakrrau āysaṃ
9 śūrī pe̮ñāṃ jsä u | ysa̮rä baiśa̮ nīhīyai
10 kaumä-gūṇvā̮ a̮va̮phadä ṣṭau jsī | na paśāvai :
ttraiṣṇījai bīrä jsä pāsa̮ ttä ttu mauñada[3]
11 | sa khu jä ñūṣṭyai pyairä bīrä jsä hatsä :
12 va̮rä ṣṭau haśmīśta natcā̮ | ṣṭä padä na byaihai
13 ttraiṣṇījsai bīrä jsä pāsa ttū mau | ñadä

[1] Independent *au* and *o*. [2] *bā* added in small hand.
[3] *ttr.* to *mauñada* deleted.

ḁysmū ñūṣṭārä tcaṃnä gūsttya nḁ byaihīdä
14 | sa khu jä syai jsīrauvä ucä śūjai kṣaijīdä
15 tcḁrkyau udäśḁ̄ | yḁ hāṣṭä vāṣṭä baysārai
16 na vä pvāñāṃ panavāṃ | padau tsūmä vḁräṣṭä līkä
17 sāhḁ ttyai pā padä na ñḁ̄pḁi | brrīyā
draumä khva hvai aṃgau baidä raijsai ārä haṃjsä
18 gūśta | thajä dīśḁ dīśe̥ ā vā rīśtä
19 raijsai kāḍārä dairä baidä | mākṣī
ysvyai kaiṇḁ ḁstaṃ daukhḁ vḁrḁ̄śḁi : vejala[1]
20 | sūjaba āstaṃnä avāmāvä ḁvāmā tsīrai
21 ālagḁ̄ryau | jsa śaikä aṃga ājsänīdä :
22 pajsāsḁ kṣḁṣṭä ysārä cai | stḁ phaidäla
23 pḁijsaigau māstḁ ttrḁ̄mīdä hada bḁhyau phai | rīdä :
vyāṣḁ rasḁya jsā kaiśtḁsādärä kaiṇḁ [tca]
24 | tcūrävāya kīthāṣṭä rahḁ kāḍa gūhḁ khaiṇḍḁ
25 brrī | yījai brrīttä jsä pajsāḍä ḁbaustḁ ṣṭä
26 raustḁ ḁbḁiña | pajsa ṣḁ raudäkä raumḁ ṣe̥ ::
27 saṃ khu jä hvai hagrrīhḁ ttairä | da bīysḁrä vī
habaḍä ḁśḁcḁ̄caugḁ gatsä tta jsaidai
28 khva jsa | viṣṭä kūṣ̥ī pe̥ṣṇaicä ṣavä hḁḍā
29 tta tta pā bīysḁrāra | parīyḁstau vḁṣayḁ :
30 sa khu jä śvai magāri hauṣkä āstai | ṣīmai
paysḁsīdai dadḁ̄ räysḁ gvaunä nḁ byaidai
31 hīya | ṣahḁ śūla ḁnvaśtārä nḁ byau[hattai][2]tta
32 ttä pā satsāra | satta gajsa na bvārai :
33 brra[3] prrahaujanau hvaṇḍau ama byeda | na tsūva :
saṃtsārū sauha baida pḁijsa naṣaima :
34 satsḁ̄ra ttrau hai | ra khu rai baida mīracai :
35 āra-mḁ̄rga bāvyara satsḁ̄ra jsa gū | syara[4]
36 cu ja ma ya pīrūyau bāḍa bīsā | hvaṇḍa :
cu ja ma satsaira basta kauma-gūṇau baida :
37 ava | māva ḅaysa parye na nḁ vījīṣṭauda :
38 bakyai[5] sauhḁ kaiṇa dū | rvā narya vavaṃda[6]
aysmū ma hvāṣṭa ṣṭai pajūā skadvā:

[1] *vejala* written vertical. [2] *hattai* deleted. [3] *brra* blurred out.
[4] Four round figures of punctuation.
[5] *kāle* below *bakyai*: read *bakalekyai*?
[6] One figure of punctuation.

39 skadai jsāṃ | bīsa ṣṭārai aysmū hīya :
40 khu ja hā pā skada na gīhīdai | aysmū
aysmū pā vī skadau haira na yūḍa īda[1]
41 | aysmūnā pūna parāhąnai bagau :
42 dāvīnai dīsa hajūttā jsā ā|ysīra :
aysmūnai bīsana ka nai daryą yūḍādū :
43 ṣąu au vaña bā|ye śarv(ā) dīrvā kīrrvā[1] :
44 |[2] nūrä vyahä seśākä[3] dāśaidai brrīyą :
45 naistą havyīśaṃcä khu | hala-baiśkvā tsaṃbai
46 khauysaṃdą nūvärä baudąhą | brrīyūnä
sa khu jī[tta]śkyą mauṇḍā phasttārą cāpąnai
47 | caistā hvąṇḍā pā ysīrä kṣąmä ṣavä hąḍā :
48 śvą ṣavä pana | mī davą śūlakä ąsthaṃjai
49 śva ṣavä sąrbai brrai bīśā | paḍaurakä
brrąvai hā hūña vąhaiysą gaumaña brrīyąkä :
50 | pharä ṣą hasta khu hvai ttaudä ąyūla hvīḍä
51 cū bai|śa padäśḍa rūvä ttīña naraumīdä
52 na ma ṣą śtākä khu | hve hīyai ąysmū
53 kaumą-gūṇā rūyą u ttī khā|ysą pajāysḍai
54 | dastą dastą baistą tcūra-śauda palyadą
55 cą ṣṭau śau aṃga hau|da daiśtą tta[4] mvīrai
56 uryaunä tcąrä tcąrä mista vī|ysāṃjai
kūṣṭa au ha vīra būśą tcarkyä yąnārai
57 | sa-kūlye paṣą jsä hā jasta vyīśamä
58 maistyai śarä | vyauha jsa aṃdavaṃda[kąkā]kāṣṭä paṣṭīda
59 paḍā śa[×]|krra jasta hatcä vyāha jsa
60 padīṣṭa ttīṣąstą sttrīyą|sttrīśvā āśą[5] :
ṣai ṣṭāṃ ja daśa-bhūme aurmaysdau jasta :
61 kaidara-dvaipa | seśāka tsvai kṣārmai na hamyai :
haiysdai mūkūvāśai hada pyaura ttraumai
62 | khu [prra] brra na byaihę ravye au nīśaidauda[5] :

[1] One figure of punctuation.
[2] Change to hand 1.
[3] *se* below.
[4] Or *na*?
[5] Figure of punctuation.

16

P 2023

1 [10 *syllables*] khu śaṃkīña ≈ ×
2 .... ≈ śauki cąmauṇḍva hārrvä raiva dr⟨i⟩-
3 ⟨ḍha būma dīvyai⟩ ≈ kaṃthą dīvyą ≈ kūṣḍį dīvyai rā-
4 jä dīvyai āstaṃna ≈ hąrābīśa ṣṭāṃ vā hī⟨yv⟩ā
5 h⟨ī⟩vy⟨ā⟩ sthānvą pąṣatta[na][1] — maṣḍilvā[2] aunaka ×
6 drau kṣai( )āṃ byaujā pūña kuśąla-mūṣṭau[3] ttā-ṃ has⟨p⟩i-
7 skyą dharmadąna pąrāṇāmau 12 ca būri maṃ ×
8 *hva*taną kṣīrä parāmąṇḍąla vī viṣ̄ūną-gūną
9 haṃdaiṣṭą pąttarre ṣṭaudai ≈ akąla brraṃthą *u*
10 akāle bąrä harabaiśą maṃ ttyai dąyai dharmadau-
11 ⟨na⟩ .. -ai jsą vyąchīyai parąvarttīyai āchai
12 ⟨na ha⟩mąvai daurbaikṣą maṃ ną hą(mā)vai ≈ śva tcā-
13 ma śąlarbe vyąchīyai pąrarvattīyai ≈ naṣąña
14 hīrąña vī tsīyai sąttu-dątta ysama-śaṃdai
15 vī ttā[4] × ⟨u⟩rmäys(d)ą sarbī sątvąną haurä haṃdą-
16 rä upąjīva bąrai pīsąña hūṣą tsīdai ×

17

P 2025

1–6 *Khotanese Texts II*, no. 79
7 ‖ byūṣṭä vasve jūhaunai bāḍä pasālī
8 cū ṣṭā pįsaittä brrāṃ | hvāṣṭāṃ aysmya jūhau -
9 bīysāña ṣṭā cįsta hvąṇḍä śūje vąlska -
seśīryau thyau puṣa spyakyāṃ dąśāṃdä
10 phūmīdä | ⟨ṣṭ⟩ā dīśę vī brravīya padämaka -
11 jūhāṃjaka thaṃjīdä | ysera ṣāca brrīyįkyi -
12 mąṣṭā tta tta setta ṣį ṣṭāṃ jabvī hūlrī -
hūvąysaña jūhaunai ttrrikṣą ma kiną ≈

[1] Blurred.
[2] *ṣḍ* for *ṇḍ*.
[3] *ṣṭ* for *ly*.
[4] *ttā* below.

13 dīśe̮ vī pastā|va g̱yasta mạgadha māsta
14 ṣeśạkāṃ va ṣe̮rīda hamāranvạ | spyakvạ ⁓
15 hvaṇḍāṃ vī m̱ūśḍa yuḍāṃda mạra pā dāśāṃ|dä ⁓
ustā karạśa paiśkyä u spūlạka khīysịra spyakye
16 | kakva tcīrauka u papūśka biṃjakye ⁓
17 tta mī bījeṣạra haṃ|da spyauysāṃ baṃhyāṃ ≈
18 paijaṃkya gvīthārä tta ma jsāṃ hada karạ|śau ≈
ṣāhạna gvīradạ tsīda hadạ spūālakāṃ :
19 uskạ | asphīräca jạhvā sphālya-g̱ūna :
20 spyakīnai kāysvä|ka bīḍä pajsạ-gū :
21 aysdyūävi ragāṃ jsa gestạ yida | dvanakye :
panāyīda spyakya khū ja bīna astạna ≈
22 | ⟨s⟩pyakīnai pyauśạkạ iheja aysbạnakvạ ≈
23 bīysạ|śta tvā uska sạha jsai hā sāśe ≈
24 nạṣṭa ttaśta spya|kyāṃ habrraista bụśau jsa ≈
25 tta āṃ bījāṣa[1] yida khū ja|stūña gaysakye ≈
26 m̱uaiśḍa uysdaitta īsījā[1] tcaimeśa|kyāṃ jsa ≈
ạysmụryau jūhạnai sāñīda pavinaka ≈
27 vaṣịcha | khvīśakyāṃ jsa raga spyakya bīysaśte ≈
28 parigeśa skāṃdaka | samū brre mạṇḍvā[2] khai tta ≈
29 ysarūnä para bahyāṃ samū gvai|va bāstāṃda ≈
ñạña spūlakīnā haphada ạṣṭakye ⁓
30 tta|rū lākṣa-gū khīysara karvīnạ ⁓
31 hanavä tta sa śūje | paujsīda paśạuda jsa ≈
32 haṃdara haṣprrīya khu brrī | vaska brrīyaka
33 ṇesta havrrīśace khu halạ-beśkvāṃ | tsaṃbe
khauysadạ nūvara bạdāha brrīyūna ⁓
34 sa | khu jīśkyi māṇḍvā phastārä cāpine ⁓
35 hadära ysānā|ra khu ṣiṣa brre hạlạ-beśkvạ ⁓
36 nāṣṭi varūśạra khu | tcījsa brrīyikyạ pijvā
37 chakīnyau daṃdākyau skauda byihä|nīdä
sa khu ja brrạ khītta skauda brrīyakä vaska ≈
38 hadä|ra ājsava śīya ttarūna spyakyị ⁓
39 padamyau phastā|rä khu brre gärśa mīrạhe̮ ⁓
40 pajarūṣṭīda śūje tta khu | śittanvạ pāyvā
kạstakä ysạnāra haṃtsi pajūṣṭā jsa

[1] *jā* with *-ai*, probably being two anusvāras for one. [2] *vā* with *ai*.

41 | yyauvaka sa̤ñīda ttu spyakūḍä pavanakä ˷
42[1] sañī | dä ūskyāṣṭä ū ysa̤nāra ttä auna ˷
43 śīya-vrrähā satta khū | dāśädai brrīyakä ˷
44 sarbä paḍaura brrīyakyä māśā | ṣṭä śva̤ ṣive ≈
45 bachadā̤ bahya ˷ karā̤śä śūjañ⟨ā⟩ | ṣṭa ˷
brrīyūnakyä cesta jīśkyi kṣaudā-bākve[2]
46 ūysdvīdi | karā̤śau jsa vīyārastū śūje ˷
47 khā̤ṣ̤īdau ttū brrīvī | nai ysaujsä n̤i̤ka-raysä[3] ≋
kaukala̤ īmūka cāṣa̤ karavī
48 stā | ryi[4] kakva papūśkyi bejakyi ysyama ˷
49 aṣṇā tcīrauka ū tta | ra ūcā̤ mūäraka
50 ga̤gā̤ tsīdä bahavyūā brrīye jsa śatca | pha ≈
hadarä kṣi̤jīda hadä bahyā śūje
51 tta ma jsāṃ ⟨bvi⟩ | jsyau jsa spyakya hañā̤ñāre ˷
52 yināri ttu ysīra byā̤ | je hvara bījā̤ṣakä ˷
53 saṃ [khu][5] khu pauśkyi ka̤jīdä ījīji | nūvare
ṣāṃdakyi rrā̤ysārä hadä hauṣṭyā bahyā ≈
54 karägaka | ka̤jīda u thvrrūcala̤sta hūḍūka ˷
55 cha rrvana pā u gesaca rū | sana dyekyi
śūje pyatsa ñada ≈ pau gahvarda ma grrausīda ≈
56 | hagrrīsīda cauṇäkya bauṇyäkya spyakakvā̤
57 ṣe̤rīda jū⟨hau⟩ | jsa khu ranīja bīna ṣkūvī
58 gūjsabrrīsīda ˷ dīśa̤ vī paskyā | ṣṭä hā̤ysa tsīda
59 baysāra nāyaca sa brrī pamäri bū | sta ≋
cu ttye na ī gūscyīnai āsparä beda ˷
60 nai ī gvaḍau śa̤ bha | vanīja mū-varga ˷
kā̤ma-gūṇā̤ hīya (pi)jsāṃ gaṃjsa na bvā̤ve
61 drrā̤ | mye bā̤ḍä vī āttamā̤tta bīysaśte ≋
62 spyakyau ājsavä bve | ysi ha̤ba̤ḍä pha̤ysdvä
63 jastuñe khaṣ̤a̤na asphīräci⟨ña⟩ | hā̤ysiñä ˷
yausa jsa varkāṃda bauśä spyakyāṃ hīya ˷
64 | arähadä va śtāka̤ [ca][5] ca ḏrrvī[6] tsāṣṭa därye īdä ≈
65 pi⟨ja⟩ | kyi gvīthā̤rä kya̤śa̤ brrīya[va][7]ka vaska
66 hagyeḍä skaudaka brraukä | la̤kīja ˷ dunaka

[1] Mark in margin.
[2] Read *bāḍve*.
[3] For *eka-raysa-*.
[4] *ryi* like *di*.
[5] Blurred out.
[6] Read *u͡vī*.
[7] *va* blurred out.

67 ttūrakä harą̄śa̮dai vaña śa̮ulą au | ṣṭakye
ğyasta b̮aysa ttadī śacä ra gū yanīdä
68 va⟨tca⟩ | ka paysaṇvakye khanai bų̄śa viṭakyį
69 nvākaka nvārī⟨da⟩ | vakṣisacą brrą̄sakyį
70 staiña vaṭakye tcana pajāḍa ⟨u͡vī⟩ | kyį
narvą̄ṇū sauhi cada ysą̄stä
71 ttye jsa pūñūdi ara | hada ca satsāra niraṃda
72 na ysīra brrī aśta na va ⟨jū⟩ | hai bvaurį
a mūśtų kīrä yų̄ḍai hadira ysaṃthvi
73 ca ma | ṣṭāṃ jūhāṃja ra vyätteva panūḍai
74 prrahūjanyāṃ hvaṇḍyā[1] | ama byäda nä tsūva
75 ṣkāṃjīnai są̄hi baida pijṣa na | ṣaitta satsą̄ra
drrau hera khū rai baida mīrrcai[2]
76 ārya-⟨mārga⟩ | bą̄vyara satsāra naraumyari
77 ką̄ma tta yi pīrū⟨yau bā⟩ | ḍa prrahajuna satva
78 cū ma kleśa̮u jsa ṣaiṣṭa kāma-gū⟨ṇāṃ⟩ | baida
avamāva b̮eysa parya na ra vījaiṣṭāda
79 dū⟨kha⟩ | są̄hi kaiṇą dūrā narya vavadi ——
80–268 *Khotanese Buddhist Texts*, no. 10.

18

P 2026

1–2 [*bases of syllables*] | hvīṃdi ttā samāhāṃ spāśą̄ñä
3 saṃ narvakalpä vasve akhauṣṭä *ṣį* | jsa b̮aysūśtä ṣṭa saṃ 11
4 khu ṣṭāṃ tvī ñatūṃ vīra b̮aysūśtä kṣimī u⟨vā⟩ | ra
na ni pyaisa byąme pha saṃ śimatha spāśä aharṣṭä
5 aciṃdya tva | hamayi nai yina hą̄murä gvą̄na 12
6 stai ṣṭą̄na ṇastä palaṃgä ⟨tsū⟩ | macä kīrä yinacä
7 apūṣṭye bhāvana gīhna ustaṃ vā ttī vara raṣṭä 13
prrą̄ttyākṣaṇä harbaiśä bva ṣį cū anābhauga carye jsa
8 ci tvā | haspaistya yināve caṃdä pve jsāve
9 u byāśḍe ṣį baiśä b̮aysū | śtāṣṭä jsāve 14
10 cai ttūśä dharma paysemdä hų̄nä mą̄ñaṃda mi | rīca
kṣāṃttä anulāṃbą̄me kiṃṇa vyachai bhų̄mä paḍauysna 15

[1] -*ā* with -*ai* for -*āṃ*. [2] Read *marrīcai*.

11 | saṃ khu paśi jsi̮na ttanī pariśudhvā kṣaittrvā
12 hīśtä ā svāhāva̮ ā ttu|ṣvā̮ maittrai vīra 16
13 hvīṃdi ttā ci gū̮nai haṃjsira vīra basta īṃ⟨dä⟩ | jaḍa satta
dā uysdīśā̮me beḍa daśta saṃñä ttyāṃ va k̮ā̮ma 17
14 | astīkavādya satta ttyāṃ strrīyi ttatve seṃdä
15 brrīye jsa āsva tsīṃdä | ttūśātte arthä nä bvāre 18
16 ttyāṃ arva aśūba hvañäre gū̮⟨na⟩|ḍa byātaji pyaṃtsä
17 agū̮nai ttyāṃ va śtāka cu baiśä hīra amya bu|tte 19
ttaraṃdarä pīśāra-vīhä: aśacāṃgyau haṃbaḍä́ by̮estä
18 | haṃdari vya prrā̮ṇā by̮āsta tta hauparahaudā ysāre 20
19 kṣaṣṭä kūla | ṣā̮ maista bihī agapī ecä kū̆ṭheṃgä
20 pīrāṃ jsa by̮āstä vara brrī|ye jsa nihvarda
ṣa̮ brrīye hīya bāta k̮ā̮myāṃ jsa ṣṭāṃ vā ysaiye 21
21 | khvai na sattā̮ña ni kaittä nai na hami brrīyā ysyā̮ñä
22 khu ji hū̮ña rū|va vicaittra dahä: strrīyi dyā̮me jsa ni īṃdä
23 bīysā̮ṇā̮me jsa nirū|dhä drā̮ma tti harbaiśä ṣkāṃje 22
24 ṣa̮ brrīyā cvai ja ni byehe na ni jsā|ve brrīye rāśa̮
satta brrīye jsa hamaṃga b̮aysūśtī naysdakä bvā̮ñä 23
25 | khavi̮nai pẹṇḍai ttye na aśtä eṣṭā̮ma sārä drā̮mä rū
26 cai tta tta butte | ttye samāhāṃ kīḍi raṣṭä 24
27 cu baiśä hīra ttūśā paysemdä c̮ā|yi mā̮ñaṃdä mirīce
28 ttye naṣā̮mi̮nai suhi:na puṣa saṃtsäräna | gū 25
29 khu prrattyākṣiṇa gaucarä yaugä samāhāṃ bhāvañä gīhna | haṃbera
30 dasau bhū̮mä tta ni abyehā̮me jsa dharma b̮aysa baiśä sā̮|ha ttye 26
ca ṣi̮ ci ttū yaugä ciri̮mä pathīsā̮ñä gūśtina mau jsa
31 | gūśti-hvārā̮ñä ṣā̮ prrara amy̮aiśd̮a hamāre staura 27
32 mau ṣa̮ u͡vī vī ×|ña pade̮me byātarji harbaiśä rūye
33 drabāḍvāṃ b̮aysāṃ hīvī | gra parau hā̮murä īṃdä 28
34 gūśta-hvārā̮ñä vīṣ̮ū̮na saṃtsera dā|rbūra ga̮śe
paṃjsa-sse śe śe sattä puḍä jsāva jīye aṃga 29
35 cu bu|ri ysama-śaṃdya satta biśä bāṃda bīṃñä barīṃdä
36 ysana brrātara | śūje pātcä ni haṃbuśtä khvai ye hvīḍä 30
37 vaña burai māta u pye ×[1] | mai ttai kīrāṃ aṃga
nai butte sa̮mai hvīḍä mera pyarä hīya gūśta 31
38 | cu hvaḍāṃdä śūje gūśta narya tsvāṃdä myāṃ dai ṣṭāre
39 kalpa puṣa pa|rya pharāka na ṣṭāṃ byehīṃdä parīya 32

[1] Broken syllable.

40 cu tta tta haiṣṭāya pathī|ya jasta-kṣīrvā tsvāṃdä auska
41 vyachāṃdä dā paramārthä parya saṃtsā|räna baiśä 33
cu ttye ḇaysūśtä kṣimī varttạñä vasve parāhä:
42 ka|rma-paha dasau maista ṣavi haḍā ānạ śtāka 34
43 mauta-varāthạ|ñä girye-varạñä ci buri hamāṃde
44 baudhasattä paṃtsạñä baiśä khu ⟨bu⟩|ri ārä na pette 35
ttaraṃdarä pathaṃka śtāka biśạ ṣị ānạ tcere
45 | aysmūna asaidäna ceṃda ṣạ parāhä: saṃvarä maistä 36
46 kūṣṭi | lauvya gvāra hvāñāre ā khanā būśä vaṭākye
47 baudhasattä ni tsūñī| hāṣṭa 37[1] haṃgä nai mụñạñä tsāṣṭä
48 paḍāṃjsya harbaiśä ḇaysa | cu vaña haiysdāṃjsva pātcä
49 ttana [×] dāna ḇaysūśtä bausta 38[2] uysdī|śāṃdī[3] jsā vāṣṭạ
tta tta paste sarvaña sūttra cu burä ttrasahasrrye vīra
50 ga|ga ñāya grīcau sya cadạ tta ḇeysa hamāre 39
51 hū pañe sarvaña[4] ḇaysa | vasva karvīnā paṣạ
khu ye ttyā ḇaysau biśạ pajsa īda paṣạ jsa hatsa
52 da|daka pha ṣṭāna pabasta cada tta grīca hamāre 40
53 haḍa khapa vāsta pamū|ha upakaraṇạ ṣada jsa he
54 khva rä jsāna āysana ⟨hai⟩śẹ . . . | ranīnā vasva vamāna
55 ttye tta puña buḍärä hamāre āsā paramārtha | vīra 41
parạmārtha bāvaña ṣṭāna
56 kuṣṭa na rū aśta na saña na vā sa⟨ṃ⟩|tsārä na kṣāṃca
ṣạ anạpattya-kṣātta agunai tsāṣṭạ naṣạda 42[5]
57 ṣạ bvau|ma cu paysaida ṣạ rä jsāna bvāma pārusta
58 varä drạma na bīde | sa khu dai āca (na) pasūśte 43[6]
sarava ḇeysūśtä harśtä ttaña beḍa vasva akhauṣṭa
59 kū|ṣṭa na rū aśtạ na saña na vā satsārä na kṣāṃca ⟨44⟩
60 ausde[7] cī vā sarbe aharīna ttāra | jaida
ā khu caittāmaṃ räna satva baiśạ sūhya padīme ——

[*Space*]

61 | || namau karạkasūdạ jasta ḇeysi namasū nauda ||
namau kanakamaunạ jasta ḇeysa namạsū nauda ||

[1] Numeral set after third *pāda* instead of fourth.
[2] Numeral placed after third *pāda*.
[3] Different hand from *śāṃ*.
[4] *ña* below.
[5] 42 below *da ṣạ*.
[6] 43 written below *dai*.
[7] *ste* with *t* changed to *d*, for *au(rmay)sde*.

62 | kāśava̯ jasta b̯eysi namasūṃ nauda̯ ||
63 sīhä: gauṣa̯ dādäb̯esvara̯rā̯ja jasta b̯eysi namasū | nauda̯ ||
rūja̯ jasta̯ b̯eyse nama̯sū nauda̯ ||
dīpaṃkarä jasta b̯eysa na̯masū nauda ||
64 kauḍāṃ jasta b̯e|ysi namasū nauda ||
brrūya bīsai jasta b̯eysa namasū nauda̯ ||
65 khāṃhyape̯ vī jasta b̯eysa̯ nama|sū nauda ||

[*Space*]

66 | || sarbada dīśa̯ hālaiyāṣṭä bīsā sakhā̯ra̯mau hālai[1] u damarā̯ṣ̯au
67 hālai u ārñānā | hālai u pe̯mau hālai u besā hālai u araṇä-dī̯ṣ̯āṃ hālai
68 u dīyagarau hālai u pīḍā | bvākaḍā prrasthā̯rmaḍā beysūñū prrabaibai-
69 kā̯yā b̯eysā hālai arga[2] śaräṇāva | tsū nama̯sū vanū aunū nauda̯ 1
70 dahä: kṣanye dīśa̯ hālaiyāṣṭä bīsā sakhā̯ra̯mau hā|lai u ārñā̯nāṃ hālai u besā bauspājā hālai u pe̯mau hālai u dīya̯garau hālai (u)
71 | pīḍāṃ bvā̯kaḍau prrastharmaḍāṃ b̯eysūñā prraibaibau hālai u ara̯ṇa̯-
72 dī̯ṣ̯au hāle u drrayā | ranā hālai aurga śaraṇāva tsū[3] aunū vanū na̯ma̯sū nā̯ḍa 2
73 pūrvye dīśa̯ hālaiyāṣṭa bī|sau sakhā̯rmā hālai u aurñānā hālai u
74 besau bauspājā hālai u pe̯mau hālai pīḍāṃ bvā|kaḍā prrastharmaḍāṃ dīya̯garāṃ u araṇā-dīśa̯u hālai u drrayau raṃnā hālai u be̯ysū⟨ñā⟩
75 | prraba̯ibau hālai u da̯marāśa̯u hālai aurga drrūnā śarṇāva tsū ānū
76 namasū nauda | 3
uttarye dīśa̯ hālaiyāṣṭä sakhā̯rmā hālaiyāṣṭä u ārñānāṃ hālai u
77 damarā̯ṣ̯⟨au⟩ | hālai u pe̯mau hālai u dīya̯garau hālai u dīyagarāṃ
78 besā hālai u drrayā ranāṃ hā|lai u pīḍāṃ bvā̯kaḍāṃ prrastharmaḍāṃ
79 u prrabaiba-kā̯yau be̯ysuñā sthyapā[4] caittāṃ u | bauspājāṃ hālai u
80 dīya̯garā hālai be̯ysauñā prrabebau hālaiyāṣṭä aurga tsū | va̯nū śaräṇāva tsū aunū namasū nauda 4
81 da̯rye anāha̯ ysa̯ma-śadai vī bīsā | be̯ysūña prrabaiba̯-kā̯yā ja̯sta be̯ysa
82 namasū u pūñūda̯ hajva kaḍauna-|maittra parehadā̯ jā̯yarä nama̯sū
83 u darye anā̯ha ysama̯-śadai vī bīsā be|sa u be̯ysa u pema u ara̯ṇä-
84 sthāna u ārñāna u anā̯ha̯ ysama̯-śadai vī bī|sā sakhā̯rama u namau
85 drrabā̯ḍa ja̯sta̯ be̯ysa nama̯sū daśvā dīśvā bīsā | u daśva̯ dīśy̯ā bīsā
86 drrabāḍva haṣṭā ara̯ṇa-sthānūā bīsā baudasatta namasū (nau)|da u drabāḍa kṣasa̯ maista mahāsthīrä namasū u drraise pajsā[5] kṣaṣṭä

[1] *lai* below. [2] Read *aurga*. [3] *tsū* below.
[4] *sthya* for *sthū*. [5] *pajsā* written below.

87 mahā-ṣāvāṃ u drra | bā̯ḍa̯ pacābaiña saidya-vaidyā̯ḍa̯rä deva̯-raṣa̯iya

88 namasū u drrabā̯ḍa pū | ñūdä śarärana pīsā kaḍāna-mittra nama̯sū u drrayi rana (na)masū ——

89 | || sādathyeda [*Chinese. Figures of two Buddhas.*]

[*Space*]

90 | ≈ ca bāḍa aysmya hagetta kūra kā̯ma sañä

91 tta bāḍa satsāra va | ṣṭa byāṃda tcana na gava̯ gesti 1

92 asada kauma kūra ṣa̯ satsāra pa | didā̯
vasva kā̯ma raṣṭa ṣa̯ naravāṇa padīme 2

93 ysarūña | āche āstana saña-māttra-darma

94 ṣa̯ śā ka̯ma kūra na va ha⟨ṃ⟩ | dara̯ hira aśta 3[1]

95 tvā ṣa mī kāma tta tta sāśa khvā na thū ya sa | ña vī
kūra kā̯ma u raṣṭa ṣa̯ śā ttadī prrara śuḍa

96 aysmya gu⟨.⟩e | ca ṣṭāṃ kaumi ysyā̯ñi da 4

97 daru śira vasūja sa [khu] khu āya | ña śā̯ma
ttena rānāṃ haspūnaka kūṣṭe dyāda hvāṣṭa hve

98 khu kū | ra hetta spāṣṭau haspīsadāṃ śūra 5

99 sumīra garu śaśvā tta tte | āvya bāvyarä[2]
sumīrä śaśvā̯ṇa̯ñä ttrāyi hatcä tcauryau dvīpyau 6
u ——

[*Space*]

100 || syādathidaṃ aṇi ma̯ṇi ⁀ akhe makhe ⁀ samaṃttamūkhe ⁀ sattyā-rā̯me ⁀ saumeyū-

101 ktte ⁀ narūhtte: ⁀ narūhtta:prrabhe ⁀ ele mele ⁀ hile kalpe ⁀ kalyä̈tte[3] ⁀ kalpase ⁀

102 sāre sārava̯tte ⁀ halahalī ⁀ halīle ⁀ halā halīle ⁀ halā halīle ⁀ vaṃde ⁀

103 vatte ⁀ caraṇe ⁀ carācaraṇe ⁀ aṃcale ⁀ atte ⁀ aṃttatte ⁀ karaṇe ⁀ ara̯ṇe ⁀ a-

104 sa̯tte ⁀ narava̯ktte ⁀ naravarttane ⁀ naramūktte ⁀ naidhya̯tte ⁀ naidhyaste nadhare ⁀ na̯rahāre

105 na̯rahāra-vamale ⁀ narahāra-śudhane ⁀ śudhane ⁀ śīla-śudhana ⁀ prrakatta-varṇe ⁀ prra(ka)-

106 tta-dīpane ⁀ bhāvābhā̯vane ⁀ a̯saṃge dame same va̯pūla-prrabhe ⁀ saṃkarṣaṇe ⁀ dare

107 dhadhare ⁀ mahādhadhare ⁀ dīpane ⁀ bhāvābhāva̯ne ⁀ asaṃge ⁀ asaṃga-va̯hāre ⁀ a-

[1] 1, 2, 3 written below. [2] Small *rä*. [3] *ly* for *lp*.

108 ga̮nīhāre ⁓ samatta̮mūkhe ⁓ nirahāre̮ ⁓ nirhāra-yuktte ⁓ narhāra-vamale ⁓ narhāra-

109 śudhane ⁓ draiḍha-saṃdhe ⁓ sūsthatte ⁓ saume ⁓ saumavatte ⁓ staṃbhavatte ⁓ draiḍha-sthaume ⁓

110 sthā̮maprrāptte ⁓ samaṃttaprrabhe ⁓ va̮mala-prrabhe ⁓ va̮mala-raśme ⁓ samaṃttamūkhe ⁓ sarva-ttrau-

111 ṇḍadhagatte ⁓ anāchida-prrattabhā̮na-dhāraṇe ⁓ nadhāna-dhāraṇe ⁓ dhāraṇa-mū-

112 khānesaṃdhe sarva-budhā-bhā̮ṣa̮tte ⁓ sarva-budhādhaiṣṭatte ⁓ na-dhā̮na-gauttre sva̮-

113 hā ⁓ —— [*Chinese*]

114 || nama̮ha̮ sarva-baudha baudhasatvebhya ⁓ ttad-yathā baudha baudha baudha ⁓ sarvalaukāra̮-

115 vrraga̮ttā ⁓ dharmacakrra-vrragā̮ttā ⁓ mārä-saña-vrraga̮ttā ⁓ abaiṣāya-vrragāttā ⁓ tta-

116 d-yathā anaṃdedyā-prrattīye ⁓ nama̮rūda̮-prrattīye ⁓ bava̮-prrattī-ye ⁓ jāra-prrattī-

117 ye ⁓ naraudha-prrattīye ⁓ ttad-yathā mara̮naṃ hara ⁓ baudha-sattyena ⁓ dharma-sattyena ⁓ sa-

118 ga-sattyena ⁓ deva-sattyena ⁓ nāga-sattyena ⁓ yakṣa-sattyena ⁓ rākṣa(sa)-sattyena ⁓ aysu̮-

119 ra-sattyena ⁓ garūṇḍa-sattyena ⁓ kedhara-sattyena ⁓ mahaurga-sattyena ⁓ sarva-pa̮ṣa-bha-

120 ṣa-sattyenä sūhā ≈ ——

121 ≈ nama ≈ sarva-budha-bau ——

19

P 2027

1–66 in *Khotanese Texts II*, no. 49.

67 ≈ namau vipaśau nauma jasta ḇeysa̮ na̮masau ≈

68 namau śaikhau namau jasta ḇaiysa | namasau ≈
namau veśūbau[1] nauma jasta̮ ḇeysa̮ nama̮sau ≈

[1] *ve* below.

69 namau karakąsū | dau nauma jasta beysą namąsau ≈
70 namau kanąkamūnau nauma jasta | ḇeysą namasau ≈
namau kāśapau naumą jasta ḇe(ysa) namąsau ≈
71 | namau śākyamūnau nauma jasta ḇeysa namasau ≈
72 harbaiśa ṣṭāṃ ją | sta ḇeysa vanau namasau naudą ≈
73 harbaiśa ṣṭāṃ ttradvai ttrīyąṇī | ḇeysāṃ dā vinau namąsau naudi ≈
74 harbaiśa ṣṭāṃ ttradvai ttrīyau | ṇī bīsaṃgīne rana vänau namąsau nauda ≈
75 harbaiśa ṣṭau ttā | pajsama pūjā-karma hąiśąu ≈
harbaiśa ṣṭau karma baśdai dīśąu
76 | harbaiśa ṣṭāṃ pūña kūśala-mūla ysvāṃ bvejāṃ anūmaudau ≈
77 | harbaiśa ṣṭāṃ jasta baiysa maista rraispūra tcū-syau hye
78 dāvīna parau | paryąme hālai ājaṣąu ≈
79 harbaiśa ṣṭāṃ jasta ḇeysą maistą | rrįspūra hye jsīña dījsąmai h(ā)lai namadrau ≈
80 harbaiśa ṣṭau pū | ña kūśala-mūla pajvā gavū satvau jsa habajsya yinau ≈
81 habī | kṣau ḇeysūśta ṣṭau parṇąmau ≈
82 ttyāṃ pūñā kūśala-mūlā hīyi pai | ṣkeci ≈
ttyau pūñā kūśala-mūlā hīyi dāśauma ≈
83 ttyau pūñāṃ | kūśala-mūlā hīyā hāva anūśāsą ≈
84 badäcąrye nū ha | rbaiśa uspūra hamaude ——
85 symbol.

[*Space*]

86 ≈ haṃ tcya kīmą ḍā tcya : ——

[*Space*]

20

P 2029

a 1, 2 cvai sāji vāśi cvä jsa āsā yaṃde ⌢ śę ysaṃthi pariśaudhvā | kṣittrvā hīśtä nauda || || ——
3 || syādathedaṃ ąṇe mąṇe ⌢ akhe makhe ⌢ simaṃttamūkhe ⌢
4, 5 | sattyārąme ⌢ sąmeyūrtte ⌢ niyūrtte ⌢ niyūrttiprribhe ⌢ | ele mele hele ⌢ kalpāṃtte ⌢ kalpatte ⌢ sāre ⌢ sāravatte ⌢

[*Space*]

6, 7 hala hala ⌢ halīle ⌢ halīle ⌢ halā halīle ⌢ halā ha|līle ⌢ caṃde ⌢
8 caṃdatte ⌢ cire cire ⌢ cirāciriṇe ⌢ aci|le ⌢ acile ⌢ aṃtte
9 aṃttatte ⌢ karaṇe ⌢ karaṇe ⌢ asaṃtte ⌢ a|saṃtte ⌢ nirivartte ⌢
10 niravartte ⌢ nidhyaṃtte ⌢ nidhyaṃste ⌢ nidhare ⌢ | nidhare ⌢
11 nirahāra-vimale ⌢ nirahāra-śudhane ⌢ śīla-śudha|ne ⌢ prrikạtta-varṇe ⌢ prrikạtta-dīpane ⌢ bhāve ⌢ bhāvena

b 12, 13 | asaṃge ⌢ asaṃge ⌢ asiga-vihāre ⌢ asaṃga-nīhāre ⌢ sa|maṃtta-mukhe ⌢ yūrtte niruktte ⌢ samaṃttaprribhẹ ⌢ vimala-prribhe ⌢ |
14, 15 vimala-raśme ⌢ simaṃttamukhe ⌢ sarvi-ttrāṇ̣ādagatte ⌢ anā|chida-prrittadhāriṇe ⌢ dhāriṇamukhạṇe ⌢ saṃdhe ⌢ sarvibaudha-|
16 bhāṣattā ⌢ sarva-baudhiṣṭatte ⌢ nidhạnagūptte svāhā || ||

[*Space*]

17 drayi yạna tti paṃdāta hvañāre ⌢
18 nauhä: vīri ttaṃdī viri śā | hami gūscya ⌢
ṣị buri hve śāstārä haṃbịstāna sūtträ ⌢
19 saṃdau|ṣṭa baudhasatva ṣāvā biśä ⌢
20 jasta hvaṃdä nāti aysūra kiṃna|ra yaḳṣa ⌢
simāsye sūttri biśī ysịnī dāṃdä[1] ⌢
21 sadharma-pụ|ṇdarī ttye sūttri vīra
vistārī arthä rriysī biśä vā ttraṃdä ⌢

21

P 2742

1, 2 || sedama na(ma)sūmā ṣada jsa brrīyạ ajalakä jsāṇa|kye ṣṭauna aysa
3 hūyī kīma-cūna drrabāḍva hạrabaiśa[2] be|ysa baudasattvau jsa hamīḍa
4 dārāña namasūmā ūvā|rä paramārtha cū beysa hvauda cū baiśa
5, 6 jastau karma kī|ḍeśạ dūkha ysatha pveṇạ ḫarīysa ge bīsagīja | ūvārä
7 kūṣṭa ārä-paudagalä haṣṭa kūṣṭa pūñāṃ | vīvā byehīda ttarä jsā
8 namasū nauda ttaña nvaiya na|masū pātca kūla jasta beysa cū vaña
9 ttye badrrai-ka|lpa parījīda sattva pharākä cū bū[× ×]rä jsāṃ īde |
10, 11 ḫeca būśūña pūjākarma ⌢ väña ṣṭāṃ haiysda vī aysa | hūyī kīma-

[1] Sic *dāṃ*, but P 2782. 58 *nāṃdä*. [2] *ra* below.

12 tcūna ṣada jsa ttāṣṭa ⁀ drabāḍau b̮aysāṃ hai|ṣ̮ū prraṇahauna samā-
syāṃdā II II

13 sidhamä ą̄rga tsū nama|sū naudä drabāḍvą harbaiśa b̮aysä ttrrīyą̄ṇī

14 dā | ahärīna[1] b̮aysą̄na parṣa tcahaura

15 sarbadä hālaiyā|ṣṭa[2] akṣą̄bą namasū b̮aysa majūśrī āstana phara

16 | kūla namasū naudä

17 ravye pa namasū b̮aysa rahna|ketta uvāra ākāśagarba paḍauysna

18 harbīśe parṣą | jsa hatsa :

19 ñūhūjsada hālaiyāṣṭą namäsū aramyāyä | beysa daṃde ra vara paṣą

20 pharākä khvai na hakhīysa na ñā|pe lą̄kyeśvara āstana mista daśa-

21 būmā tta baudasatva | vīysą̄nvā dyaurā-[ā]ārä bīśū namasū ną̄da

22 uttarye dī|śą namasū beysa ttu daudavesvarä nāma uvāra samatta-

23 ba|drra paḍauysana harbīśe paṣą jsa ḫatca

24 paḍą̄ysye vīdaśą jsa | ną̄da namasūmā sarvaña beysa dharaṇa-

25 dhara nāma uvāra | harbīśe paṣą jsa hatca

26 śẹye vīdaśą hālaiyāṣṭa na[3] | namasū sarvaña beysa nārāya peñāṃ

27 mista harbīśe paṣą | jsa hatsa

28 ñūhūjsadye vīdaśą jsa nauda namasū sarvaña beysa | cadrra-
prrabha nāma uvārä ḫarbīśe paṣą jsa hatsa

29 tcūramye vīda|śą jsa ną̄da namasūmā sarvaña beysa śauttrraidrrai

30 nąma uvā|rä harbīśe paṣą jsa hatsa uskyāṣṭa dīśą namäsū nąda

31 badrrą|śrrī [rī] sarvaña beysa nāṣṭa dīśą namasū beysa verauca

32 paṣą | jsa hatsa cū būre ysama-śadyą yāva śararaṇą[4] satva pūñūda

33 be|ysūña-vūysā mista harbīśe namasū nąḍą II II

34 sedhama
dvāsa | kūla jasta beysa raḫanāttamä nąma bīśū namasū naudä

35 | haṣṭūse kūla jasta b̮aysa rahnāśaikha nā(ma) bīśū namasū naudä

36 | haṣṭūsa kula jasta b̮aysa bīśū namasū naudä rahnābhāsa nauma

37, 8 baista kūla jasta beysa śą̄matha nāmä biśū namäsū | nauda

39 ḫaṣṭūsa kūla jasta beysa rahanābhāsakitta naumä | bīśū namasū nąda

40 besta kūla jasta beysa kāśava nā|ma bīśū namasū nauda

41 kṣa-se kūla jasta beysa vamala-|prrabhāsa nāma bīśū namasū nauda

42 sparanau kūla jasta | beysa śākyamūnau (nāma) bīśū namasū nauda

43 dvī-sa kūla jasta beysa va|paśa nauma bīśū namasū nauda

44 dvī-sa ysāra jasta beysa | kauṭīña nauma bīśū namasū nauda

[1] Two dots : below *ha*. [2] *hā* below.
[3] *na* of *namasū* written twice. [4] Second *ra* below.

45 haṣṭā kūla jasta beysa sū | prrabhausadharmauttara nąma bīśū namasū nauda
46 pa-se jasta beysa | prrattāpana nāma bīśū namasū nauda
47 pa-ysārä jasta beysa prrā | dyątta nauma bīśū namasū nauda
48 haṣṭā ysāra jasta beysa nā | gauttama nāma[1] bīśū namasū nauda
49 pa-ysārä jasta beysa ādettya nā | ma bīśū namasū nauda
50 haṣṭā ysāra jasta beysa sālarāya | nāma bīśū namasū nauda
51 haṣṭa-se jasta beysa śamatha ną | ma bīśū namasū nauda
52 dasau ysārä jasta beysa prrasanna-vada | na-u[pa]ttapala-gadhakūṭa nauma bīśū namasū nauda :
53 bīśīda | beysa ḫamāre tcahause kūla pīrma haṣṭūsa lakṣa
54 byura hau | da ysārä ḫaṣṭase cva ye nāma pyūṣḍe ṣą na drrayvā
55 avāyvā ysatha | na byehe na ra narye jsāve na prrīyvā
56 na ttrrīṣ̨ū cva sāje hvāñe | samādauna jsa bāyī ṣą b̮aysūśta jsa avīsädai hame
57 namau kṣaimākara | jasta b̮iysä namasū nauda :
58 namau dvīyaśāya bīsai jasta b̮aysa nama | sū nauda :
namą meysakau jasta b̮eysa namasū :
59 nąmau mūraucä jasta b̮e | ysa namasū :
namau ranaumala jasta b̮iysa namasū :
60 nąmau aparmata-gūṇa- | rahnavyūha-ttejąrāja-kalpą nąma ttathāgatą[2] :
61 namą sahasrramaya-garrja | ta-rāja jasta b̮eysa namasū nądä :
62 namą sūvarṇątama[2]-prrabhāsa-śrī | ⟨jasta b̮eysa namasū :⟩
63 namą bahavaidha-ttejārāja-śrrī-narbhāsa | ⟨nāma ttathāgatą⟩

22

P 2782

01 [*bases of akṣaras*]
02 : bau hau ma sū
[*Space*]

[1] *nāma* below. [2] *ta* rather like *bha*.

1 || sidhamä
ekayāṃ bārrai śau b̮aysūñä paṃde ⌒
aurga ī ttye hālai ṣadyāyä vaṃña ⌒
2 rri|hāsä kāḍi mistä tvari py̮īstai arthi ⌒
drayi paṃdāvū haṃgrathūṃ śau ⌒
3 tta-ṃ pyūṣṭä hamye[1] mahā-śāstā|ri
śi̮ña beḍa gridhikūṭä gari vī āstai ye
mista[2] rraṣa̮yi ga̮ bisaṃgīṃjūai karvi̮nā mi[×]sta ⌒
4 | phara ysāra baudhasatvi tvari uvāra
ttyāṃ hālai hauda-padya saṃpattä hve ⌒
5 gaṃbīra | hve vara dva kīḍa[3] mista rrihāsa ⌒
drayi vari śāṃ-tt-ū nirivā̮ṇva kaṃtha ⌒
6 pasve biśa mā̮ | ñaṃdū auvima hvava ⌒
ttye pasve biśa jsi ci āṃ saṃtsārä sūśti
7 pahaisīṃdä ṣāvā | kiḍa ṃuśd̮ūṃ baka ⌒
ṃuśd̮īṃje pyaura jsi hā tti jasta b̮aysa ⌒
8 niśīṃdä satvāṃ biṃdä | dāvi̮ne bārä ⌒
pūra aurmaysdāṃ mā̮ñaṃdä b̮āyi harū̮ñīṃdä ⌒
9 paṃda rrā̮śīṃdä | hamaṃgä nirivā̮ṇāṣṭa ⌒
paḍā biśä satva parījīṃdä dukhyau jsa ⌒
10 aysmvi̮nā bhā|jina haṃberīṃdä dāna ⌒
sa̮dharma-puṇḍarī ṣi̮ sūttri uvāri ⌒
[4]paḍauysä parivartti[4]
11 | mahā-vittūlya-sūttri̮nai raṃnä ⌒
paḍauysä parivarttä ṣi̮ mari tcūraṃ nasä ⌒
12 ḍyau tceyi-|śi̮ñä ūdiśāyi ttā āsñi biraṣṭä ⌒
śe̮ vīra paṃ-sse mari ṣāvā ṇesta ⌒
13 ha|rbiśūṃ vyārye mari sarvaṃñi b̮aysä ⌒
ahari̮nāṃ bvāñi ṣi̮ mari mistä rrihāsä
14 | k̮ṣasūṃ ra mista rriṣi̮yi rāhūlä bāja ⌒
uysdīśu̮mūṃ ttā sa[5][vi]ña b̮aysūñä paṃde
15 | tti khu sāṭhīkāṃ va nirmya kaṃtha ⌒
bitsāṃgyi ūdiśāyi mari dva hve yā̮na ⌒
16 tti ṣā|vā stāvi dukhyau śy̮a vī ṣṭā̮na ⌒
tti tta khu myāṃ cauṣkä bañīṃdä raṃnä avīhä: ⌒

[1] *hamye mahā* below, and *jsa* below *hā*. [2] *ye mista* below. [3] *kīḍa* below.
[4–4] Set inside rectangle. [5] *sa* written under blurred *vi*.

17 hūsaṃdai | hvaṇḍye biṃdä hayū̥nakyau jsa ~
tti tta ṣi̥ ḇaysū̥ñi gautträ ṣāvāṃ biṃda ~
18 cirya | pīrūyū prrarai ni ri bvāre ~
tti tta khu kauṭi̥ñä sthīri rāhulä nvaiya ~
19 ḁnaṃ | dä pūrṇi tti mari ṣāvā hvata ~
ttyāṃ paḍauysḁñä jsi vyārye ttū̥ ḇaysä ~
20 paṃ | dāṃ ṣi̥ śau hami bhāvyarai arthä ~
cirāṃ mḁñaṃdä huṣṭyi śaṃde vīra
21 vira ṣaka | la brriṃji khu mi̥ ūtci udiśä ~
ni va byehīṃdä ūtci stāsīṃdä saṃ ~
22 tti tta | ttuśā-dastā tsīṃdä ttarina tti hāysa ~
tti tta ttu mḁñaṃdä ci au[1] vara ttu[2] dā pvāre ~
[3]ḇaysūśtḁ kṣḁmä u ttu nayi ni bvāre[3]
23 | biysḁnḁma vū̥[4] vira ttye[5] duṣkari tvare
tti khu ṣakala brriṃjvā karä ūtci ni byide ~
24 | sadharma-pu̥ṇḍarī ttye sūtträ vīra ~
vistārī dā ṣṭi u mira haṃbistä hvīṃde
25 | śe̥ cutturi-bhāgä niraṃdä[6] ṣḁ[7] sūttri̥nai raṃnä ~
26 kuṣṭi mistāṃ ṣāvāṃ vyārḁma | hvava ~
myāṃ parṣi̥ vāvāra[8] dimarāśḁ niraṃdä
hauda-raṃnī auski āśḁṣṭä sa
27 | viri sādhäkāri niraṃdä visve bijāṣāna ~
28 āśi̥ bi̥nḁñä u spye bā | ḍāṃdä baysgä ~
daśau diśḁu jsai hā āta[9] pacaḍna ~
29 nirimāṇḁ-kāya ḇaysa | u baudhasatva ~
ttye ri jsāṃ sthūpä[10] dimirrāśḁ sthūpa[11] dyḁme kiṃṇa ~
30 śāstārä pa | sti parya kalpa pharāka ~
aciṃdya ttḁma khu aysä mari vye[12] rre vyeṃ[13] ~
31 devidattä dye ṣi̥[14] nḁma[15] | riṣḁyä ~
ttye jsai[16] ra aysa[17] pyūṣṭeṃ a ttu sūtträ ūvāri ~
32 bhaiṣajirrāji paḍau | ysḁñä jsa pātcä
tti khu haṣṭä kūla baudhasatva panava[18] ~

[1] *au* below.
[2] *ttu* deleted.
[3–3] *ḇaysūśtḁ* to *bvāre* interlinear, marked to follow *pvāre*.
[4] *vūṃ* deleted.
[5] *ttye* below.
[6] *niraṃdä* deleted.
[7] *ṣḁ* below.
[8] *ra* below.
[9] *ta* below.
[10] *sthūpä* deleted.
[11] *sthūpa* below.
[12] *vye* below.
[13] *vyeṃ* deleted.
[14] *dye ṣi̥* deleted.
[15] *nḁma* below.
[16] *jsa* with *-ai* and *-ā*.
[17] *ra aysa* below.
[18] *pa* under a blurred *akṣara*.

33 tti vira ūtsāhi: puḍāṃ|dä vasve[1] ūvārä
dijsā̮ma̮ mihe ttu sūtträ ustaṃ bāḍä[2] ~
34 śaṃde jsa vāṣṭä baudhasatva | niraṃda ~
tti pā utsā(hi) yuḍāṃdä utsā ūvārä
35 ācāri gaurava jsa | drai padya ūvāri
phara[3] ysāra kūla ahakhīysa aṇa̮scya
hakhīysa vaṣṭa vasvai paryai śā śā ge̮
rrak̮ṣā̮mä ttu[4] sūttri birāṣ̮ā̮mī jsiṃṇä
36 ṣi̮ jastāṃ b̮aysāṃ tti khu | cauṣkaña raṃnä ~
ttu sūträ hvā̮ñā̮ma ustimāṃjsī bāḍä[5]
ttī jastä b̮aysä tsāṣṭä paṃjsāsä kalpa
37 avyāyā̮me jsa si|māhāṃ vī ṇe̮stä ~
ttye parṣi̮ ri dyau parṣyau jsi[6] pa̮ñāṃ jsa[7] ttu kālä
38 khuai parya kalpa khu[8] ū|staṃ stye pajāṣṭe
khū vā vi dihye: pyāsti sarvaṃñä b̮aysä
39 parinärvūṃ pūryau | vīji mā̮ñaṃdä vaṃña ~
haṃgārūṃ jsi̮na mihā vā imi ditta ~
40 ci ttu arthä | [....][9] puñai ysyāre pharāki ~
ttye paraṃbarai jsai animaudyarä vā pä[10] biśä bī ×[11]
41 paṃ|jsāsä na̮si[12] u ni na pīttä avāyä ~
42 k̮ṣa iṃdrāṃ jsāṃ visūsīṃdä ū vā paṃjsāsäna | pacaḍana
ṣi̮ miri ttye kra̮mna tvari mistä rrihāsä ~
43 sadharma-|pu̮ṇḍarī ttye sūttri vīra
vistārī dā ṣṭi u miri haṃbistä hvīṃde ~
44 śe̮ citturi-|bhāgä niraṃdä sūttrī arthäna ~
hvaṃnī hauna khu ttye dā arthi bvāre ~
45 sidhā-| paribhuttä vā parivarttä pacīḍa
46 aysūṣkä mari vīvā nāṃdä maṃ vī sa|tva ~
46a aysū[13] saṃ styūdä u mittri bhāvyeṃ dāvū *bhava* hveṃ[14] yuḍeṃ
46b ttye biśā̮ prrahālī distä hauva dide | mista ~
sadā-parabhūttä dharmapā̮ṇai ṣṭā̮na ~
uysdīśa̮ dārañä vinīyāṃ pa̮na̮

[1] Under blurred *ūtsā*. [2] *ustaṃ bāḍä* below. [3] *phara* to *ge̮* below.
[4] *ttu* below. [5] *ttu* to *bāḍä* below, marked to follow *raṃnä*.
[6] *parṣyau jsi* circled. [7] *pa̮ñāṃ jsa* below. [8] Blurred out.
[9] Blurred out. [10] *vā pä* deleted. [11] *biśä bī* × below.
[12] With *na pī* below. [13] *aysū* to *pana* interlinear marked to follow *satva*.
[14] *u* to *hveṃ* deleted =47, and *bare* below *-dä u*.

cu mi ahḁmañāṃdä satva ṣṭikūla puḍāṃdä
47 saṃ mittra bhāvyeṃ dā bhḁva | hveṃ ~
usta vā prrīyi-darśa ṣṭḁna ttu kālä
48 ḇuśañāṃ jsa alīyä[1] padī | yeṃ tvā kāyi
si khvaṃ dāvīji mista rrūṃdā sarbe
49 śẹ pūrva-yaugä ṣi̥ | pātca miri ttiṃdä biraṣṭi ~
gadigẹsvari baudhasatvä vā pacīḍa[2] pātcä[3]
50 prrahālyai dhyḁñe | laukyeśvari-rrāji
śūbi vyūhä: ñūysdyi[4] m̱uśḏi[5] ūdiśi[6] bustuṃ biśä ~
51 ttye sūtträ | hīvī arthä biśä aharḭna ~
ttiña myḁña samaṃttabhadrä mḁñaṃdä pātcä
52 | ttyāṃ dharma-puṇyāṃ āyḁme kiṇa ~
ci ttu sūttri hvḁñīṃde u[7] ci ri dijsāṃde ~
53 tti | khu ysārä tvaḍa ḇaysa diṃdä[8] pacaḍna ~
pana vā śāstārä dharmāysñyi ḁna
baudhasatvḁnī hā ysḭnī bāste[9]
54 | pichaṣṭū ttu sūtträ nāsīrau ttāṣṭä ~
55 śau nauhi : mihā-simṳdrä biśūñā[10] | ñāvāṃ[11] tsūmaci
ṣi̥ ūtca simḁdrāṣṭä jsāti u viri śau rraysä hvīṃde ~
56 | tti tta drayi yḁna tti paṃdāvi hviñāre ~
57 nauhä: vī tta[12] ri ttaṃdī viri[13] śā hami | gūstya ~
ṣi̥ buri hve śāstārä haṃḇistāna sūtträ ~
58 saṃdauṣṭa tta[14] baudhasatva ṣā | vā dīve[15] jasta
hvaṃdä nāta aysūra kiṃnara yaḵṣa ~
59 simāsye sūtträ bi | śai ysḭnī nāṃdä ~
sḁdharma-puṇḍarī ttye sūtträ vīra
60 vistārī arthä rriysī | biśä vā ttraṃdä ~
cvai sāji vāśi̥ cvaṃ jsa āsā yaṃde ~
61 śẹ ysaṃthä pari | śaudhvā ḵṣittrvā hīśtä
nauda || ||

[1] *alīyä* deleted. [2] *pacīḍa* below, with *badhasa* under *baudhasatvä*.
[3] *pātcä* deleted. [4] *ñyūysdi* below. [5] *m̱uśḏi* deleted.
[6] With *udeśi* below *udiśi* and *bustu* below *bustuṃ*. [7] *u* below.
[8] *diṃdä* deleted and *dada* under *ḇaysa*.
[9] *baudhasatvḁnī* to *bāste* interlinear, marked to follow *ḁna*, and with *dada* above *hā*.
[10] *ñā* deleted.
[11] With *ṣa ekayāṃ* below marked to follow *simṳdrä*.
[12] *tta* deleted. [13] *viri* below. [14] *tta* below.
[15] *dīve* deleted with *biśä* below.

śī yāṃmaji ḍyau si-khūṃ palyesi śiḍā
62 ‖ syādathidaṃ a̧ṇe ma̧ṇe ⌢ akhe makhe ⌢ simaṃttamūkhe ⌢
sattyāra̧me ⌢ sau-
63 meyūrtte ⌢ niyūrtte ⌢ [sima][1] niyūrtti-prribhe ⌢ ele mele [cile][1]
hele ⌢ ka-
64 lpāṃtte ⌢ kalpatte ⌢ sāre ⌢ sāravatte[2] ⌢ hala halī ⌢ halīla ⌢
halīle ⌢ halā halīle ⌢ ha-
65 lā halīle ⌢ caṃde ⌢ caṃdatte ⌢ cira ⌢ cirāṇe ⌢ aṃcale ⌢ acale ⌢
66 aṃtte ⌢ aṃttatte ⌢ karaṇe ⌢ karaṇe ⌢ asaṃtte ⌢ asaṃtte ⌢
nirivartte ⌢ nirava-[3]
67 rtte ⌢ nidhyaṃtte ⌢ nidhyaṃste ⌢ nidire ⌢ nidire ⌢ nirahāra-
vamale ⌢ nirahā-
68 ra-śudhane ⌢ śīla-śudhane ⌢ prraka̧tta-varṇe[4] prraka̧tta-dīpane ⌢
bhāve ⌢ bhāvena ⌢ asaṃge ⌢
69 asaṃge ⌢ asaṃgavihāre ⌢ asaṃganīhāre ⌢ samaṃttamukhe[5] ⌢
yūktte ⌢
70 nirūktte ⌢ samaṃttaprrabhe ⌢ vimalaprrabhe ⌢ vimalaraśme ⌢
sa̧maṃttamukhe ⌢ sa-
71 rvattra̧ṇādagatte ⌢ anāchida ⌢ prrittadhāra̧ṇe ⌢ dhāriṇa-
mukhāye ⌢
72 saṃdhe ⌢ sarva-baudha-bhāṣattā ⌢ sarva-baudhadhiṣṭatte ⌢
nidhāna-gūptte svāhā :
73 oṃ[6] : salā-spāna : chaitta-pū hḍa : saṅga ragyaisa kī : śpyarṇna ⌢
vadaka̧ caka ṇana-
74 pa śpyaṇna raśa ḍa thāṃ : skatta̧ mī thūna ya̧ṇa : cha̧sa hacī paḍa
hasa
75 vadaka̧ pātta kī skatta̧ : mī tsaḍa : salā-spāna : thūha̧sa ttaga̧
mīga ḍa : salā-
76 spāna chaina-pau yī śa̧ sṇa : nasa : thu saṃ vla dai haṃ ma mīva
dai : kuai phasa-pha
77 saśīna hacai sapaḍa : śñūūṃ naṃ : hū sāṃ ḍa ş̣īna chīsa : vada
caka ṇana-pa :
78 pha-spa ja spaḍa kī : ş̣aḍa thāṃ du : chīva : ḍaha̧sa : śa̧ṇa̧ śkya
vla yī ḍa sale

[1] *sima, cile* deleted. [2] *sāre, sāravatte* below. [3] *ra* below.
[4] *prraka̧tta-varṇe* below.
[5] Caret mark, but no signs below.
[6] 73–80 Tibetan. Large *oṃ* before beginning of line.

79 | ttṣ̮āna machīsa : pha-spa ja śpa̮ gī śa̮ḍa thāna kuna̮ : hapūḍa du phīna
80 baśñīḍa ttai tcūka sama :
namau beśa[ ][1] vara[ ][1]sya da ha dya : auma ai
81 drai[2] aidrāttapadīye svāhā : ——
82 tta būre āśa̮rya cu caigvā tsīda āśa̮rī dharmaidrākara-pūña
83 sarva-janā̮na karaume ——
84 nama sarva nami sarva-baudha-baudhasattaibhye
85 namā̮ gīnauna vairaucanāyā ttathāga | ttāya :
namā̮ āra-samadrāya : baudhasattūāya māhā-sattuāya :
86 yāvatta | kīcetta daśa daśi lya kai ——

23

P 2790

1–126 in *Khotanese Texts II*, no. 60.
127 • • cu saṃtsārä ṣṭe ⌢ ttye jsa maṃ ttairṣṭhaṃda ḡyasta b̮eysi na
128 purrdāṃdä cu ha[3] | varrjā̮mai ttaraṃdarä ye u sarvajña b̮vā̮ma
129 harbaiśä tta anā | stana-kālva ḡyasta b̮eysi anaicä rā̮śä tsūāṃdä saṃtsārai
130 tta tta grū | sīdä cu harbīśāṃ dūkhāṃ kāṣṭyāṃ gy̮ā̮ysā̮ṃ padīmākä ṣṭe
131 u | mistye sauhä : janākä saṃtsera tsūmaṃdāṃ satvāṃ buḍa hīrattara
132 | hamāra cu na k̮ṣamīdä[4] ṣai khu tta ḡyasta b̮eysi anaicä rā̮śä
133 tsū̮(maṃ) | dä īde cu hara saṃtsā̮rū ge̮sä vaska pyauca tvā ma
134 pastāṃdä | paśāve cu maistye dai pyauca ṣā̮ cu mista utca cu mistye uca
135 | pyauca ṣā̮ cū bāys̮vā śara hauvi[na][5] cu gy̮āysä kāṣṭya hīye pyau
136, 7 | ca ṣā̮ cu b̮eysāṃ dā ⌢ ttye prracai maharaṃgä uhya : stä pūnä | jsa [rī
138 b̮vā̮ma][6] u haiśtä hīvī nauhä : jsa ṣi̮ aśtä u saṃtsārä jsa | phījāma[7] ṣa̮
139 neśtä cu saṃgīnai ṣṭa tha vaña prrahījaṃ hvę ṣṭa tvī | vīnau ttakye
b̮eysāṃ dā ciṃdä u bhāvä ttya[8] vīnau ttakye
Recto (behind lines 135–9)
140, 1 ra haṃda hye : na hame vaña tta mūnā āysāṃja spāśä | u purāṃ
142 dvarāṃ hīyi cu kāṣṭya duk̮ha̮ ttu tta nvītha cu hamye | ×mākä daukhä
143 ttu ra nva būḍa na padīmä khu ra tta ttuña baida gā | rī na jsāte e̮ṣṭa
144 tta va haṃdaryau puśä u hamaiyi na hanāśa

[1–1] Marks from line below. [2] *drai* blurred. [3] *ha* deleted.
[4] *kṣ̮ī* with *ī* deleted. [5] *na* deleted. [6] *dukhä* above *stä pū*; *rī b̮vā̮ma* deleted.
[7] *jā* struck through. [8] *ttya* deleted.

24

P 2798

1–122 Alphabets.

123–212 in *Khotanese Buddhist Texts*, no. 14.

213 thyina hīṅi nāmyi kṣuṅi[1] aśi salya muñaji māśta ṣ̨i byāvi-

214 | ja pīḍaki ttye prracina ce

Repeated with *thyina* in 214, and *thina* in 216, 217, 219, 220.

221, 2 a hāṃ gula | sai hvaḍa ttyi kaṅa[1]

a hāṃ hvaḍa ca tha lyai ri ——

223 | || tha || thina hīṅi nāmyi[2] ka ṣa[3]

25

P 2800

1, 2 || śairä paryạra vasve : aysmū paryạrä paśta sä jạsta | beysa ārava

3, 4 tsāṃ : dā ārava tsāṃ bīsa | ga ārava tsāṃ bīsagīje ge ārava tsāṃ | śẹ

5 jūna daidä jūṇạ ạysa tta-tta-nāmana | dạ̄nava jasta beysa dā bīsagīnai

6, 7 ra | na ārava paryāṃ ạhavāysye mạ na ttā | drrayvā maiśtvā ạvāyvā

8, 9 ysatha byehau | ma nāve vīnā prraṇihaunā parya paśta | sa khu ṣṭāṃ

10, 11 vaysña śạrye ṣạda jsa hana | madāṃ drayāṃ saskārāṃ jsa jasta be | ysa

12, 13 [pa][4] paḍạ̄ysạ̄ñạ jsä bīsagīje | ge parysya udiśāyạ ttu hvạḍa | khạṣṭạ

14 paiṇvā haiṣ̨āṃ ttāṃ būra ṣṭāṃ daśau | maiśtāṃ baśḍ̨āṃ jsạ pathīsāṃ

15, 16 dasau raṣṭāṃ | maista śǟḍe samādāye parehau[5] tta | khu drai-padyạ[6]

17, 18 ttaradarana : tcạ̄-padya | bīśạna : drai-padya ạysmūna khu paḍā | na

19 pastāṃda paśte tta śẹna tta daidana uve | ttu ṣṭāṃ hvaḍa khạṣṭa

20, 21 baiśa-paḍā hīye | ttravargye āyạ̄nye bvaiysye jsīna paba | ạskhajsạ̄me

22, 23 bāja haiṣ̨āṃ ttana saba | jī ttana haurana ttana parāhana khvaṃ | jsa

ttā ha bāḍä[7] yanāṃ kṣa pārạ̄me da

[*Space*]

[1] *ṅ* for *ṇ*. [2] *nāmyi* below. [3] Full *ka* over *ṣa* for *kṣa*.
[4] Blurred. [5] *hau* over *ra*. [6] With *-ā* deleted.
[7] With *ä* over *-ā*.

26

Rāma

P 2801

<table>
<tr><td>1</td><td>‖ siddhaṃ</td><td></td></tr>
<tr><td></td><td>tta tta khu bhadrai kalpa ⁀</td><td>krrakasūṃdä sarvaṃña b̮aysä ⁀</td></tr>
<tr><td>2</td><td>kanakamu̮nä kāśa | vä b̮aysä ⁀</td><td>b̮aysūśtä busta dūrä ⁀</td></tr>
<tr><td></td><td>haudamye salye ṣi̮ ttyāṃ ⁀</td><td>sadharmä aṃdarahī:</td></tr>
<tr><td>3</td><td>| śākyämu̮nä sarvaṃña b̮aysä ⁀</td><td>śara bāḍa karya sahye: ⁀</td></tr>
<tr><td>4</td><td>śūka ttye śāṣ̮aṃ kiṃṇa ⁀</td><td>khvaṃ | eṣṭa b̮uysye bāḍna ⁀</td></tr>
<tr><td></td><td>paḍāṃda hīṃdva k̮ṣīra ⁀</td><td>mahaiśvara bahya̮: tta-gauttrai ⁀</td></tr>
<tr><td>5</td><td>ma̮ṇavai ṣṭā | ye śau ⁀</td><td>phara śāstra sīya u ṣṭīka ⁀</td></tr>
<tr><td>6</td><td>ṣi̮ vā ttī carya ūsthīye ⁀</td><td>mahaiśvarä pajsaṃ prra | caina ⁀</td></tr>
<tr><td></td><td>garvā ttraṃdä ma̮ṇḍalä ṣkāṃde ⁀</td><td>salī parye dvāsä pabastä ⁀</td></tr>
<tr><td>7</td><td>khu ṣṭāṃ vara pajsaṃ | yuḍe ⁀</td><td>hamye ttye pajsaṃ ūspurä ⁀</td></tr>
<tr><td></td><td>vistāvai pyaṃtsä pīchaṣṭä ⁀</td><td>mahaiśvarä deta</td></tr>
<tr><td>8[1]</td><td></td><td>raṣa̮ | yä jastāṃ mūrä ⁀</td></tr>
<tr><td></td><td>pajaista-ṃ jsa brraṃma saidä ⁀</td><td>hauḍai ra di̮nva gūha: ⁀</td></tr>
<tr><td>9</td><td>upakaraṇa prra | cāṃ vaska ⁀</td><td>cvai k̮ṣāṃda tta ttai hamīya ⁀</td></tr>
<tr><td>10</td><td>ṣi̮ mi̮ ttī gūttairä nvaiya ⁀</td><td>nārä nāta jva̮me va | ska ⁀</td></tr>
<tr><td></td><td>bāśa̮ tsve nera jsa haṃtsa ⁀</td><td>phara bāḍa vara ṣṭāṃ mūṃde ⁀</td></tr>
<tr><td>11</td><td>ttiña k̮ṣīrä śūrä pūṃñūṃdä</td><td>| rre ṣṭā ye daśarathä na̮ma ⁀</td></tr>
<tr><td>12</td><td>ttye hīvī pūrä ysā śūrä ⁀</td><td>ṣi̮ cu sahasrrabāhä: | na̮ma hamye ⁀</td></tr>
<tr><td></td><td>ṣi̮ ṣṭāṃ rre rruśtä yuḍe ⁀</td><td>a̮mācāṃ hārvāṃ haṃtsa ⁀</td></tr>
<tr><td>13</td><td>ṣi̮ vā rre byaha buḍe</td><td>| pharākye hīña jsa haṃtsa ⁀</td></tr>
<tr><td></td><td>hasūrä jsāṃ vara vaṣṭä ā</td><td>kūṣṭa mūṃda brraṃma ysāḍä ⁀</td></tr>
<tr><td>14</td><td>brraṃ | ma̮ṇāṃ padaṃja ṣa̮ ⁀</td><td>khvaṃ kya̮śa̮ hīsīṃdä satta ⁀</td></tr>
<tr><td>15</td><td>āgaṃdūka vrraitti yanīṃdä ⁀</td><td>na pa | śīṃdä avajsama hāysa ⁀</td></tr>
<tr><td></td><td>ṣi̮ mi̮ saṃ aysmya hi̮ña ⁀</td><td>ciṃda̮mana ciṃdye tvā ⁀</td></tr>
<tr><td>16</td><td>rre parye | ava̮jsaṃ kya̮śa̮ ⁀</td><td>khu vā ttī paskyāṣṭä īste ⁀</td></tr>
<tr><td>17</td><td>yanūmī brru̮na pajsaṃ ⁀</td><td>ciṃda̮manä jsai | ṣä hamīra ⁀</td></tr>
<tr><td></td><td>hvaḍa khaṣṭa ysaujsa prraṇi̮tta ⁀</td><td>saṃ khu rre āṣaṃ yaṃde ⁀</td></tr>
<tr><td>18</td><td>bāysa jsāṃ raṣṭa ṣi̮ | śirkä ⁀</td><td>rruṃda va kūṣṭa ye khāṣ̮e ⁀</td></tr>
</table>

[1] Alignment at times uncertain. A half line seems to be missing.

khu hā rre paskyāṣṭä īṣṭä –
19 | namaṃdrye brraṃma rruṃdä –
20 śūka ye brraṃma ysāḍä –
cḁyä ṣṭāṃ yaṃda ṣi̥ ysāḍä –
21 ama ra ṣṭāṃ ciṃ | dyarä ni̥ –
22 yuḍāṃdä hā vūīyä rruṃdä –
jsaiṇa vīra khvai ye bvāṃ –
numadru̥na paḍā tsūñai –
ustaṃ vā bvḁma pḁtte (–)
23 khve na ya paḍā phara –
na jsāṃ pā prracā haiysda –
24 saiddha śarā | tta tta vā byaude –
25 ḁmāca hārva hvāṣṭa –
tti ra khu mī khaysḁ parye –
26 svaṃna hā hārva haṣṭe –
īṇāva parśḁrä yāṃdä –
27 rausta tvā brraṃma gū | ha: –
pajī tsve haḍai haḍai –
28 ṣḁi tta hve khu ra maṃ jvai –
29 gūḍa hā brraṃma prrara –
sahasrrabāhä: rruṃdāṃ rre –
30 hamyai drāṃ mai | ysdyūṃ pūra –
31 paraśva rḁmä brraṃmanaṣai –
kārṣḁ va ca burai śtāka –
32 garvā ttraṃdä mḁṇḍalä ṣkāṃde
bīda tvā saidä śarā
33 ṣḁsta | paraśḁ āvai nvaiya –
34 pūṣa pastā kuṣḍḁ vīrāṣṭa –
tta bajsḁna śaṃdā hvaste –
35 naḍa na | ḍāṃ vaska vadiṃdä –
36 narada hārva spāṣṭāṃdä –
cu ṣṭāṃ vā śaṃdā dyū –
37 ṣi̥ mu sa | ttä hera īṃdä śau –
38 rre ttiṃdä śaṃdā spāṣṭe –
py̥aisyarai kūṣṭa yai satta –

stā khajauttä pavaṃ biṃda
vistā rre tti pasta ciṃdye –
na ma distä | khaysḁ ūryāṃ –
ḁmāca hārva brraṣṭe –
didrāṃ herä ca ma na ye –
mahe pu̥sḁma | na jasta –
caṃda[1] ñaśä īye hy̥e –
jauya [×] usta tsu̥ñai –
brraṣṭāṃdä brraṃmaṃ ysāḍä
| rre baḍa byaha vaña –
gūḍa hā brraṃma prrara –
gūha: hā pyaṃtsä najsauṣṭe –
aurāsä tta tta | hvāṃdä rruṃdä –
rre[2] bvestä kūṣḍi vīrāṣṭa
aḍa gūha: jaitta | vāṣṭä –
naiśtä nḁma salā na śtāka –
hamye drāṃ maiysdyūṃ kṣu̥na –
hūṣāvai pūrakä ky̥āśḁ –
cve na khāysä ne jsāṃ bīsä –
adā | yuḍä mḁnī rre –
gūha: ysye tcaṃnḁ jveṃ –
vistā ṣīkä aysmya vīra –
saṃ ttanī prracā | hauṣṭe
ṣi̥ pā saṃ ttū padī tsve –
| dvāsamye salye ṣi̥ pātcä
āvāhye: brrahmāṃ: jastä –
ṣi̥ mī saṃ paraṣ̥ä usthīye –
| vara vīra kūṣḍi vistā –
rathä dirye mista tta hve –
khvai bvāra naḍa ye dahä: –
mū gra | hastä āsta ṣi̥ sattä –
haṃdāra hvaṃdä tta hvāṃdä –
auraṣṭāṃdä hārva rruṃdä –
pyāsta hā pa | rau tta paste –
khu vā tsvai ca ttū bijeṣa –

[1] *caṃda* to *pḁtte* below with mark to insert after *bvāṃ*.
[2] *rre* to *vīrāṣṭa* below marked to follow *parye*.

39	ṣị hā saṃ mistä | tti hve lau vā ā ⌢	paraśva rḁ̄mä brraṃmanaṣai ⌢
40	ca ttū puḍä mū̥nai pye ⌢	ca vā ysyai | mū̥nā gūha: [āma][1] ⌢
	narḁ̄ma vā phara vā īdä ⌢	āmarṣḁ-prrāpttai ṣṭḁ̄na ⌢
41	rre pa|sta hastä vā bāyara ⌢	dū̥na ra jsāṃ rri̥jsä pū̥na
42	īṃda maṃ dasta pharāka	ṣye̥ ṇḁ̄[×]|yūṃ śaṃde biṃdä ⌢
	naraṃdä hā pyaṃtsāṣṭä rre ⌢	hastä biṃdä hī̥ña jsa haṃtsa ⌢
43	rruṃda | ysīra śūrī pḁjsä ⌢	vañai saṃ biṃda paśū
44	baysgä pū̥nī̥nai bārä ⌢	paraśva rḁ̄|mä ttye jsāṃ ya ⌢
	āhau:rrji sidhä śarā ⌢	bachaṃdā śūje kyḁ̄śḁ ⌢
45	paraśva rḁ̄mä | hastä śḁ̄ṇḍä murrde ⌢	pḁraśḁnai bāysve krrīye ⌢
46	rre pastä jsī̥na paśāte ⌢	para|śva rḁ̄ma paskyāṣṭä īṣṭä ⌢
	k̥ṣīrañvā kaṃthvā tsve ⌢	rruṃda jse brraṃmana ṇḁ̄ste ⌢
47	sa|hasrrabāhä: pūra harya ⌢	dī śaṃde pacena pyūva ⌢
48	cvaṃ pacā pāḍā rī̥na	| dvāsamye salye tta ṣīka ⌢
49	pūnä hīye rrūṃdakyä nvaiya ⌢	natca khu̥ne vāṣṭä na|raṃda ⌢
	tti ṣīka śau rḁ̄mä hamye ⌢	śe̥ ra jsāṃ rraiṣmaṃ nḁ̄ma ⌢
50	busta baiśä prracai vī|rä	paraśva rḁ̄mä cvāṃ jse pyarä ⌢
51	khu pyūṣṭāṃdä kṣīrva hvḁṇḍä ⌢	rrḁ̄mä hamye | śūrāṃ myḁ̄ña
	cu bura saṃ uhyasta īye ⌢	vilau pū̥nä gvḁ̄na na tsīya ⌢
52	| rraiṣmaṃ ṣị ñḁnau rrḁ̄ṣḁ ⌢	tti mī̥ dva haṃtsa panava ⌢
53	kūysdāṃdä paraśva rḁ̄mä ⌢	brra|ṣṭāṃdä kūṣṭa tta daitte ⌢
	garvā aśtä vara ṣṭāṃ mū̥ñye ⌢	tti khu āta śūje pyaṃtsa ⌢
54	na | paysāṃdāṃdä hvastäna parya ⌢	tti khu āta haṃdä garāṃ ⌢
55	paraśva rḁ̄mä kū|ṣṭa ya mūṃja ⌢	ttūśā diśḁna na ja vaṣṭīya ⌢
56	bijeṣyāṃdä brrātara hatsa ⌢	a|ḍarä ye cvāṃ pyaṃtsa ā ⌢
	varī saṃ paskyāṣṭä īṣṭä ⌢	tti khu haṃgvāṃdä śūje
57	draya | hvāṃdai vara ṣṭḁ̄na salāta ⌢	ysīra ysaiṣḁga cvaṃ ya haṃtsa ⌢
58	rḁ̄mä paraśva | rḁ̄mä biysīye ⌢	haṃgrautta śaṃdya hvaste ⌢
59	vahaṃdä nāṣṭä audä tcījsāṃ ⌢	va|ḍāṣṭai pū̥na jsa uhya:ste ⌢
60	paraśva rḁ̄mä uysna narada ⌢	hamye va jabvī dara ttūryāṃ diśta ⌢
	saṃ ttanī brraṃmana jsāṃdä	haṣṭū ysāra pharāka ⌢
61	kṣīrañvā brraṣṭāṃda sa|tta ⌢	śūra tta kūṣṭa īṃdä mū̥ ⌢
	tti ra khu mī samavāyä khaste ⌢	rak̥ṣaysāṃ ṇḁ̄styā jiṃga ⌢

[1] *āma* blurred out.

<table>
<tr><td>62</td><td>| daśagraivä rakṣaysä ysāta ~</td><td>dūva śā rrī̥ña jsa hvḁ̄ṣṭye ~</td></tr>
<tr><td>63</td><td>spāṣṭāṃdī jauttaiṣä nvaiya</td><td>hauḍāṃ|dī vyāraṇä tvā ~</td></tr>
<tr><td></td><td>tvā kaṃtha jiṃdä padaśḍ̥ä ~</td><td>padī̥mai raysau ttūśā ~</td></tr>
<tr><td>64</td><td>daśagraiva ra|kṣaysä paste ~</td><td>savayai pyḁnarä śī̥ña ~</td></tr>
<tr><td>65</td><td>parauśḁrä miśtaña ttāja ~</td><td>jiṃga saṃ ttūrye | śtāka ~</td></tr>
<tr><td></td><td>pyaṃdāṃdī ra miśta savaya ~</td><td>nīśāṃdī miśtaña ttāja ~</td></tr>
<tr><td>66</td><td>na vahaṃda pī|rma ka tsvā ~</td><td>· vira biṃdä ttāja gvahḁña ~</td></tr>
<tr><td>67</td><td>raṣḁyä ye śāstrī daśtä ~</td><td>vrraittavaśtara|ṇyāṃ bvākä ~</td></tr>
<tr><td></td><td>khu dye ttū sava parauṣṭḁ̈ ~</td><td>bīysīyai natcai vistāte ~</td></tr>
<tr><td>68</td><td>uysgaustai spāṣṭai ttū</td><td>| cu ṣi̥ hirä aśtä mara ~</td></tr>
<tr><td></td><td>ṣi̥ va śā jīśaka ya ~</td><td>raṣḁyī muṣḍ̥i jsa pāḍe ~</td></tr>
</table>

27

P 2781

<table>
<tr><td>69 (1)</td><td>u | khu hamya kṣuṃdḁ-bāḍva ~</td><td>ttiña bḁḍa jsāṃ hā āva ~</td></tr>
<tr><td>70 (2)</td><td>rriṣma rḁ̄mä tti haṃtsa ~</td><td>khu dyāṃdä | tvā strīya da śirka ~</td></tr>
<tr><td></td><td>parauṣṭūṃ aysmū pḁjsä ~</td><td>brrīye jsa basta vistāta ~</td></tr>
<tr><td>71 (3)</td><td>na na tsvāṃ⟨dä⟩[1] | saṃ vara ṇḁ̄sta ~</td><td>pajaistāṃdä nāra ja tvā ~</td></tr>
<tr><td>72 (4)</td><td>bāstāṃdä di̥śa vī hāysa ~</td><td>śe̥ bāysa | hastarä myḁ̄ña ~</td></tr>
<tr><td></td><td>haṃtsa jsa samāṃ yuḍāṃdä ~</td><td>prrahanauśtä agapya ñaśa ~</td></tr>
<tr><td>73 (5)</td><td>karavī̥nā | karā yuḍāṃdä ~</td><td>haṃdrauysī murä na aśtä</td></tr>
<tr><td>74 (6)</td><td>cu hā tvā byāśḍ̥a karā ~</td><td>mara mū̥ña | myḁ̄ña kare ~</td></tr>
<tr><td></td><td>gi̥jä murä cu vara paśāṃdä</td><td>ttye jsa va bu̥ñakya pherde ~</td></tr>
<tr><td>75 (7)</td><td>aravī na pa|śä[2] [vä][3] hūgvḁ̄na ~</td><td>khu śau ttraima haṃtse kiṃṇa ~</td></tr>
<tr><td></td><td>vīra va paraśi̥ viśtīya ~</td><td></td></tr>
<tr><td>76 (8)</td><td>khu mḁ̄nī | śūje vīra ~</td><td>kṣārma gaṃjsa na hama hūgvḁ̄na ~</td></tr>
<tr><td>77 (9)</td><td>śe̥ ra jsāṃ khu ṣä viśtīya ~</td><td>vara vī|ra tta tta ya haṭha ~</td></tr>
<tr><td></td><td>bisavḁ̄nū khu ṣä usthīye ~</td><td>śūje nḁ kṣārmä padiṃde ~</td></tr>
<tr><td>78 (10)</td><td>| ṣḁ haṭha na hamya raṣṭa ~</td><td>jaṣṭāṃdī ttū vara ṣṭḁ̄na ~</td></tr>
<tr><td>79 (11)</td><td>ssa ṭci̥mḁña ahā vijsyāṃde ~</td><td>| tta tta ra vā haudva ttī ~</td></tr>
<tr><td></td><td>bāysañvā byaha yanīra ~</td><td>kṣ̥īrañvā kūysdāṃdä śūra</td></tr>
</table>

[1] *dä* broken out. [2] *pa* broken. [3] *vä* deleted.

80 (12)	| ttiña bạḍa jsāṃ hā ā ⌢	daśagraiva rakṣaysä pīrma ⌢
81 (13)	haṃdrauysī āśạ pathī ⌢	spā | ṣṭa vā śaṃde biṃdāṣṭä ⌢
	vara strīya ṣṭīya da śirka ⌢	vahaiṣṭa hā śadyāṣṭä ttī
82 (14)	| karä hā na byāṣṭä yuḍe ⌢	strīya jsāṃ hāṣṭä na tsvā ⌢
83 (15)	parajausta mura jsa haṃtsa	| ttī vistā pạjsa khajauttä ⌢
	gaijä murä haṃthrrī kṣụna ⌢	ṣ̣ai vaska haṃphve mụṇḍa ⌢
84 (16)	ttra | lị̄nā hụ̄ña jsa rausta ⌢	murä rauṭe jsa ttramaste ⌢
85 (17)	garkhä hamye jsị̄na paśāte ⌢	| ṣụ̄rä jsāṃ saṃvarä nāte ⌢
86 (18)	laṣṭa pāttara dīśta biysīye ⌢	hāṣṭä tsve piṇḍvā | kiṃna ⌢
	nūḍā hā pịṇḍvā strīya ⌢	biysīyai dastäna tvā ⌢
87 (19)	haṃdrauysī āśạ pa | nạ | ⌢	ttä ra khu mī rriṣmaṃ rrạ̄mä ⌢
	āta vara haudva daṃña ⌢	na va ya sījsa bīśa ⌢
88 (20)	īṃ | garśä nvāśāṃdä ysairkä ⌢	dyakya hvastāṃdä u ysairä ⌢
89 (21)	natca-ụna hamya śatcaṃ | pha ⌢	tti ra khu mī jabyị̄ darä
90 (22)	raistāṃdä kūysdāṃdä biśä ⌢	pạjsārga kāṣcya jsa | tsvāṃdä ⌢
	nai busta kūṣṭai vịjsyāṃ ⌢	tti khu āta makalāṃ ḳṣīra ⌢
91 (23)	vara makala ṣṭā ye | mistä ⌢	ysāḍakä haphva-jseṃ ⌢
	tta tta nvastä śaṃde biṃda ⌢	khu ja garä hīya ttraikha ⌢
92 (24)	| brraṣṭāṃdai khu ra ṣṭāṃ jvī ⌢	khu hamyai da ysaṃgarä ñaśä ⌢
93 (25)	ṣa tta hve uma	ca vaña cai | staka ṣṭīrau ⌢
	haṃgrīhya : rä brraukala maṃ ⌢	vaṣkaista haudva pasta ⌢
94 (26)	ḳṣārma bīdāṃdä | pharākä ⌢	ṣūrī vạ aphārä hamye ⌢
95 (27)	ysāḍä makala hautaṃ ye ⌢	hāysa tsvāṃdä | kṣārmana haṃtsa ⌢
	śūje jsa hva hva tsvāṃdä ⌢	murrdāṃdä diśạ vī tcaḍä ⌢
96 (28)	bāysạ | ña caṃbva kuṣḍa ⌢	paśạ kālä naḍa dyāṃdä grạña ⌢
97 (29)	cu ṣṭāṃ ve kuṃjsa ttị̄ma ⌢	dvāsa | mye salye tta ṣika ⌢
	vara āva śūje pyaṃtsä ⌢	kāṣcya ja vara śūje kỵāśạ ⌢
98 (30)	ṇạ̄ | sta ciṃdạ̄mana vīra ⌢	pātca ttikye diśạ vī ṣṭạ̄na ⌢
99 (31)	kūṣṭa makala ṣṭā ye ysāḍä ⌢	| makala dyāṃdä brrātara jauysa ⌢
100 (32)	tta-ṃ hvāṃdä sa jau ra na jvīrau ⌢	vistarana hvạ̄ | ñarä vāṣṭä ⌢
	tti hā ttī gūḍāṃdä raṣṭä ⌢	mahe dva brrātara ṣṭāṃ ⌢
101 (33)	ysāḍa pye jsị̄na | paśāte ⌢	rruśta kaṇāṃ śavakṣä panạ ⌢
102 (34)	śau sūgrīvä nạ̄ma makalä ⌢	śẹ ra jsāṃ | naṇḍä makalä ⌢
103 (35)	hama-śạ̄mä śūje mūṃdāṃdä ⌢	naṇḍä makala jsạ̄nẹ nạ̄ | stä ⌢
	ama śūra ṣṭīrau haṃtsa ⌢	aḍarä vā gīhya : rä jse ⌢
104 (36)	aysāṃ śirkạ̄ña yanūṃ	| khu aysä byehị̄me rruśtä ⌢
	śūka ttyāṃ makalāṃ biṃda ⌢	amājai parau yanūṃ ⌢

105 (37) | tti makala śūje mūṃdāṃdä ⌢ na ñāpye kāṃ jve āste ⌢
106 (38) ttai hvāṃda sä āyeṃ bą | ña ⌢ paysą̄ña hama aḍārä jsanāṃ ⌢
107 (39) uhya : stai pū̧na jsa rą̄mä ⌢ muḍä pastä | pyeha : jsa śaṃdya ⌢
naṇḍa makala aska jsā rruśta ⌢ yūḍa pajsaṃ rriṣma rrą̄mä ⌢
108 (40) ttai | hvāṃ : dä sä mą̄nī pā ⌢ ysīra aśtä khīrai kāṣcya ⌢
109 (41) sījsa kiṇa cvai na vijsyāṃ ⌢ ama | diśyā vidaśyā tsūta ⌢
paṃmarai bvīrau aśka ⌢ · naṇḍa makalä parau tta paste ⌢
110 (42) jaṃbvī | ya sījsa panaṣṭa ⌢ hauda haḍā kūśarä yāṃdä ⌢
111 (43) khvai byehya : rä phara vā yaṃda ⌢ ttī na byehā : va sījsa ⌢ |
nai ra jsāṃ paṃmara bvāta ⌢ haṃgrīsyarä harbaiśä vāṣṭä
112 (44) ṭcịṃąñūṃ thaṃjūṃ baiśä ṣāṃdāṃ va khāysa ja haurūṃ ⌢
113 (45) makala baiśä diśą vī tsvāṃ | dä ⌢ kūysdāṃdä pharai na busta ⌢
114 (46) kūṣṭai byehą̄ : mana sījsa ⌢ (hauda) haḍā ja haṃgāṃ | ā ⌢
viñāṃ svī ṭcịṃąña thajīṃdä ⌢ laphūṣa śā makala panava ⌢
115 (47) phūḍa śā sū̧ | nāha : kūysdā ⌢ vara jsāṃ va sū̧nāhä : biṃdä ⌢
116 (48) auska vī ṣavarakä ye ⌢ śe ṣāṃ | da hīvī ttī ⌢
ṣāṃdä tsvā khāysä va baṣṭa ⌢ bịnāsā ṣāṃdala ṣīka ⌢
117 (49) mera va | nvāśāṃdä kṣū̧na ⌢ ṣą tti hvā ą̄ṣṭyarä ttā ⌢
118 (50) makalī̧ña ṭcịṃąña gṛą̄me ⌢ svī hva | ḍa khaysą hamye ⌢
119 (51) ttai hvādä sa kūṣṭa vā byeha : ⌢ ma[×]kalī̧ña ṭcịṃąña | gṛą̄me ⌢
ṣą tta hvā sījsa panaṣṭa ⌢ sījsa jsāṃ dajagraiva hauṣṭe
120 (52) lagāpūrä [kī][1] | kīthai bāste ⌢ āḍa ra makala hamāre
121 (53) tcịmañūṃ thaṃjīṃdä ttyāṃ ⌢ cī phūṣa maka | la ttū hirä pyūṣṭā ⌢
varī saṃ natcāṣṭä naraṃda saṃduṣta maśpya tsvā ⌢
122 (54) na kaistā | mistä tta hvā ⌢ phūṣa makala butta hirä
123 (55) nai ṣa haḍa gyāre ⌢ ṣai khvai gyarī rruṃdä | pyaṃtsai gyare ⌢
hadarai makalakä pyūṣṭe ⌢ varī hā ḳvą̄ṣą̄ṣṭä haiṣṭä ⌢
124 (56) ttai hve | sä maṃ vā gyara ⌢ ca ttū pyūṣṭāyä da śirkä ⌢
125 (57) makala hvā biṃdāṃ byūṣṭä ⌢ sī | jsa kiṇa paṃmare bve ⌢
erkañai haṃphve styūdä ⌢ pū̧mye vai ṭcịṃąña tturä ⌢
126 (58) ttai hve | sa maṃ vā gyara ⌢ padā a rruṃdä vī tsūṃ ⌢
127 (59) sarvaṃdai nāsūṃ stą̄na ⌢ haṃtsakā gāṃ | gāṃ tsvāṃdä ⌢
biṃda ttāja raṃgä vistāva ⌢ makala hā na darvā ūca ⌢

[1] *kī* of *kīthai* written twice.

128 (60) ṣai ma | kalä dasta jsa bīysīye ⌢ aysā ttā ttrvāyūṃ ūca ⌢
129 (61) tha jsāṃ vā raṣṭakä gyara ⌢ gū | ḍā hā makalakä pyaṃtsä ⌢
130 (62) ṣūrä ttraṃdä makala na ttrvāstī ⌢ aḍārina ttājä khu | ā ⌢
harbīśai hāmurä tsve ⌢ varī hā paskyāṣṭä īṣṭä ⌢
131 (63) ttai hve sa ūtca parāṃdeṃ ⌢ | khu na pyāmana haudva ūca ⌢
132 (64) parya ṇāśta sve biṃdä maṃ vañā ttā ttrvāyūṃ ū | ca ⌢
myāṃ ttāja khvai ājiṃde ⌢ vara ṣṭānai tta tta hve hāṣṭä ⌢
133 (65) aḍa hirä cvaṃ vā hvā | yä ⌢ harbīśūṃ hāmurä tsve ⌢
māta maṃ brra vī pajsa ⌢ ca ttū ṣṭāṃ rahāsä paciña
134 (66) | ca burä ye pvīstä rahāsä harbīśī gūḍā hāṣṭä ⌢
135 (67) aḍāri ttāja khu ā varai | ṇāsta ṣūrä parye ⌢
khu haṃgya rriṣma rrāma gūḍā hā raṣṭa phara ⌢
136 (68) bijeṣyāṃdä | brrātara haṃtsa ⌢
hīna hā bāyāṃ baysga ⌢ sarautāṃ āstaṃ birga ⌢
137 (69) jabvīya pa | rau paśāṃdä ⌢ haṃgrīsyarä harbaiśä vāṣṭa ⌢
138 (70) jabvīyā [×] makalā haṃtsa ⌢ katha | biśä jiṇä [× ×] būrvāṃ ⌢
139 (71) tvā rakṣaysāṃ hīya auska ⌢ usthīyāṃda hīna bīysāṃ | ja ⌢
pastāva mistye vyūha: na ⌢ mahā-samudri raṃgä vī āva ⌢
140 (72) vara ṇāsta na ttraṃ | da hamya ⌢ bijeṣyāṃdä vara ṣṭāṃ ttī ⌢
khu ttrāmāṃ mahā-samādrä ⌢
141 (73) naṇḍä makala va | ra ṣṭāṃ hve ⌢ vilakä ṣṭāṃ sīyeṃ ka ⌢
142 (74) brraṃmanāṃ pārṣa yuḍeṃ ⌢ passeyāṃ haṃ bāḍä | biśä
pīsā namañū vā vāṣṭä khu ma jsa vā hatsā yaṃde ⌢
143 (75) bāñāṃ jsa hā | ṣṭä u vāṣṭä ⌢ parauṣṭūṃ aysmū ūvī ⌢
144 (76) tta ra khu mī pīsai bustä ⌢ makala ṣikä āra | hanaṣṭe ⌢
jaysarūmā tvāva-ṃ hauḍe ūca tvī maraṃ hamāte ⌢
145 (77) brraṃmanāṃ tta | ka bura krrāra ⌢ cu varttīṃdä avarī yāṃdä ⌢
146 (78) ysīrä ttū[1] gūha: ra jsīṃdä pī | sāna avajsama yaṃde ⌢
ttī rahāsa nvīḍä natcāṣṭä ⌢ tta varttāña tcaura ṣakṣāte
147 (79) | audä maraṃ khvai na hatcyāre khvaṃ mijṣye haudā ysairä ⌢
148 (80) hamyeṃ drāṃ kamala hana | haysgama byaudeṃ pajsa ⌢
kiṇa ttraikṣa maraṃ jsa mīre ⌢ māṇavāṃ ṣanāṃ yuḍeṃ ⌢
149 (81) | habā dyāṃ pīsai kiṃṇa ⌢ khvai vasuśtä aysmū vāṣṭä ⌢
150 (82) khvaṃ īśä śā paraṃjsa ⌢ | ttai māṇavā ṣanāṃ yuḍāṃdä ⌢
151 (83) nai patsa śāvai haura ⌢ āhaurrda ma paskyāṣṭä | ttū ⌢
ca burä hīra īde garkha ⌢ saṃgä hīśaṃ ttralau śā ⌢

[1] *ttra* altered to *ttū*.

152 (84) ūca tvī na vahanīṃde ⁀ | na jsāṃ tha vahạnā gvạna ⁀
ttai hvāṃdä vaña ttā saṃ ⁀ hī ṇạya sagyau ūca ⁀
153 (85) | khu mī hī ṇạstä yuḍe ⁀ hịna jsāṃ harbiśä ttraṃda ⁀
154 (86) hī ūstaṃ buṣṭāṃdä | biśä khu na pahaiśtä hịna naṃaṣä ⁀
155 (87) tti ra khu mī ịñaka āva ⁀ naysdä lagā-|pūrä kaṃthe ⁀
tta ttai dyāṃdä aḍavā daitte ⁀ āṣanvā pyaurvā āṣa ⁀
156 (88) nīśāṃda ha|lahaja biysāṃja ⁀ pajsabrrīyāṃdä cakrra u kūsa ⁀
157 (89) padāṃdāṃdä būysa ṣve | śaṃga ⁀ makalạnä hīvī chadä
hvīyaṣāṃ hīvī rathä ⁀ birgāṃ ttralaphāṃ
158 (90) ttyāṃ | hīvī nāya maysairkä ⁀ hastạna hīvī bāsä
159 (91) aśāṃ hīvī rachanai ⁀ bī|rīysya śaṃdā mista ⁀
gara trrairkhya[1] harbaiśa vaṣṭe ⁀ burṣṭe nāṣṭi śadya paste ⁀
160 (92) cī ra|kṣaysa ttū hirä busta ⁀ jaṃbvīyā āva bīysaurrja ⁀
161 (93) auraṣṭāṃdä vara ṣṭāṃ ttī | daśagraiva rakṣaysä[2] rruṃdä ⁀
rriṣma rrạma jsa haṃtsa hịna ājiṃdāṃdä[3]
161a [*in margin beginning opposite line* 65] yūttä paḍä hīvī cu ā hā aysạnā
ṣkịma sa yūtta paḍä hīvī vā ttākye ttune *v*au ūcä vahä

28

P 2783

162 (1) | gaistä pyāstyūṃ tvare ⁀
panạ rathä nvāsä u dạmä ⁀ nadāṃ ṣkalä śaṃdā tsau ⁀
163 (2) | bīsaijāṃdä rakṣaysa biśä ⁀ nai busta cāṣṭa ra tsāṃ ⁀
164 (3) ạmāca miśtara dva ⁀ gra | hvāṃdä pū ttā jasta ⁀
jabvīyā thyautta rruṃde ⁀ strīyāṃ kiṇa janave jāṃdä ⁀
165 (4) | paḍāṃda jabvī myạña ⁀ rre ṣṭā ye nahauṣa purä ⁀
166 (5) ṣị ṣṭāṃ rre paṃcābhaijña ra ×[4] | jsa ātaṃ aude ⁀
khu phara bye ttrīyaṣūnạna ⁀ hauḍāṃdai āvaṃ ttye ⁀
167 (6) phara bustä | ttrīyaṣūnạna ⁀ nahauṣä rre parau tta paste ⁀
168 (7) aysa ṣṭāṃ jastvā sarbūṃ ⁀ aśa pa|sta haiysda vi[× ×]ścarä ⁀
hūvathāta tcarṣva ttuṃna ⁀ ṣạ vā rre ūryạña tsve
169 (8) | haryūnāṃ tcarkyāṃ kiṃṇa ⁀ dī bahya: pārautta śe ⁀

[1] Perhaps the scribe intended *ttairkhya*.
[2] The hook below broken away.
[3] Here a lacuna ?
[4] One *akṣara* broken away.

170 (9) māṃjā̤na khụ̄naka dye ⌢ ha|ysgamastä māṃjä naradä
pyaṃtsī hā muṃjakä ā ⌢ brraṣṭai sa kūṣṭa āṃ tsai
171 (10) haysga|mastä ma vā gvera ⌢ ṣa̤i tta hve sä nāra̤ ysā
172 (11) puṣṭaka va āṃ tsūṃ ⌢ dahaka-ṃ sa|ttakä ṣṭe ⌢
khvaṃ na hama ṣkūṭa ragai ⌢ rruṃdä khā̤nai hamye ttanī ⌢
173 (12) bijāṣnai ṣa | khatta ṣi̤ mistä ⌢ rruṃda [×] ky̤āṣ̤ä ⌢ rrīnaka ya
174 (13) dvyāṃ tci̤mañāṃ jsa hamaṃga | ṣai tta hvā khvai ṣa na ra ttrvā-
yīdä
būśarā būśa vaṭākye ⌢ ca ttū dyai khana vī ttrāṃ
175 (14) gy̤a | vā mṳ̄ña pyaṃtsä ⌢ rruṃda jsāṃ śā tta tta ye
176 (15) khu gy̤arī varī ṣi̤ mīḍe ⌢ na ra bustä khu | yanū vaṃña ⌢
āṣṭaṃda gy̤ara ṣi̤ ttī ⌢ samai byaṃdā jāṃdä rri̤ne ⌢
177 (16) nvaiya hā rruṃ|dä va ttī yūṣä̤ ājiṃdāṃdä ttī ⌢
ttī ṃ̤āva ja ṣṭā ya śā kṣuṃdai ra tta tta hvā ttī ⌢
178 (17) | maṃ āṃ aḍa yūṣi̤ kṣame ⌢ asthaṃja vā śau tturä vāṣṭä ⌢
179 (18) ṃ̤āvī ra tta tta hve hāṣṭä ⌢ | aḍa bīhī ttuda ṣṭa yūṣi̤ ⌢
khu hā pī mīra vara ṣṭāṃ ⌢ kṣuṃdaive kāṃ hama ttī (⌢)
180 (19) | ttai hvā sä śvera mira ⌢ saṃ khu a byehūṃ: yūṣi̤ ⌢
181 (20) aysdrauttä ṃ̤ā hā pūṣa pastä | muḍä tti khu ysagarä kurä ⌢
182 (21) rre ṃ̤ā naṣphūsta natcāṣṭä ⌢ sava hā ṃ̤āva ja | biṃda :⌢
pharākyāṃ ṃ̤āvāṃ haṃtsa ⌢ yūṣi̤ hvaḍā ttye ṃ̤ā biṃdä ⌢
183 (22) arañī dye | vara ṣṭā rre ⌢ ṣi̤ vā rre pasta nariṃde ⌢
184 (23) hasta-śela hastāṃ spāṣṭe ⌢ cu ṣṭāṃ hvaḍāṃ|dä rrīysū tte ⌢
aśa ra aśpara hvaḍāṃdä ⌢ khaḍara jsāṃ hauṣka hvaḍāṃdä ⌢
185 (24) | khara tti jsāṃ hvāta hvaḍāṃdä ⌢ strīya khara kharä ttī hvā ⌢
186 (25) aḍa aśparä khaḍa|rāṃ pyaṃtsä ⌢ ma vaska hauśa̤ra ttiṃdä ⌢
187 (26) hvāta ṣṭāṃ na hvaḍä yanū ⌢ kharaì ra tta tta | hve hāṣṭä ⌢
khaḍarä ttyāṃ prrara viśṳ̄na ⌢ kiṇa mahā gūjsarīṃdä pa̤jsa ⌢
188 (27) | mire a ahvañe ṣṭā̤na ⌢ ṣai tta hvā śvera mira ⌢
189 (28) sa khu a aśparä byehūṃ: ⌢ | khu hā haiṣṭa ⌢ khaḍarāṃ
pana ⌢
190 (29) haṣkaistai brraihā: khaḍarä ⌢ hatcastai mūḍä | pastä śaṃdya ⌢
eha: ṣṭā̤nai vā ṣi̤ khara ⌢ aśpara thīyā ttye hvaḍā ⌢
191 (30) u | haṃdarye ī khari tsvā ⌢ rre spāṣṭa kīthāṣṭä by̤āstä ⌢
192 (31) pātca naḍa maśpya tsve | kharāṃ biṃdä hvāṣä buḍe ⌢
193 (32) biṃda maśpa va ttī ⌢ būysa ṣṭā ye tvara pharā|kye ⌢
śā būysa caukalä tta hvā ⌢ ma vaska vā śau tturä thā ⌢

194 (33)	hvāṣä varā | kharä biṃdä ṣṭānä ⁀	caukalī tta tta hve hāṣṭä
195 (34)	aḍä āṃ naḍa na vijsya ā ⁀	nva | kharāṃ śau phvai dīśtä ⁀
	ṣị mahā śau phvai dyū ⁀	māstaiva-ṃ biśa bya hauṣ̱e ⁀
196 (35)	| ttai hvā sa śvera dyū ⁀	paḍā vā hvāṣa varā
197 (36)	khu tha mirā śvera mira ⁀	saṃ khu a bye|hūṃ: hvāṣä ⁀
	caukalī tta tta hve hāṣṭä ⁀	a na a nahauṣa pūrre ṣṭe ⁀
198 (37)	ca vaña śe strī|ya udaiśä ⁀	hajaiṣḍi jīyakä rrūyä ⁀
	rre pyūṣṭa ysīrai niśāte ⁀	
199 (38)	ttā-ṃ ṣä | pyūṣṭä ṣaiṣa jsāṃ rre ⁀	śaysdä hamye strīya ūdaiśä ⁀
200 (39)	śakrra jastä alye | kiṇä	stẹñe gụ̄nā cairä hamya ⁀
201 (40)	āmāca hā tta tta [hvā][1] ttī ⁀	haṣḍi yuḍāṃ|dä prraulye biṃdä ⁀
	āyanā vāṣ̱āṃdä yāṃdä ⁀	na haṃgūṣṭa ysura yuḍa pạjsa ⁀
202 (41)	khvai | busta na ja ṣṭāṃ nāste ⁀	ṣị dāya mājai rre ⁀
203 (42)	jaṃbvīyāṃ vīrāṣṭä ttī ⁀	pastrīya hāṣṭä pahai|ya ⁀
	khvai bustä tta hā pahaiya ⁀	rahāśä mụ̄nā hvāṣṭa ⁀
204 (43)	hạśa sa uska bīraṣ̱ä ⁀	vira | mạṇḍalä ṣkāṃda maysairkä ⁀
	ūpavāysä hauda haḍa ⁀	si pātte laṣṭạ̄na vā ⁀
205 (44)	rahä | sarba śakrrä hīvī ⁀	vālāhyāṃ: aśāṃ jsa haustä ⁀
206 (45)	biṃda śī paṣcī dīsä ⁀	khu ttū bye|hị: ne dīśta ⁀
	pūrrūṃ tvā hị̄na biysāṃja ⁀	dīsai vā dāśe dyāṃ ⁀
	gva aśāṃ hīya ttī ⁀	
207 (46)	| jaṃbvīyā jsāṃ hā ttraṃda	biśä laṃgāpūrä kīthe ⁀
208 (47)	haṃdarai pỵāhna: varaira ⁀	stụ̄nä hạ|śä hīye kasvā ⁀
	haṃdarai dīśira ⁀	haṃdarai hāṣṭä gvahaṃda ⁀
209 (48)	ysura na yuḍa saṃ tta | tta ṇạ̄stä ⁀	rriṣma rrāmä tta hvāṃdä ⁀
210 (49)	ca ttū īṃdä cu vā na pyāye ⁀	tta-ṃ hvāṃdä si u|pavāysä yaṃde ⁀
	vīsamāṃ hị̄ña jsa purrdä ⁀	ttye vaska mī hā ttī ⁀
211 (50)	naṇḍä makalä | haśa gvahaṃdä ⁀	varai yuḍa nera jsa bụ̄ñe ⁀
212 (51)	khvai daśagrīvä rakṣaysä dye ⁀	nera jsạ | bụ̄ñe yaṃde ⁀
	ysurä yuḍä āphiḍä pạjsä ⁀	saidä ṣại ttūśị̄ma tsve ⁀
213 (52)	raha: vahaṃdä | dīsai pyū ⁀	khvai busta sä[na ṣṭāṃ][2] nyauṣṭūṃ biśnä ⁀
214 (53)	ttī auska pyaurvā sa ⁀	myāṃ samụ|dra ṣṭạ̄nai ṣị vā ⁀

[1] *hvā* deleted. [2] *na ṣṭāṃ* deleted.

ba̮-vūḍä ājavaiṣi̮ thīye ⌒   cvai skauya sattāṃ biṃda ⌒
215 (54) tta tta bī | sīra khu bura ⌒   khvai busta maṃdrāṃ bvāka ⌒
216 (55) gvīhä: rrūṃ ṣa̮stāṃdä tte ⌒   biṃda hā saṃkhai | stāṃdä ⌒
ājavaiṣä̮ gā̮ma pahai ⌒   pātcä hā daśagraiva ttī ⌒
217 (56) prraharaṃ nīśāta | prrāsä ⌒   hairthamai rā̮mä hīye ⌒
218 (57) ttera biṃdä ttraṃdä ṣi̮ ttīñä ⌒   ṣye̮ ṇā̮stä śaṃde | biṃdä ⌒
hamīḍakä makala u hva̮ṇḍä   haysgama bīdāṃdä pa̮jsa ⌒
219 (58) tta tta hvāṃdä śū | je pyaṃtsä ⌒   rrā̮mä haṃjsaiṣḍi mirāṃ ⌒
220 (59) hamīḍaka harbaiśä vaṃña ⌒   rakṣaysāṃ deta ha | myadūṃ ⌒
ṣanāṃ yuḍāṃdä jīvai vījä ⌒   khu hama rrā̮ma drū̮nai thyau ⌒
221 (60) ṣa̮-ṃ tta hve eṣṭyara | ttā aysai vā jehūṃ: thyau ⌒
hamavaṃdä garä vī aśtä ⌒   amrratta saṃjīva arva ⌒
222 (61) navi̮ | mye diśa̮ hālai ⌒   āṣeṃjä aśtä maysairka ⌒
223 (62) sūpī[ra]yāṃ[1] gūhāṃ: kṣīra ⌒   vara bise | uca jsa haṃtsa ⌒
raysāyaṃ śū̮hyāṃ: ttū ⌒   ttye jsa hama drū̮nai thyau ⌒
224 (63) naṇḍä makala bāysvā | hauta ⌒   ṣi̮ mi̮ ttī parvachä tsve (⌒)
hamavaṃdä garä vī ā ⌒   arve nāma hā̮murä tsvā ⌒
225 (64) ṣi̮ mi̮ ttī arve udaiśä ⌒   gara ttrairkha pārṣṭa maysairka ⌒
226 (65) pūṣai būḍa raysga vī hā | raysāyaṃ śū̮stāṃdä thyau ⌒
hūḍāṃdä rā̮mä ttanī ⌒   prraharaṃ cvai ye prrāsä ⌒
227 (66) ṣa̮i bura mū̮ | ñaṃdä bī ⌒   hamya vī drū̮nā rrā̮mä ⌒
228 (67) haṃdrauysī pyaurvā āśa̮ ⌒   daśagraivä rakṣaysä | ṇā̮stä ⌒
sījsa jsāṃ era bīysīye[2]   haṃga̮stä rā̮mä ttanī ⌒
ṣye̮ ṇā̮sta pūnyau ttū ⌒   na vā pastä saṃ tta tta ṇā̮stä ⌒
229 (68) | spāṣṭāṃdī jauttaiśä nvaiya ⌒   jīya̮ draivī kūṣṭa aśtä mū̮ ⌒
230 (69) dyāṃdai sa pai hīvī ⌒   hva | radai āṣṭī biṃda ⌒
ttai hvāṃdä sä khu da śūrä ā̮va ⌒   hvaraṃdai pai hīvī āṣṭī
231 (70) thaṃ | jä mā̮ñāṃ va ⌒   ṣi̮ hā pai hā̮ṣṭä haraṣṭe ⌒
232 (71) uhyastai pū̮na jsa rrā̮mä ⌒   pastä vā | pya̮hä: na śaṃdya ⌒
garśa jsai bastāṃdä thyau ⌒   tcaṃgalai ṇā̮stāṃdä dva ⌒
233 (72) ṣi̮ vā ttī aṣṭa pa | haisä ⌒   haṃdrauysī ā̮śā̮ṣṭä raysga ⌒
haṃgaistä naṇḍä makalä   ṣa̮i nāṣṭä śaṃdya hvaste (⌒)
234 (73) | varai āṣṭaṃdāṃdä jsa̮nä ⌒   ṣanāṃ yuḍa vara ṣṭāṃ ttī ⌒
235 (74) na ma jsanyarä bāja̮ nāsyarä ⌒ | harye vara ṣṭā̮na ajsa ⌒
ttī rrā̮mä rraiṣma haṃtsa ⌒   sījsa va ha̮tha prracaina ⌒
236 (75) ssa-salä | mūḍai vistāṃdä ⌒   rrā̮mä tta hve a dīda śūrūṃ ⌒

[1] *ra* deleted.   [2] *sījsa* to *bīysīye* below.

237 (76) khu ṣṭāṃ śau sattä vijsye ysurrjä ~ | cvaṃ ṣṭāṃ vā biṃdāṣṭä jsāte ~
238 (77) ysīra-ṃ ṣṭāṃ biśä tta tta rīysde ~   khu ja kattalä bahyä | bāgara rīysde ~
rraiṣma tta tta hve hāṣṭä   dī śaṃde a̮jsa ysīrä ~
239 (78) ña̮nau va biśä | maṃ rrāṣ̮a ~   śā mūra khvaṃ hy̮e heḍä ~
240 (79) ṣa̮-ṃ pharākä hastarä saittä ~   sījsa hā pyā | stā hāṣṭä ~
hagargvā būśä vaṭākye ~   na-ṃ vijsye hairṣṭai vīra ~
241 (80) naḍa vijsye ttadī ttū ~ | cvaṃ hvā̮ña śirkä salā ~
ssa sala mūḍai būjve ~   prra̮ña jsāṃ pastāṃdä sījse ~
242 (81) khu | hvā saṃ tta ttai hamye ~   vahaṃda varī śadya nāṣṭä ~
243 (82) baka kai drauta biysīya ~ | īṣṭa vā hī̮ña jsa haṃtsa ~
244 (83) mahā-samu̮drä raṃgä vī āta ~   vara nāta ysurä yu | ḍāṃdä ~
hvīyaṣā agapya ñaśa ~   bidä samu̮drä khu mūrīṃdä saṃ ~
245 (84) vara mī | hā ttanī niśāṃdä ~   biṃda padva ajaṃ śaśvāṃ ~
246 (85) nāta biśä bhavana paśāṃdä | dīṣ̮a vīdaṣ̮a vīra pahaiya ~
247 (86) āta vā jaṃbvī vīra biśa   pūrauysa rmā thyau | rāhä:
maraṇa-ṃ dū sa̮nä na purrdāṃdä   ttye jsai ṣä ñauṣṭa̮ ~
248 (87) aṃbharīṣä u mahāde | ta ~   [u][1] tty̮āna āstaṃna pharāka ~
249 (88) rruda ya śūra pūñūṃda ~   cvāṃ saittä ṣamanyau | vaṃña ~
cvāṃ rra̮mä ye rraiṣma haṃtsa ~   ṣa̮-ṃ vaña maittrai āste ~
250 (89) aysa pātcä śākya | mu̮nä sarvaṃña b̮aysä ~   diśagraita rakṣaysä hā ~
251 (90) b̮aysä pyatsä jsa̮nakya | n̮a̮stä ~   [tta][2] ṣi̮ hā tta tta hasḍi yuḍe ~
252 (91) tta-ṃ tta̮ma ttuṣye b̮aysa   cu ma rra̮mä | pūnyāṃ baista ~
vaña ma ttā parīja ttrvāya ~   khu ja ra bve ysaṃthāṃ jiṃga ~
253 (92) | ttye ṣa jsi̮na hama dāya ~   b̮uysä jve pharāka bāḍa ~
254 (93) vañāṃ mī udvīya | śtāka   b̮aysūśtāṣṭä a̮usa yanīrau ~
255 (94) artha-bhaugä hvāṣṭa̮ña   suhä: nāṃ | spyārä hairṣṭai vīra ~
hū ttaṃdī pūña tsīṃdä kīra

[1] Deleted *u*.
[2] Deleted *tta*.

29

P 2834

1 /// *circa* 26 *akṣaras* /// kalyāṇa-maittra *ū*
2 /// *circa* 26 *akṣaras* /// × kāla pīsāṃ na
3 /// *circa* 12 *akṣaras* /// × /// 7 akṣaras /// × × .. na daunaka lakṣaṇa
4 /// *circa* 12 *akṣaras* /// sahyāña || : || viṣṇa-vakrrārmī dvīlai nāgaina pāṃ
5 /// *circa* 12 *akṣaras* /// yināṃdä || : || ——
6–57 *Tale of Nanda.*[1]

30

P 2855[2]

1 || syād yathyiṃ ——

[*Space*]

2, 3 || syād yathyịdaṃ ‿ ạṇe ‿ maṇe ‿ akhe ‿ makhe ‿ simaṃtta | mūkhe ‿
4 sạttyārạ̄me ‿ sạ̄me ‿ yuhte ‿ nirūhte ‿ ni | rūhtä-prrabhe ‿ ele ‿ mele ‿
5 hele ‿ kạlpe ‿ kalpāṃtte ‿ kạ | lpäse ‿ säre ‿ särävatte ‿ hale ‿ halā
6, 7 halīla ‿ ha | līla ‿ halā halīla ‿ cade ‿ cīditte ‿ cirā ciräṇe ‿ | icile ‿ ạnatte ‿
8 attatte ‿ karṇe ‿ ikirṇe ‿ asaṃtte ‿ ni | rmatte ‿ nirvattane ‿ nari-
9 mūhä : tte ‿ naidyatte ‿ naidyasta naidyada | re ‿ narähārę ‿ narähārä-
10 vimile ‿ nīrähārä-śaudäne ‿ | śāṃbine ‿ śīlä-śāṃbine ‿ : prrikättä-
11 varrṇe ‿ : prrikätta-dīpä | ne ‿ bāve ‿ vibāvane ‿ isaṃge ‿ dime ‿
12 dädäme ‿ : säme ‿ | vapula-prrabhe ‿ säkạṣäṇẹ ‿ dare ‿ dadare ‿
13 mähā[da]dadä | re ‿ dīpäne ‿ bāve ‿ väbhāvine ‿ rahagę[3] bhävane ‿
14, 15 mähā | bhäväne ‿ krraṭäne ‿ mähākrriṭine ‿ : yạśävätte ‿ ni | rähere ‿ :
16 cale ‿ acale ‿ mạcale ‿ sämạcile ‿ drai | ṇḍạsthaitte ‿ sụ̄sthaitte ‿ asagä-
17 vyahāre ‿ asaṃga-nīrä | häre ‿ sạmaṃtta-mūkhi närähāre ‿ nīrähārä-
18, 19 yụ | hte ‿ nīrähārä-vamäle ‿ nīrähāra-śaubhine ‿ śaubhi | ne ‿ śīle-
20 śaubhane ‿ draiṇḍạsthaitte ‿ sụ̄sthette[4] ‿ sthạ̄me ‿ sthạ̄mäva | tte ‿
draiṇḍạsthạ̄me ‿ sthạ̄maprrāpätte ‿ mähāprribhe ‿ : samataprrabe[5]

[1] *Khotanese Buddhist Texts*, pp. 45–7.
[2] Punctuation in red ink.
[3] *rahagę* deleted.
[4] *tte* below in red.
[5] *samataprrabe* below.

21 vamä | la-prribhe ‿ vamalä-raśme : varva-ttrāṇ̮ūgąrbhe[1] ‿ : anā-
22, 3 chaidya- | prrittäbhāväne ‿ : dāraṇę ‿ : nadäräṇę ‿ : mukhaunūsai | de ‿
24 sarva-baudhā-bhāṣätte ‿ : sarva-baudhādaiṣṭätte ‿ : na | dąnä-
dāräṇe ‿ : nädąnä-grąttre ‿ : sarva-dharma-vīśaudä

Verso (*after six lines of Tibetan*)

25 || anaṃttä-mūka-(nirä)hārä-dārąñä vā pīrra[2] uspūrä khve suha : na jsāve ⸗

26 || anaṃttä-mūkä ——

31

P 2889

1 (*bases of akṣaras*)

2, 3 mācāṃga papala kṣa mācāṃga drąma ttīma dva serą ‿ śakara ha | 8[3]
sera [××][4] hauṣkyä ttrahi ‿ īrade mījsāka[5] mauva paurgä mauna |
4, 5 pāchai ‿ magāra gvīhą rrumna gūmalyąñą bedę kūṣṭä parkū | nąñä [×][6]
6 ayṣāya gąṇā gīchanā mi(jsā)ka hụraṣṭä śī śaśvāṃ | hīnāṃ ganāṃ bā
7 āra ‿ kāṃbā ‿ kūjsa ‿ kūṣṭa aśvagadha | bara śīje ‿ īrade tta hamaga
8 śtāka u paiṇḍę pāchai ×[6] | jsa khāysąña bañąña ‿ ——

[*Space*]

9 || tira bū̮ kalyāṇī rūṃ va arvi tsīda : kauṣṭą
10 —— sū̮kṣamela —— tagarą | tālīsapattrą —— dattą —— devadāra
11 —— elavājsąka —— cada —— nīlą | tpąla —— rrū̮nai —— vīśāla
—— brrąhata dvą —— haledrrą —— ysālva :

12, 13 | sū̮mana śāravą cadana śārava : sālaparṇą prraiśnaparṇą | haraiṇvą pūṣṭąra vaiysa khīysarą

14[7] | || tcūciva ha:ḍaḍī śa-hvyāṃ: hai:ttāva tvaṃcīkä ḍinä-bīrä śa-ttā ṣī-ttā

15 | prraṃkuyą haṃdryi va yausa tcīratsa śikalakä mąkṣī gulä śikara

[*Space*]

[1] *varva-* for *sarva-*.
[2] *pī* like *ṣī* and *rra* like *u*.
[3] *ha* 8 for *haṣṭa* 'eight'.
[4] Two uncertain signs.
[5] *mī* changed from *mi*.
[6] Unclear syllables.
[7] Thinner script.

32

P 2891

1 [*beginning lost*] | jastūñ⟨ä⟩ ttaradarakä[1]
bidä ṣṭāve drūnai tsāṣṭä ttī jsāṃ nvaśtakä
2 a ṣṭāṃ maṃ prrīśa[2] ṣṭą̄ | nä pąjsa pachīśę
khvaṃ vā jastä pasta parau gūma[rai]ttīrä[3] ṣṭāna ⁓
3 astä ma | hā jsa haṃtca gīra parya tsve ⁓
buvaṃ vā ttraṃdä įhä: ttī jsāṃ śau yakṣä
4 cvaṃ vā śąikä | salā naraṃdä a tsūṃ gīra ⁓
a ja tta ciṃdyai na jve tsūṃ pā gīra ⁓
5 laṣṭä asthaṃjūṃ śīña dīśta | pāttara ⁓
paṃda pęṇa[4] tsūṃ pamañauvą̄ ṣądyūṃ
prraṇīttä varą̄ṣ̌ūṃ samāhaunvā jāyūṃ
6 | gvāra na baustūṃ si pada daṃdä brrūṣki ṣṭe ⁓
u͡vera ū͡vatca saṃgvā tsvā nvaśtakä ttraṃdūṃ ⁓
7 | ysarñvā bura gvārai yiṃ daukhäna bīdai
8 maṃ ysīra tta tta ya si pada biśä ṣą̄ ka | ṣṭe
savūṃ vā ysarrñvą̄ tcaḍä berajä vīrä
9 rrai tsvai śau bvaiysä aspaurä spa | räbistä cūḍą̄ :
aśä stā brraihä: kaṣṭä mūlą pattīye :
10 hauṣṭū stai ṣṭāna | ttarañä ttī jsā ttaudiñä :
bvaiysä aśä jä satharä dūrä ttī jsāṃ sagūḍä
11 | aśä hā tsīyi ragya jsä ākṣūṃ pāstāgä ⁓
12 drai cūḍą̄ nāṣṭä khu jsā āvū | ttą̄jä :
ṣūrä utcä ttaudä ṣį jāphau jsä haṣūḍä :
13 ṣakala brraijä hauṣ̌ä rau | vä bvaiysä sūnāhe :
staurä[5] ñaśä ysagarä gaysä kāṃhuña baysgye
14 | misti sagä cū maṃ būjsana hāysdä grūsīdä ⁓
15 haje vī įrmä yakṣä | kvā u dī sthyāṃ
ttaurä hūṣadai avajsamya[6] u kauṣdyą̄ :
16 hīṣ̌ä gala ttaudä | herä hvālai kauṣḍau :

[1] Tops of *ja* and *ra* lost; *raṃ* possible.
[2] *prrī* below.
[3] *rai* blurred.
[4] *p* not certain.
[5] -*ä* written twice.
[6] *va* not clear.

baysga cauṣi ttauda brrathä drvanaka gūnä :
17 sa|va tcaimeñä hamye pada spavä savū
śau maistä kauṣḍi nāṣṭä vahaiṣṭūṃ ⁓
18 | [dra] ttraṃdū tvą̄ sīma gvagalījä u haiysgä ≈
19 hāysä jsa vą̄ daistä drajä | bīse ttraikhye:
varava ye kaista jsārä sīyā kuśāṃ banai
20 śau mistä [pī][1] | pīcä paskīnā tcą̄śvą̄ u krraigä
majṣyī jsaiṇi aysdaurä[2] maṃ haḍä
21 saṃ|gū rūna sastä hvaṇḍvä āvūṃ :
hama haṃdāṃ ttadī[3] ttū jīye caidyai ≈
22 | ttradū ×[4] mista kasājsä naurä nasä nąhä: :
23 mista ttraikhye gvagye ba|ysgyä hvālai phyaṣṭe :
jūṣḍyą̄nāṃ khaiṇḍä saga dī pai baysgä :
24 vaṣṭi [bī][5] | bīmi haiysgä padä anvaśtä
25 ūtcä pyā thaṃjai sagä vīrä nīṣi jsā prru|ya
ttaurä saṃ ragye cąṇi̯ vīrāṣṭä ttraṃdū
26 drą̄ma ttraikhyä cvä sa pīrākä | na pīḍä īdä :
āvaṣ̨ä mū ttīña narrvāṃdä mārą̄-pyaryau
27 hala vāsye bī|mila phastadā sagä :
dī pai jsā vaṣṭä ragä būña būña gatsä :
28 vara mī | saṃ śakrrä hīye aidre śṭą̄kä
29 ā jä rraidäpāla cū saṃ raysgä vī pa|rsūṃ :
sarbä vahaiysä padä vaṣṭä hala vāsacä :
30 pemä mase saṃgä | ḅvaiysä gesa va thą̄rsä
paha jsa nūḍä utcäla kauysä dīrą jūṣṭä :
31 ba|ysga aysbą̄nä sagīnä ṣperīdä pyestyūṃ:
32 ttye[6] hīvī ṣkala sa khu prrī|yi bīsaijīdä :
padvala kūve raṣṭä ttą̄jä pharākye :
33 āstāpha stū|rāṃ hīyi cū varä bījsāttą
34 ttye herä prracaiñä cū padä pejsä brrūṣki | yi :
ttū karä a kuṣṭä caidyai jūdai ṣṭänä :
35 hīsūṃ ttye nauhye padä mārā-|pyaryau :[7]
jairmä aśä sāgī aula ṣą kaṇä mīḍe :
36 samaina baustū si pa|ḍą̄ daukhä kāṃ barūṃ :

[1] *pī* written twice.
[2] *d* certain.
[3] *tta* below, and *-ī* over *-ai*.
[4] Uncertain syllable, perhaps *nū*.
[5] *bī* written twice for *bīmi*.
[6] *ttye* with *-āṃ*, for *ttye* or *ttyāṃ*.
[7] One dot omitted.

jastä ba̮ysä ārava tsvai sa byūrä jū̮nä
37 cvaidä | mistä mvaiśḍä bīśāṃ satvāṃ vīrä :
38 parädīvyai ysairkä khu ma jsä dyaiyi | ttā̮mä
tta dakhä spāśīyi ttraiḵṣä mūñä baidä :
39 bīmvā ttarä baysgä ca tta | tta straihä :
u kṣvīrä strīyi bījeṣīrä khu kakva jä bījeṣe :
40 kamala rā̮hä | ysīrä dūvā ttī jsä gesā
drā̮cä uysnä be udaśāyi cvaṃ vā khaste :
41 śa̮ | hama ttājä drai-se kṣaṣṭä ⌢ daiśa̮i[1] ttraṃdūṃ
42 mvaiśā̮ aśä bvaina mvaiśā̮ pā|yai tsīnä : ——
43 (*tops of akṣaras*)

33

P 2892

1–165 Siddhasāra.
165 drraubha ⌢ "ŏ" kyeśä ⌢ hūlaihä: hame ⌢ ttupī ⌢ hū̮laihä: hīvī[2] bā̮na̮
166 hame ⌢ kūrṅālūkä ⌢ byiha̮ dū̮nai hame ⌢ yasīkä ⌢ ṇveysdyä hame
167 kapäha:kä ⌢ hūlaihä: hīvī tturakä hame ⌢ yihärähā : kä ⌢ hūlai-
168 hä: mūṇūkä[3] hame ⌢ kyeśä yūkī ⌢ paraiṣkhārä [×] baṃda hame ⌢
169 baḫa:rai ⌢ duṇä hīvī thaṃnä hame ⌢ saḍī ⌢ brrā̮nä hame ⌢ ttuttasī
170 || yūguṇa ⌢ ttī̮nä ⌢ ttīysgī̮nä ⌢ yaiḫä: ⌢ aḫä:ysī ⌢ sakalä drrūkä
171 īḍaihä: adrri̮mä ⌢ yapī ⌢ e̮mäysīhä: ⌢ kā̮mūlä drrūysi ⌢ kālū̮nä
172 ttākä ⌢ ttīḍī ⌢ ūttuhä: ⌢ kiraihä: ⌢ kūdäsäḫā̮:nä ⌢ tterkākä
173 tteḫa:kä ⌢ ūlū̮nä ⌢ keysä ⌢ ttāḍai ⌢ tto̮mau ⌢ aḍi̮nä ⌢ ttulū̮nä
skai gahe rahā chaskāṃ ttāra haṃdrrāṃgä glsana
174 kaśī ⌢ kapa̮kä ⌢ kīräpīkä ⌢ yi̮ttī karäkä ⌢ yūrū̮mä kärakä ⌢ i̮ṅä ⌢
brraukalä tciṃmūlä hā̮ne jastā śīyä tceṃ halaśä
175 yū̮ṅakä ⌢ ttīśättaḫä: ⌢ aysaihä: ⌢ yiṅakä ⌢ kasa̮ihä: ⌢ eḫi̮:nä
vatcä ysīmä haskä
176 auv̮ūärūhä: ⌢ sa̮ṅäraikä ⌢ cattäkīrä ⌢ yi̮ḍädī ⌢ cattā ⌢ ūvūnä ⌢ arthä[4]
vahaiysä ṣakye sarbe
177 ärttä āyai ⌢ e̮ṅä ⌢ ttimäḫa:kä ⌢ cīkī̮nä ⌢ yari̮nä ⌢ e̮śu̮nä ⌢
namūsthāṃ phattanai[5]
178 käḍai ⌢ bīḍakä ⌢ äya ⌢ yūysī ⌢ būysäsakä ⌢ kākuysä ⌢ sa̮-

[1] *śa* with *-ai* and *-ä*.
[2] *hī* below.
[3] *ṇ*, not *ṅ*.
[4] *arthä* deleted.
[5] *tt* not clear, perhaps for *ta*.

179 ṅärä sahä: ‿ ya̯nä ‿ ārttä̯nä yūysä ‿ ttīysä ‿ bauḫū̯:nä ‿ yāda
180 bakañākä ‿ eḫau:cakä ‿ aupäka ‿ yūrakä ‿ baḫai:rä ‿ ttirakä
181 a̯uttä ‿ sūva̯cā ‿ karnai ‿ bīdī ‿ bauḫa̯:nä ‿ yūmūrä ‿ karäḫā:ka[1] ‿
182 sarkāñakä ‿ baḫä:räsähä: ‿ a̯uyä ettī ‿ auysa̯nä ‿ yūrägakä ‿ ī-
183 ḍäpacākä ‿ ā̯ñācä ‿ ba̯uḫūrä ‿ ya̯nättai ‿ kausärai ‿ e̯yä ‿ ba̯iki̯-
184 nä ‿ tta̯uśä ‿ sapäha:kä ——

34

P 2893

1 *traces of akṣaras*
2 *illegible letters*
3 // 10 *letters* // . . . . dä -ya nāṃdä laṣṭa hai . . .
4 // 2 *letters* // 〈 〉ī ba̯ysä hauva prrabhāva . . -y śaṃdā cī d sta〈 〉i nāṃ . . .
5 // 1 *letter* // 〈 〉i . tsve . r basta palaśä pyāly . s tv ‿ . js g ña kī mārnī p v -ai tt .
6 sta × × × va maṃ ǣyastä śārapūttra sthīrä : pūñardaṃ nāma bhūmaprāpattai sthīr〈ä〉
7 ttiña beḍa vā vara ttī haṣṭa-pacīḍa śira baudhasatva ca ḵṣīrī nāṃdi dīśa̯ ayai-
8 ṣcyā〈ṃ〉dä kuṣṭa ā̯ma mūṃja satvā̯ni ṃūśdä udaiśä hye: suhi kiṃṇi bisanā̯ña vās〈ä〉
9 āryāmittrai ysūṣṭe bhaiṣajyarāji banācvā vī mūṃja ttūla sagapālāṃ kiḍa sa-
10 maṃttabhadra u 〈kṣittigarbha〉 ra ñā̯nagīrai ys(ī)nī āryāvalaukitteśvara baudhasa-
11 tvā ṣa̯ jusña parīja vinīyā harahausta attrāsta ‿ baudhasatva maṃjāśrī ṣe̯ kāśavittra ttri-
12 ṇa-śela āsta biśe parṣa̯na haṃtsa māṇabhāva ñānīthāṃ ṣi̯ kāṃśavittrī ādakarmya
13 āmūha nāve ‿ ākāśagarbha ra jsāṃ ṣi̯ baudhasatvä sakāyagīra satvaparipākä udaiśa va-

[1] *ka* below.

14 krra dyā̮ñe haṣṭa vā parvālā hauvana mista ∽ pīchaṣṭu ba̮ysna kṣīra ysīnī nāṃdä biśa va-

15 ra śāśa̮ṃ sarva-saṃga prravaiya rruṃdä āstaṃna hvāṣṭa ṣada karīha vrrīśamaṃ saṃñī aparājai ja-

16 sta gaganasvarä svarṇamāla grrahava̮ḍatti ∽ nvaiya hā aṃgūśa̮ stānāva̮ parṣa̮na hatsa ttyā-

17 na āstaṃna mista uvāra drai byūra hauvana pa-ysāra pa[ca]cīḍa[1] pa-se ra hauda tta

18 parvālā biśna ∽ haṣṭusä ysāra nāgarāja balauda śāsanābhaprrāptta ra hvaṃ k̮ṣīra dījsā-

19 ta nā cadyi nā japa mū̮ne būstu ysāra- salū kṣaudi sṃma̮nāva padaidāya sudū jīyaka

20 yāvajī cadyi droma hera cuḍa iḍāya[2] ca na pamūḍa ka bistä ysāra daśa-bhū̮mā m̮ūśd̮a

21 byauda ∽ tta pā ttū hvaṃ kṣī(ri) āysdaḍa dījsāre ∽ ttī jasta ba̮ysa ca k̮ṣīra sīma dījsāre

22 vā dirṣṭāśaya asadarṇa satva ni byehīda biśna ka vā̮nīha uvāśa̮ prrabiṃba-kā-

23 ya biśä dīśa̮ ve thā̮na ca ṣi̮ rājagrā̮mai śāstāra ṣṭa vaṃña ṣa̮ vā vaiśāla rāmagrā̮-

24 maka ṣṭāna mvaiśd̮a kiṃṇä usahye: ttye k̮ṣīra prraci̮(na khu) na bvīdä sā̮nāṃ āchai jsa ttū kāla ṇi-

25 tcaṃpha bāḍä khu k̮ṣīra ākṣū jīye grahavattä nāvāṃ rre ttū pūṣa bāyi pajsamai-

26 na hī̮ña bhavaña varai pharāka biśū̮ña brrū̮na pajsama saṃskāra ca ṣi̮ dikabanī

27 śāstāra ṣṭa vaṃña ṣi̮ vā veśāla rā̮magrā̮maka ṣṭā̮na mvaiśd̮a kiṃṇa usahye ttye k̮ṣīra prraci̮na ∽ khu na bvīṃ-

28 da sā̮nāṃ āchai jsa ttū kāla ṇetcaṃpha kāla khu k̮ṣīri ākṣū̮ dū jīye ∽ grahavada(tti) nātāṃ re ttu pūṣa

29 bāye pajsamaina hīña bhavaña varai pharāka ∽ biśū̮ña brrū̮na pajsama saṃskāra haiśe̮ ∽ ca ṣa̮ ditkaba-

30 nī śāstāra ṣṭa uvāra ∽ nā̮ma̮na prrabhūttaraśū bvaijsaudi ∽ ṣi̮ vā sāketta ṣṭā̮na ā̮rmvā tsve da̮ṇḍa ∽ ttairṣcaṃda

31 tti ∽ na ekä ka pa rā de na : maitrāvardana stā kṣā tta saha saṃ na sa rā na sa da sta a × d

[1] *ca* blurred.   [2] With *lā* deleted above *ḍā*; and independent *i*.

32 ·· viña ttā hva hva biśụ̄ñāṃ āchāṃ va pịṇḍạ̄ hvañāre u yauga :: ——
33 ·· halīrai ⌢ vihīlai ⌢ aumalai ⌢ hamaṃga . vīśṭạ̄ña ⌢ nauka ārạ̄ña
34 mākṣīna paherạ̄ñä | saṃdvena tciṃña rāẖä jidä ::
35 phaja vaha pau ⌢ hauṣka gūra ⌢ kuṃjsa ⌢ būysị̄ña pī ⌢ | hamaṃga
vīstạ̄ña ⌢ u kūṭạ̄ña ṣị paiṇḍai-tciña bañạ̄ña ::
36 khu beva jsa tciña rā | ẖa hạme ṣị pẹśā āphiḍe tcịmeñvā vī hạ̄ nestra-
37 makauṭe[1] hạmāre garkhye drạ̄ma | siphāṃ vaṣṭe ⌢ jsiṇūṃ jsa ni
38 vījseṣḍe ⌢ ṣại va pẹṇḍai ⌢ sauthara spyakä ⌢ bā ttīma ⌢ | hạmaṃ(ga)
vīśṭạ̄ña ⌢ ttīlaka hā haumai vimathạ̄ña ⌢ ẖugalakä hạ̄ ṣẹ pẹṇḍai
39 padīmạ̄ | ña ⌢ ttaṃgalakạ̄ña pẹmakạ̄ña ñūṣṭyạ̄ña ⌢ grạ̄makä kacau
40 ysaiysai u pạśā tceña ni | śạ̄ña jatte ::
41 khu pettana u hụ̄ña āphārä va tciṃña rāẖa hạme ṣạ śya haḍ(ā)
āphe | ḍe ⌢ ṭcịmañī heṃjä hamāre ⌢ ysīḍaurgä vījaiṣḍe ṣị va pẹṇḍai ⌢
42 halīrai ⌢ vihīlai ⌢ au | malai ⌢ duma-hauṣṭa gūra ⌢ kūṃjsa ⌢ hamaṃga
43 vīśṭạ̄ña ⌢ kūṭạ̄ña ⌢ ṣvīdana peṇḍai | pāche ⌢ grrāṃ grāṃ parye śva
haḍā tciña niśạ̄ñä jatte ::
44 cū śilīṣụmạ jsi tciṃ | ña rāẖa hame ṣị ysaiysai[2] āpheḍe tcimạñī
45 garkhyä hạmāre u kyahāre ⌢ hauvi vī | ṣṣaidä ⌢ drạ̄mī hera haṃ-masä
46 caṃbūlạ maṃ ṣṭāre ⌢ āṣkī jsāve ṣại va pẹṇḍai | kuṃjsa ⌢ kuṃbā ⌢
47 śā śā hāḍa nauka ārạ̄ñä ⌢ u ttī ysīḍā spye śā hāḍe ⌢ nauka | kuṭāñä ⌢
48 drai vasīya uci jsa jṣạ̄ñạ̄ña ⌢ daṃdä khū ra va śau vasī harśtä | ttī pẹ
ysụ̄ñạ̄ña ⌢ u paskyāṣṭä hā tcirai ⌢ ṣị kuṃjsa ⌢ kuṃbā ⌢ hā tcerai ⌢
49 ṣị ẖugä | pẹṇḍai pāchai ⌢ drai haḍā vaṣṭä ysaiysai u pẹśā grāṃ grāṃ
50 dasau jūna tciṃ | ña nīśạ̄ñä jatte ::
51 cū drayau dūṣyạu jsa ṭciña rrāẖä hạme ⌢ ṣại va yaugä ⌢ ttri | phala ⌢
52 halīrai ⌢ vihīle ⌢ aumalai ⌢ vinau gachạ̄kāṃ śā śā mācāṃgye | nauka
kūṭạ̄ña ⌢ drai vasīya ūcä jsi jṣạ̄ñạ̄ñä khū ra va śau vasī harśtä |
53 ysụ̄ñạ̄ñä ⌢ na ạ̄naẖạ̄ dvī prūyi maṃgārä gvīẖa rūṃ tcerai ⌢ hauda
54 khaśạ | pẹśā khāśạ̄ñä jatte ::
55 ṣị būri ṭciṃñạ̄ṣṭä rūṃ va arva jsāve ⌢ vạ̄mī | nai rūṃ śā prūye ⌢
56 aviṣgị̄nai rūṃ śā prūye ⌢ gvīẖa dvī prūye ⌢ gūrvāṃ gi | chanāṃ
mijsạ̄kāṃ jsa rūṃ dvī prūye ⌢ haryāsä kuṃjsạna ruṃ śau śiṃgä ⌢
57 kapū | ra hālai akṣarä ⌢ kụrkāṃ śau akṣari ⌢ yausa śau akṣarä hālai[3] ⌢
58 yausa hālai | akṣari ⌢ cigāṃ būśạ̄nai śā mācāṃgye ⌢ hạma ysā śikarä
59 śau akṣä ⌢ nīra lạ | vaṃgä ⌢ dvī mācāṃgye ⌢ mahābuṃjä śau sirä ⌢

[1] *stra* for *ttra*.
[2] Second *ysai* below with caret above.
[3] *yausa* to *hālai* deleted.

60 bakä kūṭạña ‿ drai hạmạ̄kä ‿ ū | ci jsä jṣạ̄ñạ̄ñä ‿ daṃdä khū ra va śau
61 hạmākä harśtä ‿ ysụ̄ṇạ̄ñä paskyāṣṭä ṣị | kaṣạ̄ hạ̄ña tcirā ‿ kaṣạña
62 ciṃgāṃ būśạ̄nai ‿ kurkāṃ ‿ lavagä ‿ haṃtsä jṣạ̄ñạ̄ | ñä ‿ daṃdä khū ra ruṃ harśtä ‿ khū naysdä vaḫä hame ‿ ttī hā kapūrä ‿ yausa ‿
63 śika | ra tcirai ‿ khū śau dva jūṃ haṃtsä jīṣḍị thaṃjạ̄ña ‿ ysụ̄mạ̄ñä ‿
64 pẹṣ̣ā ḳṣi kạnai haysgvā | paśạ̄ñä ‿ kamalä pāstāṃgä biysaṃjạ̄ñä ‿ tti
65 vā ḇvejse ‿ khu bẹva jsä ṭcịmeñạ | āphīrārai jahāre ‿ kạmala rrāḫä jidä ‿ khū ṭcaiṃẹña ṣṣaidä ‿ khū ttī jsiṃ | ṇä ni vijsyä ‿ myāṃ ttira
66 vīna jiṃdä ‿ cū saṃ beva jsä ṭciṃeña āphīrārai ‿ | biśūṃ va śira
67 īṃdä : :
68 tti vā khāysạ̄ña pịṇḍạ̄ ‿ āḍa hạ̄mai ‿ vịyaji ‿ rā | jā-nämva ḇiḫạ̄ya ‿
69 hạmaṃgä viśṭạ̄ñä ‿ nauka ārạ̄ñä ‿ mauna pāchai ‿ biṃdä | halīrai
70 parkụ̄ṇāñä ‿ darye jsahāra nīśạ̄ñä ‿ petta śliṣmī khāysạ̄ñä u | ahạña ạ̄ma naṣpaśḏe : :
71 haryāsa sacha mauna pāchai ‿ ṣị pẹṇḍai ura biṃ | dä nīśạ̄ñä paṣkạ̄sā jiṃdä : :
72 paḍā śā ṣavä khāysạ̄ña hạ̄ma śīya ttrahe | bañạ̄ñä ‿ u biṃdä śīya
73 namva sauyạ̄ña ‿ u ttī ustaṃ ṣị pẹṇḍai bañạ̄ | ñä : :
bāṇva ṣavarä ‿ dva bāga ‿ hạmārnai phaura dva bāga ‿ huṣkyä
74 ttrahe dva bā | gä ‿ rrājā-namva dva bāgä ‿ āḍa hạ̄mai śau bāgä ‿
75 nauka ārạ̄ñä hatsä ‿ pẹ | ṇḍai padịmạ̄ñä khāysạ̄ña āchā jiṃdä ‿ haśä u dūvarä : :
76 ahaysnāva ysa | raṃjsạ ‿ būysịñä padī ṣū hīya ranūṣkä ‿ mau hīya
77 purgä ‿ rūsāḍä ‿ [ṣa][1] | hạmagä vīśṭạ̄ña ‿ hatsä kūṭạ̄ñä ‿ pẹṇḍai
78 padīmạ̄ña ‿ bi[sai][2]dai śī ḇū parkū | ṇạ̄ña ‿ khāysạ̄ña bañạ̄ñä ‿ haśä tcaḇeje : :
79 aysāya ‿ u gụṇāṃ u gīchạ | nā mījsạ̄ka ‿ hūraṣṭä ‿ śī śaśvāṃ ‿
80 hịnạ̄ ‿ ganạ̄nai bā ttịma ‿ āra ‿ kuṃbā ‿ | kuṃjsa ‿ kuṣṭä ‿ aśvagaṃdhạ ‿ bara śīṃje ‿ īraṃde ‿ biśa hạmaṃgä vīśṭạ̄ñä ‿
81 nauka | kūṭạ̄ñä ‿ pẹṇḍaitūṃ jsa padịmạ̄ñä ‿ uci jsa pāchai ‿ khā-
82 ysạ̄ña hạ̄ma bā | va paśtä ‿ haśä jiṃdä ‿ u bāva śilīṣụmajsa āchā u phāḫä : :
83 ttī vā ha | śi va pẹṇḍạ̄ ‿ huṣkyi ttrahe ‿ kuṃjsārgyä ‿ mauna pāche ‿ ṣị sālyẹ haśa va pẹṇḍai : :
84 | ayṣ̣āyä nauka kuṭạ̄ñä ‿ uci jsä jṣạ̄ñạ̄ñä ‿ hạ̄mai hā vamathạ̄ñä ‿ ṣẹ
85 pẹ | ṇḍai sāḍa hasve jiṃdä : :

[1] Unclear. [2] Blurred *sai*.

86 jsanaspāra ⌢ jbdrre[1] ⌢ huṣkyi ttrahe ⌢ bāṇva ṣavarä ⌢ | b̮ahauya ⌢
87 hamaṃgä vīśtā̮ña ⌢ nauka ārā̮ñä ⌢ mauna u namvena pāchai haśa | va
pe̮ṇḍai ::
88 ṣvīdana rūsāḍä ⌢ paherā̮ñä ⌢ āḍa gūrva ⌢ ā vā khāhāṃ hīye | ūci
jsa heṃje haśä bidä nīśā̮ñä tcab̮eje ::
89 kuṃjsa ⌢ kuṃbā ⌢ ysarūṃ māṃgä ⌢ | rīysū ⌢ ysīḍā spye ⌢ mahā-
90 buṃji ⌢ hamaṃgä vīśtā̮ña ⌢ naukä ārā̮ñä ⌢ ṣvīdina | pe̮ṇḍe pāche ⌢
gvīḫa rūṃna ⌢ gūmalyā̮ñä ⌢ saṃdve̮na haśä jiṃdä ⌢ bina hū̮ñä
91 va | sūje ::
mākṣī̮na vasva uysmä paherā̮ñä ⌢ ā vā veśtīñe ā n(au)ka[2] kūṭāñä ⌢
92 mā̮ | kṣī̮na paherā̮ñä cu jara strīśtä ⌢ vara baññā̮ñä ṣa̮i vasū̮je ::
93 halīrai ⌢ vihī | lai ⌢ ā̮malai ⌢ śī sū̮maṃ spye ⌢ halaidrä ⌢ śīlā-jattä ⌢
94 dū̮ma-hauṣṭä gūra ⌢ biśa ha̮ | maṃgä vīśtā̮ñä mākṣī̮na paherā̮ña ⌢ jara
95 vī baññā̮ñä ⌢ phāḫi uysänä āphārä | jiṃdä ::
96 śī pau phaji pajsā̮ñä ⌢ cipaññā̮ñä ⌢ biṃdai śikarä parkūnā̮ña ⌢ u
ha | laidrä ⌢ jara biṃdä baññā̮ñä ⌢ jara vasū̮je ::
97 rrustiri āṣkä ⌢ u śīṃji āṣkä ⌢ | ysarūṃ māṃgä krriṃgīñä [hā?][3]
98 āḫa ⌢ ha̮maṃgä vīśtā̮ñä ⌢ ārā̮ña ⌢ buysī̮ña ṣvīdä | na pi̮ṇḍai pāchai
[ja][4] jara biṃdä baññā̮ñä ::
99 nīyakä ⌢ ahauḍi vārrjä biṃdä būṣvā̮ña | u bidai hā hama ysā śikarä
100 parkūnā̮ñä ⌢ ṣi̮ pi̮ṇḍai paṃjsä haḍā vaṣṭä jarrä biṃdä ⌢ baññā̮ñä ⌢ cū
buri va jara̮ña āchā īṃde ⌢ biśī vasū̮sīṃdä ::
101 rūva ⌢ rrustarä ⌢ | rū̮nai ⌢ rrīysva gūrva ⌢ būysī̮ñä pī ⌢ hauṣkä
102 gurä ⌢ biśä ha̮maṃgä viśtā̮ñä naukä | kūṭā̮ñä ⌢ ṣi̮ jarä biṃdāṣṭä
103 pi̮ṇḍai ⌢ rrū̮nä ttīṃ ⌢ y̮iyajä ⌢ ha̮magä vīśtā̮ñä ⌢ kū | ṭā̮ñä ⌢ maṃgārä
mauna paherā̮ña ⌢ khvai va bāva pa̮jsa īṃ ttī kūjsävī[na][5]nai rūṃna
104 ⌢ | ā vā gy̮īḫä: rūṃna ⌢ mūrā̮ñä ⌢ jarra vī baññā̮ña ⌢ jara vī ttraikṣä
vī̮nä jiṃdä ::
105 ttīra | ahāḍä hīya ṣara ⌢ gulä ⌢ sūdākṣīrä ⌢ rrustirä āṣkä ⌢ ba-
106 lāttakye ⌢ padīya | āste ⌢ caittrai hīya grūṣkä ⌢ b̮a̮nījāṃ grūṣkyāṃ
107 hīvī kṣārä ⌢ hamaṃgä vīśtā̮ñä | nauka kūṭā̮ñä ⌢ tcāra jsä peṃḍai
108 padīmā̮ñä ⌢ jara vī ⌢ khāysā̮ña ⌢ phiysgā̮ña ⌢ | ga̮uma jidä ⌢ u haśä
jiṃdä ⌢ u parigrahä ⌢ u vāttäṣṭhī̮lai biśä jiṃdä ::
109 tti vā | ṣpaijai biṃdāṣṭä pi̮ṇḍā̮ ::

[1] Or *d* in place of *j* ?
[2] *ā n(au)ka* not clear.
[3] Blurred syllable.
[4] *ja* blurred.
[5] *na* blurred.

110 īraṃde gurmạñä ⌢ nauka ārạñä ⌢ khyera ṣvīdi jsi peṃ | ḍai pāchai ⌢
kujsavīnai rūṃna gumalyạñä ⌢ bidai kuṣṭä parkūṇạñä ⌢ u spajūṃ ⌢
111 ṣpaijai | bidä bañạñä ::
112 īraṃde dūmä-hauṣṭä gūra ⌢ pattaudä gạṇā mījsākä ⌢ hamaṃ | gä
vīśtạña ⌢ nauka ārạñä ⌢ haṃtsä pāchai ⌢ ṣpaijai biṃdä bañạñä ::
113 gạṇā | mījsākä ⌢ gīchạnā mījsạkä ⌢ śīṃja āṣkä ⌢ kuṃjsa ⌢ aśä sahä̱
114 hīya ranū | ṣkä ⌢ khū ra vastạña bīsā garṣva ⌢ rrājā-namva ⌢ hạmaṃgä
115 vīśtạñä ⌢ nauka ārạñä | mauna pāchai ⌢ ṣpaijai vī bañạñä parigrahä
jiṃdä u kasai vīśte ::
116 dājsaṃ | dai[1] ⌢ mījsạka ⌢ haṃga ⌢ āra ⌢ [a][2] pauṣṭarä ⌢ biśi
117 hạmaṃgä vīśtạñä ⌢ nauka kū | ṭạñä ⌢ rrāji-namve jsa ṣị peṃḍai
pāchai ⌢ ṣpạijai vī bañạñä ⌢ kasai vīśte ::
118 | hajārnā spye ⌢ tcyāṃśvīna ⌢ rrāje-namvena ṣị pịṇḍai pāchai ⌢ u
119 hạmai hā vamathau | ñä ⌢ ṣị piṃḍai ṣpạijai biṃḍä bañạñä ⌢ maṃgārä
kasai vīśte ::
120 kuṣṭä ⌢ āra ⌢ spaju | bā ttīṃ ⌢ gūrve īraṃde ⌢ kuṃjsa ⌢ hamaṃgä
121 vīśtạñä ⌢ naukä ārạñä ⌢ khyerye [×][3] | tcāri jsi mūrạñä ⌢ hạugä
122 peṃḍai padịrnạñä ⌢ grāṃ grāṃ pṣạijai[4] biṃdä bañạñä | ṣpạijai vī
khaiya jiṃdä ::
tti vā nihāṣṭä peṃḍā ::
123 rrvīysva gūrva ⌢ halaidrä ⌢ | śikarä ⌢ huṣkä gūrä ⌢ hamaṃgä
124 vīśtāñä ⌢ naukä kūṭạñä ⌢ ūlịñye tcāri jsä | ṣị pịṇḍai pihẹrạñä ⌢ neha
bañạñä ⌢ aha vasūje ::
125 gūra ⌢ śī pau ⌢ tti hạ | maṃgä kūṭạñä ⌢ śikarä ⌢ sadalūṃ ⌢ hạ-
126 maṃgä vīśtạñä ⌢ pātcä ārạñä ⌢ gyī | hạ ruṃna mūrạñä ⌢ neha
bañạñä ⌢ ṣị ahe vasūjạkä pịṇḍai ::
127 kuṃjsa ⌢ śika | rä ⌢ ttirṣcya ⌢ hạmaṃgä vīśtạñä ⌢ nauka ārạñä ⌢
128 gvīhạ rūṃna ⌢ māḳṣịna paherạña | niha bañạñä ⌢ ṣị ahạnāṣṭä
pẹṇḍai ::
129 dūmi-hauṣṭä gūra ⌢ ttyāṃ ma dạna thaṃ | jạña (ka)stūra būhana
130 6 haṃtsä naukä kūṭạñä ⌢ gvīhä rūṃna mūrạñyä ⌢ ṣị piṃdạ | kä nehạ
bañạñä ⌢ aha vasụje ⌢ u khāysä vī raiṣä padịme ::
131 dụmi-hauṣṭä gūra ⌢ | tharkä mījsā ⌢ kuṃjsa ⌢ bara śīṃje ⌢ āḍä
132 hạmaṃgä vīśtạñä naukä kūṭạñä ⌢ pau hīye | ucä jsä paherạñä ⌢ nihạ
bañạñä ṣẹ peṃḍai vā tta pittä jiṃdä ū dūvarä ::

[1] So with *ā*.
[2] *a* blurred.
[3] Blurred *akṣara*.
[4] *pṣ* for *ṣp*.

133 ysa | rūṃ māgä ⁀ dvyī mācāṃgye ⁀ vį̄na gīchąkāṃ halīrā dvyī
134 mācāṃgye ⁀ spajū hālā mā | cāṃgye ⁀ nauka ārąña ⁀ gvīhä rūṃnä
135 paherąñä ⁀ niha bañąñä ahe va piṃḍai | kālī naiśtä ⁀ cī bāḍä
hąmāve : :
136 tti vā naraiya va u nāṣṭä āchąna pį̄ṇḍā ⁀ cu | saṃbhārä vahaiysāre ⁀
mistye hvąṇḍe ⁀ ā valakyä ṣīkä ⁀ ṣąi va paiḍai ⁀ hainai caṃdä[1] ⁀
137 | kuṣṭä ⁀ sidalūṃ ⁀ kąṇḍārya ⁀ lākṣä ⁀ kastīrä[2] biśä hąmaṃgä
138 vīśtąñä ⁀ naukä kūṭą | ñä ⁀ sauttäna u kaujsąvīnai rūṃna ṣį pimḍai
pāchai hā bañąñä jatte : :
139 ttī vā pātcä ttyau | hąmyau arvyau jsa u suttäna kuṃjsąvīnai rūṃ
140 pāchai makṣąñū jsä u khāśąñä ⁀ narai | ya jiṃdä : :
vasve hąmai haṃtsä mį̄jsąkį̄nai rūṃna mūrąñä ⁀ u ṣį peṃḍai hūṣya
141 bañą | ñä naraiye jatte : :
142 ttī pātcä nīysva jṣąñąñä u ṣį pęṇḍai ⁀ hā nīśąñä ⁀ u mījsä | kį̄nai
rūṃ gūmalyąñä ⁀ hūṣya bąñāñä naraiya jeṃdä : :
143 cū saṃbhāra hasvīṃdä ⁀ ṣąi | peṃḍai ⁀ halīrai ⁀ vihīlai ⁀ ąmalai ⁀
144 hamaṃgä vīśtąñä ⁀ naukä kūṭąña ⁀ pahe | rąñä ⁀ cu saṃbhārä sāḍä
145 hąmāṃde varaṃ[×][3] grāṃ grāṃ bañąñä ⁀ cū ttaudä īṃde varä | pvā
bąñąñä : :
146 kalarbä bāta ⁀ rūṃña jṣąñąñä ⁀ u kūṭąñä ⁀ dahį̄ñä ⁀ gūnai | biṃdä
bañąñä ūpadeśä jeṃdä : :
147 ysīḍā spye ⁀ į̄raṃde ⁀ kuṃjsa ⁀ sauhį̄ya | rrauṭā ⁀ hąmaṃgä
148 vīśtąñä ulį̄ñe tcāra jsä u khyerye tcārä jsä mūrąñä pę | mą jsä ñūṣṭyąñä
grāṃ grāṃ pheysgąñä nīśąñä brūṣkyä vį̄nä jiṃdä : :
149 bā ttį̄ma | sauhīya rrauṭā ⁀ kuṣṭä ⁀ sidalūṃ ⁀ tti hamaṃgä vīśtąñä ⁀
150 nauka ārą | ñä ⁀ ysūnąñä ⁀ kuṃjsavį̄nai rūṃna ⁀ śāvį̄ña bąjinakąñä ⁀
151 dūra padį̄mąñä | ⁀⁀ cū na myąnāṣṭä hasvā īṃde ⁀ varä saṃkhilyąñä ⁀
152 cū vą saṃ ⁀ khu nvaśtä himāve | vara biśä ⁀ śera īṃdä : :
153 cū pyatsī ūski vaśe ⁀ kąśte ⁀ u vīnai hąme ⁀ ṣąi peṃ | ḍai ⁀ ttīrä
ahauḍä[4] hīya ṣarä ⁀ ṣį hvī ṣvį̄danä ⁀ bīnąyi vīśtąñä ⁀ u dva ⁀ pį̄ṇḍā
154 | padį̄mąña ⁀ grāṃ grāṃ śau phiysgąña nīśąñä ⁀ u śau hā tvī tvī
155 āyvąñä uskä vaśe prra | hāje : :
saunai phąrä ⁀ naṃvīṃje uci jsä pāchai ⁀ piṃḍaiyūṃ jsä padī-
156 mąñä ⁀ kūjsą | vīnai rūṃna gūmalyąñä ⁀ khu saṃbhārä hasvīṃdä ⁀
varä bañąñä : :

[1] For *caṃdaṃ*.
[2] With -*ī*-.
[3] Blurred syllable.
[4] *a*- written below.

157 khu nimaitträ | na pḁname u ṣḁi aspaśd̥e ::
158 du̥ma-hauṣṭä gūrä ⌒ tharkä mi̥jsā ⌒ b̥igajä pī ⌒ kuṃjsä ⌒ | īraṃde ⌒
phaji vah̥a pau ⌒ ūli̥ña tcārä ⌒ [×][1] hamaṃgä vīśtḁñä ⌒ haṃtsä
159 kūṭḁ | ñä mūrḁñä ⌒ ṣi̥ peṃḍai mijṣḁṃ phaiysgḁñä bañḁñä ⌒ pūrḁña
āchḁ jiṃdä ::
160 b̥ijāsi̥ | ña tcārä ⌒ caurṣī̥ ⌒ tharka mījsā ⌒ papala ⌒ ttaugarä khāṣḁñä ⌒
161 namaitträ pḁname ⌒ da | hä pūra padi̥me ::
tti vā arrjä va piṃḍḁ ⌒ cuvaṃ ⌒ pr̥yaṃgä ⌒ vaṇḍaṃgä ⌒ vḁmīrāṃ ⌒
162 | yausa ⌒ siṃjsūrä ⌒ hḁmaṃgä vīśtḁñä ⌒ ṅaukä ārḁñä ⌒ nīyakänä ṣi̥
163 peṃḍai pahairḁ | ñä ⌒ cū brrāṃgä narḁme ⌒ vara bḁñḁñä ⌒ krreṃgä
rūya arrjä jeṃdä u pīrḁnä jeṃdä ::
164 | hu̥ṣkyä ttrahe kūṭḁñä ⌒ maṃgärä rūṃna jṣyḁñḁñä krregä rūya
165 bañḁñä ⌒ vīśtä arrja jeṃ | dä ::
aṃgu̥ṣḍi ⌒ kuṃjsavīnai ru̥ñya jṣḁñḁñä ⌒ ū krreṃga rūya bañḁñä ⌒
166 u nih̥ä saṃkhalyḁ | ñä ⌒ arrjä uysbāyi thaṃje̥ ::
nūvara-ysā basḁkä hīvī saṃnä birṣṭä ḁysaṃ ⌒ u rrājā-namva ⌒
167 | hamaṃgä vīśtḁñä ⌒ kūṭḁñä ⌒ kujsavīnai rūṃna pāchai arrjä biṃdä ⌒
168 bañḁñä ⌒ hu̥ña vī | śte u arrjä jeṃdä ::
169 mūla hḁhvḁñä ⌒ ū śī pḁna hatsä kūṭḁñä ⌒ arrjä biṃdāṣṭä peṃ | ḍai ::
pātca mūla sūttauña nīśḁña hahvḁña ⌒ u mākṣi̥na mūrḁñä ⌒ arrjä
170 biṃdä bañḁ | ñä ::
tti vā ḁsyāṃ va yaugä u pe[ṇḍā][2]ṇḍā ranīkä ttä cu jsiṇä ḁsye
171 sarbīṃdä ⌒ u pi̥jsa | kyihāre ⌒ humari biysaṃjāre ttyāṃ va ttīrā-
172 dḁnīnai rūṃ pajsḁñä ⌒ u kūṭya jastä ḁni | ttīrā-dḁnä śtākä drrai
173 śiṃga ⌒ u kah̥ä dva śiṃga ⌒ puṣṭattākavi dva śiṃga ⌒ sali̥cä hā | lai
śiṃgä ⌒ ṣi̥ biśä śūjina haṃbrrīhḁñä ⌒ darä akūṭye bagala pyḁṇḁñä ⌒
174 bagala hīvī | tturä gūrvyau hḁcänyau jsä styu̥dä pūṇvḁña ⌒ styūdi
175 śaṃdai dīrḁ ju̥ṣṭi̥nainai[3] gatsä padī | mḁñä ⌒ u ṣi̥ hā bagalä pāstuṃgä
176 vīśtḁñä ⌒ dīnai hā grīṃja lakḁna vīśtāña ⌒ ā vā mistä | gītserä ⌒ kuṣṭä
hā ṣi̥ ruṃ ttḁśtä ⌒ u ttye bagala bidä saṃñyau jsa dai tcerai ⌒ daṃdä
177 khu ṣi̥ bagala bī | se herä biśä su̥śtä ::
śe̥ ranīkāṃ va yaugä ⌒ ysaṃgarä puṣṭārä tcārbä ⌒ jseṇä jseṇä gvāśḁu-
178 | ñä bagi̥la pyanḁñä tta tta pāchai khu ri tti̥rā-dḁni̥nai rūṃ u kaura
179 hvāṣi hyḁñḁñä ⌒ kujsavi̥ | nai rrūṃnä paherḁñä kuṣṭä ranīkāṃ bidä
saṃkhalyḁña ⌒ pīrmāttaṃ yaugä ::

[1] Blurred syllable. [2] Blurred out.
[3] Omit one *nai*.

180 būysi̮ña pī ⌢ | rrustarä ⌢ rrūva ⌢ drā̮ma ttī̮ma ⌢ huṣka gūra ⌢
181 ha̮maṃga vīśtā̮ña naukä [×][1] kūṭā̮ña gy̮īḫä rūṃ̮na | mūrā̮ñä ⌢ nuvara-
narve āsī ā viraṃ biṃdä bañā̮ñä ⌢ ysū śa̮ule ⌢ u haṃbrrauñe : :
182 mijȩ-jū̮ | na sachi perä u ahaysnāva ysaraṃ̮jsä ⌢ pattā̮dä hā̮mai
183 hamaṃgä vīśtā̮ñä u hvī ṣvī̮danä | paiṇḍai padī̮mā̮ñä ⌢ stā̮ṃgä āsī
haṃdäve : :
184 mahābā̮ṃji jiṣṭye kaṣȩna kūṭye ga̮usäna pai | ḍai pāchai stana-
vrridhi tcab̮aje u haṃby̮a : :
185 dājsaṃdai ttī̮ma ⌢ āra tcyā̮ña sū̮maṃ ⌢ aṣṇūha ⌢ ha | maṃgä naukä
ārā̮ña ḫvī ṣvī̮danä pȩṇḍai padī̮mā̮ñä ⌢ haṃb̮va tcab̮eje ⌢ u hami ttā̮ña
186 haśä | : :
kā̮ṃjsa̮ ⌢ kāṃbā ⌢ tcyā̮ñä sū̮maṃ ⌢ kuṣṭä ⌢ gā̮ṇā mījsā̮kä ⌢ āḍa
187 gūrva ⌢ sadalūṃ ⌢ ā | ra drrā̮ma ttī̮ma ⌢ huṣka mūrau ⌢ aṣṇūha ⌢
188 bijūha ⌢ mūlaṣki̮ñä padīya gaysä virä | ysaṃbaste ⌢ hamaṃgä ⌢
189 vīśtā̮ñä ⌢ naukä ārrā̮ñä ⌢ ttīra ñyena ā vā āhvarai raysäna ṣi̮ | pȩṇḍai
tcerai ⌢ gā̮mi ⌢ habva ⌢ haśä ā̮sye haṃdeve : :
190 śiji āṣkä ⌢ rū̮nai ⌢ mahābāṃji ⌢ | ha̮maṃgä vīśtā̮ñä ⌢ nauka kūṭā̮ñä
191 mākṣīna paherā̮ñä ⌢ vīranāṃ biṃdä bañā̮ñä haṃbrrau | ñākä [piṃ]
piṇḍai : :
hā̮mai ⌢ śī b̮u̮ ⌢ gvīḫi rūṃ ⌢ mauna mūrā̮ñä ⌢ ṣi̮ durṣṭi āsyau
192 bidāṣṭä | peṇḍai : :
ṣi̮ välū̮ttä ā̮sī̮ biṃdāṣṭä piṇḍai ⌢ avaṣāya̮ ⌢ gy̮ai ⌢ raḫi piṇä ⌢ śīya
193 b̮a | ḫauyä ⌢ rrustarä ⌢ hinā̮ aṣṇū̮ha ⌢ hamaṃgä vīśtā̮ña kūṭā̮ñä ⌢
194 gy̮īḫä rūṃna paherā̮ | ñä ⌢ ā vā gy̮īḫa ysā̮ysä hīye ucä jsa ⌢ ā vā
195 ttraikṣä mauva sauttäna ⌢ duṣṭi ā̮sī biṃdi ba | ñā̮ñä : :
padīya būhane dūmi-hauṣṭä gūra ⌢ pattaudä gāṇā mījsākä ⌢
196 ha̮maṃgä vīśtau | ñä ⌢ kūṭā̮ñä haṃtsä mūrrā̮ña ⌢ ṣi̮ pȩṇḍai styūdä āsī
haṃdeve : :
197 śī pau hīye ājve ⌢ | svaṃ̮na-gīrai ⌢ pī hamaṃgä vīśtā̮ñä kūṭā̮ñä
198 haṃtsä mūrā̮ñä ⌢ ṣi̮ piṇḍai nālā-virä | jeṃdä : :
du̮mi-hauṣṭä gūra ⌢ būhane ⌢ padīya gā̮ṇāṃ mījsākä ⌢ ha̮maṃgä
199 vīśtā̮ñä haṃ | tsä mūrā̮ñä ⌢ kūṭā̮ñä ṣi̮ piṇḍai ysvaurgä āsī̮ naṣkirrdä : :
200 kapāysä ttīṃ kūṭā̮ñä ⌢ cvai vā | haṃdäna bīsai ysīḍai ysīrakä narā̮me
201 ṣi̮ hy̮ī ṣvīdänä paherā̮ñä ⌢ rranī̮kāṃ bidä saṃkha | lyāña : :
śȩ yaugä ⌢ kūṭya rruṣṭārā̮nä śau śiṃgä ⌢ kūṭye mahābāṃji śau
202 śiṃgä ⌢ ūtcä śau | ṣaṃgä ⌢ haṃtsä hauña tcirā̮ daṃdä jṣā̮ñā̮ñä khū

[1] Blurred syllable.

203 ra va drrai śiṃgä hạrśä thaṃjā̧ña ysū̧nā̧ñä ṣị | pẹsva utcä hā̧ñä tcerai
paskyā̧ṣṭä ⌢ ū śau śiṃgä hā[1] kahīnai rrūṃ tcerai ⌢ daṃdä pāchai khu
204 ra va rūṃ | harśtä ⌢ thaṃjā̧ñä rranīkạ jsä gūmalyā̧ñä ⌢ u kuṣṭä ⌢ u
biśä jāre ::
205 saunūṣkä ⌢ haṃtsä | hvī ṣvī̧däna thāsakāñä daṃdä jṣā̧ñā̧ñä ⌢ khū
206 haṃtsä haṃbirtte khū drāṃ hạmi khū hạnājä | ttī hā vasve kā̧ṃjsạ-
vīnai rūṃ tcirai ⌢ kuṣṭä ⌢ āstaṃna rranīkāṃ bidä saṃkhalyā̧ñä
jatte ::
207 •• tti vā vāśärūṃ va pịṇḍā̧ ⌢ mahābāṃji ⌢ ysīḍā spye ⌢ ttä haṃtsä
208 jṣā̧ñā̧ñä ⌢ āḍä hā̧mai ⌢ | gvīḥi saṃnä hamaṃgä vīśtā̧ñä ⌢ ttye kaṣẹna
209 pẹṇḍai pāchai u rūṃna gū̧malyā̧ña vāśärūṃ | vī bañā̧ñạ ::
laṃgära[2] bāvä mahābāṃjä ⌢ hā̧mai ⌢ hạmaṃgä śtākä naukä ārā̧ñä
210 hvi ṣvīdä|na pāchai ⌢ vāśärūṃ vī bañā̧ñä ::
211 hīṣạ hīyä rranū[ṣṭä][3] ṣkä śī pau ⌢ ysīḍā [spye][4] spye ⌢ mahābāṃ|ji ⌢
tti haṃtsä [×][5] jṣā̧ñā̧ñä ⌢ kuṃjsä ⌢ pattaudä hā̧mai ⌢ pattaudä āḍä ⌢
212 tti pātcä hamaṃgä śtā|kä ⌢ ttye kaṣẹ jsa ṣị pẹṇḍai pāchai u yamai
213 rūṃna gūmalyā̧ñä ⌢ saṃdvẹna vāśärūṃ u hasvai | jeṃdä ::
jīvakä ⌢ raṣabha[ka][6] kä ⌢ laṃgara bātä ⌢ mahābauji ⌢ ụṣtä bāva ⌢
214 sạcha bā̧|ta ciruttä ⌢ hạmaṃgä śtā[×]kä ⌢ naukä kuṭā̧ñä ⌢ ṣvīda jsä
215 peṃḍai pāchai ⌢ hạmarvā vāśūruṃ | jidä ::
mida ⌢ mahāmidä ⌢ kākauṭä ⌢ kṣīravākauṭä[7] ⌢ jīvakä ⌢ raṣa-bhakä ⌢
216 mūdgä-|parṇä ⌢ māṣaparṇä ⌢ jīva[ttä][8] ttä ⌢ mahābāṃji ⌢ hạmaṃgä
217 śtākä ⌢ nauka ārā̧ñä ⌢ ci|rụttäna ⌢ gvīḥi ⌢ rūṃna u ṣvī̧dä ⌢ ṣị pịṇḍai
218 tcirai hạmirvā bañā̧ñä ⌢ vāśarūṃ jiṃdä | u hạmirvā vīne ::
gvīḥi kāṃjsavīnai rrūṃ ⌢ mijsä ⌢ pī ⌢ īraṃde ⌢ kuṃjsa ⌢ kapāysä
219 ttī hī|ysämau ⌢ bātā̧ ⌢ kuṣṭä ⌢ āra ⌢ halaidrä ⌢ aṃguṣḍi ⌢ suttä ⌢
220 ūtca ⌢ hā̧mai ⌢ biśä hạ|maṃgä vīśtā̧ñä naukä kūṭā̧ñä ⌢ ṣị pịṇḍai
221 hạmarvā bañā̧ñä ⌢ vāśärūṃ jeṃdä : | ::
aśvagaṃdhạ ⌢ pyāśä tcāra ⌢ khyerä tcārä ⌢ ulī̧ña tcārä ⌢ tharkä
222 mījsā ⌢ īraṃde ⌢ haṃga ⌢ biśa hạmaṃgä śtākä kūṭā̧ña ⌢ ttyau arvyau
223 jsä ṣị peṃḍai pāchai ⌢ kūṣṭä hạmarvā vī̧na īde ⌢ | vara bañā̧ñä
jihāre ::
khyera saṃna ⌢ namva mau ⌢ rūṃ ⌢ haṃtsä ū(ci) ysūyā̧ña ⌢
224 āyvā̧ñä ⌢ | grāṃ grāṃ hạmarrvā̧ bañā̧ñä vāśärūṃ jeṃdä ::

[1] Read *hā(lai)* ?
[2] *ra* below; read *laṃgarä*.
[3] *ṣṭä* blurred.
[4] *spye* blurred.
[5] Blurred syllable.
[6] *ka* blurred.
[7] Read *kā* for *vā*.
[8] *ttä* blurred.

225 kāṃjsa ārą̄ñä ṣyīdana pāchai kūṣṭä hami|rvā vį̄na varä bañą̄ñä
vāśärūṃ va piṃḍai : :
226 gąnaṃ kūṭą̄ña ⌢ u mahābāṃji ⌢ hąmaṃgä vīśtą̄ñä | u hyī ṣyīdanä
pāchai ⌢ hamarvā bañą̄ñä ⌢ vāśärūṃ vą paiṇḍai : :
227 kaujsa ⌢ kāṃbą̄ ⌢ rrīysų̄ | bi[śä][1]śä hąmaṃgä śtą̄kä ⌢ kūṭą̄ña ⌢
228 namvena ṣį pęṇḍai pāchai ⌢ hąmarrvą̄ vāśärų̄na jiṃ ⌢|dä : :
traulä ⌢ śīlājatti ⌢ aśvägaṃdhä ⌢ hamaṃgä naukä ārą̄ña ⌢ gitsīrį̄ña ⌢
229 bājinañä ≈ | jṣą̄ñą̄ñä ⌢ khu baysgä hąme vara saṃkhalyą̄ñä ⌢ kuṣṭä
vį̄na īṃde ⌢ vāśärūṃ jiṃdä : :
230 | kāṃjsa kūṭą̄ña ⌢ kāṃjīna ⌢ ā vā bīśį̄nä vara saṃkhalyą̄ñä ⌢ kuṣṭä
231 vį̄na īṃde ⌢ vā|śarūṃ jiṃdä : :
drrą̄ma ⌢ hą̄mai ⌢ saṃdalūṃ ⌢ gvīhä rūṃ ⌢ kāṃjsavį̄nai rūṃ ⌢
232 ganą̄nai bā ⌢ hą|maṃgä śtākä ⌢ hatsä kuṭą̄ñä ⌢ greña bājinañä
233 jṣą̄ñāñä ⌢ baysgä saṃkhalyą̄|ñä ⌢ āvaṃjsä ⌢ peṃḍai padį̄mą̄-[×][2] ñä ⌢
vara bañą̄ñä ⌢ kūṣṭä vį̄ne ⌢ vāśärūṃ jiṃdä : :
234 | ·· viña ttā bīśų̄ña ⌢ biśų̄ñä ⌢ piṃḍā hvą̄ñäre ⌢ u yaugä : :
235 kahä ≈ kāṃjsa ⌢ kāṃ|bā ⌢ pattaudä hą̄mai ⌢ pattaudä yiyaji ⌢
236 hauṣkyä ttrahe ⌢ biśä hąmaṃgä śtākä ⌢ u ārą̄|ñä paherą̄ñä ⌢ u naṣīyūṃ
237 jsä pāchai ⌢ u ttī ṣį naṣī ⌢ paskyą̄ṣṭä ārą̄ña ⌢ ysūną̄ñä | ttīra ñeną jsä
pattrūṣa pāchai ⌢ u na ą̄nahā anarva māśąkä tcerą̄ ⌢ u drą̄ma ṣikä ⌢
238 | ū ahi: ṣį vą dāttä ⌢ hauji pajsą̄ñä ⌢ ārą̄ñä ⌢ hā tcirā ṣį pattrūṣä
239 hverai | avīysārä bąñe : :
śau kabä sperka jṣą̄ñą̄ñä ⌢ ttilakä hā gyīha rūṃ tcerā u mākṣī ⌢
240 | khāśą̄ñä phāhä: uysąnä āphārä jeṃdä : :
241 rrustirą̄nä cipañą̄ñä kamäñä | bañą̄ñä paysau pettä ⌢ jīye utcī
narą̄me : :
242 ttį̄rä ahauḍä hīye ttį̄me ⌢ ląvaṃ|gä ⌢ byārä bana ⌢ jiląbhaṃgä ⌢ tti
243 biśä hąmaṃgä vīśtą̄ñä ⌢ kūṭą̄ñä grą̄mye ū|ci jsä haṃthrrają̄ñä ⌢ u dva
244 drrai jų̄na tta tta ysų̄ną̄ñä ⌢ khū va hera vī kalamakyä na ha tsīṃ|dä ⌢
śau vasī haṃbāyi khāṣą̄ñä pęjsä bąmą̄ñe : :
245 mauva sauttana hugä būna padį̄mą̄|ñä ṣų̄ñyā bañą̄ñä ⌢ maṃgārä
ṣų̄ñä rrāhi: jeṃdä : :
246 cu paijvā vį̄na u maysdä|rvā ⌢ vį̄nä ṣai va paiṇḍai ⌢ ysarūṃ
247 māṃgä ⌢ naukä ārą̄ña ysų̄ną̄ñä śau bāgä ṣį vīśtą̄ñä | ysālva mahā-
bāṃjä ⌢ sijsąnā spye ⌢ kujsa ⌢ tti pātcä hamaṃgä vīśtą̄ñä ⌢ naukä
248 ārą̄ñä haṃ|brrīhą̄ñä khyera ṣvīdāna ⌢ pį̄ṇḍai padīmą̄ñä ⌢ pāchai ⌢

[1] Blurred *śä*.

[2] Blurred syllable.

249 gvīḫä ⁀ rūṃna gūmalyā̮ña ⁀ paijvā ba̮|ñā̮ñä audä svā̮milau vī būre ⁀
ysairbanvā vī̮na jiṃdä ::
250 cu pe̮jsä ttarä ⁀ ttye śe̮ye haḍai | ya̮mai rrūṃna cegāṃ būśā̮nai
paśā̮ñä ttarī̮ jī̮ye ::
251 kujsa ⁀ hauṣka gūra ⁀ mahābāṃ|jä ⁀ āḍä ⁀ hā̮mai ⁀ hamaṃgä ⁀
252 vīśtā̮ñä ⁀ ārā̮ña̮ mauna ṣi̮ piṃḍai pāchai ⁀ śī pau ⁀ pha|ji pajsā̮ñä
bītcañā̮ñä u ttye pe̮ṇḍai bidä starāñä ⁀ gvīḫa rūna gūmilyā̮ñä ⁀
253 brre|ḫä: biṃdä bañā̮ña ⁀ brraha rāḫä jiṃdä ⁀ ttī kaṃiña bañī
254 kamala rrāḫä: jeṃdä bi̮na hū̮na|ña vasūje ::
paṃjalau ⁀ kuṣṭi ⁀ āra ⁀ punarṇava ⁀ ttāgarä ⁀ devadārä ⁀ ṣala ⁀
255 kujsa ⁀ kāṃ|bā ⁀ śaśvāṃ ⁀ īraṃde ⁀ biśä ha̮maṃgä vīśtā̮ñä ⁀ gvīḫä:
256 rūṃ ⁀ kujsavīnai [×][1] rrūṃ ⁀ mau ⁀ ṣvīdä ⁀ | ñye ⁀ biśä pātcä
ha̮maṃgä ⁀ śtā̮kä ⁀ haṃtsä haṃbrrīhā̮ñä ṣi̮ peṃḍai pāchai ⁀ āhusāñe
257 bi ⁀|nāṃ āchāṃ vī biśä vi̮ haṃbūsaṃ ::
ttrahāṃ padī̮yāṃ ba̮nījāṃ grūṣkyāṃ hīvī kṣārä nauka ārā̮ñä ⁀
258 | ttīra ñena paherā̮ñä ⁀ ṣi̮ piṃḍai ysauṇvañä ⁀ hasvai jiṃdä ⁀ gvīḫä:
259 ṣū ra̮ṇā̮ñä | cu pe̮jsä haikä ⁀ ttye ranūṣkyänä padvāñä ⁀ khvai ṣa̮
du̮mi ehi haysgvā̮ ttrā̮me jatte ::
260 | ysīḍā[2] spye ⁀ mahābāṃji ⁀ tti śau śau serä śtākä ⁀ ysīra kūṭā̮ñä ⁀
261 u drrai śigä ucäna | ⟨da⟩dä jṣā̮ñā̮ñä khu śva̮ jīye ttī askināñä paskyā̮ṣṭä
262 hā̮ñāṣṭä ⁀ ysū̮nā̮ñä ⁀ ttī̮ kujsa | ⟨..⟩ bā ⁀ śā śā (ā)ḍä vīśtā̮[×]ña ⁀
263 naukä ārāñä ⁀ hā tcerā ttye ucäna pāchai u ttilakä ⁀ | ⟨..⟩ danaji
hā̮mai vamathā̮ñä ṣi̮ piṃḍai padīmā̮ña ḫugä ⁀ gvīḫä rūṃna ⁀ gū-
264 malyā̮ñä | ⟨...⟩ × ārrdä hauṣka ysvālva parkūnā̮ñä ⁀ ttai vā ḫujsai
265 haijä ha̮śä jidä ⁀ ttauda ⁀ hū̮ña va | ⟨....⟩ bāva niṣa̮ime ⁀ vīnāṃ
bidä vīna jiṃdä ⁀ uci ttī drāṃ tciña rāḫä ha̮māve ⁀ cu ṣṣī | ⟨....⟩-e
266 ysai tciṃeña ṣaidä ⁀ u haune streha ha̮māre ⁀ u heṃja ha̮māre ⁀ u
267 raijsai | ⟨....⟩ × pe̮śā hā̮ ⁀ paiḍai nīśā̮ña ⁀ hauda haṣṭä jūṃ grāṃ
grāṃ ⁀ tcaura piṃḍakä padī̮

[1] Blurred syllable. [2] *ḍā* below.

35

P 2896

1 [*vertical, from bottom to top*] tta rrvī vī vara ttu haṣḍi yani
2–15 in *Khotanese Buddhist Texts*, no. 7.
16 rrvī vī vara tta ha ——
17 ·· rrvī vī vara tta haṣḍa yani ——
[*Space*][1]
18 rraspūra thaya tcū[2] rrī[3] rrvī vī vara tta haṣḍa yani ñaśa[4] bīsa painaka ma vā parrau naiśta
19 pāṃ śu sa caiga ——
[*Space*]
20 ≈ rrvī vī varä tta haṣḍä yane ——
21 —— ñaśä bīsa śvakala ñaśi bī-
22 si aśtu ā̦rä īḍai ca māṃ vara tcū khāṃ būka paka ttai hūḍai
23 [*in margin*] uvāryāṃ garkhyau vi̦sthāryau pūñāṃ kūśala mūla
24 .. rrispūra[5] ⟨rr⟩vi rrvī vī ——
25 ǁ pvisu ttā ṣau saihyi hāysye dīśa̦ vī hāysye dīśa̦ vīra̦ naysda̦ grāṃ
26 | aysmū jsa̦ rrvīyi dī mvę̄śt̨e tta tsāṣṭa̦ka̦ ṣṭa̦ve prra̦mau ttā cīka gūlai
27 drū | nā pvisu khvi tta̦ ttye pa̦ṣ̌āṃjsī śaikye ba̦ḍa̦ vī g̱yastāṃ biysau jsa
28 a | yīkṣye ttye kāla vī ṣṭāve aysmya̦ tsāṣṭa̦ baimāña̦ drūnai a ma pā
29, 30 | hayu puñūda drūnaka mūdai bāḍa hīya̦ pa̦ravālā diva | tta kāka
31 tca̦ra lāka̦pāla vrrīśa̦mamaṃ jsā[6] hatca̦ ka̦kai divā śai | rka aha̦ṣṭa̦ ṣīya
32 haḍāya bāḍi hūṣa tsī sa khu hauṣka | bāśa̦ dai ma jsāṃ tta̦ pūña[7]
33 spyādi raysga̦ vī ga̦maña khu ja ttā hīsu | kṣīra cvā vau va̦ska hagūjū
34 śairka ha̦yu hīya dyāma brra | ma̦nāña māśa cvā vaṃ khāṣ̌ā hatca[8]
35[9] rri̦spūra | ≈ rrvī vī daśa —— rri̦spūra thaya tcūna
35*a* [*margin*] pvaisū ttā ni ra mūvara iysāṃgyau śva prrūī ǁ a ṣa ma aśtu āra īḍai hvanya kṣīra ca maṣyāṃ bāstau ttaña ṣacū g̱yītha
36 prrūī[10] ysathvāṃjsūāṃ kīrā kaṇa khu īḍai ā yse ——

[1] *ñaśa* in middle of the space.
[2] *thaya tcū* thin script, see line 35.
[3] *rrī* below.
[4] *ñaśa* starting lower than *yani*.
[5] *rrva* below *rriṃ*.
[6] With *-ā* deleted.
[7] *ña* below.
[8] *rra* below *ha*.
[9] Several Chinese signs.
[10] Three times with top towards margin across lines 35 and 36, in different hand.

37 | ≈ na kṣama khva hąysä paśąṃ ysīra na de re na kṣama khva hada
brra paśta vī nąma

38 | ysaira jsāna paśū hamāra pāna paśū ttadī ttu rrvai kaṇa hva khu
ṇī paśä

39 | ·· uvāryau garkhyau vaisthāryau pūñā kuśalä mūlyä̆ sagrāvāsyau

40 prraṇahaunyau jsa | haphve śakrra āstana saidraupạidrau jastā hīye
nąsi jsa hamya pajsyau jastā

41 | beysau jsa āhaurrda[1] jastyā jsa haura śarā byauda-līka sarasve

42 ğyaśta hīye ttīśą jsa | vīvace rä daśvą̄ būmvā ramaṃca pūñūda
bvaumaya bīka (ka)lyā̆ṇa ysīra māñada

43 | vasve cakrravarttā gūttairą jsa ysāva vrrīśama yakṣąna rrūda hīye

44 gūttairä jsa nara|da ñąpacā baudasatvąnā bvaijsyau gūṇā ṣahānyau

45 jsa haphva udaya-gara ttrai|khvā nūvarą naṣkąscye aurmaysda

46 mąñadä aurmaysda [×][2] gauṣprrīsaca[3] auna aurmaysda ttrāma|cāṣṭä
hāysye dīśą vī auna śau haḍā ysārą jūna jūhānai aysmū jsa pharākä

47 | drūnā pvaisāma hūñū —— ayi ttagąraimä[4] ——

48 | ·· rrispūrä painąkä u rrispūrą capąstaka aurga drūnā pvaisāma
ha(ṣ)ḍa yane ——

49–55 [*Love poem, above p.* 36, no. 11.]

56 ——[5] rrịspūra painaka vī ⌢ ——

57 | uvāryāṃ garkhyā vịsthāryau pūñāṃ kūśala-mūlyāṃ sagrā(vā)syau

58 maistye prra|māṃ ttaihai: ḍaina ąrrga drūnā hasḍa yane ——

59 | —— rrịspūra śvakalau khu tta viña

60 | —— gū rrvī[6]

61 rrịspūra thaya tcụna rrịspūra painaka rraispūra

62 capastaka rrịspū|ra śvakalau ——

63 ·· rrvī ——

64 || rrvī vī vara tta haṣḍa yani ——

65, 66 —— ñaśą bīsa[7] hūrāsanī sagai —— | ñaśa vā bīsa parą̄ ni (pa)sta

67 sa hīyi cīga kṣīra bāya[8] khu mara āvū ṣacū mara ma[śā][9]|śā bīsa
narada tsvadū[10] nąma ysīratha jsa nai jsau au byihū vaña rrvī jsa

68 āspā|va khu tsvā[tsva]dū byehū gąśta
|| rrvī vī vara tta haṣḍa yane ——

[1] *ā*- below.
[2] Blurred syllable.
[3] *ca* below.
[4] Turkish *Ai tängrim*.
[5] At beginning of line, drawing of a horse.
[6] *rrvī* below.
[7] *sa* below.
[8] *bāya* below.
[9] Blurred *śā*.
[10] With *tsva* below.

69 : dauna datvā sūkhī bevatte
dauna datvā vīśārada tta[1]
70 daunena pū | janau bavitte
deveṣau manūjeṣa ca
udagatte pacama sūryā
71 kṣī | yette jala-sāgara
sagasya dayatte dauna
ttena śaka ——

36

P 2897

1–3 /// hąśta | /// | /// *de* ramanī :
4 tcaṣvai *amā*na dra d | . . . . . . *raṣṭa*
hūvasve bvaijai ṣą sūhāva najava[2]
5 ysaura | . . . . dā jsaiṇa vī ranau [ra][3] uḍa :
6 ysa[nä][3]ranā pacaḍ*ana* | . .
⟨mū⟩ra kakye mūra sye
7 mūrą hayarīda nva kṣama āṣai | jvā
kūmada[4] ca ma byā vara ttaña kṣaidra[5] ≈
8 aśvagarbīnai | × gala[6] ysaranā ṣaica
bāgara aijsījai ysyaikya sakījai ≈
9 kū | ṣṭa va ārai phara se-ysāra baudhasatta
10 avarajsa pedai : daśana-mą | rga kīḍa gūstya :
vara va āstai cattaumana ra(na) śama vaiysa :
11 baida | aramyāya baiysa : phara se-ysāra baudhasatta hajsa :
12 kṣamaja | beysa × cvau(n)ā bvaujsā
āṣaṇa sūhaja[7] na hamya u͡vaira
13 vaña śāsta | na bīśvā bāḍvā
baiysana hvānaka śama nāvai nauda || ——
14–44 in *Khotanese Texts II*, p. 114, no. 61.

[1] With *ñaśa bīsa tsvadū* written above *vīśārada*.
[2] Read *janava*.
[3] Deleted *ra* and *nä*.
[4] Third *akṣara* uncertain.
[5] *dra* for *ttra*.
[6] First *akṣara* uncertain; *ba*?
[7] *sūhaja* written close above *ṇa na*.

37

P 2906

1 se-ysāra gaga ñāya gr⟨ī⟩ca //// (12 *akṣaras*)

2 daśvā̮ dīs̮vā̮ vada̮śvā̮ drrabvā̮ḍva ttaiṣkṣāda̮ haiysdaujsya jasta b̮aysa namasū ⟨||⟩

3 | pātca̮ ttu padī paḍā̮ bīsai ha̮maga haṃkhīysa̮ jsa [ha][1]

4 ustimaujsya̮ ja̮sta b̮a|ysa namasū naudä ||

na̮mau da̮śäba̮la kā̮lakṣaittri nā̮ma ja̮sta̮ b̮eysa nama⟨sū⟩

5 || na̮mau dādäbesvarä jasta̮ b̮eysa̮ na̮masū

6 || na̮mau śauttaidrrai ja̮sta̮ b̮eysa̮ | na̮masū

|| namau dairnedirä ja̮stä b̮eysä näma̮sūṃ

7 || na̮mau caṃdiprrabha ja⟨sta⟩ | b̮eysa̮[2] na̮masū

8 || na̮mau ra̮hnakūsū̮ma-sāgūrä-veṇḍūrya-ka̮na̮ka-sū⟨va|rṇa-kāṃca⟩-näprrabhāsä-śarī nā̮ma jastä b̮eysa̮ na̮masū

9 na̮mau baṃdi|ra ⟨jasta⟩ b̮⟨e⟩ysa[3] na⟨masū⟩ ||

namau kṣaiprakärä jastä b̮eysä na̮ma̮sū

10 || na̮mau bā|ṣma jasta b̮eysa na̮masū

|| na̮mau dvā̮sä kūla ja̮sta̮ b̮eysä na̮masū

11 | daśvā dīśvā bīsā drrabāḍva jasta b̮eysa namasū ttaikṣadä sāmūha

12 | siddhaṃ

aurga tsūṃ namasūṃ nauda

13 dribāḍva harbaiśä b̮aysa ttriyā̮ṇī ⟨dā⟩ | aharī̮na b̮aysā̮na parṣa̮ tcahaura 1

14 sarbaṃdä hālaiyāṣṭä ahä:kṣau|bhä namasūṃ

b̮aysä maṃjuśrī āstaṃ parṣa̮ phara kūla namasūṃ nauda 2

15 rav⟨y⟩e | pa namasūṃ b̮aysä ttu rahnakettä uvārä ākāśagarbhä

16 paḍauysna harbi⟨śä⟩ | parṣā̮ jsa haṃtsa 3

17 paḍauysye vidis̮i jsa nā̮da namasū̮mä sarvañä b̮a|⟨ysa dharaṇ⟩iṃ-⟨dhar⟩ä ⟨nāma⟩ uvārä harbiśe parṣā̮ jsa haṃtsa 4

18 śe̮ vidi|s̮i hāleyāṣṭä namasūmä sarvaṃñä b̮aysä nārāyaṃ pa̮ñau

19 maistä | harbiśe parṣā̮ jsa haṃtsa 5

20 ñuhūjsaṃce vidis̮i jsa nā̮da namasū̮mä | sarvañä b̮aysä caṃdaprrabhä nā̮ma uvārä harbiśe parṣā̮ jsa haṃtsa 6

[1] Blurred *akṣara*. [2] Hook broken out. [3] *e* and hook broken out.

21 | tcūramye vidiśa̮ jsa nauda namasū̮mä sarvaṃñä b̮aysä śauttemdrai
22 nā̮ma | uvārä harbiśe parśi̮ jsa haṃtsa 7
23 uskyāṣṭä diśa̮ namasūṃ nauda bha|draśrī sarvaṃñä b̮aysä
24 nāṣṭa diśa̮ namasūṃ b̮aysä viraucaṃ parṣi̮ jsa | haṃtsa 8
25 ci buri ysama-śaṃdya yāva śiraraṇa satta puñauda b̮aysū|ña-vūysā
maista harbiśūṃ namasūṃ nauda 9
26 utvaḍa namasūṃ ttū darma|kāyä vasve akhauṣṭä sarvasatvā̮nä
27 biśānä auṣkä sattā̮nvā ṣṭū|kä 10
khu ji carau pyīstä pace haṃgustä na vā harū̮ñe
28 aysgustä ṣṭā̮ṃ | saṃ ttäña beḍa hamye kṣa̮nä rrūṃdä īṃdä 11
29 kā̮ma tti ci dyāṃdä hama|ye ttū dharmakāyä vasve
parya saṃtsārna biśä b̮aysūśtä bausta durā 12
30 | ttye nayä jsa ye ttiña b̮aḍa b̮aysū̮ña-vūysai śau
31 mahāyāṃ dā vī ṣadä | ⟨ś⟩au-⟨n⟩au⟨h⟩ä b̮aysūśtä kūśe̮ 14[1]
tta ttai kṣa̮mä kāṭhaiśä satta mahā⟨yā⟩ṃ
32 | /// (*tops of akṣaras*) naravāṇä kī⟨ṃtha⟩ /// (4 *akṣaras*)

Recto in margin

33 || uvāryau garkhā vaisthāryau puñā kuśala-mūlyā[2] sagrā̮vāsyau jsa u prraṇahaunyau mistye haurä vara̮śa̮me jsa puñūdä bvaumayi ⌢ śāśa̮nasthā vīśeṣa̮kyau bvaijsā jsa haphve ⌢ drravadye śaikṣa vī ādara̮vada ⌢ śairkye ṣauma × ///

38

P 2910

1 ce cū dū*khya* saida hama
2 orga tsū namasū nauda drabāḍa ha|rbeśa baysa ttrīyāṇī dā aharīna
3 b̮aysona paṣa̮ tcaho|ra sarbada hāle[ha][3]yāṣṭa akṣoba namasū
4 b̮aysa | majaśūrya ā[sta][3]stana ——
5 | sa̮dha̮ma̮
6 aurga tsū nämasū nauda̮ dra̮bādū harbaiśa : | b̮aiysa : ttrīyauṇī dā
7 aharīna̮ ≈ b̮aiysā̮na̮ paṣa̮ | tcahaurai ≈
8 sarbada hālaiyāṣṭa̮ ≈ akṣūba na̮masū | baiysa majaśūrī āstaṃnä
9 paṣa̮i ⌢ phara̮ kūla na̮|masū nauda̮ ≈

[1] 14 for 13. [2] -ā written twice. [3] *ha* and *sta* blurred.

10 ravye pa nąmasū ḇaiysą : ttu rahnakai | ttą uvārą ≈ ākāśagąrba [ba][1]
11 paḍauysną ≈ harbīśai pa | ṣą jsą hatcą ≈
12 ñuhūjsadi hālaiyāṣṭą ≈ armyāyi nä | masū ḇaiysa ≈ cada vara paṣ̨ą
13 pharāka : khvai na ha | khīysąnä ñāpąi : lākyaiśvurą āstaną maista :
14, 15 dä | śa-būmyā tta baudhasatta ne[2] vī ysą̄va dyaunūā ārai ≈ | harbīśa nąmasū nauda :
16 uttarye dīśą jsa namąsū | nauda : ḇaiysa daudūbaisvara nauma :
17 samaṃttabadrą pa | ḍauysanä : harbīśe paṣ̨a jsa hatca ≈ paḍauysye
18, 19 vīdą | śą jsa nauda ≈ namąsūmā sarvaña ḇaiysa : darąṇaida | nauma uvāra : harbīśa nimasū naudą :
20 śąi vīdaśą hā | laiyāṣṭą : namasūmā sarvaña baiysa ≈ nārāyi pąiñą̄
21 | maista ≈ harbīśai paṣą jsa hatca ≈
22 ñuhūjsadye vīdaśą jsa | nauda ≈ namasų̄mā sąrvaña baiysa :
23 cadraprraba nauma | uvāra ≈ harbīśai paṣą jsa hatca :
24 tcūrmye vīdaśą jsa nauda | namasūmā sarvaña ḇaiysa : śauttaidrai
25 nauma uvāra : ha | rbīśai paṣą jsa hatca :
26 uskyāṣṭa dīśą jsa nauda : badraśrī | sarvaña baiysą :
27 nāṣṭa dīśą jsa namasū baiysą : vairauca | paṣą jsa ḫatca :
28 cu būra ysama-śadya yāva : śarara | ṇą satva pūñūdä : baiysūña-
29 vūāysā maista : harbī | śa nąmasū nauda :
30 utvaḍa namasū ttu dharmakāyi va | svai akhauṣṭą : sarvasątvą̄na
31 bīśaunä : auṣką saṃtvą̄nūā | ṣṭų̄ka ≈
32 khva ja carau pvīsta pacai ≈ hagausta [na] na vā ha | rūñai ≈
33 uysagausta ṣṭāṃ sa ttaña baiḍa : hamyai kṣąṇa | rūdā īda ≈
34 kauma cu dyauda hamayi ≈ ttu darma | kāyi vasvai :
35 parya saṃtsāraną baiśa : baiysūsta | ƀaus⟨t⟩a dūrā ≈
36 ttye naḍa ye ttaña baiḍa : baiysūña-vūā | ⟨ysai śau⟩
37 ⟨ma⟩hāyāṃ dā vī ṣada ≈ śau-nauḫą baiysū | śta kūśai ≈

[1] *ba* blurred. [2] Small inserted *ne*.

39

P 2925

1 [*vertical*] ×× prrimaha nāgadaprrabha nāpa
2 thaya uvāra rana b*au* gai da haña nara ——
3 : maudrai prrināha[1] gai[2] nā prra da bha bha prra da pai tta gai
nā prrihauma[3]
4 ba prramayihana bagavada prraśana ba pa va pa va
5 na ba :

[*Monogram*]

[*Space*]

6 || avamāyā bvaijsā aumauna śāśạña parāha: hajvättai jsa :
7 | khū kīvakṣa samūdrra sagrāvāsyā bīśā satvā ysīra brrī
8 aidrā | jsa naṣạgaista khū dai hauṣkāña bāśạ
9 drrayvā pīlyā artha ausairma [ba][4] | bāyāka
ttī jsāṃ bāvāvā avaṣṭa ṣīya haḍạya
10 śvṛrai u mālai | ṣṭīka ttī jsā jāvā
ttyau ysyai hūrāka sa khū ācārī prrabhä : ——
11 | khvai baustīya pūra caigvā au tsai śau vai :
12 vadrramai paṣvīnaca jīyai | vī :
hūña a sa khauṣīna ttāṣṭa hālai kū tsai ⌢
13 aśta ka vā jasta ḅai | ysa ṃvaiśạ īnīra : :
14 rasābūga krrīyāvādī uchaidaśta vīnāya | ka[5]
jaṭasvī ca ttapasvī ca garba āśvaistamvaiva ca : :
15 prrabha ttā tsai | ttāṣṭa : ṣācū kīthāṣṭa : gīhyara vā jasta padārāysā
16 khva vā byai | hai pada kamacū kīthāṣṭa ama jsā ttyai gīsta jsa maista
17 ḅaiysūśta bvī | ryaụ : :
18 vara hīyā guṇā būhattā: svāpatta aga śakhaupamāya | cabū ja du
19 ttā śīla rāṣṭa paiṇḍama sayattā : khva ṣa ttaya | ttrakṣa kīra hadara-
20 ysathva prraṇahānau jsa ysatha kamacū nāvai va | ra jsā va thā ysāvī
valakā ——
21 : prraṇahaunau jsa ca vā bastāya | ma va : saskāra drraya sūbāva

[1] *nā* for *mā*.
[2] Syllables in reverse order = *nāgaidaprrabha*.
[3] Read *prrimauha*.
[4] *ba* blurred.
[5] Top of *ka* lost.

22 hatca khū samīda śa bvauña | parāvrrītta[1] yanārai[2] hamyai dāvīnai ḇaiysai :

23 pharāya hvaṇḍa | ttakyai janavai vīra : na ṣä va basta aysamū ha

24 bāḍa śā ṣavai a|ysamū va tvī baida basta valakā nā pai : ca ṣṭā brrīyā

25 tta tta ysaiya | śųḍa śųḍa : aikatträ vālapathai-bābaudrrāyāvatta-

26 vālaga nadī | yakṣaittāpacattāvalattaiṣau ttai ca lakṣaṇa śvauña-sūbāva[3] :

27 | sauha kaiṇā saiśai ysīra ysūṣṭa ysīra bīsī sauha tta na dyai

28 kā|ṣṭa tvā tta bīdī śā māśta sauha na yai gvaṣṭī mā jsa hīya daśta

29 | bai khaṣṭai na ṣṭau gvaśtai :

30 darmāyattāmaiva ttathā babūrāttā|ttāpīnaudyāya vīttąmahaṣāvai-

31 duyasapalaina sūsaina | pūnairaba[4]būsūraida īvaudarīkṣai :

32 byaḍauśą vauma vī parauysa|dā jīya :
naiśtara satsaira jva gaja ma vāthajai :

33 khva ṣa vā | hīsī ṣąka ca ma ysīra aśta

34 ṣą ma vąthajai khū durauśą ttraha | thaja :
prrimayihana bagavada prrana[5] | : ——

35 | ⌢ ⌢ paijsą ttą ąmä nāye ttvī vī hūśąiną

36 ce ttā ttyai vīrä | na vā pastāyą sāṣṭe
ma na ttara ye na pāpe jsą bīnāvū

37 | thā vajūttąyą[6] thą jsā vā na naradī ⌢ ⌢

38 ma ṣą ysīraka | derä dedąyą nāse

39 cai būrai sä ⌢ hūñīne baiśā ttą ttą ī|dą
khvai pā hūñū ga[ri]rmą[7]-māṣṭai kaśą nūyą

40 pātca kąśa jsāvä | garma-mąṣṭai nūtte ::
ttuña ma satsaira vīnau ttuñai jīyaka saiyai

41 | śau śau hada hvai brrauda ysūṣkyaira

42 ā vā va byāva na tsā śą ha|ḍā sa jña[8]
prrañaittā haṣḍā yanū hakṣa pīra :

43 ysai ysai pa|namā aysai byāva hamaunai :

44 paiśą nūyā pātcai byāva hamau|nai
naista pana vīrai haumaura na tsīnai :

45 auda mara vai sa [9]hau hau | × haumąra na ×[9] ñauysaira hamaunai :

[1] ī over *ai*.
[2] *-ai* and *-ā* together.
[3] Or *śau-*?
[4] *ba* below.
[5] Badly formed letters as in line 4.
[6] *jū* for *jña*.
[7] *ri* deleted.
[8] *jña* for *jū*.
[9–9] deleted.

46 saiśākau myauña | gulīnai saka pauṇḍai
caistau myauña sahattau prraysā :
47 ṣacū | au jsā va śaika vaisthārī jña[1] :
48 brrai kṣaudai nvāśa ysaikä ysīra byā|jai yai :
khū ttā sāśu ttāṣṭa janavai hālai haudvī va tcaimaña
49 ā|ṣkyau jsa habaḍai hūḍai [×][2] ga śu-kyaina vakṣvai
50 āṣkälakyau jsa jūdai | auna ttraikṣa bīdai kāṣṭa :
51 paisa pharāka hasta yai cau a ttara | yaiñīnau
ttāṃ nvaiśa̱ aravauna hamīya khvau vaña jvīhūna
52 mau | byaihyara īñaka ama jūhai jsa jagya haudvī raustai :
53 haurau dyāvai | khvau jūhai jsa a mīrai : ——
54 | aysamū ṣṭau kauma paimaiśja guthalaka :
55 garkhai ṣṭau thūya | pajsa gai vī śuka :
kaumyai gai vī būḍa kauma īyai aysmū
56 valra baitta paijsa kaumau udaśāya :
57 [3]mau prri ha gai pai da nā prra | nā bha[3]
(*inverted*) prrimauha nāgaidaprrabha .[4]
: nāgaidaprrabha prrimauha :
58 ana pamūlḍaida hairtha vīra ṣa̱ika vā carya nai tta mūña bai ——

[*Space*]

59[5] || sidhamai
60 aivamayā śutam ikasmī samayai ≈ yai bhagavau rā|jagrrahai viharati smī gṛdakūṭi paravattai mahattā bhaikṣū-saṃgai|na sādhama anakaśtaiśtai baudhisatvai śatta-sahasryai : sarvai kūmārakal|ttattai : ttattra khalū ba[×][6]gavau śakrrau : dai ——

40

P 2927

1 : ṣacu śī ca[7] pū[8] sa tca tcūka : na × ///
2 ra : pīka ẖara pvaina dū ///
3 siddhaṃ̱ sa siddhaṃ̱[9]

[1] *jña* for *jū*.
[2] Syllable blurred out.
[3–3] Syllables in wrong order =*prrimauha nāgai pai da prrabha nā . . .*
[4] Dot as mark of punctuation.
[5] *Kauśika-prajñā-pāramitā*, see P 5537.
[6] Incomplete *akṣara*.
[7] *ca* below.
[8] Or *sū*?
[9] *siddhaṃ̱* below.

4 || ysani gni kva≈yi yaṃ kivi ṣ̮ī ≈ pūṃ cvāṃ tva ≈ hyāṃ ×[1] ttu[2]
5,6 tti | hvani ⌢ śe̮vū lva̮ni ⌢ hyāṃ śī ××[3] gani lai ×[3] hīhä | śī kvä ⌢ yi
7 ñāṃ kyāṃ va ci hvani ⌢ baha: cāṃ ⌢ śī | tcavi gne || || ttai hvī śau
8 hūṃ śau hvani yi yīva ḍai yā tcī sana | cha pa hva śvaina gva ha̮ṃ
9 ū͡vana hvā kyaiva hvī śa̮iva lva̮na kīma tcaiva mau | ba mau ga tcī
10 pana yi yāva sī lana sī rcāṃ ḍai yā chī lana kī tcau | ṣ̮īyi khī lva rcāṃva
kai yā a ca ya || ||

11 a la ḫā rama̮   śaika na na | nai tsāṣṭa
ū ḍaiyi ḫā rma :   bīśāṣṭa va : śaika na nai ::
12 ñau ca ḫā rma | hūśa̮ina va śaika na nai
ṣacu tta śe ḍe la ḫvera
13 na lvaye phī | na
ḍaina ca gvaiyi śai yu
ttai śīyi ba yā ca
14 khava ttau | tcīya be
tcayi le hvara na lva   ttā hāyse dīśa vīra[4] ysāra jsā āstya
15 hvayi leyi yā sa | rśayi   ñau ysera bīsai
rrvai sū[5]
16 a la ḫā rma   śaika na na nai tsāṣṭa
ū ḍai ḫā rma   biśa va śai(ka) nai
17 ñau tcai | ḫā rma   hūṣīna va śaika tta nai :
18 nama ṣ̮ī ḫā rma   pūrau dvarau va śaika | na nai :
19 ṣ̮īma nai mai hū   vañā maṃ hvāṣṭā hīyai mve|śḏa jsa
ysīma ḫaura || || śaika ttai :
khu na hvapa :   pastai va̮ stāva nai
20,1 ṣ̮īna ba chu|ḫa śai   hvaṇḍa vā u stura svaḫakṣai jsa ā|va
pī śaina ttāṃ le rma :   nai ||
22 kva śa̮ina ḫā yīma tcī   hvāṣṭa hīye mveśḏa | jsa vā beśa
ttā le   āvadū || ||
23 na kha layi kvana   kūṣṭa pastai | yai ||
ṣ̮īna :
īva śama kava hvana   aśtu tta gīryai-va̮rāṃ aśta ——
24 | tcai yai   vara baiva aśca ||
25 yāva śama   śaika būka | caraumyai guna jsa
haira śtą ṣṭāvai bema aśta ——

[1] Blurred form of following sign. [2] Or *rma*?
[3] Blurred out. [4] *ra* below. [5] *sū* uncertain.

26,7 | tsai dīśa̮ hāle kūṣṭa brrīyika mūñai padi tsū[1] hā | bvī caḇe jūhā
28 spyakye ttyai hera prracaina cva tta aña | rrva brraṣṭi prraṇahānai
29 vaska bañū a̮ḍāña ysīthā|ṣṭa || ||
ysa̮nījai je(na)y̮ai vī caigau bāḍä vī ysāvū
30 satsai|ra vīnau sauhau:[2] khū mūñū sāha :
31 ttu īnū ca ma mūña | ysīra baiśta
aḍa̮ña ysītha ba ūtca pū ṣṭa̮vai || ||
32 | tcāṃ tcaiyāṣṭa kūysa bina ra tcaiyāṣṭa kūysai nauhya :
33 | bīsā ṣe cha tta pā tcaiyāṣṭa kūysi gvaḍināṃ
34 ttradū kṣū|na mauḍä naradū ava̮idanya[3] nairamāna mava̮
sāṣṭā || ||
35, 6 | arana ttra̮mū arañīnai pāsūra na ra pā āyvena āyā|ṣṭa
37 pāṣ̮arai a̮[×]nāraṣṭā na ka ma āḍāra bevai da̮|yi
khvai ṣṭāna kṣamū na va̮ caudana ṇeye || || ——
38 | ma ttakye tcaimeśkya u͡vīśakya[4] aidrai
39 aysmū ysaira hīye ysīrja | bā[×]vanvī beda
40 ba̮ste na ṣṭā va̮ pana satta ysīruāṃ mā|rai
ahvaña̮ dakha ṣṭāre kūysa brruṣka aysmva || ||
41 | hvaṇḍa tta hūñīda saga jsa styudyera hera naiśta
42 styudyai ra ma | naiśta khū vīna āste hvī ysera daukha hamāvai
43 na va̮ ṣke|tta na̮ vā beṣḍi sauha: hamāvai natca̮ṣṭa vā na
44 narau|ma̮ || ||
śadaka bīnamīye brrī sa̮tta vahanī
45 ā vā vai | jīyi drai a̮iha: askhaysī
46 hamāra brra hvaṇḍa u | gva̮ysāra avīpa
47 na mīrāṃ brra satta ttyai jsa ttraikṣyaira daukha | naiśta || ||
a ṣṭā ma ṣacu tsū drai māśta hāle
48 thā jsā ma kau|madau gvatha̮na gucha̮
49 khve brrī ṣṭa̮nai vaijala̮kāṃ hūśa̮i cū|ba
ka nūyi pāysvīra ka pe̮ ma na hara̮śa̮ ——
50 | śaika ba̮ḍä pvāṣ̮ī ṣṭai śaika pasālī
51 habaḍa ñauva̮ jsa | uska jsāva
brre bīśa̮ṣṭa aysdyuvai ragyau jsa
52 khvaiśkya sā|ña pana̮ye panāyidī

[1] Like *k* over *jsū*.
[2] *-au* blurred, perhaps deleted.
[3] Two slanting dots ˙. over *nya*.
[4] *śa* with blurred *ky* below, for *śkya*.

53 pyāśa̮ka khū ja bīna a | stāna || ||
a [×] tsū hāysa pada ṣacu burakyai
54 valakāṃ | hūśe̮na na mase śa āhālaña
55 prraṇahāna tvī vīyi | valakāṃ hūśe̮na
ttuñe jūẖe: jsa mīre ī tvī hīsū

41

P 2928

1,2 thyaina śīva dīde kṣuṇa gūha salyę rarūya māśta dasa | mye haḍai ṣa
3 byāvaja pīḍaka ttye prracaina cū va [tha][1] thaya ttīka | pūña-badrra ——

[*Space*]

4 | tta pyūṣṭa hame hada bāḍą   tta tta śākyamauna sarvaña | beysa
5 śrrāvasta kṣīrai ṣa mūde   jattavaña baiṣṭyau hatca
6–7 | ttana bāḍna hada śā bīsaḏārai   śrāvasta kīthe ysanauśca | yūḍe
8 u nāra nāve nva gūttaira   tta tta khū padaja ṣta mī | stye
9 nera jsa hatca tcarkye haryauna   vara ṣṭe dadą khū urau | da hamyą
ṣą̄ majṣye[2] vara ttaña beḍa[3]   haṣṭa nā[4] dasau māśca khve parye
10 ysā ṣa pacīḍa | daẖa pūra   dya vī śairka uspūryau aidrrā jsa
11 khū ścāka | aidrrau jsa brra vī bure   cha ttarū vaiysna hamaga
12 habāna pa | kṣau śairka   rau[×]daṣai māñada dyena
13 jāttamaka beḍai ttye | yūḍauda   nvą gūttere[5] nauma
14 tta tta hūṣā parbautta vāṣṭā   sa khū | vaiysa pvāvaña uca
hadarye bāḍena bīsadārai[6]   nera jsa pyāste
ttai hve sa ma vaña ysā   pūraka bvaijsyā byā
15 cū ttī hū naṣpau | ṣṭa hūysīnātta   ttare pamye śara vāsta prrahauna
16 u | dahauna ālaṃgāra   ẖayūnyau hatca
17 narada bīna | ña   tta tta jsā tsve ayevī
18 vara ttaña beḍa   māśa ye ha | da maista
kuṣṭa mūda agrakuleka   alakṣaṃ aumācą skarba

[1] Blurred. [2] ṣ uncertain. [3] *ṣā* to *beḍa* below.
[4] *nā* for *nau*. [5] *tte* below.
[6] *bīsadārai* to *cū* below, marked to follow *bāḍena*.

19	I ttuka ca mara māja	kṣīra ttu gūhau grūsīda
20	sa tta aumāca ṣṭa	I vana ye hīña bīśa
21	vara ttaña beḍa eysāja	hairtha vīra baysā I nya sava
22	ttanī ca byāśā brrūka ayāṣṭi	ttana cū ysama-śadya̮ nai I śte
	[ya] byamā-jsera strrīyā satta	vījaiṣṭā śakalaka dyena
23,4	bīsa I dārāṣai ttaña beḍa bīhī būra	śairka-vamye ālagre hūysīnā I tta
	tta brrīvīnai be-vūḍa pūna	ysaira baida baista avyāca
25	spya I kīnai tceṣū grā[×]na	haraṣṭā ttye baidāṣṭa
26	khu ṣa̮ cakrraka spāṣṭa	na I ṣkaṣṭa ca ṣa̮ vā nīśāva
27	mū ttu grauna dye ttaña beḍa	eysāja cū I byūca ṣṭīya
28	tta tta hālā̦ natcāṣṭa narada	bīhī būra tcaṣva̮ dye I na
	drauma sa khū ye pīchaṣṭa̮	dyaunaca brrīyā spāśa
29	tta tta bai I śmäśvarmai s̮ūste	ā kaumadeva hamaiya̮
30	strrīyānyau bvaijsyā I byauda	khattā vī hā brrīya̮ khū dye
31	dīda dyena agajsa tvā strrīya	I ṣa̮ vara ttū bāḍa bū raustai
32	aysmū pejsa ttye vīrāṣṭa	brrīye thau I ña na na parye
	sa vara ṇesta ttye pa	byūka va rame baida
33	bīnau I na ṣkvīda damīda	spāśāra śūje ysairka
34	ṣa̮ mī eysāja ttū bāḍa	I śāma ttyau haṣṭā ysāra
	ttye cakṣaka vīrāṣṭa̮	skāda[1] yāna mūṣe
35	mara hū I sa mahā jsa	prraysīnīme ṣṭau maista
36	vaña khaysa khāśe̮ sauha	aumā I ca kṣa haḍā ḫagana
37	kūṣḍau vī īrauda mūñe	ttu būra eysāja jsa ha I [tca][2] tca
	sauḫa varāśa̮ aysmū nvaiya	sadāṣṭa hamye bīhī
38	ttai hve sa I ttā tta tta hama	bīka ttanī dva pajūṣṭa̮ vachauste
39	ttai hve sa śau hā I pūṣa̮ heśa̮	eysāja śe̮ ttu tha nāsa mahā ma peśā
40	ttai da[3] sa dā laka I ṣa̮ vīra spāśa	ṣā̮ ttrā kha [ga] gaumaña tsvā
41	ttu pajūṣṭa haiṣṭā[4] hāṣṭa	tte hvā sa ttu jsā śau ma hūḍe
	ca ṣa̮ ṣṭa̮ dīśca ——	

[*At right side three akṣaras st- -ā haṃ followed by the figure for* 8.]

[1] *skāda* below. [2] Incomplete *tca* blurred.
[3] *ttai da* below. [4] *ṣṭā* small inserted below.

42

P 2929

1, 2 ārya-chaṃnahyāñāṃ harąbīśāṃ ṣṭāṃ vā dąsau dīśą | vīra auṇadā ≈
3 dràbą̄ḍa ttaikṣaṃdą saumāhvą jastą̄na | jastą ḅęysą ą̄spāvą nąsau ≈
4 ḅęśą mąista mahā | brrūmą-prrāpattą̄ baudąsatvą ≈ arąhaṃdą ≈ u
5, 6 prrą | ttīką saṃbauda ≈ hvana kṣīrä hīyi kąka nīvą̄ | ysva āysdąrą̄
7 dęvattą parvą̄lā ≈ pajsaṃ ą̄ṣą | nạ ≈ hąrąbīśa ṣṭāṃ vą̄ nąmądrrāṃ
8 ą̄chą̄yau ≈ ca | būrä tta baiysūñyai ṣkūi vīrä ≈ ayīkṣyą ≈ daṃtta-[1]
9, 10 cai | tta sthūpą dąmarą̄ṣą īdai ≈ ją̄tta-caitti ą̄staṃ | na tcaurä mąistą
11 caitta ≈ hąṣṭą baudąsątta baivąna ≈ | ahąrīnaką grū caṃdą̄ną para-
12 ṇāmä ≈ baiysū ≈ | ña raną ≈ u bīsaṃgīnai räna ≈ u dą̄vīnai rana
13, 14 ā | staṃna ≈ cą bą̄rä vañä haiysdą vī daivattą parvą̄lā | īdai ≈ ttą tta
15 khu ą̄rāvąlākyaittaiş́vąrä baudasatta | ą̄rą̄ majvāśūrī baudasątta āryau
16, 17 kṣattagąrbą | baudąsatta ≈ ą̄ryą̄ sąmattrra-bhądrra baudąsątta ≈ ą̄ | ryą̄
18 mąittrai baudąsątta ≈ ą̄ryą̄ väjäräpauña ≈ | baudasattä ≈ pąḍauysāña
19, 20 jsä daivatta pąravą̄ | lā īdai ≈ hąräbīśą ṣṭā vą̄ īmūjsī hąḍą̄ | jsa tta-tta-
21 nąmaṃ ⟨d⟩aunavą ≈ vīrą̄ṣṭą -āṃ × -ā -au | namadrrau ≈ kṣa maistā[2]
bauj⟨s⟩ā ——

43

P 2933

1 ⟨tcū⟩ | rä-y[3]sanya h⟨ī⟩na b⟨i⟩ysajä ⌒
pharä ysārä ją̄ysa gūny- vā ⌒
2 b⟨ai⟩śä hī | nä-bāyā hvāṣṭa ⌒
aurmaysdą̄nāṃ hīye bveyą
3 pyaurya baiśä varä ttaña | beḍä ⌒
ttye hīña hīye vyūhi ⌒
nähīśanā khva ye garä spāśa ⌒
4 ṣai | ṣä ūysarä jastāṃ vaska ⌒
ṇetsāṃdä ją̄yą̄ṣṭi vaysña ⌒

[1] *daṃ* is certain. [2] *stā* uncertain. [3] *y* uncertain.

5 ysa̮nā | ve ṣṭä tta tta au pātcä
ṣā̮ hīna ysaunāvä vāṣṭi ⌢
6 gaga ñā raga[1] baidā ā | vä
aḍārai nāṣṭa naradä ⌢
phara ysārä brrama pyatsä
7 hagrrāṃdä da | sta ūskyāṣṭa ⌢
āstadaudä āśrīvāde ⌢
pūrä jasta baiśe saunä
8 | ṣā̮ śadā samaudra ṇestya ⌢
jastūñe sauhi ⌢ hamāve ⌢
9 hūṣe tsī ttī | śa̮ hauvä ⌢
ṣa̮ mahā-kaphainä re
tta caidye hīña ysīrāṣṭi ⌢
10 khu ṣa̮ re | ⟨. . .⟩ × piṃ × ṣ⟨ṭ⟩āve ⌢
-o -e -ī -ī × × -au -e
-e jsä su bī ///

44

P 2936

1 [*bases of akṣaras*]
2 × -i va ≂
tturka vīysañä vāḍä bada-jīvā spyaką ⌢
3 ysīrañä bīsā raṃna | × avatsä vīya ⌢
naiśta ṣä satsera daṃdä brrī satta khu tha ṣṭa ⌢
4 hvū̮:ś̮ęnā brrī | haṃgūjsana -e ā
śaṃdaka bīnämāve brrī satta vahanī ⌢
5 ā vā vā vai jī | ⟨yi drai a̮iha: askh⟩auysī ⌢
hamārä brra sattu gvaysārä avīpa ⌢
6 na mīrā[2] brra satta | ⟨ttye jsa⟩ ttraikṣyera dakha naiśtä ≂
mūraka bīśaurakä ci dīdä kṣavū drāhe ⌢
7 | /// -ṃ ṣi paijalakvā gūśta kalai ṣṭe ⌢
khve tta jūhyī:me byeāhe ve ra hamā

[1] *raga* below.

[2] *-ā* with *-e*.

8 | /// raka drạmakya khāvarä ma bīysaṃja styūdä ≈
9 saṃgịnai vaṣḍi ṣị | /// v ṣṭāṃ eṣṭe ≈
ā vā vạ kauthaira hịśaṃ jsä vadaidi ṣṭe ≈
10 śau-kṣịrä ṣṭāṃ hvā | mārä pya sauhä: īnāre
aysai na ḅve jūhau naiśte īñakä tsūṃ ⌒ 20
11 a ṣṭāṃ maṃ ttuñye | jūhai jsa vañä mīre ⌒
paskyāṣṭạ̄ ttuñe jūhai jsa svī būjve ⌒
12 ttye herä prracainä | ce ttā kỵeṣ̣ä nä āvụ̄ṃ ⌒
haure dyāve khve jūhai jsa a mīre ≈ ——

[*Space*]

45

P 2942

1 uvāryau vistāryā pūñā jsa haphva :
2 hāysye dīśa vī naysda grā aysmū | jsa :
ysāra jūna brāva tsveva ṣīyi haḍāyi ≈
3 pūñūda bvaumayi bī|ka maista thyena ṣī : ⌒
ana maista haḫäśa u kīma ḍī pyaina ≈
4 ranạ varai | kūla pauśana ṣanīraka ≈
cā kraśīsa āstanūāva hamīḍa
5 hvauṣṭa drūnā | ttā haṣḍä yinau brīyạ thauña ≈
6 jsīnīvau[1] nāsīda harbaiśạ ḅeysạ | :
haṣṭạ baudhisatva [ha][2] hatca [pa][3] parvālau jsa :
7 asūlaka baudhasạtta gva|ka hīyāda :
padārāysạ cvau bāyīda[4] pada[5] śairka ≈
8 khvau tta vaña haysda | vīra[6] uvārạ ttaraṃdarä :
drūnai ṣṭāve nūśta ttī jsā ḅemaiña :
9 aṇẹscyạ rāśạ | cakrravartta caiga rauda hyai :
haphautta tsīye parau khū byava rauḍai ≈⌒
10 vaña ttā | śau haṣḍä yinau jūhai udaśāyi :

[1] *js*, not *ys* as always elsewhere.
[2] *ha* blurred.
[3] *pa* blurred.
[4] *hū* below *bā*, *rī* above *yī* for *hūrīda*.
[5] *pada* below.
[6] *ra* below.

11 ñaśa prravai hvarä ga u javaidrākī | rä-sīẖa :
cā amaga kharaśau u vailaka paḍai :
12 ñāṃ tcauma kāṣṭa pąijsa | pharāka byaudauda ≈
vaña jsau ttā śkaisana pamauḍa yuḍaudū ≈
13 ttye prracaina | cū caigvā na rä hīsau:
pūñāṃ prracainau jsīna vāra na tsīye ≈
14 janavai | vī ttā pārs̨a harbaiśa dāśau ≈ ——

[*Space*]

15 ṣai hamąḍā jasta b̨eysą mąhāparnarvāṃ pastą dyauñe :
16 cū ną.rą vā | maẖai ja[6][1]bvīyāṃ satva baką bvaumąyi ≈
17 ma ṣąika ysīra salā cū pya | ra kaiṇą pyūṣṭai :
18 hamye kṣaṇą jsīna śtākä yi khva narābāsa vī | tsīye ≈
cū hvī yserą ṣṭe ṣą vīśąrä raną mauñāda ṣṭai
19 ttye prracaina cū | na narauśta u na bvaysdaiyai ≈

[*Space*]

46

P 3510

c Recto (in margin) 1

Verso

1 saddhaṃ
aurga[2] ttā ī drrayāṃ ranā hālai ⌢
2 tta tta muhu jsa | pyūṣṭa śe stye gyastąnä gyasta b̨aysa rājagṛaihä
3 pasta mū | de gṛddhakūṭą śarä[3] vīra ⌢ mistye ąśiryāṃ jsa bisaṃgäna haṃtsa

d Recto (in margin) 2

1, 2 u avamāta sa-ysāryau baudhisatvyau jsa hatsa ⌢ ttina haḍi | ra
3 vātcä bāḍnä ⌢ gyastä b̨aysä nąva[4] būña pasta hajsa | ra harūñąmai nąma dāyī pacaḍä samāhāṃ samā-

Verso

1, 2 vaje ⌢ ttina ra jsąna bāḍä jsa āryąvalokyatteśvarä | baudhisatva

[1] The numeral 6 blurred.
[2] Independent *au-*.
[3] Read *garä*.
[4] *va* small inserted.

3 mista ḇaysūña-vūysai ∽ gaṃbhīrya (ha)jvatte|vīje pārḁ̄me vī tsū-
maṃcä ṣṭḁ̄na haḍi vā sḁtta tta u-

g Recto (in margin) 3

1 ye ∽ cū paṃjsa skaṃ(dha) tta ra jsḁ̄na hīya va uysḁ̄nauña jsa
ttuśā | haḍi vā sḁtta tta uyyḁ̄ñä ttī śirḁ ḁ̄śirī śāripūttra | ḇaysū̥ñe
2,3 hauva jsa ∽ āryāvalokyatteśvarä b(au)dhisatvä mistä

Verso

1 ḇaysū̥ña-vūysai jsa pyḁ̄ste u tta ttai hve si kḁ̄mä cankai ja na
2,3 bi|sīvrrḁ̄ṣā gaṃbhīrye hajvattetīje pārḁ̄me kūśḁ̄mavä kṣḁ|mä ṣṭḁ̄na
ttye ma khū sājḁ̄ñä ∽ tta tta hva ṣṭḁ̄na āryāvalokyatteśvarä

f Recto (in margin) 4

1,2 baudhisatva mistä ḇaysūña-vūysai jsa pyāste u tta ttai hve | si
3 kḁ̄mä cankai ja na bisīvrrḁ̄ṣā gaṃbhīrye hajvattetī|je pārāme tsūme
kūśḁ̄mavä kṣḁmä ṣṭḁ̄na ttye ma khū sājḁ̄ñä

Verso

1,2 tta tta hva ṣṭḁ̄na āryāvalokyatteśvarä baudhasatvä mistä ḇa|ysūña-
3 vūysai ḁ̄śirī śāriputträ jsa pyāste u tta tta hve | si kḁ̄mä cankai jä na
śāriputtra bisīvrrāṣai au[1] bisīvrrāṣai-

a Recto 5

a1 ñi jsa vā ∽ gaṃbhīrye hajvattevīji pārḁ̄me tsūme kūśāmatä ttye
2,3 | haḍi vā sḁtta tta ūyḁ̄ñä ci paṃjsa skadha tta uysḁ̄ñe|njsa (ska)dha
ttuśā dyāña ∽ rū ttuśai ttuśāttā haḍa vā sa rū ∽ rū jsa hāḍi

Verso

1 ni hva ttuśāttā ∽ u ttuśātte jsa ni hva rū cū saṃ ṣi̥ rū ttuśai ∽
2,3 ttu|śāttā haḍi vā saṃ rū ∽ tta tta pā saṃ varḁ̄śāma syḁ̄ma ṣkau|ji
aysmū ttu nijsaḍā ∽ tta tta pā śāriputtra harbiśä dharma ttuśā ∽

b Recto

1,2 baudhisatvä mista ḇaysūña-vūysai ḁ̄śirī śāriputträ jsa pyā|ste ∽
3 u tta tta hve si kḁ̄mä cankai jä na śḁ̄riputtra bisīvrrā|ṣaiñi jsä vā ∽
gaṃbhī(rye hajvattevīji pārḁ̄me tsūme kūśāmatä ttye) drraisamye
haḍi cū ḇaysūña parāya ∽

[*Small script interlinear*]

4 hḁ̄damye haḍai khū tti[2] baiśä kūśḁla dāśe ∽ pustyau ttai beḍä baiśä
kha ma yūḍāṃdū ≈

[1] Independent *au*. [2] *tti* below.

5 pūstya ma haṃkhīysna tcahaisä ṣṭāre ⁓ pūñau kūśala-mūl(au) jsa satva ḇaysa
6 hamāṃde || ⁓ ——

Verso

1,2 dā sājāṃ hạ̄dhiä haḍā vairṣ̤ä pattajāṃ ⁓ bīsagyä parṣ̤eṃ | haḍi
3 khāysä śä hvạrau haṭhvā śavvā[1] maṃ kaśạ̄ | me byaṃdī rrāṣ̤ä || ||

[*Smaller script*]

hạ̄damye haḍai khū baiśä kū(śala dā)śe ⁓ pūstyāṃ ttai beḍä baiśä
4 kha ma | yūḍāṃdū

e Recto

1,2 a-uysạ̄nā apanava anarūjya ⁓ anau āyauysä pahai | ṣṭa-āyauysa ⁓
3 anau hīvyañāme anau hīvyauṣṭe ⁓ ttye prra | caina haiysdä vīra śāriputtra ttu[2]śätte jsa na rū ni varāṣ̤āma ⁓

Verso blank

47

P 3513, 1–12

Recto blank

Verso

1 sidhaṃ
dvāsä kūla jasta ḇaysa ratnauttama nạ̄ma biśū namasūṃ nauda ——
2 haṣṭū | sä kūla jasta ḇaysa ratnāvabhāsa nạ̄ma biśū[3] namasūṃ nauda[4] ——
3 bi | stä kūla jasta ḇaysa śikha n. b. n. n. ——
4 bistä kūla jasta | ḇaysa kāśava ... —— (*as before*)
2r 1 kṣise kūla jasta ḇaysa vimala-prrabhā | sa ... ——
2 sparanau kūla jasta ḇaysa śākyamūna ... ——
3 haṣṭase ysāri jasta ḇaysa iṃdrradhvaja ... ——
haṣṭase jasta ḇaysa sūprrabhāsa ... ——
4 nau kūla jasta ḇaysa kṛkasūṃda ... ——
2v 1 haṣṭūsä kūla jasta | ḇaysa kanakamūna ... ——
2 drraise kūla jasta ḇaysa avabhā | saśrya ...[5] ——

[1] Read *gavvā*. [2] *ttu* subscript. [3] Else *biśūṃ*, except 3 v 3.
[4] *nạ̄da* in 2 r 2. [5] Here *namasū* without *-ṃ*.

3 sparibistä kūla jasta ba̱ysa pūṣya ... ——
4 dvāsä kūla jasta ba̱ysa vipaśya ... ——
dvī ysāri kūla jasta ba̱ysa kauṭiña ... ||

3r 1 | haṣṭā kūla jasta ba̱ysa svabhāva-dharmauttara ... ——
2 haṣṭā kū|la jasta ba̱ysa caṃdrra-sūrya-prradīpa ... ——
3 paṃ-ysā|ri jasta ba̱ysa prrādyā̱tta ... ——
4 paṃ-se jasta ba̱ysa | prratā̱pa̱na ... ——

3v 1 haṣṭā ysāri jasta ba̱ysa nāga ... || ——
2 paṃ-ysāri jasta ba̱ysa sālarāja ... || ——
haṣṭase jasta ba̱ysa śamatha ... —— ||
3 dasau ysāra jasta ba̱ysa prrasaṃna-vadana-utpala-ga̱ndhakūṭa ...[1]
4 biśīda jasta ba̱ysa himāri haṃba̱ci jsa tcahause kūla pīrma

4r 1 | haṣṭūsä lakṣa byūrä hauda ysāri haṣṭase cvaṃ ye nā̱ma byehi pyūṣṭi
2 ṣi̱ drrayāṃ avā|yāṃ paṃdi basti ni ni narya jsāti ni prrīyvā ni
3 ttrīyaśū̱ṃ cvaṃ sāji samāda̱na̱ jsa | bāyi ṣi̱ ba̱ysūśti jsa avīsadai hami
ni vara bya̱mā tcerā || ——
4 namau | uttaraprradīpä jastä ba̱ysä cvai nā̱ma hū̱ñe ni ni garkhyāṃ
āchyau jsa haṃthrrīśtä || ——

4v 1 | namau jā̱tte-saumya-gandhāvabhāsa-śrī nā̱ma jastä ba̱ysä cvai
2 nā̱ma hvā̱ñi ni ni strīya himi | || ——
namau jñānaulakä jastä ba̱ysä cvai nā̱ma hvā̱ñe ni avīśä mahā-narī
3 | ysaṃthä nāsti —— ||
4 namau aṣaṃgarājä nā̱ma jastä ba̱ysä cvai nā̱ma hvā̱|ñi amauvuā
byaugvā baṃdana-śālvā ni kaśti || ——

5r 1 namau anantayaśä nā̱ma jastä ba̱a|ysä cvai nā̱ma hvā̱ñi biśau gaṃjsyāṃ
jsa pahaiṣṭā himi || ——
2 namau merä nā̱ma jastä ba̱a|ysä cvai nā̱ma hvā̱ñi narya ysaṃthä ni
byehi || ——
3 namau mahāmerä nā̱ma ja|stä ba̱ysä cvai nā̱ma hū̱ñi prrīyvā ra
ysaṃthä ni nāste || ——
4 namau amittame|rä nā̱ma jastä ba̱ysä cvai nā̱ma hvā̱ñi ttrīyaśū̱ṃ ra
ysaṃthä ni nāsti || ——

5v 1 namau a|mittamerä nā̱ma jastä ba̱ysä cvai nā̱ma hvā̱ñi ttrīyaśū̱ṃ
ysaṃthä ni nāsti ||

[1] Here *namasū* without *-ṃ*.

5v 2 namau | akṣubha jastä ḇaysä cvai ną̄ma hvą̄ñi ḇiśai bīsaṃgą̄nī hvaḍä
3 khaṣṭä anāva | rąṇä gvaśti deśanai himi || ——
4 namau ratnakettä jastä ḇaysä cvai ną̄ma hų̄ | ñi ttiri brrų̄ñaṃdai himi
khu raṃnīnai daśą || ——

6r 1 namau armyāyä jastä ḇaysä cvai ną̄ | ma hų̄ñi haṣṭä kūla kalpa
haṃjsauda karma baśdę ttai biśä jāri maraṃ ve sūhāva ysaṃthä
2 | nāsti || ——
namau dūṃdubhisvarä jastä ḇaysä cvai ną̄ma hų̄ñi ttirī śirkä
3 | bījāṣä himi khu jastų̄ñä kūsä pą̄hi || ——
4 namau ratna-kusūma-guṇa- | sāgara-vaiṇḍūrya-kanaka-giri-sūvarṇa-
kāṃcana-prrabhāsa-śrī ną̄ma jastä ḇaysä cvai ną̄ma

6v 1 | hvą̄ñi harbiśāṃ barījāṃ siją̄ma byehi tsā himi sūhye || ——
2 namau sūdarśaṃ jastä | ḇaysä cvai ną̄ma hvą̄ñi kalpasthyavī karma
jāri dyena śirkä himi prraysā || ——
3 namau veraucaṃ jastä ḇaysä cvai ną̄ma hvą̄ñi dāvīnai ttaraṃdarä
byehi || ——
4 namau gandhauttamą jastä ḇaysä cvai ną̄ma hvą̄ñi ysaṃthvāvī

7r 1 tturrna vasva upalą spye hīya | būśä narą̄me ni ni kūṭheṃgvā
ysaiye || ——
2 namau aparimita-gūṇa-ratna-śrī-vyūha-tte | jarāja-kalpą ną̄ma tathā-
gatau || ——
3 namau sarvadharma-prratibhāsa-hyūha[1]-śrī ną̄ma | tathāgatau || ——
namau aparimita-prratibhāsa-vyūha-saṃcīrṇa-būdhau nāma
4 | tathāgatau || ——
namau sahasrra-megha-garjita-svara-rājau ną̄ma tathāgatau || ——

7v 1 namau | svavarṇottama-prrabhāsa-śrī ną̄ma ttathāgatau ——
2 namau bahū-vividdha-tejaurāja-śrī-nirbhā | sau ną̄ma ttathāga-
tau || ——

7v 3 namau asaṃkhyeya-kalpakauṭī-samūdānītta-būdhau ną̄ma tathā-
| gatau || ——
namau śubha-kanaka-gagana-nirnāda-nirbhāsau ną̄ma ttathāga-
tau || ——

v 4 namau sarvadharma-naya-vikurvata-tejau ną̄ma ttathāgatau || ——

[1] *hyū* for *vyū*.

8r 1 namau gūṇa-saṃkusūmitau | nā̦ma tathāgatau || ——
cū ṣi̦ cū ttyāṃ jastāṃ ḇaysāṃ nā̦mi sāji vā̦ṣi o[1] vā pyūṣḍi śe śe
2 | ḇaysä nā̦mi hvā̦ñā̦me jsa kalpasthya karma jāre śe̦ ysaṃthāna
ḇaysūśtä būste || ——
3 | namau samādhi-hastaura-śrī nā̦ma jastä ḇaysä namasūṃ || ——
4 namau sa | mādhi-hastautara-padmautara-nakṣatra-rāyä nā̦ma jastä
ḇaysä namasūṃ || ——

8v 1 namau pa | dmautara-śrī nā̦ma jastä ḇaysä naṃasūṃ || ——
2 namau padmahastā nā̦ma jastä ḇaysä nama | sūṃ || ——
namau sūrya-mā̦ṇḍala-prrabhāsauttamą-śrī nā̦ma tathāgatau || ——
3 | namau sarva-sūryauttamāgni-paripūrṇa-lakṣaṇa-kāya-gātträ
4 nā̦ma jastä ḇaysä | namasūṃ || ——
namau eka-ratna-chatträ[2] nā̦ma jastä ḇaysä namasūṃ || ——

9r 1 namau sa | rva-samādhi-uttama-vikrrā̦mo nā̦ma jastä ḇaysä nama-
sūṃ || ——
2 namau ratna-kusūmita-sa | maṃttāvabhāsa-śrī nā̦ma jastä ḇaysä na-
masūṃ || ——
3 namau ratnauttamo nā̦ma ja | stä ḇaysä namasūṃ || ——
4 || namau sarvaratna-prratimā̦ṇḍata-rūpadhārī nā̦ma | jastä ḇaysä
namasūṃ || ——
namau anūttara-padma-vikrrā̦mä nā̦ma jastä ḇaysä namasū || ——

9v 1 | namau anaṃtta-gandhauttama-rāyä nā̦ma jastä ḇaysä nama-
sūṃ || ——
2 namau ratnapa | dma-vikrrā̦mä nā̦ma jastä ḇaysä namasūṃ || ——
3 namau ratna-mā̦ṇḍala-tteja-sa | mūdgata-prrabhāsauttama-śrī nā̦ma
jastä ḇaysä namasūṃ || ——

9v 4 namau ratna-ga | rbhä nā̦ma jastä ḇaysä namasūṃ || ——

10r 1 cū ṣi̦ ttyāṃ jastāṃ ḇaysāṃ nā̦mi parī pī̦ḍi au[3] | vāśe̦ anaṃttaryā̦nī
karmāṃ deśana himi didirū jsa pariloka bā̦nya satva parsīdä khu
2 gaṃgä | nyāya gruīcyau sya ni vara byā̦mā tcerā ≈ ——
3 nam(au) sarvasatva-pāpa-dhana-vajrrā | ya tathāgatāya tad-yathā
auṃ[3] vajrre vajrre samaya-vajrre vajrra-samaṃtta-śikha | re svāhā
|| ——
4 namau avaivartakau nā̦ma tathāgatau || ——

[1] Independent *o*. [2] Independent *e*. [3] Independent *au*.

10v 1 namau dharmarājau ną̄ | ma tathāgattau || ——
namau sų̄darśanau ną̄ma tathāgatau || ——
2 namau jautti-saumya-gąndhāva|bhāsa śrī ną̄ma ttathāgatau || ——
namau aṣaṃga-kauśau ną̄ma tathāgatau || ——
3 namau avabhāsa-śrī ną̄ma tathāgatau || ——
4 namau prrajñākūṭau ną̄ma tathā | gatau || ——
namau aśaukau ną̄ma tathāgatau || ——

11r 1 namau sāleṃdra-rājau ną̄ma tathā | gatau || ——
namau balanaṃdau ną̄ma tathāgatau || ——
2 namau aparājita-dhvajau ną̄ma | tathāgatau ——
namau acittya-gūṇa-prrabhā-śrī ną̄ma tathāgatau ——
3 na | mau samertha-kalpą ną̄ma tathāgatau || ——
4 namau guṇedra-kalpą ną̄ma ta | thāgatau || ——
namau vimala-prrabhāsau ną̄ma tathāgatau || ——

11v 1 namau vimala-kī | rrta-rāją̄ ną̄ma tathāgatau || ——
namau vaśavarta-rāją̄ ną̄ma tathāgatau || ——
2 | namau vajrra-sīhau ną̄ma tathāgatau || ——
3 namau utara-prradīpa-citra-prra | bha-ratna-kusų̄ma-nayana-kana-
4 ka- ⁀ kanabha-gāttra-vairaucana-raśmi-prratimą | ṇḍita-aprratihata-
12r 1 cakṣu-daśa-diśa-sarvalokadhātu-avabhāsa-ketu-rāją̄ ną̄ma | tathā-
gatau arha-sąmyak-saṃbaudhau || ——
2 namau kamala-dala-vimala-nakṣattra-rāja- | saṃkusūmitābhijñą̄ ną̄ma
tathāgatau || ||

48

P 4089*b*[1]

1 /// [8 *or* 9 *akṣaras*] /// stye ysāra b̨vaiyą aurmaysdą māñadä ⁀ hāysye
2, 3 | /// ḍā ysāra jūna byāva-tsvava-līkä ⁀ syau thi cū | /// d⟨rū⟩nā
4 py̨esauma haṣḍi yane ≈ ñaśa prravai | /// khu tta vaña ttye g̨yastāṃ
5 b̨eysā jsa ayīṣṭe spyau | /// -e . -ā -ī ///
6[2] rya garkhya pūñāṃ kūśala-mūlyāṃ jsa haphve maistye bvą̄me

[1] Verso to *Khotanese Buddhist Texts*, no. 10, p. 20–1.
[2] Reversed to lines 1–5.

7 haura varāś̮aume | saida śerä byūda-līkä : hāysye dīśa̮ vī naysdä
8 jūhaunai aysmūä jsa śau × | ñana byāva-tsva-līkä : mastye janava
9 kaḍyāṇye rīña jastūña aysmū ārā | × aidrrā jsä pūñūda bvā̮maya :
10 maistye syau khara painakä ā̮rgä drrū⟨nā⟩ | pvaisūä : ——
11 ñaśa hve pye ma tcū yāṃ : māva paḍä kä : | sagīle ⁀ tcvale : dvīle :
12 khve na ttye śairkye jūhaunai spyā̮ysa̮ haṣprrīsaṃdai kāla | ṣṭāve
tsāṣṭa drrūnai ttye kaṃṇa mamauñāṃ tvāra aysmyä śairkä ṣṭe phara
13 b̮eḍena | hamāve pūña kūśala-mūla hā spyāṃde khve ma saṃ thyā̮
14 raysgä vī ma janave vī | pakūṣḍä ssä byūryau pāysā̮ hadara vya rrvīye
15 gakhye my̮aiśḍä jsa hagrrau|na magalīya dyā̮ma byehaudye : mau-
16 ñā̮ma vañä baiśa pañe śaika ṣṭe tsā | × nai daukhau rama ttu nai ṣṭe
17 saṃ khu tta drrūnaka parī mūde ttī jsāṃ tta maistye ja|stū ārāhye
ya khu jsāṃ vā sī ja va hā vasva kṣaijsä hīśa ⁀ vaña ttā a bvaiya[1]
18 | haḍa naradä śkyesa ttā na dāśaudū pamara ttuśai pī(ḍa)ka kaṃṇa
19 ttā ysā̮ra na × | × khu vā na dāśā ā veñā hadara vyä ttā haḍa tsīde
20 ādara īnāṃ khu ttā ha|jsāṃda īnāṃ vāṣṭa vā pā śaika vaśu̮ hīye phara
21 īna ce jsāṃ ttā śtāka | pātca vā pīḍakaña vīśtä ūme ttā hajsā̮māṃ :
22 hamārīja māś⟨ta⟩ | ×× -ā ārgä d⟨rū⟩nā p⟨y̮⟩aisāṃ [*tops of akṣaras*]

49

P 5536

Recto

01 paiha̮ pa̮na : hauśa hūlāṃ pvaiskha hvaṣī pāraka ——
1, 2 sidhamä *n*ämäsūmä ṣada jsa brrīya ajalakä jsāṇakye ṣṭau|na aysa
3 hūyī kīmä-tcūnä drrebāḍuä ha̮räbaiśai beysä *u* | baudhasatvāṃ jsa
hamīḍä *s*äjäña
4 namasū tvā uvārä parä|märtha cū beysa hvauda cū baiśa jastau
5 kärma kīḍeśa̮ dū|kha ysatha̮ pveṇa ha̮rīysa ge bīsagīja uvārä kūṣṭa
6 ā|räpaudagala̮ has*ṭa* ××× ñāṃ vīvä byehīda tturä jsā

Verso

7 | namäsū nāda ⟨....⟩ namasū
8 pātca kula̮ jasta be|ysa cū vaṃña ⟨....⟩ yā parījīda satva pharāka
9, 10 | cū būrä jsā ⟨........⟩ jsā . × . × -au | haiysda vī ×

[1] Broken *akṣara*.

50

P 5536*b*

a1 /// *pv*anä ⁀
2 /// hāysye dīṣ̨ä vī grānä
3 /// hąṣḍi yane *ñ*aśi bīśä kīmä
4 /// ḇiṃdą sättą*n*vā drrayvā saṃskā⟨rvā⟩
5 /// mye kaṃṇa mąña śe bīśą jästāṃ ḇe⟨ysāṃ⟩
6 /// ṣṭą saṃ khu tta drrūnā parīya mude maṃ
7 /// ye viska tta vā[1] ādąrä parīya yū⟨ḍe⟩
b /// dä dyau ///

51

P 5537[2]

1 s⟨i⟩ddhama
na(mau) sarva-satvebhya ǁ eva[3] ma(yā) śrūtam ika(s)mī sa-
2 mayi bhagąvau rājagahi viharati (s)mi gradhakvaṭyi pa-
3 rv[ū]a(ta) sa(ṃ)gh[at]ena sā(r)dham anekaiś ci baudhasatva-śata-
4 bh(i)kṣu-śata-sahasra sarvai kumāraka-bhūte tadrra
5 khal(u) ba(ga)vā śakyau devānā[nā](m) (indram) āma(ṃ)tray(at)e sma kauśika
6 arthata p(r)ajñā-pāramitā(yā) artha ǁ tatha ——
7 arthava p(r)ajñā-[sta]pāramitā [stita] vyavāstita
8 ⁀ rrv(ī) vī haṣḍa yanuṃ ña(śa) bīsa idhyapyadhī ava[ra]l(au)[ka]-
9 ka-sīmāya aunaka vyayāsavā pārama tcarma-
10 ja prraumāha idrrapradīpa himāña ——
11 kauṭyām ivam ivāya(ṃ) kauśaka p(r)ājñā-pāra-
12 mittāy(ā) artha tad yathā sarva-dharmam ivatvā p(r)a-
13 jñā-pāramitā samā sarva-dharmā v(i)viktatvā prijyā-
14 pāramitā v(i)vikta sarva-dharmācalatvā prajñā-
15 pāramitācalā sarva-dharmāmanyatatvā prajñā

[1] *vā* below.
[2] Unpractised hand of a learner. From 25 copy written by teacher, imitated by pupil. Text full of repetitions, with many omissions.
[3] *e* vowel over independent *e* = *ai*.

16 na sa(ṃk)l(e)śatau na vyāvadānat(au) (nāvyava)d(ā)natau na [dana] (u)t(s)argatau
17 nā[tsa]tsa(rgatau) ayāgatau nāyāgat(au) na (saṃ)kaḍ(e)śa[pa?]-
18 t(au) na pratyaya k(au)ṭyām ivam ivāya(ṃ) kauśa(ka) pra-
19 jñā-pāramitā na
rrv(ī vī) ha(ṣ)ḍa yanä ñaśa bī-
20 sa riddhapadhapa aval(au)ka-sīmāya ānaka
21 bisādha sājāme va(s)kā dhakhakarai [sasa?]
22 buḍa
sa p(ā)ramitāy(ā) aratha sarava-dharm(ā) [sa]ṇā(ṃ) pra-
23 jñā-[pa]pāramitā gagana-kalpatvāda ——
24[1] khva ma ysimaśa —— ḍa ḍa yvīyi pā hvaṇā ——
25[2] khva[3] ma ysimaśadya hvīyiṣāṃ hvạṇḍāṃ hvīya
26 khva ma ysimaśadya hvīyiṣā hvaṇḍā hvī ——
27[4] ñāpāma hamya cū mārā-pyarana bīśvā
28 = 27
29[4] bāḍvā pajsamaḍa dīryāṃda viña pā ja-
30 = 29
31[4] navai jsa hvaṇḍa mārā-pyarau biṃdä ṣada
32 = 31
33[4] garkhūṣṭānā biḍa ttu ysithāi śaika hame
34 = 33
35[4] ū ysithvā jsāṃ paraśudä būdä-kṣai-
36[4] ttra vajaiṣḍe ——
37 khva ma ysimaśadya hvīyiṣā hvaṇḍā hvīya
38 ñāpāma hamya ca mārā-pyarani bīśvā
39 bāḍvā pajsamaḍa mārā-(pya)rani bīsadhārā
40 p(ā) parau janavai jsa hvaṃḍa vara pyaukala hamyī havi
41 pa va *t*sāña mara [ba] bīsadārā pyaukala ha-
42 mī janavai jsa [jsa] hvaṇḍa mārā-pyarau bida ṣada
43 garkhūṣ(ṭ)änā bi[da]ḍa ttu ysīthā śairka ha-
44 mi ū ysithvā jsāṃ paraśūdä būda-kṣai(ttra) ——
45 parau janavi jsa hvaḍā vara pyaukara hamya [ha]
46 parā janavi jsa hvaḍā vara p(yau)ka(ra) ——
47 bāḍvā pajsamaḍa dīryāda viña pā j[s]anavi

[1] Pupil's writing (*ī* written upside down).
[2] Teacher's hand.
[3] *ma* above *khva*.
[4] Well written.

48 jsa hvaḍo mārā-pyarāau bida ṣada ga[khu]rkhuṣṭa-
49 nā bava[1] tt(u) ysathāi[2] śirka hami ū ysi-
50 thvā jsi pāraśūaidi būdi-kṣaittra vajaiṣḍi ——
51 uvāro visthā[ra]rya puña kuśala-mūlā ——
52 na (saṃ)kal(e)śatau na vyāvadānat(au) na utsargatau na utsarga
52a [*interlinear*] [ga]tau nā [kī] kuiśli[3] ci p(r)adyaya-
53 tau nāprat(y)aya k[rr]a[rma?]rmatau nādharmath(au) na bhūva kauśa-
54 dyā[4] naubhūta
rrv(ī) vī ha(ṣ)ḍa yani ña(śa) bīsa idyapyadī
55 aparāka dā va(s)ka dakhakarä būḍa īḍa vaña
56 rrū(ī) jsa āspāva khū na va mvaśta na harasta biysā
57 : rrv(ī) vī ha(ṣ)ḍa y(an)i ñaśa ——
58 bīsa idya[pa]pyadhī hāysa vā pada pharāka bā*ya*[5] pasta
59 da va(ña) janavi jsä hyaḍa vara cū ama pyīrau ña(śa) b(ī)sa naḍīrau ñā bi
60 [×] māśta pastādu [ma] b(i)di misti kṣyaḍa hvavu ××[6]
61 ī āstanaka kṣā kṣyaḍa rāśya pasta ——
62[7] ña ra va ja māśta nāmyā h(ī)ya bīsadārā pyākara
63 vañā bida mū(śḍa) pastādū bīdi ī āstanaka *ma hva*
64 janava jsa hvaḍau vara cu ama pyīrau u ñaśa bīsa ḍī
65 ga(r)khūṣṭänā biḍa khu *ttu* ysi[ba]thāi[2] śairka ha-
66 mi ū ysithvā jsā paraśūdhi [vījiṣḍi] būda-
67 kṣai(ttra) rrv(ī) vī haṣḍa yini ña(śa) bīsa idyapyadī aval(au)ka-sīmā-
68 [ba]ha[8] ānaka biys(ā) dā sājāmä va(s)ka dakhakaryi
69 būḍi vaña r(v)ī jsa āspāva khū na va muś(ḏ)a na haraste
70 khva ma ysimaśadya hvīyaṣā hvaṇḍā hvīya
71 thū na va rakṣay(s)a vaña mistä hami śāva nā
72 [×] mista gyasta īnā śāva kaha tha(ya) tīka biraṣṭa
73 śyara va sya ——
74 ñāpāma hamya cū mārā-pyaranä bīśvā
75 bā(ḍvā) pajsamaḍa dīry(ā)da viña pā jä(na)vä ha(ṣ)ḍa y(an)i
75a [*interlinear*] rr(vī) vī ha(ṣḍa) ——
76 rrvī vī haṣḍä yanai tcarmaj̨ą prramāhą ai ṣḍa ṣḍa[9] ya

[1] *bava* for *bida*. [2] With *-ā* and *-i*. [3] For *kuśala*?
[4] *dyā* for *kyā* or *lyā*? [5] *ya* not clear. [6] Two unknown signs.
[7] 62–4 reversed writing, hence in order 64, 63, 62.
[8] *ha* for *ya*. [9] Or *ṣṭu ṣṭu*.

52

P 5538*b*

1 [*small*] kīma dī *na dī* ttai-ṣī pya ——

2 vī rrvī vī ḫaṣḍi yane eva ha mayikasmī samaye śarāvasta kītha ā(sta)

3 vye jīva rrespūra bā̱ṣa anāhap⟨iṇḍī⟩ sakhyerma —— rrvī vī (ha)ṣḍa yane rrispūra

[*Space*]

4 bye rī ttaṇḍä na yā̱lāśta hūña aprracaina yā̱ × rma × kamacū bīṣā̱ haḍa na āta hī⟨v⟩ī

5 au × sī cī ve hā *ka tta ce pa ve* yi ——

6 ‖ kīma sī ce ⁀[1] ādarä parya̱ īḍe khu thyau ha̱stama ḫeysū(śta) ḫye ⁀ ttī hā u͡vī na īnā[2] ttī ttā × *sa̱* × *skra*

7 u × -ī × × × ādara parya īḍe ⁀ vaṃña sāja khu me pīsā kaḍā̱namittrā ṣṭā̱re tta ādara hā

8 dīśä ——

9 śā̱bana svastī kuśala śarīrä ⁀ śaika tta tta nai tsā̱ṣṭa ttava prrasadaina

10 kūśala ⁀ ttūñe mvai | ⟨ś⟩ḏ⟨i⟩ jsa ma śaika ttai ⁀ tta⟨va śā̱ba⟩na astī ⁀

11 tvī tta śaika tta nai ⁀ kasmīṃ sthane agatta ⁀ kūṣṭa | aunaka vā pastai

12 āvai ⁀ gaustana-deśa agatta ⁀ hvanya kṣīra ānaka vā̱ āvūṃ ⁀ | hīdūka-deśe kī kale agatta ⁀ hīdva kṣīra aunaka vā ca bā̱ḍa pastai āvai ⁀

13 | sabatsara-dvaya babūva ⁀ dvī salī hamye ⁀ gā̱stana-deśai kūtrra

14 sthanai ttaiṣṭatta ⁀ | hvanya kṣīra kūṣṭa pastai mūdai ⁀ sagarmai

15 ttaiṣṭatta ⁀ sakhyairma mūdai ⁀ kasmī sagarmai ⁀ | kauña sakhyairma pastai mūṃda ⁀ rajsa śā̱bana drraiṣṭa ⁀ rai ttā śaika sā̱ṣṭa nai ⁀

16 śā̱bana | drraiṣṭa ⁀ śaika sāṣṭai ⁀ īdanī kūtrra gatsasī ⁀ vaṇā̱ṃ kūṣṭa

17 tsai ⁀ caina-daiśa gatsamī ⁀ | caiga kṣīra tsū ⁀ caina-[×]deśa̱ kī karma

18 astī ⁀ caiga kṣīra va cī kīra ⁀ majāśrruī | baudasatva paśamī ⁀

19 majā̱śrruī baudasatva sāśūṃ ⁀ pūna kī kala mattra agatsa | sī ⁀ ca bā̱ḍa (ma)ra vā ge̱sa ⁀ sarba cīna-deśa paśamī paśtatta agatsamī ⁀

20 | caiga kṣīra sāśū paskāṣṭa vā gesū ⁀ matrra kīca ttaiṣṭa a̱ika dvaya

21 masa ⁀ laka | mara parya mūṃdai śā̱ dvī māśta ⁀ matrra rajsa daivī

22 ṣadavada ⁀ mara bīsai rai jaśta | ṣadā̱ ⁀ na ttaiṣṭamī ⁀ na mūñūṃ ⁀

23 śīgrraṃ gatsamī ⁀ gā̱ma tsū ⁀ pathvyā̱pakarṇa parī | pūrṇa astī athā̱

[1] ⁀ for ≂ of MS. [2] With *dadā* below.

24 na ˷ padā̮ya bīsā̮ tta ūpakarṇa īda nai ˷ mama pathyā̮|pakarṇa na
kṣamattī ˷ ma padā̮ya bīsā ū̮pakarṇa na kṣamīda ˷ a̮ika dvaya aśvena
25 ga|tsamī ˷ śau dva aśa hamai tsū ˷ pūstaka astī atha na ˷ pūstya tta
26 īda ā (ne ˷) pūstaka astī ˷ īda | kīma pūstaka astī sūtrra avīdarma
27 vīnaya vajrra-yāna ˷ a̮ittana madyai kīma pūstaka astī ˷ | sūtrra
avīdarma vīnīva vajrra-yā̮na ˷ ttakyāṃ harda vya tta kāṃ pūstye
28 aśta ˷ ttava kīma pūstaka kṣa|mattī ˷ tvī au kā̮manai pūstye kṣamai ˷
29 mama vajrra-yā̮na kṣamattī śaikṣapaya ˷ vajrra-yā̮na | kṣamai parya vā
pūṣṭai ˷ śaikṣapayamī ˷ pūśū ttā ˷ aha śīgrra gā̮tsamī kī kala śaikṣapa-
30 |yamī ˷ a gā̮maña tsū ca bā̮ḍe ttā pūśū ˷ yava matrra ttaiṣṭasi
31 ttavatta kala śaikṣapaya | kūṣṭa būra parī tsūe parya vā pūṣṭai ˷
32 śaikṣaya ˷ 'sāja ˷ rajsa-kūlai nmatrrīyattī ˷ kūṣḍa̮ vī|rā̮ṣṭau nama-
drrīda ˷ ūttaiṣṭavada tta gatsamī ˷ parsa ttā tsāṃ ˷ aha̮ vatcana na
33 jsanamī rajsa | pūratta śā̮bana śā̮bana kathaya ˷ a ā pha̮ra na bvai thā̮
34 hā jasta pyatsa śaika bījaiṣa̮ | matrra kīcatta ttava[1] ttaiṣṭa yavatta
vatcana jsa(na)sī ˷ mara laka mūña pha̮ra bva̮ ˷ matrra baikṣū darma
35 jsana|ttī atha na ˷ mara bīsā̮ āśa̮ dā̮ bvā̮ra ā (ne) ˷ kījatta alpa
36 jsanattī ˷ bakala bvā̮rai ˷ | darma alpa jsanattī śīlavatta atha dūśīla ˷
37 dā bakalaka bvārai paraiha dā̮ ā avarai|ha dā̮ ˷ śīla pūnä na astī
38 dūśīla baikṣū ˷ parāha naiśta avaraiha dā āṣa̮ ˷ īdanī kala | astī aha
gatsamī ˷ vaña baiḍa̮ hamye a tsū ˷ ttava gatsa vajñapūttī karayaṃ ˷
39 thā̮ tsa aurāśa | hā̮ ˷ vījñapūttī krratta rajsakīya tcakrra babūva kīja
40 ttaiṣṭa ˷ auraṣṭai hā̮ parau tta pasta sa laka mūña ˷ | mama karma na
astī matrra na ttaiṣṭamī ˷ mama kīra naiśta mara ma na mūñū ˷
41 kamacū daiśe rajsa śā̮bana pūja krra|tta dana kī labada ˷ kamacū
bīsai ttā re śaika sāṣṭa nai aśtū byaudai ˷ ttava agatta attīva śā̮bana
42 | karma krratta ˷ thā̮ vā ge̮sā vī śaika kīra hamye ˷ mama caitta
43 prrabūtta sadūṣṭā ˷ mama aysmya pha̮|rāka sadauṣṭā hamye ˷ [×]
dva baikṣū caina-daśa gatta atha na ˷ dva ttaiṣya caiga kṣīra tsvāṃda
44 ā ne ˷ | gatta ˷ tsvāda ˷ hīdūka ttaiṣī agatta pūratta gatsamī ˷ hīdū
45 ttaiṣī pasta āvai pyatsā̮śa̮ tsau ˷ | aha ttava pūratta dūra na agatta
46 rauṣa na karaya ˷ hā̮ysa ttā pyatsā na āvū ysāra na īna ˷ | mahatta
prrasada ˷ pajsa ttā pachīṣ̮au ˷ aha grra[×]he gatsamī ˷ a bīśa tsū ˷
47 grrahe kī ka|rma astī ˷ bīśa cī kīra ˷ kīja karma astī ˷ laka kīra aśta ˷
48 śīgrra [×] gatsa ˷ gāmaña tsa ˷ | śīgrra agatsa ˷ gaumaña vā̮ ge̮sa ˷
49 bhakatta labada ˷ atha na ˷ khāysa byaudai ā ne ˷ labada ˷ | byaudai ˷

[1] *ttava* above *catta*.

naitrra agatta sūpamī ⌢ hūna ā hūsāṃ ⌢ bhakatta būja ⌢ khāysa
50 hvara ⌢ prrattūṣye prra | būtta na kathaiyą ⌢ ysai ysai būḍą p̱harāka
51 na bījaiṣa ⌢ śattī ttaiṣṭa ⌢ tsāṣṭa (mū)ña ⌢ attaśtamū | ttaśta na gatsa ⌢
ttāṣṭa vāṣṭa na tsa ⌢ lajsa na astī ⌢ kṣāramai tta naiśta ā (ne) ⌢ agaṇī
52 prrajsvalaya ⌢ | dai hą vīśta ⌢ nīlajsą pūrūṣą ⌢ akṣąrma hve ⌢ narī ⌢
53 maṇḍe ⌢ ūpasthayaka ⌢ baiṣṭa vakṣāyai[1] | aẖa vaṇaya ⌢ gvūsa vą ⌢
rajsa-kūla gatsa kuśla[2] varatta prraitsaya ⌢ kūṣḍą vī tsa ⌢ tsāṣṭā
54 drrūnā | hą pvaisa ⌢ gatta ⌢ tsvai ⌢ mrraiṣa na kathaiyą ⌢ yāla na
55 hūña ⌢ na gatta ⌢ na tsvai ⌢ śvūrṇa kī katha | yattī ⌢ hagū aśtū
bījaiṣīda ⌢ cainadaiśa kīma[3] prrattyaya na gatta ⌢ caiga kṣīra aśtai kaṇa
56 na tsve ⌢ | ttaiṣī avaṇītta ⌢ ttątta prrattaya na gatta ⌢ ttaiṣī gąṣṭe tta
57 tta na tsvai ⌢ kṣūtta pīvasa astī athą na ⌢ bīną | sai ttara tta aśta ā ne ⌢
kṣūtta pīvasa na astī ⌢ naiśta ma ⌢ garabī pūrūṣa ⌢ maisalā hve ⌢
58 agadū | ka baikṣū ⌢ agatta ⌢ iṇāvaka ąṣī ā ⌢ kīma prratyaya agatta ⌢
59 aśtai keṇa ā ⌢ na jsanamī ⌢ | na bvai ⌢ kīma kṣamattī ⌢ aśtū vai
kṣamai ⌢ bauṭa baikṣū ⌢ ttąẖatta ąṣī ⌢ mrraiṣavadī ⌢ yālajsa ⌢
60 | prraitsamī ⌢ pvaisūmai ⌢ prrai[×]tsa ⌢ pvaise ⌢ mama drraiṣṭa baya
61 karayattī gatta ⌢ māṃ hą dyauda pvaistai | tsvauda ⌢ [×] vīrūpa
satva pūratta paśattī ⌢ arīśą satta pyatsa sąśīda ⌢ paśtatta na paśattī ⌢
62 paskī | nąṣṭa na sąśīda ⌢ satya na kathaiyattī ⌢ rasṭa na bījaiṣe ⌢
63 alapa [lī] karaiyattī ⌢ haura mąra pa | dīmai ⌢ na [×] na karaiyattī ⌢
na padīmai ⌢ prrabhūtta narī prrīya ⌢ p̱harąka maṇḍī brrai ⌢
64 prrabhatta atta | śtąmuttaśta gatsattī ⌢ pharąka hąṣṭa vāṣṭa jsāvai ⌢
65 maithūna-darma karaiyattī ⌢ mahatta śrreṣṭī ⌢ maista hvā | ṣṭa ⌢
ttava[4] ttīḍaskara dadą ⌢ thą hakhīśą ⌢ tta mūnūṣa mama ttīḍaskara
66 datta ⌢ aśū[ca][5]ca hīna satva ⌢ | asūrai ñaśa satta ⌢ ūṇamatta ⌢
67 grrąhasta ⌢ barja ⌢ nāra ⌢ agarīka ⌢ gąkṣai ⌢ kaṣṭa bajana alnīya ⌢
hamāka vā bara ⌢ bauṭa baikṣū rąga babūva ttąẖatta ąṣī āchanai
68 hamye ⌢ | namattranaka pūrūṣa agatsattī ⌢ namadrrąka hve hīṣṭą ⌢
69 dana prratsadaya ⌢ haira pacana ⌢ | bagąpattra ⌢ khąlavī ⌢ ttava
ttasya pūrūṣa lakūṭa dadą ⌢ ttakye satta daula hūra ⌢ na ttaṇḍaya ⌢
70 na | dvya ⌢ samaśana ⌢ gūṇaṃba ⌢ dveṣī ⌢ ysaiṣṭa ⌢ prravarṇa
71 prravara ⌢ pamūha pajsa ⌢ prravarṇa ūttaraya ⌢ | pūmaha [na][6] hajsa ⌢
pūratta mūnūṣa astī bahai kathaiyattī ⌢ natca gvairrīda ⌢ karattī ⌢

[1] *vakṣāyai* below.
[2] Or *kuśala* with *śa* written close.
[3] Small *ma* inserted.
[4] *ttava* below.
[5] *ca* deleted.
[6] *na* blurred.

72 [×] g̮aihe ⌢ | ghaṇṭa ⌢ g̮ai ⌢ mattapītta ⌢ mā̮vapye̮ ⌢ ū̮padyaya ⌢
73 pīse ā̮ṣ̮ī ⌢ būdha̮ ⌢ b̮eysa ⌢ keśa avattaraya | tcajsa vā̮ hā̮ja ⌢
prrapalana ⌢ pahai ⌢ paśtatta pūna agatta ⌢ paskyā̮ṣ̮ṭa ā ⌢ śaiṣya ⌢
74 baiṣṭa ⌢ maṣī-bhajana ⌢ | narā̮ṃja ⌢ vrrīdha ⌢ ysagara ⌢ dīrga ⌢
bvaiysa ⌢ rasva ⌢ mvaiysgä ⌢ svamī ⌢ hīyai ⌢ vīrūpa satva mūkha ⌢
75 | mama rā̮ṣ̮a na astī kaiśa na ū̮tpaṇ̮ḍ̮ayamī ⌢ mama ysā̮ra naiśta tcajsai na
76 thaṃjū ⌢ kī kala ttava vīrūpa kathai | yasī ⌢ ca bā̮ḍ̮a thā̮ arī̮ṣ̮a bījaiṣā̮ ⌢
77 ttatta kala mama rā̮ṣ̮a agatsattī ⌢ ttai b̮eḍa ma ysā̮ra hamai | krraiṣṇa ⌢
hīrāsa ⌢ śvaitta ⌢ śī ⌢ pītta ⌢ ysīḍai ⌢ rahta ⌢ hainai ⌢ harītta ⌢
78 ysarū ⌢ nīla ⌢ āṣai ⌢ lāhītta ⌢ dajsa ⌢ | vara badaya ⌢ vara baña ⌢
ūdūgaṭaya ⌢ vara prrahā̮ja ⌢ adūna ⌢ vaña ⌢ adya ⌢ īmūṃjsū ⌢
79 dvaya ttrīya dīna ⌢ | dva drrai haḍā̮ ⌢ madīlīyana rajsa-pāttra grīḫa
80 na adīka astī ⌢ a̮iṣī pūrūṣa lābī astī ⌢ ṣaika hve | ttraikṣa ttai ⌢ bala
ajñana ⌢ jsaiṇa satta na bauttai ⌢ ada gatta ⌢ nā̮ṣ̮ṭa vahaiṣṭa ⌢ ū̮rda
81 agatta ⌢ ū̮skyā̮ṣ̮ṭa sarba ⌢ abya | ttara prravrrīśa ⌢ hadara trrā̮mau ⌢
baihai neṣkamamī ⌢ natcā̮ṣ̮ṭa narāmau ⌢ aśva a̮ika grrāṇ̮ṇayamī ⌢ śā
82 aśa gīnāṃ ⌢ aha | pūna gatsamī ⌢ a pā tsū ⌢ ttava na gatsa ⌢ thā na
83 tsa ⌢ rajsavarī ⌢ haḍa ⌢ śīgrra gatsattī ⌢ gā̮maña tsīda ⌢ | cīrakala
caina-daiśa na ttaiṣṭa ⌢ bvaiysa va caiga kṣīra na mūña ⌢ vīrūpa
84 vastū ⌢ arī̮ṣ̮a haira ttai ⌢ | dīrga gatta ⌢ bvaiysa tsvāda ⌢ adūna
85 agatsattī ⌢ vaña haiśta ⌢ sūca anaya ⌢ sūttra ⌢ saujsaña ācana vā̮ ba | ra ⌢
sūtḫana ⌢ kaumadai ⌢ patraṇa ⌢ haiya ⌢ malīna karapaṭa̮ ⌢ [ha]
86 pakhalaya[1] rrīmajsa pamūha ttai haysña ⌢ malīna na astī ⌢ rī | ma
maṃ naiśta ⌢ yā̮ga asana kījatta dada̮ ⌢ aśpara vā laka hūra ⌢ anaya ⌢
87 hūrū ttā̮ ⌢ a̮ṇ̮ḍ̮a̮ ⌢ ṣaga ⌢ mīṇaya ⌢ | pīma̮ ⌢ mūṃjsana ⌢ kalye ⌢
mū̮ddha ⌢ ñūśka ⌢
88 [*reversed at end of roll*] vīpaśa śaika vīśvaba karasūda kanakamā̮na
kā̮śaba śā̮kyamā̮na

53

FM 25, 1[2]

a 1 hasp⟨ä⟩jīmä[3] ttānu śära hautana tcera
u cäro padajsāña nauvaretcaholsä pabanä jīvätä
ttītä ttye palye ttānu *cä*roṇu puñyau jsa jsīnai hūṣṭä 1

[1] *pakhalaya* below *ha*. [2] Bhaiṣajyaguru-vaiḍūryaprabha-sūtr.
[3] Top of *spä* lost.

2 hā yi × × ⟨pa⟩|śīndä varä ṣṭāna ttītä dukhyau jsa
ttänai byevīndä parrīyu harbiśyau haysgamatyau jsa 2
trāṇamuktä vā būtäsatvä ānandä ttītä tta hvate se ⌒
3 cu ttutu ttīśondu balondu sūtru | hvate balysä uysguste 3
yäḍe uysnaurāṇu biśānu ce buro pyūẏāte ttu sūtru
biśī dīra härа jyāre puṣo parśti biśyau dukhyau jsa 4
4 ttiña parṣo āysdarrgye ⟨dvā⟩su | yakṣānu rrunde balonda
ttītä āysarnna vahäṣṭa dasta hā haṃju yäḍāndä 5
patä balysu jsonauta västāta tta pā haṣḍä yäḍāndä ⌒
5 buhu dvāsu hautana yakṣa ku halci kā|miña kṣīra 6
kīntha biśa āvuṯo bāśa ⌒ garuẏo ulatāñe saṃkherma
o[1] rrayso *bīñä* ku āvye ⌒ buhu nä rakṣāmä biśīnda 7
b1 cu buro tvī bäṣṭe tcahaur-pandiya ce sājītä | dṛjsāte
ttutu sūtru cu halci āt- -*u*ta niśtä cu va ne byevä 8
ānandä vātcu trāṇamuktu būtasatvu tta brraṣṭe
cu buro ttä ttä yakṣa duvāsu kho nä nāma vā mama hvāña 9
2 paḍā | k⟨ä⟩mīr = ro vaśärä mekhalä tcūramä andālä
pūhä vā anilä sanilä ⌒ kṣeima *r*u indālä rro nāma 70
haṣṭamä rro pāyälä nomä mahurä cändālä rro nāma ⌒
3 śau yakṣä pāyälä | *c*au *dvā*saṃ yakṣä bikalä nāma
trāṇamuktä vā būtäsatvä ānandä ttītä hvate se
ttätä hautana yakṣa ci ro paḍā nāma hvataimä 2
4 hvatä tāmye parṣa hauda ysāre ttä ⌒ | biśī vaysña hamālä
dasta hā haṃju yädāndä ⟨kama⟩la hanatāndä biśīnda 3
pyūṣṭāndä cu gyastä balysä kho hvate ttye balysi padaṃgyo
5 bhaiṣajyagurä prraṇähāna paḍājsy × × | × teta 4
biśä tta ttätu būtāña aṃga ⌒ karaṇa varä ṣṭāna paśāndä
ne mara pharu tsīndä saṃtsera thatau byevīndä parrīyu 5
ce ju ṣä ḥve ītä ce āchaina vītanaustä d⟨u⟩khol⟨ttä⟩

[1] Independent *o*.

54

Godfrey 3

a1 /// ra ××× nāma bodhisatväna 2
caturanda-saṃkusumittä nāma bodhisatväna 3
2 /// ×××× pradīpä nāma bodhisatväna 4
3 anantāvalokitta-sarvaviṣayasa | /// ⟨nā⟩ma bodhisatväna 5
merukūṭātyuḍgattä nāma bodhisatväna 6
4 abhi | /// saṃjananä nāma bodhisatväna 7
5 vimala-bāhu-apratihata-raśmi | /// ⟨bo⟩dhisatväna 8
sarvasatvāśaya-viniścitārtha-pāragata-ggāmä nāma bodhisal⟨tväna 9⟩

b1 /// dṛḍha-prrāptä nāma bodhisatvina 10
2 sarvaruta-ravitayomastara-*vy* . | /// nāma bodhisatväna 11
brahmasvara-tteja-atyudgattä nāma bodhisatväna 12
3 kīrtisva | /// nana-apratihata-buddhi nāma bodhisatvina 13
4 sarvakula-ratna-saṃca⟨ya⟩ | /// ⟨nāma⟩ bodhisatväna 14
u maṃjuśrīna alysānaina 15
5 ttyau paḍauysyau kṣaṣṭä yse⟨ryau⟩ | /// sa -au -ī × mai
āśirī śśāriputrä palśārä haḍai samāhā*nä*na panatä ⁓

55

Paris Z[1]

1 ⟨a⟩|ysmū jsa ṣacu auna aurga drūnā pvaisauma haṣḍä yanai:
2 phara sī bvāmaya ha|jū vāysya aysmū
draya pīla sīye śāsttra ṭhīka vībāṣai abīdarma
3 yą|gaśāstra haṣṭa yaugasthana
ttu tta bauttai sa khu hīya nąma
4 dravīlai prrañeṃda|pauña bvaijsīnai rana :
draiye pīla sīye baida prrakaraṇa haṣṭa

[1] See *Khotanese Texts II*, no. 1. 36 ff.

5 svārtha parā I rtha vīra hajū nḁ̄hauysa naṣḁgaista :
6 śāstrvā bīsai artha bāye daśa I khaiṇḍa aiha̮
dravīle savanaittapauña hūṣai tsīye jsīna :
7 jsaiṇa ca I rya jsāṃ vai ahaṣṭa sakra varttai
8 sīye draiye pīla śā[stra]stra prrakaraṇa ṭhī I ka
9 sājai pūśai ahaṣṭa bāvana yadai prrañavarda jaista hayū ā I dara tta
10 ye parāha̮ paraustai vasvai ba̮ysa parauya sakra ṣḁumaña carya I ttā
11 hūṣa bāstai āstāka mūdai valeka auna vaña būrai cau I sa ye śaika
12 vīśḁ hajsauye baśa : vairṣ̥a jī nauma jaista hayū I baiysūśta ttā bvā :
13 valaka auna khu tsūai jsaṇa padaja ṣaumaña sa I kra yāda tvā hūṣa
14 bāstai sīye jsāṃ dā draina pīlvā ṣadyāya I tsāṣṭaka bv(ā)maya dahū
15 paiña haira jsa dyaunaisū jaista hayū[1] I śakalaka śaumai brraura ña-
16 haluā khanadai u prraysā baiysāṃ dā sīme jsa[2] I draina pīlā ṣadyāya :
17 vajrrayḁ̄na sīye ahaṣṭa ṣīya ha I ḍāya ṣa[dya]dya śakalaka padī ḁ̄ṣ̥ī hīya
18 śauttaidrākara jī nau I ma jasta hayū bvajsāṃ haphva : khva tta vaña
19 ttyai śaikṣa jastāṃ be̮ys(ā)ṃ jsa I ayīkṣai vaṣḁ̄vāysaujsī kāla vīra
20 uvārrvā drayvā saskhārrvā tcaurya I mahābuvau[3] hīye avīysamḁ̄śa tta
jsāṃ vīysama na ṣṭāṃdai[4] hīye avīysamḁ̄śta hada vya śairka[5] ṣṭāvai
21 tsāṣṭa drūnai I ttyai kaiṇa ma ña(śa) prravai sthaira aysmyai śairka ṣṭai
22 phar(ā)ka bāḍa phar(ā)ka salī I vautta sa śaikyaira hamāvai : ñaśai prravai
23 āśarī[6] dharmaidrākarapūña pūña I spaudai khu maistāṃ hayūnau hīya
24 thau raysga vīra avaphada brruna I magalīya dy(ā)ma byaihūdai : ——

[*Space*]

56

Khadaliq I. 119

Folio 29

Recto

1 ttu balysūñavūyso āysda yanāre thīyo haspījīndä ttye dārañe
2 byehāṣce kä I ḍäna ⌢ kāmi haṣṭa paḍā raucä nāma jastaṣṣai 1 veraucanä
3 nāma gyastaṣṣai 2 I prañāprabhä nāma gyastaṣṣai 3 u sūryagarbhä

[1] *ha'* below.
[2] *jsa* below, between *sī* and *me*.
[3] *-au* deleted.
[4] *hīye avīysamḁ̄śa* to *ṣṭāṃdai* deleted.
[5] *hīye* to *śairka* below.
[6] *āśarī* struck through.

4 nāma gyastaṣṣai 4 u sattyä nā | ma gyastaṣṣai 5 u abhiprāya-paripūraṇä
5 nāma gyastaṣṣai 6 u nakṣatra- | rājä nāma jastaṣṣei 7 u cāritramata
nāma gyastaṣṣai 8 || ttäte haṣṭa gyasta-

Verso

1 ṣṣā ttättu bodhisatvä ānatä yanīndä u haspījīndī ttye dārañe
2 byehāṣce | käḍäna ce tvo dārañu vätä haspäsaṃdai hīṭhei hämāñu sa-
3 gauravä śe | rākä ⁓ cändäkī ye vätä śśäru yīndä ṣī bvāñä u bustä ṣṭānī
4 ne hāmu | ru ne tcerä śtä ⁓ gaṃbhīrye dätä vamaseme käḍäna ācya-
5 vaṃdä hämāñu ⁓ | biśī hära ahämäta nväśtāña ⁓ kho jve haṃdarye
heḍä cindä hanu nasu yīndä ⁓

57

Khadaliq 1. 158

1, 2 : rruśta vīra baste ≂ paje*nu* kūmi-guṇyau jsa × × × ⟨ha⟩ṣṭi ma | nāta :
3 sūhava̤na āyīmāmane ≂ nivā hīye śukye ahvyāñe | saṃtsārū baṃdani-
4 śāla[1] guchā̤me ūdiśāyi ≂ śrāviki-prratīka-bu | dha-yā parrīya[2] bha-
5 vāgra āstanaka audi avīśa būre ysyāme ysi | rūña maraṃ rāśa̤
6 tsūti ≂ drahiṣkalī ysimaśaṃde ≂ hye suhi śire | kiṇa ≂ drayau ttira-
7 diryau jsa haṃphva ≂ biśi pīrmāttạma ḇaysāni ḇa | ysūśti kūṣā̤ṃ ≂
8 hvāñari ma ni ttā ≂ hvā[ra]ñari ≂ cu būrā̤ṃ ji ttāha*re* | ḇaysūśti vaski
9 upakạrṇä śtāki himā̤ṃde ≂ tti khu ysīri ā̤jsạ raṃna mura | mīrāḫe ≂
harbīśū raṃna maura aspūrri himā̤ṃde ≂ ma na ttā haṃdirye rrā̤ṣi
10 | himāmane ≂ ma braṃga̤rā ≂ ma dīri-gūttirya ≂ ma kastara ≂ ma na
11 ttā agyau prrattya | gyau jsi vārūḍya himāmane ≂ baiśi ysaṃthi va
12 ṣṭāṃ ttā hīya dasteṃ raṇạ caṃdā | va̤ña mvīri māñaṃdạ himā̤ṃde ≂
13 avā̤māvāṃ[3] ttạta ≂ himāte ≂ avimāvi patsā̤ | ma : avimātạ dāḵṣaṇya ≂
14 ma ni ttā hīsi rrā̤ṣi himā̤mane ≂ ma ni ttā ḇa | ysūñä aysmū panāśā̤mani
15 ma ṃāśḏi : ma prraṇạhā̤na ≂ baiśä ysaṃthi vaṣṭi | ttā sūdhā̤na ẹysānai
16 māñaṃdä rraṣṭạ sadabhūtti[4] pīsā kalyā̤ninaittri byehā̤ | mine ≂
17 ttrā̤mū ārāhye yinā̤mane khu namau mahāsthā̤niprrāpta baudhisa | tva
≂ cirā̤mi āryāva̤laukyitteśvarä baudhasatva ṃāśḏä : ākāśā̤garbhi

[1] Top not clear.
[2] Top lost.
[3] Or *avimāvā̤ṃ* if the second -*ā*- has been deleted.
[4] *da* below.

18 hau|vą ≈ ksittigarbhi cąrya : simattibhadri vimūha ≈ majiśrī prraṇą-
19 hąna ≈ u | ma ttā mąnī himāṃde ≈ dädirū jsą ttā rraysgi vī vinīyą
20 ttrvāsti yiną|mane khu namau bhaiṣająrāji baudhasatva ttrāste ≈
21 ttrāmą ttā sątvā bā|ji karmi āvarṇa kauce : baśde ṣądāvā dīśę
22 yinąmane ≈ khu namau | akṣubi jasti ḅaysi dīśę ≈ ttrąmą ttā satvā bāji
dukha karye bu[1]

58

Khadaliq 1. 221

1 [*bases of Khadaliq* 1. 158]
2 ḍi yināmine khu namau mahākārṇakä śākyamāṃ jastąna jasta ḅaysi
3 | budä baudhasatvä cäryāyi jsąna ≈ dädäri ttā rraysgą vī ḅaysūśtā-
4 |ṣṭa aviṣī byehāmane ≈ khu namau āryāmaittrai baudhisatva bīde :
5 ttrą|mū ttā baudhakṣaittri himāne khu svahāvą lauvidā ≈ ttiri ṣṭā
6 pūña-|kuśila-mūla namau armyāyi jasti ḅaysa[2] vari ysīnīyi bāyāṃ
7 mariṇa-|kālā byāti himāde : simattiveraucināṃ baidi ṃāśḍiji ḅāyi
8, 9 bī|rāśī ≈ vīnā naṣąmāṃde dāvījā tcamąña vasūsīde ≈ ttye adheṣṭą|na ≈
hūna[3] mąñadi baiśi çāyi mīrīci mąñaṃdi sąrvadharmi ttuśā paysā-
10 nąma|ne ≈ upā[la]yi-kau[la]śila nąma pārąme haṃbīrāṃde dasau
11 | bhųmi dasau pąñä ≈ vigihi baudhadharma haṃbīrāṃde ≈ haṃbaḍa
12 āvaṃ|ni baiśi sarvasątva uysdaura[4] ysimaśadya ḅaysi himāṃde ≈ ttą
hvąñari tti pā
12*a* [*interlinear at end of line*] dvīlai cadrākara-bhadrrasīhe
13 | mehe tta-tti-nąmani dąnive ḅaysi himāmane || ≈ ——
14 || āśąryį āysdi yinīryau : tti-tti-nąmani dąnive ṣṭąre kalyąna-maittri
15, 16 āśąrī | paḍauysąña jsi : simagri kāśivitrī bisaṃgą paha ūsihyādi | pūjā-
karmyau jsi hva hvą ṣṭāṃ āśąryą ttiraṃdarą drūnā parīdą brrīṣṭi :
17, 18 | aysmya jsā ṣṭā ≈ suḥi sīravā saṃdurṣṭī prravārṇaji bāḍi pa|chīṣāre ≈
19 kimi jsi bīsaṃgīji gę jsi[5] āśąrya : mari ūvārye | mahācaitti paṃna
20 byaudāṃdi dye : dąnive audi tti pastāṃdi asthīye | si : mānī vā jsāṃ
21 pā drayvā ramnvā ūvārä vistārya padya pūña-kū|śila-mūla śiḍe
22 deyidharma kṣamīdi yūḍe ≈ ūtvaḍire jsa bī|saṃgīji gę parysi viri ≈ ttye
23 haira[6] prracāyiną paḍāṃda bīsaṃgąni ā|śąrya nimadrrādi : uvārąna

[1] *buḍi*, continued in Khadaliq 1. 221. 1. [2] *ḅaysa* below.
[3] *hūna* below. [4] sic *d*; below. [5] *jsi* over *maṃ*. [6] *ra* below.

24 b̮aysūñi aysmyani : nemaṃdrūni pa | stāṃdi ahavāysye : khīnā ni
25 miñāṃdi ≈ kīḍa būrāṃ jsa̮ ṣṭāṃ pa | tsa̮brrīyā pachīṣ̮āre ⌢ viñā ṣṭāṃ
26 himadā hamadā[1] ttāṣṭi parīdi nimaṃ | dre : styaji kāla parīdi ārauśȩ
27 ≈ pārṣ̮a pa̮jsaṃ dāśe ≈ bīsaṃgni | vā jsāṃ pā āśa̮rya ttāṣṭi pūṣi
28 parsyari ≈ caityi-vaṃda̮nāṣṭi ttiri | vā jsāṃ pā tti namau jastāṃ b̮aysāṃ
29 baudhasa̮tvāṃ : devattāṃ parvālā ≈ | pa̮jsa̮mi pūjā-karma armūvyari
30 parṇāmyari : ttāṣṭi pūṣi parsyari | saṃgasthāñāṣṭi ≈ ttiri vā jsāni pā tta
31 hva hva sthā̮nave āysnā | vīrä pārihīryau ≈ dānivā gīḫani pārṣ̮a
32 pa̮jsaṃ pajāysīryau: | sarvūpaka̮rṇi pȩṇḍvāna ≈ dā̮nive vā jsā̮ni pā
33 audi tti pastāṃdi | asthīye ≈ vima tvā śaṃdai pūña-kūśila-mūla himya
34, 5 īde ≈ | cira ḫaitti drayvā ranvā pūña-kūśila-mūla yuḍādū ā̮ma -e | ci ma ttyāṃ dva padya [pū][2] pu̮ṇyä jñāni-saṃbhārāṃ sa̮⟨ma⟩grī ttāṃ
36 pūñāṃ kūśila-mūlā[3] hīya tvārā himya | ī ≈ audi bvaśte b̮aysūśti
37 būre jsā ṣṭā pūña-kūśila-mūla | ttāhire sima̮gri kāśivitrī bīsaṃgna
38 haṃbrrīhāre ≈ × ⟨. . .⟩ | āśa̮rī āstaṃna yāvi audi sa̮rva nivāña
39 būre ≈ ⟨jsā ṣṭā?⟩ | pūña-kūśilamūla ≈ [blurred *akṣaras*]

59

Khadaliq VI 4. 1

a1 /// tva spa̮tte hāve ci dīru̮ye auṣṭä spa̮tte hāvī ⌢ ci pīru̮ye
2 ⟨auṣṭä spa̮tte⟩ /// di ci biṣ̮ā spatti b̮inai maraṃ paṃmarāñi ⌢ ci haṃgari spa-
3 ⟨tti⟩ /// spa̮tti āchai paṃmarāñä ⌢ ci phaṃnai spalāte tta bvā̮ña
4 /// stā spa̮tti tta bvāñä kalahāra-ṃ hime ⌢ ci hvaraṃdai sve spa-
5 ⟨tti⟩ /// cu ysiri spa̮tte girye parā thyau hime ⌢ ci hvaraṃdai bāysu̮
6 /// haṃgūjsa hime ⌢ ci hvaraṃdai pa̮vai spa̮tti strīyānī bye
b1 /// hvaraṃdai hālai kamalä spa̮tti bvāña si śira ≈ khu syaṃdai
2 /// ⟨spa⟩lāte bvāñä si śira ā̮ma byehūṃ ⌢ ci vā syaṃdai gu̮ spa-
3 ⟨tti⟩vara hīsīdi kuṣṭä pajsaṃ byehe ci syaṃca paysanva spatti bvā̮-
4 ⟨ñä⟩ /// ⟨ha⟩ysgy⟨e⟩ spalāri bvā̮ña si ysañau hayūñau śiri salā
5 /// d⟨ai⟩ braukalä spalāte bvāñä si haṃgrīma pūrūṃ ⌢ ci syaṃdai
6 /// bvāñe si sāñyau jsa pūrūṃ ⌢ ci syaṃdai hālai tcȩmä spattä strīye

[1] *hamadā* below. [2] *pū* deleted. [3] *sa̮⟨ma⟩grī* to *mūlā* below.

60

Balawaste 0152

Folio

a 1 /// ṣṭa aysmūna ⌒ cu ṣa hasta

2 /// aysmūna sūrättete jsa ā̤re ⌒ hu-

3 /// m*a* jsa anāphäḍa dvāredärśyau hudahī-

4 /// × ttuvare hastaru bärūñäre kho ysarrne nä|⟨kä⟩

b 1 /// × ḍe buśānei ⌒ aysmū sīru hamändä ⌒ ttye

2 /// śäryau vāysañyau tcabrītä väcätryau rata|⟨nyau⟩

3 /// -ā pajustä ratanīnyau gā̤kyau pa-

4 /// mä balysa dästa ⌒ praysā-

61

Balawaste 0154

1 /// ⟨śaṃd⟩ā haṃbujsai haṣḍä yani ——

2 /// ṣī maṃjsa ma śirkä pyāsti 20 1 ⟨haḍā?⟩tūṃ

3 /// × nāṃ gvārä au ysä ma śi byaudeṃ vaña buri

4 /// × varä na pharāka śirka paysā̤nūṃ u ysirūvai

5 /// -ra[1] ttā maṃ va hvaṃḍä āta khvaṃ ye ī thvai bustī ū samūvā ga-

6 rśä khaste śau haḍātūṃ ma brāṃba ni darrvai ci a mūri bāsteṃ īme a jūṃdai yeṃ

7 tvī beṃdeṃ ni ŋāya khu hamadā a hvaṃḍä ⟨ts?⟩eya tvī vā natca sījyāṃ varä burä

8 paśā̤ñä yeṃ haṣṭa māśtä anvaśtā yuḍa ya cve biśa diryeṃ khu vā hamaiyi ni tsvai

9 śe hvaṃḍye dīśte vā paṃjsa śeṃga ⟨..⟩ ⟨ham⟩īḍä haurā̤ñä ye dire vā anāspeti

10 paśā̤ñä yeṃ pa̤jsūṃ vā uṣṭaṃ ⟨h⟩imya × × -e āṃ pā viśeṣā̤ bve ci ma ttara śirkä spāṣṭai

[1] *pra* or *pu*?

11 mūraṃ tta biysīyai haṣṭase u haṣṭasetūṃ jsāṃ puñaśūra̮na puḍa u 1000 śūrabu-

12 da -e ⟨...⟩ × . ×× ⟨......⟩ hvarakaṃ īra-puña̮ñi haura 1000

13 /// /// -au -i -i hvaraki jsāṃ hā bya̮mā jänava

14 /// /// × vā māṃ cāṃ-ṣī

62

Farhad Beg 05

Folio

*a*1 /// stä ṣṭānä suhauttä u hā ysāḍä ṣṭānä ///

2 /// ku hūḍu yīndä numānī ne[1] hämäte ⁓ × ///

3 /// mäte u tsättara : ṣẹịṣä karmä tcamna ///

4 /// ⟨hau⟩ru heḍä ustamātu tcaramu śye ///

*b*1 /// × häte ṣa̮ṣä karmä tcamäna ḫve cä ///

2 /// suhauttä hämäte ⁓ kye ṣä ḫve kuī ye ///

3 /// ⟨hau⟩ru hūḍu tīndä ttīyä sīrä hämäte ///

4 /// ⁓ u ku ysāḍä hämäte ttīyä vā × ///

63

Iledong 04

Folio

*a*1 /// ⟨hī⟩ñe jsa haṃtsa sarva*sa* ///

2 /// ⟨suva⟩rṇa-bhāsauttamä sūttrāṇu ///

3 /// ṇä tsūta rakṣe käḍāna ——

4 /// ⟨sū⟩ttrāṇu rrundänu dijsāka ///

5 /// ysama-śśandai ///

6 /// vā -e × y ///

*b*1 /// dijsāka × ///

2 /// tunä tsāṣṭ- ///

[1] *ne* below.

3 /// avihīläta ahva⟨ ⟩ ///
4 /// ⟨rru⟩ndänu rrundä vista(rna) birā⟨śä⟩ ///
5 /// ⟨hva⟩raṃdā ysānve śśando vi⟨stāndä⟩ ///
6 /// ggāhyau gyastu balysu ///

64

Iledong 05

a 1 /// ⟨ba⟩ṣṭarrda dätaimä u
2 /// mä ‿ u hauda riṃchā
3 /// -ätaimä ‿ uskyāṣṭä di|⟨śä?⟩
4 /// × ṣṭu diśä jsa kūlu se
5 /// × × ysava biśśä hau
6 /// -āṇaṃdā ci āṇa

b 1 /// ⟨ba⟩lysa tta braṣṭemä
2 /// × balysa tta hvāndä se ‿
3 /// × tta ttītä aysu gya|⟨sta⟩
4 /// × tä gyasta balysa tta bra⟨ṣṭ-⟩
5 /// × gyastä balysä ‿ ttä mä gya⟨sta⟩
6 /// ⟨ba⟩lysä ce biśśä kleśa tvī

65

Iledong 06[1]

a 1 /// ⟨ā⟩ysda yande kāmo diśo nvā-
2 ⟨śtäte⟩ /// ⟨biśśū⟩nīna suhāvätānäna su-
3 ⟨häta⟩ /// ⟨dīn⟩āryau ysīrrna mūryau mārā-
4 ⟨hyau⟩ /// ⟨uvat⟩āryau tsāta ⟨ttä⟩ uysnora hä|⟨māre⟩

b 1 /// śrī-mahādīvata vara drai gyū-
2 ⟨na⟩ /// ⟨hau⟩rā u väkṣīvyo nyānartha
3 ⟨yanāña⟩ /// -*ā* huṣṭä raysä śaṃdye sīra
4 /// -ä u vicitra ro handa-

[1] See *Khotanese Texts I*, 53 *r* 2 on p. 237.

66

Iledong 015

1 || mäḍāṃ jasta varata haṣḍị yane ——

2 spā sude ci vā jasta parau pastai hauḍe si ādatana yu ×

67

Iledong 023

a1 /// lsatetu[1] kūśāmä u cu mä tceru × × × × × ///

2 /// × aysmū balysūśtu varāṣṭo käḍe sthīdu[2] västāte × ///

3 /// ⟨a⟩ysmūna uysnora hayūna mañäte u na × × ///

4 /// panamäte ‿ khanaṃce tcīre jsa paḍā dākṣāṇyau päta

5 /// × u ṣä tcūramä -ä aväṣkälsto hīśäḍośtu därysde u

6 /// × -ä u ka vānä cu × na vätä u nai paphīndä pyū̥-

7 ⟨ṣṭe⟩ /// ⟨patta⟩rre k⟨ä⟩ḍe ga*rkh*e vajäṣḍe ‿ u cu handara balysūña ///

b1 /// biśä kīre × *pa*ḍa[3] häru balysūñīneina aysmūna hī[4] ///

2 /// × biṣ̥yo śäru̥o gaṭuo ysaṃthu byehu ‿ u kai biśa uysnora väta ///

3 /// ⟨ka⟩rīttätä väta u cu jāna samāda vätä ka ne ttye käḍana ///

4 /// × daśtatete jsa ārsta väta u ⟨. . . .⟩ daśtatete jsa ///

5 /// gya hīśäḍostä väta u tta biśu uṣṭañä abätandä ///

6 /// × biśūnya hära däde ne yandä hämäte u ka rā × × ///

7 /// buljsa pyūṣḍe ‿ u ka dīraṃgāryau hayūna y- ///

68

Iledong 026

a1 samagr̥ saṃgapālānajä b̥isaṃgä śaṃdā haṃbujsai haṣḍā yani ——

2 aysä miḍi ḡyastä ka tta ra āśiryāṃ hva hva ttaraṃdara drūnai ṣṭāte u aysmya

[1] *ls* or *lys* possible. [2] *du* for *ru*?

[3] *ḍa*, not *ḍā*. [4] *h* uncertain.

3 tsāṣṭā aysä saṃduṣṭūṃ ⁀ vaña āṃ ttā ṣiṇau yani haspisca hasta padī byi-

4 haṃjarä u kṣīra byāta yanīrau cu ma kṣīra vaśū̯na hira haṃjsiṣṭa ṣṭāde khu

5 vyachīdä u muhu tta pātcä hasta padī byāta yanīrau u prrattilā̯ma

b1 p sa ×× .. pusūṃ ×××× mara ×××× vyachīdä u khu mara

2 kṣīra tsāṣṭā himi u pātcä tta ṣau viṣṇadatta tta byāta yanīrau khu thyau b̯e-

3 mañe jsa mara hīśtä ⁀ ——

69

Ch. 00217 (Stein 117. 1–3)[1]

1 recto [*cat-headed ravisher*]

1 || mattrra̯naṃdī nā̯ma susi rūna

2 ṣṣīkä biṣā̯ thaṃje u eha khavä narāme

verso [*bird-headed*]

1 || śakunī nā̯ma mura rūna dīra

2 īdä aviysärä padīme

2 recto [*cock-headed*]

1 ⟨k⟩irakapaṃdanī nā̯ma krriga rūna dīra īra[2] eha

2 • ⟨bi⟩ś‹ā̯›[3] uspaśde kaṃthapāṇī[4] nāma

verso [*wolf-headed*]

1 mukhamaṃda nā̯ma ttavai padīme eha

2 ⟨gan⟩ānai hime

3 recto [*stag-headed*]

1 || miṃkhalaca nā̯ma gūysna rūna dīrä

2 īdä mṛgarāja nāma

3 verso [*ox-headed*]

1 || maṃgica nāma

2 miṃjuka nāma gūha rū⟨na⟩

[1] Facsimile in Eiichi Matsumoto, *Tonkôga no kenkyû*, 1937.
[2] For *īdä*.
[3] Subscript hook lost.
[4] *kaṃthapāṇī* in different hand.

70

S 5212*a*[1]

1 || śu tta ma la :
kī pa[2] tca hvana
2 ttai ma tcīna
bīka ñau tca la
3 va ṣī yau | va śyai yaiva ra
ṣī yīra :
4 yauva śa ma na :
caina tta ma la :
5 tta ma hvana śī la
yama tta ma[3] la
ba la :
6 pa lai yana
ī kha che hvana
7 u ḍa kyaura
sū tta ma la
bauva
8 ana ḍa kha | ra :
ṣ̄ī ba la
tcīva tta ma la

utca vā bara :
khāysa vā pajsa :
| sūraka vā pajsa
maṇḍai vā kūṣ̄a śā :

hairai kṣamī hairai hūrrū :
| aśtuau vai kṣaimai :
nama vą̄ bara :
khā | ysā vā bara :
namva vā bara :
tsa vā
| vā ā : :
śau tturaka khaysa pajāysa :
| parya tta paryai :
ttaradya vā bara :
naiśta ma :
kūṣṭau parī tsvai :
parya vā ttraidai :
mau vā bara

[*Space*]

9 [*Tibetan script*] oṃ bod.skad

71

S 6701

1 —— ttara dāśa beysūśta

[*Space*]

2 . vaña ttā śa ——

[*Space*]

[1] S 5212*b* in *Khotanese Texts II*, no. 72, p. 130.
[2] *pa* below.
[3] *ma* small inserted.

3 || khu ttyāṃ gaḍanau pajsa kṣamī ⌢ jastyāṃ bęysāṃ u bauda

[*Space*]

4 ≈ khu ttyāṃ gäḍạnau pajsaṃ kṣamī ⌢ jastyāṃ ḅeysāṃ u
5 baudhasatvāṃ aurga tsvą̄ñai u śakrra jastaṣau a-
6 ysūrāṃ āstanä mistą hauvanau raudāṃ ⌢ dā jsa haphva
7 ttyāṃ harabaiśa ą̄rga tsvauñai vasvą-varą̄hąu parī-
8 yastāṃ jsa vadīda nva padaṃjä bīsai ṣį pūsai khu
9 au vaña īmījsū ttyau gaḍanāṃ jsa ttu pvaisai pvaisū
10 hīye nva kṣama khva ma aysmyą ṣṭāvai na śuka hī- ⌢
11 yi jīyį udaśāya ⌢ khu au ttū pvaisū khva masa
12 hąmą̄ve naiṣkaistą jsa vā parayą uysdīśai

[*Space*]

13 [*large, isolated signs*] nā nā nā

[*Space*]

14 uca hīvī vā pina-paka hīyį vāṣī thaṃ-pastą
15 devatta ≈ śade jsa vā vīśų dā na naraume cū būre
16 kṣamī tte baiśa nva aysmūi hamāre ≈ ąuską aunā
17 kaidä āysdiḍā dījsą̄re cū būra caidā nva kṣame
18 ttā naiṣkalīda ≈ ttī ttye nva pvaisai tsvai jaste baiśa nva
19 aysmūi āvama habairīda uską̄tta bīsā vā jsāṃ
20 kąida khvai japha na hamāre u hąivai hame ≈ ha-
21 rabeśe hīra hvara cī hamāre khu ttī maṇḍai kai-
22 ṇą pvaisā ttī va byada pastą u ttī haḍa asta śarka
23 ṣṭe
24 [*large isolated signs*] sarau sarau sarau

[*Space*]

72

Dandan-uilik III 12[1]

1 /// *r* /// *śā* t *tty* . . ///
2 -enä va tty⟨e⟩ yuḍāṃdi sarvaṃdāti ///
3 lattärhaṃnä nāri ḳṣamī ne nä rrą̄ṣai kh⟨va⟩ṃ m⟨i⟩jṣę kṣuṃd⟨ai⟩ ***n r***
4 ⟨. .⟩ pātcī rrą̄ṣa cuai va dūvaka yaśāśāri khattunä nāṃ

[1] Facsimile, *Ancient Khotan*, plate CX.

5 ⟨...⟩ spāta pāḍi khu mästa häme ttītī lattärhaṃnä
6 /// ×īyaṃ u ṣąi hamayä kṣuṃdai heḍi cu ri au staṃ bā
7 /// ×ätä cu ri ttū ṣ̥ūstau pademḍi gvā(rä) byūhī rruī
8 /// ⟨mū⟩ri heḍi u dirsä daula nāste ttī ri
9 /// × lattärhaṃnä haṃguṣṭä viśte ttä
10 /// ×nä —— lattä | rhaṃ haṃ | gu | ṣṭä[1]

73

Paris W

1 || ḫvāṃ: śāṃ khįñä pasti pīḍe ⁀ ḫuysye jsįña
2 priyaugä udiśāyä ⁀ sahaicä salya
3 didye māśta 10mye haḍai nauda ⁀ ——

74

P 2900

1 : namau bagävätte śākyemaunasyą ttathāgattasya namau cūttirä-
2 mahārā | jasya vrrīśämaṇḍasya ttathāgattasya baiśvämarasyą maḫiśu-
3 rasyą a | parājittasya sañasyą mauṇḍibadrrųsya bīnāyekasya
4 ttadīthā | byade byade byade-bal(e)na prrattī[tta]kä-sabude-balena
5, 6 ari | hadi-balena satta-bal(e)na cahamārauye-balena ari | (ha)di-balena[2]
7 sa sara sariṇi vittāla badanä ḫeḫe hū | hū auḫeni mauḫai vāriṇi sari-
8 viṣādauṣpa cittąna badani | syahā
9 namau b(u)dadāya namau b(u)[3] namāṃ byadāya namau dari | māya
namau sagāya namau samya-sabyadāya ttadīthā ——

75

P 5535

1 || namau rahną: ttrīyāya ⁀ namahä: caṇḍavajrrapāṇīye ⁀ mahāyakṣa-
2 sį | nādhapattīye ⁀ namau vajrrakrraudhāya ⁀ āgradhaṣṭaudakabhī-

[1] Mark below. [2] *aridi-balena* deleted.
[3] *namau b.n. b(u)* deleted.

3 ravāya ⌢ a | samūsalapariśapārśvidīpttakhaṇḍagavajrrihastāya ⌢ ttad
4 yathā aumä | pada pada ⌢ dhāva dhāva ⌢ amrratta-kụṇḍala ⌢ khakha
5 khakha ⌢ khāha khā | ha ⌢ ttiṣṭi ttiṣṭa ⌢ baṃdha baṃdha ⌢ hana
6 hana ⌢ daha daha ⌢ paca paca ⌢ garji | garji ⌢ ttarji ttarja ⌢ viṣphauṭīyi
7 viṣphauṭīya ⌢ sarva-vigna[1]-vināyikạ̄nāṃ ⌢ | murdhaṃ ttāṇḍiya vajrreṇa
8 ⌢ mahāgaṇapattajīvattinakarāya hūṃ phaṭä | svāhā || ——
9 Chinese.

SUPPLEMENT

76

Khot. (IO) 159, 1+2+3

Saṃghāṭa-sūtra

Recto

1 | (8 *akṣaras*) ⟨ba⟩lysāna cīya hatcaste u àuṣku byāta yīndä tta ne dukhä ne aysmya udvīya ham⟨ä⟩t⟨ä⟩ |

2 | (4 *akṣaras*) ⟨cā⟩lsto tsīmä u ce ro mamä trāyākä hämäte ttīyä ṣä hve' aysmyata kei'tä se tsīmä aysu paṃ ×

3 | (4 *akṣaras*) ggaruvo × tr⟨āmī⟩mä ku vara jīvätäna parsīmä ku ne ne ju ye mamä trāyākä śtä tta rro hvāñätä se

4 | ⌢ y⟨ä⟩ḍ⟨ai⟩mä mästa dīre käḍäyāne aysu trāmä hämätāmä kho ju sūta dīra stuna ⌢ ne ne mara ysāne ysama-

5 | śaṃdya lovä baña ⌢ ne ne mä ysānä paralova aśtä karä ⌢ haṃdaro biśe ju mamä ysānä niśtä karä nätca ka ne

6 | aysu gvārna lovä baña ⌢ ārre jsa yäḍaimä dīra käḍägāne aysu ttāna hā tsīmä naryo käḍe dīro gato ⌢ haṃda-

Verso

1 | ru ysaṃthu mamä mästa bera dukha ⌢ ku ttu n⟨e⟩ ju ne bve se ku mä hīsāñu × -m- ⌢ gyastai pyū⟨v-⟩' . tty⟨e⟩ hva'⟨n⟩d⟨ä⟩ *cv*⟨e?⟩ ttä dukha ×

2 | bremätä bette käḍägāne *ttä*täna hamu anāspetä ṣä paralovä mamä òṣku mä narya mamä tsuño bera dukha ⌢ ja-

3 | ḍä hve⟨'⟩ tsīmä dukha barämä vīyane store ka ne mä ne ttrāyākä ne ārūvo karä 4 dukhäna paśīmä puṣo jī ×

[1] *vi* below.

4 I (3 *akṣaras*) *a*ysu mātaru pätaru jsatämä ttätä mä paṃjsa yäḍa ana[na]nantarya ⌢ garu vīrä sarbīmä samu ne

5 I (3 *akṣaras*) × mä cu *ño* jūmä aysu 5 gyastai hvāñīndä ma jaḍa hv⟨e⟩' tta yana ⌢ ma ne yanu pātcu dīru käḍägāne

6 I (5 *akṣaras*) × karma hve' ⌢ ttausau pātcu uysānye cūḍe yana 6 naryau ysaṃthä kye uysāno jsande hve⟨'⟩ *pātc*⟨u⟩

Saṃghāṭa-sūtra, Gilgit MS 37

34 Recto

1 stūpa-bhedaṃ ca paṃcānantaryāṇi ca karmāṇi samanusmarati ⌢ sa tato duḥkhaṃ nirveda-cittam u-

2 tpādayaṭi kutrāhaṃ yāsyāmi ko me tratā bhaviṣyati ⌢ sa evaṃ cintayati gamiṣyāmy a-

3 haṃ parvata-giri-kandareṣu praviśāmi tatra me kāla-kriyā bhaviṣyati na ca me iha ka-

4 ś cit trātāsti ⌢ āha ca ⌢ kṛtaṃ me pāpakaṃ karma dagdha-sthūṇāṃ nirantaraṃ nemaṃ loke

5 śobhayiṣye na śobh[iṣy]āmi paratra ca ⌢ antargṛhe na śobhāmi na śobhāmi ca bā-

6 hire ⌢ doṣa-hetoḥ kṛtaṃ pāpaṃ tena yāsyāmi durgatim paratra duḥkhitaḥ kutra vasiṣyāmīha durgatau ⌢ śṛṇvanti devatā-vācā aśru-kaṇṭhaṃ prarodati ⌢

Verso

1 aho nirāśāf[1] palralokaṃ prayāsyāmīha durgatim II taṃ devatā āha ≈

2 mūḍho si gaccha puruṣa maivaṃ cintaya I duḥkhitaḥ śaraṇaṃ na ca me trāṇaṃ duḥkhāṃ vindāmi vedanāṃ

3 mātṛ-ghātaṃ pitṛ-ghātaṃ pancālnantaryāñ ca me kṛtam parvate mūrdhni gacchāmi tata ātmā⟨naṃ⟩ tyajāmy ahaṃ

4 mā gaccha mūḍha pu I ruṣa karma mā kuru pāpakaṃ ⌢ bahu tvayā kṛtaṃ pāpaṃ vyāpannena hi cetasā ≈

5 kurvanti I ye ātma-ghātaṃ narakaṃ yānti duḥkhitāḥ

[1] Upadhmānīya.

77

Khot. (IO) 159, 4

Saṃghāṭa-sūtra

Recto

1 | ⟨trīyaś⟩ūnya śamalauvya dāruṇa niṣ⟨ṭh⟩u⟨ra⟩ × dukha h⟨ämä⟩|⟨ta⟩
2 | dä (*c.* 13 *akṣaras*) naryau trīyaśūnä prīvo' dukha ne dyāma u ne nä ttä be- |
3 re . × v⟨ī⟩tane pārahā × tt- y⟨ä⟩t⟨e⟩ ka uysn⟨o⟩rāṇu mātā-pätara ce balysāña paroya sīrata ne vä |
4 śt⟨e⟩ tta ttä hvāñīdä se tta muhu vaṃña pūryau cu yanāṃä u gāhäna ro tta hvāñīndä ttū saṃghāṭu dātä dānavatä da-
5 ṣikä parstä pīḍe × × ṣva jsei' āchei ŏśä āchei na puva'ṇa hämāre ◡ na ro haḍe hīśtä maraṇä pūryau āchei ma puv'ata'

Verso

1 tta parrīyu hämä*t*⟨e⟩ u maṃ pūryau āchyau puva'ṇyau jsa ttārä haḍe dairyä se mā vīyau ne maraṇa dye āte || biśä nä
2 ⟨. .⟩ ạṅga maraṇu dyāmu uysyānye ne ne vaṃña bajāṣa ne pyūvā'-mane guvyau jsa tcemanyo rūva ne ne dyāmä 3
3 (4 *akṣaras*) ⟨bi⟩śä ne buvi ⟨n⟩e × ⟨n⟩e . . . -ī -ä hamara gūsīndä samu kho cakalä ttaraṃdarä mā ttrā-
4 (8 *akṣaras*) ye (*c.* 12 *akṣaras*) × -tau hvatemä ko ne puva'ta maraṇū ju pūräna |
5 (*c.* 21 *akṣaras*) × -au āchei tīndä mātä ⟨.⟩ *h*amara ⟨. .⟩

Saṃghāṭa-sūtra, Gilgit MS 37

72 Recto

1 naraka-tiryagyoni-yamalokopapattiṃ ghorāṃ dāruṇān dṛṣṭvā maraṇa-
2 kāla-samaye evaṃ bhavati ◡ ko me trātā bhaved yad ahaṃ naraka-tiryak-preta-yamaloka-vi-
3 ṣayaṃ na paśyeyaṃ na ca tāṃ duḥkhāṃ vedanāṃ vedayeyaṃ ◡ tasyaivaṃ pralapataḥ paraloka-
4 m ākramataḥ tau mātā-pitarāv evam āhatuḥ kiṃ kariṣyāma putraka ≈ gāthābhiś cā-

72 Recto (*contd*)

5 ddhyabhāṣataḥ
grahītuṃ śakyate naiva vyādhi-duḥkhaṃ mahābhayam -
6 nāsti te maraṇam pultra glānasya maraṇād bhayaṃ -
mokṣo bhaviṣyate tubhyaṃ vyādher hi bhaya-bhairavān
7 dhṛtiṃ kurulṣva he putra tataḥ siddhir bhaviṣyati -

Verso

1 niruddhyate me vijñānaṃ kāyo me pīḍyate bhṛśaṃ
sarve aṅgāṇi duḥkhaṃti mṛtyuṃ paśyati ātmanaḥ
2 na paśyataś cakṣuṣī me karṇau | me na śṛṇonti ca -
śrotraṃ punar na lapsyāmi na kāyaḥ saṃsahiṣyati -
3 aṅgam aṅgāni duḥkhanti | kāṣṭhā iva acetanāḥ
visvādayasi me amba nāgataṃ maraṇaṃ tava ≈
mātā āha -
4 vaktuṃ | nārhasi putraivaṃ mā me trāsa-parāṃ kuru -
kāyaṃ tava jvarākrāntaṃ viprakarāṇi paśyasi - putra āha -

78

Kha 1.219, 1[1]

Recto

1 / *r*rā /
2 / bäysä⟨r⟩*gyū* /
3 / mä hā āt⟨ä⟩ /
4 / *n*ä rrūvāsa b⟨iśśä⟩ /
5 / ⟨u⟩*l*atāñe baly⟨s⟩ä *ha* /
6 (*lost*)

Verso

1 / te /
2 / ta bärṣṭa ⟨t⟩ta /
3 / ⟨uskyā⟩lsto ṣṣonda p⟨u⟩ /
4 / j⟨u⟩ ye daso j⟨s⟩ī /
5 / ⟨ysa⟩nuva ś⟨ś⟩ä /
6 / -ä × /

[1] Variant to E 21.30–41.

79

Ch. 0046 a

1 | ka kā ke kī kū k⟨au⟩ k⟨au⟩ ka⟨ṃ⟩ ka va vā v⟨e⟩ vī vū vai vau vau vaṃ va |

2 ya yā ye yī yū yai yau yau yaṃ ya kha khā khe khī khū khai

3 khau khau khaṃ kha ca cā ce cī cū cai cau cau caṃ ca la lā ——

4 le lī lye le lā lā laṃ la la ysa ysā yse ysī ysū ysai ysau

5 ysau ysaṃ ysa ba bā be bī bū bai bau bau ——

6 baṃ ba tta ttā tte ttī ttū ttai ttau ttau ttaṃ tta ——

7 ra rā re rī ru rai rau rau raṃ ra śa śā śe śī śu śai śau śau śaṃ śa pa pā

8 p(e) pī pū pai pau pau paṃ pa ga gā ge gī gū gai gau gau gaṃ ga ——

9 ṣa ṣā ṣe ṣī ṣū ṣai ṣau ṣau ṣaṃ ṣa ——

10 ña ñā ñe ñī ñū ñai ñā ñau ñaṃ ña kṣa kṣā kṣe kṣī kṣū kṣai kṣau kṣau kṣa⟨ṃ⟩ kṣa

11 ha hā he hī hū hai hau hau haṃ ha cha chā che chī chū chai chau chau

12 chaṃ cha dha dhā dhe dhī dhū dhai dhau dhau dhaṃ dha pha phā phe phī phū phai

13 phau phau phaṃ pha tha thā the thī thū thai thau thau tha⟨ṃ⟩ tha 'a 'ā 'ī 'e 'ai 'au 'au 'a⟨ṃ⟩ 'a

14 tta ttā tte ttī ttu ttai ttau ttau ttaṃ tta ——

15 da dā de dī dū dai dau dau da⟨ṃ⟩ da ——

16 bha bhā bhe ⟨bhī⟩ bhu bhai bhau bhau bhaṃ bha na nā ne nī nu nai nau nau naṃ na ——

17 sedhame 'a 'ā 'e 'ī 'ā ū 'e va 'ai 'auva 'au 'a⟨ṃ⟩ 'a ka kha ga gaha ja ca cha

18 ja jaha ña tta the da dha na pa pha ba bha ma ya ra la va śa ṣaṃ sa ha kṣa

[*Space*]

80

Ch. 0046 b

Recto baudhasatta

Chinese text

Verso

1 ka kha ke ḳī kū kai kau k⟨au⟩ ka⟨ṃ⟩ ka va vā *ve* v⟨ī⟩
2 vū vai vau vau vaṃ va ≈ ya yā ye yī yū ——
3 yai yau yau ya⟨ṃ⟩ ya kha khā khe khī khū khai khau /
4 khau khaṃ kha ≈ ca cā ce cī cū cai cau cau caṃ ca ——
5 la lā le lī lūe la ——

81

Ch. 0046 c

1 || parau mista tcāṃ tte hvāṃ' u hūśai'na khvau tta ṣṭe |
2 sa thū mista rraispūra pūyaṃ śī kvaina ——
3 ttaugä 'eysa vaijalaka svahąka ——
4 cā krraśīsa amaga[1] svanī u kva ṣanīraka
5 kīma ttehą śaną yā kī tsena la pha drū /
6 (1 *akṣara*) kvā sa gu sera hvā hvai jvai ——

82

Ch. 0050 a[2]

1 (*bases*)
2 ye mve'śdalalaka sī 'īraudrū pīsai vā baiṣṭe khuā vāśe karastā hīya mv⟨e⟩'-
3 śa' haraysde ——

[*Space*]

[1] Or *gu*?
[2] See also Khot. (IO) C, KT 5. 311.

4 ll mista tcau hvāṃ' u hūśai' na ——
5 —— haṣḍi yane ñaśa bī⟨sa⟩
6 kīma tteha śanä ñaśau bīsā hvāṃ' pajsaṃ hamye sa ke' sa jara tte hv̌āṃ hī⟨ya⟩
7 mve' śdalalaka sī 'īraudrū pīsai vā baiṣṭe khuā vāśe karastā hīya
8 mvai' śa' haraysde ——

[*Space*]

83

Ch. 0050 b

1.1 mista tcau tte hvāṃ' u hūśai'na ——
2 —— hạṣḍi yane ñaśa bī⟨sa⟩
3 kīma ttehä śana ñaśau bīsā vā parau hạmye sa ke' sa jara tte hvāṃ' hīye m⟨ve⟩'-
4 śdalalaka sī 'īraudrū pīsai hvāṃ' baiṣṭe khuā vāśe karastā hīya mvai'śda hara-
5 ysde ——
6 ll mista tcau tte hvāṃ' u hūśai'na ——
7 —— haṣḍi yane ñaśa bīsa
8 . -e . . . . -au -ī -ā -ā . -au -i -e × . . × . .
2.1 mista tcau tta mista tcau tte hvāṃ' u hūśai'na —— haṣḍa yane ña⟨śa bīsa⟩
2 kīma tte śana ñaśau bīsā parau hamye sa ka' sā jara tte hvā hī⟨ye⟩
3 mve⟨'⟩śdalalaka sī ⟨'īrau⟩dū u pīsai hvā' baiṣṭa khuā vāśāṃ karastā ——
4 mve'śdalalaka sī 'īraudū u pīsai hv́āṃ' baiṣṭa khuā vāśe karastā hīye
5 (*lost*)

84

Ch. xc 002[1]

u āysāja gatcastä līka sadhaṃ

[1] JRAS 1911, 453.

85

MT c 0025[1]

1 | praṇihạ̄ni cvā jsi yiḍeṃ haṃda ysaṃthi ṣṭāṃ pīrụ̄yvā ysaṃthvā *kṣạ̄ma pīsai* |

86

MT 0489[2]

1 || hiyaudi āmāca |
2 de vāṃ na ñāṃ tcīṣ⟨ī?⟩ |
3 ne dva ṣaṃga ysāri × |
4 ysaṃthi haurūṃ × |
5 ⟨. .⟩ di de × |

87

MT a 1 0035

Two columns

<table>
<tr><td>*a* 1</td><td>(*left column lost*)</td><td>⟨puña?⟩de nam⟨au⟩ḍ⟨i⟩
sāthara jsajsa sahadāysa pasā</td></tr>
<tr><td>2</td><td>(*left column half lost*) × -'
sa⟨ṃ⟩gabude</td><td>——</td></tr>
<tr><td>3</td><td>paḍ⟨au⟩ysāña paraṃ pīsai rāsa</td><td>—— śe'ña paraṃ baraṃ
pīsai śattā ——</td></tr>
<tr><td>4</td><td>pīsạị ṣilā || jsajsa ——</td><td>pīsai puska | sahadaysi ——</td></tr>
<tr><td>5</td><td>sahadatti || pīsai sāthare ——</td><td>śi'lebasī sahadatti || 'auṣi ——</td></tr>
<tr><td>6</td><td>sūdele || u*rrv*edi ——</td><td>pīsai vidyela ||
pīsai saṃgau ——</td></tr>
<tr><td>7</td><td>pīsai smaṃlā | valārrja ——</td><td>pīsai vismade ——</td></tr>
<tr><td>8</td><td>pīsai sahadāysi ——</td><td>pīsai viśa're ——
pīsai sagalakaṃ</td></tr>
</table>

[1] Facsimile, *Saka Documents III*, plate 61.
[2] Facsimile, *Saka Documents III*, plate 59.

9	puñasaga ——	puñade ——
10	kāśide ——	pīsai kāśade pī[ñi]sai
		saṃgabudi ——
11	śerīde ——	⟨pīs⟩ai
12	’īrū ——	(*tops*)
13	. -i × ///	(*traces*)

Two columns

b 1	(*left column blank*)	ā’ysaṃ dva kūsi 5 ṣaṃga ṣīlāṃ jisti ——
2	(*left blank*)	ā’ysaṃ 2 kūsi ’īrū jisti ——

3 rrusi tcahau kūsi mvīkāṃ puñadi jïsti u × ṣaga —— ā’ysaṃ 2 kūsi vismidi jisti ——

4 rrusi śau kūsi × sahavari jisti —— ā’ysaṃ 5 ṣaga sahadatti jisti ——

5 rrusi 10 5 ṣaṃgaṃ sātha jisti ——

6 rrusi śau kūsi vilaucaṃ jisti ——

7 rrusi dva kūsi ’īrū jisti ——

8 pātci rrusa śau dva[1] kūsi sahadaraṃ jisti —— biśe taṃka rrusi hamye 10 5 kūsi 8

9 rrusi śau kūsa namauḍi sāthari jisti —— ṣaṃga vīni · ysaṃthạ mānagä ——

10 rrusi drrai kūsi ṣīlā jisti ——

11 rrusi śau ṣīlā pu⟨ñadi?⟩ jisti ——

[*Space*]

88

Ch. 00272

Gostana-Sanskrit text

67 - - rahna-drrīya prraṇamyādau ≂ grrathab = īttrra hrratta prrattai ≂

68 śāstrraṃ allpa prravakṣaumi I grrathattau mahad-arthatta ittai : ——

Normalized Bud. Sanskrit gives here: ratna-trayaṃ praṇamya - ādau I grantham itra hitaṃ prati II śāstram alpaṃ pravakṣyāmi granthato mahad-arthata iti

——

83 ≂ yas = tueśarāṃbaira parahnaṃ vayauūka vabairanau napūlaka

[1] *dva* below *śau*.

84 baladupadīś ta dąrī-krraitvą prrīya-prraṇaiyaṇaupada-
85 m = āttabaudī ≈ dharmatta daiśī ca ca śamāya namaus = ⟨t⟩ū ttasamī
86 yaṃ prrāpya durgatta yā bayā narauttarauttarau bhavattai narvātta ca aṣṭą-
87 pathāṃ sarvāṃ bhavatta baudā ≈ ttasāra-sāgara-samāttara-ṇaika settau ≈ yasmī gūṇa adaśīya lakṣaṇa-dākṣaṇīya-
89 kąryą krrattą prrathavąū prrathana bhavatta sarvāṃ manąnamatta-
90 tta sūgatta-prraśasta-aṣṭąr⟨y⟩a-paugala-vaśaiṣa-krrattau
91 tta vāṃ I sā

———

97 yas = tue[1] śarābaira para yūva yūauka vabairanau vapūlaka

89

Tarishlak 1.009

Picture with brāhmī script, facsimile Serindia XII.

1 āśi'rī mittrabha-
2 *dr*i pasti pīḍi
3 -āṃnai[2] ysīnī
4 *h*atsa va*l*ayaina

90

Picture, The Louvre, facsimile in Eiichi Matsumoto, Tonkō-ga no kenkyū, Study of the paintings of Tunhuang, 1937, CXXXI.

1 ⟨spā⟩ta vā tte (*figura*) yaṭī pastä pīḍe ——
2 ⟨ . ⟩ *be*ysau hīyi jūhai ų̄dąśāyä ——
3 ⟨ . . . ⟩ × × jsa beysuśta brrīya

[1] Unskilled copy of line 83; below *stue stui* is written twice.
[2] Uncertain initial consonant.

91

MT piece x (facsimile, *Saka Documents* III, plate 68)

1 | || kaspakyi vī bisai veṃjilakä jsārä nātä nau kūsi saṃ ttī kūsa nau 20 2mye kṣuṇä mūtca- |
2 ci māśtä 10 8mye haḍai ttiña haṃkhīśi' kṣe' kūsä kūṣḍvī bisai ye 4 stūrä u dva stūrä
3 ṣau śūresa hīyai (*mark*) desä (*oblique*)

92

MT a ii 0094 (facsimile, *Saka Documents* III, plate 64)

1 (*c.* 15 *akṣaras*) ⟨braṃ⟩ khaysdy⟨e⟩ ⟨mā⟩śta c- ttrrā × |
2 (c. 9 *akṣaras*) (*traces of* 6 *akṣaras*) || braṃkhaysdye 20mye haḍai ttye
3 prracaina × × × × -ai ye māśte 10 ba × × × || ——
4 ya k- tcana māśte tta parī —— × × khu parau pvīry⟨au⟩
5 × × × × ra ki × × ha -ai × × × byehe × × māśte 20
6 mye haḍai parau tsve pa salye (*mark*) ——

93

MT c iii 0081 (facsimile, *Saka Documents* III, plate 58)

1 || hārū sividatta nāra ạysāṃji pụsūṃ /
2 kūra ājeṃ*my*aṃ saṃdurṣṭa hima ——